Exam 70-640: *TS: Windows Server® 2008 Active Directory®, Configuring*

Objective	Chapter	Lesson
Configuring Domain Name System (DNS) for Active Directory (16 percent)		
Configure zones.	9	1
Configure DNS server settings.	9	2
Configure zone transfers and replication.	9	2
Configuring the Active Directory Infrastructure (25 percent)		
Configure a forest or a domain.	1, 10, 12	Chapter 1, Lessons 1, 2 Chapter 10, Lessons 1, 2 Chapter 12, Lessons 1, 2
Configure trusts.	12	2
Configure sites.	11	1, 2
Configure Active Directory replication.	8, 10, 11	Chapter 8, Lesson 3 Chapter 10, Lesson 3 Chapter 11, Lesson 3
Configure the global catalog.	11	2
Configure operations masters.	10	2
Configuring Additional Active Directory Server Roles (9 percent)		
Configure Active Directory Lightweight Directory Service (AD LDS).	14	1, 2
Configure Active Directory Rights Management Service (AD RMS).	16	1, 2
Configure the read-only domain controller (RODC).	8	3
Configure Active Directory Federation Services (AD FS).	17	1, 2
Creating and Maintaining Active Directory Objects (24 percent)		
Automate creation of Active Directory accounts.	3, 4, 5	Chapter 3, Lessons 1, 2 Chapter 4, Lessons 1, 2 Chapter 5, Lessons 1, 2
Maintain Active Directory accounts.	2, 3, 4, 5	Chapter 2, Lessons 2, 3 Chapter 3, Lessons 1, 2, 3 Chapter 4, Lessons 1, 2, 3 Chapter 5, Lessons 1, 2, 3
Create and apply Group Policy objects (GPOs).	6	1, 2, 3
Configure GPO templates.	6, 7	Chapter 6, Lessons 1, 2, 3 Chapter 7, Lessons 1, 2, 3
Configure software deployment GPOs.	7	3
Configure account policies.	8	1
Configure audit policy by using GPOs.	7, 8	Chapter 7, Lesson 4 Chapter 8, Lesson 2
Maintaining the Active Directory Environment (13 percent)		
Configure backup and recovery.	13	2
Perform offline maintenance.	13	1
Monitor Active Directory.	6, 11, 13	Chapter 6, Lesson 3 Chapter 11, Lesson 3 Chapter 13, Lesson 1

D1477941

Objective	Chapter	Lesson
Configuring Active Directory Certificate Services (13 percent)		
Install Active Directory Certificate Services.	15	1
Configure CA server settings.	15	2
Manage certificate templates.	15	2
Manage enrollments.	15	2
Manage certificate revocations.	15	2

MCTS Self-Paced Training Kit (Exam 70-640): Configuring Windows Server® 2008 Active Directory®

Dan Holme,
Nelson Ruest, and
Danielle Ruest

PUBLISHED BY
Microsoft Press
A Division of Microsoft Corporation
One Microsoft Way
Redmond, Washington 98052-6399

Printed and bound in the United States of America.

1 2 3 4 5 6 7 8 9   QWT   3 2 1 0 9 8

Distributed in Canada by H.B. Fenn and Company Ltd.

A CIP catalogue record for this book is available from the British Library.

Microsoft Press books are available through booksellers and distributors worldwide. For further information about international editions, contact your local Microsoft Corporation office or contact Microsoft Press International directly at fax (425) 936-7329. Visit our Web site at www.microsoft.com/mspress. Send comments to tkinput@microsoft.com.

Acquisitions Editor: Ken Jones
Developmental Editor: Laura Sackerman
Project Editor: Maureen Zimmerman
Editorial Production: nSight, Inc.
Technical Reviewers: Bob Hogan, Bob Dean; Technical Review services provided by Content Master, a member of CM Group, Ltd.
Cover: Tom Draper Design

SubAssy Part No. X14-33179
Body Part No. X14-33191
Section No. X14-33182

About the Authors

Dan Holme

Dan Holme, a graduate of Yale University and Thunderbird, has spent more than a decade as a consultant and trainer, delivering solutions to tens of thousands of IT professionals from the most prestigious organizations and corporations around the world. Dan's company, Intelliem, specializes in boosting the productivity of IT professionals and end users by creating advanced, customized solutions that integrate clients' specific design and configuration into productivity-focused tools, training, and knowledge management services. Dan is also a contributing editor for *Windows IT Pro* magazine, an MVP (Office SharePoint Server), and the community lead of *officesharepointpro.com*. From his base in beautiful Maui, Dan travels around the globe supporting customers and delivering Windows technologies training. Immediately following the release of this Training Kit, he will be preparing for the Beijing Olympic Games as the Windows Technologies Consultant for NBC television, a role he also played in Torino in 2006.

Danielle Ruest

Danielle Ruest is passionate about helping people make the most of computer technology. She is a senior enterprise workflow architect and consultant with over 20 years of experience in project implementations. Her customers include governments and private enterprises of all sizes. Throughout her career, she has led change-management processes, developed and delivered training, provided technical writing services, and managed communications programs during complex technology implementation projects. More recently, Danielle has been involved in the design and support of test, development, and production infrastructures based on virtualization technologies. She is an MVP for the Virtual Machine product line.

Nelson Ruest

Nelson Ruest is passionate about doing things *right* with Microsoft technologies. He is a senior enterprise IT architect with over 25 years of experience. He was one of Canada's first Microsoft Certified Systems Engineers (MCSEs) and Microsoft Certified Trainers. In his IT career, he has been a computer operator, systems administrator, trainer, Help desk operator, support engineer, IT manager, project manager, and now, IT architect. He has also taken part in numerous migration projects, where he was responsible for everything from project management to systems design in both the private and public sectors. He is an MVP for the Windows Server product line.

Nelson and Danielle work for Resolutions Enterprises, a consulting firm focused on IT infrastructure design. Resolutions Enterprises can be found at *http://www.reso-net.com*. Both are authors of multiple books, notably the free *The Definitive Guide to Vista Migration* (*http://www.realtime-nexus.com/dgvm.htm*) and *Microsoft Windows Server 2008: The Complete Reference* (McGraw-Hill Osborne, 2008) (*http://www.mhprofessional.com/product.php?cat=112&isbn=0072263652*).

Tony Northrup

Tony Northrup, MVP, MCSE, MCTS, and CISSP, is a Windows consultant and author living in Phillipston, Massachusetts. Tony started programming before Windows 1.0 was released but has focused on Windows administration and development for the past 15 years. He has written more than a dozen books covering Windows networking, security, and development. Among other titles, Tony is coauthor of *Microsoft Windows Server 2003 Resource Kit* (Microsoft Press, 2005) and *Windows Vista Resource Kit* (Microsoft Press, 2007).

When he's not consulting or writing, Tony enjoys photography, remote-controlled flight, and golf. Tony lives with his cat, Sam, and his dog, Sandi. You can learn more about Tony by visiting his technical blog at *http://www.vistaclues.com* or his personal Web site at *http://www.northrup.org*.

Contents at a Glance

1   Installation 1

2   Administration 33

3   Users. 85

4   Groups 139

5   Computers. 187

6   Group Policy Infrastructure 229

7   Group Policy Settings 289

8   Authentication 355

9   Integrating Domain Name System with AD DS. 393

10   Domain Controllers 459

11   Sites and Replication 507

12   Domains and Forests 555

13   Directory Business Continuity 607

14   Active Directory Lightweight Directory Services 685

15   Active Directory Certificate Services and Public Key
Infrastructures 723

16   Active Directory Rights Management Services 781

17   Active Directory Federation Services 825

       Answers 875

       Index 921

Table of Contents

Introduction . . . .**xxix**

    Making the Most of the Training Kit xxx

    Setup and Hardware Requirements xxx

    Software Requirements and Setup xxxi

    Using the CD xxxi

        How to Install the Practice Tests xxxii

        How to Use the Practice Tests xxxii

    How to Uninstall the Practice Tests xxxiii

    Microsoft Certified Professional Program xxxiv

    Technical Support xxxiv

1   **Installation** **1**

    Before You Begin 2

    Lesson 1: Installing Active Directory Domain Services 3

        Active Directory, Identity and Access 3

        Beyond Identity and Access 8

        Components of an Active Directory Infrastructure 8

        Preparing to Create a New Windows Server 2008 Forest 11

        Adding the AD DS Role Using the Windows Interface 12

        Creating a Domain Controller 13

        Creating a Windows Server 2008 Forest 14

        Lesson Summary 21

        Lesson Review 21

What do you think of this book? We want to hear from you!

Microsoft is interested in hearing your feedback so we can continually improve our books and learning resources for you. To participate in a brief online survey, please visit:

www.microsoft.com/learning/booksurvey/

Lesson 2: Active Directory Domain Services on Server Core 23
Understanding Server Core. 23
Installing Server Core. 24
Performing Initial Configuration Tasks 25
Adding AD DS to a Server Core Installation. 26
Removing Domain Controllers 26
Installing a Server Core Domain Controller 27
Lesson Summary. 29
Lesson Review 30
Chapter Review. 31
Key Terms. 31
Case Scenario 32
Case Scenario: Creating an Active Directory Forest 32
Take a Practice Test. 32

2   **Administration. 33**
Before You Begin 33
Lesson 1: Working with Active Directory Snap-ins. 35
Understanding the Microsoft Management Console 35
Active Directory Administration Tools. 36
Finding the Active Directory Administrative Tools 37
Adding the Administrative Tools to Your Start Menu. 37
Running Administrative Tools with Alternate Credentials 37
Creating a Custom Console with Active Directory Snap-ins 38
Saving and Distributing a Custom Console 39
Creating and Managing a Custom MMC 40
Lesson Summary. 44
Lesson Review 45
Lesson 2: Creating Objects in Active Directory. 46
Creating an Organizational Unit. 46
Creating a User Object. 48
Creating a Group Object 50
Creating a Computer Object. 52
Finding Objects in Active Directory. 54

Finding Objects by Using *Dsquery* 59

Understanding DNs, RDNs, and CNs. 60

Creating and Locating Objects in Active Directory. 61

Lesson Summary. 67

Lesson Review 67

Lesson 3: Delegation and Security of Active Directory Objects. 69

Understanding Delegation 69

Viewing the ACL of an Active Directory Object. .70

Object, Property, and Control Access Rights 72

Assigning a Permission Using the Advanced Security Settings Dialog Box. . . .72

Understanding and Managing Permissions with Inheritance 73

Delegating Administrative Tasks with the Delegation Of Control Wizard 74

Reporting and Viewing Permissions 75

Removing or Resetting Permissions on an Object 75

Understanding Effective Permissions 76

Designing an OU Structure to Support Delegation 77

Delegating Administrative Tasks 78

Lesson Summary. 79

Lesson Review 80

Chapter Review. 81

Key Terms 81

Case Scenario 82

Case Scenario: Organizational Units and Delegation 82

Suggested Practices. 82

Maintain Active Directory Accounts 82

Take a Practice Test 84

3   Users. 85

Before You Begin 86

Lesson 1: Automating the Creation of User Accounts. 87

Creating Users with Templates. 87

Using Active Directory Command-Line Tools 88

Creating Users with *Dsadd* 89

Importing Users with *CSVDE* 90

Importing Users with *LDIFDE* 90

Automating the Creation of User Accounts 93

Lesson Summary. 96

Lesson Review 96

Lesson 2: Creating Users with Windows PowerShell and VBScript 98

Introducing Windows PowerShell 98

Understanding Windows PowerShell Syntax, Cmdlets, and Objects 99

Getting Help 101

Using Variables 102

Using Aliases 102

Namespaces, Providers, and PSDrives. 103

Creating a User with Windows PowerShell. 103

Importing Users from a Database with Windows PowerShell 106

Executing a Windows PowerShell Script 108

Introducing VBScript 108

Creating a User with VBScript. 109

VBScript vs. Windows PowerShell. 109

Creating Users with Windows PowerShell and VBScript. 110

Lesson Summary. 112

Lesson Review 112

Lesson 3: Supporting User Objects and Accounts 114

Managing User Attributes with Active Directory Users and Computers 114

Understanding Name and Account Attributes. 118

Managing User Attributes with *Dsmod* and *Dsget* 121

Managing User Attributes with Windows PowerShell and VBScript. 123

Administering User Accounts 124

Supporting User Objects and Accounts 130

Lesson Summary. 133

Lesson Review 133

Chapter Review. 135

Key Terms. 135

Case Scenario 136

Case Scenario: Import User Accounts. 136

Suggested Practices. 136

    Automate the Creation of User Accounts. 136

    Maintain Active Directory Accounts 137

Take a Practice Test 137

4　Groups **139**

Before You Begin 139

Lesson 1: Creating and Managing Groups 141

    Managing an Enterprise with Groups 141

    Defining Group Naming Conventions 143

    Understanding Group Types. 145

    Understanding Group Scope 145

    Converting Group Scope and Type. 149

    Managing Group Membership 151

    Developing a Group Management Strategy 153

    Creating and Managing Groups 155

    Lesson Summary. 156

    Lesson Review. 157

Lesson 2: Automating the Creation and Management of Groups 159

    Creating Groups with *Dsadd*. 159

    Importing Groups with *CSVDE*. 160

    Managing Groups with *LDIFDE* 161

    Retrieving Group Membership with *Dsget*. 162

    Changing Group Membership with *Dsmod*. 162

    Moving and Renaming Groups with *Dsmove* 163

    Deleting Groups with *Dsrm* 163

    Managing Group Membership with Windows PowerShell and VBScript . . . 164

    Automating the Creation and Management of Groups. 165

    Lesson Summary. 167

    Lesson Review. 167

Lesson 3: Administering Groups in an Enterprise. 169

    Best Practices for Group Attributes 169

    Protecting Groups from Accidental Deletion. 171

    Delegating the Management of Group Membership. 172

Understanding Shadow Groups 176

Default Groups 177

Special Identities 179

Administering Groups in an Enterprise 180

Lesson Summary 181

Lesson Review 182

Chapter Review 184

Key Terms 184

Case Scenario 185

Case Scenario: Implementing a Group Strategy 185

Suggested Practices 185

Automating Group Membership and Shadow Groups 186

Take a Practice Test 186

5   Computers 187

Before You Begin 188

Lesson 1: Creating Computers and Joining the Domain 189

Understanding Workgroups, Domains, and Trusts 189

Identifying Requirements for Joining a Computer to the Domain 190

Computers Container 190

Creating OUs for Computers 190

Delegating Permission to Create Computers 192

Prestaging a Computer Account 192

Joining a Computer to the Domain 193

Importance of Prestaging Computer Objects 195

Creating Computers and Joining the Domain 198

Lesson Summary 201

Lesson Review 202

Lesson 2: Automating the Creation of Computer Objects 203

Importing Computers with *CSVDE* 203

Importing Computers with *LDIFDE* 204

Creating Computers with *Dsadd* 205

Creating Computers with *Netdom* 205

Creating Computers with Windows PowerShell 206

Creating Computers with VBScript 208

Create and Manage a Custom MMC. 209

Lesson Summary. 211

Lesson Review 212

Lesson 3: Supporting Computer Objects and Accounts 213

Configuring Computer Properties. 213

Moving a Computer. 214

Managing a Computer from the Active Directory Users and
Computers Snap-In 215

Understanding the Computer's Logon and Secure Channel. 216

Recognizing Computer Account Problems 216

Resetting a Computer Account 217

Renaming a Computer 218

Disabling and Enabling Computer Accounts. 219

Deleting Computer Accounts. 220

Recycling Computers. 220

Supporting Computer Objects and Accounts 221

Lesson Summary. 222

Lesson Review 223

Chapter Review. 224

Key Terms 224

Case Scenarios 224

Case Scenario 1: Creating Computer Objects and Joining the Domain 225

Case Scenario 2: Automating the Creation of Computer Objects 225

Suggested Practices. 225

Create and Maintain Computer Accounts 225

Take a Practice Test 227

6   Group Policy Infrastructure **229**

Before You Begin 230

Lesson 1: Implementing Group Policy 231

An Overview and Review of Group Policy 231

Group Policy Objects. 237

Policy Settings. 241

Administrative Templates Node 244

Implementing Group Policy 248

Lesson Summary 252

Lesson Review 253

Lesson 2: Managing Group Policy Scope 255

GPO Links 255

GPO Inheritance and Precedence 257

Using Security Filtering to Modify GPO Scope 262

WMI Filters 264

Enabling or Disabling GPOs and GPO Nodes 266

Targeting Preferences 267

Group Policy Processing 268

Loopback Policy Processing 270

Configuring Group Policy Scope 272

Lesson Summary 275

Lesson Review 276

Lesson 3: Supporting Group Policy 277

Resultant Set of Policy 277

Examining Policy Event Logs 281

Configuring Group Policy Scope 281

Lesson Summary 284

Lesson Review 285

Chapter Review 286

Key Terms 286

Case Scenario 287

Case Scenario: Implementing Group Policy 287

Suggested Practices 287

Create and Apply Group Policy Objects (GPOs) 287

Take a Practice Test 288

7   Group Policy Settings 289

Before You Begin 289

Lesson 1: Delegating the Support of Computers 291

Understanding Restricted Groups Policies 291

Delegating Administration Using Restricted Groups Policies
with the Member Of Setting. 294

Delegating Membership Using Group Policy 295

Lesson Summary. 298

Lesson Review 298

Lesson 2: Managing Security Settings 300

Configuring the Local Security Policy 300

Managing Security Configuration with Security Templates. 302

The Security Configuration Wizard 309

Settings, Templates, Policies, and GPOs 314

Managing Security Settings 315

Lesson Summary. 320

Lesson Review 321

Lesson 3: Managing Software with Group Policy Software Installation 322

Understanding Group Policy Software Installation. 322

Preparing an SDP 325

Creating a Software Deployment GPO 325

Managing the Scope of a Software Deployment GPO. 327

Maintaining Applications Deployed with Group Policy 327

GPSI and Slow Links. 329

Managing Software with Group Policy Software Installation 329

Lesson Summary. 332

Lesson Review 332

Lesson 4: Auditing. 335

Audit Policy 335

Auditing Access to Files and Folders. 337

Auditing Directory Service Changes 341

Auditing. 342

Lesson Summary. 346

Lesson Review 346

Chapter Review. 348

Key Terms 349

Case Scenarios 350

Case Scenario 1: Software Installation with Group Policy
Software Installation. 350

Case Scenario 2: Security Configuration. 350

Suggested Practices 351

Restricted Groups 351

Security Configuration 352

Take a Practice Test. 354

8   Authentication. 355

Before You Begin 356

Lesson 1: Configuring Password and Lockout Policies. 357

Understanding Password Policies. 357

Understanding Account Lockout Policies 359

Configuring the Domain Password and Lockout Policy 360

Fine-Grained Password and Lockout Policy 360

Understanding Password Settings Objects 361

PSO Precedence and Resultant PSO 362

PSOs and OUs 362

Configuring Password and Lockout Policies 363

Lesson Summary. 366

Lesson Review 367

Lesson 2: Auditing Authentication 368

Account Logon and Logon Events. 368

Configuring Authentication-Related Audit Policies. 369

Scoping Audit Policies 370

Viewing Logon Events 371

Auditing Authentication 371

Lesson Summary. 372

Lesson Review 373

Lesson 3: Configuring Read-Only Domain Controllers 374

Authentication and Domain Controller Placement in a Branch Office 374

Read-Only Domain Controllers 375

Deploying an RODC. 377

Password Replication Policy 380

Administer RODC Credentials Caching 381

Administrative Role Separation 383

Configuring Read-Only Domain Controllers 383

Lesson Summary 386

Lesson Review 387

Chapter Review 389

Key Terms 389

Case Scenarios 390

Case Scenario 1: Increasing the Security of Administrative Accounts 390

Case Scenario 2: Increasing the Security and Reliability of
Branch Office Authentication 391

Suggested Practices 391

Configure Multiple Password Settings Objects 391

Recover from a Stolen Read-Only Domain Controller 392

Take a Practice Test 392

9   Integrating Domain Name System with AD DS 393

DNS and IPv6 395

The Peer Name Resolution Protocol 397

DNS Structures 398

The Split-Brain Syndrome 400

Before You Begin 403

Lesson 1: Understanding and Installing Domain Name System 406

Understanding DNS 406

Windows Server DNS Features 414

Integration with AD DS 417

Installing the DNS Service 419

Lesson Summary 429

Lesson Review 429

Lesson 2: Configuring and Using Domain Name System 431

Configuring DNS 431

Forwarders vs. Root Hints 439

Single-Label Name Management 441

DNS and DHCP Considerations 443

Working with Application Directory Partitions 445

Administering DNS Servers. 448

Finalizing a DNS Server Configuration in a Forest. 450

Lesson Summary. 452

Lesson Review 452

Chapter Review. 455

Key Terms. 456

Case Scenario 456

Case Scenario: Block Specific DNS Names. 456

Suggested Practices 456

Working with DNS 456

Take a Practice Test. 457

10   Domain Controllers **459**

Before You Begin 459

Lesson 1: Installing Domain Controllers. 461

Installing a Domain Controller with the Windows Interface 461

Unattended Installation Options and Answer Files. 462

Installing a New Windows Server 2008 Forest. 464

Installing Additional Domain Controllers in a Domain. 465

Installing a New Windows Server 2008 Child Domain 467

Installing a New Domain Tree. 468

Staging the Installation of an RODC 469

Installing AD DS from Media 472

Removing a Domain Controller 473

Installing Domain Controllers 474

Lesson Summary. 476

Lesson Review 477

Lesson 2: Configuring Operations Masters 478

Understanding Single Master Operations. 478

Forest-Wide Operations Master Roles. 480

Domain-Wide Operations Master Roles 480

Placing Operations Masters. 483

Identifying Operations Masters 484

Transferring Operations Master Roles. 485

Recognizing Operations Master Failures 486

Seizing Operations Master Roles 487

Returning a Role to Its Original Holder. 488

Transferring Operations Master Roles. 489

Lesson Summary. 491

Lesson Review. 492

Lesson 3: Configuring DFS Replication of SYSVOL. 494

Raising the Domain Functional Level 494

Understanding Migration Stages. 495

Migrating SYSVOL Replication to DFS-R 496

Configuring DFS Replication of SYSVOL. 497

Lesson Summary. 502

Lesson Review. 502

Chapter Review. 504

Key Terms 504

Case Scenario 504

Case Scenario: Upgrading a Domain 505

Suggested Practices. 505

Upgrade a Windows Server 2003 Domain. 505

Take a Practice Test 506

11   Sites and Replication 507

Before You Begin 508

Lesson 1: Configuring Sites and Subnets. 509

Understanding Sites. 509

Planning Sites 510

Defining Sites 512

Managing Domain Controllers in Sites. 515

Understanding Domain Controller Location 516

Configuring Sites and Subnets. 519

Lesson Summary. 520

Lesson Review. 521

Lesson 2: Configuring the Global Catalog and Application Directory Partitions . 522

    Reviewing Active Directory Partitions 522

    Understanding the Global Catalog 523

    Placing GC Servers 523

    Configuring a Global Catalog Server. 524

    Universal Group Membership Caching 524

    Understanding Application Directory Partitions 525

    Replication and Directory Partitions 527

    Lesson Summary. 529

    Lesson Review 529

Lesson 3: Configuring Replication. 531

    Understanding Active Directory Replication 531

    Connection Objects 532

    The Knowledge Consistency Checker 533

    Intrasite Replication 534

    Site Links. 535

    Bridgehead Servers. 538

    Configuring Intersite Replication 539

    Monitoring Replication 543

    Configuring Replication. 545

    Lesson Summary. 547

    Lesson Review 547

Chapter Review. 550

Key Terms. 551

Case Scenario 551

    Case Scenario: Configuring Sites and Subnets 551

Suggested Practices. 553

    Monitor and Manage Replication 553

Take a Practice Test. 554

12   Domains and Forests 555

Before You Begin 555

Lesson 1: Understanding Domain and Forest Functional Levels 557

    Understanding Functional Levels. 557

Domain Functional Levels. 557

Forest Functional Levels 560

Raising the Domain and Forest Functional Levels. 563

Lesson Summary. 565

Lesson Review 565

Lesson 2: Managing Multiple Domains and Trust Relationships 567

Defining Your Forest and Domain Structure 567

Moving Objects Between Domains and Forests 572

Understanding Trust Relationships 576

Authentication Protocols and Trust Relationships. 579

Manual Trusts 583

Administering Trusts 590

Securing Trust Relationships. 591

Administering a Trust Relationship 595

Lesson Summary. 601

Lesson Review 602

Chapter Review. 604

Chapter Summary 604

Case Scenario 605

Case Scenario: Managing Multiple Domains and Forests. 605

Suggested Practices. 605

Configure a Forest or Domain 605

Take a Practice Test 606

13   Directory Business Continuity

13   Directory Business Continuity **607**

Before You Begin 608

Lesson 1: Proactive Directory Maintenance and Data Store Protection. 610

Twelve Categories of AD DS Administration 612

Performing Online Maintenance 622

Performing Offline Maintenance. 623

Relying on Built-in Directory Protection Measures. 624

Relying on Windows Server Backup to Protect the Directory. 629

Performing Proactive Restores. 638

Protecting DCs as Virtual Machines 648

Working with the AD DS Database 650

Lesson Summary. 657

Lesson Review 658

Lesson 2: Proactive Directory Performance Management 660

Managing System Resources. 660

Working with Windows System Resource Manager 672

AD DS Performance Analysis. 675

Lesson Summary. 680

Lesson Review 680

Chapter Review. 682

Key Terms. 683

Case Scenario 683

Case Scenario: Working with Lost and Found Data 683

Suggested Practices 684

Proactive Directory Maintenance. 684

Take a Practice Test. 684

14   Active Directory Lightweight Directory Services. 685

Before You Begin 687

Lesson 1: Understanding and Installing AD LDS. 690

Understanding AD LDS 690

AD LDS Scenarios 692

Installing AD LDS 694

Installing AD LDS 696

Lesson Summary. 699

Lesson Review 699

Lesson 2: Configuring and Using AD LDS 701

Working with AD LDS Tools. 701

Creating AD LDS Instances 703

Working with AD LDS Instances. 709

Working with AD LDS Instances. 714

Lesson Summary. 718

Lesson Review 719

Chapter Review. 720

Chapter Summary 720

Key Terms 721

Case Scenario 721

    Case Scenario: Determine AD LDS Instance Prerequisites 721

Suggested Practices. 721

    Work with AD LDS Instances 722

Take a Practice Test 722

15   Active Directory Certificate Services and Public Key Infrastructures. . 723

Before You Begin 727

Lesson 1: Understanding and Installing Active Directory Certificate Services. . . . 730

    Understanding AD CS 731

    Installing AD CS 740

    Installing a CA Hierarchy. 742

    Lesson Summary. 750

    Lesson Review 751

Lesson 2: Configuring and Using Active Directory Certificate Services 753

    Finalizing the Configuration of an Issuing CA. 753

    Finalizing the Configuration of an Online Responder 759

    Considerations for the Use and Management of AD CS 763

    Working with Enterprise PKI. 765

    Protecting Your AD CS Configuration. 766

    Configuring and Using AD CS 767

    Lesson Summary. 773

    Lesson Review. 774

Chapter Review. 776

Key Terms 777

Case Scenario 777

    Case Scenario: Manage Certificate Revocation. 777

Suggested Practices. 778

    Working with AD CS 778

Take a Practice Test 779

16   Active Directory Rights Management Services 781

Before You Begin 784

Lesson 1: Understanding and Installing Active Directory Rights
Management Services 786

Understanding AD RMS. 786

Installing Active Directory Rights Management Services. 794

Installing AD RMS. 802

Lesson Summary. 807

Lesson Review 808

Lesson 2: Configuring and Using Active Directory Rights Management Services. 809

Configuring AD RMS 810

Creating a Rights Policy Template 819

Lesson Summary. 820

Lesson Review 821

Chapter Review. 822

Key Terms. 823

Case Scenario 823

Case Scenario: Prepare to Work with an External AD RMS Cluster 823

Suggested Practices 823

Work with AD RMS. 824

Take a Practice Test. 824

17   Active Directory Federation Services. 825

The Purpose of a Firewall 826

Active Directory Federation Services. 827

Before You Begin 829

Lesson 1: Understanding Active Directory Federation Services. 832

The AD FS Authentication Process. 833

Working with AD FS Designs. 836

Understanding AD FS Components. 838

Installing Active Directory Federation Services 845

Prepare an AD FS Deployment. 849

Lesson Summary. 852

Lesson Review. 853

Lesson 2: Configuring and Using Active Directory Federation Services. 854

Finalize the Configuration of AD FS 854

Using and Managing AD FS 855

Finalizing the AD FS Configuration. 857

Lesson Summary. 869

Lesson Review. 870

Chapter Review. 871

Key Terms 872

Case Scenario 872

Case Scenario: Choose the Right AD Technology 872

Suggested Practices. 873

Prepare for AD FS. 873

Take a Practice Test 873

Answers. 875

Index 921

What do you think of this book? We want to hear from you!

Microsoft is interested in hearing your feedback so we can continually improve our books and learning resources for you. To participate in a brief online survey, please visit:

www.microsoft.com/learning/booksurvey/

Heartfelt Thanks

Nelson, Danielle, Tony, and I would like to pay tribute to the incredible folks at Microsoft Press for giving us the opportunity to contribute to the Windows Server 2008 training and certification effort. Starting with Laura Sackerman and Ken Jones: you pulled us together in 2007 and created a framework that was both comfortable and effective, bringing out the best in us as authors and resulting in what we believe is a tremendous resource for the Windows IT professional community. Thanks for giving us the chance to write about a technology we love! Maureen Zimmerman, your tireless attention to detail and nurturing of the process brought us, and this training kit, across a finish line that at times seemed elusive. I know I owe you special thanks for your faith in me and your support and "props" along the way. Bob Hogan, you kept us honest and contributed great ideas to the cause. Kerin Forsyth, you make us sound better than we really are. Bob Dean, we all are grateful that with your efforts, the practice test questions for this training kit are first class. And Chris Norton, without you, there wouldn't be a page to look at, let alone hundreds of pages of valuable training and reference. Thanks to all of you, from all of us!

Finally, my own deepest gratitude goes to my Einstein, and we all thank our families, our friends, and our muses who make it possible and worthwhile.

Introduction

This training kit is designed for IT professionals who support or plan to support Microsoft Windows Server 2008 Active Directory Domain Services (AD DS) and who also plan to take the Microsoft Certified Technology Specialist (MCTS) 70-640 examination. It is assumed that, before you begin using this kit, you have a solid foundation-level understanding of Microsoft Windows client and server operating systems and common Internet technologies. The MCTS exam, and this book, assume that you have at least one year of experience administering AD DS.

The material covered in this training kit and on the 70-640 exam builds on your understanding and experience to help you implement AD DS in distributed environments that can include complex network services and multiple locations and domain controllers. By using this training kit, you will learn how to do the following:

- Deploy Active Directory Domain Services, Active Directory Lightweight Directory Services, Active Directory Certificate Services, Active Directory Federation Services, and Active Directory Rights Management Services in a forest or domain.
- Upgrade existing domain controllers, domains, and forests to Windows Server 2008.
- Efficiently administer and automate the administration of users, groups, and computers.
- Manage the configuration and security of a domain by using Group Policy, fine-grained password policies, directory services auditing, and the Security Configuration Wizard.
- Implement effective name resolution with Domain Name System (DNS) on Windows Server 2008.
- Plan, configure, and support the replication of Active Directory data within and between sites.
- Add, remove, maintain, and back up domain controllers.
- Enable authentication between domains and forests.
- Implement new capabilities and functionality offered by Windows Server 2008.

Find additional content online   As new or updated material that complements your book becomes available, it will be posted on the Microsoft Press Online Windows Server and Client Web site. Based on the final build of Windows Server 2008, the type of material you might find includes updates to book content, articles, links to companion content, errata, sample chapters, and more. This Web site will be available soon at *http://www.microsoft.com/learning/books/online/serverclient* and will be updated periodically.

Making the Most of the Training Kit

This training kit will prepare you for the 70-640 MCTS exam, which covers a large number of concepts and skills related to the implementation and administration of AD DS on Windows Server 2008. To provide you with the best possible learning experience, each lesson in the training kit includes content, practices, and review questions, and each chapter adds case scenario exercises and suggested practices. The companion CD provides links to external resources and dozens of sample questions.

We recommend that you take advantage of each of these components in the training kit. Some concepts or skills are easiest to learn within the context of a practice or sample questions, so these concepts and skills might be introduced in the practices or sample questions and not in the main body of the lesson. Don't make the mistake of reading the lessons and not performing the practices or of performing practices and taking sample exams without reading the lessons. Even if you do not have an environment with which to perform practices, at least read and think through the steps so that you gain the benefit of the new ideas they introduce.

Setup and Hardware Requirements

Practice exercises are a valuable component of this training kit. They enable you to experience important skills directly, reinforce material discussed in lessons, and even introduce new concepts. Each lesson and practice describes the requirements for exercises. Although many lessons require only one computer, configured as a domain controller for a sample domain named *contoso.com*, some lessons require additional computers acting as a second domain controller in the domain, as a domain controller in another domain in the same forest, as a domain controller in another forest, or as a server performing other roles.

The chapters that cover AD DS (chapters 1–13) require, at most, three machines running simultaneously. Chapters covering other Active Directory roles require up to seven machines running simultaneously to provide a comprehensive experience with the technology.

It is highly recommended that you use virtual machines rather than physical computers to work through the lessons and practices. Doing so will reduce the time and expense of configuring physical computers. You can use Virtual PC 2007 or later or Virtual Server 2005 R2 or later, which you can download for free at *http://www.microsoft.com/downloads*. You can use other virtualization software instead, such as VMware Workstation or VMware Server, which can be downloaded at *http://www.vmware.com*. Refer to the documentation of your selected virtualization software for guidance regarding the creation of virtual machines for Windows Server 2008.

Windows Server 2008 can run comfortably with 512 megabytes (MB) of memory in small environments such as the sample *contoso.com* domain. As you provision virtual machines, be sure to give each machine at least 512 MB of RAM. It is recommended that the physical host running the virtual machines have sufficient physical RAM for the host operating system and each of the concurrently running virtual machines. If you encounter performance bottlenecks while running multiple virtual machines on a single physical host, consider running virtual machines on different physical hosts. Ensure that all virtual machines can network with each other. It is highly recommended that the environment be totally disconnected from your production environment.

The authors recommend that you preserve each of the virtual machines you create until you have completed the training kit. After each chapter, create a backup or snapshot of the virtual machines used in that chapter so that you can reuse them as required in later exercises.

Software Requirements and Setup

You must have a copy of Windows Server 2008 to perform the exercises in this training kit. Several exercises require Windows Server 2003, and some optional exercises require Windows Vista.

Evaluation versions of Windows Server 2008 can be downloaded from *http://www.microsoft.com /downloads*. To perform the exercises in this training kit, you can install either the Standard or Enterprise editions, and you can use either 32-bit or 64-bit versions, according to the hardware or virtualization platform you have selected. Chapter 1, "Installation," includes setup instructions for the first domain controller in the *contoso.com* domain, which is used throughout this training kit. Lessons that require an additional computer provide guidance regarding the configuration of that computer.

Using the CD

A companion CD, included with this training kit, contains the following:

- **Practice tests** You can reinforce your understanding of how to configure Windows Server 2008 by using electronic practice tests you customize to meet your needs from the pool of Lesson Review questions in this book. Alternatively, you can practice for the 70-640 certification exam by using tests created from a pool of 200 realistic exam questions, which give you many practice scenarios to ensure that you are prepared.
- **An eBook** An electronic version (eBook) of this book is included for when you do not want to carry the printed book with you. The eBook is in Portable Document Format (PDF), and you can view it by using Adobe Acrobat or Adobe Reader.
- **Sample chapters** Sample chapters from other Microsoft Press titles on Windows Server 2008 are offered on the CD. These chapters are in PDF.

> **Digital Content for Digital Book Readers:** If you bought a digital-only edition of this book, you can enjoy select content from the print edition's companion CD. Visit **http://go.microsoft.com/fwlink/?LinkId=114977** to get your downloadable content. This content is always up-to-date and available to all readers.

How to Install the Practice Tests

To install the practice test software from the companion CD to your hard disk, do the following:

1. Insert the companion CD into your CD drive and accept the license agreement. A CD menu appears.

   NOTE If the CD menu does not appear

   If the CD menu or the license agreement does not appear, AutoRun might be disabled on your computer. Refer to the Readme.txt file on the CD-ROM for alternate installation instructions.

2. Click Practice Tests and follow the instructions on the screen.

How to Use the Practice Tests

To start the practice test software, follow these steps.

1. Click Start\All Programs\Microsoft Press Training Kit Exam Prep.

   A window appears that shows all the Microsoft Press training kit exam prep suites installed on your computer.

2. Double-click the lesson review or practice test you want to use.

   NOTE Lesson reviews vs. practice tests

   Select the (70-640) TS: Configuring Windows Server 2008 Active Directory *lesson review* to use the questions from the "Lesson Review" sections of this book. Select the (70-640) TS: Configuring Windows Server 2008 Active Directory *practice test* to use a pool of 200 questions similar to those that appear on the 70-640 certification exam.

Lesson Review Options

When you start a lesson review, the Custom Mode dialog box appears so that you can configure your test. You can click OK to accept the defaults, or you can customize the number of questions you want, how the practice test software works, which exam objectives you want the questions to relate to, and whether you want your lesson review to be timed. If you are retaking a test, you can select whether you want to see all the questions again or only the questions you missed or did not answer.

After you click OK, your lesson review starts.

- To take the test, answer the questions and use the Next and Previous buttons to move from question to question.
- After you answer an individual question, if you want to see which answers are correct—along with an explanation of each correct answer—click Explanation.
- If you prefer to wait until the end of the test to see how you did, answer all the questions and then click Score Test. You will see a summary of the exam objectives you chose and the percentage of questions you got right overall and per objective. You can print a copy of your test, review your answers, or retake the test.

Practice Test Options

When you start a practice test, you choose whether to take the test in Certification Mode, Study Mode, or Custom Mode.

- **Certification Mode** Closely resembles the experience of taking a certification exam. The test has a set number of questions. It is timed, and you cannot pause and restart the timer.
- **Study Mode** Creates an untimed test in which you can review the correct answers and the explanations after you answer each question.
- **Custom Mode** Gives you full control over the test options so that you can customize them as you like.

In all modes, the user interface when you are taking the test is basically the same but with different options enabled or disabled, depending on the mode. The main options are discussed in the previous section, "Lesson Review Options."

When you review your answer to an individual practice test question, a "References" section is provided that lists where in the training kit you can find the information that relates to that question and provides links to other sources of information. After you click Test Results to score your entire practice test, you can click the Learning Plan tab to see a list of references for every objective.

How to Uninstall the Practice Tests

To uninstall the practice test software for a training kit, use the Add Or Remove Programs option (Windows XP) or the Programs And Features option (Windows Vista) in Windows Control Panel.

Microsoft Certified Professional Program

The Microsoft certifications provide the best method to prove your command of current Microsoft products and technologies. The exams and corresponding certifications are developed to validate your mastery of critical competencies as you design and develop or implement and support solutions with Microsoft products and technologies. Computer professionals who become Microsoft certified are recognized as experts and are sought after industry-wide. Certification brings a variety of benefits to the individual and to employers and organizations.

MORE INFO All the Microsoft certifications

For a full list of Microsoft certifications, go to *http://www.microsoft.com/learning/mcp/default.asp*.

Technical Support

Every effort has been made to ensure the accuracy of this book and the contents of the companion CD. If you have comments, questions, or ideas regarding this book or the companion CD, please send them to Microsoft Press by using either of the following methods:

- E-mail: tkinput@microsoft.com
- Postal mail at:

  Microsoft Press
  Attn: *MCTS Self-Paced Training Kit (Exam 70-640): Configuring Windows Server 2008 Active Directory*, Editor
  One Microsoft Way
  Redmond, WA 98052-6399

For additional support information regarding this book and the CD-ROM (including answers to commonly asked questions about installation and use), visit the Microsoft Press Book and CD Support Web site at *http://www.microsoft.com/learning/support/books*. To connect directly to Microsoft Knowledge Base and enter a query, visit *http://support.microsoft.com/search*. For support information regarding Microsoft software, connect to *http://support.microsoft.com*.

Chapter 1
Installation

Active Directory Domain Services (AD DS) and its related services form the foundation for enterprise networks running Microsoft Windows as, together, they act as tools to store information about the identities of users, computers, and services; to authenticate a user or computer; and to provide a mechanism with which the user or computer can access resources in the enterprise. In this chapter, you will begin your exploration of Windows Server 2008 Active Directory by installing the Active Directory Domain Services role and creating a domain controller in a new Active Directory forest. You will find that Windows Server 2008 continues the evolution of Active Directory by enhancing many of the concepts and features with which you are familiar from your experience with Active Directory.

This chapter focuses on the creation of a new Active Directory forest with a single domain in a single domain controller. The practice exercises in this chapter will guide you through the creation of a domain named *contoso.com* that you will use for all other practices in this training kit. Later, in Chapter 8, "Authentication," Chapter 10, "Domain Controllers," and Chapter 12, "Domains and Forests," you will learn to implement other scenarios, including multidomain forests, upgrades of existing forests to Windows Server 2008, and advanced installation options. In Chapter 14, "Active Directory Lightweight Directory Services," Chapter 15, "Active Directory Certificate Services and Public Key Infrastructures," Chapter 16, "Active Directory Rights Management Services," and Chapter 17, "Active Directory Federation Services," you will learn the details of other Active Directory services such as Active Directory Lightweight Directory Services, Active Directory Certificate Services and public key infrastructure, Active Directory Rights Management Service, and Active Directory Federated Services.

Exam objectives in this chapter:
- Configuring the Active Directory Infrastructure
  - ❑ Configure a forest or a domain.

Lessons in this chapter:
- Lesson 1: Installing Active Directory Domain Services 3
- Lesson 2: Active Directory Domain Services on Server Core 23

Before You Begin

To complete the lessons in this chapter, you must have done the following:

■ Obtained two computers on which you will install Windows Server 2008. The computers can be physical systems that meet the minimum hardware requirements for Windows Server 2008 found at *http://technet.microsoft.com/en-us/windowsserver/2008/bb414778.aspx*. You will need at least 512 MB of RAM, 10 GB of free hard disk space, and an x86 processor with a minimum clock speed of 1GHz or an x64 processor with a minimum clock speed of 1.4 GHz. Alternatively, you can use virtual machines that meet the same requirements.

■ Obtained an evaluation version of Windows Server 2008. At the time of writing, links to evaluation versions are available on the Windows Server 2008 Home Page at *http://www.microsoft.com/windowsserver2008*.

Real World

Dan Holme

Domain controllers perform identity and access management functions that are critical to the integrity and security of a Windows enterprise. Therefore, most organizations choose to dedicate the role of domain controller, meaning that a domain controller does not provide other functions such as file and print servers. In previous versions of Windows, however, when you promote a server to a domain controller, other services continue to be available whether or not they are in use. These additional unnecessary services increase the need to apply patches and security updates and expose the domain controller to additional susceptibility to attack. Windows Server 2008 addresses these concerns through its role-based architecture, so that a server begins its life as a fairly lean installation of Windows to which roles and their associated services and features are added. Additionally, the new Server Core installation of Windows Server 2008 provides a minimal installation of Windows that even forgoes a graphical user interface (GUI) in favor of a command prompt. In this chapter, you will gain firsthand experience with these important characteristics of Windows Server 2008 domain controllers. These changes to the architecture and feature set of Windows Server 2008 domain controllers will help you and other enterprises further improve the security, stability, and manageability of your identity and access management infrastructure.

Lesson 1: Installing Active Directory Domain Services

Active Directory Domain Services (AD DS) provides the functionality of an identity and access (IDA) solution for enterprise networks. In this lesson, you will learn about AD DS and other Active Directory roles supported by Windows Server 2008. You will also explore Server Manager, the tool with which you can configure server roles, and the improved Active Directory Domain Services Installation Wizard. This lesson also reviews key concepts of IDA and Active Directory.

After this lesson, you will be able to:
- Explain the role of identity and access in an enterprise network.
- Understand the relationship between Active Directory services.
- Configure a domain controller with the Active Directory Domain Services (AD DS) role, using the Windows interface.

Estimated lesson time: 60 minutes

Active Directory, Identity and Access

As mentioned in the introductions to the chapter and this lesson, Active Directory provides the IDA solution for enterprise networks running Windows. IDA is necessary to maintain the security of enterprise resources such as files, e-mail, applications, and databases. An IDA infrastructure should do the following:

- **Store information about users, groups, computers, and other identities**   An identity is, in the broadest sense, a representation of an entity that will perform actions on the enterprise network. For example, a user will open documents from a shared folder on a server. The document will be secured with permissions on an access control list (ACL). Access to the document is managed by the security subsystem of the server, which compares the identity of the user to the identities on the ACL to determine whether the user's request for access will be granted or denied. Computers, groups, services, and other objects also perform actions on the network, and they must be represented by identities. Among the information stored about an identity are properties that uniquely identify the object, such as a user name or a security identifier (SID), and the password for the identity. The *identity store* is, therefore, one component of an IDA infrastructure. The Active Directory data store, also known as the directory, is an identity store. The directory itself is hosted on and managed by a domain controller—a server performing the AD DS role.

- **Authenticate an identity**   The server will not grant the user access to the document unless the server can verify the identity presented in the access request as valid. To validate the identity, the user provides secrets known only to the user and the IDA infrastructure. Those secrets are compared to the information in the identity store in a process called *authentication*.

Kerberos Authentication in an Active Directory Domain

In an Active Directory domain, a protocol called Kerberos is used to authenticate identities. When a user or computer logs on to the domain, Kerberos authenticates its credentials and issues a package of information called a ticket granting ticket (TGT). Before the user connects to the server to request the document, a Kerberos request is sent to a domain controller along with the TGT that identifies the authenticated user. The domain controller issues the user another package of information called a service ticket that identifies the authenticated user to the server. The user presents the service ticket to the server, which accepts the service ticket as proof that the user has been authenticated.

These Kerberos transactions result in a single network logon. After the user or computer has initially logged on and has been granted a TGT, the user is authenticated within the entire domain and can be granted service tickets that identify the user to any service. All of this ticket activity is managed by the Kerberos clients and services built into Windows and is transparent to the user.

- **Control access**   The IDA infrastructure is responsible for protecting confidential information such as the information stored in the document. Access to confidential information must be managed according to the policies of the enterprise. The ACL on the document reflects a security policy composed of permissions that specify access levels for particular identities. The security subsystem of the server in this example is performing the access control functionality in the IDA infrastructure.
- **Provide an audit trail**   An enterprise might want to monitor changes to and activities within the IDA infrastructure, so it must provide a mechanism by which to manage auditing.

AD DS is not the only component of IDA that is supported by Windows Server 2008. With the release of Windows Server 2008, Microsoft has consolidated a number of previously separate components into an integrated IDA platform. Active Directory itself now includes five technologies, each of which can be identified with a keyword that identifies the purpose of the technology, as shown in Figure 1-1.

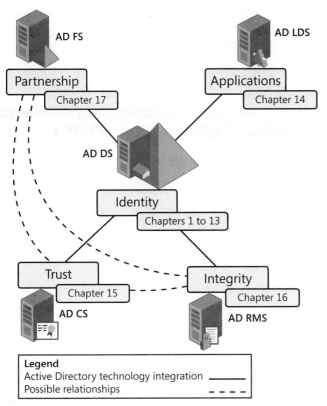

Figure 1-1   The integration of the five Active Directory technologies

These five technologies comprise a complete IDA solution:

■ **Active Directory Domain Services (Identity)**   AD DS, as described earlier, is designed to provide a central repository for identity management within an organization. AD DS provides authentication and authorization services in a network and supports object management through Group Policy. AD DS also provides information management and sharing services, enabling users to find any component—file servers, printers, groups, and other users—by searching the directory. Because of this, AD DS is often referred to as a network operating system directory service. AD DS is the primary Active Directory technology and should be deployed in every network that runs Windows Server 2008 operating systems. AD DS is covered in chapters 1 through 13.

For a guide outlining best practices for the design of Active Directory, download the free "Chapter 3: Designing the Active Directory" from *Windows Server 2003, Best Practices for Enterprise Deployments* at *http://www.reso-net.com/Documents/007222343X_Ch03.pdf*.

MORE INFO   AD DS design

For updated information on creating an Active Directory Domain Services design, look up *Windows Server 2008: The Complete Reference*, by Ruest and Ruest (McGraw-Hill Osborne, in press).

- **Active Directory Lightweight Directory Services (Applications)**   Essentially a standalone version of Active Directory, the Active Directory Lightweight Directory Services (AD LDS) role, formerly known as Active Directory Application Mode (ADAM), provides support for directory-enabled applications. AD LDS is really a subset of AD DS because both are based on the same core code. The AD LDS directory stores and replicates only application-related information. It is commonly used by applications that require a directory store but do not require the information to be replicated as widely as to all domain controllers. AD LDS also enables you to deploy a custom schema to support an application without modifying the schema of AD DS. The AD LDS role is truly lightweight and supports multiple data stores on a single system, so each application can be deployed with its own directory, schema, assigned Lightweight Directory Access Protocol (LDAP) and SSL ports, and application event log. AD LDS does not rely on AD DS, so it can be used in a standalone or workgroup environment. However, in domain environments, AD LDS can use AD DS for the authentication of Windows security principals (users, groups, and computers). AD LDS can also be used to provide authentication services in exposed networks such as extranets. Once again, using AD LDS in this situation provides less risk than using AD DS. AD LDS is covered in Chapter 14.

- **Active Directory Certificate Services (Trust)**   Organizations can use Active Directory Certificate Services (AD CS) to set up a certificate authority for issuing digital certificates as part of a public key infrastructure (PKI) that binds the identity of a person, device, or service to a corresponding private key. Certificates can be used to authenticate users and computers, provide Web-based authentication, support smart card authentication, and support applications, including secure wireless networks, virtual private networks (VPNs), Internet Protocol security (IPSec), Encrypting File System (EFS), digital signatures, and more. AD CS provides an efficient and secure way to issue and manage certificates. You can use AD CS to provide these services to external communities. If you do so, AD CS should be linked with an external, renowned CA that will prove to others you are who you say you are. AD CS is designed to create trust in an untrustworthy world; as such, it must rely on proven processes that certify that each person or computer that obtains a certificate has been thoroughly verified and approved. In internal networks, AD CS can integrate with AD DS to provision users and computers automatically with certificates. AD CS is covered in Chapter 15.

  For more information on PKI infrastructures and how to apply them in your organization, visit *http://www.reso-net.com/articles.asp?m=8* and look for the "Advanced Public Key Infrastructures" section.

- **Active Directory Rights Management Services (Integrity)** Although a server running Windows can prevent or allow access to a document based on the document's ACL, there have been few ways to control what happens to the document and its content after a user has opened it. Active Directory Rights Management Services (AD RMS) is an information-protection technology that enables you to implement persistent usage policy templates that define allowed and unauthorized use whether online, offline, inside, or outside the firewall. For example, you could configure a template that allows users to read a document but not to print or copy its contents. By doing so, you can ensure the integrity of the data you generate, protect intellectual property, and control who can do what with the documents your organization produces. AD RMS requires an Active Directory domain with domain controllers running Windows 2000 Server with Service Pack 3 (SP3) or later; IIS; a database server such as Microsoft SQL Server 2008; the AD RMS client that can be downloaded from the Microsoft Download Center and is included by default in Windows Vista and Windows Server 2008; and an RMS-enabled browser or application such as Microsoft Internet Explorer, Microsoft Office, Microsoft Word, Microsoft Outlook, or Microsoft PowerPoint. AD RMS can rely on AD CS to embed certificates within documents as well as in AD DS to manage access rights. AD RMS is covered in Chapter 16.

- **Active Directory Federation Services (Partnership)** Active Directory Federation Services (AD FS) enables an organization to extend IDA across multiple platforms, including both Windows and non-Windows environments, and to project identity and access rights across security boundaries to trusted partners. In a federated environment, each organization maintains and manages its own identities, but each organization can also securely project and accept identities from other organizations. Users are authenticated in one network but can access resources in another—a process known as single sign-on (SSO). AD FS supports partnerships because it allows different organizations to share access to extranet applications while relying on their own internal AD DS structures to provide the actual authentication process. To do so, AD FS extends your internal AD DS structure to the external world through common Transmission Control Protocol/Internet Protocol (TCP/IP) ports such as 80 (HTTP) and 443 (Secure HTTP, or HTTPS). It normally resides in the perimeter network. AD FS can rely on AD CS to create trusted servers and on AD RMS to provide external protection for intellectual property. AD FS is covered in Chapter 17.

Together, the Active Directory roles provide an integrated IDA solution. AD DS or AD LDS provides foundational directory services in both domain and standalone implementations. AD CS provides trusted credentials in the form of PKI digital certificates. AD RMS protects the integrity of information contained in documents. And AD FS supports partnerships by eliminating the need for federated environments to create multiple, separate identities for a single security principal.

Beyond Identity and Access

Active Directory delivers more than just an IDA solution, however. It also provides the mechanisms to support, manage, and configure resources in distributed network environments.

A set of rules, the *schema*, defines the classes of objects and attributes that can be contained in the directory. The fact that Active Directory has user objects that include a user name and password, for example, is because the schema defines the *user* object class, the two attributes, and the association between the object class and attributes.

Policy-based administration eases the management burden of even the largest, most complex networks by providing a single point at which to configure settings that are then deployed to multiple systems. You will learn about such policies, including Group Policy, audit policies, and fine-grained password policies in Chapter 6, "Group Policy Infrastructure," Chapter 7, "Group Policy Settings," and Chapter 8.

Replication services distribute directory data across a network. This includes both the data store itself as well as data required to implement policies and configuration, including logon scripts. In Chapter 8, Chapter 11, "Sites and Replication," and Chapter 10, you will learn about Active Directory replication. There is even a separate partition of the data store named *configuration* that maintains information about network configuration, topology, and services.

Several components and technologies enable you to query Active Directory and locate objects in the data store. A partition of the data store called the *global catalog* (also known as the *partial attribute set*) contains information about every object in the directory. It is a type of index that can be used to locate objects in the directory. Programmatic interfaces such as Active Directory Services Interface (ADSI) and protocols such as LDAP can be used to read and manipulate the data store.

The Active Directory data store can also be used to support applications and services not directly related to AD DS. Within the database, application partitions can store data to support applications that require replicated data. The domain name system (DNS) service on a server running Windows Server 2008 can store its information in a database called an Active Directory integrated zone, which is maintained as an application partition in AD DS and replicated using Active Directory replication services.

Components of an Active Directory Infrastructure

The first 13 chapters of this training kit will focus on the installation, configuration, and management of AD DS. AD DS provides the foundation for IDA in and management of an enterprise network. It is worthwhile to spend a few moments reviewing the components of an Active Directory infrastructure.

NOTE **Where to find Active Directory details**

For more details about Active Directory, refer to the product help installed with Windows Server 2008 and to the TechCenter for Windows Server 2008 located at *http://technet.microsoft.com/en-us /windowsserver/2008/default.aspx.*

- **Active Directory data store** As mentioned in the previous section, AD DS stores its identities in the directory—a data store hosted on domain controllers. The directory is a single file named Ntds.dit and is located by default in the %SystemRoot%\Ntds folder on a domain controller. The database is divided into several partitions, including the schema, configuration, global catalog, and the domain naming context that contains the data about objects within a domain—the users, groups, and computers, for example.

- **Domain controllers** Domain controllers, also referred to as DCs, are servers that perform the AD DS role. As part of that role, they also run the Kerberos Key Distribution Center (KDC) service, which performs authentication, and other Active Directory services. Chapter 10 details the roles performed by DCs.

- **Domain** One or more domain controllers are required to create an Active Directory *domain.* A domain is an administrative unit within which certain capabilities and characteristics are shared. First, all domain controllers replicate the domain's partition of the data store, which contains among other things the identity data for the domain's users, groups, and computers. Because all DCs maintain the same identity store, any DC can authenticate any identity in a domain. Additionally, a domain is a scope of administrative policies such as password complexity and account lockout policies. Such policies configured in one domain affect all accounts in the domain and do not affect accounts in other domains. Changes can be made to objects in the Active Directory database by any domain controller and will replicate to all other domain controllers. Therefore, in networks where replication of all data between domain controllers cannot be supported, it might be necessary to implement more than one domain to manage the replication of subsets of identities. You will learn more about domains in Chapter 12.

- **Forest** A *forest* is a collection of one or more Active Directory domains. The first domain installed in a forest is called the *forest root domain.* A forest contains a single definition of network configuration and a single instance of the directory schema. A forest is a single instance of the directory—no data is replicated by Active Directory outside the boundaries of the forest. Therefore, the forest defines a security boundary. Chapter 12 will explore the concept of the forest further.

- **Tree** The DNS namespace of domains in a forest creates trees within the forest. If a domain is a subdomain of another domain, the two domains are considered a tree. For example, if the *treyresearch.net* forest contains two domains, *treyresearch.net* and *antarctica.treyresearch.net,* those domains constitute a contiguous portion of the DNS namespace, so they are a single tree. If, conversely, the two domains are *treyresearch.net* and *proseware.com*, which are not contiguous in the DNS namespace, the domain is considered to have two trees. Trees are the direct result of the DNS names chosen for domains in the forest.

Figure 1-2 illustrates an Active Directory forest for Trey Research, which maintains a small operation at a field station in Antarctica. Because the link from Antarctica to the headquarters is expensive, slow, and unreliable, Antarctica is configured as a separate domain. The DNS name of the forest is *treyresearch.net*. The Antarctica domain is a child domain in the DNS namespace, *antarctica.treyresearch.net*, so it is considered a child domain in the domain tree.

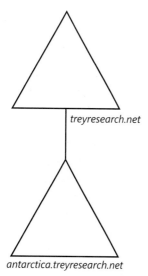

treyresearch.net

antarctica.treyresearch.net

Figure 1-2   An Active Directory forest with two domains

■ **Functional level**   The functionality available in an Active Directory domain or forest depends on its *functional level*. The functional level is an AD DS setting that enables advanced domain-wide or forest-wide AD DS features. There are three domain functional levels, Windows 2000 native, Windows Server 2003, and Windows Server 2008 and two forest functional levels, Microsoft Windows Server 2003 and Windows Server 2008. As you raise the functional level of a domain or forest, features provided by that version of Windows become available to AD DS. For example, when the domain functional level is raised to Windows Server 2008, a new attribute becomes available that reveals the last time a user successfully logged on to a computer, the computer to which the user last logged on, and the number of failed logon attempts since the last logon. The important thing to know about functional levels is that they determine the versions of Windows permitted on domain controllers. Before you raise the domain functional level to Windows Server 2008, all domain controllers must be running Windows Server 2008. Chapter 12, details domain and forest functional levels.

■ **Organizational units**   Active Directory is a hierarchical database. Objects in the data store can be collected in containers. One type of container is the object class called *container*. You have seen the default containers, including Users, Computers, and Builtin, when you open the Active Directory Users and Computers snap-in. Another type of container is the organizational unit (OU). OUs provide not only a container for objects but also a scope with which to manage the objects. That is because OUs can have objects called Group Policy objects (GPOs) linked to them. GPOs can contain configuration settings that will then be applied automatically by users or computers in an OU. In Chapter 2, "Administration," you will learn more about OUs, and in Chapter 6, you will explore GPOs.

■ **Sites**   When you consider the network topology of a distributed enterprise, you will certainly discuss the network's sites. Sites in Active Directory, however, have a very specific meaning because there is a specific object class called *site*. An Active Directory site is an object that represents a portion of the enterprise within which network connectivity is good. A site creates a boundary of replication and service usage. Domain controllers within a site replicate changes within seconds. Changes are replicated between sites on a controlled basis with the assumption that intersite connections are slow, expensive, or unreliable compared to the connections within a site. Additionally, clients will prefer to use distributed services provided by servers in their site or in the closest site. For example, when a user logs on to the domain, the Windows client first attempts to authenticate with a domain controller in its site. Only if no domain controller is available in the site will the client attempt to authenticate with a DC in another site. Chapter 11 details the configuration and functionality of Active Directory sites.

Each of these components is discussed in detail later in this training kit. At this point, if you are less familiar with Active Directory, it is important only that you have a basic understanding of the terminology, the components, and their relationships.

Preparing to Create a New Windows Server 2008 Forest

Before you install the AD DS role on a server and promote it to act as a domain controller, plan your Active Directory infrastructure. Some of the information you will need to create a domain controller includes the following:

■ The domain's name and DNS name. A domain must have a unique DNS name, for example, *contoso.com*, as well as a short name, for example, CONTOSO, called a NetBIOS name. NetBIOS is a network protocol that has been used since the first versions of Microsoft Windows NT and is still used by some applications.

■ Whether the domain will need to support domain controllers running previous versions of Windows. When you create a new Active Directory forest, you will configure the functional level. If the domain will include only Windows Server 2008 domain controllers, you can set the functional level accordingly to benefit from the enhanced features introduced by this version of Windows.

■ Details for how DNS will be implemented to support Active Directory. It is a best practice to implement DNS for your Windows domain zones by using Windows DNS Service, as you will learn in Chapter 9, "Integrating Domain Name System with AD DS"; however, it is possible to support a Windows domain on a third-party DNS service.

■ IP configuration for the domain controller. Domain controllers require static IP addresses and subnet mask values. Additionally, the domain controller must be configured with a DNS server address to perform name resolution. If you are creating a new forest and will run Windows DNS Service on the domain controller, you can configure the DNS address to point to the server's own IP address. After DNS is installed, the server can look to itself to resolve DNS names.

■ The user name and password of an account in the server's Administrators group. The account must have a password—the password cannot be blank.

■ The location in which the data store (including *Ntds.dit*) and system volume (SYSVOL) should be installed. By default, these stores are created in %SystemRoot%, for example, C:\Windows, in the NTDS and SYSVOL folders, respectively. When creating a domain controller, you can redirect these stores to other drives.

MORE INFO   Deployment of AD DS

This list comprises the settings that you will be prompted to configure when creating a domain controller. There are a number of additional considerations regarding the deployment of AD DS in an enterprise setting. See the Windows Server 2008 Technical Library at *http://technet2.microsoft.com/windowsserver2008/en/library/bab0f1a1-54aa-4cef-9164-139e8bcc44751033.mspx* for more information.

Adding the AD DS Role Using the Windows Interface

After you have collected the prerequisite information listed earlier, you are ready to add the AD DS role. There are several ways to do so. In this lesson, you will learn how to create a domain controller by using the Windows interface. In the next lesson, you will learn to do so using the command line.

Windows Server 2008 provides role-based configuration, installing only the components and services required for the roles a server plays. This role-based server management is reflected in the new administrative console, Server Manager, shown in Figure 1-3. Server Manager consolidates the information, tools, and resources needed to support a server's roles.

You can add roles to a server by using the Add Roles link on the home page of Server Manager or by right-clicking the Roles node in the console tree and choosing Add Roles. The Add Roles Wizard presents a list of roles available for installation and steps you through the installation of selected roles.

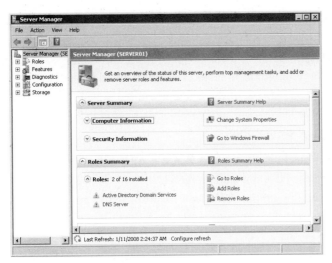

Figure 1-3   Server Manager

Practice It   Exercise 3, "Install a New Windows Server 2008 Forest with the Windows Interface," at the end of this lesson guides you through adding the AD DS role, using the Windows interface.

Creating a Domain Controller

After you add the AD DS role, the files required to perform the role are installed on the server; however, the server is not yet acting as a domain controller. You must subsequently run the Active Directory Domain Services Installation Wizard, which can be launched using the *Dcpromo.exe* command, to configure, initialize, and start Active Directory.

Practice It   Exercise 4, "Install a New Windows Server 2008 Forest," at the end of this lesson guides you through configuration of AD DS, using the Active Directory Domain Services Installation Wizard.

> **Quick Check**
> - You want to use a new server running Windows Server 2008 as a domain controller in your Active Directory domain. Which command do you use to launch configuration of the domain controller?
>
> **Quick Check Answer**
> - *Dcpromo.exe*

PRACTICE # Creating a Windows Server 2008 Forest

In this practice, you will create the AD DS forest for Contoso, Ltd. This forest will be used for exercises throughout this training kit. You will begin by installing Windows Server 2008 and performing post-installation configuration tasks. You will then add the AD DS role and promote the server to a domain controller in the *contoso.com* forest, using the Active Directory Domain Services Installation Wizard.

▶ **Exercise 1   Install Windows Server 2008**

In this exercise, you will install Windows Server 2008 on a computer or virtual machine.

1. Insert the Windows Server 2008 installation DVD.

    If you are using a virtual machine (VM), you might have the option to mount an ISO image of the installation DVD. Consult the VM Help documentation for guidance.

2. Power on the system.

    If the system's hard disk is empty, the system should boot to the DVD. If there is data on the disk, you might be prompted to press a key to boot to the DVD.

    If the system does not boot to the DVD or offer you a boot menu, go to the BIOS settings of the computer and configure the boot order to ensure that the system boots to the DVD.

    The Install Windows Wizard appears, shown in Figure 1-4.

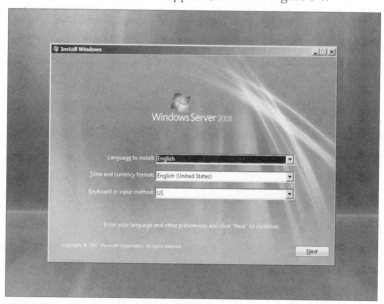

Figure 1-4   The Install Windows Wizard

3. Select the language, regional setting, and keyboard layout that are correct for your system and click Next.

4. Click Install Now.

   You are presented with a list of versions to install, as shown in Figure 1-5. If you are using an x64 computer, you will be presented with x64 versions rather than with x86 versions.

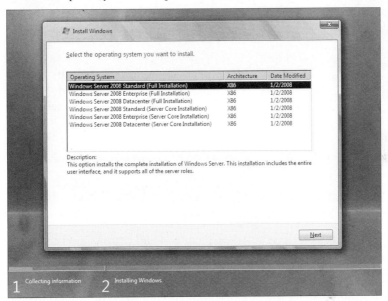

Figure 1-5   The Select The Operating System You Want To Install page

5. Select Windows Server 2008 Standard (Full Installation) and click Next.

6. Select the I Accept The License Terms check box and click Next.

7. Click Custom (Advanced).

8. On the Where Do You Want to Install Windows page, select the disk on which you want to install Windows Server 2008.

   If you need to create, delete, extend, or format partitions or if you need to load a custom mass storage driver to access the disk subsystem, click Driver Options (Advanced).

9. Click Next.

   The Installing Windows dialog box appears, shown in Figure 1-6. The window keeps you apprised of the progress of Windows installation.

   Installation of Windows Server 2008, like that of Windows Vista, is image-based. Therefore, installation is significantly faster than previous versions of Windows even though the operating systems themselves are much larger than earlier versions. The computer will reboot one or more times during installation.

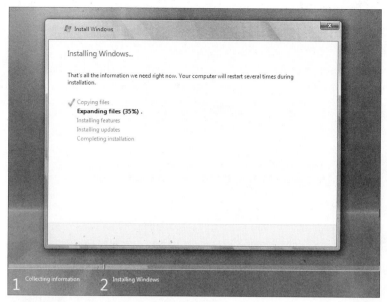

Figure 1-6   The Installing Windows page

When the installation has completed, you will be informed that the user's password must be changed before logging on the first time.

10. Click OK.

11. Type a password for the Administrator account in both the New Password and Confirm Password boxes and press Enter.

    The password must be at least seven characters long and must have at least three of four character types:

    ❑ Uppercase: A–Z

    ❑ Lowercase: a–z

    ❑ Numeric: 0–9

    ❑ Nonalphanumeric: symbols such as $, #, @, and !

NOTE   Do not forget this password

Without it, you will not be able to log on to the server to perform other exercises in this training kit.

---

12. Click OK.

    The desktop for the Administrator account appears.

▶ **Exercise 2   Perform Post-Installation Configuration**

In this exercise, you will perform post-installation configuration of the server to prepare the server with the name and TCP/IP settings required for exercises in this training kit.

1. Wait for the desktop for the Administrator account to appear.

   The Initial Configuration Tasks window appears, as shown in Figure 1-7. This tool is designed to make it easy for you to perform best practice, post-installation configuration tasks.

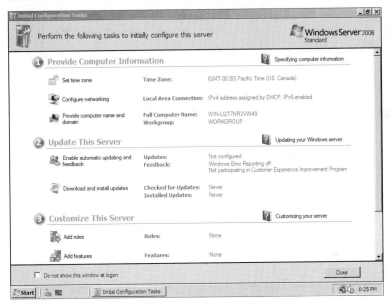

Figure 1-7   The Initial Configuration Tasks window

2. Use the Initial Configuration Tasks window to configure the following settings:
   - ❏ Time zone: as appropriate for your environment.
   - ❏ Computer name: SERVER01. Do not restart until instructed to do so later in this exercise.

3. Click the Configure Networking link in the Initial Configuration Tasks window and make sure the server's IP configuration is appropriate for your environment.

4. If the server has connection to the Internet, it is highly recommended to click the Download And Install Updates link so that you can update the server with the latest security updates from Microsoft.

5. After the server is updated, restart the server.

   The remaining exercises in this training kit will create a domain using IP addresses in the 10.0.0.11–10.0.0.20 range, with a subnet mask of 255.255.255.0. If these addresses are used in your production environment, and if the server is connected to your production

environment, you must change the IP addresses in this book accordingly so that the
contoso.com domain you create in these practices does not conflict with your production network.

6. In the Initial Configuration Tasks window, click the Configure Networking link.

    The Network Connections dialog box appears.

7. Select Local Area Connection.

8. On the toolbar, click Change Settings Of This Connection.

9. Select Internet Protocol Version 4 (TCP/IPv4) and click Properties.

    Windows Server 2008 also provides native support for Internet Protocol Version 6
    (TCP/IPv6).

10. Click Use The Following IP Address. Enter the following configuration:

    ❑   IP address: **10.0.0.11**

    ❑   Subnet mask: **255.255.255.0**

    ❑   Default gateway: **10.0.0.1**

    ❑   Preferred DNS server: **10.0.0.11**

11. Click OK, and then click Close.

12. Note the Add Roles and Add Features links in the Initial Configuration Tasks window.

    In the next exercise, you will use Server Manager to add roles and features to SERVER01.
    These links are another way to perform the same tasks.

    The Initial Configuration Tasks window will appear each time you log on to the server.

13. Select the Do Not Show This Window At Logon check box to prevent the window from
    appearing.

    If you need to open the Initial Configuration Tasks window in the future, you do so by
    running the *Oobe.exe* command.

14. Click the Close button at the bottom of the Initial Configuration Tasks window.

    Server Manager appears. Server Manager enables you to configure and administer the
    roles and features of a server running Windows Server 2008. You will use Server Manager
    in the next exercise.

NOTE   Create a snapshot of your virtual machine

If you are using a virtual machine to perform this exercise, and if the virtual machine
enables you to create point-in-time snapshots of the machine's state, create a snapshot at
this time. This baseline installation of Windows Server 2008 can be used to perform the
exercises in this chapter, which enable you to experiment with the variety of methods of
adding the AD DS role.

▶ **Exercise 3   Install a New Windows Server 2008 Forest with the Windows Interface**

In this exercise, you will add the AD DS role to the server you installed and configured in Exercise 1, "Install Windows Server 2008," and Exercise 2, "Perform Post-Installation Configuration."

1. If Server Manager is not open, open it from the Administrative Tools program group.
2. In the Roles Summary section of the home page, click Add Roles.

   The Add Roles Wizard appears.
3. Click Next.
4. On the Select Server Roles page, select the check box next to Active Directory Domain Services. Click Next.
5. On the Active Directory Domain Services page, click Next.
6. On the Confirm Installation Selections page, click Install.

   The Installation Progress page reports the status of installation tasks.
7. On the Installation Results page, confirm that the installation succeeded and click Close.

   In the Roles Summary section of the Server Manager home page, you'll notice an error message indicated by a red circle with a white x. You'll also notice a message in the Active Directory Domain Services section of the page. Both of these links will take you to the Active Directory Domain Services role page of Server Manager, shown in Figure 1-8. The message shown reminds you that it is necessary to run *Dcpromo.exe*, which you will do in the next exercise.

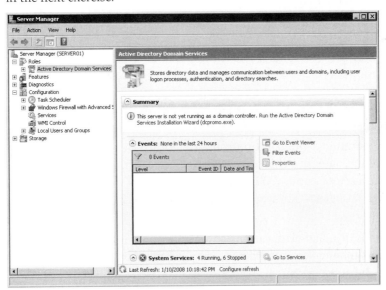

Figure 1-8   The Active Directory Domain Services roles page in Server Manager

▶ **Exercise 4   Install a New Windows Server 2008 Forest**

In this exercise, you will use the Active Directory Domain Services Installation Wizard (*Dcpromo.exe*) to create a new Windows Server 2008 forest.

1. Click Start, click Run, type **Dcpromo.exe**, and then click OK.

NOTE   *Dcpromo* will add the AD DS role if necessary

In the previous exercise, you added the AD DS role by using Server Manager. However, if you run *Dcpromo.exe* on a server that does not yet have the AD DS role installed, *Dcpromo.exe* will install the role automatically.

The Active Directory Domain Services Installation Wizard appears. In Chapter 10, you will learn about advanced modes of the wizard.

2. Click Next.

3. On the Operating System Compatibility page, review the warning about the default security settings for Windows Server 2008 domain controllers, and then click Next.

4. On the Choose a Deployment Configuration page, select Create A New Domain In A New Forest, and click Next.

5. On the Name The Forest Root Domain page, type **contoso.com**, and then click Next.

   The system performs a check to ensure that the DNS and NetBIOS names are not already in use on the network.

6. On the Set Forest Functional Level page, choose Windows Server 2008, and then click Next.

   Each of the functional levels is described in the Details box on the page. Choosing Windows Server 2008 forest functional level ensures that all domains in the forest operate at the Windows Server 2008 domain functional level, which enables several new features provided by Windows Server 2008. You will learn about functional levels in Chapter 12.

   The Additional Domain Controller Options page appears. DNS Server is selected by default. The Active Directory Domain Services Installation Wizard will create a DNS infrastructure during AD DS installation. The first domain controller in a forest must be a global catalog (GC) server and cannot be a read-only domain controller (RODC).

7. Click Next.

   A Static IP assignment warning appears. Because discussion of IPv6 is beyond the scope of this training kit, you did not assign a static IPv6 address to the server in Exercise 2. You did assign a static IPv4 address in Exercise 2, and later exercises will use IPv4. You can, therefore, ignore this warning in the context of the exercise.

8. Click Yes, The Computer Will Use A Dynamically Assigned IP Address (Not Recommended).

A warning appears that informs you that a delegation for the DNS server cannot be created. In the context of this exercise, you can ignore this error. Delegations of DNS domains will be discussed in Chapter 9.

9. Click Yes to close the Active Directory Domain Services Installation Wizard warning message.

10. On the Location For Database, Log Files, And SYSVOL page, accept the default locations for the database file, the directory service log files, and the SYSVOL files and click Next.

    The best practice in a production environment is to store these files on three separate volumes that do not contain applications or other files not related to AD DS. This best practices design improves performance and increases the efficiency of backup and restore.

11. On the Directory Services Restore Mode Administrator Password page, type a strong password in both the Password and Confirmed Password boxes. Click Next.

    Do not forget the password you assigned to the Directory Services Restore Mode Administrator.

12. On the Summary page, review your selections.

    If any settings are incorrect, click Back to make modifications.

13. Click Next.

    Configuration of AD DS begins. The server will require a reboot when the process is completed. Optionally, select the Reboot On Completion check box.

Lesson Summary

- Active Directory services comprise an integrated solution for identity and access in enterprise networks.
- Active Directory Domain Services (AD DS) provide the directory service and authentication components of IDA. Additionally, AD DS facilitates management of even large, complex, distributed networks.
- Windows Server 2008 systems are configured based on the roles they play. You can add the AD DS role by using Server Manager.
- Use *Dcpromo.exe* to configure AD DS and create a domain controller.

Lesson Review

You can use the following questions to test your knowledge of the information in Lesson 1, "Installing Active Directory Domain Services." The questions are also available on the companion CD if you prefer to review them in electronic form.

NOTE   **Answers**

Answers to these questions and explanations of why each answer choice is right or wrong are located in the "Answers" section at the end of the book.

---

1. Which of the following are required to create a domain controller successfully? (Choose all that apply.)

    A. A valid DNS domain name

    B. A valid NetBIOS name

    C. A DHCP server to assign an IP address to the domain controller

    D. A DNS server

2. Trey Research has recently acquired Litware, Inc. Because of regulatory issues related to data replication, it is decided to configure a child domain in the forest for Litware users and computers. The Trey Research forest currently contains only Windows Server 2008 domain controllers. The new domain will be created by promoting a Windows Server 2008 domain controller, but you might need to use existing Windows Server 2003 systems as domain controllers in the Litware domain. Which functional levels will be appropriate to configure?

    A. Windows Server 2008 forest functional level and Windows Server 2008 domain functional level for the Litware domain

    B. Windows Server 2008 forest functional level and Windows Server 2003 domain functional level for the Litware domain

    C. Windows Server 2003 forest functional level and Windows Server 2008 domain functional level for the Litware domain

    D. Windows Server 2003 forest functional level and Windows Server 2003 domain functional level for the Litware domain

Lesson 2: Active Directory Domain Services on Server Core

Many organizations want to implement the maximum available security for servers acting as domain controllers because of the sensitive nature of information stored in the directory—particularly user passwords. Although the role-based configuration of Windows Server 2008 reduces the security surface of a server by installing only the components and services required by its roles, it is possible to reduce its servers and security surface further by installing Server Core. A Server Core installation is a minimal installation of Windows that forgoes even the Windows Explorer GUI and the Microsoft .NET Framework. You can administer a Server Core installation remotely, using GUI tools; however, to configure and manage a server locally, you must use command-line tools. In this lesson, you will learn to create a domain controller from the command line within a Server Core installation. You will also learn how to remove domain controllers from a domain.

After this lesson, you will be able to:

- Identify the benefits and functionality of installing Server Core.
- Install and configure Server Core.
- Add and remove Active Directory Domain Services (AD DS), using command-line tools.

Estimated lesson time: 60 minutes

Understanding Server Core

Windows Server 2008 (Server Core Installation), better known as Server Core, is a minimal installation of Windows that consumes about 3 GB of disk space and less than 256 MB of memory. Server Core installation limits the server roles and features that can be added but can improve the security and manageability of the server by reducing its attack surface. The number of services and components running at any one time are limited, so there are fewer opportunities for an intruder to compromise the server. Server Core also reduces the management burden of the server, which requires fewer updates and less maintenance.

Server Core supports nine server roles:

- Active Directory Domain Services
- Active Directory Lightweight Directory Services (AD LDS)
- Dynamic Host Configuration Protocol (DHCP) Server
- DNS Server
- File Services
- Print Server

- Streaming Media Services
- Web Server (IIS) (as a static Web server—ASP.NET cannot be installed)
- Hyper-V (Windows Server Virtualization)

Server core also supports these 11 optional features:

- Microsoft Failover Cluster
- Network Load Balancing
- Subsystem for UNIX-based applications
- Windows Backup
- Multipath I/O
- Removable Storage Management
- Windows Bitlocker Drive Encryption
- Simple Network Management Protocol (SNMP)
- Windows Internet Naming Service (WINS)
- Telnet client
- Quality of Service (QoS)

Installing Server Core

You can install Server Core by using the same steps presented in Exercise 1 of Lesson 1. The differences between a full installation and a Server Core installation are, first, that you select Server Core Installation in the Installing Windows Wizard shown in Figure 1-9, and that when the installation is complete and you log on, a command prompt appears rather than the Windows Explorer interface.

NOTE   The blank initial Administrator password

When you install Windows Server 2008 from the installation DVD, the initial password for the Administrator account is blank. When you log on to the server for the first time, use a blank password. You will be prompted to change the password on first log on.

Practice It   Exercise 1, "Install Server Core," in the practice at the end of this lesson, steps you through the installation of Server Core.

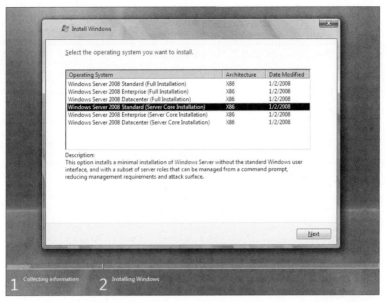

Figure 1-9   The Operating Systems selection page of the Install Windows Wizard

Performing Initial Configuration Tasks

On a full installation of Windows Server 2008, the Initial Configuration Tasks window appears to guide you through post-installation configuration of the server. Server Core provides no GUI, so you must complete the tasks by using command-line tools. Table 1-1 lists common configuration tasks and the commands you can use. To learn more about any command, open a command prompt and type the name of the command followed by /?.

Table 1-1   Server Core Configuration Commands

Task	Command
Change the Administrator password	When you log on with Ctrl + Alt + Del, you will be prompted to change the password. You can also type the following command: *Net user administrator **
Set a static IPv4 configuration	*Netsh interface ipv4*
Activate Windows Server	*Cscript c:\windows\system32\slmgr.vbs −ato*
Join a domain	*Netdom*
Add Server Core roles, components, or features	*Ocsetup.exe* package or feature Note that the package or feature names are case sensitive.

Table 1-1   Server Core Configuration Commands

Task	Command
Display installed roles, components, and features	*Oclist.exe*
Enable Remote Desktop	*Cscript c:\windows\system32\scregedit.wsf /AR 0*
Promote a domain controller	*Dcpromo.exe*
Configure DNS	*Dnscmd.exe*
Configure DFS	*Dfscmd.exe*

Practice It   Exercise 2, "Perform Post-Installation Configuration on Server Core," in the practice at the end of this lesson, steps you through the initial configuration of a Server Core installation of Windows Server 2008.

The *Ocsetup.exe* command is used to add supported Server Core roles and features to the server. The exception to this rule is AD DS. Do not use *Ocsetup.exe* to add or remove AD DS. Use *Dcpromo.exe* instead.

Adding AD DS to a Server Core Installation

Because there is no Active Directory Domain Services Installation Wizard in Server Core, you must use the command line to run *Dcpromo.exe* with parameters that configure AD DS. To learn about the parameters of *Dcpromo.exe*, open a command line and type **dcpromo.exe /?**. Each configuration scenario has additional usage information. For example, type **dcpromo.exe /?:Promotion** for detailed usage instructions for promoting a domain controller.

MORE INFO   Unattended installation parameters

You can find a listing of unattended installation parameters at *http://technet2.microsoft.com /windowsserver2008/en/library/bcd89659-402d-46fb-8535-8da1feb8d4111033.mspx*.

Practice It   You will add AD DS to a Server Core installation during Exercise 3, "Create a Domain Controller with Server Core," in the practice at the end of this lesson.

Removing Domain Controllers

Occasionally, you might have a reason to take a domain controller offline for extended maintenance or to remove it permanently. It is important that you remove a domain controller correctly so that the information about the domain controller is cleaned up in Active Directory.

To remove a domain controller, use the *Dcpromo.exe* command. If you run the command on a domain controller by using the Windows interface, the Active Directory Domain Services Installation Wizard will step you through the process. If you want to use the command line or are removing AD DS from a Server Core installation, type **dcpromo.exe /?:Demotion** for usage information regarding parameters for the demotion operation.

Practice It   In Exercise 4, "Remove a Domain Controller," in the practice at the end of the lesson, you will remove a domain controller by using the *Dcpromo.exe* command.

When you demote a domain controller, you must provide a password that will be assigned to the local Administrator account of the server after demotion.

PRACTICE **Installing a Server Core Domain Controller**

In this exercise, you will add a domain controller to the *contoso.com* forest you created in the Lesson 1 practice. To increase the security and reduce the management overhead of the new DC, you will promote a server running Server Core to a domain controller. Before performing the exercises in this practice, you must have completed the practice in Lesson 1.

▶ **Exercise 1   Install Server Core**

In this exercise, you will install Server Core on a computer or virtual machine.

1. Insert the Windows Server 2008 installation DVD.

    If you are using a VM, you might have the option to mount an ISO image of the installation DVD. Consult the VM Help documentation for guidance.

2. Power on the system.

    If the system's hard disk is empty, the system should boot to the DVD. If there is data on the disk, you might be prompted to press a key to boot to the DVD.

    If the system does not boot to the DVD or offer you a boot menu, go to the BIOS settings of the computer and configure the boot order to ensure that the system boots to the DVD.

3. Select the language, regional setting, and keyboard layout that are correct for your system and click Next.

4. Click Install Now.

5. Select Windows Server 2008 Standard (Server Core Installation) and click Next.

6. Select the I Accept The License Terms check box and click Next.

7. Click Custom (Advanced).

8. On the Where Do You Want To Install Windows page, select the disk on which you want to install Windows Server 2008.

    If you need to create, delete, extend, or format partitions, or if you need to load a custom mass storage driver to access the disk subsystem, click Driver Options (Advanced).

9. Click Next.

10. When installation has completed, log on to the system.

    The initial password for the Administrator account is blank

11. You will be prompted to change the password. Enter a password for the Administrator account in both the New Password and Confirm Password boxes and press Enter.

    The password must be at least seven characters long and must have at least three of four character types:

    ❑ Upper case: A–Z

    ❑ Lower case: a–z

    ❑ Numeric: 0–9

    ❑ Nonalphanumeric: symbols such as $, #, @, and !

NOTE   Do not forget this password

Without it, you will not be able to log on to the server to perform other exercises in this training kit.

---

12. Click OK.

    The command prompt for the Administrator account appears.

▶ **Exercise 2   Perform Post-Installation Configuration on Server Core**

In this exercise, you will perform post-installation configuration of the server to prepare it with the name and TCP/IP settings required for the remaining exercises in this lesson.

1. Rename the server by typing **netdom renamecomputer %computername% /newname: SERVER02**. You will be prompted to press **Y** to confirm the operation.

2. Set the IPv4 address of the server by typing each of the following commands:

    ```
    netsh interface ipv4 set address name="Local Area Connection"
    source=static address=10.0.0.12 mask=255.255.255.0
    gateway=10.0.0.1 1

    netsh interface ipv4 set dns name="Local Area Connection"
    source=static address=10.0.0.11 primary
    ```

3. Confirm the IP configuration you entered previously with the command **ipconfig /all**.

4. Restart by typing **shutdown –r –t 0**.

5. Log on as Administrator.

6. Join the domain with the command **netdom join %computername% /domain: contoso.com**.

7. Restart by typing **shutdown –r –t 0**, and then log on again as Administrator.

8. Display installed server roles by typing oclist.

    Note the package identifier for the DNS server role: DNS-Server-Core-Role.

9. Type **ocsetup** and press Enter.

   Surprise! There is a minor amount of GUI in Server Core.

10. Click OK to close the window.

11. Type **ocsetup DNS-Server-Core-Role**.

    Package identifiers are case sensitive.

12. Type **oclist** and confirm that the DNS server role is installed.

▶ **Exercise 3   Create a Domain Controller with Server Core**

In this exercise, you will add the AD DS role to the Server Core installation, using the *Dcpromo.exe* command.

1. Type **dcpromo.exe /?** and press Enter.

   Review the usage information.

2. Type **dcpromo.exe /?:Promotion** and press Enter.

   Review the usage information.

3. Type the following command to add and configure the AD DS role:

```
dcpromo /unattend /replicaOrNewDomain:replica
/replicaDomainDNSName:contoso.com /ConfirmGC:Yes
/UserName:CONTOSO\Adminsitrator /Password:* /safeModeAdminPassword:P@ssword
```

4. When prompted to enter network credentials, type the password for the Administrator account in the *contoso.com* domain and click OK.

   The AD DS role will be installed and configured, and then the server will reboot.

▶ **Exercise 4   Remove a Domain Controller**

In this exercise, you will remove AD DS from the Server Core installation.

1. Log on to the Server Core installation as Administrator.

2. Type **dcpromo /unattend /AdministratorPassword:***password* where *password* is a strong password that will become the local Administrator password of the server after AD DS has been removed. Press Enter.

Lesson Summary

- Windows Server 2008 Server Core Installation, better known simply as Server Core, is a minimal installation of Windows that supports a subset of server roles and features.

- Server Core can improve the security and manageability of Windows servers.

- The *Ocsetup.exe* command is used to add and remove Server Core roles except for AD DS, which is added by using *Dcpromo.exe*.

- You can fully configure an automated promotion or demotion operation by using the *Dcpromo.exe /unattend* command with parameters appropriate for the operation.

Lesson Review

You can use the following questions to test your knowledge of the information in Lesson 2, "Active Directory Domain Services on Server Core." The questions are also available on the companion CD if you prefer to review them in electronic form.

NOTE   Answers

Answers to these questions and explanations of why each answer choice is right or wrong are located in the "Answers" section at the end of the book.

---

1. You are logged on as Administrator to SERVER02, one of four domain controllers in the *contoso.com* domain that run Server Core. You want to demote the domain controller. Which of the following is required?

   A. The local Administrator password

   B. The credentials for a user in the Domain Admins group

   C. The credentials for a user in the Domain Controllers group

   D. The address of a DNS server

2. SERVER02 is running Server Core. It is already configured with the AD DS role. You want to add Active Directory Certificate Services (AD CS) to the server. What must you do?

   A. Install the Active Directory Certificate Services role.

   B. Install the Active Directory Federated Services role.

   C. Install the AD RMS role.

   D. Reinstall the server as Windows Server 2008 (Full Installation).

Chapter Review

To further practice and reinforce the skills you learned in this chapter, you can perform the following tasks:

- Review the chapter summary.
- Review the list of key terms introduced in this chapter.
- Complete the case scenario. This scenario sets up a real-world situation involving the topics of this chapter and asks you to create a solution.
- Take a practice test.

Chapter Summary

- Active Directory services perform identity access and management functions to support an organization's network.
- A domain controller hosts the Active Directory data store and related services. Domain controllers are created by adding the AD DS role and then configuring AD DS by using *Dcpromo.exe*.
- Server Core enables you to reduce the management costs and increase the security of your domain controllers.

Key Terms

Use these key terms to understand better the concepts covered in this chapter.

- **authentication**   The mechanism by which an identity is validated by comparing secrets such as passwords provided by the user or computer compared to secrets maintained in the identity store.
- **domain**   An administrative unit of Active Directory. Within a domain, all domain controllers replicate information about objects such as users, groups, and computers in the domain.
- **forest**   The boundary of an instance of Active Directory. A forest contains one or more domains. All domains in the forest replicate the schema and configuration partitions of the directory.
- **forest root domain**   The first domain created in a forest.
- **functional level**   A setting that determines which features of Active Directory are enabled within a domain or forest. The functional level limits the versions of Windows that can be used by domain controllers in a domain or forest.
- **global catalog (or partial attribute set)**   A partition of the Active Directory data store that contains a subset of attributes for every object in the Active Directory forest. The global catalog is used for efficient object queries and location.

- **identity store**   A database of information regarding users, groups, computers, and other security principals. Attributes stored in an identity store include user names and passwords.
- **Kerberos**   A standard protocol used by Active Directory for authentication.
- **schema**   A definition of the attributes and object classes supported by Active Directory.
- **site**   An Active Directory object that represents a portion of the network with reliable connectivity. Within a site, domain controllers replicate updates within seconds, and clients attempt to use the services within their site before obtaining the services from other sites.

Case Scenario

In the following case scenario, you will apply what you've learned about Server Core installation and related Active Directory Domain Services. You can find answers to these questions in the "Answers" section at the end of this book.

Case Scenario: Creating an Active Directory Forest

You have been asked to create a new Active Directory forest for a new research project at Trey Research. Because of the sensitive nature of the project, you must ensure that the directory is as secure as possible. You are considering the option of using a Server Core installation on the two servers that will act as domain controllers.

1. Can you create an Active Directory forest by using only Server Core servers?
2. Which command will you use to configure static IP addresses on the servers?
3. Which command will you use to add the DNS server role?
4. Which command will you use to add Active Directory Domain Services?

Take a Practice Test

The practice tests on this book's companion CD offer many options. For example, you can test yourself on just one exam objective, or you can test yourself on all the 70-640 certification exam content. You can set up the test so that it closely simulates the experience of taking a certification exam, or you can set it up in study mode so that you can look at the correct answers and explanations after you answer each question.

MORE INFO   **Practice tests**

For details about all the practice test options available, see the "How to Use the Practice Tests" section in this book's introduction.

Chapter 2
Administration

Most administrators first experience Active Directory Domain Services (AD DS) by opening Active Directory Users And Computers and creating user, computer, or group objects within the organizational units (OUs) of a domain. Such tasks are fundamental to the job requirements of an IT professional in an Active Directory environment, so now that you have created a domain in Chapter 1, "Installation," you can address the tools, tips, and best practices regarding the creation of these objects. Later chapters will explore each of these object classes in detail.

In this chapter, you will also look at two important, higher-level concerns within an enterprise: how to locate objects in the directory and how to ensure that Active Directory is secure while enabling support personnel to perform the tasks required of their roles.

Exam objectives in this chapter:
- Creating and Maintaining Active Directory Objects
  - Maintain Active Directory accounts

Lessons in this chapter:
- Lesson 1: Working with Active Directory Snap-ins 35
- Lesson 2: Creating Objects in Active Directory 46
- Lesson 3: Delegation and Security of Active Directory Objects 69

Before You Begin

To complete the lessons in this chapter, you must have installed Windows Server 2008 on a physical computer or virtual machine. The machine should be named SERVER01 and should be a domain controller in the *contoso.com* domain. The details for this setup are presented in Chapter 1.

Real World

Dan Holme

You are certainly familiar with administrative tools, such as the Active Directory Users and Computers snap-in, and the basic skills required to create organizational units, users, computers, and groups. This chapter reviews those tools and skills so that you can fill in any gaps in your knowledge. More important, however, this chapter introduces ways you can elevate your productivity and effectiveness as an administrator. I find that many administrators continue to use the default consoles and, therefore, have to open multiple tools to do their jobs, instead of creating a single, customized Microsoft Management Console (MMC) that contains all the snap-ins they need. I also see administrators diving deep into their OU structure to locate and manage objects rather than taking advantage of the power of Saved Queries to virtualize the view of their domains. Although this chapter covers only one exam objective, "Maintain Active Directory accounts," the tips and guidance I provide here is some of the most valuable in the book because it will enable you to work more efficiently and more securely every day in the real world of your enterprise.

Lesson 1: Working with Active Directory Snap-ins

The Active Directory administrative tools, or snap-ins, expose the functionality you require to support the directory service. In this lesson, you will identify and locate the most important Active Directory snap-ins. You will also learn how to work effectively with them, using alternate credentials, and how to build custom consoles that can be distributed to administrators in your organization.

After this lesson, you will be able to:
- Work with Microsoft Management Console.
- Identify the most important Active Directory administrative snap-ins.
- Install the Remote Server Administration Tools (RSAT) on Windows Server 2008 and Windows Vista.
- Launch administrative tools with alternate credentials, using Run As Administrator.
- Create, manage, and distribute a custom MMC.

Estimated lesson time: 35 minutes

Understanding the Microsoft Management Console

Windows administrative tools share a common framework called the Microsoft Management Console (MMC). The MMC displays tools in a customizable window with a left pane that displays the console tree (similar to the Windows Explorer tree) and a center pane that displays details. An Actions pane on the right exposes commands, called actions by MMC. Figure 2-1 shows an example.

To control the visibility of the left and right panes, use the Show/Hide Console Tree and Show/Hide Action Pane buttons or the *Customize* command on the View menu.

Administrative tools, called *snap-ins*, use the console tree and details pane of the console to provide administrative functionality. You can think of an MMC as a tool belt to which you can attach one or more tools (snap-ins). Snap-ins cannot be launched directly; they can function within the context of an MMC only. Most of the tools in the Administrative Tools folder constitute a single console with a single snap-in. These tools include Event Viewer, Services, and Task Scheduler. Other tools, such as Computer Management, are consoles that contain multiple snap-ins, including some that exist as standalone consoles. For example, the Computer Management console contains Event Viewer, Services, and Task Scheduler.

As you are administering Windows with snap-ins, you will be performing commands, called *actions* by the MMC, that you can find in the console's Action menu, on the context menu that appears when you right-click, and in the Actions pane on the right side of the console. Most experienced administrators find the context menu to be the most productive way to perform actions in an MMC snap-in. If you use the context menu exclusively, you can turn off the Actions pane so that you have a larger area to display information in the details pane.

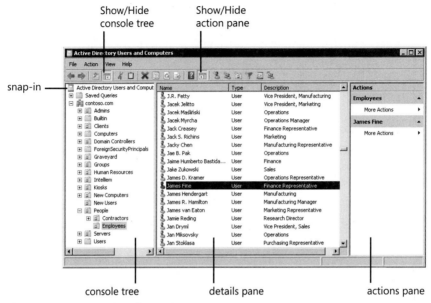

Figure 2-1 An MMC and snap-in

There are two types of MMC: preconfigured and custom. Preconfigured consoles are installed automatically when you add a role or feature, to support administration of that role or feature. They function in user mode, so you cannot modify them or save them. The user, however, can create custom consoles to provide exactly the tools and functionality required. In the following sections, you will look at both preconfigured and custom consoles.

Active Directory Administration Tools

Most Active Directory administration is performed with the following snap-ins and consoles:

- **Active Directory Users and Computers** Manage most common day-to-day resources, including users, groups, computers, printers, and shared folders. This is likely to be the most heavily used snap-in for an Active Directory administrator.
- **Active Directory Sites and Services** Manage replication, network topology, and related services. You will use this snap-in heavily in Chapter 11, "Sites and Replication."
- **Active Directory Domains and Trusts** Configure and maintain trust relationships and the domain and forest functional levels. This tool will be discussed in Chapter 13, "Domains and Forests."

- **Active Directory Schema**   Examine and modify the definition of Active Directory attributes and object classes. This schema is the "blueprint" for Active Directory. It is rarely viewed and even more rarely changed. Therefore, the Active Directory Schema snap-in is not installed by default.

Active Directory snap-ins and consoles are installed when you add the AD DS role to a server. Two commonly used Active Directory administrative tools are added to Server Manager when you install the AD DS role: the Active Directory Users and Computers snap-in and the Active Directory Sites and Services snap-in. However, to administer Active Directory from a system that is not a domain controller, you must install the RSAT, a feature that can be installed from the Features node of Server Manager on Windows Server 2008. It can be downloaded from Microsoft and installed on clients running Windows Vista Service Pack 1.

Finding the Active Directory Administrative Tools

You can find two Active Directory snap-ins in Server Manager by expanding Roles and Active Directory Domain Services. All tools, however, can be found in the Administrative Tools folder, which itself is found in Control Panel. In the classic view of Control Panel, you will see the Administrative Tools folder displayed. Using the Control Panel Home view, you can find administrative tools in System And Maintenance.

Adding the Administrative Tools to Your Start Menu

By default, administrative tools are not added to the Start menu on Windows Vista clients. You can make the administrative tools easier to access by adding them to your Start menu.

1. Right-click the Start button and choose Properties.
2. Click Customize.
3. If you are using the default Start menu, scroll to System Administrative Tools and select Display On The All Programs Menu And The Start Menu or Display On The All Programs Menu. If you are using the Classic Start menu, select Display Administrative Tools.
4. Click OK twice.

Running Administrative Tools with Alternate Credentials

Many administrators log on to their computers by using their administrative accounts. This practice is dangerous because an administrative account has more privileges and access to more of the network than a standard user account. Therefore, malware that is launched with administrative credentials can cause significant damage. To avoid this problem, do not log on as an administrator. Instead, log on as a standard user and use the Run As Administrator feature to launch administrative tools in the security context of an administrative account:

1. Right-click the shortcut for an executable, Control Panel applet, or MMC that you want to launch, and then choose Run As Administrator. If you do not see the command, try holding down the Shift key and right-clicking.

   The User Account Control dialog box appears, as shown in Figure 2-2.

Figure 2-2   The User Account Control dialog box prompting for administrative credentials

2. Enter the user name and password of your administrative account.
3. Click OK.

If you will be running an application regularly as an administrator, create a new shortcut that preconfigures Run As Administrator. Create a shortcut and open the Properties dialog box for the shortcut. Click the Advanced button and select Run As Administrator. When you launch the shortcut, the User Account Control dialog box will appear.

Creating a Custom Console with Active Directory Snap-ins

It's easier to administer Windows when the tools you need are in one place and can be customized to meet your needs. You can achieve this by creating a custom administrative MMC which, continuing our tool belt metaphor, is a tool belt made just for you. When you create a custom MMC, you can:

■ Add multiple snap-ins so that you do not have to switch between consoles to perform your job tasks and so that you have to launch only one console with Run As Administrator.
■ Save the console to be used regularly.
■ Distribute the console to other administrators.
■ Centralize consoles in a shared location for unified, customized administration.

To create a custom MMC, open an empty MMC by clicking the Start button. Then, in the Start Search box, type **mmc.exe** and press Enter. The *Add/Remove Snap-in* command in the File menu enables you to add, remove, reorder, and manage the console's snap-ins.

Practice It   Exercise 1, "Create a Custom MMC," Exercise 2, "Add a Snap-in to an MMC," and Exercise 3, "Manage the Snap-ins of an MMC," in the practice at the end of this lesson step you through the skills related to creating a custom MMC with multiple snap-ins.

Saving and Distributing a Custom Console

If you plan to distribute a console, it is recommended to save the console in user mode. To change a console's mode, choose Options from the File menu. By default, new consoles are saved in author mode, which enables adding and removing snap-ins, viewing all portions of the console tree, and saving customizations. User mode, by contrast, restricts the functionality of the console so that it cannot be changed. There are three types of user modes, described in Table 2-1. User Mode – Full Access is commonly selected for a console provided to skilled administrators with diverse job tasks requiring broad use of the console snap-ins. User Mode – Limited Access (multiple window and single window) is a locked-down mode and is, therefore, selected for a console provided to administrators with a more narrow set of job tasks.

Table 2-1   MMC Console Modes

Mode	Use when
Author	You want to continue customizing the console.
User Mode – Full Access	You want users of the console to be able to navigate between and use all snap-ins. Users will not be able to add or remove snap-ins or change the properties of snap-ins or the console.
User Mode – Limited Access, multiple window	You want users to navigate to and use only the snap-ins that you have made visible in the console tree, and you want to preconfigure multiple windows that focus on specific snap-ins. Users will not be able to open new windows.
User Mode – Limited Access, single window	You want users to navigate to and use only the snap-ins that you have made visible in the console tree within a single window.

After a console is no longer saved in author mode, you—the original author—can make changes to the console by right-clicking the saved console and choosing Author.

Practice It   Exercise 4, "Prepare a Console for Distribution to Users," in the practice at the end of the lesson, guides you through saving a console in user mode so that it can be locked down for deployment to other administrators.

Consoles are saved with the .msc file extension. The default location to which consoles are saved is the Administrative Tools folder, but not the folder in Control Panel. Rather, they are saved in the Start menu folder of your user profile: *%userprofile%*\AppData\Roaming \Microsoft\Windows\StartMenu.

This location is problematic because it is secured with permissions so that only your user account has access to the console. The best practice is to log on to your computer with an account that is not privileged and then run administrative tools such as your custom console with alternate credentials that have sufficient privilege to perform administrative tasks. Because two accounts will be involved, saving the console to the Start menu subfolder of one account's user profile will mean additional navigation, at a minimum, and access-denied errors in a worst-case scenario.

Save your consoles to a location that can be accessed by both your user and your administrative credentials. It is recommended to save consoles to a shared folder on the network so that you can access your tools when you are logged on to other computers. Optionally, the folder can be made accessible by other administrators to create a centralized store of customized consoles. You can also save consoles to a portable device such as a USB drive, or you can even send a console as an e-mail attachment.

It is important to remember that consoles are basically a set of instructions that are interpreted by *mmc.exe*—instructions that specify which snap-ins to add and which computers to manage with those snap-ins. Consoles do not contain the snap-ins themselves. Therefore, a console will not function properly if the snap-ins it contains have not been installed, so be sure you have installed appropriate snap-ins from RSAT on systems on which you will use the console.

> ## Quick Check
> - Describe the difference between a console saved in user mode and in author mode.
>
> ### Quick Check Answer
> - Author mode enables a user to add and remove snap-ins and thoroughly customize the console. User mode prevents users from making changes to the console.

PRACTICE Creating and Managing a Custom MMC

In this practice, you will create a custom MMC. You will add, remove, and reorder snap-ins. You will then prepare the console for distribution to other administrators.

▶ **Exercise 1   Create a Custom MMC**

In this exercise, you will create a custom MMC with the Active Directory Users and Computers, Active Directory Schema, and Computer Management snap-ins. These tools are useful for administering Active Directory and domain controllers.

1. Log on to SERVER01 as Administrator.

2. Click the Start button and, in the Start Search box, type **mmc.exe** and press Enter.

   An empty MMC appears. By default, the new console window is not maximized within the MMC. Maximize it to take advantage of the application's full size.

3. Choose Add/Remove Snap-in from the File menu.

   The Add Or Remove Snap-ins dialog box, shown in Figure 2-3, appears.

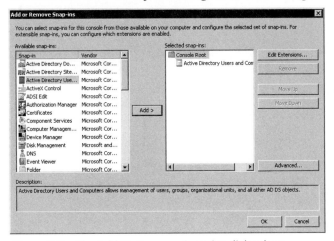

Figure 2-3   The Add Or Remove Snap-ins dialog box

If you do not see the snap-ins listed that you want, be sure you've installed the RSAT.

4. In the Add Or Remove Snap-ins dialog box, select Active Directory Users And Computers from the Available Snap-ins list.

5. Click the Add button to add it to the Selected Snap-ins list.

   Notice that the Active Directory Schema snap-in is not available to add. The Active Directory Schema snap-in is installed with the Active Directory Domain Services role with the RSAT, but it is not registered, so it does not appear.

6. Click OK to close the Add Or Remove Snap-ins dialog box.

7. Click the Start button. In the Start Search box, type **cmd.exe**.

8. At the command prompt, type the **regsvr32.exe schmmgmt.dll** command.

   This command registers the dynamic link library (DLL) for the Active Directory Schema snap-in. This is necessary to do one time on a system before you can add the snap-in to a console.

9. A prompt will appear that indicates the registration was successful. Click OK.

10. Return to your custom MMC and repeat steps 2–6 to add the Active Directory Schema snap-in.

11. Choose Add/Remove Snap-in from the File menu.

12. In the Add Or Remove Snap-ins dialog box, select Computer Management from the Available Snap-ins list.

13. Click the Add button to add it to the Selected Snap-ins list.

    When a snap-in supports remote administration, you are prompted to select the computer you wish to manage, as shown in Figure 2-4.

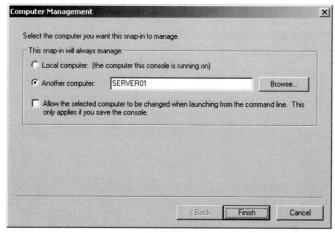

Figure 2-4   Selecting the computer to be managed by a snap-in

- ❑ To manage the computer on which the console is running, select Local Computer. This does not refer solely to the computer on which you are creating the console. If you launch the console from another computer, the console will manage that computer.

- ❑ To specify a single computer that the snap-in should manage, select Another Computer. Then, enter the computer's name or click Browse to select the computer.

14. Choose Another Computer and type **SERVER01** as the computer name.

15. Click Finish.

16. Click OK to close the Add Or Remove Snap-ins dialog box.

17. Choose Save from the File menu and save the console to your desktop with the name **MyConsole.msc**.

18. Close the console.

▶ **Exercise 2   Add a Snap-in to an MMC**

In this exercise, you will add Event Viewer to the console you created in Exercise 1. Event Viewer is useful to monitor activity on domain controllers.

1. Open MyConsole.msc.

   If you did not save the console to your desktop in Exercise 1, and instead saved the console to the default location, you will find it in the Start\All Programs\Administrative Tools folder.

2. Choose Add/Remove Snap-in from the File menu.

3. In the Add Or Remove Snap-ins dialog box, select Event Viewer from the Available Snap-ins list.

4. Click the Add button to add it to the Selected Snap-ins list.

   You will be prompted to select a computer to manage.

5. Choose Another Computer and type **SERVER01** as the computer name.

6. Click OK.

7. Click OK to close the Add Or Remove Snap-ins dialog box.

8. Save and close the console.

▶ **Exercise 3   Manage the Snap-ins of an MMC**

In this exercise, you will change the order of snap-ins and delete a snap-in. You will also learn about extension snap-ins.

1. Open MyConsole.msc.

2. Choose Add/Remove Snap-in from the File menu.

3. In the list of Selected snap-ins, select Event Viewer.

4. Click the Move Up button.

5. Select Active Directory Schema.

6. Click the Remove button.

7. In the list of Selected snap-ins, select Computer Management.

8. Click Edit Extensions.

   Extensions are snap-ins that exist within another snap-in to provide additional functionality. The Computer Management snap-in has many familiar snap-ins as extensions, each of which you can enable or disable.

9. Select Enable Only Selected Extensions.

10. Deselect Event Viewer. You have already added Event Viewer as a standalone snap-in for the console.

11. Click OK to close the Extensions For Computer Management dialog box.

12. Click OK to close the Add Or Remove Snap-in dialog box.

13. Save and close the console.

▶ **Exercise 4   Prepare a Console for Distribution to Users**

In this exercise, you will save your console in user mode so that users cannot add, remove, or modify snap-ins. Keep in mind that MMC users are typically administrators themselves.

1. Open MyConsole.msc.

2. Choose Options from the File menu.

3. In the Console Mode drop-down list, choose User Mode – Full Access.

4. Click OK.

5. Save and close the console.

6. Open the console by double-clicking it.

7. Click the File menu. Note that there is no *Add/Remove Snap-in* command.

8. Close the console.

9. Right-click the console and choose Author.

10. Click the File menu. In author mode, the *Add/Remove Snap-in* command appears.

11. Close the console.

Lesson Summary

- Windows administrative tools are snap-ins that can be added to an MMC. Active Directory Users And Computers and other Active Directory management snap-ins are also added to Server Manager and are contained in preconfigured consoles in the Administrative Tools folder.

- Administrators should not log on to their computers with administrative credentials. Instead, they should use a standard user account for logon and launch administrative tools by using the *Run As Administrator* command.

- Create a custom MMC that contains all the snap-ins you require to perform your job tasks. Such a console can be saved to a location where you, and possibly other administrators, can access it and launch it with administrative credentials. Ideally, this should be the only tool you need to run as administrator if it is fully customized to your needs.

- It is recommended that you save a console in user mode so that changes cannot be made to the console or its snap-ins.

- Consoles require that the appropriate administrative tools have been installed. Otherwise, console snap-ins will not function properly.

Lesson Review

You can use the following questions to test your knowledge of the information in Lesson 1, "Working with Active Directory Snap-ins." The questions are also available on the companion CD if you prefer to review them in electronic form.

NOTE Answers

Answers to these questions and explanations of why each answer choice is right or wrong are located in the "Answers" section at the end of the book.

1. You are a support professional for Contoso, Ltd. The domain's administrators have distributed a custom console with the Active Directory Users and Computers snap-in. When you open the console and attempt to reset a user's password, you receive Access Denied errors. You are certain that you have been delegated permission to reset passwords for users. What is the best solution?

   A. Close the custom console and open Server Manager. Use the Active Directory Users and Computers snap-in in Server Manager.

   B. Close the custom console and open a command prompt. Type **dsa.msc**.

   C. Close the custom console, and then right-click the console and choose Run As Administrator. Type the credentials for your secondary administrative account.

   D. Close the custom console, and then right-click the console and open a command prompt. Use the *DSMOD USER* command with the *−p* switch to change the user's password.

Lesson 2: Creating Objects in Active Directory

Active Directory is a directory service, and it is the role of a directory service to maintain information about enterprise resources, including users, groups, and computers. Resources are divided into OUs to facilitate manageability and visibility—that is, they can make it easier to find objects. In this lesson, you will learn how to create OUs, users, groups, and computers. You will also learn important skills to help you locate and find objects when you need them.

If you are experienced with Active Directory, you will be able to review the first few sections in this lesson quickly, but you might want to pay particular attention to the later sections, beginning with "Find Objects in Active Directory," because they will help you make better use of Active Directory tools.

The practice exercises at the end of this lesson will be important for you to complete because they create some of the objects that will be used in future practices.

> **After this lesson, you will be able to:**
> - Create users, groups, computers, and organizational units.
> - Disable protection to delete an organizational unit.
> - Customize and take advantage of views and features of the Active Directory Users and Computers snap-in to work effectively with objects in the directory.
> - Create saved queries to provide rule-based views of objects in the directory.
>
> **Estimated lesson time: 45 minutes**

Creating an Organizational Unit

Organizational units (OUs) are administrative containers within Active Directory that are used to collect objects that share common requirements for administration, configuration, or visibility. What this means will become clearer as you learn more about OU design and management. For now, just understand that OUs provide an administrative hierarchy similar to the folder hierarchy of a disk drive: OUs create *collections* of objects that belong together for *administration*. The term *administration* is emphasized here because OUs are not used to assign permissions to resources—that is what groups are for. Users are placed into groups that are given permission to resources. OUs are administrative containers within which those users and groups can be managed by administrators.

To create an organizational unit:

1. Open the Active Directory Users And Computers snap-in.
2. Right-click the Domain node or the OU node in which you want to add the new OU, choose New, and then select Organizational Unit.

3. Type the name of the organizational unit.

    Be sure to follow the naming conventions of your organization.

4. Select Protect Container From Accidental Deletion.

    You'll learn more about this option later in this section.

5. Click OK.

    OUs have other properties that can be useful to configure. These properties can be set after the object has been created.

6. Right-click the OU and choose Properties.

    Follow the naming conventions and other standards and processes of your organization. You can use the *Description* field to explain the purpose of an OU.

    If an OU represents a physical location, such as an office, the OU's address properties can be useful.

    The Managed By tab can be used to link to the user or group that is responsible for the OU. Click the Change button underneath the Name box. By default, the Select User, Contact, Or Group dialog box that appears does not, despite its name, search for groups; to search for groups, you must first click the Object Types button and select Groups. You'll learn about the Select Users, Contacts, Or Groups dialog box later in this lesson. The remaining contact information on the Managed By tab is populated from the account specified in the Name box. The Managed By tab is used solely for contact information—the specified user or group does not gain any permissions or access to the OU.

7. Click OK.

The Windows Server 2008 administrative tools add a new option: the Protect Container From Accidental Deletion. This option adds a safety switch to the OU so that it cannot be accidentally deleted. Two permissions are added to the OU: Everyone::Deny::Delete and Everyone::Deny::Delete Subtree. No user, not even an administrator, will be able to delete the OU and its contents accidentally. It is highly recommended that you enable this protection for all new OUs.

If you want to delete the OU, you must first turn off the safety switch. To delete a protected OU, follow these steps:

1. In the Active Directory Users And Computers snap-in, click the View menu and select Advanced Features.

2. Right-click the OU and choose Properties.

3. Click the Object tab.

    If you do not see the Object tab, you did not enable Advanced Features in step 1.

4. Clear the check box labeled Protect Object From Accidental Deletion.

5. Click OK.

6. Right-click the OU and choose Delete.

7. You will be prompted to confirm that you want to delete the OU. Click Yes.

8. If the OU contains any other objects, you will be prompted by the Confirm Subtree Deletion dialog box to confirm that you want to delete the OU and all the objects it contains. Click Yes.

Quick Check

■ You attempt to delete an OU and receive an insufficient privileges error. You are logged on as a member of Domain Admins, so you are certain you should have permission to delete an OU. What is happening and what must you change to delete the OU?

Quick Check Answer

■ The OU is protected from accidental deletion. You must deselect the option to protect the object from accidental deletion. The option is located on the Object tab of the OU's Properties dialog box, which is accessible only when Advanced Features is enabled.

Creating a User Object

To create a new user in Active Directory, perform the following steps. Be certain to follow the naming conventions and processes specified by your organization.

1. Open the Active Directory Users And Computers snap-in.

2. In the console tree, expand the node that represents your domain (for instance, *contoso.com*) and navigate to the OU or container (for example, Users) in which you want to create the user account.

3. Right-click the OU or container, choose New, and then select User.

    The New Object – User dialog box appears, as shown in Figure 2-5.

4. In First Name, type the user's first name.

5. In Initials, type the user's middle initial(s).

    Note that this property is, in fact, meant for the initials of a user's middle name, not the initials of the user's first and last name.

6. In Last Name, type the user's last name.

7. The *Full Name* field is populated automatically. Make modifications to it if necessary.

    The *Full Name* field is used to create several attributes of a user object, most notably the common name (CN), and to display name properties. The CN of a user is the name displayed in the details pane of the snap-in. It must be unique within the container or OU. Therefore, if you are creating a user object for a person with the same name as an existing user in the same OU or container, you will need to enter a unique name in the *Full Name* field.

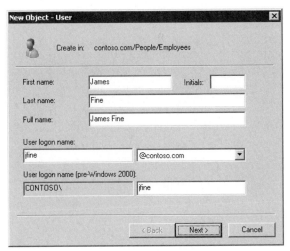

Figure 2-5   New Object – User dialog box

8. In User Logon Name, type the name that the user will log on with and, from the drop-down list, select the user principle name (UPN) suffix that will be appended to the user logon name following the @ symbol.

    User names in Active Directory can contain some special characters (including periods, hyphens, and apostrophes), which enable you to generate accurate user names such as O'Hara and Smith-Bates. However, certain applications can have other restrictions, so it is recommended to use only standard letters and numerals until you have fully tested the applications in your enterprise for compatibility with special characters in logon names.

    The list of available UPN suffixes can be managed using the Active Directory Domains And Trusts snap-in. Right-click the root of the snap-in, Active Directory Domains And Trusts, choose Properties, and then use the UPN Suffixes tab to add or remove suffixes. The DNS name of your Active Directory domain will always be available as a suffix and cannot be removed.

9. In the User logon name (Pre-Windows 2000) box of the Active Directory Users And Computers snap-in, enter the pre-Windows 2000 logon name, often called the down-level logon name.

    In Chapter 3, "Users," you will learn about the two different logon names.

10. Click Next.

11. Enter an initial password for the user in the Password and Confirm Password boxes.

12. Select User Must Change Password At Next Logon.

    It is recommended that you always select this option so that the user can create a new password unknown to the IT staff. Appropriate support staff members can always reset the user's password at a future date if they need to log on as the user or access the user's resources. However, only users should know their passwords on a day-to-day basis.

13. Click Next.
14. Review the summary and click Finish.

    The New Object – User interface enables you to configure a limited number of account-related properties such as name and password settings. However, a user object in Active Directory supports dozens of additional properties. These can be configured after the object has been created.
15. Right-click the user object you created and choose Properties.
16. Configure user properties.

    Be certain to follow the naming conventions and other standards of your organization.

    You will learn more about many of the user properties in Chapter 3 and Chapter 8, "Authentication."
17. Click OK.

Creating a Group Object

Groups are an important class of object because they are used to collect users, computers, and other groups to create a single point of management. The most straightforward and common use of a group is to grant permissions to a shared folder. If a group has been given read access to a folder, for example, then any of the group's members will be able to read the folder. You do not have to grant read access directly to each individual member; you can manage access to the folder simply by adding and removing members of the group.

To create a group:

1. Open the Active Directory Users And Computers snap-in.
2. In the console tree, expand the node that represents your domain (for instance, *contoso.com*) and navigate to the OU or container (such as Users) in which you want to create the group.
3. Right-click the OU or container, choose New, and then select Group.

   The New Object – Group dialog box appears, as shown in Figure 2-6.
4. Type the name of the new group in the Group Name box.

   Most organizations have naming conventions that specify how group names should be created. Be sure to follow the guidelines of your organization.

   By default, the name you type is also entered as the pre-Windows 2000 name of the new group. It is very highly recommended that you keep the two names the same.
5. Do not change the name in the Group Name (Pre-Windows 2000) box.
6. Choose the Group type.
   - ❑ A Security group can be given permissions to resources. It can also be configured as an e-mail distribution list.

❑ A Distribution group is an e-mail–enabled group that cannot be given permissions to resources and is, therefore, used only when a group is an e-mail distribution list that has no possible requirement for access to resources.

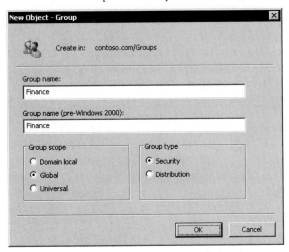

Figure 2-6 The New Object – Group dialog box

7. Select the Group Scope.

   ❑ A Global group is used to identify users based on criteria such as job function, location, and so on.

   ❑ A Domain local group is used to collect users and groups who share similar resource access needs, such as all users who need to be able to modify a project report.

   ❑ A Universal group is used to collect users and groups from multiple domains.

   Group scope will be discussed in more detail in Chapter 4, "Groups."

   Note that if the domain in which you are creating the group object is at a mixed or interim domain functional level, you can select only Domain Local or Global scopes for security groups. Domain functional levels will be discussed in Chapter 13, "Domains and Forests."

8. Click OK.

   Group objects have a number of properties that are useful to configure. These can be specified after the object has been created.

9. Right-click the group and choose Properties.

10. Enter the properties for the group.

   Be sure to follow the naming conventions and other standards of your organization.

   The group's Members and Member Of tabs specify who belongs to the group and what groups the group itself belongs to. Group membership will be discussed in Chapter 4.

The group's *Description* field, because it is easily visible in the details pane of the Active Directory Users And Computers snap-in, is a good place to summarize the purpose of the group and the contact information for the individual(s) responsible for deciding who is and is not a member of the group.

The group's *Notes* field can be used to provide more detail about the group.

The Managed By tab can be used to link to the user or group that is responsible for the group. Click the Change button underneath the Name box. To search for a group, you must first click the Object Types button and select Groups. The Select User, Contact, Or Group dialog box will be discussed later in this lesson.

The remaining contact information on the Managed By tab is populated from the account specified in the Name box. The Managed By tab is typically used for contact information so that if a user wants to join the group, you can decide who in the business should be contacted to authorize the new member. However, if you select the Manager Can Update Membership List option, the account specified in the Name box will be given permission to add and remove members of the group. This is one method to delegate administrative control over the group. Other delegation options are discussed in Lesson 3.

11. Click OK.

Creating a Computer Object

Computers are represented as accounts and objects in Active Directory, just as users are. In fact, behind the scenes, a computer logs on to the domain just as a user does. The computer has a user name—the computer's name with a dollar sign appended, for instance, DESKTOP101$—and a password that is established when you join the computer to the domain, and it's changed automatically every thirty days or so thereafter. To create a computer object in Active Directory:

1. Open the Active Directory Users And Computers snap-in.
2. In the console tree, expand the node that represents your domain (such as *contoso.com*) and navigate to the OU or container (for instance, Users) in which you want to create the computer.
3. Right-click the OU or container, choose New, and then select Computer.
   The New Object – Computer dialog box appears, as seen in Figure 2-7.
4. In the Computer Name box, type the computer's name.
   Your entry will automatically populate the Computer Name (Pre-Windows 2000) box.
5. Do not change the name in the Computer Name (Pre-Windows 2000) box.
6. The account specified in the *User Or Group* field will be able to join the computer to the domain. The default value is Domain Admins. Click Change to select another group or user.

Generally, you will select a group that represents your deployment, desktop support, or help desk team. You can also select the user to whom the computer is assigned. You will explore the issues related to joining the computer to the domain in Chapter 5, "Computers."

7. Do not select the check box labeled Assign This Computer Account As A Pre-Windows 2000 Computer unless the account is for a computer running Microsoft Windows NT 4.0.

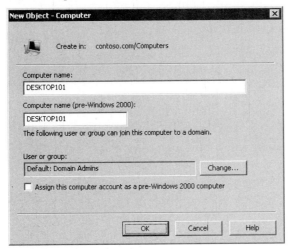

Figure 2-7   The New Object – Computer dialog box

8. Click OK.

Computer objects have a number of properties that are useful to configure. These can be specified after the object has been created.

9. Right-click the computer and choose Properties.

10. Enter the properties for the computer.

Be sure to follow the naming conventions and other standards of your organization.

The computer's *Description* field can be used to indicate who the computer is assigned to, its role (for instance, a training-room computer), or other descriptive information. Because Description is visible in the details pane of the Active Directory Users And Computers snap-in, it is a good place to store the information you find most useful to know about a computer.

There are several properties that describe the computer, including DNS Name, DC Type, Site, Operating System Name, Version, and Service Pack. These properties will be populated automatically when the computer joins the domain.

The Managed By tab can be used to link to the user or group responsible for the computer. Click the Change button underneath the Name box. To search for groups, you must first click the Object Types button and select Groups. The Select Users, Contacts,

Or Groups dialog box is discussed later in this lesson. The remaining contact information on the Managed By tab is populated from the account specified in the Name box. The Managed By tab is typically used for contact information. Some organizations use the tab to indicate the support team (group) responsible for the computer. Others use the information to track the user to whom the computer is assigned.

11. Click OK.

Finding Objects in Active Directory

You have learned how to create objects in Active Directory, but what good is information in a directory service if you can't get it out of the directory as well? You will need to locate objects in Active Directory on many occasions:

- **Granting permissions**   When you configure permissions for a file or folder, you must select the group (or user) to which permissions should be assigned.
- **Adding members to groups**   A group's membership can consist of users, computers, groups, or any combination of the three. When you add an object as a member of a group, you must select the object.
- **Creating links**   Linked properties are properties of one object that refer to another object. Group membership is, in fact, a linked property. Other linked properties, such as the *Managed By* attribute discussed earlier, are also links. When you specify the *Managed By* name, you must select the appropriate user or group.
- **Looking up an object**   You can search for any object in your Active Directory domain.

There are many other situations that will entail searching Active Directory, and you will encounter several user interfaces. In this section, you'll learn some techniques for working with each.

Controlling the View of Objects in the Active Directory Users and Computers Snap-in

The details pane of the Active Directory Users and Computers snap-in can be customized to help you work effectively with the objects in your directory. Use the *Add/Remove Columns* command on the View menu to add columns to the details pane. Not every attribute is available to be displayed as a column, but you are certain to find columns that will be useful to display such as User Logon Name. You might also find columns that are unnecessary. If your OUs have only one type of object (user or computer, for example), the Type column might not be helpful.

When a column is visible, you can change the order of columns by dragging the column headings to the left or right. You can also sort the view in the details pane by clicking the column: the first click will sort in ascending order, the second in descending order, just like Windows Explorer. A common customization is to add the Last Name column to a view of users so they can be sorted by last name. It is generally easier to find users by last name than by the Name column, which is the CN and generally first name/last name.

Using Saved Queries

Windows Server 2003 introduced the Saved Queries node of the Active Directory Users and Computers snap-in. This powerful function enables you to create rule-driven views of your domain, displaying objects across one or more OUs. To create a saved query:

1. Open the Active Directory Users And Computers snap-in.

   Saved Queries is not available in the Active Directory Users And Computers snap-in that is part of Server Manager. You must use the Active Directory Users And Computers console or a custom console with the snap-in.

2. Right-click Saved Queries, choose New, and then select Query.

3. Type a name for the query.

4. Optionally, enter a description.

5. Click Browse to locate the root for the query.

   The search will be limited to the domain or OU you select. It is recommended to narrow your search as much as possible to improve search performance.

6. Click Define Query to define your query.

7. In the Find Common Queries dialog box, select the type of object you want to query.

   The tabs in the dialog box and the input controls on each tab change to provide options that are appropriate for the selected query.

8. Click OK.

After your query is created, it is saved within the instance of the Active Directory Users And Computers snap-in, so if you open the Active Directory Users And Computers console (*dsa.msc*), your query will be available the next time you open the console. If you created the saved query in a custom console, it will be available in that custom console. To transfer saved queries to other consoles or users, you can export the saved query as an XML file and then import it to the target snap-in.

The view in the details pane of the saved query can be customized as described earlier, with specific columns and sorting. A very important benefit of saved queries is that the customized view is specific to each saved query. When you add the Last Name column to the "normal" view of an OU, the Last Name column is actually added to the view of *every* OU, so you will see an empty Last Name column even for an OU of computers or groups. With saved queries, you can add the Last Name column to a query for user objects and other columns for other saved queries.

Saved queries are a powerful way to virtualize the view of your directory and monitor for issues such as disabled or locked accounts. Learning to create and manage saved queries is a worthwhile use of your time.

MORE INFO   Saved queries

The following site is highly recommended for details and examples of saved queries: *http://www.petri.co.il/saved_queries_in_windows_2003_dsa.htm*.

Using the Select Users, Contacts, Computers, Or Groups Dialog Box

When you add a member to a group, assign a permission, or create a linked property, you are presented with the Select Users, Contacts, Computers, Or Groups dialog box shown in Figure 2-8. This dialog box is referred to as the *Select dialog box* throughout this training kit. If you'd like to see an example, open the properties of a group object, click the Members tab, and then click the Add button.

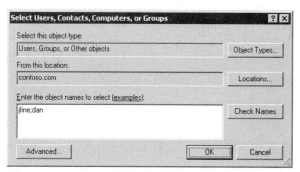

Figure 2-8   Select Users, Contacts, Computers, Or Groups dialog box

If you know the names of the objects you need, you can type them directly into the Enter The Object Names To Select text box. Multiple names can be entered, separated by semicolons, as shown in Figure 2-8. When you click OK, Windows looks up each item in the list and converts it into a link to the object, then closes the dialog box. The Check Names button also converts each name to a link but leaves the dialog box open, as shown in Figure 2-9.

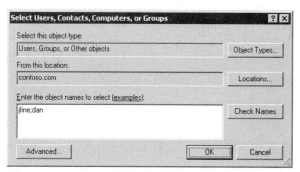

Figure 2-9   Names resolved to links using the Check Names button

You do not need to enter the full name; you can enter partial names instead. For example, Figure 2-8 shows the names jfine and dan. When you click OK or Check Names, Windows will attempt to convert your partial name to the correct object. If there is only one matching object, such as the logon name jfine, the name will be resolved as shown in Figure 2-9. If there are multiple matches, such as the name Dan, the Multiple Names Found box, shown in Figure 2-10, appears. Select the correct name(s) and click OK. The selected name appears as shown in Figure 2-9.

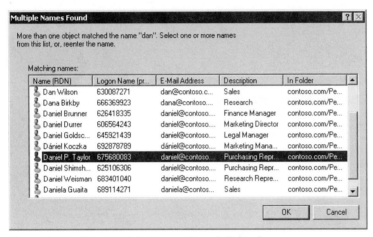

Figure 2-10   The Multiple Names Found dialog box

By default, the Select dialog box searches the entire domain. If you are getting too many results and wish to narrow the scope of your search, or if you need to search another domain or the local users and groups on a domain member, click Locations.

Additionally, the Select dialog box, despite its full name—Select Users, Contacts, Computers, Or Groups—rarely searches all four object types. When you add members to a group, for example, computers are not searched by default. If you enter a computer name, it will not be resolved correctly. When you specify Name on the Managed By tab, groups are not searched by default. You must make sure that the Select dialog box is scoped to resolve the types of objects you want to select. Click the Object Types button, use the Object Types dialog box shown in Figure 2-11 to select the correct types, and then click OK.

If you are having trouble locating the objects you want, click the Advanced button on the Select dialog box. The advanced view, shown in Figure 2-12, enables you to search both name and description fields as well as disabled accounts, nonexpiring passwords, and stale accounts that have not logged on for a specific period of time. Some of the fields on the Common Queries tab might be disabled, depending on the object type you are searching. Click the Object Types button to specify exactly the type of object you want.

Figure 2-11   The Object Types dialog box

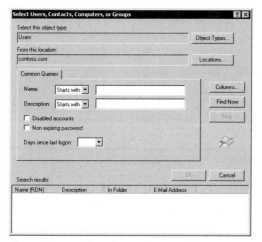

Figure 2-12   The advanced view of the Select dialog box

Using the *Find* Commands

Windows systems also provide the Active Directory query tool, called the Find box by many administrators. One way to launch the Find box is to click the Find Objects In Active Directory Domain Services button on the toolbar in the Active Directory Users And Computers snap-in. The button and the resulting Find box are shown in Figure 2-13.

Use the Find drop-down list to specify the type(s) of objects you want to query or select Common Queries or Custom Search. The In drop-down list specifies the scope of the search. It is recommended that, whenever possible, you narrow the scope of the search to avoid the performance impact of a large, domain-wide search. Together, the Find and the In lists define the scope of the search.

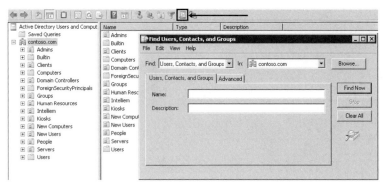

Figure 2-13   The Find box

Next, configure the search criteria. Commonly used fields are available as criteria based on the type of query you are performing. For the most complete, advanced control over the query, choose Custom Search in the Find drop-down list. If you choose Custom Search and then click the Advanced tab, you can build powerful LDAP queries. For example, the query **OU=*main*** searches for any OU with a name that contains *main* and would return the Domain Controllers OU. Without the custom search, you can search based on the text at the *beginning* of the name only; the custom search with wildcards enables you to build a "contains" search.

When you have specified your search scope and criteria, click Find Now. The results will appear. You can then right-click any item in the results list and perform commands such as *Move*, *Delete*, and *Properties*.

The Find box also appears in other Windows locations, including the Add Printer Wizard when locating a network printer. The Network folder also has a Search Active Directory button. You can add a custom shortcut, perhaps to your Start menu or desktop, to make searches even more accessible. The target of the shortcut should be *rundll32 dsquery,OpenQueryWindow*.

Finding Objects by Using *Dsquery*

Windows provides command-line utilities that perform functionality similar to that of user interface tools, such as the Active Directory Users and Computers snap-in. Many of those commands begin with the letters DS, so they are often referred to as *the DS commands. Dsquery* can locate objects in Active Directory.

Dsquery, like other DS commands, is well documented. Type **dsquery.exe /?** to learn its syntax and usage. Most DS commands are used by specifying the object class you want the command to work against. For example, you would type **dsquery user** to look for a user, whereas *Dsquery computer, Dsquery group*, and *Dsquery ou* would query for their respective object types. Following the object type specifier, you can use switches to indicate the criteria for the query. Each object can be located by its name, for example, with the *-name* switch. Most objects can be queried based on the description (-*desc*). Security principals can be located based on their pre-Windows 2000 logon name (-*samid*). To learn which properties may be queried, type **dsquery objecttype /?**.

For example, if you want to locate all users whose names begin with "Jam," you would type **dsquery user -name jam***. After the property switch, *name* in this case, you can enter the criteria, which are not case sensitive and can include wildcards such as the asterisk, which represents any zero or more characters. The *Dsquery* command returns matching objects with their distinguished names (DNs) by default, as you can see in Figure 2-14.

```
c:\>dsquery user -name jam*
"CN=James  D. Kramer,OU=Employees,OU=People,DC=contoso,DC=com"
"CN=James Fine,OU=People,DC=contoso,DC=com"
"CN=James Hendergart,OU=Employees,OU=People,DC=contoso,DC=com"
"CN=James R. Hamilton,OU=Employees,OU=People,DC=contoso,DC=com"
"CN=James van Eaton,OU=Employees,OU=People,DC=contoso,DC=com"
"CN=Jamie Reding,OU=Employees,OU=People,DC=contoso,DC=com"
```

Figure 2-14   The *Dsquery* command

If DNs are not the way you'd like to see the results, add the −*o* switch to the *Dsquery* command. You can add -*o samid*, for example, to return the results with pre-Windows 2000 logon names, or -*o upn* to return the list as user logon names, called UPNs.

Understanding DNs, RDNs, and CNs

DNs are a kind of path to an object in Active Directory. Each object in Active Directory has a completely unique DN. Our user, James Fine, has the DN CN=James Fine,OU=People,DC=contoso,DC=com.

You can see what is happening: the DN is a path starting at the object and working up to the top-level domain in the *contoso.com* DNS namespace. As mentioned earlier, CN stands for common name, and when you create a user, the Full Name box is used to create the CN of the user object. OU means organizational unit, not surprisingly. And DC means domain component.

The portion of the DN prior to the first OU or container is called the *relative distinguished name*, or RDN. In the case of James Fine, the RDN of the object is CN=James Fine. Not every RDN is a CN. The DN of the People OU is OU=People,DC=contoso,DC=com. The RDN of the People OU is, therefore, OU=People.

Because the DN of an object must be unique within the directory service, the RDN of an object must be unique within its container. That's why if you hire a second James Fine, and if both user objects should be in the same OU, you will have to give that user a different CN. The same logic applies as files in a folder: you cannot have two files with identical names in a single folder.

You will encounter DNs regularly as you work with Active Directory, just as you encounter file paths regularly if you work with files and folders. It's very important to be able to read them and interpret them.

PRACTICE **Creating and Locating Objects in Active Directory**

In this practice, you will create and then locate objects in Active Directory. You will create OUs, users, groups, and computers. You will then create a saved query and customize the view of that saved query. The objects you create in this practice will be used in other practices in this training kit.

▶ **Exercise 1   Create Organizational Units**

The default Users and Computers containers are provided to facilitate the setup of and migration to an Active Directory domain. It is recommended that you create OUs that reflect your administrative model and that you use these OUs to create and manage objects in your directory service. In this exercise, you will create OUs for the example domain, *contoso.com*. These OUs will be used in practices and exercises later in this training kit.

1. Log on to SERVER01 as Administrator.
2. Open the Active Directory Users And Computers snap-in.
3. Expand the Domain node.
4. Right-click the Domain node, choose New, and then select Organizational Unit.
5. Type the name of the organizational unit: **People**.
6. Select Protect Container From Accidental Deletion.
7. Click OK.
8. Right-click the OU and choose Properties.
9. In the *Description* field, type **Non-administrative user identities**.
10. Click OK.
11. Repeat steps 2–10 to create the following OUs.

OU Name	OU Description
Clients	Client computers
Groups	Non-administrative groups
Admins	Administrative identities and groups
Servers	Servers

▶ **Exercise 2   Create Users**

Now that you have created OUs in the *contoso.com* domain, you are ready to populate the directory service with objects. In this exercise, you will create several users in two of the OUs you created in Exercise 1, "Create Organizational Units." These user objects will be used in practices and exercises later in this training kit.

1. Log on to SERVER01 as Administrator and open the Active Directory Users And Computers snap-in.

2. Follow the procedure in the "Creating a User Object" section earlier in the chapter and create the following users in the People OU. For each user, create a complex, secure password. Remember the passwords you assign—you will be logging on as these user accounts in other exercises and practices in this training kit.

3. In the console tree, expand the Domain node, *contoso.com*, and select the People OU.

4. Right-click the People OU, choose New, and then select User.

   The New Object – User dialog box appears.

5. In First Name, type the user's first name: **Dan**.

6. In Last Name, type the user's last name: **Holme**.

7. In User Logon Name, type the user's logon name: **dholme**.

8. In the User Logon Name (Pre-Windows 2000) text box, enter the pre-Windows 2000 logon name: **dholme**.

9. Click Next.

10. Enter an initial password for the user in the Password and Confirm Password boxes.

    The default password policy for an Active Directory domain requires a password of seven or more characters. Additionally, the password must contain three of four character types: upper case (A–Z), lower case (a–z), numeric (0–9), and nonalphanumeric (for example, ! @ # $ %). The password cannot contain any of the user's name or logon name attributes.

    Remember the password you assign to this user; you will be logging on as this user account in other exercises and practices in this training kit.

    Many training resources suggest using a generic password such as P@ssword. You may use a generic password for the practices in this training kit; however, it is recommended that you create unique passwords, even in a practice, so that you are using best practices even in a lab environment.

11. Select User Must Change Password At Next Logon.

12. Click Next.

13. Review the summary and click Finish.

14. Right-click the user object you created and choose Properties.

15. Examine the attributes that can be configured in the Properties dialog box. Do not change any of the user's properties at this time.

16. Click OK.

17. Repeat steps 3–12 and create the following users in the People OU.
    - ❑ James Fine
        - First name: James
        - Last name: Fine

- ● Full name: James Fine
- ● User logon name: jfine
- ❑ Barbara Mayer
  - ● First name: Barbara
  - ● Last name: Mayer
  - ● Full name: Barbara Mayer
  - ● User logon name: bmayer
  - ● Pre-Windows 2000 logon name: bmayer
- ❑ Barbara Moreland
  - ● First name: Barbara
  - ● Last name: Moreland
  - ● Full name: Barbara Moreland
  - ● User logon name: bmoreland
  - ● Pre-Windows 2000 logon name: bmoreland

18. Repeat steps 3–12 and create a user account for yourself in the People OU. For the user logon name, use your first initial and last name, for example, dholme for Dan Holme. Create a complex, secure password and remember it because you will be logging on as this account in other exercises and practices in this training kit.

19. Repeat steps 3–12 and create an administrative account for yourself in the Admins OU. This account will be given administrative privileges. Create the user object in the Admins OU rather than in the People OU. For the user logon name, use your first initial and last name, followed by _admin, for instance, dholme_admin for Dan Holme's administrative account. Create a complex, secure password and remember it because you will be logging on as this account in other exercises and practices in this training kit.

▶ **Exercise 3   Create Computers**

Computer accounts should be created before joining machines to the domain. In this exercise, you will create several computers in two of the OUs you created in Exercise 1. These computer objects will be used in practices and exercises later in this training kit.

1. Log on to SERVER01 as Administrator and open the Active Directory Users And Computers snap-in.

2. In the console tree, expand the Domain node, *contoso.com*, and select the Servers OU.

3. Right-click the Servers OU, choose New, and then select Computer.
   The New Object – Computer dialog box appears.

4. In the Computer Name box, type the computer's name: **FILESERVER01**.
   Your entry will automatically populate the Computer Name (Pre-Windows 2000) box.

5. Do not change the name in the Computer Name (Pre-Windows 2000) box.

6. Take note of the account specified in the User Or Group Field text box. Do not change the value at this time.

7. Do not select the check box labeled Assign This Computer Account As A Pre-Windows 2000 Computer.

8. Click OK.

9. Right-click the computer and choose Properties.

10. Examine the properties that are available for a computer. Do not change any attributes at this time.

11. Click OK.

12. Repeat steps 3–8 to create computer objects for the following computers:
    - ❏   SHAREPOINT02
    - ❏   EXCHANGE03

13. Repeat steps 3–8 and create the following computers in the Clients OU rather than in the Servers OU.
    - ❏   DESKTOP101
    - ❏   DESKTOP102
    - ❏   LAPTOP103

▶ **Exercise 4   Create Groups**

It is a best practice to manage objects in groups rather than to manage each object individually. In this exercise, you will create several groups in two of the OUs you created in Exercise 1. These groups will be used in practices and exercises later in this training kit.

1. Log on to SERVER01 as Administrator and open the Active Directory Users And Computers snap-in.

2. In the console tree, expand the Domain node, *contoso.com*, and select the Groups OU.

3. Right-click the Groups OU, choose New, and then select Group.

    The New Object – Group dialog box appears.

4. Type the name of the new group in the Group Name text box: **Finance**.

5. Do not change the name in the Group Name (Pre-Windows 2000) box.

6. Select the Group Type: Security.

7. Select the Group Scope: Global.

8. Click OK.

    Group objects have a number of properties that are useful to configure. These can be specified after the object has been created.

9. Right-click the group and choose Properties.

10. Examine the properties available for the group. Do not change any attributes at this time.

11. Click OK.

12. Repeat steps 3–8 to create the following global security groups in the Groups OU:
    - ❑ Finance Managers
    - ❑ Sales
    - ❑ APP_Office 2007

13. Repeat steps 3–8 to create the following global security groups in the Admins OU rather than in the Groups OU.
    - ❑ Help Desk
    - ❑ Windows Administrators

▶ **Exercise 5   Add Users and Computers to Groups**

Now that you have created groups, you can add objects as members of the groups. In this exercise, you will add users and computers to groups. Along the way, you will gain experience with the Select dialog box that is used in some procedures to locate objects in Active Directory.

1. Log on to SERVER01 as Administrator and open the Active Directory Users And Computers snap-in.

2. Open the properties of your administrative account in the Admins OU.

3. Click the Member Of tab.

4. Click the Add button.

5. In the Select Groups dialog box, type the name **Domain Admins**.

6. Click OK.

7. Click OK again to close the account properties.

8. Open the properties of the Help Desk group in the Admins OU.

9. Click the Members tab.

10. Click the Add button.

11. In the Select dialog box, type **Barb**.

12. Click Check Names.

    The Multiple Names Found box appears.

13. Select Barbara Mayer and click OK.

14. Click OK to close the Select dialog box.

15. Click OK again to close the group properties.

16. Open the properties of the APP_Office 2007 group in the Groups OU.

17. Click the Members tab.

18. Click the Add button.

19. In the Select dialog box, type **DESKTOP101**.

20. Click Check Names.

    A Name Not Found dialog box appears, indicating that the object you specified could not be resolved.

21. Click Cancel to close the Name Not Found box.

22. In the Select box, click Object Types.

23. Select Computers as an object type and click OK.

24. Click Check Names. The name will resolve now that the Select box is including computers in its resolution.

25. Click OK.

▶ **Exercise 6   Find Objects in Active Directory**

When you need to find an object in your domain's directory service, it is sometimes more efficient to use search functionality than to click through your OU structure to browse for the object. In this exercise, you will use three interfaces for locating objects in Active Directory.

1. Log on to SERVER01 and open the Active Directory Users And Computers snap-in.

2. Click the Find Objects In Active Directory Domain Services button.

3. Make sure the In drop-down list is set to *contoso.com* (the domain name).

4. In the Name box, type **Barb**.

5. Click Find Now.

6. The two users named Barbara should appear in the Search results.

7. Close the Find box.

8. Open Network from the Start menu.

9. Click Search Active Directory.

10. Repeat steps 3–7.

11. In the Active Directory Users And Computers snap-in, right-click the Saved Queries node, choose New, and then choose Query.

    If Saved Queries is not visible, close the console and open the Active Directory Users And Computers console from the Administrative Tools folder of Control Panel.

12. In the Name box, type **All Users**.

13. In the Description box, type **Users for the entire domain**.

14. Click Define Query.

15. On the Users tab, in the Name box, choose Has A Value.

16. Click OK twice to close the dialog boxes.

    The results of the saved query appear. Note that it shows the users from both the People OU and the Admins OU.

17. Choose View, and then click Add/Remove Columns.

18. In the Available columns list, select Last Name and click the Add button.

19. In the Displayed columns list, select Type and click the Remove button.

20. Click OK.

21. Drag the Last Name column heading so that it is between Name and Description.

22. Click the Last Name column heading so that users are sorted alphabetically by last name.

Lesson Summary

■ Organizational units (OUs) are administrative containers that collect objects sharing similar requirements for administration, configuration, or visibility. They provide a way to access and manage a collection of users, groups, computers, or other objects easily. An OU cannot be given permission to a resource such as a shared folder.

■ When you create an object such as a user, computer, or group, you are able to configure only a limited number of its properties while creating it. After creating the object, you can open its properties and configure the attributes that were not visible during creation.

■ Object properties such as Description, Managed By, and Notes can be used to document important information about an object.

■ By default, OUs are created with protection, which prevents the accidental deletion of the OU. To disable protection, you must turn on Advanced Features from the View menu. Then, in the properties of the OU, click the Object tab to deselect protection.

Lesson Review

You can use the following questions to test your knowledge of the information in Lesson 2, "Creating Objects in Active Directory." The questions are also available on the companion CD if you prefer to review them in electronic form.

NOTE Answers

Answers to these questions and explanations of why each answer choice is right or wrong are located in the "Answers" section at the end of the book.

---

1. You have opened a command prompt, using Run As Administrator, with credentials in the Domain Admins group. You use the *Dsrm* command to remove an OU that had been created accidentally by James, a member of the Administrators group of the domain. You receive the response: Dsrm Failed: Access Is Denied. What is the cause of the error?

    A. You must launch the command prompt as a member of Administrators to perform Active Directory tasks.

    B. Only Administrators can delete OUs.

    C. Only the owner of the OU can delete an OU.

    D. The OU is protected from deletion.

Lesson 3: Delegation and Security of Active Directory Objects

In previous lessons of this chapter, you've learned how to create users, groups, computers, and OUs and how to access the properties of those objects. Your ability to perform those actions was dependent on your membership in the Administrators group of the domain. You would not want every user on your help desk team to be a member of the domain's Administrators group just to reset user passwords and unlock user accounts. Instead, you should enable the help desk and each role in your organization to perform the tasks that are required of the role and no more. In this lesson, you'll learn how to delegate specific administrative tasks within Active Directory, which is achieved by changing the access control lists (ACLs) on Active Directory objects.

After this lesson, you will be able to:
- Describe the business purpose of delegation.
- Assign permissions to Active Directory objects by using the security editor user interfaces and the Delegation of Control Wizard.
- View and report permissions on Active Directory objects by using user interface and command-line tools.
- Evaluate effective permissions for a user or group.
- Reset the permissions on an object to its default.
- Describe the relationship between delegation and OU design.

Estimated lesson time: 35 minutes

Understanding Delegation

In most organizations, there is more than one administrator, and as organizations grow, administrative tasks are often distributed to various administrators or support organizations. For example, in many organizations, the help desk is able to reset user passwords and unlock the accounts of users who are locked out. This capability of the help desk is a delegated administrative task. The help desk cannot, usually, create new user accounts, but it can make specific changes to existing user accounts.

All Active Directory objects, such as the users, computers, and groups you created in the previous lesson, can be secured using a list of permissions, so you could give your help desk permission to reset passwords on user objects. The permissions on an object are called *access control entries* (ACEs), and they are assigned to users, groups, or computers (called *security principals*). ACEs are saved in the object's discretionary access control list (DACL). The DACL is a part of the object's ACL, which also contains the system access control list (SACL) that includes auditing settings. This might sound familiar to you if you have studied the permissions on files and folders—the terms and concepts are identical.

The delegation of administrative control, also called the delegation of control or just delegation, simply means assigning permissions that manage access to objects and properties in Active Directory. Just as you can give a group the ability to change files in a folder, you can give a group the ability to reset passwords on user objects.

Viewing the ACL of an Active Directory Object

At the lowest level is the ACL on an individual user object in Active Directory. To view the ACL on an object:

1. Open the Active Directory Users And Computers snap-in.
2. Click the View menu and select Advanced Features.
3. Right-click an object and choose Properties.
4. Click the Security tab.

   If Advanced Features is not enabled, you will not see the Security tab in an object's Properties dialog box.

   The Security tab of the object's Properties dialog box is shown in Figure 2-15.

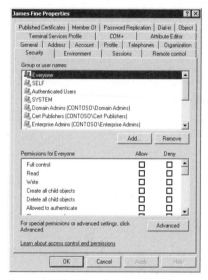

Figure 2-15   The Security tab of an Active Directory object's Properties dialog box

5. Click the Advanced button.

   The Security tab shows a very high-level overview of the security principals that have been given permissions to the object, but in the case of Active Directory ACLs, the Security tab is rarely detailed enough to provide the information you need to interpret or manage the ACL. You should always click Advanced to open the Advanced Security Settings dialog box.

The dialog box showing Advanced Security Settings for an object appears, shown in Figure 2-16.

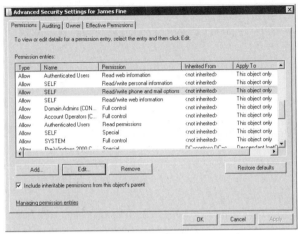

Figure 2-16   The Advanced Security Settings dialog box for an Active Directory object

The Permissions tab of the Advanced Security Settings dialog box shows the DACL of the object. You can see in Figure 2-16 that ACEs are summarized on a line of the Permission entries list. In this dialog box, you are not seeing the granular ACEs of the DACL. For example, the permission entry that is selected in Figure 2-16 is actually composed of two ACEs.

6.   To see the granular ACEs of a permission entry, select the entry and click Edit.

The Permission Entry dialog box appears, detailing the specific ACEs that make up the entry, as in Figure 2-17.

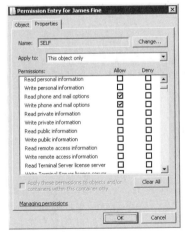

Figure 2-17   The Permission Entry dialog box

Quick Check

- You want to view the permissions assigned to an OU. You open the OU's Properties dialog box and there is no Security tab visible. What must you do?

Quick Check Answer

- In the Active Directory Users And Computers snap-in, click the View menu and select Advanced Features.

Object, Property, and Control Access Rights

The DACL of an object enables you to assign permissions to specific properties of an object. As you saw in Figure 2-17, you can allow (or deny) permission to change phone and e-mail options. This is in fact not just one property; it is a property set that includes multiple specific properties. Property sets make it easier to manage permissions to commonly used collections of properties. But you could get even more granular and allow or deny permission to change just the mobile telephone number or just the home street address.

Permissions can also be assigned to manage control access rights, which are actions such as changing or resetting a password. The difference between those two control access rights is important to understand. If you have the right to *change* a password, you must know and enter the current password before making the change. If you have the right to *reset* a password, you are not required to know the previous password.

Finally, permissions can be assigned to objects. For example, the ability to change permissions on an object is controlled by the Allow::Modify Permissions ACE. Object permissions also control whether you are able to create child objects. For example, you might give your desktop support team permissions to create computer objects in the OU for your desktops and laptops. The Allow::Create Computer Objects ACE would be assigned to the desktop support team at the OU.

The type and scope of permissions are managed using the two tabs, Object and Properties, and the Apply To drop-down lists on each tab.

Assigning a Permission Using the Advanced Security Settings Dialog Box

Imagine a scenario in which you want to allow the help desk to change the password on James Fine's account. In this section, you will learn to do it the most complicated way first: by assigning the ACE on the DACL of the user object. Later, you'll learn how to perform the delegation by using the Delegation Of Control Wizard for the entire OU of users, and you'll see why this latter practice is recommended.

1. Open the Active Directory Users And Computers snap-in.
2. Click the View menu and select Advanced Features.
3. Right-click an object and choose Properties.
4. Click the Security tab.
5. Click the Advanced button.
6. Click the Add button.

   If you have User Account Control enabled, you might need to click Edit and, perhaps, enter administrative credentials before the Add button will appear.
7. In the Select dialog box, select the security principal to which permissions will be assigned.

   It is an important best practice to assign permissions to groups, not to individual users. In your example, you would select your Help Desk group.
8. Click OK.

   The Permission Entry dialog box appears.
9. Configure the permissions you want to assign.

   For our example, on the Object tab, scroll down the list of Permissions and select Allow::Reset Password.
10. Click OK to close each dialog box.

Understanding and Managing Permissions with Inheritance

You can imagine that assigning the help desk permission to reset passwords for each individual user object would be quite time-consuming. Luckily, you don't have to and, in fact, it's a terrible practice to assign permissions to individual objects in Active Directory. Instead, you will assign permissions to organizational units. The permissions you assign to an OU will be inherited by all objects in the OU. Thus, if you give the help desk permission to reset passwords for user objects, and you attach that permission to the OU that contains your users, all user objects within that OU will inherit that permission. With one step, you'll have delegated that administrative task.

Inheritance is an easy concept to understand. Child objects inherit the permissions of the parent container or OU. That container or OU in turn inherits its permissions from its parent container, OU, or, if it is a first-level container or OU, from the domain itself. The reason child objects inherit permissions from their parents is that, by default, each new object is created with the Include Inheritable Permissions From This Object's Parent option enabled. You can see the option in Figure 2-16.

Note, however, that as the option indicates, only *inheritable* permissions will be inherited by the child object. Not every permission, however, is inheritable. For example, the permission to reset passwords assigned to an OU would not be inherited by group objects because group objects do not have a password attribute. So inheritance can be scoped to specific object classes: passwords are applicable to user objects, not to groups. Additionally, you can use the Apply To box of the Permission Entry dialog box to scope the inheritance of a permission. The conversation can start to get very complicated. What you should know is that, by default, new objects inherit inheritable permissions from their parent object—usually an OU or container.

What if the permission being inherited is not appropriate? Two things can be done to modify the permissions that a child object is inheriting. First, you can disable inheritance by deselecting the Include Inheritable Permissions From This Object's Parent option in the Advanced Security Settings dialog box. When you do, the object will no longer inherit any permissions from its parent—all permissions will be explicitly defined for the child object. This is generally not a good practice because it creates an exception to the rule that is being created by the permissions of the parent containers.

The second option is to allow inheritance but override the inherited permission with a permission assigned specifically to the child object—an explicit permission. Explicit permissions always override permissions that are inherited from parent objects. This has an important implication: an explicit permission that *allows* access will actually override an inherited permission that *denies* the same access. If that sounds counterintuitive to you, it is not: the rule is being defined by a parent (deny), but the child object has been configured to be an exception (allow).

Exam Tip   Look out for scenarios in which access or delegation are not performing as expected either because inheritance has been broken—the child is no longer inheriting permissions from its parent—or because the child object has an explicit permission that overrides the permissions of the parent.

Delegating Administrative Tasks with the Delegation Of Control Wizard

You've seen the complexity of the DACL, and you've probably gleaned that managing permissions by using the Permission Entry dialog box is not a simple task. Luckily, the best practice is not to manage permissions by using the security interfaces but, rather, to use the Delegation of Control Wizard. The following procedure details the use of the wizard.

1. Open the Active Directory Users And Computers snap-in.
2. Right-click the node (Domain or OU) for which you want to delegate administrative tasks or control and choose Delegate Control.

    In this example, you would select the OU that contains your users.

    The Delegation of Control Wizard is displayed to guide you through the required steps.

3. Click Next.

   You will first select the administrative group to which you are granting privileges.

4. On the Users or Groups page, click the Add button.

5. Use the Select dialog box to select the group and click OK.

6. Click Next.

   Next, you will specify the specific task you wish to assign that group.

7. On the Tasks To Delegate page, select the task.

   In this example, you would select Reset User Passwords and Force Password Change at Next Logon.

8. Click Next.

9. Review the summary of the actions that have been performed and click Finish.

   The Delegation of Control Wizard applies the ACEs that are required to enable the selected group to perform the specified task.

Reporting and Viewing Permissions

There are several other ways to view and report permissions when you need to know who can do what. You've already seen that you can view permissions on the DACL by using the Advanced Security Settings and Permission Entry dialog boxes.

Dsacls.exe is also available as a command-line tool that reports on directory service objects. If you type the command, followed by the distinguished name of an object, you will see a report of the object's permissions. For example, this command will produce a report of the permissions associated with the People OU:

```
dsacls.exe "ou=People,dc=contoso,dc=com"
```

Dsacls can also be used to set permissions—to delegate. Type **dsacls.exe /?** for help regarding the syntax and usage of *Dsacls*.

Removing or Resetting Permissions on an Object

How do you remove or reset permissions that have been delegated? Unfortunately, there is no undelegate command. You must use the Advanced Security Settings and Permission Entry dialog boxes to remove permissions. If you want to reset the permissions on the object back to the defaults, open the Advanced Security Settings dialog box and click Restore Defaults. The default permissions are defined by the Active Directory schema for the class of object. After you've restored the defaults, you can reconfigure the explicit permissions you want to add to the DACL. *Dsacls* also provides the */s* switch to reset permissions to the schema-defined defaults, and the */t* switch makes the change for the entire tree—the object and all its child objects. For example, to reset permissions on the People OU and all its child OUs and objects, you would type:

```
dsacls "ou=People,dc=contoso,dc=com" /resetDefaultDACL
```

Understanding Effective Permissions

Effective permissions are the resulting permissions for a security principal, such as a user or group, based on the cumulative effect of each inherited and explicit ACE. Your ability to reset a user's password, for example, can be due to your membership in a group that was allowed Reset Password permission on an OU several levels above the user object. The inherited permission assigned to a group to which you belong resulted in an effective permission of Allow::Reset Password. Your effective permissions can be complicated when you consider allow and deny permissions, explicit and inherited ACEs, and the fact that you might belong to multiple groups, each of which might be assigned different permissions.

Permissions, whether assigned to your user account or to a group to which you belong, are equivalent. In the end, an ACE applies to you, the user. The best practice is to manage permissions by assigning them to groups, but it is also possible to assign ACEs to individual users or computers. Just because a permission has been assigned directly to you, the user, doesn't mean that permission is either more important or less important than a permission assigned to a group to which you belong.

Permissions that allow access (allow permissions) are cumulative. When you belong to several groups, and those groups have been granted permissions that allow a variety of tasks, you will be able to perform all the tasks assigned to all those groups as well as tasks assigned directly to your user account.

Permissions that deny access (deny permissions) override an equivalent allow permission. If you are in one group that has been allowed the permission to reset passwords, and another group that has been denied permission to reset passwords, the deny permission will prevent you from resetting passwords.

NOTE Use Deny permissions sparingly

It is generally unnecessary to assign deny permissions. If you simply do not assign an allow permission, users cannot perform the task. Before assigning a deny permission, check to see whether you could achieve your goal by removing an allow permission instead. Use deny permissions rarely and thoughtfully.

Each permission is granular. Even though you've been denied the ability to reset passwords, you might still have the ability, through other allow permissions, to change the user's logon name or e-mail address.

Finally, you learned earlier in this lesson that child objects inherit the inheritable permissions of parent objects by default and that explicit permissions can override inheritable permissions. This means that an explicit allow permission will actually override an inherited deny permission.

Unfortunately, the complex interaction of user, group, explicit, inherited, allow, and deny permissions can make evaluating effective permissions a bit of a chore. There is an Effective Permissions tab in the Advanced Security Settings dialog box of an Active Directory object, but the tab is practically useless; it does not expose enough permissions to provide the kind of detailed information you will require. You can use the permissions reported by the *Dsacls* command or on the Permissions tab of the Advanced Security Settings dialog box to begin evaluating effective permissions, but it will be a manual task.

MORE INFO   Role-based access control

The best way to manage delegation in Active Directory is through role-based access control. Although this approach will not be covered on the certification exam, it is well worth understanding for real-world implementation of delegation. See *Windows Administration Resource Kit: Productivity Solutions for IT Professionals*, by Dan Holme (Microsoft Press, 2008) for more information.

Designing an OU Structure to Support Delegation

OUs are, as you now know, administrative containers. They contain objects that share similar requirements for administration, configuration, and visibility. You now understand the first of those requirements: administration. Objects that will be administered the same way, by the same administrators, should be contained within a single OU. By placing your users in a single OU called "People," you can delegate the help desk permission to change all users' passwords by assigning one permission to one OU. Any other permissions that affect what an administrator can do to a user object will be assigned at the People OU. For example, you might allow your HR managers to disable user accounts in the event of an employee's termination. You would delegate that permission, again, to the People OU.

Remember that administrators should be logging on to their systems with user credentials and launching administrative tools with the credentials of a secondary account that has appropriate permissions to perform administrative tasks. Those secondary accounts are the administrative accounts of the enterprise. It is not appropriate for the frontline help desk to be able to reset passwords on such privileged accounts, and you probably would not want HR managers to disable administrative accounts. Therefore, administrative accounts are being administered differently than nonadminstrative user accounts. That's why you have a separate OU, Admins, for administrative user objects. That OU will be delegated quite differently than the People OU.

Similarly, you might delegate the desktop support team the ability to add computer objects to the Clients OU, which contains your desktops and laptops, but not to the Servers OU, where only your Server Administration group has permissions to create and manage computer objects.

The primary role of OUs is to scope delegation efficiently, to apply permissions to objects and sub-OUs. When you design an Active Directory environment, you always begin by designing an OU structure that will make delegation efficient—a structure that reflects the administrative model of your organization. Rarely does object administration in Active Directory look like your organizational chart. Typically, all normal user accounts are supported the same way, by the same team, so user objects are often found in a single OU or in a single OU branch. Quite often, an organization that has a centralized help desk function to support users will also have a centralized desktop support function, in which case, all client computer objects would be within a single OU or single OU branch. However, if desktop support is decentralized, you would be likely to find that the Clients OU is divided into sub-OUs representing geographic locations so that each location is delegated to allow the local support team to add computer objects to the domain in that location.

Design OUs, first, to enable the efficient delegation of objects in the directory. Once you have achieved that design, you will refine the design to facilitate the configuration of computers and users through Group Policy, which will be discussed in Chapter 6, "Group Policy Infrastructure." Active Directory design is an art and a science.

PRACTICE Delegating Administrative Tasks

In this practice, you will manage the delegation of administrative tasks within the *contoso.com* domain and view the resulting changes to ACLs on Active Directory objects. Before performing the exercises in this practice, you must perform the practice in Lesson 2, "Practice: Creating and Locating Objects in Active Directory." The OUs created in that practice are required for these exercises.

▶ **Exercise 1   Delegate Control for Support of User Accounts**

In this exercise, you will enable the Help Desk to support users by resetting passwords and unlocking user accounts in the People OU.

1. Log on to SERVER01 as Administrator and open the Active Directory Users And Computers snap-in.
2. Expand the Domain node, *contoso.com*, right-click the People OU, and choose Delegate Control to launch the Delegation Of Control Wizard.
3. Click Next.
4. On the Users Or Groups page, click the Add button.
5. Using the Select dialog box, type **Help Desk**, and then click OK.
6. Click Next.

7. On the Tasks To Delegate page, select the Reset User Passwords And Force Password Change At Next Logon task.

8. Click Next.

9. Review the summary of the actions that have been performed and click Finish.

▶ **Exercise 2   View Delegated Permissions**

In this exercise, you will view the permissions you assigned to the Help Desk.

1. Log on to SERVER01 as Administrator and open the Active Directory Users And Computers snap-in.

2. Right-click the People OU and choose Properties.

   Note that the Security tab is not visible. If Advanced Features is not enabled, you will not see the Security tab in an object's Properties dialog box.

3. Click OK to close the Properties dialog box.

4. Click the View menu and select Advanced Features.

5. Right-click the People OU and choose Properties.

6. Click the Security tab.

7. Click the Advanced button.

8. In the Permission Entries list, select the first permission assigned to the Help Desk.

9. Click the Edit button.

10. In the Permission Entry dialog box, locate the permission that is assigned, and then click OK to close the dialog box.

11. Repeat steps 8–10 for the second permission entry assigned to the Help Desk.

12. Repeat steps 2–11 to view the ACL of a user in the People OU and to examine the inherited permissions assigned to the Help Desk.

13. Open the command prompt, type **dsacls "ou=people,dc=contoso,dc=com"**, and press Enter.

14. Locate the permissions assigned to the Help Desk.

Lesson Summary

- Delegation of control in Active Directory enables an organization to assign specific administrative tasks to appropriate teams and individuals.
- Delegation is the result of permissions, or ACEs, on the DACL of Active Directory objects.
- The DACL can be viewed and modified using the Advanced Security Settings of the object's Properties dialog box.
- The Delegation of Control Wizard simplifies the underlying complexity of object ACLs by enabling you to assign tasks to groups.

- Permissions on an object can be reset to their defaults by using the Advanced Security Settings dialog box or *Dsacls* with the */resetDefaultDACL* switch.

- It is a best practice to delegate control by using organizational units. Objects within the OUs will inherit the permissions of their parent OUs.

- Inheritance can be modified by disabling inheritance on a child object or by applying an explicit permission to the child object that overrides the inherited permission.

- Effective permissions are the result of user, group, allow, deny, inherited, and explicit permissions. Deny permissions override allow permissions, but explicit permissions override inherited permissions. Therefore, an explicit allow permission will override an inherited deny permission.

Lesson Review

You can use the following questions to test your knowledge of the information in Lesson 3, "Delegation and Security of Active Directory Objects." The questions are also available on the companion CD if you prefer to review them in electronic form.

NOTE   Answers

Answers to these questions and explanations of why each answer choice is right or wrong are located in the "Answers" section at the end of the book.

---

1. You want to enable your help desk to reset user passwords and unlock user accounts. Which of the following tools can be used? (Choose all that apply.)

   A. The Delegation of Control Wizard

   B. DSACLS

   C. DSUTIL

   D. The Advanced Security Settings dialog box

Chapter Review

To further practice and reinforce the skills you learned in this chapter, you can perform the following tasks:

- Review the chapter summary.
- Review the list of key terms introduced in this chapter.
- Complete the case scenario. This scenario sets up a real-world situation involving the topics of this chapter and asks you to create a solution.
- Complete the suggested practices.
- Take a practice test.

Chapter Summary

- The Active Directory Users and Computers snap-in, which is part of Server Manager and of the Active Directory Users and Computers console, can be also be added to custom consoles and distributed to administrators.
- As you create objects with the Active Directory Users and Computers snap-in, you are able to configure a limited number of initial properties. After an object is created, you can populate a much larger set of properties. These properties can be used in saved queries to provide customizable views of your enterprise objects.
- Organizational units should be used to delegate administrative control so that teams in your enterprise can perform the tasks required of their role. With inheritance enabled, objects will inherit the permissions of their parent OUs.

Key Terms

Use these key terms to understand better the concepts covered in this chapter.

- **delegation** Assignment of an administrative task. Delegation within Active Directory is achieved by modifying the DACL of an object. A common example is delegation of the ability to reset user passwords to a help desk role. By assigning the help desk the Allow::Reset Passwords control access right on an OU, members of the help desk role will be able to reset passwords for all user objects within the OU.
- **saved query** A view of Active Directory objects based on search criteria. Saved Queries, a node within the Active Directory Users and Computers snap-in, allow enables you to specify the type and properties of objects that you want to look for. Results are returned in the details pane of the snap-in.

Case Scenario

In the following case scenario, you will apply what you've learned about Active Directory snap-ins and object creation, delegation, and security. You can find answers to these questions in the "Answers" section at the end of this book.

Case Scenario: Organizational Units and Delegation

You are an administrator at Contoso, Ltd. Contoso's Active Directory was created when the organization was very small. One OU was created for users and one for computers. Now, the organization spans five geographic sites around the world, with over 1,000 employees. At each site, one or two members of desktop support personnel provide help to users with desktop applications and are responsible for installing systems and joining them to the domain. In addition, a small team at headquarters occasionally installs systems, joins them to the domain, and ships them to the site. If a user has forgotten his or her password, a centralized help desk telephone number is directed to one of the support personnel members on call, regardless of which site the user is in. Answer the following questions for your manager, who is concerned about manageability and least privilege, and explain how delegation would be managed:

1. Should computer objects remain in a single OU, or should the objects be divided by site? If divided, should the site OUs be under a single parent OU?
2. Should the ability to manage computer objects in sites be delegated directly to the user accounts of the desktop support personnel, or should groups be created, even though those groups might have only one or two members?
3. Should users be divided by site or remain within a single OU?

Suggested Practices

To help you successfully master the exam objectives presented in this chapter, complete the following tasks.

Maintain Active Directory Accounts

In this practice, you will validate that delegation has been successful, and you will experience what happens when an administrator attempts to perform a task that has not been delegated. You will also experience the results of inheritance and of OU protection.

To perform this practice, you must have performed the practices in Lesson 2 and Lesson 3. Specifically, ensure that:

- There is a user account in the Admins OU.
- There is a Help Desk group in the Admins OU.
- There is a user account for Barbara Mayer and at least one other user account in the People OU.
- The user Barbara Mayer is a member of the Help Desk group.
- The Help Desk group has been delegated the Reset User Passwords and Force Password Change at Next Logon permissions for the People OU.

In addition, make sure that the Domain Users group is a member of the Print Operators group, which can be found in the Builtin container. This will enable all sample users in the practice domain to log on to the SERVER01 domain controller. This is important for the practices in this training kit, but you should not allow users to log on to domain controllers in your production environment, so do not make Domain Users members of the Print Operators group in your production environment.

- **Practice 1**   Log on to SERVER01 as Barbara Mayer. She is a member of the Help Desk group. Validate that she can reset the password of users other than her own in the People OU. Then attempt to change the password of a user account in the Admins OU. Investigate the results.

- **Practice 2**   Log on to SERVER01 as Administrator. Create a new OU within the People OU, called Branch. When you create the Branch OU, ensure that the Protect Container From Accidental Deletion option is selected because you will delete this OU after this practice. Create a user account in the OU. Open the DACL of the user object in the Advanced Security Settings dialog box. Note the permissions assigned to the Help Desk. Are they explicit or inherited? If inherited, where are they inherited from? Open the DACL of the Branch OU in the Advanced Security Settings dialog box. Deselect the Include Inheritable Permissions From This Object's Parent option.

  Log off and log on as Barbara Mayer. Validate that she can reset the password of a user in the People OU. Now attempt to reset the password of the user in the Branch OU. Access is denied.

  Log off and log on as Administrator. Troubleshoot Barbara's lack of access by restoring inheritance to the Branch OU. Log off and log on as Barbara to validate the results. Can she successfully reset the password of a user in the Branch OU?

- **Practice 3**   Log on to SERVER01 as Barbara Mayer. Attempt to delete the Branch OU. Access is denied. Log off and log on as Administrator. Attempt to delete the Branch OU. Access is denied. Open the properties of the Branch OU. Look for the Object tab. If it is not visible, turn on the Advanced Features view of the Active Directory Users And Computers snap-in. On the Object tab, unprotect the Branch OU. Finally, delete the Branch OU and the user account within it.

Take a Practice Test

The practice tests on this book's companion CD offer many options. For example, you can test yourself on just one exam objective, or you can test yourself on all the 70-640 certification exam content. You can set up the test so that it closely simulates the experience of taking a certification exam, or you can set it up in study mode so that you can look at the correct answers and explanations after you answer each question.

MORE INFO   Practice tests

For details about all the practice test options available, see the "How to Use the Practice Tests" section in this book's introduction.

Chapter 3
Users

Chapter 1, "Installation," introduced Active Directory Domain Services (AD DS) as an identity and access solution. User accounts stored in the directory are the fundamental component of identity. Because of their importance, knowledge of user accounts and the tasks related to support them is critical to the success of an administrator in a Microsoft Windows enterprise.

Your ability to work effectively with user accounts can make a big difference in your overall productivity. Skills that are effective to create or modify a single user account, such as the procedures described in Chapter 2, "Administration," can become clumsy and inefficient when you are working with large numbers of accounts, such as when creating the accounts of newly hired employees.

In this chapter, you will learn how to apply tools and techniques to automate the creation and management of users and to locate and manipulate user objects and their attributes. Along the way, you will be introduced to Microsoft Windows PowerShell, which represents the future of command line–based and automated administration for Windows technologies. You will learn a variety of options for performing each of the most common administrative tasks.

The certification exam will expect you to have a very basic understanding of the purpose and syntax of command-line utilities, Windows PowerShell, and Microsoft Visual Basic Script (VBScript). However, this chapter goes beyond the expectations of the exam to provide a solid introduction to scripting and automation. Practice what you learn in this chapter, not because you'll need to be a scripting guru to pass the exam but because the more you can automate those tedious administrative tasks, the more you can elevate your productivity and your success.

Exam objectives in this chapter:
- Creating and Maintaining Active Directory Objects
    - ❑ Automate creation of Active Directory accounts.
    - ❑ Maintain Active Directory accounts.

Lessons in this chapter:
- Lesson 1: Automating the Creation of User Accounts. 87
- Lesson 2: Creating Users with Windows PowerShell and VBScript 98
- Lesson 3: Supporting User Objects and Accounts. 114

Before You Begin

To complete the practices in this chapter, you must have created a domain controller named SERVER01 in a domain named *contoso.com*. See Chapter 1 for detailed steps for this task.

Real World

Dan Holme

It's really amazing to stop and consider how much of our time as Windows administrators is spent performing basic tasks related to user objects. Each day in an enterprise network brings with it a unique set of challenges related to user management. Employees are hired, moved, married, and divorced, and most eventually leave the organization. As human beings, they make mistakes like forgetting passwords or locking out their accounts by logging on incorrectly.

Administrators must respond to all these changes, and user accounts are so complicated, with so many properties, that even the most well-intentioned administrators often stray from the procedures and conventions they've established. I believe that the key to efficient, effective, consistent, and secure user environments begins with raising the skill set of administrators.

Lesson 1: Automating the Creation of User Accounts

In Chapter 2, you learned how to create a user account in the Active Directory Users and Computers snap-in. Although the procedures discussed in Chapter 2 can be applied to create a small number of users, you will need more advanced techniques to automate the creation of user accounts when a large number of users must be added to the domain. In this lesson, you will learn several of these techniques.

After this lesson, you will be able to:
- Create users from user account templates.
- Import users with *CSVDE*.
- Import users with *LDIFDE*.

Estimated lesson time: 30 minutes

Creating Users with Templates

Users in a domain often share many similar properties. For example, all sales representatives can belong to the same security groups, log on to the network during similar hours, and have home folders and roaming profiles stored on the same server. When you create a new user, you can simply copy an existing user account rather than create a blank account and populate each property.

Since the days of Microsoft Windows NT 4.0, Windows has supported the concept of user account templates. A user account template is a generic user account prepopulated with common properties. For example, you can create a template account for sales representatives that is preconfigured with group memberships, logon hours, a home folder, and roaming profile path.

NOTE Disable template user accounts

The template account should not be used to log on to the network, so be sure to disable the account.

To create a user based on the template, select Copy from the shortcut menu. The Copy Object – User Wizard appears. You are prompted for the name, logon name, and password settings of the new user. A number of properties of the template are copied to the new user account. After a user account is created, you can view its properties, grouped by tab, in the Properties dialog box. Some of the tabs and properties that appear are the following:

- **General**   No properties are copied from the General tab
- **Address**   P.O. box, city, state or province, zip or postal code, and country or region. Note that the street address itself is not copied
- **Account**   Logon hours, logon workstations, account options, and account expiration
- **Profile**   Profile path, logon script, home drive, and home folder path

- **Organization**   Department, company, and manager
- **Member Of**   Group membership and primary group

NOTE   What you see isn't all you get

User accounts have additional properties that are not visible on the standard tabs in the Active Directory Users and Computers snap-in. These hidden attributes include useful properties such as assistant, division, employee type, and employee ID. To view these properties, click the View menu in the Active Directory Users and Computers snap-in and select the Advanced Features option. Then open the properties of a user account and click the Attribute Editor tab. Several of these attributes, including assistant, division, and employee type, are also copied from a template to a new account.

What Is Copied Is Not Enough

Many administrators consider the list of copied attributes to be somewhat limited. For example, you might want the job title and street address attributes to be copied. You can actually modify the Active Directory schema to include additional attributes when duplicating a user. See Knowledge Base article 827832 at *http://support.microsoft .com/kb/827832* for instructions.

However, you will be well served to use more advanced methods for automating the creation of user accounts. Later in this chapter, you will learn to use directory service (DS) commands, Comma-Separated Values Data Exchange (CSVDE), LDAP Data Interchange Format Data Exchange (LDIFDE), and Windows PowerShell to automate administrative tasks. With these tools, you will have full control over the process used to provision a new account.

Using Active Directory Command-Line Tools

In Chapter 2, you were introduced to *Dsquery.exe*, one of a suite of Active Directory command-line tools collectively called *DS commands*. The following DS commands are supported in Windows Server 2008:

- **Dsadd**   Creates an object in the directory.
- **Dsget**   Returns specified attributes of an object.
- **Dsmod**   Modifies specified attributes of an object.
- **Dsmove**   Moves an object to a new container or OU.
- **Dsrm**   Removes an object, all objects in the subtree beneath a container object, or both.
- **Dsquery**   Performs a query based on parameters provided at the command line and returns a list of matching objects. By default, the result set is presented as the distinguished

names (DNs) of each object, but you can use the *−o* parameter with modifiers such as *dn*, *rdn*, *upn*, or *samid* to receive the results as DNs, relative DNs, user principal names (UPNs), or pre-Windows 2000 logon names (security accounts manager [SAM] IDs).

Most of the DS commands take two modifiers after the command itself: the object type and the object's DN. For example, the following command adds a user account for Mike Fitzmaurice:

```
dsadd user "cn=Mike Fitzmaurice,ou=People,dc=contoso,dc=com"
```

The object type, *user*, immediately follows the command. After the object type is the object's DN. When the object's DN includes a space, surround the DN with quotes. The following command removes the same user:

```
dsrm user "cn=Mike Fitzmaurice,ou=People,dc=contoso,dc=com"
```

DS commands that read or manipulate attributes of objects include *Dsquery.exe*, *Dsget.exe*, and *Dsmod.exe*. To specify an attribute, include it as a parameter after the object's DN. For example, the following command retrieves the home folder path for Mike Fitzmaurice:

```
dsget user "cn=Mike Fitzmaurice,ou=People,dc=contoso,dc=com" -hmdir
```

The parameter of a DS command that represents an attribute, for example, *hmdir*, is not always the same as the name of the attribute in the Active Directory Users and Computers snap-in or in the schema.

Creating Users with *Dsadd*

Use the *Dsadd* command to create objects in Active Directory. The *DSADD USER UserDN* command creates a user object and accepts parameters that specify properties of the user. The following command shows the basic parameters required to create a user account:

```
dsadd user "User DN" -samid pre-Windows 2000 logon name
-pwd {Password | *} -mustchpwd yes
```

The *pwd* parameter specifies the password. If it is set to an asterisk (*), you are prompted for a user password. The *mustchpwd* parameter specifies that the user must change the password at next logon.

DSADD USER accepts a number of parameters that specify properties of the user object. Most parameter names are self-explanatory: *-email*, *-profile*, and *-company*, for example. Type **DSADD USER /?** or search the Windows Server 2008 Help And Support Center for thorough documentation of the *DSADD USER* parameters.

The special token *$username$* represents the SAM ID in the value of the *-email*, *-hmdir*, *-profile*, and *-webpg* parameters. For example, to configure a home folder for a user when creating the user with the *DSADD USER* command shown earlier, add the following parameter:

```
-hmdir \\server01\users\$username$\documents
```

Importing Users with *CSVDE*

CSVDE is a command-line tool that imports or exports Active Directory objects from or to a comma-delimited text file (also known as a comma-separated value text file, or .csv file). Comma-delimited files can be created, modified, and opened with tools as familiar as Notepad and Microsoft Office Excel. If you have user information in existing Excel or Microsoft Office Access databases, you will find that *CSVDE* is a powerful way to take advantage of that information to automate user account creation.

The basic syntax of the *CSVDE* command is:

```
csvde [-i] [-f Filename] [-k]
```

The *i* parameter specifies import mode; without it, the default mode of *CSVDE* is export. The *-f* parameter identifies the file name to import from or export to. The *-k* parameter is useful during import operations because it instructs *CSVDE* to ignore errors including Object Already Exists, Constraint Violation, and Attribute Or Value Already Exists.

The import file itself is a comma-delimited text file (.csv or .txt) in which the first line defines the imported attributes by their Lightweight Directory Access Protocol (LDAP) attribute names. Each object follows, one per line, and must contain exactly the attributes listed on the first line. Here's a sample file:

```
DN,objectClass,sAMAccountName,sn,givenName,userPrincipalName
"cn=Lisa Andrews,ou=People,dc=contoso,dc=com",user,lisa.andrews,
Lisa,Andrews,lisa.andrews@contoso.com
```

This file, when imported by the *CSVDE* command, will create a user object for Lisa Andrews in the People OU. The user logon names, last name and first name, are configured by the file. You cannot use the *CSVDE* to import passwords, and without a password, the user account will be disabled initially. After you have reset the password, you can enable the object.

In Chapter 4, "Groups," and Chapter 5, "Computers," you will use *CSVDE* to import computers and groups. For more information about *CSVDE*, including details regarding its parameters and usage to export directory objects, type **csvde /?** or search the Windows Server 2008 Help and Support Center.

Importing Users with *LDIFDE*

You can also use *Ldifde.exe* to import or export Active Directory objects, including users. The Lightweight Directory Access Protocol Data Interchange Format (LDIF) is a draft Internet standard for file format that can be used to perform batch operations against directories that conform to the LDAP standards. LDIF supports both import and export operations as well as batch operations that modify objects in the directory. The *LDIFDE* command implements these batch operations by using LDIF files.

The LDIF file format consists of a block of lines that, together, constitute a single operation. Multiple operations in a single file are separated by a blank line. Each line comprising an operation consists of an attribute name followed by a colon and the value of the attribute. For example, suppose you wanted to import user objects for two sales representatives, named April Stewart and Tony Krijnen. The contents of the LDIF file would look similar to the following example:

```
DN: CN=April Stewart,OU=People,DC=contoso,DC=com
changeType: add
CN: April Stewart
objectClass: user
sAMAccountName: april.stewart
userPrincipalName: april.stewart@contoso.com
givenName: April
sn: Stewart
displayName: Stewart, April
mail: april.stewart@contoso.com
description: Sales Representative in the USA
title: Sales Representative
department: Sales
company: Contoso, Ltd.

DN: CN=Tony Krijnen,OU=People,DC=contoso,DC=com
changeType: add
CN: Tony Krijnen
objectClass: user
sAMAccountName: tony.krijnen
userPrincipalName: tony.krijnen@contoso.com
givenName: Tony
sn: Krijnen
displayName: Krijnen, Tony
mail: tony.krijnen@contoso.com
description: Sales Representative in The Netherlands
title: Sales Representative
department: Sales
company: Contoso, Ltd.
```

Each operation begins with the *DN* attribute of the object that is the target of the operation. The next line, *changeType*, specifies the type of operation: *add*, *modify*, or *delete*.

As you can see, the LDIF file format is not as intuitive or familiar as the comma-separated text format. However, because the LDIF format is also a standard, many directory services and databases can export LDIF files.

After creating or obtaining an LDIF file, you can perform the operations specified by the file by using the *LDIFDE* command. From a command prompt, type **ldifde /?** for usage information. The two most important switches for the *LDIFDE* command are:

- *-i* Turn on Import mode. Without this parameter, *LDIFDE* exports information.
- *-f Filename* The file from which to import, or to which to export.

For example, the following command will import objects from the file named Newusers.ldf:

```
ldifde -i -f newusers.ldf
```

The command accepts a variety of modifications using parameters. The most useful parameters are summarized in Table 3-1.

Table 3-1   *LDIFDE* Parameters

Command	Usage
General parameters	
-i	Import mode. (The default is Export mode.)
-f filename	Import or export file name.
-s servername	The domain controller to bind to for the query.
-c FromDN ToDN	Convert occurrences of *FromDN* to *ToDN*. This is useful when importing objects from another domain, for example.
-v	Turn on Verbose mode.
-j path	Log file location.
-?	Help.
Export-specific parameters	
-d RootDN	The root of the LDAP search. The default is the root of the domain.
-r Filter	LDAP search filter. The default is (objectClass=*), meaning all objects.
-p SearchScope	The scope, or depth, of the search. Can be *subtree* (the container and all child containers), *base* (the immediate child objects of the container only), or *onelevel* (the container and its immediate child containers).
-l list	Comma-separated list of attributes to include in export for resulting objects. Useful if you want to export a limited number of attributes.
-o list	List of attributes (comma-separated) to omit from export for resulting objects. Useful if you want to export all but a few attributes.
Import-specific parameters	
-k	Ignore errors and continue processing if Constraint Violation or Object Already Exists errors appear.

Exam Tip   For the 70-640 certification exam, you should understand that both *CSVDE* and *LDIFDE* are able to import and export objects by using their respective file formats. Both commands are in the export mode by default and require the *-i* parameter to specify import mode. Only *LDIFDE* is capable of modifying existing objects or removing objects. Neither command enables you to import a user's password. Only *Dsadd* supports specifying the password. If you import users with *CSVDE* or *LDIFDE*, the accounts will be disabled until you reset their passwords and enable the accounts.

PRACTICE Automating the Creation of User Accounts

In this practice, you will create a number of user accounts with automated methods discussed in this lesson. To perform the exercises in this practice, you will need the following objects in the *contoso.com* domain:

- A first-level OU named People
- A first-level OU named Groups
- A global security group in the Groups OU named Sales

▶ **Exercise 1   Create Users with a User Account Template**

In this exercise, you will create a user account template that is prepopulated with properties for sales representatives. You will then create a user account for a new sales representative by copying the user account template.

1. Log on to SERVER01 as Administrator.
2. Open the Active Directory Users And Computers snap-in and expand the domain.
3. Right-click the People OU, choose New, and then select User.
4. In the First Name box, type **_Sales**, including the underscore character.
5. In the Last Name box, type **Template**.
6. In the User Logon Name box, type **_salestemplate**, including the underscore character. Click Next.
7. Type a complex password in the Password and Confirm Password boxes.
8. Select the Account Is Disabled check box. Click Next. Click Finish.

    Notice that the underscore character at the beginning of the account's name ensures that the template appears at the top of the list of users in the People OU. Notice also that the icon of the user object includes a down arrow, indicating that the account is disabled.
9. Double-click the template account to open its Properties dialog box.
10. Click the Organization tab.
11. In the Department box, type **Sales**.
12. In the Company box, type **Contoso, Ltd.**
13. Click the Member Of tab.
14. Click the Add button.
15. Type **Sales**, and then click OK.
16. Click the Profile tab.
17. In the Profile Path box, type **\\server01\profiles\%username%**.
18. Click OK.

    You have now created a template account that can be copied to generate new user accounts for sales representatives. Next, you will create an account based on the user account template.

19. Right-click _Sales Template and choose Copy.

The Copy Object – User dialog box appears.

20. In the First Name box, type **Jeff**.

21. In the Last Name box, type **Ford**.

22. In the User Logon Name box, type **jeff.ford**. Click Next.

23. Type a complex password in the Password and Confirm Password boxes.

24. Clear the Account Is Disabled check box.

25. Click Next, and then click Finish.

26. Open the properties of the Jeff Ford account and confirm that the attributes you configured in the template were copied to the new account.

▶ Exercise 2   Create a User with the *Dsadd* Command

In this exercise, you will use the *Dsadd* command to create a user account for Mike Fitzmaurice in the People OU.

1. Open a command prompt.

2. Type the following command on one line, and then press Enter:

```
dsadd user "cn=Mike Fitzmaurice,ou=People,dc=contoso,dc=com"
-samid mike.fitz –pwd * -mustchpwd yes –hmdir
\\server01\users\%username%\documents -hmdrv U:
```

3. You will be prompted to enter a password for the user twice. Type a password that is complex and at least seven characters long.

4. Open the Active Directory Users And Computers snap-in and open the properties of Mike's user account. Confirm that the properties you entered on the command line appear in the account.

▶ Exercise 3   Import Users with *CSVDE*

In the previous two exercises, you created users one at a time. In this exercise, you will use a comma-delimited text file to import two users.

1. Open Notepad and enter the following three lines. Each of the following bullets represents one line of text. Do not include the bullets in the Notepad document.

   ❑ DN,objectClass,sAMAccountName,sn,givenName,userPrincipalName

   ❑ "cn=Lisa Andrews,ou=People,dc=contoso,dc=com",user,lisa.andrews, Lisa,Andrews,lisa.andrews@contoso.com

   ❑ "cn=David Jones,ou=People,dc=contoso,dc=com",user,david.jones, David,Jones,david.jones@contoso.com

2. Save the file to your Documents folder with the name **Newusers.txt**.

3. Open a command prompt.

4. Type **cd %userprofile%\Documents** and press Enter.

5. Type **csvde -i -f newusers.txt -k** and press Enter.

   The three users are imported. If you encounter any errors, examine the text file for typographical problems.

6. Open the Active Directory Users And Computers snap-in and confirm that the users were created successfully.

   If you have had the Active Directory Users And Computers snap-in open during this exercise, you might have to refresh your view to see the newly created accounts.

7. Examine the accounts to confirm that first name, last name, user principal name, and pre-Windows 2000 logon name are populated according to the instructions in NewUsers.txt.

▶ **Exercise 4   Import Users with *LDIFDE***

Like *CSVDE*, *LDIFDE* can be used to import users. The LDIF file format, however, is not a typical delimited text file. In this exercise, you will use *LDIFDE* to import two users.

1. Open Notepad and type the following lines. Be sure to include the blank line between the two operations.

   ```
   DN: CN=April Stewart,OU=People,DC=contoso,DC=com
   changeType: add
   CN: April Stewart
   objectClass: user
   sAMAccountName: april.stewart
   userPrincipalName: april.stewart@contoso.com
   givenName: April
   sn: Stewart
   displayName: Stewart, April
   mail: april.stewart@contoso.com
   description: Sales Representative in the USA
   title: Sales Representative
   department: Sales
   company: Contoso, Ltd.

   DN: CN=Tony Krijnen,OU=People,DC=contoso,DC=com
   changeType: add
   CN: Tony Krijnen
   objectClass: user
   sAMAccountName: tony.krijnen
   userPrincipalName: tony.krijnen@contoso.com
   givenName: Tony
   sn: Krijnen
   displayName: Krijnen, Tony
   mail: tony.krijnen@contoso.com
   description: Sales Representative in The Netherlands
   title: Sales Representative
   department: Sales
   company: Contoso, Ltd.
   ```

2. Save the file to your Documents folder with the name **Newusers.ldf**. Surround the file name with quotes; otherwise, Notepad will add a .txt extension.

Although you can import LDIF files with any extension, it is convention to use the .ldf extension.

3. Open a command prompt.

4. Type **cd %userprofile%\Documents** and press Enter.

5. Type **ldifde -i -f newusers.ldf -k** and press Enter.

   The two users are imported. If you encounter any errors, examine the text file for typographical problems.

6. Open the Active Directory Users And Computers snap-in and confirm that the users were created successfully.

   If you have had the Active Directory Users And Computers snap-in open during this exercise, you might have to refresh your view to see the newly created accounts.

7. Examine the accounts to confirm that user properties are populated according to the instructions in Newusers.ldf.

Lesson Summary

- You can copy a user account in Active Directory to create a new account. A small subset of account properties are copied. To create a user account template, create a user and pre-populate the appropriate attributes. Then, disable the template account so that it cannot be used for authentication. Copy the template as a basis for new user accounts.

- The *Dsadd* command enables you to create user objects from the command line, with parameters that specify properties of the user.

- You can import a comma-delimited text file of users and their properties with the *CSVDE* command.

- Use *LDIFDE* to perform operations in Active Directory, including adding, changing, and removing users. The LDIF file that specifies such operations is a standard format that enables the interchange of data between directories.

Lesson Review

You can use the following questions to test your knowledge of the information in Lesson 1, "Automating the Creation of User Accounts." The questions are also available on the companion CD if you prefer to review them in electronic form.

NOTE   Answers

Answers to these questions and explanations of why each answer choice is right or wrong are located in the "Answers" section at the end of the book.

---

1. You are an administrator at a large university, and you have just been sent an Excel file containing information about 2,000 students who will enter the school in two weeks. You want to create user accounts for the new students with as little effort as possible. Which of the following tasks should you perform?

    A. Create a user account template and copy it for each student.

    B. Run *LDIFDE -i.*

    C. Use *CSVDE -i.*

    D. Run the *DSADD USER* command.

2. You are an administrator at a large university. Which command can be used to delete user accounts for students who graduated?

    A. *LDIFDE*

    B. *Dsmod*

    C. *DEL*

    D. *CSVDE*

Lesson 2: Creating Users with Windows PowerShell and VBScript

In Lesson 1, you learned how to use command-line tools to add or import user accounts. In this lesson, you will discover two of the most powerful tools for performing and automating administrative tasks: Windows PowerShell and VBScript. Both of these tools enable you to create scripts that can automate the creation of user accounts. Windows PowerShell also enables you to create users from a twenty-first century command shell that lives up to its middle name, *Power*.

After this lesson, you will be able to:

- Install the Windows PowerShell feature on Windows Server 2008.
- Identify key elements of the Windows PowerShell syntax, including cmdlets, variables, aliases, namespaces, and providers.
- Create a user in Windows PowerShell.
- Create a user in VBScript.

Estimated lesson time: 75 minutes

Introducing Windows PowerShell

Windows PowerShell is a powerful tool for performing and automating administrative tasks in Windows Server 2008.

Exam Tip   This section introduces you to Windows PowerShell so that you can become familiar with this important administrative tool. You are not expected to create Windows PowerShell scripts on the 70-640 exam; however, you should be able to recognize cmdlets used for basic Active Directory tasks such as those described in this training kit. If you want to learn to administer using Windows PowerShell, refer to *Windows PowerShell Scripting Guide* by Ed Wilson (Microsoft Press, 2008).

Windows PowerShell is both a command-line shell and a scripting language including more than 130 command-line tools called *cmdlets* (pronounced, "command-lets") that follow extremely consistent syntax and naming conventions and can be extended with custom cmdlets. Unlike traditional command shells such as *Cmd.exe* in Windows or BASH in Unix that operate by sending a text command a separate process or utility and then returning the results of that command as text, Windows PowerShell performs direct manipulation of Microsoft .NET Framework objects at the command line.

Windows PowerShell is installed as a feature of Windows Server 2008. Open Server Manager and click the Add Features link to install Windows PowerShell. After you have installed Windows PowerShell, you can open it from the Start menu. It is likely that you will use Windows

PowerShell often enough to warrant creating a shortcut in a more accessible location. Right-click Windows PowerShell in the Windows PowerShell program group and choose Pin To Start Menu. The Windows PowerShell command shell looks very similar to the command prompt of *Cmd.exe* except that the default background color is dark blue, and the prompt includes *PS*. Figure 3-1 shows the Windows PowerShell.

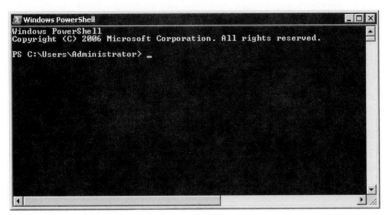

Figure 3-1 The Windows PowerShell console

NOTE   One Windows, one shell

Windows PowerShell enables you to use launch programs and execute commands that are identical to those in the command shell. Therefore, Windows PowerShell is backward compatible for administrators. If you use Windows PowerShell, you can perform administrative tasks either with familiar *Cmd.exe* commands or with Windows PowerShell directives.

Understanding Windows PowerShell Syntax, Cmdlets, and Objects

In traditional shells such as *Cmd.exe*, you issue commands such as *dir* or *copy* that access utilities built into the shell, or you call executable programs such as *attrib.exe* or *xcopy.exe*, many of which accept parameters from the command line and return feedback in the form of output, errors, and error codes.

In Windows PowerShell, you issue directives by using cmdlets. A cmdlet is a single-feature command that manipulates an object. Cmdlets use a Verb-Noun syntax—a verb and a noun separated by a hyphen. Examples include Get-Service and Start-Service.

NOTE   Cmdlets support direct entry and scripting

Cmdlets can be typed into the Windows PowerShell interactively or saved in script files (*.PS1) that are then executed by Windows PowerShell.

What Is an Object?

An object is a programming construct. From a technical perspective, a .NET object is an instance of a .NET class that consists of data and the operations associated with that data. Think of an object as a virtual representation of a resource of some kind. For example, when you use the Get-Service *cmdlet* in Windows PowerShell, the cmdlet returns one or more objects representing services. Objects can have *properties* that represent data, or attributes, maintained by the resource. An object representing a service, for example, has properties for the service name and its startup state. When you get a property, you are retrieving the data of the resource. When you set a property, you are writing that data to the resource.

Objects also have *methods*, which are actions that you can perform on the object. The service object has *start* and *stop* methods, for example. When you perform a method on the object that represents the resource, you perform the action on the resource itself.

These cmdlets do not pass commands or parameters to other utilities or programs but, rather, operate on .NET objects directly. If you type the cmdlet Get-Service, Windows PowerShell returns a *collection* of objects for all services. It presents the results of the cmdlet as a table showing the service, its name, and its display name, as shown in Figure 3-2.

Figure 3-2   The Get-Service cmdlet

These simple commands can be used together by combining or *pipelining* to create more complex directives. For example, pipelining the Get-Service cmdlet to the Format-List cmdlet produces a different result, as Figure 3-3 shows.

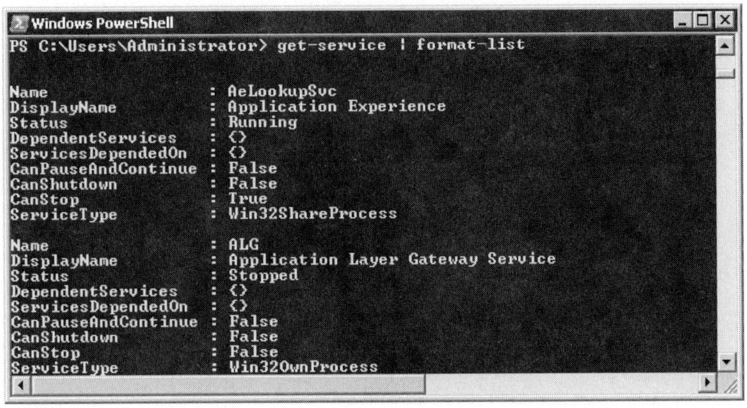

Figure 3-3   The Format-List cmdlet operating on the collection generated by Get-Service

Notice that the Format-List cmdlet produces far more detail than the default output of the Get-Service cmdlet. This reveals an important point. The Get-Service cmdlet is not just returning a static list of three attributes of services; it is returning objects representing the services. When those objects are pipelined, or passed, to the Format-List cmdlet, Format-List is able to work directly with those objects and display all the attributes of the services.

NOTE   Subtle but important difference

This is quite different from the standard Windows command shell, in which the output of one command piped to another command can be only text. If this were *Cmd.exe*, a *"format list"* command could reformat only the three pieces of information provided by a *"get-service"* command.

The Format-List cmdlet makes decisions about which attributes to display. You can direct it to show all properties by adding a parameter, *property*, with a value of all represented by an asterisk (*). The following command will list all available properties of all services:

```
get-service | format-list -property *
```

Getting Help

The Windows PowerShell Get-Help cmdlet is the best place to start looking for information, especially when you are just getting started with Windows PowerShell. The simplest form of help is provided by typing the Get-Help cmdlet followed by the cmdlet name you want help with, for example:

```
get-help get-service
```

You can get more detailed help by adding the *detailed* or *full* parameters, for example, *get-help get-command -detailed* or *get-help get-command -full*.

Using Variables

If you are repeatedly issuing a path or object definition, you can assign it to a variable to reduce your level of effort. Variables in Windows PowerShell always begin with a dollar sign ($). For example, you can assign the variable $DNS to represent the object retrieved by the Get-Service DNS cmdlet:

```
$DNS=get-service DNS
```

When you assign an object to a variable, you create an *object reference*. You can retrieve properties of the object by using dot (.) properties. For example, to return the status of the DNS service, type the following:

```
$DNS.status
```

A special *pipeline variable* can be used as a placeholder for the current object within the current pipeline. The pipeline variable is $_. For example, to get a list of all running services, type the following:

```
get-service | where-object { $_.status -eq "Running" }
```

This directive retrieves all services and pipes the objects to the Where-Object cmdlet, which evaluates each object in the pipeline to determine whether the object represented by the pipeline variable $_ has a status property equal to *Running*.

Using Aliases

An *alias* is an alternative way to refer to a cmdlet. For example, the Where-Object *cmdlet* previously shown has an alias of, simply, Where, so the code shown previously could be shortened to the following:

```
get-service | where { $_.status -eq "Running" }
```

Many of the Windows PowerShell cmdlets have already been assigned aliases. For example, the cmdlet that displays the contents of a folder on a disk is Get-ChildItem. This cmdlet has been given the alias Dir, equivalent to the Windows command shell command, and the alias Ls, for users more accustomed to a UNIX shell.

How do you determine which cmdlet is behind an alias? Type **alias**, as in the following example:

```
alias dir
```

The output will reveal that Dir is an alias for Get-ChildItem.

Whereas Windows PowerShell provides aliases for command-shell commands, Windows PowerShell cmdlets do not take the same parameters as *Cmd.exe* commands. For example, to retrieve a directory of folders and all subfolders at the command prompt, type **dir /s**. In Windows PowerShell, type **dir -recurse**.

Namespaces, Providers, and PSDrives

Cmdlets operate against objects in a namespace. A folder on a disk is an example of a namespace—a hierarchy that can be navigated. Namespaces are created by providers, which you can think of as drivers. For example, the file system has a Windows PowerShell provider, as does the registry, so Windows PowerShell can directly access and manipulate objects in the namespaces of those providers.

You are certainly familiar with the concept of representing the namespace of a disk volume with a letter or representing a shared network folder's namespace as a mapped drive letter. In Windows PowerShell, namespaces from any provider can be represented as *PSDrives*. Windows PowerShell automatically creates a PSDrive for each drive letter already defined by Windows.

Windows PowerShell takes this concept to the next level by creating additional PSDrives for commonly required resources. For example, it creates two drives, *HKCU* and *HKLM*, for the HKEY_CURRENT_USER and HKEY_LOCAL_MACHINE registry hives. Now you can navigate and manipulate the registry as easily as you can a file system. Type the following in the Windows PowerShell:

```
cd hklm:\software
dir
```

Drives are also created for aliases, environment, certificates, functions, and variables. To list the PSDrives that have been created, type **get-psdrive**.

Creating a User with Windows PowerShell

You are now ready to learn how to apply Windows PowerShell to create a user in Active Directory. The most basic Windows PowerShell script to create a user will look similar to the following:

```
$objOU=[ADSI]"LDAP://OU=People,DC=contoso,DC=com"
$objUser=$objOU.Create("user","CN=Mary North")
$objUser.Put("sAMAccountName","mary.north")
$objUser.SetInfo()
```

This code exemplifies the four basic steps to creating an object in Active Directory with Windows PowerShell:

1. Connect to the container—for example, the OU—in which the object will be created.
2. Invoke the *Create* method of the container with the object class and relative distinguished name (RDN) of the new object.
3. Populate attributes of the object with its *Put* method.
4. Commit changes to Active Directory with the object's *SetInfo* method.

Each of these steps is examined in detail in the following sections.

Connecting to an Active Directory Container

To create an object such as a user, you ask the object's container to create the object. So you begin by performing an action—a method—on the container. The first step, then, is to connect to the container. Windows PowerShell uses the Active Directory Services Interface (ADSI) type adapter to tap into Active Directory objects. A *type adapter* is a translator between the complex and sometimes quirky nature of a .NET Framework object and the simplified and consistent structure of Windows PowerShell. To connect to an Active Directory object, you submit an LDAP query string, which is simply the LDAP:// protocol moniker followed by the DN of the object. So the first line of code is as follows:

```
$objOU=[ADSI]"LDAP://OU=People,DC=contoso,DC=com"
```

Windows PowerShell uses the ADSI type adapter to create an object reference to the People OU and assigns it to a variable. The variable name *objOU* reflects programming standards that suggest a three-letter prefix to identify the type of variable, but variable names can be anything you'd like as long as they start with a dollar sign.

Invoking the *Create* Method

At this point, the variable $objOU is a reference to the People OU. You can now ask the container to create the object, using the container's *Create* method. The *Create* method requires two parameters, passed as arguments: the object class and the RDN of the object. An object's RDN is the portion of its name beneath its parent container. Most object classes use the format CN=*object name* as their RDNs. The RDN of an OU, however, is OU=*organizational unit name*, and the RDN of a domain is DC=*domain name*. The following line, then, creates a user object with the RDN specified as *CN=Mary North*.

```
$objUser=$objOU.Create("user","CN=Mary North")
```

The resulting object is assigned to the variable $objUser, which will represent the object and enable you to manipulate it.

Populating User Attributes

It's important to remember that the new object and the changes you make are not saved until you commit the changes, and you cannot commit the changes successfully until all required attributes are populated. The required attribute for user objects is the pre-Windows 2000 logon name. The LDAP name for this attribute is *sAMAccountName*. Therefore, the next line of code assigns the *sAMAccountName* to the object, using the *Put* method. *Put* is a standard method for writing a property of an object. *Get* is a standard method for retrieving a property. The resulting code is:

```
$objUser.Put("sAMAccountName","mary.north")
```

There are other mandatory attributes for a user object, including its security identifier (SID), but those attributes are created automatically by Active Directory when you commit a new user to the directory.

Committing Changes with the *SetInfo* Method

To commit the changes, use the Active Directory object's *SetInfo* method, as in the following line of code:

```
$objUser.SetInfo()
```

Populating Additional User Attributes

The preceding commands create a user with only the mandatory *sAMAccountName* attribute configured. You should populate other user attributes when creating a user object. You just learned to use the *Put* method of a user object to write a property. All you have to do is use the same method repeatedly, specifying each attribute you want to add. Examine the following code:

```
$objUser.put("sAMAccountName",$samAccountName)
$objUser.put("userPrincipalName",$userPrincipalName)
$objUser.put("displayName",$displayName)
$objUser.put("givenName",$givenName)
$objUser.put("sn",$sn)
$objUser.put("description",$description)
$objUser.put("company",$company)
$objUser.put("department",$department)
$objUser.put("title",$title)
$objUser.put("mail",$mail)
$objUser.SetInfo()
```

Each of these commands populates an attribute of a user with the value stored in a variable. Don't forget to use the *SetInfo()* method of the user object to commit the changes to Active Directory! Until you use *SetInfo()*, the changes you make are occurring only in your local copy of the object. The *SetInfo()* method evaluates your object's properties for validity. If you configured an invalid value for an attribute, you will receive an error on the *SetInfo()* line. Using the *GetInfo()* method of the user object reloads the original object, effectively undoing all your changes.

If you're not sure what the LDAP name for an attribute is, click the Attribute Editor tab of a user account in the Active Directory Users And Computers snap-in. The tab is visible when you select Advanced Features from the View menu. The Attribute Editor shows all attributes of an object, including their LDAP names and values. You can also use either of these commands to show properties that are populated for a user object:

```
$objUser.psbase.properties
$objUser | get-member
```

NOTE   **Multivalued attributes are different**

Although most user attributes are single valued, some are multivalued. If an attribute takes multiple values, use the *PutEx()* method of the user object. Perform a search on the Internet with the following keywords: *PowerShell user array PutEx*, and you will find numerous community resources that will help you learn the nuances of working with multivalued attributes.

And what about the user's password? You do not use *Put* to set a user's password. Instead, you use the *SetPassword* method, as in the following command:

```
$objUser.SetPassword("COmp!exP@sswOrd")
```

Unfortunately, *SetPassword* can be used only *after* you've created the user and invoked the *SetInfo()* method. That means, in fact, you are creating the account before assigning it a password. That's not a bug or a limitation of Windows PowerShell—it's a reality of Kerberos and LDAP. However, it's secure because the account is created in the disabled state.

You must then enable the account. The status of an account is a flag that is also not manipulated with the *Put* command. Instead, you use the following command:

```
$objUser.psbase.InvokeSet("AccountDisabled",$false)
$objUser.SetInfo()
```

Importing Users from a Database with Windows PowerShell

Although you will not be expected to understand database imports with Windows PowerShell for the 70-640 examination, learning how to do so can be a tremendous benefit to your efforts to automate the creation of users. As you'll see, it takes only a few lines of additional code with the powerful cmdlets of Windows PowerShell.

Assume that you receive an Excel worksheet from the human resources department with information about newly hired employees. Excel can save the file as a comma-delimited text file (.csv), which can be imported by Windows PowerShell. The first line of the .csv file must have field names followed by the information about each user. As a simple example, consider the following .csv file saved as Newusers.csv:

Newusers.csv
```
cn,sAMAccountName,FirstName,LastName
John Woods,john.woods,Johnathan,Woods
Kim Akers,kim.akers,Kimberly,Akers
```

Notice that the field names do not have to match the LDAP attribute names. They will be mapped to attribute names by the script.

Windows PowerShell can import this data source with one command:

```
$dataSource=import-csv "newusers.csv"
```

After you import the data source, you must loop through each record in the data source. This is performed with a *foreach* block, which takes the following format:

```
foreach($dataRecord in $datasource)
{
    # do whatever you want to do
}
```

The ForEach cmdlet loops through each object or record in the data source and assigns the current object to the *$dataRecord* variable, so the *$dataRecord* variable represents the current record. You can now look at the actual fields in each record, which become properties of the *$dataRecord* variable. For example, the first name of the first user is:

```
$dataRecord.FirstName
```

You can assign it to a variable:

```
$givenName = $dataRecord.FirstName
```

Again, it is not necessary for the variable or the field name to match the LDAP attribute name. The mapping is performed when you write the variable containing the value to the attribute itself:

```
$objUser.Put("givenName",$givenName)
```

The LDAP attribute, *givenName*, is in quotes. Only when you refer to the actual attribute of an object must you use the correct name. It certainly makes it easier to follow the code, however, if data source field names and variable names reflect the attribute names.

Putting it together, you can create a user import script:

Userimport.ps1

```
$objOU=[ADSI]"LDAP://OU=People,DC=contoso,DC=com"
$dataSource=import-csv "NewUsers.csv"
foreach($dataRecord in $datasource) {
    #map variables to data source
    $cn=$dataRecord.cn
    $sAMAccountName=$dataRecord.sAMAccountName
    $givenName=$dataRecord.FirstName
    $sn=$dataRecord.LastName
    $displayName=$sn + ", " + $givenName
    $userPrincipalName=$givenName + "." + $sn + "@contoso.com"

    #create the user object
    $objUser=$objOU.Create("user","CN="+$cn)
    $objUser.Put("sAMAccountName",$sAMAccountName)
    $objUser.Put("userPrincipalName",$userPrincipalName)
    $objUser.Put("displayName",$displayName)
    $objUser.Put("givenName",$givenName)
    $objUser.Put("sn",$sn)
    $objUser.SetInfo()
```

```
    $objUser.SetPassword("COmp!exP@sswOrd")
    $objUser.psbase.InvokeSet("AccountDisabled",$false)
    $objUser.SetInfo()
}
```

The first line of the script connects to the container, the OU in which all new users will be created. The next two lines connect to the data source and loop through each record, assigning each record to a variable, *$dataRecord*. The *foreach* block does two things. First, it maps fields in the data source to variables. Then it creates a user.

Notice that some variables are constructed by concatenating (appending) two fields. The *$displayName* variable takes the *LastName, FirstName* format, and the *$userPrincipalName* variable takes the *FirstName.LastName@contoso.com* format.

The user is created by invoking the *Create* method of the OU. Attributes of the user are populated and committed, and then the password is set and the account is enabled. Voilà!

Executing a Windows PowerShell Script

By default, Windows PowerShell prevents the execution of scripts as a security measure. To run a script that you have created, you must change the execution policy of Windows PowerShell with the following command:

```
set-executionpolicy remotesigned
```

The execution policy specifies which scripts can be run. The command just shown configures Windows PowerShell so that it will run local scripts but will require scripts from remote sources to be signed. Changing the execution policy has security implications, so you should read the information about running Windows PowerShell scripts at *http://www.microsoft.com/technet/scriptcenter/topics/winpsh/manual/run.mspx#EXC*.

After you've set the execution policy, you can run your script. but do not run it by name alone—you will receive an error. You must specify the path to the script! A shortcut is to use the *.\scriptname* notation, which indicates the current directory, so the following command will execute the user import script:

```
.\UserImport.ps1
```

Introducing VBScript

VBScript is a scripting language that supports the automation of administrative tasks on all current versions of Windows. VBScript files are text files typically edited with Notepad or a script editor and saved with a .vbs extension. To execute a script, you can double-click it, which opens the script, using *Wscript.exe*. Alternatively, from the command line, you can run the script with *Cscript.exe*, using the following syntax:

```
cscript.exe scriptname
```

Both *Wscript.exe* and *Cscript.exe* are components of the Windows Scripting Host (WSH), which is the automation framework installed on all current versions of Windows that supports several scripting languages, including VBScript.

Creating a User with VBScript

Because VBScript also uses the ADSI interface to manipulate Active Directory, the process for creating a user in VBScript is identical to the process in Windows PowerShell. A simple script for creating a user follows:

```
Set objOU=GetObject("LDAP://OU=People,DC=contoso,DC=com")
Set objUser=objOU.Create("user","CN=Mary North")
objUser.Put "sAMAccountName","mary.north"
objUser.SetInfo()
```

The script first connects to the container, the OU in which the user will be created. VBScript uses the GetObject statement to connect to an ADSI object by its distinguished name. When you assign an object to a variable in VBScript, you use the Set statement to create the object reference.

The second line of code invokes the *Create* method of the OU to create an object of a specific class and with a specific relative distinguished name, just as in the Windows PowerShell example. Because the result of the method is an object, you again have to use the Set statement to assign the object reference to a variable.

The third line uses the *Put* method of the user object, but VBScript does not use parentheses to pass the parameters to the argument. The fourth line is identical to Windows PowerShell; it commits the changes. Save the script as Newuser.vbs and execute it from the command shell, or from Windows PowerShell, with this command:

```
cscript.exe newusers.vbs
```

VBScript vs. Windows PowerShell

VBScript has two major advantages over Windows PowerShell. The first is the fact that VBScript scripts can be run on all current versions of Windows using the WSH, whereas Windows PowerShell must be downloaded and installed on versions of Windows prior to Windows Server 2008 and requires .NET Framework 2.0 or greater. The second advantage of VBScript is that it has been around for many years, so there is an extraordinary amount of experience, knowledge, and community-posted information on the Internet.

However, WSH does not provide a shell for directly executing commands. Additionally, VBScript as a language is not a particularly rich scripting language and does not fully use the .NET Framework. Although the WSH exists on Windows Server 2008 and VBScript is still supported, the way of the future is Windows PowerShell. That is why it was presented first in this lesson.

The disadvantages of Windows PowerShell are the inverse of the VBScript advantages. The very fact that Windows PowerShell is new means that it is a product still in development. In the previous sections, you learned to create user accounts with Windows PowerShell. The techniques and code you learned are fairly complex in the bigger picture of Windows PowerShell. In fact, they are almost identical to VBScript.

That's because in the current version of Windows PowerShell, there is very limited support for Active Directory administration. Unlike Windows Management Interface (WMI) and Microsoft Exchange Server, which have very rich Windows PowerShell providers, Active Directory support is limited to the ADSI type adapter, which is quirky and awkward and, ultimately, relies on ADSI just as VBScript does. In future versions of Windows PowerShell, an Active Directory provider will be introduced that will make working with Active Directory objects as easy as working with files in a file system.

Remember that on the 70-640 exam, you are not expected to create scripts in either Windows PowerShell or VBScript. Be able to recognize a script that follows the correct process to create a user: Connect to the OU, create the object, populate its properties, and then commit the changes.

PRACTICE Creating Users with Windows PowerShell and VBScript

In this practice, you will create a number of user accounts with automated methods discussed in this lesson. To perform the exercises in this practice, you will need the first-level OU object, named People, in the *contoso.com* domain.

▶ **Exercise 1   Install Windows PowerShell**

In preparation for exercises that use Windows PowerShell for administrative tasks, you will install the Windows PowerShell feature in this exercise.

1. Open Server Manager.
2. Click the Features node in the console tree.
3. Click the Add Features link.
4. Select Windows PowerShell from the Features list. Click Next.
5. Click Install.
6. When the installation is complete, click Close.
7. Right-click Windows PowerShell in the Windows PowerShell program group and choose Pin To Start Menu.

▶ **Exercise 2   Create a User with Windows PowerShell**

Now that Windows PowerShell is installed, you will use it to create a user in Active Directory.

1. Open Windows PowerShell.
2. Connect to the People OU by typing the following command:

```
$objOU=[ADSI]"LDAP://OU=People,DC=contoso,DC=com"
```

3. Create a user object in the OU by typing the following command:

   ```
   $objUser=$objOU.Create("user","CN=Mary North")
   ```

4. Assign the mandatory attribute, the user's pre-Windows 2000 logon name, by typing the following command:

   ```
   $objUser.Put("sAMAccountName","mary.north")
   ```

5. Commit the changes to Active Directory by typing the following command:

   ```
   $objUser.SetInfo()
   ```

6. Confirm that the object was created by typing the following command:

   ```
   $objUser.distinguishedName
   ```

   The user's distinguished name should be returned.

7. Examine the user attributes that Active Directory configured automatically by typing the following command:

   ```
   $objUser | get-member
   ```

   This command pipes the object representing the user to the Get-Member cmdlet, which enumerates, or lists, the populated attributes.

▶ Exercise 3 **Create a New User with a Windows PowerShell Script**

In Exercise 2, "Create a User with Windows PowerShell," you created a user by entering commands directly into Windows PowerShell. In this exercise, you will create a Windows PowerShell script that automates the creation of a user.

1. Open Notepad.

   Type the following lines of code:

   ```
   $objOU=[ADSI]"LDAP://OU=People,DC=contoso,DC=com"
   $objUser=$objOU.Create("user","CN=Scott Mitchell")
   $objUser.Put("sAMAccountName","scott.mitchell")
   $objUser.SetInfo()
   ```

2. Save the script in your Documents folder as "Newuser.ps1", including the quotes so that Notepad does not add a .txt extension.

3. Open Windows PowerShell.

4. Type **get-childitem** and press Enter.

   The Get-ChildItem cmdlet enumerates all child objects of the object currently in the pipe. At the Windows PowerShell prompt, the current directory is in the pipe.

5. Type **dir** and press Enter.

   The *dir* alias refers to the Get-ChildItem cmdlet.

6. Type **cd documents** and press Enter.

   You should now be in your Documents folder.

7. Enable script execution by typing the following command:

    ```
    set-exceutionpolicy remotesigned
    ```

8. Execute the script by typing .\newuser.ps1 and pressing Enter.

    The .\ notation provides the current path as the path to the script. Without .\, an error is thrown.

9. Confirm that the user was created successfully in Active Directory.

▶ Exercise 4   Create a New User with a VBScript Script

In this exercise, you will create a VBScript script that automates the creation of a user.

1. Open Notepad.

2. Type the following lines of code:

    ```
    Set objOU=GetObject("LDAP://OU=People,DC=contoso,DC=com")
    Set objUser=objOU.Create("user","CN=Linda Mitchell")
    objUser.Put "sAMAccountName","linda.mitchell"
    objUser.SetInfo()
    ```

3. Save the script in your Documents folder as "Newuser.vbs", including the quotes so that Notepad does not add a .txt extension.

4. Open the command prompt.

5. Type cd %userprofile%\documents and press Enter.

6. Execute the script by typing cscript.exe newuser.vbs.

7. Confirm that the user was created successfully in Active Directory.

Lesson Summary

■ Windows PowerShell provides support for performing administrative tasks from a command line and from scripts. Windows PowerShell is a feature of Windows Server 2008 and can be downloaded for Windows Server 2003, Windows Vista, and Windows XP.

■ VBScript is a scripting language that can be processed by the Windows Scripting Host, a component that exists in all current versions of Windows.

■ To create an Active Directory object by using Windows PowerShell or VBScript, you connect to the container—the OU, for example—and then create the object, populate its properties, and commit changes to Active Directory with the *SetInfo* method.

Lesson Review

You can use the following questions to test your knowledge of the information in Lesson 2, "Creating Users with Windows PowerShell and VBScript." The questions are also available on the companion CD if you prefer to review them in electronic form.

---

1. You want to create a user object with Windows PowerShell. Which of the following must you do?

   A. Use the Create-User cmdlet.

   B. Use the *NewUser* method of ADSI.

   C. Invoke the *Create* method of an OU.

   D. Use the *set objUser=CreateObject* statement.

2. You want to create a user object with a single command. Which of the following should you do?

   A. Use the Create-Item cmdlet.

   B. Use the *SetInfo* method.

   C. Use the *Create* method of an OU.

   D. Use the *Dsadd* command.

3. Which of the following lines of Windows PowerShell code are necessary to create a user object in the People OU? (Choose all that apply. Each correct answer is a part of the solution.)

   A. `$objUser=$objOU.Create("user","CN=Jeff Ford")`

   B. `$objUser.SetInfo()`

   C. `$objUser=CreateObject("LDAP://CN=Jeff Ford,OU=People,DC=contoso,DC=com")`

   D. `$objOU=[ADSI]"LDAP://OU=People,DC=contoso,DC=com"`

Lesson 3: Supporting User Objects and Accounts

The first two lessons of this chapter detailed the methods with which to create user accounts. That is only the first step in the life cycle of a user in a domain. After creating the user, you must configure attributes that define both the properties of the security principal (the account) and properties that manage the user. You must also know how and when to administer the account—to perform password resets and to unlock the account. Finally, you must be able to move the user between OUs and, eventually, deprovision the account by disabling or deleting it. This lesson will cover the procedures used to support a user object through its life cycle—procedures you can perform using both the Windows interface and the command line or automation tools.

After this lesson, you will be able to:
- Identify the purpose and requirements of user account attributes and user name properties.
- View and modify hidden attributes of user objects.
- Modify attributes of multiple users simultaneously.
- Manage users with the Active Directory Users And Computers snap-in, DS commands, Windows PowerShell, and VBScript.
- Perform common administrative tasks to support user accounts.

Estimated lesson time: 90 minutes

Managing User Attributes with Active Directory Users and Computers

When you create a user with the Active Directory Users and Computers snapin New Object–User Wizard, you are prompted for some common properties, including logon names, password, and user first and last names. A user object in Active Directory, however, supports dozens of additional properties that you can configure at any time with the Active Directory Users and Computers snap-in.

To read and modify the attributes of a user object, right-click the user and choose Properties. The user's Properties dialog box appears, as shown in Figure 3-4. Attributes of a user object fall into several broad categories that appear on tabs of the dialog box:

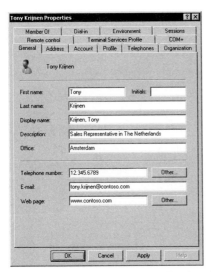

Figure 3-4   The Properties dialog box for a user

■ **Account attributes: the Account tab**   These properties include logon names, password, and account flags. Many of these attributes can be configured when you create a new user with the Active Directory Users and Computers snap-in. The "Account Properties" section details account attributes.

■ **Personal information: the General, Address, Telephones, and Organization tabs**   The General tab exposes the name properties that are configured when you create a user object, as well as basic description and contact information. The Address and Telephones tabs provide detailed contact information. The Telephones tab is also where Microsoft chose to put the *Notes* field, which maps to the *info* attribute and is a very useful general-purpose text field that is underused by many enterprises. The Organization tab shows job title, department, company, and organizational relationships.

■ **User configuration management: the Profile tab**   Here you can configure the user's profile path, logon script, and home folder.

■ **Group membership: the Member Of tab**   You can add the user to and remove the user from groups and change the user's primary group. Group memberships and the primary group will be discussed in Chapter 5, "Computers."

■ **Terminal services: the Terminal Services Profile, Environment, Remote Control, and Sessions tabs**   These four tabs enable you to configure and manage the user's experience when the user is connected to a Terminal Services session.

MORE INFO   **Terminal Services settings**

For more information about configuring Terminal Services settings, see *MCTS: Configuring Windows Server 2008 Applications Infrastructure*, by J.C. Mackin and Anil Desai (Microsoft Press, 2008).

- **Remote access: the Dial-in tab**   You can enable and configure remote access permission for a user on the Dial-in tab.
- **Applications: the COM+ tab**   This tab enables you to assign the users to an Active Directory COM+ partition set. This feature facilitates the management of distributed applications and is beyond the scope of the 70-640 exam.

Viewing All Attributes

A user object has even more properties than are visible in its Properties dialog box. Some of the so-called hidden properties can be quite useful to your enterprise. To uncover hidden user attributes, you must turn on the Attribute Editor, a new feature in Windows Server 2008. Click the View menu and select the Advanced Features option. Then open the Properties dialog box of the user, and the Attribute Editor tab will be visible, as shown in Figure 3-5.

Figure 3-5   The Attribute Editor tab

The Attribute Editor displays all the system attributes of the selected object. The Filter button enables you to choose to see even more attributes, including backlinks and constructed attributes. Backlinks are attributes that result from references to the object from other objects. The easiest way to understand backlinks is to look at an example: the *memberOf* attribute. When a user is added to a group, it is the group's *member* attribute that is changed—the distinguished name of the user is added to this multivalued attribute. Therefore, the *member* attribute of a group is called a *forward link* attribute. A user's *memberOf* attribute is updated automatically by Active Directory when the user is referred to by a group's *member* attribute. You do not ever write directly to the user's *memberOf* attribute; it is dynamically maintained by Active Directory.

A *constructed* attribute is one of the results from a calculation performed by Active Directory. An example is the *tokenGroups* attribute. This attribute is a list of the security identifiers (SIDs) of all the groups to which the user belongs, including nested groups. To determine the value of *tokenGroups*, Active Directory must calculate the effective membership of the user, which takes a few processor cycles. Therefore, the attribute is not stored as part of the user object or dynamically maintained. Instead, it is calculated when needed. Because of the processing required to produce constructed attributes, the Attribute Editor does not display them by default. They also cannot be used in LDAP queries.

As you can see in Figure 3-5, some attributes of a user object could be quite useful, including *division*, *employeeID*, *employeeNumber*, and *employeeType*. Although the attributes are not shown on the standard tabs of a user object, they are now available through the Attribute Editor, and they can be accessed programmatically with Windows PowerShell or VBScript.

MORE INFO   Hidden attributes of objects

For more information on using hidden attributes of objects and extending the schema with custom attributes, see *Windows Administration Resource Kit: Productivity Solutions for IT Professionals* by Dan Holme (Microsoft Press, 2008).

Managing Attributes of Multiple Users

The Active Directory Users and Computers snap-in enables you to modify the properties of multiple user objects simultaneously. Select several user objects by holding the Ctrl key as you click each user or using any other multiselection technique. Be certain that you select only objects of one class, such as users. After you have multiselected the objects, right-click any one of them and choose Properties.

When you have multiselected the user objects, a subset of properties is available for modification.

- **General**   Description, Office, Telephone Number, Fax, Web Page, E-mail
- **Account**   UPN Suffix, Logon Hours, Computer Restrictions (logon workstations), all Account Options, Account Expires
- **Address**   Street, P.O. Box, City, State/Province, ZIP/Postal Code, Country/Region
- **Profile**   Profile Path, Logon Script, and Home Folder
- **Organization**   Title, Department, Company, Manager

Exam Tip   Be sure to know which properties can be modified for multiple users simultaneously. Exam scenarios and simulations that suggest a need to change many user object properties as quickly as possible are often testing your understanding of multiselecting. In the real world, remember that you can and should use automation tools such as Dsmod, Windows PowerShell, and VBScript.

Understanding Name and Account Attributes

Two sets of attributes tend to appear on the certification exams and to present challenges to Windows administrators: name attributes and account attributes.

User Object Names

Several attributes are related to the name of a user object and an account. It is important to understand the distinctions between them.

- A user's *sAMAccountName* attribute (the pre-Windows 2000 logon name) must be unique for the entire domain. Many organizations use initials or some combination of first and last name to generate the *sAMAccountName*. That approach can be problematic because an organization of any size is likely to have users with names similar enough that the rules for generating the *sAMAccountName* would generate a duplicate name, so exceptions have to be built into the system and, eventually, the rules are riddled with exceptions. This problem is solved if the employee number or some other unique attribute of the users is used for the *sAMAccountName*. If you have the ability to direct the naming conventions at your organization, a unique, name-independent logon name is recommended.

- The *userPrincipalName* (UPN) attribute consists of a logon name and a UPN suffix which is, by default, the DNS name of the domain in which you create the object. The UPN must be unique for the entire forest. E-mail addresses, which must be unique for the whole world, certainly meet that requirement. Consider using e-mail addresses as UPNs. If your Active Directory domain name is not the same as your e-mail domain name, you must add the e-mail domain name as an available UPN suffix. To do this, open the Active Directory Domains And Trusts snap-in, right-click the root of the snap-in, and choose Properties.

- The RDN must be unique within an OU. For users, this means the *cn* attribute must be unique within the OU. This can be a tricky one. If you have a single, flat OU for users that already contains a user named Scott Miller, and you hire a second Scott Miller, his user object cannot have the same common name as the first. Unfortunately, there's no perfect answer to this problem for all organizations. Design a naming standard that applies a single rule for all CNs. Perhaps the CN should include an employee's number— for example, *Scott Miller (645928)*. If your OU structure for user accounts is flat, be prepared to address this challenge.

  Additionally, many organizations choose to configure the *cn* attribute as *LastName, First-Name* because by doing so, you can sort users by last name in the Active Directory Users and Computers snap-in. This is not a recommended method to achieve the goal. Instead of using a last-name-first format for *cn*, add the Last Name column to your view in the Active Directory Users And Computers snap-in by clicking the View menu and choosing Add/Remove Columns. Then click the Last Name column header to sort by last name.

■ The *displayName* attribute appears in the Exchange global address list (GAL). It can be easier to locate users in the GAL if they are sorted by last name, so you can create a naming convention for your organization that specifies that the *displayName* attribute takes the *LastName, FirstName* syntax.

Account Properties

On the Account tab of a user's Properties dialog box, shown in Figure 3-6, are the attributes directly related to the fact that a user is a security principal, meaning that it is an identity to which permissions and rights can be assigned. Other security principals include computers, groups, and the *inetOrgPerson* object class.

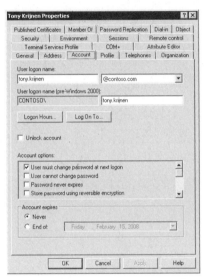

Figure 3-6   Account properties of a user object

Several of the account properties are worth highlighting because they are potentially quite useful and are not self-explanatory. Table 3-2 describes these properties.

Table 3-2   User Account Properties

Property	Description
Logon Hours	Click Logon Hours to configure the hours during which a user is allowed to log on to the network.
Log On To	Click Log On To if you want to limit the workstations to which the user can log on. This is called Computer Restrictions in other parts of the user interface and maps to the *userWorkstations* attribute. You must have NetBIOS over TCP/IP enabled for this feature to restrict users, because it uses the computer name rather than the Media Access Control (MAC) address of its network card to restrict logon.

Table 3-2 **User Account Properties**

Property	Description
User Must Change Password At Next Logon	Select this check box if you want the user to change the password you have entered the first time he or she logs on. You cannot select this option if you have selected Password Never Expires. Selecting this option will automatically clear the mutually exclusive option User Cannot Change Password.
User Cannot Change Password	Select this check box if you have more than one person using the same domain user account (such as Guest) or to maintain control over user account passwords. This option is commonly used to manage service account passwords. You cannot select this option if you have selected User Must Change Password At Next Logon.
Password Never Expires	Select this check box if you never want the password to expire. This option will automatically clear the User Must Change Password At Next Logon setting because they are mutually exclusive. This option is commonly used to manage service account passwords.
Account Is Disabled	Select this check box to disable the user account, for example, when creating an object for a newly hired employee who does not yet need access to the network.
Store Password Using Reversible Encryption	This option, which stores the password in Active Directory without using Active Directory's powerful, nonreversible encryption hashing algorithm, exists to support applications that require knowledge of the user password. If it is not absolutely required, do not enable this option because it weakens password security significantly. Passwords stored using reversible encryption are similar to those stored as plaintext. Macintosh clients using the AppleTalk protocol require knowledge of the user password. If a user logs on using a Macintosh client, you will need to select this option.
Smart Card Is Required For Interactive Logon	Smart cards are portable, tamper-resistant hardware devices that store unique identification information for a user. They are attached to, or inserted into, a system and provide an additional, physical identification component to the authentication process.
Account Is Trusted For Delegation	This option enables a service account to impersonate a user to access network resources on behalf of a user. This option is not typically selected, certainly not for a user object representing a human being. It is used more often for service accounts in three-tier (or multitier) application infrastructures.
Account Expires	Use the Account Expires controls to specify when an account expires.

NOTE   **Configure highly complex passwords for service accounts**

Services require credentials with which to access system resources. Many services require a domain user account with which to authenticate, and it is common to specify that the account password never expires. In such situations, be sure you use a long, complex password. If the service account is used by services on a limited number of systems, you can increase the security of the account by configuring the Log On To property with the list of systems using the service account.

Managing User Attributes with *Dsmod* and *Dsget*

The *Dsmod* and *Dsget* commands are two Active Directory command-line tools, called DS commands. You encountered *Dsquery* in Chapter 2 and *Dsadd* in Lesson 1 of this chapter.

Dsmod

Dsmod modifies the attributes of one or more existing objects. DS commands were introduced in Lesson 1. Like other DS commands, the *Dsmod* basic syntax is:

```
dsmod user UserDN ... parameters
```

The *UserDN* parameter specifies the distinguished name of the user to modify. The remaining parameters indicate the attribute to change and the new value. For example, the following command changes the *Office* attribute of Tony Krijnen:

```
dsmod "cn=Tony Krijnen,ou=People,dc=contoso,dc=com" –office "Amsterdam"
```

The attribute parameters do not map directly to the names of LDAP attributes of a user object. For example, the *dept* parameter of the *DSMOD USER* command modifies the *department* attribute of a user object. Additionally, *DSMOD USER* can modify only a subset of user attributes. Type **DSMOD USER /?** for usage information and a list of supported parameters.

Piping Multiple DNs to *Dsmod*

The *UserDN* parameter of the *Dsmod* command does not have to be entered directly into the command line. There are two other ways to pipe DNs to it. The first is to enter the DNs into the console. Let's assume you need to change the *office* attribute of two users, Linda Mitchell and Scott Mitchell, to reflect their relocation to the Sydney office. At the command prompt, type the following command:

```
dsmod user –office "Sydney"
```

The *UserDN* parameter is missing. The console (the command prompt) waits for you to enter DNs of users. Enter one per line, surrounded with quotes, pressing Enter at the end of each DN. After entering the last DN and pressing Enter, press Ctrl+Z at the beginning of the next line and press Enter to indicate that you are finished. The command will then execute against each of the DNs you have entered.

A more sophisticated way to send DNs to the *Dsmod* command is by piping the results of a *Dsquery* command. *Dsquery* was covered in Chapter 2; it searches Active Directory for specified criteria and returns the DNs of matching objects. For example, to change the *office* attribute of Linda and Scott Mitchell's accounts to Sydney, use the following command:

```
dsquery user -name "* Mitchell" | dsmod user -office "Sydney"
```

The *DSMOD USER* command searches Active Directory for users whose names end with *Mitchell*. The resulting objects' DNs are then piped to *DSMOD USER*, which changes the *office* attribute to *Sydney*.

As another example, assume you want to assign all users a home folder on SERVER01. The following command changes the *homeDirectory* and *homeDrive* attributes of user objects in the People OU:

```
dsquery user "ou=People,dc=contoso,dc=com" | dsmod user
-hmdir "\\server01\users\%username%\documents" -hmdrv "U:"
```

As mentioned in Lesson 1, the special *%username%* token can be used to represent the *sAMAccountName* of user objects when using DS commands to configure the value of the *-email*, *-hmdir*, *-profile*, and *-webpg* parameters.

Dsget

The *Dsget* command gets and outputs selected attributes of one or more objects. Its syntax, like that of *Dsmod*, is:

```
dsget user UserDN... parameters
```

You can supply the DNs of one or more user objects by specifying them on the command line, separated by spaces; by entering them in the console; or by piping the results of a *DSQUERY USER* command. Unlike *Dsadd* and *Dsmod*, *Dsget* takes only a parameter and not an associated value. For example, *Dsget* takes the *samid* parameter like *Dsadd* does, but it does not take a value. Instead, it reports the current value of the attribute. For example, to display the pre-Windows 2000 logon name of Jeff Ford in the People OU, use the following command:

```
dsget user "cn=Jeff Ford,ou=People,dc=contoso,dc=com" -samid
```

To display the pre-Windows 2000 logon names of all users in the Sydney office, use this command:

```
dsquery user -office "Sydney" | dsget user -samid
```

Managing User Attributes with Windows PowerShell and VBScript

To read an attribute of a user object with Windows PowerShell or VBScript, you use the ADSI to connect to the user object, a process called *binding*. In Lesson 2, you connected to an OU to create an object. After the object exists, you connect directly to the object. One way to do so is with the Active Directory services path (*aDSPath*) of the object, which is the "LDAP://" protocol moniker followed by the distinguished name of the object.

The Windows PowerShell command for connecting to the user account of Jeff Ford in the People OU is:

```
$objUser=[ADSI]"LDAP://cn=Jeff Ford,ou=People,dc=contoso,dc=com"
```

The VBScript equivalent is:

```
Set objUser=GetObject("LDAP://cn=Jeff Ford,ou=People,dc=contoso,dc=com"
```

Remember that Windows PowerShell specifies the ADSI type adapter, and VBScript uses *GetObject*. VBScript uses the Set statement to assign an object reference to a variable. Windows PowerShell does not use the Set statement and prefixes all variables with a dollar sign.

After you have a variable that references the object, you can get its properties. For example, in Windows PowerShell, type the following to report the user's *sAMAccountName* attribute:

```
$objUser.Get("sAMAccountName")
```

In VBScript, you must indicate that you want to output the attribute. A common way to do that is with the WScript.Echo statement, as follows:

```
WScript.Echo objUser.Get("sAMAccountName")
```

You will often see a shorthand form called the *.property* (pronounced "dot-property") format, such as *$objUser.sAMAccountName* in Windows PowerShell and *objUser.sAMAccountName* in VBScript. Although this method works most of the time, it is recommended to specify the *Get* method, particularly when working with Active Directory objects in Windows PowerShell.

If you want to modify an attribute, you need to perform three steps:

1. Connect to the user object.
2. Modify an attribute.
3. Commit the change.

You've already seen how to connect to the object. The second step is to change the attribute. Most attributes are simple, single-valued attributes and can be changed with the *Put* method of the object. For example, in Windows PowerShell:

```
$objUser.put("company","Contoso, Ltd.")
```

and in VBScript:

```
objUser.put "company","Contoso, Ltd."
```

The only difference here is that VBScript does not use parentheses to pass the parameters to the *Put* method.

You can set multiple attributes during the second step. After all attributes have been specified, you must commit the changes to the directory with *SetInfo*. The Windows PowerShell version is:

```
$objUser.SetInfo()
```

The VBScript version is identical, except for the variable name:

```
objUser.SetInfo()
```

Putting the three steps together, you have a Windows PowerShell script:

```
$objUser=[ADSI]"LDAP://cn=Jeff Ford,ou=People,dc=contoso,dc=com"
$objUser.put("company","Contoso, Ltd.")
$objUser.SetInfo()
```

In VBScript, the code is as follows:

```
Set objUser=GetObject("LDAP://cn=Jeff Ford,ou=People,dc=contoso,dc=com"
objUser.put "company","Contoso, Ltd."
objUser.SetInfo()
```

What if you want to delete an attribute entirely? You must first connect to the object. Then you can set an attribute to a blank string, "" if it is a string attribute or to *0* if it is a numeric attribute and *0* if 0 is an appropriate representation of "empty." However, you can also delete the attribute entirely, assuming it is not a mandatory attribute. To do so, you must use the *PutEx* method of the user object. To delete the *office* attribute, for example, you would use the following code in Windows PowerShell:

```
$objUser.PutEx(1, "office", 0)
$objUser.SetInfo()
```

In VBScript, you would use the following lines to delete an attribute:

```
objUser.PutEx 1, "office", 0
objUser.SetInfo()
```

Administering User Accounts

The primary purpose of user objects in Active Directory is to support authentication of a human being or of a service. Accounts are provisioned, administered, and, eventually, deprovisioned. The most common administrative tasks related to user accounts are resetting a password, unlocking an account, disabling, enabling, deleting, moving, and renaming user objects.

The following sections will examine each of these tasks and how they can be performed using the Windows interface, Windows PowerShell, VBScript, or the command prompt. Each of these tasks requires you to have appropriate permissions to the user objects. Delegating administrative permissions was discussed in Chapter 2.

Resetting a User's Password

If the user forgets his or her password and attempts to log on, he or she will receive a logon message, as shown in Figure 3-7.

Before the user can log on successfully, you will have to reset that password. You do not need to know the user's old password to do so. Simply right-click the user's object in Active Directory and choose Reset Password. The Reset Password dialog box, shown in Figure 3-8, appears. Enter the new password in both the New Password and Confirm Password boxes. It is a best practice to select the User Must Change Password At Next Logon option so that the user's password is known only to the user.

Figure 3-7   A logon message notifying a user that the user name or password is invalid

Figure 3-8   The Reset Password dialog box

You can also use a DS command to reset a user's password and, optionally, to force the user to change that password at the next logon. Type the following command:

```
dsmod user UserDN -pwd NewPassword -mustchpwd yes
```

Using Windows PowerShell, type the following commands:

```
$objUser=[ADSI]"LDAP://UserDN"
$objUser.SetPassword("NewPassword")
```

Note that, unlike other attributes, you do not use *SetInfo* after using *SetPassword* to configure the user's password. However, if you want to force the user to change passwords at the next logon, you do as follows:

```
$objUser.Put ("pwdLastSet",0)
$objUser.SetInfo()
```

In VBScript, the code is very similar:

```
Set objUser=GetObject("LDAP://UserDN")
objUser.SetPassword "NewPassword"
objUser.Put "pwdLastSet",0
objUser.SetInfo
```

It is even possible to import passwords, using *LDIFDE*, a command introduced in Lesson 1. See Knowledge Base article 263991 at *http://support.microsoft.com/default.aspx?scid=kb;en-us;263991* for information.

Unlocking a User Account

In Chapter 8, "Authentication," you will learn to configure password and account lockout policies. A lockout policy is designed to prevent an intruder from attempting to penetrate the enterprise network by logging on repeatedly with various passwords until he or she finds a correct password. When a user attempts to log on with an incorrect password, a logon failure is generated. When too many logon failures occur within a specified period of time defined by the lockout policy, the account is locked out. The next time the user attempts to log on, a notification clearly states the account lockout.

NOTE   Watch for drives mapped with alternate credentials

A common cause of account lockout is a drive mapped with alternate credentials. If the alternate credentials' password is changed, and the Windows client attempts repeatedly to connect to the drive, that account will be locked out.

Your lockout policy can define a period of time after which a lockout account is automatically unlocked. But when a user is trying to log on and discovers he or she is locked out, it is likely he or she will contact the help desk for support. You can unlock a user account by right-clicking the account, choosing Properties, clicking the Account tab, and selecting the Unlock Account check box.

Windows Server 2008 also adds the option to unlock a user's account when you choose the *Reset Password* command. Select the Unlock The User's Account check box, shown in Figure 3-8. This method is particularly handy when a user's account has become locked out because the user did, in fact, forget the password. You can now assign a new password, specify that the user must change the password at next logon, and unlock the user's account in one dialog box.

Unfortunately, neither the command line nor Windows PowerShell provides a native tool for unlocking accounts. To unlock a user with VBScript, use the following code:

```
Set objUser = GetObject("LDAP://UserDN")
objUser.IsAccountLocked = False
objUser.SetInfo
```

Disabling and Enabling a User Account

User accounts are security principals—identities that can be given access to network resources. Because each user is a member of Domain Users and of the Authenticated Users special identity, each user account has at least read access to a vast amount of information in Active Directory and on your file systems unless you have been severe and unusually successful at locking down access control lists (ACLs).

Therefore, it is important not to leave user accounts open. That means you should configure password policies and auditing—both discussed in Chapter 8—and procedures to ensure that accounts are being used appropriately. If a user account is provisioned before it is needed, or if an employee will be absent for an extended period of time, disable the account.

To disable an account in the Active Directory Users And Computers snap-in, right-click a user and choose Disable. From the command line, you can use *Dsmod.exe*, as in the following example:

```
dsmod user UserDN -disabled yes
```

With Windows PowerShell, as you learned in Lesson 2, you must use a roundabout method to set the flag:

```
$objUser=[ADSI]"LDAP://UserDN"
$objUser.psbase.InvokeSet('Account Disabled',$true)
$objUser.SetInfo()
```

VBScript is more straightforward:

```
Set objUser = GetObject("LDAP://UserDN")
objUser.AccountDisabled=TRUE
```

Enabling an account is just a matter of *yes* to *no* for the *Dsmod.exe* command:

```
dsmod user UserDN -disabled no
```

In the Windows PowerShell commands shown earlier, change *$true* to *$false* and, in VBScript, change *TRUE* to *FALSE*.

Deleting a User Account

When an account is no longer necessary, you can delete it from your directory. However, it is critical to consider that after the account has been deleted, it is eventually purged entirely from the directory. You cannot simply re-create a new account with the same name as a deleted account and hope it has the same group memberships and access to resources; it will not. The loss of the user's SID and of its group memberships can cause significant problems if, later, you realize you need the account.

Therefore, many organizations choose to deprovision a user account in stages. First, the account is disabled. After a period of time, it is deleted. Active Directory actually maintains a subset of the account's properties—most notably its SID—for a period of time called the *tombstone lifetime*, 60 days by default. After that time, the account's record is removed from the directory.

You can also consider recycling a user account. If a user leaves your organization, it's possible you will eventually hire a replacement who will need very similar resource access, group memberships, and user rights as the previous user. You can disable the account until a replacement is found and then rename the account to match the new user's name. The previous user's SID, group memberships, and resource access are thereby transferred to the replacement.

To delete a user account in Active Directory, select the user and press Delete or right-click the user and choose Delete. You will be prompted to confirm your choice because of the significant implications of deleting a security principal.

You can delete objects from Active Directory by using the *Dsrm* command, another of the DS commands. *Dsrm* uses a simple syntax:

```
dsrm UserDN
```

Notice that *Dsrm* is not followed by the *user* object class as are the other DS commands.

To delete a user from Active Directory, using Windows PowerShell, you connect to the parent container—the OU—and use the container's *Delete* method. This might seem slightly strange, but it parallels the fact that you use the container's *Create* method to create a user. The following two Windows PowerShell commands will delete a user:

```
$objOU = [ADSI]"LDAP://organizational unit's DN"
$objOU.Delete("user","CN=UserCN")
```

VBScript uses the same approach, with its unique syntax:

```
Set objOU = GetObject(LDAP://organizational unit's DN")
objOU.Delete "user","CN=UserCN"
```

Moving a User Account

If you need to move a user object in Active Directory, you can drag and drop it in the Active Directory Users and Computers snap-in. However, it is more accurate to right-click the user and choose the *Move* command. Keep in mind that when you move a user, you might change the Group Policy objects (GPOs) that apply to that user. GPOs are discussed in Chapter 6, "Group Policy Infrastructure."

To move a user with a command-line tool, use *Dsmove*. *Dsmove* uses the following syntax:

```
dsmove UserDN -newparent TargetOUDN
```

Dsmove does not specify a *user* object class. Instead, it simply indicates the DN of the user to move and, in the *TargetOUDN* placeholder, the distinguished name of the OU to which the user will be moved.

To move a user in Windows PowerShell, you must use the *psbase.MoveTo* method. The following two lines of code will move a user:

```
$objUser=[ADSI]"LDAP://UserDN"
$objUser.psbase.MoveTo("LDAP://TargetOUDN")
```

This is another example of a workaround required because this version of Windows PowerShell does not deliver an Active Directory provider. Some day in the future, you will be able to use the Move-Item cmdlet as you can with the file system and registry providers, but not yet.

In VBScript, you use an approach that seems a bit backward. You connect to the target container and then you grab the user object and move it to the container. The following two lines of code do the trick:

```
Set objOU = GetObject("LDAP://TargetOUDN")
objOU.MoveHere "LDAP://UserDN", vbNullString
```

The intrinsic constant *vbNullString* passes *Null* to the *MoveHere* method, instructing it that you want the object to keep its current CN.

Renaming a User Account

In the "User Object Names" section, you learned about many of the names associated with a user account. When a user account needs to be renamed, there can be one or more attributes you must change. To rename a user in Active Directory, right-click the user and choose Rename. Type the new common name (CN) for the user and press Enter. The Rename User dialog box appears and prompts you to enter the Full Name (which maps to the *cn* and *name* attributes), First Name, Last Name, Display Name, User Logon Name, and User Logon Name (Pre-Windows 2000).

From a command prompt, you can use *Dsmod.exe* with the following syntax:

```
dsmod user UserDN [-upn UPN][-fn FirstName][-mi Initial][-ln LastName]
[-dn DisplayName][-email EmailAddress]
```

You cannot change the *samAccountName* attribute by using *Dsmod.exe*, and you cannot change the CN of the object by using *Dsmod.exe*.

To change the CN of an object from a command shell, you must use Windows PowerShell or VBScript. In Windows PowerShell, two lines of code work:

```
$objUser=[ADSI]"LDAP://UserDN"
$objUser.psbase.rename("CN=New CN")
```

You can also change other name attributes, using the *Put* method of the user object.

To rename a user with VBScript, use a variation of the *MoveHere* method shown in the previous section:

```
Set objOU = GetObject("LDAP://CurrentOUDN")
objOU.MoveHere "LDAP://UserDN", "CN=New CN"
```

In these two lines, you connect to the user's current OU and use the *MoveHere* method of the OU to apply a new CN to the user.

PRACTICE Supporting User Objects and Accounts

In this practice, you will perform procedures that reflect common tasks required to support users in an enterprise environment. To perform the exercises in this practice, you should have performed the practices in Lesson 1 and Lesson 2 so that the following user objects exist in the People OU:

- Tony Krijnen
- Linda Mitchell
- Scott Mitchell
- April Stewart

▶ **Exercise 1   View All Attributes of a User**

In this exercise, you will discover the Attribute Editor and use it to reveal and modify user attributes that are not visible in the Active Directory Users and Computers snap-in.

1. Log on to SERVER01 as Administrator and open the Active Directory Users And Computers snap-in.

2. In the People OU, right-click Tony Krijnen and choose Properties.

3. Examine the tabs of the Properties dialog box.

   What attributes are visible? Do you see any that you have not seen before? Do you see any attributes that, if configured, can provide useful information to your enterprise?

4. Click the Telephones tab and enter information into the *Notes* field. Click OK.

5. Click the View menu and select Advanced Features.

6. Open the properties of Tony Krijnen again and click the Attribute Editor tab.

7. Scroll to locate the *info* attribute.

   What do you see there?

8. Locate the *division* attribute, double-click it, type **Subsidiary**, and then click OK.

9. Locate the *employeeID* attribute, double-click it, type **104839**, and then click OK.

10. Examine other attributes that are visible in the Attribute Editor.

    What attributes do you see that are not visible in the Active Directory Users and Computers snap-in? Can any of the hidden attributes, if configured, provide useful information to your enterprise?

11. Click OK to close the Properties dialog box.

▶ **Exercise 2 Manage Attributes of Multiple Objects**

In this exercise, you will select multiple objects and configure properties of the objects.

1. In the People OU, select Scott Mitchell.

2. Hold the Ctrl key and select Linda Mitchell and April Stewart.

   You should have three users selected now.

3. Right-click any of the selected users and choose Properties.

   A Properties dialog box appears with a subset of user properties that can be applied to multiple users simultaneously.

4. On the General tab, select the Office check box and type **Miami** in the Office text box.

5. Click the Account tab.

   In this scenario, these three users work on weekdays. They are not allowed to log on during the weekend.

6. Select the Logon Hours check box, and then click the Logon Hours button.

7. Click Sunday and click the Logon Denied button.

8. Click Saturday and click the Logon Denied button. Then click OK.

   Additionally, the three users are allowed to log on to only specific computers in the enterprise.

9. Select the Computer Restrictions check box, and then click the Log On To button.

10. Select The Following Computers option.

11. In the Computer Name box, type **DESKTOP101** and click Add.

12. Repeat the process to add **DESKTOP102** and **DESKTOP103**. Then click OK.

13. On the Address tab, select the Street, City, State/Province, and ZIP/Postal Code check boxes. Enter fictitious address information in these boxes.

14. Click the Profile tab and configure the **\\server01\%username%\documents** home folder.

15. Click the Organizational tab and configure the company name, **Contoso, Ltd**.

16. Click OK.

17. Open the user objects to confirm that the changes were applied.

▶ **Exercise 3   Manage User Attributes with DS Commands**

In this scenario, Linda and Scott Mitchell are relocating from Miami to Sydney. They will be taking three weeks to perform the relocation. You will manage their accounts through the process.

1. Open Windows PowerShell.

   Windows PowerShell can launch executables just like the command prompt.

2. Spend some time considering how you could, with a single command, change the *office* attribute of the two users to *Sydney* and disable the accounts so that the accounts cannot be used while the employees are away. What command would you issue?

3. Type the following command and press Enter:

   `dsquery user –name "* Mitchell" | dsmod user –office "Sydney" –disabled yes`

4. In the Active Directory Users And Computers snap-in, open the user accounts to confirm the changes were made.

5. You need to make a record of the users' pre-Windows 2000 logon names and user principal names. What single command could you enter to show you that information?

6. Type the following command and press Enter:

   `dsquery user –name "* Mitchell" | dsget user –samid –upn`

   The Mitchells have arrived in Sydney. It is now time to enable their accounts.

7. In Windows PowerShell, type the following lines:

   ```
   $objUser = [ADSI]"LDAP://CN=Linda Mitchell,OU=People,DC=contoso,DC=com"
   $objUser.psbase.InvokeSet('AccountDisabled',$false)
   $objUser.SetInfo()
   ```

8. In the Active Directory Users And Computers snap-in, confirm that Linda Mitchell's account is once again enabled.

9. Right-click Scott Mitchell's account and choose Enable Account.

▶ **Exercise 4   Reset a Password and Unlock a User Account**

While he was relocating from Miami to Sydney, Scott Mitchell forgot his password. After you enabled his account, he attempted to log on several times with an incorrect password, and then his account was locked. In this exercise, you will reset Scott's password and unlock his account.

1. In the Active Directory Users And Computers snap-in, select the People OU.

2. In the details pane, right-click Scott Mitchell's account and choose Reset Password.

3. Enter a new password for Scott in the New Password and Confirm Password boxes.

4. Ensure that the User Must Change Password At Next Logon check box is selected.

5. Select the Unlock The User's Account check box.

6. Click OK.

Lesson Summary

- Use the Attribute Editor to view and modify all attributes of a user object.
- User account properties can restrict the workstations to which a user logs on, the hours during which logon is allowed, and the date that the account will expire on.
- You can modify the attributes of multiple objects simultaneously by using *Dsmod.exe* or by multiselecting objects in the Active Directory Users And Computers snap-in. However, the properties you can change with each method are limited. You can use a script, for example, a VBScript or Windows PowerShell script, to modify attributes of objects as well.
- When you delete a user account, you cannot create an account with the same name; the new account will not belong to the same groups or have the same resource access. You will have to rebuild those memberships and permissions for the new account.

Lesson Review

You can use the following questions to test your knowledge of the information in Lesson 3, "Supporting User Objects and Accounts." The questions are also available on the companion CD if you prefer to review them in electronic form.

NOTE Answers

Answers to these questions and explanations of why each answer choice is right or wrong are located in the "Answers" section at the end of the book.

1. You want to set the Office property of ten users in two different OUs. The users currently have the Office property configured as *Miammi*. You recently discovered the typographic error and want to change it to *Miami*. What can you do to make the change? (Choose all that apply.)
   A. Select all ten users by holding the Ctrl key and opening the Properties dialog box.
   B. Use *Dsget* and *Dsmod*.
   C. Use *Dsquery* and *Dsmod*.
   D. Use Get-Item and Move-Item.
2. You want to move a user from the Paris OU to the Moscow OU. Which tools can you use? (Choose all that apply.)
   A. Move-Item
   B. The *MoveHere* method of the Moscow OU
   C. *Dsmove*
   D. *Redirusr.exe*
   E. Active Directory Migration Tool

3. A user reports that she is receiving a logon message that states, "Your account is configured to prevent you from using the computer. Please try another computer." What should you do to enable her to log on to the computer?

   A. Click the Log On To button on the Account tab of her user account.

   B. Click the Allowed To Join Domain button in the New Computer dialog box.

   C. Use the *Dsmove* command.

   D. Give her the right to log on locally, using the local security policy of the computer.

Chapter Review

To further practice and reinforce the skills you learned in this chapter, you can perform the following tasks:

- Review the chapter summary.
- Review the list of key terms introduced in this chapter.
- Complete the case scenario. This scenario sets up a real-world situation involving the topics of this chapter and asks you to create a solution.
- Complete the suggested practices.
- Take a practice test.

Chapter Summary

- A variety of tools are at your disposal for managing user objects through the life cycle of the account.
- VBScript and Windows PowerShell are powerful ways to automate administrative tasks. Although neither tool is the solution for all problems, there are more samples and resources for administering Active Directory with VBScript than with Windows PowerShell. However, the future of command-based administration and automation is clearly in Windows PowerShell.
- Because users are security principals, it is particularly important to manage accounts carefully and to be comfortable with the tasks, including resetting passwords; unlocking, enabling, and disabling accounts; moving and renaming accounts; and, eventually, deleting accounts.
- If you have a data source of user information, it is likely that you will be able to import it into Active Directory with *CSVDE*, Windows PowerShell, or VBScript.

Key Terms

Use these key terms to understand better the concepts covered in this chapter.

- **method**   In the context of programming or scripting, an action performed on an object. For example, you can use the *SetPassword* method of a user object to perform a secure password reset. You can use the *Create* method of a container object in Active Directory to create a new user, group, or computer.
- **object**   In the context of programming or scripting, a data structure that represents a system resource. For example, an object might represent a user account in Active Directory. Objects expose properties or attributes, methods or actions.

Case Scenario

In the following case scenario, you will apply what you've learned about creating and maintaining user accounts. You can find answers to these questions in the "Answers" section at the end of this book.

Case Scenario: Import User Accounts

You are an administrator at a large university. Each term, you receive a file containing information about incoming students. Your job is to create a user account for each of the new students. The file you receive is created in Excel, and it contains name and contact information for each student. The user accounts you create must have logon names, display names, and e-mail addresses that follow the naming conventions established for the university. For example, logon names are constructed using the student's last name followed by the first letter of his or her first name. E-mail addresses are constructed to follow the first.last@domain.edu format. Your manager has asked you to have all accounts created four weeks before the beginning of the new term. In the past, you have created the accounts manually. This year, you want to automate the creation of the user accounts.

1. Which tool discussed in this chapter should you use to import the user accounts from the database? Why do you believe that tool is better than the other available user import tools?

2. What can you do to increase the security of the accounts you are creating, considering that they will be created four weeks before they are used for the first time?

3. After creating the accounts, you realize that you forgot to populate the *company* attribute with the name of your university. All the new student accounts are in a single year. What can you do quickly to populate that attribute, using the Active Directory Users and Computers snap-in or the command prompt?

Suggested Practices

To help you successfully master the exam objectives presented in this chapter, complete the following tasks.

Automate the Creation of User Accounts

In the first practice, you will use one method to create a large number of user accounts. In the second practice, which is optional and advanced, you will use a different method.

■ **Practice 1**   Create an Excel worksheet that will serve as a database of user accounts. In the first row of the worksheet, type the following LDAP attribute names, one attribute per column: *distinguishedName*, *objectClass*, *givenName*, *sn*, *sAMAccountName*. Populate the file with sample data. Remember that *givenName* is the user's first name, and *sn* is the user's last name. Use the sample in Exercise 3, "Import Users with *CSVDE*," of Lesson 1 if you need assistance. Save the file as a comma-separated text file. Use the *CSVDE* command to import the file.

■ **Practice 2**   In Chapter 2, you examined a script that can use a .csv file to create users. Modify the script to import users from your .csv file. Construct attributes such as *user-PrincipalName* and *displayName* in the script, as the sample in Chapter 2 illustrated.

Maintain Active Directory Accounts

In this practice, you will apply the methods presented in Chapter 3, "Users," for managing user accounts.

■ **Practice**   Chapter 3 illustrated a number of options for performing administrative tasks to support user accounts. It will be an extremely valuable learning experience to step through the examples provided in the chapter and apply them, hands on. Treat each of the commands and scripts illustrated in this chapter as a practice.

Take a Practice Test

The practice tests on this book's companion CD offer many options. For example, you can test yourself on just one exam objective, or you can test yourself on all the 70-640 certification exam content. You can set up the test so that it closely simulates the experience of taking a certification exam, or you can set it up in study mode so that you can look at the correct answers and explanations after you answer each question.

MORE INFO   **Practice tests**

For details about all the practice test options available, see the "How to Use the Practice Tests" section in this book's introduction.

Chapter 4

Groups

Although users and computers, and even services, change over time, business roles and rules tend to remain more stable. Your business probably has a finance role, which requires certain capabilities in the enterprise. The user or users who perform that role will change, but the role will remain. For that reason, it is not practical to manage an enterprise by assigning rights and permissions to individual user, computer, or service identities. Management tasks should be associated with groups. In this training kit, you will use groups to identify administrative and user roles, to filter Group Policy, to assign unique password policies, to assign rights and permissions, and more. To prepare for those tasks, in this lesson you will learn how to create, modify, delete, and support group objects in an Active Directory Domain Services (AD DS) domain.

Exam objectives in this chapter:
- Creating and Maintaining Active Directory Objects
  - ❑ Automate creation of Active Directory accounts.
  - ❑ Maintain Active Directory accounts.

Lessons in this chapter:
- Lesson 1: Creating and Managing Groups 141
- Lesson 2: Automating the Creation and Management of Groups 159
- Lesson 3: Administering Groups in an Enterprise 169

Before You Begin

This chapter applies Microsoft Windows PowerShell, Microsoft VBScript, Comma-Separated Values Data Exchange (*CSVDE*), and LDAP Data Interchange Format Data Exchange (*LDIFDE*) to the task of automating computer account creation. Read Lesson 1, "Automating the Creation of User Accounts," and Lesson 2, "Creating Users with Windows PowerShell and VBScript," of Chapter 3, "Users," prior to reading this chapter.

In addition, to perform exercises in this chapter, you must have created a domain controller named SERVER01 in a domain named *contoso.com*. See Chapter 1, "Installation," for detailed steps for this task.

Real World

Dan Holme

Efficient and effective group management is a tremendous enabler for security, consistency, and productivity in an IT environment. As a consultant, I spend a lot of time with clients, aligning technology with their business needs. In the case of Microsoft Windows technologies, that entails defining and implementing business roles and rules so that administration can be defined, documented, and automated. And that process often requires improving clients' group management knowledge, technologies, and processes. Many IT professionals have come into Windows Server 2008 Active Directory with former practices that do not take advantage of groups as fully as possible. In fact, I've seen so much wasted productivity and decreased security due to poor group management that I dedicated two chapters of my book, *Windows Administration Resource Kit: Productivity Solutions for IT Professionals* (Microsoft Press, 2008), to improving and automating group management. In this lesson, you will learn what you need to know for the certification exam, and I share with you a few of the tips and best practices you'll need to make the most of groups in a production environment. I highly recommend reading the resource kit for more information, guidance, and fantastic tools related to group management.

Lesson 1: Creating and Managing Groups

You are certainly familiar with the purpose of groups: to collect items and manage them as a single entity. The implementation of group management in Active Directory is not intuitive because Active Directory is designed to support large, distributed environments, so it includes seven types of groups: two types of domain groups with three scopes each and local security groups. In this lesson, you will learn the purpose each of these groups serves, and you'll learn to align your business requirements with the potentially complex options that Active Directory provides.

> **After this lesson, you will be able to:**
> - Create groups by using the Active Directory Users and Computers snap-in.
> - Manage and convert group type and scope.
> - Identify the types of objects that can be members of groups of various scopes.
> - Manage group membership.
> - Develop a group management strategy.
>
> **Estimated lesson time: 45 minutes**

Managing an Enterprise with Groups

Groups are security principals with a security identifier (SID) that, through their *member* attribute, collect other security principals (users, computers, contacts, and other groups) to facilitate management.

Imagine that all 100 users in the sales department require read-level access to a shared folder on a server: It is not manageable to assign permissions to each user individually. When new salespeople are hired, you will have to add the new accounts to the access control list (ACL) of the folder. When accounts are deleted, you will have to remove the permissions from the ACL, or else you will be left with the missing account entry on the ACL, shown in 4-1, which results from a SID on the ACL that refers to an account that cannot be resolved. Imagine now that all 100 users in the sales department require access to 10 shared folders on three servers. The management challenges just increased significantly.

You have, no doubt, learned that although assigning permissions to a resource to an individual identity—user or computer—is possible, the best practice is to assign a single permission to a group and then to manage access to the resource simply by changing membership of the group.

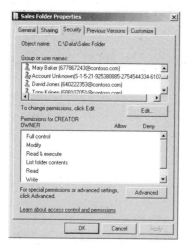

Figure 4-1   An ACL with a SID that refers to an account that can no longer be resolved

So, to continue the example, you could create a group called Sales and assign the group the Allow Read permission on the 10 shared folders on the three servers. Now, you have a *single point of management*. The Sales group effectively manages access to the shared folder. You can add new sales users to the group, and they will gain access to the 10 shared folders. When you delete an account, it is automatically deleted from the group, so you will not have irresolvable SIDs on your ACLs. There's an extra benefit also: because your ACL will remain stable with the Sales group having Allow Read permission, your backups will be easier. When you change the ACL of a folder, the ACL propagates to all child files and folders, setting the Archive flag and thereby requiring a backup of all files, even if the contents of the files have not changed.

Imagine, now, that it is not only salespeople who require read access to the folders. Marketing department employees and the sales consultants hired by your organization also require Read permission to the same folders. You could add those groups to the ACL of the folders, but soon you will end up with an ACL with multiple permissions, this time assigning the Allow Read permission to multiple groups instead of multiple users. To give the three groups permission to the 10 folders on the three servers, you will have to add 30 permissions! The next group that requires access will require 10 more changes to grant permissions to the ACLs of the 10 shared folders. What if eight users, who are not salespeople, marketing employees, or consultants, have business need for Read access to the 10 folders? Do you add their individual user accounts to the ACLs?

You can see quickly that using only one type of group—a group that defines the business roles of users—is not enabling effective management of access to the 10 folders. The solution is to recognize that two types of management must exist to manage this scenario effectively. You must manage the users as collections, based upon their business roles, and you must manage access to the 10 folders. The 10 folders are also a collection of items: They are a single resource that just happens to be distributed across 10 folders on three servers. You are trying to manage Read access to that resource collection. You need a single point of management with which to manage access to the resource collection.

This requires another group—a group that represents read access to the 10 folders on the three servers. Imagine that a group is created called ACL_Sales Folders_Read. This group will be assigned the Allow Read permission on the 10 folders. The sales, marketing, and consultants groups, along with the eight individual users, will all be members of the ACL_Sales Folders_Read group. As additional groups or users require access to the folders, they will be added to that group. It also becomes much easier to report who has access to the folders. Instead of having to examine the ACLs on each of the 10 folders, you simply examine the membership of the ACL_Sales Folders Read group.

This approach to managing the enterprise with groups is called *role-based management*. You define roles of users based on business characteristics—for example, department or division affiliation such as sales, marketing, and consultants—and you reflect your business rules such as which roles and individuals can access the 10 folders.

You can achieve both management tasks, using groups in a directory. Roles are represented by groups that contain users, computers, and other roles. That's right—roles can include other roles. For example, a Managers role might include the Sales Managers, Finance Managers, and Production Managers roles. Rules, such as the rule that defines Read access to the 10 folders, are represented by groups as well. Rule groups contain role groups and, occasionally, individual users or computers such as the eight users in the example.

To achieve manageability of an enterprise of any size or complexity, you will need to manage groups effectively and have an infrastructure of groups that provide single points of management for roles and rules. That means, technically, that you will need groups that can include as members users, computers, other groups, and, possibly, security principals from other domains.

For more information about role-based management, see *Windows Administration Resource Kit: Productivity Solutions for IT Professionals*.

Defining Group Naming Conventions

To create a group by using the Active Directory Users And Computers snap-in, simply right-click the OU in which you want to create a group, choose New, and select Group. The New Object – Group dialog box, shown in Figure 4-2, enables you to specify fundamental properties of the new group.

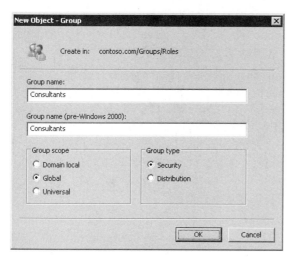

Figure 4-2   The New Object – Group dialog box

The first properties you must configure are the group's names. A group, like a user or computer, has several names. The first, shown in the Group Name box in Figure 4-2, is used by Windows 2000 and later systems to identify the object—it becomes the *cn* and *name* attributes of the object. The second, the pre-Windows 2000 name, is the *sAMAccountName* attribute, used to identify the group to computers running Microsoft Windows NT 4.0 and to some devices such as network attached storage (NAS) devices running non-Microsoft operating systems. The *cn* and *name* attributes must be unique only within the container—the OU—in which the group exists. The *sAMAccountName* must be unique in the entire domain. Technically, the *sAMAccountName* could be a different value than the *cn* and *name*, but it is highly discouraged to do so. Pick a name that is unique in the domain and use it in both name fields in the New Object – Group dialog box.

The name you choose should help you manage the group and manage your enterprise on a day-to-day basis. It is recommended to follow a naming convention that identifies the type of group and the purpose of the group. The example in the previous section used a group name, ACL_Sales Folder_Read. The prefix indicates that the group is used to assign permissions to a folder: It is used on access control lists. The main part of the name describes the resource that is being managed with the group: the sales folder. The suffix further defines what is being managed by the group: read access. A delimiter—in this case, an underscore—is used to separate parts of the name. Note that the delimiter is not used between the words *Sales* and *Folder*. Spaces are acceptable in group names—you will just need to enclose group names in quotes when you refer to them on command lines. You can create scripts that use the delimiter to deconstruct group names to facilitate auditing and reporting. Keep in mind that role groups that define user roles will often be used by nontechnical users. For example, you might e-mail enable the Sales group so that it can be used as an e-mail distribution list. Therefore, it is recommended that you do not use prefixes on role group names—keep the names user-friendly and descriptive.

For more information about managing groups effectively, see *Windows Administration Resource Kit: Productivity Solutions for IT Professionals.*

Understanding Group Types

There are two types of groups: security and distribution. When you create a group, you make the selection of the group type in the New Object – Group dialog box.

Distribution groups are used primarily by e-mail applications. These groups are not security enabled; they do not have SIDs, so they cannot be given permissions to resources. Sending a message to a distribution group sends the message to all members of the group.

Security groups are security principals with SIDs. These groups can, therefore, be used as permission entries in ACLs to control security for resource access. Security groups can also be used as distribution groups by e-mail applications. If a group will be used to manage security, it must be a security group.

Because security groups can be used for both resource access and e-mail distribution, many organizations use only security groups. However, it is recommended that if a group will be used only for e-mail distribution, you should create the group as a distribution group. Otherwise, the group is assigned a SID, and the SID is added to the user's security access token, which can lead to unnecessary token bloat.

Understanding Group Scope

Groups have members: users, computers, and other groups. Groups can be members of other groups, and groups can be referred to by ACLs, Group Policy object (GPO) filters, and other management components. *Group scope* affects each of these characteristics of a group: what it can contain, what it can belong to, and where it can be used. There are four group scopes: global, domain local, local, and universal.

The characteristics that define each scope fall into these categories:

- **Replication**   Where is the group defined and to what systems is the group replicated?
- **Membership**   What types of security principals can the group contain as members? Can the group include security principals from trusted domains?

  In Chapter 12, "Domains and Forests," you will learn about trust relationships, or *trusts*. A trust enables a domain to refer to another domain for user authentication, to include security principals from the other domain as group members, and to assign permissions to security principals in the other domain. The terminology used can be confusing. If Domain A trusts Domain B, then Domain A is the *trusting* domain and Domain B is the *trusted* domain. Domain A accepts the credentials of users in Domain B. It forwards requests by Domain B users to authenticate to a domain controller in Domain B because it *trusts* the identity store and authentication service of Domain B. Domain A can add

Domain B's security principals to groups and ACLs in Domain A. See Chapter 12 for more detail.

Exam Tip   In the context of group membership, remember that if Domain A trusts Domain B, Domain B is *trusted*, and its users and global groups can be members of domain local groups in Domain A. Additionally, Domain B's users and global groups can be assigned permissions to resources in Domain A.

■ **Availability**   Where can the group be used? Is the group available to add to another group? Is the group available to add to an ACL?

Keep these broad characteristics in mind as you explore the details of each group scope.

Local Groups

Local groups are truly local—defined on and available to a single computer. Local groups are created in the security accounts manager (SAM) database of a domain member computer. Both workstations and servers have local groups. In a workgroup, you use local groups to manage security of resources on a system. In a domain, however, managing the local groups of individual computers becomes unwieldy and is, for the most part, unnecessary. It is not recommended to create custom local groups on domain members. In fact, the Users and Administrators local groups are the only local groups that you should be concerned with managing in a domain environment. To summarize:

■ **Replication**   A local group is defined only in the local SAM database of a domain member server. The group and its membership are not replicated to any other system.
■ **Membership**   A local group can include as members:
   ❑ Any security principals from the domain: users, computers, global groups, or domain local groups.
   ❑ Users, computers, and global groups from any domain in the forest.
   ❑ Users, computers, and global groups from any trusted domain.
   ❑ Universal groups defined in any domain in the forest.
■ **Availability**   A local group has only computer-wide scope. It can be used in ACLs on the local computer only. A local group cannot be a member of any other group.

Domain Local Groups

Domain local groups are used primarily to manage permissions to resources. For example, the ACL_Sales Folder_Read group discussed earlier in the lesson would be created as a domain local group. Domain local groups have the following characteristics:

- **Replication**   A domain local group is defined in the domain naming context. The group object and its membership (the *member* attribute) are replicated to every domain controller in the domain.
- **Membership**   A domain local group can include as members:
    - ❑ Any security principals from the domain: users, computers, global groups, or other domain local groups.
    - ❑ Users, computers, and global groups from any domain in the forest.
    - ❑ Users, computers, and global groups from any trusted domain.
    - ❑ Universal groups defined in any domain in the forest.
- **Availability**   A domain local group can be added to ACLs on any resource on any domain member. Additionally, a domain local group can be a member of other domain local groups or even computer local groups.

The membership capabilities of a domain local group are identical to those of local groups, but the replication and availability of the domain local group makes it useful across the entire domain. The domain local group is, therefore, well suited for defining business management rules, such as access rules, because the group can be applied anywhere in the domain, and it can include members of any type within the domain and members from trusted domains as well.

Global Groups

Global groups are used primarily to define collections of domain objects based on business roles. Role groups, such as the Sales and Marketing groups mentioned earlier, as well as roles of computers such as a Sales Laptops group, will be created as global groups. Global groups have the following characteristics:

- **Replication**   A global group is defined in the domain naming context. The group object, including the *member* attribute, is replicated to all domain controllers in the domain.
- **Membership**   A global group can include as members users, computers, and other global groups in the same domain only.
- **Availability**   A global group is available for use by all domain members as well as by all other domains in the forest and all trusting external domains. A global group can be a member of any domain local or universal group in the domain or in the forest. It can also be a member of any domain local group in a trusting domain. Finally, a global group can be added to ACLs in the domain, in the forest, or in trusting domains.

As you can see, global groups have the most limited membership (only users, computers, and global groups from the same domain) but the broadest availability across the domain, the forest, and trusting domains. That is why they are well suited to defining roles, because roles are generally collections of objects from the same directory.

Universal Groups

Universal groups are useful in multidomain forests. They enable you to define roles, or to manage resources, that span more than one domain. The best way to understand universal groups is through an example. Trey Research has a forest with three domains: Americas, Asia, and Europe. Each domain has user accounts and a global group called Regional Managers that includes the managers of that region. Remember that global groups can contain only users from the same domain. A universal group called Trey Research Regional Managers is created, and the three Regional Managers groups are added as members. The Trey Research Regional Managers group, therefore, defines a role for the entire forest. As users are added to any one of the Regional Managers groups, they will, through group nesting, be a member of the Trey Research Regional Managers.

Trey Research is planning to release a new product that requires collaboration across its regions. Resources related to the project are stored on file servers in each domain. To define who can modify files related to the new product, a universal group is created called *ACL_New Product_Modify*. That group is assigned the Allow Modify permission to the shared folders on each of the file servers in each of the domains. The Trey Research Regional Managers group is made a member of the ACL_New Product_Modify group, as are various global groups and a handful of users from each of the regions.

As you can see from this example, universal groups can help you represent and consolidate groups that span domains in a forest and help you define rules that can be applied across the forest. Universal groups have the following characteristics:

- **Replication**   A universal group is defined in a single domain in the forest but is replicated to the global catalog. You will learn more about the global catalog in Chapter 10, "Domain Controllers." Objects in the global catalog will be readily accessible across the forest.

- **Membership**   A universal group can include as members users, global groups, and other universal groups from any domain in the forest.

- **Availability**   A universal group can be a member of a universal group or domain local group anywhere in the forest. Additionally, a universal group can be used to manage resources, for example, to assign permissions anywhere in the forest.

Summarizing Group Membership Possibilities

Both on the 70-640 examination and in day-to-day administration, it is important for you to be completely familiar with the membership characteristics of each group scope.

Table 4-1 summarizes the objects that can be members of each group scope.

Table 4-1   Group Scope and Members

Group Scope	Members from the same domain	Members from another domain in the same forest	Members from a trusted external domain
Local	Users Computers Global groups Universal groups Domain local groups Local users defined on the same computer as the local group	Users Computers Global groups Universal groups	Users Computers Global groups
Domain Local	Users Computers Global groups Domain local groups Universal groups	Users Computers Global groups Universal groups	Users Computers Global groups
Universal	Users Computers Global groups Universal groups	Users Computers Global groups Universal groups.	N/A
Global	Users Computers Global groups	N/A	N/A

Quick Check
- Which types of objects can be members of a global group in a domain?

Quick Check Answer
- Global groups can contain only users, computers, and other global groups from the same domain.

Converting Group Scope and Type

If, after creating a group, you determine that you need to modify the group's scope or type, you can do so. Open the Properties dialog box of an existing group and, on the General tab, shown in Figure 4-3, you will see the existing scope and type. At least one more scope and type are available to be selected.

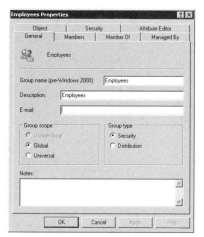

Figure 4-3   The General tab of a group's Properties dialog box

You can convert the group type at any time by changing the selection in the Group Type section of the General tab. Be cautious, however. When you convert a group from security to distribution, any resources to which the group had been assigned permission will no longer be accessible in the same way. After the group becomes a distribution group, users who log on to the domain will no longer include the group's SID in their security access tokens.

You can change the group scope in one of the following ways:

- Global to universal
- Domain local to universal
- Universal to global
- Universal to domain local

The only scope changes that you cannot make directly are from global to domain local or domain local to global. However, you can make these changes indirectly by first converting to universal scope and then converting to the desired scope, so all scope changes are possible.

Remember, however, that a group's scope determines the types of objects that can be members of the group. If a group already contains members or is a member of another group, you will be prevented from changing scope. For example, if a global group is a member of another global group, you cannot change the first group to universal scope, because a universal group cannot be a member of a global group. An explanatory error message will display such as that shown in Figure 4-4. You must correct the membership conflicts before you can change the group's scope.

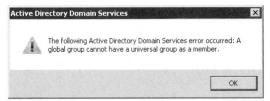

Figure 4-4 The error produced when a group's membership will not allow a change of scope

The *Dsmod* command, introduced in Chapter 3, can be used to change group type and scope by using the following syntax:

```
dsmod group GroupDN –secgrp { yes | no } –scope { l | g | u }
```

The *GroupDN* is the distinguished name of the group to modify. The following two parameters affect group scope and type:

■ **-secgrp { yes | no }** specifies group type: security (*yes*) or distribution (*no*).

■ **-scope { l | g | u }** determines the group scope: domain local (*l*), global (*g*), or universal (*u*).

Managing Group Membership

When you need to add or remove members of a group, you have several methods by which to do so. First, you can open the group's Properties dialog box and click the Members tab. To remove a member, simply select the member and click Remove. To add a member, click the Add button. The Select Users, Computers, Or Groups dialog box appears, as shown in Figure 4-5.

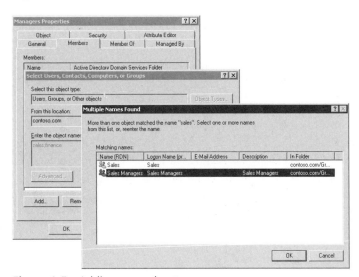

Figure 4-5 Adding a member to a group

Several tips are worth mentioning about this process:

- In the Select dialog box, in the Enter The Object Names box, you can type multiple accounts separated by semicolons. For example, in Figure 4-5, both *sales* and *finance* were entered. They are separated by a semicolon.

- You can type partial names of accounts—you do not need to type the full name. Windows searches Active Directory for accounts that begin with the name you entered. If there is only one match, Windows selects it automatically. If there are multiple accounts that match, the Multiple Names Found dialog box appears, enabling you to select the specific object you want. This shortcut—typing partial names—can save time adding members to groups and can help when you don't remember the exact name of a member.

- By default, Windows searches only for users and groups that match the names you enter in the Select dialog box. If you want to add computers to a group, you must click the Options button and select Computers.

- By default, Windows searches only domain groups. If you want to add local accounts, click the Locations button in the Select dialog box.

- If you cannot find the member you want to add, click the Advanced button in the Select dialog box. A more powerful query window will appear, giving you more options for searching Active Directory.

You can also add an object to a group in the Active Directory Users And Computers snap-in by opening the properties of the object and clicking its Member Of tab. Click the Add button and select the group. Similarly, you can right-click one or more selected objects and use the *Add To Group* command.

The *Member* and *MemberOf* Attributes

When you add a member to a group, you change the group's *member* attribute. The *member* attribute is a multivalued attribute. Each member is a value represented by the distinguished name (DN) of the member. If the member is moved or renamed, Active Directory automatically updates the *member* attributes of groups that include the member.

When you add a member to a group, the member's *memberOf* attribute is also updated, indirectly. The *memberOf* attribute is a special type of attribute called a *backlink*. It is updated by Active Directory when a forward link attribute, such as *member*, refers to the object. When you add a member to a group, you are always changing the *member* attribute. Therefore, when you use the Member Of tab of an object to add to a group, you are actually changing the group's *member* attribute. Active Directory updates the *memberOf* attribute automatically.

Helping Membership Changes Take Effect Quickly

When you add a user to a group, the membership does not take effect immediately. Group membership is evaluated at logon for a user (at startup for a computer). Therefore, a user will have to log off and log on before the membership change becomes a part of the user's token.

Additionally, there can be a delay while the group membership change replicates. Replication will be discussed in Chapter 11, "Sites and Replication." This is particularly true if your enterprise has more than one Active Directory site. You can facilitate the speed with which a change affects a user by making the change on a domain controller in the user's site. Right-click the domain in the Active Directory Users And Computers snap-in and choose Change Domain Controller.

Developing a Group Management Strategy

Adding groups to other groups—a process called *nesting*—can create a hierarchy of groups that support your business roles and rules. Now that you have learned the business purposes and technical characteristics of groups, it is time to align the two in a strategy for group management.

Earlier in this lesson, you learned which types of objects *can* be members of each group scope. Now it is time to identify which types of objects *should* be members of each group scope. This leads to the best practice for group nesting, known as AGDLA:

- **A**ccounts (user and computer identities) are members of
- **G**lobal groups that represent business roles. Those role groups (global groups) are members of
- **D**omain **L**ocal groups that represent management rules—which have Read permission to a specific collection of folders, for example. These rule groups (domain local groups) are added to
- **A**ccess control lists (ACLs), which provide the level of access required by the rule.

In a multidomain forest, there are universal groups, as well, that fit in between global and domain local. Global groups from multiple domains are members of a single universal group. That universal group is a member of domain local groups in multiple domains. You can remember the nesting as AGUDLA.

This best practice for implementing group nesting translates well even in multidomain scenarios. Consider Figure 4-6, which represents a group implementation that reflects not only the technical view of group management best practices (AGDLA) but also the business view of role-based, rule-based management.

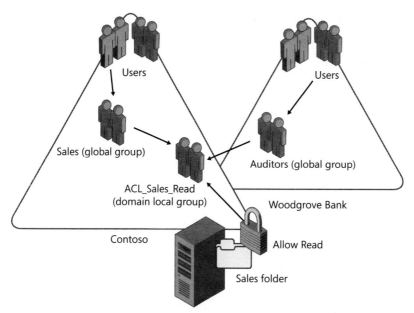

Figure 4-6   A group management implementation

Consider the following scenario. The sales force at Contoso, Ltd., has just completed their fiscal year. Sales files from the previous year are in a folder called Sales. The sales force needs read access to the Sales folder. Additionally, a team of auditors from Woodgrove Bank, a potential investor, require Read access to the Sales folder to perform the audit. The steps to implement the security required by this scenario are as follows:

1. Assign users with common job responsibilities or other business characteristics to role groups implemented as global security groups.

    This happens separately in each domain. Sales people at Contoso are added to a Sales role group. Auditors at Woodgrove Bank are added to an Auditors role group.

2. Create a group to represent the business rule regarding who can access the Sales folder with Read permission.

    This is implemented in the domain containing the resource to which the rule applies. In this case, it is the Contoso domain in which the Sales folder resides. The rule group is created as a domain local group.

3. Add the role groups to whom the business rule applies to the rule group.

    These groups can come from any domain in the forest or from a trusted domain such as Woodgrove Bank. Global groups from trusted external domains, or from any domain in the same forest, can be a member of a domain local group.

4. Assign the permission that implements the required level of access.

    In this case, grant the Allow Read permission to the domain local group.

This strategy results in single points of management, reducing the management burden. There is one point of management that defines who is in Sales or who is an Auditor. Those roles, of course, are likely to have a variety of permissions to resources beyond simply the Sales folder. There is another single point of management to determine who has Read access to the Sales folder. The Sales folder might not just be a single folder on a single server; it could be a collection of folders across multiple servers, each of which assigns Allow Read permission to the single domain local group.

PRACTICE **Creating and Managing Groups**

In this practice, you will create groups, experiment with group membership, and convert group type and scope. Before performing the exercises in this practice, you need to create the following objects in the *contoso.com* domain:

- A first-level OU named Groups
- A first-level OU named People
- User objects in the People OU for Linda Mitchell, Scott Mitchell, Jeff Ford, Mike Fitzmaurice, Mike Danseglio, and Tony Krijnen

▶ **Exercise 1   Create Groups**

In this exercise, you will create groups of different scopes and types.

1. Log on to SERVER01 as Administrator and open the Active Directory Users And Computers snap-in. Select Groups OU in the console tree.
2. Right-click Groups OU, choose New, and then select Group.
3. In the Group Name box, type **Sales**.
4. Select the Global group scope and Security group type. Click OK.
5. Right-click the Sales group and choose Properties.
6. Click the Members tab.
7. Click the Add button.
8. Type **Jeff; Tony** and click OK.
9. Click OK to close the Properties dialog box.
10. Repeat steps 2–4 to create two global security groups named **Marketing** and **Consultants**.
11. Repeat steps 2–4 to create a domain local security group named **ACL_Sales Folder_Read**.
12. Open the properties of the ACL_Sales Folder_Read group.
13. Click the Member tab.
14. Click Add.
15. Type **Sales;Marketing;Consultants** and click OK.
16. Click Add.

17. Type **Linda** and click OK.
18. Click OK to close the Properties dialog box.
19. Open the Properties dialog box of the Marketing group.
20. Click the Member tab and click Add.
21. Type **ACL_Sales Folder_Read** and click OK.

    You are unable to add a domain local group to a global group.

22. Cancel out of all open dialog boxes.
23. Create a folder named **Sales** on the C drive.
24. Right-click the Sales folder, choose Properties, and click the Security tab.
25. Click Edit, and then click Add.
26. Click Advanced, and then click Find Now.

    Notice that by using a prefix for group names, such as the *ACL_* prefix for resource access groups, you can find them quickly, grouped together at the top of the list.

27. Cancel out of all open dialog boxes.
28. Right-click Groups, choose New, and then select Group.
29. In the Group Name box, type **Employees**.
30. Select the Domain Local group scope and the Distribution group type. Click OK.

▶ **Exercise 2   Convert Group Type and Scope**

In this exercise, you will learn how to convert group type and scope.

1. Right-click the Employees group and choose Properties.
2. Change the group type to Distribution.
3. Click Apply.

   Consider: Can you change the group scope from Domain Local to Global? How?

4. Change the group scope to Universal. Click Apply.
5. Change the group scope to Global. Click Apply.
6. Click OK to close the Properties dialog box.

Lesson Summary

- There are two types of groups: security and distribution. Security groups can be assigned permissions although distribution groups are used primarily as e-mail distribution lists.
- In addition to local groups, which are maintained only in the local SAM database of a domain member server, there are three domain group scopes: global, domain local, and universal.

- The group scope affects the group's replication, the types of objects that can be members of the group, and the group's availability to be a member of another group or to be used for management tasks such as assigning permissions.
- You can convert group type and scope after creating the group.

Lesson Review

You can use the following questions to test your knowledge of the information in Lesson 1, "Creating and Managing Groups." The questions are also available on the companion CD if you prefer to review them in electronic form.

NOTE Answers

Answers to these questions and explanations of why each answer choice is right or wrong are located in the "Answers" section at the end of the book.

---

1. A new project requires that users in your domain and in the domain of a partner organization have access to a shared folder on your file server. Which type of group should you create to manage the access to the shared folder?

    A. Universal security group

    B. Domain local security group

    C. Global security group

    D. Domain local distribution group

2. Your domain includes a global distribution group named Company Update. It has been used to send company news by e-mail to its members. You have decided to allow all members to contribute to the newsletter by creating a shared folder on a file server. What must you do to allow group members access to the shared folder?

    A. Change the group scope to domain local.

    B. Change the group scope to universal.

    C. Add the group to the Domain Users group.

    D. Use *Dsmod* with the *−secgrp yes* switch.

3. You have created a global security group in the *contoso.com* domain named Corporate Managers. Which members can be added to the group? (Choose all that apply.)

    A. Sales Managers, a global group in the *fabrikam.com* domain, a trusted domain of a partner company

    B. Sales Managers, a global group in the *tailspintoys.com* domain, a domain in the *contoso.com* forest

C. Linda Mitchell, a user in the *tailspintoys.com* domain, a domain in the *contoso.com* forest

D. Jeff Ford, a user in the *fabrikam.com* domain, a trusted domain of a partner company

E. Mike Danseglio, a user in the *contoso.com* domain

F. Sales Executives, a global group in the *contoso.com* domain

G. Sales Directors, a domain local group in the *contoso.com* domain

H. European Sales Managers, a universal group in the *contoso.com* forest

Lesson 2: Automating the Creation and Management of Groups

In Lesson 1, you learned the steps for creating groups, choosing group scope and type, and configuring group membership, using the Active Directory Users and Computers snap-in. When you need to create more than one group at a time, or when you want to automate group creation, you must turn to other tools. Chapter 3 introduced you to command-line and automation tools, including *CSVDE*, *LDIFDE*, *Dsadd*, Windows PowerShell, and VBScript. These tools can also be used to automate the creation and management of group objects. In this lesson, you'll learn how to manage the life cycle of group objects, from birth to death, using command-line and automation tools.

After this lesson, you will be able to:

- Create groups with *Dsadd*, *CSVDE*, and *LDIFDE*.
- Modify groups' membership with *Dsmod*, *LDIFDE*, Windows PowerShell, and VBScript.
- Enumerate group membership with *Dsget*.
- Move and delete groups with *Dsmove* and *Dsrm*.

Estimated lesson time: 45 minutes

Creating Groups with *Dsadd*

The *Dsadd* command, introduced in Chapter 3, enables you to add objects to Active Directory. To add a group, type the command **dsadd group *GroupDN***, where *GroupDN* is the DN of the group, such as "CN=Finance Managers,OU=Groups,DC=contoso,DC=com." Be certain to surround the DN with quotes if the DN includes spaces. For example, to create a new global security group named Marketing in the Groups OU of the *contoso.com* domain, the command would be:

```
dsadd group "CN=Marketing,OU=Groups,DC=contoso,DC=com"
   -samid Marketing -secgrp yes -scope g
```

You can also provide the *GroupDN* parameter by one of the following ways:

- By piping a list of DNs from another command such as *Dsquery*.
- By typing each DN on the command line, separated by spaces.
- By leaving the DN parameter empty, at which point you can type the DNs one at a time at the keyboard console of the command prompt. Press Enter after each DN. Press Ctrl + Z and Enter after the last DN.

Because you can include more than one DN on the command line, separated by a space, you can generate multiple groups at once with *Dsadd*. The *Dsadd* command can also configure group attributes of the groups you create with the following optional parameters:

- **−secgrp** { **yes** | **no** } specifies group type: security (*yes*) or distribution (*no*).
- **−scope** { **l** | **g** | **u** } determines the group scope: domain local (*l*), global (*g*), or universal (*u*).
- **−samid** *Name* specifies the *sAMAccountName* of the group. If not specified, the name of the group from its DN is used. It is recommended that the *sAMAccountName* and the group name be the same, so you do not need to include this parameter when using *Dsadd*.
- **−desc** *Description* configures the group's description.
- **−members** *MemberDN* adds members to the group. Members are specified by their DNs in a space-separated list.
- **−memberof** *GroupDN* ... makes the new group a member of one or more existing groups. The groups are specified by their DNs in a space-separated list.

Importing Groups with *CSVDE*

Chapter 3 also introduced you to *CSVDE*, which imports data from comma-separated values (.csv) files. It is also able to export data to a .csv file. The following example shows a .csv file that will create a group, Marketing, and populate the group with two initial members, Linda Mitchell and Scott Mitchell.

```
objectClass,sAMAccountName,DN,member
group,Marketing,"CN=Marketing,OU=Groups,DC=contoso,DC=com",
    "CN=Linda Mitchell,OU=People,DC=contoso,DC=com;CN=Scott Mitchell,
    OU=People,DC=contoso,DC=com"
```

The objects listed in the *member* attribute must already exist in the directory service. Their DNs are separated by semicolons within the *member* column.

You can import this file into Active Directory by using the command:

```
csvde -i -f "Filename" [-k]
```

The −*i* parameter specifies import mode. Without it, *CSVDE* uses export mode. The −*f* parameter precedes the filename, and the −*k* parameter ensures that processing continues even if errors are encountered.

Exam Tip *CSVDE* can be used to create objects, not to modify existing objects. You cannot use *CSVDE* to import members to existing groups.

Managing Groups with *LDIFDE*

LDIFDE, as you learned in Chapter 3, is a tool that imports and exports files in the Lightweight Directory Access Protocol Data Interchange Format (LDIF) format. LDIF files are text files within which operations are specified by a block of lines separated by a blank line. Each operation begins with the DN attribute of the object that is the target of the operation. The next line, *changeType*, specifies the type of operation: *add*, *modify*, or *delete*.

The following LDIF file creates two groups, Finance and Research, in the Groups OU of the *contoso.com* domain:

```
DN: CN=Finance,OU=Groups,DC=contoso,DC=com
changeType: add
CN: Finance
description: Finance Users
objectClass: group
sAMAccountName: Finance

DN: CN=Research,OU=Groups,DC=contoso,DC=com
changeType: add
CN: Research
description: Research Users
objectClass: group
sAMAccountName: Research
```

Convention would suggest saving the file with an .ldf extension, for example Groups.ldf. To import the groups into the directory, issue the *Ldifde.exe* command as shown here:

```
ldifde -i -f groups.ldf
```

Modifying Group Membership with *LDIFDE*

LDIFDE can also be used to modify existing objects in Active Directory, using LDIF operations with a *changeType* of *modify*. To add two members to the Finance group, the LDIF file would be:

```
dn: CN=Finance,OU=Groups,DC=contoso,DC=com
changetype: modify
add: member
member: CN=April Stewart,OU=People,dc=contoso,dc=com
member: CN=Mike Fitzmaurice,OU=People,dc=contoso,dc=com
-
```

The *changeType* is set to *modify*, and then the change operation is specified: *add* objects to the *member* attribute. Each new member is then listed on a separate line that begins with the *member* attribute name. The change operation is terminated with a line containing a single dash. Changing the third line to the following would remove the two specified members from the group:

```
delete: member
```

Retrieving Group Membership with *Dsget*

The *Dsmod* and *Dsget* commands discussed in Chapter 3 are particularly helpful for managing the membership of groups. There is no option in the Active Directory Users and Computers snap-in to list all the members of a group, including nested members. You can see only direct members of a group on the group's Members tab. Similarly, there is no way to list all the groups to which a user or computer belongs, including nested groups. You can see only direct membership on the user's or computer's Member Of tab.

The *Dsget* command enables you to retrieve a complete list of a group's membership, including nested members, with the following syntax:

```
dsget group "GroupDN" -members [-expand]
```

The *expand* option performs the magic of expanding nested groups' members.

Similarly, the *Dsget* command can be used to retrieve a complete list of groups to which a user or computer belongs, again by using the *expand* option in the following commands:

```
dsget user "UserDN" -memberof [-expand]
dsget computer "ComputerDN" -memberof [-expand]
```

The *memberof* option returns the value of the user's or computer's *memberOf* attribute, showing the groups to which the object directly belongs. By adding the *expand* option, those groups are searched recursively, producing an exhaustive list of all groups to which object the user belongs in the domain.

Changing Group Membership with *Dsmod*

The *Dsmod* command was applied in Lesson 1 to modify the scope and type of a group. The command's basic syntax is:

```
dsmod group "GroupDN" [options]
```

You can use options such as *samid* and *desc* to modify the *sAMAccountName* and *description* attributes of the group. Most useful, however, are the options that enable you to modify a group's membership:

- **–addmbr "*Member DN*"**   Adds members to the group
- **–rmmbr "*Member DN*"**   Removes members from the group

As with all DS commands, *Member DN* is the distinguished name of another Active Directory object, surrounded by quotes if the DN includes spaces. Multiple *Member DN* entries can be included, separated by spaces. For example, to add Mike Danseglio to the Research group, the *Dsmod* command would be:

```
dsmod group "CN=Research,OU=Groups,DC=contoso,DC=com"
    -addmbr "CN=Mike Danseglio,OU=People,DC=contoso,DC=com"
```

You can use *Dsget* in combination with *Dsmod* to copy group membership. In the following example, the *Dsget* command is used to get information about all the members of the Sales group and then, by piping that list to *Dsmod*, to add those users to the Marketing group:

```
dsget group "CN=Sales,OU=Groups,DC=contoso,DC=com" -members |
    dsmod group "CN=Marketing,OU=Groups,DC=contoso,DC=com" -addmbr
```

Moving and Renaming Groups with *Dsmove*

The *Dsmove* command, also discussed in Chapter 3, enables you to move or rename an object within a domain. You cannot use it to move objects between domains. Its basic syntax is:

```
dsmove ObjectDN [-newname NewName] [-newparent TargetOUDN]
```

The object is specified by using its distinguished name in the *ObjectDN* parameter. To rename the object, specify its new common name as the value of the *newname* parameter. To move an object to a new location, specify the distinguished name of the target container as the value of the *newparent* parameter.

For example, to change the name of the Marketing group to Public Relations, type:

```
dsmove "CN=Marketing,OU=Groups,DC=contoso,DC=com"
    -newname "Public Relations"
```

To then move that group to the Marketing OU, type:

```
dsmove "CN=Public Relations,OU=Groups,DC=contoso,DC=com"
    -newparent "OU=Marketing,DC=contoso,DC=com"
```

NOTE   You're not limited to the command line

You can also move or rename a group in the Active Directory Users And Computers snap-in by right-clicking the group and choosing Move or Rename from the context menu.

Deleting Groups with *Dsrm*

Dsrm can be used to delete a group or any other Active Directory object. The basic syntax of *Dsrm* is:

```
dsrm ObjectDN ... [-subtree [-exclude]] [-noprompt] [-c]
```

The object is specified by its distinguished name in the *ObjectDN* parameter. You will be prompted to confirm the deletion of each object unless you specify the *noprompt* option. The *-c* switch puts *Dsrm* into continuous operation mode, in which errors are reported, but the command keeps processing additional objects. Without the *-c* switch, processing halts on the first error.

To delete the Public Relations group, type:

```
dsrm "CN=Public Relations,OU=Marketing,DC=contoso,DC=com"
```

You can also delete a group in the Active Directory Users And Computers snap-in by right-clicking the group and choosing the *Delete* command.

NOTE   Know the impact before deleting a group

When you delete a group, you are removing a point of management in your organization. Be certain you have evaluated the environment to verify that there are no permissions or other resources that rely on the group. Deleting a group is a serious action with potentially significant consequences. It is recommended that, before you delete a group, you record its membership and remove all members for a period of time to determine whether the members lose access to any resources. If anything goes wrong, simply re-add the members. If the test succeeds, then delete the group.

Managing Group Membership with Windows PowerShell and VBScript

It is unlikely that you will need to understand the intricacies of managing group membership for the 70-640 examination, and an exhaustive discussion of scripting groups is beyond the scope of this book. See *Windows Administration Resource Kit: Productivity Solutions for IT Professionals* for detailed discussions about automating group management with VBScript.

However, it doesn't hurt to know the basics. In both VBScript and Windows PowerShell, there are several ways to manipulate group membership—a group's *member* attribute—but the most common and effective involve these steps:

1. Determine the *aDSPath* of the member. The *aDSPath* takes the form, *LDAP://*<DN of member>.

2. Connect to the group.

3. Use the *Add* or *Remove* method of the group object, specifying the *aDSPath* of the member.

A Windows PowerShell script that adds Mike Danseglio to the Research group would, therefore, be:

```
$MemberADSPath = "LDAP://CN=Mike Danseglio,OU=People,DC=contoso,DC=com"
$objGroup = [ADSI]"LDAP://CN=Research,OU=Groups,DC=contoso,DC=com"
$objGroup.Add ($MemberADSPath)
```

In VBScript, the script would be:

```
MemberADSPath = "LDAP://CN=Mike Danseglio,OU=People,DC=contoso,DC=com"
Set objGroup = GetObject("LDAP://CN=Research,OU=Groups,DC=contoso,DC=com")
objGroup.Add MemberADSPath
```

To remove members, use the *Remove* method instead of the *Add* method. The remainder of each script remains the same.

PRACTICE **Automating the Creation and Management of Groups**

In this practice, you will use DS commands, *CSVDE*, and *LDIFDE* to perform group management tasks. Before performing the exercises in this practice, you need to create the following objects in the *contoso.com* domain:

- A first-level OU named Groups
- A first-level OU named People
- User objects in the People OU for Linda Mitchell, Scott Mitchell, Jeff Ford, Mike Fitzmaurice, Mike Danseglio, April Stewart, and Tony Krijnen.

In addition, *delete* any groups with the following names: Finance, Accounting.

▶ **Exercise 1   Create a Group with *Dsadd***

In this exercise, you will use *Dsadd* to create a group. *Dsadd* can create a group, and even populate its membership, with a single command.

1. Log on to SERVER01 as Administrator.
2. Open a command prompt and type the following command on one line. Then press Enter:

```
dsadd group "CN=Finance,OU=Groups,DC=contoso,DC=com"
    -samid Finance -secgrp yes -scope g
```

3. Open the Active Directory Users And Computers snap-in and confirm that the group was created successfully. If the Active Directory Users And Computers snap-in was open prior to performing step 2, refresh the view.

▶ **Exercise 2   Import Groups with *CSVDE***

1. Log on to SERVER01 as Administrator.
2. Open Notepad and type the following lines. Each bullet is one line of text in Notepad but do not include the bullets:
   - objectClass,sAMAccountName,DN,member
   - group,Accounting,"CN=Accounting,OU=Groups,DC=contoso,DC=com",
     "CN=Linda Mitchell,OU=People,DC=contoso,DC=com;
     CN=Scott Mitchell,OU=People,DC=contoso,DC=com"
3. Save the file to your Documents folder with the name "**Importgroups.csv**" including the quotes so that Notepad doesn't add a .txt extension.
4. Open a command prompt and type the following command:

```
csvde -i -f "%userprofile%\importgroups.csv"
```

5. Open the Active Directory Users And Computers snap-in and check to confirm that the groups were created successfully. You might need to refresh the view if the Active Directory Users And Computers snap-in was open prior to performing the step.

▶ **Exercise 3   Modify Group Membership with *LDIFDE***

CSVDE cannot modify the membership of existing groups, but *LDIFDE* can. In this exercise, you will use *LDIFDE* to modify the group membership of the Accounting group you imported in Exercise 2, "Import Groups with *CSVDE*."

1. Open Notepad and type the following lines:

    ```
    dn: CN=Accounting,OU=Groups,DC=contoso,DC=com
    changetype: modify
    add: member
    member: CN=April
    Stewart,OU=People,dc=contoso,dc=com
    member: CN=Mike Fitzmaurice,OU=People,dc=contoso,dc=com
    -

    dn: CN= Accounting,OU=Groups,DC=contoso,DC=com
    changetype: modify
    delete: member
    member: CN=Linda Mitchell,OU=People,dc=contoso,dc=com
    -
    ```

    Be sure to include the dashes after each block and the blank line between the two blocks.

2. Save the file to your Documents folder as "**Membershipchange.ldf**" including the quotes, so that Notepad does not add a .txt extension.

3. Open a command prompt.

4. Type the following command and press Enter:

    ```
    ldifde -i -f "%userprofile%\documents\membershipchange.ldf"
    ```

5. Using the Active Directory Users And Computers snap-in, confirm that the membership of the Accounting group changed according to the instructions of the LDIF file. It should now include April Stewart, Mike Fitzmaurice, and Scott Mitchell.

▶ **Exercise 4   Modify Group Membership with *Dsmod***

In this exercise, you will add a user and a group to the Finance group, using the *Dsmod* command.

1. Open a command prompt.

2. Type the following command to change the membership of the Finance group:

    ```
    dsmod group "CN=Finance,OU=Groups,DC=contoso,DC=com" -addmbr "CN=Tony
    Krijnen,OU=People,DC=contoso,DC=com"
    "CN=Accounting,OU=Groups,DC=contoso,DC=com"
    ```

3. In the Active Directory Users And Computers snap-in, confirm that the membership of the Finance group consists of Tony Krijnen and the Accounting group.

▶ **Exercise 5   Confirm Group Membership with *Dsget***

Evaluating effective group membership is difficult with the Active Directory Users and Computers snap-in but is easy with the *Dsget* command. In this exercise, you will look at both the full membership of a group and the group memberships of a user.

1. Open a command prompt.

2. List the direct members of the Accounting group by typing the following command and then pressing Enter:

   ```
   dsget group "CN=Accounting,OU=Groups,DC=contoso,DC=com" -members
   ```

3. List the direct members of the Finance group by typing the following command and then pressing Enter:

   ```
   dsget group "CN=Finance,OU=Groups,DC=contoso,DC=com" -members
   ```

4. List the full list of members of the Finance group by typing the following command and then pressing Enter:

   ```
   dsget group "CN=Finance,OU=Groups,DC=contoso,DC=com" -members -expand
   ```

5. List the direct group membership of Scott Mitchell by typing the following command and then pressing Enter:

   ```
   dsget user "CN=Scott Mitchell,OU=People,DC=contoso,DC=com" -memberof
   ```

6. List the full group membership of Scott Mitchell by typing the following command on one line and then pressing Enter:

   ```
   dsget user "CN=Scott Mitchell,OU=People,DC=contoso,DC=com"
      -memberof -expand
   ```

Lesson Summary

- You can create groups with *Dsadd*, *CSVDE*, and *LDIFDE*.
- *LDIFDE* and *Dsmod* can modify the membership of existing groups.
- The *Dsget* command can list the full membership of a group or the full list of groups to which a user belongs, including nested groups.

Lesson Review

You can use the following questions to test your knowledge of the information in Lesson 2, "Automating the Creation and Management of Groups." The questions are also available on the companion CD if you prefer to review them in electronic form.

NOTE Answers

Answers to these questions and explanations of why each answer choice is right or wrong are located in the "Answers" section at the end of the book.

---

1. Which of the following can be used to remove members from a group? (Choose all that apply.)

   A. Remove-Item

   B. *Dsrm*

   C. *Dsmod*

   D. *LDIFDE*

   E. *CSVDE*

2. You are using *Dsmod* to add a domain local group named GroupA to a global group named GroupB. You are receiving errors. Which command will solve the problem so that you can then add GroupA to GroupB? (Choose all that apply.)

   A. *Dsrm.exe*

   B. *Dsmod.exe*

   C. *Dsquery.exe*

   D. *Dsget.exe*

3. Your management has asked you to produce a list of all users who belong to the Special Project group, including those users belonging to groups nested into Special Project. Which of the following can you use?

   A. Get-Members

   B. *Dsquery.exe*

   C. *LDIFDE*

   D. *Dsget.exe*

Lesson 3: Administering Groups in an Enterprise

Lesson 1 and Lesson 2 prepared you to perform daily administrative tasks related to groups in Active Directory. You learned to create, modify, and delete groups, using a variety of tools and procedures. This lesson rounds out your exploration of groups by preparing you to take advantage of useful group attributes for documenting groups, to delegate the management of group membership to specific administrative teams or individuals, and to break away from reliance on some of the Active Directory and Windows default groups.

After this lesson, you will be able to:
- Document the purpose of a group by using the group's attributes.
- Prevent a group from being accidentally deleted.
- Delegate management of a group's membership.
- Create a shadow group.
- Recognize and manage default domain groups.
- Assign permissions to special identities.

Estimated lesson time: 45 minutes

Best Practices for Group Attributes

Creating a group in Active Directory is easy. It is not so easy to make sure that the group is used correctly over time. You can facilitate the correct management and use of a group by documenting its purpose to help administrators understand how and when to use the group. There are several best practices, which, although they are unlikely to be addressed by the certification exam, will prove immensely useful to your enterprise group administration:

- **Establish and adhere to a strict naming convention** Lesson 1 addressed a suggested naming convention. In the context of ongoing group administration, establishing and following group naming standards increases administrative productivity. Using prefixes to indicate the purpose of a group, and a consistent delimiter between the prefix and the descriptive part of the group names, can help locate the correct group for a particular purpose. For example, the prefix APP can be used to designate groups that are used to manage applications, and the prefix ACL can be used for groups that are assigned permissions on ACLs. With such prefixes, it becomes easier to locate and interpret the purpose of groups named APP_Accounting versus ACL_Accounting_Read. The former is used to manage the deployment of the accounting software, and the latter provides read access to the accounting folder. Prefixes also help group the names of groups in the user interface. Figure 4-7 shows an example. When attempting to locate a group to use in assigning permissions to a folder, you can type the prefix *ACL_* in the Select dialog box and click OK. A Multiple Names Found dialog box appears showing only the *ACL_* groups in the directory, thereby ensuring that permissions will be assigned to a group that is designed to manage resource access.

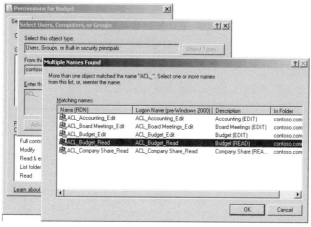

Figure 4-7   Selecting a group by using a group prefix to narrow down to the correct type of group

- **Summarize a group's purpose with its *description* attribute**   Use the *description* attribute of a group to summarize the group's purpose. Because the Description column is enabled by default in the details pane of the Active Directory Users and Computers snap-in, the group's purpose can be highly visible to administrators.

- **Detail a group's purpose in its Notes**   When you open a group's Properties dialog box, the *Notes* field, at the bottom of the General tab, can be used to document the group's purpose. For example, you can list the folders to which a group has been given permission, as shown in Figure 4-8.

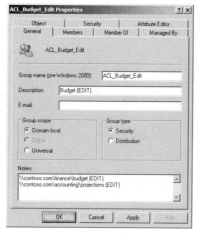

Figure 4-8   A group's Properties dialog box, showing the *Notes* field used to detail the group's purpose

Protecting Groups from Accidental Deletion

Deleting a group has a high impact on administrators and, potentially, on security. Consider a group that has been used to manage access to resources. If the group is deleted, access to that resource is changed. Either users who should be able to access the resource are suddenly prevented from access, creating a denial-of-service scenario, or if you had used the group to deny access to a resource with a Deny permission, inappropriate access to the resource becomes possible.

Additionally, if you re-create the group, the new group object will have a new SID, which will not match the SIDs on ACLs of resources. Instead, you must perform object recovery to reanimate the deleted group before the tombstone interval is reached. When a group has been deleted for the tombstone interval—60 days by default—the group and its SID are permanently deleted from Active Directory. When you reanimate a tombstoned object, you must re-create most of its attributes, including, significantly, the *member* attribute of group objects. That means you must rebuild the group membership after restoring the deleted object. Alternatively, you can perform an authoritative restore or, in Windows Server 2008, turn to your Active Directory snapshots to recover both the group and its membership. Authoritative restore and snapshots are discussed in Chapter 13, "Maintenance, Backup, and Recovery."

MORE INFO   Recovering deleted groups

You can learn more about recovering deleted groups and their memberships in Knowledge Base article 840001, which you can find at *http://support.microsoft.com/kb/840001/en-us*.

In any event, it is safe to say that recovering a deleted group is a skill you should hope to use only in disaster recovery fire drills, not in a production environment. Protect yourself from the potentially devastating results of group object deletion by protecting each group you create from deletion. Windows Server 2008 makes it easy to protect any object from accidental deletion. To protect an object, follow these steps:

1. In the Active Directory Users And Computers snap-in, click the View menu and make sure that Advanced Features is selected.
2. Open the Properties dialog box for a group.
3. On the Object tab, select the Protect Object From Accidental Deletion check box.
4. Click OK.

   This is one of the few places in Windows where you actually have to click OK. Clicking Apply does not modify the ACL based on your selection.

The Protect Object From Accidental Deletion option applies an access control entry (ACE) to the ACL of the object that explicitly denies the Everyone group both the Delete permission and the Delete Subtree permission. If you really do want to delete the group, you can return to the Object tab of the Properties dialog box and clear the Protect Object From Accidental Deletion check box.

Delegating the Management of Group Membership

After a group has been created, you might want to delegate the management of the group's membership to a team or an individual who has the business responsibility for the resource that the group manages. For example, assume that your finance manager is responsible for creating next year's budget. You create a shared folder for the budget and assign Write permission to a group named *ACL_Budget_Edit*. If someone needs access to the budget folder, he or she contacts the help desk to enter a request, the help desk contacts the finance manager for business approval, and then the help desk adds the user to the ACL_Budget_Edit group. You can improve the responsiveness and accountability of the process by allowing the finance manager to change the group's membership. Then, users needing access can request access directly from the finance manager, who can make the change, removing the intermediate step of the help desk. To delegate the management of a group's membership, you must assign to the finance manager the Allow Write Member permission for the group. The *member* attribute is the multivalued attribute that is the group's membership. There are several ways to delegate the Write Member permission. Two of them are covered in the following sections.

Delegating Membership Management with the Managed By Tab

The easiest way to delegate membership management of a single group is to use the Managed By tab. The Managed By tab of a group object's Properties dialog box, shown in Figure 4-9, serves two purposes. First it provides contact information related to the manager of a group. You can use this information to contact the business owner of a group to obtain approval prior to adding a user to the group.

The second purpose served by the Managed By tab is to manage the delegation of the *member* attribute. Note the check box shown in Figure 4-9. It is labeled Manager Can Update Membership List. When selected, the user or group shown in the Name box is given the WriteMember permission. If you change or clear the manager, the appropriate change is made to the group's ACL.

NOTE   Click OK

This is another of the strange and rare places where you must actually click OK to implement the change. Clicking Apply does not change the ACL on the group.

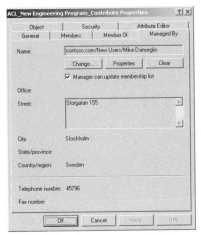

Figure 4-9   The Managed By tab of a group's Properties dialog box

It is not quite so easy to insert a group into the Managed By tab of another group. When you click the Change button, the Select User, Contact, Or Group dialog box appears, shown in Figure 4-10. If you enter the name of a group and click OK, an error occurs. That's because this dialog box is not configured to accept groups as valid object types, even though *Group* is in the name of the dialog box itself. To work around this odd limitation, click the Object Types button, and then select the check box next to Groups. Click OK to close both the Object Types and Select dialog boxes. Be sure to select the Manager Can Update Membership List check box if you want to assign the WriteMember permission to the group. When a group is used on the Managed By tab, no contact information is visible because groups do not maintain contact-related attributes.

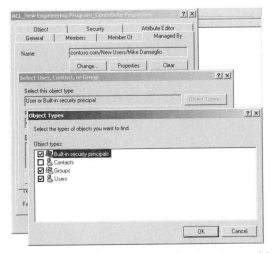

Figure 4-10   Selecting a group for the Managed By tab

Delegating Membership Management Using Advanced Security Settings

You can use the Advanced Security Settings dialog box to assign the Allow Write Member permission directly. You can assign the permission for an individual group or for all the groups in an OU.

Delegate the management of membership for an individual group

1. In the Active Directory Users And Computers snap-in, click the View menu and make sure Advanced Features is selected.
2. Right-click the groups' OU and choose Properties.
3. Click the Security tab.
4. Click the Advanced button.
5. In the Advanced Security Settings dialog box, click the Add button.

   If the Add button is not visible, click the Edit button, and then click the Add button.
6. In the Select dialog box, enter the name for the group to whom you want to grant permission or click Browse to search for the group. When you are finished, click OK.

   The Permission Entry dialog box appears.
7. Click the Properties tab.
8. In the Apply To drop-down list, choose This Object And All Descendant Objects.
9. In the Permissions list, select the Allow check boxes for the Read Members and Write Members permissions.

   By default, all users have the Read Members permission, so that permission is not required. However, role-based access control is best implemented by assigning all the permissions required to achieve the desired capability rather than relying on permissions assigned indirectly.

   Figure 4-11 shows the resulting Permission Entry dialog box.

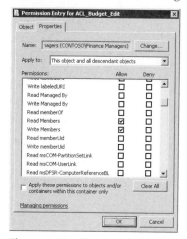

Figure 4-11   The Permission Entry dialog box showing the delegation of group membership management for a group

10. Click OK to close each of the security dialog boxes.

Delegate the ability to manage membership for all groups in an OU

1. In the Active Directory Users And Computers snap-in, click the View menu and make sure Advanced Features is selected.

2. Right-click the groups' OU and choose Properties.

3. Click the Security tab.

4. Click the Advanced button.

5. In the Advanced Security Settings dialog box, click the Add button.
    If the Add button is not visible, click the Edit button, and then click the Add button.

6. In the Select dialog box, enter the name for the group to whom you want to grant permission or click Browse to search for the group. When you are finished, click OK.
    The Permission Entry dialog box appears.

7. Click the Properties tab.

8. In the Apply To drop-down list, choose Descendant Group Objects. If you are using earlier versions of the Active Directory Users And Computers snap-in, choose Group Objects.

9. In the Permissions list, select the Allow check boxes for the Read Members and Write Members permissions.
    By default, all users have the Read Members permission, so that permission is not required. However, role-based access control is best implemented by assigning all the permissions required to achieve the desired capability rather than relying on permissions assigned indirectly.
    Figure 4-12 shows the resulting Permission Entry dialog box.

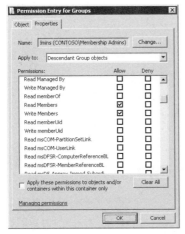

Figure 4-12   The Permission Entry dialog box showing the delegation of group membership management for all groups in the Groups OU

10. Click OK to close each of the security dialog boxes.

Understanding Shadow Groups

Most management of an enterprise is implemented with groups. Groups are assigned permission to resources. Groups can be used to filter the scope of Group Policy objects. Groups are assigned fine-grained password policies. Groups can be used as collections for configuration management tools such as Microsoft System Center Configuration Manager. The list goes on. OUs, however, are not used as frequently to manage the enterprise, and in some cases, they cannot be used. For instance, OUs cannot be assigned permissions to resources, nor can they be assigned fine-grained password policies (discussed in Chapter 8, "Authentication"). Instead, the primary purpose of an OU is to provide a scope of management for the delegation of administrative permissions for the objects in that OU. In other words, an OU of users enables you to delegate to your help desk the ability to reset passwords for all users in the OU. OUs are administrative containers.

The reason for this separation of purpose between OUs and groups is that OUs do not provide the same flexibility as groups. A user or computer (or other object) can only exist within the context of a single OU whereas a security principal can belong to many groups. Therefore, groups are used for aligning identities with the capabilities required by those identities.

Sometimes, you might want to manage using an OU when it is not possible. For example, you might want to give all users in an OU access to a folder. Or you might want to assign a unique password policy to users in an OU. You cannot do so directly, but you can achieve your goal by creating what is called a *shadow group*. A shadow group is a group that contains the same users as an OU. More accurately, a shadow group contains users that meet a certain criterion.

The easiest way to create a shadow group is to create the group; then, in the OU containing the users, press Ctrl + A to select all users. Right-click any selected user and choose Add To Group. Type the name of the group and click OK.

Exam Tip   On the 70-640 exam, be prepared to see the term *shadow group* in use. Know that it means a group that contains, as members, the users in an OU.

Unfortunately, Windows does not yet provide a way to maintain the membership of a shadow group dynamically. When you add or remove a user to or from the OU, you must also add or remove the user to or from the shadow group.

MORE INFO   **Maintaining shadow groups dynamically**

See *Windows Administration Resource Kit: Productivity Solutions for IT Professionals* for scripts that will help maintain shadow groups dynamically.

Default Groups

A number of groups are created automatically on a server running Windows Server 2008. These are called *default local groups*, and they include well-known groups such as Administrators, Backup Operators, and Remote Desktop Users. Additional groups are created in a domain, in both the Builtin and Users containers, including Domain Admins, Enterprise Admins, and Schema Admins. The following list provides a summary of capabilities of the subset of default groups that have significant permissions and user rights related to the management of Active Directory:

- **Enterprise Admins (Users container of the forest root domain)**   This group is a member of the Administrators group in every domain in the forest, giving it complete access to the configuration of all domain controllers. It also owns the Configuration partition of the directory and has full control of the domain naming context in all forest domains.

- **Schema Admins (Users container of the forest root domain)**   This group owns and has full control of the Active Directory schema.

- **Administrators (Builtin container of each domain)**   This group has complete control over all domain controllers and data in the domain naming context. It can change the membership of all other administrative groups in the domain, and the Administrators group in the forest root domain can change the membership of Enterprise Admins, Schema Admins, and Domain Admins. The Administrators group in the forest root domain is arguably the most powerful service administration group in the forest.

- **Domain Admins (Users container of each domain)**   This group is added to the Administrators group of its domain. Therefore, it inherits all the capabilities of the Administrators group. It is also, by default, added to the local Administrators group of each domain member computer, giving Domain Admins ownership of all domain computers.

- **Server Operators (Builtin container of each domain)**   This group can perform maintenance tasks on domain controllers. It has the right to log on locally, start and stop services, perform backup and restore operations, format disks, create or delete shares, and shut down domain controllers. By default, this group has no members.

- **Account Operators (Builtin container of each domain)**   This group can create, modify, and delete accounts for users, groups, and computers located in any organizational unit in the domain (except the Domain Controllers OU) as well as in the Users and Computers container. Account Operators cannot modify accounts that are members of the Administrators or Domain Admins groups, nor can they modify those groups. Account Operators can also log on locally to domain controllers. By default, this group has no members.

- **Backup Operators (Builtin container of each domain)**   This group can perform backup and restore operations on domain controllers as well as log on locally and shut down domain controllers. By default, this group has no members.
- **Print Operators (Builtin container of each domain)**   This group can maintain print queues on domain controllers. It can also log on locally and shut down domain controllers.

The default groups that provide administrative privileges should be managed carefully because they typically have broader privileges than are necessary for most delegated environments and because they often apply protection to their members.

The Account Operators group is a perfect example. If you examine its capabilities in the preceding list, you will see that its rights are very broad, indeed. It can even log on locally to a domain controller. In very small enterprises, such rights will probably be appropriate for one or two individuals who might be domain administrators anyway. In enterprises of any size, the rights and permissions granted to Account Operators are usually far too broad.

Additionally, Account Operators is, like the other administrative groups listed previously, a *protected group*. Protected groups are defined by the operating system and cannot be unprotected. Members of a protected group become protected. The result of protection is that the permissions (ACLs) of members are modified so that they no longer inherit permissions from their OU but, rather, receive a copy of an ACL that is quite restrictive. For example, if Jeff Ford is added to the Account Operators group, his account becomes protected and the help desk, which can reset all other user passwords in the People OU, cannot reset Jeff Ford's password.

MORE INFO   Protected accounts

For more information about protected accounts, see Knowledge Base article 817433 at *http://support.microsoft.com/?kbid=817433*. If you want to search the Internet for resources, use the keyword *adminSDHolder*.

For these reasons—overdelegation and protection—strive to avoid adding users to the groups listed previously that do not have members by default: Account Operators, Backup Operators, Server Operators, and Print Operators. Instead, create custom groups to which you assign permissions and user rights that achieve your business and administrative requirements. For example, if Scott Mitchell should be able to perform backup operations on a domain controller but should not be able to perform restore operations that could lead to database rollback or corruption and should not be able to shut down a domain controller, don't put Scott in the Backup Operators group. Instead, create a group and assign it only the Backup Files And Directories user right; then add Scott as a member.

MORE INFO   Default group capabilities information

There is an exhaustive reference to the default groups in a domain and to the default local groups on Microsoft TechNet. If you are not familiar with the default groups and their capabilities, you should prepare for the examination by reading them. The default domain groups reference is at *http:// technet2.microsoft.com/WindowsServer/en/library/1631acad-ef34-4f77-9c2e-94a62f8846cf1033.mspx*, and the default local groups reference is at *http://technet2.microsoft.com/WindowsServer/en/library/ f6e01e51-14ea-48f4-97fc-5288a9a4a9b11033.mspx*.

Special Identities

Windows and Active Directory also support *special identities*, groups for which membership is controlled by the operating system. You cannot view the groups in any list in the Active Directory Users and Computers snap-in, for example. You cannot view or modify the membership of these special identities, and you cannot add them to other groups. You can, however, use these groups to assign rights and permissions. The most important special identities, often referred to as groups for convenience, are described in the following list:

- **Anonymous Logon**   Represents connections to a computer and its resources that are made without supplying a user name and password. Prior to Microsoft Windows Server 2003, this group was a member of the Everyone group. Beginning in Windows Server 2003, this group is no longer a default member of the Everyone group.
- **Authenticated Users**   Represents identities that have been authenticated. This group does not include Guest, even if the Guest account has a password.
- **Everyone**   Includes Authenticated Users and Guest. On computers running versions of Windows earlier than Windows Server 2003, this group includes Anonymous Logon.
- **Interactive**   Represents users accessing a resource while logged on locally to the computer hosting the resource, as opposed to accessing the resource over the network. When a user accesses any given resource on a computer to which the user is logged on locally, the user is automatically added to the Interactive group for that resource. Interactive also includes users logged on through a remote desktop connection.
- **Network**   Represents users accessing a resource over the network, as opposed to users who are logged on locally at the computer hosting the resource. When a user accesses any given resource over the network, the user is automatically added to the Network group for that resource.

The importance of these special identities is that they enable you to provide access to resources based on the type of authentication or connection rather than on the user account. For example, you could create a folder on a system that allows users to view its contents when logged on locally to the system but does not allow the same users to view the contents from a mapped drive over the network. This would be achieved by assigning permissions to the Interactive special identity.

PRACTICE **Administering Groups in an Enterprise**

In this practice, you will perform best-practices group management tasks to improve the administration of groups in the *contoso.com* domain. To perform the exercises in this practice, you will need the following objects in the *contoso.com* domain:

- A first-level OU named Groups.
- A global security group named Finance in the Groups OU.
- A first-level OU named People.
- A user account named Mike Danseglio in the People OU. Populate the user account with sample contact information: address, phone, and e-mail. Make sure the account is *not* required to change the password at the next logon.

In addition, ensure that the Domain Users group is a member of the Print Operators group, which can be found in the Builtin container. This will enable all sample users in the practice domain to log on to the domain controller, SERVER01. This is important for the practices in this training kit, but you should not allow users to log on to domain controllers in your production environment, so do not make Domain Users members of the Print Operators group in your production environment.

▶ **Exercise 1   Create a Well-Documented Group**

In this exercise, you will create a group to manage access to the Budget folder, and you will follow the best-practices guidelines presented in this lesson.

1. Log on to SERVER01 as Administrator and open the Active Directory Users And Computers snap-in.
2. Select the Groups OU in the console tree.
3. Right-click the Groups OU, choose New, and then select Group.
   The New Object – Group dialog box appears.
4. In the Group Name box, type **ACL_Budget_Edit**.
5. Select Domain Local in the Group Scope section and Security in the Group Type section, and then click OK.
6. Click the View menu and ensure that Advanced Features is selected.
7. Right-click the ACL_Budget_Edit group and choose Properties.
8. Click the Object tab.
9. Select the Protect Object From Accidental Deletion check box and click OK.
10. Open the group's Properties again.
11. In the Description box, type **BUDGET (EDIT)**.

12. In the *Notes* field, type the following paths to represent the folders that have permissions assigned to this group:

    \\server23\data$\finance\budget
    \\server32\data$\finance\revenue projections

13. Click OK.

▶ **Exercise 2   Delegate Management of Group Membership**

In this exercise, you will give Mike Danseglio the ability to manage the membership of the ACL_Budget_Edit group.

1. Open the Properties dialog box of the ACL_Budget_Edit group.
2. Click the Managed By tab.
3. Click the Change button.
4. Type the user name for Mike Danseglio and click OK.
5. Select the Manager Can Update Membership List check box. Click OK.

▶ **Exercise 3   Validate the Delegation of Membership Management**

In this exercise, you will test the delegation you performed in Exercise 2, "Delegate Management of Group Membership," by modifying the membership of the group as Mike Danseglio.

1. Open a command prompt.
2. Type the following command: **runas /user:Username cmd.exe**, where *Username* is the user name for Mike Danseglio.
3. When prompted, enter the password for Mike Danseglio.

   A new command prompt window appears, running as Mike Danseglio.
4. Type the following command and press Enter:

   ```
   dsmod group "CN=ACL_Budget_Edit,OU=Groups,DC=contoso,DC=com" -addmbr
   "CN=Finance,OU=Groups,DC=contoso,DC=com"
   ```

5. Close the command prompt.
6. In the Active Directory Users And Computers snap-in, examine the membership of the ACL_Budget_Edit group and confirm that the Finance group was added successfully.

Lesson Summary

- Use the *Description* and *Notes* fields in a group's Properties dialog box to document the purpose of the group.
- The Managed By tab enables you to specify a user or group that is responsible for a group. You can also select the Manager Can Update Membership List check box to delegate membership management to the user or group indicated on the Managed By tab.
- To delegate the management of group membership, you grant the Allow Write Members permission.

■ Use the Protect Object From Accidental Deletion check box to prevent the potential security and management problems created when a group is accidentally deleted.

■ Windows Server 2008 and Active Directory contain default groups with significant permissions and user rights. You should not add users to the default domain groups that do not already have members (Account Operators, Backup Operators, Print Operators, and Server Operators), and you should seriously restrict membership in other service administration groups (Enterprise Admins, Domain Admins, Schema Admins, and Administrators).

■ Special identities such as Authenticated Users, Everyone, Interactive, and Network can be used to assign rights and permissions. Their membership is determined by the operating system and cannot be viewed or modified.

Lesson Review

You can use the following questions to test your knowledge of the information in Lesson 3, "Administering Groups in an Enterprise." The questions are also available on the companion CD if you prefer to review them in electronic form.

NOTE   Answers

Answers to these questions and explanations of why each answer choice is right or wrong are located in the "Answers" section at the end of the book.

1. Your company is conducting a meeting for a special project. The data is particularly confidential. The team is meeting in a conference room, and you have configured a folder on the conference room computer that grants permission to the team members. You want to ensure that team members access the data only while logged on to the computer in the conference room, not from other computers in the enterprise. What must you do?

   A. Assign the Allow Read permission to the Interactive group.

   B. Assign the Allow Read permission to the team group.

   C. Assign the Deny Traverse Folders permission to the team group.

   D. Assign the Deny Full Control permission to the Network group.

2. You want to allow a user named Mike Danseglio to add and remove users from a group called Special Project. Where can you configure this permission?

   A. The Members tab of the group

   B. The Security tab of Mike Danseglio's user object

   C. The Member Of tab of Mike Danseglio's user object

   D. The Managed By tab of the group

3. Which of the following groups can shut down a domain controller? (Choose all that apply.)

   A. Account Operators

   B. Print Operators

   C. Backup Operators

   D. Server Operators

   E. Interactive

Chapter Review

To further practice and reinforce the skills you learned in this chapter, you can perform the following tasks:

- Review the chapter summary.
- Review the list of key terms introduced in this chapter.
- Complete the case scenario. This scenario sets up a real-world situation involving the topics of this chapter and asks you to create a solution.
- Complete the suggested practices.
- Take a practice test.

Chapter Summary

- Group scopes (global, universal, domain local, and universal) define group characteristics related to membership, replication, and availability of the group.
- In an enterprise, role-based management suggests that groups should be viewed as either defining a role or defining a business rule. Role groups are generally implemented as global groups, and rules are defined using domain local groups.
- A group's *member* attribute is a multivalued attribute containing the DNs of the group's members. Each member's *memberOf* attribute is automatically updated to reflect changes in membership. When you add a user to a group, you are always changing the group's *member* attribute. The *memberOf* attribute, which is read-only, is called a backlink.
- You can delegate the management of group membership by assigning the Allow Write Members permission, which grants write permission to the *member* attribute.
- Directory Services tools such as *Dsquery*, *Dsget*, and *Dsmod* can be used to list, create, and modify groups and their membership.
- *CSVDE* and *LDIFDE* can import and export groups. Additionally, *LDIFDE* can modify the membership of existing groups.
- The *Dsadd*, *Dsmove*, and *Dsrm* commands can add, move, and delete groups, respectively.

Key Terms

Use these key terms to understand better the concepts covered in this chapter.

- **backlink**   A type of read-only attribute that is automatically updated when its corresponding forward link attribute changes. For example, a group's *member* attribute is a forward link attribute, paired with the *memberOf* attribute. When a group's *member* attribute is changed to reflect an update in the group's membership, the *memberOf* attribute of affected objects is automatically updated by Active Directory.

- **shadow group**   A group that contains all users in an OU, or all users that meet a specific criteriona. A shadow group is a concept, not a type of group; you must create a shadow group manually, add all users to it, and update its membership according to changes in your environment.
- **special identities**   Users and groups that are dynamically maintained by the operating system, such as Authenticated Users, Everyone, and Anonymous Logon. You can assign rights and permissions to special identities, but you cannot view or manage their membership.

Case Scenario

In the following case scenario, you will apply what you've learned about administering groups in an enterprise. You can find answers to these questions in the "Answers" section at the end of this book.

Case Scenario: Implementing a Group Strategy

You are an administrator at Trey Research. A new product development initiative called Sliced Bread is underway, and there is confidential information about the project in shared folders on three servers in three different sites. Users in Research, Marketing, and Finance need access to the project data. Additionally, the CEO and her assistant need access. Of these, only Marketing and Research require Write access. Several interns are currently working in the Marketing department, and you want to prevent them from gaining access. Finally, a team of auditors from Woodgrove Bank, an investor in Trey Research, need Read access as well. You have a trust relationship configured so that the Trey Research domain trusts the Woodgrove Bank domain.

1. What types and scopes of groups do you create to represent the user roles in Trey Research? What type and scope of group do you ask administrators at Woodgrove Bank to create to represent the auditors' role?
2. What types and scopes of groups do you create to manage Read and Write access to the Sliced Bread folders?
3. Describe the nesting of users and groups you implement to achieve the security required by this project.

Suggested Practices

To help you successfully master the exam objectives presented in this chapter, complete the following tasks.

Automating Group Membership and Shadow Groups

In this practice, you will create a shadow group to reflect the user accounts in the People OU. You will apply the *Dsquery* and *Dsmod* commands to keep the membership up to date.

To perform this practice, you must have the following objects in the *contoso.com* domain:

- A first-level OU named Groups
- An OU named People
- Several sample user accounts in the People OU
- **Practice 1**   In the Groups OU, create a global security group named People. Then click the People OU in the tree pane of the Active Directory Users And Computers snap-in. Click any user in the details pane and press Ctrl + A to select all. Right-click any selected user and choose Add To Group. Add the users to the People group. Examine the Members tab of the People group to confirm that all users were added successfully.
- **Practice 2**   Open a command prompt. Delete the People group you created in Practice 1. Type the following two commands to create the People shadow group:

```
dsadd group "CN=People,OU=Groups,DC=contoso,DC=com" -secgrp yes -scope g
dsquery user "OU=People,DC=contoso,DC=com" |
    dsmod group "CN=People,OU=Groups,DC=contoso,DC=com" -addmbr
```

- **Practice 3**   In a command prompt, type the following two commands to remove all members of the group and repopulate it with the current users in the People OU:

```
dsget group "CN=People,OU=Groups,DC=contoso,DC=com" -members |
    dsmod group "CN=People,OU=Groups,DC=contoso,DC=com" -rmmbr
dsquery user "OU=People,DC=contoso,DC=com" |
    dsmod group "CN=People,OU=Groups,DC=contoso,DC=com" -addmbr
```

Take a Practice Test

The practice tests on this book's companion CD offer many options. For example, you can test yourself on just one exam objective, or you can test yourself on all the 70-640 certification exam content. You can set up the test so that it closely simulates the experience of taking a certification exam, or you can set it up in study mode so that you can look at the correct answers and explanations after you answer each question.

MORE INFO   **Practice tests**

For details about all the practice test options available, see the "How to Use the Practice Tests" section in this book's introduction.

Chapter 5

Computers

Computers in a domain are security principals, like users are. They have an account with a logon name and password that Microsoft Windows changes automatically every 30 days or so. They authenticate with the domain. They can belong to groups, have access to resources, and be configured by Group Policy. And, like users, computers sometimes lose track of their passwords, requiring a reset, or have accounts that need to be disabled or enabled.

Managing computers—both the objects in Active Directory Domain Services (AD DS) and the physical devices—is part of the day-to-day work of most IT professionals. New systems are added to the organization, computers are taken offline for repairs, computers are exchanged between users or roles, and older equipment is retired or upgraded, leading to the acquisition of replacement systems. Each of these activities requires managing the identity of the computer represented by its object, or account, and Active Directory.

Unfortunately, most enterprises do not invest the same kind of care and process in the creation and management of computer accounts as they do for user accounts, even though both are security principals. In this chapter, you will learn how to create computer objects, which include attributes required for the object to be an account. You will learn how to support computer accounts through their life cycle, including configuration, troubleshooting, repairing, and deprovisioning computer objects. You will also deepen your understanding of the process through which a computer joins a domain, so that you can identify and avoid potential points of failure.

Exam objectives in this chapter:
- Creating and Maintaining Active Directory Objects
    - Automate creation of Active Directory accounts.
    - Maintain Active Directory accounts.

Lessons in this chapter:
- Lesson 1: Creating Computers and Joining the Domain 189
- Lesson 2: Automating the Creation of Computer Objects 203
- Lesson 3: Supporting Computer Objects and Accounts. 213

Before You Begin

This chapter applies Microsoft Windows PowerShell, Microsoft VBScript, *CSVDE*, and *LDIFDE* to the task of automating computer account creation. Please read Lesson 1, "Automating the Creation of User Accounts," and Lesson 2, "Creating Users with Windows PowerShell and VBScript," of Chapter 3, "Users," prior to reading this chapter.

Real World

Dan Holme

"Computers are people, too," or at least in Active Directory they are. In fact, computers have the *objectClass* attribute of *user*. They have accounts, just as users do. They can even forget their passwords, like users do. Because computers are security principals and can be used to scope Group Policy (as you'll learn in the next chapter), it is important to treat computer accounts with the same care as you'd treat user accounts.

I'm sure you've run into a situation when you had to remove a computer from a domain and then had it rejoin the domain. As you will see in Lesson 3, "Supporting Computer Objects and Accounts," that's a bad practice, equivalent to deleting and re-creating a user's account just because the user forgot his or her password. That's just one example of scenarios I see regularly, in which administrators are a bit less careful with computer accounts than they probably should be.

In this lesson, you'll learn the best practices for supporting computer accounts with the same level of respect as other security principals (including users and groups) in the domain. You'll also learn how to use command-line tools, VBScript, and Windows PowerShell scripts to automate the creation and management of computer objects. You'll see a lot of similarities to the procedures discussed in Chapter 3. Why? Because computers are people, too!

Lesson 1: Creating Computers and Joining the Domain

The default configuration of Windows Server 2008—as well as of Microsoft Windows Server 2003, Windows Vista, Windows XP, and Windows 2000—is that the computer belongs to a workgroup. Before you can log on to a computer with a domain account, that computer must belong to the domain. To join the domain, the computer must have an account in the domain which, like a user account, includes a logon name (*sAMAccountName*), a password, and a security identifier (SID) that uniquely represent the computer as a security principal in the domain. Those credentials enable the computer to authenticate against the domain and to create a secure relationship that then enables users to log on to the system with domain accounts. In this lesson, you will learn the steps to prepare the domain for a new computer account, and you will explore the process through which a computer joins the domain.

> **After this lesson, you will be able to:**
> - Design an OU structure for computers.
> - Create computer objects in the domain.
> - Delegate the creation of computer objects.
> - Join computers to the domain.
> - Redirect the default computer container.
> - Prevent nonadministrative users from creating computers and joining the domain.
>
> **Estimated lesson time: 45 minutes**

Understanding Workgroups, Domains, and Trusts

In a workgroup, each system maintains an identity store of user and group accounts against which users can be authenticated and access can begin. The local identity store on each computer is called the Security Accounts Manager (SAM) database. If a user logs on to a workgroup computer, the system authenticates the user against its local SAM database. If a user connects to another system, to access a file for example, the user is re-authenticated against the identity store of the remote system. From a security perspective, a workgroup computer is, for all intents and purposes, a standalone system.

When a computer joins a domain, it delegates the task of authenticating users to the domain. Although the computer continues to maintain its SAM database to support local user and group accounts, user accounts will typically be created in the central domain directory. When a user logs on to the computer with a domain account, the user is now authenticated by a domain controller rather than by the SAM. Said another way, the computer now *trusts* another authority to validate a user's identity. Trust relationships are generally discussed in the context of two domains, as you will learn in Chapter 12, "Domains and Forests," but there is also a trust between each domain member computer and its domain that is established when the computer joins the domain.

Identifying Requirements for Joining a Computer to the Domain

Three things are required for you to join a computer to an Active Directory domain:

- A computer object must be created in the directory service.
- You must have appropriate permissions to the computer object. The permissions allow you to join a computer with the same name as the object to the domain.
- You must be a member of the local Administrators group on the computer to change its domain or workgroup membership.

The next sections examine each of these requirements.

Computers Container

Before you create a computer object in the directory service—the first of the three requirements for joining a computer to the domain—you must have a place to put it. When you create a domain, the Computers container is created by default (CN=Computers, . . .). This container is not an organizational unit (OU); it is an object of class *container*. There are subtle but important differences between a container and an OU. You cannot create an OU within a container, so you cannot subdivide the Computers OU, and you cannot link a Group Policy object to a container. Therefore, it is highly recommended to create custom OUs to host computer objects instead of using the Computers container.

Creating OUs for Computers

Most organizations create at least two OUs for computer objects: one to host computer accounts for clients—desktops, laptops, and other user systems—and another for servers. These two OUs are in addition to the Domain Controllers OU created by default during the installation of Active Directory. In each of these OUs, computer objects are created. There is no technical difference between a computer object in a clients OU and a computer object in a servers or domain controllers OU; computer objects are computer objects. But separate OUs are typically created to provide unique scopes of management so that you can delegate management of client objects to one team and server objects to another.

Your administrative model might necessitate further dividing your client and server OUs. Many organizations create sub-OUs beneath a server OU to collect and manage specific types of servers, for example, an OU for file and print servers and an OU for database servers. By doing so, the team of administrators for each type of server can be delegated permissions to manage computer objects in the appropriate OU. Similarly, geographically distributed organizations with local desktop support teams often divide a parent OU for clients into sub-OUs for each site. This approach enables each site's support team to create computer objects in the site for client computers and join computers to the domain by using those computer objects. This is an example only; what is most important is that your OU structure reflects your administrative model so that your OUs provide single points of management for the delegation of administration.

Figure 5-1 illustrates a typical OU design for an organization whose server administration teams are focused on specific types of servers and whose desktop support teams are focused on clients in specific geographical areas.

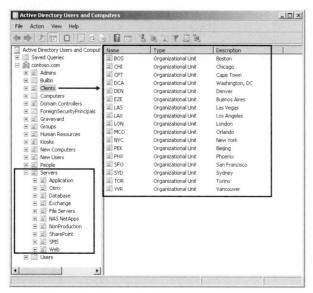

Figure 5-1   A common OU design illustrating site-based administration of clients and role-based administration of servers

Additionally, separate OUs enable you to create different baseline configurations, using different Group Policy objects (GPOs) linked to the client and the server OUs. Group Policy, discussed in detail in Chapter 6, "Group Policy Infrastructure," enables you to specify configuration for collections of computers by linking GPOs that contain configuration instructions to OUs. It is common for organizations to separate clients into desktop and laptop OUs. GPOs specifying desktop or laptop configuration can then be linked to appropriate OUs.

If your organization has decentralized, site-based administration and wants to manage unique configurations for desktops and laptops, you face a design dilemma. Should you divide your clients OU based on administration and then subdivide desktops and laptops, or should you divide your clients OU into desktop and laptop OUs and then subdivide based on administration? The options are illustrated in Figure 5-2. Because the primary design driver for Active Directory OUs is the efficient delegation of administration through the inheritance of access control lists (ACLs) on OUs, the design on the left would be recommended.

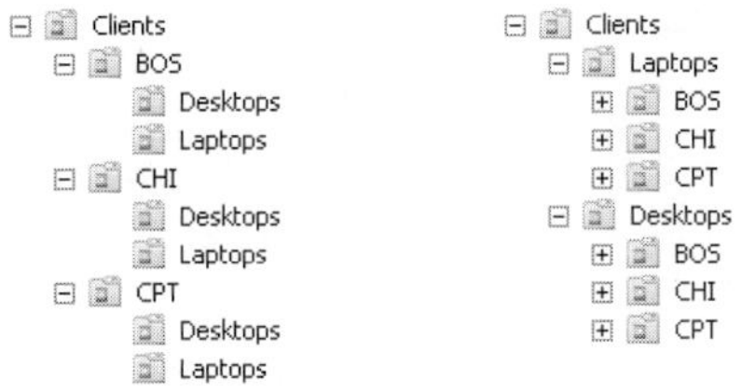

```
⊟ ▣ Clients              ⊟ ▣ Clients
   ⊟ ▣ BOS                  ⊟ ▣ Laptops
      ▣ Desktops              ⊞ ▣ BOS
      ▣ Laptops               ⊞ ▣ CHI
   ⊟ ▣ CHI                    ⊞ ▣ CPT
      ▣ Desktops           ⊟ ▣ Desktops
      ▣ Laptops               ⊞ ▣ BOS
   ⊟ ▣ CPT                    ⊞ ▣ CHI
      ▣ Desktops              ⊞ ▣ CPT
      ▣ Laptops
```

Figure 5-2   OU design options

Delegating Permission to Create Computers

By default, the Enterprise Admins, Domain Admins, Administrators, and Account Operators groups have permission to create computer objects in any new OU. However, as discussed in Chapter 4, "Groups," it is recommended that you tightly restrict membership in the first three groups and that you do not add administrators to the Account Operators group.

Instead, delegate the permission to create computer objects to appropriate administrators or support personnel. The permission required to create a computer object is Create Computer Objects. This permission, assigned to a group for an OU, allows members of the group to create computer objects in that OU. For example, you might allow your desktop support team to create computer objects in the clients OU and allow your file server administrators to create computer objects in the file servers OU.

Practice It   Exercise 3, "Delegate the Ability to Create Computer Objects," at the end of this lesson, steps you through the procedure required to delegate the creation of computer objects.

Prestaging a Computer Account

After you have been given permission to create computer objects, you can do so by right-clicking the OU and choosing Computer from the New menu. The New Object – Computer dialog box, shown in Figure 5-3, appears.

Enter the computer name, following the naming convention of your enterprise, and select the user or group that will be allowed to join the computer to the domain with this account. The two computer names—Computer Name and Computer Name (Pre-Windows 2000)—should be the same; there is rarely, if ever, a justification for configuring them separately.

NOTE   The New Object – Computer Wizard over-delegates

The permissions that are applied to the user or group you select in the New Object – Computer Wizard are more than are necessary simply to join a computer to the domain. The selected user or group is also given the ability to modify the computer object in other ways. For guidance regarding a least-privilege approach to delegating permission to join a computer to the domain, see *Windows Administration Resource Kit: Productivity Solutions for IT Professionals* by Dan Holme (Microsoft Press, 2008).

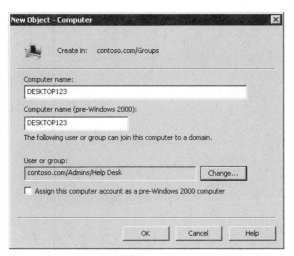

Figure 5-3   The New Object – Computer dialog box

The process you have completed to create a computer account before joining the computer to the domain is called *prestaging* the account. The advantage of performing this procedure is that the account is in the correct OU and is, therefore, delegated according to the security policy defined by the ACL of the OU and is within the scope of GPOs linked to the OU before the computer joins the domain. Prestaging is highly recommended for reasons discussed in the "Importance of Prestaging Computer Objects" section.

Joining a Computer to the Domain

By prestaging the computer object, you fulfill the first two requirements for joining a computer to a domain: the computer object exists, and you have specified who has permissions to join a computer with the same name to the domain. Now, a local administrator of the computer can change the computer's domain membership and enter the specified domain credentials to complete the process successfully. To join a computer to the domain, follow these steps:

1. Log on to the computer with credentials that belong to the local Administrators group on the computer.

    Only local administrators can alter the domain or workgroup membership of a computer.

2. Open the System properties, using one of the following methods:
    - ❑ Windows XP, Windows Server 2003: Right-click My Computer and choose Properties.
    - ❑ Windows Vista, Windows Server 2008: Right-click Computer; choose Properties; and then, in the Computer Name, Domain, And Workgroup Settings section, click Change Settings. Click if prompted.

3. Click the Computer Name tab.

4. Click Change.

5. Under Member Of, select Domain.

6. Type the name of the domain you want to join.

NOTE   Use the full DNS name of the domain

Use the full DNS name of the Active Directory domain. Not only is this more accurate and more likely to succeed, but if it does not succeed, it indicates a possible problem with DNS name resolution that should be rectified before joining the computer to the domain.

---

7. Click OK.

8. Windows prompts for the credentials of your user account in the domain.

   The domain checks to see whether a computer object already exists with the name of the computer. One of the following three things happens:

   - If the object exists and a computer with that name has already joined the domain, an error message is returned, and you cannot join the computer to the domain.

   - If the object exists and it is prestaged—a computer with the same name has not joined the domain—the domain confirms that the domain credentials you entered have permission to join the domain using that account. These permissions are discussed in the "Prestaging a Computer Account" section.

   - If the computer account is not prestaged, Windows checks to see whether you have permissions to create a new computer object in the default computer container. If you do have permissions to create a new computer object in the default computer container, the object is created with the name of the computer. This method of joining a domain is supported for backward compatibility, but is not recommended. It is recommended to prestage the account as indicated earlier and as detailed in the next section, "The Importance of Prestaging Computer Objects."

   The computer then joins the domain by assuming the identity of its Active Directory object. It configures its SID to match the domain computer account's SID and sets an initial password with the domain. The computer then performs other tasks related to joining the domain. It adds the Domain Admins group to the local Administrators group and the Domain Users group to the local Users group.

9. You are prompted to restart the computer. Click OK to close this message box.

10. Click Close (in Windows Vista) or OK (in Windows XP) to close the System Properties dialog box.

11. You are prompted, again, to restart the computer, after which the system is fully a member of the domain, and you can log on using domain credentials.

The *Netdom.exe* command enables you to join a computer to the domain from the command line. The basic syntax of the command is:

```
netdom join MachineName /Domain:DomainName [/OU:"DN of OU"]
    [/UserO:LocalUsername] [/PasswordO:{LocalPassword|*} ]
    [/UserD:DomainUsername] [/PasswordD:{DomainPassword|*} ]
    [/SecurePasswordPrompt] [/REBoot[:TimeInSeconds]]
```

It can be useful to join a computer to a domain from the command line, first, because it can be included in a script that performs other actions. Second, *Netdom.exe* can be used to join a computer *remotely* to the domain. Third, *Netdom.exe* enables you to specify the OU for the computer object. The command's parameters are, for the most part, self-explanatory. *UserO* and *PasswordO* are credentials that are members of the workgroup computer's local Administrators group. Specifying * for the password causes *Netdom.exe* to prompt for the password on the command line. *UserD* and *PasswordD* are domain credentials with permission to create a computer object, if the account is not prestaged, or to join a computer to a prestaged account. The *REBoot* parameter causes the system to reboot after joining the domain. The default timeout is 30 seconds. The *SecurePasswordPrompt* parameter displays a pop-up for credentials when * is specified for either *PasswordO* or *PasswordD*.

Importance of Prestaging Computer Objects

The best practice is to prestage a computer account prior to joining the computer to the domain. Unfortunately, Windows enables you to join a computer to a domain without following best practices. You can log on to a workgroup computer as a local administrator and change the computer's membership to the domain. Then, on demand, Windows creates a computer object in the default computer container, gives you permission to join a computer to that object, and joins the system to the domain.

There are three problems with this behavior of Windows. First, the computer account created automatically by Windows is placed in the default computer container, which is not where the computer object belongs in most enterprises. Second, you must move the computer from the default computer container into the correct OU, which is an extra step that is often forgotten. Third, any user can join a computer to the domain—no domain-level administrative permissions are required. Because a computer object is a security principal, and because the creator of a computer object owns the object and can change its attributes, this exposes a potential security vulnerability. The next sections detail these disadvantages.

Configuring the Default Computer Container

When you join a computer to the domain and the computer object does not already exist in Active Directory, Windows automatically creates a computer account in the default computer container, which is called Computers (CN=Computers,DC=*domain*, by default). The problem with this relates to the discussion of OU design earlier in the lesson. If you have implemented the best practices described there, you have delegated permissions to administer computer objects in specific OUs for clients and servers. Additionally, you might have linked GPOs to those OUs to manage the configuration of these computer objects. If a new computer object is created outside of those OUs, in the default computer container, the permissions and configuration it inherits from its parent container will be different than what it should have received. You will then need to remember to move the computer from the default container to the correct OU after joining the domain.

Two steps are recommended to reduce the likelihood of this problem. First, always try to prestage computer accounts. If an account is prestaged for a computer in the correct OU, then when the computer joins the domain, it will use the existing account and will be subject to the correct delegation and configuration.

Second, to reduce the impact of systems being joined to the domain without a prestaged account, change the default computer container so that it is not the Computers container itself but, instead, is an OU that is subject to appropriate delegation and configuration. For example, if you have an OU called Clients, you can instruct Windows to use that OU as the default computer container, so that if computers are joined to the domain without prestaged accounts, the objects are created in the Clients OU.

The *Redircmp.exe* command, available on domain controllers, redirects the default computer container with the following syntax:

```
redircmp "DN of OU for new computer objects"
```

Now, if a computer joins the domain without a prestaged computer account, Windows creates the computer object in the specified organizational unit.

Redirecting the Default User Container

The same concepts apply to the creation of user accounts. By default, if a user account is created using an earlier practice that does not specify the OU for the account, the object is created in the default user container (CN=Users,DC=*domain*, by default). The *Redirusr.exe* command, available on domain controllers, can redirect the default container to an actual OU that is delegated and configured appropriately. *Redirusr*, like *Redircmp*, takes a single parameter: the distinguished name of the OU that will become the default user container.

Exam Tip   The *Redircmp.exe* command redirects the default computer container to a specified OU. *Redirusr.exe* does the same for the default user container. You might see these two commands used as *distracters*—presented as potential (but incorrect) answers to questions that have nothing to do with the default computer or user containers. As you look at any exam question, evaluate the possible answers to determine whether the answers are proposing to use real commands but in the wrong application of those commands.

Restricting the Ability of Users to Create Computers

When a computer account is prestaged, the permissions on the account determine who is allowed to join that computer to the domain. When an account is not prestaged, Windows will, by default, allow any authenticated user to create a computer object in the default computer container. In fact, Windows will allow any authenticated user to create up to ten computer objects in the default computer container. The creator of a computer object, by default, has permission to join that computer to the domain. It is through this mechanism that any authenticated user can join ten computers to the domain without any explicit permissions to do so.

The ten-computer quota is configured by the *ms-DS-MachineAccountQuota* attribute of the domain. It allows any authenticated user to join a computer to the domain, no questions asked. This is problematic from a security perspective because computers are security principals, and the creator of a security principal has permission to manage that computer's properties. In a way, the quota is like allowing any domain user to create ten user accounts, without any controls.

It is highly recommended that you close this loophole so that nonadministrative users cannot join computers to the domain. To change the *ms-DS-MachineAccountQuota* attribute, follow these steps:

1. Open ADSI Edit from the Administrative Tools folder.
2. Right-click ADSI Edit and choose Connect To.
3. In the Connection Point section, choose Select A Well Known Naming Context and, from the drop-down list, choose Default Naming Context.
4. Click OK.
5. Expand Default Naming Context.
6. Right-click the dc=contoso,dc=com domain folder, for example, and choose Properties.
7. Select ms-DS-MachineAccountQuota and click Edit.
8. Type **0**.
9. Click OK.

The Authenticated Users group also is assigned the user right to add workstations to the domain, but you do not have to modify this right if you have changed the default value of the *ms-DS-MachineAccountQuota* attribute.

After you have changed the *ms-DS-MachineAccountQuota* attribute to zero, you can be assured that the only users who can join computers to the domain are those who have been specifically delegated permission to join prestaged computer objects or to create new computer objects.

> **Quick Check**
> - What two things determine whether you can join a computer account to the domain?
>
> **Quick Check Answer**
> - To join a computer to a prestaged account, you must be given permission on the account to join it to the domain. If the account is not prestaged, the *ms-DS-MachineAccountQuota* attribute will determine the number of computers you can join to the domain in the default computer container without explicit permission.

After you've eliminated this loophole, you must make sure you have given appropriate administrators explicit permission to create computer objects in the correct OUs, as described in the "Delegating Permission to Create Computers" section; otherwise, the error message shown in Figure 5-4 will appear.

Figure 5-4   An error message appearing when a user has exceeded the default computer account quota specified by the *ms-DS-MachineAccountQuota* attribute

PRACTICE Creating Computers and Joining the Domain

In this practice, you will implement best practices for creating computers and joining systems to the domain. You will begin by creating an OU structure to host new computer objects. You will then create prestaged computer objects and delegate permission to join the computers to the domain. You will delegate permission to create computer objects, using the *Dsacls.exe* command, and you will redirect the default computer container.

Before performing the exercises, you must create the following objects in the *contoso.com* domain:

- A first-level OU named Admins with a sub-OU named Groups.
- A global security group in the Admins\Groups OU named Server Admins.
- A global security group in the Admins\Groups OU named Help Desk.
- A first-level OU named People.
- A user in the People OU named Jeff Ford. The user is a member of Domain Users and Server Admins.
- A user in the People OU named Linda Mitchell. The user is a member of Domain Users and Help Desk.

In addition, make sure that the Domain Users group is a member of the Print Operators group, which can be found in the Builtin container. This will enable all sample users in the practice domain to log on to the SERVER01 domain controller. This is important for the practices in this training kit, but you should not allow users to log on to domain controllers in your production environment, so do not make Domain Users members of the Print Operators group in your production environment.

▶ **Exercise 1 Create OUs for Client and Server Computer Objects**

Before you can create computer accounts, you must create OUs for the objects. In this exercise, you will create OUs for server and computer objects.

1. Log on to SERVER01 as Administrator.
2. Open the Active Directory Users And Computers snap-in and expand the domain.
3. Right-click the *contoso.com* domain, choose New, and then select Organizational Unit.
4. Type **Clients** and click OK.
5. Right-click the *contoso.com* domain, choose New, and then select Organizational Unit.
6. Type **Servers** and click OK.

▶ **Exercise 2 Create Computer Objects**

After an OU has been created for computer objects, you can prestage accounts for computers that will join the domain. In this exercise, you will prestage an account for a client and an account for a server and delegate the ability to join the computer to the domain.

1. Right-click the Clients OU, choose New, and then select Computer.
2. The New Object – Computer dialog box appears, as shown in Figure 5-3.
3. Type the computer's name in the Computer Name box: **DESKTOP101**.
4. Click the Change button next to the User Or Group box.
5. In the Select User Or Group dialog box that appears, type the name of the user or group that will be allowed to join the computer to the domain: **Help Desk**. Click OK.

6. Click OK to close the New Object – Computer dialog box.

7. Right-click the Servers OU, choose New, and then select Computer.

8. The New Object – Computer dialog box appears, as shown in Figure 5-3.

9. Type the computer's name in the Computer Name box: **SERVER02**.

10. Click the Change button next to the User Or Group box.

11. In the Select User Or Group dialog box that appears, enter the name of the user or group that will be allowed to join the computer to the domain: **Server Admins**. Click OK.

12. Click OK to close the New Object – Computer dialog box.

▶ **Exercise 3   Delegate the Ability to Create Computer Objects**

You must have permission to create computer objects to create accounts as you did in Exercise 2, "Create Computer Objects." The Administrator account has such permissions, but you might want to delegate the ability to create computer accounts to other groups. In this exercise, you will delegate least-privilege permissions to create computer objects.

1. On SERVER01, open the Active Directory Users And Computers snap-in.

2. Click the View menu and ensure that Advanced Features is selected.

3. Right-click Clients and choose Properties.

4. Click the Security tab.

5. Click Advanced.

6. Click Add.

7. Type **Help Desk** and click OK.

8. Click the Object tab.

9. In the Apply To drop-down list, choose This Object And All Descendant Objects.

10. In the Permissions list, select the check box for Allow next to the Create Computer Objects.

11. Click OK three times to close all dialog boxes.

12. You can test your delegation by launching a command prompt as Linda Mitchell and performing Exercise 1, "Create a Computer with *Dsadd*," in Lesson 2, "Automating the Creation of Computer Objects."

▶ **Exercise 4   Redirect the Default Computer Container**

It is recommended to redirect the default computer container so that any new computer objects generated by joining a computer to the domain without a prestaged account will be created in a managed OU rather than in the Computers container. In this exercise, you will use *Redircmp.exe* to redirect the default computer container.

1. On SERVER01, open a command prompt.

2. Type the following command and press Enter:

```
redircmp "OU=Clients,DC=contoso,DC=com"
```

▶ **Optional Exercise 5   Join a Computer to the Domain**

In this exercise, you will join a computer to the domain. This requires a second system, which would be either a server named SERVER02 running Windows Server 2008 or a client named DESKTOP101 running Windows Vista. If the computer has another name, you must either rename it or create a computer object for it in the correct OU, using the steps in Exercise 2 as a reference.

1. Log on to the workgroup computer with credentials that belong to the local Administrators group on the computer.

2. Open the System properties, using one of the following methods:
   ❑ Open System from Control Panel.
   ❑ Right-click Computer in the Start menu.
   ❑ Press the Windows key and the Pause key.

3. In the Computer Name, Domain, And Workgroup Settings section, click Change Settings. Click Continue if prompted.

4. Click the Computer Name tab.

5. Click Change.

6. Under Member Of, select Domain.

7. Type the name of the domain you want to join: **contoso.com**.

8. Click OK.

   The computer attempts to contact the domain. Windows prompts for the credentials of your user account in the domain.

9. Enter domain credentials and click OK.
   ❑ If you are joining SERVER02 to the domain, enter the credentials of Jeff Ford, who belongs to the Server Admins group.
   ❑ If you are joining DESKTOP101 to the domain, enter the credentials of Linda Mitchell, who belongs to the Help Desk group.

10. You are prompted to restart the computer. Click OK to close this message box.

11. Click Close to close the System Properties dialog box.

12. You are prompted, again, to restart the computer.

Lesson Summary

■ The Computers container does not support linking Group Policy objects or creating child OUs. Create an OU structure to reflect the administrative model of your organization.

■ Always prestage computer accounts, which means that you create a computer object in Active Directory prior to joining the system to the domain.

- To join the domain successfully, you must be a local Administrator of the computer, a computer account must be created, and you must provide domain credentials that have permission on the computer object to join the domain.
- You use *Redircmp.exe* to redirect the default computer container to an OU that has been delegated and configured to meet your business requirements.
- The *ms-DS-MachineAccountQuota* allows all authenticated users to join up to ten systems to the domain. Windows will create computer objects for the systems in the default computer container. Reduce this quota to zero to prevent nonadministrative users from creating security principals.

Lesson Review

You can use the following questions to test your knowledge of the information in Lesson 1, "Creating Computers and Joining the Domain." The questions are also available on the companion CD if you prefer to review them in electronic form.

NOTE   Answers

Answers to these questions and explanations of why each answer choice is right or wrong are located in the "Answers" section at the end of the book.

---

1. You want to require all new computer accounts created when computers join the domain to be placed in the Clients OU. Which command should you use?

   A. *Dsmove*

   B. Move-Item

   C. *Netdom*

   D. *Redircmp*

2. You want to prevent nonadministrative users from joining computers to the domain. What should you do?

   A. Set *ms-DS-MachineAccountQuota* to zero.

   B. Set *ms-DS-DefaultQuota* to zero.

   C. Remove the Add Workstations To Domain user right from Authenticated Users.

   D. On the domain, deny the Authenticated Users group the Create Computer Objects permission.

3. You want to join a remote computer to the domain. Which command should you use?

   A. *Dsadd.exe*

   B. *Netdom.exe*

   C. *Dctest.exe*

   D. *System.cpl*

Lesson 2: Automating the Creation of Computer Objects

The steps you learned in Lesson 1 for creating a computer account become burdensome if you must create dozens or even hundreds of computer accounts at the same time. Commands such as *CSVDE*, *LDIFDE*, and *Dsadd*, as well as VBScript and Windows PowerShell scripts, can import and automate the creation of computer objects. Scripts can also enable you to *provision* computer objects, that is, to perform business logic such as the enforcement of computer naming conventions. In this lesson, you will learn to import, automate, and provision computer objects. You will build upon the knowledge of these commands that you gained from reading Lesson 1 and Lesson 2 of Chapter 3, which are a prerequisite for this lesson.

After this lesson, you will be able to:
- Use *CSVDE* and *LDIFDE* to import computers.
- Create computers with *Dsadd*.
- Create computers with *Netdom*.
- Create computers with Windows PowerShell.
- Create computers with VBScript.

Estimated lesson time: 30 minutes

Importing Computers with *CSVDE*

You were introduced to the *Comma-Separated Values Data Exchange* (CSVDE) command in Lesson 1 of Chapter 3. *CSVDE* is a command-line tool that imports or exports Active Directory objects from or to a comma-delimited text file (also known as a comma-separated value text file, or .csv file). The basic syntax of the *CSVDE* command is:

```
csvde [-i] [-f "Filename"] [-k]
```

The *–i* parameter specifies import mode; without it, the default mode of *CSVDE* is export. The *–f* parameter identifies the file name to import from or export to. The *–k* parameter is useful during import operations because it instructs *CSVDE* to ignore errors including Object Already Exists, Constraint Violation, and Attribute Or Value Already Exists.

Comma-delimited files can be created, modified, and opened with tools as familiar as Notepad and Microsoft Office Excel. The first line of the file defines the attributes by their Lightweight Directory Access Protocol (LDAP) attribute names. Each object follows, one per line, and must contain exactly the attributes listed on the first line. A sample file is shown in Excel in Figure 5-5.

When importing computers, be sure to include the *userAccountControl* attribute and set it to 4096. This attribute ensures that the computer will be able to join the account. Also include the pre-Windows 2000 logon name of the computer, the *sAMAccountName* attribute, which is the name of the computer followed by a dollar sign ($) as shown in Figure 5-5.

	A	B	C	D	E
1	DN	objectClass	name	userAccountControl	sAMAccountName
2	CN=DESKTOP103,OU=Clients,DC=contoso,DC=con	computer	DESKTOP103	4096	DESKTOP103$
3	CN=DESKTOP104,OU=Clients,DC=contoso,DC=con	computer	DESKTOP104	4096	DESKTOP104$
4	CN=SERVER02,OU=Servers,DC=contoso,DC=com	computer	SERVER02	4096	SERVER02$

Figure 5-5   A .csv file, opened in Excel, that will create three computer accounts

---

MORE INFO   In Chapter 3 and Chapter 4, you used the *CSVDE* command to import users and groups. For more information about *CSVDE*, including details regarding its parameters and usage to export directory objects, type csvde /? or search the Windows Server 2008 Help and Support Center.

Importing Computers with *LDIFDE*

Chapter 3 also introduced you to *Ldifde.exe*, which imports data from files in the Lightweight Directory Access Protocol Data Interchange Format (LDIF) format. LDIF files are text files within which operations are specified by a block of lines separated by a blank line. Each operation begins with the *DN* attribute of the object that is the target of the operation. The next line, *changeType*, specifies the type of operation: *add*, *modify*, or *delete*.

The following listing is an LDIF file that will create two server accounts:

```
dn: CN=SERVER10,OU=Servers,DC=contoso,DC=com
changetype: add
objectClass: top
objectClass: person
objectClass: organizationalPerson
objectClass: user
objectClass: computer
cn: SERVER10
userAccountControl: 4096
sAMAccountName: SERVER10$

dn: CN= SERVER11,OU= Servers,DC=contoso,DC=com
changetype: add
objectClass: top
objectClass: person
objectClass: organizationalPerson
objectClass: user
objectClass: computer
cn: SERVER11
userAccountControl: 4096
sAMAccountName: SERVER11$
```

The basic syntax of the *LDIFDE* command is similar to that of the *CSVDE* command:

```
ldifde [-i] [-f "Filename"] [-k]
```

By default, *LDIFDE* is in export mode. The −*i* parameter specifies import mode. You must specify the −*f* mode to identify the file you are using for import or export. *LDIFDE* will stop when it encounters errors unless you specify the −*k* parameter, in which case, *LDIFDE* continues processing.

Exam Tip   Remember that the default mode of *CSVDE* and *LDIFDE* is export. You must use the −*i* parameter to import objects.

Creating Computers with *Dsadd*

The *Dsadd* command has been used in previous chapters to create objects in Active Directory. To create computer objects, simply type **dsadd computer *ComputerDN*** where ComputerDN is the distinguished name (DN) of the computer, such as CN=Desktop123,OU=Desktops,DC =contoso,DC=com.

If the computer's DN includes a space, surround the entire DN with quotation marks. The *ComputerDN* parameter can include more than one distinguished name for new computer objects, making *Dsadd Computer* a handy way to generate multiple objects at once. The parameter can be entered in one of the following ways:

- By piping a list of DNs from another command such as *Dsquery*.
- By typing each DN on the command line, separated by spaces.
- By leaving the *DN* parameter empty, at which point, you can type the DNs, one at a time, at the keyboard console of the command prompt. Press Enter after each DN. Press Ctrl+Z and Enter after the last DN.

The *Dsadd Computer* command can take the following optional parameters after the DN parameter:

- -samid *SAMName*
- -desc *Description*
- -loc *Location*

Creating Computers with *Netdom*

The *Netdom* command is also able to perform a variety of domain account and security tasks from the command line. In Lesson 1, you learned to use *Netdom* to join a computer to the domain. You can also use it to create a computer account by typing the following command:

```
netdom add ComputerName /domain:DomainName [/ou:OUDN]
[/userd:User /PasswordD:Password]
```

This command creates the computer account for *ComputerName* in the domain indicated by the *domain* parameter, using the credentials specified by *UserD* and *PasswordD*. The *ou* parameter causes the object to be created in the OU specified by the *OUDN* distinguished name following the parameter. If no *OUDN* is supplied, the computer account is created in the default computer container. The user credentials must have permissions to create computer objects.

Creating Computers with Windows PowerShell

Chapter 3 introduced you to Windows PowerShell, the new administrative and automation shell for Windows platforms. You learned how to create users in that chapter. As with user objects, you can create computer objects by following these high-level steps:

1. Connect to the container (the OU) in which you want to create a computer.
2. Use the *Create* method of the container to create the computer.
3. Populate mandatory attributes.
4. Commit your changes.

To connect to an OU in Windows PowerShell, type the following at a PowerShell prompt:

```
$objOU = [ADSI]"LDAP://DN of OU"
```

The command creates an object reference stored in the *$objOU* variable that represents the OU. You can now invoke the methods of the OU, using the *$objOU* variable. To create a computer, use the *Create* method by typing the following:

```
$objComputer = $objOU.Create("computer","CN=Computer CN")
```

Next, you must configure two attributes. The first is the computer's pre-Windows 2000 logon name, the *sAMAccountName* attribute, which is the computer's name appended with a dollar sign ($). The second is the computer's *userAccountControl* attribute, which must be set to 4096 (0x1000 in hexadecimal). The *userAccountControl* attribute is a series of flags, 1 bit each. This bit indicates that the account is for a domain member. Without it, a computer will not be able to join the domain by using the account. To set these two attributes, type the following:

```
$objComputer.Put("sAMAccountName", "ComputerName$")
$objComputer.Put("userAccountControl", 4096)
```

You can set other attributes at this time as well. For example, you can set *description* or *info*. When you have finished configuring attributes, you must commit your changes with the following code.

```
$objComputer.SetInfo()
```

Importing Computers from a Database with Windows PowerShell

On the 70-640 examination, it is highly unlikely that you will need to know how to connect to a database and create computers with Windows PowerShell. However, such knowledge can be a tremendous benefit in your production environment. Assume you receive a list of computers that are being shipped from your vendor. You want to prestage computer accounts for those systems.

You can easily do so with a Windows PowerShell script. With scripts, you can also perform business logic such as enforcing naming standards. In this section, you will learn how to do so.

Windows PowerShell can connect to and expose a data source such as a .csv file, which you can create in Excel. So, for example, you could paste the asset tags from the list of computers you received from your vendor into an Excel worksheet, as shown in Figure 5-6, and save the worksheet as a .csv file with a name such as Assets.csv.

	A	B
1	AssetTag	Type
2	A849XD	Desktop
3	D82KE8	Desktop
4	ELW938	Laptop
5	XKD8G0	Laptop
6	93JX9D	Laptop
7	SJ0GJ3	Laptop

Figure 5-6   A simple Excel data source of computer asset tags

Assume that you want to import these computers into your domain, and you want them to follow two rules. First, laptops and desktops are in separate OUs, specifically the Laptops OU and the Desktops OU, under your Clients OU. Second, your computer naming convention is to prefix the asset tag with an L or a D, for laptop or desktop, respectively. For example, the computer name for the first computer listed in Figure 5-6 would be DA849XD. These two simple rules are examples of what would be called *logic* in the context of programming.

A script that would import computers from the file would look similar to the following code. Line numbers have been added to facilitate discussing the code.

```
1. $dataSource=import-csv "Assets.csv"
2. foreach($dataRecord in $datasource) {
3.     #map variables to data source
4.     $AssetTag = $dataRecord.AssetTag
5.     $Type = $dataRecord.Type

6.     #determine name
7.     $ComputerName = $Type.substring(0,1) + $AssetTag
8.     $sAMAccountName=$ComputerName + "$"
9.     #determine OU
10.    $strOUADsPath = "LDAP://OU=" + $Type + "s" + `
11.         ",OU=Clients,DC=contoso,DC=com"

12.    #create the computer object
13.    $objOU=[ADSI]$strOUADsPath
14.    $objComputer=$objOU.Create("computer","CN="+$ComputerName)
15.    $objComputer.Put("sAMAccountName",$sAMAccountName)
16.    $objComputer.Put("userAccountControl",4096)
17.    $objComputer.SetInfo()
18. }
```

Lines 13–17 are identical to the commands shown in the previous section, except that in line 13, a variable is used rather than a hard-coded path to the OU. These lines are part of a block of code, bounded by lines 2 and 18, that are repeated for each record in the data source. The data source is defined in line 1, using the same Import-Csv cmdlet you learned about in Chapter 3. Line 2 uses a *foreach* collection (*foreach* is an alias for ForEach-Object) to loop through each record in the data source.

Lines 4 and 5 assign the two fields in each record to variables. Lines 6–11 perform the business logic. Line 7 creates the computer name, using the first character of the *Type* field (a *D* or an *L*) and appending *AssetTag*. Line 8 creates the *sAMAccountName* attribute by adding a dollar sign to the computer name. Line 10 creates the path to the OU for the object. The back tick mark at the end of line 10 is a line continuation character; it means that the code continues on line 11. Therefore, lines 10 and 11 are actually a single line of code. The logic indicated that a Desktop asset *Type* goes into the Desktops OU, so the type has an *s* added to it.

As you can see from this script, it is possible and not terribly difficult to create a data-driven provisioning system for new computer objects. Define your data sources and define your business logic, and Windows PowerShell scripts can do the rest.

Creating Computers with VBScript

VBScript uses the same Active Directory Services Interface (ADSI) as does Windows PowerShell to manipulate Active Directory objects, so the steps to create a computer are identical: connect to the container, create the object, populate its attributes, and commit the changes. The following code will create a computer in the domain:

```
Set objOU = GetObject("LDAP://DN of OU")
Set objComputer = objOU.Create("computer","CN=Computer CN")
objComputer.Put "sAMAccountName", "ComputerName$"
objComputer.Put "userAccountControl", 4096
objComputer.SetInfo
```

The code is very similar to the Windows PowerShell commands in lines 13–17 of the script presented in the previous section.

NOTE   VBScript does databases

In the previous section, you learned how to use a .csv file as a data source for a Windows PowerShell script. VBScript can also load and use data from .csv files, but it is not as elegant as the Windows PowerShell Import-Csv cmdlet.

PRACTICE **Create and Manage a Custom MMC**

In this practice, you will implement automation to import and create computers in the *contoso.com* domain. Before performing the exercises in this practice, be sure that you have the following objects in the *contoso.com* domain.

■ A first-level OU called Clients
■ A first-level OU called Servers

You must also have installed the Windows PowerShell feature. The practice in Chapter 3, Lesson 2 has instructions.

▶ **Exercise 1   Create a Computer with *Dsadd***

The *Dsadd* command enables you to add a computer from the command line. An advantage of the *Dsadd* command is that it requires only the computer's DN. It creates the *sAMAccountName* and *userAccountControl* attributes automatically. In this exercise, you will create a computer with *Dsadd.exe*.

1. Log on to SERVER01 as Administrator.
2. Open a command prompt.
3. Type the following command and press Enter:

   ```
   dsadd computer "CN=DESKTOP152,OU=Clients,DC=contoso,DC=com"
   ```

4. Using the Active Directory Users And Computers snap-in, verify that the computer was created successfully.

▶ **Exercise 2   Import Computers by Using *CSVDE***

When you want to create more than a few computers, you might find it easier to import the computer objects from a data source such as a .csv file. In this exercise, you will use *CSVDE* to import computer accounts from a .csv file.

1. Open Notepad.
2. Type the following lines into Notepad. Each bullet is one line. Do not include the bullets in the Notepad file.
   ❑ DN,objectClass,name,userAccountControl,sAMAccountName
   ❑ "CN=DESKTOP103,OU=Clients,DC=contoso,DC=com",computer, DESKTOP103,4096,DESKTOP103$
   ❑ "CN=DESKTOP104,OU=Clients,DC=contoso,DC=com",computer, DESKTOP104,4096,DESKTOP104$
   ❑ "CN=SERVER02,OU=Servers,DC=contoso,DC=com",computer, SERVER02,4096,SERVER02$
3. Save the file to your Documents folder with the name "**Computers.csv**" including the quotes so that Notepad does not add a .txt extension.

4. Open a command prompt.

5. Type the following command, and then press Enter:

```
csvde -i -f "%userprofile%\documents\computers.csv"
```

6. Open the Active Directory Users And Computers snap-in and verify that the computer objects were created successfully.

▶ **Exercise 3   Import Computers from an LDIF File**

LDIF files are not as familiar to most administrators as .csv files, but they are powerful and relatively easy to master. In this exercise, you will create an LDIF file and import it by using *Ldifde.exe*.

1. Open Notepad.

2. Enter the following into Notepad, making certain to include a blank line between the two operations (before the *dn* line for *SERVER11*):

```
dn: CN=SERVER10,OU=Servers,DC=contoso,DC=com
changetype: add
objectClass: top
objectClass: person
objectClass: organizationalPerson
objectClass: user
objectClass: computer
cn: SERVER10
userAccountControl: 4096
sAMAccountName: SERVER10$

dn: CN= SERVER11,OU=Servers,DC=contoso,DC=com
changetype: add
objectClass: top
objectClass: person
objectClass: organizationalPerson
objectClass: user
objectClass: computer
cn: SERVER11 userAccountControl: 4096
sAMAccountName: SERVER11$
```

3. Save the file to your Documents folder with the name "Computers.ldf" including the quotation marks so Notepad doesn't add a .txt extension.

4. Open a command prompt.

5. Type the following command, and then press Enter:

```
ldifde -i -f "%userprofile%\documents\computers.ldf"
```

6. Open the Active Directory Users And Computers snap-in and verify that the computers were created successfully.

▶ **Exercise 4   Create a Computer with Windows PowerShell**

Windows PowerShell enables you to use ADSI to create and manipulate Active Directory objects. In this exercise, you will create a computer with Windows PowerShell.

1. Open Windows PowerShell.

2. Type the following commands, pressing Enter after each:

```
$objOU = [ADSI]"LDAP://OU=Clients,DC=contoso,DC=com"
$objComputer = $objOU.Create("computer","CN=DESKTOP154")
$objComputer.Put("sAMAccountName", "DESKTOP154$")
$objComputer.Put("userAccountControl", 4096)
$objComputer.SetInfo()
```

3. Open the Active Directory Users And Computers snap-in and confirm that DESKTOP154 was created in the Clients OU.

▶ **Exercise 5   Create a Computer with VBScript**

You can also use VBScript to create a computer. In this exercise, you will create a computer by writing a VBScript and executing it.

1. Open Notepad.

2. Type the following code into Notepad:

```
Set objOU = GetObject("LDAP://OU=Clients,DC=contoso,DC=com ")
Set objComputer = objOU.Create("computer","CN= DESKTOP155")
objComputer.Put "sAMAccountName", " DESKTOP155$"
objComputer.Put "userAccountControl", 4096
objComputer.SetInfo
```

3. Save the file to your Documents folder with the name "**CreateComputer.vbs**" including the quotes so that Notepad doesn't add a .txt extension.

4. Open a command prompt and type the following command:

```
cscript "%userprofile%\documents\createcomputer.vbs"
```

5. Open the Active Directory Users And Computers snap-in and verify that the computer was created successfully.

Lesson Summary

- Use *CSVDE* to import computers from comma-delimited text files, which can be edited using tools as simple as Notepad or Excel.
- Use *LDIFDE* to import LDIF files containing computer add operations.
- *Dsadd* can add a computer to the domain with a single command.
- VBScript and Windows PowerShell can add computers, using ADSI.

Lesson Review

You can use the following questions to test your knowledge of the information in Lesson 2, "Automating the Creation of Computer Objects." The questions are also available on the companion CD if you prefer to review them in electronic form.

---

1. Your manager has just asked you to create an account for DESKTOP234. Which of the following enables you to do that in one step?

    A. *CSVDE*

    B. *LDIFDE*

    C. *Dsadd*

    D. Windows PowerShell

    E. VBScript

2. Your hardware vendor has just given you an Excel worksheet containing the asset tags of computers that will be delivered next week. You want to create computer objects for the computers in advance. Your naming convention specifies that computers' names are their asset tags. Which of the following tools can you use to import the computers? (Choose all that apply.)

    A. *CSVDE*

    B. *LDIFDE*

    C. *Dsadd*

    D. Windows PowerShell

    E. VBScript

Lesson 3: Supporting Computer Objects and Accounts

A computer account begins its life cycle when it is created and when the computer joins the domain. Day-to-day administrative tasks include configuring computer properties; moving the computer between OUs; managing the computer itself; renaming, resetting, disabling, enabling, and, eventually, deleting the computer object. This lesson looks closely at the computer properties and procedures involved with these tasks and will equip you to administer computers in a domain.

After this lesson, you will be able to:

- Configure the properties of a computer running Active Directory.
- Move a computer between OUs.
- Rename a computer.
- Disable and enable computer accounts.
- Reset the secure channel of a domain member computer.
- Perform administrative tasks with the Active Directory Users and Computers snap-in, command-line commands, VBScript, and Windows PowerShell.

Estimated lesson time: 45 minutes

Configuring Computer Properties

When you create a computer object, you are prompted to configure only the most fundamental attributes, including the computer name and the delegation to join the computer to the domain. Computers have several properties that are not visible when creating the computer object, and you should configure these properties as part of the process of staging the computer account.

Open a computer object's Properties dialog box to set its location and description, configure its group memberships and dial-in permissions, and link it to the user object of the user to whom the computer is assigned. The Operating System tab is read-only. The information will be blank until a computer has joined the domain, using that account, at which time, the client publishes the information to its account.

Several object classes in Active Directory support the *managedBy* attribute that is shown on the Managed By tab. This linked attribute creates a cross-reference to a user object. All other properties—the addresses and telephone numbers—are displayed directly from the user object. They are not stored as part of the computer object itself.

On the Member Of tab of a computer's Properties dialog box, you can add the computer to groups. The ability to manage computers in groups is an important and often underused feature of Active Directory. A group to which computers belong can be used to assign resource access permissions to the computer or to filter the application of a GPO.

As with users and groups, it is possible to multiselect more than one computer object and subsequently manage or modify properties of all selected computers simultaneously.

Configuring Computer Attributes with *Dsmod*

The *Dsmod* command, which you learned about in Chapter 3 and Chapter 4, is able to modify only the *description* and the *location* attributes. It uses the following syntax:

```
dsmod computer "DN of Computer" [-desc Description] [-loc Location]
```

Configuring Computer Attributes with Windows PowerShell or VBScript

In Windows PowerShell and VBScript, you can change attributes of a computer with three steps:

1. Connect to the computer using ADSI and the *aDSPath* attribute of the computer in the form "LDAP://*Distinguished Name of Computer*."
2. Use the *Put* method of the computer object to set single-valued attributes.
3. Use the *SetInfo* method to commit changes to the object.

The Windows PowerShell commands are as follows:

```
$objComputer = [ADSI]"LDAP://DN of Computer"
$objComputer.Put ("property", value)
$objComputer.SetInfo()
```

The VBScript code follows this format:

```
Set objComputer = GetObject("LDAP://DN of Computer")
objComputer.Put "property",
value objComputer.SetInfo
```

In both cases, if the value is a text value, it must be surrounded by quotes.

Moving a Computer

Many organizations have multiple OUs for computer objects. Some domains, for example, have computer OUs based on geographic sites, as shown in Figure 5-2. If you have more than one OU for computers, it is likely that someday you will need to move a computer between OUs.

You can move a computer in the Active Directory Users and Computers snap-in using either drag and drop or the *Move* command, available when you right-click a computer.

You must have appropriate permissions to move an object in Active Directory. Default permissions allow Account Operators to move computer objects between containers, including the Computers container and any OUs *except* into or out of the Domain Controllers OU. Administrators, which include Domain Admins and Enterprise Admins, can move computer objects between any containers, including the Computers container, the Domain Controllers OU, and any other OUs. There is no way to delegate the specific task of moving an object in Active Directory. Instead, your ability to move a computer is derived from your ability to delete an object in the source container and create an object in the destination container. When you move the object, you are not actually deleting and re-creating it; those are just the permissions that are evaluated to allow you to perform a move.

The *Dsmove* command allows you to move a computer object or any other object. The syntax of *Dsmove* is:

```
dsmove ObjectDN [-newname NewName] [-newparent ParentDN]
```

The *newname* parameter enables you to rename an object. The *newparent* parameter enables you to move an object. To move a computer named DESKTOP153 from the Computers container to the Clients OU, you would type the following:

```
dsmove "CN=DESKTOP153,CN=Computers,DC=contoso,DC=com" -newparent
"OU=Clients,DC=contoso,DC=com"
```

To move a computer in Windows PowerShell, you must use the *psbase.MoveTo* method. The following two lines of code will move a computer:

```
$objUser=[ADSI]"LDAP://ComputerDN "
$objUser.psbase.MoveTo("LDAP://TargetOUDN")
```

With VBScript, you connect to the source container and use the container's *MoveHere* method:

```
Set objOU = GetObject("LDAP://TargetOUDN")
objOU.MoveHere "LDAP://ComputerDN", vbNullString
```

Before you move a computer, consider the implications to delegation and configuration. The target OU might have different permissions than the originating OU, in which case, the object will inherit new permissions affecting who is able to manage the object further. The target OU might also be within the scope of different GPOs, which would change the configuration of settings on the system itself.

Managing a Computer from the Active Directory Users and Computers Snap-In

One of the beneficial but lesser used features of the Active Directory Users and Computers snap-in is the *Manage* command. Select a computer in the Active Directory Users and Computers snap-in, right-click it, and choose Manage. The Computer Management console opens, focused on the selected computer, giving you instant access to the computer's event logs, local users and groups, shared folder configuration, and other management extensions. The tool is launched with the credentials used to run the Active Directory Users and Computers snap-in, so you must be running the Active Directory Users and Computers snap-in as a member of the remote computer's Administrators group to gain the maximum functionality from the Computer Management console.

Understanding the Computer's Logon and Secure Channel

Every member computer in an Active Directory domain maintains a computer account with a user name (*sAMAccountName*) and password, just like a user account does. The computer stores its password in the form of a local security authority (LSA) secret and changes its password with the domain every 30 days or so. The Netlogon service uses the credentials to log on to the domain, which establishes the secure channel with a domain controller.

Recognizing Computer Account Problems

Computer accounts and the secure relationships between computers and their domain are robust. However, certain scenarios might arise in which a computer is no longer able to authenticate with the domain. Examples of such scenarios include:

- After reinstalling the operating system on a workstation, the workstation is unable to authenticate even though the technician used the same computer name. Because the new installation generated a new SID and because the new computer does not know the computer account password in the domain, it does not belong to the domain and cannot authenticate to the domain.

- A computer is completely restored from backup and is unable to authenticate. It is likely that the computer changed its password with the domain after the backup operation. Computers change their passwords every 30 days, and Active Directory remembers the current and previous password. If the restore operation restored the computer with a significantly outdated password, the computer will not be able to authenticate.

- A computer's LSA secret gets out of synch with the password known by the domain. You can think of this as the computer forgetting its password, although it did not forget its password; it just disagrees with the domain over what the password really is. When this happens, the computer cannot authenticate and the secure channel cannot be created.

The most common signs of computer account problems are:

- Messages at logon indicate that a domain controller cannot be contacted, that the computer account might be missing, that the password on the computer account is incorrect, or that the trust (another way of saying "the secure relationship") between the computer and the domain has been lost. An example is shown in Figure 5-7.

Figure 5-7   An error message indicating a failed secure channel

- Error messages or events in the event log indicating similar problems or suggesting that passwords, trusts, secure channels, or relationships with the domain or a domain controller have failed. One such error is NETLOGON Event ID 3210: Failed To Authenticate, which appears in the computer's event log.

- A computer account is missing in Active Directory.

Resetting a Computer Account

When the secure channel fails, you must reset it. Many administrators do so by removing the computer from the domain, putting it in a workgroup, and then rejoining the domain. This is not a good practice because it has the potential to delete the computer account altogether, which loses the computer's SID and, more important, its group memberships. When you rejoin the domain, even though the computer has the same name, the account has a new SID, and all the group memberships of the previous computer object must be re-created.

NOTE   Do not remove a computer from the domain and rejoin it

If the trust with the domain has been lost, do not remove a computer from the domain and rejoin it. Instead, reset the secure channel.

To reset the secure channel between a domain member and the domain, use the Active Directory Users and Computers snap-in, *Dsmod.exe*, *Netdom.exe*, or *Nltest.exe*. By resetting the account, the computer's SID remains the same and it maintains its group memberships.

- **The Active Directory Users and Computers snap-in**   Right-click a computer and choose Reset Account. Click Yes to confirm your choice. The computer will then need to be rejoined to the domain, requiring a reboot.

- *Dsmod*   Type the command, **dsmod computer "*Computer DN*" −reset**. You will have to rejoin the computer to the domain and reboot the computer.

- *Netdom*   Type the command **netdom reset MachineName /domain DomainName / UserO UserName /PasswordO** {*Password* | *}** where the credentials belong to the local Administrators group of the computer. This command resets the secure channel by attempting to reset the password on both the computer and the domain, so it does not require rejoining or rebooting.

■ *Nltest*   On the computer that has lost its trust, type the command **nltest /server:*Server Name* /sc_reset:*DOMAIN\DomainController***, for example, *nltest /server:SERVER02 / sc_reset:CONTOSO\SERVER01*. This command, like *Netdom.exe*, attempts to reset the secure channel by resetting the password both on the computer and in the domain, so it does not require rejoining or rebooting.

Because *Nltest.exe* and *Netdom.exe* reset the secure channel without requiring a reboot, try those commands first. Only if not successful should you use the *Reset Account* command or *Dsmod* to reset the computer account.

Quick Check

■ A user complains that when she attempts to log on, she receives an error message indicating the trust with the domain has been lost. You want to attempt to reset the secure channel without rebooting her system. Which two commands can you use?

Quick Check Answer

■ The *Netdom.exe* and *Nltest.exe* commands reset the secure channel without requiring you to rejoin the computer to the domain and, therefore, they require no reboot.

Renaming a Computer

When you rename a computer, you must be careful to do it correctly. Remember that the computer uses its name to authenticate with the domain, so if you rename only the domain object, or only the computer itself, they will be out of synch. You must rename the computer in such a way that both the computer and the domain object are changed.

You can rename a computer correctly by logging on to the computer itself, either locally or with a remote desktop session. Open the System properties from Control Panel and, in the Computer Name, Domain, And Workgroup Settings section, click Change Settings. Click Continue if prompted, and then click the Change button on the Computer Name tab.

From the command prompt, you can use the *Netdom* command with the following syntax:

```
netdom renamecomputer MachineName /NewName:NewName
    [/UserO:LocalUsername] [/PasswordO:{LocalPassword|*} ]
    [/UserD:DomainUsername] [/PasswordD:{DomainPassword|*} ]
    [/SecurePasswordPrompt] [/REBoot[:TimeInSeconds]]
```

In addition to specifying the computer to rename (*MachineName*) and the desired new name (*NewName*), you must have credentials that are a member of the local Administrators group on the computer and credentials that have permission to rename the domain computer object. By default, *Netdom.exe* will use the credentials with which the command is executed. You can specify credentials, using *UserO* and *PasswordO* for the credentials in the computer's local Administrators group, and *UserD* and *PasswordD* for the domain credentials with permission to rename the computer object. Specifying * for the password causes *Netdom.exe* to prompt for the password on the command line. The *SecurePasswordPrompt* parameter displays a pop-up for credentials when * is specified for either *PasswordO* or *PasswordD*. After you rename a computer, you must reboot it. The *REBoot* parameter causes the system to reboot after 30 seconds unless otherwise specified by *TimeInSeconds*.

When you rename a computer, you can adversely affect services running on it. For example, Active Directory Certificate Services (AD CS) relies on the server's name. Be certain to consider the impact of renaming a computer before doing so. Do not use these methods to rename a domain controller.

Disabling and Enabling Computer Accounts

If a computer is taken offline or is not to be used for an extended period of time, consider disabling the account. This recommendation reflects the security principle that an identity store allows authentication only of the minimum number of accounts required to achieve the goals of an organization. Disabling the account does not modify the computer's SID or group membership, so when the computer is brought back online, the account can be enabled.

You can disable a computer by right-clicking it and choosing Disable Account. A disabled account appears with a down-arrow icon in the Active Directory Users and Computers snap-in, as shown in Figure 5-8.

DESKTOP153

Figure 5-8   A disabled computer account

While an account is disabled, the computer cannot create a secure channel with the domain. The result is that users who have not previously logged on to the computer, and who, therefore, do not have cached credentials on the computer, will be unable to log on until the secure channel is reestablished by enabling the account.

To enable a computer account, simply select the computer and choose the *Enable Account* command from the context menu.

To disable or enable a computer from the command prompt, use the *Dsmod* command. The syntax used to disable or enable computers is:

```
DSMOD COMPUTER ComputerDN -DISABLED YES
DSMOD COMPUTER ComputerDN -DISABLED NO
```

Deleting Computer Accounts

You have learned that computer accounts, like user accounts, maintain a unique SID, which enables an administrator to grant permissions to computers. Also like user accounts, computers can belong to groups. Therefore, like user accounts, it is important to understand the effect of deleting a computer account. When a computer account is deleted, its group memberships and SID are lost. If the deletion is accidental, and another computer account is created with the same name, it is nonetheless a new account with a new SID. Group memberships must be reestablished, and any permissions assigned to the deleted computer must be reassigned to the new account. Delete computer objects only when you are certain that you no longer require those security-related attributes of the object.

To delete a computer account using Active Directory Users and Computers, right-click the computer object and, from the context menu, choose the *Delete* command. You will be prompted to confirm the deletion and, because deletion is not reversible, the default response to the prompt is No. Select Yes, and the object is deleted.

The *Dsrm* command introduced in Chapter 3 enables you to delete a computer object from the command prompt. To delete a computer with *Dsrm*, type:

```
DSRM ObjectDN
```

where *ObjectDN* is the distinguished name of the computer, such as "CN=Desktop154, OU=Clients,DC=contoso,DC=com." Again, you will be prompted to confirm the deletion.

Recycling Computers

If a computer account's group memberships and SID, and the permissions assigned to that SID, are important to the operations of a domain, you do not want to delete that account. So what would you do if a computer was replaced with a new system with upgraded hardware? Such is another scenario in which you would reset a computer account.

Resetting a computer account resets its password but maintains all the computer object's properties. With a reset password, the account becomes, in effect, available for use. Any computer can then join the domain using that account, including the upgraded system. In effect, you've recycled the computer account, assigning it to a new piece of hardware. You can even rename the account. The SID and group memberships remain.

As you learned earlier in this lesson, the *Reset Account* command is available in the context menu when you right-click a computer object. The *Dsmod* command can also be used to reset a computer account by typing **dsmod computer "***ComputerDN***" -reset.**

PRACTICE Supporting Computer Objects and Accounts

In this practice, you will support and troubleshoot computer accounts with the skills you learned in this chapter. To perform the exercises in this practice, you must have the following objects in the *contoso.com* domain.

- A first-level OU named Clients.
- Two computer objects, DESKTOP154 and DESKTOP155, in the Clients OU.
- An OU named Desktops and an OU named Laptops in the Clients OU.
- A first-level OU named People.
- User accounts in the People OU for Linda Mitchell and Scott Mitchell. Populate sample contact information for the accounts: address, telephone, and e-mail.
- A first-level OU named Groups.
- A group in the Groups OU named Sales Desktops.

▶ Exercise 1   Manage Computer Objects

In this exercise, you will perform several common administrative tasks related to computers as you support the computers assigned to Linda Mitchell and Scott Mitchell, two salespeople at Contoso, Ltd.

1. Log on to SERVER01 as Administrator.
2. Open the Active Directory Users And Computers snap-in.
3. Select the Clients OU.
4. In the details pane, right-click DESKTOP154 and choose Properties.
5. Click the Managed By tab.
6. Click the Change button.
7. Type the user name for Scott Mitchell and click OK.

   The Managed By tab reflects the contact information you populated in Scott Mitchell's user object.
8. Click the Properties button.

   The Properties button on the Managed By tab takes you to the object referred to by the *managedBy* attribute.
9. Click OK to close each dialog box.
10. Repeat steps 4–9 to associate DESKTOP155 with Linda Mitchell.
11. In the console details pane of the Clients OU, select both DESKTOP154 and DESKTOP155.
12. Drag both objects into the Desktops OU. Click Yes to confirm your action.
13. In the console tree, select the Desktops OU.
14. In the details pane, select both DESKTOP154 and DESKTOP155.

15. Right-click one of the two selected computers and choose Properties.

    The Properties For Multiple Items dialog box appears.

16. Select the Change The Description Text For All Selected Objects check box and type **Sales Desktop**. Click OK.

17. With both computers selected, right-click one of the selected computers and choose Add To A Group.

18. Type **Sales Desktops** and click OK.

    A success message appears.

19. Click OK.

20. In the console tree, select the Domain Controllers OU.

21. In the details pane, right-click SERVER01 and choose Manage.

22. The Computer Management console appears, focused on SERVER01.

▶ **Exercise 2   Troubleshoot Computer Accounts**

In this exercise, you will simulate resetting the secure channel on a domain member. If you have a second computer joined to the *contoso.com* domain, you can use its name in step 4 of this exercise to actually perform a secure channel reset.

1. Open a command prompt.

2. The *Nltest* command can test the secure channel and perform a number of useful domain-related tests. Type **nltest /?** and review the options supported by *Nltest.exe*.

3. The *Netdom* command performs a number of tasks related to computers and to the domain. Type **netdom /?** and review the options supported by *Netdom.exe*.

4. Simulate resetting a computer's secure channel by typing **netdom reset desktop154**. You will receive an error, The RPC Server Is Not Available, because the system is not online.

Lesson Summary

- You can configure computer properties by using the Active Directory Users and Computers snap-in, *Dsmod*, Windows PowerShell, or VBScript.

- Computers maintain accounts that, like users, include a SID and group memberships. Be careful about deleting computer objects. Disabling computer objects allows you to enable the objects again when the computer needs to participate in the domain.

- When a computer's secure channel is broken, you can use the *Reset Account* command in the Active Directory Users and Computers snap-in, the *Dsmod* command, *Netdom.exe*, or *nltest.exe* to reset the secure channel.

Lesson Review

You can use the following questions to test your knowledge of the information in Lesson 3, "Supporting Computer Objects and Accounts." The questions are also available on the companion CD if you prefer to review them in electronic form.

NOTE Answers

Answers to these questions and explanations of why each answer choice is right or wrong are located in the "Answers" section at the end of the book.

---

1. A server administrator reports Failed To Authenticate events in the event log of a file server. What should you do?
   A. Reset the server account.
   B. Reset the password of the server administrator.
   C. Disable and enable the server account.
   D. Delete the account of the server administrator.

2. A computer has permissions assigned to its account to support a system service. It also belongs to 15 groups. The computer is being replaced with new hardware. The new hardware has a new asset tag, and your naming convention uses the asset tag as the computer name. What should you do? (Choose all that apply. Each correct answer is a part of the solution.)
   A. Delete the computer account for the existing system.
   B. Create a computer account for the new system.
   C. Reset the computer account for the existing system.
   D. Rename the computer account for the existing system.
   E. Join the new system to the domain.

3. Your enterprise recently created a child domain to support a research project in a remote location. Computer accounts for researchers were moved to the new domain. When you open Active Directory Users And Computers, the objects for those computers are displayed with a down-arrow icon. What is the most appropriate course of action?
   A. Reset the accounts.
   B. Disable the accounts.
   C. Enable the accounts.
   D. Delete the accounts.

Chapter Review

To further practice and reinforce the skills you learned in this chapter, you can perform the following tasks:

- Review the chapter summary.
- Review the key term introduced in this chapter.
- Complete the case scenarios. These scenarios set up real-world situations involving the topics of this chapter and ask you to create a solution.
- Complete the suggested practices.
- Take a practice test.

Chapter Summary

- Computers maintain accounts which, like users, include a logon name, security identifier (SID), and password. Computer accounts must, therefore, be created, managed, and supported with the same level of care as user accounts.
- You can create computer accounts, using the Active Directory Users and Computers snap-in, *Dsadd*, *Netdom.exe*, Windows PowerShell, and VBScript.
- You should prestage computer accounts before joining computers to the domain.
- You must have permissions on the Active Directory OU to create a computer object, and you must have permissions on the computer object to join a computer to the domain.
- If a computer's secure channel is broken and it loses its trust with the domain, you should reset the account, using *Netdom.exe*, *Nltest.exe*, *Dsmod*, or the Active Directory Users and Computers snap-in.

Key Terms

Use this key term to understand better the concepts covered in this chapter.

- **secure channel**   The encrypted communications stream between a computer and the domain. The secure channel is established by the Netlogon service, which authenticates to the domain, using the computer's user name and password.

Case Scenarios

In the following case scenarios, you will apply what you've learned about creating and supporting computer objects, automating their creation, and joining domains. You can find answers to these questions in the "Answers" section at the end of this book.

Case Scenario 1: Creating Computer Objects and Joining the Domain

During your security audit, you discover a number of computers in the Computers container. This is against your procedures, which dictate that a computer account should be pre-staged in the Clients OU. You are concerned about this fact because the Computers container is not within the scope of Group Policy objects that apply your corporate security baseline settings. You want to restrict administrators and users from adding computers to the Computers container.

1. Under what circumstances are computers added to the Computers container?
2. How can you ensure that computers are added to the Clients OU by default?
3. What can you do to prevent nonadministrative users from joining computers to the domain?

Case Scenario 2: Automating the Creation of Computer Objects

You recently ordered 100 laptops to support expansion of your remote sales force. The vendor sent you a list of asset tags as an Excel file. You want to create computer accounts for the systems, using the asset tags as the computer names.

1. Which tool will you use to import the computers?
2. You import the computers into a single, new OU. You want to disable all the accounts with a single command line. What command can you use?
3. You open one of the imported objects in the Active Directory Users and Computers snap-in and realize you forgot to configure the *Description* attribute to be *Sales Laptop*. How can you configure the description for all 100 systems within the Active Directory Users and Computers snap-in?

Suggested Practices

To help you successfully master the exam objectives presented in this chapter, complete the following tasks.

Create and Maintain Computer Accounts

In this practice, you will perform key administrative tasks that support the life cycle of a computer in a domain.

To perform this practice, you must have the following objects in the *contoso.com* domain:

- A first-level OU named Clients
- A first-level OU named Servers
- A first-level OU named Admins with a child OU named Groups

- A group named Help Desk in the Admins OU
- A first-level OU named People
- A user account for Linda Mitchell and April Stewart in the People OU
- Linda Mitchell as a member of the Help Desk group

Finally, you will need a second computer that can be used to join the domain. The computer can be a system running either Windows Server 2008 or Windows Vista, and it must be in a workgroup. Name the computer **DESKTOP555**.

- **Practice 1**   Log on to SERVER01 as Administrator and, in the Clients OU, create a computer account for DESKTOP555. In the User Or Group section, click Change and select the Help Desk group so that the Help Desk group can join the computer to the domain.

- **Practice 2**   Log on to DESKTOP555 as Administrator. Join the domain. When prompted for domain credentials, enter the user name and password for Linda Mitchell. Restart the system and log on as the domain user April Stewart.

- **Practice 3**   Open the Active Directory Users And Computers snap-in, right-click DESKTOP555, and choose Reset Account. This completely breaks the secure channel between DESKTOP555 and the domain. Attempt to log on to DESKTOP555 as Linda Mitchell. You will receive an error message explaining that the trust with the domain has been broken. Because you used the *Reset Account* command to break the secure channel, you will not be successful using *Netdom.exe* or *Nltest.exe* to repair the secure channel. Under normal troubleshooting scenarios, you should try those tools first. In this case, rejoin the computer to the domain.

- **Practice 4**   Remove DESKTOP555 from the domain, putting it back in a workgroup. Be certain its account has been deleted from Active Directory. Use the *Redircmp.exe* command to redirect the default computer container to the Clients OU. Log on to DESKTOP555 as Administrator and join the domain. When prompted for credentials, enter those of April Stewart as standard user. The computer will join the domain with a new object in the Clients OU. Remove the computer from the domain again. Follow the procedures in Lesson 1 in the "Restricting the Ability of Users to Create Computers" section to reduce *ms-DS-MachineAccountQuota* to zero. Then try to join DESKTOP555 to the domain again with April Stewart's standard user credentials. Your attempt should be prevented with the warning message shown in Figure 5-4.

Take a Practice Test

The practice tests on this book's companion CD offer many options. For example, you can test yourself on just one exam objective, or you can test yourself on all the 70-640 certification exam content. You can set up the test so that it closely simulates the experience of taking a certification exam, or you can set it up in study mode so that you can look at the correct answers and explanations after you answer each question.

MORE INFO   Practice tests

For details about all the practice test options available, see the "How to Use the Practice Tests" section in this book's introduction.

Chapter 6
Group Policy Infrastructure

In Chapter 1, "Installation," you learned that Active Directory Domain Services (AD DS) provides the foundational services of an identity and access solution for enterprise networks running Microsoft Windows and that AD DS goes further to support the management and configuration of even the largest, most complex networks. Chapter 2, "Administration," Chapter 3, "Users," Chapter 4, "Groups," and Chapter 5, "Computers," focused on the administration of Active Directory directory service security principals: users, groups, and computers. Now you will begin an examination of the management and configuration of users and computers by using Group Policy. Group Policy provides an infrastructure within which settings can be defined centrally and deployed to users and computers in the enterprise.

In an environment managed by a well-implemented Group Policy infrastructure, little or no configuration needs to be made by directly touching a desktop. All configuration is defined, enforced, and updated using settings in Group Policy objects (GPOs) that affect a portion of the enterprise as broad as an entire site or domain or as narrow as a single organizational unit (OU) or group. In this chapter, you will learn what Group Policy is, how it works, and how best to implement Group Policy in your organization. The remaining chapters in this training kit will apply Group Policy to specific management tasks such as security configuration, software deployment, password policy, and auditing.

Exam objectives in this chapter:
- Creating and Maintaining Active Directory Objects
    - Create and apply Group Policy objects (GPOs).
    - Configure GPO templates.
- Maintaining the Active Directory Environment
    - Monitor Active Directory.

Lessons in this chapter:
- Lesson 1: Implementing Group Policy. 231
- Lesson 2: Managing Group Policy Scope. 255
- Lesson 3: Supporting Group Policy 277

Before You Begin

To complete the practices in this chapter, you must have created a domain controller named SERVER01 in a domain named *contoso.com*. See Chapter 1 for detailed steps for this task.

Real World

Dan Holme

Many of my clients are attempting to do more with less: to increase security, decrease costs, and increase user productivity. All these goals are easier to achieve when you are able to manage change and configuration in your organization. When a new security concern arises, you want to be able to respond quickly to plug any holes. When help desk logs indicate a high number of calls from users requiring help to configure something on their systems, you want to be able to deploy a change centrally that proactively helps users work more effectively. If a new piece of software is required to win new business, you want to deploy it quickly. These are just a few examples of the types of change and configuration management I see tackled every day in enterprises large and small. Group Policy is a phenomenal technology that can deliver a great amount of value to an organization. Too often, I see Group Policy underused or poorly designed. In this chapter, you will learn the workings of Group Policy. Not only will your knowledge help you answer a number of Group Policy questions on the certification exam, but your expertise in Group Policy will be a great asset to your IT organization.

Lesson 1: Implementing Group Policy

A Group Policy infrastructure has a lot of moving parts. It is important that you understand not only what each part does but also how the parts work together and why you might want to assemble them in various configurations. In this lesson, you will get a comprehensive overview of Group Policy: its components, its functions, and its inner workings.

After this lesson, you will be able to:
- Identify the components of Group Policy.
- Explain the fundamentals of Group Policy processing.
- Create, edit, and link Group Policy objects.
- Create the central store for administrative templates.
- Search for specific policy settings in a GPO.
- Create a GPO from a Starter GPO.

Estimated lesson time: 90 minutes

An Overview and Review of Group Policy

Group Policy is a feature of Windows that enables you to manage change and configuration for users and computers from a central point of administration. If you are less familiar with the concepts of Group Policy, it is helpful to keep in mind at all times that Group Policy is all about configuring a setting for one or more users or one or more computers. There are thousands of configuration settings that can be managed with Group Policy, using one infrastructure that is administered with one set of tools.

Policy Settings

The most granular component of the Group Policy is an individual *policy setting*, also known simply as a *policy*, that defines a specific configuration change to apply. For example, a policy setting exists that prevents a user from accessing registry editing tools. If you define that policy setting and apply it to the user, the user will be unable to run tools such as *Regedit.exe*. Another policy setting is available that allows you to disable the local Administrator account. You can use this policy setting to disable the Administrator account on all user desktops and laptops, for example.

These two examples illustrate an important point: that some policy settings affect a user, regardless of the computer to which the user logs on, and other policy settings affect a computer, regardless of which user logs on to that computer. Policy settings such as the setting that prevents access to registry editing tools are often referred to as *user configuration settings* or *user settings*. The policy setting that disables the Administrator account and similar settings are often referred to as *computer configuration settings* or *computer settings*.

Group Policy Objects (GPOs)

Policy settings are defined and exist within a *Group Policy object (GPO)*. A GPO is an object that contains one or more policy settings and thereby applies one or more configuration settings for a user or computer.

Creating and Managing GPOs

GPOs can be managed in Active Directory by using the Group Policy Management console (GPMC), shown in Figure 6-1. They are displayed in a container named Group Policy Objects. Right-click the Group Policy Objects container and choose New to create a GPO.

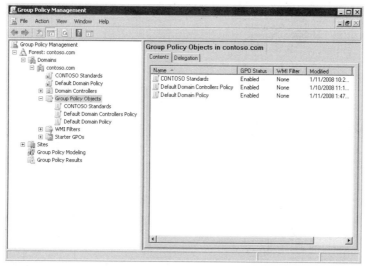

Figure 6-1   The Group Policy Management console

Editing a GPO

To modify the settings of a GPO, right-click the GPO and choose Edit. The GPO opens in the Group Policy Management Editor (GPME) snap-in, formerly known as the Group Policy Object Editor (GPO Editor), shown in Figure 6-2.

The GPME displays the thousands of policy settings available in a GPO in an organized hierarchy that begins with the division between computer settings and user settings: the Computer Configuration node and the User Configuration node. The next levels of the hierarchy are two nodes called Policies and Preferences. You will learn about the difference between these two nodes as this lesson progresses. Drilling deeper into the hierarchy, the GPME displays folders, also called nodes or policy setting groups. Within the folders are the policy settings themselves. Prevent Access To Registry Editing Tools is selected in Figure 6-2. To define a policy setting, double-click the policy setting. The policy setting's Properties dialog box appears, as shown in Figure 6-3.

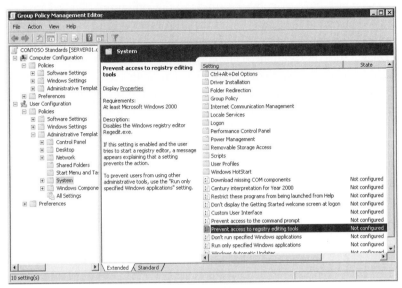

Figure 6-2   Group Policy Management Editor

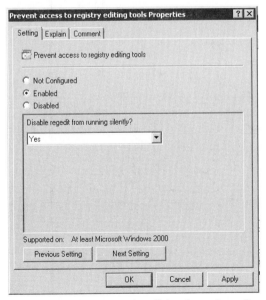

Figure 6-3   The Properties dialog box of a policy setting

Configuring a Policy Setting

A policy setting can have three states: Not Configured, Enabled, and Disabled. As you can see in Figure 6-2, in a new GPO every policy setting is Not Configured. This means that the GPO will not modify the existing configuration of that particular setting for a user or computer. If you enable or disable a policy setting, a change will be made to the configuration of users and computers to which the GPO is applied. The effect of the change depends on the policy setting itself. For example, if you enable the Prevent Access To Registry Editing Tools policy setting, users will be unable to launch the *Regedit.exe* Registry Editor. If you disable the policy setting, you ensure that users can launch the Registry Editor. Notice the double negative in this policy setting: You disable a policy that prevents an action, so you allow the action.

NOTE   Understand and test all policy settings

Many policy settings are complex, and the effect of enabling or disabling them might not be immediately clear. Also, some policy settings affect only certain versions of Windows. Be sure to review a
policy setting's explanatory text in the GPME detail pane, shown in Figure 6-2, or on the Explain tab
of the policy setting's Properties dialog box seen in Figure 6-3. Additionally, always test the effects
of a policy setting, and its interactions with other policy settings, before deploying a change in the
production environment.

Some policy settings bundle several configurations into one policy and might require additional parameters. In Figure 6-3, you can see that by enabling the policy to restrict registry editing tools, you can also define whether registry files can be merged into the system silently,
using *regedit /s*.

Scope

Configuration is defined by policy settings in Group Policy objects. However, the configuration changes in a GPO do not affect computers or users in your enterprise until you have specified the computers or users to which the GPO applies. This is called *scoping* a GPO. The *scope*
of a GPO is the collection of users and computers that will apply the settings in the GPO.

You can use several methods to manage the scope of GPOs. The first is the *GPO link*. GPOs can
be linked to sites, domains, and OUs in Active Directory. The site, domain, or OU then
becomes the maximum scope of the GPO. All computers and users within the site, domain, or
OU, including those in child OUs, will be affected by the configurations specified by policy settings in the GPO. A single GPO can be linked to more than one site or OU.

You can further narrow the scope of the GPO with one of two types of filters: *security filters* that
specify global security groups to which the GPO should or should not apply, and *Windows
Management Instrumentation (WMI) filters* that specify a scope, using characteristics of a system
such as operating system version or free disk space. Use Security filters and WMI filters to narrow or specify the scope within the initial scope created by the GPO link.

Scoping GPOs is detailed in Lesson 2, "Managing Group Policy Scope."

Resultant Set of Policy

Computers and users within the scope of a GPO will apply the policy settings specified in the GPO. An individual user or computer is likely to be within the scope of multiple GPOs linked to the sites, domain, or OUs in which the user or computer exists. This leads to the possibility that policy settings might be configured differently in multiple GPOs. You must be able to understand and evaluate the *Resultant Set of Policy (RSoP)*, which determines the settings that are applied by a client when the settings are configured divergently in more than one GPO. RSoP will be examined in Lesson 3, "Supporting Group Policy."

Group Policy Refresh

When are policies applied? Policy settings in the Computer Configuration node are applied at system startup and every 90–120 minutes thereafter. User Configuration policy settings are applied at logon and every 90–120 minutes thereafter. The application of policies is called *Group Policy refresh.*

Manually Refreshing Group Policy with GPUpdate

When you are experimenting with Group Policy or trying to troubleshoot Group Policy processing, you might need to initiate a Group Policy refresh manually so that you do not have to wait for the next background refresh. The *Gpupdate.exe* command can be used to initiate a Group Policy refresh. Used on its own, *Gpupdate.exe* triggers processing identical to a background Group Policy refresh. Both computer policy and user policy is refreshed. Use the */target:computer* or */target:user* parameter to limit the refresh to computer or user settings, respectively. During background refresh, by default, settings are applied only if the GPO has been updated. The */force* switch causes the system to reapply all settings in all GPOs scoped to the user or computer. Some policy settings require a logoff or reboot before they actually take effect. The */logoff* and */boot* switches of *Gpupdate.exe* cause a logoff or reboot, respectively, if settings are applied that require one. In Windows 2000, the *Secedit.exe* command was used to refresh policy, so you might encounter a mention of the *Secedit.exe* command on the exam.

Group Policy Client and Client-Side Extensions

And how, exactly, are the policy settings applied? When Group Policy refresh begins, a service running on all Windows systems (called the Group Policy client in Windows Vista and Windows Server 2008) determines which GPOs apply to the computer or user. It downloads any GPOs that it does not already have cached. Then a series of processes called *client-side extensions* (CSEs) do the work of interpreting the settings in a GPO and making appropriate changes to the local computer or to the currently logged-on user. There are CSEs for each major category of policy setting. For example, a CSE applies security changes, a CSE executes startup and logon scripts, a CSE installs software, and a CSE makes changes to registry keys and values. Each version of Windows has added CSEs to extend the functional reach of Group Policy. Several dozen CSEs are now in Windows Server 2008. One of the more important concepts to remember about Group Policy is that it is really client driven. The Group Policy client pulls the GPOs from the domain, triggering the CSEs to apply settings locally. Group Policy is not a "push" technology.

The behavior of CSEs can be configured using Group Policy, in fact. Most CSEs will apply settings in a GPO only if that GPO has changed. This behavior improves overall policy processing by eliminating redundant applications of the same settings. Most policies are applied in such a way that standard users cannot change the setting on their system–they will always be subject to the configuration enforced by Group Policy. However, some settings can be changed by standard users, and many can be changed if a user is an Administrator on that system. If users in your environment are administrators on their computers, consider configuring CSEs to reapply policy settings even if the GPO has not changed. That way, if an administrative user changes a configuration so that it is no longer compliant with policy, the configuration will be reset to its compliant state at the next Group Policy refresh.

NOTE   Configure CSEs to reapply policy settings even if the GPO has not changed

You can configure CSEs to reapply policy settings, even if the GPO has not changed, at background refresh. To do so, configure a GPO scoped to computers and define the settings in the Computer Configuration\Policies\Administrative Templates\System\ Group Policy node. For each CSE you want to configure, open its policy processing policy setting, for example, Registry Policy Processing for the Registry CSE. Click Enabled and select the check box labeled Process Even If The Group Policy Objects Have Not Changed.

An important exception to the default policy processing settings is settings managed by the Security CSE. Security settings are reapplied every 16 hours even if a GPO has not changed.

NOTE   The Always Wait For Network At Startup And Logon policy setting

It is highly recommended that you enable the Always Wait For Network At Startup And Logon policy setting for all Windows XP and Windows Vista clients. Without this setting, by default, Windows XP and Windows Vista clients perform only background refreshes, meaning that a client might start up and a user might log on without receiving the latest policies from the domain. The setting is located in Computer Configuration\Policies\Administrative Templates\System\Logon. Be sure to read the policy setting's explanatory text.

Slow Links and Disconnected Systems

One of the tasks that can be automated and managed with Group Policy is software installation. Group Policy Software Installation (GPSI) is supported by the software installation CSE. You can configure a GPO to install one or more software packages. Imagine, however, if a user were to connect to your network over a slow connection. You would not want large software packages to be transferred over the slow link because performance would be problematic.

The Group Policy client addresses this concern by detecting the speed of the connection to the domain and determining whether the connection should be considered a slow link. That determination is then used by each CSE to decide whether to apply settings. The software extension, for example, is configured to forgo policy processing so that software is not installed if a slow link is detected. By default, a link is considered to be slow if it is less than 500 kilobits per second (kbps).

If a user is working disconnected from the network, the settings previously applied by Group Policy will continue to take effect, so a user's experience is identical whether on the network or working away from the network. There are exceptions to this rule, most notably that startup, logon, logoff, and shutdown scripts will not run if the user is disconnected.

If a remote user connects to the network on a Windows Vista or Windows Server 2008 system, the Group Policy client wakes up and determines whether a Group Policy refresh window has been missed. If so, it performs a Group Policy refresh to obtain the latest GPOs from the domain. Again, the CSEs determine, based on their policy processing settings, whether settings in those GPOs are applied.

Group Policy Objects

Now that you have a broad-stroke understanding of Group Policy and its components, you can look more closely at each component. In this section, you will examine GPOs in detail. To manage configuration for users and computers, you create GPOs that contain the policy settings you require. Each computer has several GPOs stored locally on the system—the *local GPOs*—and can be within the scope of any number of domain-based GPOs.

Local GPOs

Computers running Windows 2000, Windows XP, and Microsoft Windows Server 2003 each have one local GPO, which can manage configuration of that system. The local GPO exists whether or not the computer is part of domain, workgroup, or a non-networked environment. It is stored in %SystemRoot%\System32\GroupPolicy. The policies in the local GPO affect only the computer on which the GPO is stored. By default, only the Security Settings policies are configured on a system's local GPO. All other policies are set at Not Configured.

When a computer does not belong to an Active Directory domain, the local policy is useful to configure and enforce configuration on that computer. However, in an Active Directory domain, settings in GPOs that are linked to the site, domain, or OUs will override local GPO settings and are easier to manage than GPOs on individual computers.

Windows Vista and Windows Server 2008 systems have multiple local GPOs. The Local Computer GPO is the same as the GPO in previous versions of Windows. In the Computer

Configuration node, configure all computer-related settings. In the User Configuration node, configure settings you want to apply to all users on the computer. The user settings in the Local Computer GPO can be modified by the user settings in two new local GPOs: Administrators and Non-Administrators. These two GPOs apply user settings to a logged-on user who is a member of the local Administrators group or is not, respectively. You can further refine user settings with a local GPO that applies to a specific user account. User-specific local GPOs are associated with local, not domain, user accounts.

RSoP is easy for computer settings: the Local Computer GPO is the only local GPO that can apply computer settings. User settings in a user-specific GPO will override conflicting settings in the Administrators and Non-Administrators GPOs, which themselves override settings in the Local Computer GPO. The concept is simple: the more specific the local GPO, the higher the precedence of its settings.

To create and edit local GPOs, click the Start button and, in the Start Search box, type **mmc.exe**. An empty Microsoft Management console (MMC) opens. Click File and choose Add/Remove Snap-in. Select the Group Policy Object Editor and click Add. A dialog box will appear, prompting you to select the GPO to edit. The Local Computer GPO is selected by default. If you want to edit another local GPO, click the Browse button. On the Users tab, you will find the Non-Administrators and Administrators GPOs and one GPO for each local user. Select the GPO and click OK. Click Finish and then OK to close each of the dialog boxes, and the Group Policy Object editor will be added, focused on the selected GPO.

Keep in mind that local GPOs are designed for nondomain environments. Configure them for your computer at home, for example, to manage the settings for your spouse or children. In a domain environment, settings in domain-based GPOs override conflicting settings in local GPOs, and it is a best practice to manage configuration by using domain-based GPOs.

Domain-Based GPOs

Domain-based GPOs are created in Active Directory and stored on domain controllers. They are used to manage configuration centrally for users and computers in the domain. The remainder of this training kit refers to domain-based GPOs rather than to local GPOs, unless otherwise specified.

When AD DS is installed, two default GPOs are created:

- **Default Domain Policy**   This GPO is linked to the domain and has no security group or WMI filters. Therefore, it affects all users and computers in the domain (including computers that are domain controllers). This GPO contains policy settings that specify password, account lockout, and Kerberos policies. As discussed in Chapter 8, "Authentication," modify the existing settings to align with your enterprise password and account lockout policies but do not add unrelated policy settings to this GPO. If you need to configure other settings to apply broadly in your domain, create additional GPOs linked to the domain.

- **Default Domain Controllers Policy**   This GPO is linked to the Domain Controllers OU. Because computer accounts for domain controllers are kept exclusively in the Domain Controllers OU, and other computer accounts should be kept in other OUs, this GPO affects only domain controllers. The Default Domain Controllers GPO should be modified to implement your auditing policies, as discussed in Chapter 7, "Group Policy Settings," and in Chapter 8. It should also be modified to assign user rights required on domain controllers.

Creating, Linking, and Editing GPOs

To create a GPO, right-click the Group Policy Objects container and choose New. You must have permission to the Group Policy Objects container to create a GPO.

By default, the Domain Admins group and the Group Policy Creator Owners group are delegated the ability to create GPOs. To delegate permission to other groups, select the Group Policy Objects container in the GPME console tree and then click the Delegation tab in the console details pane.

After you have created a GPO, you can create the initial scope of the GPO by linking it to a site, domain, or OU. To link a GPO, right-click the container and choose Link An Existing GPO. Note that you will not see your sites in the Sites node of the GPMC until you right-click Sites, choose Show Sites, and select the Sites you want to manage. You can also create and link a GPO with a single step by right-clicking a site, domain, or OU and choosing Create A GPO In This Domain And Link It Here.

You must have permission to link GPOs to a site, domain, or OU. In the GPMC, select the container in the console tree and then click the Delegation tab in the console details pane. From the Permission drop-down list, select Link GPOs. The users and groups displayed hold the permission for the selected OU. Click the Add or Remove buttons to modify the delegation.

To edit a GPO, right-click the GPO in the Group Policy Objects container and choose Edit. The GPO is opened in the GPME. You must have at least Read permission to open the GPO in this way. To make changes to a GPO, you must have Write permission to the GPO. Permissions for the GPO can be set by selecting the GPO in the Group Policy Objects container and then clicking the Delegation tab in the details pane.

The GPME will display the name of the GPO as the root node. The GPME also displays the domain in which the GPO is defined and the server from which the GPO was opened and to which changes will be saved. The root node is in the *GPOName [ServerName]* format. In Figure 6-2, the root node is CONTOSO Standards [SERVER01.contoso.com] Policy. The GPO name is CONTOSO Standards, and it was opened from SERVER01.contoso.com, meaning that the GPO is defined in the *contoso.com* domain.

GPO Storage

Group Policy settings are presented as GPOs in Active Directory user interface tools, but a GPO is actually two components: a Group Policy Container (GPC) and Group Policy Template (GPT). The GPC is an Active Directory object stored in the Group Policy Objects container within the domain naming context of the directory. Like all Active Directory objects, each GPC includes a globally unique identifier (GUID) attribute that uniquely identifies the object within Active Directory. The GPC defines basic attributes of the GPO, but it does not contain any of the settings. The settings are contained in the GPT, a collection of files stored in the SYSVOL of each domain controller in the %SystemRoot%\SYSVOL\Domain\Policies*GPO GUID* path, where *GPO GUID* is the GUID of the GPC. When you make changes to the settings of a GPO, the changes are saved to the GPT of the server from which the GPO was opened.

By default, when Group Policy refresh occurs, the CSEs apply settings in a GPO only if the GPO has been updated. The Group Policy client can identify an updated GPO by its version number. Each GPO has a version number that is incremented each time a change is made. The version number is stored as an attribute of the GPC and in a text file, GPT.ini, in the GPT folder. The Group Policy client knows the version number of each GPO it has previously applied. If, during Group Policy refresh, it discovers that the version number of the GPC has been changed, the CSEs will be informed that the GPO is updated.

Quick Check

- Describe the default Group Policy processing behavior, including refresh intervals and CSE application of policy settings.

Quick Check Answer

- Every 90–120 minutes, the Group Policy Client service determines which GPOs are scoped to the user or computer and downloads any GPOs that have been updated, based on the GPOs' version numbers. CSEs process the policies in the GPOs according to their policy processing configuration. By default, most CSEs apply policy settings only if a GPO has been updated. Some CSEs also do not apply settings if a slow link is detected.

GPO Replication

The two parts of a GPO are replicated between domain controllers by using distinct mechanisms. The GPC in Active Directory is replicated by the Directory Replication Agent (DRA), using a topology generated by the Knowledge Consistency Checker (KCC). You will learn more about these services in Chapter 11, "Sites and Replication." The result is that the GPC is replicated within seconds to all domain controllers in a site and is replicated between sites based on your intersite replication configuration, which will also be discussed in Chapter 11.

The GPT in the SYSVOL is replicated using one of two technologies. The File Replication Service (FRS) is used to replicate SYSVOL in domains running Windows Server 2008, Windows Server 2003, and Windows 2000. If all domain controllers are running Windows Server 2008, you can configure SYSVOL replication, using Distributed File System Replication (DFS-R), a much more efficient and robust mechanism.

Because the GPC and GPT are replicated separately, it is possible for them to become out of synch for a short time. Typically, when this happens, the GPC will replicate to a domain controller first. Systems that obtained their ordered list of GPOs from that domain controller will identify the new GPC, will attempt to download the GPT, and will notice the version numbers are not the same. A policy processing error will be recorded in the event logs. If the reverse happens, and the GPO replicates to a domain controller before the GPC, clients obtaining their ordered list of GPOs from that domain controller will not be notified of the new GPO until the GPC has replicated.

You can download from the Microsoft Download Center the Group Policy Verification Tool, *Gpotool.exe*, which is part of Windows Resource Kits. This tool reports the status of GPOs in the domain and can identify instances in which, on a domain controller, the GPC and the GPT do not have the same version. For more information about *Gpotool.exe*, type **gpotool /?** at the command line.

Exam Tip   *Gpotool.exe* is used to troubleshoot GPO status, including problems caused by the replication of GPOs, leading to inconsistent versions of a GPC and GPT.

Policy Settings

Group Policy settings, also known simply as policies, are contained in a GPO and are viewed and modified using the GPME. In this section, you will look more closely at the categories of settings available in a GPO.

Computer Configuration and User Configuration

There are two major divisions of policy settings: computer settings, contained in the Computer Configuration node, and user settings, contained in the User Configuration node. The Computer Configuration node contains the settings that are applied to computers, regardless of who logs on to them. Computer settings are applied when the operating system starts up and during background refresh every 90–120 minutes thereafter. The User Configuration node contains settings that are applied when a user logs on to the computer and during background refresh every 90–120 minutes thereafter.

Within the Computer Configuration and User Configuration nodes are the Policies and Preferences nodes. Policies are settings that are configured and behave similarly to the policy settings in earlier versions of Windows. Preferences are introduced in Windows Server 2008. The following sections examine these nodes.

Software Settings Node

Within the Policies nodes within Computer Configuration and User Configuration are a hierarchy of folders containing policy settings. Because there are thousands of settings, it is beyond the scope of the exam and of this training kit to examine individual settings. It is worthwhile, however, to define the broad categories of settings in the folders. The first of these nodes is the Software Settings node, which contains only the Software Installation extension. The Software Installation extension helps you specify how applications are installed and maintained within your organization. It also provides a place for independent software vendors to add settings. Software deployment with Group Policy is discussed in Chapter 7.

Windows Settings Node

In both the Computer Configuration and User Configuration nodes, the Policies node contains a Windows Settings node that includes the Scripts, Security Settings, and Policy-Based QoS nodes.

The *Scripts* extension enables you to specify two types of scripts: startup/shutdown (in the Computer Configuration node) and logon/logoff (in the User Configuration node). Startup/shutdown scripts run at computer startup or shutdown. Logon/logoff scripts run when a user logs on or off the computer. When you assign multiple logon/logoff or startup/shutdown scripts to a user or computer, the scripts CSE executes the scripts from top to bottom. You can determine the order of execution for multiple scripts in the Properties dialog box. When a computer is shut down, the CSE first processes logoff scripts, followed by shutdown scripts. By default, the timeout value for processing scripts is 10 minutes. If the logoff and shutdown scripts require more than 10 minutes to process, you must adjust the timeout value with a policy setting. You can use any ActiveX scripting language to write scripts. Some possibilities include Microsoft Visual Basic, Scripting Edition (VBScript), Microsoft JScript, Perl, and Microsoft MS DOS style batch files (.bat and .cmd). Logon scripts on a shared network directory in another forest are supported for network logon across forests.

The Security Settings node allows a security administrator to configure security, using GPOs. This can be done after, or instead of, using a security template to set system security. For a detailed discussion of system security and the Security Settings node, refer to Chapter 7.

The Policy-Based QoS node defines policies that manage network traffic. For example, you might want to ensure that users in the Finance department have priority for running a critical network application during the end-of-year financial reporting period. Policy-Based QoS enables you to do that.

In the User Configuration node only, the Windows Settings folder contains the additional Remote Installation Services, Folder Redirection, and Internet Explorer Maintenance nodes.

Remote Installation Services (RIS) policies control the behavior of a remote operating system installation, using RIS. Folder Redirection enables you to redirect user data and settings folders (AppData, Desktop, Documents, Pictures, Music, and Favorites, for example) from their default user profile location to an alternate location on the network, where they can be centrally managed. *Internet Explorer Maintenance* enables you to administer and customize Microsoft Internet Explorer.

Administrative Templates Node

In both the Computer Configuration and User Configuration nodes, the Administrative Templates node contains registry-based Group Policy settings. There are thousands of such settings available for configuring the user and computer environment. As an administrator, you might spend a significant amount of time manipulating these settings. To assist you with the settings, a description of each policy setting is available in two locations:

- On the Explain tab in the Properties dialog box for the setting. In addition, the Settings tab in the Properties dialog box for the setting lists the required operating system or software for the setting.
- On the Extended tab of the GPME. The Extended tab appears on the bottom of the right details pane and provides a description of each selected setting in a column between the console tree and the settings pane. The required operating system or software for each setting is also listed.

The Administrative Templates node is discussed in detail in the "Administrative Templates" section.

Preferences Node

Underneath both Computer Configuration and User Configuration is a Preferences node. New to Windows Server 2008, preferences provide more than 20 CSEs to help you manage an incredible number of additional settings, including:

- Applications such as Microsoft Office 2003 and Office 2007
- Mapped drives
- Registry settings
- Power options
- Folder options
- Regional options
- Starch menu options

Preferences also enables you to deploy the following:

- Files and folders
- Printers

- Scheduled tasks
- Network connections

Many enterprises will also benefit from Preferences because the options can be used to enable or disable hardware devices or classes of devices. For example, you can use Preferences to prevent USB hard drives, including personal media players, from being connected to computers.

The new version of the GPME that supports configuring Preferences is available for download for Windows Vista SP1 from the Microsoft Download Center at *http://www.microsoft.com /downloads*. To apply preferences, systems require the preferences CSEs, which Windows Server 2008 includes. CSEs for Windows XP, Windows Server 2003, and Windows Vista can be downloaded from the Microsoft Download Center.

The interface you use to configure many preferences looks identical to the Windows user interface in which you would make the change manually. Figure 6-4 shows a Folder Options (Windows XP) preference *item*—a collection of settings that are processed by the preferences CSE. You will recognize the similarity to the Folder Options application in Control Panel.

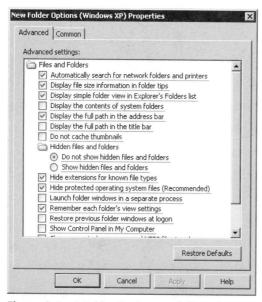

Figure 6-4   A Folder Options preference item

Administrative Templates Node

Policies in the Administrative Templates node in the Computer Configuration node modify registry values in the HKEY_LOCAL_MACHINE (HKLM) key. Policies in the Administrative Templates node in the User Configuration node modify registry values in the

HKEY_CURRENT_USER (HKCU) key. Most of the registry values that are modified by the default policies are located in one of the following four reserved trees:

- HKLM\Software\Policies (computer settings)
- HKCU\Software\Policies (user settings)
- HKLM\Software\Microsoft\Windows\CurrentVersion\Policies (computer settings)
- HKCU\Software\Microsoft\Windows\CurrentVersion\Policies (user settings)

An *administrative template* is a text file that specifies the registry change to be made and that generates the user interface to configure the Administrative Templates policy settings in the GPME. Figure 6-3 shows the properties dialog box for the Prevent Access To Registry Editing Tools. The fact that the setting exists, and that it provides a drop-down list with which to disable *Regedit.exe* from running silently, is determined in an administrative template. The registry setting that is made based on how you configure the policy is also defined in the administrative template.

You can add new administrative templates to the GPME by right-clicking the Administrative Templates node and choosing Add/Remove Templates. Some software vendors provide administrative templates as a mechanism to manage the configuration of their application centrally. For example, you can obtain administrative templates for all recent versions of Microsoft Office from the Microsoft Downloads Center. You can also create your own custom administrative templates. A tutorial on creating custom administrative templates is beyond the scope of this training kit.

In versions of Windows prior to Windows Vista, an administrative template had an .adm extension. ADM files have several drawbacks. First, all localization must be performed within the ADM file. That is, if you want to create an ADM file to help deploy configuration in a multilingual organization, you would need separate ADM files for each language to provide a user interface for administrators who speak that language. If you were to decide later to make a modification related to the registry settings managed by the templates, you would need to make the change to each ADM file.

The second problem with ADM files is the way they are stored. An ADM file is stored as part of the GPT in the SYSVOL. If an ADM file is used in multiple GPOs, it is stored multiple times, contributing to SYSVOL bloat. There were also challenges maintaining version control over ADM files.

In Windows Vista and Windows Server 2008, an administrative template is a pair of XML files, one with an .admx extension that specifies changes to be made to the registry and the other with an .adml extension that provides a language-specific user interface in the GPME. When changes need to be made to settings managed by the administrative template, they can be made to the single ADMX file. Any administrator who modifies a GPO that uses the template accesses the same ADMX file and calls the appropriate ADML file to populate the user interface.

NOTE   No need to take sides

ADM and ADMX/ADML administrative templates can coexist.

Central Store

As was previously stated, ADM files are stored as part of the GPO itself. When you edit a GPO that uses administrative templates in the ADM format, the GPME loads the ADM from the GPC to produce the user interface. When ADMX/ADML files are used as administrative templates, the GPO contains only the data that the client needs for processing Group Policy, and when you edit the GPO, the GPME pulls the ADMX and ADML files from the local workstation.

This works well for smaller organizations, but for complex environments that include custom administrative templates or that require more centralized control, Windows Server 2008 introduces the central store. The central store is a single folder in SYSVOL that holds all the ADMX and ADML files that are required. After you have set up the central store, the GPME recognizes it and loads all administrative templates from the central store instead of from the local computer.

To create a central store, create a folder called PolicyDefinitions in the *FQDN*\SYSVOL *FQDN*\Policies path. For example, the central store for the *contoso.com* domain would be \\contoso.com\SYSVOL\contoso.com\Policies\PolicyDefinitions. Then, copy all files from the %SystemRoot%\PolicyDefinitions folder of a Windows Server 2008 system to the new SYSVOL PolicyDefinitions folder. These will include the .admx files and the .adml files in a language-specific subfolder of %SystemRoot%\PolicyDefinitions. For example, English (United States) ADML files are located in %SystemRoot%\PolicyDefinitions\en-us. Copy them into *FQDN* \SYSVOL*FQDN*\Policies\PolicyDefinitions\en-us. If additional languages are required, copy the folder that contains the ADML files to the central store. When you have copied all ADMX and ADML files, the PolicyDefinitions folder on the domain controller should contain the ADMX files and one or more folders containing language-specific ADML files.

Exam Tip   If logging on to a domain controller, locally or by using Remote Desktop, the local path to the PolicyDefinitions folder is %SystemRoot%\SYSVOL\domain\Policies\PolicyDefinitions.

Filtering Administrative Template Policy Settings

A weakness of the Group Policy editing tools in previous versions of Windows is the inability to search for a specific policy setting. With thousands of policies to choose from, it can be difficult to locate exactly the setting you want to configure. The new GPME in Windows Server 2008 solves this problem for Administrative Template settings: you can now create filters to locate specific policy settings.

To create a filter, right-click Administrative Templates and choose Filter Options. To locate a specific policy, select Enable Keyword Filters, enter the words with which to filter, and select the fields within which to search. Figure 6-5 shows an example of a search for policy settings related to the screen saver.

In the top section of the Filter Options dialog box shown in Figure 6-5, you can filter the view to show only policy settings that are configured. This can help you locate and modify settings that are already specified in the GPO.

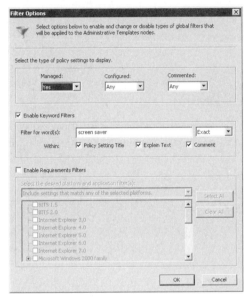

Figure 6-5   Filtering the Administrative Templates policy settings

Commenting

You can also search and filter based on policy-setting comments. Windows Server 2008 enables you to add comments to policy settings in the Administrative Templates node. Double-click a policy setting and click the Comment tab. It is a best practice to add comments to configured policy settings as a way to document the justification for a setting and its intended effect. You should also add comments to the GPO itself. Windows Server 2008 enables you to attach comments to a GPO. In the GPME, right-click the root node in the console tree and choose Properties; then click the Comment tab.

Starter GPOs

Another new Group Policy feature in Windows Server 2008 is starter GPOs. A starter GPO contains Administrative Template settings. You can create a new GPO from a starter GPO, in which case, the new GPO is prepopulated with a copy of the settings in Starter GPO. A starter

GPO is, in effect, a template. Unfortunately, Microsoft had already been using the term *template* in the context of administrative templates, so another name had to be found. When you create a new GPO, you can still choose to begin with a blank GPO, or you can select one of the preexisting starter GPOs or a custom starter GPO.

NOTE   **When you need more than administrative template settings**

Starter GPOs can contain only Administrative Templates policy settings. You can also copy and paste entire GPOs in the Group Policy Objects container of the Group Policy Management console so that you have a new GPO with all the settings of the source GPO. To transfer settings between GPOs in different domains or forests, right-click a GPO and choose Back Up. In the target domain, create a new GPO, right-click it, and choose Import Settings. You will be able to import the settings of the backed-up GPO.

Managed and Unmanaged Policy Settings

There is a nuance to the registry policy settings configured by the Administrative Templates node that is important to understand: the difference between managed and unmanaged policy settings. The registry policy settings that have been discussed so far and that are encountered in the practices of this chapter are examples of managed policy settings. A managed policy setting effects a configuration change of some kind when the setting is applied by a GPO. When the user or computer is no longer within the scope of the GPO, the configuration reverts to its original state automatically. For example, if a GPO prevents access to registry editing tools and then the GPO is deleted, disabled, or scoped so that it no longer applies to users, those users will regain access to registry editing tools at the next policy refresh.

In contrast, an unmanaged policy setting makes a change that is persistent in the registry. If the GPO no longer applies, the setting remains. This is often called *tattooing* the registry. To reverse the effect of the policy setting, you must deploy a change that reverts the configuration to the desired state.

By default, the GPME hides unmanaged policy settings to discourage you from implementing a configuration that is difficult to revert. However, you can make many useful changes with unmanaged policy settings, particularly for custom administrative templates to manage configuration for applications. To control which policy settings are visible, right-click Administrative Templates and choose Filter Options. Make a selection from the Managed drop-down list.

PRACTICE Implementing Group Policy

In this practice, you will implement configuration in the *contoso.com* domain by using Group Policy. You will create, configure, and scope GPOs. You will also gain hands-on experience with the new features of Group Policy in Windows Server 2008.

▶ **Exercise 1   Create, Edit, and Scope a Group Policy Object**

In this exercise, you will create a GPO that implements a setting mandated by the corporate security policy of Contoso, Ltd., and scope the setting to all users and computers in the domain.

1. Log on to SERVER01 as Administrator.
2. Open the Group Policy Management console from the Administrative Tools folder.
3. Expand Forest, Domains, the *contoso.com* domain, and the Group Policy Objects container.
4. Right-click the Group Policy Objects Container in the console tree and choose New.
5. In the Name box, type **CONTOSO Standards**. Click OK.
6. Right-click the CONTOSO Standards GPO and choose Edit.

    Group Policy Management Editor appears.
7. Right-click the root node of the console, CONTOSO Standard, and choose Properties.
8. Click the Comment tab and type **Contoso corporate standard policies. Settings are scoped to all users and computers in the domain. Person responsible for this GPO: *your name*.** Then click OK.

    In this scenario, the Contoso corporate IT security policy specifies that computers cannot be left unattended and logged on for more than 10 minutes. To meet this requirement, you will configure the screen saver timeout and password-protected screen saver policy settings. You will use the new search capability of Windows Server 2008 Group Policy to locate the policy settings.
9. Expand User Configuration\Policies\Administrative Templates.
10. Spend a few moments browsing the settings beneath this node. Review the explanatory text of policy settings that sound interesting to you. Do not make any configuration changes.
11. Right-click Administrative Templates in the User Configuration node and choose Filter Options.
12. Select the Enable Keyword Filters check box.
13. In the Filter for Word(s) text box, type **screen saver**.
14. In the drop-down list next to the text box, choose Exact.
15. Click OK.

    Administrative Templates policy settings are filtered to show only those that contain the words *screen saver*.
16. Browse to examine the screen saver policies that you have found.
17. In the Control Panel\Display node, click the policy setting Screen Saver Timeout. Note the explanatory text in the left margin of the console's details pane.
18. Double-click the policy setting Screen Saver Timeout.

19. Review the explanatory text on the Explain tab.

20. Click the Setting tab and select Enabled.

21. In the Seconds box, type **600**.

22. On the Comment tab, type **Corporate IT Security Policy implemented with this policy in combination with Password Protect the Screen Saver.**

23. Click OK.

24. Double-click the Password Protect The Screen Saver policy setting.

25. Select Enabled.

26. On the Comment tab, type **Corporate IT Security Policy implemented with this policy in combination with Screen Saver Timeout.**

27. Click OK.

28. Close the GPME.

    Changes you make in the GPME are saved in real time. There is no Save command.

29. In the Group Policy Management console, right-click the *contoso.com* domain and choose Link An Existing GPO.

30. Select the CONTOSO Standards GPO and click OK.

▶ **Exercise 2   View the Effects of Group Policy Application**

In this exercise, you will experience the effect of the Group Policy setting you configured in Exercise 1, "Create, Edit, and Scope a Group Policy Object," and you will practice triggering a manual policy refresh, using *Gpupdate.exe*.

1. On SERVER01, right-click the desktop and choose Personalize.

2. Click Screen Saver.

3. Note that you can change the screen saver timeout and the option to display the logon screen on resume. Close the Screen Saver Settings dialog box.

4. Open a command prompt and type **gpupdate.exe /force /boot /logoff**.

    These options of the *Gpupdate.exe* command invoke the most complete Group Policy refresh. Wait until both user and computer policies have been updated.

5. Return to the Screen Saver Settings dialog box. Note that you can no longer change the screen saver timeout or resume option.

▶ **Exercise 3   Explore a GPO**

Now that you've seen a GPO in action, you will explore the GPO itself to learn about the inner workings of Group Policy.

1. In the Group Policy Management console, select the CONTOSO Standards GPO in the Group Policy Objects container.

2. On the Scope tab, notice that the GPO reports its links in the Links section.

3. Click the Settings tab to see a report of the policy settings in the GPO.

If you have Internet Explorer Enhanced Security Configuration (ESC) enabled, you will be prompted to confirm that you want to add *about:security_mmc.exe* to your Trusted Sites zone.

4. Click the Show All link at the top of this settings report to expand all sections of the report. Notice that the policy setting comments you added are part of the settings report.

5. Point at the text for the policy Screen Saver Timeout. Notice that the policy title is actually a hyperlink. Click the link to reveal the explanatory text for the policy setting.

6. Click the Details tab. Notice that your GPO comments appear on this tab along with GPO version information.

7. Write down the Unique ID shown on the Details tab.

8. Open the following folder: \\contoso.com\SYSVOL\contoso.com\Policies.

9. Double-click the folder with the same name as the GPO's Unique ID.

   This is the GPT of the GPO.

▶ **Exercise 4   Explore Administrative Templates**

Administrative templates provide the instructions with which the GPME creates a user interface to configure Administrative Templates policy settings and specify the registry changes that must be made based on those policy settings. In this exercise, you will examine an administrative template.

1. Open the %SystemRoot%\PolicyDefinitions folder.

2. Open the en-us folder or the folder for your region and language.

3. Double-click ControlPanelDisplay.adml. Choose the Select A Program From A List Of Installed Programs option and click OK. Choose to open the file with Notepad and click OK.

4. Turn on Word Wrap from the Format menu.

5. Search for the ScreenSaverIsSecure text.

6. Note the label for the setting and, on the next line, the explanatory text.

7. Close the file and navigate up to the PolicyDefinitions folder.

8. Double-click ControlPanelDisplay.admx. Choose the Select A Program From A List Of Installed Programs option and click OK. Choose to open the file with Notepad and click OK.

9. Search for the text shown here:

```
<policy name="ScreenSaverIsSecure" class="User"
displayName="$(string.ScreenSaverIsSecure)"
explainText="$(string.ScreenSaverIsSecure_Help)"
key="Software\Policies\Microsoft\Windows\Control Panel\Desktop"
valueName="ScreenSaverIsSecure">
        <parentCategory ref="Display" />
        <supportedOn ref="windows:SUPPORTED_Win2kSP1" />
        <enabledValue>
```

```
      <string>1</string>
    </enabledValue>
    <disabledValue>
       <string>0</string>
    </disabledValue>
  </policy>
```

10. Identify the parts of the template that define the following:

   ❑ The name of the policy setting that appears in the GPME

   ❑ The explanatory text for the policy setting

   ❑ The registry key and value affected by the policy setting

   ❑ The data put into the registry if the policy is enabled

   ❑ The data put into the registry if the policy is disabled

▶ **Exercise 5   Creating a Central Store**

In this exercise, you will create a central store of administrative templates to centralize the management of templates.

1. In the Group Policy Management console, right-click CONTOSO Standards and choose Edit.

2. Expand User Configuration\Policies\Administrative Template.

3. Note that the node reports Policy Definitions (ADMX Files) Retrieved From The Local Machine.

4. Close the GPME.

5. Open the following folder: \\contoso.com\SYSVOL\contoso.com\Policies.

6. Create a folder named **PolicyDefinitions**.

7. Copy the contents of %SystemRoot%\PolicyDefinitions to the folder you created in the previous step.

8. In the Group Policy Management console, right-click CONTOSO Standards and choose Edit.

9. Expand User Configuration\Policies\Administrative Template.

10. Note that the node reports Policy Definitions (ADMX Files) Retrieved From The Central Store.

Lesson Summary

- GPOs contain policy settings that define configuration. When GPOs are scoped to a site, domain, or OU, users and computers within the scope of the GPO apply its policy settings.

- Processes on Windows clients determine the GPOs that must be downloaded and applied. Group Policy processing occurs at startup and every 90–120 minutes thereafter for computer settings and at logon and every 90–120 minutes thereafter for user settings.

- By default, CSEs apply settings only if the GPO has changed, except for Security settings, which are applied every 16 hours, whether or not the GPO is changed. CSEs can be configured to reapply settings at each policy refresh and to apply or skip policy application if a slow link is detected.

- Windows Server 2008 introduces Group Policy Preferences, which add more than 20 CSEs to manage a wide variety of user and computer settings.

- Administrative templates (.adm or .admx/.adml files) define the user interface and registry changes for policy settings in the Administrative Templates node of the GPO.

- You can centralize the management of administrative templates by creating a central store.

- Windows Server 2008 also adds the ability to attach comments to GPOs and policy settings and to create new GPOs based on starter GPOs that contain a baseline of Administrative Templates policy settings.

Lesson Review

You can use the following questions to test your knowledge of the information in Lesson 1, "Implementing Group Policy." The questions are also available on the companion CD if you prefer to review them in electronic form.

NOTE   Answers

Answers to these questions and explanations of why each answer choice is right or wrong are located in the "Answers" section at the end of the book.

1. Litware, Inc., has three business units, each represented by an OU in the *litwareinc.com* domain. The business unit administrators want the ability to manage Group Policy for the users and computers in their OUs. Which actions do you perform to give the administrators the ability to manage Group Policy fully for their business units? (Choose all that apply. Each correct answer is a part of the solution.)

   A. Copy administrative templates from the central store to the PolicyDefinitions folder on the administrators' Windows Vista workstations.

   B. Add business unit administrators to the Group Policy Creator Owners group.

   C. Delegate Link GPOs permission to the administrators in the *litwareinc.com* domain.

   D. Delegate Link GPOs permission to the each business unit's administrators in the business unit's OU.

2. You are an administrator at Contoso, Ltd. The *contoso.com* domain has a child domain, *es.contoso.com*, for the branch in Spain. Administrators of that domain have asked you to provide a Spanish-language interface for Group Policy Management Editor. How can you provide Spanish-language versions of administrative templates?

   A. Log on to a domain controller in the *es.contoso.com* domain, open %SystemRoot% \SYSVOL\domain\Policies\PolicyDefinitions, and copy the ADM files to the ES folder.

   B. Copy ADML files to the \\es.contoso.com\SYSVOL\es.contoso.com\policies\ PolicyDefinitions\es folder.

   C. Log on to a domain controller in the *es.contoso.com* domain, open %System-Root%\SYSVOL\domain\Policies\PolicyDefinitions, and copy the ADMX files to the ES folder.

   D. Install the Boot.wim file from the Windows Server 2008 CD on a domain controller in the child domain.

3. You are an administrator at Contoso, Ltd. At a recent conference, you had a conversation with administrators at Fabrikam, Inc. You discussed a particularly successful set of configurations you have deployed using a GPO. The Fabrikam administrators have asked you to copy the GPO to their domain. Which steps can you and the Fabrikam administrators perform?

   A. Right-click the Contoso GPO and choose Save Report. Create a GPO in the Fabrikam domain, right-click it, and choose Import.

   B. Right-click the Contoso GPO and choose Back Up. Right-click the Group Policy Objects container in the Fabrikam domain and choose Restore From Backup.

   C. Right-click the Contoso GPO and choose Back Up. Create a GPO in the Fabrikam domain, right-click it, and choose Paste.

   D. Right-click the Contoso GPO and choose Back Up. Create a GPO in the Fabrikam domain, right-click it, and choose Import Settings.

Lesson 2: Managing Group Policy Scope

A GPO is, by itself, just a collection of configuration instructions that will be processed by the CSEs of computers. Until the GPO is scoped, it does not apply to any users or computers. The GPO's scope determines which computers' CSEs will receive and process the GPO, and only the computers or users within the scope of a GPO will apply the settings in that GPO. Several mechanisms are used to scope a GPO:

- The GPO link to a site, domain, or OU and whether that link is enabled
- The Enforce option of a GPO
- The Block Inheritance option on an OU
- Security group filtering
- WMI filtering
- Policy node enabling or disabling
- Preferences targeting
- Loopback policy processing

You must be able to define the users or computers to which configuration is deployed, and therefore, you must master the art of scoping GPOs. In this lesson, you will learn each of the mechanisms with which you can scope a GPO and, in the process, the concepts of Group Policy application, inheritance, and precedence.

After this lesson, you will be able to:
- Manage GPO links.
- Evaluate GPO inheritance and precedence.
- Understand the Block Inheritance and Enforced link options.
- Use security filtering to narrow the scope of a GPO.
- Apply a WMI filter to a GPO.
- Implement loopback policy preferences.

Estimated lesson time: 90 minutes

GPO Links

A GPO can be linked to one or more Active Directory sites, domains, or OUs. After a policy is linked to a site, domain, or OU, the users or computers and users in that container are within the scope of the GPO, including computers and users in child OUs.

As you learned in Lesson 1, you can link a GPO to the domain or to an OU by right-clicking it and choosing Link An Existing GPO. If you have not yet created a GPO, you can choose Create A GPO In This Domain, And Link It Here. You can choose the same commands to link a GPO to a site, but by default, your Active Directory sites are not visible in the GPME; you must first right-click Sites and choose Show Sites.

Site-Linked GPOs and Domain Controller Placement

A GPO linked to a site affects all computers in the site without regard to the domain to which the computers belong (as long as all computers belong to the same Active Directory forest). Therefore, by linking a GPO to a site, that GPO can be applied to multiple domains within a forest. Site-linked GPOs are stored on domain controllers in the domain in which the GPO was created. Therefore, domain controllers for that domain must be accessible for site-linked GPOs to be applied correctly. If you implement site-linked policies, you must consider policy application when planning your network infrastructure. Either place a domain controller from the GPO's domain in the site to which the policy is linked or ensure that WAN connectivity provides accessibility to a domain controller in the GPO's domain.

When you link a GPO to a site, domain, or OU, you define the initial scope of the GPO. Select a GPO and click the Scope tab to identify the containers to which the GPO is linked. In the details pane of the GPMC, the GPO links are displayed in the first section of the Scope tab, as seen in Figure 6-6.

Figure 6-6   A GPO's links displayed on the Scope tab of the GPMC

The impact of the GPO's links is that the Group Policy client will download the GPO if either the computer or the user objects fall within the scope of the link. The GPO will be downloaded only if it is new or updated. The Group Policy client caches the GPO to make policy refresh more efficient.

Linking a GPO to Multiple OUs

You can link a GPO to more than one site, domain, or OU. It is common, for example, to apply configuration to computers in several OUs. You can define the configuration in a single GPO and link that GPO to each OU. If you later change settings in the GPO, your changes will apply to all OUs to which the GPO is linked.

Deleting or Disabling a GPO Link

After you have linked a GPO, the GPO link appears in the GPMC underneath this site, domain, or OU. The icon for the GPO link has a small shortcut arrow. When you right-click the GPO link, a context menu appears, as shown in Figure 6-7.

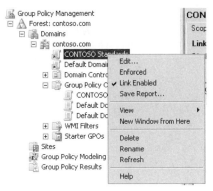

Figure 6-7   The context menu of a GPO link

You can delete a GPO link by choosing Delete from the context menu. Deleting a GPO link does not delete the GPO itself, which remains in that Group Policy Objects container. Deleting the link does change the scope of the GPO so that it no longer applies to computers and users within a site, domain, or OU to which it was previously linked.

You can also modify a GPO link by disabling it. Right-click the GPO link and deselect the Link Enabled option. Disabling the link also changes the scope of the GPO so that it no longer applies to computers and users within that container. However, the link remains so that it can be easily re-enabled.

GPO Inheritance and Precedence

A policy setting can be configured in more than one GPO, and GPOs can be in conflict with one another. For example, a policy setting can be enabled in one GPO, disabled in another GPO, and not configured in a third GPO. In this case, the *precedence* of the GPOs determines which policy setting the client applies. A GPO with higher precedence will prevail over a GPO with lower precedence. Precedence is shown as a number in the GPMC. The smaller the number—that is, the closer to 1—the higher the precedence, so a GPO with a precedence of 1 will prevail over other GPOs. Select the domain or OU and then click the Group Policy Inheritance tab to view the precedence of each GPO.

When a policy setting is enabled or disabled in a GPO with higher precedence, the configured setting takes effect. However, remember that policy settings are set to Not Configured by default. If a policy setting is not configured in a GPO with higher precedence, the policy setting (either enabled or disabled) in a GPO with lower precedence will take effect.

A site, domain, or OU can have more than one GPO linked to it. The link order of GPOs determines the precedence of GPOs in such a scenario. GPOs with higher-link order take precedence over GPOs with lower-link order. When you select an OU in the GPMC, the Linked Group Policy Objects tab shows the link order of GPOs linked to that OU.

The default behavior of Group Policy is that GPOs linked to a higher-level container are inherited by lower-level containers. When a computer starts up or a user logs on, the Group Policy client examines the location of the computer or user object in Active Directory and evaluates the GPOs with scopes that include the computer or user. Then the client-side extensions apply policy settings from these GPOs. Policies are applied sequentially, beginning with the policies linked to the site, followed by those linked to the domain, followed by those linked to OUs—from the top-level OU down to the OU in which the user or computer object exists. It is a layered application of settings, so a GPO that is applied later in the process, because it has higher precedence, will override settings applied earlier in the process. This default order of applying GPOs is illustrated in Figure 6-8.

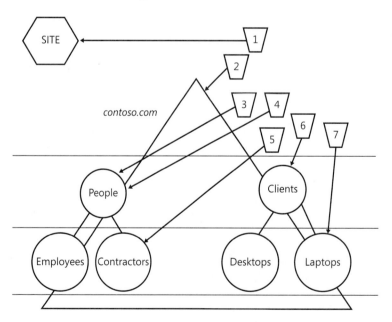

GPO processing order for the Contractors OU = 1, 2, 3, 4, 5
GPO processing order for the Laptops OU = 1, 2, 6, 7

Figure 6-8   Default processing of site, domain, and OU GPOs

Exam Tip Be certain to memorize the default domain policy processing order: site, domain, OU; remember that domain policy settings are applied after and, therefore, take precedence over settings in local GPOs.

This sequential application of GPOs creates an effect called *policy inheritance*. Policies are inherited, so the resultant set of group policies for a user or computer will be the cumulative effect of site, domain, and OU policies.

By default, inherited GPOs have lower precedence than GPOs linked directly to the container. In a practical example, you might configure a policy setting to disable the use of registry-editing tools for all users in the domain by configuring the policy setting in a GPO linked to the domain. That GPO, and its policy setting, will be inherited by all users within the domain. However, you probably want administrators to be able to use registry-editing tools, so you will link a GPO to the OU that contains administrators' accounts and configure the policy setting to allow the use of registry-editing tools. Because the GPO linked to the administrators' OU takes higher precedence than the inherited GPO, administrators will be able to use registry-editing tools.

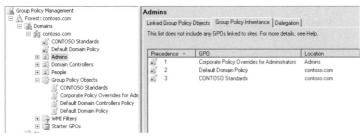

Figure 6-9   The Group Policy inheritance tab

Figure 6-9 shows this example. A policy setting that restricts registry-editing tools is defined in the CONTOSO Standards GPO, linked to the *contoso.com* domain. In the Corporate Policy Overrides For Administrators GPO, a policy setting specifically allows the use of registry-editing tools. The administrator's GPO is linked to the Admins OU. When you select an OU such as the Admins OU, the details pane of the GPMC displays a Group Policy Inheritance tab that reveals GPO precedence for that OU. You can see that the Corporate Policy Overrides For Administrators GPO has precedence. Any setting in that GPO that is in conflict with a setting in CONTOSO Standards will be applied from the administrators GPO. Therefore, users in the Admins OU will be able to use registry editing tools, although users elsewhere in the domain will not be able to. As you can see from this simple example, the default order of precedence ensures that the policy that is closest to the user or computer prevails.

Precedence of Multiple Linked Group Policy Objects

An OU, domain, or site can have more than one GPO linked to it. In the event of multiple Group Policy objects, the objects' *link order* determines their precedence. In Figure 6-10, two GPOs are linked to the People OU. The object higher on the list, with a link order of 1, has the highest precedence. Therefore, settings that are enabled or disabled in the Power User Configuration GPO will have precedence over these same settings in the Standard User Configuration GPO.

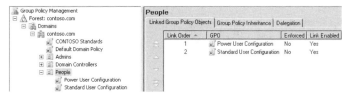

Figure 6-10   GPO link order

Blocking Inheritance

A domain or OU can be configured to prevent the inheritance of policy settings. To block inheritance, right-click the domain or OU in the GPME and choose Block Inheritance.

The Block Inheritance option is a property of a domain or OU, so it blocks *all* Group Policy settings from GPOs linked to parents in the Group Policy hierarchy. When you block inheritance on an OU, for example, GPO application begins with any GPOs linked directly to that OU–GPOs linked to higher-level OUs, the domain, or the site will not apply.

The Block Inheritance option should be used sparingly, if ever. Blocking inheritance makes it more difficult to evaluate Group Policy precedence and inheritance. In the section, "Using Security Filtering to Modify GPO Scope," you will learn how to scope a GPO so that it applies to only a subset of objects or so that it is prevented from applying to a subset of objects. With security group filtering, you can carefully scope a GPO so that it applies to only the correct users and computers in the first place, making it unnecessary to use the Block Inheritance option.

Enforcing a GPO Link

In addition, a GPO link can be set to Enforced. To do this, right-click a GPO link and choose Enforced from the context menu shown in Figure 6-7. When a GPO link is set to Enforced, the GPO takes the highest level of precedence; policy settings in that GPO will prevail over any conflicting policy settings in other GPOs. In addition, a link that is enforced will apply to child containers even when those containers are set to Block Inheritance. The Enforced option causes the policy to apply to all objects within its scope. Enforced will cause policies to override any conflicting policies and will apply regardless of whether a Block Inheritance option is set.

In Figure 6-11, Block Policy Inheritance has been applied to the Clients OU. As a result, GPO 1, which is applied to the site, is blocked and does not apply to the Clients OU. However, GPO 2, linked to the domain with the Enforced option, does apply. In fact, it is applied last in the processing order, meaning that its settings will override those of GPOs 6 and 7.

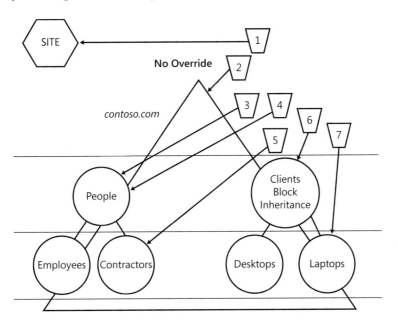

GPO processing order for the Contractors OU = 1, 3, 4, 5, 2
GPO processing order for the Laptops OU = 6, 7, 2

Figure 6-11 Policy processing with Block Inheritance and Enforced options

When you configure a GPO that defines configuration mandated by your corporate IT security and usage policies, you want to ensure that those settings are not overridden by other GPOs. You can do this by enforcing the link of the GPO. Figure 6-12 shows just this scenario. Configuration mandated by corporate policies is deployed in the CONTOSO Corporate IT Security & Usage GPO, which is linked with an enforced link to the *contoso.com* domain. The icon for the GPO link has a padlock on it—the visual indicator of an enforced link. On the People OU, the Group Policy Inheritance tab shows that the GPO takes precedence even over the GPOs linked to the People OU itself.

To facilitate evaluation of GPO precedence, you can simply select an OU (or domain) and click the Group Policy Inheritance tab. This tab will display the resulting precedence of GPOs, accounting for GPO link, link order, inheritance blocking, and link enforcement. This tab does not account for policies that are linked to a site, nor does it account for GPO security or WMI filtering.

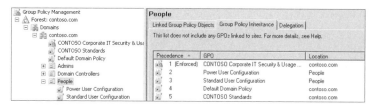

Figure 6-12   The precedence of the GPO with an enforced link

Exam Tip   Although it is recommended to use the Block Inheritance and Enforced options spar-ingly in your Group Policy infrastructure, the 70-640 exam will expect you to understand the effect of both options.

Using Security Filtering to Modify GPO Scope

By now, you've learned that you can link a GPO to a site, domain, or OU. However, you might need to apply GPOs only to certain groups of users or computers rather than to all users or computers within the scope of the GPO. Although you cannot directly link a GPO to a security group, there is a way to apply GPOs to specific security groups. The policies in a GPO apply only to users who have Allow Read and Allow Apply Group Policy permissions to the GPO.

Each GPO has an access control list (ACL) that defines permissions to the GPO. Two permis-sions, Allow Read and Allow Apply Group Policy are required for a GPO to apply to a user or computer. If a GPO is scoped to a computer, for example, by its link to the computer's OU, but the computer does not have Read and Apply Group Policy permissions, it will not download and apply the GPO. Therefore, by setting the appropriate permissions for security groups, you can filter a GPO so that its settings apply only to the computers and users you specify.

By default, Authenticated Users are given the Allow Apply Group Policy permission on each new GPO. This means that by default, *all* users and computers are affected by the GPOs set for their domain, site, or OU regardless of the other groups in which they might be members. Therefore, there are two ways of filtering GPO scope:

- Remove the Apply Group Policy permission (currently set to Allow) for the Authenti-cated Users group but do not set this permission to Deny. Then determine the groups to which the GPO should be applied and set the Read and Apply Group Policy permissions for these groups to Allow.

- Determine the groups to which the GPO should not be applied and set the Apply Group Policy permission for these groups to Deny. If you deny the Apply Group Policy permission to a GPO, the user or computer will not apply settings in the GPO, even if the user or computer is a member of another group that is allowed the Apply Group Policy Permission.

Filtering a GPO to Apply to Specific Groups

To apply a GPO to a specific security group, select the GPO in the Group Policy Objects container in the GPMC. In the Security Filtering section, select the Authenticated Users group and click Remove. Click OK to confirm the change and then click Add. Select the group to which you want the policy to apply and click OK. The result will look similar to Figure 6-13—the Authenticated Users group is not listed, and the specific group to which the policy should apply is listed.

NOTE Use global security groups to filter GPOs

GPOs can be filtered only with global security groups—not with domain local security groups.

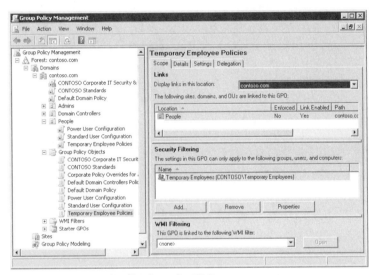

Figure 6-13 Security filtering of a GPO

Filtering a GPO to Exclude Specific Groups

Unfortunately, the Scope tab of a GPO does not allow you to exclude specific groups. To exclude a group—that is, to deny the Apply Group Policy permission—you must click the Delegation tab. Click the Advanced button, and the Security Settings dialog box appears. Click the Add button in the Security Settings dialog box, select the group you want to exclude from the GPO, and click OK. The group you selected is given the Allow Read permission by default. Deselect that permission check box and select the Deny Apply Group Policy. Figure 6-14 shows an example that denies the Help Desk group the Apply Group Policy permission and, therefore, excludes the group from the scope of the GPO.

When you click the OK button in the Security Settings dialog box, you will be warned that Deny permissions override other permissions. Because of this, it is recommended that you use

Deny permissions sparingly. Microsoft Windows reminds you of this best practice with the warning message and by the far more laborious process to exclude groups with the Deny Apply Group Policy permission than to include groups in the Security Filtering section of the Scope tab.

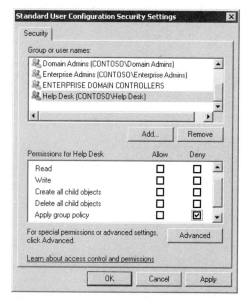

Figure 6-14   Excluding a group from the scope of a GPO with the Deny Apply Group Policy permission

---

NOTE   Deny permissions are not exposed on the Scope tab

Unfortunately, when you exclude a group, the exclusion is not shown in the Security Filtering section of the Scope tab. This is yet one more reason to use Deny permissions sparingly.

WMI Filters

Windows Management Instrumentation (WMI) is a management infrastructure technology that enables administrators to monitor and control managed objects in the network. A WMI query is capable of filtering systems based on characteristics, including RAM, processor speed, disk capacity, IP address, operating system version and service pack level, installed applications, and printer properties. Because WMI exposes almost every property of every object within a computer, the list of attributes that can be used in a WMI query is virtually unlimited. WMI queries are written using WMI query language (WQL).

You can use a WMI query to create a WMI filter, with which a GPO can be filtered. A good way to understand the purpose of a WMI filter, both for the certification exams and for real-world implementation, is through examples. Group Policy can be used to deploy software applications and service packs—a capability that is discussed in Chapter 7. You might create a GPO to deploy an application and then use a WMI filter to specify that the policy should apply only to computers with a certain operating system and service pack, Windows XP SP3, for example. The WMI query to identify such systems is:

```
Select * FROM Win32_OperatingSystem WHERE Caption="Microsoft
Windows XP Professional" AND CSDVersion="Service Pack 3"
```

When the Group Policy client evaluates GPOs it has downloaded to determine which should be handed off to the CSEs for processing, it performs the query against the local system. If the system meets the criteria of the query, the query result is a logical *True*, and the CSEs will process the GPO.

WMI exposes *namespaces*, within which are classes that can be queried. Many useful classes, including *Win32_Operating System*, are found in a class called *root\CIMv2*.

To create a WMI filter, right-click the WMI Filters node in the GPME and choose New. Type a name and description for the filter, and then click the Add button. In the Namespace box, type the namespace for your query. In the Query box, enter the query. Then click OK.

To filter a GPO with a WMI filter, click the Scope tab of a GPO, click the WMI drop-down list, and select the WMI filter. A GPO can be filtered by only one WMI filter, but that WMI filter can be a complex query, using multiple criteria. A single WMI filter can be linked to, and thereby used to filter, one or more GPOs. The General tab of a WMI filter, shown in Figure 6-15, displays the GPOs that use the WMI filter.

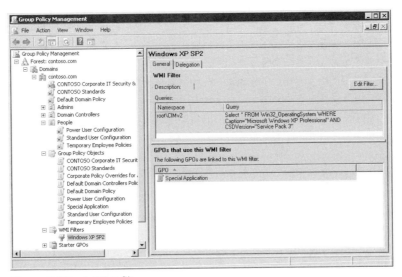

Figure 6-15 A WMI filter

There are three significant caveats regarding WMI filters. First, the WQL syntax of WMI queries can be challenging to master. You can often find examples on the Internet when you search using the keywords *WMI filter* and *WMI query* along with a description of the query you want to create.

MORE INFO WMI filter examples

You can find examples of WMI filters at *http://technet2.microsoft.com/windowsserver/en/library /a16cffa4-83b3-430b-b826-9bf81c0d39a71033.mspx?mfr=true*. You can also refer to the Windows Management Instrumentation (WMI) software development kit (SDK), located at *http:// msdn2.microsoft.com/en-us/library/aa394582.aspx*.

Second, WMI filters are expensive in terms of Group Policy processing performance. Because the Group Policy client must perform the WMI query at each policy processing interval, there is a slight impact on system performance every 90–120 minutes. With the performance of today's computers, the impact might not be noticeable, but you should certainly test the effects of a WMI filter prior to deploying it widely in your production environment.

Third, WMI filters are not processed by computers running Windows 2000. If a GPO is filtered with a WMI filter, a Windows 2000 system ignores the filter and processes the GPO as if the results of the filter were *True*.

Exam Tip   Although it is unlikely that you will be asked to recognize WQL queries on the 70-640 exam, you should be familiar with the basic functionality of WMI queries as discussed in this section. Be certain to remember that Windows 2000 systems will apply settings in GPOs with WMI filters because Windows 2000 ignores WMI filters during policy processing.

Enabling or Disabling GPOs and GPO Nodes

You can prevent the settings in the Computer Configuration or User Configuration nodes from being processed during policy refresh by changing GPO Status. On the Details tab of a GPO, shown in Figure 6-16, click the GPO Status drop-down list and choose one of the following:

- **Enabled**   Both computer configuration settings and user configuration settings will be processed by CSEs during policy refresh.
- **All Settings Disabled**   CSEs will not process the GPO to policy refresh.
- **Computer Configuration Settings Disabled**   During computer policy refresh, computer configuration settings in the GPO will be applied. The GPO will not be processed during user policy refresh.
- **User Configuration Settings Disabled**   During user policy refresh, user configuration settings in the GPO will be applied. The GPO will not be processed during computer policy refresh.

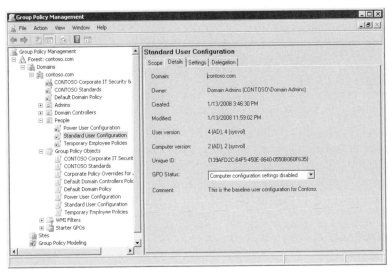

Figure 6-16   The Details tab of a GPO

You can configure GPO Status to optimize policy processing. If a GPO contains only user set-tings, for example, setting GPO Status to disable computer settings will prevent the Group Pol-icy client from attempting to process the GPO during computer policy refresh. Because the GPO contains no computer settings, there is no need to process the GPO, and you can save a few cycles of the processor.

NOTE   Use disabled GPOs for disaster recovery

You can define a configuration that should take effect in case of an emergency, security incident, or other disasters in a GPO and link the GPO so that it is scoped to appropriate users and computers. Then, disable the GPO. In the event that you require the configuration to be deployed, simply enable the GPO.

Targeting Preferences

Preferences, which are new to Windows Server 2008, have a built-in scoping mechanism called *item-level targeting*. You can have multiple preference items in a single GPO, and each preference item can be targeted or filtered. So, for example, you could have a single GPO with a preference that specifies folder options for engineers and another item that specifies folder options for sales people. You can target the items by using a security group or OU. There are over a dozen other criteria that can be used, including hardware and network characteristics, date and time, LDAP queries, and more.

NOTE   Preferences can target within a GPO

What's new about preferences is that you can target multiple preferences items within a single GPO instead of requiring multiple GPOs. With traditional policies, you often need multiple GPOs filtered to individual groups to apply variations of settings.

Like WMI filters, item-level targeting of preferences requires the CSE to perform a query to determine whether to apply the settings in a preferences item. You must be aware of the potential performance impact of item-level targeting, particularly if you use options such as LDAP queries, which require processing time and a response from a domain controller to process. As you design your Group Policy infrastructure, balance the configuration management benefits of item-level targeting against the performance impact you discover during testing in a lab.

Group Policy Processing

Now that you have learned more about the concepts, components, and scoping of Group Policy, you are ready to examine Group Policy processing closely. As you read this section, keep in mind that Group Policy is all about applying configurations defined by GPOs, that GPOs are applied in an order (site, domain, and OU), and that GPOs applied later in the order have higher precedence; their settings, when applied, will override settings applied earlier. The following sequence details the process through which settings in a domain-based GPO are applied to affect a computer or user:

1. The computer starts, and the network starts. Remote Procedure Call System Service (RPCSS) and Multiple Universal Naming Convention Provider (MUP) are started. The Group Policy client is started.

2. The Group Policy client obtains an ordered list of GPOs scoped to the computer.

   The order of the list determines the order of GPO processing, which is, by default, local, site, domain, and OU:

   a. Local GPOs. Each computer running Windows Server 2003, Windows XP, and Windows 2000 has exactly one GPO stored locally. Windows Vista and Windows Server 2008 have multiple local GPOs. The precedence of local GPOs is discussed in the "Local GPOs" section in Lesson 1.

   b. Site GPOs. Any GPOs that have been linked to the site are added to the ordered list next. When multiple GPOs are linked to a site (or domain or OU), the *link order*, configured on the Scope tab, determines the order in which they are added to the list. The GPO that is highest on the list, with the number closest to 1, has the highest precedence, and is added to the list last. It will, therefore, be applied last, and its settings will override those of GPOs applied earlier.

   c. Domain GPOs. Multiple domain-linked GPOs are added as specified by the link order.

NOTE Domain-linked policies are not inherited by child domains

Policies from a parent domain are not inherited by a child domain. Each domain maintains distinct policy links. However, computers in several domains might be within the scope of a GPO linked to a site.

---

    d. OU GPOs. GPOs linked to the OU highest in the Active Directory hierarchy are added to the ordered list, followed by GPOs linked to its child OU, and so on. Finally, the GPOs linked to the OU that contains the computer are added. If several group policies are linked to an OU, they are added in the order specified by the link order.

    e. Enforced GPOs. These are added at the end of the ordered list, so their settings will be applied at the end of the process and will, therefore, override settings of GPOs earlier in the list and in the process. As a point of trivia, enforced GPOs are added to the list in reverse order: OU, domain, and then site. This is relevant when you apply corporate security policies in a domain-linked, enforced GPO. That GPO will be at the end of the ordered list and will be applied last, so its settings will take precedence.

3. The GPOs are processed synchronously in the order specified by the ordered list. This means that settings in the local GPOs are processed first, followed by GPOs linked to the site, the domain, and the OUs containing the user or computer. GPOs linked to the OU of which the computer or user is a direct member are processed last, followed by enforced GPOs.

As each GPO is processed, the system determines whether its settings should be applied based on the GPO status for the computer node (enabled or disabled) and whether the computer has the Allow Group Policy permission. If a WMI filter is applied to the GPO, and if the computer is running Windows XP or later, it performs the WQL query specified in the filter.

4. If the GPO should be applied to the system, CSEs trigger to process the GPO settings. Policy settings in GPOs will overwrite policies of previously applied GPOs in the following ways:

    ❑ If a policy setting is configured (set to Enabled or Disabled) in a GPO linked to a parent container (OU, domain, or site), and the same policy setting is Not Configured in GPOs linked to its child container, the resultant set of policies for users and computers in the child container will include the parent's policy setting. If the child container is configured with the Block Inheritance option, the parent setting is not inherited unless the GPO link is configured with the Enforced option.

    ❑ If a policy setting is configured (set to Enabled or Disabled) for a parent container, and the same policy setting *is* configured for a child, the child container's setting

overrides the setting inherited from the parent. If the parent GPO link is configured with the Enforced option, the parent setting has precedence.

❑ If a policy setting of GPOs linked to parent containers is Not Configured, and the
child OU setting is also Not Configured, the resultant policy setting is the setting
that results from the processing of local GPOs. If the resultant setting of local
GPOs is also Not Configured, the resultant configuration is the Windows default
setting.

5. When the user logs on, steps 2, 3, and 4 are repeated for user settings. The client obtains
an ordered list of GPOs scoped to the user, examines each GPO synchronously, and
hands over GPOs that should be applied to the appropriate CSEs for processing. This
step is modified if User Loopback Group Policy Processing is enabled. Loopback policy
processing is discussed in the next section.

**NOTE   Policy settings in both the Computer Configuration and User Configuration
nodes**

Most policy settings are specific to either the User Configuration or Computer Configuration
node. A small handful of settings appear in both nodes. Although in most situations the setting in the Computer Configuration node will override the setting in the User Configuration
node, it is important to read the explanatory text accompanying the policy setting to understand the setting's effect and its application.

---

6. Every 90–120 minutes after computer startup, computer policy refresh occurs, and steps
2, 3, and 4 are repeated for computer settings.

7. Every 90–120 minutes after user logon, user policy refresh occurs, and steps 2, 3, and 4
are repeated for user settings.

NOTE   Settings might not take effect immediately

Although most settings are applied during a background policy refresh, some CSEs do not
apply the setting until the next startup or logon event. Newly added startup and logon script
policies, for example, will not run until the next computer startup or logon. Software installation, discussed in Chapter 7, will occur at the next startup if the software is assigned in computer settings. Changes to folder redirection policies will not take effect until the next logon.

Loopback Policy Processing

By default, a user's settings come from GPOs scoped to the user object in Active Directory.
Regardless of which computer the user logs on to, the resultant set of policies that determine
the user's environment will be the same. There are situations, however, when you might want
to configure a user differently, depending on the computer in use. For example, you might
want to lock down and standardize user desktops when users log on to computers in closely
managed environments such as conference rooms, reception areas, laboratories, classrooms,

and kiosks. Imagine a scenario in which you want to enforce a standard corporate appearance for the Windows desktop on all computers in conference rooms and other public areas of your office. How could you centrally manage this configuration, using Group Policy? Policy settings that configure desktop appearance are located in the User Configuration node of a GPO. Therefore, by default, the settings apply to users, regardless of which computer they log on to. The default policy processing does not give you a way to scope user settings to apply to computers, regardless of which user logs on. That's where loopback policy processing comes in.

Loopback policy processing alters the default algorithm used by the Group Policy client to obtain the ordered list of GPOs that should be applied to a user's configuration. Instead of user configuration being determined by the User Configuration node of GPOs that are scoped to the user object, user configuration can be determined by the User Configuration node policies of GPOs that are scoped to the *computer* object.

The User Group Policy Loopback Processing Mode policy, located in the Computer Configuration\Policies\Administrative Templates\System\Group Policy folder in Group Policy Management Editor, can be, like all policy settings, set to Not Configured, Enabled, or Disabled. When enabled, the policy can specify Replace or Merge mode.

- **Replace**   In this case, the GPO list for the user (obtained in step 5 in the "Group Policy Processing" section) is replaced in its entirety by the GPO list already obtained for the computer at computer startup (during step 2). The settings in the User Configuration policies of the computer's GPOs are applied to the user. Replace mode is useful in a situation such as a classroom, where users should receive a *standard configuration* rather than the configuration applied to those users in a less managed environment.

- **Merge**   In this case, the GPO list obtained for the computer at computer startup (step 2 in the "Group Policy Processing" section) is appended to the GPO list obtained for the user when logging on (step 5). Because the GPO list obtained for the computer is applied later, settings in GPOs on the computer's list have precedence if they conflict with settings in the user's list. This mode would be useful to apply *additional settings* to users' typical configurations. For example, you might allow a user to receive his or her typical configuration when logging on to a computer in a conference room or reception area but replace the wallpaper with a standard bitmap and disable the use of certain applications or devices.

Exam Tip   The 70-640 exam is likely to include several questions that test your knowledge of Group Policy scope. Sometimes, questions that seem to be addressing the technical details of a policy setting are, in fact, testing your ability to scope the setting to appropriate systems. When you encounter Group Policy questions, ask yourself, "Is this really about a specific policy setting, or is it about the scope of that setting?"

PRACTICE Configuring Group Policy Scope

In this practice, you will follow a scenario that builds upon the GPO you created and configured in Lesson 1. In each vignette, you will refine your application of Group Policy scoping. Before performing these exercises, complete the exercises in Lesson 1.

▶ **Exercise 1   Create a GPO with a Policy Setting That Takes Precedence over a Conflicting Setting**

Imagine you are an administrator of the *contoso.com* domain. The CONTOSO Standards GPO, linked to the domain, configures a policy setting that requires a ten-minute screen saver time-out. An engineer reports that a critical application that performs lengthy calculations crashes when the screens saver starts, and the engineer has asked you to prevent the setting from applying to the team of engineers that use the application every day.

1. Log on to SERVER01 as Administrator.
2. Open the Active Directory Users And Computers snap-in and create a first-level OU called People and a child OU called Engineers.
3. Open the GPMC.
4. Right-click the Engineers OU and choose Create A GPO In This Domain, And Link It Here.
5. Enter the name **Engineering Application Override** and click OK.
6. Expand the Engineers OU, right-click the GPO, and choose Edit.
7. Expand User Configuration\Policies\Administrative Templates\Control Panel\Display.
8. Double-click the Screen Saver Timeout policy setting.
9. Click Disabled, and then click OK.
10. Close the GPME.
11. In the GPMC, select the Engineers OU, and then click the Group Policy Inheritance tab.
12. Notice that the Engineering Application Override GPO has precedence over the CONTOSO Standards GPO.

    The setting you configured, which explicitly disables the screen saver, will override the setting in the CONTOSO Standards GPO.

▶ **Exercise 2   Configure the Enforced Option**

You want to ensure that all systems receive changes to Group Policy as quickly as possible. To do this, you want to enable the Always Wait For The Network Group Policy setting described in Lesson 1. You do not want any administrators to override the policy; it must be enforced for all systems.

1. In the GPMC, right-click the *contoso.com* domain and choose Create A GPO In This Domain, And Link It Here.
2. Enter the name **Enforced Domain Policies** and click OK.
3. Right-click the GPO and choose Edit.

4. Expand Computer Configuration\Policies\Administrative Templates\System\Logon.

5. Double-click the Always Wait For The Network At Computer Startup And Logon policy setting.

6. Select Enabled and click OK.

7. Close the GPME.

8. Right-click the Enforced Domain Policies GPO and choose Enforced.

9. Select the Engineers OU, and then click the Group Policy Inheritance tab.

   Note that your enforced domain GPO has precedence even over GPOs linked to the Engineers OU. Settings in a GPO such as Engineering Application Override cannot successfully override settings in an enforced GPO.

▶ **Exercise 3 Configure Security Filtering**

As time passes, you discover that a small number of users must be exempted from the screen saver timeout policy configured by the CONTOSO Standards GPO. You decide that it is no longer practical to use overriding settings. Instead, you will use security filtering to manage the scope of the GPO.

1. Open the Active Directory Users And Computers snap-in and create an OU called Groups. Within it, create a global security group named **GPO_CONTOSO Standards_Exceptions**.

2. In the GPMC, select the Group Policy Objects container.

3. Right-click the Engineering Application Override GPO and choose Delete. Click Yes to confirm your choice.

4. Select the CONTOSO Standards GPO in the Group Policy Objects container.

5. Click the Delegation tab.

6. Click the Advanced button.

7. In the Security Settings dialog box, click the Add button.

8. Type the name of the group and click OK.

9. In the permissions list, scroll down and select the Deny permission for Apply Group Policy. Then click OK.

10. Click Yes to confirm your choice.

11. Note the entry shown on the Delegation tab in the Allowed Permissions column for the GPO_CONTOSO Standards_Exceptions group.

12. Click the Scope tab and examine the Security Filtering section.

    The default security filtering of the new GPO is that the Authenticated Users group has the Allow Apply Group Policy permission, so all users and computers within the scope of the GPO link will apply the settings in the GPO. Now, you have configured a group with the Deny Apply Group Policy permission, which overrides the Allow permission. If any user requires exemption from the policies in the CONTOSO Standards GPO, you can simply add the computer to the group.

▶ **Exercise 4   Loopback Policy Processing**

Recently, a salesperson at Contoso, Ltd., turned on his computer to give a presentation to an important customer, and the desktop wallpaper was a picture that exhibited questionable taste on the part of the salesperson. The management of Contoso, Ltd., has asked you to ensure that the laptops used by salespeople will have no wallpaper. It is not necessary to manage the wallpaper of salespeople when they are logged on to desktop computers at the office. Because policy settings that manage wallpaper are user configuration settings, but you need to apply the settings to sales laptops, you must use loopback policy processing. In addition, the computer objects for sales laptops are scattered across several OUs, so you will use security filtering to apply the GPO to a group rather than to an OU of sales laptops.

1. Open the Active Directory Users And Computers snap-in and create a global security group called **Sales Laptops** in the Groups OU. Also create an OU called Clients for client computer objects.

2. In the GPMC, right-click the Group Policy Objects container and choose New.

3. In the Name box, type **Sales Laptop Configuration** and click OK.

4. Right-click the GPO and choose Edit.

5. Expand User Configuration\Policies\Administrative Templates\Desktop\Desktop.

6. Double-click the Desktop Wallpaper policy setting.

7. Click the Explain tab and review the explanatory text.

8. Click the Comment tab and type **Corporate standard wallpaper for sales laptops**.

9. Click the Settings tab.

10. Select Enabled.

11. In the Wallpaper Name box, type **c:\windows\web\Wallpaper\server.jpg**.

12. Click OK.

13. Expand Computer Configuration\Policies\Administrative Templates\System\Group Policy.

14. Double-click the User Group Policy Loopback Processing Mode policy setting.

15. Click Enabled and, in the Mode drop-down list, select Merge.

16. Click OK and close the GPME.

17. In the GPMC, select the Sales Laptop Configuration GPO in the Group Policy Objects container.

18. On the Scope tab, in the Security Filtering section, select the Authenticated Users group and click the Remove button. Click OK to confirm your choice.

19. Click the Add button in the Security Filtering section.

20. Type the group name, **Sales Laptops**, and click OK.

21. Right-click the Clients OU and choose Link An Existing GPO.

22. Select Sales Laptop Configuration and click OK.

    You have now filtered a GPO so that it applies only to objects in the Sales Laptops group. You can add computer objects for sales laptops as members of the group, and those laptops will be within the scope of the GPO. The GPO configures the laptops to perform loopback policy processing in Merge mode. When a user logs on to one of the laptops, user configuration settings scoped to the user are applied and then user configuration settings in GPOs scoped to the computer are applied, including the Sales Laptop Configuration GPO.

Lesson Summary

- The initial scope of the GPO is established by GPO links. A GPO can be linked to one or more sites, domains, or OUs. The scope of the GPO can be further refined using security filtering or WMI filters.

- CSEs apply GPOs in the following order: local GPOs, GPOs linked to the site in which a user or computer logs on, GPOs linked to the user or computer domain, and then GPOs linked to OUs. The layered application of policy settings creates the effect of policy inheritance.

- Policy inheritance can be blocked by configuring the Block Inheritance option on a domain or OU.

- A GPO link can be set to Enforced. The settings in an enforced GPO are applied to computers and users within the scope of the GPO, even if the Block Inheritance option is set. Additionally, settings in an enforced GPO take precedence, so they will override conflicting settings.

- You can use security filtering to specify the groups to which a GPO will apply or the groups that will be exempted from the GPO. Only global security groups can be used to filter GPOs.

- Under normal policy processing, during user policy refresh (at logon and every 90–120 minutes thereafter), the system applies user configuration policy settings from GPOs scoped to the logged-on user.

- Loopback policy processing causes the system to change the way it applies GPOs during user policy refresh. In Merge mode, after applying settings from GPOs scoped to the logged on user, the system applies policy settings from GPOs scoped to the computer. These settings take precedence over conflicting settings from user GPOs. In loopback processing Replace mode, user configuration settings from GPOs scoped to the logged-on user are not applied. Instead, only user configuration settings from GPOs scoped to the computer are applied.

Lesson Review

You can use the following questions to test your knowledge of the information in Lesson 2, "Managing Group Policy Scope." The questions are also available on the companion CD if you prefer to review them in electronic form.

NOTE   Answers

Answers to these questions and explanations of why each answer choice is right or wrong are located in the "Answers" section at the end of the book.

---

1. You want to deploy a GPO named Northwind Lockdown that applies configuration to all users at Northwind Traders. However, you want to ensure that the settings do not apply to members of the Domain Admins group. How can you achieve this goal? (Choose all that apply.)

   A. Link the Northwind Lockdown GPO to the domain, and then right-click the domain and choose Block Inheritance.

   B. Link the Northwind Lockdown GPO to the domain, right-click the OU that contains the user accounts of all users in the Domain Admins group, and choose Block Inheritance.

   C. Link the Northwind Lockdown GPO to the domain, and then assign the Domain Admins group the Deny Apply Group Policy permission.

   D. Link the Northwind Lockdown GPO to the domain, and then configure security filtering so that the GPO applies to Domain Users.

2. You want to create a standard lockdown desktop experience for users when they log on to computers in your company's conference and training rooms. You have created a GPO called Public Computers Configuration with desktop restrictions defined in the User Configuration node. What additional steps must you take? (Choose all that apply. Each correct answer is a part of the solution.)

   A. Enable the User Group Policy Loopback Processing Mode policy setting.

   B. Link the GPO to the OU containing user accounts.

   C. Select the Block Inheritance option on the OU containing conference and training room computers.

   D. Link the GPO to the OU containing conference and training room computers.

Lesson 3: Supporting Group Policy

Group Policy application can be complex to analyze and understand, with the interaction of multiple settings in multiple GPOs scoped using a variety of methods. You must be equipped to effectively evaluate and troubleshoot your Group Policy implementation, to identify potential problems before they arise, and to solve unforeseen challenges. Microsoft Windows provides two tools that are indispensible for supporting Group Policy: Resultant Set of Policy (RSOP) and the Group Policy Operational Logs. In this lesson, you will explore the use of these tools in both proactive and reactive troubleshooting and support scenarios.

After this lesson, you will be able to:

- Analyze the set of GPOs and policy settings that have been applied to a user or computer
- Proactively model the impact of Group Policy or Active Directory changes on resultant set of policy
- Locate the event logs containing Group-Policy related events

Estimated lesson time: 30 minutes

Resultant Set of Policy

In Lesson 2, you learned that a user or computer can be within the scope of multiple GPOs. Group Policy inheritance, filters, and exceptions are complex, and it's often difficult to determine just which policy settings will apply. *Resultant Set of Policy (RSoP)* is the net effect of GPOs applied to a user or computer, taking into account GPO links, exceptions such as Enforced and Block Inheritance, and the application of security and WMI filters. RSoP is also a collection of tools that help you evaluate, model, and troubleshoot the application Group Policy settings. RSoP can query a local or remote computer and report back the exact settings that were applied to the computer and to any user who has logged on to the computer. RSoP can also model the policy settings that are anticipated to be applied to a user or computer under a variety of scenarios, including moving the object between OUs or sites or changing the object's group membership. With these capabilities, RSoP can help you manage and troubleshoot conflicting policies.

Windows Server 2008 provides the following tools for performing RSoP analysis:

- The Group Policy Results Wizard
- The Group Policy Modeling Wizard
- *Gpresult.exe*

Generating RSoP Reports with the Group Policy Results Wizard

To help you analyze the cumulative effect of GPOs and policy settings on a user or computer in your organization, the Group Policy Management console includes the Group Policy Results Wizard. If you want to understand exactly which policy settings have applied to a user or computer and why, the Group Policy Results Wizard is the tool to use.

The Group Policy Results Wizard is able to reach into the WMI provider on a local or remote computer running Window Vista, Windows XP, Windows Server 2003, and Windows Server 2008. The WMI provider can report everything there is to know about the way Group Policy was applied to the system. It knows when processing occurred, which GPOs were applied, which GPOs were not applied and why, errors that were encountered, the exact policy settings that took precedence, and their source GPO.

There are several requirements for running the Group Policy Results Wizard:

- You must have administrative credentials on the target computer.
- The target computer must be running Windows XP or later. The Group Policy Results Wizard cannot access Windows 2000 systems.
- You must be able to access WMI on the target computer. That means that it must be powered on, connected to the network, and accessible through ports 135 and 445.

NOTE Enable remote administration of client computers

Performing RSoP analysis by using Group Policy Results Wizard is just one example of remote administration. Windows XP SP2, Windows Vista, and Windows Server 2008 include a firewall that prevents unsolicited inbound connections even from members of the Administrators group. Group Policy provides a simple way to enable remote administration. In the Computer Configuration\Policies\Administrative Templates\Network\Network Connections\Windows Firewall\Domain Profile folder, you will find a policy setting named Windows Firewall: Allow Inbound Remote Administration Exception. When you enable this policy setting, you can specify the IP addresses or subnets from which inbound remote administration packets will be accepted. As with all policy settings, review the explanatory text on the Explain tab and test the effect of the policy in a lab environment before deploying it in production.

- The WMI service must be started on the target computer.
- If you want to analyze RSoP for a user, that user must have logged on at least once to the computer. It is not necessary for the user to be currently logged on.

After you have ensured that the requirements are met, you are ready to run an RSoP analysis. Right-click Group Policy Results in the GPMC and choose Group Policy Results Wizard. The wizard prompts you to select a computer. It then connects to the WMI provider on that computer and provides a list of users that have logged on to it. You can then select one of the users or opt to skip RSoP analysis for user configuration policies.

The wizard produces a detailed RSoP report in a dynamic HTML format. If Internet Explorer ESC is enabled, you will be prompted to allow the console to display the dynamic content. Each section of the report can be expanded or collapsed by clicking the Show or Hide link or by double-clicking the heading of the section. The report is displayed on three tabs:

- **Summary**   The Summary tab displays the status of Group Policy processing at the last refresh. You can identify information that was collected about the system, the GPOs that were applied and denied, security group membership that might have affected GPOs filtered with security groups, WMI filters that were analyzed, and the status of CSEs.
- **Settings**   The Settings tab displays the resultant set of policy settings applied to the computer or user. This tab shows you exactly what has happened to the user through the effects of your Group Policy implementation. A tremendous amount of information can be gleaned from the Settings tab, but some data isn't reported, such as IPSec, wireless, and disk quota policy settings.
- **Policy Events**   The Policy Events tab displays Group Policy events from the event logs of the target computer.

After you have generated an RSoP report with the Group Policy Results Wizard, you can right-click the report to rerun the query, print the report, or save the report as either an XML file or an HTML file that maintains the dynamic expanding and collapsing sections. Either file type can be opened with Internet Explorer, so the RSoP report is portable outside the GPMC. If you right-click the node of the report itself, underneath the Group Policy Results folder in the console tree, you can switch to Advanced View. In Advanced View, RSoP is displayed using the RSoP snap-in, which exposes all applied settings, including IPSec, wireless, and disk quota policies.

Generating RSoP Reports with *Gpresult.exe*

The *Gpresult.exe* command is the command-line version of the Group Policy Results Wizard. *Gpresult* taps into the same WMI provider as the wizard, produces the same information, and, in fact, enables you to create the same graphical reports. *Gpresult* runs on Windows Vista, Windows XP, Windows Server 2003, and Windows Server 2008. Windows 2000 includes a *Gpresult.exe* command, which produces a limited report of Group Policy processing but is not as sophisticated as the command included in later versions of Windows.

When you run the *Gpresult* command, you are likely to use the following options:

- **/s *computername***   Specifies the name or IP address of a remote system. If you use a dot (.) as the computer name, or do not include the /s option, the RSoP analysis is performed on the local computer.
- **/scope [user | computer]**   Displays RSoP analysis for user or computer settings. If you omit the /scope option, RSoP analysis includes both user and computer settings.
- **/user *username***   Specifies the name of the user for which RSoP data is to be displayed.
- **/r**   Displays a summary of RSoP data.

- **/v** Displays verbose RSoP data that presents the most meaningful information.
- **/z** Displays super verbose data, including the details of all policy settings applied to the system. Often, this is more information than you will require for typical Group Policy troubleshooting.
- **/u** *domain\user* **/p** *password* Provides credentials that are in the Administrators group of a remote system. Without these credentials, *Gpresult* runs using the credentials with which you are logged on.
- **[/x | /h]** *filename* Saves the reports in XML or HTML format, respectively. These options are available in Windows Vista SP1 and Windows Server 2008.

Quick Check

- You want to perform RSoP analysis on a remote system. Which two tools can you use?

Quick Check Answer

- The Group Policy Results Wizard and *Gpupdate.exe* can be used to perform your top analysis on a remote system.

Troubleshooting Group Policy with the Group Policy Results Wizard and *Gpresult.exe*

As an administrator, you will likely encounter scenarios that require Group Policy troubleshooting. You might need to diagnose and solve problems, including:

- GPOs are not applied at all.
- The resultant set of policies for a computer or user are not those that were expected.

The Group Policy Results Wizard and *Gpresult.exe* will often provide the most valuable insight into Group Policy processing and application problems. Remember that these tools examine the WMI RSoP provider to report exactly what happened on a system. Examining the RSoP report will often point you to GPOs that are scoped incorrectly or policy processing errors that prevented the application of GPOs settings.

Performing What-If Analyses with the Group Policy Modeling Wizard

If you move a computer or user between sites, domains, or OUs, or change its security group membership, the GPOs scoped to that user or computer will change and, therefore, the RSoP for the computer or user will be different. RSoP will also change if slow link or loopback processing occurs or if there is a change to a system characteristic that is targeted by a WMI filter.

Before you make any of these changes, you should evaluate the potential impact to the RSoP of the user or computer. The Group Policy Results Wizard can perform RSoP analysis only on what has actually happened. To predict the future and to perform what-if analyses, you can use the Group Policy Modeling Wizard.

Right-click the Group Policy Modeling node in the GPMC. Choose Group Policy Modeling Wizard and perform the steps in the wizard. Modeling is performed by conducting a simulation on a domain controller, so you are first asked to select a domain controller that is running Windows Server 2003 or later. You do not need to be logged on locally to the domain controller, but the modeling request will be performed on the domain controller. You are then asked to specify the settings for the simulation:

- Select a user or computer object to evaluate or specify the OU, site, or domain to evaluate.
- Choose whether slow link processing should be simulated.
- Specify to simulate loopback processing and, if so, choose Replace or Merge mode.
- Select a site to simulate.
- Select security groups for the user and for the computer.
- Choose which WMI filters to apply in the simulation of user and computer policy processing.

When you have specified the settings for the simulation, a report is produced that is very similar to the Group Policy Results report discussed earlier. The Summary tab shows an overview of which GPOs will be processed, and the Settings tab details the policy settings that will be applied to the user or computer. This report, too, can be saved by right-clicking it and choosing Save Report.

Examining Policy Event Logs

Windows Vista and Windows Server 2008 improve your ability to troubleshoot Group Policy not only with RSoP tools but also with improved logging of Group Policy events. In the System log, you will find high-level information about Group Policy, including errors created by the Group Policy client when it cannot connect to a domain controller or locate GPOs. The Application log captures events recorded by CSEs. A new log, called the Group Policy Operational Log, provides detailed information about Group Policy processing. To find these logs, open the Event Viewer snap-in or console. The System and Application logs are in the Windows Logs node. The Group Policy Operational Log is found in Applications And Services Logs\Microsoft\Windows\GroupPolicy\Operational. This log will not be available until after you use the Group Policy Modeling Wizard initially.

PRACTICE Configuring Group Policy Scope

In this practice, you will follow a scenario that builds upon the GPOs you created and configured in Lesson 1 and Lesson 2. You will perform RSoP results and modeling analysis and examine policy-related events in the event logs. To perform these exercises, you must have completed the practices in Lesson 1 and Lesson 2.

▶ **Exercise 1   Use the Group Policy Results Wizard**

In this exercise, you will use the Group Policy Results Wizard to examine RSoP on SERVER01. You will confirm that the policies you created in Lesson 1 and Lesson 2 have applied.

1. Log on to SERVER01 as Administrator.
2. Open a command prompt and type **gpupdate.exe /force /boot** to initiate a Group Policy refresh. Wait for the process host to reboot. Make a note of the current system time; you will need to know the time of the refresh in Exercise 3, "View Policy Events."
3. Log on to SERVER01 as Administrator and open the Group Policy Management console.
4. Expand Forest.
5. Right-click Group Policy Results and choose Group Policy Results Wizard.
6. Click Next.
7. On the Computer Selection page, select This Computer and click Next.
8. On the User Selection page, select Display Policy Settings For, select Select A Specific User, and select CONTOSO\Administrator. Then click Next.
9. On the Summary Of Selections page, review your settings and click Next.
10. Click Finish.

    The RSoP report appears in the details pane of the console.
11. On the Summary tab, click the Show All link at the top of the report.
12. Review the Group Policy Summary results. For both user and computer configuration, identify the time of the last policy refresh and the list of allowed and denied GPOs. Identify the components that were used to process policy settings.
13. Click the Settings tab and click the Show All link at the top of the page. Review the settings that were applied during user and computer policy application and identify the GPO from which the settings were obtained.
14. Click the Policy Events tab and locate the event that logs the policy refresh you triggered with the *Gpupdate.exe* command in step 2.
15. Click the Summary tab, right-click the page, and choose Save Report. Save the report as an HTML file to your Documents folder with a name of your choice.
16. Open the saved RSoP report from your Documents folder.

▶ **Exercise 2   Use the *Gpresult.exe* Command**

In this exercise, you will perform RSoP analysis from the command line, using *Gpresult.exe*.

1. Open a command prompt.
2. Type **gpresult /r** and press Enter.

   RSoP summary results are displayed. The information is very similar to the Summary tab of the RSoP report produced by the Group Policy Results Wizard.

3. Type **gpresult /v** and press Enter.

   A more detailed RSoP report is produced. Notice many of the Group Policy settings applied by the client are listed in this report.

4. Type **gpresult /z** and press Enter.

   The most detailed RSoP report is produced.

5. Type **gpresult /h:"%userprofile%\Documents\RSOP.html"** and press Enter.

   An RSoP report is saved as an HTML file to your Documents folder.

6. Open the saved RSoP report from your documents folder. Compare the report, its information, and its formatting to the RSoP report you saved in the previous exercise.

▶ **Exercise 3   View Policy Events**

As a client performs a policy refresh, Group Policy components log entries to the Windows event logs. In this exercise, you will locate and examine Group Policy–related events.

1. Open the Event Viewer console from the Administrative Tools folder.

2. Expand Windows Logs\System.

3. Locate events with GroupPolicy as the Source. You can even click the Filter Current Log link in the Actions pane and then select GroupPolicy in the Event Sources drop-down list.

4. Review the information associated with GroupPolicy events.

5. Click the Application node in the console tree underneath Windows Logs.

6. Sort the Application log by the Source column.

7. Review the logs by Source and identify the Group Policy events that have been entered in this log.

   Which events are related to Group Policy application, and which are related to the activities you have been performing to manage Group Policy?

8. In the console tree, expand Applications And Services Logs\Microsoft\Windows \GroupPolicy\Operational.

9. Locate the first event related in the Group Policy refresh you initiated in Exercise 1, "Use the Group Policy Results Wizard," with the *Gpupdate.exe* command. Review that event and the events that followed it.

▶ **Exercise 4   Perform Group Policy Modeling**

In this exercise, you will use Group Policy modeling to evaluate the potential effect of your policy settings on users who log on to sales laptops.

1. Open the Active Directory Users And Computers snap-in.

2. Create a user account for Mike Danseglio in the People OU.

3. Create an OU in the domain called **Clients**.

4. Create a computer account in the Clients OU called **LAPTOP101**.

5.   Add LAPTOP101 and Domain Users to the Sales Laptops group.

It is an underdocumented fact that when you combine the loopback processing with security group filtering, the application of user settings during policy refresh uses the credentials of the computer to determine which GPOs to apply as part of the loopback processing, but the logged-on user must also have the Apply Group Policy permission for the GPO to be successfully applied.

6.   In the Group Policy Management console, expand Forest.

7.   Right-click Group Policy Modeling and choose Group Policy Modeling Wizard.

8.   Click Next.

9.   On the Domain Controller Selection page, click Next.

10.   On the User And Computer Selection page, in the User Information section, click the User button, click Browse, and then select Mike Danseglio.

11.   In the Computer Information section, click the Computer button, click Browse, and select LAPTOP101 as the computer.

12.   Click Next.

13.   On the Advanced Simulation Options page, select the Loopback Processing check box and select Merge.

Even though the Sales Laptop Configuration GPO specifies the loopback processing, you must instruct the Group Policy Modeling Wizard to consider loopback processing in its simulation.

14.   Click Next.

15.   On the Alternate Active Directory Paths page, click Next.

16.   On the User Security Groups page, click Next.

17.   On the Computer Security Groups page, click Next.

18.   On the WMI Filters For Users page, click Next.

19.   On the WMI Filters For Computers page, click. Next.

20.   Review your settings on the Summary Of Selections page. Click Next, and then click Finish.

Lesson Summary

■   RSoP reports can be generated in the Windows interface by using the Group Policy Results Wizard, a component of the GPMC. RSoP reports reveal the actual results of policy processing at the last policy refresh.

■   RSoP reports can be generated from the command line, using *Gpresult.exe*. The */scope* option can be used to generate a report containing only user or computer settings. The */s* switch can be used to run *Gpresult.exe* against a remote system.

- The Group Policy Modeling Wizard enables you to simulate the application of Group Policy to evaluate the possible effect of changes to your Group Policy infrastructure or of moving users and computers between OUs and groups.
- Group Policy components create entries in the Windows event logs.

Lesson Review

You can use the following questions to test your knowledge of the information in Lesson 3, "Supporting Group Policy." The questions are also available on the companion CD if you prefer to review them in electronic form.

NOTE   Answers

Answers to these questions and explanations of why each answer choice is right or wrong are located in the "Answers" section at the end of the book.

---

1. A user calls the help desk at your organization and reports problems that you suspect might be related to changes that were recently made to Group Policy. You want to examine information regarding Group Policy processing on her system. Which tools can you use to gather this information remotely? (Choose all that apply.)

    A. Group Policy Modeling Wizard

    B. Group Policy Results Wizard

    C. *Gpupdate.exe*

    D. *Gpresult.exe*

    E. *Msconfig.exe*

2. You are the administrator at Contoso, Ltd. The *contoso.com* domain has five GPOs linked to the domain, one of which configures the password-protected screen saver and screen saver timeout required by corporate policy. Some users report that the screen saver is not launching after 10 minutes as expected. How do you know when the GPO was applied?

    A. Run *Gpresult.exe* for the users.

    B. Run *Gpresult.exe –computer*.

    C. Run *Gpresult –scope computer*.

    D. Run *Gpupdate.exe /Target:User*.

Chapter Review

To further practice and reinforce the skills you learned in this chapter, you can perform the following tasks:

■ Review the chapter summary.

■ Review the list of key terms introduced in this chapter.

■ Complete the case scenario. This scenario sets up a real-world situation involving the topics of this chapter and asks you to create a solution.

■ Complete the suggested practices.

■ Take a practice test.

Chapter Summary

■ Group Policy enables you to manage and change configuration centrally in an enterprise environment.

■ There are thousands of policy settings that can be configured within a GPO. By default, these policy settings are set to Not Configured. When a setting is enabled or disabled, it effects a change.

■ GPOs can be scoped to apply to users and computers with a variety of mechanisms, including links to sites, domains, and OUs. You can also filter GPOs with security groups and WMI filters.

■ You can support and troubleshoot Group Policy with tools, including RSoP tools and event logs.

Key Terms

Use these key terms to understand better the concepts covered in this chapter.

■ **Group Policy object (GPO)**   A collection of policy settings that determine configuration.

■ **policy setting or policy**   A configuration or change within a Group Policy object.

■ **Resultant Set of Policies (RSoP)**   The net effect of policy settings applied by Group Policy, accounting for GPO scope links, security filters, WMI filters, and options such as Block Inheritance and Enforced.

■ **scope**   In the context of Group Policy, the users or computers to which a GPO applies.

Case Scenario

In the following case scenario, you will apply what you've learned about implementing GPOs, managing Group Policy scope, and supporting Group Policy. You can find answers to these questions in the "Answers" section at the end of this book.

Case Scenario: Implementing Group Policy

You are an administrator at Northwind Traders. Your company is converting to a new enterprise resource planning (ERP) application and, in the process, will be conducting a large number of training sessions. You are responsible for configuring the computers in the training rooms, and you want to provide a single, consistent user experience for any student who logs on to the systems. For example, you want to implement a specific desktop wallpaper, prevent users from accessing registry editing tools, and disable the password-protected screen saver policy that is implemented by a GPO linked to the domain.

1. Are the policy settings that will configure the desired desktop environment found in the Computer Configuration or the User Configuration node of a GPO?
2. After you configure the settings, should you link the GPO to the OU containing user accounts or to the OU containing the training computers?
3. What must you do to ensure that the settings are applied when users log on to computers in the training rooms and not when they log on to their normal computers?
4. What setting must be configured to prevent policy settings that normally apply to users from being applied when the users log on to training computers?
5. What must you do to prevent the domain's screen saver policies from applying to training room computers?

Suggested Practices

To help you successfully master the exam objectives presented in this chapter, complete the following tasks.

Create and Apply Group Policy Objects (GPOs)

In this practice, you will configure the environment proposed in the case scenario. You will create an OU for training room computers and configure a standard user desktop experience for those computers, using loopback Group Policy processing. You will also prevent a domain policy from applying to training room computers. You will confirm your work by performing RSoP analysis.

- **Practice 1**   Create an OU called **Training Room**. Create several sample computer objects within the OU. Then, create a global security group called **Training Room Computers** and add the computer objects as members of the group.
- **Practice 2**   Create a GPO called **Training Room Configuration**. In the GPO, enable a policy that prevents access to registry editing tools and configure a standard desktop wallpaper. Both of these settings are user configuration settings in the Administrative Templates node. If you need assistance finding them, filter the settings with keywords. In the Computer Configuration node, locate the administrative templates setting that enables loopback policy processing. Enable this setting and choose to implement loopback processing in Replace mode.
- **Practice 3**   Link the Training Room Configuration GPO to the Training Room OU.
- **Practice 4**   In Lesson 1, you created the CONTOSO Standards GPO and configured it to implement screen saver policy settings. If you no longer have this GPO, perform Exercise 1 of Lesson 1. Using the Delegation tab of the GPO, add a permission that denies the Training Room Computers group the Apply Group Policy permission.
- **Practice 5**   Use the Group Policy Modeling Wizard to evaluate RSoP for a user logging on to one of the sample computers. Be sure in the wizard to select the option to simulate loopback processing and Replace mode.

Take a Practice Test

The practice tests on this book's companion CD offer many options. For example, you can test yourself on just one exam objective, or you can test yourself on all the 70-640 certification exam content. You can set up the test so that it closely simulates the experience of taking a certification exam, or you can set it up in study mode so that you can look at the correct answers and explanations after you answer each question.

MORE INFO   **Practice tests**

For details about all the practice test options available, see the "How to Use the Practice Tests" section in this book's introduction.

Chapter 7
Group Policy Settings

Group Policy can be used to manage the configuration of an enormous variety of components and features of Microsoft Windows. In the previous chapter, you learned how to configure a Group Policy infrastructure. In this chapter, you will learn to apply that infrastructure to manage several types of configuration related to security and software installation. You will also discover tools, such as the Security Configuration Wizard, that make it easier to determine which settings should be configured based on a server's roles. Finally, you will learn how to configure auditing of files and folders and of Active Directory Domain Services (AD DS) changes.

Exam objectives in this chapter:

- Creating and Maintaining Active Directory Objects
    - ❑ Create and apply Group Policy objects (GPOs).
    - ❑ Configure GPO templates.
    - ❑ Configure audit policy by using GPOs.

Lessons in this chapter:

- Lesson 1: Delegating the Support of Computers 291
- Lesson 2: Managing Security Settings 300
- Lesson 3: Managing Software with Group Policy Software Installation 322
- Lesson 4: Auditing. 335

Before You Begin

To complete the practices in this chapter, you must have created a domain controller named SERVER01 in a domain named *contoso.com*. See Chapter 1, "Installation," for detailed steps to perform this task.

Real World

Dan Holme

I am often brought in by clients to perform "sanity checks" on their Active Directory implementations. These sanity checks involve an examination of Group Policy settings and a discussion of how to take better advantage of Group Policy to manage change and configuration. It amazes me that a full eight years after the introduction of Group Policy, many organizations do not yet use its full capability, particularly in the area of security. Three of the four lessons in this chapter focus on the interaction between security configuration and Group Policy. Configuration such as the membership of the Administrators group and assignment of user rights, service startup modes, and audit policies can be effectively managed with Group Policy. What you will learn in this chapter will not only help you pass the 70-640 exam; it will also help you increase the manageability and security of your entire enterprise. This includes Active Directory itself. For the past eight years, I've constantly been asked, "How can I know what changes have been made by administrators in Active Directory?" Now, thanks to the new Directory Service Changes auditing in Windows Server 2008, you can simply check your security log. Even if you are already using policy to manage your security configuration, this new feature, along with the vastly improved Security Configuration Wizard, will surely take your security management capabilities to a higher level.

Lesson 1: Delegating the Support of Computers

Many enterprises have one or more members of personnel dedicated to supporting end users, a role often referred to as the *help desk, desktop support*, or just *support*. Help desk personnel are often asked to perform troubleshooting, configuration, or other support tasks on client computers, and these tasks often require administrative privileges. Therefore, the credentials used by support personnel must be at the level of a member of the local Administrators group on client computers, but desktop support personnel do not need the high level of privilege given to the Domain Admins group, so it is not recommended to place them in that group. Instead, configure client systems so that a group representing support personnel is added to the local Administrators group. Restricted groups policies enable you to do just that, and in this lesson, you will learn how to use restricted groups policies to add the help desk personnel to the local Administrators group of clients and, thereby, to delegate support of those computers to the help desk. The same approach can be used to delegate the administration of any scope of computers to the team responsible for those systems.

> **After this lesson, you will be able to:**
> - Delegate the administration of computers.
> - Use Group Policy to modify or enforce the membership of groups.
>
> **Estimated lesson time: 30 minutes**

Understanding Restricted Groups Policies

When you edit a Group Policy object (GPO) and expand the Computer Configuration node, the Policies node, the Windows Settings node, and the Security Settings node, you will find the Restricted Groups policy node, shown in Figure 7-1.

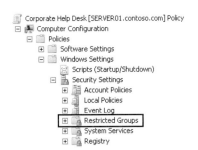

Figure 7-1   The Restricted Groups policy node of a Group Policy object

Restricted groups policy settings enable you to manage the membership of groups. There are two types of settings: This Group Is A Member Of (the Member Of setting) and Members Of This Group (the Members setting). Figure 7-2 shows examples.

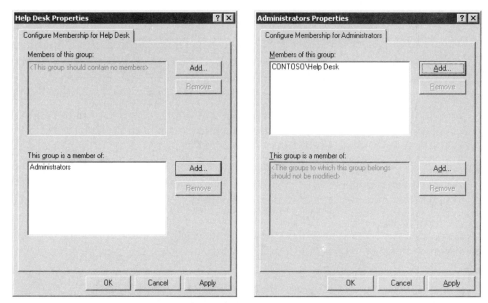

Figure 7-2   Member Of and Members restricted groups policies

It's very important to understand the difference between these two settings. A Member Of setting specifies that the group specified by the policy is a member of another group. On the left side of Figure 7-2, you can see a typical example: The CONTOSO\Help Desk group is a member of the Administrators group. When a computer applies this policy setting, it ensures that the Help Desk group from the domain becomes a member of its local Administrators group. If there is more than one GPO with restricted groups policies, each Member Of policy is applied. For example, if a GPO linked to the Clients organizational unit (OU) specifies CONTOSO\Help Desk as a member of Administrators, and a second GPO linked to the NYC OU (a sub-OU of the Clients OU) specifies CONTOSO\NYC Support as a member of Administrators, a computer in the NYC OU will add both the Help Desk and NYC Support groups to its Administrators group in addition to any existing members of the group such as Domain Admins. This example is illustrated in Figure 7-3. As you can see, restricted groups policies that use the Member Of setting are cumulative.

Figure 7-3   Results of restricted groups policies using the Member Of setting

The second type of restricted groups policy setting is the Members setting, which specifies the entire membership of the group specified by the policy. The right side of Figure 7-2 shows a typical example: the Administrators group's Members list is specified as CONTOSO\Help Desk. When a computer applies this policy setting, it ensures that the local Administrators group's membership consists *only* of CONTOSO\Help Desk. Any members not specified in the policy are removed, including Domain Admins. The Members setting is the authoritative policy—it defines the final list of members. If there is more than one GPO with restricted group policies, the GPO with the highest priority will prevail. For example, if a GPO linked to the Clients OU specifies the Administrators group membership as CONTOSO\Help Desk, and another GPO linked to the NYC OU specifies the Administrators group membership as CONTOSO\NYC Support, computers in the NYC OU will have only the NYC Support group in their Administrators group. This example is illustrated in Figure 7-4.

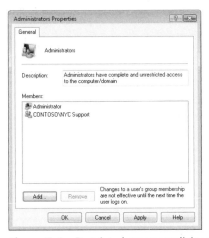

Figure 7-4   Restricted groups policies using the Members setting

In your enterprise, be careful to design and test your restricted groups policies to ensure that they achieve the desired result. Do not mix GPOs that use the Member Of and the Members settings—use one approach or the other.

Exam Tip   On the 70-640 exam, be able to identify the differences between restricted groups policies that use the Member Of setting and those that use the Members setting. Remember that Member Of settings are cumulative and that if GPOs use the Members setting, only the Members setting with the highest GPO processing priority will be applied, and its list of members will prevail.

Delegating Administration Using Restricted Groups Policies with the Member Of Setting

You can use restricted groups policies with the Member Of setting to manage the delegation of administrative privileges for computers by following these steps:

1. In Group Policy Management Editor, navigate to Computer Configuration\Policies\Windows Settings\Security Settings\Restricted Groups.
2. Right-click Restricted Groups and choose Add Group.
3. Click the Browse button and, in the Select Groups dialog box, type the name of the group you want to add to the Administrators group, for example, **CONTOSO\Help Desk**, and click OK.
4. Click OK to close the Add Group dialog box.
   A Properties dialog box appears.
5. Click the Add button next to the This Group Is A Member Of section.
6. Type **Administrators** and click OK.
   The Properties group policy setting should look something like the left side of Figure 7-2.
7. Click OK again to close the Properties dialog box.

Delegating the membership of the local Administrators group in this manner adds the group specified in step 3 to that group. It does not remove any existing members of the Administrators group. The group policy simply tells the client, "Make sure this group is a member of the local Administrators group." This allows for the possibility that individual systems could have other users or groups in their local Administrators group. This group policy setting is also cumulative. If multiple GPOs configure different security principals as members of the local Administrators group, all will be added to the group.

To take complete control of the local Administrators group, follow these steps:

1. In Group Policy Management Editor, navigate to Computer Configuration\Windows Settings\Security Settings\Restricted Groups.
2. Right-click Restricted Groups and choose Add Group.

3. Type **Administrators** and click OK.

   A Properties dialog box appears.

4. Click the Add button next to the Members Of This Group section.

5. Click the Browse button and type the name of the group you want to make the sole member of the Administrators group—for example, **CONTOSO\Help Desk**—and click OK.

6. Click OK again to close the Add Member dialog box.

   The group policy setting Properties should look something like the right side of Figure 7-2.

7. Click OK again to close the Properties dialog box.

When you use the Members setting of a restricted groups policy, the Members list defines the final membership of the specified group. The steps just listed result in a GPO that authoritatively manages the Administrators group. When a computer applies this GPO, it will add all members specified by the GPO and will remove all members not specified by the GPO, including Domain Admins. Only the local Administrator account will not be removed from the Administrators group because Administrator is a permanent and nonremovable member of Administrators.

Quick Check

- You want to add a group to the local Administrators group on computers without removing accounts that already exist in the group. Describe the restricted groups policy you should create.

Quick Check Answer

- Create a restricted groups policy for the group you wish to add. Use the Member Of policy setting (This Group Is A Member Of) and specify Administrators.

PRACTICE Delegating Membership Using Group Policy

In this practice, you will use Group Policy to delegate the membership of the Administrators group. You will first create a GPO with a restricted groups policy setting that ensures that the Help Desk group is a member of the Administrators group on all client systems. You will then create a GPO that adds the NYC Support group to Administrators on clients in the NYC OU. Finally, you will confirm that in the NYC OU, both the Help Desk and NYC Support groups are administrators.

To perform this practice, you will need the following objects in the *contoso.com* domain:

- A first-level OU named Admins with a sub-OU named Admin Groups.
- A global security group named Help Desk in the Admins\Admin Groups OU.
- A global security group named NYC Support in the Admins\Admin Groups OU.

- A first-level OU named Clients.
- An OU named NYC in the Clients OU.
- A computer object named DESKTOP101 in the NYC OU.

▶ **Exercise 1   Delegate the Administration of All Clients in the Domain**

In this exercise, you will create a GPO with a restricted groups policy setting that ensures that the Help Desk group is a member of the Administrators group on all client systems.

1. In the Group Policy Management console, expand Forest\Domains\contoso.com. Select the Group Policy Objects container.
2. Right-click the Group Policy Objects container and choose New.
3. In the Name box, type **Corporate Help Desk** and click OK.
4. Right-click the GPO and choose Edit.
5. In Group Policy Management Editor, navigate to Computer Configuration\Policies\Windows Settings\Security Settings\Restricted Groups.
6. Right-click Restricted Groups and choose Add Group.
7. Click the Browse button and, in the Select Groups dialog box, type **CONTOSO\Help Desk** and click OK.
8. Click OK to close the Add Group dialog box.
9. Click the Add button next to the This Group Is A Member Of section.
10. Type **Administrators** and click OK.

    The group policy setting Properties should look like the left side of Figure 7-2.
11. Click OK again to close the Properties dialog box.
12. Close Group Policy Management Editor.
13. In the Group Policy Management console, right-click the Clients OU and choose Link An Existing GPO.
14. Select the Corporate Help Desk GPO and click OK.

▶ **Exercise 2   Delegate the Administration of a Subset of Clients in the Domain**

In this exercise, you will create a GPO with a restricted groups policy setting that adds the NYC Support group to the Administrators group on all client systems in the NYC OU.

1. In the Group Policy Management console, expand Forest\Domains\Contoso.com. Select the Group Policy Objects container.
2. Right-click the Group Policy Objects container and choose New.
3. In the Name box, type **New York Support** and click OK.
4. Right-click the GPO and choose Edit.
5. Repeat steps 5–12 of Exercise 1, "Delegate the Administration of All Clients in the Domain," except type **CONTOSO\NYC Support** as the group name in step 7.

6. In the Group Policy Management console, right-click the Clients\NYC OU and choose Link An Existing GPO.

7. Select the New York Support GPO and click OK.

▶ **Exercise 3   Confirm the Cumulative Application of Member Of Policies**

You can use Group Policy Modeling to produce a report of the effective policies applied to a computer or user. In this exercise, you will use Group Policy Modeling to confirm that a computer in the NYC OU will include both the Help Desk and NYC Support groups in its Administrators group.

1. In the Group Policy Management console, expand Forest and select the Group Policy Modeling node.

2. Right-click the Group Policy Modeling node and choose Group Policy Modeling Wizard.

3. Click Next.

4. On the Domain Controller Selection page, click Next.

5. On the User And Computer Selection page, in the Computer Information section, click the Browse button.

6. Expand the domain and the Clients OU, and then select the NYC OU.

7. Click OK.

8. Select the Skip To The Final Page Of This Wizard Without Collecting Additional Data check box.

9. Click Next.

10. On the Summary Of Selections page, click Next.

11. Click Finish.

    The Group Policy Modeling report appears.

12. Click the Settings tab.

13. Double-click Security Settings.

14. Double-click Restricted Groups.

    You should see both the Help Desk and NYC Support groups listed. Restricted groups policies using the This Group Is A Member Of setting are cumulative. Notice the report does not specify that the listed groups belong to Administrators. This is a limitation of the report.

▶ **Optional Exercise 4   Confirm the Membership of the Administrators Group**

If your test environment includes a computer named DESKTOP101 that is a member of the *contoso.com* domain, you can start the computer, log on as the domain's Administrator, and open the Computer Management console from the Administrative Tools folder in Control Panel. In Computer Management, expand the Local Users And Groups node and, in the Groups folder, open the Administrators group. You should see the following members listed:

- CONTOSO\Help Desk, applied by the Corporate Help Desk GPO
- CONTOSO\NYC Support, applied by the New York Support GPO
- Domain Admins, made a member of Administrators when the computer joined the domain
- The local Administrator account, a default member that cannot be removed

Lesson Summary

- To delegate support of computers in your domain, you must manage the membership of the Administrators groups on those systems.
- GPOs using the Member Of setting of restricted groups policies can add domain groups to the Administrators group. Member Of settings are cumulative, so multiple GPOs can add groups to Administrators.
- A GPO using the Members setting of restricted groups policies can define the membership of the Administrators group. The Members setting is final and authoritative. If more than one GPO applies to a computer, only the GPO with the highest precedence will determine the membership of the Administrators group.

Lesson Review

You can use the following questions to test your knowledge of the information in Lesson 1, "Delegating the Support of Computers." The questions are also available on the companion CD if you prefer to review them in electronic form.

NOTE   Answers

Answers to these questions and explanations of why each answer choice is right or wrong are located in the "Answers" section at the end of the book.

---

1. The *contoso.com* domain contains a GPO named Corporate Help Desk, linked to the Clients OU, and a GPO named Sydney Support linked to the Sydney OU within the Clients OU. The Corporate Help Desk GPO includes a restricted groups policy for the CONTOSO\Help Desk group that specifies This Group Is A Member Of Administrators. The Sydney Support GPO includes a restricted groups policy for the CONTOSO\Sydney Support group that specifies This Group Is A Member Of Administrators. A computer named DESKTOP234 joins the domain in the Sydney OU. Which of the following accounts will be a member of the Administrators group on DESKTOP234? (Choose all that apply.)

        A. Administrator

        B. Domain Admins

        C. Sydney Support

        D. Help Desk

        E. Remote Desktop Users

2. The *contoso.com* domain contains a GPO named Corporate Help Desk, linked to the Clients OU, and a GPO named Sydney Support linked to the Sydney OU within the Clients OU. The Corporate Help Desk GPO includes a restricted groups policy for the Administrators group that specifies the Members Of This Group setting to be CONTOSO\Help Desk. The Sydney Support GPO includes a restricted groups policy for the Administrators group that specifies the Members Of This Group setting to be CONTOSO\Sydney Support. A computer named DESKTOP234 joins the domain in the Sydney OU. Which of the following accounts will be a member of the Administrators group on DESKTOP234? (Choose all that apply.)

        A. Administrator

        B. Domain Admins

        C. Sydney Support

        D. Help Desk

        E. Remote Desktop Users

3. The *contoso.com* domain contains a GPO named Corporate Help Desk, linked to the Clients OU, and a GPO named Sydney Support linked to the Sydney OU within the Clients OU. The Corporate Help Desk GPO includes a restricted groups policy for the Administrators group that specifies the Members Of This Group setting to be CONTOSO\Help Desk. The Sydney Support GPO includes a restricted groups policy for the CONTOSO\Sydney Support group that specifies This Group Is A Member Of Administrators. A computer named DESKTOP234 joins the domain in the Sydney OU. Which of the following accounts will be a member of the Administrators group on DESKTOP234? (Choose all that apply.)

        A. Administrator

        B. Domain Admins

        C. Sydney Support

        D. Help Desk

        E. Remote Desktop Users

Lesson 2: Managing Security Settings

Security is a primary concern for all Windows administrators. Windows Server 2008 includes numerous settings that affect the services that are running, the ports that are open, the network packets that are allowed into or out of the system, the rights and permissions of users, and the activities that are audited. There is an enormous number of settings that can be managed, and unfortunately, there is no magic formula that applies the perfect security configuration to a server. The appropriate security configuration for a server depends on the roles that server plays, the mix of operating systems in the environment, and the security policies of the organization, which themselves depend on compliance regulations enforced from outside the organization.

Therefore, you must work to determine and configure the security settings that are required for servers in your organization, and you must be prepared to manage those settings in a way that centralizes and optimizes security configuration. Windows Server 2008 provides several mechanisms with which to configure security settings on one or more systems. In this lesson, you will discover these mechanisms and their interactions.

After this lesson, you will be able to:
- Configure security settings on a computer using the Local Security Policy.
- Create and apply security templates to manage security configuration.
- Analyze security configuration based on security templates.
- Create, edit, and apply security policies using the Security Configuration Wizard.
- Deploy security configuration with Group Policy.

Estimated lesson time: 60 minutes

Configuring the Local Security Policy

Each server running Windows Server 2008 maintains a collection of security settings that can be managed using the local GPO. You can configure the local GPO by using the Group Policy Object Editor snap-in or the Local Security Policy console. The available policy setting categories are shown in Figure 7-5.

This lesson focuses on the mechanisms with which to configure and manage security settings rather than on the details of the settings themselves. Many of the settings—including account policies, audit policy, and user rights assignment—are discussed elsewhere in this training kit.

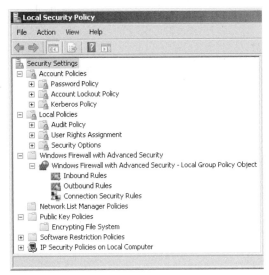

Figure 7-5   The security settings available in the local GPO

Because domain controllers (DCs) do not have local user accounts—only domain accounts—the policies in the Account Policies container of the local GPO on DCs cannot be configured. Instead, account policies for the domain should be configured as part of a domain-linked GPO such as the Default Domain Policy GPO. Account policies are discussed in the first lesson of Chapter 8, "Authentication."

The settings found in the local Security Settings policies are a subset of the policies that can be configured using domain-based Group Policy, shown in Figure 7-6. As you learned in Chapter 6, "Group Policy Infrastructure," it is a best practice to manage configuration by using domain-based Group Policy rather than on a machine-by-machine basis using local Group Policy. This is particularly true for domain controllers. The Default Domain Controllers Policy GPO is created when the first domain controller is promoted for a new domain. It is linked to the Domain Controllers OU and should be used to manage baseline security settings for all DCs in the domain so that DCs are consistently configured.

Figure 7-6   Security settings in a domain-based GPO

Managing Security Configuration with Security Templates

The second mechanism for managing security configuration is the security template. A security template is a collection of configuration settings stored as a text file with the .inf extension. As you can see in Figure 7-7, a security template contains settings that are a subset of the settings available in a domain-based GPO but a somewhat different subset than those managed by the local GPO. The tools used to manage security templates present settings in an interface that enables you to save your security configurations as files and deploy them when and where they are needed. You can also use a security template to analyze the compliance of a computer's current configuration against the desired configuration.

Figure 7-7   Security settings in a security template

There are several advantages to storing security configuration in security templates. For example, because the templates are plaintext files, you can work with them manually as with any text file, cutting and pasting sections as needed. Further, templates make it easy to store security configurations of various types so that you can easily apply different levels of security to computers performing different roles.

Security templates enable you to configure any of the following types of policies and settings:

- **Account Policies**   Enables you to specify password restrictions, account lockout policies, and Kerberos policies
- **Local Policies**   Enables you to configure audit policies, user rights assignments, and security options policies
- **Event Log Policies**   Enables you to configure maximum event log sizes and rollover policies
- **Restricted Groups**   Enables you to specify the users who are permitted to be members of specific groups
- **System Services**   Enables you to specify the startup types and permissions for system services
- **Registry Permissions**   Enables you to set access control permissions for specific registry keys
- **File System Permissions**   Enables you to specify access control permissions for NTFS files and folders

You can deploy security templates in a variety of ways, using Active Directory Group Policy Objects, the Security Configuration And Analysis snap-in, or *Secedit.exe*. When you associate a security template with an Active Directory object, the settings in the template become part of the GPO associated with the object. You can also apply a security template directly to a computer, in which case, the settings in the template become part of the computer's local policies. You will learn about each of these options in this section.

Using the Security Templates Snap-in

To work with security templates, you use the Security Templates snap-in. Windows Server 2008 does not include a console with the Security Templates snap-in, so you have to create one yourself using the MMC *Add/Remove Snap-in* command. The snap-in creates a folder called Security and a subfolder called Templates in your Documents folder, and the Documents \Security\Templates folder becomes the template search path, where you can store one or more security templates.

You can create a new security template by right-clicking the node that represents your template search path—C:\Users\Documents\Administrator\Security\Templates, for example—and choosing New Template. You can also create a template that reflects the current configuration of a server; you'll learn how to do that in the "Creating a Security Template" section.

Settings are configured in the template in the same way that settings are configured in a GPO. The Security Templates snap-in is used to configure settings in a security template. It is just an editor—it does not play any role in actually applying those settings to a system. Configure security settings in a template by using the Security Templates snap-in. Although the template itself is a text file, the syntax can be confusing. Using the snap-in ensures that settings are changed using the proper syntax. The exception to this rule is adding Registry settings that are not already listed in the Local Policies\Security Option portion of the template. As new security settings become known, if they can be configured using a Registry key, you can add them to a security template. To do so, you add them to the Registry Values section of the template.

MORE INFO   **Adding custom registry settings**

The article "How to Add Custom Registry Settings to Security Configuration Editor" helps you understand how to perform this task. You can find it at *http://support.microsoft.com/?kbid=214752*.

NOTE   **Save your settings**

Be sure to save your changes to a security template by right-clicking the template and choosing Save.

When you install a server or promote it to a domain controller, a default security template is applied by Windows. You can find that template in the %SystemRoot%\Security\Templates folder. On a domain controller, the template is called DC security.inf. You should not modify this template directly, but you can copy it to your template search path and modify the copy.

NOTE   **Security templates in Windows Server 2008 and in earlier versions of Windows**

In previous versions of Windows, a number of security templates were available to modify and apply to a computer. The new role-based configuration of Windows Server 2008 and the improved Security Configuration Manager have made these templates unnecessary.

Deploying Security Templates by Using Group Policy Objects

Creating and modifying security templates does not improve security unless you apply those templates. To configure a number of computers in a single operation, you can import a security template into the Group Policy Object for a domain, site, or organizational unit object in Active Directory. To import a security template into a GPO, right-click the Security Settings node and choose Import Policy. In the Import Policy From dialog box, if you select the Clear This Database Before Importing check box, all security settings in the GPO will be erased prior to importing the template settings, so the GPO's security settings will match the template's settings. If you leave the Clear This Database Before Importing check box deselected, the GPO's security policy settings will remain and the templates settings will be imported. Any settings defined in the GPO that are also defined in the template will be replaced with the template's setting.

Security Configuration and Analysis Tool

You can use the Security Configuration and Analysis snap-in to apply a security template to a computer interactively. The snap-in also provides the ability to analyze the current system security configuration and compare it to a baseline saved as a security template. This enables you to determine quickly whether someone has changed a computer's security settings and whether the system conforms to your organization's security policies.

As with the Security Templates snap-in, Windows Server 2008 does not include a console with the Security Configuration and Analysis snap-in, so you must add the snap-in to a console yourself.

To use the Security Configuration and Analysis snap-in, you must first create a database that will contain a collection of security settings. The database is the interface between the actual security settings on the computer and the settings stored in your security templates. Create a database (or open an existing one) by right-clicking the Security Configuration And Analysis node in the console tree.

You can then import one or more security templates. If you import more than one template, you must decide whether to clear the database. If the database is cleared, only the settings in the new template will be part of the database. If the database is not cleared, additional template settings that are defined will override settings from previously imported templates. If settings in newly imported templates are not defined, the settings in the database from previously imported templates will remain. To summarize, the Security Configuration and Analysis snap-in creates a database of security settings composed of imported security template settings. The settings in the database can be applied to the computer or used to analyze the computer's compliance and discrepancies with the desired state.

IMPORTANT   Database settings vs. the computer's settings

Remember that settings in a database do not modify the computer's settings or the settings in a template until that database is either used to configure the computer or exported to a template.

Applying Security Templates to a Computer

After you have imported one or more templates to create the database, you can apply the database settings to the computer. Right-click Security Configuration And Analysis and choose Configure Computer Now. You will be prompted for a path to an error log that will be generated during the application of settings. After applying the settings, examine the error log for any problems.

> ## Quick Check
>
> - Describe the procedure used to apply a security template to a computer.
>
> ## Quick Check Answer
>
> - Use the Security Configuration and Analysis snap-in to create a database. Import the template into the database. Configure the computer by using the database.

Analyzing the Security Configuration of a Computer

Before applying the database settings to a computer, you might want to analyze the computer's current configuration to identify discrepancies. Right-click Security Configuration And Analysis and choose Analyze Computer Now. The system prompts you for the location of its error log file and then proceeds to compare the computer's current settings to the settings in the database. After the analysis is complete, the console produces a report such as the one shown in Figure 7-8.

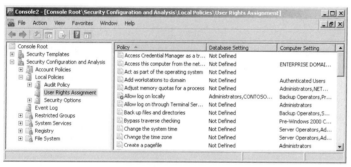

Figure 7-8 The Security Configuration and Analysis snap-in displays an analysis of the computer's configuration.

Unlike the display of policy settings in the Group Policy Management Editor, Group Policy Object Editor, Local Security Policy, or Security Templates snap-ins, the report shows for each policy the setting defined in the database (which was derived from the templates you imported) and the computer's current setting. The two settings are compared, and the comparison result is displayed as a flag on the policy name. For example, in Figure 7-8, the Allow Log On Locally policy setting is showing a discrepancy between the database setting and the computer setting. The meanings of the flags are as follows:

- **X in a red circle** Indicates that the policy is defined both in the database and on the computer but that the configured values do not match
- **Green check mark in a white circle** Indicates that the policy is defined both in the database and on the computer and that the configured values do match

- **Question mark in a white circle**   Indicates that the policy is not defined in the database and, therefore, was not analyzed or that the user running the analysis did not have the permissions needed to access the policy on the computer
- **Exclamation point in a white circle**   Indicates that the policy is defined in the database but does not exist on the computer
- **No flag**   Indicates that the policy is not defined in the database or on the computer

Correcting Security Setting Discrepancies

As you examine the elements of the database and compare its settings with those of the computer, you might find discrepancies and want to make changes to the computer's configuration or to the database to bring the two settings into alignment. You can double-click any policy setting to display its Properties dialog box and modify its value in the database. After you've made changes to the database, you can apply the database settings to the computer by performing the steps described earlier, in the section, "Applying Security Templates to a Computer."

CAUTION   Applying or exporting database changes

Modifying a policy value in the Security Configuration and Analysis snap-in changes the database value only, not the actual computer setting. For the changes you make to take effect on the computer, you must either apply the database settings to the computer using the *Configure Computer Now* command or export the database to a new template and apply it to the computer, using a GPO or the *Secedit.exe* command (discussed in the "*Secedit.exe*" section).

Alternatively, you can modify the computer's security settings directly by using the Local Security Policy console, by modifying the appropriate Group Policy Object, or by manually manipulating file system or registry permissions. After making such changes, return to the Security Configuration And Analysis snap-in and choose the *Analyze Computer Now* command to refresh the analysis of the computer's settings compared to the database.

Creating a Security Template

You can create a new security template from the database by right-clicking Security Configuration And Analysis and selecting Export Template. The template will contain the settings in the database, which have been imported from one or more security templates and which you have modified to reflect the current settings of the analyzed computer.

IMPORTANT   Exporting the database to a template

The Export Template feature creates a new template from the current database settings at the time you execute the command, not from the computer's current settings.

Secedit.exe

Secedit.exe is a command-line utility that can perform the same functions as the Security Configuration and Analysis snap-in. The advantage of *Secedit.exe* is that you can call it from scripts and batch files, enabling you to automate your security template deployments. Another big advantage of *Secedit.exe* is that you can use it to apply only part of a security template to a computer, something you cannot do with the Security Configuration and Analysis snap-in or with Group Policy Objects. For example, if you want to apply the file system's permissions from a template but leave all the other settings alone, *Secedit.exe* is the only way to do it.

To use *Secedit.exe*, you run the program from the command prompt with one of the following six main parameters, plus additional parameters for each function:

- **Configure**   Applies all or part of a security database to the local computer. You can also configure the program to import a security template into the specified database before applying the database settings to the computer.
- **Analyze**   Compares the computer's current security settings with those in a security database. You can configure the program to import a security template into the database before performing the analysis. The program stores the results of the analysis in the database itself, which you can view later, using the Security Configuration and Analysis snap-in.
- **Import**   Imports all or part of a security template into a specific security database.
- **Export**   Exports all or part of the settings from a security database to a new security template.
- **Validate**   Verifies that a security template is using the correct internal syntax.
- **Generaterollback**   Creates a security template you can use to restore a system to its original configuration after applying another template.

For example, to configure the machine by using a template called BaselineSecurity, use the following command:

```
secedit /configure /db BaselineSecurity.sdb
/cfg BaselineSecurity.inf /log BaselineSecurity.log
```

To create a rollback template for the BaselineSecurity template, use the following command:

```
secedit /generaterollback /cfg BaselineSecurity.inf
/rbk BaselineSecurityRollback.inf
/log BaselineSecurityRollback.log
```

MORE INFO   *Secedit.exe*

For full details regarding *Secedit.exe* and its switches, see *http://technet2.microsoft.com/windowsserver /en/library/b1007de8-a11a-4d88-9370-25e2445605871033.mspx?mfr=true*.

The Security Configuration Wizard

The Security Configuration Wizard can be used to enhance the security of a server by closing ports and disabling services not required for the server's roles. The Security Configuration Wizard can be launched from the home page of Server Manager, in the Security Information section, or from the Administrative Tools folder. There is also a command-line version of the tool, *scwcmd.exe*. Type **scwcmd.exe /?** at the command prompt for help on the command or see *http://technet2.microsoft.com/windowsserver2008/en/library/a222cb38-db08-4bf1-b9cf-6ec566c239e91033.mspx?mfr=true*.

The Security Configuration Wizard is a next-generation security management tool. It is more advanced than the Security Configuration and Analysis snap-in and role-based in accordance with the new role-based configuration of Windows Server 2008. The Security Configuration Wizard creates a security policy—an .xml file—that configures services, network security including firewall rules, registry values, audit policy, and other settings based on the roles of a server. That security policy can then be modified, applied to another server, or transformed into a GPO for deployment to multiple systems.

Creating a Security Policy

To create a security policy, you launch the Security Configuration Wizard from the Administrative Tools folder or the Security Information section on the home page of Server Manager. You can open the Security Configuration Wizard Help file by clicking the Security Configuration Wizard link on the first page of the wizard. Click Next and choose Create A New Security Policy. Click Next and enter the name of the server to scan and analyze. The security policy will be based on the roles being performed by the specified server. You must be an administrator on the server for the analysis of its roles to proceed. Ensure also that all applications using inbound IP ports are running prior to running the Security Configuration Wizard.

When you click Next, the Security Configuration Wizard begins the analysis of the selected server's roles. It uses a security configuration database that defines services and ports required for each server role supported by the Security Configuration Wizard. The security configuration database is a set of .xml files installed in %SystemRoot%\Security\Msscw\Kbs.

NOTE Centralizing the security configuration database

In an enterprise environment, centralize the security configuration database so that administrators use the same database when running the Security Configuration Wizard. Copy the files in the %SystemRoot%\Security\Msscw\Kbs folder to a network folder; then launch the Security Configuration Wizard with the *Scw.exe* command, using the syntax **scw.exe /kb *DatabaseLocation***. For example, the command *scw.exe /kb \\server01\scwkb* launches the Security Configuration Wizard, using the security configuration database in the shared folder scwkb on SERVER01.

The Security Configuration Wizard uses the security configuration database to scan the selected server and identifies the following:

- Roles that are installed on the server
- Roles likely being performed by the server
- Services installed on the server but not defined in the security configuration database
- IP addresses and subnets configured for the server

The information discovered about the server is saved in a file named Main.xml. This server-specific file is called the *configuration database*, not to be confused with the security configuration database used by the Security Configuration Wizard to perform the analysis. You can display this file by clicking the View Configuration Database button on the Processing Security Configuration page. The initial settings in the configuration database are called the *baseline settings*.

After the server has been scanned and the configuration database has been created, you have the opportunity to modify the database, which will then be used to generate the security policy to configure services, firewall rules, registry settings, and audit policies. The security policy can then be applied to the server or to other servers playing similar roles. The Security Configuration Wizard presents each of these four categories of the security policy in a section—a series of wizard pages.

- **Role-Based Service Configuration** The outcome of this section is a set of policies that configure the startup state of services on the server. You want to ensure that only the services required by the server's roles start and that other services do not start. To achieve this outcome, the Security Configuration Wizard presents pages that display the server roles, client features, and administration and other options detected on the scanned server. You can add or remove roles, features, and options to reflect the desired role configuration. The last page of the section, titled "Confirm Service Changes" and shown in Figure 7-9, shows the changes that will be made to services based on the roles you specify.

    The server shown in Figure 7-9 is a domain controller, and you can see that the AD DS service is currently configured to start automatically; the policy will also set the service to start automatically to support the AD DS role. However, audio is not required for a DC, so the service named Audiosrv used by the Windows Audio option will be configured by the policy as disabled.

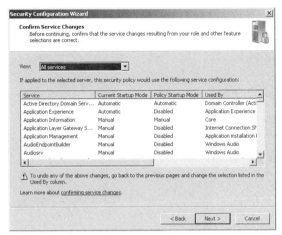

Figure 7-9   The Confirm Service Changes page of the Security Configuration Wizard

You cannot change the startup states on the Confirm Service Changes page of the Security Configuration Wizard. Instead, you must click the Back button to locate the role, service, or option indicated in the Used By column and either select or deselect that item. The service startup policies on the Confirm Service Changes page are determined by the selected roles, services, and options. Those not selected will result in service startup policy settings of disabled.

It is conceivable that the server on which you run the Security Configuration Wizard has services that are not defined by the Security Configuration Wizard security configuration database. The Select Additional Services page of the wizard enables you to include those services in the security policy so that, if the services exist on a system to which you apply the policy, those services will be started according to the startup setting in the baseline configuration database.

It is also conceivable that a server to which you apply the security policy might have services not found on the server from which you created the security policy. The Handling Unspecified Services page enables you to specify whether such services should be disabled or allowed to remain in their current startup mode.

- **Network Security**   The Network Security section produces the firewall settings of the security policy. Those settings will be applied by Windows Firewall with Advanced Security. Like the Role-Based Service Configuration section, the Network Security section displays a page of settings derived from the baseline settings in the configuration database. The settings in the Network Security section, however, are firewall rules rather than service startup modes. Figure 7-10 shows the rule that allows incoming ping requests to a domain controller. You can edit existing rules or add and remove custom rules.

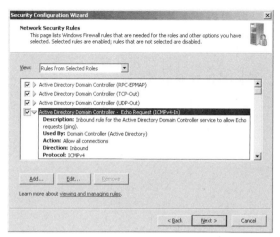

Figure 7-10 The Network Security Rules page of the Security Configuration Wizard

Windows Firewall with Advanced Security combines Internet Protocol security (IPSec) and a stateful firewall that inspects and filters all IP version 4 (IPv4) and IP version 6 (IPv6) packets, discarding unsolicited packets unless a firewall rule has been created to allow traffic explicitly to a port number, application name, or service name. The security policy generated by the Security Configuration Wizard manages firewall rules, but IPSec configuration is not provided by the Security Configuration Wizard.

- **Registry Settings** The Registry Settings section configures protocols used to communicate with other computers. These wizard pages determine server message block (SMB) packet signing, Lightweight Directory Access Protocol (LDAP) signing, LAN Manager (LM) authentication levels, and storage of password LM hash values. Each of these settings is described on the appropriate page, and a link on each page takes you to a Security Configuration Wizard Help page that details the setting.

- **Audit Policy** The Audit Policy section generates settings that manage the auditing of success and failure events and the file system objects that are audited. Additionally, the section enables you to incorporate a security template called SCWAudit.inf into the security policy. Use the Security Templates snap-in, described earlier in this lesson, to examine the settings in the template, which is located in %SystemRoot%\Security\Msscw\Kbs.

You can skip any of the last three sections you do not want to include in your security policy. When all the configuration sections have been completed or skipped, the Security Configuration Wizard presents the Security Policy section. The Security Policy File Name page, shown in Figure 7-11, enables you to specify a path, a name, and a description for the security policy.

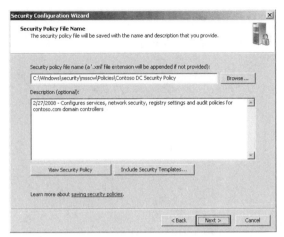

Figure 7-11 The Security Policy File Name page of the Security Configuration Wizard

Click the View Security Policy button to examine the settings of the security policy, which are very well documented by the Security Configuration Wizard. You can also import a security template into the security policy. Security templates, discussed earlier in this lesson in the "Managing Security Configuration with Security Templates" section, contain settings that are not provided by Managing Security Configuration with Security Templates, including restricted groups, event log policies, and file system and registry security policies. By including a security template, you can incorporate a richer collection of configuration settings in the security policy. If any settings in the security template conflict with the Security Configuration Wizard, the settings in the Security Configuration Wizard will take precedence. When you click the Next button, you are given the option to apply the security template to the server immediately or to apply the policy later.

Editing a Security Policy

You can edit a saved security policy by launching the Security Configuration Wizard and choosing Edit An Existing Security Policy on the Configuration Action page. Click the Browse button to locate the policy .xml file. When prompted to select a server, select the server that was used to create the security policy.

Applying a Security Policy

To apply a security policy to a server, open the Security Configuration Wizard and, on the Configuration Action page, choose Apply An Existing Security Policy. Click the Browse button to locate the policy .xml file. The server you specify on the Select Server page is the server to which the policy will be applied. Many of the changes specified in a security policy, including the addition of firewall rules for applications already running and the disabling of services, require that you restart the server. Therefore, as a best practice, it is recommended to restart a server any time you apply a security policy.

Rolling Back an Applied Security Policy

If a security policy is applied and causes undesirable results, you can roll back the changes by launching the Security Configuration Wizard and choosing Rollback The Last Applied Security Policy as the configuration action. When a security policy is applied by the Security Configuration Wizard, a rollback file is generated that stores the original settings of the system. The rollback process applies the rollback file.

Modifying Settings of an Applied Security Policy

Alternatively, if an applied security template does not produce an ideal configuration, you can manually change settings by using the Local Security Policy console discussed at the beginning of this lesson in the "Configuring the Local Security Policy" section. Thus, you can see the whole picture of security configuration, from manual settings to the generation of security templates to the creation of security policies with the Security Configuration Wizard, which can incorporate security templates, to the application of security policies and back to the manual configuration of settings.

Deploying a Security Policy Using Group Policy

You can apply a security policy created by the Security Configuration Wizard to a server by using the Security Configuration Wizard itself, by using the *Scwcmd.exe* command, or by transforming the security policy into a GPO. To transform a security policy into a GPO, log on as a domain administrator and run *Scwcmd.exe* with the *transform* command. For example, the *scwcmd transform /p:"Contoso DC Security.xml" /g:"Contoso DC Security GPO"* command will create a GPO called *Contoso DC Security GPO* with settings imported from the *Contoso DC Security.xml* security policy file. The resulting GPO can then be linked to an appropriate scope—site, domain, or OU—by using the Group Policy Management console. Be sure to type **scwcmd.exe transform /?** for help and guidance about this process.

Settings, Templates, Policies, and GPOs

As suggested in the introduction to this lesson, there are a number of mechanisms with which to manage security settings. You can use tools such as the Local Security Policy console to modify settings on an individual system. You can use security templates, which have existed since Windows 2000, to manage settings on one or more systems and to compare the current state of a system's configuration against the desired configuration defined by the template. Security policies generated by the Security Configuration Wizard are the most recent addition to the security configuration management toolset. They are role-based .xml files that define service startup modes, firewall rules, audit policies, and some registry settings. Security policies can incorporate security templates. Both security templates and security policies can be deployed using Group Policy.

The plethora of tools available can make it difficult to identify the best practice for managing security on one or more systems. Plan to use Group Policy whenever possible to deploy security configuration. You can generate a GPO from a role-based security policy produced by the Security Configuration Wizard, which itself incorporates additional settings from a security template. After the GPO has been generated, you can make additional changes to the GPO by using the Group Policy Management Editor snap-in. Settings not managed by Group Policy can be configured on a server-by-server basis, using the local GPO security settings.

PRACTICE **Managing Security Settings**

In this practice, you will manage security settings, using each of the tools discussed in this lesson. To perform the exercises in this practice, you must have the following objects in the directory service for the *contoso.com* domain:

- A first-level OU named Admins.
- An OU named Admin Groups in the Admins OU.
- A global security group named SYS_DC Remote Desktop in the Admins\ Admin Groups OU. The group must be a member of the Remote Desktop Users group. This membership gives the SYS_DC Remote Desktop group the permissions required to connect to the RDP-Tcp connection.

Alternatively, you can add the SYS_DC Remote Desktop group to the access control list (ACL) of the RDP-Tcp connection, using the Terminal Services Configuration console. Right-click RDP-Tcp and choose Properties; then click the Security tab, click the Add button, and type **SYS_DC Remote Desktop**. Click OK twice to close the dialog boxes.

▶ **Exercise 1 Configure the Local Security Policy**

In this exercise, you will use the local security policy to enable a group to log on using Remote Desktop to the domain controller named SERVER01. The local security policy of a domain controller affects only that individual DC—it is not replicated between DCs.

1. Log on to SERVER01 as Administrator.
2. Open the Local Security Policy console from the Administrative Tools folder.
3. Expand Security Settings\Local Policies\User Rights Assignment.
4. In the details pane, double-click Allow Log On Through Terminal Services.
5. Click Add User Or Group.
6. Type **CONTOSO\SYS_DC Remote Desktop** and click OK.
7. Click OK again.

    If you want to test the results of this exercise by logging on to the DC, using Remote Desktop as a member of the SYS_DC Remote Desktop group, create a user account and add it to the group. Be sure that the group is a member of Remote Desktop Users or has been given permission to connect to the RDP-Tcp connection as described earlier.

You will now remove the setting because you will manage the setting by using other tools in later exercises.

8. Double-click Allow Log On Through Terminal Services.
9. Select CONTOSO\SYS_DC Remote Desktop.
10. Click Remove.
11. Click OK.

▶ **Exercise 2 Create a Security Template**

In this exercise, you will create a security template that gives the SYS_DC Remote Desktop group the right to log on using Remote Desktop.

1. Log on to SERVER01 as Administrator.
2. Click Run from the Start menu.
3. Type **mmc** and press Enter.
4. Choose Add/Remove Snap-in from the File menu.
5. Select Security Templates from the Available Snap-ins list and click the Add button. Click OK.
6. Choose Save from the File menu and save the console to your desktop with the name **Security Management**.
7. Right-click C:\Users\Administrator\Documents\Security\Templates and choose New Template.
8. Type **DC Remote Desktop** and click OK.
9. Expand DC Remote Desktop\Local Policies\User Rights Assignment.
10. In the details pane, double-click Allow Log On Through Terminal Services.
11. Select Define These Policy Settings In The Template.
12. Click Add User Or Group.
13. Type **CONTOSO\SYS_DC Remote Desktop** and click OK.
14. Click OK.
15. Right-click DC Remote Desktop and choose Save.

▶ **Exercise 3 Use the Security Configuration and Analysis Snap-in**

In this exercise, you will analyze the configuration of SERVER01, using the DC Remote Desktop security template to identify discrepancies between the server's current configuration and the desired configuration defined in the template. You will then create a new security template.

1. Log on to SERVER01 as Administrator. Open the Security Management console you created and saved in Exercise 2, "Create a Security Template."
2. Choose Add/Remove Snap-in from the File menu.
3. Select Security Configuration And Analysis from the Available Snap-ins list and click the Add button. Click OK.

4. Choose Save from the File menu to save the modified console.

5. Select the Security Configuration And Analysis console tree node.

6. Right-click the same node and choose Open Database.

    The *Open Database* command enables you to create a new security database.

7. Type **SERVER01 Test** and click Open.

    The Import Template dialog box appears.

8. Select the DC Remote Desktop template you created in Exercise 2 and click Open.

9. Right-click Security Configuration And Analysis and choose Analyze Computer Now.

10. Click OK to confirm the default path for the error log.

11. Expand Local Policies and select User Rights Assignment.

12. Notice that the Allow Log On Through Terminal Services policy is flagged with a red circle and an X. This indicates a discrepancy between the database setting and the computer setting.

13. Double-click Allow Log On Through Terminal Services.

14. Notice the discrepancies. The computer is not configured to allow the SYS_DC Remote Desktop Users group to log on through Terminal Services

15. Notice also that the Computer Setting currently allows Administrators to log on through Terminal Services. This is an important setting that should be incorporated into the database.

16. Click the check box next to Administrators under Database Setting, and then click OK. This will add the right for Administrators to log on through Terminal Services to the database. It does not change the template, and it does not affect the current configuration of the computer.

17. Right-click Security Configuration And Analysis and choose Save.

    This saves the security database, which includes the settings imported from the template plus the change you made to allow Administrators to log on through Terminal Services. The hint displayed in the status bar when you choose the *Save* command suggests that you are saving the template. That is incorrect. You are saving the database.

18. Right-click Security Configuration And Analysis and choose Export Template.

19. Select DC Remote Desktop and click Save.

    You have now replaced the template created in Exercise 2 with the settings defined in the database of the Security Configuration and Analysis snap-in.

20. Close and reopen your Security Management console.

    This is necessary to refresh fully the settings shown in the Security Templates snap-in.

21. Expand C:\Users\Administrator\Documents\Security\Templates\DC Remote Desktop \Local Policies\User Rights Assignment.

22. In the details pane, double-click Allow Log On Through Terminal Services.

23. Notice that both the Administrators and SYS_DC Remote Desktop groups are allowed to log on through Terminal Services in the security template.

24. Right-click Security Configuration And Analysis and choose Configure Computer Now.

25. Click OK to confirm the error log path.

    The settings in the database are applied to the server. You will now confirm that the change to the user right was applied.

26. Open the Local Security Policy console from the Administrative Tools folder.

    If the console was already open during this exercise, right-click Security Settings and choose Reload.

27. Expand Security Settings\Local Policies\User Rights Assignment. Double-click Allow Log On Through Terminal Services.

28. Confirm that both Administrators and SYS_DC Remote Desktop are listed.

    The Local Security Policy console displays the actual, current settings of the server.

▶ **Exercise 4   Use the Security Configuration Wizard**

In this exercise, you will use the Security Configuration Wizard to create a security policy for domain controllers in the *contoso.com* domain based on the configuration of SERVER01.

1. Log on to SERVER01 as Administrator.

2. Open the Security Configuration Wizard from the Administrative Tools folder.

3. Click Next.

4. Select Create A New Security Policy and click Next.

5. Accept the default server name, SERVER01, and click Next.

6. On the Processing Security Configuration Database page, you can optionally click View Configuration Database and explore the configuration that was discovered on SERVER01.

7. Click Next and, on the Role Based Service Configuration section introduction page, click Next.

8. On the Select Server Roles, Select Client Features, Select Administration And Other Options, Select Additional Services, and Handling Unspecified Services pages, you can optionally explore the settings that were discovered on SERVER01, but do not change any settings. Click Next on each page.

9. On the Confirm Service Changes page, click the View drop-down list and choose All Services. Examine the settings in the Current Startup Mode column, which reflect service startup modes on SERVER01, and compare them to the settings in the Policy Startup Mode column. Click the View drop-down list and choose Changed Services. Click Next.

10. On the Network Security section introduction page, click Next.

11. On the Network Security Rules page, you can optionally examine the firewall rules derived from the configuration of SERVER01. Do not change any settings. Click Next.

12. On the Registry Settings section introduction page, click Next.

13. Click through each page of the Registry Settings section. Examine the settings, but do not change any of them. When the Registry Settings Summary page appears, examine the settings and click Next.

14. On the Audit Policy section introduction page, click Next.

15. On the System Audit Policy page, examine but do not change the settings. Click Next.

16. On the Audit Policy Summary page, examine the settings in the Current Setting and Policy Setting columns. Click Next.

17. On the Save Security Policy section introduction page, click Next.

18. In the Security Policy File Name text box, type **DC Security Policy**.

19. Click Include Security Templates.

20. Click Add.

21. Browse to locate the DC Remote Desktop template created in Exercise 3, "Use the Security Configuration And Analysis Snap-In," located in your Documents\Security \Templates folder. When you have located and selected the template, click Open.

22. Click OK to close the Include Security Templates dialog box.

23. Click View Security Policy to examine the settings in the security policy. You will be prompted to confirm the use of the ActiveX control; click Yes. Close the window after you have examined the policy, and then click Next in the Security Configuration Wizard window.

24. Accept the Apply Later default setting and click Next.

25. Click Finish.

▶ **Exercise 5   Transform a Security Configuration Wizard Security Policy to a Group Policy**

In this exercise, you will convert the security policy generated in Exercise 4, "Use the Security Configuration Wizard," to a GPO, which could then be deployed to computers by using Group Policy.

1. Log on to SERVER01 as Administrator.

2. Open the command prompt.

3. Type **cd c:\windows\security\msscw\policies** and press Enter.

4. Type **scwcmd transform /?** and press Enter.

5. Type **scwcmd transform /p:"DC Security Policy.xml" /g:"DC Security Policy"** and press Enter.

6. Open the Group Policy Management console from the Administrative Tools folder.

7. Expand the console tree nodes Forest, Domains, *contoso.com*, and Group Policy Objects.

8. Select DC Security Policy.

   This is the GPO created by the *Scwcmd.exe* command.

9. Click the Settings tab to examine the settings of the GPO.

10. Click the Show link next to Security Settings.

11. Click the Show link next to Local Policies / User Rights Assignment.

12. Confirm that the BUILTIN\Administrators and CONTOSO\SYS_DC Remote Desktop groups are given the Allow Log On Through Terminal Services user right.

    The GPO is not applied to DCs because it is not linked to the Domain Controllers OU. In this practice, do not link the GPO to the domain, site, or any OU. In a production environment, you would spend more time examining, configuring, and testing security settings in the security policy before deploying it as a GPO to production domain controllers.

Lesson Summary

- Security settings can be configured using the local GPO on an individual computer. The local GPO can be edited using the Group Policy Object Editor snap-in or the Local Security Policy console.

- Security settings can be defined in a security template with the Security Templates snap-in. Security templates can define a large number of security-related settings.

- Security templates can be used by the Security Configuration and Analysis snap-in to create a database. The snap-in can then analyze the configuration of a system for discrepancies between the computer's current settings and those specified in the database. The snap-in can also apply the database settings to the computer or export the database settings to a security template.

- *Secedit.exe* is the command-line tool that performs and extends the functionality of the Security Configuration and Analysis snap-in.

- Security policies are collections of settings created by the Security Configuration Wizard that define service startup modes, firewall rules, certain registry settings, and audit policies. The Security Configuration Wizard creates security policies based on the roles of a server.

- A security policy can incorporate the settings in a security template. In the event of conflicting settings, the settings in the security policy take precedence.

- *Scwcmd.exe* is the command-line tool that performs and extends the functionality of the Security Configuration Wizard.

- You can import a security template into a GPO.

- You can use *Scwcmd.exe transform* to convert a security policy into a GPO.

Lesson Review

You can use the following questions to test your knowledge of the information in Lesson 2, "Managing Security Settings." The questions are also available on the companion CD if you prefer to review them in electronic form.

1. You want to deploy security settings to multiple servers by using Group Policy. The settings need to apply the user rights that you have configured and validated on a server in your test environment. Which tool should you use?

   A. Local Security Policy
   B. Security Configuration And Analysis
   C. Security Configuration Wizard
   D. Security Templates

2. You want to deploy security settings to multiple servers by using Group Policy. The settings need to configure services, firewall rules, and audit policies appropriate for servers in your enterprise that act as file and print servers. Which tool would be the best choice for you to use?

   A. Local Security Policy
   B. Security Configuration And Analysis
   C. Security Configuration Wizard
   D. Security Templates

3. You created a security policy by using the Security Configuration Wizard. Now you want to deploy the settings in that security policy to the servers in your Servers OU. Which of the following steps are required? (Choose two. Each correct answer is a part of the solution.)

   A. Use *Scwcmd.exe /transform*.
   B. Create a Group Policy Object in the Group Policy Objects container.
   C. Right-click the Security Settings node of a GPO and choose Import.
   D. Link the GPO to the Servers OU.

Lesson 3: Managing Software with Group Policy Software Installation

You might be aware of several tools that can be used to deploy software within an organization, including Microsoft System Center Configuration Manager (Configuration Manager) and its predecessor, Microsoft Systems Management Server (SMS). Although these tools provide great benefits, including features to meter software use and inventory systems, you can effectively deploy most software without these tools, using only Group Policy software installation (GPSI).

After this lesson, you will be able to:
- Deploy software using GPSI to computers and users.
- Remove software installed originally with GPSI.

Estimated lesson time: 45 minutes

Understanding Group Policy Software Installation

Group Policy software installation (GPSI) is used to create a managed software environment that has the following characteristics:

- Users have access to the applications they need to do their jobs, no matter which computer they log on to.
- Computers have the required applications, without intervention from a technical support representative.
- Applications can be updated, maintained, or removed to meet the needs of the organization.

The software installation extension is one of the many client-side extensions (CSEs) that support change and configuration management using Group Policy. CSEs were discussed in Chapter 6. The extension enables you to manage the initial deployment, the upgrades, and the removal of software centrally. All configuration of the software deployment is managed within a GPO, using procedures detailed later in this lesson.

Windows Installer Packages

GPSI uses the Windows Installer service to install, maintain, and remove software. The Windows Installer service manages software, using information contained in the application's Windows Installer package. The Windows Installer package is in a file with an .msi extension that describes the installed state of the application. The package contains explicit instructions regarding the installation and removal of an application. You can customize Windows Installer packages by using one of the following types of files:

- **Transform (.mst) files**   These files provide a means for customizing the installation of an application. Some applications provide wizards or templates that permit a user to create transforms. For example, Adobe provides an enterprise deployment tool for Adobe Acrobat Reader that generates a transform. Many enterprises use the transform to configure agreement with the end user license agreement and to disable certain features of the application such as automatic updates that involve access to the Internet.

- **Patch (.msp) files**   These files are used to update an existing .msi file for security updates, bug fixes, and service packs. An .msp file provides instructions about applying the updated files and registry keys in the software patch, service pack, or software update. For example, updates to Microsoft Office 2003 and later are provided as .msp files.

NOTE   Installation of .msp and .mst files

You cannot deploy .mst or .msp files alone. They must be applied to an existing Windows Installer package.

GPSI can make limited use of non-MSI application files (.zap file), also known as down-level application packages, that specify the location of the software distribution point (SDP) and the setup command. See knowledge base article 231747 at *http://support.microsoft.com/?kbid=231747* for details. Most organizations do not use .zap files, however, because the installation of the application requires the user to have administrative privileges on the system. When GPSI installs an application by using a Windows Installer package, the user does not require administrative privileges, allowing for a more secure enterprise.

NOTE   GPSI and Windows Installer packages

GPSI can fully manage applications only if the applications are deployed using Windows Installer packages. Other tools, including Configuration Manager and SMS, can manage applications that use other deployment mechanisms.

The .msi file, transforms, and other files required to install an application are stored in a shared SDP.

Software Deployment Options

You can deploy software by assigning applications to users or computers or by publishing applications for users. You *assign* required or mandatory software to users or to computers. You *publish* software that users might find useful in performing their jobs.

Exam Tip   Know the difference between assigning applications and publishing applications.

Assigning Applications   When you assign an application to a user, the application's local registry settings, including filename extensions, are updated and its shortcuts are created on the Start menu or desktop, thus advertising the availability of the application. The application advertisement follows the user regardless of which physical computer he or she logs on to. This application is installed the first time the user activates the application on the computer, either by selecting the application on the Start menu or by opening a document associated with the application. When you assign an application to the computer, the application is installed during the computer's startup process.

Publishing Applications   When you publish an application to users, the application does not appear as if it is installed on the users' computers. No shortcuts are visible on the desktop or Start menu. Instead, the application appears as an available application for the user to install using Add Or Remove Programs in Control Panel on a Windows XP system or in Programs And Features on a Windows Server 2008 and Windows Vista system. Additionally, the application can be installed when a user opens a file type associated with the application. For example, if Acrobat Reader is advertised to users, it will be installed if a user opens a file with a .pdf extension.

Given that applications can be either assigned or published and targeted to users or computers, you can establish a workable combination to meet your software management goals. Table 7-1 details the different software deployment options.

Table 7-1   Software Deployment Options

	Publish (User Only)	**Assign (User)**	**Assign (Computer)**
After deployment of the GPO, the software is available for installation:	The next time a user logs on.	The next time a user logs on.	The next time the computer starts.
Typically, the user installs the software from:	The Control Panel Add Or Remove Programs (Windows XP) or Programs And Features (Windows Server 2008 and Windows Vista) applications.	Start menu or desktop shortcut. An application can also be configured to install automatically at logon.	The software is installed automatically when the computer starts up.
If the software is not installed and the user opens a file associated with the software, does the software install?	Yes (if auto-install is enabled).	Yes.	Does not apply; the software is already installed.

Table 7-1   Software Deployment Options

	Publish (User Only)	Assign (User)	Assign (Computer)
Can the user remove the software by using Control Panel?	Yes, and the user can choose to install it again from Control Panel.	Yes, and the software is available for installation again from the Start menu shortcuts or file associations.	No. Only a local administrator can remove the software; a user can run a repair on the software.
Supported installation files:	Windows Installer packages (.msi files), .zap files.	Windows Installer packages (.msi files).	Windows Installer packages (.msi files).

Quick Check

- You want to use GPSI to deploy an administrative tool so that it is available for administrators on any system to which they log on. You do not want the tool to install automatically because administrators do not need the tool on each computer, but you want the tool to be easily installed. Should you publish or assign the application? Describe how an administrator will install the tool.

Quick Check Answer

- Publish the application. An administrator will use the Programs And Features Control Panel application on a Windows Server 2008 and Windows Vista system or Add/Remove Programs on a Windows XP system to install the application.

Preparing an SDP

Now that you understand GPSI at a high level, you are ready to prepare the SDP. The SDP is simply a shared folder from which users and computers can install applications. Create a shared folder and create a separate folder for each application. Then copy the software package, modifications, and all other necessary files to the application folders. Set appropriate permissions on the folders that allow users or computers Read And Execute permission—the minimum permission required to install an application successfully from the SDP. The administrators of the SDP must be able to change and delete files to maintain the SDP over time.

Creating a Software Deployment GPO

To create a software deployment GPO, use the Group Policy Management console to create a new GPO or select an existing GPO. Edit the GPO, using Group Policy Management Editor. Expand the console nodes User Configuration\Policies\Software Settings\Software Installation. Alternatively, select the Software Installation node in the Computer Configuration branch. Right-click Software Installation, choose New, and then select Package. Browse to locate the .msi file for the application. Click Open. The Deploy Software dialog box appears, shown in Figure 7-12. Select Published, Assigned, or Advanced. You cannot publish an application to computers, so the option will not be available if you are creating the package in the Software Installation node in Computer Configuration.

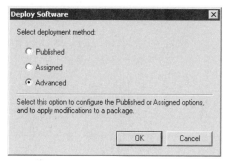

Figure 7-12   The Deploy Software dialog box

The Advanced option enables you to specify whether the application is published or assigned and gives you the opportunity to configure advanced properties of the software package. Therefore, it is recommended that you choose Advanced. The package properties dialog box then appears. Among the more important properties that you can configure are the following choices:

- **Deployment Type**   On the Deployment tab, configure Published or Assigned.
- **Deployment Options**   Based on the selected deployment type, different choices will appear in the Deployment Options section. These options, along with other settings on the Deployment tab, manage the behavior of the application installation.
- **Uninstall This Application When It Falls Out Of The Scope Of Management**   If this option is selected, the application will be automatically removed when the GPO no longer applies to the user or computer.
- **Upgrades**   On the Upgrades tab, you can specify the software that this package will upgrade. Upgrades are discussed in the "Maintaining Applications Deployed with Group Policy" section later in this lesson.
- **Categories**   The Categories tab enables you to associate the package with one or more categories. Categories are used when an application is published to a user. When the user goes to Control Panel to install a program, applications published using GPSI are presented in groups based on these categories.

  To create categories that are available to associate with packages, right-click Software Installation and choose Properties; then click the Categories tab.
- **Modifications**   If you have a transform (.mst file) that customizes the package, click the Add button to associate the transform with the package. Most tabs in the package Properties dialog box are available for you to change settings at any time. However, the Modifications tab is available only when you create the new package and choose the Advanced option shown in Figure 7-12.

Managing the Scope of a Software Deployment GPO

After you have created a software deployment GPO, you can scope the GPO to distribute the software to appropriate computers or users. In many software management scenarios, applications should be assigned to computers rather than to users. This is because most software licenses allow an application to be installed on one computer, and if the application is assigned to a user, the application will be installed on each computer to which the user logs on.

As you learned in Chapter 6, you can scope a GPO by linking the GPO to an OU or by filtering the GPO so that it applies only to a selected global security group. Many organizations have found that it is easiest to manage software by linking an application's GPO to the domain and filtering the GPO with a global security group that contains the users and computers to which the application should be deployed. For example, a GPO that deploys the XML Notepad tool (available from the Microsoft downloads site at *http://www.microsoft.com/downloads*) would be linked to the domain and filtered with a group containing developers that require the tool. The group would have a descriptive name that indicates its purpose to manage the deployment of XML Notepad—*APP_XML Notepad*, for example.

Exam Tip   On the 70-640 exam, you are likely to encounter questions that present software installation scenarios but are in fact testing your knowledge of how to scope a GPO effectively. As you read questions on the exam, try to identify what knowledge the question is really targeting.

Maintaining Applications Deployed with Group Policy

After a computer has installed an application by using the Windows Installer package specified by a GPO, the computer will not attempt to reinstall the application at each Group Policy refresh. There might be scenarios in which you want to force systems to reinstall the application. For example, small changes might have been made to the original Windows Installer package. To redeploy an application deployed with Group Policy, right-click the package in the GPO, choose All Tasks, and then select Redeploy Application.

You can also upgrade an application that has been deployed with GPSI. Create a package for the new version of the application in the Software Installation node of the GPO. The package can be in the same GPO as the package for the previous version or in any different GPO. Right-click the package and choose Properties. Click the Upgrades tab, and then click the Add button. The Add Upgrade Package dialog box appears, shown in Figure 7-13.

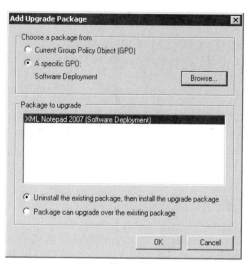

Figure 7-13   The Add Upgrade Package dialog box

Select whether the package for the previous version of the application is in the current GPO or in another GPO. If the previous package is in another GPO, click the Browse button to select that GPO. Then select the package from the Package To Upgrade list. Based on your knowledge of the application's upgrade behavior, choose one of the upgrade options shown at the bottom of Figure 7-13. Then click OK.

You can also remove an application that was deployed with GPSI. To do so, right-click the package, choose All Tasks, and then select Remove. In the Remove Software dialog box, choose one of the following two options:

- **Immediately Uninstall The Software From Users And Computers**   This option, known as *forced removal*, causes computers to remove the application. The software installation extension will remove an application when the computer restarts if the application was deployed with a package in the Computer Configuration portion of the GPO. If the package is in the User Configuration portion, the application will be uninstalled the next time the user logs on.

- **Allows Users To Continue To Use The Software, But Prevents New Installations**   This setting, known as *optional removal*, causes the software installation extension to avoid adding the package to systems that do not yet have the package installed. Computers that had previously installed the application do not forcibly uninstall the application, so users can continue using it.

If you use one of these two options to remove software using GPSI, it is important that you allow the settings in the GPO to propagate to all computers within the scope of the GPO before you delete, disable, or unlink the GPO. Clients need to receive this setting that specifies forced or optional removal. If the GPO is deleted or no longer applied before all clients have received this setting, the software is not removed according to your instructions. This is particularly important in environments with mobile users on laptop computers that might not connect to the network on a regular basis.

If, when creating the software package, you chose the Uninstall This Application When It Falls Out Of The Scope Of Management option, you can simply delete, disable, or unlink the GPO, and the application will be forcibly removed by all clients that have the installed package with that setting.

GPSI and Slow Links

When a client performs a Group Policy refresh, it tests the performance of the network to determine whether it is connected using a slow link defined by default as 500 kilobits per second (kbps). Each client-side extension is configured to process Group Policy or to skip the application of settings on a slow link. By default, GPSI does not process Group Policy settings over a slow link because the installation of software over a slow link could cause significant delays.

You can change the slow link policy processing behavior of each client-side extension, using policy settings located in Computer Configuration\Policies\Administrative Templates\System\Group Policy. For example, you could modify the behavior of the software installation extension so that it does process policies over a slow link.

You can also change the connection speed threshold that constitutes a slow link. By configuring a low threshold for the connection speed, you can convince the client-side extensions that a connection is not a slow link, even if it actually is. There are separate Group Policy Slow Link Detection policy settings for computer policy processing and user policy processing. The policies are in the Administrative Templates\System\Group Policy folders in Computer Configuration and User Configuration.

PRACTICE Managing Software with Group Policy Software Installation

In this practice, you will install, upgrade, and remove software, using GPSI. You will practice software management by using XML Notepad, a simple XML editor available from the Microsoft downloads site. To perform this practice, you must complete the following preparatory steps:

- Create a first-level OU named **Groups** and, within that OU, create an OU called **Applications**.
- In the Applications OU, create a global security group named **APP_XML Notepad** to represent the users and computer to which XML Notepad is deployed.
- Create a folder named **Software** on the C drive of SERVER01. Within that folder, create a folder named **XML Notepad**. In the XML Notepad folder, give the APP_XML Notepad

group Read And Execute permission. Share the Software folder with the share name Software and grant the Everyone group the Allow Full Control share permission.

■ Download XML Notepad from the Microsoft downloads site at *http://www.microsoft.com /downloads*. Save it to the Software\XML Notepad folder. Make a note of the version you have downloaded. At the time of writing this chapter, the current version is XML Notepad 2007.

▶ **Exercise 1   Create a Software Deployment GPO**

In this exercise, you will create a GPO that deploys XML Notepad to developers who require the application.

1. Log on to SERVER01 as Administrator.
2. Open the Group Policy Management console.
3. Right-click the Group Policy Objects container and choose New.
4. In the Name box, type the name of the application, for example **XML Notepad**, and then click OK.
5. Right-click the XML Notepad GPO and choose Edit.
6. Expand User Configuration\Policies\Software Settings.
7. Right-click Software Installation, choose New, and then select Package.
8. In the File Name text box, type the network path to the software distribution folder, for example, **\\server01\software**; select the Windows Installer package, for example, XmlNotepad.msi; and then click Open.
9. In the Deploy Software dialog box, select Advanced and click OK.
10. On the General tab, note that the name of the package includes the version, for example, XML Notepad 2007.
11. Click the Deployment tab.
12. Select Assigned.
13. Select the Install This Application At Logon check box.
14. Select Uninstall This Application When It Falls Out Of The Scope Of Management.
15. Click OK.
16. Close Group Policy Management Editor.
17. In the Group Policy Management console, select the XML Notepad GPO in the Group Policy Objects container.
18. Click the Scope tab.
19. In the Security Filtering section, select Authenticated Users and click Remove. Click OK to confirm your action.
20. Click the Add button.

21. Type the name of the group that represents users and computers to which the application should be deployed, for example **APP_XML Notepad**.

22. Click OK.

    The GPO is now filtered to apply only to the APP_XML Notepad group. However, the GPO settings will not apply until it is linked to an OU, to a site, or to the domain.

23. Right-click the domain, *contoso.com*, and choose Link An Existing GPO.

24. Select XML Notepad from the Group Policy Objects list and click OK.

    You can optionally test the GPO by adding the Administrator account to the APP_XML Notepad group. Log off and then log on. XML Notepad will be installed when you log on.

▶ **Exercise 2   Upgrade an Application**

In this exercise, you will simulate deploying an upgraded version of XML Notepad.

1. Log on to SERVER01 as Administrator.

2. Open the Group Policy Management console.

3. Right-click the XML Notepad GPO in the Group Policy Objects container and choose Edit.

4. Expand User Configuration\Policies\Software Settings.

5. Right-click Software Installation, choose New, and then select Package.

6. In the File Name text box, enter the network path to the software distribution folder, for example, **\\server01\software**; select the .msi file name; and click Open.

    This exercise will use the existing XmlNotepad.msi file as if it is an updated version of XML Notepad.

7. Click Open.

8. In the Deploy Software dialog box, select Advanced and click OK.

9. On the General tab, change the name of the package to suggest that it is the next version of the application, for example, **XML Notepad 2008**.

10. Click the Deployment tab.

11. Select Assigned.

12. Select the Install This Application At Logon check box.

13. Click the Upgrades tab.

14. Click the Add button.

15. Select the Current Group Policy Object (GPO) option.

16. In the Package To Upgrade list, select the package for the simulated earlier version, XML Notepad 2007, for example.

17. Select Uninstall The Existing Package, and then select Then Install The Upgrade Package.

18. Click OK.

19. Click OK again.

If this were an actual upgrade, the new package would upgrade the previous version of the application as clients applied the XML Notepad GPO. Because this is only a simulation of an upgrade, you can remove the simulated upgrade package.

20. Right-click the package that you just created to simulate an upgrade, choose All Tasks, and then select Remove.

21. In the Remove Software dialog box, select the Immediately Uninstall The Software From Users And Computers option.

22. Click OK.

Lesson Summary

- Group Policy Software Installation (GPSI) can be used to deploy, maintain, upgrade, and remove software.

- You can assign a software package in the Computer Configuration portion of a GPO. Client computers within the scope of the GPO will install the application at startup.

- You can assign a software package in the User Configuration portion of a GPO. The application will be installed when a user launches the application by using a shortcut in the Start menu or opens a file type associated with the application. You can optionally configure a user assigned application to install at logon.

- You can publish a software package in the User Configuration portion of a GPO. The application will be advertised in the Programs And Features Control Panel application on Windows Server 2008 and Windows Vista clients and in the Add/Remove Programs Control Panel application on Windows XP clients.

- Transforms (.mst files) can be used to modify the behavior of a Windows Installer package deployed using GPSI.

- Applications managed using GPSI can be redeployed or removed by the software installation extension.

- A software package can be configured to upgrade other applications deployed using GPSI.

- GPSI settings are not applied when a slow link is detected.

Lesson Review

You can use the following questions to test your knowledge of the information in Lesson 3, "Managing Software with Group Policy Software Installation." The questions are also available on the companion CD if you prefer to review them in electronic form.

NOTE   Answers

Answers to these questions and explanations of why each answer choice is right or wrong are located in the "Answers" section at the end of the book.

1. You want to deploy an application by using Group Policy to client computers in the headquarters and in a branch office. The branch office is connected to the headquarters with a wide area network connection that is 364 kbps. What steps must you take to deploy the software? (Choose two. Each correct answer is part of the solution.)

   A. Create a GPO that applies to all client computers in the headquarters and branch office. In the GPO, create a software package in the User Configuration node that assigns the application.

   B. Create a GPO that applies to all client computers in the headquarters and branch office. In the GPO, create a software package in the Computer Configuration node that assigns the application.

   C. In a GPO that applies to all computers, configure the slow link detection policy connection speed in the User Configuration node to 256 kbps.

   D. In a GPO that applies to computers in the branch office, configure the slow link detection policy connection speed in the Computer Configuration node to 256 kbps.

   E. In a GPO that applies to computers in the branch office, configure the slow link detection policy connection speed in the Computer Configuration node to 1,000 kbps.

2. In your domain, the Employees OU contains all user accounts. Each site has an OU within which a Sales OU contains accounts for the computers in the Sales department at that site. You want to deploy an application so that it is available to all users in the organization's Sales departments. Which methods can you use? (Choose all that apply.)

   A. Create a GPO linked to the domain. Create a group containing all Sales users. Filter the GPO so that it applies only to the group. In the GPO's User Configuration policies, create a software package that assigns the application.

   B. Create a GPO linked to each site's Sales OU. In the GPO's User Configuration policies, create a software package that assigns the application.

   C. Create a GPO linked to the domain. Create a group containing all Sales users. Filter the GPO so that it applies only to the group. In the GPO's Computer Configuration policies, create a software package that assigns the application.

   D. Create a GPO linked to each site's Sales OU. In the GPO User Configuration policies, create a software package that assigns the application. In the GPO's Computer Configuration, enable loopback policy processing in merge mode.

3. Your organization consists of ten branch offices. Within your Active Directory, an Employees OU is divided into ten child OUs containing user accounts at each branch office. You want to deploy an application to users at four branches. The application should be fully installed before the user opens the application for the first time. Which steps should you take? (Choose four. Each correct answer is a part of the solution.)

   A. Create a software deployment GPO linked to the Employees OU.

   B. Create a package in the User Configuration polices that publishes the application.

   C. Select the Install This Application At Logon deployment option.

   D. Create a shadow group that includes the users in the four branches. Filter the software deployment GPO so that it applies only to the shadow group.

   E. Create a package in the User Configuration policies that assigns the application.

   F. Select the Required Upgrade For Existing Packages option.

Lesson 4: Auditing

Auditing is an important component of security. Auditing logs specified activities in your enterprise to the Windows Security log, which you can then monitor to understand those activities and to identify issues that warrant further investigation. Auditing can log successful activities to provide documentation of changes. It can also log failed and potentially malicious attempts to access enterprise resources. Auditing involves up to three management tools: audit policy, auditing settings on objects, and the Security log. In this lesson, you will learn how to configure auditing to address several common scenarios.

> **After this lesson, you will be able to:**
> - Configure audit policy.
> - Configure auditing settings on file system and directory service objects.
> - Implement Windows Server 2008 new Directory Service Changes auditing.
> - View the Security log, using the Event Viewer snap-in.
>
> **Estimated lesson time: 45 minutes**

Audit Policy

Audit Policy configures a system to audit categories of activities. If Audit Policy is not enabled, a server will not audit those activities. Figure 7-14 shows the Audit Policy node of a GPO expanded.

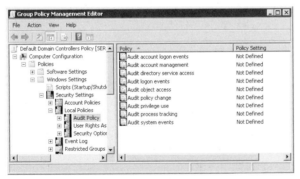

Figure 7-14   The Audit Policy node of a GPO

To configure auditing, you must define the policy setting. Double-click any policy setting and select the Define These Policy Settings check box. Then select whether to enable auditing of Success events, Failure events, or both. Table 7-2 defines each audit policy and its default settings on a Windows Server 2008 domain controller.

Table 7-2 **Audit Policies**

Audit Policy Setting	Explanation	Default Setting for Windows Server 2008 Domain Controllers
Audit Account Logon Events	Creates an event when a user or computer attempts to authenticate using an Active Directory account. For example, when a user logs on to any computer in the domain, an account logon event is generated.	Successful and failed account logons are audited.
Audit Logon Events	Creates an event when a user logs on interactively (locally) to a computer or over the network (remotely). For example, if a workstation and a server are configured to audit logon events, the workstation audits a user logging on directly to that workstation. When the user connects to a shared folder on the server, the server logs that remote logon. When a user logs on, the domain controller records a logon event because logon scripts and policies are retrieved from the DC.	Successful and failed logons are audited.
Audit Account Management	Audits events, including the creation, deletion, or modification of user, group, or computer accounts and the resetting of user passwords.	Successful account management activities are audited.
Audit Directory Service Access	Audits events that are specified in the system SACL, which is seen in an Active Directory object's Properties Advanced Security Settings dialog box. In addition to defining the audit policy with this setting, you must also configure auditing for the specific object or objects using the SACL of the object or objects. This policy is similar to the Audit Object Access policy used to audit files and folders, but this policy applies to Active Directory objects.	Successful directory service access events are audited, but few objects' SACLs specify audit settings. See the discussion in the "Auditing Directory Services Changes" section for more information.
Audit Policy Change	Audits changes to user rights assignment policies, audit policies, or trust policies.	Successful policy changes are audited.
Audit Privilege Use	Audits the use of a privilege or user right. See the explanatory text for this policy in Group Policy Management Editor (GPME).	No auditing is performed, by default.
Audit System Events	Audits system restart, shutdown, or changes that affect the system or security log.	Successful and failed system events are audited.

Table 7-2   **Audit Policies**

Audit Policy Setting	Explanation	Default Setting for Windows Server 2008 Domain Controllers
Audit Process Tracking	Audits events such as program activation and process exit. See the explanatory text for this policy in GPME.	Successful process tracking events are audited.
Audit Object Access	Audits access to objects such as files, folders, registry keys, and printers that have their own SACLs. In addition to enabling this audit policy, you must configure the auditing entries in objects' SACLs.	Successful object access events are audited.

Exam Tip   Microsoft certification exams often test your knowledge of audit policies at a high level. Commit the information in Table 7-2 to memory and you are likely to be able to answer one or more exam items correctly.

As you can see, most major Active Directory events are already audited by domain controllers, assuming that the events are successful. Therefore, the creation of a user, the resetting of a user's password, the logon to the domain, and the retrieval of a user's logon scripts are all logged.

However, not all failure events are audited by default. You might need to implement additional failure auditing based on your organization's IT security policies and requirements. Auditing failed account logon events, for example, will expose malicious attempts to access the domain by repeatedly trying to log on as a domain user account without yet knowing the account's password. Auditing failed account management events can reveal someone attempting to manipulate the membership of a security-sensitive group.

One of the most important tasks you must fulfill is to balance and align Audit Policy with your corporate policies and reality. Your corporate policy might state that all failed logons and successful changes to Active Directory users and groups must be audited. That's easy to achieve in Active Directory. But how, exactly, are you going to use that information? Verbose auditing logs are useless if you don't know how or don't have the tools to manage those logs effectively. To implement auditing, you must have the business requirement to audit, a well-configured audit policy, and the tools with which to manage audited events.

Auditing Access to Files and Folders

Many organizations elect to audit file system access to provide insight into resource usage and potential security issues. Windows Server 2008 supports granular auditing based on user or group accounts and the specific actions performed by those accounts. To configure auditing, you must complete three steps: specify auditing settings, enable audit policy, and evaluate events in the security log.

Specifying Auditing Settings on a File or Folder

You can audit access to a file or folder by adding auditing entries to its SACL. To access the SACL and its audit entries, open the Properties dialog box and click the Security tab. Then click the Advanced button and click the Auditing tab. The Advanced Security Settings dialog box of a folder named Confidential Data is shown in Figure 7-15.

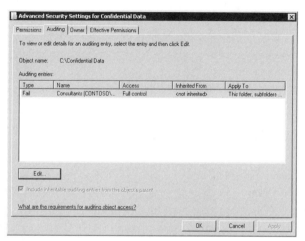

Figure 7-15   The Advanced Security Settings dialog box of a folder named Confidential Data

To add an entry, click the Edit button to open the Auditing tab in Edit mode. Click the Add button to select the user, group, or computer to audit. Then, in the Auditing Entry dialog box shown in Figure 7-16, indicate the type of access to audit.

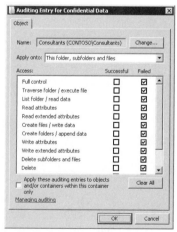

Figure 7-16   The Auditing Entry dialog box

You are able to audit for successes, failures, or both as the specified user, group, or computer attempts to access the resource by using one or more of the granular access levels.

You can audit successes for the following purposes:

- To log resource access for reporting and billing
- To monitor access that would suggest users are performing actions greater than what you had planned, indicating that permissions are too generous
- To identify access that is out of character for a particular account, which might be a sign that a user account has been breached by a hacker

Auditing failed events enables you:

- To monitor for malicious attempts to access a resource to which access has been denied.
- To identify failed attempts to access a file or folder to which a user does require access. This would indicate that the permissions are not sufficient to achieve a business requirement.

Auditing entries direct Windows to audit the successful or failed activities of a security principal (user, group, or computer) to use a specific permission. The example in Figure 7-15 audits for unsuccessful attempts by users in the Consultants group to access data in the Confidential Data folder at any level. It does that by configuring an auditing entry for Full Control access. Full Control includes all the individual access levels, so this entry covers any type of access. If a Consultant group member attempts access of any kind and fails, the activity will be logged.

Typically, auditing entries reflect the permission entries for the object. In other words, you would configure the Confidential Data folder with permissions that prevent members of the Consultants group from accessing its contents. You would then use auditing to monitor members of the Consultants group who nonetheless attempt to access the folder. Keep in mind, of course, that a member of the Consultants group can also belong to another group that does have permission to access the folder. Because that access will be successful, the activity is not logged. Therefore, if you really are concerned about keeping users out of a folder and making sure they do not access it in any way, monitor failed access attempts; however, also audit successful access to identify situations in which a user is accessing the folder through another group membership that is potentially incorrect.

NOTE Don't over-audit

Audit logs have the tendency to get quite large quite rapidly, so a golden rule for auditing is to configure the bare minimum required to achieve the business task. Specifying to audit the successes and failures on an active data folder for the Everyone group using Full Control (all permissions) would generate enormous audit logs that could affect the performance of the server and make locating a specific audited event all but impossible.

Enabling Audit Policy

Configuring auditing entries in the security descriptor of a file or folder does not, in itself, enable auditing. Auditing must be enabled by defining the Audit Object Access setting shown in Figure 7-17. After auditing is enabled, the security subsystem begins to pay attention to the audit settings and to log access as directed by those settings.

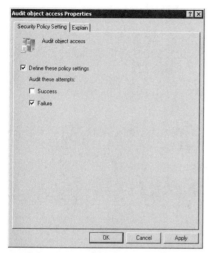

Figure 7-17 The Audit Object Access policy

The policy setting must be applied to the server that contains the object being audited. You can configure the policy setting in the server's local GPO or use a GPO scoped to the server.

You can define the policy then to audit Success events, Failure events, or both. The policy setting (shown in Figure 7-17) must specify auditing of Success or Failure attempts that match the type of auditing entry in the object's SACL (shown in Figure 7-16). For example, to log a failed attempt by a member of the Consultants group to access the Confidential Data folder, you must configure the Audit Object Access policy to audit failures, and you must configure the SACL of the Confidential Data folder to audit failures. If Audit Policy audits successes only, the failure entries in the folder's SACL will not trigger logging.

NOTE Making sure Audit Policy matches auditing entries

Remember that access that is audited and logged is the combination of the audit entries on specific files and folders and the settings in Audit Policy. If you've configured audit entries to log failures, but the policy enables only logging for successes, your audit logs will remain empty.

Evaluating Events in the Security Log

After you have enabled the Audit Object Access policy setting and specified the access you want to audit, using object SACLs, the system will begin to log access according to the audit entries. You can view the resulting events in the Security log of the server. Open the Event Viewer console from Administrative Tools. Expand Windows Logs\Security.

Exam Tip   Auditing access to objects such as files and folders requires three components. First, the Audit Object Access policy must be enabled and configured to audit Success or Failure events as appropriate for the scenario. Second, the SACL of the object must be configured to audit successful or failed access. Third, you must examine the Security log. Audit Policy is often managed using a GPO, so the GPO must be scoped to apply to the server with the file or folder, which is usually a file server rather than a domain controller. Some exam questions that appear to be testing your knowledge of auditing are actually testing your ability to scope a GPO with Audit Policy to the correct servers.

Auditing Directory Service Changes

Just as the Audit Object Access policy enables you to log attempts to access objects such as files and folders, the Audit Directory Service Access policy enables you to log attempts to access objects in Active Directory. The same basic principles apply. You configure the policy to audit success or failure. You then configure the SACL of the Active Directory object to specify the types of access you want to audit.

As an example, if you want to monitor changes to the membership of a security-sensitive group such as Domain Admins, you can enable the Audit Directory Service Access policy to audit Success events. You can then open the SACL of the Domain Admins group and configure an auditing entry for successful modifications of the group's *member* attribute. You will do this in an exercise in this lesson's practice.

In Microsoft Windows Server 2003 and Windows 2000 Server, you could audit directory service access and you would be notified that an object, or the property of an object, had been changed, but you could not identify the previous and new values of the attribute that had changed. For example, an event could be logged indicating that a particular user changed the *member* attribute of Domain Admins, but you could not determine exactly what change was made.

Windows Server 2008 adds an auditing category called Directory Service Changes. The important distinction between Directory Service Changes and Directory Service Access is that with Directory Service Changes auditing, you can identify the previous and current values of a changed attribute.

Directory Service Changes is not enabled in Windows Server 2008 by default. Instead, Directory Service Access is enabled to mimic the auditing functionality of previous versions of Windows.

To enable auditing of successful Directory Service Changes, open a command prompt on a domain controller and type this command:

```
auditpol /set /subcategory:"directory service changes" /success:enable
```

Exam Tip   The *auditpol* command is used to enable auditing of directory service changes.

You must still modify the SACL of objects to specify which attributes should be audited. Although you can use the preceding command to enable Directory Service Changes auditing in a lab and explore the events that are generated, don't implement this in a domain until you've read the documentation on TechNet, starting with the step-by-step guide found at *http://technet2.microsoft.com/windowsserver2008/en/library/a9c25483-89e2-4202-881c-ea8e02b4b2a51033.mspx*.

When Directory Service Changes auditing is enabled, and auditing entries are configured in the SACL of directory service objects, events are logged to the Security log that clearly indicate the attribute that was changed and when the change was made. In most cases, event log entries will show the previous and current value of the changed attribute.

Quick Check

- You want to audit changes to properties of user accounts provided for temporary employees. When a change is made, you want to see the previous and new value of the changed attribute. What type of auditing do you perform?

Quick Check Answer

- Directory Services Changes auditing

PRACTICE Auditing

In this practice, you will configure auditing settings, enable audit policies for object access, and filter for specific events in the Security log. The business objective is to monitor a folder containing confidential data that should not be accessed by users in the Consultants group. You will also configure auditing to monitor changes to the membership of the Domain Admins group. To perform this practice, you must complete the following preparatory tasks:

- Create a folder called Confidential Data on the C drive.
- Create a global security group called Consultants.
- Add the Consultants group to the Print Operators group.

  This is a shortcut that will allow a user in the Consultants group to log on locally to SERVER01, which is a domain controller in this exercise.

- Create a user named James Fine and add the user to the Consultants group.

▶ **Exercise 1   Configure Permissions and Audit Settings**

In this exercise, you will configure permissions on the Confidential Data folder to deny access to consultants. You will then enable auditing of attempts by consultants to access the folder.

1. Log on to SERVER01 as Administrator.
2. Open the properties of the C:\Confidential Data folder and click the Security tab.
3. Click Edit.
4. Click Add.
5. Type **Consultants** and click OK.
6. Click the Deny check box for the Full Control permission.
7. Click Apply. Click Yes to confirm the use of a Deny permission.
8. Click OK to close the Permissions dialog box.
9. Click Advanced.
10. Click the Auditing tab.
11. Click Edit.
12. Click Add.
13. Type **Consultants** and click OK.
14. In the Auditing Entry dialog box, select the check box under Failed next to Full Control.
15. Click OK to close all dialog boxes.

▶ **Exercise 2   Enable Audit Policy**

Because SERVER01 is a domain controller, you will use the existing Domain Controller Security Policy GPO to enable auditing. On a standalone server, you would enable auditing by using Local Security Policy or a GPO scoped to the server.

1. Open the Group Policy Management console and select the Group Policy Objects container.
2. Right-click the Domain Controller Security Policy and choose Edit.
3. Expand Computer Configuration\Policies\Windows Settings\Security Settings\Local Policies\Audit Policy.
4. Double-click Audit Object Access.
5. Select Define These Policy Settings.
6. Select the Failure check box.
7. Click OK, and then close the console.
8. To refresh the policy and ensure that all settings have been applied, open a command prompt and type the command **gpupdate**.

▶ **Exercise 3   Generate Audit Events**

You will now attempt to access the Confidential Data folder as a member of the Consultants group.

1. Log on to SERVER01 as James Fine.
2. Open My Computer and browse to C:\Confidential Data. Attempt to open the folder.
3. Create a text file on your desktop and attempt to cut and paste the file into the Confidential Data folder.

▶ **Exercise 4   Examine the Security Log**

You can now view the attempts by a consultant to access the Confidential Data folder.

1. Log on to SERVER01 as Administrator.
2. Open Event Viewer from the Administrative Tools folder.
3. Expand Windows Logs\Security.
4. Which types of events do you see in the Security log? Remember that policies can enable auditing for numerous security-related actions, including directory service access, account management, logon, and more. Notice that the source of events indicated in the Source column is Microsoft Windows security auditing.
5. To filter the log and narrow the scope of your search, click the Filter Current Log link in the Actions pane.
6. Configure the filter to be as narrow as possible.

   What do you know about the event you are trying to locate? You know it occurred within the last hour, that the source is Microsoft Windows security auditing, and that it is a File System event.
7. Check your work by referring to Figure 7-18.

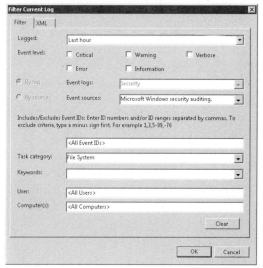

Figure 7-18   Filtering the Security Log for recent File System events

8. Click OK.

Can you more easily locate the events generated when James Fine attempted to access the Confidential Data folder?

You could not filter for the C:\Confidential Data folder name in the Filter dialog box shown in Figure 7-18. But you can locate events for that folder by exporting the file to a log analysis tool or even to a text file.

9. Click the Save Filter Log File As link in the Actions pane.
10. In the Save As dialog box, click the Desktop link in the Favorite Links pane.
11. Click the Save As Type drop-down list and choose Text.
12. In the File Name text box, type **Audit Log Export**.
13. Click Save.
14. Open the resulting text file in Notepad and search for instances of C:\Confidential Data.

▶ **Exercise 5   Use Directory Services Changes Auditing**

In this exercise, you will see the Directory Service Access auditing that is enabled by default in Windows Server 2008 and Windows Server 2003. You will then implement the new Directory Services Changes auditing of Windows Server 2008 to monitor changes to the Domain Admins group.

1. Open the Active Directory Users And Computers snap-in.
2. Click the View menu and ensure that Advanced Features is selected.
3. Select the Users container.
4. Right-click Domain Admins and choose Properties.
5. Click the Security tab, and then click Advanced.
6. Click the Auditing tab, and then click Add.
7. Type **Everyone**, and then click OK.
8. In the Auditing Entry dialog box, click the Properties tab.
9. Select the check box below Successful and next to Write Members.
10. Click OK.
11. Click OK to close the Advanced Security Settings dialog box.

    You have specified to audit any changes to the *member* attribute of the Domain Admins group. You will now make two changes to the group's membership.

12. Click the Members tab.
13. Add the user James Fine and click Apply.
14. Select James Fine, click Remove, and then click Apply.
15. Click OK to close the Domain Admins Properties dialog box.
16. Open the Security log and locate the events that were generated when you added and removed James Fine. The Event ID is 4662. Examine the information provided on the General tab.

You will be able to identify that a user (Administrator) accessed an object (Domain Admins) and used a Write Property access. The property itself is displayed as a globally unique identifier (GUID)—you cannot readily identify that the *member* attribute was changed. The event also does not detail the change that was made to the property.

You will now enable Directory Service Changes auditing, a new feature of Windows Server 2008.

17. Open a command prompt and type the following command:

```
auditpol /set /subcategory:"directory service changes" /success:enable
```

18. Open the properties of Domain Admins and add James Fine to the group.

19. Return to the Event Viewer snap-in and refresh the view of the Security log. You should see both a Directory Service Access event (Event ID 5136) and a Directory Service Changes event (Event ID 5136). If you do not see the Directory Service Changes event, wait a few moments, and then refresh the view again. It can take a few seconds for the Directory Service Changes event to be logged.

20. Examine the information in the Directory Service Changes event.

The information on the General tab clearly indicates that a user (Administrator) made a change to an object in the directory (Domain Admins) and that the specific change made was adding James Fine.

Lesson Summary

- Audit Policy defines whether success or failure events are audited. There are a number of audit policies related to specific types of activities such as account logon, object access, and directory service changes.

- To audit file system access, you must add auditing entries to the SACL of a file or folder, define the Audit Object Access policy setting, and evaluate resulting audit entries in the Security log.

- Windows Server 2008 enables a more detailed auditing of changes to objects in Active Directory. You can use the *Auditpol.exe* command to enable this new category of auditing. Events display the attribute that was changed and clearly indicate the type of change that was made or the previous and current value of the attribute.

Lesson Review

You can use the following questions to test your knowledge of the information in Lesson 4, "Auditing." The questions are also available on the companion CD if you prefer to review them in electronic form.

1. You are concerned that an individual is trying to gain access to computers by logging on with valid domain user names and a variety of attempted passwords. Which audit policy should you configure and monitor for such activities?

   A. Logon Event failures

   B. Directory Service Access failures

   C. Privilege Use successes

   D. Account Logon Event failures

   E. Account Management failures

2. You want to audit changes to attributes of user accounts used by administrators in your organization. When a change is made, you want to see both the previous and changed values of the attribute. What must you do to achieve your goal?

   A. Define Account Management audit policy.

   B. Use the *Auditpol.exe* command.

   C. Enable Privilege Use auditing.

   D. Define Directory Service Access audit policy.

3. Your organization includes 10 file servers, which have computer accounts in the Servers OU of your domain. A GPO named Server Configuration is linked to the Servers OU. On five of the servers, a folder called Confidential Data exists. You have hired a team of consultants to assist on a project, and you want to ensure that those consultants cannot access the Confidential Data folder. You configure permissions on the folder to prevent access by consultants, and you want to audit any attempt by consultants to open or manipulate the folder. Which steps must you take? (Choose three. Each correct answer is part of the solution.)

   A. Add audit entries to the Confidential Data folder to audit successful Full Control access.

   B. Evaluate entries in the Security logs on the domain controllers.

   C. Define the Audit Directory Service Access policy in the Server Configuration GPO.

   D. Define the Audit Object Access policy in the Default Domain Controllers GPO.

   E. Define the Audit Object Access policy in the Server Configuration GPO.

   F. Evaluate entries in the Security logs on each file server.

   G. Add audit entries to the Confidential Data folder to audit failed Full Control access.

Chapter Review

To further practice and reinforce the skills you learned in this chapter, you can perform the following tasks:

- Review the chapter summary.
- Review the list of key terms introduced in this chapter.
- Complete the case scenarios. These scenarios set up real-world situations involving the topics of this chapter and ask you to create a solution.
- Complete the suggested practices.
- Take a practice test.

Chapter Summary

- Group Policy can be used to configure the membership of groups, security settings, software management, and auditing.
- In addition to the Group Policy Management console and a Group Policy Management Editor, numerous tools affect Group Policy, including security templates, the Security Configuration Wizard, *Scwcmd.exe*, and *Auditpol.exe*.
- It is critical that you know how to scope GPOs effectively, both for the 70-640 exam and for the success of Group Policy in your enterprise.
- Restricted groups policies can add members to a group in a cumulative manner or can define the single, authoritative membership of a group.
- The new Security Configuration Wizard creates role-based security policies that can incorporate security templates managed by snap-ins that have existed in previous versions of Windows. The *Scwcmd.exe* command can transform a security policy into a GPO.
- Software can be assigned to users or computers or can be published to users for installation using Control Panel. Group Policy Software Installation can also manage the redeployment, upgrade, or removal of an application.
- Auditing file system access, directory service access, or directory service changes requires defining Audit Policy and auditing entries in the SACL of objects.

Key Terms

Use these key terms to understand better the concepts covered in this chapter.

- **audit policy**   A setting that configures the logging of security-related activities.
- **delegation**   An assignment of administrative responsibility. A grant of permission to perform an administrative task.
- **Extensible Markup Language (XML)**   An abbreviated version of the Standard Generalized Markup Language (SGML). XML enables the flexible development of user-defined document types and provides a nonproprietary, persistent, and verifiable file format for the storage and transmission of text and data both on and off the Internet.
- **firewall**   A hardware or software product designed to isolate a system or network from another network. Traditionally used to protect a private network from intrusion from the Internet, firewall technology is now included in Windows through Windows Firewall With Advanced Security. A firewall inspects inbound or outbound packets or both and determines, based on rules, which packets to allow to the other side of the firewall.
- **Lightweight Directory Access Protocol (LDAP)**   The primary access protocol for Active Directory. LDAP version 3 is defined by a set of Proposed Standard documents in Internet Engineering Task Force (IETF) RFC 2251.
- **local Group Policy object**   A Group Policy object (GPO) stored on each computer running Windows. Settings in a local GPO are overwritten by conflicting settings in Active Directory–based GPOs.
- **security template**   A collection of security-related configuration settings stored as a text file with a .inf extension. You can use the Security Configuration and Analysis snap-in to create a database based on the security template to analyze the compliance of a computer with the settings in the template or to apply the settings in the template to a computer.
- **service**   A process that performs a specific system function to support applications or other services. Some examples of services are Active Directory Domain Services, DFS Replication, Netlogon, Server, Task Scheduler, and Windows Event Log.
- **Windows Installer package (.msi file)**   A database that contains instructions about the installation and removal of one or more applications.
- **Windows Installer transform (.mst file)**   A file that customizes a Windows Installer package. Some applications support the use of transforms to automate or customize application installation. See Windows Installer package.

Case Scenarios

In the following case scenarios, you will apply what you've learned about managing security settings, Group Policy with software installation, and auditing. You can find answers to these questions in the "Answers" section at the end of this book.

Case Scenario 1: Software Installation with Group Policy Software Installation

You are an administrator at Contoso, Ltd. You will be deploying a new application to the users in your mobile sales force, and you would like to do so using Group Policy software installation (GPSI). In your Active Directory, all users are in the Employees OU, and all client computer accounts are in the Clients OU. The application is licensed per machine. When sales personnel are at the office, they log on to other systems such as computers in conference rooms. You want to ensure that the application is installed only on the sales force's desktops and laptops—not on other computers. You have created a transform that automates installation of the application's Windows Installer package.

1. Should the package for the application be created in the Computer Configuration node or User Configuration node of a GPO? Why?
2. When you create the package, should you choose Publish, Assign, or Advanced? Why?
3. How should you scope the GPO so that it applies only to the mobile sales force users?

Case Scenario 2: Security Configuration

You are an administrator at Contoso, Ltd. You maintain twenty servers for the Human Resources department—servers that are distributed across seven global sites. The Salaries folder is replicated to a server in each site. Because the folder contains highly sensitive information about employee compensation, you have been asked to secure it thoroughly and audit inappropriate attempts to access it. You have applied NTFS permissions that allow only appropriate HR personnel access to the Salaries folders—even the Administrators groups on the servers do not have access. Of course, members of a server's Administrators group can always take ownership of a resource and give themselves permissions, but that can be audited as well. To improve the security of these servers and their sensitive data further, you want to ensure that only your user account and that of the vice president of HR are administrators of the server—the vice president's account is to be used as a backup when you are not available. You want to deploy this configuration to all seven servers without having to reproduce each step manually. You are not delegated permissions to create or modify Group Policy objects in your organization.

1. You must audit inappropriate attempts to access the Salaries folder. You are also to audit any access to the folder by members of the Administrators group on the server, including attempts to take ownership of the folder. What auditing entries should you configure on the Salaries folder?

2. What policy setting should you configure to enforce the limited membership of the Administrators group? Can you remove the Administrator account with this policy?

3. Which audit policies should you configure?

4. How can you deploy this configuration to the seven servers without Group Policy?

5. Can policy settings in Active Directory–based GPOs override your settings? If so, how can you monitor the servers occasionally to ensure that your configuration is not being changed?

Suggested Practices

To help you successfully master the exam objectives presented in this chapter, complete the following tasks.

Restricted Groups

In this practice, you will create a best practices framework for the delegation of support for client computers. You will configure the Administrators group on client computers so that it includes the corporate Help Desk and a support group specific to a geographical site. Administrators will not include Domain Admins.

To perform this practice, you must have the following objects in the Active Directory domain:

- A first-level OU named Admins.
- Two child OUs in the Admins OU: Identities and Groups.
- A global security group named Help Desk in the Admins\ Admin Groups OU.
- A global security group named NYC Support in the Admins\ Admin Groups OU.
- One or more user accounts representing corporate help desk personnel in the Admins\Identities OU. These users are members of the Help Desk group.
- One or more users representing members of the New York desktop support team in the Admins\Identities OU. These users are members of the NYC Support group.
- A first-level OU named Clients.
- An OU named NYC in the Clients OU.
- A computer object named DESKTOP101 in the Clients\NYC OU.
- **Practice 1**   In this practice, you will create intermediate groups to manage the delegation of administration. Create two domain local security groups in the Admins\Groups OU: SYS_Clients_Admins and SYS_NYC_Admins. Add the Help Desk group as a member of SYS_Clients_Admins and add the NYC Support group as a member of SYS_NYC_Admins.
- **Practice 2**   Create a GPO that defines the membership of Administrators as *only* the SYS_Clients_Admins group. Refer to the steps in Exercise 2, "Delegate the Administration of a Subset of Clients in the Domain," of Lesson 1 if you need help. In this practice,

however, you must create a restricted groups policy for Administrators that uses the Members Of This Group setting and specifies SYS_Clients_Admins. Scope the GPO to apply to all computers in the Clients OU.

- **Practice 3**   This practice is identical to Exercise 3, "Confirm the Cumulative Application of Member Of Policies," of Lesson 1. Create a GPO that ensures that the SYS_NYC_Admins group is a member of Administrators. Create a restricted group policy for SYS_NYC_Admins that uses the This Group Is A Member Of setting and specifies Administrators. Scope the GPO to apply to all computers in the NYC OU.

- **Practice 4**   Use Resultant Set of Policy (RSoP) Modeling and verify that the Administrators group contains SYS_Clients_Admins and SYS_NYC_Admins. Refer to Exercise 3 in Lesson 1 for the required steps if you need assistance. If you have a test computer named DESKTOP101 joined to the domain, refer to Optional Exercise 4, "Confirm the Membership of the Administrators Group," in Lesson 1 for the required steps to log on and validate the membership of the Administrators group. On DESKTOP101, you will see that the Administrators group no longer includes Domain Admins.

This practice appears similar to the practice in Lesson 1, but it varies in two significant ways. First, Practice 2 uses the Members setting of a restricted groups policy, which has the effect of removing the Domain Admins group from the local Administrators group. This is a best practice because the Domain Admins group should be used only for directory service and domain controller–related administration, not for universal system support. Second, in Lesson 1, you used Group Policy to add the Help Desk and NYC Support groups directly to the Administrators group of clients. In this practice, you added the intermediate groups—SYS_Clients_Admins and SYS_NYC_Admins—to the Administrators group on client systems, so the help desk and NYC support teams are still members, but indirectly. The advantage of the indirect structure is that if other groups need to be members of the Administrators group, you do not need to change your policies and configuration—you simply add them to the domain local group. If, for example, you deploy an application that requires local administrative credentials on all clients, you do not need to touch each system, and you do not need to change your GPOs. You simply add the application's account to the SYS_Clients_Admins group. Similarly, if a team of auditors is assigned to examine all computers in New York, you add the team to the SYS_NYC_Admins group. No change to security configuration or GPOs is required.

Security Configuration

In this practice, you will implement a security configuration similar to that proposed in Case Scenario 2, "Security Configuration." Review Case Scenario 2 before proceeding. You will need the following objects in Active Directory to perform these practices:

- A first-level OU named Admins with a sub-OU named Admin Groups
- A group in the Admin Groups OU named HR Server Admins

- A first-level OU named Groups
- A group in the Groups OU named Human Resources

In addition, you will need a folder named Salaries on the C drive of SERVER01.

- **Practice 1**   In the Security Templates snap-in, create a new security template called **HR Server**. In the Local Policies\Audit Policy node, configure Audit Object Access to audit success and failure events and configure Audit Privilege Use to audit successes. In the Restricted Groups node, add a new restricted group policy for Administrators that defines Members Of This Group as HR Server Admins. In Active Directory Users And Computers, make a note of the current membership of the Administrators group (in the BUILTIN OU) so that you can restore the membership to this state after the practice. Save the template by right-clicking HR Server and choosing Save.

- **Practice 2**   Case Scenario 2 suggested that you would manually configure permissions and auditing entries on the Salaries folder. Windows provides file system policies that enable you to configure permissions and auditing entries through policies so that you do not have to do so manually and so that security can be reapplied and enforced through policy. In the HR Server security template, right-click the File System node and choose Add File. In the dialog box that appears, type **C:\Salaries** in the Folder text box and click OK. In the Database Security dialog box, remove all entries and add a permission for Human Resources that gives the group Full Control permission. That should be the only permission applied. Click the Advanced button and click the Auditing tab. Add an auditing entry for Everyone that audits failed full-control access. Add a second auditing entry for Administrators that audits successful full-control access. Click OK to close all dialog boxes, accepting all defaults that are presented. Save the template by right-clicking HR Server and choosing Save.

- **Practice 3**   In the Security Configuration And Analysis snap-in, open a new database named **HR Server Configuration**. Import the HR Server template you created in Practices 1 and 2. Right-click Security Configuration And Analysis and choose Analyze Computer Now. Click OK. Examine the three nodes of security settings that you modified: Audit Policy, Restricted Groups, and File System. Locate the discrepancies between the computer's current settings and the settings in the template.

- **Practice 4**   Right-click Security Configuration And Analysis and choose Configure Computer Now. Click OK. Confirm the changes that were made by examining the membership of the Administrators group in the BUILTIN OU and by examining the security and auditing settings on the C:\Salaries folder.

Be sure to reset the membership of the Administrators group to the original members you recorded in Practice 1. If you did not record the original membership of the group, make sure that Enterprise Admins and Domain Admins are members.

Take a Practice Test

The practice tests on this book's companion CD offer many options. For example, you can test yourself on just one exam objective, or you can test yourself on all the 70-640 certification exam content. You can set up the test so that it closely simulates the experience of taking a certification exam, or you can set it up in study mode so that you can look at the correct answers and explanations after you answer each question.

MORE INFO   Practice tests

For details about all the practice test options available, see the "How to Use the Practice Tests" section in this book's introduction.

Chapter 8
Authentication

When a user logs on to an Active Directory Domain Services (AD DS) domain, she enters her user name and password, and the client uses those credentials to *authenticate* the user—to validate the user's identity against her Active Directory account. In Chapter 3, "Users," you learned how to create and manage user accounts and their properties, including their passwords. In this chapter, you will explore the domain-side components of authentication, including the policies that specify password requirements and the auditing of authentication-related activities. You will also discover two new options, password settings objects (PSOs) and read-only domain controllers (RODCs).

Exam objectives in this chapter:
- Creating and Maintaining Active Directory Objects
    - Configure account policies.
    - Configure audit policy by using GPOs.
- Configuring the Active Directory Infrastructure
    - Configure Active Directory replication.
- Configuring Additional Active Directory Server Roles
    - Configure the read-only domain controller (RODC).

Lessons in this chapter:

- Lesson 1: Configuring Password and Lockout Policies. 357
- Lesson 2: Auditing Authentication 368
- Lesson 3: Configuring Read-Only Domain Controllers 374

Before You Begin

To complete the lessons in this chapter, you must have installed a domain controller named SERVER01 in the *contoso.com* domain.

Real World

Dan Holme

As I work with clients to implement AD DS, I must constantly balance the need to maintain high levels of security with the need to continue conducting the client's business. With versions of Microsoft Windows prior to Windows Server 2008, I constantly ran into two scenarios in which this balance was particularly difficult to reach. The first relates to the security of user accounts with high levels of privilege within the enterprise. Such accounts are particularly attractive to hackers, so they should be locked down with particularly lengthy and complex passwords. In earlier versions of Windows, only one password policy could be applied to all accounts in the domain. Therefore, I either had to apply the highly restrictive password policy to all users in the domain, which was never a palatable solution, or ask administrators to follow the more restrictive policy but with no way to require compliance. Windows Server 2008 introduces fine-grained password policies that can be used to apply more or less restrictive passwords after requirements to groups or users in a domain.

Branch offices were also highly problematic because I had to balance the user's need to be authenticated quickly and reliably against the branch office's desire to centralize control over the physical security of domain controllers. Placing a domain controller in a branch office would clearly improve performance for users in the office but would also typically expose the domain controller to lower levels of security than those maintained at the data center. Coming to the rescue once again, Windows Server 2008 can act as a read-only domain controller, authenticating users and the branch office without storing all domain user credentials, thus reducing the risk to the enterprise in the event of a stolen branch office domain controller.

If you have worked with Active Directory for any period of time, you already appreciate the value of fine-grained password policies and read-only domain controllers. If you are new to Active Directory, you are lucky to be able to work with these much-anticipated new features.

Lesson 1: Configuring Password and Lockout Policies

In a Windows Server 2008 domain, users are required to change their password every 42 days, and a password must be at least seven characters long and meet complexity requirements including the use of three of four character types: uppercase, lowercase, numeric, and nonalphanumeric. Three password policies—maximum password age, password length, and password complexity—are among the first policies encountered by administrators and users alike in an Active Directory domain. Rarely do these default settings align precisely with the password security requirements of an organization. Your organization might require passwords to be changed more or less frequently or to be longer. In this lesson, you'll learn how to implement your enterprise's password and lockout policies by modifying the Default Domain Policy Group Policy object (GPO).

There are exceptions to every rule, and you likely have exceptions to your password policies. To enhance the security of your domain, you can set more restrictive password requirements for accounts assigned to administrators, for accounts used by services such as Microsoft SQL Server, or for a backup utility. In earlier versions of Windows, this was not possible; a single password policy applied to all accounts in the domain. In this lesson, you will learn to configure fine-grained password policies, a new feature in Windows Server 2008 that enables you to assign different password policies to users and groups in your domain.

> **After this lesson, you will be able to:**
> - Implement your domain password policy.
> - Configure and assign fine-grained password policies.
>
> **Estimated lesson time: 45 minutes**

Understanding Password Policies

Your domain's password policy is configured by a GPO scoped to the domain. Within the GPO, in the Computer Configuration\Policies\Windows Settings\ Security Settings\ Account Policies \Password Policy node, you can configure the policy settings that determine password requirements. The Password Policy node is shown in Figure 8-1.

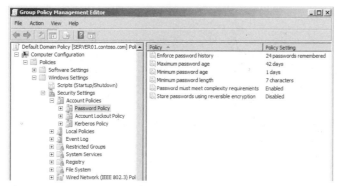

Figure 8-1   The Password Policy node of a GPO

You can understand the effects of the policies by considering the life cycle of a user password. A user will be required to change his or her password within the number of days specified by the Maximum Password Age policy setting. When the user enters a new password, the length of the new password will be compared to the number of characters in the Minimum Password Length policy. If the Password Must Meet Complexity Requirements policy is enabled, the password must contain at least three of four character types:

- Uppercase—for example, A–Z
- Lowercase—for example, a–z
- Numeric—0–9
- Nonalphanumeric—symbols such as !, #, %, or &

If the new password meets requirements, Active Directory puts the password through a mathematical algorithm that produces a representation of the password called the *hash code*. The hash code is unique; no two passwords can create the same hash code. The algorithm used to create the hash code is called a one-way function. You cannot put the hash code through a reverse function to derive the password. The fact that a hash code, and not the password itself, is stored in Active Directory helps increase the security of the user account.

Occasionally, applications require the ability to read a user's password. This is not possible because, by default, only the hash code is stored in Active Directory. To support such applications, you can enable the Store Passwords Using Reversible Encryption policy. This policy is not enabled by default, but if you enable the policy, user passwords are stored in an encrypted form that can be decrypted by the application. Reversible encryption significantly reduces the security of your domain, so it is disabled by default, and you should strive to eliminate applications that require direct access to passwords.

Additionally, Active Directory can check a cache of the user's previous hash codes to make sure that the new password is not the same as the user's previous passwords. The number of previous passwords against which a new password is evaluated is determined by the Enforce Password History policy. By default, Windows maintains the previous 24 hash codes.

If a user is determined to reuse a password when the password expiration period occurs, he or she could simply change the password 25 times to work around the password history. To prevent that from happening, the Minimum Password Age policy specifies an amount of time that must pass between password changes. By default, it is one day. Therefore, the determined user would have to change his or her password once a day for 25 days to reuse a password. This type of deterrent is generally successful at discouraging such behavior.

Each of these policy settings affects a user who changes his or her password. The settings do not affect an administrator using the Reset Password command to change another user's password.

Understanding Account Lockout Policies

An intruder can gain access to the resources in your domain by determining a valid user name and password. User names are relatively easy to identify because most organizations create user names from an employee's e-mail address, initials, combinations of first and last names, or employee IDs. When a user name is known, the intruder must determine the correct password by guessing or by repeatedly logging on with combinations of characters or words until the logon is successful.

This type of attack can be thwarted by limiting the number of incorrect logons that are allowed. That is exactly what account lockout policies achieve. Account lockout policies are located in the node of the GPO directly below Password Policy. The Account Lockout Policy node is shown in Figure 8-2.

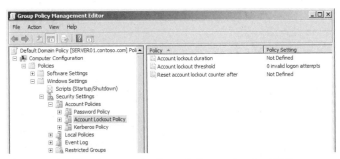

Figure 8-2 The Account Lockout Policy node of a GPO

Three settings are related to account lockout. The first, Account Lockout Threshold, determines the number of invalid logon attempts permitted within a time specified by the Account Lockout Duration policy. If an attack results in more unsuccessful logons within that timeframe, the user account is locked out. When an account is locked out, Active Directory will deny logon to that account, even if the correct password is specified.

An administrator can unlock a locked user account by following the procedure you learned in Chapter 3. You can also configure Active Directory to unlock the account automatically after a delay specified by the Reset Account Lockout Counter After policy setting.

Configuring the Domain Password and Lockout Policy

Active Directory supports one set of password and lockout policies for a domain. These policies are configured in a GPO that is scoped to the domain. A new domain contains a GPO called the Default Domain Policy that is linked to the domain and that includes the default policy settings shown in Figure 8-1 and Figure 8-2. You can change the settings by editing the Default Domain Policy.

Practice It   You can practice configuring a domain's password and lockout policies in Exercise 1, "Configure the Domain's Password and Lockout Policies," in the practice for this lesson.

The password settings configured in the Default Domain Policy affect all user accounts in the domain. The settings can be overridden, however, by the password-related properties of the individual user accounts. On the Account tab of a user's Properties dialog box, you can specify settings such as Password Never Expires or Store Passwords Using Reversible Encryption. For example, if five users have an application that requires direct access to their passwords, you can configure the accounts for those users to store their passwords, using reversible encryption.

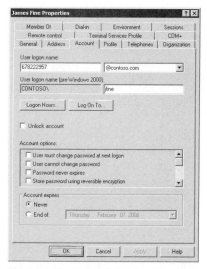

Figure 8-3   Password-related properties of a user account

Fine-Grained Password and Lockout Policy

You can also override the domain password and lockout policy by using a new feature of Windows Server 2008 called *fine-grained password and lockout policy*, often shortened to simply *fine-grained password policy*. Fine-grained password policy enables you to configure a policy that applies to one or more groups or users in your domain. To use fine-grained password policy, your domain must be at the Windows Server 2008 domain functional level described in Chapter 12, "Domains and Forests."

This feature is a highly anticipated addition to Active Directory. There are several scenarios for which fine-grained password policy can be used to increase the security of your domain. Accounts used by administrators are delegated privileges to modify objects in Active Directory; therefore, if an intruder compromises an administrator's account, more damage can be done to the domain than could be done through the account of a standard user. For that reason, consider implementing stricter password requirements for administrative accounts. For example, you might require greater password length and more frequent password changes.

Accounts used by services such as SQL Server also require special treatment in a domain. A service performs its tasks with credentials that must be authenticated with a user name and password just like those of a human user. However, most services are not capable of changing their own password, so administrators configure service accounts with the Password Never Expires option enabled. When an account's password will not be changed, make sure the password is difficult to compromise. You can use fine-grained password policies to specify an extremely long minimum password length and no password expiration.

Understanding Password Settings Objects

The settings managed by fine-grained password policy are identical to those in the Password Policy and Accounts Policy nodes of a GPO. However, fine-grained password policies are not implemented as part of Group Policy, nor are they applied as part of a GPO. Instead, there is a separate class of object in Active Directory that maintains the settings for fine-grained password policy: the *password settings object* (PSO).

Exam Tip   There can be one, and only one, authoritative set of password and lockout policy settings that applies to all users in a domain. Those settings are configured in the Default Domain Policy GPO. Fine-grained password policies, which apply to individual groups or users in the domain, are implemented using PSOs.

Most Active Directory objects can be managed with user-friendly graphical user interface (GUI) tools such as the Active Directory Users and Computers snap-in. You manage PSOs, however, with low-level tools, including ADSI Edit.

MORE INFO   Password Policy Basic

Although it will not be addressed on the 70-640 exam, it is highly recommended that you use Password Policy Basic by Special Operations Software to manage fine-grained password policy. The GUI tool can be downloaded free from *http://www.specopssoft.com*.

You can create one or more PSOs in your domain. Each PSO contains a complete set of password and lockout policy settings. A PSO is applied by linking the PSO to one or more global security groups or users. For example, to configure a strict password policy for administrative accounts, create a global security group, add the service user accounts as members, and link a PSO to the group. Applying fine-grained password policies to a group in this manner is more manageable than applying the policies to each individual user account. If you create a new service account, you simply add it to the group, and the account becomes managed by the PSO.

PSO Precedence and Resultant PSO

A PSO can be linked to more than one group or user, an individual group or user can have more than one PSO linked to it, and a user can belong to multiple groups. So which fine-grained password and lockout policy settings apply to a user? One and only one PSO determines the password and lockout settings for a user; this PSO is called the *resultant PSO*. Each PSO has an attribute that determines the precedence of the PSO. The precedence value is any number greater than 0, where the number 1 indicates highest precedence. If multiple PSOs apply to a user, the PSO with the highest precedence (closest to 1) takes effect. The rules that determine precedence are as follows:

- If multiple PSOs apply to groups to which the user belongs, the PSO with the highest precedence prevails.
- If one or more PSOs are linked directly to the user, PSOs linked to groups are ignored, regardless of their precedence. The user-linked PSO with highest precedence prevails.
- If one or more PSOs have the same precedence value, Active Directory must make a choice. It picks the PSO with the lowest globally unique identifier (GUID). GUIDs are like serial numbers for Active Directory objects—no two objects have the same GUID. GUIDs have no particular meaning—they are just identifiers—so choosing the PSO with the lowest GUID is, in effect, an arbitrary decision. Configure PSOs with unique, specific precedence values so that you avoid this scenario.

These rules determine the resultant PSO. Active Directory exposes the resultant PSO in a user object attribute, so you can readily identify the PSO that will affect a user. You will examine that attribute in the practice at the end of this lesson. PSOs contain all password and lockout settings, so there is no inheritance or merging of settings. The resultant PSO is the authoritative PSO.

PSOs and OUs

PSOs can be linked to global security groups or users. PSOs cannot be linked to organizational units (OUs). If you want to apply password and lockout policies to users in an OU, you must create a global security group that includes all the users in the OU. This type of group is called a *shadow group*—its membership shadows, or mimics, the membership of an OU.

> ## Quick Check
> - You want to require that administrators maintain a password of at least 15 characters and change the password every 45 days. The administrators' user accounts are in an OU called Admins. You do not want to apply the restrictive password policy to all domain users. What do you do?
>
> ## Quick Check Answer
> - Create a global security group that contains all users in the Admins OU. Create a PSO that configures the password policies and link the PSO to the group.

Shadow groups are conceptual, not technical objects. You simply create a group and add the users that belong to the OU. If you change the membership of the OU, you must also change the membership of the group.

MORE INFO **Shadow groups**

Additional information about PSOs and shadow groups is available at *http://technet2.microsoft.com /windowsserver2008/en/library/2199dcf7-68fd-4315-87cc-ade35f8978ea1033.mspx?mfr=true.*

MORE INFO **Maintaining shadow group membership with scripts**

You can use scripts to maintain the membership of shadow groups dynamically so that they always reflect the users in OUs. You can find example scripts in *Windows Administration Resource Kit: Productivity Solutions for IT Professionals* by Dan Holme (Microsoft Press, 2008).

PRACTICE **Configuring Password and Lockout Policies**

In this practice, you will use Group Policy to configure the domain-wide password and lockout policies for *contoso.com*. You will then secure administrative accounts by configuring more restrictive, fine-grained password and lockout policies.

▶ **Exercise 1   Configure the Domain's Password and Lockout Policies**

In this exercise, you will modify the Default Domain Policy GPO to implement a password and lockout policy for users in the *contoso.com* domain.

1. Log on to SERVER01 as Administrator.
2. Open the Group Policy Management console from the Administrative Tools folder.
3. Expand Forest, Domains, and *contoso.com*.
4. Right-click Default Domain Policy underneath the *contoso.com* domain and choose Edit. You might be prompted with a reminder that you are changing the settings of a GPO.

5. Click OK.

    The Group Policy Management Editor appears.

6. Expand Computer Configuration\Policies\Security Settings\Account Policies, and then select Password Policy.

7. Double-click the following policy settings in the console details pane and configure the settings indicated:

    ❑ Maximum Password Age: 90 Days

    ❑ Minimum Password Length: 10 characters

8. Select Account Lockout Policy in the console tree.

9. Double-click the Account Lockout Threshold policy setting and configure it for 5 Invalid Logon Attempts. Then click OK.

10. A Suggested Value Changes window appears. Click OK.

    The values for Account Lockout Duration and Reset Account Lockout Counter After are automatically set to 30 minutes.

11. Close the Group Policy Management Editor window.

▶ **Exercise 2   Create a Password Settings Object**

In this exercise, you will create a PSO that applies a restrictive, fine-grained password policy to users in the Domain Admins group. Before you proceed with this exercise, confirm that the Domain Admins group is in the Users container. If it is not, move it to the Users container.

1. Open ADSI Edit from the Administrative Tools folder.

2. Right-click ADSI Edit and choose Connect To.

3. In the Name box, type **contoso.com**. Click OK.

4. Expand *contoso.com* and select DC=contoso,DC=com.

5. Expand DC=contoso,DC=com and select CN=System.

6. Expand CN=System and select CN= Password Settings Container.

    All PSOs are created and stored in the Password Settings Container (PSC).

7. Right-click the PSC, choose New, and then select Object.

    The Create Object dialog box appears. It prompts you to select the type of object to create. There is only one choice: msDS-PasswordSettings—the technical name for the object class referred to as a PSO.

8. Click Next.

    You are then prompted for the value for each attribute of a PSO. The attributes are similar to those found in the GPO you examined in Exercise 1.

9. Configure each attribute as indicated in the following list. Click Next after each attribute.

    ❑ Common Name: **My Domain Admins PSO**. This is the friendly name of the PSO.

    ❑ msDS-PasswordSettingsPrecedence: **1**. This PSO has the highest possible precedence because its value is the closest to 1.

❑ msDS-PasswordReversibleEncryptionEnabled: **False**. The password is not stored using reversible encryption.

❑ msDS-PasswordHistoryLength: **30**. The user cannot reuse any of the last 30 passwords.

❑ msDS-PasswordComplexityEnabled: **True**. Password complexity rules are enforced.

❑ msDS-MinimumPasswordLength: **15**. Passwords must be at least 15 characters long.

❑ msDS-MinimumPasswordAge: **1:00:00:00**. A user cannot change his or her password within one day of a previous change. The format is d:hh:mm:ss (days, hours, minutes, seconds).

❑ MaximumPasswordAge: **45:00:00:00**. The password must be changed every 45 days.

❑ msDS-LockoutThreshold: **5**. Five invalid logons within the time frame specified by XXX (the next attribute) will result in account lockout.

❑ msDS-LockoutObservationWindow: **0:01:00:00**. Five invalid logons (specified by the previous attribute) within one hour will result in account lockout.

❑ msDS-LockoutDuration: **1:00:00:00**. An account, if locked out, will remain locked for one day or until it is unlocked manually. A value of zero will result in the account remaining locked out until an administrator unlocks it.

The attributes listed are required. After clicking Next on the *msDS-LockoutDuration* attribute page, you will be able to configure the optional attribute.

10. Click the More Attributes button.

11. In the Edit Attributes box, type **CN=DomainAdmins,CN=Users,DC=contoso,DC=com** and click OK.

Click Finish.

▶ **Exercise 3   Identify the Resultant PSO for a User**

In this exercise, you will identify the PSO that controls the password and lockout policies for an individual user.

1. Open the Active Directory Users And Computers snap-in.

2. Click the View menu and make sure that Advanced Features is selected.

3. Expand the *contoso.com* domain and click the Users container in the console tree.

4. Right-click the Administrator account and choose Properties.

5. Click the Attribute Editor tab.

6. Click the Filter button and make sure that Constructed is selected.

The attribute you will locate in the next step is a *constructed* attribute, meaning that the resultant PSO is not a hard-coded attribute of a user; rather, it is calculated by examining the PSOs linked to a user in real time.

7. In the Attributes list, locate *msDS-ResultantPSO*.

8. Identify the PSO that affects the user.

The My Domain Admins PSO that you created in Exercise 2, "Create a Password Settings Object," is the resultant PSO for the Administrator account.

▶ **Exercise 4   Delete a PSO**

In this exercise, you will delete the PSO you created in Exercise 2 so that its settings do not affect you in later exercises.

1. Repeat steps 1–6 of Exercise 2 to select the Password Settings container in ADSI Edit.

2. In the console details pane, select CN=My Domain Admins PSO.

3. Press Delete.

4. Click Yes.

Lesson Summary

- Password policy settings determine when a password can or must be changed and what the requirements of the new password are.

- Account lockout settings cause Active Directory to lock out a user account if a specified number of invalid logons occurs within a specified period of time. Lockout helps prevent intruders from repeatedly attempting to log on to a user account in an effort to guess the user's password.

- A domain can have only one set of password and lockout policies that affect all users in the domain. These policies are defined using Group Policy. You can modify the default settings in the Default Domain Policy GPO to configure the policies for your organization.

- Windows Server 2008 gives you the option to specify different password and lockout policies for global security groups and users in your domain. Fine-grained password policies are deployed not with Group Policy but with password settings objects.

- If more than one PSO applies to a user or to groups to which a user belongs, a single PSO, called the resultant PSO, determines the effective password and lockout policies for the user. The PSO with the highest precedence (precedence value closest to 1) will prevail. If one or more PSOs are linked directly to the user rather than indirectly to groups, group-linked PSOs are not evaluated to determine the resultant PSO, and the user-linked PSO with the highest precedence will prevail.

Lesson Review

You can use the following questions to test your knowledge of the information in Lesson 1, "Configuring Password and Lockout Policies." The questions are also available on the companion CD if you prefer to review them in electronic form.

NOTE Answers

Answers to these questions and explanations of why each answer choice is right or wrong are located in the "Answers" section at the end of the book.

---

1. You are an administrator at Tailspin Toys. Your Active Directory domain includes an OU called Service Accounts that contains all user accounts. Because you have configured service accounts with passwords that never expire, you want to apply a password policy that requires passwords of at least 40 characters. Which of the following steps should you perform? (Choose all that apply. Each correct answer is part of the solution.)

   A. Set the Minimum Password Length policy in the Default Domain Policy GPO.
   B. Link a PSO to the Service Accounts OU.
   C. Create a group called Service Accounts.
   D. Link a PSO to the Service Accounts group.
   E. Add all service accounts as members of the Service Accounts group.

2. You want to configure account lockout policy so that a locked account will not be unlocked automatically. Rather, you want to require an administrator to unlock the account. Which configuration change should you make?

   A. Configure the Account Lockout Duration policy setting to 100.
   B. Configure the Account Lockout Duration policy setting to 1.
   C. Configure the Account Lockout Threshold to 0.
   D. Configure the Account Lockout Duration policy setting to 0.

3. As you evaluate the password settings objects in your domain, you discover a PSO named PSO1 with a precedence value of 1 that is linked to a group named Help Desk. Another PSO, named PSO2, with a precedence value of 99, is linked to a group named Support. Mike Danseglio is a member of both the Help Desk and Support groups. You discover that two PSOs are linked directly to Mike. PSO3 has a precedence value of 50, and PSO4 has a precedence value of 200. Which PSO is the resultant PSO for Mike?

   A. PSO1
   B. PSO2
   C. PSO3
   D. PSO4

Lesson 2: Auditing Authentication

In Chapter 7, "Group Policy Settings," you learned to configure auditing for several types of activities, including access to folders and changes to directory service objects. Windows Server 2008 also enables you to audit the logon activity of users in a domain. By auditing successful logons, you can look for instances in which an account is being used at unusual times or in unexpected locations, which might indicate that an intruder is logging on to the account. Auditing failed logons can reveal attempts by intruders to compromise an account. In this lesson, you will learn to configure logon auditing.

After this lesson, you will be able to:
- Configure auditing of authentication-related activity.
- Distinguish between account logon and logon events.
- Identify authentication-related events in the Security log.

Estimated lesson time: 30 minutes

Account Logon and Logon Events

This lesson examines two specific policy settings: Audit Account Logon Events and Audit Logon Events. It is important to understand the difference between these two similarly named policy settings.

When a user logs on to any computer in the domain using his or her domain user account, a domain controller authenticates the attempt to log on to the domain account. This generates an account logon event on the domain controller.

The computer to which the user logs on—for example, the user's laptop—generates a logon event. The computer did not authenticate the user against his or her account; it passed the account to a domain controller for validation. The computer did, however, allow the user to log on interactively to the computer. Therefore, the event is a logon event.

When the user connects to a folder on a server in the domain, that server authorizes the user for a type of logon called a network logon. Again, the server does not authenticate the user; it relies on the ticket given to the user by the domain controller. But the connection by the user generates a logon event on the server.

Exam Tip   Be certain that you can distinguish between *account logon events* and *logon events*. The simplest way to remember the difference is that an account logon event occurs where the account lives: on the domain controller that authenticates the user. A logon event occurs on the computer to which the user logs on interactively. It also occurs on the file server to which the user connects using a network logon.

Configuring Authentication-Related Audit Policies

Account logon and logon events can be audited by Windows Server 2008. The settings that manage auditing are located in a GPO in the Computer Configuration\Policies\Windows Settings \Security Settings\Local Policies\Audit Policy node. The Audit Policy node and the two settings are shown in Figure 8-4.

Figure 8-4 Authentication-related policy settings

To configure an audit policy, double-click the policy, and its properties dialog box appears. The Audit Account Logon Events Properties dialog box is shown in Figure 8-5.

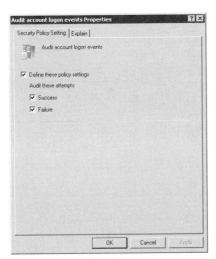

Figure 8-5 The Audit Account Logon Events Properties dialog box

The policy setting can be configured to one of the following four states:

- **Not defined** If the Define These Policy Settings check box is cleared, the policy setting is not defined. In this case, the server will audit the event based on its default settings or on the settings specified in another GPO.
- **Defined for no auditing** If the Define These Policy Settings check box is selected, but the Success and Failure check boxes are cleared, the server will not audit the event.
- **Audit successful events** If the Define These Policy Settings check box is selected, and the Success checkbox is selected, the server will log successful events in its Security log.

- **Audit failed to events**   If the Define These Policy Settings check box is selected, and the Failure check box is selected, the server will log unsuccessful events in its Security log.

A server's audit behavior is determined by the setting that wins based on the rules of policy application discussed in Chapter 6, "Group Policy Infrastructure."

Scoping Audit Policies

As with all policy settings, be careful to scope settings so that they affect the correct systems. For example, if you want to audit attempts by users to connect to file servers in your enterprise, you can configure logon event auditing in a GPO linked to the OU that contains your file servers. Alternatively, if you want to audit logons by users to desktops in your human resources department, you can configure logon event auditing in a GPO linked to the OU containing human resources computer objects. Remember that domain users logging on to a client computer or connecting to a server will generate a logon event—not an account logon event—on that system.

Only domain controllers generate account logon events for domain users. Remember that an account logon event occurs on the domain controller that authenticates a domain user, regardless of where that user logs on. If you want to audit logons to domain accounts, scope account logon event auditing to affect only domain controllers. In fact, the Default Domain Controllers GPO that is created when you install your first domain controller is an ideal GPO in which to configure account logon audit policies.

In the previous section, you learned that if an event auditing policy is not defined, the system will audit based on the settings in other GPOs or on its default setting. In Windows Server 2008, the default setting is to audit successful account logon events and successful logon events, so both types of events are, if successful, entered in the server's Security log. If you want to audit failures or turn off auditing, you will need to define the appropriate setting in the audit policy.

Quick Check

- You are concerned that an intruder is attempting to gain access to your network by guessing a user's password. You want to identify the times at which the intruder is trying to log on. What type of event should you audit? Should you configure the policy setting in the Default Domain Policy or in the Default Domain Controllers Policy?

Quick Check Answer

- Enable auditing of failed account logon events (not logon events) in the Default Domain Controllers GPO. Only domain controllers generate account logon events related to the authentication of domain users. The Default Domain Controllers GPO is scoped correctly to apply only to domain controllers.

Viewing Logon Events

Account logon and logon events, if audited, appear in the Security log of the system that generated the event. Figure 8-6 shows an example. Thus, if you are auditing logons to computers in the human resources department, the events are entered in each computer's Security log. Similarly, if you are auditing unsuccessful account logons to identify potential intrusion attempts, the events are entered in each domain controller's Security log. This means, by default, you will need to examine the Security logs of all domain controllers to get a complete picture of account logon events in your domain.

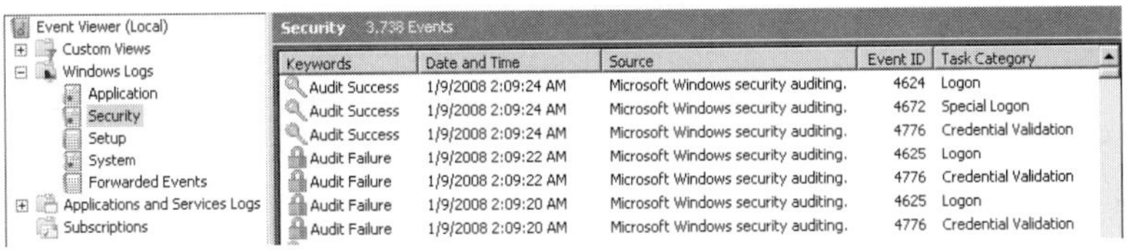

Figure 8-6   Authentication events in the Security log

As you can imagine, in a complex environment with multiple domain controllers and many users, auditing account logons or logons can generate a tremendous number of events. If there are too many events, it can be difficult to identify problematic events worthy of closer investigation. Balance the amount of logging you perform with the security requirements of your business and the resources you have available to analyze logged events.

PRACTICE **Auditing Authentication**

In this practice, you will use Group Policy to enable auditing of logon activity by users in the *contoso.com* domain. You will then generate logon events and view the resulting entries in the event logs.

▶ **Exercise 1   Configure Auditing of Account Logon Events**

In this exercise, you will modify the Default Domain Controllers Policy GPO to implement auditing of both successful and failed logons by users in the domain.

1. Open the Group Policy Management console.
2. Expand Forest\Domains\Contoso.com\Domain Controllers.
3. Right-click Default Domain Controllers Policy and select Edit.
    Group Policy Management Editor appears.
4. Expand Computer Configuration\Policies\Windows at Settings\Security Settings\Local Policies, and then select Audit Policy.
5. Double-click Audit Account Logon Events.
6. Select the Define These Policy Settings check box.
7. Select both the Success and Failure check boxes. Click OK.

8. Double-click Audit Logon Events.

9. Select the Define These Policy Settings check box.

10. Select both the Success and Failure check boxes. Click OK.

11. Close Group Policy Management Editor.

12. Click Start and click Command Prompt.

13. Type **gpupdate.exe /force**.

   This command causes SERVER01 to update its policies, at which time the new auditing settings take effect.

▶ **Exercise 2   Generate Account Logon Events**

In this exercise, you will generate account logon events by logging on with both incorrect and correct passwords.

1. Log off of SERVER01.

2. Attempt to log on as Administrator with an incorrect password. Repeat this step once or twice.

3. Log on to SERVER01 with the correct password.

▶ **Exercise 3   Examine Account Logon Events**

In this exercise, you will view the events generated by the logon activities in Exercise 2.

1. Open Event Viewer from the Administrative Tools folder.

2. Expand Windows Logs, and then select Security.

3. Identify the failed and successful events.

Lesson Summary

- Account logon events occur on a domain controller as it authenticates users logging on anywhere in the domain.

- Logon events occur on systems to which users log on, for example, to their individual desktops and laptops. Logon events are also generated in response to a network logon, for example, when a user connects to a file server.

- By default, Windows Server 2008 systems audit successful account logon and logon events.

- To examine account logon events in your domain, you must look at the individual event logs from each domain controller.

Lesson Review

You can use the following questions to test your knowledge of the information in Lesson 2, "Auditing Authentication." The questions are also available on the companion CD if you prefer to review them in electronic form.

1. You want to obtain a log that will help you isolate the times of day that failed logons are causing a user's account to be locked out. Which policy should you configure?
   A. Define the Audit Account Logon Events policy setting for Success events in the Default Domain Policy GPO.
   B. Define the Audit Account Logon Events policy setting for Failure events in the Default Domain Policy GPO.
   C. Define the Audit Logon Events policy setting for Success events in the Default Domain Policy GPO.
   D. Define the Audit Logon Events policy setting for Failure events in the Default Domain Policy GPO.

2. You want to keep track of when users log on to computers in the human resources department of Adventure Works. Which of the following methods will enable you to obtain this information?
   A. Configure the policy setting to audit successful account logon events in the Default Domain Controllers GPO. Examine the event log of the first domain controller you installed in the domain.
   B. Configure the policy setting to audit successful logon events in a GPO linked to the OU containing user accounts for employees in the human resources department. Examine the event logs of each computer in the human resources department.
   C. Configure the policy setting to audit successful logon events in a GPO linked to the OU containing computer accounts in the human resources department. Examine the event logs of each computer in the human resources department.
   D. Configure the policy setting to audit successful account logon events in a GPO linked to the OU containing computer accounts in the human resources department. Examine the event logs of each domain controller.

Lesson 3: Configuring Read-Only Domain Controllers

Branch offices present a unique challenge to an enterprise's IT staff: if a branch office is separated from the hub site by a wide area network (WAN) link, should you place a domain controller (DC) in the branch office? In previous versions of Windows, the answer to this question was not a simple one. Windows Server 2008, however, introduces a new type of DC—the read-only domain controller (RODC)—that makes the question easier to answer. In this lesson, you will explore the issues related to branch office authentication and DC placement, and you will learn how to implement and support a branch-office RODC.

> **After this lesson, you will be able to:**
> - Identify the business requirements for RODCs.
> - Install an RODC.
> - Configure password replication policy.
> - Monitor the caching of credentials on an RODC.
>
> **Estimated lesson time: 60 minutes**

Authentication and Domain Controller Placement in a Branch Office

Consider a scenario in which an enterprise is characterized by a hub site and several branch offices. The branch offices connect to the hub site over WAN links that might be congested, expensive, slow, or unreliable. Users in the branch office must be authenticated by Active Directory to access resources in the domain. Should a DC be placed in the branch office?

In branch office scenarios, many IT services are centralized in a hub site. The hub site is carefully maintained by the IT staff and includes secure facilities for services. The branch offices, however, offer inadequate security for servers and might have insufficient IT staff to support the servers.

If a DC is not placed in the branch office, authentication and service ticket activities will be directed to the hub site over the WAN link. Authentication occurs when a user first logs on to his or her computer in the morning. *Service tickets* are a component of the Kerberos authentication mechanism used by Windows Server 2008 domains. You can think of a service ticket as a key issued by the domain controller to a user. The key allows the user to connect to a service such as the File and Print services on a file server. When a user first tries to access a specific service, the user's client requests a service ticket from the domain controller. Because users typically connect to multiple services during a workday, service ticket activity happens regularly. Authentication and service ticket activity over the WAN link between a branch office and a hub site can result in slow or unreliable performance.

If a DC is placed in the branch office, authentication is much more efficient, but there are several potentially significant risks. A DC maintains a copy of all attributes of all objects in its domain, including secrets such as information related to user passwords. If a DC is accessed or stolen, it becomes possible for a determined expert to identify valid user names and passwords, at which point the entire domain is compromised. At a minimum, you must reset the passwords of every user account in the domain. Because the security of servers at branch offices is often less than ideal, a branch office DC poses a considerable security risk.

A second concern is that the changes to the Active Directory database on a branch office DC replicate to the hub site and to all other DCs in the environment. Therefore, corruption to the branch office DC poses a risk to the integrity of the enterprise directory service. For example, if a branch office administrator performs a restore of the DC from an outdated backup, there can be significant repercussions for the entire domain.

The third concern relates to administration. A branch office domain controller might require maintenance, for example, a new device driver. To perform maintenance on a standard domain controller, you must log on as a member of the Administrators group on the domain controller, which means you are effectively an administrator of the domain. It might not be appropriate to grant that level of capability to a support team at a branch office.

Read-Only Domain Controllers

These concerns—security, directory service integrity, and administration—left many enterprises with a difficult choice to make, and there was no best practices answer. The RODC is designed specifically to address the branch office scenario. An RODC is a domain controller, typically placed in the branch office, that maintains a copy of all objects in the domain and all attributes except secrets such as password-related properties. When a user in the branch office logs on, the RODC receives the request and forwards it to a domain controller in the hub site for authentication.

You are able to configure a password replication policy (PRP) for the RODC that specifies user accounts the RODC is allowed to cache. If the user logging on is included in the PRP, the RODC caches that user's credentials, so the next time authentication is requested, the RODC can perform the task locally. As users who are included in the PRP log on, the RODC builds its cache of credentials so that it can perform authentication locally for those users. These concepts are illustrated in Figure 8-7.

Because the RODC maintains only a subset of user credentials, if the RODC is compromised or stolen, the effect of the security exposure is limited; only the user accounts that had been cached on the RODC must have their passwords changed. Writable domain controllers maintain a list of all cached credentials on individual RODCs. When you delete the account of the stolen or compromised RODC from Active Directory, you are given the option to reset the passwords of all user accounts that were cached on the RODC. The RODC replicates changes to Active Directory from DCs in the hub site. Replication is one way (from a writable domain controller to a RODC); no changes to the RODC are replicated to any other domain controller. This eliminates the exposure of the directory service to corruption resulting from changes made to a compromised branch office DC. Finally, RODCs, unlike writable DCs, have a local Administrators group. You can give one or more local support personnel the ability to maintain an RODC fully, without granting them the equivalence of domain administrators.

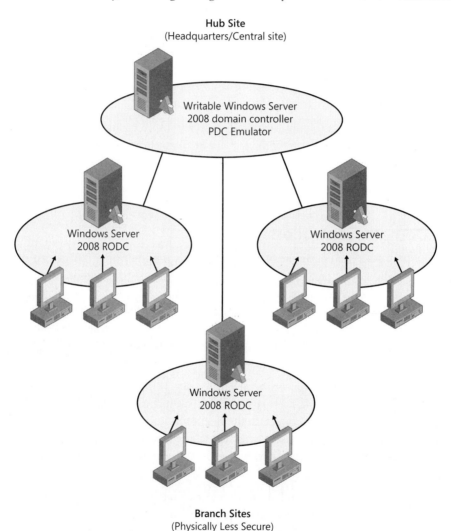

Figure 8-7   A branch office scenario supported by RODCs

Deploying an RODC

The high-level steps to install an RODC are as follows:

1. Ensure that the forest functional level is Windows Server 2003 or higher.
2. If the forest has any DCs running Microsoft Windows Server 2003, run *Adprep /rodcprep*.
3. Ensure that at least one writable DC is running Windows Server 2008.
4. Install the RODC.

Each of these steps is detailed in the following sections.

Verifying and Configuring Forest Functional Level of Windows Server 2003 or Higher

Functional levels enable features unique to specific versions of Windows and are, therefore, dependent on the versions of Windows running on domain controllers. If all domain controllers are Windows Server 2003 or later, the domain functional level can be set to Windows Server 2003. If all domains are at Windows Server 2003 domain functional level, the forest functional level can be set to Windows Server 2003. Domain and forest functional levels are discussed in detail in Chapter 12.

RODCs require that the forest functional level is Windows Server 2003 or higher. That means that all domain controllers in the entire forest are running Windows Server 2003 or later. To determine the functional level of your forest, open Active Directory Domains And Trusts from the Administrative Tools folder, right-click the name of the forest, choose Properties, and verify the forest functional level, as shown in Figure 8-8. Any user can verify the forest functional level in this way.

If the forest functional level is not at least Windows Server 2003, examine the properties of each domain to identify any domains for which the domain functional level is not at least Windows Server 2003. If you find such a domain, you must ensure that all domain controllers in the domain are running Windows Server 2003. Then, in Active Directory Domains And Trusts, right-click the domain and choose Raise Domain Functional Level. After you have raised each domain functional level to at least Windows Server 2003, right-click the root node of the Active Directory Domains And Trusts snap-in and choose Raise Forest Functional Level. In the Select An Available Forest Functional Level drop-down list, choose Windows Server 2003 and click Raise. You must be an administrator of a domain to raise the domain's functional level. To raise the forest functional level, you must be either a member of the Domain Admins group in the forest root domain or a member of the Enterprise Admins group.

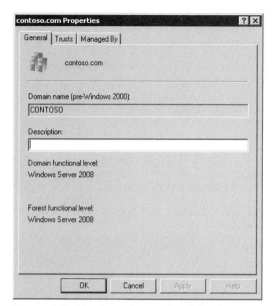

Figure 8-8 The forest Properties dialog box

Running *Adprep /rodcprep*

If you are upgrading an existing forest to include domain controllers running Windows Server 2008, you must run *Adprep /rodcprep*. This command configures permissions so that RODCs are able to replicate DNS application directory partitions. DNS application directory partitions are discussed in Chapter 9, "Integrating Domain Name System with AD DS." If you are creating a new Active Directory forest and it will have only domain controllers running Windows Server 2008, you do not need to run *Adprep /rodcprep*.

You can find this command in the *cdrom*\Sources\Adprep folder of the Windows Server 2008 installation DVD. Copy the folder to the domain controller acting as the schema master. The schema master role is discussed in Chapter 10, "Domain Controllers." Log on to the schema master as a member of the Enterprise Admins group, open a command prompt, change directories to the Adprep folder, and type **adprep /rodcprep**.

Placing a Writable Windows Server 2008 Domain Controller

An RODC must replicate domain updates from a writable domain controller running Windows Server 2008. It is critical that an RODC is able to establish a replication connection with a writable Windows Server 2008 domain controller. Ideally, the writable Windows Server 2008 domain controller should be in the closest site—the hub site. In Chapter 11, "Sites and Replication," you'll learn about Active Directory replication, sites, and site links. If you want the RODC to act as a DNS server, the writable Windows Server 2008 domain controller must also host the DNS domain zone.

> ## Quick Check
> - Your domain consists of a central site and four branch offices. A central site has two domain controllers. Each branch office site has one domain controller. All domain controllers run Windows Server 2003. Your company decides to open a fifth branch office, and you want to configure it with a new Windows Server 2008 RODC. What must you do before introducing the first RODC into your domain?
>
> ## Quick Check Answer
> - You must first ensure that the forest functional level is Windows Server 2003. Then, you must upgrade one of the existing domain controllers to Windows Server 2008 so that there is one writable Windows Server 2008 domain controller. You must also run *Adprep /rodcprep* from the Windows Server 2008 installation DVD.

Installing an RODC

After completing the preparatory steps, you can install an RODC. An RODC can be either a full or Server Core installation of Windows Server 2008. With a full installation of Windows Server 2008, you can use the Active Directory Domain Services Installation Wizard to create an RODC. Simply select Read-Only Domain Controller (RODC) on the Additional Domain Controller Options page of the wizard, as shown in Figure 8-9.

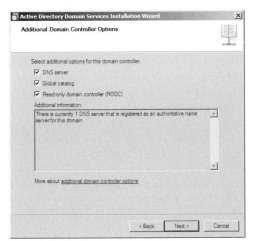

Figure 8-9 Creating an RODC with the Active Directory Domain Services Installation Wizard

Practice It   Exercise 1, "Install an RODC," in the practice at the end of this lesson walks you through the use of the Active Directory Domain Services Installation Wizard to create an RODC.

Alternatively, you can use the *Dcpromo.exe* command with the */unattend* switch to create the RODC. On a Server Core installation of Windows Server 2008, you must use the *Dcpromo.exe* */unattend* command.

It is also possible to delegate the installation of the RODC, which enables a user who is not a domain administrator to create the RODC, by adding a new server in the branch office and running *Dcpromo.exe*. To delegate the installation of an RODC, pre-create the computer account for the RODC in the Domain Controllers OU and specify the credentials that will be used to add the RODC to the domain. That user can then attach a server running Windows Server 2008 to the RODC account. The server must be a member of a workgroup—not of the domain—when creating an RODC by using delegated installation.

MORE INFO   Options for installing an RODC

For details regarding other options for installing an RODC, including delegated installation, see "Step-by-Step Guide for Read-only Domain Controllers" at *http://technet2.microsoft.com /windowsserver2008/en/library/ea8d253e-0646-490c-93d3-b78c5e1d9db71033.mspx?mfr=true.*

Password Replication Policy

Password Replication Policy (PRP) determines which users' credentials can be cached on a specific RODC. If PRP allows an RODC to cache a user's credentials, then authentication and service ticket activities of that user can be processed by the RODC. If a user's credentials cannot be cached on an RODC, authentication and service ticket activities are referred by the RODC to a writable domain controller.

A PRP of an RODC is determined by two multivalued attributes of the RODC computer account. These attributes are commonly known as the Allowed List and the Denied List. If a user's account is on the Allowed List, the user's credentials are cached. You can include groups on the Allowed List, in which case all users who belong to the group can have their credentials cached on the RODC. If the user is on both the Allowed List and the Denied List, the user's credentials will not be cached—the Denied List takes precedence.

Configure Domain-Wide Password Replication Policy

To facilitate the management of PRP, Windows Server 2008 creates two domain local security groups in the Users container of Active Directory. The first, named Allowed RODC Password Replication Group, is added to the Allowed List of each new RODC. By default, the group has no members. Therefore, by default, a new RODC will not cache any user's credentials. If there are users whose credentials you want to be cached by all domain RODCs, add those users to the Allowed RODC Password Replication Group.

The second group is named Denied RODC Password Replication Group. It is added to the Denied List of each new RODC. If there are users whose credentials you want to ensure are never cached by domain RODCs, add those users to the Denied RODC Password Replication Group. By default, this group contains security-sensitive accounts that are members of groups including Domain Admins, Enterprise Admins, and Group Policy Creator Owners.

NOTE   Computers are people, too

Remember that it is not only users who generate authentication and service ticket activity. Computers in a branch office also require such activity. To improve performance of systems in a branch office, allow the branch RODC to cache computer credentials as well.

Configure RODC-Specific Password Replication Policy

The two groups described in the previous section provide a method to manage PRP on all RODCs. However, to support a branch office scenario most efficiently, you need to allow the RODC in each branch office to cache user and computer credentials in that specific location. Therefore, you need to configure the Allowed List and the Denied List of each RODC.

To configure an RODC PRP, open the properties of the RODC computer account in the Domain Controllers OU. On the Password Replication Policy tab, shown in Figure 8-10, you can view the current PRP settings and add or remove users or groups from the PRP.

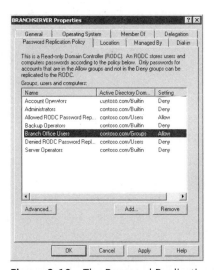

Figure 8-10   The Password Replication Policy tab of an RODC

Administer RODC Credentials Caching

When you click the Advanced button on the Password Replication Policy tab shown in Figure 8-10, an Advanced Password Replication Policy dialog box appears. An example is shown in Figure 8-11.

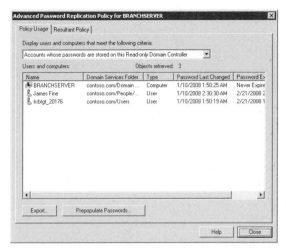

Figure 8-11   The Advanced Password Replication Policy dialog box

The drop-down list at the top of the Policy Usage tab enables you to select one of two reports for the RODC:

- **Accounts Whose Passwords Are Stored On This Read-Only Domain Controller**   Displays the list of user and computer credentials that are currently cached on the RODC. Use this list to determine whether credentials are being cached that you do not want to be cached on the RODC; modify the PRP accordingly.

- **Accounts That Have Been Authenticated To This Read-Only Domain Controller**   Displays the list of user and computer credentials that have been referred to a writable domain controller for authentication or service ticket processing. Use this list to identify users or computers that are attempting to authenticate with the RODC. If any of these accounts are not being cached, consider adding them to the PRP.

In the same dialog box, the Resultant Policy tab enables you to evaluate the effective caching policy for an individual user or computer. Click the Add button to select a user or computer account for evaluation.

You can also use the Advanced Password Replication Policy dialog box to prepopulate credentials in the RODC cache. If a user or computer is on the allow list of an RODC, the account credentials can be cached on the RODC but will not be cached until the authentication or service ticket events cause the RODC to replicate the credentials from a writable domain controller. By prepopulating credentials in the RODC cache for users and computers in the branch office, for example, you can ensure that authentication and service ticket activity will be processed locally by the RODC even when the user or computer is authenticating for the first time. To prepopulate credentials, click the Prepopulate Passwords button and select the appropriate users and computers.

Administrative Role Separation

RODCs in branch offices can require maintenance such as an updated device driver. Additionally, small branch offices might combine the RODC with the file server role on a single system, in which case it will be important to be able to back up the system. RODCs support local administration through a feature called *administrative role separation*. Each RODC maintains a local database of groups for specific administrative purposes. You can add domain user accounts to these local roles to enable support of a specific RODC.

You can configure administrative role separation by using the *Ddsmgmt.exe* command. To add a user to the Administrators role on an RODC, follow these steps:

1. Open a command prompt on the RODC.
2. Type **dsmgmt** and press Enter.
3. Type **local roles** and press Enter.

   At the *local roles* prompt, you can type **?** and press Enter for a list of commands. You can also type **list roles** and press Enter for a list of local roles.
4. Type **add** *username* **administrators**, where *username* is the pre-Windows 2000 logon name of a domain user, and press Enter.

You can repeat this process to add other users to the various local roles on an RODC.

MORE INFO Improving authentication and security

RODCs are a valuable new feature for improving authentication and security in branch offices. Be sure to read the detailed documentation on the Microsoft Web site at *http://technet2.microsoft.com /windowsserver2008/en/library/ea8d253e-0646-490c-93d3-b78c5e1d9db71033.mspx*.

PRACTICE **Configuring Read-Only Domain Controllers**

In this practice, you will implement read-only domain controllers in a simulation of a branch office scenario. You will install an RODC, configure password replication policy, monitor credential caching, and prepopulate credentials on the RODC. To perform this practice, you must complete the following preparatory tasks:

- Install a second server running Windows Server 2008. Name the server **BRANCH-SERVER**. Set the server's IP configuration as follows:
  - ❑ IP Address: 10.0.0.12
  - ❑ Subnet Mask: 255.255.255.0
  - ❑ Default Gateway: 10.0.0.1
  - ❑ DNS Server: 10.0.0.11 (the address of SERVER01)

- Create the following Active Directory objects:
    - ☐ A global security group named Branch Office Users
    - ☐ A user named James Fine, who is a member of Branch Office Users
    - ☐ A user named Adam Carter, who is a member of Branch Office Users
    - ☐ A user named Mike Danseglio, who is not a member of Branch Office Users
- Add the Domain Users group as a member of the Print Operators group.

IMPORTANT A word about permission levels

This is a shortcut that allows standard user accounts to log on to the domain controllers that you will use in these exercises. In a production environment, it is not recommended to allow standard users to log on to domain controllers.

▶ **Exercise 1   Install an RODC**

In this exercise, you will configure the BRANCHSERVER server as an RODC in the *contoso.com* domain.

1. Log on to BRANCHSERVER as Administrator.
2. Click Start and click Run.
3. Type **dcpromo** and click OK.

   A window appears that informs you the Active Directory Domain Services binaries are being installed. When installation is completed, the Active Directory Domain Services Installation Wizard appears.
4. Click Next.
5. On the Operating System Compatibility page, click Next.
6. On the Choose A Deployment Configuration page, select the Existing Forest option, and then select Add A Domain Controller To An Existing Domain. Click Next.
7. On the Network Credentials page, type **contoso.com**.
8. Click the Set button.
9. In the User Name box, type **Administrator**.
10. In the Password box, type the password for the domain's Administrator account. Click OK.
11. Click Next.
12. On the Select A Domain page, select *contoso.com* and click Next.
13. On the Select A Site page, select Default-First-Site-Name and click Next.

    In a production environment, you would select the site for the branch office in which the RODC is being installed. Sites are discussed in Chapter 11.
14. On the Additional Domain Controller Options page, select Read-Only Domain Controller (RODC). Also ensure that DNS Server and Global Catalog are selected. Then click Next.

15. On the Delegation Of RODC Installation And Administration page, click Next.
16. On the Location For Database, Log Files, And SYSVOL page, click Next.
17. On the Directory Services Restore Mode Administrator Password page, type a password in the Password and Confirm Password boxes, and then click Next.
18. On the Summary page, click Next.
19. In the progress window, select the Reboot On Completion check box.

▶ **Exercise 2   Configure Password Replication Policy**

In this exercise, you will configure PRP at the domain level and for an individual RODC. PRP determines whether the credentials of a user or computer are cached on an RODC.

1. Log on to SERVER01 as Administrator.
2. Open the Active Directory Users And Computers snap-in.
3. Expand the domain and select the Users container.
4. Examine the default membership of the Allowed RODC Password Replication Group.
5. Open the properties of the Denied RODC Password Replication Group.
6. Add the DNS Admins group as a member of the Denied RODC Password Replication Group.
7. Select the Domain Controllers OU.
8. Open the properties of BRANCHSERVER.
9. Click the Password Replication Policy tab.
10. Identify the PRP settings for the two groups, Allowed RODC Password Replication Group and Denied RODC Password Replication Group.
11. Click the Add button.
12. Select Allow Passwords For The Account To Replicate To This RODC and click OK.
13. In the Select Users, Computers, Or Groups dialog box, type **Branch Office Users** and click OK.
14. Click OK.

▶ **Exercise 3   Monitor Credential Caching**

In this exercise, you will simulate the logon of several users to the branch office server. You will then evaluate the credentials caching of the server.

1. Log on to BRANCHSERVER as James Fine, and then log off.
2. Log on to BRANCHSERVER as Mike Danseglio, and then log off.
3. Log on to SERVER01 as Administrator and open the Active Directory Users And Computers snap-in.
4. Open the properties of BRANCHSERVER in the Domain Controllers OU.

5. Click the Password Replication Policy tab.

6. Click the Advanced button.

7. On the Policy Usage tab, in the Display Users And Computers That Meet The Following Criteria drop-down list, select Accounts Whose Passwords Are Stored On This Read-Only Domain Controller.

8. Locate the entry for James Fine.

    Because you had configured the PRP to allow caching of credentials for users in the Branch Office Users group, James Fine's credentials were cached when he logged on in step 1. Mike Danseglio's credentials are not cached.

9. In the drop-down list, select Accounts That Have Been Authenticated To This Read-Only Domain Controller.

10. Locate the entries for James Fine and Mike Danseglio.

11. Click Close, and then click OK.

▶ **Exercise 4   Prepopulate Credentials Caching**

In this exercise, you will prepopulate the cache of the RODC with the credentials of a user.

1. Log on to SERVER01 as Administrator and open the Active Directory Users And Computers snap-in.

2. Open the properties of BRANCHSERVER in the Domain Controllers OU.

3. Click the Password Replication Policy tab.

4. Click the Advanced button.

5. Click the Prepopulate Passwords button.

6. Type **Adam Carter** and click OK.

7. Click Yes to confirm that you want to send the credentials to the RODC.

8. On the Policy Usage tab, select Accounts Whose Passwords Are Stored On This Read-Only Domain Controller.

9. Locate the entry for Adam Carter.

    Adam's credentials are now cached on the RODC.

10. Click OK.

Lesson Summary

- RODCs contain a read-only copy of the Active Directory database.
- An RODC replicates updates to the domain from a writable domain controller using inbound-only replication.

- Password replication policy defines whether the credentials of the user or computer are cached on an RODC. The Allowed RODC Password Replication Group and Denied RODC Password Replication Group are in the Allowed List and Denied List, respectively, or in each new RODC. You can, therefore, use the two groups to manage a domain-wide password replication policy. You can further configure the individual PRP of each domain controller.

- An RODC can be supported by configuring administrator role separation to enable one or more users to perform administrative tasks without granting those users permissions to other domain controllers or to the domain. The *Dsmgmt.exe* command implements administrator role separation.

- An RODC requires a Windows Server 2008 writable domain controller in the same domain. Additionally, the forest functional level must be at least Windows Server 2003, and the *Adprep /rodcprep* command must be run prior to installing the first RODC.

Lesson Review

You can use the following questions to test your knowledge of the information in Lesson 3, "Configuring Read-Only Domain Controllers." The questions are also available on the companion CD if you prefer to review them in electronic form.

NOTE Answers

Answers to these questions and explanations of why each answer choice is right or wrong are located in the "Answers" section at the end of the book.

---

1. Your domain consists of five domain controllers, one of which is running Windows Server 2008. All other DCs are running Windows Server 2003. What must you do before installing a read-only domain controller?

    A. Upgrade all domain controllers to Windows Server 2008.

    B. Run *Adprep /rodcprep.*

    C. Run *Dsmgmt.*

    D. Run *Dcpromo /unattend.*

2. During a recent burglary at a branch office of Tailspin Toys, the branch office RODC was stolen. Where can you find out which users' credentials were stored on the RODC?

    A. The Policy Usage tab

    B. The membership of the Allowed RODC Password Replication Group

    C. The membership of the Denied RODC Password Replication Group

    D. The Resultant Policy tab

3. Next week, five users are relocating to one of the ten overseas branch offices of Litware, Inc. Each branch office contains an RODC. You want to ensure that when the users log on for the first time in the branch office, they do not experience problems authenticating over the WAN link to the data center. Which steps should you perform? (Choose all that apply.)

    A. Add the five users to the Allowed RODC Password Replication Group.

    B. Add the five users to the Password Replication Policy tab of the branch office RODC.

    C. Add the five users to the Log On Locally security policy of the Default Domain Controllers Policy GPO.

    D. Click Prepopulate Passwords.

Chapter Review

To further practice and reinforce the skills you learned in this chapter, you can perform the following tasks:

- Review the chapter summary.
- Review the list of key terms introduced in this chapter.
- Complete the case scenarios. These scenarios set up real-world situations involving the topics of this chapter and ask you to create a solution.
- Complete the suggested practices.
- Take a practice test.

Chapter Summary

- Windows Server 2008 enables you to specify password and account lockout settings for the entire domain by modifying the Default Domain Policy GPO. You can then use fine-grained password and lockout policies contained in password settings objects (PSOs) to configure specific policies for groups or individual users.
- When a domain user logs on to a computer in a domain, the computer generates a logon event, and the domain generates an account logon event. These events can be audited to monitor authentication activity. By default, Windows Server 2008 audits successful account logon and logon events.
- Read-only domain controllers (RODCs) provide valuable support for branch office scenarios by authenticating users in the branch office. RODCs reduce the security risk associated with placing a domain controller in a less secure site. You can configure which credentials an RODC will cache. You can also delegate administration of the RODC without granting permissions to other domain controllers or to the domain.

Key Terms

Use these key terms to understand better the concepts covered in this chapter.

- **password replication policy (PRP)**   A policy that determines which user credentials can be cached on a read-only domain controller. An RODC PRP includes an Allowed List and a Denied List. Credentials of users on the Allowed List can be cached by the RODC. If a user is on both the Allowed List and the Denied List, the user's credentials are not cached.
- **password settings object (PSO)**   A collection of settings that define password requirements and account lockout policies for a subset of users in a domain. PSOs can be

applied to groups and individual users in a domain to configure policies that are different from the domain-wide password and lockout policies defined by Group Policy.

- **read-only domain controller (RODC)**   A domain controller that maintains a copy of Active Directory with all objects and attributes except for user credentials. An RODC obtains domain updates from a writable domain controller using inbound-only replication. RODCs are particularly well suited for branch office scenarios.
- **resultant PSO**   The password settings object that applies to a user. The resultant PSO is calculated by examining the precedence value of all PSOs linked to a user's groups and directly to the user.

Case Scenarios

In the following case scenarios, you will apply what you've learned about fine-grained password policies and RODCs. You can find answers to these questions in the "Answers" section at the end of this book.

Case Scenario 1: Increasing the Security of Administrative Accounts

You are an administrator at Contoso, Ltd., which recently won a contract to deliver an important and secret new product. The contract requires that you increase the security of your Active Directory domain. You must ensure that accounts used by domain administrators are at least 25 characters long and are changed every 30 days. You believe it would not be reasonable to enforce such strict requirements on all users, so you wish to limit the scope of the new password requirements to only domain administrators. Additionally, you are required by the contract to monitor attempts by potential intruders to gain access to the network by using an administrative account.

1. Your domain currently contains four Windows Server 2003 domain controllers and eight Windows Server 2008 domain controllers. What must you do before you are able to implement fine-grained password policies that meet the requirements of the new contract?

2. Which tool do you use to configure fine-grained password and lockout policies?

3. You return from a vacation and discover that other administrators have created several new password settings objects (PSOs) with precedence values ranging from 10–50. You want to ensure that the PSO you created for domain administrators has the highest precedence so that it always takes effect for those users. What value should you assign to the precedence of your PSO?

4. How will you configure the domain to monitor attempts by potential intruders to gain access to the network by using an administrative account? Which GPO will you modify? Which settings will you define?

Case Scenario 2: Increasing the Security and Reliability of Branch Office Authentication

You are an administrator at Contoso, Ltd. You maintain the domain's directory service on four domain controllers at a data center in your main site. The domain controllers run Windows Server 2003. Contoso has decided to open a new office overseas. Initially, the office will have ten salespeople. You are concerned about the speed, expense, and reliability of the connection from the branch office to the data center, so you decide to place a read-only domain controller in the branch office.

1. What must you do to your existing domain controllers and to functional levels before you can install an RODC?

2. Due to customs regulations, you decide to ask one of the employees in the branch office to purchase a server locally. Can you allow the employee to create an RODC without giving the user domain administrative credentials?

3. You want the same user to be able to log on to the RODC to perform regular maintenance. Which command should you use to configure administrator role separation?

Suggested Practices

To help you successfully master the exam objectives presented in this chapter, complete the following tasks.

Configure Multiple Password Settings Objects

In this practice, you will experience the effects of PSO precedence by creating several PSOs that apply to a single user and evaluating the resultant PSO for that user.

To perform this practice, create the following objects in the *contoso.com* domain:

- A global security group named **Human Resources**
- A global security group named **Secure Users**
- A user account named **James Fine** that is a member of both the Human Resources and Secure Users groups
- **Practice 1**   Create a PSO named *PSO1* that is linked to the Human Resources group. Give *PSO1* a precedence value of 10. You can use any valid settings for the other attributes of the PSO. Create a second PSO named *PSO2* and give it a precedence value of 5. You can use any valid settings for the other attributes of the PSO. Use the steps in Exercise 2, "Create a Password Settings Object," of Lesson 1 as a reference if you require any reminders for creating a PSO.

- **Practice 2** Identify the PSO that affects James Fine. Use the steps in Exercise 3, "Identify the Resultant PSO for a User," of Lesson 1 as a guide to evaluating resultant PSOs. Which PSO applies to James Fine?

- **Practice 3** Create a PSO named *PSO3* that is linked to James Fine's user account. Give *PSO3* a precedence value of *20*. You can use any valid settings for the other attributes of the PSO. Use the steps in Exercise 2 of Lesson 1 as a reference if you require any reminders for creating a PSO. Use the steps in Exercise 3 of Lesson 1 as a guide to evaluating resultant PSO. Identify the PSO that affects James Fine.

Recover from a Stolen Read-Only Domain Controller

In this practice, you will learn how to recover if an RODC is stolen or compromised, by simulating the loss of the server named BRANCHSERVER. To perform this practice, you must have completed the practice in Lesson 3, "Configuring Read-Only Domain Controllers."

When an RODC is stolen or compromised, any user credentials that had been cached on the RODC should be considered suspect and should be reset. Therefore, you must identify the credentials that had been cached on the RODC and reset the passwords of each account.

- **Practice 1** Determine the user and computer accounts that had been cached on BRANCHSERVER by examining the Policy Usage tab of the BRANCHSERVER Advanced Password Replication Policy dialog box. Use the steps in Exercise 3, "Monitor Credential Caching," of Lesson 3 if you require reminders for how to identify accounts whose passwords were stored on the RODC. Export the list to a file on your desktop.

- **Practice 2** Open the Active Directory Users And Computers snap-in and, in the Domain Controllers OU, select BRANCHSERVER. Press the Delete key and click Yes. Examine the options you have for automatically resetting user and computer passwords.

Take a Practice Test

The practice tests on this book's companion CD offer many options. For example, you can test yourself on just one exam objective, or you can test yourself on all the 70-640 certification exam content. You can set up the test so that it closely simulates the experience of taking a certification exam, or you can set it up in study mode so that you can look at the correct answers and explanations after you answer each question.

MORE INFO   **Practice tests**

For details about all the practice test options available, see the "How to Use the Practice Tests" section in this book's introduction.

Chapter 9

Integrating Domain Name System with AD DS

Without the Domain Name System (DNS), using the Internet would not be easy. Oh, you could still use the Internet because the underlying technology for the Internet is really TCP/IP, but going to *http://207.46.198.248* isn't quite like going to *http://Technet.microsoft.com*, especially when you have to type the address in your browser. When you look up a new technology such as Windows Server 2008 in Windows Live Search and receive a collection of IP addresses hosting information as the result of your query, it doesn't inspire confidence that these sites are safe to navigate to. IP addresses do not mean much to humans whereas domain names do.

This is why users rely so much on DNS: it translates IP addresses into common terms or domain names that humans can relate to more easily. In fact, DNS is at the very core of the TCP/IP protocol, whether it is IPv4—the traditional, 32-bit addressing scheme—or IPv6, the new, 128-bit addressing scheme that is built into Windows Server 2008. Each time you set up a system in a network, it will be identified by its IP address or addresses. In a Windows Server 2008 network running Active Directory Domain Services (AD DS), each of the devices linked to the directory will also be linked to the DNS name resolution system and will rely on it to identify each of the services it interacts with.

For example, when you boot a computer that is part of a domain, a standard process takes place. This process begins by the identification of service location records (SRV) from a DNS server to identify the closest domain controller (DC). Then, after DNS has done its work, the authentication process between the computer and the DC can begin. However, without the name resolution for the SRV by DNS, it would be difficult for AD DS to authenticate a member computer.

Because it provides the translation of IP addresses to names, DNS enables programming standards through common names in applications. When programmers know they need a process that will support the discovery of a specific service, they use a common name for that service; then, when the customer implements the DNS service along with the new application, DNS will render the common name to the actual IP address assigned to the computer hosting the service.

In addition, because it is a technology designed to manage naming on the Internet, DNS is one of the technologies contained within Windows Server 2008 that enables you to extend the authority of your network to the outside world. Like Active Directory Certificate Services

(AD CS), Active Directory Rights Management Services (AD RMS), Active Directory Light-weight Directory Services (AD LDS), and Active Directory Federation Services (AD FS), DNS is integrated with AD DS, but it can also run independently in a perimeter network and beyond. (See Figure 9-1.) When it does so, it enables other organizations and individuals to locate you from anywhere in the world. When they find you, they can interact with you or the applications you might share with customers, partners, mobile users, and anyone else through some form of electronic communication.

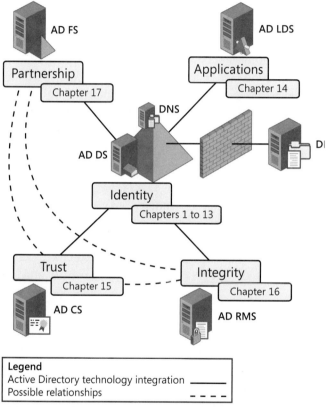

Figure 9-1   DNS extends your organization's authority beyond the borders of your internal network

Whether it communicates on the Internet or in your internal network, DNS always relies on TCP/IP port 53. All clients and servers are tuned to this port to locate and identify information about the computer names they need to interact with.

The naming structure supported by DNS is hierarchical. Names begin with a root and extend from the root when additional tiers are added to the hierarchy. The actual root of the DNS hierarchy is the dot (.) itself. However, this dot is not used in Internet naming. Commonly, standard root names are registered on the Internet and include names such as .com, .biz., .net,

.info, .name, .ms, .edu, .gov, .org, and so on. Organizations can link to the Internet through the binding of a common name with the root name. For example, *Microsoft.com* is two levels down from the root name but three levels down from the actual DNS root, as shown in Figure 9-2. *Technet.microsoft.com* is three levels down from the name but four from the DNS root and so on. AD DS relies on this hierarchy to create the domain structure of a forest.

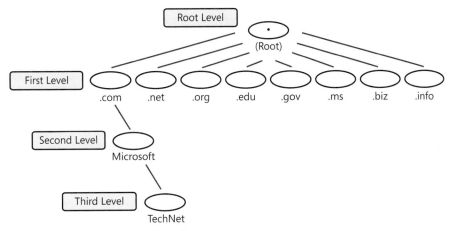

Figure 9-2   The DNS hierarchy of the Internet

DNS and IPv6

In Windows Server 2008, DNS has been updated to integrate with IPv6. Unlike IPv4, which is composed of four octets of binary digits to form the 32-bit IP address, IPv6 uses eight 16-bit pieces to form the 128-bit IP that is usually displayed in hexadecimal format. For example, FE80:: refers to the autogenerated link-local IPv6 address Windows Vista or Windows Server 2008 will assign to your computer if you rely on the Dynamic Host Configuration Protocol (DHCP) and there is no available DHCP server to respond with an actual address. The FE80:: address is the same as the Automatic Private IP Addressing (APIPA) address your system will generate if the same thing happens with an IPv4 address allocation.

In IPv6, each time a 16-bit address piece is composed of all zeros, you can concatenate the address and represent it with two colons (::). The two colons will represent any number of 16-bit sections that are composed of all zeros as long as they are contiguous. This facilitates writing out IPv6 addresses; otherwise, IPv6 notation could become quite complex.

Like IPv4, IPv6 provides several types of addresses:

- **Link-local**   Addresses that enable direct neighbors to communicate with each other. Any computer on the same network segment will be able to communicate with any other by using this address type. This is the address type assigned by default when IPv6 is turned on but does not use a static address and cannot communicate with a dynamic address provider such as a DHCPv6 server. These addresses are similar to the 169.254.0.0/16 addresses used by the APIPA process.

- **Site-local** Addresses that support private address spaces and you can use internally without having your own IPv6 address allocation. Site-local addresses can be routed, but should never have a routed connection to the Internet. They are similar to the 10.0.0.0/8, 172.16.0.0/12, and 192.168.0.0/16 addresses organizations use internally with IPv4.

- **Global unicast** Addresses that are entirely unique and can be used on the Internet to identify an interface. These addresses are routable on the Internet and enable direct communication to any device. These are comparable to the public IPv4 addresses organizations use on the Internet today.

The boon of IPv6 is the sheer number of addresses it provides. With the world population booming, the number of services and devices requiring IP addresses increasing, and the number of IPv4 addresses dwindling, it is time for the IP infrastructure of the Internet to evolve to the next level. By providing 340 billion billion billion billion—or 2^{128} addresses—IPv6 should support the next stage of the Internet for a long time. All you have to do is compare it to the 4 billion IPv4 addresses to see the difference.

Table 9-1 outlines the most common IPv6 address types.

Table 9-1   Common IPv6 Address Types

Address Type	Format	Description
Unspecified	::	Indicates the absence of an address. Comparable to 0.0.0.0 in IPv4.
Loopback	::1	Indicates the loopback interface and enables a node to send packets to itself. Comparable to 127.0.0.1 in IPv4.
Link-local	FE80::	Local network browsing address only. Comparable to APIPA or addresses in the 169.254.0.0/16 range in IPv4. Unroutable by IPv6 routers.
Site-local	FEC0::	Site-level internal address space. Routable but not to the Internet. Comparable to addresses in the 10.0.0.0/8, 172.16.0.0/12, and 192.168.0.0/16 ranges in IPv4.
Global unicast	All others	Unique addresses assigned to specific interfaces.

To comply with Internet standards and support the move to IPv6, DNS in Windows Server 2008 has been updated to support the longer address form of the IPv6 specification. IPv6 is installed and enabled by default in both Windows Vista and Windows Server 2008. This means that you can use this technology, at least internally, with little risk. It will be some time before all the elements that require an IPv6 connection to the Internet—intrusion detection systems, firewalls, anti-spam filtering, and so on—have been upgraded to support secure IPv6 transmissions.

MORE INFO   IPv6

For more information on IPv6, go to *http://www.microsoft.com/technet/network/ipv6/ipv6rfc.mspx.*

The Peer Name Resolution Protocol

Because they fully support IPv6, Windows Server 2008 and Windows Vista also include a secondary name resolution system called Peer Name Resolution Protocol (PNRP). Unlike DNS, which relies on a hierarchical naming structure, PNRP relies on peer systems to resolve the location of a computer system. Basically, PNRP is a referral system that performs lookups based on known data. For example, if you need to look up Computer A and you are near Computers B and C, your system will ask Computer B if it knows Computer A. If Computer B says yes, it will provide you with a link to Computer A. If not, your system will ask Computer C if it knows Computer A and then use the same process as with Computer B. If neither Computer B nor Computer C knows Computer A, your system will send a request to other computers near it until it finds one that knows of Computer A.

PNRP includes several features that are different from the DNS service:

- It is a distributed naming system that does not rely on a central server to locate objects. It is almost entirely serverless, but in some instances, servers are required to develop the name resolution process by themselves. Windows Server 2008 includes PNRP server components as an add-on feature.

- PNRP can scale to billions of names, unlike the DNS service, which will host only a small number of names and will then rely on another DNS server to locate the names over which it is not authoritative.

- Because it is distributed and relies on clients as much as servers, PNRP is fault tolerant. Several computers can host the same name, providing multiple paths to that name.

- Name publication is instantaneous, free, and does not require administrative intervention in the way DNS does.

- Names are updated in real time, unlike DNS, which relies heavily on caching to improve performance. Because of this, PNRP does not return stale addresses the way a DNS server, especially an earlier, nondynamic DNS server, can.

- PNRP also supports the naming of services as well as of computers because the PNRP name includes an address, a port, and a potential payload such as a service's function.

■ PNRP names can be protected through digital signatures. Protecting the names in this way ensures that they cannot be spoofed or replaced with counterfeit names by malicious users.

To provide resolution services, PNRP relies on the concept of a cloud. Two different clouds can exist. The first is the global cloud and includes the entire IPv6 global address scope, which encompasses the entire Internet. The second is a link-local cloud and is based on the link-local IPv6 address scope. Local links usually represent a single subnet. There can be several link-local clouds but only a single global cloud.

Just as the world has not fully moved to IPv6 yet, it also hasn't moved to PNRP and continues to rely on DNS to provide name resolution services. However, PNRP is an important new technology that will have a greater and greater impact on Internet operation as organizations move to IPv6.

MORE INFO   **PNRP**

For more information on PNRP, go to *http://technet.microsoft.com/en-us/library/bb726971.aspx.*

DNS Structures

DNS has been around since the Internet was first developed and has evolved with it. Because of this, the DNS service in Windows Server 2008 can provide a number of roles. There are three possible types of DNS servers:

■ **Dynamic DNS servers**   Servers that are designed to accept name registrations from a wide variety of devices through dynamic updates are deemed to be dynamic DNS (DDNS) servers. DDNS is designed to enable devices—clients and servers—to self register to the DNS server so that other devices can locate them. When the DNS service runs on a DC and is integrated with the directory service, it runs in DDNS mode, enabling computers that use DHCP to register their own names within it automatically. This enables AD DS to locate the client when it needs to send it management data such as Group Policy objects (GPOs). DDNS servers are read-write servers, but they accept registrations from known entities only.

Exam Tip   Note that the exam does not include direct references to dynamic DNS. It will, however, refer to dynamic updates as well as to Active Directory–integrated DNS zones. Any time a DNS server is updated automatically through authorized clients, it is a DDNS. Keep this in mind when taking the exam.

■ **Read-write DNS servers**   Earlier DNS servers that are not running in dynamic mode but that will accept writes from known sources such as authorized operators are deemed read-write DNS servers. The most common type of read-write DNS server is the primary

DNS server. Primary DNS servers are usually deployed in perimeter networks and are not integrated with AD DS.

■ **Read-only DNS servers**   DNS servers that hold a read-only copy of DNS data that originates from another location are deemed read-only DNS servers. In Windows Server 2008, there are two types of read-only DNS servers. The first is the secondary DNS server. Secondary DNS servers are linked to primary DNS servers and will accept and host DNS data provided by the primary parent server. They make data available locally but cannot be modified because they support only one-way replication from the primary. A second type of read-only DNS server in Windows Server 2008 is the DNS server that runs on a read-only DC (RODC). These servers run primary read-only zones when integrated with RODCs.

Using these three types of DNS servers, you can construct a name resolution strategy that meets all your naming requirements. (See Figure 9-3.) For example, you could pair DDNS servers with every domain controller in your network because the DNS data is usually integrated with the directory store. Because it is contained in the directory store, the DNS data is replicated to every DC in a domain and sometimes in a forest through the same mechanism that replicates directory traffic. This means each DC has a local copy of DNS data. Installing the DNS service on the DC automatically gives it access to this data and can provide local rather than remote name resolution services, avoiding wide area network (WAN) traffic. In addition, you can use the RODC DNS service in read-only mode in unsecured locations within your network, locations that warrant local services but do not have local administrative staff. You can also use the standalone primary DNS service in perimeter networks. These servers contain few records but support access to any application or service you host in your perimeter. Last, you could use read-only secondary DNS servers in unsecured locations facing the Internet.

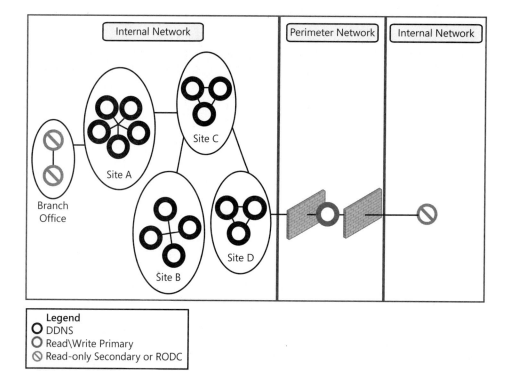

Figure 9-3   DNS server placement in a Windows Server 2008 network: DDNS follows DCs, primaries are protected, and RODCs are internal, whereas secondaries are external

---

MORE INFO   **Domain Name System**

For more information on DNS, go to *http://technet2.microsoft.com/windowsserver2008/en/servermanager/dnsserver.mspx*.

The Split-Brain Syndrome

One of the most basic tenets of internetworking is the segregation of the internal network from the Internet. Small and large organizations alike will endeavor to protect their internal network through a variety of systems and technology. The most common protection mechanism is the firewall, which protects your network by blocking entry of undesirable traffic through the control of TCP/IP ports. Accepted ports are open and all unacceptable ports are closed. It's as simple as that.

Similarly, when you work with Windows Server 2008 and especially with AD DS, you will need to work with two namespaces. Because AD DS directories are based on the DNS hierarchical naming system, you must use a properly formed DNS name, often called a fully qualified domain name (FQDN), to name your directory forests and the domains they contain. Frequently, organizations use the same name they use to represent themselves on the Internet.

For example, this book suggests names such as *contoso.com* or *woodgrovebank.com* as potential names for your internal networks. This is by no means a best practice. This book uses these names because they are legally acceptable names that Microsoft Press is allowed to use to represent fictitious organizations. However, using the same name internally for your AD DS directory structure as you use for your external exposure to the Internet means you must implement a split-brain DNS service.

That's because you need to maintain two namespaces for two purposes all across a firewall. Nothing could be more complex. Your users must be able to locate both internal and external resources that rely on the same name. If Contoso, Ltd., used *contoso.com* for both its internal and its external namespaces in real life, its DNS administrators would need to manage the separation manually between internal and external name resolution mechanisms.

However, if Contoso used *contoso.com* exclusively for its external presence and used a corresponding name with a different extension, for example, .net, for its internal AD DS namespace, the DNS administrators would have to do nothing to segregate the two namespaces. The very fact that they use different roots automatically segregates the names and the two DNS services that would be used to support them. The only thing that needs to transit through the firewall is standard name references you would normally use for any name that is not located within your network.

In addition, it is very easy for Contoso to buy and maintain all the possible combinations of its Internet name, including common roots such as .com, .net, .info, .ms, .ws, and more. This way, Contoso knows it can use any of the names it owns for any forest implementation, production, testing, development, or staging or for whichever purpose it needs it and never conflict with anyone else even if it faces a merger or an acquisition.

Issues that commonly arise around this topic are often based on the ownership of the DNS service. Traditionally, network operators own previous DNS services and, very often, these DNS services are maintained in environments that are not Microsoft Windows–based. However, Windows and, especially, AD DS are designed to rely very tightly on the Windows DNS service. Although it is possible to use Windows with non-Windows DNS servers, it is not recommended because it requires so much more work. When you use the Windows DNS service and integrate it with your AD DS service, everything becomes automatic. When you don't, everything remains manual and, very often, you'll find that specific components don't work because the manual configuration was not completed or was misconfigured by non-Windows system administrators.

If you are in this situation and you must run two DNS technologies, the best and ideal network configuration is to use a whole-brain approach and rely on two different namespaces, integrate the internal namespace with Windows DNS servers running on DCs, and simply link the two namespaces through standard DNS resolution mechanisms. This will provide you with the implementation that will require the least amount of administrative effort and ensure that all services work at all times. (See Figure 9-4.)

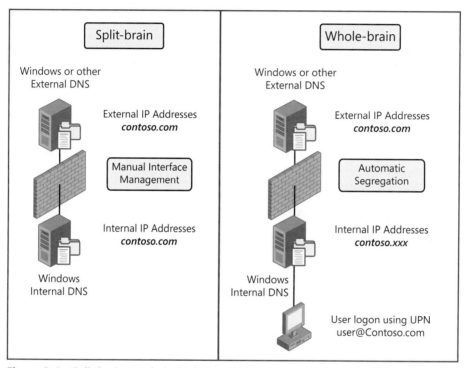

Figure 9-4   Split-brain vs. whole-brain DNS structures

Further, you needn't worry about users. If you are using a different namespace internally, but you want them to log on with the external network name, for example, *contoso.com*, just add it as the preferred user principal name (UPN) suffix in your directory. DNS will be simpler to manage, your internal network will be protected from external access, and your users won't know the difference!

MORE INFO   Split-brain DNS

For more information on split-brain DNS setups, go to *http://www.microsoft.com/serviceproviders/ resources/techresarticlesdnssplit.mspx.*

Exam objectives in this chapter:

■ Configuring Domain Name System (DNS) for Active Directory

  ❑ Configure zones.

  ❑ Configure DNS server settings.

  ❑ Configure zone transfers and replication.

Lessons in this chapter:

■ Lesson 1: Understanding and Installing Domain Name System 406

■ Lesson 2: Configuring and Using Domain Name System. 431

Before You Begin

To complete the lessons in this chapter, you must have done the following:

■ Installed Windows Server 2008 on a physical or virtual computer that should be named SERVER10 and should be a standalone server. This computer will host the DNS server and DC service you will install and create through the exercises in this chapter. Assign an IPv4 address from one of the private ranges, for example, 192.168.x.x, and map its DNS server address to its own address.

■ Installed Windows Server 2008 on a physical or virtual computer that should be named SERVER20 and should be a standalone server. This computer will host the DNS server and DC service you will install and create through the exercises in this chapter. Assign an IPv4 address from one of the private ranges, for example, 192.168.x.x, and map its DNS server address to the address you assigned to SERVER10.

■ Installed Windows Server 2008 on a physical or virtual computer that should be named SERVER30 and should be a standalone server. This computer will host the DNS server and DC service you will install and create through the exercises in this chapter. Assign an IPv4 address from one of the private ranges, for example, 192.168.x.x, and map its DNS server address to the address you assigned to SERVER10.

We strongly recommend using virtual machines (VMs) in support of the exercises. The DC and DNS server roles are ideal for virtualization through either Microsoft Virtual Server 2005 R2 or Windows Server 2008 Hyper-V.

Real World

Danielle Ruest and Nelson Ruest

In late 2002, we were putting finishing touches to our second book: *Windows Server 2003, Best Practices for Enterprise Deployments* for McGraw-Hill Osborne. This book was based on our experiences with customers in designing and deploying Windows 2000–based Active Directory (AD) structures. One feature that intrigued us the most was the new application directory partition feature in Microsoft Windows Server 2003. According to the documentation provided with the beta versions, application directory partitions would be used to store DNS data within the directory and control their replication scope.

As our customers would create best-practices forests, using a forest root domain and a single, global child production domain, we discovered that when you created the forest root domain, DNS data was properly located within the forest root domain partition, but when you created a child domain, the data would not be stored automatically within the child domain partition. This caused a serious problem with DNS data. All our customers would use a two-DC forest root to keep it as secure as possible and to control access to forest root administration tightly. Because of this, the forest root DCs would always be located within central headquarter sites. The child production domain, however, would be highly distributed and include domain controllers within each remote site that had more than a certain number of users.

Because DNS data for the child domain was actually included in the forest root domain partition and not in the child partition, each client had to perform DNS lookups over the WAN to contact the forest root DCs. However, if DNS data was to be stored in the directory and made available to DCs, it should be in the local DC, not in a remote DC.

We discovered that we could change the replication scope of the child domain DNS data after the directory service was deployed, but we have always been proponents of doing things right in the first place, not correcting them afterward. This meant we needed to find a way to make sure the DNS data would be stored in the proper location during installation rather than later.

We contacted the Microsoft Active Directory development team and reported this DNS behavior as a bug, and they agreed that this should be corrected at installation, not afterward. Further research demonstrated that because a child domain namespace is an extension of the root domain's namespace, the child domain name would resolve properly during the verification checks the Active Directory Installation Wizard performed. Because of this, the wizard would store the data within the forest root domain. In fact, the wizard was behaving properly; we just didn't give it enough information.

Further investigation revealed that if you created a manual DNS delegation before creating the child domain, the wizard would locate the data properly within the child domain partition—the manual delegation would point to a server that did not exist yet because the child domain was not created. For example, if you had a root domain named *treyresearch.net* and a child domain that would be named *intranet.treyresearch.net*, you would point the delegation to a server named *servername*.intranet.treyresearch.net. Because no server of that name existed until the child domain was actually created, the delegation would contain dummy data and would be called a dummy DNS delegation. When the wizard would run, it would find this server in DNS and try to use it to resolve the child domain's DNS name. The resolution would fail and force the wizard to install DNS during the creation of the domain and create the appropriate DNS data partition.

The Active Directory Domain Services Installation Wizard now properly creates delegations for child domains. Many AD implementations based on Windows Server 2003 did not locate DNS data in the proper partition during installation, and only IT administrators who knew how to use the dummy delegation before creating a child domain were aware of the issue. Windows Server 2008 has resolved this problem.

Lesson 1: Understanding and Installing Domain Name System

Domain name resolution is a complex process that relies on a naming hierarchy to match IP addresses, both IPv4 and IPv6, to system names. DNS name resolution also supports the identification of service locations. This is how the AD DS logon process works. In fact, DNS plays an essential role in this process and, because of this, services such as those provided by AD DS would simply not be possible without the DNS service.

To do this, the DNS service relies on name records. Records can be inscribed manually, such as in a primary DNS server that provides read-write services. However, writes are supported only from administrators, or they can be inscribed automatically such as with dynamic DNS servers that accept name records from devices. Smart devices such as computers running editions of Windows 2000, Windows XP, Windows 2003, Windows Vista, or Windows Server 2008 can register their own names within a DDNS, but devices running earlier operating systems such as Microsoft Windows NT cannot. Former devices will rely on the DHCP to perform the inscription for them; however, this is a less secure implementation of a DDNS infrastructure.

DNS contains a host of record types that can be used to provide name resolution for specific service types or specific computer types. In addition, these records are stored within DNS zones—special placeholders that provide a given name resolution functionality for a specific namespace.

Understanding the various components of the Windows Server 2008 DNS service is critical to understanding how it works and how it should be used.

MORE INFO   DNS in Windows Server 2008

For more information on DNS in Windows Server 2008, go to *http://technet2.microsoft.com/ windowsserver2008/en/servermanager/dnsserver.mspx*.

> **After this lesson, you will be able to:**
> - Understand when to use DNS.
> - Install DNS.
> - Locate and view the DNS installation.
>
> **Estimated lesson time: 70 minutes**

Understanding DNS

The first thing to understand when working with DNS is how it works to resolve a name. You already know that DNS relies on a hierarchy of servers because a DNS server cannot hold all possible name records within itself. Because of this, the DNS service relies on name referrals to perform name resolution. (See Figure 9-5.)

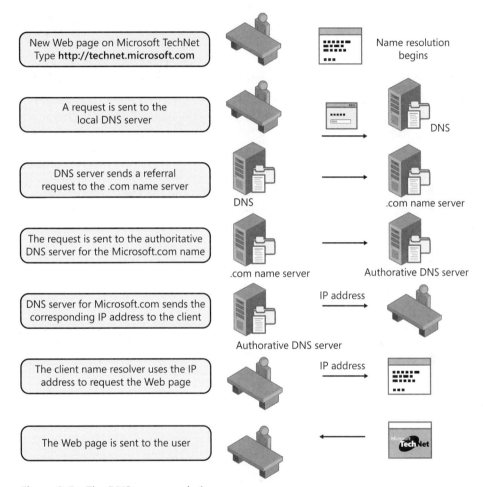

Figure 9-5   The DNS name resolution process

Here's how name resolution works:

1. You try to look up a Web page on the Microsoft TechNet Web site. To do so, you type *http://technet.microsoft.com* in the address bar of your browser and press Enter. That's when name resolution begins.

2. Your computer sends out a request to its local DNS server or at least to one of the servers listed in its IP configuration settings for the name.

3. If this server does not include the name in its own database or cache, it sends a referral request to the name server. Because the Microsoft site name ends in .com, the DNS server sends the referral to the .com name server.

4. The .com name server is the authority for all names that end in the .com suffix. This server knows the location of all DNS servers that are the final authorities for a particular name ending with .com. In this case, it sends the request to the authoritative DNS server for the *microsoft.com* name.

5. The DNS server for *microsoft.com* sends the corresponding IP address for the requested page to the client computer.

6. The name resolver on the client uses the IP address to request the actual page from its Internet provider.

7. If the page is not already in the local cache of the Internet provider, it requests the actual page and sends it to the client.

This name resolution procedure occurs within seconds, and the Web page appears almost as fast as you type it, depending on the speed of your connection and the current load of the requested server. That's what happens when you look at the green progress bar at the bottom of your browser. The actual progress also includes downloading content such as text and graphics to your own computer.

DNS is a system that does not and cannot work alone. It must rely on other servers to operate. In addition, the DNS service includes a terminology of its own. Table 9-2 outlines the most common terms you will encounter when working with DNS.

Table 9-2 DNS Terms and Concepts

Term	Description
Active Directory Integrated (ADI) zone	When a DNS zone is integrated with Active Directory, it is hosted in the AD DS database, *NTDS.dit*, and is replicated throughout the directory with other directory data.
Aging	DNS records are associated with an age or a Time to Live (TTL). When the record lasts beyond its age, it is no longer valid and can result in false positives, giving users the impression they are going to a specific location when the location is no longer valid.
Application directory partitions	When DNS data is stored within AD DS directory databases, it is replicated by default with the directory data it is associated with. However, you can define a custom replication scope for DNS data. For example, DNS data that belongs to a root domain for a forest must be made available to the entire forest whereas DNS data for a specific domain is really required only for that domain. You control DNS data replication scopes through application directory partitions.

Table 9-2   DNS Terms and Concepts

Term	Description
DDNS	This is a DNS service that can be automatically updated by the clients that rely on it. In Windows Server 2008, you install DDNS whenever you choose to install the DNS service with AD DS. Because all the clients in a DDNS implementation have AD DS accounts, they are deemed secure clients and are authorized to update the DNS server with their record information.
DNS Notify	Traditional or former DNS servers manage data in local files. These files are located on the primary server. They are then transferred through a polling and zone transfer mechanism to read only secondary servers. However, large zones will often require frequent record updating. This could lead to incorrect records located within the secondary server. To correct this situation, DNS uses a special notification process that notifies slave servers that an update is available, which then prompts a zone transfer to the read-only servers.
Domain DNS zone	This is the zone that contains the records for a particular domain, either a root or a child domain, within an AD DS forest structure.
Forest DNS zone	This is the zone that contains the records that pertain to an entire forest within an AD DS forest structure.
Forward lookup	DNS supports two types of lookups: forward or reverse. A forward lookup relies on a client providing an FQDN to the server. The server then matches this FQDN to the corresponding IP address.
Forward lookup zone	This comprises DNS containers—databases or text files—that include name resolutions for forward lookups.
Forwarders	DNS servers have two mechanisms for name resolution: forwarders or root hints. DNS servers that provide name resolution services to the internal network will often rely on forwarders to forward any request they cannot resolve on their own to a trusted external DNS server. Windows Server 2008 also includes the ability to rely on conditional forwarders or forwarders that are used only when specific conditions are met in a request. For example, if the name is for an internal domain, but not one managed by this server, it can automatically forward the request to the internal name server for that domain.
GlobalNames Zone (GNZ)	NetBIOS names are single-label names that do not use the FQDN format. For example, down-level computer names are single-label names. Traditionally, these names are managed by Windows Internet Name Service (WINS). In an effort to remove this prior service from a Windows-based network, Microsoft has implemented the GlobalNames Zone in DNS in Windows Server 2008. GNZs can contain single-label names and replace WINS in a Windows-based network.

Table 9-2   DNS Terms and Concepts

Term	Description
Legacy DNS	Nondynamic DNS servers that rely on manual updating of zone records are deemed legacy DNS servers. Because it complies with the set of request for comments (RFC) that define and standardize the DNS protocol on the Internet, Windows Server 2008 can support former DNS services as well as the dynamic DNS service required by AD DS. Legacy DNS servers host either primary or secondary zones.
Name recursion	Name resolutions can be either iterative or recursive. In an iterative request, each DNS server holds only part of the answer for a query and must rely on other DNS servers to complete the query. In a recursive query, the DNS server will hold the complete answer and provide it to the requester. Because of record aging, it is possible for a recursive query to respond with an erroneous IP address.
Primary zones	These are zones that contain read-write information for a particular domain. Primary zones are stored on nondynamic or dynamic DNS servers. When stored on nondynamic DNS servers, primary zones are contained within text files and are edited manually by an administrator. When stored on DDNS servers, primary zones are contained within Active Directory and are updated either automatically by each record holder or manually by an administrator.
Resource records	These are the name records contained within DNS databases. Resource records usually link an IP address with an FQDN.
Reverse lookup	DNS supports two types of lookups: forward or reverse. A reverse lookup relies on a client providing an IP address and requesting the FQDN that corresponds to the address.
Reverse lookup zone	This zone comprises DNS containers—databases or text files—that include name resolutions for reverse lookups for a particular domain.
Root hints	DNS servers have two mechanisms for name resolution: forwarders or root hints. DNS servers that provide name resolution services to the internal network but also have a direct connection to the Internet can rely on root hints to locate authoritative servers for root names such as .com, .org, .net, and so on in the Internet and provide resolution services to internal clients. By default, Windows Server 2008 DNS servers rely on root hints for external name resolution. These hints are regularly updated through Microsoft Windows Update. Root hints are contained within a special file named Cache.dns, which can also be used to reset root hints in the event of issues with the external name resolution process.

Table 9-2   DNS Terms and Concepts

Term	Description
Round robin	DNS services can be used to provide some form of high availability. This is done by creating multiple records for the same resource, each with a different IP address. When queried, the DNS server will provide the first address, then the second address, then the third, and so on, balancing the load between multiple servers that host the same service. For example, Microsoft Exchange Server 2007 Edge Transport Server—servers that face the Internet to accept and send internal e-mail—rely on the round robin process to provide e-mail load balancing.
Secondary zone	A secondary zone is a read-only zone obtained from a primary DNS server. Secondary zones provide local DNS resolution in highly distributed networks.
Server scavenging	A feature that was introduced with the dynamic DNS service released with Windows 2000 Server. Because records have an age or time to live, they can become stale when they extend beyond their expected duration. Server scavenging will scour the DNS database to locate records that have aged beyond their usefulness and automatically remove them.
Single-label names	NetBIOS names that do not use the FQDN format. For example, down-level computer names are single-label names. These names include 16 characters and do not support special characters such as dots. Only the first 15 characters of a single-label name can be used because the sixteenth character is reserved by the system to complete the name. Traditionally, these names are managed by WINS. In Windows Server 2008, you can rely on the GNZ in DNS to replace WINS.
Start of Authority (SOA) record	This is a special DNS record that outlines domain information such as the update schedule for the records it contains, the intervals other DNS servers should use to verify updates, and the date and time of the last update as well as other information such as contacts for the domain and so on. Only one SOA record can be contained within a specific zone file. Each zone file should contain a particular SOA record.
Stub zone	This is a special zone type that contains only the records of other DNS servers that maintain the actual zone itself. This can speed name resolution and reduce the likelihood of errors because stub zones are used as referrals to other, authoritative DNS servers for a zone.
TTL	Each DNS record is given a TTL value. This value determines the valid duration of the record. When it expires, the record can be deleted through scavenging. However, if the record is still valid before its TTL value expires, you can renew the record and, therefore, renew its TTL value.

Table 9-2   DNS Terms and Concepts

Term	Description
Zone delegations	Delegations are used to help you manage different namespace sections better. For example, Microsoft might want to delegate different sections of its namespace, notably the MSDN or TechNet sections of *Microsoft.com*, to have them administered by other divisions in the company. When managing DNS namespaces in AD DS, you must delegate new domain-based zones when you create the domain; otherwise, the zone will be managed at the forest level and not at the domain level as it should be. In Windows Server 2003, this delegation had to be created manually before creating the domain. In Windows Server 2008, the Active Directory Domain Services Installation Wizard will perform the delegation automatically when you create a child domain.
Zone scavenging	Scavenging scours the DNS server to remove stale or outdated records whose age has gone beyond their TTL value. Zone scavenging applies when scavenging is applied to a single zone as opposed to the entire server.
Zone transfers	These are the transactions DNS servers use to replicate information from one server to another. Full zone transfers transfer the entire content of a zone to one or more other DNS servers. Incremental transfers send only a subset of the data. Traditionally, full transfers are referred to as Asynchronous Full Transfer (AXFR) whereas incremental transfers are dubbed Incremental Zone Transfer (IXFR). Windows Server 2008 also supports secure zone transfers, which are performed through AD DS multimaster replication.

The Windows Server 2008 DNS service supports three zone types, as shown in Figure 9-6:

- **Primary Zone**   Zones that can be integrated with AD DS or that can be of the former, standard type. These zones are authoritative for the namespace they contain. Primary zones are read-write zones except when located on RODCs.
- **Secondary Zone**   Zones that are of the former, standard type and are only a replica of the data maintained by a primary or authoritative server for a namespace. When you create a secondary zone, you must tell DNS the address of the primary zone or source of the zone data.
- **Stub Zone**   Zones that are nothing but pointers to other, authoritative servers for the namespace they maintain. Once again, when you create a stub zone, you must specify a list of server(s) that are authoritative for the namespace.

Each zone type can be stored either in a text file or within an Active Directory directory store partition.

Exam Tip   Keep these zone types in mind for the exam. You can change from one zone type to another in DNS, but remember that the most useful zone type is the primary zone. This is the type used by AD DS when you integrate the DNS service with it.

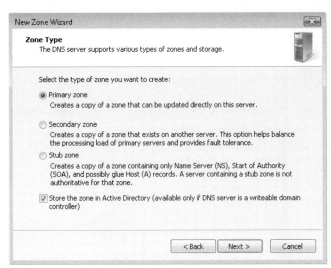

Figure 9-6   The New Zone Wizard enables you to create any of the three supported zones

Zones are containers that include information about the objects they manage. This information is in the form of records. DNS can contain several types of records. Table 9-3 outlines the most common record types used in DNS in Windows Server 2008.

Table 9-3   DNS Record Types in Windows Server 2008

Record Type	Usage
Alias (CNAME)	Used to create an alternate record or alias DNS name for a name that is already specified as another record type in a specific zone. This is also known as a canonical name (CNAME). For example, if you want to create a record such as *intranet.contoso.com* to point to a server or server farm hosting Microsoft Office SharePoint Server, you would create it as an alias record. This facilitates usage by providing a more functional name than the server name.
Host (A or AAAA) records	The most common record type in DNS. They represent computer objects in the namespace and are used to resolve a specific IP address to a device.

Table 9-3 DNS Record Types in Windows Server 2008

Record Type	Usage
Mail exchanger (MX)	Routes e-mail messages to a specific namespace. For example, the MX record for *contoso.com* would indicate that all e-mail directed to *contoso.com* should pass through the host or hosts identified by this record.
Pointer (PTR)	Points to a specific location within the namespace. PTR records are usually used to provide reverse lookup capabilities within the namespace.
Service location (SRV)	Indicates the location of a specific TCP/IP service. For example, if you want to use Microsoft Office Communications Server, you must create a session initiation protocol (SIP) service location record to indicate to all the devices that rely on this service where it is situated in your network. Similarly, AD DS creates several service location records in support of the logon or the Group Policy distribution processes. Service location records usually consist of the IP address for the server as well as the TCP/IP port on which the service is available.

The records in Table 9-3 provide the main functionality of DNS in a Windows Server 2008 implementation.

Exam Tip Table 9-3 lists the most common record types. However, review all the record types the Windows Server 2008 DNS server supports in preparation for the exam.

Windows Server DNS Features

The Windows Server 2008 DNS server complies fully with the RFC generated by the Internet Engineering Task Force (IETF, found at *http://www.ietf.org*) for Internet technology standards, but, in addition, it also includes a series of features that are designed to support the network operating system (NOS) features of AD DS. The DNS server in Windows Server 2008 can also operate with non-Windows-based DNS servers because it complies with all the RFCs related to the DNS service.

When the DNS service is integrated with AD DS, you can store DNS data in different locations within the directory database. DNS data can be stored within the domain partition of the directory. You choose this option for data that references the domain itself. For example, a child domain within a forest would normally have its data stored within its own domain partition to make the data available to all DNS servers in the domain. You can also store data within application directory partitions. Unlike domain partitions, application directory partitions have a controllable replication scope. For example, forest DNS data is stored in an application directory partition that spans the entire forest, making this data available to any DNS server within the forest. By default, Windows Server DNS creates two application directory partitions to host DNS data in each forest. These partitions are respectively named

ForestDnsZones and DomainDnsZones. In addition, DomainDnsZones is created in each child domain within a forest to host data for that domain.

Exam Tip   DNS replication scopes are a key section of the exam. Examine them in your DNS server implementations and understand the contents of each scope type.

In addition, the DNS service in Windows Server 2008 has been improved to support background zone loading. When a DNS server hosts a large number of zones and records hosted in AD DS, it might take time for the server to boot because, traditionally, it needs to load all zone data before servicing requests. By using background loading, the DNS service can begin to respond to requests more quickly as it continues to load zone data in the background after the computer is started and logon is initiated.

To support the new read-only domain controller role, DNS has been updated to provide read-only DNS data for primary zones hosted on the RODC. This further secures the role and ensures that no one can create records from potentially unprotected servers to spoof the network.

Exam Tip   Remember that DNS zones in RODCs are read-only *primary* DNS zones. Traditionally, read-only zones are secondary zones.

In an effort to support the removal of the WINS service from networks while still providing support for single-label names or names that do not include the parent name in their own (for example, SERVER10 instead of SERVER10.Contoso.com), DNS has been updated to include a GNZ. This zone can be used to host a small number of names with static IP addresses.

Exam Tip   Keep in mind that you use GNZs to replace WINS implementations but only when you have a small number of single-label names to manage. Single-label or NetBIOS names are often required for previous applications that cannot work with the more complex FQDN structure. In fact, single-label names stem from older Windows NT–based networks or applications. In most cases, organizations should have been able to deprecate these applications and remove them from their networks, but some exceptions might remain. GNZs are designed to support these few remaining applications. However, if an organization needs to run a multitude of single-label names, you will need to implement the WINS service along with DNS.

Finally, in an effort to provide further protection against spoofing, DNS now supports the addition of global query block lists. When clients use protocols such as the Web Proxy Automatic Discovery Protocol (WPAD) or the Intra-site Automatic Tunnel Addressing Protocol (ISATAP) and rely on DNS to resolve host names, they can be vulnerable to malicious users who take advantage of dynamic updates to register computers that are not legitimate hosts.

WPAD is normally the protocol Web browsers rely on to discover network proxy server settings. Spoofing this address could lead users to malicious servers that impersonate legitimate proxy servers and potentially compromise a network. ISATAP is a transition protocol that enables IPV4 and IPv6 networks to work together. It does this by encapsulating IPv6 packets in IPv4 format to transmit them through routers. It does not support dynamic router discovery. Instead, it relies on a potential routers list to identify potential ISATAP routers. If this list is compromised, IPv6 packets could be routed to malicious routers and compromised in turn.

You can reduce the potential for these vulnerabilities by using global query block lists that contain specific blocked address ranges. Only the leftmost portion of an FQDN is included in global query block lists. When the DNS server receives a query that includes this name, it returns an answer as if no record existed. By default, the DNS server will generate this list at installation or during an upgrade of an existing DNS service. If either of the two protocols exists, the one that exists will not be blocked. If they do not exist, they will both be blocked. In addition, you can add your own names to this list to block names you do not want to be operational in your network.

MORE INFO Global query block lists

For more information on global query block lists, search for DNS global query block lists on the Microsoft Web site. You can download a document on the subject.

In short, the DNS service in Windows Server 2008 provides full support for all the standard features you would expect in a DNS server but also includes custom features that are available in Windows only.

Quick Check

1. What are the most common address types in IPv6 and which type is used by default on Windows Server 2008 and Windows Vista systems?
2. What is a major difference between the PNRP and DNS?
3. Which are the two types of read-only DNS servers supported by Windows Server 2008?
4. What is the first step in an AD DS logon process?
5. Which type of delegations can the Active Directory Domain Services Installation Wizard automatically remove?

Quick Check Answers

1. The most common IPv6 address types are link-local, site-local, and global unicast. By default, Windows Server 2008 and Windows Vista are designed to use dynamic IPv6 addresses. However, when no DHCPv6 servers are present in a network, IPv6 automatically assigns a link-local address to the interface.

2. One major difference between PNRP and DNS is the number of records each can contain. PNRP can scale to contain millions of name records; DNS is much more modest and relies on a hierarchy of servers to validate names.

3. The DNS server supports two read-only modes in Windows Server 2008. The first is the traditional, or legacy, secondary DNS. Secondary DNS servers are subordinate to one or more primary servers and contain only a copy of the information provided to them by a read-write source. The second type of read-only server is the one included in an RODC. This DNS server, however, includes *primary* read-only zones.

4. The first step in an AD DS logon process is a DNS request sent to locate the SRV for the closest domain controller. When this record is resolved, the logon process can begin through exchanges with the domain controller.

5. The Active Directory Domain Services Installation Wizard supports the removal of any delegation you have control over. This means it will properly remove child domain delegations, but it cannot remove top-level delegations because the root servers are on the Internet, and you do not have access to these servers.

Integration with AD DS

Because of its special Windows features, always deploy the Windows DNS server when you deploy AD DS. You can rely on a third-party DNS server to provide name resolution support for AD DS also, but it is significantly more work to set up and prepare this DNS server than to use the one built into Windows. When you use the Windows DNS server with AD DS, all DNS content is configured by default. This is why DNS installation is integrated with the domain controller promotion wizard. Installing DNS with AD DS performs several tasks that are usually completely transparent to the administrator running the wizard. These operations occur only during the creation of a forest, a domain tree within an existing forest, or a new domain within an existing forest.

If the AD DS deployment is for a forest root domain, DNS will create placeholders for the forward lookup zones (FLZ), the reverse lookup zones (RLZ) and conditional forwarders (CF). Then, it will generate two new zones within the FLZ. The first will be a container for the entire forest for the namespace you created during the installation of AD DS. This zone is usually named _msdcs.*domainname*. For example, for the *contoso.com* domain, this zone is called *_msdcs.contoso.com*. In addition, it creates a zone within the FLZ for the root domain itself, as shown in Figure 9-7.

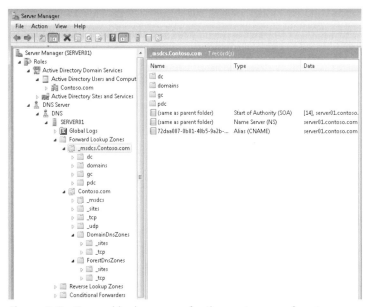

Figure 9-7 Forward lookup zones for the *contoso.com* forest

When the AD DS process creates a domain tree in an existing forest, it requires a manual delegation before the domain tree is created. Because the name of the domain tree is different from the root domain name—it must be different because that is the definition of a tree within a forest—the wizard cannot create the delegation on its own. When two DNS namespaces are different, neither has the authority to delegate information for the other, hence the need for a manual delegation. Then, after the delegation has been created, the AD DS Installation Wizard will create the DNS namespace and store it appropriately within the domain tree's new domain partition.

When the AD DS process creates a child domain in an existing forest, it automatically creates a delegation within the top-level root domain and then properly stores the DNS data for the child domain in the child domain's partition.

To remove a domain, you must run the Active Directory Domain Services Installation Wizard once again to remove the domain controller role, and then you can remove the AD DS role. However, because there is no interface to access the wizard anywhere, you must type **Dcpromo.exe** in the Search box of the Start menu to launch the wizard. When you remove the DC role, it will also remove DNS data created for a domain if this DC is the last DC in a domain. Also, if the DC is a global catalog (GC) server, it will give you a warning during the demotion because GCs support the search function in AD DS. During the removal of the DC role, you will be prompted to remove DNS delegations, as shown in Figure 9-8. If this is a top-level domain such as a forest or tree root domain, make sure you clear this option; otherwise, you will receive an error because the wizard will ask you for credentials to delete the delegation. Because you do not have root-level credentials (for names such as .com, .net, .org, and so on), you cannot provide them and, therefore, cannot delete (or create, for that matter) root-level delegations. However, if it is a child domain, select to delete the DNS delegation and it will work properly.

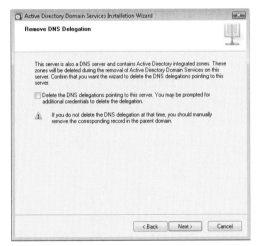

Figure 9-8   Removing DNS delegations with the AD DS Installation Wizard

PRACTICE Installing the DNS Service

In this practice, you will install the DNS service. In the first exercise, you will install the DNS service in standalone mode to explore how you would create a legacy primary server. Then, you will install AD DS and create a root domain in a new forest. This will create forest DNS zones in the DNS server. In the third exercise, you will create a manual zone delegation to prepare for the integration of a new domain tree into your new forest. Then, you will install AD DS and create a new domain tree within the same forest as the first server. This creates tree-based zones in DNS by relying on the delegation you created. Finally, you will install AD DS and create a child domain to view child domain zones in DNS. Note that in this case, the wizard will properly create the appropriate delegations for the child domain. This exercise requires that SERVER10, SERVER20, and SERVER30 be running.

▶ **Exercise 1   Install a Primary DNS Server**

In this exercise, you will use a standalone computer to install the DNS service and view how it operates in nondynamic mode. This exercise is performed on SERVER10.

1. Log on to Server10 with the local administrator account.

2. In Server Manager, right-click the Roles node and select Add Roles.

3. Review the Before You Begin page and click Next.

4. On the Select Server Roles page of the Add Roles Wizard, select DNS Server and click Next.

5. Review the information in the DNS Server page and click Next.

6. Review your choices and click Install.

7. Examine the installation results and click Close.

    Your installation is complete.

8. Move to the DNS Server node in Server Manager and expand all its sections. You might need to close and reopen Server Manager to refresh the nodes.

    As you can see, the DNS installation creates all the containers required to run the DNS service in Windows Server 2008, but because this is the process you would normally use to install a legacy DNS server, no information is created within the DNS container structure. (See Figure 9-9.) Legacy DNS servers require manual input for the creation of zone information. You can automate the input process, but because Windows does not know why you want to use this DNS server, it does not create data for you.

9. Explore the DNS Server container structure before you move on to Exercise 2, "Install AD DS and Create a New Forest."

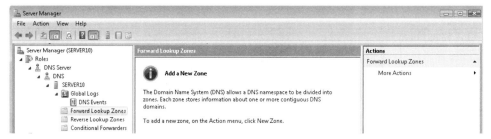

Figure 9-9   Viewing the default DNS server containers

▶ Exercise 2   Install AD DS and Create a New Forest

In this exercise, you will use a standalone computer to install the AD DS role and then create a new forest. After AD DS is installed, you will use the Active Directory Domain Services Installation Wizard to create a root domain in a new forest.

1. Log on to Server10 with the local administrator account.

2. In Server Manager, right-click the Roles node and select Add Roles.

3. Review the Before You Begin screen and click Next.

4. On the Select Server Roles page of the Add Roles Wizard, select Active Directory Domain Services and click Next.

5. Review the information on the Active Directory Domain Services page and click Next.

6. Confirm your choices and click Install.

7. Examine the installation results and click Close.

    Your installation is complete.

8. Next, click the Active Directory Domain Services node in Server Manager.

9. Click Run The Active Directory Domain Services Installation Wizard in the details pane. This launches the Active Directory Domain Services Installation Wizard.

10. Click Next.

11. Review the information on the Operating System Compatibility page and click Next.

12. On the Choose A Deployment Configuration page, choose Create A New Domain In A New Forest and click Next.

13. On the Name The Forest Root Domain page, type **treyresearch.net** and click Next.

     You use a name with the .net extension because you do not want to use a split-brain DNS model. Trey Research uses a public name with the .com extension on the Internet but a name with the .net extension internally. Trey Research has purchased both domain names and knows that because it owns them, no one can use the names for AD DS structures. If Trey Research ever faces a merger or acquisition, it will be much easier for the company to integrate its own forest with another to streamline IT operations for the new organization.

14. On the Set Forest Functional Level page, select Windows Server 2008 from the drop-down list and click Next.

15. On the Additional Domain Controller Options page, verify that DNS Server and Global Catalog are both selected and click Next. Note that the DNS Server service is already installed on this server.

16. If you did not assign a static IP address, the Active Directory Domain Services Installation Wizard will give you a warning because you are using a dynamic IP address. Click the Yes, The Computer Will Use A Dynamically Assigned IP Address (Not Recommended) option.

17. The Active Directory Domain Services Installation Wizard will warn you that it cannot create a delegation for this server. Click Yes.

     You get this error message for two reasons. First, because you assigned this server's own IP address as the DNS server in its network configuration, you cannot reach a proper DNS server to create the delegation. Second, even if you could reach a proper DNS server, you are using a name based on a top-level root name (.net), and you would not have the authorization to create the delegation in the server hosting root addresses for the that extension.

18. On the Location For Database, Log Files And SYSVOL page, accept the default locations and click Next.

19. On the Directory Services Restore Mode Administrator Password page, type a strong password, confirm it, and click Next.

20. Confirm your settings on the Summary page and click Next.

21. Select the Reboot On Completion check box and wait for the operation to complete.

22.   After the computer has been rebooted, log on with the newly created domain credentials (TreyResearch\Administrator) and move to the DNS Server node in Server Manager.

Review the changes the AD DS setup created within the forward lookup zones of this new forest. Note that DNS data is divided into two sections, one that affects the entire forest and another that affects only the root domain, as shown in Figure 9-10.

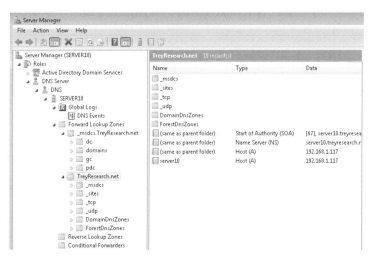

Figure 9-10   Active Directory Domain Services entries for a new forest

▶ **Exercise 3   Create a Manual Zone Delegation**

In this exercise, performed on SERVER10, you will use the newly created domain controller for the *treyresearch.net* domain to create a manual DNS zone delegation. This delegation will be used in Exercise 4, "Install AD DS and Create a New Domain Tree," to load DNS data for a domain tree. It will not contain any data when you create it and will point to a nonexistent server—a server that is not yet created; this is called a dummy DNS delegation. Also, because a domain tree uses a different DNS name than the forest, you will need to create a new FLZ for the tree; otherwise, you would not be able to use the new name in the delegation.

1.   Log on to Server10 with the domain administrator account.

2.   In Server Manager, expand the DNS Server node and click the Forward Lookup Zones node.

3.   Right-click Forward Lookup Zones and select New Zone.

     This launches the New Zone Wizard.

4.   Click Next.

5. On the Zone Type page, select Primary Zone and make sure the Store The Zone In Active Directory check box is selected. Click Next.

   You must create a new zone to host the delegation because if you tried to store the delegation in an existing zone, it would automatically add the name suffix for this zone. Because a domain tree is distinguished from the forest namespace by its name suffix, you must create a new zone to host it.

6. On the Active Directory Zone Replication Scope page, select To All DNS Servers In This Domain: *treyresearch.net* and click Next. This will place the DNS data in the DomainDnsZones application directory partition for the *treyresearch.net* domain.

7. On the Zone Name page, type **northwindtraders.com** and click Next.

   Trey Research has decided to expand its operations and create a new division that will be focused on new sportswear related to Trey's latest discoveries and inventions. Because of this, they need to create a new domain tree in their existing forest.

   IMPORTANT   Using name extensions other than .com

   You would normally use a name extension other than .com to protect your internal network from possible name conflicts and to avoid the split-brain syndrome, but using a .com extension is valid for the purposes of this exercise.

   ---

8. On the Dynamic Update page, select Allow Only Secure Dynamic Updates (Recommended For Active Directory) and click Next.

   Dynamic updates are not really required for this zone because it will host a delegation only, but using this setting will allow for eventual growth if the Trey Research strategy for this domain changes in the future.

9. Click Finish to create the zone.

10. Move to the *northwindtraders.com* zone and select it.

    The DNS server is peculiar in that it does not provide you with context menu options until you have selected the item first. You need to select the item with the left mouse button, and then you can use the right mouse button to view the context menu.

11. Right-click the *northwindtraders.com* zone and select New Delegation.

    This launches the New Delegation Wizard.

12. Click Next.

13. On the Delegated Domain Name page, type **SERVER20**, which should list SERVER20 .northwindtraders.com as the FQDN, and click Next.

14. On the Name Servers page, click Add and type the FQDN of the server you will create for this zone.

    The value should be SERVER20.northwindtraders.com.

15. Move to the IP Addresses Of This NS Record section of the dialog box, click <Click Here To Add An IP Address>, and then type the IP address you assigned to SERVER20. Click OK.

16. Click Next and then Finish to create the delegation.

    The dialog box will give you an error because the *northwindtraders.com* domain is not yet created, and a server with an FQDN of SERVER20.northwindtraders.com does not yet exist, hence the dummy delegation name for this type of delegation.

IMPORTANT   Add name servers to a delegation

In a production environment, you should have at least two or more name servers for this delegation. In this exercise, one is enough, but when you create any AD DS domain, always create at least two DCs. You should, therefore, return to this delegation after the second server is created and add it to the delegation to provide fault tolerance for it.

▶ **Exercise 4   Install AD DS and Create a New Domain Tree**

In this exercise, you will use a standalone computer to install the AD DS role and then create a new domain tree in an existing forest. This exercise is performed on SERVER20, but SERVER10 must also be running. After AD DS is installed, you will use the Active Directory Domain Services Installation Wizard to create a new domain tree in an existing forest.

1. Log on to SERVER20 with the local administrator account.

2. In Server Manager, right-click the Roles node and select Add Roles.

3. Review the Before You Begin screen and click Next.

4. On the Select Server Roles page of the Add Roles Wizard, select Active Directory Domain Services and click Next.

5. Review the information on the Active Directory Domain Services page and click Next.

6. Confirm your choices and click Install.

7. Examine the installation results and click Close. Your installation is complete.

8. Next, click the Active Directory Domain Services node in Server Manager.

9. Click Run The Active Directory Domain Services Installation Wizard in the details pane.

10. This launches the Active Directory Domain Services Installation Wizard. Select the Use Advanced Mode Installation check box, and then click Next.

    This option enables you to create a new domain tree.

11. Review the information on the Operating System Compatibility page and click Next.

12. On the Choose A Deployment Configuration page, select Existing Forest, select Create A New Domain In An Existing Forest, select the Create A New Domain Tree Root Instead Of A New Child Domain check box, and click Next.

13. On the Network Credentials page, type **treyresearch.net**, and then click Set to enter alternate credentials. Type **treyresearch.net\administrator** or the equivalent account name and the password. Click OK, and then click Next.

14. On the Name The New Domain Tree Root page, type **northwindtraders.com** and click Next.

15. On the Domain NetBIOS Name page, accept the proposed name and click Next.

    This page appears because you are running the wizard in advanced mode. Note that the name does not include the final *s* because it is limited to fifteen characters. The sixteenth is always reserved by the system.

16. On the Select A Site page, accept the default and click Next. This page also appears because you are running the wizard in advanced mode.

17. On the Additional Domain Controller Options page, verify that the DNS Server check box is selected. Select the Global Catalog check box, and then click Next.

    Note that one authoritative DNS server has been found for this domain. This is the server in your delegation and is the server you are now creating.

18. If you did not assign a static IP address, the Active Directory Domain Services Installation Wizard will give you a warning because you are using a dynamic IP address. Click the Yes, The Computer Will Use A Dynamically Assigned IP Address (Not Recommended) option.

    The AD DS Installation Wizard will warn you that it has detected an existing DNS infrastructure for this domain and, because of this, you now have two choices: to attempt to create a DNS delegation or to omit it. See Figure 9-11.

19. Select No, Do Not Create The DNS Delegation and click Next.

    You select No because you already created the delegation manually. The wizard cannot create this delegation because it would attempt to create it in a .com root name DNS server, and you do not have access rights to this server.

20. On the Source Domain Controller page, verify that Let The Wizard Choose An Appropriate Domain Controller is selected and click Next.

21. On the Location For Database, Log Files And SYSVOL page, accept the default locations and click Next.

22. On the Directory Services Restore Mode Administrator Password page, type a strong password, confirm it, and click Next.

23. Confirm your settings on the Summary page and click Next. Select the Reboot On Completion check box and wait for the operation to complete.

24. When the computer has been rebooted, log on with the new domain credentials (NorthwindTraders\Administrator or equivalent) and move to the DNS Server node in Server Manager. Review the changes the AD DS setup created within the FLZs of this new domain tree. Note that DNS data includes a container for this tree only and not for the domain. (See Figure 9-12.)

Any child domains created under this tree root would also create delegations of their own and would be listed in this zone.

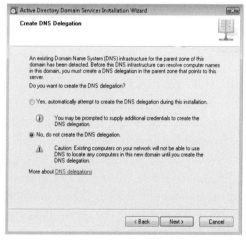

Figure 9-11   The Create DNS Delegation page

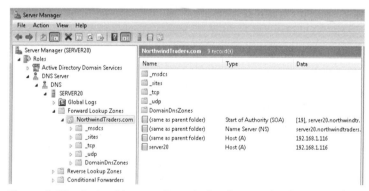

Figure 9-12   Active Directory Domain Services entries for a new domain tree in an existing forest

▶ **Exercise 5   Install AD DS and Create a Child Domain**

In this exercise, you will use a standalone computer to install the AD DS role and then create a new child domain. This exercise is performed on SERVER30. After AD DS is installed, you will use the Active Directory Domain Services Installation Wizard to create a child domain in the Trey Research forest.

1. Log on to SERVER30 with the local administrator account.
2. In Server Manager, right-click the Roles node and select Add Roles.
3. Review the Before You Begin screen and click Next.
4. On the Select Server Roles page of the Add Roles Wizard, select Active Directory Domain Services and click Next.
5. Review the information in the AD DS page and click Next.
6. Confirm your choices and click Install.
7. Examine the installation results and click Close.
    Your installation is complete.
8. Next, click the Active Directory Domain Services node in Server Manager.
9. Click Run The Active Directory Domain Services Installation Wizard in the details pane.
    This launches the Active Directory Domain Services Installation Wizard.
10. Click Next.
11. Review the information on the Operating System Compatibility page and click Next.
12. On the Choose a Deployment Configuration page, choose Existing Forest and Create A New Domain In An Existing Forest and click Next.
13. On the Network Credentials page, type **treyresearch.net** and click Set to add proper credentials.
14. In the Network Credentials dialog box, type **treyresearch\administrator** or equivalent, type the password, click OK, and click Next.
15. On the Name The New Domain page, type **treyresearch.net** as the FQDN of the parent domain, type **intranet** in the single label of the child domain field, and click Next.
    The complete FQDN should be *intranet.treyresearch.net*.
    When you create a global child production domain, you name it with an appropriate name such as Intranet. This provides a clear demarcation for users and clearly shows that they are in an internal, protected network.
16. On the Select a Site page, use the default settings and click Next.

17. On the Additional Domain Controller Options page, verify that the DNS Server check box is selected and select the Global Catalog check box. Click Next.

     Note that there are no authoritative DNS servers for this domain name.

     If you did not assign a static IP address, the Active Directory Domain Services Installation Wizard will give you a warning because you are using a dynamic IP address.

18. Click the Yes, The Computer Will Use A Dynamically Assigned IP Address (Not Recommended) option.

19. On the Location For Database, Log Files And SYSVOL page, accept the default locations and click Next.

20. On the Directory Services Restore Mode Administrator Password page, type a strong password, confirm it, and click Next.

21. Confirm your settings on the Summary page and click Next.

     Note that in this case, the wizard will create a DNS delegation for this domain. (See Figure 9-13.) This is because the parent domain is authoritative for the *treyresearch.net* zone and can, therefore, create a proper delegation for the child domain.

22. Select the Reboot On Completion check box and wait for the operation to complete.

23. When the computer has been rebooted, log on with the newly created domain credentials (Intranet\Administrator or equivalent) and move to the DNS Server node in Server Manager.

24. Review the changes the AD DS setup created within the FLZs of this new domain. Note that DNS data is in only one section that affects this particular domain, as shown in Figure 9-14. Also, if you return to SERVER10, you will see that a new DNS delegation (a gray icon instead of yellow) has been created for this child domain in the *treyresearch.net* FLZ.

Figure 9-13   The Active Directory Domain Services Installation Summary page

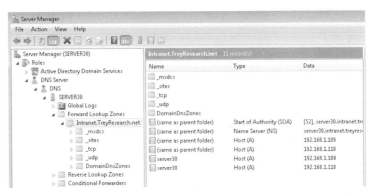

Figure 9-14   Active Directory Domain Services entries for a new child domain in an existing forest

Lesson Summary

- DNS is a name resolution system that relies on a hierarchical naming structure to map IP addresses to FQDNs, which are in the *object.namespace.rootname* format.

- AD DS also relies on a hierarchical structure. In fact, the AD DS forest structure is based entirely on the hierarchical structure found in DNS.

- Because Windows Server 2008 has been updated to support IPv6, and IPv6 is installed by default with link-local addresses, the DNS server in Windows Server 2008 provides support for the longer 128-bit address format used by IPv6.

- DNS Server can host three types of zones. Primary zones are read-write zones that contain data in support of name resolution for a given namespace. Secondary zones are read-only zones that contain a copy of a primary zone. Stub zones are pointers to other DNS servers and contain only the authoritative servers for the namespace they point to. Each zone type can be integrated with AD DS to be stored in the directory database.

Lesson Review

You can use the following questions to test your knowledge of the information in Lesson 1, "Understanding and Installing Domain Name System." The questions are also available on the companion CD if you prefer to review them in electronic form.

NOTE   Answers

Answers to these questions and explanations of why each answer choice is right or wrong are located in the "Answers" section at the end of the book.

---

1. You are an administrator for Contoso, Ltd. Your organization has decided to move to Windows Server 2008 and, because of your past experience, you have decided to create a new server implementation instead of upgrading your existing infrastructure. After the new infrastructure has been created, you will move all data–accounts, directory settings, and more–to the new forest you will implement with Windows Server 2008. You have been asked to create the initial forest structure. This forest includes a root domain, a global child production domain, and a domain tree. The forest is named with a .net extension, and the domain tree uses a .ms extension to differentiate it from the production forest. You successfully create the forest root domain and the child domain, but when you come to the domain tree, you find that you cannot locate the domain tree option. What could be the problem?

    A. You cannot create a domain tree with the Active Directory Domain Services Installation Wizard. You must use the command-line *Dcpromo.exe* command to do so.

    B. You are not logged on with the appropriate credentials.

    C. You must return to the Welcome page of the wizard to select the Advanced mode of the wizard.

    D. The server you are using is not a member of the forest root domain.

2. You are an administrator for Contoso, Ltd. Your organization has decided to move to Windows Server 2008 and, because of your past experience, you have decided to create a new server implementation instead of upgrading your existing infrastructure. After the new infrastructure has been created, you will move all data–accounts, directory settings, and more–to the new forest you will implement with Windows Server 2008. You have been asked to create the initial forest structure. This forest includes a root domain, a global child production domain, and a domain tree. The forest is named with a .net extension, and the domain tree uses a .ms extension to differentiate it from the production forest. You successfully create the forest root domain and the child domain, but when you come to the domain tree, you find that you cannot create the delegation, no matter which options you try or which credentials you provide. What could be the problem? (Choose all that apply.)

    A. You must select the advanced mode of the wizard to create the delegation.

    B. You must create a manual delegation before creating the domain tree.

    C. You must tell the wizard to create the delegation during the creation of the domain tree and provide appropriate credentials.

    D. You must tell the wizard to omit the creation of the delegation during the creation of the domain tree.

    E. You must create the delegation manually after the domain tree has been created.

Lesson 2: Configuring and Using Domain Name System

When you install the DNS Server role with AD DS, there is little configuration to be done. FLZs are created automatically; replication is configured automatically because it rides on the AD DS multimaster replication system, and you don't even need to add records because all computer systems running Windows 2000 or later can register and update their own records in the dynamic DNS AD DS requires.

However, some operations are not performed automatically. For example, the DNS server configuration does not, by default, include RLZs. It is a good idea to add them to support reverse lookups. In addition, the DNS server needs configuration finalization. For example, you must set it to support record scavenging, automatically deleting outdated records.

It is also a very good idea to review all the DNS server content to become familiar with it and ensure that all data and values correspond to your actual requirements.

> **After this lesson, you will be able to:**
> - Finalize the configuration of your DNS servers.
> - Administer DNS servers and DNS replication.
>
> **Estimated lesson time: 40 minutes**

Configuring DNS

The DNS configuration involves several activities. These include:

- Considering the security of your DNS servers to reduce their attack surface.
- Configuring scavenging settings for the server as a whole.
- Finalizing the configuration of your FLZs.
- Creating RLZs.
- Adding custom records to FLZs for specific services and resources.

It is also a good idea to make sure your DNS replication is working properly and that all DNS data is being replicated properly.

Security Considerations for the DNS Server Role

DNS servers that are exposed to the Internet are notorious targets for malicious users. The most common attack is a denial-of-service (DoS) attack that floods the DNS service with so many requests that the service cannot respond to valid requests. Another common attack form occurs when an attacker tries to obtain all the data contained within a DNS server, intending to use it to identify the object a network contains. This is called *footprinting the network*. Two more attack types attempt to modify data within the DNS server or redirect user queries from a valid DNS server to another DNS server that would be under the control of the attacker. The latter usually occurs through the modification of DNS data contained within the DNS cache. Remember that DNS uses in-memory caching to increase the speed of responses to queries. When this data is corrupted, users can receive invalid responses to their queries.

This is why it is important to apply common security measures to your DNS installations. When you use a whole-brain approach to DNS configuration and you rely on DNS integration with AD DS in your internal network, your internal DNS servers are much less prone to attack because they do not share a namespace with the outside world and are, therefore, protected from external access by firewalls, which do not allow external users to access your internal DNS servers. This does not mean that internal servers do not need protection. Any time an untrusted user can connect to your network either through the wired connections or through wireless access, your infrastructure is at risk. This is why extensive screening is a good practice whenever you allow someone you are not familiar with to connect to your network. It is not because you are inside the firewall that everything is protected by default.

Consider a different security approach with internal vs. external DNS servers. When servers are in an external or perimeter network, they should be highly secured. One good protection method is to use a secondary or subordinate server only whenever the server is exposed to the outside world. Then, you configure the zone updates to occur only from known sources that are included within DNS itself.

In internal networks, tie the DNS Server role to the DC role and ensure that they support secure dynamic updates only. This will help protect them from obtaining or transmitting erroneous data. Verify DNS data on a regular basis to validate it and monitor your DNS event logs to identify potential security issues quickly if they arise.

Exam Tip   The exam focuses on DNS usage with AD DS. Because of this, it does not cover external or standalone DNS servers. If you find you need to configure an external DNS server, you can look up more information on DNS security at *http://technet2.microsoft.com/windowsserver/en/library /fea46d0d-2de7-4da0-9c6f-2bb0ae9ca7e91033.mspx?mfr=true*.

Working with DNS Server Settings

DNS stores name records for a specific period of time. Each name record is assigned a TTL value. When this value expires, the record should be removed to avoid providing false positive results to users performing lookups on the name. Fortunately, the DNS server in Windows Server 2008 can perform this task automatically through server or zone scavenging. When applied to the server, scavenging cleans all active zones on the server. When applied to a particular zone, only the records for the zone are scavenged.

Configuring Scavenging for All Zones   To set scavenging for an entire server, you must assign the setting through the server's action menu.

1. Right-click the server name in the DNS node of Server Manager and choose Set Aging/ Scavenging For All Zones.

2. Select the Scavenge Stale Resource Records check box to enable the feature.

   No-Refresh Interval refers to the time between the most recent refresh of a record stamp and the moment when the system allows the timestamp to be refreshed again. Refresh Interval refers to the earliest moment when a record may be updated or when it may be scavenged if no updates have been applied. The default value of seven days is sufficient for most networks.

3. Leave the default values as is and click OK.

4. Because you set the values for existing zones, DNS also enables you to set it for any future zone you create, including Active Directory–integrated zones. Select the Apply These Settings To The Existing Active Directory-Integrated Zones check box and click OK.

Your DNS zones are set to remove stale records. Make sure you apply these settings to every DNS server in your network. Make this part of your default configuration for DNS servers. If you need to modify the setting for a single zone, you must use the Properties dialog box for that zone. Zone scavenging is performed by using the General tab and clicking the Aging button.

You'll note that in the server's context menu, you can also manually initiate scavenging by clicking Scavenge Stale Resource Records. You use this operation when you discover that your servers are sending out stale data.

If you do discover that records are stale, you can also use the *Clear Cache* command from the same context menu. Because the DNS server relies heavily on the in-memory cache to improve performance, you might have scavenged records from the database but find they are still in the cache, which might still be providing false positives.

Finalizing FLZ Configuration   When you examine the Properties dialog box for a FLZ, you'll find that there are several options you can set for each zone. Make a point of examining these options and configure the following settings for each production DNS zone as a best practice:

- On the General tab, make sure each internal DNS zone is Active Directory-Integrated, uses the proper replication scope, and supports Secure Only dynamic updates.
    - ❑ Domain-based DNS zones should replicate to all DNS servers in the domain. Each DC that also hosts the DNS role will include the zone.
    - ❑ Forest DNS zones should replicate to all DNS servers in the forest.
    - ❑ If you maintain Windows 2000 Server DCs in your network, you must use the To All Domain Controllers In This Domain (For Windows 2000 Compatibility) option because Windows 2000 Server does not support application directory partitions.
    - ❑ You can also set replication to custom application directory partitions, but you must create the partition first.

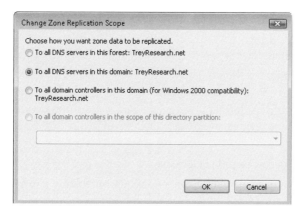

- On the Name Servers tab, ensure that each DNS zone includes at least two name severs. Just as you would create at least two DCs for each domain, create two DNS servers for each zone as a best practice.

- On the WINS tab, assign WINS lookups only if you cannot use GNZs and you must deploy WINS. This lesson will discuss single-label name management further in a later section.

- On the Zone Transfers tab, set the name servers to which you allow this zone to be transferred upon request. If this zone is integrated with Active Directory, zone transfers are not required. This tab is mostly used for previous DNS server installations.

- On the Security tab, review the default security settings. These settings use the appropriate configuration for most networks, but in highly secure implementations, they might need to be revised and modified.

- The final tab is the SOA. SOA records identify the zone and its related information such as owner, operator, update schedules, and so on. These records include the following information:

  ❑ Serial Number, which is assigned when your zone is created. You can increment the serial number if you need to change its value.

  ❑ Primary Server is the master server for this zone. This is usually the server where the zone was first created.

  ❑ Responsible Person should list the operator name for this server. Normally, this is a standard term such as Hostmaster or Operations. By default, Windows Server 2008 assigns hostmaster.*dnszonename* where dnszonename is the FQDN of the zone. Responsible Person entries are based on Responsible Person records. These records are not created by default. Create a proper Responsible Person record for each zone or, at the very least, for each master DNS server and assign it to this value.

  ❑ The SOA lists the various intervals and time-based settings for the record. These include the Refresh Interval, the Retry Interval, the Expires After setting, and the

Minimum (Default) TTL for the record. Default values are acceptable for most record types.

❑ The last value of the SOA is the TTL For This Record. Note that it is assigned to the same value as the Minimum (Default) TTL value listed above it in the dialog box.

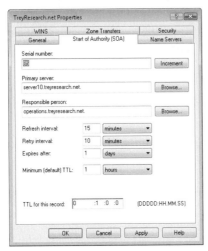

Finalize these settings for each zone you manage on your DNS servers.

Creating a Responsible Person Record   As mentioned earlier, each zone should be assigned a Responsible Person (RP) as a best practice. This means you need at least one RP record in your DNS configuration. Use the context menu for the zone you want to host this record in to create the record. Keep in mind that you will require different items for the creation of this record. These include:

- **A common group name**   This name will be displayed in the record.
- **A group mailbox in the directory**   It is best to use a group mailbox to make sure the messages sent to this address are treated in a timely fashion.
- **A text record to include with the Responsible Person record**   The text record can indicate information about your organization and its DNS management policies.

Use the following procedure to create the RP record. Begin with the Text Record.

1. Right-click the zone name and choose Other New Records.
2. In the Select A Resource Record Type list, scroll down to select Text (TXT) and click Create Record.
3. In the New Resource Record dialog box, type the name of the record, for example, **Disclaimer**, and move to the Text entry box.
4. Type your message. Click OK to create the record. This returns you to the Resource Record Type dialog box.

This should include information about who you are and what your DNS management practices are. You might consider preparing the message in a word processor and then pasting it in this dialog box because the text box does not include any proofing capabilities.

5. In the Select A Resource Record Type list, scroll up to select Responsible Person (RP) and click Create Record.

6. In the New Resource Record dialog box, type the name of the record in the Host Or Domain text box, for example, **Operations**, and click Browse to locate the mailbox of the responsible person. You can also type the address if you know it.

7. Click Browse to locate your newly created text record. Navigate to the zone you are working with to locate the text record, select it, and click OK.

8. Click OK to create the record. Click Done to close the Resource Record Type dialog box.

9. Return to the zone Properties dialog box or double-click the Start Of Authority record to assign the RP record to the SOA record.

Perform these operations for each zone you manage. It is always better to configure the zone completely than to have to figure out what to do if issues arise and nothing is configured.

Creating Reverse Lookup Zones

Small networks with few computers, for example, fewer than 500, might not require RLZs. These zones are used to provide resolution from an IP address to a name instead of a name to an IP address. These are most often used by applications. For example, a secure Web application will use a reverse lookup to verify that the computer it is communicating with is actually the right computer and not another computer impersonating it. If you do not have any such application in your network, then you can safely do without RLZs.

However, clients that have the ability to update their own DNS records dynamically will also create a PTR record—a reverse record that maps the IP address to the name—and try to store it within the RLZ that corresponds to the FLZ their name record is located in. If there is no RLZ, these records will never be generated.

MORE INFO   **How dynamic updates work**

For more information on dynamic updates and how they work, go to *http://technet2.microsoft.com/ windowsserver/en/library/e760737e-9e55-458d-b5ed-a1ae9e04819e1033.mspx?mfr=true.*

If you need RLZs, create them for the corresponding FLZs. Create a zone for each named FLZ. In an Active Directory–integrated DNS implementation, you would create a RLZ for each domain DNS zone. In a multidomain forest, this would include the root domain, any child domain, and any domain trees. Use the following procedure:

1. Move to the Reverse Lookup Zone section of the DNS node in Server Manager.

2. Right-click Reverse Lookup Zone and select New Zone.

3. Review the information on the Welcome page and click Next.

4. Select Primary Zone, make sure the Store The Zone In Active Directory check box is selected, and click Next.

5. Because RLZs are tied to a specific domain name, apply To All DNS Servers In This Domain and click Next.

6. On the Reverse Lookup Zone Name page, select either IPv4 or IPv6 and click Next.

   Remember that reverse lookups map an IP address to a name. You need to create an RLZ for the type of IP addressing you are using in the network. If you are using both IPv6 and IPv4, you must create two zones.

   You generate the zone name on the next page. This page will differ, depending on the IP version you are using.

7. If you are using IPv4, type the network ID for the zone. Note that as you type the network address, the name is automatically generated in the lower part of the page under Reverse Lookup Zone Name.

8. Click Next.

   If you are using IPv6, you can add up to eight zones at once. Remember that IPv6 addresses use hexadecimal format. For example, if you are using site-local addresses in your network, you might type **fe80::/64** as the address scope. This will automatically generate the zone name in the Reverse Lookup Zones section of the page. If one zone is all you need, you can move on from this page.

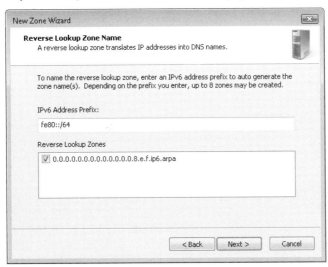

9. On the next page, select which type of dynamic update you want to allow. In most cases, select Allow Only Secure Dynamic Updates and click Next. Click Finish to create the zone.

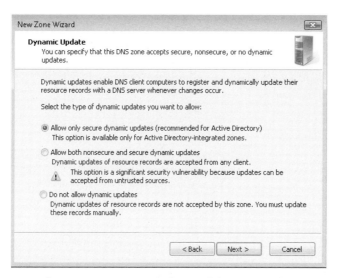

As soon as the zones are created, they will begin supporting record hosting when the next dynamic update refresh occurs on your client systems.

Exam Tip   Practice working with zones and zone properties because they are an important part of the exam topics.

Quick Check

1. Why should you configure scavenging and aging on a DNS server?
2. When should you create reverse lookup zones?

Quick Check Answers

1. Every DNS name record is assigned a TTL value when created. This value determines when the information in the record is no longer valid. If the record is not renewed, then it becomes a stale record. Aging and scavenging on the DNS server will automatically remove stale records to limit the possibility of false positives when users request data from the DNS server.

2. Reverse lookup zones are mostly useful for secure Web applications, which must validate the IP address provided by the systems they communicate with. If a network does not include any such application, then reverse lookup zones are not required.

Creating Custom Records

The last step in a DNS server configuration is the creation of custom records for the FLZs. Custom records are created manually and will provide a variety of services in your network. For example, you might need to create the following:

- An MX record to point to your e-mail servers.
- An alias record such as intranet.*domainname* to point to an Office SharePoint Server server farm to support collaboration in your network.
- SRV records for various services in your network. For example, you must create SIP records for Microsoft Office Communication Server deployments.

Time will tell which custom records you need. In an internal network, manually created records should be infrequent because of the dynamic update process initiated by client systems.

Exam Tip Practice record creation because it is also an important topic on the exam.

Forwarders vs. Root Hints

Name resolution is performed by two main methods. DNS servers will either contain root hints that enable them to identify and locate authoritative DNS servers for root names or rely on forwarders to link them to another server that will perform the lookup for them.

By default, Windows DNS Server relies on root hints to perform lookups. This means that if your users need to perform a lookup on the Internet, your DNS servers will communicate with the name servers. In smaller organizations, this is quite acceptable because even if your DNS servers expose themselves by communicating directly with the Internet, they are the ones who initiate the communication. External systems reply to the initiated communication only and cannot initiate the communication themselves.

However, in highly secure networks, you might prefer to rely on forwarders instead of root hints. For example, you might place two standalone DNS servers in your perimeter network and link the internal DNS servers to these servers through forwarders. Each time the internal servers need to resolve an Internet name, they link to one of the servers in the perimeter and ask it to perform the lookup for them. This way, the only servers to communicate outside the network are the more secure standalone servers in the perimeter.

Forwarders are configured as part of the properties of the DNS server and are accessed from the Forwarders tab in the DNS server Properties dialog box. (See Figure 9-15.) If you are configuring forwarders for security purposes, make sure you uncheck the Use Root Hints option if no forwarders are available; otherwise, your internal DNS servers will communicate directly with the Internet if your servers in the perimeter do not respond.

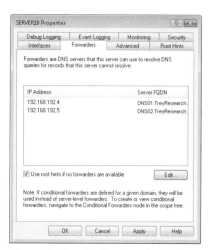

Figure 9-15   Configuring forwarders in DNS

You can also use conditional forwarders in your DNS configuration. Conditional forwarders are used to forward DN requests when specific conditions are met. For example, if you want to link two namespaces but only when users request a particular name, you would use conditional forwarders.

For example, consider the following scenario. Your network includes two forests. The first is the production forest, the one that contains all the accounts users use to work together in your organization. The second is a special forest that was created to test the AD DS integration of third-party applications with the AD DS forest schema before they are deployed in your production forest. Because of the schema changes, you do not want to link your forests together through a forest trust. Therefore, you create conditional forwarders in each forest so that users in the production domain, mostly developers and IT professionals, can link from the production to the staging domain.

Conditional forwarders include their own container in DNS Server.

1. To create a new conditional forwarder, right-click the Conditional Forwarders node and select New Conditional Forwarder.
2. Type the name of the DNS domain you want to forward to.
3. Click <Click Here To Add An IP Address Or DNS Name> and type the server's IP address.
4. Add at least two servers to the list.
5. As a best practice, store the conditional forwarder in Active Directory and determine which replication scope to apply to the forwarder. Click OK.

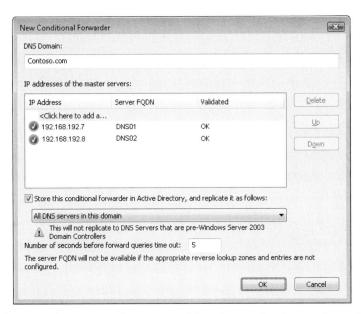

In the preceding example, you would replicate the data only to the production domain because you do not need to replicate it to the entire forest. In other cases, you might need to replicate it to the entire forest.

Note that when you create a conditional forwarder, it creates a new container for the domain you will forward to under the Conditional Forwarders node. From now on, each time your users request a name resolution that contains this domain name, your DNS servers will automatically forward it to the DNS servers you provided in the list.

Single-Label Name Management

When you want to manage single-label names, you will need to create a GNZ manually. A single GNZ is required for each forest. The basic process of creating a GNZ requires five steps, but it involves an operation on each DNS server in the forest. If you are using AD DS–integrated DNS servers and each of your DCs is also running the DNS service, you must perform this operation on each DC. This means using domain administrator credentials to complete the operation.

- Create the GlobalNames FLZ.
- Set its replication scope to all DNS servers in the forest.
- Do not enable dynamic updates for this zone.
- Enable GNZ support on each DNS server in the forest.
- Add single-label names to the DNS zone.

Configuration is performed through the command line because there is no graphical interface to access this feature. However, you can create the GNZ through Server Manager, but enabling

GNZ support in a DNS server requires a modification of the Windows Registry. This modification is performed with the *Dnscmd.exe* command and uses the following format:

```
dnscmd /config /enableglobalnamessupport 1
```

This command needs to be run on each DNS server in the forest. If you need to support single-label names and you do not want to use WINS, you might want to make this command part of your standard DNS server installation and configuration process. You need to restart the DNS service when the command has been run.

After you have enabled GNZ support, you can begin to add records. GNZ names are aliases because each object in your network already has a host name in DNS. You create an alias and point it to the corresponding FQDN for the object. GNZ aliases, like WINS names, cannot have more than 15 characters—they actually use 16 characters, but the system reserves the last character. If you want to create the names through a command file, use the following command format for each name:

```
dnscmd dnsservername /recordadd globalnames singlelabelname cname
correspondingdnsname
```

Where *dnsservername* is the name of the DNS server that you are adding the name to, the *singlelabelname* is the 15-character name you want to add, and *correspondingdnsname* is the FQDN of the object whose GNZ name you are adding.

MORE INFO   GlobalNames zones

For more information on GNZs, view the DNS GlobalNames Zone Deployment document at *http://www.microsoft.com/downloads/details.aspx?FamilyID=1c6b31cd-3dd9-4c3f-8acd-3201 a57194f1&displaylang=en*.

DNS and WINS

If you are in a network that requires a multitude of single-label names and you cannot provide support for them through a GNZ because there are simply too many names to manage, install the WINS service on at least two servers in your network. WINS will then automatically generate and manage names for each object in the network. Remember that WINS services are a feature of Windows Server 2008, not a role, and that it is an outdated technology that has not been updated since the original release of Windows Server 2003.

If you do deploy WINS, remember that:

- WINS does not appear in Server Manager. To administer WINS, you must use the WINS console in the Administrative Tools program group.
- WINS supports IPv4 addresses only and will not be updated to support IPv6.

■ You need at least two WINS servers to provide fault tolerance for single-label names in your network. These two servers should be configured to use push/pull synchronization to make sure both name databases are synchronized at all times.

■ You need to ensure that the values for WINS are specified in the DHCP settings you send to computers requiring dynamic IPv4 addresses. Two settings are required. The first lists the name servers and the second identifies which type of node each client will work with.

  ❏ 044 WINS/NBNS Servers identifies which servers host the WINS service.

  ❏ 046 WINS/NBT Node Type identifies how nodes interact with WINS. The most commonly used node type is 0x8 or the Hybrid node type. This minimizes the amount of broadcasting required in single-label name networks.

■ You can also integrate WINS and DNS by modifying the properties of an FLZ. This property sheet includes a WINS tab that is unused unless you have WINS servers in your network. (See Figure 9-16.) This feature is useful in networks in which many clients rely on WINS and it is possible that some of the client device names will not be present in DNS. However, all Windows operating systems since Windows 2000 can participate in a dynamic DNS infrastructure. Networks that run earlier clients than Windows 2000 are becoming very rare.

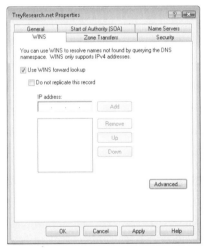

Figure 9-16   Linking DNS with WINS to provide both FQDN and single-label name resolution

DNS and DHCP Considerations

When you work with dynamic DNS and you integrate the DNS service with the AD DS directory store, you must change the traditional approach network administrators use to configure DHCP settings that are provided to each client device that relies on dynamic IP addresses, whether they are IPv4 or IPv6.

Traditionally, network administrators provide as few as two central DNS servers in the server options of the DHCP settings. This provides all client devices with the DNS addresses they need to resolve both internal and external FQDNs, but because the servers were centrally located, any client that was in a remote site would need to perform a DNS lookup over the WAN.

However, with the integration of DNS and especially DNS data with the directory store, DNS data is now available wherever there is a DC and, to provide authentication services wherever clients are located, DCs are distributed throughout a network. In fact, some organizations have DCs available wherever there are at least 20 clients. With the advent of server virtualization through Hyper-V as well as DC hardening through the RODC, DCs can be even more prevalent in networks. This means that DNS data, even read-only DNS data, will be available in each remote site or branch office. Clients can use servers in their local site to perform FQDN lookups.

However, for clients to perform the lookup locally, they must know about the presence of local DNS servers. Imagine the following scenario:

- A client in a remote site uses a dynamic IP address allocated through DHCP.
- There are two DCs in the remote site.
- DNS is integrated with the directory and is replicated with the domain partition.
- DHCP sends out values for only two DNS servers in a central site.
- When the client boots in the morning, it performs a DNS lookup to locate its closest DC to log on.
- The DNS lookup occurs over the WAN to request the name resolution from one of the two central DCs.
- The central DNS servers look up the client's site and find that there are two local DCs to support logon.
- The DNS server returns the location of the closest DC to the client, once again over the WAN.
- The client contacts its local DC to log on.

In this scenario, the client cannot log on if there is no WAN connectivity even though the DNS data is stored locally within the two DCs!

Because of this, DHCP options must be modified as follows:

- The server scope should continue to provide at least two addresses for centrally located DNS servers for redundancy purposes. If the local DCs is down, clients will still be able to log on, albeit over the WAN.
- Each individual address scope should include options for name resolution servers, and these records should point to the DCs that are local to the site the scope is assigned to. This means adding the *006 DNS Servers* value to each individual scope in DHCP.

- All DCs should also be running the DNS Server role. That's all you have to do. If a DNS zone is stored in the AD DS directory store, it will be made available to the DNS service as soon as you install the DNS Server role on the DC. There is nothing more to configure except global DNS server settings.

Keep this in mind when planning to integrate DNS with DHCP.

Working with Application Directory Partitions

In certain circumstances, you will want to create custom application directory partitions in support of DNS data replication. Remember that application directory partitions control the replication scope of the data they contain. The DNS server creates two application directory partitions when it is installed with AD DS in a forest, one for forest data and one for domain data in each domain, but under certain conditions, these two scopes might not be appropriate, especially in complex forests.

Consider this scenario. Your forest includes three domains: the forest root, a global child production domain, and a development domain. You created the development domain because your developers have special access right requirements and you do not want to grant them these access rights in the production domain. All production domain users except for system administrators have standard user access rights. In the development domain, however, you can grant developers higher access rights—rights to create, modify, or delete objects—because this domain does not affect production operations.

In addition, you created only a single account for each developer. This account is located in the global child production domain and has standard user rights, but through the transitive trusts inherent in each forest, developers can use their accounts from the production domain to access objects in the development domain where their production domain accounts have higher access rights.

By default, name resolution between the two child domains passes through the forest root domain. Developers access this domain on a constant basis every day, so to provide them with faster name resolution, you create a custom application directory partition to share the DNS records between the development and the production domains. This means that because the data is available in the partition, production DNS servers will not need to pass through the forest root domain to resolve development domain names. (See Figure 9-17.)

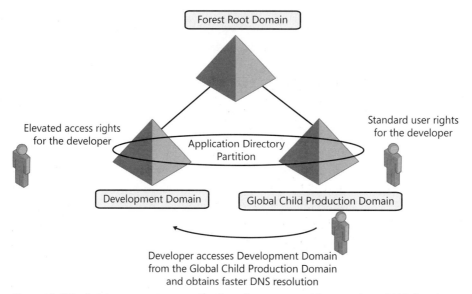

Figure 9-17 Relying on custom application directory partitions to share DNS data between two child domains

Creating and Assigning Custom Application Directory Partitions

Custom application directory partitions are created through the command line with the *Dnscmd.exe* command. There is no interface for creating these partitions. However, after they are created, the partitions can be assigned through the graphical interface. You can perform each operation through the command line if you prefer. You must perform three tasks:

- Create the partition.
- Enlist DNS servers into the partition.
- Assign the zones whose replication scope you want to change to the newly created partition.

To create an application directory partition, you must be a member of the Enterprise Admins groups because you must have full access to the forest.

1. Log on to a DNS server with an account that is a member of the Enterprise Admins group for the forest.

2. Launch an elevated command prompt through the context menu and the *Run as* administrator command.

3. Type the following command:

   dnscmd *dnsservername* /createdirectorypartition *partitionfqdn*

   where the *dnsservername* is the FQDN of your DNS server or its IP address, and *partitionfqdn* is the FQDN of the partition you want to create.

For example, if you want to create a new partition on SERVER10 and name it partition01.treyresearch.net, you would use the following command:

```
dnscmd server10.treyresearch.net /createdirectorypartition
partition01.treyresearch.net
```

4. Enlist the server into the partition. Once again, you use the *Dnscmd.exe* command. Type the following command:

   dnscmd *dnsservername* /enlistdirectorypartition *partitionfqdn*

   You need to repeat this command for each DNS server you want to enlist into the partition. Note that the server you use to create the partition is enlisted by default. In the preceding scenario, you would need to enlist all the DNS servers for the production domain as well as all the DNS servers for the development domain into the partition. For example, if you want to enlist SERVER30—a server of the child domain—as an additional server into the new partition named partition01.treyresearch.net, you would use the following command:

   ```
   dnscmd server30.intranet.treyresearch.net /enlistdirectorypartition
   partition01.treyresearch.net
   ```

   Now you can change the replication scope of the zones you want to make available to the members of the new application directory partition.

5. Return to the DNS node in Server Manager, right-click the name of the zone you want to change, and select Properties.

6. On the General tab, click the Change button to change the replication scope.

7. In the Change Zone Replication Scope dialog box, select To All Domain Controllers In The Scope Of This Directory Partition and click the drop-down list to select your new partition. Click OK twice.

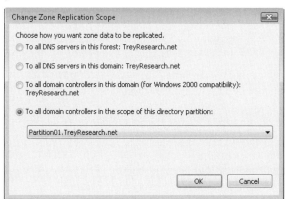

Be careful when you work with application directory partitions because many of the commands are manually entered. If you make a mistake, you could damage the replication scope of your servers and, therefore, disable name resolution.

MORE INFO Application directory partitions

For more information on application directory partitions, go to *http://technet2.microsoft.com/windowsserver2008/en/library/2e2e0678-1775-4cdd-8779-32d5c281540f1033.mspx?mfr=true*.

Exam Tip Replication scopes and application directory partitions are an important part of the exam. Be sure you understand them fully.

Administering DNS Servers

You've already seen several tools in operation through practices and detailed step-by-step lists. However, you might need to work with other tools when working with your DNS servers. Table 9-4 outlines the different tools you can use to support DNS operations and management.

Table 9-4 Common DNS Administration Tools

Tool	Task	Location
DNS Manager	Perform initial configuration of a new server. Connect to and manage a local DNS server. Add and remove forward and reverse lookup zones. Add, remove, and update resource records in zones. Modify how zones are stored and replicated between servers. Modify how server processes queries and handles dynamic update. Modify security for specific zones or resource records. Perform maintenance. Monitor contents of the server cache. Tune advanced server options. Configure and perform aging and scavenging of stale resource records.	Administrative Tools program group or Server Manager
Dnscmd	Manage all aspects of DNS servers. This is the most powerful command-line tool for DNS administration. Common switches include: ■ */info* to obtain server information. ■ */config* to modify server configuration parameters. ■ */statistics* to obtain operational statistics from a server. ■ */clearcache* to clear and reset the cache. ■ */startscavenging* to initiate a scavenging operation. ■ */directorypartitioninfo* for information about partitions. ■ */exportsettings* to create a backup file of your server's settings.	Command line

Table 9-4 **Common DNS Administration Tools**

Tool	Task	Location
Dnslint	Diagnose common DNS name resolution issues. Common switches include: ■ */d* to request domain name resolution tests. ■ */ql* to verify DNS query tests from a list. ■ */ad* to verify records specifically related to Active Directory.	
Event Viewer	There are two options for monitoring DNS servers: ■ Default logging of DNS server event messages to the DNS server log. ■ Debug options for trace logging to a text file on the DNS server. This option is enabled through the DNS server's Properties dialog box and is disabled by default. Use it only for debugging purposes.	Server Manager
Ipconfig	Display and modify IP configuration details. Common switches include: ■ */all* to display all network configuration settings on a system. ■ */renew* to request a dynamic IPv4 address renewal from DHCP. ■ */renew6* to request a dynamic IPv6 address renewal from DHCP. ■ */release* to release a dynamic IPv4 address. ■ */release6* to release a dynamic IPv6 address. ■ */flushdns* to clear the DNS resolver cache on a system. ■ */registerdns* to renew a dynamic DNS registration for a system.	Command line
Nslookup	Perform query testing of the DNS domain namespace. *Nslookup* is also a command interpreter that is entered by simply typing **nslookup** at the command line. Type **exit** to return to the command line. However, it can also be used directly. To do so, type **nslookup** followed by the hostname or the IP address of the computer you are looking for.	Command line
System Monitor	Create charts and graphs of server performance trends. Determine performance benchmarks.	Server Manager, Diagnostics, Reliability, and Performance

Exam Tip   Run through each of these tools. DNS operation is an important part of the exam.

Little will go wrong with your internal DNS implementations if you follow the guidelines outlined here. However, there is always the possibility of uncontrolled issues. This is why you should become familiar with the tools listed in Table 9-4. Examine DNS events and understand them.

MORE INFO   DNS troubleshooting and potential resolutions

For more information on DNS troubleshooting and potential resolutions to DNS issues, go to *http://technet2.microsoft.com/windowsserver2008/en/library/8e3f7e44-91dd-44c4-81cf-158cea7089021033.mspx?mfr=true*. To obtain *Dnslint.exe*, go to *http://support.microsoft.com/kb/321045*.

PRACTICE **Finalizing a DNS Server Configuration in a Forest**

In this practice, you will work with the DNS service to finalize its configuration. First, you will enable single-label name management in the Trey Research forest. Then you will create single-label names to populate your GNZ. Finally, you will modify a global query block list to protect your servers from dynamic entry spoofing.

▶ **Exercise 1   Single-Label Name Management**

In this exercise, you will create and configure a GNZ for the *treyresearch.net* forest. This operation is manual and will require domain administrator credentials because your DNS servers are running on DCs. This exercise will require SERVER10, SERVER20, and SERVER30.

1. Log on to SERVER10 with treyresearch\administrator.
2. In Server Manager, select the Forward Lookup Zones node in the DNS role.
3. Right-click Forward Lookup Zone to select New Zone from the context menu.
4. Review the welcome information and click Next.
5. Select Primary Zone and make sure you select the Store The Zone In Active Directory check box. Click Next.
6. On the next page, select To All DNS Servers In This Forest:TreyResearch.net and click Next.
7. On the Zone Name page, type **GlobalNames** and click Next.
8. On the Dynamic Update page, select Do Not Allow Dynamic Updates and click Next.

   You do not allow dynamic updates in this zone because all single-label names are created manually in DNS.
9. Click Finish to create the zone.

   Now, enable GNZ support on this DNS server. You need to do this through an elevated command line.
10. From the Start menu, right-click Command Prompt to select Run As Administrator.
11. Type the following command:

    ```
    dnscmd /config /enableglobalnamessupport 1
    ```

12. Close the command prompt and return to Server Manager. Right-click SERVER10 under the DNS node, select All Tasks, and choose Restart to recycle the DNS service on this server.

13. Repeat steps 10–12 on SERVER20 and SERVER30.

14. Return to SERVER10 to add single-label names.

▶ **Exercise 2   Create Single-Label Names**

In this exercise, you will create single-label names within the GNZ on SERVER10. This operation is manual and will require domain administrator credentials because your DNS servers are running on DCs. You will add a single-label record for each of your three servers.

1. Log on to SERVER10 with treyresearch\administrator.

2. In Server Manager, select the GlobalNames FLZ node in the DNS role.

3. Right-click GlobalNames to select New Alias (CNAME) from the context menu.

4. In the *Alias Name* field, type **SERVER10**, move to *Fully Qualified Domain Name (FQDN) For Target Host* field, and type **SERVER10.treyresearch.net**.

   Remember that like WINS names, single-label DNS names cannot have more than 15 characters—they actually use 16 characters, but the system reserves the last character. Also, single-label or NetBIOS names tend always to be in uppercase. Use uppercase to create your single-label names as a best practice.

5. Do not select the Allow Any Authenticated User To Update All DNS Records With The Same Name. This Setting Applies Only To DNS Records For A New Name check box.

6. Click OK to create the single-label name.

7. Use the command line to create the other two single-label names you need. From the Start menu, right-click Command Prompt to select Run As Administrator.

8. Type the following commands:

   ```
   dnscmd server10.treyresearch.net /recordadd globalnames server20 cname
   server20.northwindtraders.com

   dnscmd server10.treyresearch.net /recordadd globalnames server30 cname
   server30.intranet.treyresearch.net
   ```

9. Close the command prompt and return to the GNZ in Server Manager to view the new records. Use the Refresh button to update the details view.

   If you have many names to add, you might want to script this operation to simplify it.

▶ **Exercise 3   Modify a Global Query Block List**

In this exercise, you will modify an existing global query block list on SERVER10. This operation is manual and will require domain administrator credentials because your DNS server is running on a DC. You will add a special DNS name, **manufacturing**, to the list to block name resolution for any object that uses this name.

1. Log on to SERVER10 with treyresearch\administrator.
2. Use the command line to modify the block list. From the Start menu, right-click Command Prompt to select Run As Administrator.
3. Type the following commands:

```
dnscmd /config /globalqueryblocklist wpad isatap manufacturing
```

   You must add the existing names in the block list, WPAD and ISATAP, to the command to ensure that they continue to be blocked. Make a note of the new name to ensure that you continue to block it if you need to add another name at a later date.
4. Close the command prompt.

   Your block list is configured.

Lesson Summary

- After the DNS server is installed, its configuration must be completed. DNS configuration settings include a review of the security parameters, scavenging and aging settings, zone configuration, and possible RLZ creations.
- Each forward lookup or stub zone includes a SOA record. This record should be properly configured to include the e-mail address of the responsible parties for DNS operation as well as information about your DNS operating standards.
- If you require single-label name management in your network, you will need to determine whether you will be using GNZs or the WINS service. GNZs are used when only a select list of names is required. If a multitude of names is required, you must deploy WINS.
- By default, DNS servers rely on root hints for name resolution. You can also use forwarders, which direct the DNS server to another DNS server under special circumstances.
- By default, replication scopes for DNS data integrated with Active Directory will automatically span the proper number of DNS servers. However, under special circumstances, you can create manual application directory partitions to control the replication scope more precisely.

Lesson Review

You can use the following questions to test your knowledge of the information in Lesson 2, "Configuring and Using Domain Name System." The questions are also available on the companion CD if you prefer to review them in electronic form.

1. You are the DNS administrator for the *contoso.com* internal forward lookup zone. You have been asked to complete the configuration of this zone now that it has been created. What should you do? (Choose all that apply).

   A. Configure scavenging for the zone.

   B. Validate the replication scope for the zone.

   C. Create custom records for the zone.

   D. Create a text (TXT) record for the zone.

   E. Assign an e-mail address to the zone.

   F. Delete unused records in the zone.

   G. Create a reverse lookup zone for the zone.

2. You are a system administrator for the *treyresearch.net* domain. Your organization has decided to create a new development domain to segregate development from the production domain. Because of compliance issues, all users of the production domain except operational staff must be granted only standard user rights. This means that for developers to be able to work, they must be granted rights other than in the production domain. However, because developers will be using the new domain on a regular basis, it has been determined that a new application directory partition must be created to support faster DNS name resolution between the two domains. All forward lookup zones are Active Directory–integrated zones. You must assign this new partition to a forward lookup zone. However, when you go to assign it, it is not available. What could be the problem? (Choose all that apply.)

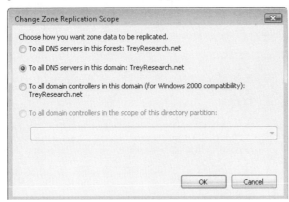

A.   You must log on with domain administrator credentials.

B.   You must enlist the server you are using in the partition.

C.   You must log on with enterprise administrator credentials.

D.   You must use the command line to assign the zone to the partition.

E.   You cannot change the replication scope of a forward lookup zone after it is created.

Chapter Review

To further practice and reinforce the skills you learned in this chapter, you can perform the following tasks:

- Review the chapter summary.
- Review the list of key terms introduced in this chapter.
- Complete the case scenario. This scenario sets up a real-world situation involving the topics of this chapter and asks you to create a solution.
- Complete the suggested practices.
- Take a practice test.

Chapter Summary

- The most common types of DNS structures are the dynamic DNS server, the primary DNS server, and the secondary DNS server. Dynamic DNS servers will accept automatic name registration from authorized entities within their network. Primary DNS servers are read-write servers that are usually maintained by authorized administrators. Names can be entered manually or through automated processes but are not entered dynamically. Secondary DNS servers are usually subordinate servers that include read-only data that has originated from another DNS server, usually a primary DNS server. DNS in Windows Server 2008 also includes another type of read-only DNS server, the read-only DC DNS server, which hosts read-only *primary* DNS zones.

- A typical Windows Server 2008 DNS scenario can include up to four DNS server deployments. The first and most prolific is the dynamic DNS server, which is integrated with every DC in the network. Read-write DCs will also contain read-write DNS servers. In remote sites that do not have local administrative staff but require a DC for availability purposes, read-only DCs will also include read-only DNS servers. External networks will include at least one primary standalone DNS, which will be maintained manually. If more DNS servers are required, they should be secondary, read-only DNS servers. Read-only DNS servers are more secure than read-write servers and should be deployed in areas that demand the highest security levels.

- To support further the move to IPv6, Windows Server 2008 also supports the Peer Name Resolution Protocol and includes a PRNP server that can help promote name resolution. PNRP and DNS do not work the same way and do not include the same features. However, most organizations will continue to rely on DNS to support name resolution for the time being. For example, AD DS hierarchies are not supported in PNRP. This is a good reason to continue using DNS for the time being.

Key Terms

Use these key terms to understand better the concepts covered in this chapter.

- **record**   A valid entry in a DNS zone that provides a correspondence between an IPv4 or IPv6 address and a fully qualified domain name.
- **zone**   A special container in DNS that includes records that will resolve to valid IP addresses. Zones address a specific namespace and only one namespace.

Case Scenario

In the following case scenario, you will apply what you've learned about Domain Name System services. You can find answers to the questions in this scenario in the "Answers" section at the end of this book.

Case Scenario: Block Specific DNS Names

In the past, Trey Research has had problems with the Biometrics and the Biology departments when unauthorized users in these departments set up their own non-Windows servers to run their research programs. These servers were set up with little or no care for security and were quickly taken over by malicious users. After they were compromised, the servers started sending out dynamic updates for the Biometrics department, spoofing valid addresses. Now, Trey Research wants to ensure that this can never occur again. They have taken administrative measures to ensure that if other non-Windows operating systems are needed, they are installed according to proper IT guidelines.

Which other technical measure could Trey Research take to ensure that these two departments do not cause issues with DNS name resolution in the internal network?

Suggested Practices

To help you successfully master the exam objectives presented in this chapter, complete the following tasks.

Working with DNS

DNS in Windows Server 2008 is tightly integrated with Active Directory Domain Services. Therefore, you should practice working with dynamic DNS systems that support AD DS. Use the following practices to do so.

- **Practice 1**   Practice installing and uninstalling DNS both on its own and through the Active Directory Domain Services Installation Wizard in as many scenarios as possible. In addition, create manual delegations and compare their interaction with the installation process to the automatically created delegations the wizard generates. This will familiarize you with the various pages presented by the wizards.

- **Practice 2**   Work with zones, creating each of the three supported zone types one after the other. Try as many configuration options as possible. Then, create as many different record types as possible. This will familiarize you with the different dialog boxes and wizards used to configure zones and records.

- **Practice 3**   Work with the command-line tools and try as many different switches as possible for each tool. The *Dnscmd.exe* command, especially, will be present on the exam. Familiarity with this command will help you understand its function better.

- **Practice 4**   Work with the DNS event log and tracing log and examine their content. Familiarity with DNS logging is essential for any DNS operator.

Take a Practice Test

The practice tests on this book's companion CD offer many options. For example, you can test yourself on just one exam objective, or you can test yourself on all the 70-640 certification exam content. You can set up the test so that it closely simulates the experience of taking a certification exam, or you can set it up in study mode so that you can look at the correct answers and explanations after you answer each question.

MORE INFO   **Practice tests**

For details about all the practice test options available, see the "How to Use the Practice Tests" section in this book's introduction.

Chapter 10

Domain Controllers

Domain controllers (DCs) host the directory service and perform the services that support identity and access management in a Microsoft Windows enterprise. To this point in the training kit, you have learned to support the logical and management components of an Active Directory Domain Services (AD DS) infrastructure: users, groups, computers, and Group Policy. Each of these components is contained in the directory database and in SYSVOL on domain controllers. In this chapter, you will begin your exploration of the service-level components of Active Directory, starting with the domain controllers themselves. You will learn how to add Windows Server 2008 domain controllers to a forest or domain, how to prepare a Microsoft Windows Server 2003 forest or domain for its first Windows Server 2008 DC, how to manage the roles performed by DCs, and how to migrate the replication of SYSVOL from the File Replication Service (FRS) used in previous versions of Windows to the Distributed File System Replication (DFS-R) mechanism that provides more robust and manageable replication.

Exam objectives in this chapter:
- Configure a forest or a domain.
- Configure Active Directory replication.
- Configure operations masters.

Lessons in this chapter:

- Lesson 1: Installing Domain Controllers. 461
- Lesson 2: Configuring Operations Masters. 478
- Lesson 3: Configuring DFS Replication of SYSVOL 494

Before You Begin

To complete the practices in this chapter, you must have created a domain controller named SERVER01 in a domain named *contoso.com* and a member server, with a full installation, joined to the domain named SERVER02. See Chapter 1, "Installation," for detailed steps for this task.

Real World

Dan Holme

Active Directory enables you to configure a domain and a forest with a single domain controller. But that's not enough. Domain controllers provide functionality critical to the identity and access management requirements of an enterprise, and if a domain controller fails, you must have a way to provide continuity of service. That's why it's very important to have at least two DCs in a domain. As soon as you start adding DCs to a domain, you start needing to consider replication, and in this chapter, you'll learn about one of the exciting new features of Windows Server 2008: DFS-R of SYSVOL. FRS, used by previous versions of Windows and supported by Windows Server 2008 for backward compatibility, has been a notorious weak spot prone to problems and difficult to troubleshoot. To take advantage of this feature, all domain controllers must be running Windows Server 2008, so you'll need to know how to prepare an existing forest for its first Windows Server 2008 DC—another objective of this chapter. Finally, as you add domain controllers to an enterprise, you need to consider the placement of single master operations, which are special roles assigned to one DC in a forest or domain. By the time you're through with this chapter, you'll have the skills to improve the redundancy, performance, and manageability of multiple domain controllers in your enterprise.

Lesson 1: Installing Domain Controllers

In Chapter 1, you used the Add Roles Wizard in Server Manager to install Active Directory Domain Services (AD DS). Then you used the Active Directory Domain Services Installation Wizard to create the first DC in the *contoso.com* forest. Because DCs are critical to authentication, it is highly recommended to maintain at least two domain controllers in each domain in your forest to provide a level of fault tolerance in the event that one DC fails. You might also need to add domain controllers to remote sites or create new domains or trees in your Active Directory forest. In this lesson, you will learn user-interface, command-line, and unattended methods for installing domain controllers in a variety of scenarios.

After this lesson, you will be able to:

- Install a DC, using the Windows interface, *Dcpromo.exe* command-line parameters, or an answer file for unattended installation.
- Add Windows Server 2008 DCs to a domain or forest with Windows Server 2003 and Windows 2000 Server DCs.
- Create new domains and trees.
- Perform a staged installation of a read-only domain controller.
- Install a DC from installation media to reduce network replication.
- Remove a domain controller.

Estimated lesson time: 60 minutes

Installing a Domain Controller with the Windows Interface

If you want to use the Windows interface to install a domain controller, there are two major steps. First, you must install the AD DS role, which, as you learned in Chapter 1, can be accomplished using the Add Roles Wizard in Server Manager. After the AD DS role installation has copied the binaries required for the role to the server, you must install and configure AD DS by launching the Active Directory Domain Services Installation Wizard, using one of these methods:

- Click Start and, in the Start Search box, type **dcpromo** and click OK.
- When you complete the Add Roles Wizard, click the link to launch the Active Directory Domain Services Installation Wizard.
- After adding the AD DS role, links will appear in Server Manager that remind you to run the Active Directory Domain Services Installation Wizard. Click any of those links.

The Active Directory Domain Services Installation Wizard is shown in Figure 10-1.

Figure 10-1   The Active Directory Domain Services Installation Wizard

---

NOTE   All-in-one wizard

Microsoft documentation for Windows Server 2008 emphasizes the role-based model, so it recommends you add the AD DS role and then run *Dcpromo.exe* (the Active Directory Domain Services Installation Wizard). However, you can simply run *Dcpromo.exe* and, as a first step, the wizard detects that the AD DS binaries are not installed and adds the AD DS role automatically.

Unattended Installation Options and Answer Files

You can also add or remove a domain controller at the command line, using unattended installation supported by the Windows Server 2008 version of *Dcpromo.exe*. Unattended installation options provide values to the Active Directory Domain Services Installation Wizard. For example, the NewDomainDNSName option specifies a fully qualified domain name (FQDN) for a new domain.

These options can be provided at the command line by typing **dcpromo /*unattendOption*:*value*,** for example, **dcpromo /newdomaindnsname:contoso.com**. Alternatively, you can provide the options in an unattended installation answer file. The answer file is a text file that contains a section heading, [DCINSTALL], followed by options and their values in the *option=value* form. For example, the following file provides the NewDomainDNSName option:

```
[DCINSTALL]
NewDomainDNSName=contoso.com
```

The answer file is called by adding its path to the *unattend* parameter, for example:

```
dcpromo /unattend:"path to answer file"
```

The options in the answer file can be overridden by parameters on the command line. For example, if the NewDomainDNSName option is specified in the answer file and the */New-DomainDNSName* parameter is used on the command line, the value on the command line takes precedence. If any required values are neither in the answer file nor on the command line, the Active Directory Domain Services Installation Wizard will prompt for the answers, so you can use the answer file to partially automate an installation, providing a subset of configuration values to be used during an interactive installation.

The wizard is not available when running *Dcpromo.exe* from the command line in Server Core. In that case, the *Dcpromo.exe* command will return with an error code.

For a complete list of parameters that you can specify as part of an unattended installation of AD DS, open an elevated command prompt and type the following command:

```
dcpromo /?[:operation]
```

where *operation* is one of the following:

- **Promotion** returns all parameters you can use when creating a domain controller.
- **CreateDCAccount** returns all parameters you can use when creating a prestaged account for a read-only domain controller (RODC).
- **UseExistingAccount** returns all parameters you can use to attach a new DC to a prestaged RODC account.
- **Demotion** returns all parameters you can use when removing a domain controller.

MORE INFO *Dcpromo* **parameters and unattended installation**

For a complete reference of *Dcpromo* parameters and unattended installation options, see *http://go.microsoft.com/fwlink/?LinkID=101181*.

NOTE **Generate an answer file**

When you use the Windows interface to create a domain controller, the Active Directory Domain Services Installation Wizard gives you the option, on the Summary page, to export your settings to an answer file. If you need to create an answer file for use from the command line, for example, on a Server Core installation, you can use this shortcut to create an answer file with the correct options and values.

Installing a New Windows Server 2008 Forest

Chapter 1 discussed the installation of the first Windows Server 2008 DC in a new forest, using the Windows interface. Exercise 3, "Install a New Windows Server 2008 Forest with the Windows Interface," and Exercise 4, "Install a New Windows Server 2008 Forest," of Lesson 1, "Installing Active Directory Domain Services," in that chapter detailed the steps to add the AD DS role to a server by using Server Manager and then to run *Dcpromo.exe* to promote the server to a domain controller. When creating a new forest root domain, you must specify the forest root Domain Name System (DNS) name, its NetBIOS name, and the forest and domain functional levels. The first domain controller cannot be a read-only domain controller and must be a global catalog (GC) server. If the Active Directory Domain Services Installation Wizard detects that it is necessary to install or configure DNS, it does it automatically.

You can also use an answer file by typing **dcpromo /unattend:"*path to answer file*"**, where the answer file contains unattended installation options and values. The following example contains the minimum parameters for an unattended installation of a new Windows Server 2008 domain controller in a new forest:

```
[DCINSTALL]
ReplicaOrNewDomain=domain
NewDomain=forest
NewDomainDNSName=fully qualified DNS name
DomainNetBiosName=domain NetBIOS name
ForestLevel={0=Windows 2000 Server Native;
             2=Windows Server 2003 Native;
             3=Windows Server 2008}
DomainLevel={0=Windows Server 2000 Native;
             2=Windows Server 2003 Native;
             3=Windows Server 2008}
InstallDNS=yes
DatabasePath="path to folder on a local volume"
LogPath="path to folder on a local volume"
SYSVOLPath="path to folder on a local volume"
SafeModeAdminPassword=password
RebootOnCompletion=yes
```

You can also specify one or more unattended installation parameters and values at the command line. For example, if you don't want the Directory Services Restore Mode password in the answer file, leave the entry blank and specify the */SafeModeAdminPassword:password* parameter when you run *Dcpromo.exe*.

You can also include all options on the command line itself. The following example creates the first domain controller in a new forest in which you don't expect to install any Windows Server 2003 domain controllers:

```
dcpromo /unattend /installDNS:yes /dnsOnNetwork:yes
    /replicaOrNewDomain:domain /newDomain:forest
    /newDomainDnsName:contoso.com /DomainNetbiosName:contoso
```

```
/databasePath:"e:\ntds" /logPath:"f:\ntdslogs" /sysvolpath:"g:\sysvol"
/safeModeAdminPassword:password /forestLevel:3 /domainLevel:3
/rebootOnCompletion:yes
```

Installing Additional Domain Controllers in a Domain

If you have a domain with at least one domain controller running Windows 2000 Server, Windows Server 2003, or Windows Server 2008, you can create additional domain controllers to distribute authentication, create a level of fault tolerance in the event any one DC fails, or provide authentication in remote sites.

Installing the First Windows Server 2008 Domain Controller in an Existing Forest or Domain

If you have an existing forest with domain controllers running Windows Server 2003 or Windows 2000 Server, you must prepare them prior to creating your first Windows Server 2008 domain controller. That's because there are objects and attributes that Windows Server 2008 adds to the directory that previous versions of Windows don't understand. Therefore, the schema must be updated. The schema is the definition of the attributes and object classes that can exist within a domain. It is like the catalog for what can be created in other directory partitions. To prepare the forest schema for Windows Server 2008, follow these steps:

1. Log on to the schema master as a member of the Enterprise Admins, Schema Admins, and Domain Admins groups.

   Lesson 2, "Configuring Operations Masters," discusses operations masters and provides steps for identifying which domain controller is the schema master.

2. Copy the contents of the \Sources\Adprep folder from the Windows Server 2008 DVD to a folder on the schema master.

3. Open a command prompt and change directories to the Adprep folder.

4. Type **adprep /forestprep** and press Enter.

5. If you plan to install an RODC in any domain in the forest, type **adprep /rodcprep** and press Enter.

NOTE   RODCPREP, anytime

You can also run *Adprep /rodcprep* at any time in a Windows 2000 Server or Windows Server 2003 forest. It does not have to be run in conjunction with */forestprep*; however, you must run it and allow its changes to replicate throughout the forest prior to installing the first RODC. You can run *Adprep /rodcprep* from any DC as long as you are logged on as a member of the Enterprise Admins group.

Exam Tip The *Adprep /rodcprep* command is required before installing an RODC into any domain in an existing forest with Windows Server 2003 or Windows 2000 Server domain control- lers. It is not necessary if the forest is a new forest consisting only of Windows Server 2008 domain controllers.

You must allow time for the operation to complete. After the changes have replicated through- out the forest, you can continue to prepare the domains for Windows Server 2008. To prepare a Windows 2000 Server or Windows Server 2003 domain for Windows Server 2008, perform these steps:

1. Log on to the domain infrastructure operations master as a member of Domain Admins. Lesson 2 provides steps for identifying which domain controller is the infrastructure operations master.

2. Copy the contents of the \Sources\Adprep folder from the Windows Server 2008 DVD to a folder on the infrastructure master.

3. Open a command prompt and change directories to the Adprep folder.

4. Type **adprep /domainprep /gpprep** and press Enter.
   On Windows Server 2003, you might receive an error message stating that updates were unnecessary. You can ignore this message.

Allow the change to replicate throughout the forest before you install a domain controller that runs Windows Server 2008.

Installing an Additional Domain Controller

Additional domain controllers can be added by installing AD DS and launching the Active Directory Domain Services Installation Wizard. You are prompted to choose the deployment configuration; to enter network credentials; to select a domain and site for the new DC; and to configure the DC with additional options such as DNS Server, Global Catalog, or Read-Only Domain Controller. The remaining steps are the same as for the first domain controller: con- figuring file locations and the Directory Services Restore Mode Administrator password.

If you have one domain controller in a domain, and if you select the Use Advanced Mode Installation check box on the Welcome To The Active Directory Domain Services Installation Wizard page, you are able to configure advanced options, which are:

■ **Install From Media** By default, a new domain controller replicates all data for all direc- tory partitions it will host from other domain controllers during the Active Directory Domain Services Installation Wizard. To improve the performance of installation, par- ticularly over slow links, you can use installation media created by existing domain controllers. Installation media is a form of backup. The new DC is able to read data from the installation media directly and then replicate only updates from other domain controllers. Install From Media (IFM) is discussed in the "Installing AD DS from Media" section.

- **Source Domain Controller** If you want to specify the domain controller from which the new DC replicates its data, you can click Use This Specific Domain Controller.

NOTE *Dcpromo /adv* is still supported

In Windows Server 2003, *Dcpromo /adv* was used to specify advanced installation options. The *adv* parameter is still supported; it simply pre-selects the Use Advanced Mode Installation check box on the Welcome page.

To use *Dcpromo.exe* with command-line parameters to specify unattended installation options, you can use the minimal parameters shown in the following example:

```
dcpromo /unattend /replicaOrNewDomain:replica
    /replicaDomainDNSName:contoso.com /installDNS:yes /confirmGC:yes
    /databasePath:"e:\ntds" /logPath:"f:\ntdslogs" /sysvolpath:"g:\sysvol"
    /safeModeAdminPassword:password /rebootOnCompletion:yes
```

If you are not logged on to the server with domain credentials, specify the *userdomain* and *username* parameters as well. A minimal answer file for an additional domain controller in an existing domain is as follows:

```
[DCINSTALL]
ReplicaOrNewDomain=replica
ReplicaDomainDNSName=FQDN of domain to join
UserDomain=FQDN of domain of user account
UserName=DOMAIN\username (in Administrators group of the domain)
Password=password for user specified by UserName (* to prompt)
InstallDNS=yes
ConfirmGC=yes
DatabasePath="path to folder on a local volume"
LogPath="path to folder on a local volume"
SYSVOLPath="path to folder on a local volume"
SafeModeAdminPassword=password
RebootOnCompletion=yes
```

Installing a New Windows Server 2008 Child Domain

If you have an existing domain, you can create a new child domain by creating a Windows Server 2008 domain controller. Before you do, however, you must run *Adprep /forestprep,* as described in the "Installing the First Windows Server 2008 Domain Controller in an Existing Forest or Domain" section.

Then install AD DS and launch the Active Directory Domain Services Installation Wizard and, on the Choose A Deployment Configuration page, click Existing Forest and Create A New Domain In An Existing Forest. You are prompted to select the domain functional level.

Because it is the first DC in the domain, it cannot be an RODC, and it cannot be installed from media. If you select the Use Advanced Mode Installation check box on the Welcome page, the wizard presents you with a Source Domain Controller page on which you specify a domain controller from which to replicate the configuration and schema partitions.

Using *Dcpromo.exe*, you can create a child domain with the minimal options shown in the following command:

```
dcpromo /unattend /installDNS:yes
    /replicaOrNewDomain:domain /newDomain:child
    /ParentDomainDNSName:contoso.com
    /newDomainDnsName:subsidiary.contoso.com /childName:subsidiary
    /DomainNetbiosName:subsidiary
    /databasePath:"e:\ntds" /logPath:"f:\ntdslogs" /sysvolpath:"g:\sysvol"
    /safeModeAdminPassword:password /forestLevel:3 /domainLevel:3
    /rebootOnCompletion:yes
```

The following answer file reflects the same minimal parameters:

```
[DCINSTALL]
ReplicaOrNewDomain=domain
NewDomain=child
ParentDomainDNSName=FQDN of parent domain
UserDomain=FQDN of user specified by UserName
UserName= DOMAIN\username (in Administrators group of ParentDomainDNSName)
Password=password for user specified by UserName or * for prompt
ChildName=single-label prefix for domain
          (Child domain FQDN will be ChildName.ParentDomainDNSName)
DomainNetBiosName=Domain NetBIOS name
DomainLevel=domain functional level (not lower than current forest level)
InstallDNS=yes
CreateDNSDelegation=yes
DNSDelegationUserName=DOMAIN\username with permissions to create
                     DNS delegation, if different than UserName, above
DNSDelegationPassword=password for DNSDelegationUserName or * for prompt
DatabasePath="path to folder on a local volume"
LogPath="path to folder on a local volume"
SYSVOLPath="path to folder on a local volume"
SafeModeAdminPassword=password
RebootOnCompletion=yes
```

Installing a New Domain Tree

You learned in Chapter 1 that in an Active Directory forest, a tree is composed of one or more domains that share contiguous DNS namespace. So, for example, the *contoso.com* and *subsidiary. contoso.com* domains would be in a single tree. Additional trees are simply additional domains that are not in the same namespace. For example, if Contoso, Ltd., bought Tailspin Toys, the *tailspintoys.com* domain would be in a separate tree in the domain. There is very little functional difference between a child domain and a domain in another tree, and the process for creating a new tree is, therefore, very similar to creating a child domain.

First, you must run *Adprep /forestprep*, as described in the "Installing the First Windows Server 2008 Domain Controller in an Existing Forest or Domain" section. Then you can install AD DS and run the Active Directory Domain Services Installation Wizard. You must select Use Advanced Mode Installation on the Welcome page of the wizard. On the Choose A Deployment Configuration page, click Existing Forest, select Create A New Domain In An Existing Forest, and select Create A New Domain Tree Root Instead Of A New Child Domain. The rest of the process is identical to creating a new child domain.

The following options provided as parameters to *Dcpromo.exe* create a new tree for the *tailspintoys.com* domain within the *contoso.com* forest:

```
dcpromo /unattend /installDNS:yes
    /replicaOrNewDomain:domain /newDomain:tree
    /newDomainDnsName:tailspintoys.com /DomainNetbiosName:tailspintoys
    /databasePath:"e:\ntds" /logPath:"f:\ntdslogs" /sysvolpath:"g:\sysvol"
    /safeModeAdminPassword:password /domainLevel:2
    /rebootOnCompletion:yes
```

The domain functional level is configured at 2—Windows Server 2003 Native—so the domain could include Windows Server 2003 domain controllers. An unattended installation answer file that creates the same new tree would look similar to the following:

```
[DCINSTALL]
ReplicaOrNewDomain=domain
NewDomain=tree
NewDomainDNSName=FQDN of new domain
DomainNetBiosName=NetBIOS name of new domain
UserDomain=FQDN of user specified by UserName
UserName= DOMAIN\username (in Administrators group of ParentDomainDNSName)
Password=password for user specified by UserName or * for prompt
DomainLevel=domain functional level (not lower than current forest level)
InstallDNS=yes
ConfirmGC=yes
CreateDNSDNSDelegation=yes
DNSDelegationUserName=account with permissions to create DNS delegation
                        required only if different than UserName, above
DNSDelegationPassword=password for DNSDelegationUserName or * for prompt
DatabasePath="path to folder on a local volume"
LogPath="path to folder on a local volume"
SYSVOLPath="path to folder on a local volume"
SafeModeAdminPassword=password
RebootOnCompletion=yes
```

Staging the Installation of an RODC

As you remember from Chapter 8, "Authentication," RODCs are designed to support branch office scenarios by providing authentication local to the site while mitigating the security and data integrity risks associated with placing a DC in a less well-controlled environment. Many times, there are few or no IT support personnel in a branch office. How, then, should a domain controller be created in a branch office?

To answer this question, Windows Server 2008 enables you to create a staged, or delegated, installation of an RODC. The process includes two stages:

- **Create the account for the RODC**   A member of Domain Admins creates an account for the RODC in Active Directory. The parameters related to the RODC are specified at this time: the name, the Active Directory site in which the RODC will be created, and, optionally, the user or group that can complete the next stage of the installation.

- **Attach the server to the RODC account**   After the account has been created, AD DS is installed, and the RODC is attached to the domain. These steps can be the users or groups specified when the RODC account was prestaged; these users do not require any privileged group membership. A server can also be attached by a member of Domain Admins or Enterprise Admins, but the ability to delegate this stage to a nonprivileged user makes it much easier to deploy RODCs in branches without IT support. The domain controller will replicate its data from another writable DC in the domain, or you can use the IFM method discussed in the "Installing AD DS from Media" section.

NOTE   **Promote from a workgroup**

When you create an RODC by using the staged approach—when you attach an RODC to a pre-staged account—the server must be a member of a workgroup, not of the domain, when you launch *Dcpromo.exe* or the Active Directory Domain Services Installation Wizard. The wizard will look in the domain for the existing account with its name and will attach to that account.

Creating the Prestaged Account for the RODC

To create the account for the RODC, using the Active Directory Users and Computers snap-in, right-click the Domain Controllers OU and choose Pre-Create Read-Only Domain Controller Account. A wizard appears that is very similar to the Active Directory Domain Services Installation Wizard. You are asked to specify the RODC name and site. You are also able to configure the password replication policy, as detailed in Chapter 8.

On the Delegation Of RODC Installation And Administration page, you can specify one security principal—user or group—that can attach the server to the RODC account you create. The user or group will also have local administrative rights on the RODC after the installation. It is recommended that you delegate to a group rather than to a user. If you do not specify a user or group, only members of the Domain Admins or Enterprise Admins groups can attach the server to the account.

MORE INFO   Creating prestaged RODC accounts

You can create prestaged RODC accounts by using *Dcpromo.exe* with numerous parameters or by creating an answer file for *Dcpromo.exe*. The steps for doing so are detailed at *http://technet2.microsoft.com/windowsserver2008/en/library/f349e1e7-c3ce-4850-9e50-d8886c866b521033.mspx?mfr=true*.

Attaching a Server to the RODC Account

After you have prestaged the account, the server can be attached to it. You cannot simply launch the Active Directory Domain Services Installation Wizard. You must do so by typing **dcpromo /useexistingaccount:attach**. The wizard prompts for network credentials and then finds the RODC account in the domain indicated by the credentials. Remaining steps are similar to other domain controller promotion operations.

To use an answer file, provide the following options and values:

```
[DCINSTALL]
ReplicaDomainDNSName=FQDN of domain to join
UserDomain=FQDN of user specified by UserName
UserName=DOMAIN\username (in Administrators group of the domain)
Password=password for user specified by UserName
InstallDNS=yes
ConfirmGC=yes
DatabasePath="path to folder on a local volume"
LogPath="path to folder on a local volume"
SYSVOLPath="path to folder on a local volume"
SafeModeAdminPassword=password
RebootOnCompletion=yes
```

Run *Dcpromo* with the unattend:"answer file path" and the UseExistingAccount:Attach options, as in the following example:

```
dcpromo /useexistingaccount:attache /unattend:"c:\rodcanswer.txt"
```

All the options just shown in the answer file can also be specified or overridden directly on the command line. Just type a command similar to the following:

```
dcpromo /unattend /UseExistingAccount:Attach /ReplicaDomainDNSName:contoso.com
    /UserDomain:contoso.com /UserName:contoso\dan /password:*
    /databasePath:"e:\ntds" /logPath:"f:\ntdslogs" /sysvolpath:"g:\sysvol"
    /safeModeAdminPassword:password /rebootOnCompletion:yes
```

> ## Quick Check
>
> - You administer a domain containing Windows Server 2003 domain controllers. You want to allow a manager at a remote site to promote a member server at a remote site to an RODC. You do not want to give the manager administrative credentials in the domain. What steps must you and the manager take?
>
> ## Quick Check Answer
>
> - You must run *Adprep /rodcprep* to prepare the domain for the RODC. You must then prestage the RODC account, delegating to the manager the ability to attach the domain controller to the account. The manager will run *Dcpromo.exe* with the UseExistingAccount option to attach the server, but first, the server must be removed from the domain and placed in a workgroup.

Installing AD DS from Media

When you add domain controllers to a forest, data from existing directory partitions are replicated to the new DC. In an environment with a large directory or where bandwidth is constrained between a new DC and a writable DC from which to replicate, you can install AD DS more efficiently by using the IFM option. Installing from media involves creating *installation media*—a specialized backup of Active Directory that can be used by the Active Directory Domain Services Installation Wizard as a data source for populating the directory on a new DC. Then the new DC will replicate only updates from another writable DC, so if the installation media is recent, you can minimize the impact of replication to a new DC.

Remember that it is not only the directory that must be replicated to a new DC but SYSVOL as well. When you create your installation media, you can specify whether to include SYSVOL on the installation media.

Using IFM also enables you to control the timing of impact to your network bandwidth. You can, for example, create installation media and transfer it to a remote site during off hours, then create the domain controller during normal business hours. Because the installation media is from the local site, impact to the network is reduced, and only updates will be replicated over the link to the remote site.

To create installation media, open a command prompt on a writable domain controller, running Windows Server 2008. The installation media is compatible across platforms. Run *Ntdsutil.exe* and then, at the ntdsutil prompt, type the **activate instance ntds** command and then the **ifm** command. At the *ifm:* prompt, type one of the following commands, based on the type of installation media you want to create:

- **create sysvol full** *path*   Creates installation media with SYSVOL for a writable domain controller in the folder specified by *Path*

- **create full** *path*   Creates installation media without SYSVOL for a writable domain controller or an Active Directory Lightweight Directory Services (AD LDS) instance in the folder specified by *Path*
- **create sysvol rodc** *path*   Creates installation media with SYSVOL for a read-only domain controller in the folder specified by *Path*
- **create rodc** *path*   Creates installation media without SYSVOL for a read-only domain controller in the folder specified by *Path*

When you run the Active Directory Domain Services Installation Wizard, select the Use Advanced Mode Installation check box, and you will be presented the Install From Media page later in the wizard. Choose Replicate Data From Media At The Following Location. You can use the ReplicationSourcePath installation option in an answer file or on the *Dcpromo.exe* command line.

Practice It   Exercise 3, "Create Installation Media," in the practice at the end of this lesson, steps you through the process of creating installation media with *Ntdsutil.exe*.

Removing a Domain Controller

You can remove a domain controller by using *Dcpromo.exe*, either to launch the Active Directory Domain Services Installation Wizard or from a command prompt, specifying options at the command line or in an answer file. When a domain controller is removed while it has connectivity to the domain, it updates the forest metadata about the domain controller so that the directory knows the DC has been removed.

MORE INFO   **Removing a domain controller**

For detailed steps for removing a domain controller, see *http://technet2.microsoft.com /windowsserver2008/en/library/9260bb40-a808-422f-b33b-c3d2330f5eb81033.mspx.*

If a domain controller must be demoted while it cannot contact the domain, you must use the forceremoval option of *Dcpromo.exe*. Type **dcpromo /forceremoval**, and the Active Directory Domain Services Installation Wizard steps you through the process. You are presented warnings related to any roles the domain controller hosts. Read each warning and, after you have mitigated or accepted the impact of the warning, click Yes. You can suppress warnings, using the demotefsmo:yes option of *Dcpromo.exe*. After the DC has been removed, you must manually clean up the forest metadata.

MORE INFO   **Performing metadata cleanup**

See article 216498 in the Microsoft Knowledge Base for information about performing metadata cleanup. The article is located at *http://go.microsoft.com/fwlink/?LinkId=80481.*

PRACTICE **Installing Domain Controllers**

In this practice, you will perform the steps required to install an additional domain controller in the *contoso.com* domain. You will install AD DS and configure an additional DC, using the Active Directory Domain Services Installation Wizard. *You will not complete the installation.* Instead, you will save the settings as an answer file. You will then use the settings to perform an unattended installation, using the *Dcpromo.exe* command with installation options.

To perform this exercise, you will need a second server running Windows Server 2008 full installation. The server must be named SERVER02, and it should be joined to the *contoso.com* domain. Its configuration should be as follows:

- Computer Name: SERVER02
- Domain Membership: *contoso.com*
- IPv4 address: 10.0.0.12
- Subnet Mask: 255.255.255.0
- Default Gateway: 10.0.0.1
- DNS Server: 10.0.0.11

▶ **Exercise 1   Create an Additional DC with the Active Directory Domain Services Installation Wizard**

In this exercise, you will use the Active Directory Domain Services Installation Wizard (*Dcpromo.exe*) to create an additional domain controller in the *contoso.com* domain. You will not complete the installation, however. Instead, you will save the settings as an answer file, which will be used in the next exercise.

1. Log on to SERVER02 as CONTOSO\Administrator.
2. Click Start, click Run, type **Dcpromo.exe**, and press Enter.
3. Click Next.
4. On the Operating System Compatibility page, review the warning about the default security settings for Windows Server 2008 domain controllers, and then click Next.
5. On the Choose A Deployment Configuration page, select Existing Forest, select Add A Domain Controller To An Existing Domain, and then click Next.
6. On the Network Credentials page, type **contoso.com** in the text box, select My Current Logged On Credentials, and then click Next.
7. On the Select A Domain page, select *contoso.com* and click Next.
8. On the Select A Site page, select Default-First-Site-Name and click Next.

    The Additional Domain Controller Options page appears. DNS Server and Global Catalog are selected by default.

9. Clear the Global Catalog and DNS Server check boxes, and then click Next.

    An Infrastructure Master Configuration Conflict warning appears. You will learn about the infrastructure master in Lesson 2, so you will ignore this error.

10. Click Do Not Transfer The Infrastructure Master Role To This Domain Controller. I Will Correct The Configuration Later.

11. On the Location For Database, Log Files, And SYSVOL page, accept the default locations for the database file, the directory service log files, and the SYSVOL files and click Next.

    The best practice in a production environment is to store these files on three separate volumes that do not contain applications or other files not related to AD DS. This best practices design improves performance and increases the efficiency of backup and restore.

12. On the Directory Services Restore Mode Administrator Password page, type a strong password in both the Password and Confirmed Password boxes. Click Next.

    Do not forget the password you assigned to the Directory Services Restore Mode Administrator.

13. On the Summary page, review your selections.

    If any settings are incorrect, click Back to make modifications.

14. Click Export Settings.

15. Click Browse Folders.

16. Select Desktop.

17. In the File Name box, type **AdditionalDC** and click Save.

    A message appears indicating that settings were saved successfully.

18. Click OK.

19. On the Active Directory Domain Services Installation Wizard Summary page, click Cancel.

20. Click Yes to confirm that you are cancelling the installation of the DC.

▶ **Exercise 2   Add a Domain Controller from the Command Line**

In this exercise, you will examine the answer file you created in Exercise 1, "Create an Additional DC with the Active Directory Domain Services Installation Wizard." You will use the installation options in the answer file to create a *Dcpromo.exe* command line to install the additional domain controller.

1. Open the AdditionalDC.txt file you created in Exercise 1.

2. Examine the answers in the file. Can you identify what some of the options mean?

   Tip: Lines beginning with a semicolon are comments or inactive lines that have been commented out.

3. Open a command prompt.

   You will be building a command line, using the options in the answer file. Position the windows so you can see both Notepad and the command prompt or print the answer file for reference.

4. Determine the command line to install the domain controller with the configuration contained in the answer file.

   Parameters on the command line take the form */option:value* whereas, in the answer file, they take the form *option=value*.

5. Type the following command and press Enter:

```
dcpromo /unattend /replicaornewdomain:replica
/replicadomaindnsname:contoso.com /sitename:Default-First-Site-Name
/installDNS:No /confirmGC:No /CreateDNSDelegation:No
/databasepath:"C:\Windows\NTDS" /logpath:"C:\Windows\NTDS"
/sysvolpath:"C:\Windows\SYSVOL" /safemodeadminpassword:password
/transferimroleifnecessary:no
```

where *password* is a complex password.

6. Installation will complete, and the server will reboot.

▶ **Exercise 3   Create Installation Media**

You can reduce the amount of replication required to create a domain controller by promoting the domain controller, using the IFM option. IFM requires that you provide installation media, which is, in effect, a backup of Active Directory. In this exercise, you will create the installation media.

1. Log on to SERVER01 as Administrator.
2. Open a command prompt.
3. Type **ntdsutil** and press Enter.
4. Type **activate instance ntds** and press Enter.
5. Type **ifm** and press Enter.
6. Type **?** and press Enter to list the commands available in IFM mode.
7. Type **create sysvol full c:\IFM** and press Enter.

    The installation media files are copied to C:\Ifm.

Lesson Summary

- AD DS can be installed by running *Dcpromo.exe*, which launches the Active Directory Domain Services Installation Wizard or, with the unattend option, can obtain installation options from the command line or an answer file.

- When you introduce the first Windows Server 2008 domain controller into an existing forest, you must run *Adprep /forestprep*. Before you introduce the first Windows Server 2008 DC into an existing domain, you must run *Adprep /domainprep /gpprep*.

- Before you install the first RODC in a domain containing Windows 2000 Server or Windows Server 2003 DCs, you must run *Adprep /rodcprep*.

- To perform a staged installation of an RODC, you create the account for the RODC and specify the user or group that will be able to attach the RODC to the account.

- To reduce replication requirements, you can create installation media and use the media as a source when performing a domain controller promotion.

Lesson Review

You can use the following questions to test your knowledge of the information in Lesson 1, "Installing Domain Controllers." The questions are also available on the companion CD if you prefer to review them in electronic form.

NOTE Answers

Answers to these questions and explanations of why each answer choice is right or wrong are located in the "Answers" section at the end of the book.

---

1. You are an administrator at Trey Research. The Trey Research forest consists of three domains, each of which includes two domain controllers running Windows Server 2003. You want to upgrade one of the domain controllers to Windows Server 2008. What must you do first?

   A. Upgrade the domain controller's operating system to Windows Server 2008.

   B. Run the *Adprep.exe /domainprep /gpprep* command.

   C. Run the Active Directory Domain Services Installation Wizard.

   D. Run the *Adprep.exe /forestprep* command.

   E. Run the *Adprep.exe /rodcprep* command.

2. You are an administrator at Contoso, Ltd. The domain was built using Windows Server 2008 domain controllers. You want to improve authentication at a remote site by promoting a member server at the site to a read-only domain controller. There is no IT support at the site, so you want the site's manager to perform the promotion. You do not want to give her administrative credentials in the domain. Which steps must you or the manager take? (Choose all that apply. Each correct answer is part of the solution.)

   A. Run *Adprep /rodcprep*.

   B. Create the RODC account in the Domain Controllers OU.

   C. Run *Dcpromo.exe* with the UseExistingAccount option.

   D. Remove the server from the domain.

3. You want to promote a server to act as a domain controller, but you are concerned about the replication traffic that will occur during the promotion and its impact on the slow link between the server's site and the data center where all other domain controllers are located, so you choose to promote the server, using a backup of the directory from another domain controller. What must you do to create the installation media?

   A. Run *Ntbackup.exe* and select System State.

   B. Install the Windows Server Backup Features.

   C. Run *Ntdsutil.exe* in the IFM mode and use the *Create Sysvol Full* command.

   D. Copy *ntds.dit* and SYSVOL from a domain controller to a location in the remote site.

Lesson 2: Configuring Operations Masters

In an Active Directory domain, all domain controllers are equivalent. They are all capable of writing to the database and replicating changes to other domain controllers. However, in any multimaster replication topology, certain operations must be performed by one and only one system. In an Active Directory domain, *operations masters* are domain controllers that play a specific role. Other domain controllers are capable of playing the role but do not. This lesson will introduce you to the five operations masters found in Active Directory forests and domains. You will learn their purposes, how to identify the operations masters in your enterprise, and the nuances of administering and transferring roles.

> **After this lesson, you will be able to:**
> - Define the purpose of the five single master operations in Active Directory forests.
> - Identify the domain controllers performing operations master roles.
> - Plan the placement of operations master roles.
> - Transfer and seize operations master roles.
>
> **Estimated lesson time: 45 minutes**

Understanding Single Master Operations

In any replicated database, some changes must be performed by one and only one replica because they are impractical to perform in a multimaster fashion. Active Directory is no exception. A limited number of operations are not permitted to occur at different places at the same time and must be the responsibility of only one domain controller in a domain or forest. These operations, and the domain controllers that perform them, are referred to by a variety of terms:

- *Operations masters*
- *Operations master roles*
- *Single master roles*
- *Operations tokens*
- *Flexible single master operations (FSMOs)*

Regardless of the term used, the idea is the same. One domain controller performs a function, and while it does, no other domain controller performs that function.

Not Déjà Vu

If you were an administrator in the days of Microsoft Windows NT 4.0, the concept of operations masters might sound similar to Windows NT primary domain controllers (PDCs). However, single master operations are characteristic of any replicated database, and Active Directory single master operations bear striking differences to Windows NT 4.0 PDCs:

- All Active Directory domain controllers are capable of performing single master operations. The domain controller that actually does perform an operation is the domain controller that currently holds the operation's token.

- An operation token, and thus the role, can be transferred easily to another domain controller without a reboot.

- To reduce the risk of single points of failure, the operations tokens can be distributed among multiple DCs.

AD DS contains five operations master roles. Two roles are performed for the entire forest:

- Domain naming
- Schema

Three roles are performed in each domain:

- Relative identifier (RID)
- Infrastructure
- PDC Emulator

Each of these roles is detailed in the following sections. In a forest with a single domain, there are, therefore, five operations masters. In a forest with two domains, there are eight operations masters because the three domain master roles are implemented separately in each of the two domains.

Exam Tip   Commit to memory the list of forest-wide and domain single master operations. You are likely to encounter questions that test your knowledge of which roles apply to the entire forest and which are domain specific. Exam questions are cast in scenarios and, often, the scenarios provide so much detail that you can lose sight of what is really being asked. When you read items on the certification exam, always ask yourself, "What is really being tested?" Sometimes what is being tested is different from, and simpler than, what the scenario in the question would lead you to believe.

Forest-Wide Operations Master Roles

The schema master and the domain naming master must be unique in the forest. Each role is performed by only one domain controller in the entire forest.

Domain Naming Master Role

The domain naming role is used when adding or removing domains in the forest. When you add or remove a domain, the domain naming master must be accessible, or the operation will fail.

Schema Master Role

The domain controller holding the schema master role is responsible for making any changes to the forest's schema. All other DCs hold read-only replicas of the schema. If you want to modify the schema or install an application that modifies the schema, it is recommended you do so on the domain controller holding the schema master role. Otherwise, changes you request must be sent to the schema master to be written into the schema.

Domain-Wide Operations Master Roles

Each domain maintains three single master operations: RID, Infrastructure, and PDC Emulator. Each role is performed by only one domain controller in the domain.

RID Master Role

The RID master plays an integral part in the generation of security identifiers (SIDs) for security principals such as users, groups, and computers. The SID of a security principal must be unique. Because any domain controller can create accounts and, therefore, SIDs, a mechanism is necessary to ensure that the SIDs generated by a DC are unique. Active Directory domain controllers generate SIDs by assigning a unique RID to the domain SID. The RID master for the domain allocates pools of unique RIDs to each domain controller in the domain. Thus, each domain controller can be confident that the SIDs it generates are unique.

NOTE The RID master role is like DHCP for SIDs

If you are familiar with the concept that you allocate a scope of IP addresses for the Dynamic Host Configuration Protocol (DHCP) server to assign to clients, you can draw a parallel to the RID master, which allocates pools of RIDs to domain controllers for the creation of SIDs.

Infrastructure Master Role

In a multidomain environment, it is common for an object to reference objects in other domains. For example, a group can include members from another domain. Its multivalued *member* attribute contains the distinguished names of each member. If the member in the other domain is moved or renamed, the infrastructure master of the group's domain updates the group's *member* attribute accordingly.

NOTE **The infrastructure master**

You can think of the infrastructure master as a tracking device for group members from other domains. When those members are renamed or moved in the other domain, the infrastructure master identifies the change and makes appropriate changes to group memberships so that the memberships are kept up to date.

Phantoms of the Directory

Although you are not expected to understand the internals of the infrastructure master role for the certification exam, such understanding can be helpful in the production environment. When you add a member from another domain into a group in your domain, the group's *member* attribute is appended with the distinguished name of the new member. However, your domain might not always have access to a domain controller from the member's domain, so Active Directory creates a phantom object to represent the member. The phantom object includes only the member's SID, distinguished name (DN), and globally unique identifier (GUID). If the member is moved or renamed in its domain, its GUID does not change, but its DN changes. If the object is moved between domains, its SID also changes. The infrastructure master periodically—every two days by default—contacts a GC or a DC in the member domain. At that time, the infrastructure master looks for each phantom object, using the GUID of the phantom object. It updates the DN of the phantom objects with the current DN of the object. Any change is then propagated to the *member* attribute of groups.

After a member is moved or renamed in another domain, and until the infrastructure master has updated DNs, you might look at the membership of a group using the Active Directory Users and Computers snap-in, for example, and the group might appear not to include that member. However, the member continues to belong to the group. The member's *memberOf* attribute still refers to the group, so the *memberOf* attribute and the *tokenGroups* constructed attribute are unchanged. There is no compromise to security; it is only an administrator looking at that particular group membership that would notice the temporary inconsistency.

PDC Emulator Role

The PDC Emulator role performs multiple, crucial functions for a domain:

■ **Emulates a Primary Domain Controller (PDC) for backward compatibility**   In the days of Windows NT 4.0 domains, only the PDC could make changes to the directory. Previous tools, utilities, and clients written to support Windows NT 4.0 are unaware that all Active Directory domain controllers can write to the directory, so such tools request a connection to the PDC. The domain controller with the PDC Emulator role registers itself as a PDC so that down-level applications can locate a writable domain controller. Such applications are less common now that Active Directory is nearly 10 years old, and if your enterprise includes such applications, work to upgrade them for full Active Directory compatibility.

■ **Participates in special password update handling for the domain**   When a user's password is reset or changed, the domain controller that makes the change replicates the change immediately to the PDC emulator. This special replication ensures that the domain controllers know about the new password as quickly as possible. If a user attempts to log on immediately after changing passwords, the domain controller responding to the user's logon request might not know about the new password. Before it rejects the logon attempt, that domain controller forwards the authentication request to a PDC emulator, which verifies that the new password is correct and instructs the domain controller to accept the logon request. This function means that any time a user enters an incorrect password, the authentication is forwarded to the PDC emulator for a second opinion. The PDC emulator, therefore, should be highly accessible to all clients in the domain. It should be a well-connected, high-performance DC.

■ **Manages Group Policy updates within a domain**   If a Group Policy object (GPO) is modified on two DCs at approximately the same time, there could be conflicts between the two versions that could not be reconciled as the GPO replicates. To avoid this situation, the PDC emulator acts as the focal point for all Group Policy changes. When you open a GPO in Group Policy Management Editor (GPME), the GPME binds to the domain controller performing the PDC emulator role. Therefore, all changes to GPOs are made on the PDC emulator by default.

■ **Provides a master time source for the domain**   Active Directory, Kerberos, File Replication Service (FRS), and DFS-R each rely on timestamps, so synchronizing the time across all systems in a domain is crucial. The PDC emulator in the forest root domain is the time master for the entire forest, by default. The PDC emulator in each domain synchronizes its time with the forest root PDC emulator. Other domain controllers in the domain synchronize their clocks against that domain's PDC emulator. All other domain members synchronize their time with their preferred domain controller. This hierarchical structure of time synchronization, all implemented through the Win32Time service, ensures consistency of time. Universal Time Coordinate (UTC) is synchronized, and the time displayed to users is adjusted based on the time zone setting of the computer.

MORE INFO Change the time service only one way

It is highly recommended to allow Windows to maintain its native, default time synchronization mechanisms. The only change you should make is to configure the PDC emulator of the forest root domain to synchronize with an extra time source. If you do not specify a time source for the PDC emulator, the System event log will contain errors reminding you to do so. See *http://go.microsoft.com/fwlink/?LinkId=91969*, and the articles it refers to, for more information.

■ **Acts as the domain master browser** When you open Network in Windows, you see a list of workgroups and domains, and when you open a workgroup or domain, you see a list of computers. These two lists, called *browse lists*, are created by the Browser service. In each network segment, a master browser creates the browse list: the lists of workgroups, domains, and servers in that segment. The domain master browser serves to merge the lists of each master browser so that browse clients can retrieve a comprehensive browse list.

Placing Operations Masters

When you create the forest root domain with its first domain controller, all five operations master roles are performed by the domain controller. As you add domain controllers to the domain, you can transfer the operations master role assignments to other domain controllers to balance the load among domain controllers or to optimize placement of a single master operation. The best practices for the placement of operations master roles are as follows:

■ **Co-locate the schema master and domain naming master** The schema master and domain naming master roles should be placed on a single domain controller that is a GC server. These roles are rarely used, and the domain controller hosting them should be tightly secured. The domain naming master must be hosted on a GC server because when a new domain is added, the master must ensure that there is no object of any type with the same name as the new domain. The GC's partial replica contains the name of every object in the forest. The load of these operations master roles is very light unless schema modifications are being made.

■ **Co-locate the RID master and PDC Emulator roles** Place the RID and PDC Emulator roles on a single domain controller. If the load mandates that the roles be placed on two separate domain controllers, those two systems should be physically well connected and have explicit connection objects created in Active Directory so that they are direct replication partners. They should also be direct replication partners with domain controllers that you have selected as standby operations masters.

■ **Place the infrastructure master on a DC that is not a GC** The infrastructure master should be placed on a domain controller that is not a GC server but is physically well connected to a GC server. The infrastructure master should have explicit connection objects in Active Directory to that GC server so that they are direct replication partners.

The infrastructure master can be placed on the same domain controller that acts as the RID master and PDC emulator.

NOTE **It doesn't matter if they're all GCs**

If all DCs in a domain are GC servers—which indeed is a best practices recommendation that will be discussed in Chapter 11, "Sites and Replication"—you do not need to worry about which DC is the infrastructure master. When all DCs are GCs, all DCs have up-to-date information about every object in the forest, which eliminates the need for the infrastructure master role.

- **Have a failover plan**   In following sections, you will learn to transfer single operations master roles between domain controllers, which is necessary if there is lengthy planned or unplanned downtime of an operations master. Determine, in advance, a plan for transferring operations roles to other DCs in the event that one operations master is offline.

Identifying Operations Masters

To implement your role placement plan, you must know which DCs are currently performing single master operations roles. Each role is exposed in an Active Directory administrative tool as well as in other user interface and command-line tools. To identify the current master for each role, use the following tools:

- **PDC Emulator: The Active Directory Users And Computers snap-in**   Right-click the domain and choose Operations Masters. Click the PDC tab. An example is shown in Figure 10-2, which indicates that SERVER01.contoso.com is currently the PDC operations master.

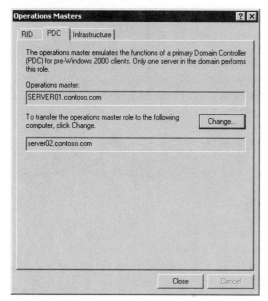

Figure 10-2 PDC Operations Master

- **RID Master: The Active Directory Users And Computers snap-in**   Right-click the domain and choose Operations Masters. Click the RID tab.
- **Infrastructure Master: The Active Directory Users And Computers snap-in**   Right-click the domain and choose Operations Masters. Click the Infrastructure tab.
- **Domain Naming: The Active Directory Domains And Trusts snap-in**   Right-click the root node of the snap-in (Active Directory Domains And Trusts) and choose Operations Master.
- **Schema Master: The Active Directory Schema snap-in**   Right-click the root node of the snap-in (Active Directory Schema) and choose Operations Master.

NOTE   **Registering the Active Directory Schema snap-in**

You must register the Active Directory Schema snap-in before you can create a custom Microsoft Management Console (MMC) with the snap-in. At a command prompt, type **regsvr32 schmmgmt.dll**.

You can also use several other tools to identify operations masters, including the following commands:

```
ntdsutil
roles
connections
connect to server DomainControllerFQDN:portnumber
quit
select operation target
list roles for connected server"
quit
quit
quit

dcdiag /test:knowsofroleholders /v

netdom query fsmo
```

Practice It   Exercise 1, "Identify Operations Masters," in the practice at the end of this lesson, steps you through the identification of operations masters.

Transferring Operations Master Roles

You can transfer a single operations master role easily. You will transfer roles in the following scenarios:

- When you establish your forest, all five roles are performed by the first domain controller you install. When you add a domain to the forest, all three domain roles are performed by the first domain controller in that domain. As you add domain controllers, you can distribute the roles to reduce single-point-of-failure instances and improve performance.

- If you plan to take a domain controller offline that is currently holding an operations master role, transfer that role to another domain controller prior to taking it offline.

- If you are decommissioning a domain controller that currently holds an operations master role, transfer that role to another domain controller prior to decommissioning. The Active Directory Domain Services Installation Wizard will attempt to do so automatically, but you should prepare for demoting a domain controller by transferring its roles.

To transfer an operations master role, follow these steps:

1. Open the administrative tool that exposes the current master.

   For example, open the Active Directory Users And Computers snap-in to transfer any of the three domain master roles.

2. Connect to the domain controller to which you are transferring the role.

   This is accomplished by right-clicking the root node of the snap-in and choosing Change Domain Controller or Change Active Directory Domain Controller. (The command differs between snap-ins.)

3. Open the Operations Master dialog box, which will show you the domain controller currently holding the role token for the operation. Click the Change button to transfer the role to the domain controller to which you are connected.

Practice It   Exercise 2, "Transfer an Operations Master Role," in the practice at the end of this lesson, steps you through the transfer of an operations master role.

When you transfer an operations master role, both the current master and the new master are online. The token is transferred, the new master immediately begins to perform the role, and the former master immediately ceases to perform the role. This is the preferred method of moving operations master roles.

It is recommended to make sure that the new role holder is up to date with replication from the former role holder before transferring the role. You can use skills introduced in Chapter 11 to force replication between the two systems.

Recognizing Operations Master Failures

Several operations master roles can be unavailable for quite some time before their absence becomes a problem. Other master roles play a crucial role in the day-to-day operation of your enterprise. You can identify problems with operations masters by examining the Directory Service event log.

However, you will often discover that an operations master has failed when you attempt to perform a function managed by the master, and the function fails. For example, if the RID master fails, eventually you will be prevented from creating new security principals.

Seizing Operations Master Roles

If a domain controller performing a single master operation fails, and you cannot bring the system back to service, you have the option of seizing the operations token. When you seize a role, you designate a new master without gracefully removing the role from the failed master.

Seizing a role is a drastic action, so before seizing a role, think carefully about whether it is necessary. Determine the cause and expected duration of the offline operations master. If the operations master can be brought online in sufficient time, wait. What is sufficient time? It depends on the impact of the role that has failed:

- **PDC emulator failure** The PDC emulator is the operations master that will have the most immediate impact on normal operations and on users if it becomes unavailable. Fortunately, the PDC Emulator role can be seized to another domain controller and then transferred back to the original role holder when the system comes back online.

- **Infrastructure master failure** A failure of the infrastructure master will be noticeable to administrators but not to users. Because the master is responsible for updating the names of group members from other domains, it can appear as if group membership is incorrect although, as mentioned earlier in this lesson, membership is not actually affected. You can seize the infrastructure master role to another domain controller and then transfer it back to the previous role holder when that system comes online.

- **RID master failure** A failed RID master will eventually prevent domain controllers from creating new SIDs and, therefore, will prevent you from creating new accounts for users, groups, or computers. However, domain controllers receive a sizable pool of RIDs from the RID master, so unless you are generating numerous new accounts, you can often go for some time without the RID master online while it is being repaired. Seizing this role to another domain controller is a significant action. After the RID master role has been seized, the domain controller that had been performing the role cannot be brought back online.

- **Schema master failure** The schema master role is necessary only when schema modifications are being made, either directly by an administrator or by installing an Active Directory integrated application that changes the schema. At other times, the role is not necessary. It can remain offline indefinitely until schema changes are necessary. Seizing this role to another domain controller is a significant action. After the schema master role has been seized, the domain controller that had been performing the role cannot be brought back online.

- **Domain naming master failure** The domain naming master role is necessary only when you add a domain to the forest or remove a domain from a forest. Until such changes are required to your domain infrastructure, the domain naming master role can remain offline for an indefinite period of time. Seizing this role to another domain controller is a significant action. After the domain naming master role has been seized, the domain controller that had been performing the role cannot be brought back online.

Although you can transfer roles by using the administrative tools, you must use *Ntdsutil.exe* to seize a role. To seize an operations master role, perform the following steps:

1. From the command prompt, type **ntdsutil** and press Enter.
2. At the ntdsutil prompt, type **roles** and press Enter.

    The next steps establish a connection to the domain controller you want to perform the single master operation role.

3. At the fsmo maintenance prompt, type **connections** and press Enter.
4. At the server connections prompt, type **connect to server** *DomainControllerFQDN* and press Enter.

    DomainControllerFQDN is the FQDN of the domain controller you want to perform the role.

    Ntdsutil responds that it has connected to the server.

5. At the server connections prompt, type **quit** and press Enter.
6. At the fsmo maintenance prompt, type **seize** *role* and press Enter.

    Role is one of the following:

    a. schema master
    b. domain naming master
    c. RID master
    d. PDC
    e. infrastructure master

7. At the fsmo maintenance prompt, type **quit** and press Enter.
8. At the ntdsutil prompt, type **quit** and press Enter.

Returning a Role to Its Original Holder

To provide for planned downtime of a domain controller if a role has been transferred, not seized, the role can be transferred back to the original domain controller.

If, however, a role has been seized and the former master is able to be brought back online, you must be very careful. The PDC emulator and infrastructure master are the only operations master roles that can be transferred back to the original master after having been seized.

NOTE   Do not return a seized schema, domain naming, or RID master to service

After seizing the schema, domain naming, or RID roles, you must completely decommission the original domain controller.

If you have seized the schema, domain naming, or RID roles to another domain controller, you must not bring the original domain controller back online without first completely decommissioning it. That means you must keep the original role holder physically discon-nected from the network, and you must remove AD DS by using the *Dcpromo /forceremoval* command. You must also clean the metadata for that domain controller as described in *http://go.microsoft.com/fwlink/?LinkId=80481*.

After the domain controller has been completely removed from Active Directory, if you want the server to rejoin the domain, you can connect it to the network and join the domain. If you want it to be a domain controller, you can promote it. If you want it to resume performing the operations master role, you can transfer the role back to the DC.

NOTE   Better to rebuild

Because of the critical nature of domain controllers, it is recommended that you completely reinstall the former domain controller in this scenario.

> ## Quick Check
> - You need to upgrade the power supply and motherboard of SERVER01, the domain controller performing the PDC Emulator operations master role. You want to ensure continuity of services provided by the PDC emulator. Describe the pro-cess of transferring the role to SERVER02, another domain controller, and trans-ferring it back after SERVER01 has been upgraded. Which tools will you use, and which steps will you perform?
>
> ## Quick Check Answer
> - Prior to performing the upgrade, make sure the standby operations master is up to date with replication from the PDC emulator. Then open the Active Directory Users And Computers snap-in, right-click the domain, and choose Change Domain Controller. Select SERVER02. Right-click the domain and choose Opera-tions Masters. Click the PDC tab and click Change. The role is transferred. When SERVER01 comes back online, right-click the domain, choose Change Domain Controller, and select SERVER01. Right-click the domain, choose Operations Mas-ters, click the PDC tab, and click Change.

PRACTICE   Transferring Operations Master Roles

In this practice, you will identify the operations masters in the *contoso.com* domain, and you will transfer an operations master to another domain controller to take the current master offline for maintenance. To perform Exercise 2 in this practice, you must have completed "Practice: Installing Domain Controllers" in Lesson 1 so that you have a second domain con-troller, SERVER02, in the domain.

▶ **Exercise 1   Identify Operations Masters**

In this exercise, you will use both user interface and command-line tools to identify operations masters in the *contoso.com* domain.

1. Log on to SERVER01 as Administrator.
2. Open the Active Directory Users And Computers snap-in.
3. Right-click the *contoso.com* domain and choose Operations Masters.
4. Click the tab for each operations master.

    The tabs identify the domain controllers currently performing the single master operations roles for the domain: PDC emulator, RID master, and Infrastructure master.

5. Click Close.
6. Open the Active Directory Domains And Trusts snap-in.
7. Right-click the root node of the snap-in, Active Directory Domains And Trusts, and choose Operations Master.

    The dialog box identifies the domain controller performing the domain naming master role.

8. Click Close.

    The Active Directory Schema snap-in does not have a console of its own and cannot be added to a custom console until you have registered the snap-in.

9. Open a command prompt, type **regsvr32 schmmgmt.dll**, and press Enter.
10. Click OK to close the message box that appears.
11. Click Start and, in the Start Search box, type **mmc.exe**, and press Enter.
12. Choose Add/Remove Snap-In from the File menu.
13. From the Available snap-ins list, choose Active Directory Schema, click Add, and then click OK.
14. Right-click the root node of the snap-in, Active Directory Schema, and choose Operations Master.

    The dialog box that appears identifies the domain controller currently performing the schema master role.

15. Click Close.
16. Open a command prompt, type the command **netdom query fsmo**, and press Enter.

    All operations masters are listed.

▶ **Exercise 2   Transfer an Operations Master Role**

In this exercise, you will prepare to take the operations master offline by transferring its role to another domain controller. You will then simulate taking it offline, bringing it back online, and returning the operations master role.

1. Open the Active Directory Users And Computers snap-in.

2. Right-click the *contoso.com* domain and choose Change Domain Controller.

3. In the list of directory servers, select server02.contoso.com and click OK.

    Before transferring an operations master, you must connect to the domain controller to which the role will be transferred.

    The root node of the snap-in indicates the domain controller to which you are connected: Active Directory Users And Computers [server02.contoso.com].

4. Right-click the *contoso.com* domain and choose Operations Masters.

5. Click the PDC tab.

    The tab indicates that SERVER01.contoso.com currently holds the role token. SERVER02.contoso.com is listed in the second dialog box. It should appear similar to Figure 10-2.

6. Click the Change button.

    An Active Directory Domain Services dialog box prompts you to confirm the transfer of the operations master role.

7. Click Yes.

    An Active Directory Domain Services dialog box confirms the role was successfully transferred.

8. Click OK, and then click Close.

9. Simulate taking SERVER01 offline for maintenance by shutting down the server.

10. Simulate bringing the server back online by starting the server.

    Remember you cannot bring a domain controller back online if the RID, schema, or domain naming roles have been seized. But you can bring it back online if a role was transferred.

11. Repeat steps 1–8, this time connecting to SERVER01 and transferring the operations master role back to SERVER01.

Lesson Summary

- Operations master roles are assigned to domain controllers to perform single master operations.

- There are five operations master roles. Two are unique to the entire forest: schema and domain naming. Three are unique to each domain: PDC Emulator, RID, and infrastructure.

- The infrastructure master must be placed on a domain controller that is not a GC unless all DCs in the domain are GC servers.

- You can transfer a role by using Windows tools or *Ntdsutil.exe*. Transferring a role is the preferred method for managing operations masters.

- You can seize a role, using *Ntdsutil.exe*. This should be done only when the former role holder cannot be brought back online in sufficient time. Only the PDC Emulator and infrastructure roles can be transferred back to the original holder when it comes back online. DCs that held schema, RID, or domain naming roles must be completely decommissioned if those roles are seized.

Lesson Review

You can use the following questions to test your knowledge of the information in Lesson 2, "Configuring Operations Masters." The questions are also available on the companion CD if you prefer to review them in electronic form.

NOTE   Answers

Answers to these questions and explanations of why each answer choice is right or wrong are located in the "Answers" section at the end of the book.

---

1. You are an administrator at Contoso, Ltd. The *contoso.com* domain consists of two sites. At the headquarters, one domain controller, named SERVER01, is a GC server and performs all five operations master roles. The second domain controller at the headquarters is named SERVER02. SERVER02 is not a GC and performs no operations master roles. At the branch office, the domain controller is named SERVER03, and it is a GC server. Which change to the operations master role placement must you make?

    A. Transfer the infrastructure master to SERVER03.

    B. Transfer the RID master to SERVER02.

    C. Transfer the schema master to SERVER02.

    D. Transfer the domain naming master to SERVER03.

    E. Transfer the infrastructure master to SERVER02.

2. You are an administrator at Contoso, Ltd. The forest consists of two domains, *contoso.com* and *windows.contoso.com*. Currently, SERVER02.windows.contoso.com performs all five operations master roles. You are going to decommission the *windows.contoso.com* domain and move all accounts into *contoso.com*. You want to transfer all operations masters to SERVER01.contoso.com. Which operations masters do you transfer? (Choose all that apply.)

    A. Infrastructure master

    B. PDC emulator

    C. RID master

    D. Schema master

    E. Domain naming master

3. You are an administrator at Contoso, Ltd. The *contoso.com* domain has five domain controllers. You want to move all domain operations masters to SERVER02.contoso.com. Which masters do you move? (Choose all that apply.)

   A. Infrastructure master

   B. PDC emulator

   C. RID master

   D. Schema master

   E. Domain naming master

Lesson 3: Configuring DFS Replication of SYSVOL

SYSVOL, a folder located at %SystemRoot%\SYSVOL by default, contains logon scripts, group policy templates (GPTs), and other resources critical to the health and management of an Active Directory domain. Ideally, SYSVOL should be consistent on each domain controller. However, changes to Group Policy objects and to logon scripts are made from time to time, so you must ensure that those changes are replicated effectively and efficiently to all domain controllers. In previous versions of Windows, the FRS was used to replicate the contents of SYSVOL between domain controllers. FRS has limitations in both capacity and performance that cause it to break occasionally. Unfortunately, troubleshooting and configuring FRS is quite difficult. In Windows Server 2008 domains, you have the option to use DFS-R to replicate the contents of SYSVOL. In this lesson, you will learn how to migrate SYSVOL from FRS to DFS-R.

> **After this lesson, you will be able to:**
> - Raise the domain functional level.
> - Migrate SYSVOL replication from FRS to DFS-R.
>
> **Estimated lesson time: 60 minutes**

Raising the Domain Functional Level

In Chapter 12, "Domains and Forests," you will learn about forest and domain functional levels. A domain's functional level is a setting that both restricts the operating systems that are supported as domain controllers in a domain and enables additional functionality in Active Directory. A domain with a Windows Server 2008 domain controller can be at one of three functional levels: Windows 2000 Native, Windows Server 2003 Native, and Windows Server 2008. At Windows 2000 Native domain functional level, domain controllers can be running Windows 2000 Server or Windows Server 2003. At Windows Server 2003 Native domain functional level, domain controllers can be running Windows Server 2003. At Windows Server 2008 domain functional level, all domain controllers must be running Windows Server 2008.

As you raise functional levels, new capabilities of Active Directory are enabled. At Windows Server 2008 domain functional level, for example, you can use DFS-R to replicate SYSVOL. Simply upgrading all domain controllers to Windows Server 2008 is not enough: You must specifically raise the domain functional level. You do this by using Active Directory Domains and Trusts. Right-click the domain and choose Raise Domain Functional Level. Then select Windows Server 2008 as the desired functional level and click Raise. After you've set the domain functional level to Windows Server 2008, you cannot add domain controllers running Windows Server 2003 or Windows 2000 Server. The functional level is associated only with domain controller operating systems; member servers and workstations can be running Windows Server 2003, Windows 2000 Server, Windows Vista, Windows XP, or Windows 2000 Workstation.

Quick Check

■ You are the administrator of Northwind Traders. The domain consists of three domain controllers. You have upgraded two of them to Windows Server 2008. The third is still running Windows Server 2003. You want to establish DFS-R as the replication mechanism for SYSVOL. What must you do?

Quick Check Answer

■ You must upgrade the third domain controller to Windows Server 2008 and then raise the domain functional level to Windows Server 2008.

Understanding Migration Stages

Because SYSVOL is critical to the health and functionality of your domain, Windows does not provide a mechanism with which to convert replication of SYSVOL from FRS to DFS-R instantly. In fact, migration to DFS-R involves creating a parallel SYSVOL structure. When the parallel structure is successfully in place, clients are redirected to the new structure as the domain's system volume. When the operation has proven successful, you can eliminate FRS.

Migration to DFS-R thus consists of four stages or *states*:

■ **0 (start)**   The default state of a domain controller. Only FRS is used to replicate SYSVOL.

■ **1 (prepared)**   A copy of SYSVOL is created in a folder called SYSVOL_DFSR and is added to a replication set. DFS-R begins to replicate the contents of the SYSVOL_DFSR folders on all domain controllers. However, FRS continues to replicate the original SYSVOL folders and clients continue to use SYSVOL.

■ **2 (redirected)**   The SYSVOL share, which originally refers to SYSVOL\sysvol, is changed to refer to SYSVOL_DFSR\sysvol. Clients now use the SYSVOL_DFSR folder to obtain logon scripts and Group Policy templates.

■ **3 (eliminated)**   Replication of the old SYSVOL folder by FRS is stopped. The original SYSVOL folder is not deleted, however, so if you want to remove it entirely, you must do so manually.

You move your domain controllers through these stages, using the *Dfsrmig.exe* command. You will use three options with *Dfsrmig.exe*:

■ **setglobalstate *state***   The setglobalstate option configures the current global DFSR migration state, which applies to all domain controllers. The state is specified by the *state* parameter, which is 0–3. Each domain controller will be notified of the new DFSR migration state and will migrate to that state automatically.

- **getglobalstate**   The getglobalstate option reports the current global DFSR migration state.

- **getmigrationstate**   The getmigrationstate option reports the current migration state of each domain controller. Because it might take time for domain controllers to be notified of the new global DFSR migration state, and because it might take even more time for a DC to make the changes required by that state, DCs will not be synchronized with the global state instantly. The getmigrationstate option enables you to monitor the progress of DCs toward the current global DFSR migration state.

If there is a problem moving from one state to the next higher state, you can revert to previous states by using the setglobalstate option. However, after you have used the setglobalstate option to specify state 3 (eliminated), you cannot revert to earlier states.

Migrating SYSVOL Replication to DFS-R

To migrate SYSVOL replication from FRS to DFS-R, perform the following steps:

1. Open the Active Directory Domains And Trusts snap-in.
2. Right-click the domain and choose Raise Domain Functional Level.
3. If the Current Domain Functional Level box does not indicate Windows Server 2008, choose Windows Server 2008 from the Select An Available Domain Functional Level list.
4. Click Raise. Click OK twice in response to the dialog boxes that appear.
5. Log on to a domain controller and open a command prompt.
6. Type **dfsrmig /setglobalstate 1**.
7. Type **dfsrmig /getmigrationstate** to query the progress of DCs toward the Prepared global state. Repeat this step until the state has been attained by all DCs.

    This can take 15 minutes to an hour or longer.

8. Type **dfsrmig /setglobalstate 2**.
9. Type **dfsrmig /getmigrationstate** to query the progress of DCs toward the Redirected global state. Repeat this step until the state has been attained by all DCs.

    This can take 15 minutes to an hour or longer.

10. Type **dfsrmig /setglobalstate 3**.

    After you begin migration from state 2 (prepared) to state 3 (replicated), any changes made to the SYSVOL folder will have to be replicated manually to the SYSVOL_DFSR folder.

11. Type **dfsrmig /getmigrationstate** to query the progress of DCs toward the Eliminated global state. Repeat this step until the state has been attained by all DCs. This can take 15 minutes to an hour or longer.

    For more information about the *Dfsrmig.exe* command, type **dfsrmig.exe /?**.

PRACTICE Configuring DFS Replication of SYSVOL

In this practice, you will experience SYSVOL replication and migrate the replication mechanism from FRS to DFS-R. You will then verify that SYSVOL is being replicated by DFS-R.

Other practices in the training kit have required Windows Server 2008 forest functional level. To perform the exercises in this practice, you will need a domain running at Windows Server 2003 domain functional level, so you must create a new forest running at Windows Server 2003 forest functional level consisting of one domain at Windows Server 2003 domain functional level and two domain controllers. To prepare for this practice, perform the following tasks:

- Install a server running Windows Server 2008 full installation. The server must be named SERVER01. Its configuration should be as follows:
    - ❑ Computer Name: SERVER01
    - ❑ Workgroup membership: WORKGROUP
    - ❑ IPv4 address: 10.0.0.11
    - ❑ Subnet Mask: 255.255.255.0
    - ❑ Default Gateway: 10.0.0.1
    - ❑ DNS Server: 10.0.0.11

    Use the procedures described in Lesson 1, "Installing Active Directory Domain Services," of Chapter 1 if you need assistance installing Windows Server 2008.

- Promote SERVER01 as a domain controller in a new forest named *contoso.com*. Select Windows Server 2003 forest and domain functional levels. Allow the Active Directory Domain Services Installation Wizard to install DNS on the domain controller.

    Use the steps in Exercise 1, "Install Windows Server 2008," of Lesson 1 of Chapter 1 if you need assistance promoting the domain controller. Be certain, however, to select Windows Server 2003 forest and domain functional levels.

- Install a second server running Windows Server 2008 full installation. The server must be named SERVER02. Its configuration should be as follows:
    - ❑ Computer Name: SERVER02
    - ❑ Workgroup membership: WORKGROUP
    - ❑ IPv4 address: 10.0.0.12
    - ❑ Subnet Mask: 255.255.255.0
    - ❑ Default Gateway: 10.0.0.1
    - ❑ DNS Server: 10.0.0.11

    Use the procedures described in Lesson 1 of Chapter 1 if you need assistance installing Windows Server 2008.

■ Promote SERVER02 as an additional domain controller in the *contoso.com* domain. Do not make it a GC or DNS server.

Use the steps in Exercise 1 of Lesson 1 of this chapter if you need assistance promoting SERVER02.

▶ **Exercise 1   Experience SYSVOL Replication**

In this exercise, you will experience SYSVOL replication by adding a logon script to the NETLOGON share and observing its replication to another domain controller.

1. Log on to SERVER01 as Administrator.
2. Open %SystemRoot%\Sysvol\Domain\Scripts.
3. Create a new text file called **Sample Logon Script**.
4. Log on to SERVER02 as Administrator.
5. Open %SystemRoot%\Sysvol\Domain\Scripts.
6. Confirm that the text file has replicated to the SERVER02 Scripts folder.

▶ **Exercise 2   Prepare to Migrate to DFS-R**

Before you can migrate replication of SYSVOL to DFS-R, the domain must contain only Windows Server 2008 domain controllers, and the domain functional level must be raised to Windows Server 2008. In this exercise, you will confirm the fact that DFS-R migration is not supported in other domain functional levels. You will also install the DFS administrative tools.

1. On SERVER01, open the Active Directory Domains And Trusts snap-in.
2. Right-click the *contoso.com* domain and choose Raise Domain Functional Level.
3. Confirm that the Current Domain Functional Level is Windows Server 2003.
4. Cancel out of the dialog box without raising the functional level.
5. Open a command prompt.
6. Type **dfsrmig /getglobalstate** and press Enter.

    A message appears informing you that *Dfsrmig* is supported only on domains at the Windows Server 2008 functional level.
7. Open the Active Directory Domains And Trusts snap-in.
8. Right-click the *contoso.com* domain and choose Raise Domain Functional Level.
9. Confirm that the Select An Available Domain Functional Level list indicates Windows Server 2008.
10. Click Raise. Click OK to confirm your change.

    A message appears informing you that the functional level was raised successfully.
11. Click OK.
12. At the command prompt, type **dfsrmig /getglobalstate** and press Enter.

    A message appears informing you that DFSR migration has not yet initialized.

▶ **Exercise 3   Migrate Replication of SYSVOL to DFS-R**

In this exercise, you will migrate SYSVOL replication from FRS to DFS-R.

1. On SERVER01, open a command prompt.

2. Type **dfsrmig /setglobalstate 0** and press Enter.

   The following message appears:

   ```
   Current DFSR global state: 'Start'
   New DFSR global state: 'Start'
   Invalid state change requested.
   ```

   The default global state is already 0, 'Start,' so your command is not valid. However, this does serve to initialize DFSR migration.

3. Type **dfsrmig /getglobalstate** and press Enter.

   The following message appears:

   ```
   Current DFSR global state: 'Start'
   Succeeded.
   ```

4. Type **dfsrmig /getmigrationstate** and press Enter.

   The following message appears:

   ```
   All Domain Controllers have migrated successfully to Global state
   ('Start').
   Migration has reached a consistent state on all Domain Controllers.
   Succeeded.
   ```

5. Type **dfsrmig /setglobalstate 1** and press Enter.

   The following message appears:

   ```
   Current DFSR global state: 'Start'
   New DFSR global state: 'Prepared'

   Migration will proceed to 'Prepared' state. DFSR service will
   copy the contents of SYSVOL to SYSVOL_DFSR
   folder.

   If any DC is unable to start migration then try manual polling.
   OR Run with option /CreateGlobalObjects.
   Migration can start anytime between 15 min to 1 hour.
   Succeeded.
   ```

6. Type **dfsrmig /getmigrationstate** and press Enter.

   A message appears that reflects the migration state of each domain controller. Migration can take up to 15 minutes. Repeat this step until you receive the following message that indicates migration has progressed to the 'Prepared' state and is successful:

   ```
   All Domain Controllers have migrated successfully to Global state
   ('Prepared').
   Migration has reached a consistent state on all Domain Controllers.
   Succeeded.
   ```

When you receive the message just shown, continue to step 7.

During migration to the 'Prepared' state, you might see one of these messages:

```
The following Domain Controllers are not in sync with Global state
('Prepared'):


Domain Controller (Local Migration State) - DC Type
=======================================================

SERVER01 ('Start') - Primary DC
SERVER02 ('Start') - Writable DC

Migration has not yet reached a consistent state on all Domain Controllers.
State information might be stale due to AD latency.
```

or

```
The following Domain Controllers are not in sync with Global state
('Prepared'):


Domain Controller (Local Migration State) - DC Type
=======================================================

SERVER01 ('Start') - Primary DC
SERVER02 ('Waiting For Initial Sync') - Writable DC

Migration has not yet reached a consistent state on all Domain Controllers.
State information might be stale due to AD latency.
```

or

```
The following Domain Controllers are not in sync with Global state
('Prepared'):


Domain Controller (Local Migration State) - DC Type
=======================================================

SERVER02 ('Waiting For Initial Sync') - Writable DC

Migration has not yet reached a consistent state on all Domain Controllers.
State information might be stale due to AD latency.
```

7. Open the Event Viewer console from the Administrative Tools program group.

8. Expand Applications And Services Logs and select DFS Replication.

9. Locate the event with event ID 8014 and open its properties.

    You should see the details shown in Figure 10-3.

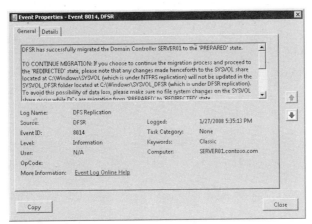

Figure 10-3 DFS-R event indicating successful migration to the 'Prepared' state

Type **dfsrmig /setglobalstate 2** and press Enter.

The following message appears:

```
Current DFSR global state: 'Prepared'
New DFSR global state: 'Redirected'

Migration will proceed to 'Redirected' state. The SYSVOL share will be
changed to SYSVOL_DFSR folder.

If any changes have been made to the SYSVOL share during the state
transition from 'Prepared' to 'Redirected', please robocopy the changes
from SYSVOL to SYSVOL_DFSR on any replicated RWDC.
Succeeded.
```

10. Type **dfsrmig /getmigrationstate** and press Enter.

A message appears that reflects the migration state of each domain controller. Migration can take up to 15 minutes. Repeat this step until you receive the following message that indicates migration has progressed to the 'Prepared' state and is successful:

```
All Domain Controllers have migrated successfully to Global state
('Redirected').
Migration has reached a consistent state on all Domain Controllers.
Succeeded.
```

When you receive the message just shown, continue to step 12.

During migration, you might receive messages like the following:

```
The following Domain Controllers are not in sync with Global state
('Redirected'):

Domain Controller (Local Migration State) - DC Type
=====================================================

SERVER02 ('Prepared') - Writable DC

Migration has not yet reached a consistent state on all Domain Controllers.
State information might be stale due to AD latency.
```

11. Type **net share** and press Enter.

12. Confirm that the NETLOGON share refers to the %SystemRoot%\SYSVOL_DFSR\Sysvol \contoso.com\Scripts folder.

13. Confirm that the SYSVOL share refers to the %SystemRoot%\SYSVOL_DFSR\Sysvol folder.

14. In Windows Explorer, open the %SystemRoot%\SYSVOL_DFSR\Sysvol\contoso.com \Scripts folder.

15. Confirm that the Sample Logon Script file was migrated to the new Scripts folder.

16. Create a new text file named **Sample Logon Script DFSR**.

17. On SERVER02, confirm that the file replicated to the %SystemRoot%\SYSVOL_DFSR \Sysvol\contoso.com\Scripts folder.

Lesson Summary

- You cannot use DFS-R to replicate SYSVOL until the domain is at Windows Server 2008 functional level.

- The *Dfsrmig.exe* command manages the migration from the FRS-replicated SYSVOL folder to the DFS-R replicated SYSVOL_DFSR folder.

- There are four migration states: Start, Prepared, Redirected, and Eliminated. You can revert to previous states until you have configured the state as Eliminated.

Lesson Review

You can use the following questions to test your knowledge of the information in Lesson 3, "Configuring DFS Replication of SYSVOL." The questions are also available on the companion CD if you prefer to review them in electronic form.

NOTE   Answers

Answers to these questions and explanations of why each answer choice is right or wrong are located in the "Answers" section at the end of the book.

1. You are an administrator at Trey Research. Your domain consists of three domain controllers, two running Windows Server 2008 and one running Windows Server 2003. The forest root domain has two domain controllers, both running Windows Server 2003. You want to replicate SYSVOL in your domain, using DFS-R. What steps must you take? (Choose all that apply. Each correct answer is part of the solution.)

    A. Upgrade the forest root domain controllers to Windows Server 2008.

    B. Configure the forest functional level to Windows Server 2008.

    C. Upgrade your Windows Server 2003 domain controller to Windows Server 2008.

    D. Configure the domain functional level of your domain to Windows Server 2008.

    E. Configure the domain functional level of the forest root domain to Windows Server 2008.

2. You want to configure Active Directory so that replication of logon scripts is managed using DFS-R. Which command do you use?

    A. *Dfsrmig.exe*

    B. *Repadmin.exe*

    C. *Dfsutil.exe*

    D. *Dfscmd.exe*

Chapter Review

To further practice and reinforce the skills you learned in this chapter, you can perform the following tasks:

- Review the chapter summary.
- Review the key term introduced in this chapter.
- Complete the case scenario. This scenario sets up a real-world situation involving the topics of this chapter and asks you to create a solution.
- Complete the suggested practices.
- Take a practice test.

Chapter Summary

- Domain controllers in an Active Directory domain replicate changes in a multimaster fashion; however, certain roles are performed by a single domain controller.
- When you add new domain controllers to a domain, you can transfer operations master roles to decrease single-point-of-failure instances, to increase performance, or to accommodate planned downtime.
- Before you add the first Windows Server 2008 domain controller to a forest, you must run *Adprep /forestprep* and *Adprep /domainprep /gpprep*.
- After all domain controllers are running Windows Server 2008, you can raise the domain functional level to Windows Server 2008, which enables you to begin migrating replication of SYSVOL to the more robust DFS-R technology.

Key Terms

Use this key term to understand better the concepts covered in this chapter.

- **operations master**   A domain controller that performs a single-master operation. There are five single-master operations: schema, domain naming, infrastructure, RID, and PDC emulator.

Case Scenario

In the following case scenario, you will apply what you've learned about installing domain controllers and configuring operations masters. You can find answers to these questions in the "Answers" section at the end of this book.

Case Scenario: Upgrading a Domain

You are a consultant who has been hired by Contoso, Ltd., to provide guidance during the upgrade of the *contoso.com* forest to Windows Server 2008 domain controllers. The forest consists of two domains, *contoso.com* and *subsidiary.contoso.com*. Both domains contain three domain controllers running Windows Server 2003.

1. What must you do before installing any Windows Server 2008 domain controllers in the *contoso.com* forest?

2. The *subsidiary.contoso.com* domain consists of three small branch offices, each with a domain controller. The management of Contoso wants all three branch office DCs to be read-only. Is this possible and, if so, how?

3. You are planning to upgrade SERVER01 in the forest root domain, which performs all forest and domain single master operations. What should you do prior to upgrading the server?

Suggested Practices

To help you successfully master the exam objectives presented in this chapter, complete the following tasks.

Upgrade a Windows Server 2003 Domain

In this practice, you will upgrade a Windows Server 2003 domain to Windows Server 2008. To perform these practices, you must have two servers available.

- **Practice 1**   Install a server running Windows Server 2003. Promote it to a domain controller in a new forest. Configure its domain and forest functional levels to Windows Server 2003.

- **Practice 2**   Run *Adprep /forestprep* and *Adprep /domainprep /gpprep* from the Windows Server 2008 installation DVD \Sources\Adprep folder.

- **Practice 3**   Install a server running Windows Server 2008 and join the domain. Promote the server to a domain controller, including DNS and global catalog.

- **Practice 4**   Transfer all operations master roles to the new domain controller.

- **Practice 5 (Option 1)**   Upgrade the first domain controller to Windows Server 2008.

- **Practice 5 (Option 2)**   Demote the Windows Server 2003 domain controller and remove it from the domain to a workgroup. Format the disk. Install Windows Server 2008 and join the domain. Promote the server to a domain controller. Transfer all operations master roles back to the system.

Take a Practice Test

The practice tests on this book's companion CD offer many options. For example, you can test yourself on just one exam objective, or you can test yourself on all the 70-640 certification exam content. You can set up the test so that it closely simulates the experience of taking a certification exam, or you can set it up in study mode so that you can look at the correct answers and explanations after you answer each question.

MORE INFO   **Practice tests**

For details about all the practice test options available, see the "How to Use the Practice Tests" section in this book's introduction.

Chapter 11
Sites and Replication

You've learned in previous chapters that domain controllers (DCs) in a Windows Server 2008 domain are peers. Each maintains a copy of the directory, each performs similar services to support authentication of security principals, and changes made on any one domain controller will be replicated to all other domain controllers. As an administrator of a Microsoft Windows enterprise, one of your tasks is to ensure that authentication is provided as efficiently as possible, and that replication between domain controllers is optimized. Active Directory Domain Services (AD DS) sites are the core component of the directory service that supports the goals of service localization and replication. In this chapter, you will learn how to create a distributed directory service that supports domain controllers in portions of your network that are separated by expensive, slow, or unreliable links. You'll learn where domain controllers should be placed and how to manage replication and service usage. You'll also learn how to control which data is replicated to each domain controller by configuring global catalogs (GCs) and application partitions.

Exam objectives in this chapter:
- Configuring the Active Directory Infrastructure
  - ❑ Configure the global catalog.
  - ❑ Configure sites.
  - ❑ Configure Active Directory replication.
- Maintaining the Active Directory Environment
  - ❑ Monitor Active Directory.

Lessons in this chapter:
- Lesson 1: Configuring Sites and Subnets 509
- Lesson 2: Configuring the Global Catalog and Application Directory Partitions . . . 522
- Lesson 3: Configuring Replication 531

Before You Begin

To complete the practices in this chapter, you must have created two domain controllers named SERVER01 and SERVER02 in a domain named *contoso.com*. See Chapter 1, "Installation," and Chapter 10, "Domain Controllers," for detailed steps for this task.

Real World

Dan Holme

As you learned in the previous chapter, it is important to have more than one domain controller in a domain to provide continuity of service in the event that one domain controller fails. That rule of thumb—at least two DCs per domain—assumes that all servers and clients in your environment are well connected to the DCs. But what happens if you have several network locations separated by links that are not LAN speed? And what must you do if those intersite links are unreliable? Well, then, you must make a determination whether to place domain controllers in remote locations and how to manage replication of the directory to those domain controllers. On the 70-640 exam, the focus on Active Directory sites is their relationship to replication, and you will certainly learn how to manage replication in this chapter. But sites are also important in highly connected environments because they enable you to manage *service localization*—that is, ensure that when a service is available from multiple servers, a client uses the most efficient server. Throughout this chapter, keep your eye on the relationship between sites and service localization as well, because although it might not be as important on the exam, it is certainly important in your production environment.

Lesson 1: Configuring Sites and Subnets

Active Directory represents human beings by user objects in the directory service. It represents machines by computer objects. It represents network topology with objects called *sites* and *subnets*. Active Directory site objects are used to manage replication and service localization and, fortunately, in many environments, the configuration of sites and subnets can be quite straightforward. In this lesson, you will learn the fundamental concepts and techniques required to configure and manage sites and subnets.

> **After this lesson, you will be able to:**
> - Identify the roles of sites and subnets.
> - Describe the process with which a client locates a domain controller.
> - Configure sites and subnets.
> - Manage domain controller server objects in sites.
>
> **Estimated lesson time: 45 minutes**

Understanding Sites

When administrators describe their network infrastructure, they often mention how many sites comprise their enterprise. To most administrators, a site is a physical location, an office or city, for example. Sites are connected by links—network links that might be as basic as dial-up connections or as sophisticated as fiber links. Together, the physical locations and links make up the network infrastructure.

Active Directory represents the network infrastructure with objects called *sites* and *site links*, and although the words are similar, these objects are not identical to the sites and links described by administrators. This lesson focuses on sites, and Lesson 3, "Configuring Replication," discusses site links.

It's important to understand the properties and roles of sites in Active Directory to understand the subtle distinction between Active Directory sites and network sites. Active Directory sites are objects in the directory, specifically in the Configuration container (CN=Configuration,DC=*forest root domain*). These objects are used to achieve two service management tasks:

- To manage replication traffic
- To facilitate service localization

Replication Traffic

Replication is the transfer of changes between domain controllers. When you add a user or change a user's password, for example, the change you make is committed to the directory by one domain controller. That change must be communicated to all other domain controllers in the domain.

Active Directory assumes there are two types of networks within your enterprise: highly connected and less highly connected. Conceptually, a change made to Active Directory should replicate immediately to other domain controllers within the highly connected network in which the change was made. However, you might not want the change to replicate immediately over a slower, more expensive, or less reliable link to another site. Instead, you might want to manage replication over less highly connected segments of your enterprise to optimize performance, reduce costs, or manage bandwidth.

An Active Directory site represents a highly connected portion of your enterprise. When you define a site, the domain controllers within the site replicate changes almost instantly. Replication between sites can be scheduled and managed.

Service Localization

Active Directory is a distributed service. That is, assuming you have at least two domain controllers, there are multiple servers (domain controllers) providing the same services of authentication and directory access. If you have more than one network site, and if you place a domain controller in each, you want to encourage clients to authenticate against the domain controller in their site. This is an example of service localization.

Active Directory sites help you localize services, including those provided by domain controllers. During logon, Windows clients are automatically directed to a domain controller in their site. If a domain controller is not available in their site, they are directed to a DC in another site that will be able to authenticate the client efficiently.

Other services can be localized as well. Distributed File System Namespaces (DFS Namespaces), for example, is a localized service. DFS clients will obtain replicated resources from the most efficient server, based on their Active Directory site. In fact, because clients know what site they are in, any distributed service could be written to take advantage of the Active Directory site structure to provide intelligent localization of service usage.

Planning Sites

Because sites are used to optimize replication and to enable service localization, you must spend time designing your Active Directory site structure. Active Directory sites might not map one to one with your network's sites. Consider two scenarios:

- You have offices in two distinct locations. You place one domain controller in each location. The locations are highly connected, and to improve performance, you decide to configure a single Active Directory site that includes both locations.
- You have an enterprise on a large, highly connected campus. From a replication perspective, the enterprise could be considered a single site. However, you want to encourage clients to use distributed services in their location, so you configure multiple sites to support service localization.

Therefore, an Active Directory site can include more than one network site or be a subset of a single network site. The key is to remember that sites serve both replication management and service localization roles. Several characteristics of your enterprise can be used to help you determine which sites are necessary:

Connection Speed

An Active Directory site represents a unit of the network that is characterized by fast, reliable, inexpensive connectivity. Much documentation suggests that the slowest link speed within a site should be no less than 512 kilobits per second (kbps). However, this guidance is not immutable. Some organizations have links as slow as 56 or even 28 kbps within a site.

Service Placement

Because Active Directory sites manage Active Directory replication and service localization, it is not useful to create a site for a network location that does not host a domain controller or other Active Directory–aware service such as a replicated DFS resource.

NOTE Sites where there are no domain controllers

Domain controllers are only one distributed service in a Windows enterprise. Other services, such as replicated DFS resources, are site-aware as well. You might configure sites to localize services other than authentication, in which case you will have sites without domain controllers.

User Population

Concentrations of users can also influence your site design, although indirectly. If a network location has a sufficient number of users for whom the inability to authenticate would be problematic, place a domain controller in the location to support authentication within the location. After a domain controller or other distributed service is placed in the location to support those users, you might want to manage Active Directory replication to the location or localize service use by configuring an Active Directory site to represent the location.

Summarizing Site Planning Criteria

Every Active Directory forest includes at least one site. The default site created when you instantiate a forest with the first domain controller is creatively named *Default-First-Site-Name*. You should create additional sites when:

- A part of the network is separated by a slow link.
- A part of the network has enough users to warrant hosting domain controllers or other services in that location.
- Directory query traffic warrants a local domain controller.
- You want to control service localization.
- You want to control replication between domain controllers.

Server Placement

Network administrators often want to know when placing a domain controller in a remote site is recommended. The answer is, "It depends." Specifically, it depends on the resources required by users in the site and the tolerance for downtime. If users in a remote site perform all work tasks by accessing resources in the data center, for example, then if the link to the remote site fails, the users cannot access the resources they require, and a local domain controller would not improve the situation. However, if users access resources in the remote site and the link fails, a local domain controller can continue to provide authentication for users and they can continue to work with their local resources.

In most branch office scenarios, there are resources in the branch office that users require to perform their work tasks. Those resources, if not stored on the user's own computer, require domain authentication of the user. Therefore, a domain controller is generally recommended. The introduction of read-only domain controllers (RODCs) in Windows Server 2008 reduces the risk and management burden of domain controllers in branch offices, so it will be easier for most organizations to deploy DCs in each network location.

Defining Sites

Sites and replication are managed using the Active Directory Sites and Services snap-in. To define an Active Directory site, you will create an object of class *site*. The site object is a container that manages replication for domain controllers in the site. You will also create one or more subnet objects. A subnet object defines a range of IP addresses and is linked to one site. Service localization is attained when a client's IP address can be associated with a site through the relationship between the subnet object and the site object.

You can create a site object by right-clicking the Sites node in Active Directory Sites And Services and choosing New Site. In the New Object – Site dialog box that appears, shown in Figure 11-1, enter a site name and select a site link. The default site link, DEFAULTIPSITELINK, will be the only site link available to you until you create additional site links as discussed in Lesson 2, "Configuring the Global Catalog and Application Directory Partitions."

Figure 11-1   The New Object – Site dialog box

After creating a site, you can right-click it and choose Rename to rename it. It is recommended that you rename the Default-First-Site-Name site to reflect a site name that is aligned with your business and network topology.

Sites are useful only when a client or server knows the site to which it belongs. This is typically achieved by associating the system's IP address with a site, and subnet objects achieve this association. To create a subnet object, right-click the Subnets node in the Active Directory Sites And Services snap-in and choose New Subnet. The New Object – Subnet dialog box shown in Figure 11-2 appears. The subnet object is defined as a range of addresses using network prefix notation. For example, to enter a subnet representing the addresses 10.1.1.1 to 10.1.1.254 with a 24-bit subnet mask, the prefix would be 10.1.1.0/24. For more information about entering addresses, click the Learn More About Entering Address Prefixes link in the New Object – Subnet dialog box.

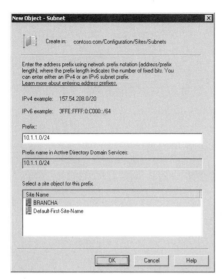

Figure 11-2   The New Object – Subnet dialog box

After entering the network prefix, select the site object with which the subnet is associated. A subnet can be associated with only one site; however, a site can have more than one subnet linked to it. The Properties dialog box of a site, shown in Figure 11-3, shows the subnets associated with the site. You cannot change the subnets in this dialog box, however; instead, you must open the properties of the subnet, shown in Figure 11-4, to change the site to which the subnet is linked.

Figure 11-3   The Properties dialog box for a site

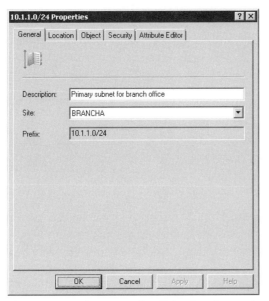

Figure 11-4   The Properties dialog box for a subnet

NOTE   Defining every IP subnet

In your production environment, be certain to define every IP subnet as an Active Directory subnet object. If a client's IP address is not included within a subnet range, the client is unable to determine which Active Directory site it belongs to, which can lead to performance and functionality problems. Don't forget backbone subnets and subnets used for remote access such as virtual private network address ranges.

Managing Domain Controllers in Sites

There are times when you might need to manage domain controllers in Active Directory sites:

■ You create a new site and move an existing domain controller to it.

■ You demote a domain controller.

■ You promote a new domain controller.

When you create your Active Directory forest, the first domain controller is automatically placed under the site object named *Default-First-Site-Name*. You can see the domain controller SERVER01.contoso.com in Figure 11-5. Additional domain controllers will be added to sites based on their IP addresses. For example, if a server with IP address 10.1.1.17 is promoted to a domain controller in the network shown in Figure 11-4, the server will automatically be added to the BRANCHA site. Figure 11-5 shows SERVER02 in the BRANCHA site.

Figure 11-5 A domain controller in a site

Each site contains a Servers container, which itself contains an object for each domain controller in the site. The Servers container in a site should show only domain controllers, not all servers. When you promote a new domain controller, the domain controller will, by default, be placed in the site associated with its IP address. However, the Active Directory Domain Services Installation Wizard will enable you to specify another site. You can also pre-create the server object for the domain controller in the correct site by right-clicking the Servers container in the appropriate site and choosing Server from the New menu.

Finally, you can move the domain controller to the correct site after installation by right-clicking the server and choosing Move. In the Move Server dialog box, select the new site and click OK. The domain controller is moved. It is a best practice to place a domain controller in the site object that is associated with the DC's IP address. If a DC is multihomed, it can belong to only one site. If a site has no domain controllers, users will still be able to log on to the domain; their logon requests will be handled by a domain controller in an adjacent site or another domain controller in the domain.

To remove a domain controller object, right-click it and choose Delete.

Understanding Domain Controller Location

You started this lesson by examining AD DS as a distributed service, providing authentication and directory access on more than one domain controller. You learned to identify where, in your network topology, to define sites and place domain controllers. Now you are ready to examine how, exactly, service localization works—how Active Directory clients become site aware and locate the domain controller in their site. Although this level of detail is unlikely to appear on the certification examination, it can be extremely helpful when you need to troubleshoot authentication of a computer or of a user.

Service Locator Records

When a domain controller is added to the domain, it advertises its services by creating Service Locator (SRV) records, also called locator records, in DNS. Unlike host records (A records), which map host names to IP addresses, SRV records map services to host names. The domain controller advertises its ability to provide authentication and directory access by registering Kerberos and LDAP SRV records. These SRV records are added to several folders within the DNS zones for the forest. The first folder is within the domain zone. It is called _tcp and it contains the SRV records for all domain controllers in the domain. The second folder is specific to this site, in which the domain controller is located, with the path _sites*sitename*_tcp, where *sitename* is the name of the site. In Figure 11-6, you can see the Kerberos and LDAP SRV records for SERVER02.contoso.com in its site, _sites\BRANCHA_tcp. You can also see the _tcp folder at the first level beneath the zone.

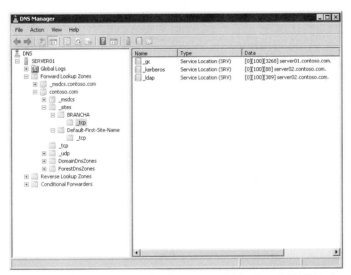

Figure 11-6   The SRV records for SERVER02 in the BRANCHA site

The same records are registered in several places in the _msdcs.*domainName* zone, for example, _msdcs.contoso.com in Figure 11-6. This zone contains records for Microsoft Domain Controller Services. The underscore characters are a requirement of RFC 2052.

Locator records contain:

- **Service name and port**   This portion of the SRV record indicates a service with a fixed port. It does not have to be a well-known port. SRV records in Windows Server 2008 include LDAP (port 389), Kerberos (port 88), Kerberos Password protocol (KPASSWD, port 464), and GC services (port 3268).

- **Protocol**   TCP or UDP will be indicated as a transport protocol for the service. The same service can use both protocols, in separate SRV records. Kerberos records, for example, are registered for both TCP and UDP. Microsoft clients use only TCP, but UNIX clients can use TCP.

- **Host name**   The name corresponds to the A (Host) record for the server hosting the service. When a client queries for a service, the DNS server returns the SRV record and associated A records, so the client does not need to submit a separate query to resolve the IP address of a service.

The service name in the SRV record follows the standard DNS hierarchy, with components separated by dots. For example, the Kerberos service of a domain controller is registered as:

```
kerberos._tcp.siteName._sites.domainName
```

Reading this SRV record name right to left like other DNS records, it translates to:

- *domainName*: the domain or zone, for example, *contoso.com*
- _sites: all sites registered with DNS
- *siteName*: the site of the domain controller registering the service
- _tcp: any TCP-based services in the site
- kerberos: a Kerberos Key Distribution Center (KDC) using TCP as its transport protocol

Domain Controller Location

Imagine a Windows client has just been joined to the domain. It restarts, receives an IP address from a DHCP server, and is ready to authenticate to the domain. How does the client know where to find a domain controller? It does not. Therefore, the client queries the domain for a domain controller by querying the _tcp folder which, you'll remember, contains the SRV records for all domain controllers in the domain. DNS returns a list of all matching DCs, and the client attempts to contact all of them on this, its first startup. The first domain controller that responds to the client examines the client's IP address, cross-references that address with subnet objects, and informs the client of the site to which the client belongs. The client stores the site name in its registry, then queries for domain controllers in the site-specific _tcp folder. DNS returns a list of all DCs in the site. The client attempts to bind with all, and the DC that responds first authenticates the client.

The client forms an affinity for this DC and will attempt to authenticate with the same DC in the future. If the DC is unavailable, the client queries the site's _tcp folder again and attempts to bind with all DCs in the site. But what happens if the client is a mobile computer—a laptop? Imagine that the computer has been authenticating in the BRANCHA site and then the user brings the computer to the BRANCHB site. When the computer starts up, it actually attempts to authenticate with its preferred DC into BRANCHA site. That DC notices the client's IP address is associated with BRANCHB and informs the client of its new site. The client then queries DNS for domain controllers in BRANCHB.

You can see how, by storing subnet and site information in Active Directory and by registering services in DNS, a client is encouraged to use services in its site—the definition of service localization.

MORE INFO   Domain controller location

For more information about domain controller location, see *http://www.microsoft.com/technet /prodtechnol/windows2000serv/reskit/distrib/dsbc_nar_jevl.mspx?mfr=true.*

Site Coverage

What happens if a site has no domain controller? Sites can be used to direct users to local copies of replicated resources such as shared folders replicated within a DFS namespace, so you might have sites without a DC. In this case, a nearby domain controller will register its SRV records in the site in a process called *site coverage*. To be precise, a site without a DC will generally be covered by a domain controller in a site with the lowest cost to the site requiring coverage. You'll learn more about site link costs in the next lesson. You can also manually configure site coverage and SRV record priority if you want to implement strict control over authentication in sites without DCs. The URL just listed contains details about the algorithm that determines which DC automatically covers a site without a DC.

PRACTICE Configuring Sites and Subnets

In this practice, you will use best practices to implement a structure of sites and subnets for the *contoso.com* domain. To perform the exercises in this practice, you must have two domain controllers, SERVER01 and SERVER02, in the domain.

▶ **Exercise 1   Configure the Default Site**

A new domain contains the Default-First-Site-Name site. In this exercise, you will rename that site and associate two subnets with the site.

1. Open the Active Directory Sites And Services snap-in.
2. Right-click Default-First-Site-Name and choose Rename.
3. Type **HEADQUARTERS** and press Enter.

   Because site names are registered in DNS, you should use DNS-compliant names that avoid special characters and spaces.
4. Right-click Subnets and choose New Subnet.
5. In the Prefix box, type **10.0.0.0/24**.
6. In the Select A Site Object For This Prefix list, select HEADQUARTERS.
7. Click OK.
8. Right-click Subnets and choose New Subnet.
9. In the Prefix box, type **10.0.1.0/24**.

10. In the Select A Site Object For This Prefix list, select HEADQUARTERS.

11. Click OK.

▶ **Exercise 2   Create an Additional Site**

Sites enable you to manage replication traffic and to localize services such as the authentication and directory access provided by domain controllers. In this exercise, you will create a second site and associate a subnet with it.

1. Open the Active Directory Sites And Services snap-in

2. Right-click Sites and choose New Site.

3. Type **BRANCHA** in the Name box.

4. Select DEFAULTIPSITELINK.

5. Click OK.

   An Active Directory Domain Services dialog box appears, explaining the steps required to complete the configuration of the site.

6. Click OK.

7. Right-click Subnets and choose New Subnet.

8. In the Prefix box, type **10.1.1.0/24**.

9. In the Select A Site Object For This Prefix list, select BRANCHA.

10. Click OK.

11. In the Active Directory Sites And Services snap-in, expand the Subnets node.

12. Right-click 10.1.1.0/24 and choose Properties.

13. In the Description box, type **Primary subnet for branch office**.

14. In the Site drop-down list, select BRANCHA.

15. Click OK.

Lesson Summary

- Sites are Active Directory objects that are used to manage directory replication and service localization.

- To configure a site, you must create a site object and associate a subnet object with the site. A site can have more than one subnet, but a subnet can belong to only one site.

- Domain controllers are placed in sites as server objects.

- Domain controllers register service locator (SRV) records to advertise their Kerberos (authentication) and directory access services. These SRV records are created in site-specific nodes within the DNS zones for the domain and forest.

- Domain members discover their site during authentication. A domain controller uses a client's IP address and the domain's site and subnet information to determine the client's site and then sends that information to the client.

Lesson Review

You can use the following questions to test your knowledge of the information in Lesson 1, "Configuring Sites and Subnets." The questions are also available on the companion CD if you prefer to review them in electronic form.

NOTE   Answers

Answers to these questions and explanations of why each answer choice is right or wrong are located in the "Answers" section at the end of the book.

---

1. Client computers in a branch office are performing poorly during logon. You notice that the computers report that their logon server is a domain controller in a remote site rather than the domain controller in the branch office itself. Which of the following could cause this problem?

    A. The branch office domain controller is not assigned to a site.

    B. The branch office site is not assigned to a site link.

    C. The branch office IP address range is not associated with the site.

    D. The branch office subnet is assigned to two sites.

2. You are adding a read-only domain controller to a branch office location. You want to ensure that clients in the branch office are likely to authenticate with the RODC. What is required? (Choose all that apply.)

    A. A subnet object with the network prefix of the branch office IP address range

    B. An account for the domain controller in the organizational unit for the site

    C. A site link transport for the site

    D. A site object for the branch office

    E. A server object in the site object for the branch office

Lesson 2: Configuring the Global Catalog and Application Directory Partitions

As soon as you have more than one domain controller in your domain, you must consider replication of the directory database between domain controllers. In this lesson, you will learn which directory partitions are replicated to each domain controller in a forest and how to manage the replication of the GC and of application partitions.

After this lesson, you will be able to:
- Define the purpose of the global catalog.
- Configure domain controllers as global catalog servers.
- Implement universal group membership caching.
- Understand the role of application directory partitions.

Estimated lesson time: 45 minutes

Reviewing Active Directory Partitions

In Chapter 1, you learned that AD DS includes a data store for identity and management, specifically the directory database, *Ntds.dit*. Within that single file are directory partitions. Each directory partition, also called a naming context, contains objects of a particular scope and purpose. Three major naming contexts have been discussed in this training kit:

- **Domain**   The domain naming context (NC) contains all the objects stored in a domain, including users, groups, computers, and Group Policy containers (GPCs).
- **Configuration**   The configuration partition contains objects that represent the logical structure of the forest, including domains, as well as the physical topology, including sites, subnets, and services.
- **Schema**   The schema defines the object classes and their attributes for the entire directory.

Each domain controller maintains a copy, or *replica*, of several naming contexts. The configuration is replicated to every domain controller in the forest, as is the schema. The domain naming context for a domain is replicated to all domain controllers within a domain but not to domain controllers in other domains, so each domain controller has at least three replicas: the domain NC for its domain, configuration, and schema.

Traditionally, replicas have been complete replicas, containing every object of an attribute, and replicas have been writable on all DCs. Beginning with Windows Server 2008, RODCs change the picture slightly. An RODC maintains a read-only replica of all objects in the configuration, schema, and domain NCs of its domain. However, certain attributes are not replicated to an RODC—specifically, secrets such as user passwords—unless the password policy of the RODC allows such replication. There are also attributes that are domain and forest secrets that are never replicated to an RODC.

Understanding the Global Catalog

Imagine a forest with two domains. Each domain has two domain controllers. All four domain controllers will maintain a replica of the schema and configuration for the forest. The domain controllers in Domain A have replicas of the domain NC for Domain A, and the domain controllers in Domain B have replicas of the domain NC for Domain B.

What happens if a user in Domain B is searching for a user, computer, or group in Domain A? The Domain B domain controllers do not maintain any information about objects in Domain A, so a domain controller in Domain B could not answer a query about objects in the domain NC of Domain A.

That's where the global catalog comes in. The *global catalog* (GC) is a partition that stores information about every object in the forest. When a user in Domain B looks for an object in Domain A, the GC provides the results of the query. To optimize efficiency of the GC, it does not contain every attribute of every object in the forest. Instead, it contains a subset of attributes that are useful for searching across domains. That is why the GC is also called the *partial attribute set* (PAS). In terms of its role supporting search, you can think of the GC as a kind of index for the AD DS data store.

Placing GC Servers

The GC improves efficiency of the directory service tremendously and is required for applications such as Microsoft Exchange Server and Microsoft Office Outlook. Therefore, you want a GC to be available to these and other applications. The GC can be served only by a domain controller and, in an ideal world, every domain controller would be a GC server. In fact, many organizations are now configuring their domain controllers as GC servers.

The potential downside to such a configuration relates to replication. The GC is another partition that must be replicated. In a single domain forest, very little overhead is actually added by configuring all domain controllers as GC servers because all domain controllers already maintain a full set of attributes for all domain and forest objects. In a large, multidomain forest, there will be overhead related to replication of changes to the partial attribute set of objects in other domains. However, many organizations are finding that Active Directory replication is efficient enough to replicate the GC without significant impact to their networks and that the benefits far outweigh such impact. If you choose to configure all DCs as GC servers, you no longer need to worry about the placement of the infrastructure operations master; its role is no longer necessary in a domain where all DCs are GC servers.

It is particularly recommended to configure a GC server on a domain controller in a site where one or more of the following is true:

- A commonly used application performs directory queries, using port 3268, the GC.
- The connection to a GC server is slow or unreliable.
- The site contains a computer running Exchange Server.

Configuring a Global Catalog Server

When you create the first domain in the forest, the first domain controller is configured as a GC. You must decide for each additional DC whether it should be a GC server. The Active Directory Domain Services Installation Wizard and the *Dcpromo.exe* command each enable you to configure a GC server when promoting a domain controller. You can also add or remove the GC from a domain controller by using Active Directory Sites And Services. Expand the site, the Servers container within the site, and the domain controller's server object. Right-click the NTDS Settings node and choose Properties. On the General tab, shown in Figure 11-7, select the Global Catalog check box. To remove the GC from a domain controller, perform the same steps, clearing the Global Catalog check box.

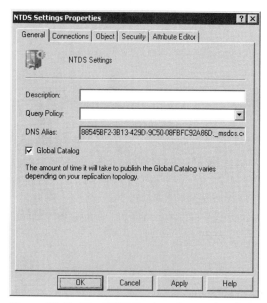

Figure 11-7   The NTDS Settings Properties dialog box, showing the Global Catalog check box

Universal Group Membership Caching

In Chapter 4, "Groups," you learned that Active Directory supports groups of universal scope. Universal groups are designed to include users and groups from multiple domains in a forest. The membership of universal groups is replicated in the GC. When a user logs on, the user's universal group membership is obtained from a GC server. If a GC is not available, universal group membership is not available. It's possible that a universal group is used to deny the user access to resources, so Windows prevents a security incident by denying domain authentication to the user. If the user has logged on to his or her computer before, he or she can log on using cached credentials, but as soon as the user attempts to access network resources, access will be denied. To summarize: if a GC server is not available, users will effectively be unable to log on and access network resources.

If every domain controller is a GC server, this problem will not arise. However, if replication is a concern, and if you have, therefore, chosen not to configure a domain controller as a GC server, you can facilitate successful logon by enabling universal group membership caching (UGMC). When you configure universal group membership caching on a domain controller in a branch office, for example, that domain controller will obtain universal group membership information from a GC for a user when the user first logs on in the site, and the domain controller will cache that information indefinitely, updating universal group membership information every eight hours. That way, if the user later logs on and a GC server is not accessible, the domain controller can use its cached membership information to permit logon by the user.

It is recommended, therefore, that in sites with unreliable connectivity to a GC server, you should configure UGMC on the site's domain controllers. To configure UGMC, open the Active Directory Sites And Services snap-in and select the site in the console tree. In the details pane, right-click NTDS Site Settings and choose Properties. The NTDS Site Settings Properties dialog box, shown in Figure 11-8, exposes the Enable Universal Group Membership Caching option. You can select the check box and specify the GC from which to refresh the membership cache.

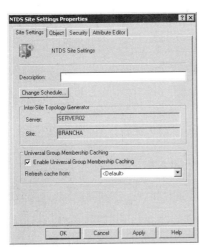

Figure 11-8   The NTDS Site Settings Properties dialog box with the option to enable Universal Group Membership Caching

Understanding Application Directory Partitions

Whereas the domain, configuration, and schema partitions of the directory are replicated to all DCs in a domain, and the configuration and schema are further replicated to all DCs in the forest, Active Directory also supports *application directory partitions*. An application directory partition is a portion of the data store that contains objects required by an application or service that is outside of the core AD DS service. Unlike other partitions, application partitions can be targeted to replicate to specific domain controllers; they are not, by default, replicated to all DCs.

Application directory partitions are designed to support directory-enabled applications and services. They can contain any type of object except security principals such as users, computers, or security groups. Because these partitions are replicated only as needed, application directory partitions provide the benefits of fault tolerance, availability, and performance while optimizing replication traffic.

The easiest way to understand application directory partitions is to examine the application directory partitions maintained by Microsoft DNS Server. When you create an Active Directory–integrated zone, DNS records are replicated between DNS servers by using an application directory partition. The partition and its DNS record objects are not replicated to every domain controller, only to those acting as DNS servers.

You can expose the application directory partitions in your forest by opening ADSI Edit. Right-click the root of the snap-in, ADSI Edit, and choose Connect To. In the Select A Well Known Naming Context drop-down list, choose Configuration and click OK. Expand Configuration and the folder representing the configuration partition, and then select the Partitions folder, CN=Partitions, in the console tree. In the details pane, you will see the partitions in your AD DS data store, as shown in Figure 11-9.

Figure 11-9   Partitions in the *contoso.com* forest

Note the two application partitions in Figure 11-9, ForestDnsZones and DomainDnsZones. Most application partitions are created by applications that require them. DNS is one example, and Telephony Application Programming Interface (TAPI) is another. Members of the Enterprise Admins group can also create application directory partitions manually by using *Ntdsutil.exe*.

An application partition can appear anywhere in the forest namespace that a domain partition can appear. The DNS partitions distinguished names—DC=DomainDnsZones,DC=contoso,DC=com, for example—place the partitions as children of the DC=contoso,DC=com domain partition. An application partition can also be a child of another application partition or a new tree in the forest.

MORE INFO **About application directory partitions**

For more information about application directory partitions, visit *http://technet2.microsoft.com /WindowsServer/en/library/ed363e83-c043-4a50-9233-763e6f4af1f21033.mspx.*

Generally speaking, you will use tools specific to the application to manage the application directory partition, its data, and its replication. For example, simply adding an Active Directory-integrated zone to a DNS server will automatically configure the domain controller to receive a replica of the DomainDns partition. With tools such as *Ntdsutil.exe* and *Ldp.exe*, you can manage application directory partitions directly.

MORE INFO **Managing application directory partitions**

To learn how to manage application directory partitions, see *http://technet2.microsoft.com /WindowsServer/en/library/920d6995-9ee9-46a7-9d1b-320e65c02d1a1033.mspx.*

It is important that you consider application partitions prior to demoting a domain controller. If a domain controller is hosting an application directory partition, you must evaluate the purpose of the partition, whether it is required by any applications, and whether the domain controller holds the last remaining replica of the partition, in which case, demoting the domain controller will result in permanently losing all information in the partition. Although the Active Directory Domain Services Installation Wizard will prompt you to remove application directory partitions, it is recommended that you manually remove application directory partitions prior to demoting a domain controller.

MORE INFO **Application directory partitions and domain controller demotion**

For more information about application directory partitions and domain controller demotion, see *http://technet2.microsoft.com/WindowsServer/en/library/1572d8a2-622c-4879-bb0b-76e26c4001291033.mspx.*

PRACTICE **Replication and Directory Partitions**

In this practice, you will configure replication of the GC and examine the DNS application directory partitions. To complete the exercises in this practice, you must have completed the Lesson 1 practice, "Configuring Sites and Subnets."

▶ **Exercise 1 Configure a Global Catalog Server**

The first domain controller in a forest acts as a GC server. You might want to place GC servers in additional locations to support directory queries, logon, and applications such as Exchange Server. In this exercise, you will configure SERVER02 to host a replica of the partial attribute set—the GC.

1. Log on to SERVER01 as Administrator.
2. Open the Active Directory Sites And Services snap-in.
3. Expand BRANCHA, Servers, and SERVER02.
4. Right-click NTDS Settings below SERVER02 and choose Properties.
5. Select Global Catalog and click OK.

▶ **Exercise 2   Configure Universal Group Membership Caching**

In sites without GC servers, user logon might be prevented if the site's domain controller is unable to contact a GC server in another site. To reduce the likelihood of this scenario, you can configure a site to cache the membership of universal groups. In this exercise, you will create a site to reflect a branch office and configure the site to cache universal group membership.

1. Right-click Sites and choose New Site.
2. In the Name box, type **BRANCHB**.
3. Select DEFAULTIPSITELINK.
4. Click OK.

    If this were a production environment, you would need to create at least one subnet object linked to the site and install a domain controller in BRANCHB.

5. Select BRANCHB in the console tree.
6. Right-click NTDS Site Settings in the details pane and choose Properties.
7. On the Site Settings tab, select the Enable Universal Group Membership Caching check box.
8. Click OK.

▶ **Exercise 3   Examine Application Directory Partitions**

In this exercise, you will explore the DomainDnsZone application directory partition, using ADSI Edit.

1. Open ADSI Edit from the Administrative Tools program group.
2. Right-click the root node of the snap-in, ADSI Edit, and choose Connect To.
3. In the Select A Well Known Naming Context drop-down list, choose Configuration. Click OK.
4. Select Configuration in the console tree, and then expand it.
5. Select CN=Configuration, DC=contoso, DC=com in the console tree, and then expand it.
6. Select CN=Partitions in the console tree.
7. Make a note of the Directory Partition Name of the DomainDnsZones partition: DC=DomainDnsZones,DC=contoso,DC=com.
8. Right-click ADSI Edit and choose Connect To.
9. Select the Select Or Type A Distinguished Name Or Naming Context option.
10. In the combo box, type **DC=DomainDnsZones,DC=contoso,DC=com**. Click OK.

11. Select Default Naming Context in the console tree, and then expand it.

12. Select and then expand DC=DomainDnsZones,DC=contoso,DC=com.

13. Select and then expand CN=MicrosoftDNS.

14. Select DC=contoso.com.

15. Examine the objects in this container. Compare them to the DNS records for the *contoso.com* domain.

Lesson Summary

- The global catalog (GC) contains a copy of every object in the forest but only a subset of object attributes. It is also called the partial attribute set (PAS).

- GC servers improve directory queries, support logon, and provide data for applications such as Exchange Server.

- The first domain controller in a forest is a GC server. You can configure a domain controller as a GC server by using the *Dcpromo.exe* command, the Active Directory Domain Services Installation Wizard, or the Active Directory Sites And Services snap-in after the domain controller has been installed.

- If a site does not contain a GC server, you can configure universal group membership caching (UGMC) to reduce the chance of a user's logon being denied when a GC server is not available.

- Application directory partitions are unique because they can be replicated to specific domain controllers throughout a forest. Active Directory integrated DNS zones are stored in application partitions.

Lesson Review

You can use the following questions to test your knowledge of the information in Lesson 2, "Configuring the Global Catalog and Application Directory Partitions." The questions are also available on the companion CD if you prefer to review them in electronic form.

NOTE Answers

Answers to these questions and explanations of why each answer choice is right or wrong are located in the "Answers" section at the end of the book.

1. A branch office is connected to the data center with a slow link that is not reliable. You want to ensure that the domain controller in the branch is able to authenticate users when it cannot contact a global catalog server. Which of the following should you configure?

   A. Read-only domain controller

   B. Application directory partition

   C. Intersite replication

   D. Universal group membership caching

2. You are the administrator at Contoso, Ltd. The Contoso forest consists of three domains, each with four domain controllers. You are preparing to demote a domain controller in the forest root domain. You want to be sure that you do not permanently destroy any Active Directory partitions. Which of the following Active Directory partitions might exist only on that domain controller? (Choose all that apply.)

   A. Schema

   B. Configuration

   C. Domain

   D. Partial attribute set

   E. Application directory partition

3. You want to configure all the existing domain controllers in your forest as global catalog servers. Which tools can you use to achieve this goal? (Choose all that apply.)

   A. *Dcpromo.exe*

   B. Active Directory Domain Services Installation Wizard

   C. Active Directory Sites and Services snap-in

   D. Active Directory Users and Computers snap-in

   E. Active Directory Domains and Trusts snap-in

Lesson 3: Configuring Replication

In Lesson 1, you learned how to create site and subnet objects that enable Active Directory and its clients to localize authentication and directory access; you decided *where* domain controllers should be placed. In Lesson 2, you configured GC servers and application directory partitions; you managed *what* will replicate between domain controllers. In this lesson, you will learn *how* and *when* replication occurs. You'll discover why the default configuration of Active Directory supports effective replication and why you might modify that configuration so that replication is equally effective but more efficient, based on your network topology.

After this lesson, you will be able to:

- Create connection objects to configure replication between two domain controllers.
- Implement site links and site link costs to manage replication between sites.
- Designate preferred bridgehead servers.
- Understand notification and polling.
- Report and analyze replication with *Repadmin.exe*.
- Perform Active Directory replication health checks with *Dcdiag.exe*.

Estimated lesson time: 90 minutes

Understanding Active Directory Replication

In previous lessons, you learned how to place domain controllers in network locations and how to represent those locations with site and subnet objects. You also learned about the replication of directory partitions (schema, configuration, and domain), the partial attribute set (GC), and application partitions. The most important thing to remember as you learn about Active Directory replication is that it is designed so that, in the end, each replica on a domain controller is consistent with the replicas of that partition hosted on other domain controllers. It is not likely that all domain controllers will have exactly the same information in their replicas at any one moment in time because changes are constantly being made to the directory. However, Active Directory replication ensures that all changes to a partition are transferred to all replicas of the partition. Active Directory replication balances accuracy (or *integrity*) and consistency (called *convergence*) with performance (keeping replication traffic to a reasonable level). This balancing act is described as *loose coupling*.

Key features of Active Directory replication are:

- Partitioning of the data store. Domain controllers in a domain host only the domain naming context for their domain, which helps keep replication to a minimum, particularly in multidomain forests. Other data, including application directory partitions and the partial attribute set (GC), are not replicated to every domain controller in the forest, by default.

- Automatic generation of an efficient and robust replication topology. By default, Active Directory will configure an effective, two-way replication topology so that the loss of any one domain controller does not impede replication. This topology is automatically updated as domain controllers are added, removed, or moved between sites.

- Attribute-level replication. When an attribute of an object is modified, only that attribute, and minimal metadata that describes that attribute, is replicated. The entire object is not replicated except when the object is created.

- Distinct control of intrasite replication (within a single site) and intersite replication (between sites).

- Collision detection and management. It is possible, although rare, that an attribute will have been modified on two different domain controllers during a single replication window. In such an event, the two changes will have to be reconciled. Active Directory has resolution algorithms that satisfy almost every such situation.

It is easier to understand Active Directory replication by examining each of its components. The following sections examine the components of Active Directory replication.

Connection Objects

A domain controller replicates changes from another domain controller because of AD DS connection objects, also called simply *connection objects*. Connection objects appear in the administrative tools in the Active Directory Sites and Services snap-in as objects contained in the NTDS Settings container of a domain controller's server object. Figure 11-10 shows an example: a connection object in SERVER02 configures replication from SERVER01 to SERVER02. A connection object represents a replication path from one domain controller to another.

Connection objects are one-way, representing inbound-only replication. Replication in Active Directory is always a pull technology. In the domain illustrated in Figure 11-10, SERVER02 pulls changes from SERVER01. SERVER02 is considered, in this example, a downstream replication partner of SERVER01. SERVER01 is the upstream partner. Changes from SERVER01 flow to SERVER02.

NOTE Force replication

You can force replication between two domain controllers by right-clicking the connection object and choosing Replicate Now. Remember replication is inbound only, so to replicate both domain controllers, you will need to replicate the inbound connection object of each domain controller.

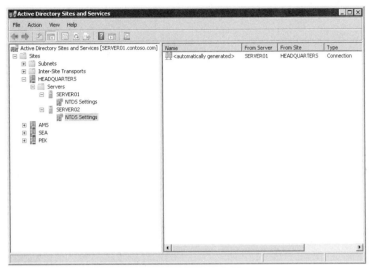

Figure 11-10   A connection object in the Active Directory Sites and Services snap-in

The Knowledge Consistency Checker

The replication paths built between domain controllers by connection objects create the replication topology for the forest. Luckily, you do not have to create the replication topology manually. By default, Active Directory creates a topology that ensures effective replication. The topology is two-way so that if any one domain controller fails, replication will continue uninterrupted. The topology also ensures that there are no more than three hops between any two domain controllers.

You'll notice in Figure 11-10 that the connection object indicates it was automatically generated. On each domain controller, a component of Active Directory called the knowledge consistency checker (KCC) helps generate and optimize the replication automatically between domain controllers within a site. The KCC evaluates the domain controllers in a site and creates connection objects to build the two-way, three-hop topology described earlier. If a domain controller is added to or removed from the site, or if a domain controller is not responsive, the KCC rearranges the topology dynamically, adding and deleting connection objects to rebuild an effective replication topology.

You can manually create connection objects to specify replication paths that should persist. Manually created connection objects are not deleted by the KCC. To create a connection object, locate the server object for the downstream replication partner—the DC that will receive changes from a source DC. Right-click the NTDS Settings container in the server object and choose New Active Directory Domain Services Connection. In the Find Active Directory Domain Controllers dialog box, select the upstream replication partner and click OK. Give the new connection object a name and click OK. Then open the properties of the connection object; use the Description field to indicate the purpose of any manually created connection object.

Within a site, there are very few scenarios that would require creating a connection object. One such scenario is standby operations masters. Operations masters are discussed in Chapter 10. It is recommended that you select domain controllers as standby operations masters to be used in the event that the operations master role must be transferred or seized. A standby operations master should be a direct replication partner with the current operations master. Thus, if a domain controller named DC01 is the RID master, and DC02 is the system that will take the RID master role if DC01 is taken offline, then a connection object should be created in DC02 so that it replicates directly from DC01.

Intrasite Replication

After connection objects between the domain controllers in a site have been established—automatically by the KCC or manually—replication can take place. Intrasite replication involves the replication of changes within a single site.

Notification

Consider the site shown in Figure 11-10. When SERVER01 makes a change to a partition, it queues the change for replication to its partners. SERVER01 waits 15 seconds, by default, to notify its first replication partner, SERVER02, of the change. *Notification* is the process by which an upstream partner informs its downstream partners that a change is available. SERVER01 waits three seconds, by default, between notifications to additional partners. These delays, called the *initial notification delay* and the *subsequent notification delay*, are designed to stagger network traffic caused by intrasite replication.

Upon receiving the notification, the downstream partner, SERVER02, requests the changes from SERVER01, and the directory replication agent (DRA) performs the transfer of the attribute from SERVER01 to SERVER02. In this example, SERVER01 made the initial change to Active Directory. It is the originating domain controller, and the change it made originates the change. When SERVER02 receives the change from SERVER01, it makes the change to its directory. The change is not called a replicated change, but it is a change nonetheless. SERVER02 queues the change for replication to its own downstream partners.

SERVER03 is a downstream replication partner of SERVER02. After 15 seconds, SERVER02 notifies SERVER03 that it has a change. SERVER03 makes the replicated change to its directory and then notifies its downstream partners. The change has made two hops, from SERVER01 to SERVER02 and from SERVER02 to SERVER03. The replication topology will ensure that there are no more than three hops before all domain controllers in the site have received the change. At approximately 15 seconds per hop, that means the change will have fully replicated in the site within one minute.

Polling

It is possible that SERVER01 might not make any changes to its replicas for quite a long time, particularly during off hours. In this case, SERVER02, its downstream replication partner, will not receive notifications from SERVER01. It is also possible that SERVER01 might be offline, which would also prevent it from sending notifications to SERVER02, so it's important for SERVER02 to know that its upstream partner is online and simply does not have any changes.

This is achieved through a process called *polling*. Polling involves the downstream replication partner contacting the upstream replication partner with a query as to whether any changes are queued for replication. By default, the polling interval for intrasite replication is once per hour. It is possible, although not recommended, to configure the polling frequency from the properties of a connection object by clicking Change Schedule.

If an upstream partner fails to respond to repeated polling queries, the downstream partner launches the KCC to check the replication topology. If the upstream server is indeed offline, the site's replication topology is rebuilt to accommodate the change.

Site Links

The KCC assumes that within a site, all domain controllers can reach each other. It builds an intrasite replication topology that is agnostic to the underlying network connectivity. Between sites, however, you can represent the network paths over which replication should occur by creating *site link* objects. A site link contains two or more sites. The intersite topology generator (ISTG), a component of the KCC, builds connection objects between servers in each of the sites to enable intersite replication—replication between sites.

Site links are greatly misunderstood, and the important thing to remember about a site link is that it represents an available path for replication. A single site link does not control the network routes that are used. When you create a site link and add sites to it, you are telling Active Directory that it can replicate between any of those sites. The ISTG will create connection objects, and those objects will determine the actual path of replication. Although the replication topology built by the ISTG will effectively replicate Active Directory, it might not be efficient, given your network topology.

An example will illustrate this concept. When you create a forest, one site link object is created: DEFAULTIPSITELINK. By default, each new site that you add is associated with the DEFAULTIPSITELINK. Consider an organization with a data center at the headquarters and three branch offices. The three branch offices are each connected to the data center with a dedicated link. You create sites for each branch office, Seattle (SEA), Amsterdam (AMS), and Beijing (PEK). The network and site topology is shown in Figure 11-11.

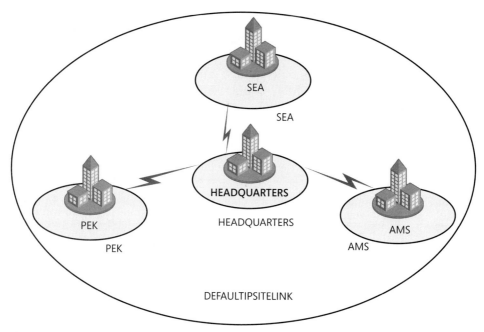

Figure 11-11   Network topology and a single site link

Because all four sites are on the same site link, you are instructing Active Directory that all four sites can replicate with each other. That means it is possible that Seattle will replicate changes from Amsterdam, Amsterdam will replicate changes from Beijing, and Beijing will replicate changes from Headquarters, which in turn replicates changes from Seattle. In several of these replication paths, the replication traffic on the network flows from one branch through the headquarters on its way to another branch. With a single site link, you have not created a hub-and-spoke replication topology even though your network topology is hub-and-spoke.

Therefore, it is recommended that you manually create site links that reflect your physical network topology. Continuing the preceding example, you would create three site links:

- HQ-AMS, including the Headquarters and Amsterdam sites
- HQ-SEA, including the Headquarters and Seattle sites
- HQ-PEK, including the Headquarters and Beijing sites

You would then delete the DEFAULTIPSITELINK. The resulting topology is shown in Figure 11-12.

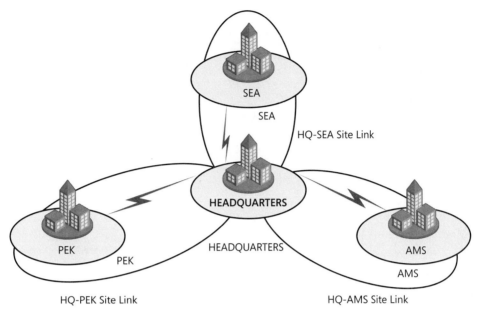

Figure 11-12   Network topology and a three-site link

After you have created site links, the ISTG will use the topology to build an intersite replication topology connecting each site. Connection objects will be built to configure the intersite replication paths. These connection objects are created automatically, and although you can create connection objects manually, few scenarios require manually creating intersite connection objects.

Replication Transport Protocols

You'll notice, in the Active Directory Sites and Services snap-in, that site links are contained within a container named IP that itself is inside the Inter-Site Transports container. Changes are replicated between domain controllers, using one of two protocols:

- **Directory Service Remote Procedure Call (DS-RPC)**   DS-RPC appears in the Active Directory Sites and Services snap-in as IP. IP is used for all intrasite replication and is the default, and preferred, protocol for intersite replication.

- **Inter-Site Messaging—Simple Mail Transport Protocol (ISM-SMTP)**   Also known simply as SMTP, this protocol is used only when network connections between sites are unreliable or are not always available.

In general, you can assume you will use IP for all intersite replication. Very few organizations use SMTP for replication because of the administrative overhead required to configure and manage a certificate authority (CA) and because SMTP replication is not supported for the domain naming context, meaning that if a site uses SMTP to replicate to the rest of the enterprise, that site must be its own domain.

Exam Tip   Although, in the production environment, you are highly unlikely to use SMTP for replication, it is possible you will encounter SMTP replication on the exam. The most important thing to remember is that if two sites can replicate only with SMTP—if IP is not an option—then those two sites must be separate domains in the forest. SMTP cannot be used to replicate the domain naming context.

Bridgehead Servers

The ISTG creates a replication topology between sites on a site link. To make replication more efficient, one domain controller is selected to be the *bridgehead server*. The bridgehead server is responsible for all replication into and out of the site for a partition. For example, if a data center site contains five DCs, one of the DCs will be the bridgehead server for the domain naming context. All changes made to the domain partition within the data center will replicate to all DCs in the site. When the changes reach the bridgehead server, those changes will be replicated to bridgehead servers in branch offices, which in turn replicate the changes to DCs in their sites. Similarly, any changes to the domain naming context in branch offices will be replicated from the branches' bridgehead servers to the bridgehead server in the data center, which in turn replicates the changes to other DCs in the data center. Figure 11-13 illustrates intrasite replication within two sites and the intersite replication using connection objects between the bridgehead servers in the sites.

To summarize, the bridgehead server is the server responsible for replicating changes to a partition from other bridgehead servers in other sites. It is also polled by bridgehead servers in other sites to determine when it has changes that they should replicate.

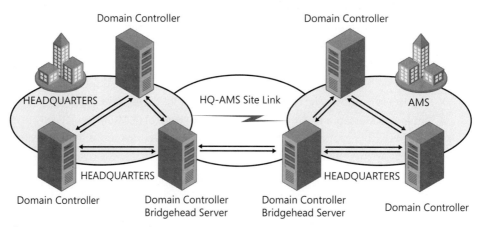

Figure 11-13   Sites, intrasite replication, bridgehead servers, and intersite replication

Bridgehead servers are selected automatically, and the ISTG creates the intersite replication topology to ensure that changes are replicated effectively between bridgeheads sharing a site link. Bridgeheads are selected per partition, so it is possible that one DC in a site might be the bridgehead server for the schema and another might be for the configuration. However, you will usually find that one domain controller is the bridgehead server for all partitions in a site unless there are domain controllers from other domains or application directory partitions, in which case bridgeheads will be chosen for those partitions.

Preferred Bridgehead Servers

You can also designate one or more *preferred bridgehead servers*. To designate a domain controller as a preferred bridgehead server, open the properties of the server object in the Active Directory Sites And Services snap-in, select the transport protocol, which will almost always be IP, and click Add.

You can configure more than one preferred bridgehead server for a site, but only one will be selected and used as the bridgehead. If that bridgehead fails, one of the other preferred bridgehead servers will be used.

It's important to understand that if you have specified one or more bridgehead servers and none of the bridgeheads is available, no other server is automatically selected, and replication does not occur for the site even if there are servers that could act as bridgehead servers. In an ideal world, you should not configure preferred bridgehead servers. However, performance considerations might suggest that you assign the bridgehead server role to domain controllers with greater system resources. Firewall considerations might also require that you assign a single server to act as a bridgehead instead of allowing Active Directory to select and possibly reassign bridgehead servers over time.

Configuring Intersite Replication

After you have created site links and the ISTG has generated connection objects to replicate partitions between bridgehead servers that share a site link, your work might be complete. In many environments, particularly those with straightforward network topologies, site links might be sufficient to manage intersite replication. In more complex networks, however, you can configure additional components and properties of replication.

Site Link Transitivity

By default, site links are transitive. That means, continuing the example from earlier, that if Amsterdam and Headquarters sites are linked, and Headquarters and Seattle sites are linked, then Amsterdam and Seattle are transitively linked. This means, theoretically, that the ISTG could create a connection object directly between a bridgehead in Seattle and a bridgehead in Amsterdam, again working around the hub-and-spoke network topology.

You can disable site link transitivity by opening the properties of the IP transport in the Inter-Site Transports container and deselecting Bridge All Site Links. Before you do this in a production environment, be sure to spend time reading the technical resources about replication in the Windows Server technical libraries on Microsoft TechNet at *http://technet.microsoft.com*.

Exam Tip   For the certification exam, you need to know that site links are transitive by default, that transitivity can be disabled, and that when transitivity is disabled, you might want to build site link bridges.

Site Link Bridges

A site link bridge connects two or more site links in a way that creates a transitive link. Site link bridges are necessary only when you have cleared the Bridge All Site Links option for the transport protocol. Remember that site link transitivity is enabled by default, in which case site link bridges have no effect.

Figure 11-14 illustrates the use of a site link bridge in a forest in which site link transitivity has been disabled. By creating a site link bridge, AMS-HQ-SEA, that includes the HQ-AMS and HQ-SEA site links, those two site links become transitive, so a replication connection can be made between a domain controller in Amsterdam and a domain controller in Seattle.

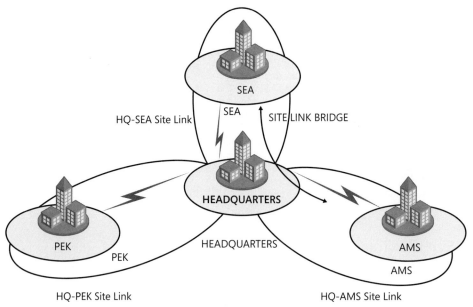

Figure 11-14   A site link bridge that includes the HQ-AMS and HQ-SEA site links

Site Link Costs

Site link costs are used to manage the flow of replication traffic when there is more than one route for replication traffic. You can configure site link cost to indicate that a link is faster, more reliable, or is preferred. Higher costs are used for slow links, and lower costs are used for fast links. Active Directory replicates using the connection with the lowest cost.

By default, all site links are configured with a cost of 100. To change the site link cost, open the properties of a site link and change the value in the Cost spin-box, shown in Figure 11-15.

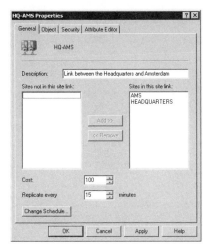

Figure 11-15   The properties of a site link

Returning to the example used earlier in the lesson, imagine if a site link was created between the Amsterdam and Beijing sites, as shown in Figure 11-16. Such a site link could be configured to allow replication between domain controllers in those two sites in the event that the links to the headquarters became unavailable. You might want to configure such a topology as part of a disaster recovery plan, for example.

With the default site link cost of 100 assigned to the AMS-PEK site link, Active Directory will replicate changes directly between Amsterdam and Beijing. If you configure the site link cost to 300, changes will replicate between Amsterdam and the Headquarters, then between the Headquarters and Beijing at a cost of 200 rather than directly over the AMS-PEK site link at a cost of 300.

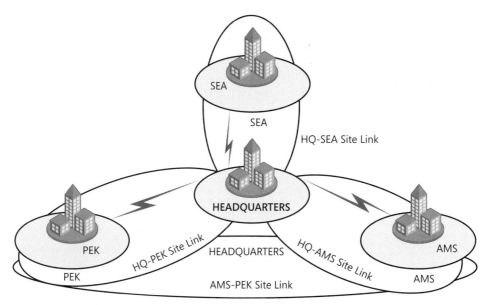

Figure 11-16 Site links and costs

Replication Frequency

Intersite replication is based only on polling; there is no notification. Every three hours, by default, a bridgehead server will poll its upstream replication partners to determine whether changes are available. This replication interval is too long for organizations that want changes to the directory to replicate more quickly. You can change the polling interval for each site link. Open the site link's properties and change the value in the Replicate Every spin-box, shown in Figure 11-15.

The minimum polling interval is 15 minutes. That means, using Active Directory's default replication configuration, a change made to the directory in one site will take several minutes before it is replicated to domain controllers in another site.

Replication Schedules

By default, replication occurs 24 hours a day. However, you can restrict intersite replication to specific times by changing the schedule attributes of a site link. Open the properties of a site link and click the Change Schedule button. Using the Schedule For dialog box shown in Figure 11-17, you can select the times during which the link is available for replication. The link shown in the figure does not replicate from 8:00 A.M. to 6:00 P.M. Monday through Friday.

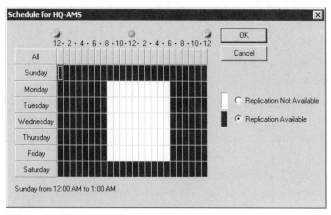

Figure 11-17   Site link schedule

You must be careful when scheduling site link availability. It is possible to schedule windows of availability that do not overlap, at which point replication will not happen. It's generally not recommended to configure link availability. If you do not require link scheduling, select the Ignore Schedules option in the properties of the IP transport protocol. This option causes any schedules for site link availability to be ignored, ensuring replication 24 hours a day over all site links.

Monitoring Replication

After you have implemented your replication configuration, you must be able to monitor replication for ongoing support, optimization, and troubleshooting. Two tools are particularly useful for reporting and analyzing replication: the Replication Diagnostics tool (*Repadmin.exe*) and Directory Server Diagnosis (*Dcdiag.exe*). This lesson introduces you to these powerful tools.

Repadmin.exe

The Replication Diagnostics tool, *Repadmin.exe*, is a command-line tool that enables you to report the status of replication on each domain controller. The information produced by *Repadmin.exe* can help you spot a potential problem before it gets out of control and troubleshoot problems with replication in the forest. You can view levels of detail down to the replication metadata for specific objects and attributes, enabling you to identify where and when a problematic change was made to Active Directory. You can even use *Repadmin.exe* to create the replication topology and force replication between domain controllers.

Like other command-line tools, you can type **repadmin /?** to see the usage information for the tool. Its basic syntax is as follows:

```
repadmin command arguments...
```

Repadmin.exe supports a number of commands that perform specific tasks. You can learn about each command by typing **repadmin /?:command**. Most commands require arguments. Many commands take a *DSA_LIST* parameter, which is simply a network label (DNS or NetBIOS name or IP address) of a domain controller. Some of the replication monitoring tasks you can perform with *Repadmin* are:

- **Displaying the replication partners for a domain controller** To display the replication connections of a domain controller, type **repadmin /showrepl DSA_LIST**. By default, *Repadmin.exe* shows only intersite connections. Add the */repsto* argument to see intersite connections as well.

- **Displaying connection objects for a domain controller** Type **repadmin /showconn DSA_LIST** to show the connection objects for a domain controller.

- **Displaying metadata about an object, its attributes, and replication** You can learn a lot about replication by examining an object on two different domain controllers to find out which attributes have or have not replicated. Type **repadmin /showobjmeta DSA_LIST Object**, where *DSA_LIST* indicates the domain controller(s) to query. (You can use an asterisk [*] to indicate all domain controllers.) *Object* is a unique identifier for the object, its DN, or its GUID, for example.

You can also make changes to your replication infrastructure by using *Repadmin*. Some of the management tasks you can perform are:

- **Launching the KCC** Type **repadmin /kcc** to force the KCC to recalculate the inbound replication topology for the server.

- **Forcing replication between two partners** You can use *Repadmin* to force replication of a partition between a source and a target domain controller. Type **repadmin /replicate Destination_DSA_LIST Source_DSA_Name Naming_Context**.

- **Synchronizing a domain controller with all replication partners** Type **repadmin /syncall DSA /A /e** to synchronize a domain controller with all its partners, including those in other sites.

Dcdiag.exe

The Directory Service Diagnosis tool, *Dcdiag.exe*, performs a number of tests and reports on the overall health of replication and security for AD DS. Run by itself, *Dcdiag.exe* performs summary tests and reports the results. On the other extreme, *Dcdiag.exe /c* performs almost every test. The output of tests can be redirected to files of various types, including XML. Type **dcdiag /?** for full usage information.

You can also specify one or more tests to perform using the */test:Test Name* parameter. Tests that are directly related to replication include:

- **FrsEvent**   Reports any operation errors in the file replication system (FRS).
- **DFSREvent**   Reports any operation errors in the DFS replication (DFS-R) system.
- **Intersite**   Checks for failures that would prevent or delay intersite replication.
- **KccEvent**   Identifies errors in the knowledge consistency checker.
- **Replications**   Checks for timely replication between domain controllers.
- **Topology**   Checks that the replication topology is fully connected for all DSAs.
- **VerifyReplicas**   Verifies that all application directory partitions are fully instantiated on all domain controllers hosting replicas.

NOTE *Repadmin.exe* and *Dcdiag.exe*

See the Help & Support Center for more information about *Repadmin.exe* and *Dcdiag.exe*.

PRACTICE **Configuring Replication**

In this practice, you will manage intrasite and intersite replication in the *contoso.com* domain. To perform the exercises in this practice, you must have completed the Lesson 1 practice as well as the Lesson 2 practice, "Replication and Directory Partitions," in this chapter.

▶ **Exercise 1   Create a Connection Object**

Configure direct replication between a domain controller that will be a standby operations master and the domain controller that is currently the operations master. Then, if the current operations master needs to be taken offline, the standby operations master is as up to date as possible with the operations master. In this exercise, you will create a connection object between SERVER01 and SERVER02, where SERVER02, the standby operations master, replicates from SERVER01, the current operations master.

1. Log on to SERVER01 as Administrator.
2. Open the Active Directory Sites And Services snap-in.
3. Expand Sites, HEADQUARTERS, Servers, and SERVER02.
4. Select the NTDS Settings node under SERVER02 in the console tree.
5. Right-click NTDS Settings and choose New Active Directory Domain Services Connection.
6. In the Find Active Directory Domain Controllers dialog box, select SERVER01 and click OK.

   Because the KCC has already created a connection from SERVER01 to SERVER02, a warning appears asking if you want to create another connection.
7. Click Yes.
8. In the New Object – Connection dialog box, type the name **SERVER01 – OPERATIONS MASTER** and click OK.

9.   Right-click the new connection object in the details pane and choose Properties.

10. Examine the properties of the connection object. Do not make any changes.

What partitions are replicated from SERVER01? Is SERVER02 a GC server?

11. Click OK to close the Properties dialog box.

12. Because the sample domain has only two DCs, and you will move the server in a later exercise, delete the connection object by right-clicking it and choosing Delete.

► **Exercise 2   Create Site Links**

In this exercise, you will create site links between the branch sites and the headquarters site.

1.   In the Active Directory Sites And Services snap-in, expand Inter-Site Transports.

2.   Select IP.

3.   Right-click DEFAULTIPSITELINK and choose Rename.

4.   Type **HQ-BRANCHA** and press Enter.

5.   Double-click HQ-BRANCHA.

6.   In the Sites In This Site Link list, select BRANCHB and click Remove. Click OK.

7.   Right-click IP and choose New Site Link.

8.   Type **HQ-BRANCHB** in the Name box.

9.   In the Sites Not In This Site Link list, select Headquarters and click Add.

10. In the Sites Not In This Site Link list, select BRANCHB and click Add.

11. Click OK.

► **Exercise 3   Designate a Preferred Bridgehead Server**

You can designate a preferred bridgehead server that will handle replication to and from its site. This is useful when you want to assign the role to a domain controller in a site with greater system resources or when firewall considerations require that the role be assigned to a single, fixed system. In this exercise, you will designate a preferred bridgehead server for the site.

1.   Expand Headquarters, Servers, and SERVER02.

2.   Right-click SERVER02 and choose Properties.

3.   In the Transports Available For Inter-Site Data Transfer list, select IP.

4.   Click Add, and then click OK.

It is recommended that if a site has a GC server, the domain controller acting as a GC server should be the preferred bridgehead server. When Active Directory designates a bridgehead server automatically, it selects a GC server if one is available.

► **Exercise 4   Configure Intersite Replication**

After you have created site links and, optionally, designated bridgehead servers, you can continue to refine and control replication by configuring properties of the site link. In this exercise, you will reduce the intersite replication polling frequency, and you will increase the cost of a site link.

1. Expand Inter-Site Transports.
2. Select the IP container in the console tree.
3. Double-click the HQ-BRANCHA site link.
4. In the Replicate Every spin-box, type **15** and click OK.
5. Double-click the HQ-BRANCHB site link.
6. In the Replicate Every box, type **15**.
7. Click the Change Schedule button.
8. Examine the Schedule For HQ-BRANCHB dialog box. Experiment with configuring the schedule but click Cancel when you are finished.
9. In the Cost spin-box, type **200**.
10. Click OK.

Lesson Summary

- Connection objects represent paths of replication between two domain controllers.
- Site links represent available network connectivity between two or more sites.
- Bridgehead servers in each site are responsible for replication to and from the site.
- The intersite topology generator (ISTG) creates connection objects between bridgehead servers that share a site link.
- If more than one connection is available, replication will proceed over the connection with the lowest cost.
- By default, site links are transitive. If you disable site link transitivity by clearing the Bridge All Site Links option in the properties of the intersite transport protocol, you might need to create site link bridges to create specific transitive links between two or more sites.

Lesson Review

You can use the following questions to test your knowledge of the information in Lesson 3, "Configuring Replication." The questions are also available on the companion CD if you prefer to review them in electronic form.

NOTE Answers

Answers to these questions and explanations of why each answer choice is right or wrong are located in the "Answers" section at the end of the book.

---

1. You are an administrator at Adventure Works. The Active Directory forest consists of three sites, Site A, Site B, and Site C. Site A and Site C are connected to Site B with a fast connection. Site A and Site C are connected to each other with a slow VPN connection. The Active Directory site link objects and their costs are as shown. You want to encourage replication to avoid the VPN connection. What should you do?

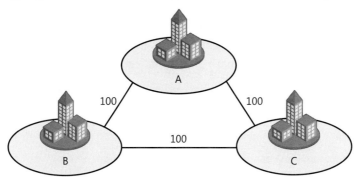

    A. Increase the cost of link A-B to 250.

    B. Increase the cost of link C-B to 250.

    C. Decrease the cost of links A-B and C-B to 75.

    D. Increase the cost of link A-C to 250.

2. You are an administrator at Adventure Works. The Active Directory forest consists of three sites, Site A, Site B, and Site C. The Active Directory site link objects and their costs are as shown. You want to ensure that all replication from Sites A and C goes to Site B before going to the other site. What should you do? (Choose all that apply. Each correct answer is part of the solution.)

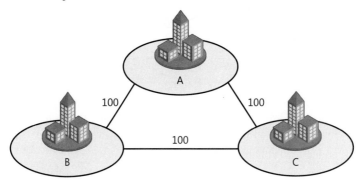

    A. Increase the cost of site link A-C to 300.

    B. Delete site link A-C.

    C. Deselect Bridge All Site Links.

    D. Reduce the costs of links A-B and B-C to 25.

3. The network infrastructure at Trey Research prevents direct IP connectivity between the data center and a research ship at sea. What must you do to support replication between the data center and the ship?

   A. Configure a separate domain in the forest for the ship.

   B. Increase the cost of the Active Directory site link containing the headquarters and the ship.

   C. Configure the domain controller on the ship as a preferred bridgehead server.

   D. Manually create a connection object between the domain controller on the ship and a domain controller at the headquarters.

4. You want to initiate replication manually between two domain controllers to verify that replication is functioning correctly. Which of the following tools can you use? (Choose all that apply.)

   A. The Active Directory Sites And Services snap-in

   B. *Repadmin.exe*

   C. *Dcdiag.exe*

   D. The Active Directory Domains And Trusts snap-in

Chapter Review

To further practice and reinforce the skills you learned in this chapter, you can perform the following tasks:

- Review the chapter summary.
- Review the list of key terms introduced in this chapter.
- Complete the case scenario. This scenario sets up a real-world situation involving the topics of this chapter and asks you to create a solution.
- Complete the suggested practices.
- Take a practice test.

Chapter Summary

- Domain controllers host replicas of Active Directory partitions: the schema, configuration, and domain naming contexts. You can configure domain controllers to host the partial attribute set (global catalog) or application directory partitions.
- Within a site, domain controllers replicate quickly, using a topology generated by the knowledge consistency checker (KCC), which is adjusted dynamically to ensure effective intersite replication.
- Between sites, the intersite topology generator (ISTG) creates a topology of connection objects between bridgehead servers in sites that share site links. Intersite replication is based on polling only, by default, with an initial frequency of every three hours.
- You can modify intersite replication behavior, including the replication frequency, site link costs, and preferred bridgehead servers.
- Advanced configuration is not generally necessary, but you can modify site link transitivity, create site link bridges, and configure site link schedules.
- The *Repadmin.exe* and *Dcdiag.exe* commands enable you to monitor and troubleshoot replication.

Key Terms

Use these key terms to understand better the concepts covered in this chapter.

- **intrasite**   Within a site.
- **intersite**   Between sites.
- **partial attribute set or global catalog (GC)**   A copy of every object from other domain naming contexts but a subset of attributes of those objects. The global catalog supports efficient forest-wide directory queries, provides universal group membership information at logon, and supports applications such as Exchange Server.
- **replica, partition, or naming context**   The top-level container of the Active Directory database. Partitions are replicated in their entirety. Every domain controller hosts a replica of the forest schema and configuration partitions. Each domain controller in a domain hosts a replica of that domain's naming context.
- **service localization**   The process by which a distributed service, available on more than one server, is provided to clients by a server in the clients' site or close to the clients' site. Domain controllers provide distributed services—authentication and directory access—and Active Directory sites and subnets localize the services so that clients use domain controllers in, or close to, their site.

Case Scenario

In the following case scenario, you will apply what you've learned about sites, subnets, partitions, and replication. You can find answers to these questions in the "Answers" section at the end of this book.

Case Scenario: Configuring Sites and Subnets

You are an administrator at Adventure Works. The Adventure Works network topology is illustrated as shown. Branch offices in Seattle, Chicago, and Miami are connected with fast, reliable links to the Denver site. Smaller branches in Portland and Fort Lauderdale are connected to Seattle and Miami, respectively. In Denver, the headquarters and the warehouse sites are connected with an extremely fast connection. There is one domain controller in each site except in the headquarters in Denver, where there are three. You are planning the Active Directory sites and replication for the domain.

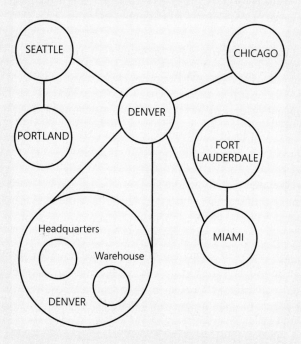

1. You want to ensure that, in Denver, any change to the directory replicates within one minute to all four domain controllers. How many Active Directory sites should you create for the Denver subnets?

2. A colleague recommends that you designate one of the domain controllers in the headquarters as a preferred bridgehead server. What are the advantages and disadvantages of doing so?

3. You want to ensure that replication follows a hub-and-spoke topology so that any change made to the directory in Denver replicates directly to all five branches and that any change made in one of the five branches replicates directly to Denver. Describe the site link changes you would make to support this goal.

4. For disaster planning purposes, you want the domain controller in the warehouse to be ready to take on forest and domain operations master roles performed by SERVER01 in the headquarters site. What change would you make to replication to support this goal?

Suggested Practices

To help you successfully master the exam objectives presented in this chapter, complete the following tasks.

Monitor and Manage Replication

In this practice, you will perform replication management and monitoring tasks, using both user interface and command-line tools. To perform these practices, you must have completed the practices in this chapter.

- **Practice 1**   Observe intersite replication by opening two instances of the Active Directory Users And Computers snap-in. In one instance, right-click the *contoso.com* domain, choose Change Domain Controller, and select SERVER01. In the other instance, right-click the *contoso.com* domain, choose Change Domain Controller, and select SERVER02. Using the SERVER01 snap-in, create an OU called People if it does not already exist. Within the People OU, create an OU called Temporary Employees. Using the SERVER02 snap-in, refresh the view to see that the objects were replicated successfully. Using the SERVER02 snap-in, create a new user named Replication Test. Confirm in the SERVER01 snap-in that the user object replicated.

- **Practice 2**   Observe the ICC and the ISTG by opening the Active Directory Sites And Services snap-in. Expand BRANCHA and Servers. Expand Headquarters and Servers. Drag SERVER02 from the HEADQUARTERS\Servers container to the BRANCHA\Servers container. In the SERVER01 Active Directory Users And Computers snap-in, create a new user object called Intersite Test 1. Examine the SERVER02 Active Directory Users And Computers snap-in. It is likely that the object replicated because the connection object between SERVER02 and SERVER01 continues to be treated as an intrasite replication connection. In the Active Directory Sites And Services snap-in, expand SERVER01, right-click NTDS Settings, choose All Tasks, and then select Check Replication Topology. Repeat the process with SERVER02. Refresh the Active Directory Sites And Services snap-in view. Select NTDS Settings in the SERVER01 container. You should see that the connection object from SERVER02 now shows that SERVER02 is in the BRANCHA site.

- **Practice 3**   Observe intersite replication and manual replication. In the SERVER01 Active Directory Users And Computers snap-in, add another user, named Intersite Test 2. In the SERVER02 snap-in, you should not see the object when you refresh the view. The servers are now replicated using intersite topology. In the Active Directory Sites And Services snap-in, select NTDS Settings under SERVER02. In the console details pane, right-click the connection object and choose Replicate Now.

Take a Practice Test

The practice tests on this book's companion CD offer many options. For example, you can test yourself on just one exam objective, or you can test yourself on all the 70-640 certification exam content. You can set up the test so that it closely simulates the experience of taking a certification exam, or you can set it up in study mode so that you can look at the correct answers and explanations after you answer each question.

MORE INFO   Practice tests

For details about all the practice test options available, see the "How to Use the Practice Tests" section in this book's introduction.

Chapter 12

Domains and Forests

In Chapter 1, "Installation," you learned that Active Directory Domain Services (AD DS) provides the foundation for an identity and access management solution, and you explored the creation of a simple AD DS infrastructure consisting of a single forest and a single domain. In subsequent chapters, you mastered the details of managing an AD DS environment. Now, you are ready to return to the highest level of an AD DS infrastructure and consider the model and functionality of your domains and forests. In this chapter, you will learn how to raise the domain and forest functionality levels within your environment, how to design the optimal AD DS infrastructure for your enterprise, how to migrate objects between domains and forests, and how to enable authentication and resource access across multiple domains and forests.

Exam objectives in this chapter:
■ Configuring the Active Directory Infrastructure
    ❑ Configure a forest or a domain.
    ❑ Configure trusts.

Lessons in this chapter:
■ Lesson 1: Understanding Domain and Forest Functional Levels 557
■ Lesson 2: Managing Multiple Domains and Trust Relationships 567

Before You Begin

To complete the practices in this chapter, you must have created two domain controllers, named SERVER01 and SERVER02, in a domain named *contoso.com*. See Chapter 1 and Chapter 10, "Domain Controllers," for detailed steps for this task.

Real World

Dan Holme

In some organizations, there is a perception that domain controllers should be the last systems to be upgraded. My experience, however, has been that domain controllers (DCs) should be among the first systems that you should upgrade (after testing the upgrade in a lab, of course). Domain controllers are the cornerstone of identity and access management in your enterprise AD DS forest. Because of that, you should ensure that, wherever possible, DCs are dedicated—serving only the AD DS role and related core services, such as DNS. If your DCs are dedicated, the risk associated with upgrading them diminishes significantly—there are far fewer moving parts that could cause problems during an upgrade. Additionally, the sooner you upgrade your DCs, the sooner you can raise the domain and forest functional levels.

Functional levels enable the newer capabilities added by Microsoft Windows Server 2003 and Windows Server 2008. In return for added functionality, you are restricted as to the versions of Microsoft Windows that are supported for the domain controllers in the domain. (Member servers and workstations can run any version of Windows.) Some of the functionality, such as linked-value replication, last logon information, read-only domain controllers, fine-grained password policies, and Distributed File System Replication (DFS-R) of System Volume (SYSVOL), have a profound impact on the day-to-day security, management, and flexibility of AD DS. I encourage you to move with a reasonable but quick pace toward upgrading your domain controllers to Windows Server 2008 so you can raise the domain and forest functional levels to take advantage of these capabilities. They make a big difference.

Lesson 1: Understanding Domain and Forest Functional Levels

As you introduce Windows Server 2008 domain controllers into your domains and forest, you can begin to take advantage of new capabilities in Active Directory directory service. Domain and forest functional levels are operating modes of domains and forests, respectively. Functional levels determine the versions of Windows that you can use as domain controllers and the availability of Active Directory features.

After this lesson, you will be able to:
- Understand domain and forest functional levels.
- Raise domain and forest functional levels.
- Identify capabilities added by each functional level.

Estimated lesson time: 45 minutes

Understanding Functional Levels

Functional levels are like switches that enable new functionality offered by each version of Windows. Windows Server 2003 added several features to Active Directory, and Windows Server 2008 continues the evolution of AD DS. These features are not backward compatible, so if you have DCs running Windows 2000 Server, you cannot enable the functionality offered by later versions of Windows, so the newer functionality is disabled. Similarly, until all DCs are running Windows Server 2008, you cannot implement its enhancements to AD DS. Raising the functional level entails two major tasks:

- All domain controllers must be running the correct version of Windows Server.
- You must manually raise the functional level. It does not happen automatically.

NOTE Functional levels, operating system versions, and domain controllers

Remember that only domain controllers determine your ability to set a functional level. You can have member servers and workstations running any version of Windows within a domain or forest at any functional level.

Domain Functional Levels

The domain functional level affects the Active Directory features available within the domain and determines the versions of Windows that are supported for domain controllers within the domain. In previous versions of Windows, domain functional levels and modes, as they were called in Windows 2000 Server, supported domain controllers running Microsoft Windows NT 4.0. That support has ended with Windows Server 2008. All domain controllers must be running Windows 2000 Server or later before you can add the first Windows Server 2008 domain controller to the domain. Windows Server 2008 Active Directory supports three domain functional levels:

- Windows 2000 Native
- Windows Server 2003
- Windows Server 2008

Windows 2000 Native

The Windows 2000 Native domain functional level is the lowest functional level that supports a Windows Server 2008 domain controller. The following operating systems are supported for domain controllers:

- Windows 2000 Server
- Windows Server 2003
- Windows Server 2008

If you have domain controllers running Windows 2000 Server or Windows Server 2003, or if you expect that you might add one or more domain controllers running those previous versions of Windows, you should leave the domain at Windows 2000 Native functional level.

Windows Server 2003

After you have removed or upgraded all domain controllers running Windows 2000 Server, the domain functional level can be raised to Windows Server 2003. At this functional level, the domain can no longer support domain controllers running Windows 2000 Server, so all domain controllers must be running one of the following two operating systems:

- Windows Server 2003
- Windows Server 2008

Windows Server 2003 domain functional level adds a number of new features offered at the Windows 2000 Native domain functional level. These features include the following:

- **Domain controller rename**   The domain management tool, *Netdom.exe*, can be used to prepare for domain controller rename.
- **The *lastLogonTimestamp* attribute**   When a user or computer logs on to the domain, the *lastLogonTimestamp* attribute is updated with the logon time. This attribute is replicated within the domain.
- **The *userPassword* attribute**   Security principals in Active Directory include users, computers, and groups. A fourth object class, *inetOrgPerson*, is similar to a user and is used to integrate with several non-Microsoft directory services. At the Windows Server 2003 domain functional level, you can set the *userPassword* attribute as the effective password on both *inetOrgPerson* and *user* objects.

- **Default user and computer container redirection**   In Chapter 5, "Computers," you learned that you can use the *Redirusr.exe* and *Redircmp.exe* commands to redirect the default user and computer containers. Doing so causes new accounts to be created in specific organizational units rather than in the Users and Computers containers.

- **Authorization Manager policies**   Authorization Manager, a tool that can be used to provide authorization by applications, can store its authorization policies in AD DS.

- **Constrained delegation**   Applications can take advantage of the secure delegation of user credentials by means of the Kerberos authentication protocol. Delegation can be configured to be allowed only to specific destination services.

- **Selective authentication**   In Lesson 2, "Managing Multiple Domains and Trust Relationships," you will learn to create trust relationships between your domain and another domain or forest. Selective authentication enables you to specify the users and groups from the trusted domain or forest who are allowed to authenticate to servers in your forest.

Windows Server 2008

When all domain controllers are running Windows Server 2008, and you are confident that you will not need to add domain controllers running previous versions of Windows, you can raise the domain functional level to Windows Server 2008. Windows Server 2008 domain functional level supports domain controllers running only one operating system—Windows Server 2008.

Windows Server 2008 domain functional level adds four domain-wide features to AD DS:

- **DFS-R of SYSVOL**   In Chapter 10, you learned to configure SYSVOL so that it is replicated with Distributed File System Replication (DFS-R) instead of with File Replication Service (FRS). DFS-R provides a more robust and detailed replication of SYSVOL contents.

- **Advanced Encryption Services**   You can increase the security of authentication with Advanced Encryption Services (AES 128 and AES 256) support for the Kerberos protocol. AES replaces the RC4-HMAC (Hash Message Authentication Code) encryption algorithm.

- **Last interactive logon information**   When a user logs on to the domain, several attributes of the user object are updated with the time, the workstation to which the user logged on, and the number of failed logon attempts since the last logon.

- **Fine-grained password policies**   In Chapter 8, "Authentication," you learned about fine-grained password policies, which enable you to specify unique password policies for users or groups in the domain.

Raising the Domain Functional Level

You can raise the domain functional level after all domain controllers are running a supported version of Windows and when you are confident you will not have to add domain controllers running unsupported versions of Windows. To raise the domain functional level, open the Active Directory Domains And Trusts snap-in, right-click the domain, and choose Raise Domain Functional Level. The dialog box shown in Figure 12-1 enables you to select a higher domain functional level.

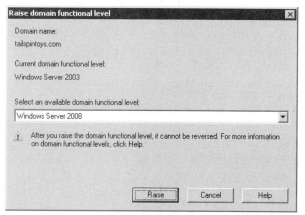

Figure 12-1   The Raise Domain Functional Level dialog box

IMPORTANT   One-way operation

Raising the domain functional level is a one-way operation. You cannot roll back to a previous domain functional level.

You can also raise the domain functional level by using the Active Directory Users And Computers snap-in. Right-click the domain and choose Raise Domain Functional Level, or right-click the root node of the snap-in and choose Raise Domain Functional Level from the All Tasks menu.

Forest Functional Levels

Just as domain functional levels enable certain domain-wide functionality and determine the versions of Windows that are supported for domain controllers in the domain, forest functional levels enable forest-wide functionality and determine the operating systems supported for domain controllers in the entire forest. Windows Server 2008 Active Directory supports three forest functional levels:

- Windows 2000

- Windows Server 2003
- Windows Server 2008

Each functional level is described in the following sections.

Windows 2000

Windows 2000 forest functional level is the baseline, default functional level. At Windows 2000 functional level, domains can be running at any supported domain functional level:

- Windows 2000 Native
- Windows Server 2003
- Windows Server 2008

You can raise the forest functional level after all domains in the forest have been raised to the equivalent domain functional level.

Windows Server 2003

After all domains in the forest are at the Windows Server 2003 domain functional level, and when you do not expect to add any new domains with Windows 2000 Server domain controllers, you can raise the forest functional level to Windows Server 2003. At this forest functional level, domains can be running at the following domain functional levels:

- Windows Server 2003
- Windows Server 2008

The following features are enabled at the Windows Server 2003 forest functional level:

- **Forest trusts**   In Lesson 2, you will learn to create trust relationships between forests.
- **Domain rename**   You can rename a domain within a forest.
- **Linked-value replication**   At Windows 2000 forest functional level, a change to a group's membership results in the replication of the entire multivalued *member* attribute of the group. This can lead to increased replication traffic on the network and the potential loss of membership updates when a group is changed concurrently at different domain controllers. It also leads to a recommended cap of 5,000 members in any one group. Linked-value replication, enabled at the Windows Server 2003 forest functional level, replicates an individual membership change rather than the entire *member* attribute. This uses less bandwidth and prevents you from losing updates when a group is changed concurrently at different domain controllers.
- **Support for read-only domain controllers**   Chapter 8 discussed read-only domain controllers (RODCs). RODCs are supported at the Windows Server 2003 forest functional level. The RODC itself must be running Windows Server 2008.

Quick Check

- You want to add an RODC to a domain with Windows Server 2003 domain controllers. The domain is at the Windows Server 2003 functional level and already includes one Windows Server 2008 domain controller. The forest is at the Windows 2000 functional level. Which two things must you do prior to adding the RODC?

Quick Check Answer

- You must raise the forest functional level to Windows Server 2003, and you must run *Adprep /rodcprep*.

- **Improved Knowledge Consistency Checker (KCC) algorithms and scalability**   The intersite topology generator (ISTG) uses improved algorithms that enable AD DS to support replication in forests with more than 100 sites. At the Windows 2000 forest functional level, you must manually intervene to create replication topologies for forests with hundreds of sites. Additionally, the election of the ISTG uses an algorithm that is more efficient than at Windows 2000 forest functional level.

- **Conversion of *inetOrgPerson* objects to *user* objects**   You can convert an instance of an *inetOrgPerson* object, used for compatibility with certain non-Microsoft directory services, into an instance of class *user*. You can also convert a *user* object to an *inetOrgPerson* object.

- **Support for *dynamicObject* auxiliary class**   The schema allows instances of the dynamic auxiliary class in domain directory partitions. This object class can be used by certain applications and by developers.

- **Support for application basic groups and LDAP query groups**   Two new group types, called *application basic groups* and *LDAP query groups*, can be used to support role-based authorization in applications that use Authorization Manager.

- **Deactivation and redefinition of attributes and object classes**   Although you cannot delete an attribute or object class in the schema, at Windows Server 2003 for forest level, you can deactivate or redefine attributes or object classes.

Windows Server 2008

The Windows Server 2008 forest functional level does not add new forest-wide features. However, after the forest is configured to Windows Server 2008 forest functional level, new domains added to the forest will operate at Windows Server 2008 domain functional level by default. At this forest functional level, all domains must be at Windows Server 2008 domain functional level, which means that all domain controllers must be running Windows Server 2008.

Raising the Forest Functional Level

Use the Active Directory Domains and Trusts snap-in to raise the forest functional level. Right-click the root node of the Active Directory Domains And Trusts snap-in, and choose Raise Forest Functional Level. The dialog box shown in Figure 12-2 enables you to choose a higher forest functional level.

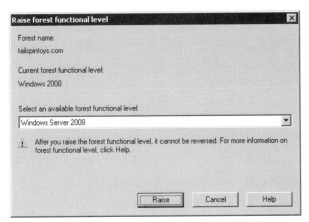

Figure 12-2   The Raise Forest Functional Level dialog box

Raise the forest functional level only when you are confident that you will not add new domains at unsupported domain functional levels. You cannot roll back to a previous forest functional level after raising it.

Exam Tip   Be sure to memorize the functionality that is enabled at each domain and forest functional level. Pay particular attention to the capabilities that affect you as an administrator.

PRACTICE Raising the Domain and Forest Functional Levels

In this practice, you will raise domain and forest functional levels. To perform the exercises in this practice, you must prepare at least one domain controller in a new domain in a new forest. Install a new full installation of Windows Server 2008.

To perform this exercise, you will need a new server running Windows Server 2008 full installation. The server must be named SERVERTST. Its configuration should be as follows:

- Computer Name: SERVERTST
- IPv4 address: 10.0.0.111
- Subnet Mask: 255.255.255.0
- Default Gateway: 10.0.0.1
- DNS Server: 10.0.0.111

Run *Dcpromo.exe* and create a new forest and a new domain named *tailspintoys.com*. Set the forest functional level to Windows 2000 and the domain functional level to Windows 2000 Native. Install DNS on the server. You will be warned that the server has a dynamic IP address. Click Yes. Also click Yes when you are informed that a DNS delegation cannot be created. Refer to Lesson 1, "Installing Active Directory Domain Services," of Chapter 1 for detailed steps to install Windows Server 2008 and to promote a domain controller as a new domain in a new forest.

In the *tailspintoys.com* domain, create two first-level organizational units (OUs) named Clients and People.

▶ **Exercise 1   Experience Disabled Functionality**

In this exercise, you will attempt to take advantage of capabilities supported at higher domain functional levels. You will see that these capabilities are not supported.

1. Log on to SERVERTST as the domain's Administrator.
2. Open a command prompt.
3. Type **redircmp.exe "ou=clients,dc=tailspintoys,dc=com"** and press Enter.

   A message appears indicating that redirection was not successful. This is because the domain functional level is not at least Windows Server 2003.
4. Type **redirusr.exe "ou=people,dc=tailspintoys,dc=com"** and press Enter.

   A message appears indicating that redirection was not successful. This is because the domain functional level is not at least Windows Server 2003.
5. Open the Active Directory Users And Computers snap-in.
6. Click the View menu, and select Advanced Features.
7. Double-click the Administrator account in the Users container.
8. Click the Attribute Editor tab.
9. Locate the *lastLogonTimestamp* attribute. Note that its value is *<not set>*.

▶ **Exercise 2   Raise the Domain Functional Level**

In this exercise, you will raise the domain functional level of the *tailspintoys.com* domain.

1. Open Active Directory Domains And Trusts.
2. Right-click the *tailspintoys.com* domain, and choose Raise Domain Functional Level.
3. Confirm that the Select An Available Domain Functional Level drop-down list indicates Windows Server 2003.
4. Click Raise. Click OK to confirm your change.

   A message appears informing you the functional level was raised successfully.
5. Click OK.

▶ **Exercise 3   Test Windows Server 2003 Domain Functional Level**

You will now discover that previously disabled functionality is now available.

1. Log off and log on as the domain Administrator.
2. Open a command prompt.
3. Type **redircmp.exe "ou=clients,dc=tailspintoys,dc=com"** and press Enter.
   A message appears indicating redirection was successful.
4. Type **redirusr.exe "ou=people,dc=tailspintoys,dc=com"** and press Enter.
   A message appears indicating redirection was successful.
5. Open the Active Directory Users And Computers snap-in.
6. Click the View menu, and ensure that Advanced Features is selected.
7. Double-click the Administrator account in the Users container.
8. Click the Attribute Editor tab.
9. Locate the *lastLogonTimestamp* attribute. Note that its value is now populated.
10. At the command prompt, type **dfsrmig /setglobalstate 0** and press Enter.
    A message appears stating that this function is available only at Windows Server 2008 domain functional level. In Chapter 10, you raised the domain functional level to Windows Server 2008 to configure DFS-R migration of SYSVOL.

Lesson Summary

- Domain and forest functional levels determine which capabilities of Active Directory are supported and which versions of Windows are supported on domain controllers.
- The Windows Server 2003 and Windows Server 2008 domain functional levels offer significant new functionality.
- The Windows Server 2003 forest functional level enables linked-value replication, supports RODCs, and provides other capabilities. The Windows Server 2008 forest functional level adds no new functionality.

Lesson Review

You can use the following questions to test your knowledge of the information in Lesson 1, "Understanding Domain and Forest Functional Levels." The questions are also available on the companion CD if you prefer to review them in electronic form.

NOTE Answers

Answers to these questions and explanations of why each answer choice is right or wrong are located in the "Answers" section at the end of the book.

---

1. You want to raise the domain functional level of a domain in the *contoso.com* forest. Which tool can you use? (Choose all that apply.)

   A. Active Directory Users And Computers

   B. Active Directory Schema

   C. Active Directory Sites And Services

   D. Active Directory Domains And Trusts

2. You are an administrator of the *contoso.com* domain. You want to add a read-only domain controller to a domain with one Windows Server 2003 domain controller and one Windows 2008 domain controller. Which of the following must be done before adding a new server as an RODC? (Choose all that apply. Each correct answer is part of the solution.)

   A. Upgrade the Windows 2003 domain controller to Windows Server 2008.

   B. Raise the domain functional level to Windows Server 2003.

   C. Raise the domain functional level to Windows Server 2008.

   D. Raise the forest functional level to Windows Server 2003.

   E. Run *Adprep /rodcprep*.

   F. Run *Adprep /forestprep*.

3. You have just finished upgrading all domain controllers in the *contoso.com* domain to Windows Server 2008. Domain controllers in the *subsidiary.contoso.com* domain will be upgraded in three months. You want to configure fine-grained password policies for several groups of users in *contoso.com*. What must you do first?

   A. Install a read-only domain controller.

   B. Run *Dfsrmig.exe*.

   C. Raise the forest functional level.

   D. Install the Group Policy Management Console (GPMC) feature.

Lesson 2: Managing Multiple Domains and Trust Relationships

Previous chapters in this training kit have prepared you to configure, administer, and manage a single domain. However, your enterprise Active Directory infrastructure might include a multidomain forest or even more than one forest. You might need to move objects between domains or restructure your domain model entirely. You might also be required to enable authentication and access to resources across domains and forests. In this lesson, you will learn the skills required to support multiple domains and forests.

After this lesson, you will be able to:
- Design an effective domain and tree structure for AD DS.
- Identify the role of the Active Directory Migration Tool and the issues related to object migration and domain restructure.
- Understand trust relationships.
- Configure, administer, and secure trust relationships.

Estimated lesson time: 60 minutes

Defining Your Forest and Domain Structure

With the perspective you have gained from the previous 11 chapters of this training kit, you are prepared to consider the design of your Active Directory forest, trees, and domains. Interestingly, the best practices guidance regarding forest and domain structure has evolved as enterprises around the world have put Active Directory into production in every conceivable configuration and as the Active Directory feature set has grown.

Dedicated Forest Root Domain

In the early days of Active Directory, it was recommended to create a dedicated forest root domain. You'll recall from Chapter 1 and Chapter 10 that the forest root domain is the first domain in the forest. A dedicated forest root domain's exclusive purpose is to administer the forest infrastructure. It contains, by default, the single master operations for the forest. It also contains highly sensitive groups, such as Enterprise Admins and Schema Admins, that can have far-reaching impact on the forest. The theory was that the dedicated forest root would enhance the security around these forest-wide functions. The dedicated forest root domain would also be less likely to become obsolete and would provide easier transfer of ownership. Underneath the dedicated forest root, according to early recommendations, would be a single global child domain with all the objects one thinks of in a domain: users, groups, computers, and so on. The structure would look something like Figure 12-3.

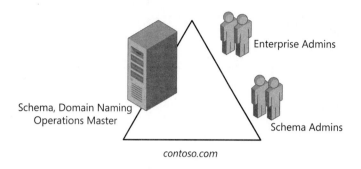

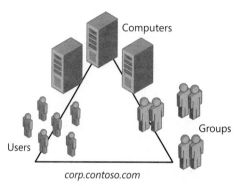

Figure 12-3   Example of a forest root domain

A Single-Domain Forest

NOTE   **Single-domain forest the new recommendation**

It is no longer recommended to implement a dedicated forest root domain for most enterprises. A single-domain forest is the most common design recommendation. There is no single design that is appropriate for every organization, so you must examine the characteristics of your enterprise against the design criteria presented later in this lesson.

After nine years on the market, Active Directory is better understood, and the former recommendation no longer applies. It is now recommended, for most organizations, to build a forest with a single domain. The experience and knowledge that have led to the change in guidance take into account that:

- There are risks and costs associated with any multidomain forest, as you'll learn later in this lesson. A single domain bears the lowest hardware and support cost and reduces certain risks.

- There are not yet tools that enable an enterprise to perform pruning and grafting of Active Directory trees. In other words, you cannot break a domain off of your tree and transplant it in the forest of another enterprise. If that were possible, a dedicated forest root that you could maintain while transferring domains in and out of your forest would make more sense.

- You can implement least-privilege security within a single domain that is at least as secure, if not more secure, than in a forest with a dedicated forest root and a child domain.

Therefore, when you consider your domain design, you should begin with the assumption that you will have a single domain in your forest.

Multiple-Domain Forests

In some scenarios, a multiple-domain forest is required. The important point to remember is that you should never create a multiple-domain forest simply to reflect the organizational structure of your business. That structure—the business units, divisions, departments, and offices—will change over time. The logical structure of your directory service should not be dependent solely on organizational characteristics.

Instead, your domain model should be derived from the characteristics of domains themselves. Certain properties of a domain affect all objects within the domain, and if that consistent effect is not appropriate for your business requirements, you must create additional domains. A domain is characterized by the following:

- **A single domain partition, replicated to all domain controllers**   The domain naming context contains the objects for users, computers, groups, policies, and other domain resources. It is replicated to every domain controller in the domain. If you need to partition replication for network topology considerations, you must create separate domains. Consider, however, that Active Directory replication is extremely efficient and can support large domains over connections with minimal bandwidth.

  If there are legal or business requirements that restrict replication of certain data to locations where you maintain domain controllers, you need to either avoid storing that data in the domain partition or create separate domains to segregate replication. In such cases, you should also ensure that the global catalog (GC) is not replicating that data.

- **A single Kerberos policy**   The default Kerberos policy settings in AD DS are sufficient for most enterprises. If, however, you need distinct Kerberos policies, you will require distinct domains.

- **A single DNS namespace**   An Active Directory domain has a single DNS domain name. If you need multiple domain names, you would need multiple domains. However, give serious consideration to the costs and risks of multiple domains before modeling your directory service domains to match arbitrary DNS name requirements.

In domains running domain functional levels lower than Windows Server 2008, a domain can support only one password and account lockout policy. Therefore, in prior versions of Windows, an organization requiring multiple password policies would need multiple domains to support that requirement. This is no longer the case in Windows Server 2008, which, at Windows Server 2008 domain functional level, can support fine-grained password policies.

Adding domains to a forest increases administrative and hardware costs. Each domain must be supported by at least two domain controllers, which must be backed up, secured, and managed. Even more domain controllers might be required to support cross-domain resource access in a geographically distributed enterprise. Additional domains can result in the need to move users between domains, which is more complicated than moving users between OUs. Group Policy objects and access control settings that are common for the enterprise will have to be duplicated for each domain.

These are just a few of the costs associated with a multiple-domain environment. There are also risks involved with having multiple domains. Most of these risks relate to the fact that a domain is not a security boundary—a forest is the security boundary. Within a forest, service administrators can cause forest-wide damage. There are several categories of vulnerability whereby a compromised administrative account, or an administrator with bad intent, could cause denial of service or damage to the integrity of the forest.

For example, an administrator in any domain can create universal groups, the membership of which is replicated to the GC. By creating multiple universal groups and overpopulating the *member* attribute, excessive replication could lead to denial of service on domain controllers acting as domain controllers in other domains. An administrator in any domain could also restore an outdated backup of the directory, which could corrupt the forest.

MORE INFO   **Security considerations for domain and forest design**

For more information about the security considerations related to domain and forest design, see "Best Practices for Delegating Active Directory Administration" at *http://technet2.microsoft.com /windowsserver/en/library/e5274d27-88e5-4043-8f12-a8fa71cbcd521033.mspx.*

Given the costs and risks of multiple domains, it is highly recommended to construct a single-domain forest. The most common driver to multiple-domain forests is a significant requirement related to the replication of the domain naming context.

In a multidomain forest, it might make sense to create a dedicated forest root domain as an empty domain to act as the trust root for the forest. Trust roots will be discussed later in this lesson.

Multiple Trees

Remember that a tree is defined as a contiguous DNS namespace. If you have more than one domain, you can decide whether those domains share a contiguous DNS namespace and form a single tree, as shown at the top of Figure 12-4, or are in a noncontiguous DNS namespace, thus forming multiple trees, as shown on the bottom of Figure 12-4.

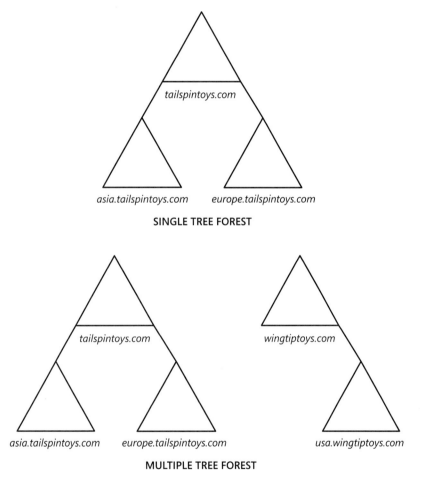

Figure 12-4 Forests with a single tree or multiple trees

Multiple Forests

A forest is an instance of Active Directory. All domains and domain controllers in a forest share replicas of the schema and configuration. Domain controllers that are GC servers host partial attribute sets for all objects in other domains in the forest. Domains in a forest share transitive, two-way trusts, meaning that all users in the domain belong to the Authenticated Users special identity in every domain. The forest's Enterprise Admins, Schema Admins, and Administrators groups in the forest root domain wield significant power over all objects in the forest.

If any of these characteristics of a forest are at odds with your business requirements, you might need multiple forests. In fact, given the market's current concerns with security, many consultants are recommending that organizations design either a single-domain forest or use multiple forests. Cross-forest trusts, discussed later in this lesson, and Active Directory Federation Services (AD FS) make it easier to manage authentication in multiple-forest enterprises.

MORE INFO   Planning the architecture

For more information about planning the architecture of an AD DS enterprise, see *http://technet2.microsoft.com/windowsserver2008/en/library/b1baa483-b2a3-4e03-90a6-d42f64b42fc31033.mspx?mfr=true.*

Moving Objects Between Domains and Forests

In multidomain scenarios, you might need to move users, groups, or computers between domains or forests to support business operations. You might need to move large quantities of users, groups, or computers between domains or forests to implement mergers and acquisitions or to restructure your domain model.

In each of these tasks, you move or copy the accounts from one domain (the *source* domain) into another domain (the *target* domain). Domain restructuring terminology, concepts, and procedures apply to *inter-forest migration* (between a Windows NT 4.0 or Active Directory source domain and an Active Directory target domain in a separate forest) and to *intra-forest migration* (that is, the restructuring or moving of accounts between domains in the same forest).

An inter-forest domain restructure preserves the existing source domain and clones (or copies) accounts into the target domain. This nondestructive method enables an enterprise to time the transition and even migrate in phases. Operations go uninterrupted because both domains are maintained in parallel to support operations for users in either domain. This method also provides a level of rollback because the original environment remains unaltered in any significant way. After the migration is complete, you can simply decommission the source domain by moving any remaining accounts, member servers, and workstations into the new domain and then taking source DCs offline, at which point, you can redeploy those DCs for roles in the new domain.

An intra-forest migration involves moving objects from the source domain to the target domain without decommissioning the source domain. After you have migrated objects, you can restructure your domains to consolidate operations and build a domain and OU structure that more accurately reflects your administrative model. Many organizations consolidate multiple domains into one Active Directory domain. This consolidation can result in cost savings and simplified administration by reducing administrative complexity and the cost of supporting your Active Directory environment.

Understanding the Active Directory Migration Tool

The Active Directory Migration Tool version 3 (ADMT v3) can perform object migration and security translation tasks. You can download ADMT v3 from *http://go.microsoft.com/fwlink/ ?LinkID=75627*. On that page, you will also find a detailed guide to the tool.

You can use ADMT to migrate objects between a source and a target domain. The migration can take place between domains in the same forest (an intra-forest migration) or between domains in different forests (an inter-forest migration). The ADMT provides wizards that automate migration tasks such as migrating users, groups, service accounts, computers, and trusts and performing security translation. You can perform these tasks, using the ADMT console or the command line, where you can simplify and automate the *Admt.exe* command with option files that specify parameters for the migration task. Then, with a simple text file, you can list objects to migrate rather than have to enter each object on the command line. ADMT also provides interfaces that enable you to script migration tasks with languages such as Microsoft VBScript. Run the ADMT console and open the online Help function for details about how to use ADMT from the command line and about scripting the ADMT.

When performing migration tasks, ADMT enables you to simulate the migration so that you can evaluate potential results and errors without making changes to the target domain. Wizards provide the Test The Migration Settings And Migrate Later option. You can then configure the migration task, test the settings, and review the log files and wizard-generated reports. After identifying and resolving any problems, you can perform the migration task. You will repeat this process of testing and analyzing results as you migrate users, groups, and computers and perform security translations.

Security Identifiers and Migration

Uninterrupted resource access is the primary concern during any migration. Further, to perform a migration, you must be comfortable with the concepts of security identifiers (SIDs), tokens, access control lists (ACLs), and *sIDHistory*.

SIDs are domain-unique values that are assigned to the accounts of security principals—users, groups, and computers, for example—when those accounts are created. When a user logs on, a token is generated that includes the primary SID of the user account and the SIDs of groups to which the user belongs. The token thus represents the user with all the SIDs associated with the user and the user's group memberships.

Resources are secured using a security descriptor (SD) that describes the permissions, ownership, extended rights, and auditing of the resource. Within the SD are two ACLs. The system ACL (SACL) describes auditing. The discretionary ACL (DACL) describes resource access permissions. Many administrators and documents refer to the DACL as the ACL. The DACL lists permissions associated with security principals. Within the list, individual access control entries (ACEs) link a specific permission with the SID of a security principal. The ACE can be an allow or deny permission.

When a user attempts to access a resource, the Local Security Authority Subsystem (LSASS) compares the SIDs in the user's token against the SIDs in the ACEs in the resource's ACL.

When you migrate accounts to a new domain, the accounts are copied or cloned from the source domain to the target domain. New SIDs are generated for the accounts in the target domain, so the SIDs of new accounts will not be the same as the SIDs of the accounts in the source domain. That is, even though the cloned accounts have the same name and many of the same properties, because the SIDs are different, the accounts are technically different and will not have access to resources in the source domain. You have two ways to address this problem: *sIDHistory* or security translation:

■ ***sIDHistory*** Enterprises typically prefer to take advantage of the *sIDHistory* attribute to perform effective domain restructuring. The capitalization, which appears odd, reflects the capitalization of the attribute in the AD schema. AD security principals (which include users, groups, and computers) have a principal SID and a *sIDHistory* attribute, which can contain one or more SIDs that are also associated with the account. When an account is copied to a target domain, the unique principal SID is generated by Active Directory in the target domain. Optionally, the *sIDHistory* attribute can be loaded with the SID of the account in the source domain. When a user logs on to an Active Directory domain, the user's token is populated with the principal SID and the *sIDHistory* of the user account and groups to which the user belongs. The LSASS uses the SIDs from the *sIDHistory* just like any other SID in the token to maintain the user's access to resources in the source domain.

- **Security translation**   Security translation is the process of examining each resource's SD, including its ACLs, identifying each SID that refers to an account in the source domain and replacing that SID with the SID of the account in the target domain. The process of remapping ACLs (and other elements in the SD) to migrated accounts in the target domain is also called re-ACLing. As you can imagine, security translation or re-ACLing would be a tedious process to perform manually in anything but the simplest environment. Migration tools such as ADMT automate security translation. ADMT can translate the SDs and policies of resources in the source domain to refer to the corresponding accounts in the target domain. Specifically, ADMT can translate:
  - ❏ File and folder permissions.
  - ❏ Printer permissions.
  - ❏ Share permissions.
  - ❏ Registry permissions.
  - ❏ User rights.
  - ❏ Local profiles, which involves changing file, folder, and registry permissions.
  - ❏ Group memberships.

In most domain restructuring and migration projects, *sIDHistory* is used to maintain access and functionality during the migration; then, security translation is performed.

MORE INFO   Domain migration

For more information about domain migration, SIDs, and SID history, see the "Domain Migration Cookbook" at *http://technet.microsoft.com/en-us/library/bb727135.aspx*.

Group Membership

The final concern related to resource access is that of group membership. Global groups can contain members only from the same domain. Therefore, if you clone a user to the target domain, the new user account cannot be a member of the global groups in the source domain to which the source user account belonged.

To address this issue in an inter-forest migration, you will first migrate global groups to the target domain. Those global groups will maintain the source groups' SIDs in their *sIDHistory* attributes, thus maintaining resource access. Then, you will migrate users. As you migrate users, ADMT evaluates the membership of the source account and adds the new account to the same group in the target domain. If the group does not yet exist in the target domain, ADMT can create it automatically. In the end, the user account in the target domain will belong to global groups in the target domain. The user and the user's groups will contain the SIDs of the source accounts in their *sIDHistory* attributes. Therefore, the user will be able to access resources in the source domain that have permissions assigned to the source accounts.

In an intra-forest migration, the process works differently. A global group is created in the target domain as a universal group so that it can contain users from both the source and the target domains. The new group gets a new SID, but its *sIDHistory* is populated with the SID of the global group in the source domain, thereby maintaining resource access for the new group. After all users have been migrated from the source to the target domain, the scope of the group is changed back to global.

Other Migration Concerns

You must address a number of issues in planning for and executing the migration of objects between domains and forests. Each of the concerns is detailed in the ADMT user guide, available from the ADMT download page listed earlier. Among the greatest concerns are:

- **Password migration**   ADMT supports migrating user passwords; however, it cannot confirm that those passwords comply with the policies of the target domain regarding password length and complexity. Nonblank passwords will migrate regardless of the target domain password policy, and users will be able to log on with those passwords until they expire, at which time a new, compliant password must be created. If you are concerned about locking down the environment at the time of migration, this might not be a satisfactory process. You might, instead, want to let ADMT configure complex passwords or script an initial password and then force the user to change the password at the first logon.

- **Service accounts**   Services on domain computers might use domain-based user accounts for authentication. As those user accounts are migrated to the target domain, services must be updated with the new service account identity. ADMT automates this process.

- **Objects that cannot be migrated**   Some objects cannot be seamlessly migrated. ADMT cannot migrate built-in groups such as Domain Admins or the domain local Administrators group. The user guide provides details for working around this limitation.

Exam Tip   For the 70-640 exam, you should recognize that the ADMT is used to copy or move accounts between domains. You should also understand that the new account in the target domain will have a new SID but that correct use of the tool can migrate group memberships and can populate *sIDHistory* with the SID of the source account.

Understanding Trust Relationships

Whenever you are implementing a scenario involving two or more AD DS domains, it is likely you will be working with *trust relationships*, or *trusts*. It is important that you understand the purpose, functionality, and configuration of trust relationships.

Trust Relationships Within a Domain

In Chapter 5, you were guided through what happens when a domain member server or workstation joins a domain. While in a workgroup, the computer maintains an identity store in the security accounts manager (SAM) database, it authenticates users against that identity store, and it secures system resources only with identities from the SAM database. When the computer joins a domain, it forms a trust relationship with the domain. The effect of that trust is that the computer allows users to be authenticated not by the local system and its local identity store but by the authentication services and identity store of the domain: AD DS. The domain member also allows domain identities to be used to secure system resources. For example, Domain Users is added to the local Users group, giving Domain Users the right to log on locally to the system. Also, domain user and group accounts can be added to ACLs on files, folders, registry keys, and printers on the system. All domain members have similar trust relationships with the domain, enabling the domain to be a central store of identity and a centralized service providing authentication.

Trust Relationships Between Domains

With that foundation, you can extend the concept of trust relationships to other domains. A trust relationship between two domains enables one domain to trust the authentication service and the identity store of another domain and to use those identities to secure resources. In effect, a trust relationship is a logical link established between domains to enable pass-through authentication.

There are two domains in every trust relationship: a trusting domain and a trusted domain. The trusted domain holds the identity store and provides authentication for users in that identity store. When a user in the directory of the trusted domain logs on to or connects to a system in the trusting domain, the trusting domain cannot authenticate that user because the user is not in its data store, so it passes the authentication to a domain controller in the trusted domain. The trusting domain, therefore, *trusts* the trusted domain to authenticate the identity of the user. The trusting domain *extends trust* to the authentication services and the identity store of the trusted domain.

Because the trusting domain trusts the identities in the trusted domain, the trusting domain can use the trusted identities to grant access to resources. Users in a trusted domain can be given user rights such as the right to log on to workstations in the trusting domain. Users or global groups in the trusted domain can be added to domain local groups in the trusting domain. Users or global groups in the trusted domain can be given permissions to shared folders by adding the identities to ACLs in the trusting domain.

The terminology can be confusing, and it is often easier to understand trust relationships with a figure. Figure 12-5 shows a simple diagram of a trust relationship. Domain A trusts Domain B. That makes Domain A the trusting domain and Domain B the trusted domain. If a user in Domain B connects to or logs on to a computer in Domain A, Domain A will pass the authentication request to a domain controller in Domain B. Domain A can also use the identities from Domain B—users and groups, for example—to grant user rights and resource access in Domain A. A user or group in Domain B can, therefore, be added to an ACL on a shared folder in Domain A. A user or group in Domain B can also be added to a domain local group in Domain A.

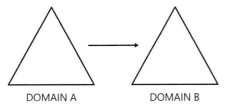

DOMAIN A   DOMAIN B

Figure 12-5   Diagram of a simple trust relationship

Exam Tip   Trust relationships are highly likely to appear on the 70-640 exam. Be certain that you completely understand the terms *trusted*, *trusting*, and *trust*. It is helpful when taking the exam to draw trust relationships so that you can more easily analyze which domain is trusted and has users and groups that the trusting domain can use to grant access to resources. Always make sure that the trust is extended from the domain with resources, such as computers and shared folders, to the domain with users.

Characteristics of Trust Relationships

Trust relationships between domains can be characterized by two attributes of the trust:

- **Transitivity**   Some trusts are not transitive, and others are transitive. In Figure 12-6, Domain A trusts Domain B, and Domain B trusts Domain C. If the trusts are transitive, then Domain A trusts Domain C. If they are not transitive, then Domain A does not trust Domain C. In most cases, you could create a third trust relationship, specifying that Domain A trusts Domain C. With transitive trusts, that third relationship is not necessary; it is implied.

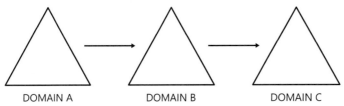

DOMAIN A   DOMAIN B   DOMAIN C

Figure 12-6   A trust relationship example

- **Direction**   A trust relationship can be one-way or two-way. In a one-way trust, such as the trust illustrated in Figure 12-5, users in the trusted domain can be given access to resources in the trusting domain, but users in the trusting domain cannot be given access to resources in the trusted domain. In most cases, you can create a second, one-way trust in the opposite direction to achieve that goal. For example, you can create a second trust relationship in which Domain B trusts Domain A. Some trust relationships are by nature two-way. In a two-way trust, both domains trust the identities and authentication services of the other domain.

- **Automatic or Manual**   Some trusts are created automatically. Other trusts must be created manually.

Within a forest, all domains trust each other. That is because the root domain of each tree in a forest trusts the forest root domain—the first domain installed in the forest—and each child domain trusts its parent domain. All trusts automatically created should never be deleted and are transitive and two-way. The net result is that a domain trusts the identity stores and authentication services of all other domains in its forest. Users and global groups from any domain in the forest can be added to domain local groups, can be given user rights, and can be added to ACLs on resources in any other domain in the forest. Trusts to other forests and to domains outside the forest must be manually established. With that summary, you can look at the details of trusts within and outside of an Active Directory forest.

Authentication Protocols and Trust Relationships

Windows Server 2003 Active Directory authenticates users with one of two protocols—Kerberos v5 or NT LAN Manager (NTLM). Kerberos v5 is the default protocol used by computers running Windows Server 2008, Windows Vista, Windows Server 2003, Windows XP, and Windows 2000 Server. If a computer involved in an authentication transaction does not support Kerberos v5, the NTLM protocol is used instead.

Kerberos Authentication Within a Domain

When a user logs on to a client running Kerberos v5, the authentication request is forwarded to a domain controller. Each Active Directory domain controller acts as a key distribution center (KDC), a core component of Kerberos. After validating the identity of the user, the KDC on the domain controller gives the authenticated user what is known as a ticket-granting ticket (TGT).

When the user needs to access resources on a computer in the same domain, the user must first obtain a valid session ticket for the computer. Session tickets are provided by the KDC of a domain controller, so the user returns to a domain controller to request a session ticket. The user presents the TGT as proof that he or she has already been authenticated. This enables the KDC to respond to the user's session ticket request without having to re-authenticate the user's identity. The user's session ticket request specifies the computer and the service the user wants to access. The KDC identifies that the service is in the same domain based on the service principal name (SPN) of the requested server. The KDC then provides the user with a session ticket for the service.

The user then connects to the service and presents the session ticket. The server is able to determine that the ticket is valid and that the user has been authenticated by the domain. This happens through private keys, a topic that is beyond the scope of this lesson. The server, therefore, does not need to authenticate the user; it accepts the authentication and identity provided by the domain with which the computer has a trust relationship.

All these Kerberos transactions are handled by Windows clients and servers and are transparent to users themselves.

Kerberos Authentication Within a Forest

Each child domain in a forest trusts its parent domain with an automatic, two-way, transitive trust called a *parent-child trust*. The root domain of each tree in a domain trusts the forest root domain with an automatic, two-way, transitive trust called a *tree-root trust*.

These trust relationships create what is referred to as the *trust path* or *trust flow* in a forest. The trust path is easy to understand with a diagram, as shown in Figure 12-7. The forest consists of two trees, the *tailspintoys.com* tree and the *wingtiptoys.com* tree. The *tailspintoys.com* domain is the forest root domain. On the top of Figure 12-7 is the forest as seen from a DNS perspective. On the bottom of the figure is the trust path. It indicates that the *wingtiptoys.com* tree root domain trusts the *tailspintoys.com* domain.

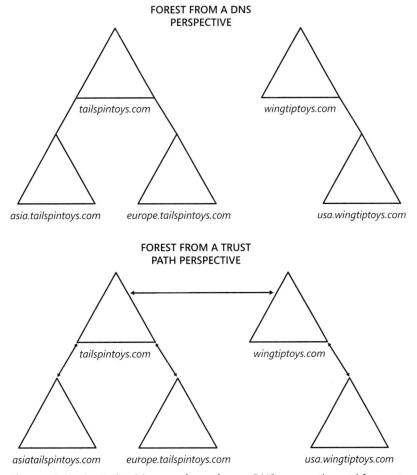

Figure 12-7 An Active Directory forest from a DNS perspective and from a trust path perspective

Kerberos authentication uses the trust path to provide a user in one domain a session ticket to a service in another domain. If a user in *usa.wingtiptoys.com* wants to access a shared folder on a server in *europe.tailspintoys.com*, the following transactions occur:

1. The user logs on to a computer in *usa.wingtiptoys.com* and is authenticated by a domain controller in *usa.wingtiptoys.com*, using the authentication process described in the previous section. The user obtains a TGT for the domain controller in *usa.wingtiptoys.com*.

   The user wants to connect to a shared folder on a server in *europe.tailspintoys.com*.

2. The user contacts the KDC of a domain controller in *usa.wingtiptoys.com* to request a session ticket for the server in *europe.tailspintoys.com*.

3. The domain controller in *usa.wingtiptoys.com* identifies, based on the SPN, that the desired service resides in *europe.tailspintoys.com*, not in the local domain.

The job of the KDC is to act as a trusted intermediary between a client and a service. If the KDC cannot provide a session ticket for the service because the service is in a trusted domain and not in the local domain, the KDC will provide the client with a *referral* to help it obtain the session ticket it is requesting.

The KDC uses a simple algorithm to determine the next step. If the KDC domain is trusted directly by the service's domain, the KDC gives the client a referral to a domain controller in the service's domain. If not, but if a transitive trust exists between the KDC and the service's domain, the KDC provides the client a referral to the next domain in the trust path.

4.   The *usa.wingtiptoys.com* is not trusted directly by *europe.tailspintoys.com*, but a transitive trust exists between the two domains, so the KDC in the *usa.wingtiptoys.com* domain gives the client a referral to a domain controller in the next domain in the trust path, *wingtiptoys.com*.

5.   The client contacts the KDC in the referral domain, *wingtiptoys.com*.

6.   Again, the KDC determines that the service is not in the local domain and that *europe.tailspintoys.com* does not trust *wingtiptoys.com* directly, so it returns a referral to a domain controller in the next domain in the trust path, *tailspintoys.com*.

7.   The client contacts the KDC in the referral domain, *tailspintoys.com*.

8.   The KDC determines that the service is not in the local domain and that *europe.tailspintoys.com* trusts *tailspintoys.com* directly, so it returns a referral to a domain controller in the *europe.tailspintoys.com* domain.

9.   The client contacts the KDC in the referral domain, *europe.tailspintoys.com*.

10.   The KDC in *europe.tailspintoys.com* returns to the client a session ticket for the service.

11.   The client contacts the server and provides the session ticket; the server provides access to the shared folder based on the permissions assigned to the user and the groups to which the user belongs.

This process might seem complicated, but recall that it is handled in a way that is completely transparent to the user.

The reverse process occurs if a user from *usa.wingtiptoys.com* logs on to a computer in the *europe.tailspintoys.com* domain. The initial authentication request must traverse the trust path to reach a KDC in the *usa.wingtiptoys.com* domain to authenticate the user.

Although it is not necessary to master the details of Kerberos authentication between domains in a forest for the 70-640 exam, it can help you in the real world to have a basic understanding that cross-domain authentication in a forest follows a trust path.

Manual Trusts

Four types of trusts must be created manually:

- Shortcut trusts
- External trusts
- Realm trusts
- Forest trusts

Each of these types of trusts will be discussed in the following sections.

Creating Manual Trust Relationships

The steps to create trusts are similar across categories of trusts. You must be a member of the Domain Admins or Enterprise Admins group to create a trust successfully.

To create a trust relationship, complete the following steps:

1. Open the Active Directory Domains And Trusts snap-in.
2. Right-click the domain that will participate in one side of the trust relationship, and choose Properties.

   You must be running Active Directory Domains And Trusts with credentials that have permissions to create trusts in this domain.
3. Click the Trusts tab.
4. Click the New Trust button.

   The New Trust Wizard guides you through the creation of the trust.
5. On the Trust Name page, type the DNS name of the other domain in the trust relationship, and then click Next.
6. If the domain you entered is not within the same forest, you will be prompted to select the type of trust, which will be one of the following:
   - ❏ Forest
   - ❏ External
   - ❏ Realm

   If the domain is in the same forest, the wizard knows it is a shortcut trust.
7. If you are creating a realm trust, you will be prompted to indicate whether the trust is transitive or nontransitive.
8. On the Direction Of Trust page, shown in Figure 12-8, select one of the following:
   - ❏ Two-Way establishes a two-way trust between the domains.
   - ❏ One-Way: Incoming establishes a one-way trust in which the domain you selected in step 2 is the trusted domain, and the domain you entered in step 5 is the trusting domain.

❑ One-Way: Outgoing establishes a one-way trust in which the domain you selected in step 2 is the trusting domain, and a domain you entered in step 5 is the trusted domain.

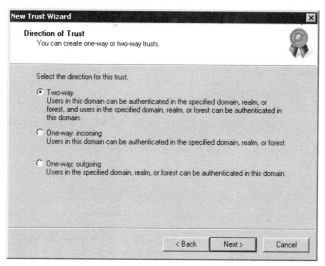

Figure 12-8 The Direction Of Trust page

9. Click Next.

10. On the Sides Of Trust page, shown in Figure 12-9, select one of the following:

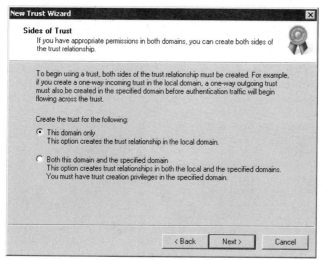

Figure 12-9 The Sides Of Trust page

❑ Both This Domain And The Specified Domain establishes both sides of the trust. This requires that you have permission to create trusts in both domains.

❑ This Domain Only creates the trust relationship in the domain you selected in step 2. An administrator with permission to create trusts in the other domain must repeat this process to complete the trust relationship.

The next steps will depend on the options you selected in steps 8 and 10. The steps will involve one of the following:

❑ If you selected Both This Domain And The Specified Domain, you must enter a user name and password with permissions to create the trust in the domain specified in step 5.

❑ If you selected This Domain Only, you must enter a trust password. A trust password is entered by administrators on each side of a trust to establish the trust. It should not be the administrators' user account passwords. Instead, it should be a unique password used only for the purpose of creating this trust. The password is used to establish the trust, and then the domains change it immediately.

11. If the trust is an outgoing trust, you are prompted to choose one of the following:

❑ Selective Authentication

❑ Domain-Wide Authentication or Forest-Wide Authentication, depending on whether the trust type is an external or forest trust, respectively.

Authentication options are discussed in the section "Securing Trust Relationships," later in this chapter.

12. The New Trust Wizard summarizes your selections on the Trust Selections Complete page. Click Next.

The Wizard creates the trust.

13. The Trust Creation Complete page appears. Verify the settings, and then click Next.

You will then have the opportunity to confirm the trust. This option is useful if you have created both sides of the trust or if you are completing the second side of a trust.

If you selected Both This Domain And The Specified Domain in step 8, the process is complete. If you selected This Domain Only in step 8, the trust relationship will not be complete until an administrator in the other domain completes the process:

■ If the trust relationship you established is a one-way, outgoing trust, then an administrator in the other domain must create a one-way, incoming trust.

■ If the trust relationship you established is a one-way, incoming trust, an administrator in the other domain must create a one-way, outgoing trust.

■ If the trust relationship you established is a two-way trust, an administrator in the other domain must create a two-way trust.

MORE INFO   **Procedures for creating trusts**

You can find detailed procedures for creating each type of trust at *http://technet2.microsoft.com /WindowsServer/en/library/f82e82fc-0700-4278-a166-4b8ab47b36db1033.mspx.*

Shortcut Trusts

In an earlier section, you followed 11 steps of the process used to grant a session ticket for a client to access a resource in another domain within a forest. Most of those steps involved referrals to domains on the trust path between the user's domain and the domain of the shared folder. When a user from one domain logs on to a computer in another domain, the authentication request must also traverse the trust path. This can affect performance, and, if a domain controller is not available in a domain along the trust path, the client will not be able to authenticate or to access the service.

Shortcut trusts are designed to overcome those problems by creating a trust relationship directly between child domains in the forest trust path. Two shortcut trusts are illustrated in Figure 12-10.

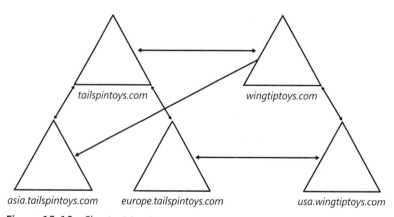

Figure 12-10   Shortcut trusts

Shortcut trusts optimize authentication and session ticket requests between domains in a multidomain forest. By eliminating the trust path, they eliminate the time required to traverse the trust path and, thereby, can significantly improve performance of session ticket requests.

Shortcut trusts can be one-way or two-way. In either case, the trust is transitive. In Figure 12-10, a one-way shortcut trust exists whereby *wingtiptoys.com* trusts *asia.tailspintoys.com*. When a user from *asia.tailspintoys.com* logs on to a computer in *wingtiptoys.com* or requests a resource in *wingtiptoys.com*, the request can be referred directly to a domain controller in the trusted domain, *asia.tailspintoys.com*. However, the reverse is not true. If a user in *wingtiptoys.com* logs on to a computer in *asia.tailspintoys.com*, the authentication request will traverse the trust path up to *tailspintoys.com* and down to *wingtiptoys.com*.

A two-way shortcut trust is illustrated between *usa.wingtiptoys.com* and *europe.tailspintoys.com*. Users in both domains can be authenticated by and can request resources from computers in the other domain, and the shortcut trust path will be used.

External Trusts

When you need to work with a domain that is not in your forest, you might need to create an external trust. An external trust is a trust relationship between a domain in your forest and a Windows domain that is not in your forest. Examples are shown in Figure 12-11.

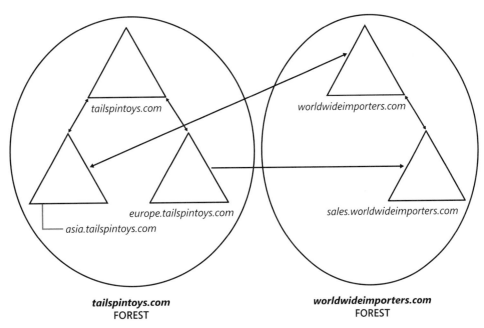

Figure 12-11 An external trust to a domain in another forest

In Figure 12-11, you can see a one-way trust between the *sales.worldwideimporters.com* domain and the *europe.tailspintoys.com* domain. The Europe domain trusts the Sales domain, so users in the Sales domain can log on to computers in the Europe domain or connect to resources in the Europe domain.

Figure 12-11 also shows a two-way trust between the *worldwideimporters.com* domain and the *asia.tailspintoys.com* domain. Users in each domain can be given access to resources in the other domain. Technically, all external trusts are nontransitive, one-way trusts. When you create a two-way external trust, you are actually creating two one-way trusts, one in each direction.

When you create an outgoing external trust, Active Directory creates a foreign security principal object for each security principal in the trusted domain. Those users, groups, and computers can then be added to domain local groups or to ACLs on resources in the trusting domain.

To increase the security of an external trust relationship, you can choose Selective Authentication on the Outgoing Trust Authentication Level page of the New Trust Wizard. Additionally, domain quarantine, also called SID filtering, is enabled by default on all external trusts. Both of these configurations are detailed in the "Securing Trust Relationships" section, later in this chapter.

Realm Trusts

When you need cross-platform interoperability with security services based on other Kerberos v5 implementations, you can establish a realm trust between your domain and a UNIX Kerberos v5 realm. Realm trusts are one-way, but you can establish one-way trusts in each direction to create a two-way trust. By default, realm trusts are nontransitive, but they can be made transitive.

If a non-Windows Kerberos v5 realm trusts your domain, the realm trusts all security principals in your domain. If your domain trusts a non–Windows Kerberos v5 realm, users in the realm can be given access to resources in your domain; however, the process is indirect. When users are authenticated by a non–Windows Kerberos realm, Kerberos tickets do not contain all the authorization data needed for Windows. Therefore, an account mapping system is used. Security principals are created in the Windows domain and are mapped to a foreign Kerberos identity in the trusted non–Windows Kerberos realm. The Windows domain uses only these proxy accounts to evaluate access to domain objects that have security descriptors. All Windows proxy accounts can be used in groups and on ACLs to control access on behalf of the non–Windows security principal. Account mappings are managed through Active Directory Users and Computers.

Forest Trusts

When you require collaboration between two separate organizations represented by two separate forests, you can consider implementing a forest trust. A forest trust is a one-way or two-way transitive trust relationship between the forest root domains of two forests. Figure 12-12 shows an example of a forest trust between the *tailspintoys.com* forest and the *worldwideimporters.com* forest.

A single forest trust relationship allows the authentication of a user in any domain by any other domain in either forest, assuming the forest trust is two-way. If the forest trust is one-way, any user in any domain in the trusted forest can be authenticated by computers in the trusting forest. Forest trusts are significantly easier to establish, maintain, and administer than are separate trust relationships between each of the domains in the forests. Forest trusts are particularly useful in scenarios involving cross-organization collaboration, mergers and acquisitions, or within a single organization that has more than one forest, to isolate Active Directory data and services.

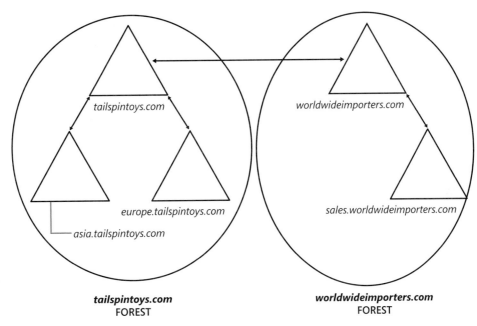

tailspintoys.com
FOREST

worldwideimporters.com
FOREST

Figure 12-12   A forest trust

When you establish a forest trust relationship, domain quarantine (also called SID filtering) is enabled by default. Domain quarantine is discussed in the "Securing Trust Relationships" section, later in this chapter. You can specify whether the forest trust is one-way, incoming or outgoing, or two-way. As mentioned earlier, a forest trust is transitive, allowing all domains in a trusting forest to trust all domains in a trusted forest. However, forest trusts are not themselves transitive. For example, if the *tailspintoys.com* forest trusts the *worldwideimporters.com* forest, and the *worldwideimporters.com* forest trusts the *northwindtraders.com* forest, those two trust relationships do not allow the *tailspintoys.com* forest to trust the *northwindtraders.com* forest. If you want those two forests to trust each other, you must create a specific forest trust between them.

Several requirements must be met before you can implement a forest trust. The forest functional level must be Windows Server 2003 or later. In addition, you must have a specific DNS infrastructure to support a forest trust.

MORE INFO   DNS requirements for a forest trust

You can learn about the DNS requirements for a forest trust at *http://technet2.microsoft.com /WindowsServer/en/library/f5c70774-25cd-4481-8b7a-3d65c86e69b11033.mspx*.

Administering Trusts

If you are concerned that a trust relationship is not functioning, you can validate a trust relationship between any two Windows domains. You cannot validate a trust relationship to a Kerberos v5 realm. To validate a trust relationship, complete the following steps.

1. Open Active Directory Domains And Trusts.
2. In the console tree, right-click the domain that contains the trust that you want to validate, and then click Properties.
3. Click the Trusts tab.
4. Select the trust you want to validate.
5. Click Properties.
6. Click Validate.
7. Do one of the following, and then click OK:
    - ❑ Click Yes, Validate The Incoming Trust. Enter credentials that are members of the Domain Admins or Enterprise Admins groups in the reciprocal domain.
    - ❑ Click No, Do Not Validate The Incoming Trust. It is recommended that you repeat this procedure for the reciprocal domain.

    You can also verify a trust from the command prompt by typing the following command:

    ```
    netdom trust TrustingDomainName /domain:TrustedDomainName /verify
    ```

There can also be reason to remove a manually created trust. To do so, follow these steps.

1. Open Active Directory Domains And Trusts.
2. In the console tree, right-click the domain that contains the trust you want to validate, and then click Properties.
3. Click the Trusts tab.
4. Select the trust you want to remove.
5. Click Remove.
6. Do one of the following, and then click OK:
    - ❑ Click Yes, Remove The Trust From Both The Local Domain And The Other Domain. Enter credentials that are members of the Domain Admins or Enterprise Admins groups in the reciprocal domain.
    - ❑ Click No, Remove The Trust From The Local Domain Only. It is recommended that you repeat this procedure for the reciprocal domain.
7. To delete a manually created trust from the command prompt, use the *Netdom.exe* command with the following syntax:

    ```
    netdom trust TrustingDomainName /domain:TrustedDomainName
        /remove [/force] /UserD:User /PasswordD:*
    ```

The *UserD* parameter is a user with credentials in the Enterprise Admins or Domain Admins group of the trusted domain. Specifying the *PasswordD:** parameter causes *Netdom.exe* to prompt you for the password to the account. The */force* switch is required when removing a realm trust.

NOTE Command-line tools to manage and test trust relationships

The Windows Domain Manager, *Netdom.exe*, and other command-line tools can be used to manage and test trust relationships. See *http://technet2.microsoft.com/windowsserver/en/library/ 108124dd-31b1-4c2c-9421-6adbc1ebceca1033.mspx?mfr=true* for details regarding these commands.

Securing Trust Relationships

When you configure a trust relationship that enables your domain to trust another domain, you open up the possibility for users in the trusted domain to gain access to resources in your domain. The following sections examine components related to the security of a trusting domain's resources.

Authenticated Users

A trust relationship itself does not grant access to any resources; however, it is likely that by creating a trust relationship, users in the trusted domain will have immediate access to a number of your domain's resources. This is because many resources are secured with ACLs that give permissions to the Authenticated Users group.

Membership in Domain Local Groups

As you learned in Chapter 4, "Groups," the best practice for managing access to a resource is to assign permissions to a domain local group. You can then nest users and groups from your domain into the domain local group and, thereby, grant them access to the resource. Domain local security groups can also include users and global groups from trusted domains as members. Therefore, the most manageable way to assign permissions to users in a trusted domain is to make them or their global groups members of a domain local group in your domain.

ACLs

You can also add users and global groups from a trusted domain directly to the ACLs of resources in a trusting domain. This approach is not as manageable as the previous method, using a domain local group, but it is possible.

Transitivity

When you create a realm trust, the trust is nontransitive by default. If you make it transitive, you open up the potential for users from domains and realms trusted by the Kerberos v5 realm to gain access to resources in your domain. It is recommended to use nontransitive trusts unless you have a compelling business reason for a transitive realm trust.

Domain Quarantine

By default, domain quarantine, also called SID filtering, is enabled on all external and forest trusts. When a user is authenticated in a trusted domain, the user presents authorization data that includes the SIDs of the user's account in the groups to which the user belongs. Additionally, the user's authorization data includes security identifiers from other attributes of the user and his or her groups.

Some of the SIDs presented by the user from the trusted domain might not have been created in the trusted domain. For example, if a user is migrated from one domain into another, a new SID is assigned to the migrated account. The migrated account will, therefore, lose access to any resources that had permissions assigned to the SID of the user's former account. To enable the user to continue to access such resources, an administrator performing a migration can specify that the *sIDHistory* attribute of the user's migrated account will include the former account's SID. When the user attempts to connect to the resource, the original SID in the *sIDHistory* attribute will be authorized for access.

In a trusted domain scenario, it is possible that a rogue administrator could use administrative credentials in the trusted domain to load SIDs into the *sIDHistory* attribute of a user that are the same as SIDs of privileged accounts in your domain. That user would then have inappropriate levels of access to resources in your domain.

Domain quarantine prevents this problem by enabling the trusting domain to filter out SIDs from the trusted domain that are not the primary SIDs of security principals. Each SID includes the SID of the originating domain, so when a user from a trusted domain presents the list of the user's SIDs and the SIDs of the user's groups, SID filtering instructs the trusting domain to discard all SIDs without the domain SID of the trusted domain.

Domain quarantine is enabled by default for all outgoing trusts to external domains and forests. Disable domain quarantine only if one or more of the following are true:

- You have extremely high levels of confidence in the administrators of the trusted domain.
- Users or groups have been migrated to the trusted domain with their SID histories preserved, and you want to grant those users or groups permissions to resources in the trusting domain based on the *sIDHistory* attribute.

To disable domain quarantine, type the following command:

```
netdom trust TrustingDomainName /domain:TrustedDomainName /quarantine:no
```

To re-enable domain quarantine, type this command:

```
netdom trust TrustingDomainName /domain:TrustedDomainName /quarantine:yes
```

Exam Tip   You might encounter either term—*domain quarantine* or *SID filtering*—on the 70-640 exam. Remember that this procedure is used so that users from a trusted domain are authorized using only the SIDs that originate in the trusted domain. An effect of domain quarantine is that the trusting domain ignores SIDs in the *sIDHistory* attribute, which typically contains the SIDs of accounts from a domain migration.

Selective Authentication

When you create an external trust or a forest trust, you can control the scope of authentication of trusted security principals. There are two modes of authentication for an external or forest trust:

- Selective authentication
- Domain-wide authentication (for an external trust) or forest-wide authentication (for a forest trust)

If you choose domain-wide or forest-wide authentication, all trusted users can be authenticated for access to services on all computers in the trusting domain. Trusted users can, therefore, be given permission to access resources anywhere in the trusting domain. With this authentication mode, you must have confidence in the security procedures of your enterprise and in the administrators who implement those procedures so that inappropriate access is not assigned to trusted users. Remember, for example, that users from a trusted domain or forest are considered Authenticated Users in the trusting domain, so any resource with permissions granted to Authenticated Users will be immediately accessible to trusted domain users if you choose domain-wide or forest-wide authentication.

If, however, you choose selective authentication, all users in the trusted domain are trusted identities; however, they are allowed to authenticate only for services on computers that you have specified. For example, imagine that you have an external trust with a partner organization's domain. You want to ensure that only users from the marketing group in the partner organization can access shared folders on only one of your many file servers. You can configure selective authentication for the trust relationship and then give the trusted users the right to authenticate only for that one file server.

To configure the authentication mode for a new outgoing trust, use the Outgoing Trust Authentication Level page of the New Trust Wizard. Configure the authentication level for an existing trust, open the properties of the trusting domain in Active Directory Domains And Trusts, select the trust relationship, click Properties, and then click the Authentication tab, shown in Figure 12-13.

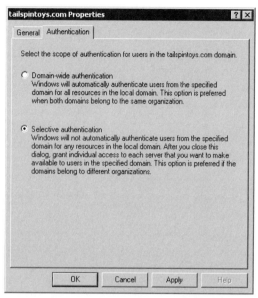

Figure 12-13   The Authentication tab of a trust relationship's Properties dialog box

After you have selected Selective Authentication for the trust, no trusted users will be able to access resources in the trusting domain, even if those users have been given permissions. The users must also be assigned the Allowed To Authenticate permission on the computer object in the domain. To assign this permission, open the Active Directory Users And Computers snap-in and make sure that Advanced Features is selected in the View menu. Open the properties of the computer to which trusted users should be allowed to authenticate—that is, the computer that trusted users will log on to or that contains resources to which trusted users have been given permissions. On the Security tab, add the trusted users or a group that contains them, and select the Allow check box for the Allowed To Authenticate permission, shown in Figure 12-14.

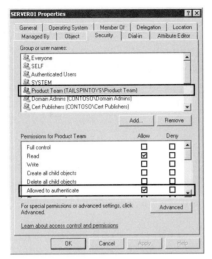

Figure 12-14   Assigning the Allowed To Authenticate permission to a trusted group

---

Quick Check
- You have configured selective authentication for an outgoing trust to the domain of a partner organization. You want to give a group of auditors in the partner organization permission to a shared folder on SERVER32. Which two permissions must you configure?

Quick Check Answer
- You must assign the auditors the Allowed To Authenticate permission for the SERVER32 computer object. You must also give the auditors NTFS permissions to the shared folder.

PRACTICE **Administering a Trust Relationship**

In this practice, you will create, secure, and administer a trust relationship between the *contoso.com* domain and the *tailspintoys.com* domain. In this scenario, Contoso, Ltd., is forming a partnership with Tailspin Toys. A team of product developers at Tailspin Toys require access to a shared folder in the Contoso domain. To perform this practice, you must have completed the practice in Lesson 1, "Understanding Domain and Forest Functional Levels," so that you have two domain controllers, one in the *contoso.com* domain and forest and one in the *tailspintoys.com* domain and forest.

▶ **Exercise 1   Configure DNS**

It is important for DNS to be functioning properly before creating trust relationships. Each domain must be able to resolve names in the other domain. In Chapter 9, "Integrating Domain Name System with AD DS," you learned how to configure name resolution. There are several ways to support name resolution between two forests. In this exercise, you will create a stub zone in the *contoso.com* domain for the *tailspintoys.com* domain and a conditional forwarder in the *tailspintoys.com* domain to resolve *contoso.com*.

1. Log on to SERVER01.contoso.com as Administrator.
2. Open DNS Manager from the Administrative Tools program group.
3. Expand SERVER01, and select Forward Lookup Zones.
4. Right-click Forward Lookup Zones, and choose New Zone.
   The Welcome To The New Zone Wizard page appears.
5. Click Next.
   The Zone Type page appears.
6. Select Stub Zone, and click Next.
   The Active Directory Zone Replication Scope page appears.
7. Click Next.
   The Zone Name page appears.
8. Type **tailspintoys.com**, and click Next.
   The Master DNS Servers page appears.
9. Type **10.0.0.111**, and press Tab.
10. Select the Use The Above Servers To Create A Local List Of Master Servers check box. Click Next, and then click Finish.
11. Log on to SERVERTST.tailspintoys.com as Administrator.
12. Open DNS Manager from the Administrative Tools program group.
13. Expand SERVERTST.
14. Right-click the Conditional Forwarders folder, and choose New Conditional Forwarder.
15. In the DNS Domain box, type **contoso.com**.
16. Select Click Here To Add An IP, and type **10.0.0.11**.
17. Select the Store This Conditional Forwarder In Active Directory, And Replicate It As Follows check box.
18. Click OK.

▶ **Exercise 2   Create a Trust Relationship**

In this exercise, you will create the trust relationship to enable authentication of Tailspin Toys users in the Contoso domain.

1. Users in *tailspintoys.com* require access to a shared folder in *contoso.com*. Answer the following questions:
    ❑   Which domain is the trusting domain, and which is the trusted domain?
    ❑   Which domain has an outgoing trust, and which has an incoming trust?

    Answers: The *contoso.com* domain is the trusting domain with an outgoing trust to the *tailspintoys.com* domain, which is the trusted domain with an incoming trust.

2. Log on to SERVER01 as the Administrator of the *contoso.com* domain.

3. Open Active Directory Domains And Trusts from the Administrative Tools program group.

4. Right-click *contoso.com*, and choose Properties.

5. Click the Trusts tab.

6. Click New Trust.

    The Welcome To The New Trust Wizard page appears.

7. Click Next.

    The Trust Name page appears.

8.   In the Name box, type **tailspintoys**. Click Next.

    Because you did not configure DNS on SERVER01 to forward queries for the *tailspintoys.com* domain to the authoritative DNS service on SERVERTST.tailspintoys.com, you must use the NetBIOS name of the *tailspintoys.com* domain. In a production environment, it is recommended to use the DNS name of the domain in this step.

    The Trust Type page appears.

9. Select External Trust, and click Next.

    The Direction of Trust page appears.

10. Select One-way: Outgoing. Click Next.

    The Sides Of Trust page appears.

11. Select This Domain Only. Click Next.

    The Outgoing Trust Authentication Level page appears.

12. Select Domain-Wide Authentication, and click Next.

    The Trust Password page appears.

13. Enter a complex password in the Trust Password and Confirm Trust Password boxes. Remember this password because you will need it to configure the incoming trust for the *tailspintoys.com* domain. Click Next.

    The Trust Selections Complete page appears.

14. Review the settings, and click Next.

    The Trust Creation Complete page appears.

15. Review the status of changes. Click Next.

    The Confirm Outgoing Trust page appears. You should not confirm the trust until both sides of the trust have been created.

16. Click Next.

    The Completing The New Trust Wizard page appears.

17. Click Finish.

    A dialog box appears to remind you that SID filtering is enabled by default.

18. Click OK.

19. Click OK to close the *contoso.com* Properties dialog box.

    Now you will complete the incoming trust for the *tailspintoys.com* domain.

20. Log on to SERVERTST.tailspintoys.com as the Administrator of the *tailspintoys.com* domain.

21. Open Active Directory Domains And Trusts from the Administrative Tools program group.

22. Right-click *tailspintoys.com*, and choose Properties.

23. Click the Trusts tab.

24. Click New Trusts.

    The Welcome To The New Trust Wizard page appears.

25. Click Next.

    The Trust Name page appears.

26. In the Name box, type **contoso**, and click Next.

    The Trust Type page appears.

27. Select External Trust, and click Next.

    The Direction Of Trust page appears.

28. Select One-way: Incoming, and click Next.

    The Sides Of Trust page appears.

29. Select This Domain Only, and click Next.

    The Trust Password page appears.

30. Enter the password you created in step 13 in the Trust Password and Confirm Trust Password boxes. Click Next.

    The Trust Selections Complete page appears.

31. Click Next.

    The Trust Creation Complete page appears.

32. Review the status of changes, and click Next.

The Confirm Incoming Trust page appears.

33. Click Next.

The Completing The New Trust Wizard page appears.

34. Click Finish.

35. Click OK to close the *tailspintoys.com* Properties dialog box.

▶ **Exercise 3   Validate the Trust**

In step 33 of the previous exercise, you had the opportunity to confirm the trust relationship. You can also confirm or validate an existing trust relationship. In this exercise, you will validate the trust between *contoso.com* and *tailspintoys.com*.

1. Log on to SERVER01.contoso.com as the Administrator of the *contoso.com* domain.

2. Open Active Directory Domains And Trusts from the Administrative Tools folder.

3. Right-click *contoso.com*, and choose Properties.

4. Click the Trusts tab.

5. Select *tailspintoys.com*, and click Properties.

6. Click Validate.

A message appears indicating that the trust has been validated and that it is in place and active.

7. Click OK.

8. Click OK twice to close the Properties dialog boxes.

▶ **Exercise 4   Provide Access to Trusted Users**

In this exercise, you will provide access to a shared folder in the Contoso domain to the product team from Tailspin Toys.

1. Create the following objects:
   - ❏ A global group named **Product Team** in the *tailspintoys.com* domain
   - ❏ A global group named **Product Developers** in the *contoso.com* domain
   - ❏ A domain local group named **ACL_Product_Access** in the *contoso.com* domain

2. Create a folder named **Project** on the C drive of SERVER01.

3. Give the ACL_Product_Access group Modify permission to the Project folder.

4. Open the Active Directory Users And Computers snap-in for *contoso.com*.

5. Open the properties of the ACL_Product_Access group.

6. Click the Members tab.

7. Click Add.

8. Type **Product Developers**, and click OK.

9. Click Add.

10. Type **TAILSPINTOYS\Product Team**, and click OK.

A Windows Security dialog box appears. Because the trust is one-way, your user account as the administrator of *contoso.com* does not have permissions to read the directory of the *tailspintoys.com* domain. You must have an account in *tailspintoys.com* to read its directory. If the trust were a two-way trust, this message would not have appeared.

11. In the User Name box, type **TAILSPINTOYS\Administrator**.

12. In the Password box, type the password for the Administrator account in *tailspintoys.com*.

13. Click OK.

14. Note that the two global groups from the two domains are now members of the domain local group in the *contoso.com* domain that has access to the shared folder.

▶ **Exercise 5   Implement Selective Authentication**

In this exercise, you will restrict the ability of users from the *tailspintoys.com* domain to authenticate with computers in the *contoso.com* domain.

1. On SERVER01.contoso.com, open Active Directory Domains And Trusts.

2. Right-click *contoso.com*, and choose Properties.

3. Click the Trusts tab.

4. Select *tailspintoys.com*, and click Properties.

5. Click the Authentication tab.

6. Click the Selective Authentication option, and then click OK twice.

   With selective authentication enabled, users from a trusted domain cannot authenticate against computers in the trusting domain, even if they've been given permissions to a folder. Trusted users must also be given the Allow To Authenticate permission on the computer itself.

7. Open the Active Directory Users And Computers snap-in for *contoso.com*.

8. Click the View menu, and ensure that Advanced Features is selected.

9. Select the Domain Controllers OU in the console tree.

10. In the details pane, right-click SERVER01, and choose Properties.

11. Click the Security tab.

12. Click Add.

13. Type **TAILSPINTOYS\Product Team**, and click OK.

    A Windows Security dialog box appears. Because the trust is one-way, your user account as the administrator of *contoso.com* does not have permissions to read the directory of the *tailspintoys.com* domain. You must have an account in *tailspintoys.com* to read its directory. If the trust were a two-way trust, this message would not have appeared.

14. In the User Name box, type **TAILSPINTOYS\Administrator**.

15. In the Password box, type the password for the Administrator account in *tailspintoys.com*.

16. Click OK.

17. In the Permissions For Product Team list, select the check box under Allow and next to Allowed To Authenticate.

18. Click OK.

Now the product team from *tailspintoys.com* can authenticate to SERVER01 and has been given permission to the shared folder through its membership in the ACL_Product_Access group. Those users cannot authenticate with any other computer in *contoso.com*, even if the group has been assigned permissions to folders on those computers. Also, no other users from *tailspintoys.com* can access resources on SERVER01.contoso.com

Lesson Summary

- The best practices design for an Active Directory forest is a single domain. However, there are requirements, particularly related to replication of the domain naming context, that might require multiple domains in a forest.

- The Active Directory Migration Tool (ADMT) is used to migrate objects between domains or for intra-forest or inter-forest domain restructure. When an account is moved to another domain, it receives a new SID. The SID of the source account can be added to the target account's *sIDHistory* attribute so that the new account maintains access to resources that had been assigned to the original account's SID. Group membership can also be maintained by the ADMT.

- Trust relationships allow users in a trusted domain to be authenticated by computers in a trusting domain and, therefore, to be added to domain local groups or to be given access to resources in the trusting domain.

- Within a forest, there are two-way, transitive trusts between each child and parent domain and between each tree root and the forest root domain. You can create shortcut trusts within a forest to improve authentication.

- You can create trusts to external domains, forests, and Kerberos v5 realms. Those trusts can be one-way or two-way. Kerberos v5 trusts can be transitive or nontransitive. Forest trusts are always transitive, and external trusts are always nontransitive.

- Selective authentication enables you to manage which trusted users and groups are allowed to authenticate against which computers in the trusting domain.

- Domain quarantine, also known as SID filtering, is enabled by default on all external and forest trusts. It prevents trusted users from presenting in their authorization data SIDs from domains other than the primary domain of the account.

Lesson Review

You can use the following questions to test your knowledge of the information in Lesson 2, "Managing Multiple Domains and Trust Relationships." The questions are also available on the companion CD if you prefer to review them in electronic form.

NOTE Answers

Answers to these questions and explanations of why each answer choice is right or wrong are located in the "Answers" section at the end of the book.

1. You are an administrator at Wingtip Toys, which has just acquired Tailspin Toys. You plan to restructure the forests of the two companies so that all objects are in the *wingtiptoys.com* domain. Until then, you want to allow users in the *wintiptoys.com* and *europe.wingtiptoys.com* domains to log on to all computers in the *tailspintoys.com* domain. Which of the following describe the trust relationship you must configure in *wingtiptoys.com*? (Choose all that apply. Each correct answer is part of the solution.)

   A. Incoming
   B. Outgoing
   C. One-way
   D. Two-way
   E. Realm
   F. Shortcut
   G. Forest
   H. External

2. You are an administrator at Wingtip Toys, which has just acquired Tailspin Toys. You have created a one-way outgoing trust to enable users in the *tailspintoys.com* domain to access resources that have been moved into the *wingtiptoys.com* domain. Some users from *tailspintoys.com* are able to access the resources successfully, but other users are reporting that they are unable to gain access to the resources. You discover that the users having problems have worked for Tailspin Toys for eight or more years and that their accounts were migrated from a Windows NT 4.0 domain. What must you do to enable them to gain access to the resources? (Choose all that apply.)

   A. Create accounts in the *wingtiptoys.com* domain with the same user names and passwords as their accounts in the *tailspintoys.com* domain.
   B. Rebuild the Windows NT 4.0 domain and upgrade a domain controller to Windows Server 2008.
   C. Run the *Netdom* trust command with the */verify* parameter.
   D. Run the *Netdom* trust command with the */quarantine:no* parameter.

3. You are an administrator of the forest shown in the following figure. Domain controllers for the *tailspintoys.com* domain are located in Los Angeles. Domain controllers for the Asia domain are in Beijing. Domain controllers for the Europe domain are in Stockholm. Users in Europe and Asia report excessive delays when attempting to open shared folders on servers in each other's domain. Performance is reasonable for accessing resources in the users' own domains. What can you do to improve performance for these users?

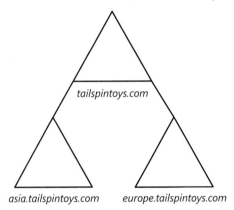

A. Reinstall the operating systems on the users' computers.

B. Change the IP address to a static address.

C. Disable dynamic updates in DNS.

D. Create a trust relationship between Europe and Asia.

Chapter Review

To further practice and reinforce the skills you learned in this chapter, you can perform the following tasks:

- Review the chapter summary.
- Complete the case scenario. This scenario sets up a real-world situation involving the topics of this chapter and asks you to create a solution.
- Complete the suggested practices.
- Take a practice test.

Chapter Summary

- Domain and forest functional levels enable features of the Active Directory that have been added by each new version of the Windows operating system. Raising the domain or forest functional level is a one-way operation. After the functional level has been raised, you can no longer add domain controllers running previous versions of Windows.

- Trust relationships between domains allow users from a trusted domain to be authenticated by computers in a trusting domain. Trusted users and groups can be added to domain local groups in the trusting domain and can be given access to resources in the trusting domain.

- Within a forest, there are two-way, transitive trusts between each child domain and its parent, and between each domain tree root domain and the forest root domain. Those trusts result in each domain in a forest trusting each other domain in the forest. You can create shortcut trusts to improve the performance and reliability of authentication within a forest.

- An external trust is created between a domain in a forest and another Windows domain. You can also create a trust with a Kerberos v5 realm.

- A cross-forest trust is established between the forest roots of two AD DS forests. It creates a trust between all domains in the two forests.

- Selective authentication can be applied in the trusting domain to control which computers allow the authentication of trusted users.

- SID filtering, or domain quarantine, is enabled by default on all external and cross-forest trusts. It prevents users in the trusted domain from presenting SIDs that were not generated in the users' primary domain.

■ The Active Directory Migration Tool (ADMT) is used to move or copy users, computers, or groups between domains. When you migrate an account, you must consider the fact that the new object will have a new SID, which can affect the object's access to resources and group membership. Use of the *sIDHistory* attribute and the migration of both users and groups can mitigate this risk.

Case Scenario

In the following case scenario, you will apply what you've learned about domain functional levels and trust relationships. You can find answers to these questions in the "Answers" section at the end of this book.

Case Scenario: Managing Multiple Domains and Forests

You are an administrator at Tailspin Toys. Your company is partnering on new product development with Wingtip Toys. You want to establish a forest trust to allow users in the *tailspintoys.com* domain to be authenticated in the *wingtiptoys.com* domain and vice versa.

1. You upgrade your domain controllers directly from Windows 2000 Server to Windows Server 2008. What must you do with the Active Directory Domains and Trusts snap-in before creating the trust relationship?
2. What type(s) of trust relationship(s) can you create in *tailspintoys.com* to achieve this goal? What must you ask administrators in *wingtiptoys.com* to do?
3. You want to control authentication so that users from *wingtiptoys.com* can access resources on only four servers in your domain. What must you do?

Suggested Practices

To help you successfully master the exam objectives presented in this chapter, complete the following tasks.

Configure a Forest or Domain

You are an administrator at Contoso, Ltd., which is expanding its operations to Europe and Asia. In this exercise, you will perform trust management tasks within a multidomain forest. These exercises require multiple domains and domain controllers. To begin the practice, you will also need two new servers, named SERVEREU.contoso.com and SERVERAS.contoso.com, with full installations of Windows Server 2008, each a member of the *contoso.com* domain.

- **Practice 1**   Promote SERVEREU.contoso.com to a domain controller in a new domain named *europe.contoso.com* in the existing *contoso.com* forest. Promote SERVERAS.contoso.com to a domain controller in a new domain named *asia.contoso.com* in the existing *contoso.com* forest. Install DNS on all servers and make sure that all forest zones are replicated to both new domain controllers. Ensure also that both domain controllers use their own DNS service to resolve names—that is, configure the DC DNS server address to point to its own IP address.

- **Practice 2**   Create a user account in the *europe.contoso.com* domain. Add the user to the Print Operators group in the Europe domain and in the Asia domain so that the user can log on to the domain controllers for the purposes of this practice. Create a shared folder on SERVERAS.asia.contoso.com and give the Europe user permission to the folder. Log on to SERVEREU.europe.contoso.com as the user and connect to the shared folder on SERVERAS.asia.contoso.com.

- **Practice 3**   Shut down SERVER01.contoso.com. Log on to SERVEREU.europe.contoso.com as the Europe user. Ping SERVERAS.asia.contoso.com. If you cannot ping the server, DNS or networking is not configured correctly. Troubleshoot the problem. When you can ping SERVERAS, attempt to connect to the shared folder. It should fail because a domain controller in the trust path is not available.

- **Practice 4**   Power on SERVER01.contoso.com. Log on to SERVEREU as the Europe administrator. Create a trust relationship with the Asia domain.

- **Practice 5**   Power down SERVER01. Log on to SERVEREU.europe.contoso.com as the Europe user. Ping SERVERAS.asia.contoso.com. If you cannot ping the server, DNS or networking is not configured correctly. Troubleshoot the problem. When you can ping SERVERAS, attempt to connect to the shared folder. The connection should succeed because the shortcut trust is in place.

Take a Practice Test

The practice tests on this book's companion CD offer many options. For example, you can test yourself on just one exam objective, or you can test yourself on all the 70-640 certification exam content. You can set up the test so that it closely simulates the experience of taking a certification exam, or you can set it up in study mode so that you can look at the correct answers and explanations after you answer each question.

MORE INFO   Practice tests

For details about all the practice test options available, see the "How to Use the Practice Tests" section in this book's introduction.

Chapter 13
Directory Business Continuity

Business continuity is a very hot topic today, especially since the recent disasters many organizations have faced all over the world. Hurricanes, tidal waves, and earthquakes are disasters on a catastrophic scale and have far-reaching impacts on organizations. Several studies have shown that up to 40 percent of small to medium-sized organizations that face a significant disaster and have no business continuity plan will fail. Don't let this happen to you. Prepare in advance and make sure you are ready for any eventuality.

Disasters don't have to be on a catastrophic scale to be devastating. A user whose Active Directory Domain Services (AD DS) account has been erased by mistake will be as devastated—albeit on a smaller scale—when he or she can't log on one morning without knowing why. That's why you need proactive plans that will keep you ready at all times and make sure you can react to any situation, disastrous or not. To do so, you need to address two key areas of business continuity: maintaining and protecting the directory and data store and managing directory performance.

Each of these areas addresses a facet of directory business continuity. A third area of business continuity, availability, is built into the AD DS operational model. Every domain controller (DC) but the read-only domain controller (RODC) includes the capability to support multi-master replication. Because of this, each time you put two or more DCs in place for the same domain, you provide high availability for the service. Therefore, simple deployment rules guide the process of maintaining directory service availability.

Exam objectives in this chapter:
- Maintaining the Active Directory Environment
    - Perform offline maintenance.
    - Configure backup and recovery.
    - Monitor Active Directory.

Lessons in this chapter:

- Lesson 1: Proactive Directory Maintenance and Data Store Protection 610
- Lesson 2: Proactive Directory Performance Management. 660

Before You Begin

To complete the lessons in this chapter, you must have done the following:

■ Installed Windows Server 2008 on a physical or virtual computer, which should be named SERVER10. This computer hosts the DNS Server role as well as the Active Directory Domain Services role and is a DC for the *treyresearch.net* forest root domain. Add a second disk to this server. Make it a dynamically expanding disk of 10 GB, format it, and name it **Data**.

■ Installed Windows Server 2008 on a physical or virtual computer, which should be named SERVER11 and should be a standalone server. This computer will host the DNS Server role and the Active Directory Domain Services role you will install and create through the exercises in this chapter. Assign an IPv4 address from one of the private ranges, for example, 192.168.x.x, and map its DNS server address to the address you assigned to SERVER10.

■ Performed the practice exercises outlined in Chapter 9, "Integrating Domain Name System with AD DS." This will have set up a multidomain directory service named *treyresearch.net*. This forest includes a forest root domain, a domain tree, and a child domain. Exercises in this chapter reuse the forest root domain created in Chapter 9.

Using virtual machines (VMs) is strongly recommended in support of the exercises. The DC and Domain Name System (DNS) server roles are ideal for virtualization through either Microsoft Virtual Server 2005 R2 or Hyper-V.

Real World

Danielle Ruest and Nelson Ruest

In 2003, we were asked to write a follow-up book to *Windows Server 2003: Best Practices for Enterprise Deployments*. This book would be a pocket guide and would focus on systems administration instead of operating system deployment.

We collected and collated tasks that should be performed on Windows Server 2003 infrastructures, depending on the different features deployed. We divided the tasks according to server role and created five categories, focusing only on roles available with the default installation files for Windows Server 2003, and we divided the list according to task frequency, finding four frequencies: daily, weekly, monthly, and ad hoc. The last would include both infrequent tasks and tasks needed to perform on a schedule longer than one month. Then, we put it all together in a single spreadsheet.

Before we started writing, we wanted to validate the task list, so we asked our clients if they would help us supplement it. Twenty-five clients, with network sizes ranging from 50 to 25,000 nodes, responded. We sent the list to each one to look it over, evaluate whether the task was appropriate, validate the schedule we suggested, and suggest any missing tasks. Clients did not know how many tasks we had listed for each server role beforehand.

Responses were quite varied, but every client came back with the same general comment: "We never knew you had to do all those things in Windows!" Of all the clients, only a handful even touched on the task list, and those were in the largest networks. We were shocked, but this taught us a valuable lesson.

When clients deploy Windows, things work for the most part and, because of this, few organizations assign staff to focus on proactive network monitoring. IT professionals are mostly overworked in almost every organization. When requests come in, they are always high priority; system administrators usually don't have time to be proactive because they are almost always in reactive mode and already working overtime.

Since our *Pocket Administrator for Windows Server 2003* has been published, we have been giving one-day Windows Server 2003 administration classes, updating them each time a new version would be released. In every case, attendees have come back to us to say that when they use our schedule, they no longer have to work overtime on a constant basis. Our new book, *Windows Server 2008: The Complete Reference*, contains the task list and has been updated accordingly.

Monitoring—especially proactive monitoring—is a very important part of any Windows Server deployment, especially in terms of AD DS or DNS, which supports it. Every organization that relies on the identity and access solution AD DS provides should take measures to verify the system's proper operation at regular intervals. Running Microsoft Windows technologies while not performing proactive management for them is not practical. They will work, but users can often leave themselves exposed to potential issues and, perhaps worse, potential security holes. This is why this might be the most important chapter in this book for you.

Lesson 1: Proactive Directory Maintenance and Data Store Protection

One of the most important concepts administrators need to understand when working with a directory service such as AD DS is the division of responsibilities they face. A directory service is very much like a Web service. IT administrators of a Web service are responsible for the management of Microsoft Internet Information Services (IIS) and the underlying operating system, not for the maintenance of the content included in the Web sites the server will host. Imagine having to change a comma here, a word there, a picture here, or a phrase there in addition to having to perform all the other work required to maintain a network environment. You would never have time to do anything else but work!

In a Web service, you must divide responsibilities based on data and service management. IT is responsible for service management whereas the users are responsible for data or content management. The same applies to the directory service. AD DS is a distributed database that contains information about the users, the computers, the servers, the services, and more that run in your network, hence its categorization as a network operating system (NOS) as well as a lightweight access directory protocol (LDAP) directory service. Because of this, administration activities are shared among several members of your organization:

- Users can update their own records. If a user uses the Search Active Directory feature to locate his or her own account record, he or she will be allowed to change information such as phone number, location, and so on.

- Security and distribution group managers, when assigned the role in AD DS, can automatically manage group content if you assign this user right to them. This is a good approach for reducing the workload system administrators face when managing a NOS directory service. How would you know whether a user should be a member of a group?

In every case, when you change group ownership, you respond to a request that was initiated by someone else. Why not cut out the middle person and make group managers directly responsible?

- Password resets are managed by the help desk. Each time a password needs to be reset, the help desk needs to get involved.

- Directory and DNS service availability is the core of the system administrator's responsibilities and should be the focus of most of his or her efforts. After all, system administrators are there to manage the availability of services and the data the directory contains, not to manage the data itself.

When you plan your proactive management strategy, focus on the service aspect of operations management and delegate data management as much as possible. AD DS delegation capabilities further enhance this model by enabling you to assign object control to others in your organization discretely. This is the approach of this chapter and the focus of this lesson.

> **After this lesson, you will be able to:**
> - Understand which administrative tasks need to be performed to maintain AD DS and DNS.
> - Understand the difference between online and offline maintenance tasks.
> - Perform offline maintenance tasks.
> - Recover data while online.
> - Recover data while offline.
>
> **Estimated lesson time: 90 minutes**

Twelve Categories of AD DS Administration

When you consider it, Active Directory administration or management covers twelve major activities. These activities and their breadth of coverage are outlined in Table 13-1, which also outlines which tasks focus on data or content management and which are concentrated on service administration.

Table 13-1   AD DS Administration Activities

Task	Description	Service	Data
User and Group Account Administration	This includes user password resets, user creation and deactivation, user group creation, and membership management. Should be delegated to the help desk.	☐	☑
Endpoint Device Administration	All computers in a Windows network environment must have a computer account. This is how they interact with the directory and how the directory interacts with them. Should be delegated to technicians.	☐	☑
Networked Service Administration	This includes publication of network file shares, printers, distributed file shares (DFS), application directory partitions, and so on. Should be delegated to the administrator of each service type.	☑	☑
Group Policy Object (GPO) Management	GPOs provide the most powerful model for object management in Windows Server 2008. Should be delegated to appropriate technicians, but a central GPO steward should control GPO proliferation.	☑	☐
DNS Administration	DNS is now tied closely to the directory, and the operation is based on a properly functioning dynamic DNS service. Because DNS is integrated with the directory, DNS administration is the responsibility of the domain administrator.	☑	☐
Active Directory Topology and Replication Management	Replication is at the very core of the directory service operation. It covers the configuration of subnets, sites, site links, site link bridges, and bridgehead servers. You should rely heavily on the Knowledge Consistency Checker (KCC)—a service that automatically generates replication topologies based on the rules and guidelines you give it—to control replication. This is the responsibility of the domain administrator.	☑	☐

Table 13-1   AD DS Administration Activities

Task	Description	Service	Data
Active Directory Configuration Management	Configuration administration involves forest, domain, and organizational unit (OU) design and implementation. It also involves Flexible Single Master of Operations (FSMO) roles, global catalog servers, and DCs, including RODCs because these servers define the configuration of each forest. One last activity that is related to configuration management is time synchronization. AD DS relies on the PDC Emulator role to synchronize time in the network. These tasks are the responsibility of the forest and domain administrators.	☑	☐
Active Directory Schema Management	AD DS is a database, albeit a distributed one. As such, it includes a database schema. Schema modifications are not done lightly because added objects cannot normally be removed although they can be deactivated, renamed, and reused. This is the responsibility of the forest administrator.	☑	☐
Information Management	This refers to the population of the directory with information about the objects it contains. User objects, shared folders, and computer objects can include owners; groups can include managers; printers and computers can include location tracking information. The Active Directory Schema Management console can be used to add or remove content from the global catalog and determine whether an object should be indexed. You can also assign NTDS quotas to make sure no one adds or extracts more information than permitted in the directory. Delegate as many of the information management tasks as possible.	☐	☑
Security Administration	Security administration covers everything from setting Domain Account policies and assigning user rights to managing trusts as well as access control list (ACL) and access control entry (ACE) administration. This is the responsibility of the domain administrator or designated operators to whom it has been delegated.	☑	☐

Table 13-1   AD DS Administration Activities

Task	Description	Service	Data
Database Management	Database management involves *Ntds.dit* maintenance and AD DS object protection as well as GPO protection. Includes managing the LostandFound and LostandFoundConfig containers, which are designed to collect homeless objects in your directory. Also includes compacting the directory database on each DC. Although AD DS regularly compacts its own database automatically, it is good practice to compact it manually. This is the responsibility of the domain administrator.	☑	☐
AD Reporting	Generate reports from your directory to know how it is structured, what it contains, and how it runs. There is no default centralized reporting tool, but you can export data at several levels of the directory. You can also generate GPO reports with the Group Policy Management console. This is the responsibility of the domain administrator and the GPO steward.	☑	☑

Depending on the size of your network, each of the activities outlined in Table 13-1 can be a job by itself. This is why you need to make sure you delegate whichever part of the work you can so that you can enlist as much help as possible to ensure that the directory service is highly available at all times. A couple of tools can help in particular situations.

Using AcctInfo.dll

When you need to manage user accounts, you'll perform activities through the Active Directory Users and Computers console. This console supports enhancements, some of which are provided by Microsoft. For example, you can add an Additional Account Info tab on the user object's properties page by downloading and registering the AcctInfo.dll on a server or workstation hosting the Active Directory Users and Computers console. AcctInfo.dll is part of the Windows Server 2003 Resource Kit along with the Account Lockout and Management tools.

IMPORTANT   Additional Account Info tab

Note that this additional tab appears in the standalone Active Directory Users and Computers console only and does not appear in the Active Directory Users and Computers node of Server Manager.

To install the Additional Account Info tab, use the following procedure. You need local administrator credentials if you are on a workstation or member server but domain administrator credentials on a DC.

1. Make sure the Remote Server Administration Tools (RSAT), especially the AD DS administration tools, are installed on your system.

2. Download Account Lockout And Management Tools from the Microsoft Web site and save them to the Documents folder on the system you want to install it to.

3. Extract the tools from the executable.

4. After the tools are extracted, locate AcctInfo.dll. It should be in your Documents folder.

5. Use an elevated command prompt to run the following command:

   `regsvr32 acctinfo.dll`

6. Click OK when you get the successful registration message and close the command prompt.

7. If the Active Directory Users and Computers console was open, close it and reopen it. This console must be re-initialized to load the new DLL.

8. Locate a user account.

9. Open its Properties dialog box.

10. Move to the Additional Account Info tab. (See Figure 13-1.) Note the information available in this screen. In addition to this information, this screen provides the following:

    ❏ Domain PW Info displays the password policy assigned to this account. Given that AD DS supports multiple password policies in a single domain, this is a useful button.

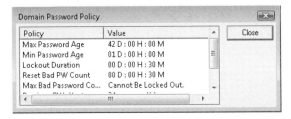

    ❏ SID History provides information on the multiple security identifiers an account might have when SID History is turned on in the domain. SID History is normally turned on when you perform a migration of accounts from one domain to the other. It enables the account object to access data from the original domain. However, in new domains, SID History is not available unless a migration occurs. It is important to turn off SID History as soon as possible after a migration occurs to avoid SID spoofing in the domain—the appropriation of an administrative SID by a malicious user. If it is turned on, you can use this button to validate that accounts have only the appropriate SIDs tied to them.

    ❏ Set PW On Site DC will enable you to reset the user's password on the user's DC to avoid replication delays and give the user immediate access to his or her new password. Use the Just Find Site button to locate the site's DC and reset the password.

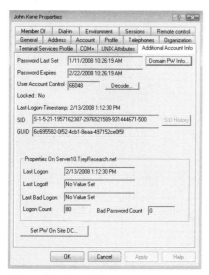

This dynamic-link library (DLL) can be quite useful to help desk staff and domain administrators alike.

Figure 13-1 Using the Additional Account Info tab in a user's Properties dialog box

---

MORE INFO **Account Lockout and Management tools**

To obtain the Account Lockout and Management tools, go to *http://www.microsoft.com/Downloads/details.aspx?FamilyID=7af2e69c-91f3-4e63-8629-b999adde0b9e&displaylang=en*.

Using Specops Gpupdate

When you work with computer objects in the directory with Active Directory Users and Computers, you can right-click the object and choose Manage to launch the Computer Management console with the computer as the focus for the console, but this does not give you access to simpler functions such as remote update of GPOs or the more common *start*, *shut down*, or *restart* commands. However, you can obtain a simple and free add-on from Special Operations Software called Specops Gpupdate. Specops Gpupdate is used here only as an example and is by no means a recommendation. This tool automatically adds functionality to the Active Directory Users and Computers console and will give you control over the following activities:

- Remotely updating GPOs on an object in the directory
- Starting computers remotely, using Wake-on-LAN if enabled locally
- Remote restarting or shutting down the selected computer
- Graphically reporting the results of an operation

In addition, Gpupdate enables you to perform these tasks on single computer objects or on a collection of objects by applying them to an entire OU. This is a good tool for administrators who must manage computers and servers remotely.

NOTE Obtaining Specops Gpupdate

To obtain the Specops Gpupdate, go to *http://www.specopssoft.com/products/specopsgpupdate /download.asp*. A one-time registration is required.

Exam Tip Note that Specops Gpupdate, while it is quite a useful tool for object management through AD DS, is not part of the exam.

If you choose to implement Specops Gpupdate, use the following procedure. You need local administrator credentials if you are on a workstation or member server but domain administrator credentials on a DC. Also, you need to be an Enterprise Administrator for the one-time Display Specifier registration in the forest.

1. Make sure the RSAT, especially the AD DS administration tools, are installed on your system.
2. Download the Specops Gpupdate tool from the Special Operations Software Web site and save it to the Documents folder on the system you want to install it to.
3. Extract the components from the executable.
4. After the components are extracted, locate the SpecopsGpupdate.msi file. It should be in your Documents folder. Double-click .msi to launch the setup.
5. Click Run in the warning dialog box.
6. Click Next at the Welcome screen.
7. Accept the license and click Next.
8. Type your full name and organization; make sure Anyone Who Uses This Computer is selected and click Next.
9. Accept the default installation location and click Next.

10. Click Next to install the application, and then click Finish when the installation is complete.

    The installation is complete, but you must add the display specifiers to the forest. This requires Enterprise Admin credentials.

11. Launch Windows Explorer and navigate to %ProgramFiles%\Common Files\Secopssoft \SpecopsADUC Extension.

12. After the Specops files are displayed in the details pane of Windows Explorer, move to the Start menu and click Run. This displays the Run dialog box.

13. Make sure the Run dialog box is empty and move to the Windows Explorer window to click and drag SpecopsAducMenuExtensionInstaller.exe into the Run dialog box.

    The command and its path should be displayed in the Run dialog box.

14. Move to the end of the text, making sure you do not change anything, and type /**add**.

    The result should be similar to "C:\Program Files\Common Files\Secopssoft\Specops-ADUC Extension\SpecopsAducMenuExtensionInstaller.exe"/add.

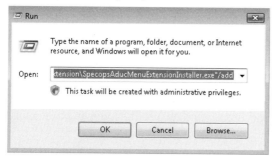

15. Press Enter to run the command.

    A command prompt will open and display command results.

16. Press any key to close the window.

Now that the display specifiers have been added, you can simply run the SpecopsGpupdate.msi file on any computer on which you want to install Specops Gpupdate by performing steps 1–10 only.

When you need to work with computer objects, you can simply use the context menu to access the new administration features on either a computer object or an organizational unit containing computer objects. (See Figure 13-2.) This tool is free and a good addition to any directory service.

Figure 13-2   The context menu commands added by Specops Gpupdate

Using AD DS Administration Tools

To perform the activities related to service administration in AD DS and DNS, you can use a series of tools. You've already seen many of these tools as you read through the previous lessons, but it is a good idea to review them here. Table 13-2 outlines which tools you can use for which task and where you can locate the tool. In this table, the focus is on service, not data administration. Many of these tools will also work with Active Directory Lightweight Directory Services (AD LDS) because it is based on the same core code as AD DS.

Table 13-2   Common Service Administration Tools

Tool	Description	Location
Active Directory Domains and Trusts	Administer trusts, domain and forest functional levels, and user principal name suffixes.	Administrative Tools program group
Active Directory Schema Snap-in	Modify the schema for AD DS directories or AD LDS instances. You must use the *Regsvr32.exe* command to register the Schmmgmt.dll first.	Custom MMC
Active Directory Sites and Services	Configure and manage replication scopes for AD DS directories and AD LDS instances.	Administrative Tools program group
Active Directory Users and Computers	Configure and manage the domain-centric FSMO roles as well as RODC features.	Administrative Tools program group
ADSI Edit	Query, view, and edit directory objects and attributes.	Administrative Tools program group
CSVDE.exe	Import data into AD DS directories or AD LDS instances.	Command line
DCDiag.exe	Diagnose AD DS directories or AD LDS instances.	Command line

Table 13-2   Common Service Administration Tools

Tool	Description	Location
Dcpromo.exe	To add or remove the DC service.	Start menu, Search
DFSRadmin.exe	Manage Distributed File System Replication, which is the system used when the forest runs in Windows Server 2008 full functional mode.	Command line
DNS Manager	Perform general maintenance of DNS servers.	Administration Tools program group or Server Manager
Dnscmd.exe	Manage all aspects of DNS servers.	Command line
DSACLS.exe	Control access control lists on directory objects.	Command line
Dsadd.exe	Add specific types of objects (users, groups, computers).	Command line
Dsamain.exe	Mount Active Directory store (.dit) backups or snapshots to identify their contents.	Command line
Dsbutil.exe (installed with AD LDS and AD DS)	Perform maintenance of the AD DS store. Configure AD LDS ports. View AD LDS instances.	Command line
Dsget.exe	View the selected properties of a specific object (user, computer).	Command line
Dsmgmt.exe	Manage application partitions and operations master roles.	Command line
Dsmod.exe	Modify an existing object of a specific type (user, computer).	Command line
Dsmove.exe	Move an object to a new location within a directory. Also rename an existing object.	Command line
Dsquery.exe	Query the directory for a specific object type according to specified criteria.	Command line
Dsrm.exe	Delete an object of a specific type or a collection of objects.	Command line
Event Viewer	Audit AD DS or AD LDS changes and log old and new values for both objects and attributes.	Administrative Tools program group
GPfixup.exe	Repair domain name dependencies in Group Policy objects. Also, relink Group Policy objects after a domain rename operation.	Command line
Group Policy Diagnostic Best Practices Analyzer	Verify the configuration of GPO as well as potential dependency errors.	Download from *microsoft.com*

Table 13-2   Common Service Administration Tools

Tool	Description	Location
Group Policy Management Console	Create, manage, back up, and restore GPOs.	Administrative Tools program group
Ipconfig	Display and modify IP configuration details.	Command line
Ksetup.exe	Configure a client to use a Kerberos v5 realm instead of an AD DS domain.	Command line
Ktpass.exe	Configure a non-Windows Kerberos service as a security principal in AD DS.	Command line
LDIFDE.exe	Import data into AD LDS instances.	Command line
Ldp.exe	Perform LDAP operations against the directory.	Start menu, Search
Movetree.exe	Move objects between domains in a forest.	Download from microsoft.com
Netdom.exe	Manage computer accounts, domains, and trust relationships.	Command line
Nltest.exe	Query replication status or verify trust relationships.	Command line
Nslookup.exe	View information on name servers to diagnose DNS infrastructure problems.	Command line
Ntdsutil.exe (installed with AD DS, not AD LDS)	Perform database maintenance on the AD DS store.	Command line
Repadmin.exe	Troubleshoot and diagnose replication between DCs that use the File Replication Service (FRS), which is the system used when the forest does not run in Windows Server 2008 full functional mode.	Command line
Server Manager	Manage existing AD DS domains or AD LDS instances.	Administrative Tools program group
System Monitor	Create charts and graphs of server performance trends. Determine performance benchmarks.	Server Manager, Diagnostics, Reliability, and Performance
Ultrasound (Ultrasound.exe)	Graphical tool to troubleshoot and diagnose replication between DCs that use FRS. Relies on Windows Management Instrumentation (WMI).	Download from microsoft.com
W32tm.exe	View settings, manage configuration or diagnose problems with Windows Time.	Command line
Windows Server Backup	Back up or restore AD DS directories or AD LDS instances and their contents.	Administrative Tools program group

---

MORE INFO   Finding and downloading tools

To locate the *Movetree.exe* command, go to *http://www.microsoft.com/downloads/details.aspx?FamilyID=96a35011-fd83-419d-939b-9a772ea2df90&DisplayLang=en*. Obtain the .cab file and extract all files named movetree.* from the file. Note that not all tools contained within this file will work with Windows Server 2008; Windows Server 2003 support tools are not supported on Windows Server 2008. For example, the *ReplMon.exe* tool simply will not launch.

To obtain Ultrasound, go to *http://www.microsoft.com/Downloads/details.aspx?FamilyID=61acb9b9-c354-4f98-a823-24cc0da73b50&displaylang=en*. Note that this tool might not be immediately available for Windows Server 2008.

To obtain the GPO Diagnostic Best Practices Analyzer for x86, go to *http://www.microsoft.com/downloads/details.aspx?FamilyID=47f11b02-8ee4-450b-bf13-880b91ba4566&DisplayLang=en*. For the x64 edition, go to *http://www.microsoft.com/downloads/details.aspx?familyid=70E0EDEC-66F7-4499-83B7-4F2009DF2314&displaylang=en*.

Performing Online Maintenance

You performed many of the activities listed in Table 13-1 as you covered other lessons. Table 13-3 maps out where you locate information about each of the 12 AD DS tasks in this book.

Table 13-3   AD DS Administration Activities

Task	Location
User and Group Account Administration	Chapter 2
	Chapter 3
	Chapter 4
Endpoint Device Administration	Chapter 5
Networked Service Administration	Chapter 4
	Chapter 7
	Chapter 10
	Chapter 11
Group Policy Object (GPO) Management	Chapter 6
	Chapter 7
Domain Name Service Administration	Chapter 9
Active Directory Topology and Replication Management	Chapter 10
	Chapter 11
Active Directory Configuration Management	Chapter 1
	Chapter 2
	Chapter 8
	Chapter 10
	Chapter 11
	Chapter 12

Table 13-3   **AD DS Administration Activities**

Task	Location
Active Directory Schema Management	Chapter 14
Information Management	Chapter 2
	Chapter 3
	Chapter 4
	Chapter 5
	Chapter 11
Security Administration	Chapter 2
	Chapter 7
	Chapter 8
	Chapter 12
Database Management	Chapter 13
Active Directory Reporting	Chapter 2
	Chapter 6
	Chapter 7
	Chapter 8
	Chapter 10
	Chapter 11
	Chapter 13

Performing Offline Maintenance

One significant change in AD DS from previous versions is the transformation of the DC role into a controllable service. In previous versions of Windows Server, the DC role was mono-lithic: to stop the service, you needed to stop the DC as a whole. This meant that when you needed to perform maintenance on the *Ntds.dit* database—the database that contains the directory store—you needed to shut down a DC and restart it in Directory Services Repair Mode. Because of this, there was no way to automate the database maintenance operations. Consequently, most domain administrators never performed any database maintenance at all. Performing no maintenance is not a valid approach to systems management.

Every database works the same way. As new records are added, the database allocates addi-tional space to store information associated with the record. However, when the record is deleted, the allocated space is not recovered. You need to perform database compaction activ-ities to recover this space. The AD DS service does perform some automatic database compac-tion, but this compaction does not recover lost space within the database; it only rearranges data to make it easier to access. To recover lost space, you must take the database offline and run a compaction and defragmentation sequence against it.

However, with AD DS and Windows Server 2008, the AD DS service is now a manageable ser-vice that can be started and stopped like all Windows Server services. This means that to perform database maintenance activities, you no longer need to shut down the DC to restart it in Directory Services Repair Mode. It also means that because the service behaves natively, you can script the defragmentation and compaction operations through basic command-line tools.

Note that to stop the AD DS service, the DC must be able to communicate with another DC that is running the service. If not, you will not be able to stop the service. AD DS includes automatic checks and verifications that ensure that at least one DC is available at all times; otherwise, no one will be able to log on to the network.

You will work with the defragmentation and compaction operation in the practice exercises at the end of this lesson.

Exam Tip   Offline defragmentation and compaction and the restartable AD DS service are important parts of the exam.

Relying on Built-in Directory Protection Measures

Data protection is also a very important aspect of proactive systems management, and it is essential for AD DS. As you know, each account stored in the AD DS database is a unique object because it is tied to a specific and unique security identifier (SID). This means that when an account is deleted, you cannot simply re-create it. Although the account will appear the same to humans, it will be a completely different object to AD DS and, as such, will not retain the properties or attributes of the formerly deleted object. Group memberships, passwords, attribute settings, and more will be completely different for the object. This is one very good reason to reassign accounts rather than re-creating them when people change positions in your network. Reassigning them automatically grants the new person the same rights as the previous account owner. Re-creating an account means you have to dig in and identify all the access rights required by the role in your network. Re-creation is a lot more work.

It is difficult to lose data within the directory because of the multimaster replication model—when a change is performed in one location, it is automatically replicated to all other locations. However, this same replication model can also cause issues. When an operator deletes an object, especially by mistake, it will be deleted in the entire directory and might need to be restored from backup to be recovered. However, AD DS includes four features that enable you to recover information without resorting to backups:

- The new object protection option, which protects objects from deletion.
- The new AD DS Access auditing feature, which logs old and new values, enabling you to return to an original value when object properties are modified.
- The tombstone container. Each object that is removed from the directory is tombstoned for a specific period of time. While the object is still in the tombstone container, it can be recovered.
- The backup and restore feature supported by Windows Server Backup.

Each of these provides a means of protecting and recovering the information in the directory database.

Protecting AD DS Objects

By default, every new object in AD DS can be protected from deletion when it is created. In every case, you must specifically assign this feature to the object. When you create objects through batch processes or through a migration process, it will not be protected unless you assign the feature during the creation process. When you create an object interactively, you must also assign protection explicitly. Object protection is assigned or removed on the Object tab, which can be viewed only when you have Advanced Features turned on in the View menu of the Active Directory Users And Computers console. (See Figure 13-3.) Note that container objects such as OUs have this option enabled by default because they form part of your directory structure.

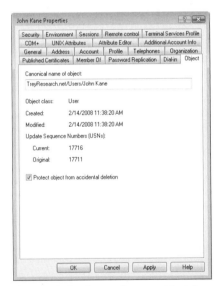

Figure 13-3   Protecting an object from deletion in AD DS

After object protection is assigned, you will not be able to delete the object accidentally. This also means that it cannot be moved from one location to the other.

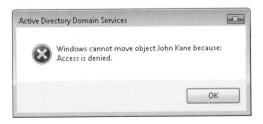

In fact, this option assigns two Deny permissions to the Everyone group: Deny Delete and Deny Delete subtree. Remember that in AD DS, deny permissions override every allow permission. The only way you can move or delete this object from this point on is if you uncheck the protection feature. This is a useful feature for organizations that delegate object administration to technical staff. In fact, you might consider making this feature part of the user account template you create to assist in the creation of user accounts in your directory.

Auditing Directory Changes

When you audit directory changes in Windows Server 2008, you automatically log old and new values of an attribute each time an object is modified. Further, because the AD DS audit policy in Windows Server 2008 now logs four subcategories of service access, you can control the assignment of this policy at a more granular level than in previous versions of Windows Server. The subcategory that controls attribute captures is Directory Service Changes. When enabled, it captures creation, modification, move, and undeletion operations on an object. Each operation is assigned a specific event ID in Directory Services Event Log.

This feature turns Event Log into a record-keeping system for directory changes, enabling you to maintain extensive records on the changes that have been made in your directory. It is also useful for fixing modifications that have been performed erroneously.

When an object is modified, at least two events are logged. The first will list the former value, and the second—most recent—will list the new value. Use the two to correct modifications that should not have been made.

Undeleting Active Directory Objects

When you mistakenly delete an Active Directory object, you can use the *Ldp.exe* command to recover it. This is performed through a procedure that exposes the deleted objects container of the directory. To undelete an object, use the following procedure on a DC. You must have domain administrator credentials to perform this operation.

1. From a command prompt, type **Ldp.exe**.
2. Click Connect from the Connection menu, type the server's fully qualified domain name (FQDN), for example, **Server10.TreyResearch.net**, and click OK.
3. Click Bind from the Connection menu, make sure the Bind As Currently Logged On User option is selected, and click OK.
4. Click Controls from the Options menu, select Return Deleted Objects from the Load Predefined drop-down list, make sure Server is selected in the Control Type section of the dialog box, and click OK.
5. Click Tree from the View menu, type the deleted object container's distinguished name (DN), and click OK.

   For example, the DN of the container in Trey Research would be cn=deleted Objects,dc =TreyResearch,dc=net.

6. In the tree pane, double-click the deleted objects container to expand its contents. Keep in mind that *Ldp.exe* will return only 1,000 objects by default.

7. Locate the object you want to restore in the tree pane and double-click it.

    This displays its information in the details pane. For example, if the object is a user account, it will begin with cn=username.

8. Right-click the object name in the tree pane and select Modify.

9. In the Modify dialog box, type **isDeleted** in the Edit Entry Attribute value, select Delete as the Operation, and click Enter.

10. In the Modify dialog box, type **distinguishedName** in the Edit Entry Attribute value, type the object's new DN in the Attribute value, select Replace as the Operation, and click Enter.

    For example, to restore John Kane's account to the People container in the Trey Research domain, the DN would be cn=John Kane,ou=People,dc=TreyResearch,dc=net.

11. Make sure the Synchronous and Extended check boxes are both selected in the bottom left of the dialog box, and then click Run. (See Figure 13-4.)

12. Use Active Directory Users And Computers to move to the OU you restored the object to. Use the refresh button to refresh the OU contents if the console was already opened.

13. Reset the newly restored object's password, group memberships, and any other values you need to reapply, and then click Enable.

    The object is restored. This procedure recovers the object and retains the original SID for the object as well, but it does not retain all group memberships and other values.

Figure 13-4   Recovering a deleted object with *Ldp.exe*

Using Quest Object Restore for Active Directory

As you can see from the previous procedure, objects are not immediately removed from the directory when they are deleted. Instead, they are tombstoned and moved to a special hidden container. You can access this container with special tools but not with the normal Active Directory consoles. You can, however, use a utility from Quest Software, Quest Object Restore for Active Directory, to access the tombstone container through a graphical console and locate objects you want to restore. This utility is free; however, it expires every six months and must be removed and reinstalled to work again. Quest Object Restore for Active Directory is used here only as an example and is by no means a recommendation.

NOTE **Obtaining Quest Object Restore**

To obtain the Quest Object Restore for Active Directory, go to *http://www.quest.com/object-restore-for-active-directory/*. A one-time registration with a business e-mail address is required.

Exam Tip Note that Quest Object Restore for Active Directory, while it is quite a useful tool for recovering deleted objects in AD DS, is not part of the exam.

Proceed as follows to download and install it. You need domain administrator credentials if you perform this on a DC or local administrator credentials if you do it on a workstation or member server.

1. Make sure the RSAT, especially the AD DS administration tools, are installed on your system.
2. Download the Quest Object Restore for Active Directory tool from the Quest Software Web site and save it to the Documents folder on the system you want to install it to.
3. Extract the components from the executable.
4. After the tools are extracted, locate the Quest Object Restore For Active Directory.msi file. It should be in your Documents folder. Double-click the .msi to launch the setup.
5. Click Run in the warning dialog box.
6. Click Next at the Welcome screen.
7. Accept the license and click Next.
8. Type your full name and organization, ensuring that Anyone Who Uses This Computer is selected, and click Next.
9. Accept the default installation location and click Next.
10. Click Next to install the application, and then click Finish when the installation is complete.

    The installation is complete.

11. To use the tool, navigate to Start\All Programs\Quest Software\Quest Object Restore For Active Directory and click Quest Object Restore For Active Directory.

    This tool runs in its own Microsoft Management console (MMC).

12. When the console is open, right-click Quest Object Restore For Active Directory and select Connect To.

13. Type the domain's FQDN or click Browse to locate it. Click OK to connect.

14. Click the domain name in the tree pane.

    This should list deleted objects in the details pane.

15. If the objects do not appear, click the Refresh button.

16. To restore an object, right-click the object name in the details pane and select Restore. (See Figure 13-5.) Click OK when the object has been restored.

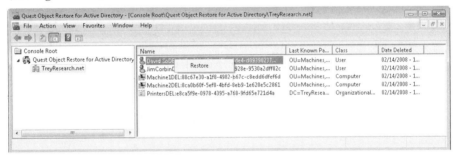

Figure 13-5   Using Quest Object Restore for Active Directory to restore objects

Basically, Quest Object Restore for Active Directory displays the tombstone container in AD DS. Because all objects are tombstoned for a period of 180 days by default, you can restore these objects any time before they are destroyed by directory database cleanup operations. However, as with the *Ldp.exe* tool, this procedure recovers the object and retains the original SID for the object as well, but it does not retain all group memberships and other values, so you must modify the object before you enable it. However, using this tool is much simpler than using the previous *Ldp.exe* procedure.

Relying on Windows Server Backup to Protect the Directory

Although you can use special tools to access the tombstone data in the directory, this does not always provide the best method for data recovery. For example, objects you restore from tombstone containers do not include all their previous attributes. Because of this, you must know ahead of time which contents and attributes were assigned to the object before deletion to be able to bring it back to its original state. However, when you restore the data from backup and reassign it to the directory, you restore all an object's attributes at once, and you do not need to reassign attributes such as group memberships and so on. This saves time after the object is restored but requires a more complex operation to perform the restore.

In addition, restoring objects in AD DS was more or less a hit-or-miss operation in previous versions of Windows Server because it was impossible to view objects within a backup data set prior to the restore. It was and continues to be impossible to restore different backup sets to different DCs and to view the data they contain. Windows Server 2008 includes a new tool, the AD DS Database mounting tool with which you can view backup data set contents prior to the restore operation. This tool can save you considerable time when you need to recover an object and help ensure that you recover the right version of the object.

When you work with Active Directory backup and restore operations, you can perform several operations:

- You can back up the entire server, including its operating system.
- You can back up only the System State Data, data that includes the server's configuration data as well as the *Ntds.dit* directory store.
- You can restore nonauthoritative data—data that will be added to the DC but updated by multimaster replication when the DC is back online.
- You can restore authoritative data—data that will be added to the DC but which will update all other DCs through multimaster replication when the DC is back online.
- You can perform Install From Media (IFM) DC setups that rely on a copy of the *Ntds.dit* from another DC to reduce the amount of replication required to create the DC during setup.

There are several ways to work with and use backup data sets when working with DCs in Windows Server 2008. However, if you are familiar with DCs from previous versions of Windows, you will find that several operations are different in Windows Server 2008.

- Backups are performed with Windows Server Backup or through its corresponding *Wbadmin.exe* command-line tool. Both are Windows Server 2008 features and must be added to the server to be made available. It is not installed by default.
- Backups are not discrete. They capture critical volumes in their entirety. On a DC, these volumes include:
    - ❑ The system volume.
    - ❑ The boot volume.
    - ❑ The volume hosting the SYSVOL share.
    - ❑ The volume that hosts the AD DS database.
    - ❑ The volume that hosts the AD DS logs.
- As with previous versions of Windows, backups can be automated or manual.
- Backups cannot be performed to tape drives or dynamic volumes, only to network drives, removable hard drives configured as basic volumes, or DVDs and CDs.
- You cannot back up individual files. Windows Server Backup supports full volume backups only.

- If you want to protect only the system state data, you must use the *Ntdsutil.exe* command-line tool. To do so, you must use the new IFM switch available in *Ntdsutil.exe* to capture this information for Install From Media installations. If the installation is for a read-only DC, this tool will automatically strip AD DS secrets from the data to create secure installation media.

- Backup operators cannot create scheduled backups; only members of the local Administrators group have this privilege in Windows Server 2008. In most cases, this means being a member of the Domain Admins group on DCs.

- If a server is down, you must use a local copy of the Windows Recovery Environment (WinRE) to restore the system. WinRE can either be installed locally or found on the Windows Server 2008 installation media.

These new capabilities affect the way you work with DCs in Windows Server 2008. Use the following recommendations when building DCs to make them easier to recover:

- Run DCs as a single-purpose server and do not add any other roles except the DNS Server role to the server.

- Run DCs as virtual machines under Windows Server 2008 Hyper-V. DCs are ideal candidates for Hyper-V because they mostly require network throughput and processing capability to manage logons. Even if your domains include thousands of users and have a high processor usage during key logon periods such as the morning and the afternoon after lunch, virtualize them and assign more resources to them.

- Do not store any other data on the DC, although you can use separate volumes for the DC database and logs if your AD DS database includes large numbers of objects.

- Transform the Windows Installation Media into an ISO file and make it available on your Hyper-V hosts so that it is readily available if you need to restore the DC. If not, install WinRE onto each DC you create. To do so, you will need access to the Windows Automated Installation Kit (WAIK).

MORE INFO **Windows Automated Installation Kit (WAIK)**

For more information about the Windows Automated Installation Kit, go to *http://go.microsoft.com/fwlink/?LinkId=90643*.

- Perform regular, automated backups of your DCs. These can be to a dedicated basic volume or to a mapped network drive.

- Protect the Directory Services Restore Mode password carefully. This password must be used to restore data to a DC and, because it is a highly privileged password, it must be protected at all times.

MORE INFO   **AD DS backup and recovery**

Find more information in "Step-By-Step Guide for Windows Server 2008 Active Directory Domain Services Backup and Recovery" at *http://technet2.microsoft.com/windowsserver2008/en /library/778ff4c7-623d-4475-ba70-4453f964d4911033.mspx*.

Working with the System State Only

On a server running the AD DS role, system state data includes the following data:

- Registry
- COM+ Class Registration database
- Boot files
- System files that are under Windows Resource Protection
- Active Directory Domain Services database
- SYSVOL directory

When other server roles are installed on a system, the system state will include the first four objects listed previously plus the following files:

- For the Active Directory Certificate Services role: AD CS database
- For the Failover Cluster feature: cluster service information
- For the Web Server role: IIS configuration files

System state information is important although it cannot be captured as is through Windows Server Backup. It can, however, be restored because Windows Server Backup supports three restore modes:

- Full server restore
- System state only restore
- Individual file or folder restore

Each mode enables you to recover the information you need when you need it. Keep in mind that backups generated by Windows Server Backup are always backed up to the same file and added to file content as changes are identified on the source system. However, each time a backup is generated, a new catalog file is created. This catalog file is used to locate data for a particular backup.

Exam Tip   Using Windows Server Backup, backing up volumes and system state data to removable media is an important part of the exam. Make sure you understand it fully.

Creating Installation From Media Data Sets

When you need to stage DCs in large networks, you might prefer to use removable media to create the initial directory content rather than filling up bandwidth to replicate directory contents during the DC installation process. To do this, you rely on Installation From Media, but to create the media, you must use the *Ntdsutil.exe* command with the IFM subcommand.

Ntdsutil.exe is a command interpreter and can be used either interactively or through a single command line that provides all options. Table 13-4 outlines the various options that are available in the IFM subcommand.

Table 13-4 *Ntdsutil.exe* **IFM Subcommand Options**

DC Type	Option	Description
Writable DC	Create Full *destination*	Create media for a normal DC or for an AD LDS instance in a destination folder.
RODC	Create RODC *destination*	Create secure media for an RODC in a destination folder.
Writable DC with SYSVOL data	Create SYSVOL Full *destination*	Create media for a normal DC, including the entire SYSVOL folder, in a destination folder.
RODC with SYSVOL data	Create SYSVOL RODC *destination*	Create media for an RODC, including the entire SYSVOL folder, in a destination folder.

Ntdsutil.exe is the only tool that supports the creation of media for installation. You will be working with this tool in the practice at the end of this lesson.

Performing a Full System Backup

Perform a full system backup in one of two ways: interactively and through a scheduled task. Each can be performed either through the graphical interface or through the command line. Begin with the graphical interface. Keep in mind that Windows Server Backup is a feature that must be installed prior to creating any backups.

Creating an Interactive Full System Backup with Windows Server Backup   Use the following procedure to protect AD DS data with Windows Server Backup. This procedure applies to both the full installation and Server Core, but when applied to Server Core, it must be performed remotely. Use the Connect To Another Computer option in the action pane to connect to a server running Server Core.

1. Log on to a DC with domain administrator credentials and launch Windows Server Backup from the Administrative Tools program group.
2. If a User Account Control dialog box appears, confirm the action and click Continue.
3. Click Backup Once in the Actions pane. This launches the Backup Once Wizard.

4. If this is the first time you run the Backup Once Wizard, choose Different Options and click Next. If not, you can also choose The Same Options.

5. Click Full Server (recommended) and click Next.

   Note that you can also check Custom, but you will not be able to omit anything other than specific volumes. You will not be able to omit folders. Remember that your DCs should be single-purpose servers and, as such, you would not need to exclude any volumes. However, if you are backing up to a local disk, you should exclude this volume from the backup operation. Note that when you use the custom option, you can select an option called Enable System Recovery, which will automatically capture all the data required to recover a full system.

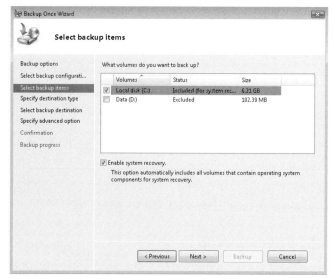

6. Choose the destination, for example, Local drives, and click Next.

   You can target DVDs, CDs, local drives, locally attached removable hard drives, or network shares.

7. If you targeted a local drive, select the drive, make sure it has enough space, and click Next.

8. On the Specify Advanced Option page, select VSS Full Backup and click Next.

   The default option, VSS copy backup, does not delete log files from the volumes and is used only if you are also using another backup product—for example, Microsoft Data Protection Manager—to back up your system. These files are then reused by the other backup tool. You select VSS Full Backup if Windows Server Backup is your only backup tool.

9. Click Backup to perform the backup.

10. Click Close.

You do not need to keep the backup window open for the backup to complete because it will continue in the background; however, it is useful to watch the progress of the backup operation.

Creating an Interactive Full System Backup with *Wbadmin.exe* You can also perform this operation at the command line through the *Wbadmin.exe* command. This procedure applies directly to either the full installation or Server Core. In the full installation, you must use an elevated command prompt—in Server Core, the command prompt is always elevated by default—and use the following command syntax:

```
wbadmin start backup -allcritical -backuptarget:location -quiet
```

where *location* is the drive letter or path to the target drive. Also, you use the –quiet option to avoid having to type **Y** for the operation to proceed.

Scheduling a Backup with Windows Server Backup Use the following procedure to protect AD DS data automatically with Windows Server Backup.

1. Log on to a DC with domain administrator credentials and launch Windows Server Backup from the Administrative Tools program group.

2. If a User Account Control dialog box appears, confirm the action and click Continue.

3. Click Backup Schedule in the Actions pane. This launches the Backup Schedule Wizard; click Next.

4. Click Full Server (Recommended) and click Next.

   Note that you can also click Custom, but this will not let you omit anything other than specific volumes, but you will not be able to omit folders. Also note that in this wizard, when you use the custom option, you will not be able to select the Enable System Recovery option.

5. On the Specify Backup Time page, choose the time of day for the backup. You can also choose to back up the system more than once a day.

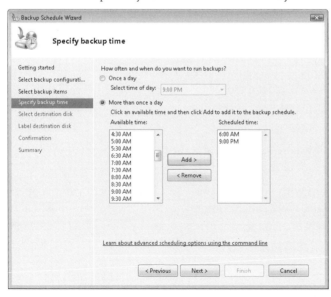

6. On the Select Destination Disk page, click Show All Available Disks, select the remote storage device, and click OK. Select the disk and click Next.

Note that you cannot use mapped network drives with Windows Server Backup when scheduling backup tasks. It will only address rewritable media such as removable hard drives. It also supports virtual hard drives as a target for backup.

IMPORTANT   Using virtual hard disks for backup

Consider using virtual hard disk (VHD) drives as backup targets because of their portability. You can store all VHDs in a central location and place them on a single removable drive to send it to an offsite location. This enables you to combine multiple backups on one disk as opposed to using multiple removable disks, one per protected system.

---

7. When you click Next, the wizard tells you that the target disk will be reformatted. Click Yes.

Windows Server Backup requires exclusive access to the target device and, therefore, must format it when the scheduled backup is created.

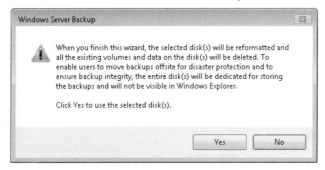

8. On the Label Destination Disk page, you must make note of the label Windows Server Backup will use for this disk before you click Next.

When you change disks, you will need to know which disk this is to perform restores. You must, therefore, label the disk accordingly.

9. Confirm your options and click Finish.

10. Click Close to create the schedule.

The target disk will be formatted, and the task will be added to the system's Scheduled Tasks list.

Scheduling a Backup with *Wbadmin.exe*   You can also perform this operation at the command line through the *Wbadmin.exe* command. In this case, you must use an elevated command prompt and rely on several commands. Begin by identifying the ID of the target disk:

```
wbadmin get disks >diskidentifers.txt
```

This will return a list of the disks attached to a system and place it in the Diskidentifiers.txt file. The *Wbadmin.exe* command relies on disk identifiers or globally unique identifiers (GUIDs) to locate a disk. You pipe the results of the command into a text file so that you can copy the target disk's GUID to the clipboard and reuse it in later commands.

To capture the disk GUID, type:

```
notepad diskidentifiers.txt
```

Highlight the disk identifier you need, including the brackets, and copy it to the clipboard. Close Notepad.

You are ready to create the schedule. Type the following commands:

```
wbadmin enable backup -addtarget:diskid –schedule:times –include:sourcedrives
```

where *diskid* is the GUID you copied. (Right-click and choose Paste to add it.) Times is the times when you want the backup to run in HH:MM 24-hour format. If more than one time is required, separate each with a comma. Source drives are the drive letters of the drives to protect. For example:

```
wbadmin enable backup -addtarget:{f0e2788d-0000-0000-0000-000000000000}
–schedule:21:00,06:00 –include:C:
```

will schedule a backup of drive C at 9:00 P.M. and 6:00 A.M. to the target drive identified by the GUID.

The result is a new scheduled task under the Microsoft\Windows\Backup node of the Task Scheduler. (See Figure 13-6.)

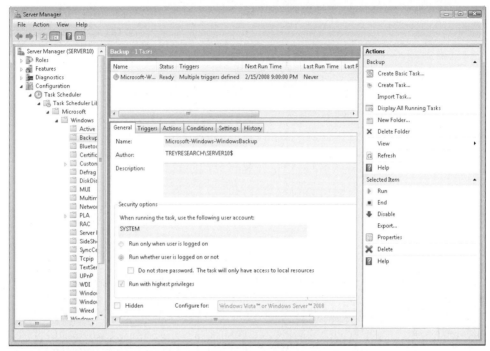

Figure 13-6   The scheduled task created by *Wbadmin.exe*

You can use this procedure to generate batch files to create these jobs, but you must pipe the results into a text file; otherwise, you will not obtain the labels for the removable disks.

Also note that the target drive will be reformatted each time the backup is run. If you need more granular schedules or if you want to change from a daily to a weekly schedule, you can modify the task in Task Scheduler after the *Wbadmin.exe* command has created it.

Performing Proactive Restores

Backup data sets are only as good as the restores and recoveries they support. This is why it is essential for you to test the restoration procedure and to test as many scenarios as possible to ensure that when you do face a disaster, you can recover the data or systems you lost by relying on your backups.

When working with a DC, there are several restoration scenarios:

- Restoring nonauthoritative data to the directory to reduce the replication required to update a DC that has been off for some time

- Restoring authoritative data because the data in the directory has been destroyed
- Restoring a complete DC from a backup

When you need to restore data to a system, you cannot do so when the DC is running, despite the fact that in Windows Server 2008, you can control the AD DS service as you would other services. In fact, you must restart the server and run WinRE, or you must restart the server in the Directory Services Restore Mode (DSRM). Each method supports different restoration procedures. DSRM supports data restores to the directory; WinRE supports the recovery of the entire system.

Restarting in DSRM

There are two ways to launch a server into DSRM. The first relies on a server reboot and, during the reboot process, pressing F8 to view startup options. This enables you to choose the Directory Services Restore Mode. Remember that you need to have access to the DSRM password to use this mode.

```
                         Advanced Boot Options

Choose Advanced Options for: Microsoft Windows Server 2008
(Use the arrow keys to highlight your choice.)

    Safe Mode
    Safe Mode with Networking
    Safe Mode with Command Prompt

    Enable Boot Logging
    Enable low-resolution video (640x480)
    Last Known Good Configuration (advanced)
    Directory Services Restore Mode
    Debugging Mode
    Disable automatic restart on system failure
    Disable Driver Signature Enforcement

    Start Windows Normally

Description: Start Windows in Directory Services Repair Mode (for Windows
             domain controllers only).



ENTER=Choose                                              ESC=Cancel
```

You can also force the reboot directly into DSRM by changing the boot order in the boot file of the OS. This is done with the *Bcdedit.exe* command. To use the command line to change the boot order, type the following command in an elevated command prompt:

```
bcdedit /set safeboot dsrepair
```

Then, when you need to restart the server normally, use the following command:

```
bcdedit /deletevalue safeboot
```

If you need to perform the operation only once, it might be best simply to rely on the F8 key at system startup.

IMPORTANT Resetting the DSRM password

Keep in mind that to reset the DSRM password—an activity you should perform on a regular basis—you must first boot into DSRM and then use the standard password changing methods.

Identifying the Appropriate Backup Data Set

One of the problems organizations who used AD DS in previous versions of Windows faced was the ability to identify properly whether the data they require is located in a particular backup data set. In Windows Server 2008, you can rely on the AD DS database mounting tool to view the contents of a data set before you perform a recovery operation. This avoids the previous hit-or-miss approach system administrators needed to rely on.

The mounting tool works with database snapshots. Snapshots can easily be created with the *Ntdsutil.exe* tool. For example, to generate regular snapshots of a directory, you would use the following command:

```
ntdsutil "activate instance NTDS" snapshot create quit quit
```

This will generate a snapshot on the same volume as the database. Be careful how you use this command because it will quickly fill up the disk on which the *Ntds.dit* database file is located.

Perform the following steps to view backup data set or snapshot contents.

1. Launch an elevated command prompt by right-clicking Command Prompt in the Start menu and choosing Run As Administrator.
2. Begin by listing the available snapshots. Snapshots are created each time a backup is run or through the *Ntdsutil.exe create* subcommand, but you need to have the snapshot GUID to mount it. Use the following command to pipe all snapshot GUIDs into a text file.

   ```
   ntdsutil "activate instance NTDS" snapshot "list all" quit quit >snapshot.txt
   ```
3. Now, look into the text file to locate and copy the GUID you need:

   ```
   notepad snapshot.txt
   ```
4. Locate the GUID you need and copy it to the clipboard. Remember to include the brackets in the selection. Minimize Notepad in case you need a different GUID.

5. Mount the snapshot you need to use. Remember to right-click and choose Paste to paste the GUID at the mount command.

```
ntdsutil
activate instance NTDS
snapshot
mount guid
quit
quit
```

Note the path listed for the mounted database.

6. Use the AD DS database mounting tool to load the snapshot as an LDAP server.

```
dsamain –dbpath c:\$snap_datetime_volumec$\windows\ntds\ntds.dit
–ldapport portnumber
```

Be sure to use ALL CAPS for the *dbpath* value and use any number beyond 50,000 for the *ldapport* value to make sure you do not conflict with AD DS. Also note that you can use the minus (–) sign or the slash (/) for the options in the command. The database will be mounted and will stay mounted until you have completed your operations. *Do not close the command prompt.* In fact, you might want to use two command prompts, one for mounting the snapshot in *Ntdsutil.exe* and one for the *Dsamin.exe* command. Then you can mount and dismount different snapshots until you locate the one that contains the information you need to recover.

7. Now use *Ldp.exe* or Active Directory Users and Computers to access the instance. For example, launch Active Directory Users And Computers from the Administrative Tools program group.

8. Right-click Active Directory Users And Computers and select Change Domain Controller.

9. In the Change Directory Server dialog box, click <Type A Directory Server Name[:Port] Here>, type the *servername:portnumber*, for example, **Server10:51000**, and press Enter. The status should be online. Click OK.

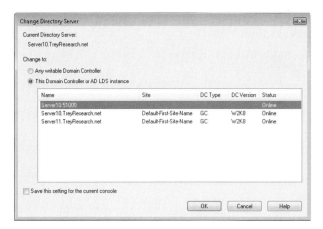

10. Search the loaded instance to locate the information you need and view its properties. If it is the instance you need, then make note of its name. Close Active Directory Users And Computers.

11. Return to the command prompt and press Ctrl+C to stop *Dsamain.exe*.

12. Unmount the database snapshot. Use the following command. Remember to paste in the GUID from the clipboard.

```
ntdsutil
activate instance NTDS
snapshot
unmount guid
quit
quit
```

13. Close the command prompt.

If the selected database snapshot was not the one you were looking for, repeat the procedure. If it was, proceed to a restore.

IMPORTANT   Using arrow keys in command prompts

Keep in mind that you can use the up and down arrow keys when you are in a command prompt to return to previous commands. Also, note that there are different buffers in the command prompt. For example, there is a buffer in the command prompt itself and then a different buffer in the *Ntdsutil.exe* command. You can use both to return to previous commands and save typing.

Performing Nonauthoritative or Authoritative Restores

As mentioned earlier, performing a restore requires you to restart the directory in DSRM. This means shutting down the DC. Remember that you can perform either nonauthoritative or authoritative restores on both the full installation or Server Core. The first addresses a DC rebuild when no data was lost because it is still found on other DCs. The second restores data that was lost and updates the Update Sequence Number (USN) for the data to make it authoritative and ensure that it is replicated to all other servers. Both use the same procedure at first. Make sure you have connected the removable media on which you stored the backup you want to restore.

1. Repair the server, if required, and start it up. During startup, press F8 to view the startup modes.

2. Select Directory Services Restore Mode and press Enter.

3. This will boot into Windows. Log on with the DSRM account and password; this should be the account displayed at the logon screen and the DSRM password you set when you created the DC.

   You can restore the data either through the command line or with Windows Server Backup. Note, however, that when you want to restore directory data, you must perform a System State restore and, to do so, you must use the command line.

4. Launch an elevated command prompt by right-clicking Command Prompt in the Start menu and choosing Run As Administrator.

5. Type the following command:

   ```
   wbadmin get versions -backuptarget:drive -machine:servername
   ```

   For example, to list the available backups located on D drive on SERVER10, type:

   ```
   wbadmin get versions -backuptarget:d: -machine:server10
   ```

   Note the version identifier information because you need the exact name for the next command.

6. To recover system state information, type the following command:

   ```
   wbadmin start systemstaterecovery -version:datetime -backuptarget:drive
   -machine:servername -quiet
   ```

   For example, to recover the system state from a backup dated 15 February, 2008, from D drive on SERVER10, type:

   ```
   wbadmin start systemstaterecovery -version:02/15/2008-19:38
   -backuptarget:d: -machine:server10 -quiet
   ```

   You use the -quiet option to avoid having to confirm the backup operation. Note that the restore will take some time to complete.

7. Close the command prompt.

   If you were performing a nonauthoritative restore, you would be finished.

8. Restart the DC in its normal operating mode.

   When you restart the server, AD DS will automatically know that it has recovered from a restore and perform an integrity check of the database as it starts.

IMPORTANT Using DFS replication

If your forest is in Windows Server 2008 functional mode, you will be using DFS replication. In this case, the restore will create a nonauthoritative version of the SYSVOL share. If you want to avoid additional replication, add the *–authsysvol* switch to the *Wbadmin.exe* command.

If, however, you are performing an authoritative restore, you must mark the data as authoritative. *Do not restart the server.* Use the following steps.

1. Type the following commands:

   ```
   ntdsutil
   authoritative restore
   restore database
   quit
   quit
   ```

2. Restart the server in normal mode.

   The restore database command marks all the data in the *Ntds.dit* database of this DC as authoritative.

   If you want to restore only a portion of the directory, use the following restore subcommand in *Ntdsutil.exe*:

   ```
   restore subtree ou=ouname,dc=dcname,dc=dcname
   ```

   where you must supply the distinguished name of the OU or object you want to restore.

After the server is restarted, the replication process will start, and the restored information that has been marked as authoritative will be replicated to all other DCs. However, it might restart several times as the restore operation updates system files. AD DS replication will bring it up to date when it has restarted for the last time either by replicating from this DC to others because the restore was authoritative or from other DCs to this one when the restore was nonauthoritative.

Exam Tip   Performing an authoritative or nonauthoritative Active Directory restore and working in Directory Services Recovery Mode are important parts of this topic on the exam.

Restoring from a Complete Backup

When the DC is completely down and needs to be rebuilt, but you have access to a full server backup, you can perform a complete system restore. You will need access to the full server backup files. If they are on a removable drive, make sure this drive is connected to the server before you begin the restore; otherwise, you will need to restart the server. If the files are on a network drive, make note of the path. Also, obtain the Windows Installation Media DVD or, if your new DC is a virtual machine, link its DVD drive to an ISO file containing the Windows Installation Media.

Full server recoveries can be performed through the graphical interface or through the command line.

Performing a Graphical Full Server Recovery   To perform a full server recovery with the graphical interface, use the following procedure. This procedure applies to both the full installation and Server Core.

1. Insert or connect the Windows Server 2008 installation DVD, restart the computer and, when prompted, press a key to start from the DVD.
2. On the initial Windows screen, accept or select Language options, the Time and Currency formats, and a Keyboard layout, and click Next.
3. In the Install Now window, click Repair Your Computer.
4. In the System Recovery Options dialog box, click anywhere to clear any operating systems that are selected for repair and click Next.

5. Under Choose A Recovery Tool, select Windows Complete PC Restore.

6. If the backup is stored on a remote server, click Cancel on the warning message.

7. Select Restore A Different Backup and click Next.

8. In the Select The Location Of The Backup page, perform the following steps, depending on whether the backup is stored locally or on a network share:

    a. If the backup is stored on the local computer, select the location of the backup and click Next.

    b. If the backup is stored on a network share, click Advanced and select Search For A Backup On The Network. Click Yes to confirm.

    c. In the Network Folder, type the path for the network share and click OK.

    d. Type the appropriate credentials and click OK.

    e. In the Select The Location Of The Backup page, select the location of the backup and click Next.

9. Select the backup to restore and click Next.

10. If you want to replace all data on all volumes, in the Choose How To Restore The Backup page, select Format And Repartition Disks.

11. To prevent volumes that are not included in the restore from being deleted and re-created, select Exclude Disks, select the disk(s) you want to exclude, and click OK.

12. Click Next and click Finish.

13. Select I Confirm That I Want To Format The Disks And Restore The Backup and click OK.

14. Reboot the server.

    It should start as a new image of the server you restored in the backup set you used.

Performing a Command-Line Full Server Recovery   To perform a full server recovery with the command line, use the following procedure. This procedure applies directly to either the full installation or Server Core.

1. Insert or connect the Windows Server 2008 installation DVD, restart the DC, and, when prompted, press a key to start from the DVD.

2. On the initial Windows screen, accept or select Language options, the Time and Currency formats, and a Keyboard layout, and click Next.

3. In the Install Now window, click Repair Your Computer.

4. In the System Recovery Options dialog box, click anywhere to clear any operating systems that are selected for repair and click Next.

5. Under Choose A Recovery Tool, select Command Prompt.

6. At the command prompt, type **diskpart** and press Enter.

7. At the diskpart prompt, type **list vol** and press Enter.

Identify the volume from the list that corresponds to the location of the full server backup you want to restore. The driver letters in WinRE do not necessarily match the volumes as they appeared in Windows Server 2008.

8. Type **exit** and press Enter.

9. At the Sources prompt, type the following command and press Enter:

```
wbadmin get versions -backuptarget:drive -machine:servername
```

For example, to list the available backups located on D drive on SERVER10, type:

```
wbadmin get versions -backuptarget:D: -machine:SERVER10
```

Note the version identifier information because you need the exact name for the next command.

10. At the command prompt, type the following command and press Enter:

```
wbadmin start systemstaterecovery -version:datetime -backuptarget:drive
-machine:servername -quiet
```

For example, to recover the system state from a backup dated 15 February, 2008, from D drive on SERVER10, type:

```
wbadmin start sysrecovery -version:02/15/2008-19:38 -backuptarget:d:
-machine:server10 -restoreallvolumes -quiet
```

You use the -quiet option to avoid having to confirm the backup operation.

11. After the recovery operation has completed, minimize the command window and, in the System Recovery Options dialog box, click Restart.

The server should restart and operate normally.

Quick Check

1. You are trying to move a group of objects from one location to the other in the directory, and you keep getting an access denied error. What could be the problem?

2. You look up a backup on one of your removable disks and discover to your dismay that the disk is completely blank. What could have happened?

3. Your forest is running in Windows Server 2008 full functional mode. Which tool should you rely on to manage replication between DCs?

4. What is the difference between reassigning a user account and re-creating the account?

5. You are trying to view directory changes in the event log. Specifically, you are searching for event IDs numbered 5136, but you can't seem to find them anywhere. What could be the problem?

Quick Check Answers

1. The objects have been assigned the *Protect From Accidental Deletion* attribute. Because of this, they cannot be moved from one location to another. You must use Advanced Features from the View menu to view the feature and then go to the object's Properties dialog box and the Object tab to clear the option before moving the objects. Make sure you recheck the option after the move has been performed.

2. When Windows Server Backup is run as a scheduled task, it always begins by formatting the target backup disk. If the task is interrupted after the formatting, for example, by a computer reboot, the backup operation would not occur, leaving the target disk blank.

3. When a forest runs in Windows Server 2008 full functional mode, replication no longer relies on the File Replication System. Instead, replication relies on the delta-based compression replication provided by the Distributed File System Replication engine. This means that you must use *DFSRadmin.exe* to manage replication.

4. When you reassign an account from one person to the other, the new person automatically gains all the access rights previously assigned to the account. When you re-create an account, you must first discover which rights need to be assigned and then assign them manually to the new account.

5. To enable directory object auditing, you must manually enable the event subcategory with the following command:

```
auditpol /set /subcategory:"directory service changes" /success:enable
```

Protecting DCs as Virtual Machines

When a server is created as a VM instead of being installed on a physical computer, it becomes nothing more than a set of files on a disk because the disk drives for the computer are hosted in virtual hard drives. DCs running both AD DS and DNS are ideal candidates for virtualization on either Microsoft Virtual Server R2 or on Hyper-V because they focus on providing a single, network-oriented service. When a machine is virtual, it becomes much easier to protect it, restore it, and otherwise manipulate it. If the server has a full system failure, just go back to an earlier version of the virtual machine and boot it up. In the case of a DC, multimaster replication will then automatically take care of the rest and bring it up to date. This is by far the most powerful business continuity scenario for DCs.

In addition, virtual machine protection is greatly facilitated by a single Windows Server 2008 feature: the Volume Shadow Copy Service (VSS). When configured, VSS automatically takes snapshots of the contents of a disk drive at regular intervals. If anything untoward occurs to any file on the disk drive, you simply rely on Previous Versions—a tab that appears in the Properties dialog box of any file or folder—to restore an older version of the file or folder quickly. Previous versions are enabled by default on Windows Server 2008 and Windows Vista.

On a virtual machine, you restore the virtual hard drives that make up the machine from a previous time or date, and your machine is back up and running. Overall, this procedure takes about five minutes. No other backup and restore scenario can compete with VSS and VMs.

VSS should be enabled on host servers that maintain and run the virtual machines in your data center. VSS can be added to either the full installation or Server Core. It takes about 10 minutes to enable VSS on any server; however, you must be prepared and have the proper disk structure. For example, a host system running Hyper-V should have at least three disk volumes:

- Drive C should be the system and boot drive and should host the Hyper-V role.
- Drive D should be the data drive that hosts the virtual machines. This drive should normally be stored on some form of shared storage to support continuity for the VMs it hosts.
- Drive E should be configured to host the VSS snapshots that will be created on an ongoing basis. Each VSS snapshot is 100 MB in size because it captures only disk pointers and not the entire disk structure. You can store up to 512 snapshots at a time. When you reach this maximum, VSS will automatically overwrite the oldest snapshots. Size this disk accordingly.

Enabling VSS involves the following steps:

1. Log on to the host server with local administration credentials.
2. Open Windows Explorer, locate drive D, right-click it, and select Properties.
3. In the Properties dialog box, select the Shadow Copies tab.
4. Begin by specifying VSS settings. Click the Settings button.
5. In the Settings dialog box, use the drop-down list to select D: Drive. Set the limit for the copy as appropriate (the default should be fine) and change the schedule if required. Click OK.
6. Select D: from the Select Volume list and click Enable. In the Enable Shadow Copies dialog box, click Yes.

    Begin with the default schedule at first; you can always change it later. The VSS service is now enabled.
7. Click Create Now to take the first snapshot. This generates the first protection set for the VMs.
8. Click OK to close the D drive Properties dialog box.

You can also perform this operation through the command line. If your host servers are running Server Core—as they should be to minimize host server CPU overhead—you will need to perform this operation either remotely or through the command line. Use the following commands:

```
vssadmin add shadowstorage /for=d: /on=e: /maxsize=6000mb
vssadmin create shadow /for=d:
vssadmin list shadowstorage
vssadmin list shadows
```

The first command sets up the shadow copies according to the default schedule. The second creates the first shadow copy. The next two list the associations and then available shadow copies.

Shadow copy schedules are scheduled tasks. To control the scheduled task and modify its schedule, rely on the *Schtasks.exe* command or use the Task Scheduler remotely in the Computer Management console.

To access previous versions of a file or a folder, open Windows Explorer, connect to a shared folder, in this case the default share created by the system, D$, and locate either the file or, if the file is gone, the folder in which it was stored; right-click it to select Properties, move to the Previous Versions tab, select the version you need, and click Restore. Close the Properties dialog box. You can also copy and compare files.

Monitor VSS usage to determine whether the default schedule is appropriate. Review how you use the VSS service to see whether you need to modify the default schedule. As you can see, VSS rivals any other backup and restore process for virtual machines.

MORE INFO   Providing high availability for virtual machines

A discussion on how to provide high availability for virtual machines is beyond the scope of this book. However, if you are interested in preparing host servers running Server Core and Hyper-V, look up *Microsoft Windows Server 2008: The Complete Reference* by Ruest and Ruest (McGraw-Hill Osborne, 2008). This book outlines how to build a complete dynamic infrastructure based on Windows Server 2008.

PRACTICE Working with the AD DS Database

In this practice, you will work with a variety of utilities to protect and manage the AD DS database. First, you will generate a backup of directory data and then use this backup to create a new DC, using offline data to speed the process and reduce replication over the network. Then you will work with the AD DS database to perform a manual defragmentation and compaction and then automate the process. Finally, you will rely on the Group Policy Management Console (GPMC) to protect Group Policy objects. This practice relies on SERVER10 and SERVER11, which you prepared in the Before You Begin section at the beginning of this chapter.

▶ **Exercise 1   Use *Ntdsutil.exe* to Capture System State Data**

In this exercise, you will use the *Ntdsutil.exe* command to capture the data required to perform an installation from media for a DC.

1. Log on to SERVER 10 with the domain administrator account.

2. Verify that this server includes a formatted D drive and create a folder named **IFM** on this drive.

3. Launch an elevated command prompt by right-clicking Command Prompt in the Start menu and choosing Run As Administrator.

4. Type the following commands:

```
ntdsutil
activate instance NTDS
ifm
create sysvol full d:\ifm
```

The system should display a Creating Snapshot message while the operation is in progress and then list a series of other information as it completes the operation. Note that the system defragments the newly captured snapshot.

5. Type:

```
quit
quit
```

6. Use Windows Explorer to view the results of the snapshot you created with *Ntdusutil.exe*.

7. Share the IFM folder by right-clicking the folder and choosing Share.

8. In the drop-down list, choose Everyone, click Add, and assign the Contributor role in the Permission Level column.

9. Click Share to create the share.

10. Click Done.

Your IFM data is now ready to use to stage a new DC.

▶ **Exercise 2   Create a DC from Backup Data**

In this exercise, you will install a new DC in the *treyresearch.net* domain, using IFM data.

1. Log on to SERVER 11 with the local administrator account.

2. Launch Windows Explorer and create a new folder on the C drive, called IFM.

3. Move to the address bar in Windows Explorer, type **\\server10\ifm**, and press Enter.

4. If the credentials dialog box appears, type **TreyResearch\Administrator** or equivalent and the required password.

    If you use the same account name and password on both servers, even though SERVER11 is not a member of the domain, you will not be prompted for credentials because of pass-through authentication.

5. Copy the entire contents from the IFM folder on SERVER10 to the C:\IFM folder on SERVER11.

6. Verify that all items have been copied.

7. Install the Active Directory Domain Services role. In Server Manager, right-click the Roles node and select Add Roles.

8. Review the Before You Begin page of the wizard and click Next.

9. On the Select Server Roles page of the Add Roles Wizard, select Active Directory Domain Services and click Next.

10. Review the information on the Active Directory Domain Services page and click Next.

11. Review your choices and click Install.

12. Examine the installation results and click Close.

    Your installation is complete.

13. Click the Active Directory Domain Services node in Server Manager.

14. Click Run The Active Directory Domain Services Installation Wizard in the details pane.

    This launches the Active Directory Domain Services Installation Wizard.

15. Make sure you select the Use Advanced Mode Installation check box before you click Next.

    You need this option to install from media.

16. Review the information on the Operating System Compatibility page and click Next.

17. On the Choose A Deployment Configuration page, choose Existing Forest, select Add A Domain Controller To An Existing Domain, and click Next.

18. On the Network Credentials page, type **treyresearch.net**.

    Because you logged on locally to the server and this account does not have access rights to the *treyresearch.net* domain, you must provide alternate credentials.

19. Click Set. Type **treyresearch.net\administrator** or the equivalent account name and add the password. Click OK, and then click Next.

20. On the Select A Domain page, click *treyresearch.net* (forest root domain) and click Next.

21. On the Select A Site page, accept the default and click Next.

    This page also appears because you are running the wizard in advanced mode.

22. On the Additional Domain Controller Options page, verify that DNS Server and Global Catalog are both selected and click Next.

If you did not assign a static IP address, the AD DS Active Directory Domain Services Installation Wizard will give you a warning because you are using a dynamic IP Address.

23. Click the Yes, The Computer Will Use A Dynamically Assigned IP Address (Not Recommended) option.

   The Active Directory Domain Services Installation Wizard will warn you that it cannot create a delegation for the domain.

24. Click Yes.

25. On the Install From Media page, click Replicate Data From Media At The Following Location, type **C:\IFM** or click Browse to locate the IFM folder on the C drive, and click Next.

   Note that it indicates that the media must have been created from a writable DC because you did not select the RODC mode for this DC.

26. On the Source Domain Controller page, accept the defaults and click Next.

27. On the Location For Database, Log Files And SYSVOL page, accept the default locations and click Next.

28. Type a strong password, confirm it, and click Next.

29. Confirm your settings on the Summary page and click Next. Select Reboot On Completion and wait for the operation to complete.

   Your new DC has been created from local media. This cuts down replication and then updates the data through replication after the DC has been created.

▶ **Exercise 3   Perform Database Maintenance**

In this exercise, you will perform interactive database maintenance, using the restartable Active Directory Domain Services mode. You can perform this operation now because there are two DCs in the *treyresearch.net* domain. You must have at least two DCs to be able to use restartable AD DS.

1. Log on to SERVER11 with the domain administrator account.
2. Use Windows Explorer to create a **C:\Temp** and a **C:\OrignalNTDS** folder.

   You will use these folders as temporary locations for the compacted and the original database.
3. In Server Manager, expand the Configuration node and click Services.
4. Locate the Active Directory Domain Services service (it should be first on the list) and right-click it to select Stop.
5. In the Stop Other Services dialog box, click Yes.

   The server will stop the service.

   Remember that if the service cannot contact another writable DC, it will not be able to stop; otherwise, no one would be able to log on to the domain.
6. Launch an elevated command prompt by right-clicking Command Prompt in the Start menu and choosing Run As Administrator.
7. Begin by compacting the database. Type the following commands:

```
ntdsutil
activate instance NTDS
files
compact to C:\temp
```

   The *Ntdsutil.exe* will compact the database and copy it to the new location. In very large directories, this operation can take some time.

8. Type the following after the compaction operation is complete:

    ```
    quit
    quit
    ```

9. Now, delete all the log files. Type the following:

    ```
    cd %systemroot%\ntds
    del *.log
    ```

    You delete the log files because you will be replacing the *Ntds.dit* file with the newly com-
    pacted file, and the existing log files will not work with the newly compacted database.

10. Now, back up the *Ntds.dit* file to protect it in case something goes wrong. Type the following:

    ```
    copy ntds.dit \originalntds
    ```

11. Copy the newly compacted database to the original NTDS folder. Making sure you are
    still within the %SystemRoot%\NTDS folder, type the following:

    ```
    copy c:\temp\ntds.dit
    y
    ```

12. Finally, verify the integrity of the new *Ntds.dit* file.

    After this is done, you will also perform a semantic database analysis to verify the data
    within the database. Type the following:

    ```
    ntdsutil
    activate instance NTDS
    files
    integrity
    quit
    semantic database analysis
    go fixup
    quit
    quit
    ```

    Note that if the integrity check fails, you must recopy the original *Ntds.dit* back to this
    folder because the newly compacted file is corrupt. If you do not do so, your DC will no
    longer be operational.

13. Return to Server Manager, expand the Configuration node, and click Services.

14. Locate the Active Directory Domain Services service (it should be first on the list) and
    right-click it to select Start.

    Your server is back online and ready to deliver authentication services to the network. It
    can take several minutes for the dependent services to restart. Delete the Ntds.dit
    located in the Original NTDS folder because it is no longer valid.

▶ **Exercise 4 Automate Database Maintenance**

You can script the entire database compaction operation from the command line if you want
to automate it. You should, however, make sure all the operational results are captured in a text
file so that you can review them if something goes wrong.

1. Log on to SERVER11 with the domain administrator account.

2. Also, make sure both a **C:\Temp** folder and a **C:\NTDS** folder exist on your server and that both folders are empty.

    You will use this folder as a temporary location for the compacted database. You are ready to automate the compaction process.

3. Move to the C:\Temp folder and right-click in the details pane to select New; then click Text Document.

4. Name the Text document **Compaction.cmd**.

    If you cannot see the .txt extension of the file, click Folder Options from the Tools menu in Windows Explorer. On the View tab, clear Hide Extensions For Known File Types and click OK. Remove the .txt extension on your file name. Confirm the removal.

5. Right-click Compaction.cmd and choose Edit. Type the following commands:

    ```
    del C:\temp\*.dit
    del C:\originalntds\*.dit
    net stop ntds /y
    ntdsutil "activate instance NTDS" files "compact to C:\temp" quit quit
    \cd \windows\ntds
    del *.log
    copy ntds.dit \originalntds
    del ntds.dit
    copy c:\temp\ntds.dit
    ntdsutil "activate instance NTDS" files integrity quit "semantic database
    analysis" "go fixup" quit quit
    net start ntds
    ```

6. Save and close the Compaction.cmd file.

    Note that you can add a pause command after each command in your text file to verify the proper operation of the commands while testing.

7. Test the file by launching an elevated command prompt by right-clicking Command Prompt in the Start menu and choosing Run As Administrator.

8. Type:

    ```
    cd \temp
    compaction
    ```

9. If at any time the file does not work, use Ctrl+C to cancel the batch file and correct the errors.

    If the file works properly, you can use it to automate the compaction process.

10. Remove any pause statements you entered in the file and save it again.

    You can reuse this command file each time you want to run the compaction on your systems. It is recommended that you run this command file interactively to address any errors or issues during the process. Be very wary of putting this file into a scheduled task. You should never run compaction in unattended mode because errors could destroy your DC.

11. If a DC is nonfunctioning, you can use the following command to remove the DC role:

    `dcpromo /forceremoval`

12. Run the Active Directory Domain Services Installation Wizard again to re-create the DC. Perform the *Ntds.dit* compaction operation at least once a month.

▶ **Exercise 5   Protect Group Policy Objects**

In this exercise, you will use the GPMC to back up GPOs.

1. Log on to SERVER11 with the domain administrator account.
2. Verify the existence of a folder named Temp on the C drive.
3. Launch the GPMC from the Administrative Tools program group.
4. Expand Forest\Domains*domainname*\Goup Policy Objects.
5. Right-click Group Policy Objects and select Back Up All.
6. Type the location as **C:\Temp** or use the Browse button to locate the folder.
7. Type a description, in this case, **First GPO Backup** and click Back Up.

    The GPO backup tool will show the progress of the backup.
8. Click OK after the backup is complete.

    Your GPOs are now protected.
9. Back up the Temp folder.

    You can rely on this folder to copy the GPOs from one domain to another if you wish. Perform this operation at least once a week.

Exam Tip   Backing up and restoring GPOs are both important parts of the exam. Practice these operations thoroughly to prepare for this topic.

Lesson Summary

- To maintain your directory service, you must perform proactive maintenance tasks. These tasks fall into twelve categories, many of which should be delegated to others. Domain administrators are responsible for the AD DS service and should focus on core directory operations such as database administration tasks.

- Several tools are available for AD DS administration. The most commonly used tools are the three main Active Directory consoles: Active Directory Users and Computers, Active Directory Sites and Services, and Active Directory Domains and Trusts.

- With Windows Server 2008, AD DS is now a manageable service like all other servers and can be started and stopped without having to restart the server in Directory Services Restore Mode.

- When you delete an object in AD DS, you must restore the object to re-create its properties. If you simply re-create the object, it will not have the same SID and, therefore, will not retain any of the deleted object's properties. Restoring an object restores the original SID and, therefore, will automatically restore most of the access rights associated with the object.

- There are several ways to protect information in the directory:
  - ❏ You can protect objects from deletion.
  - ❏ You can audit AD DS changes to view previous and changed values when changes are made.
  - ❏ You can rely on the tombstone container to recover deleted objects.
  - ❏ You can rely on backup and restore to recover lost information.
- To restore objects from the deleted objects container in AD DS, you must use a tool that will expose this container and enable you to modify the state of the object. Two tools are available for this operation: *Ldp.exe* and Quest Object Restore for Active Directory. After the object is restored, you must reassign its password, group memberships, and other informational attributes and then enable the object.
- When you restore an object from backup, the object is restored with all its previous attributes. No additional changes are required.

Lesson Review

You can use the following questions to test your knowledge of the information in Lesson 1, "Proactive Directory Maintenance and Data Store Protection." The questions are also available on the companion CD if you prefer to review them in electronic form.

NOTE   Answers

Answers to these questions and explanations of why each answer choice is right or wrong are located in the "Answers" section at the end of the book.

---

1. You are a systems administrator for *contoso.com*. You have been requested to compact the database on one of the two DCs for the forest root domain. However, when you try to stop the AD DS service, you find that you cannot stop it on the server you are working on. What could be the problem?
   - A. You cannot stop the AD DS service on a Windows Server 2008 DC.
   - B. Someone else is working on another DC in this domain.
   - C. You must restart the server in Directory Services Restore Mode.
   - D. You must use the *net stop* command to stop the AD DS service.

2. You are the network administrator of a large network. One of your DCs recently failed. You need to restore the DC to a working state. You have several backups of the server that were created with Windows Server Backup. Which of the following steps should you perform? (Choose all that apply.)

A. Restart the server in Directory Services Restore Mode.

B. Perform an authoritative restore using the *Ntdsutil.exe* command.

C. Reinstall Windows Server 2008.

D. Restart the server in WinRE.

E. Perform a nonauthoritative restore using the *Ntdsutil.exe* command.

F. Perform a full server recovery using the command line.

Lesson 2: Proactive Directory Performance Management

The second activity you must master to maintain your DCs proactively is performance management. When you use proper installation and creation procedures, your DCs should just work. Remember that the Domain Controller role is now in its fifth iteration since it appeared in Microsoft Windows NT, and it has evolved with the different releases of the Microsoft server operating system. This means that it is now a very solid and stable service.

However, you'll find that despite this stability, things can still go wrong, whether they are related to system or human errors. And when they do, you need to be ready to identify the issues quickly and take appropriate steps to correct the situation. When you perform proactive performance management, you are forewarned when untoward events might occur. This is the crux of this lesson.

> **After this lesson, you will be able to:**
> - Work with system performance indicators.
> - Use the Windows Server performance and reliability tools.
> - Use the Windows System Resource Monitor.
> - Generate and view performance reports.
>
> **Estimated lesson time: 45 minutes**

Managing System Resources

Windows Server includes several tools that help identify potential issues with system resources. When systems are not configured properly and are not assigned appropriate resources such as CPU, RAM, or disk space, systems monitoring will help you identify where bottlenecks occur. When you identify these bottlenecks, you then assign additional resources to the system. If the system is physical, this most often means shutting down the system; installing new resources, for example, additional memory chips; and then restarting the system. If the system is virtual, then depending on the virtualization engine you use, you might be able to allocate new resources while the virtual machine is still running. If not, shut it down; allocate new resources, for example, an additional CPU and additional RAM; and then restart it. After the system is restarted, monitor its performance again to identify whether the new resources solved the problem.

The tools you can rely on to identify performance bottlenecks in Windows Server 2008 include:

- Task Manager, which displays current system resource usage.
- Event Viewer, which logs specific events, including performance related events.

- Reliability Monitor, which tracks changes brought to the system, enabling you to identify whether a change could be the cause of a new bottleneck.
- Performance Monitor, which collects data in either real time or at specific intervals to identify potential issues.
- Windows System Resource Manager (WSRM), which can be used to profile specific applications to indicate which resources they need at which time. You can also use it to manage application resource allocation based on the profiles you generate.

You can use other tools as well, such as Microsoft System Center Operations Manager, to monitor the state of a system continuously and automatically correct well-known issues. Operations Manager relies on custom management packs to monitor specific applications.

Using Task Manager

The simplest of all tools to use is Task Manager. This tool provides real-time system status information and covers several key aspects of a system's performance, including:

- Running applications
- Running processes
- Running services
- Performance, including CPU and memory usage
- Networking, including network interface card (NIC) utilization
- Currently logged-on users

You can access Task Manager in a variety of ways, the most common of which is to right-click the taskbar and select Task Manager. Another common method is to use the Ctrl+Alt+Delete key combination and click Task Manager when the menu choices appear. For example, this is how you would access Task Manager on Server Core because it does not include a taskbar. You can also type **Taskmgr.exe** at a command prompt.

When you access information regarding system performance, the Performance tab is the most useful tab. (See Figure 13-7.) This displays complete information about your system's key resource usage. It details physical and kernel memory usage. This tab also includes a button that gives you access to Resource Monitor. Clicking this button will launch Resource Monitor while keeping Task Manager open.

Resource Monitor is a *super* Task Manager because it brings together the CPU, disk, memory, and network usage graphs in a single view. (See Figure 13-8.) In addition, it includes expandable components for each resource, displaying details of each component so that you can identify which processes might be the culprit if issues are evident. These two tools are ideal for on-the-spot verifications of resource usage. You should rely on them if you need to identify immediately whether something is wrong with a server.

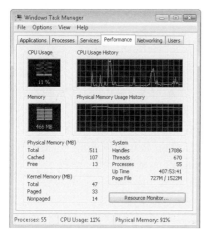

Figure 13-7 Viewing real-time performance information in Task Manager

For example, if the system does not have enough memory, you will immediately see that memory usage is constantly high. In this case, Windows will be forced to use on-disk virtual memory and will need to swap or page memory contents constantly between physical and virtual memory. Constant paging is a typical issue that servers with insufficient physical memory face and is often indicated by slow system behavior. One good indicator of insufficient memory is slow Server Manager operation.

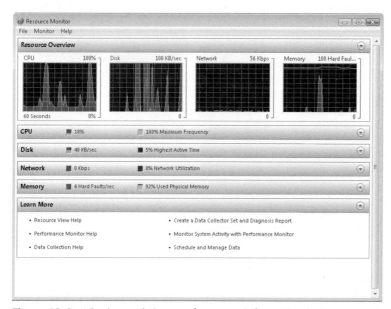

Figure 13-8 Viewing real-time performance information in Resource Monitor

---

MORE INFO   Resource Monitor

For more information on Resource Monitor, see Scenario 1 in "Windows Server 2008 Performance and Reliability Monitoring Step-by-Step Guide" at *http://technet2.microsoft.com/windowsserver2008 /en/library/7e17a3be-f24e-4fdd-9e38-a88e2c8fb4d81033.mspx?mfr=true.*

Working with Event Viewer

Another excellent indicator of system health is Windows Event Log. Windows maintains several event logs to collect information about each of the services running on a server. By default, these include the Application, Security, Setup, System, and Forwarded Events logs, all located in the Windows Logs folder. However, on a DC, you will also have additional logs that are specifically related to AD DS operation. These will be located in the Applications and Services Logs folder and will include:

- DFS Replication, which is available in domains and forests operating in Windows Server 2008 full functional mode. If you are running your domains or forests in one of the earlier modes, the log will be for the FRS replication service.
- Directory Service, which focuses on the operations that are specifically related to AD DS.
- DNS Server, which lists all events related to the naming service that supports AD DS operation.

However, one of the best features of Event Log is related to Server Manager. Because it acts as the central management location for each of the roles included in Windows Server 2008, Server Manager provides custom log views that percolate all the events related to a specific server role. For example, if you click the Active Directory Domain Services role, Server Manager will provide you with a log view that includes, among other things, a summary view of key events related to this service. (See Figure 13-9.)

Event Log lists three types of events: Information, Warning, and Errors. By default, the summary view displayed under the server role will list Errors with a high priority, Warnings with a medium priority, and Information messages with the lowest priority. Therefore, Errors will always appear at the top of the summary, alerting you immediately if there is an issue with your system. To drill down and see the event details, either double-click the event itself or move to the Event Viewer section under the Diagnostics node of the tree pane in Server Manager.

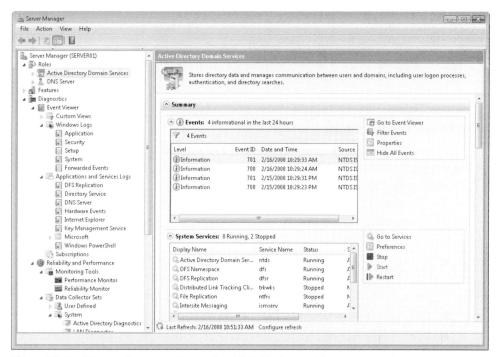

Figure 13-9   Viewing Summary Events for AD DS in Server Manager

---

MORE INFO   **Active Directory Services events and errors**

To learn about specific events and errors related to Active Directory Services roles go to *http://technet2.microsoft.com/windowsserver2008/en/library/67928ddc-3c01-4a4a-a924-f964908b072b1033.mspx.*

Events provide much more information in Windows Server 2008 and Windows Vista than ever before. In previous versions of Windows, events were arcane items that provided very little information about an issue. Today, you get a full explanation on an event in Event Viewer, and you can link to an online database maintained by Microsoft for each event. You can look up an event in this database by clicking the Event Log Online Help link in the event's Properties dialog box. You will be prompted to send information about the event to Microsoft. Click Yes if you want information specifically about this event.

This database does not provide information about every event in Windows, but it covers the most frequently viewed events. You can also use third-party event log databases to view information about events.

MORE INFO   Windows event IDs

To access a free database of Windows event IDs, go to *http://kb.prismmicrosys.com/index.asp*.

The more information you know about Windows events, the easier it will be to deal with the issue. You can rely on the Microsoft online event database and free third-party event databases as well as supplement this information with online searches through tools such as Windows Live Search to locate information about an issue. Searching on the event ID will return the most results.

MORE INFO   New features of Event Log

For more information on working with Event Log, download "Tracking Change" in Windows Vista, a multi-page article on the new features of Event Log and how it can be integrated with Task Manager to automate actions based on specific events as well as forward key events to a central collection system at *http://www.reso-net.com/download.asp?Fichier=A195*.

Working with Windows Reliability Monitor

Another useful tool to identify potential issues on a system is Reliability Monitor. This tool, located under the Diagnostic\Reliability and Performance\Monitoring Tools node in Server Manager, is designed to track changes that are made to a system. Each time a change is performed on the system, it is logged in Reliability Monitor. (See Figure 13-10.) Tracked changes include system changes, software installs or uninstalls, application failures, hardware failures, and Windows failures.

If an issue arises, one of the first places you should check is Reliability Monitor because it tracks every change to your system and reveals what might have happened to make your system unresponsive. For example, if the change is a new driver for a device, it might be a good idea to roll back the device installation and see whether the system becomes more responsive. Verify Reliability Monitor whenever an issue affecting performance arises on a server.

Exam Tip   Work with Task Manager, Event Viewer, and Reliability Monitor. All are important parts of the exam.

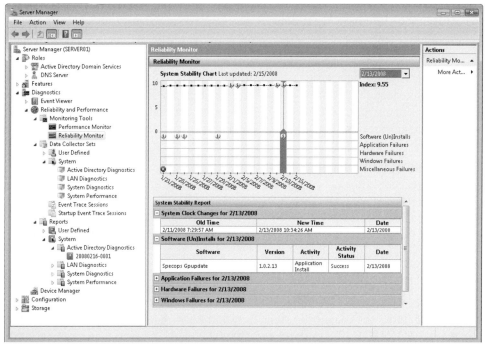

Figure 13-10   Viewing system changes in Reliability Monitor

Working with Windows Performance Monitor

Sometimes problems and issues are not immediately recognizable and require further research to identify them. In this case, you need to rely on Performance Monitor. This tool, located under the Diagnostic\ Reliability and Performance\Monitoring Tools node in Server Manager, is designed to track performance data on a system. You use Performance Monitor to track particular system components either in real time or on a scheduled basis.

If you are familiar with previous versions of Windows Server, you'll quickly note that Windows Server 2008 Performance Monitor brings together several tools you might be familiar with: Performance Logs and Alerts, Server Performance Advisor, and System Monitor. If you are new to Windows Server with the 2008 release, you'll quickly find that when it comes to performance management and analysis, Performance Monitor is the tool to use. Using Performance Monitor, you create interactive collections of system counters or create reusable data collector sets. Performance Monitor is part of Windows Reliability and Performance Monitor (WRPM). Table 13-5 outlines each of the tools in WRPM that support performance monitoring and the access rights required to work with them.

Table 13-5   WRPM Tools and Access Rights

Tool	Description	Required Membership
Monitoring Tools, Performance Monitor	To view performance data in real time or from log files. The performance data can be viewed in a graph, histogram, or report.	Local Performance Log Users group
Monitoring Tools, Reliability Monitor	To view the system stability and the events that affect reliability.	Local Administrators group
Data collector sets	Groups data collectors into reusable elements that can be used to review or log performance. Contains three types of data collectors: performance counts, event trace data, and system configuration information.	Local Performance Log Users group with the Log on as a batch user right
Reports	Includes preconfigured performance and diagnosis reports. Can also be used to generate reports from data collected using any data collector set.	Local Performance Log Users group with the Log on as a batch job user right

Windows Server 2008 includes a new built-in group called Performance Log Users, which allows server administrators who are not members of the local Administrators group to perform tasks related to performance monitoring and logging. For this group to be able to initiate data logging or modify data collector sets, it must have the Log On As A Batch Job user right. Note that this user right is assigned to this group by default.

In addition, Windows Server 2008 will create custom Data Collector Set templates when a role is installed. These templates are located under the System node of the Data Collector Sets node of WRPM. For example, with the AD DS role, four collector sets are created:

■ The Active Directory Diagnostics set collects data from registry keys, performance counters, and trace events related to AD DS performance on a local DC.

■ The LAN Diagnostics set collects data from network interface cards, registry keys, and other system hardware to identify issues related to network traffic on the local DC.

■ The System Diagnostics set collects data from local hardware resources to generate data that helps streamline system performance on the local DC.

■ The System Performance set focuses on the status of hardware resources and system response times and processes on the local DC.

Of the four, the most useful for AD DS is the first. This should be the data set you rely on the most. You can create your own personalized data set. If you do, focus on the items in Table 13-6 as the counters you should include in your data set.

Table 13-6   Monitor Common Counters for AD DS

Counter	Description	Reason
Network Interface: Bytes Total/Sec	Rate at which bytes are sent and received over each network adapter, including framing characters.	Track network interfaces to identify high usage rates per NIC. This helps you determine whether you need to segment the network or increase bandwidth.
Network Interface: Packets Outbound Discarded	Number of outbound packets that were chosen to be discarded even though no errors had been detected to prevent transmission.	Long queues of items indicate that the NIC is waiting for the network and is not keeping pace with the server. This is a bottleneck.
NTDS: DRA Inbound Bytes Total/Sec	Total bytes received through replication. It is the sum of both uncompressed and compressed data.	If this counter does not have any activity, it indicates that the network could be slowing down replication.
NTDS: DRA Inbound Object Updates Remaining in Packet	Number of object updates received through replication that have not yet been applied to the local server.	The value should be low on a constant basis. High values show that the server is not capable of adequately integrating data received through replication.
NTDS: DRA Outbound Bytes Total/Sec	Total bytes sent per second. It is the sum of both uncompressed and compressed data.	If this counter does not have any activity, it indicates that the network could be slowing down replication.
NTDS: DRA Pending Replication Synchronizations	The replication backlog on the server.	The value should be low on a constant basis. High values show that the server is not capable of adequately integrating data received through replication.
NTDS: DS Threads In Use	Number of threads in use by AD DS.	If there is no activity, the network might be preventing client requests from being processed.
NTDS: LDAP Bind Time	Time required for completion of the last LDAP binding.	High values indicate either hardware or network performance problems.
NTDS: LDAP Client Sessions	Number of connected LDAP client sessions.	If there is no activity, the network might be causing problems.
NTDS: LDAP Searches/Sec	Number of LDAP searches per second.	If there is no activity, the network might be causing problems.
NTDS: LDAP Successful Binds/Sec	Number of successful LDAP binds per second.	If there is no activity, the network might be causing problems.
NTDS: LDAP Writes /Sec	Number of successful LDAP writes per second.	If there is no activity, the network might be causing problems.

Table 13-6   **Monitor Common Counters for AD DS**

Counter	Description	Reason
Security System-Wide Statistics: Kerberos Authentications	Number of Kerberos authentications on the server per second.	If there is no activity, the network might be preventing authentication requests from being processed.
Security System-Wide Statistics: NTLM Authentication	Number of NTLM authentications on the server per second.	If there is no activity, the network might be preventing authentication requests from being processed.
DFS Replicated Folders: All Counters	Counters for staging and conflicting data.	If there is no activity, the network might be causing problems.
DFS Replication Connections: All Counters	Counter for incoming connections.	If there is no activity, the network might be causing problems.
DFS Replication Service Volumes: All Counters	Counters for update sequence number (USN) journal records and database processing on each volume.	If there is no activity, the processor might be causing problems.
DNS: All Counters	DNS Object Type handles the Windows NT DNS service on your system.	If there is no activity, the network might be causing problems, and clients might not be able to locate this DC.

To add counters to Performance Monitor, simply click the plus (+) sign in the toolbar at the top of the details pane. This displays the Add Counters dialog box. (See Figure 13-11.) Scroll through the counters to identify which ones you need. In some cases, you will need subcounters under a specific heading (as shown in Table 13-6); in others, you need the entire subset of counters. When you need a subcounter, click the down arrow beside the heading, locate the subcounter, and click Add. When you need the entire counter, click the counter and click Add. This adds the counter with a star heading below it, indicating that all subcounters have been added.

IMPORTANT   **The Windows Server 2008 interface**

When using the classic interface in Windows Server 2008, subcounters are accessed by clicking plus signs. When using the Desktop Experience feature in Windows Server 2008, which simulates the Vista interface, subcounters are accessed through down arrows.

To obtain information about a counter, click Show Description. Then, when you click any counter or subcounter, a short description will appear at the bottom of the dialog box.

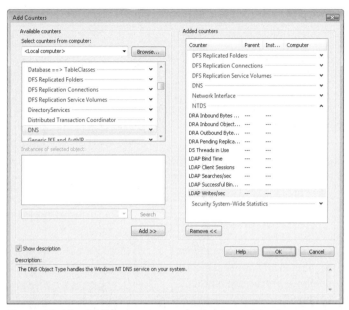

Figure 13-11   Adding counters to Performance Monitor

As soon as you are finished adding counters and you click OK, Performance Monitor will start tracking them in real time. Each counter you added will be assigned a line of a specific color. To remove a counter, click the counter, and then click the Delete button (X) on the toolbar at the top of the details pane.

You can start and stop Performance Monitor much like a media player, using the same type of buttons. When Performance Monitor runs, it automatically overwrites data as it collects more; therefore, it is more practical for real-time monitoring.

If you want to capture the counters you added into a custom data set, right-click Performance Monitor and select New; then choose New Data Collector Set. Follow the prompts to save your counter selections so that you can reuse them later.

Exam Tip   Work with Performance Monitor because it is an important part of the exam. Also, note that there is no Server Performance Advisor (SPA) in Windows Server 2008. This Windows Server 2003 tool has been rolled into Windows Reliability and Performance Monitor. Don't get caught on questions regarding SPA on the exam.

Creating Baselines for AD DS and DNS

For long-term system monitoring, you must create data collector sets. These sets run automated collections at scheduled times. When you first install a system, it is a good idea to create a performance baseline for that system. Then as load increases on the system, you can compare the current load with the baseline and see what has changed. This helps you identify whether additional resources are required for your systems to provide optimal performance. For example, when working with DCs, it is a good idea to log performance at peak and nonpeak times. Peak times would be when users log on in the morning or after lunch, and nonpeak times would be periods such as mid-morning or mid-afternoon. To create a performance baseline, you need to take samples of counter values for 30 to 45 minutes for at least a week during peak, low, and normal operations. The general steps for creating a baseline include:

1. Identify resources to track.
2. Capture data at specific times.
3. Store the captured data for long-term access.

IMPORTANT Performance monitoring affects performance

Taking performance snapshots also affects system performance. The object with the worst impact on performance is the logical disk object, especially if logical disk counters are enabled. However, because this affects snapshots at any time, even with major loads on the server, the baseline is still valid.

You can create custom collector sets, but with Windows Server 2008, use the default templates that are added when the server role is installed to do so. For example, to create a baseline for a DC, simply create a user-defined data collector set that is based on the Active Directory Diagnostics template and run it on a regular basis.

Then, when you are ready to view the results of your collection, you can rely on the Reports section of the Windows Reliability and Performance node. Right-click the collector set for which you want to view the report (either User Defined or System) and select Latest Report. This will generate the report if it isn't already available and provide extensive information on the status of your DC. (See Figure 13-12.)

MORE INFO Performance Monitor scenarios

For more information on Performance Monitor, see the scenarios in the Windows Server 2008 Performance and Reliability Monitoring Step-by-Step Guide at *http://technet2.microsoft.com /windowsserver2008/en/library/7e17a3be-f24e-4fdd-9e38-a88e2c8fb4d81033.mspx?mfr=true*.

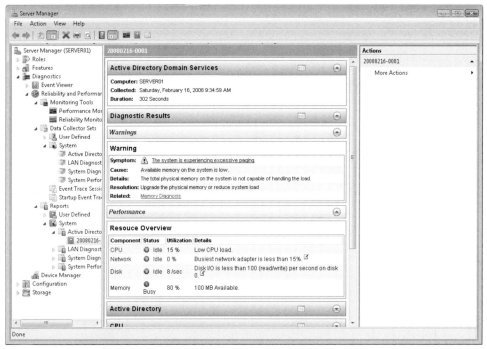

Figure 13-12   Viewing an Active Directory diagnostics report

Working with Windows System Resource Manager

Windows Server 2008 includes an additional tool for system resource management, WSRM, a feature that can be added through Add Features in Server Manager. WSRM can be used in two manners. First, it can be used to profile applications. This means that it helps identify how many resources an application requires on a regular basis. When operating in this mode, WSRM logs events in the application event log only when the application exceeds its allowed limits. This helps you fine-tune application requirements.

The second mode offered by WSRM is the manage mode. In this mode, WSRM uses its allocation policies to control how many resources applications can use on a server. If applications exceed their resource allocations, WSRM can even stop the application from executing and make sure other applications on the same server can continue to operate. However, WSRM will not affect any application if combined processor resources do not exceed 70 percent utilization. This means that when processor resources are low, WSRM does not affect any application.

WSRM also supports Alerts and Event Monitoring. This is a powerful tool that is designed to help you control processor and memory usage on large multiprocessing servers. By default, the WSRM includes four built-in management policies, but it also includes several custom resources you can use to define your own policies. Basically, WSRM will ensure that high-priority applications will always have enough resources available to them for continued operation, making it a good tool for DCs.

IMPORTANT DCs and WSRM

If you use single-purpose DCs, you will not need WSRM as much as if you use multipurpose DCs. Multipurpose DCs will usually run other workloads at the same time as they run the AD DS service. Using WSRM in this case can ensure that the AD DS service is available during peak hours by assigning it more resources than other applications. However, consider your choices carefully when deciding to create a multipurpose DC. DCs are secure servers by default and should remain this way at all times. If you add workloads to a DC, you will need to grant access rights to the DC to application administrators, administrators that do not need domain administration access rights.

Use WSRM to first evaluate how your applications are being used; then apply management policies. Make sure you thoroughly test your policies before applying them in your production environment. This way, you will be able to get a feel for WSRM before you fully implement it in your network. When you're ready, you can use WSRM Calendar to determine when which policy should be applied.

IMPORTANT WSRM resource requirements

If you are managing several servers with WSRM, you might need to dedicate resources to it because it is resource-intensive. You might consider placing it on a dedicated management server if this is the case.

Quick Check

1. You want to view potential error messages about the directory service. Where can you find this information?
2. You are using WSRM to control processor and memory resources for several applications on a server. However, after investigation, you see that none of your policies are applied. What could be the problem?
3. What are the objects you can use to allocate resources in WSRM?

Quick Check Answers

1. View potential error messages about the directory service in Event Log. You can view this information in two places. The first is by clicking the server role name in the tree pane of Server Manager. This will display a summary view of directory service events. The second is by going to the Directory Service log itself, under Event Viewer. This will display all the events related to the directory service.
2. WSRM will not apply any policies if the processor usage does not reach 70 percent.
3. WSRM resource allocations can be assigned to three objects: processes, users, or IIS application pools.

WSRM can be used for the following scenarios:

- Use predefined or user-defined policies to manage system resources. Resources can be allocated on a per-process, per-user, or per-IIS application pool basis.
- Rely on calendar rules to apply your policies at different times and dates without any manual intervention.
- Automate the resource policy selection process based on server properties, events, or even changes to available physical memory or processor count.
- Collect resource usage information in local text files or store them in a SQL database. You can also create a central WSRM collection system to collate resource usage from several systems running their own instances of WSRM.

Table 13-7 outlines the default policies included in WSRM as well as the custom resources you can use to create custom policies.

Table 13-7 WSRM Policies and Custom Resources

Built-in Policy	Description
Equal per process	Assigns each application an equal amount of resources.
Equal per user	Groups processes assigned to each user who is running them and assigns equal resources to each group.
Equal per session	Allocates resources equally to each session connected to the system.
Equal per IIS application pool	Allocates resources equally to each running IIS application pool.
Custom Resource	**Description**
Process Matching Criteria	Used to match services or applications to a policy. Can be selected by file name, command, specified users, or groups.
Resource Allocation Policies	Used to allocate processor and memory resources to the processes that match criteria you specify.
Exclusion lists	Used to exclude applications, services, users, or groups from management by WSRM. Can also use command-line paths to exclude applications from management.
Scheduling	Use a calendar interface to set time-based events to resource allocation. Supports policy-based workloads because you can set policies to be active at specific times of day, specific days, or other schedules.
Conditional policy application	Used to set conditions based on specific events to determine whether policy will run.

WSRM can completely control how applications can and should run.

PRACTICE AD DS Performance Analysis

In this practice, you will use both WRPM and WSRM to view the performance of your servers. First, you will create a custom collector set. After the collector set is created, you will run it and view the diagnostics report. In the second exercise, you will install WSRM to view the policies it provides. These exercises rely on SERVER10, but SERVER11 should also be running.

▶ **Exercise 1   Create a Data Collector Set**

A data collector set is the core building block of performance monitoring and reporting in WRPM. You can create a combination of data collectors and save them as a single data collector set.

1. Log on to SERVER10 with the domain Administrator account.

   You need to be a member only of the Performance Log Users group with the Log On As A Batch Job user right, but for the purpose of these exercises, you will use the domain administrator account.

2. In Server Manager, expand Diagnostics\Reliability and Performance\Data Collector Sets, right-click User Defined, select New, and then select Data Collector Set.

3. On the Template page, type **Custom AD DS Collector Set**, make sure Create From A Template (Recommended) is selected, and click Next.

4. On the next page, select the Active Directory Diagnostics template and click Next.

5. By default, the wizard selects %systemdrive%\PerfLogs\Admin as the root directory; however, you might prefer to keep your collector sets on a separate drive if it exists. In this case, click Browse, choose drive D, and create a new folder named **AD DS Collector Sets**. Press Enter and click OK to close the dialog box, and then click Next.

6. On the Create The Data Collector Set page, in the *Run As* field, type the account name and the password to run the data collector set. Leave the defaults and click Finish.

   When you create collector sets for long-term use, use a special account that is both a member of the Performance Log Users group and has the Log On As A Batch Job user right to run your collector sets. Note that the Performance Log Users group has this right assigned to it by default.

   When you finish the New Collector Set Wizard, you are given three options:

   - Open Properties Data For This Data Collector Set to view the properties of the data collector set or to make additional modifications
   - Start This Data Collector Set Now to run the data collector set immediately
   - Save And Close to save the data collector set without starting the collection

   Your custom data collector set has been created. Notice that it is stopped. To schedule the Start condition for your data collector set, use the following procedure.

7. Right-click Custom AD DS Collector Set and click Properties.

8. Click the Schedule tab and click Add to create a start date, time, or day schedule.

9. In the Folder Action dialog box, make sure that today's date is the beginning date, select the Expiration Date check box, and set it as one week from today. Also, make sure that the report time is set to the current time. Click OK.

   You must set the start date of the schedule to *now* for the collection set to work. If not, you will not be able to generate reports in later steps.

   Note that you can create quite a modular schedule in this dialog box. Also, note that selecting an expiration date will not stop data collection in progress on that date. It will only prevent new instances of data collection from starting after the expiration date. You must use the Stop Condition tab to configure how data collection is stopped.

10. Click the Stop Condition tab, select the Overall Duration check box, make sure it lists 5 minutes, and select the Stop When All Data Collectors Have Finished check box. Click OK.

    You select the Stop When All Data Collectors Have Finished check box to enable all data collectors to finish recording the most recent values before the data collector set is stopped if you have also configured an overall duration.

    You can also set limits on your collection. However, note that when an overall duration is configured, it will override any limits you set. If you do want to set limits, make sure the Overall Duration check box is cleared and define the following limits:

    - Use When A Limit Is Reached, Restart The Data Collector Set to segment data collections into separate logs.
    - To configure a time period for data collection to write to a single log file, select the Duration check box and set its value.
    - To restart the data collector set or to stop collecting data when the log file reaches a specific limit, select the Maximum Size check box and set its value.

Collector sets will generate a large amount of data if you allow them to run unmonitored. To configure data management for a data collector set, use the following procedure.

11. Right-click Custom AD DS Data Collector Set and click Data Manager.

12. On the Data Manager tab, you can accept the default values or change them according to your data retention policy. Keep the defaults.

   ❑ Select the Minimum Free disk or Maximum Folders check boxes to delete previous data according to the resource policy you choose from the drop-down list (Delete Largest or Delete Oldest).

   ❑ Select the Apply Policy Before The Data Collector Set Starts check box to delete previous data sets according to your selections before the data collector set creates its next log file.

   ❑ Select the Maximum Root Path Size check box to delete previous data according to your selections when the root log folder size limit is reached.

13. On the Actions tab, you can set specific data management actions for this collector set. Note that three policies already exist. Click the 1 Day(s) policy and click Edit.

    Folder actions enable you to choose how data is archived before it is permanently deleted. You can decide to disable the Data Manager limits in favor of managing all data according to these folder action rules. For example, you could copy all collection sets to a central file share before deleting them on the local server.

14. Click OK and OK again.

    Your collector set is ready to run. Wait until the scheduled time occurs for the report to run. However, if you want to view an immediate report, proceed as follows:

15. Right-click the Active Directory Diagnostics template collector set under Data Collector Sets, System and click Latest Report.

    If no report exists, this will launch the data collector set and begin the collection of information from your server. The set should run for five minutes and then stop. If a report exists, it will move you to the Reports node and display it.

16. If the report does not exist and you expand the Reports section of WRPM, you will see that the collection set is generating a report. Click the report name.

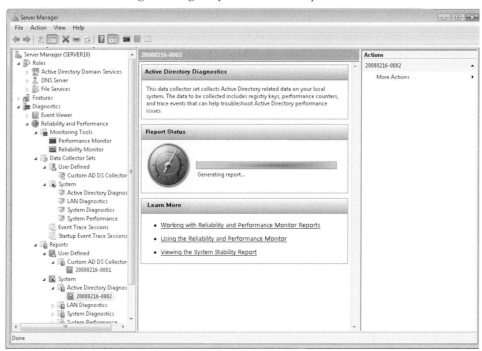

17. View the report that was generated by your collector set. Click Report Name under the collector set name in System reports.

   You can also use the other default templates to generate reports on the spot. For example, if you want to run a report from the Systems Diagnostics template, right-click the template name under the System node and select Latest Report. If no report exists, it will run the collector set and then display the report in the details pane.

▶ **Exercise 2   Install WSRM**

In this exercise, you will install the WSRM service and view how it operates. This exercise is performed on SERVER10; ensure that it is running.

1. Log on to Server10 with the domain Administrator account.

2. In Server Manager, right-click the Features node and select Add Features.

3. On the Select Features page of the Add Features Wizard, select Windows System Resource Manager and click Next.

4. Server Manager prompts you to add Windows Internal Database. Click Add Required Features. Click Next.

   Note that Windows Internal Database is a locally used database only and will not accept remote connections. To collect data from other servers, you must use Microsoft SQL Server 2005 or later.

5. Review the information on the Confirm Installation Selections page and click Install.

6. Examine the installation results and click Close.

   Your installation is complete.

7. You can now use WSRM on this system. Windows System Resource Manager is a standalone console that can be found in the Administrative Tools program group.

8. When you open the console, it will ask you which computer to connect to. Select This Computer and click Connect.

   Now you can tour the WSRM interface. (See Figure 13-13.) Note that it uses the standard Microsoft Management Console format. Explore the various features of this console.

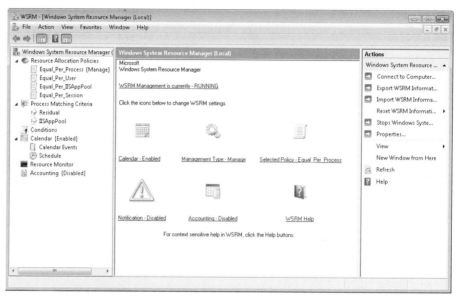

Figure 13-13   Using Windows System Resource Monitor

Lesson Summary

- In Windows Server 2008, you can use a series of tools to manage and monitor resource usage on a computer. These include Task Manager, Event Logs, Reliability Monitor, and Performance Monitor.

- Performance Monitor is now the single tool that regroups other tools used in previous versions of Windows. These tools included Performance Logs and Alerts, Server Performance Advisor, and System Monitor.

- You can use Windows System Resource Manager to control how resources behave on a scheduled basis. In fact, it provides two functions. It can monitor resource usage over time and log activity. Then, it can be used to control access to resources based on specific policies.

Lesson Review

You can use the following questions to test your knowledge of the information in Lesson 2, "Proactive Directory Performance Management." The questions are also available on the companion CD if you prefer to review them in electronic form.

NOTE Answers

Answers to these questions and explanations of why each answer choice is right or wrong are located in the "Answers" section at the end of the book.

1. You are the systems administrator for *contoso.com*. You have been assigned the task of verifying data collector sets on a DC. You did not create the collector sets. When you check the collector sets, you find that they are continuously running and that the allocated storage area is full. What could be the problem? (Choose all that apply.)

    A. The collector sets do not have an expiration date.

    B. The collector sets have not been set to run on a schedule.

    C. The collector sets do not have a stop condition.

    D. The collector sets have been scheduled improperly.

2. You are a systems administrator at *contoso.com*. As you log on to a DC to perform maintenance, you get the impression that server response is sluggish. You want to verify what is going on. Which tool should you use? (Choose all that apply.)

    A. Reliability Monitor

    B. Event Viewer

    C. Task Manager

    D. Performance Monitor

Chapter Review

To further practice and reinforce the skills you learned in this chapter, you can perform the following tasks:

- Review the chapter summary.
- Review the list of key terms introduced in this chapter.
- Complete the case scenario. This scenario sets up a real-world situation involving the topics of this chapter and asks you to create a solution.
- Complete the suggested practices.
- Take a practice test.

Chapter Summary

- Active Directory Domain Services is a set of complex services that interact with each other to provide a highly available identity and access solution. Because of this, there are several aspects to AD DS administration. In fact, twelve activities are required to manage the environment both online and offline, although many of the twelve can be delegated to others.
- As domain administrators, operators of the directory service must concentrate on making sure the AD DS service is always available and runs at its optimum performance. Many of the operations required to do this involve offline database administration tasks. With the release of Windows Server 2008, these tasks can now be performed without having to shut down the server because the AD DS service can now be started and stopped like any other service.
- There are several ways to protect AD DS data in Windows Server 2008 and several ways to restore it. One easy way to restore data is to recover it from the Deleted Items container, but when you do so, you must update the recovered item and then enable it.
- Two tools support backups of directory data in Windows Server 2008. *Ntdsutil.exe* will support both the creation of offline installation media and the protection of the system state data required by the DC. Windows Server Backup will protect entire volumes of the system and will even protect and support the restore of an entire computer system.
- Because the DC role is one that is ideal for virtualization, you can also protect DCs by using simple services such as the Volume Shadow Copy Service on host servers. This protects the virtual hard drives that comprise the virtual machine the DC is running on.
- When performance issues arise, Windows Server 2008 provides a series of tools for analysis and problem correction. These include both real-time and scheduled analysis tools. Real-time tools include Task Manager, Resource Monitor, and Performance Monitor. Scheduled or tracking tools include Event Log, Reliability Monitor, and scheduled data collection sets in Performance Monitor.

- Windows Server 2008 also includes a powerful tool by which you can manage policy-based workloads, Windows System Resource Manager. You must first use it to analyze running processes and then assign policies to these processes.

Key Terms

Use these key terms to understand better the concepts covered in this chapter.

- **compaction**   The process of recovering free space from a database. When database records are created, a specific amount of space is allocated in the database—enough to contain all of the record's possible values. When the record is deleted, the space is not recovered unless a compaction operation is performed.

- **data collector set**   A collection of values collated from the local computer, including registry values, performance counters, hardware components, and more that provides a diagnostic view into the behavior of a system.

- *Ntds.dit*   The database that contains the directory store. This database is located on every DC and, because of multimaster replication, is updated at all times by all other DCs except RODCs.

- **tombstone**   The container to which each deleted object in the directory is automatically moved. This container retains objects for a period of 180 days to ensure that all possible replications involving this object have been performed. You can use this container to recover objects before the end of the 180 days.

Case Scenario

In the following case scenario, you will apply what you've learned about subjects of this chapter. You can find answers to the questions in this scenario in the "Answers" section at the end of this book.

Case Scenario: Working with Lost and Found Data

You are a domain administrator with Contoso, Ltd. During a routine verification, you notice that some of the accounts that should be contained within a specific OU have disappeared. You know that a local technician was assigned to work on these accounts recently because none of them had any information tied to them. In addition, new accounts needed to be created in this OU. The technician was assigned to add information such as the user's address, manager, and office location in each of the accounts. You contact the technician and verify that he made the modifications as expected.

You examine your directory event logs to locate the answer. Fortunately, you configured a central collection server to which you forward AD DS events from all the DCs in your domain. After some time, you discover that another administrator from a remote office was working on the same OU at the same time as the technician. More examination shows that the administrator moved the OU from its original location and then moved it back at the same time as the technician was working on the accounts.

Where are the accounts you cannot find?

Suggested Practices

To help you successfully master the exam objectives presented in this chapter, complete the following tasks.

Proactive Directory Maintenance

Working with AD DS means working with a central repository that provides two key services: user authentication and object management, hence the classification of AD DS as a NOS directory service. To become even more familiar with the exam objectives covered by this chapter, perform the following additional practices.

- **Practice 1**   Practice working with the various backup and restore tools found in Windows Server 2008. If you can, perform a complete server backup and then a complete server restore. Work with the DSRM and practice changing the DSRM password as well as performing nonauthoritative and authoritative restores. Make sure you examine as many of the different options available to you in each of the supported DC backup and restore scenarios as possible.

- **Practice 2**   Work with the DC monitoring tools. Use Task Manager, Event Viewer, and the Windows Reliability and Performance Monitor views. Try as many of the various options as possible to become familiar with how they work. Look up the suggested article for Event Log management and apply its principles to your DCs.

- **Practice 3**   Work with Windows System Resource Manager. WSRM includes many options. Examine as many as possible and test out their operation. Try assigning different policies to your DCs to see how they affect system operation. View the event logs to see how WSRM logs information about the system.

Take a Practice Test

The practice tests on this book's companion CD offer many options. For example, you can test yourself on just one exam objective, or you can test yourself on all the 70-640 certification exam content. You can set up the test so that it closely simulates the experience of taking a certification exam, or you can set it up in study mode so that you can look at the correct answers and explanations after you answer each question.

MORE INFO   Practice tests

For details about all the practice test options available, see the "How to Use the Practice Tests" section in this book's introduction.

Chapter 14

Active Directory Lightweight Directory Services

Of the five different Active Directory technologies available in Windows Server 2008, the one that most resembles Active Directory Domain Services (AD DS) is Active Directory Lightweight Directory Services (AD LDS). That's because AD LDS is really nothing more than a subset of AD DS functionality. Both use the same core code, and both provide a very similar feature set.

AD LDS, formerly called Active Directory Application Mode (ADAM), is a technology that is designed to support directory-enabled applications on an application-by-application basis and without having to modify the database schema of your network operating system (NOS) directory running on AD DS. AD LDS is a boon to administrators who want to use directory-enabled applications without integrating them in their NOS directory.

Active Directory Domain Services can also support the use of directory-enabled applications. One very good example is Microsoft Exchange Server 2007. All user information in Exchange Server is provided by the directory. When you install Exchange Server into your network, it begins by extending the AD DS schema, practically doubling its size. As you know, schema modifications are not to be taken lightly because, when you add an object or an attribute to the AD DS schema, it will be added forever; it cannot be removed. You can deactivate or rename and reuse these objects, but who wants defunct objects in their NOS directory? Adding to the schema for an application such as Exchange Server is appropriate because it provides a core networking service: e-mail.

MORE INFO   **Best practices for Active Directory design**

For a guide outlining best practices for the design of Active Directory as well as AD DS schema management guidelines, download the free "Chapter 3: Designing the Active Directory" from *Windows Server 2003: Best Practices for Enterprise Deployments*, available at *http://www.reso-net.com/Documents/007222343X_Ch03.pdf*.

For information on creating a new forest as well as migrating its contents from one forest to another, look up *Windows Server 2008: The Complete Reference* by Ruest and Ruest (McGraw-Hill Osborne, 2008). This book outlines how to build a complete infrastructure based on Microsoft Windows Server and how to migrate all of its contents from one location to another.

However, when it comes to other applications, especially applications that are provided by third-party software manufacturers, carefully consider whether you should integrate them into your AD DS directory. Remember, your production AD DS structure will be with you for a very long time. You don't want to find yourself in a situation in which you integrated a product to your directory and then, several years later when the third-party manufacturer is out of business, have to figure out what to do with the extensions this product added to your AD DS structure, increasing replication timings and adding unused content in the directory.

This is why AD LDS is such a boon. Because it can support multiple AD LDS instances on a single server (unlike AD DS, which can support only one instance of a directory on any given server), AD LDS can meet the requirements of any directory-enabled application and even provide instances on an application-by-application basis. In addition, you do not need Enterprise Administrator or Schema Administrator credentials to work with AD LDS, as you would with AD DS. No, AD LDS runs on member or standalone servers and requires only local administration access rights to manage it. Because of this, it can also be used in a perimeter network to provide application or Web authentication services. AD LDS is one of the four Active Directory technologies that enable you to extend your organization's authority beyond the firewall and into the Internet cloud. (See Figure 14-1.)

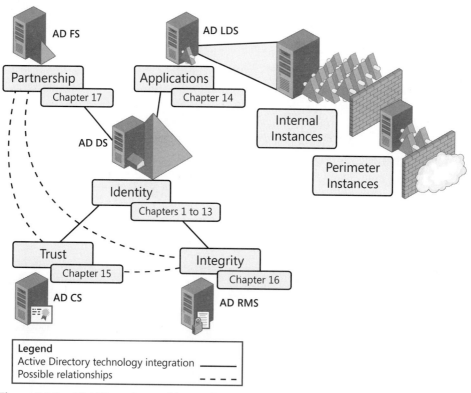

Figure 14-1   AD LDS can be used internally or externally in support of applications

Exam objectives in this chapter:

■ Configuring Additional Active Directory Server Roles

  ❑ Configure Active Directory Lightweight Directory Service (AD LDS).

Lessons in this chapter:

■ Lesson 1: Understanding and Installing AD LDS 690

■ Lesson 2: Configuring and Using AD LDS 701

Before You Begin

To complete the lessons in this chapter, you must have done the following:

■ Installed Windows Server 2008 on a physical or virtual computer, which should be named SERVER01 and should be a domain controller in the *contoso.com* domain. The details for this setup are presented in Chapter 1, "Installation," and Chapter 2, "Administration."

■ Installed Windows Server 2008 on another physical or virtual computer. The machine should be named SERVER03 and should be a member server within the *contoso.com* domain. This computer will host the AD LDS instances you will install and create through the exercises in this chapter. Make sure this computer also includes a D drive to store the data for the AD LDS instances. Ten GB is recommended for the size of this drive.

■ Installed Windows Server 2008 on a third physical or virtual computer. The computer should be named SERVER04 and should be a member server within the *contoso.com* domain. This computer will be used to configure replication scopes for AD LDS. Make sure this computer also includes a D drive to store the data for the AD LDS instances. Ten GB is recommended for the size of this drive.

Real World

Danielle Ruest and Nelson Ruest

In late 2003, we were asked by Redmond Magazine (then MCP Magazine) to put together a review of the various products on the market that would assist system administrators to manage Active Directory environments. We were thrilled by the request because Active Directory was one of our favorite technologies. Besides being a true Lightweight Directory Access Protocol (LDAP) directory service, Active Directory is also a very powerful NOS directory that can manage millions of objects. In addition, Active Directory includes Group Policy, a very powerful object management platform that extends the NOS capabilities of the directory service. Finally, through Group Policy Software Delivery, you could manage the delivery of Windows Installer–based software packages throughout the entire structure of the directory. There was no doubt, for us, that Active Directory was one of the best products ever to come out of Redmond's development labs.

After scouring the Internet and polling our customers, we came up with a short list that included six products that would assist in managing Active Directory environments:

- Quest FastLane Active Roles
- Aelita Enterprise Directory Manager
- NetIQ Security Administration Suite
- Javelina ADvantage
- NetPro Active Directory Lifecycle Suite
- Bindview Secure Active Directory LifeCycle Suite

Of the six, only four were available for the article. Bindview declined to give us an evaluation copy of their product, so we had to omit this by default. NetPro, which seemed to have a great set of tools, wasn't ready to go to market yet, so we had to omit this product as well. We did, however, have a chance to write about NetPro's suite of Active Directory products later (see *http://mcpmag.com/reviews/products/article.asp?EditorialsID=454*), and it did very well indeed. So, we were left with four products to write about. The result was an article titled "The 12 Mighty Labors of Active Directory Management" (see *http://mcpmag.com/Features/article.asp?EditorialsID=359*). Readers everywhere seemed to like the article quite a bit. But we received some very biting comments from a couple of sources about one key point we made in the article.

Two of the four products we reviewed, the NetIQ and the Quest FastLane, modified the database schema for Active Directory to work. At that time, we had consulted in quite a few Active Directory implementations, and each one faced one single difficult question: how to manage schema modifications? That's because, when the schema is modified, you can't undo it. Of course, in Windows Server 2003, Microsoft allowed you to deactivate or rename and reuse schema modifications, but for our customers and for us, that was a poor second choice. It's best to leave the schema alone, if at all possible. In addition, Microsoft had just released ADAM in support of organizations that needed to integrate applications to a directory service but didn't want to modify the schema of their NOS directory.

In the end, we chose the Aelita product as the best choice for one major reason: Aelita had opted to store all of its database requirements in Microsoft SQL Server instead of modifying the Active Directory schema, yet its tool was as powerful as the other two major contenders. Javelina's tool didn't really compete with the others because it was not designed to support the same functions.

To make a long story short, about two months after we published the article, Quest bought Aelita and transformed Enterprise Directory Manager (EDM) into the next version of Active Roles. The original Active Roles, which was produced by FastLane, a small company from Ottawa, Canada, which was also bought by Quest, was rolled into EDM. The new version of Active Roles no longer required schema modifications to be implemented, yet still offered a powerful set of Active Directory management features. Did our article have anything to do with this? Who knows? One thing is sure: no one should ever take a NOS directory schema modification lightly, not when you have powerful tools like ADAM, now AD LDS, at your fingertips.

Lesson 1: Understanding and Installing AD LDS

Even though it is based on the same code as AD DS, AD LDS is much simpler to work with. For example, when you install AD LDS on a server, it does not change the configuration of the server in the same way AD DS does when you create a domain controller. AD LDS is an application and nothing more. When you install it, you are not required to reboot the server because the application installation process only adds functionality to the server and does not change its nature.

However, before you begin, you must first understand what makes up an AD LDS instance, how AD LDS instances should be used, and what their relationship is or can be with AD DS directories. Then you can proceed to the installation of the AD LDS service.

After this lesson, you will be able to:

- Understand when to use AD LDS.
- Install AD LDS onto a member server.
- Locate and view the AD LDS directory store.

Estimated lesson time: 30 minutes

Understanding AD LDS

Like AD DS, AD LDS instances are based on the Lightweight Directory Access Protocol (LDAP) and provide hierarchical database services. Unlike relational databases, LDAP directories are optimized for specific purposes and should be used whenever you need to rely on fast lookups of information that will support given applications. Table 14-1 outlines the major differences between an LDAP directory and a relational database such as Microsoft SQL Server. This comparison helps you understand when to choose an LDAP directory in support of an application over a relational database.

Table 14-1   Comparing LDAP Directories to Relational Databases

LDAP Directories	Relational Databases
Fast read and searches.	Fast writes.
Hierarchical database design often based on the Domain Name System (DNS) or the X.500 naming system.	Structured data design relying on tables containing rows and columns. Tables can be linked together.
Relies on a standard schema structure, a schema that is extensible.	Does not rely on schemas.
Decentralized (distributed) and relies on replication to maintain data consistency.	Centrally located data repositories.

Table 14-1   Comparing LDAP Directories to Relational Databases

LDAP Directories	Relational Databases
Security is applied at the object level.	Security is applied at the row or column level.
Because the database is distributed, data consistency is not absolute—at least not until replication passes are complete.	Because data input is transactional, data consistency is absolute and guaranteed at all times.
Records are not locked and can be modified by two parties at once. Conflicts are managed through update sequence numbers (USNs).	Records are locked and can be modified by only one party at a time.

Table 14-1 provides guidelines for selection of the right database for an application.

In addition, AD LDS is based on AD DS, but it does not include all the features of AD DS. Table 14-2 outlines the differences in features between AD LDS and AD DS.

Table 14-2   Comparing AD LDS with AD DS

Feature	AD LDS	AD DS
Includes more than one instance on a server.	☑	☐
Includes independent schemas for each instance.	☑	☐
Runs on client operating systems such as Windows Vista or Windows Server 2008 member servers.	☑	☐
Runs on domain controllers.	☑	☑
Directory partitions can rely on X.500 naming conventions.	☑	☐
Can be installed or removed without a reboot.	☑	☐
Service can be stopped or started without reboot.	☑	☑
Supports Group Policy.	☐	☑
Includes a global catalog.	☐	☑
Manages objects such as workstations, member servers, and domain controllers.	☐	☑
Supports trusts between domains and forests.	☐	☑
Supports and integrates with public key infrastructures (PKIs) and X.509 certificates.	☐	☑
Supports DNS service (SRV) records for locating directory services.	☐	☑
Supports LDAP application programming interfaces (APIs).	☑	☑
Supports Active Directory Services Interface (ADSI) API.	☑	☑
Supports the Messaging API (MAPI).	☐	☑
Supports object-level security and delegation of administration.	☑	☑

Table 14-2   Comparing AD LDS with AD DS

Feature	AD LDS	AD DS
Relies on multimaster replication for data consistency.	☑	☑
Supports schema extensions and application directory partitions.	☑	☑
Can install a replica from removable media.	☑	☑
Can include security principals to provide access to a Windows Server network.	☐	☑
Can include security principals to provide access to applications and Web Services.	☑	☑
Is integrated into the Windows Server 2008 backup tools.	☑	☑

As you can see from the contents of Table 14-2, there are several similarities and differences between AD LDS and AD DS. For example, it is easy to see why Exchange Server must integrate with AD DS as opposed to relying on AD LDS because Exchange Server requires access to the global catalog service to run. Without it, e-mail users could not look up recipients. Because AD LDS does not support the global catalog, Exchange Server cannot rely on it. However, Exchange Server is an application that requires access to directory data in each site of the domain or forest. As such, it also relies on your domain controller positioning to ensure that each user can properly address e-mails.

AD LDS, however, provides much of the same functionality as AD DS. For example, you can create instances with replicas distributed in various locations in your network, just as with the location of domain controllers, and then use multimaster replication to ensure data consistency. In short, AD LDS is a lightweight, portable, and more malleable version of the directory service offered by AD DS.

AD LDS Scenarios

Now that you have a better understanding of AD LDS and its feature set, you can begin to identify scenarios in which you would need to work with this technology. Consider these scenarios when you decide whether to rely on AD LDS or AD DS.

- When your applications need to rely on an LDAP directory, consider using AD LDS instead of AD DS. AD LDS can often be hosted on the same server as the application, providing high-speed and local access to directory data. This would reduce replication traffic because all required data is local. In addition, you can bundle the AD LDS instance with the application when you deploy it. For example, if you have a human resources application that must rely on custom policies to ensure that users can access only specific content when their user object contains a set of particular attributes, you can store these attributes and policies within AD LDS.

- Rely on AD LDS to provide data associated with user accounts in AD DS but requiring extensions to the AD DS schema to support it. Using AD LDS in this scenario provides the additional user data without modifying the AD DS schema. For example, if you have a centralized application that provides a photograph of each employee in your organization and associates that photograph with the user's AD DS account, you can store the photographs in an AD LDS instance. By storing the photographs in AD LDS in a central location, they are associated with the user accounts in AD DS, but because they are in AD LDS, they are not replicated with all other AD DS data, reducing bandwidth requirements for replication.

- Rely on an AD LDS instance to provide authentication services for a Web application such as Microsoft SharePoint Portal Server in a perimeter network or extranet. AD LDS can query the internal AD DS structure through a firewall to obtain user account information and store it securely in the perimeter network. This avoids having to deploy AD DS in the perimeter or having to include domain controllers from the internal network in the perimeter. Note that you can also rely on Active Directory Federation Services (AD FS) to provide this access. AD FS is discussed in further detail in Chapter 17, "Active Directory Federation Services."

- Consolidate various identity repositories into a single directory store. Using a metadirectory service such as Microsoft Identity Integration Server (MIIS), Microsoft Identity Lifecycle Manager (MILM), or the free Identity Integration Feature Pack (IIFP), you can obtain data from various sources and consolidate it within an AD LDS instance. MIIS and MILM support the provisioning of data from a wide variety of sources such as AD DS forests, SQL Server databases, third-party LDAP services, and much more. IIFP is a subset of MIIS and supports data integration between AD DS, AD LDS, and Exchange Server. Using these solutions reduces your identity management overhead by designating a single master source and provisioning all other repositories from this source.

MORE INFO **MIIS, MILM, and IIFP**

For more information on MIIS, go to *http://www.microsoft.com/technet/miis/evaluate /overview.mspx*.

For more information on MILM, go to *http://www.microsoft.com/windowsserver/ilm2007 /default.mspx*.

For more information on and to download IIFP, go to *http://www.microsoft.com/downloads /details.aspx?familyid=d9143610-c04d-41c4-b7ea-6f56819769d5&displaylang=en*.

- Provide support for departmental applications. In some cases, departments might require additional identity information, information that is of no relevance to any other department within the organization. By integrating this information in an AD LDS instance, the department has access to it without affecting the directory service for the entire organization.

- Provide support for distributed applications. If your application is distributed and requires access to data in several locations, you can also rely on AD LDS because AD LDS provides the same multimaster replication capabilities as AD DS.

- Migrate legacy directory applications to AD LDS. If your organization is running legacy applications that rely on an LDAP directory, you can migrate the data to an AD LDS instance and standardize it on Active Directory directory technologies.

- Provide support for local development. Because AD LDS can be installed on client workstations, you can provide your developers with portable single-instance directories they can use to develop custom applications that require access to identity data. Developing with AD LDS is much simpler and easier to manage and contain than developing with AD DS.

- In addition, when evaluating directory-enabled commercial applications, you should always give preference to an application that will rely on AD LDS or its predecessor, ADAM, before selecting one that relies on AD DS schema modifications. Deploying commercial applications with portable directories is much easier and has much less impact on your network than deploying applications that will modify your NOS directory schema forever.

Each of these scenarios represents a possible use of AD LDS. Typical applications should include white-page directories, security-oriented applications and network configuration, and policy store applications.

As you can see, AD LDS is much more portable and malleable than AD DS will ever be. Whenever you need to think about schema modifications in AD DS, think of AD LDS instead. On almost every occasion, AD LDS will provide a better choice because AD DS should always be reserved as a NOS directory and should include integration only with applications that add functionality to the NOS directory functions.

MORE INFO   AD LDS

For more information on AD LDS, go to *http://technet2.microsoft.com/windowsserver2008/en /library/b7fb96ec-3f3f-4860-a1ab-eb43e54bbefc1033.mspx.*

Exam Tip   Pay attention to the scenarios outlined previously in this chapter. Although few exam questions are about AD LDS, you can be sure that when they do arise, they will be related to choosing AD LDS over other Active Directory technologies.

Installing AD LDS

As part of Windows Server 2008, AD LDS can be installed and configured in both the full installation and in Server Core. In addition, AD LDS is an ideal candidate for virtualization through Windows Server 2008 Hyper-V. Because of its light requirements, AD LDS can easily run within a virtual instance of the Windows Server 2008 operating system and should be considered as such unless the application that is tied to the AD LDS instance has specific requirements for physical installation.

In addition, avoid installing AD LDS on domain controllers as much as possible. Although AD LDS can fully coexist with the domain controller (DC) role, and even the read-only domain controller (RODC) role, domain controllers should be considered special roles within your network and should be tied only to the DNS service and nothing else, if at all possible. Because DCs are also good candidates for virtualization, any network that can rely on host servers running Hyper-V and virtualized instances of other services should virtualize DCs as much as possible. With a virtual DC, it is much easier to ensure that no other roles are hosted on the server because all other roles can also be virtualized within their own instances of Windows Server 2008.

Also, consider running AD LDS in scenarios in which high security is required. A good example is one in which you need to run an authentication directory service in extranets or perimeter networks. Relying on Server Core installations within these environments can help reduce the attack surface of servers you expose outside of your corporate network.

Identifying AD LDS Requirements

As mentioned earlier, AD LDS has very light installation requirements. They include:

- A supported operating system such as Windows Server 2008, Standard Edition, Enterprise Edition, or Datacenter Edition.
- An account with local administration access rights.

Removing AD LDS from a server requires two activities:

- First, uninstall any instance of AD LDS you created after the role installation, using Programs And Features in Control Panel.
- Second, use Server Manager to remove the AD LDS role.

As you can see, both installation and removal requirements are straightforward. The major caveat is that you ensure that all instances have been removed from a server before you remove the role.

Exam Tip   Keep in mind that you need to remove all instances of AD LDS from a server before you can remove the role from the server.

Installing AD LDS on Server Core

Installing AD LDS is very similar to installing AD DS. First you must install the server role; then you must create the AD LDS instances you want to use. Installing AD LDS on the full installation of Windows Server 2008 is covered in the practice later in this lesson.

The installation process for AD LDS is as simple on Server Core as it is on a full installation of Windows Server 2008. Use the following process:

1. Log on with local administrative credentials to a Windows Server 2008 member or standalone server running Server Core.

2. Begin by identifying the service name for AD LDS. Use the following command:

    ```
    oclist | more
    ```

    Using the pipe symbol (|) followed by the *more* command enables you to view contents one screen at a time. Press the spacebar to move from one screen to the next. Use Ctrl+C to cancel the command after you have found the name of the role. This name should appear in the first screen of information and should be DirectoryServices-ADAM-ServerCore.

3. Proceed to the installation of the role. Use the following command:

    ```
    start /w ocsetup DirectoryServices-ADAM-ServerCore
    ```

    Role names are case-sensitive, so ensure that you type the role name exactly as displayed; otherwise, the command will not work. Also, using the *start /w* command ensures that the command prompt does not return until the role installation is complete.

If you run the *oclist* command once again, you will see that the AD LDS role has been added to this server. You can also navigate to the %SystemRoot%\ADAM folder to view the new AD LDS files. Your server is ready to host AD LDS instances.

PRACTICE Installing AD LDS

In this practice, you will install the AD LDS role on a server running the full installation of Windows Server 2008. Then you will browse the contents of the installation folder to identify which files have been installed.

▶ Exercise 1   Install AD LDS

In this exercise, you will install the AD LDS server role.

1. Make sure your Active Directory Domain Server, SERVER01.contoso.com, is running, and start your member servers, SERVER03.contoso.com and SERVER04.contoso.com.

2. Log on to SERVER03.contoso.com with the Contoso\Administrator account.

    You do not need domain administrator rights to work with AD LDS. Because each AD LDS installation is independent of AD DS, you need only local administrator rights to work with it, but using the domain administrator account is acceptable for the purpose of this exercise.

3. In Server Manager, right-click the Roles node, and then select Add Roles.

4. Review the Before You Begin screen, and then click Next.

5. In the Select Server Roles dialog box, select Active Directory Lightweight Directory Services, and then click Next.

6. Review the information in the Active Directory Lightweight Directory Services window, and then click Next.

7. Confirm your choices, and then click Install.

8. Review the installation results, and then click Close.

9. Repeat the operation on SERVER04.contoso.com.

AD LDS is installed on both member servers.

The AD LDS installation installs the service and generates a directory store called Adamntds.dit located in the %SystemRoot%\Adam folder. It also adds the tools to configure and manage AD LDS.

MORE INFO   AD LDS installation process

For a step-by-step guide to the installation of AD LDS, go to *http://technet2.microsoft.com /windowsserver2008/en/library/141900a7-445c-4bd3-9ce3-5ff53d70d10a1033.mspx?mfr=true.*

When the installation is complete, the role appears in Server Manager. (See Figure 14-2.)

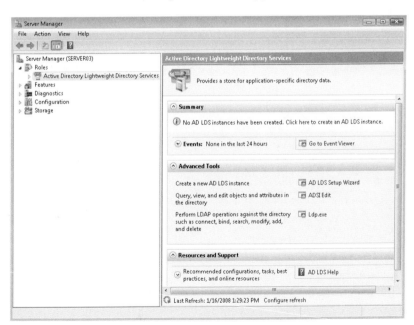

Figure 14-2   Viewing the AD LDS role within Server Manager

▶ **Exercise 2   Review the Installed AD LDS Files**

In this exercise, you will review the files AD LDS installs on servers.

1. Log on to your member server, SERVER03.contoso.com, using the Contoso\Administrator account.

2. Open a Windows Explorer window. From the Start menu, right-click Computer, and then select Explore.

3. Navigate to the %SystemRoot%\ADAM folder.

4. Review the files created by the AD LDS installation process.

   On a full installation of Windows Server 2008, AD LDS creates the ADAM folder and populates it with 20 files and two subfolders. The two subfolders include localization information. In this case, they are in U.S. English. As shown in Figure 14-3, the files contained in the ADAM folder include:

   ❑ The AD LDS program files, including .dll, .exe, .cat, .ini, and .xml files.

   ❑ The AD LDS directory store, Adamntds.dit.

   ❑ Lightweight directory format (.ldf) files that are used to populate AD LDS instances when they are created.

You will be working with these file types when you begin to configure AD LDS in the next lesson.

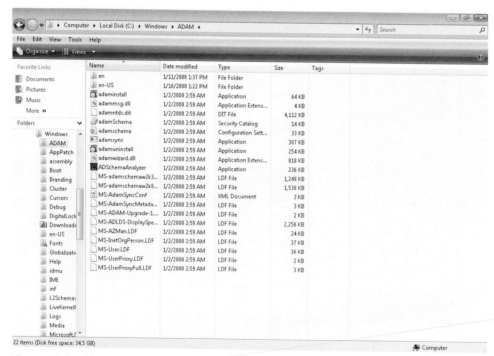

Figure 14-3   AD LDS installs into the %SystemRoot%\Adam folder and creates the AD LDS database

The installation of AD LDS on Server Core does not include the same files and folders as the installation on a full installation of Windows Server 2008. Server Core creates only one folder for localization, whereas the full installation creates two. In addition, the full installation includes an additional tool: the Active Directory Schema Analyzer, which is not installed on Server Core. (See Figure 14-4.)

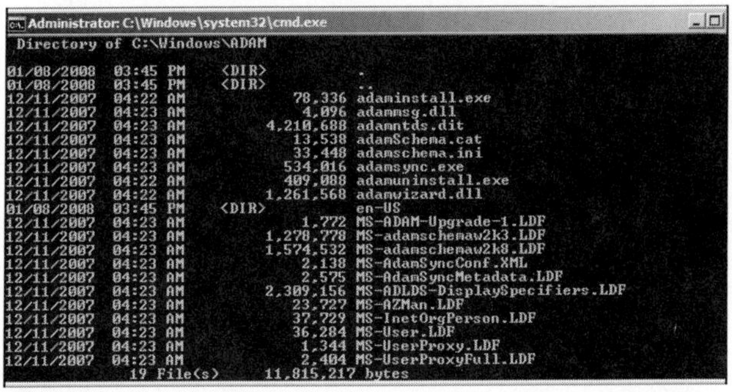

Figure 14-4   The AD LDS Installation on Server Core only includes 19 files and one single sub-folder

Lesson Summary

- As its name suggests, AD LDS is a lightweight version of AD DS. AD LDS supports all the features of AD DS except for the network operating system capabilities. As such, it is a directory service that can be tied to applications and support their need for custom configurations and authentication services in insecure environments such as perimeter networks.
- The installation requirements for AD LDS are very simple: all you need is a server running a supported version of Windows Server 2008. This server can be a member, a stand-alone server, or even a domain controller, although you should endeavor to keep your DCs separate from all other roles.
- To install AD LDS, you select the role in the Add Roles Wizard. The installation process is probably the most basic installation process of all the roles in Windows Server 2008.
- To remove AD LDS, you must first remove all instances through Programs And Features in Control Panel and then remove the role in Server Manager.

Lesson Review

You can use the following questions to test your knowledge of the information in Lesson 1, "Understanding and Installing AD LDS." The questions are also available on the companion CD if you prefer to review them in electronic form.

NOTE   Answers

Answers to these questions and explanations of why each answer choice is right or wrong are located in the "Answers" section at the end of the book.

1. You are a server administrator for *contoso.com*. This morning, your boss came in with a new request. You need to repurpose SERVER04 with a new role as soon as possible. SERVER04 currently hosts five AD LDS instances. You must uninstall AD LDS from this server. You log on to SERVER04 with local administrative rights and launch an elevated command prompt. You use the *ocsetup* command with the */uninstall* switch, and it does not work. Which of the following options should you use to resolve the problem?

   A. You must restart the server to make sure all running setup processes are complete and then run the *uninstall* command again.

   B. You must use Server Manager to remove all AD LDS instances and the role.

   C. You must uninstall all existing instances of AD LDS first, using Programs And Features in Control Panel, and then execute *ocsetup /uninstall* from the command prompt.

   D. You must use the *oclist* command to verify the syntax of the option you are trying to remove with the *ocsetup* command. You retry the *ocsetup* command with the correct syntax.

Lesson 2: Configuring and Using AD LDS

Now that you have installed AD LDS, you can begin to work with it to store directory-related data for various applications. The first thing you should do is become familiar with the AD LDS tool set. After you understand which tools you can use to manage AD LDS, you can begin to create your first instances. After you've created your instances, you can secure them to ensure that they are properly protected. You'll then move on to the creation of replicas for these instances so that you can install them on various other systems and control replication so that instances located on different computers can be updated through multimaster replication.

This lesson will show you the value AD LDS offers when you combine it with applications and integrate it with the other Active Directory technologies contained within Windows Server 2008.

> **After this lesson, you will be able to:**
> - Create AD LDS instances.
> - Work with AD LDS tools.
> - Work with application partitions.
> - Manage replication between AD LDS instances.
>
> **Estimated lesson time: 30 minutes**

Working with AD LDS Tools

You can work with AD LDS through a selection of tools, many of which will be familiar to you because they are the same tools you use for AD DS administration. Table 14-3 outlines each of these tools and the purpose it serves when managing the AD LDS service.

Table 14-3   AD LDS Tools and AD DS Tools

Tool Name	Usage	Location
Active Directory Schema Snap-in	Modify the schema for AD LDS instances. You must use the *Regsvr32.exe* command to register the Schmmgnt.dll first.	Custom MMC
Active Directory Sites and Services	Configure and manage replication scopes for AD LDS instances. AD LDS instances must be updated to support replication objects first.	Administrative Tools program group
AD LDS Setup	Create AD LDS instances.	Administrative Tools program group
ADAMInstall.exe	Command-line tool for the creation of AD LDS instances.	%SystemRoot% \ADAM folder

Table 14-3   AD LDS Tools and AD DS Tools

Tool Name	Usage	Location
ADAMSync.exe	Command-line tool for synchronizing data from AD DS forest to AD LDS instance. AD LDS instance must be updated to AD DS schema first.	%SystemRoot% \ADAM folder
ADAMUninstall.exe	Command-line tool for the removal of AD LDS instances.	%SystemRoot% \ADAM folder
ADSchemaAnalyzer.exe	Command-line tool for copying schema contents from AD DS to AD LDS or from one AD LDS instance to another. Supports third-party LDAP directory schema copies.	%SystemRoot% \ADAM folder
ADSI Edit	Interactively manage AD LDS content through ADSI.	Administrative Tools program group
CSVDE.exe	Import data into AD LDS instances.	Command line
DSACLS.exe	Control access control lists on AD LDS objects.	Command line
DSAMain.exe	Mount Active Directory store (.dit) backups or snapshots to identify their contents.	Command line
DSDBUtil.exe	Perform database maintenance, configure AD LDS ports, and view existing instances. Also, create one-step installations for transporting AD LDS instances through the Install from Media (IFM) generation process.	Command line
Dcdiag.exe	Diagnose AD LDS instances. Must use the /n:*NamingContext* switch to name the instance to diagnose.	Command line
DSMgmt.exe	Supports application partition and AD LDS policy management.	Command line
Event Viewer	To audit AD LDS changes and log old and new values for both objects and attributes.	Administrative Tools program group
LDAP Data Interchange Format (LDIF) Files	AD LDS installations can dynamically import LDIF files (.ldp) during instance creation, automatically configuring the instance.	%SystemRoot% \ADAM folder
LDIFDE.exe	Import data into AD LDS instances.	Command line
LDP.exe	Interactively modify content or AD LDS instances through LDAP.	Command line
Ntdsutil.exe	Manage AD LDS instances but only if AD DS is also installed. (Not recommended; use *DSDBUtil.exe* instead.)	Command line

Table 14-3   AD LDS Tools and AD DS Tools

Tool Name	Usage	Location
RepAdmin.exe	Analyze replication to view potential issues.	Command line
Server Manager	Manage existing AD LDS instances.	Administrative Tools program group
Windows Server Backup	Back up or restore AD LDS instances and their contents.	Administrative Tools program group

You'll use a variety of the tools listed in Table 14-3 to perform the configuration and administration operations required when you run AD LDS services.

MORE INFO   AD LDS auditing

For more information on auditing AD LDS instances or AD DS domains, go to *http://go.microsoft.com/fwlink/?LinkId=94846*.

Creating AD LDS Instances

The AD LDS role installation process is very similar to the AD DS installation process. You begin by installing the AD LDS binaries, and then, after they are installed, you create AD LDS instances to use the service. In the same way, when you deploy AD DS, you begin by installing the binaries, and then you use the Active Directory Domain Services Installation Wizard to create the AD DS instance you will use. Because of their same roots, many of the tools you use to manage them are the same.

Preparing for AD LDS Instance Creation

You create AD LDS instances by using the Active Directory Lightweight Directory Services Setup Wizard. However, you need to prepare several items before you create the instance. These items include:

- A data drive created for your server. Because this server will be hosting directory stores, place these stores on a drive that is separate from the operating system.

- The name you will use to create the instance. Use meaningful names, for example, the name of the application that will be tied to this instance, to identify instances. This name will be used to identify the instance on the local computer as well as to name the files that make up the instance and the service that supports it.

- The ports you intend to use to communicate with the instance. Both AD LDS and AD DS use the same ports for communication. These ports are the default LDAP (389) and LDAP over the Secure Sockets Layer (SSL), or Secure LDAP (636), ports. AD DS uses two additional ports, 3268, which uses LDAP to access the global catalog, and 3269, which uses Secure LDAP to access the global catalog. Because AD DS and AD LDS use the same ports, this is another good reason for not running both roles on the same server. However, when the wizard detects that ports 389 and 636 are already in use, it proposes 50,000 and 50,001 for each port and then uses other ports in the 50,000 range for additional instances.

Quick Check

1. Which ports are used to work with AD LDS instances?
2. How do the ports in an AD LDS instance differ from ports used by AD DS?

Quick Check Answers

1. The ports used by an AD LDS instance can be the standard LDAP port, 389, or the LDAP over SSL or Secure LDAP port, 636. In addition, AD LDS can use any port over 1025. However, use ports in the 50,000 range as a best practice.
2. Both AD DS and AD LDS can use ports 389 (LDAP) or 636 (Secure LDAP). In addition, AD DS uses ports 3268 (LDAP) and 3269 (Secure LDAP) to communicate with the global catalog service. However, reserve ports 389 and 636 for AD DS as a best practice.

IMPORTANT   Using ports 389 and 636

If you are creating AD LDS instances within a domain, do not use ports 389 or 636 even if you are not creating the first instance on a domain controller. AD DS uses these ports by default, and, because of this, some consoles, such as those using the Active Directory Schema snap-in, will not bind to local instances because they bind to the AD DS directory by default. As a best practice, always use ports beyond the 50,000 range for your AD LDS instances.

Exam Tip   Make note of the default ports because they are sure to be on the exam even though you should avoid them in production environments.

- The Active Directory application partition name you intend to use for the instance. You must use a distinguished name (DN) to create the partition. For example, you could use CN=AppPartition1,DC=Contoso,DC=com. Depending on how you intend to use the instance, you might or might not need the application partition. Application partitions control the replication scope for a directory store. For example, when you integrate DNS data within the directory, AD DS creates an application partition to make DNS data available to appropriate DCs. Application partitions for AD LDS can be created in one of three ways: when you create the instance, when you install the application that will be tied to the instance, or when you create the partition manually through the *LDP.exe* tool. If your application will not create application partitions automatically, create them with the wizard.

- A service account to run the instance. You can use the Network Service account, but if you intend to run multiple instances, it might be best to use named service accounts for each instance. Remember to follow the service accounts guidelines and requirements as listed here:
  - ❏ Create a domain account if you are in a domain; otherwise, use a local account (for example, in a perimeter network).
  - ❏ Name the account with the same name you gave to the instance.
  - ❏ Assign a complex password to this account.
  - ❏ Set User Cannot Change Password in the account properties. You assign this property to ensure that no one can appropriate the account.
  - ❏ Set Password Never Expires in the account properties. You assign this property to ensure that the service does not fail because of a password policy.
  - ❏ Assign the Log On As A Service User right in the Local Security Policy of each computer that will host this instance.
  - ❏ Assign the Generate Security Audits User right in the Local Security Policy of each computer that will host this instance to support account auditing.
- A group that will contain the user accounts that will administer the instance. The best practice for permission assignments is always to use groups even if only one account is a member of the group. If personnel changes, you can always add or change group members without having to add or change permissions. Create a domain group if you are in a domain; otherwise, create a local group. Name the group the same as the instance. This way, it will be easy to track the group's purpose. Add your own account to the group as well as to the service account you created earlier.
- Any additional LDIF files you need for the instance. Place these files into the %SystemRoot% \ADAM folder. These files will be imported during the creation of the instance. Importing LDIF files extends the schema of the instance you are creating to support additional operations. For example, to synchronize AD DS with AD LDS, you would import the MS-AdamSyncMetadata.ldf file. If your application requires custom schema modifications, create the LDIF file ahead of time and import it as you create the instance. Note that you can always import LDIF files after the instance is created. Default LDIF files are listed in Table 14-4.

Make note of these values because you will need them to both create and then manage the instance.

Table 14-4   Default AD LDS LDIF Files

File Name	Purpose
MS-ADAM-Upgrade-1.ldf	To upgrade the AD LDS schema to the latest version.
MS-adamschemaw2k3.ldf	Required as a prerequisite for synchronizing an instance with Active Directory in Windows Server 2003.

Table 14-4   Default AD LDS LDIF Files

File Name	Purpose
MS-adamschemaw2k8.ldf	Required as a prerequisite for synchronizing an instance with Active Directory in Windows Server 2008.
MS-AdamSyncMetadata.ldf	Required to synchronize data between an AD DS forest and an AD LDS instance through ADAMSync.
MS-ADLDS-DisplaySpecifiers.ldf	Required for the Active Directory Sites and Services snap-in operation.
MS-AZMan.ldf	Required to support the Windows Authorization Manager.
MS-InetOrgPerson.ldf	Required to create *inetOrgPerson* user classes and attributes.
MS-User.ldf	Required to create user classes and attributes.
MS-UserProxy.ldf	Required to create a simple *userProxy* class.
MS-UserProxyFull.ldf	Required to create a full *userProxy* class. MS-UserProxy.ldf must be imported first.

After you have all these items in hand, you are ready to create your instance. Make sure the account you use has local administrative rights. There are two ways to create instances. The first is through the Active Directory Lightweight Services Setup Wizard, and the second is through the command line. You will use the wizard during the practice in this lesson. Using the command line is explained in a later section.

Performing an Unattended AD LDS Instance Creation

You can also perform unattended AD LDS instance creations. For example, to create instances on Server Core installations, you must use an unattended instance creation process because there is no graphical interface to run the wizard. Unattended instance creations are also useful when you need to create an instance for a distributed application on multiple servers. Make sure you prepare all the prerequisites for the instance as outlined in the "Preparing for AD LDS Instance Creation" section earlier in this lesson.

The %SystemRoot%\ADAM folder includes an additional command, *AdamInstall.exe*, which can be run to perform unattended instance setups. As with the *Dcpromo.exe* command, this command requires a text file as input for the creation of the instance. You can run *AdamInstall.exe* on either a full installation or Server Core. Begin by creating this text file.

1. Launch Notepad

2. Type the text for the answer file. Include the following items:

```
[ADAMInstall]
InstallType=Unique
```

```
InstanceName=InstanceName
LocalLDAPPortToListenOn=PortNumber
LocalSSLPortToListenOn=PortNumber
NewApplicationPartitionToCreate=PartitionName
DataFilesPath=D:\ADAMInstances\InstanceName\Data
LogFilesPath=D:\ADAMInstances\InstanceName\Data
ServiceAccount=DomainorMachineName\AccountName
ServicePassword=Password
Administrator=DomainorMachineName\GroupName
ImportLDIFFiles="LDIFFilename1" "LDIFFilename2" "LDIFFilename3"
SourceUserName=DomainorMachineName\AccountName
SourcePassword=Password
```

Replace all names in italics with the appropriate values. Refer to the "Preparing for AD LDS Instance Creation" section earlier in this lesson to identify the required values. Use caution with this file because it includes passwords, and these passwords are displayed in clear text. The passwords are removed as soon as the file is used by the AD LDS instance creation tool.

3. Save the file in the %SystemRoot%\ADAM folder, and name it with the name of the instance you want to create.

4. Close Notepad.

MORE INFO   AD LDS instance creation

For more information on AD LDS instance creation, go to *http://technet2.microsoft.com/ windowsserver2008/en/library/141900a7-445c-4bd3-9ce3-5ff53d70d10a1033.mspx?mfr=true.*

Now you're ready to create your instance. Remember that you need local administrative rights.

1. Open an elevated command prompt from the Start menu by right-clicking Command Prompt and selecting Run As Administrator.

2. In the command prompt window, move to the %SystemRoot%\ADAM folder. Type the following command, and then press Enter.

   `cd windows\adam`

3. Type the following command. Use quotation marks for the file name if it includes spaces.

   `adaminstall /answer:filename.txt`

4. Close the command prompt window.

Your instance is ready. You can verify that the instance files have been created by going to the target folder and viewing its contents.

Migrating a Previous LDAP Instance to AD LDS

You can also migrate existing LDAP directories to AD LDS or upgrade instances of ADAM to AD LDS. You can do this by importing the contents of the older instances into a new instance of AD LDS.

Importing data can be done either when you create the instance or after the instance is created. Both processes use the same approach because both rely on LDIF files or files with the .ldf extension. If you choose to import data after the instance is created, you will need to use the *LDIFDE.exe* command. Keep in mind that you must first export the data from the previous instance and place it into a file in LDIF format before you can import the data.

You can use *LDIFDE* to export contents from legacy instances. Remember that you need local administrative rights as well as administrative rights to the instance to perform these operations. Also make sure you run the command prompt with elevated credentials. Use the following command structure:

```
ldifde -f filename -s servername:portnumber -m -b username domainname password
```

In this command structure, *filename* is the name of the file to create (use quotation marks if the path includes spaces); *servername* is the name of the server hosting the instance; *portnumber* is the communications port; *username*, *domainname*, and *password* are the credentials of an instance administrator.

Use a similar command to import the data into the new instance:

```
ldifde -i -f filename -s servername:portnumber -m -b username domainname password
```

Note that to import passwords from the legacy instance, you must use the −h switch. This switch will encrypt all passwords, using simple authentication and security layer (SASL).

Quick Check

1. What are the three ways to create application partitions for AD LDS instances?
2. What is the purpose of the LDIF files included with AD LDS?
3. How can you debug an AD LDS instance creation process that goes awry?

Quick Check Answers

1. There are three ways to create application partitions for AD LDS instances:
   - ❑ They can be created during the creation of an instance with AD LDS Setup.
   - ❑ They can be created through the installation of the application that will be tied to an AD LDS instance.
   - ❑ They can be created manually through the *LDP.exe* tool.

> 2. The LDIF files included with AD LDS serve several purposes, depending on the actual file, but generally they are used to extend the schema of an instance to support specific functionality.
>
> 3. AD LDS creates log files during the creation of the instance. These files are located in the %SystemRoot%\Debug folder and are named ADAMSetup.log and ADAMSetup_loader.log. You can review them to find and resolve issues during the creation of the instance.

MORE INFO *LDIFDE*

For more information on the *LDIFDE.exe* command, go to *http://technet2.microsoft.com/win-dowsserver/en/library/32872283-3722-4d9b-925a-82c516a1ca141033.mspx?mfr=true*. Also, refer to Chapter 3, "Users," for additional information on *LDIFDE*.

Working with AD LDS Instances

Table 14-3, presented earlier, lists all the various tools you can use to work with AD LDS instances. Of these, the most useful are the graphical tools such as ADSI Edit, *LDP.exe*, the Schema snap-in, and Active Directory Sites and Services. They control how you view and edit content in your instances. Command-line tools are more useful for automating processes and data input for AD LDS instances.

Using ADSI Edit to Work with Instances

ADSI Edit is a general administration tool for AD LDS instances. Each time you want to work with an instance, you must first connect and bind to the instance. Remember that you must be administrator of the instance to perform administrative operations on them. Use the following procedure:

1. Launch ADSI Edit from the Administrative Tools program group.
2. In the tree pane, right-click ADSI Edit, and then select Connect To. This opens the Connection Settings dialog box. Type in the following values as shown in Figure 14-5:
   - ❏ Name: should be the name of the instance to which you want to connect.
   - ❏ Connection Point: choose Select Or Type A Distinguished Name Or Naming Context, and type the distinguished name of the instance.
   - ❏ Computer: choose Select Or Type A Domain Or Server, and type the server name with the port number, for example, SERVER03:50000.
   - ❏ Computer: select the Use SSL-Based Encryption check box if you are using a Secure LDAP port.

3.   Click OK.

This connects you to the instance. Expand all entries to view the instance contents. Explore the context menus to understand the operations you can perform with ADSI Edit on AD LDS instances.

Figure 14-5   Connecting to an AD LDS instance with ADSI Edit

Now that you are bound to the instance, you can create and manage objects within the instance. Use the following procedure:

1.   Right-click the application partition distinguished name, select New, and choose Object. This opens the Create Object dialog box, which lists all the available object classes in the instance's schema.

2.   Begin by creating a user group. Scroll to the Group object, select it, and then click Next.

3.   Type the name of the group, for example, **AD LDS Users**, and then click Next.

4.   On the next screen of the dialog box, you can click More Attributes to assign more values to this new object. For example, you can assign a description to the group. From the Select A Property To View drop-down list, select adminDescription. Type a description in the *Edit Attribute* field, for example, **Group to contain AD LDS users**, click Set, and then click OK.

5.   Click Finish to create the group. By default, this creates a security group.

6.   Now create a user. Right-click the application partition distinguished name, select New, and then choose Object.

7.   Scroll to the User object, select it, and then click Next.

8.   Type the name of the user, and then click Next.

9. Once again, you can click More Attributes to assign more values to this new object.

10. Click Finish to create the user.

11. Now add the user to the group. Locate the group in the details pane, and right-click it to select Properties.

12. In the Properties dialog box, locate the member property, and then click Edit.

13. In the Multi-Valued Distinguished Name With Security Principal Editor dialog box, click Add DN.

14. In the Add Distinguished Name dialog box, type the distinguished name of the user you created. For example, type **cn=John Kane,cn=Instance01,dc=contoso,dc=com**. Click OK. The user is now listed in the members list.

15. Click OK to complete the operation.

If you view the properties of the group again, you will see that your user has been added to the group. It is quite cumbersome to add users and groups to an instance in this manner, but you can use it for single modifications. Ideally, you will create user and group lists and then use either *CSVDE.exe* or *LDIFDE.exe* to add them in batches. Refer to Chapter 3 to review the automation of user creation and to Chapter 4, "Groups," to review the automation of group creation for more information.

Using *LDP.exe* to Work with Instances

Similarly, the *LDP.exe* console enables you to view and edit instance contents. As with the ADSI Edit tool, you must connect and then bind to the instance you need to work with. Remember that you must be administrator of the instance to perform administrative operations on it. Use the following procedure:

1. Launch *LDP.exe* from the command line or from Server Manager under the Active Directory Lightweight Directory Service, Advanced Tools section.

2. Click Connection from the Connect menu.

3. Type the name of the server you want to connect to and the port number to use. Select SSL if you are using a Secure LDAP port. Click OK.

4. Click Bind from the Connect menu.

5. If your account has the required permissions, select Bind As Currently Logged On User. If not, select Bind With Credentials, and type the appropriate credentials. Click OK.

6. Click Tree from the View menu. This will fill the tree pane.

7. In the BaseDN dialog box, click the down arrow to view the list of distinguished names, and select the name of your instance. Click OK.

   From this point, you can use the tree pane to identify where you want to work inside the instance. Explore the various menus to see which operations you can perform with *LDP.exe*, and then close *LDP.exe*.

MORE INFO Using *LDP.exe* with AD LDS instances

For more information on using *LDP.exe* with AD LDS instances, see *http://technet2.microsoft.com/ windowsserver2008/en/library/141900a7-445c-4bd3-9ce3-5ff53d70d10a1033.mspx*.

Using the Schema Snap-in to Work with Instances

You can also use the Active Directory Schema snap-in to create custom consoles to manage AD LDS instance schemas. Remember that to use this snap-in, you must first register it on the server. Use the following command in an elevated command prompt:

```
regsvr32 schmmgmt.dll
```

You're now ready to load the Schema snap-in and view the schema of your instances. Remember to use administrative credentials for the instance.

1. Click Start, and then type **mmc** in the Search box. Press Enter.
2. In the empty MMC, click Add/Remove Snap-in from the File menu.
3. Locate the Active Directory Schema snap-in in the Available Snap-ins list, click Add, and then click OK.
4. Save the console with an appropriate name. Make sure you save it in an appropriate location.
5. The Schema snap-in binds to the Active Directory Domain Services directory by default. To bind to an AD LDS instance, right-click Active Directory Schema in the tree pane, and select Change Active Directory Domain Controller.
6. In the Change Directory Server dialog box, select This Domain Controller Or AD LDS Instance, click <Type A Directory Server Name[:Port] Here>, type the server name with the port number separated by a colon, and then press Enter. Click OK.
7. In the warning dialog box, click Yes to change servers.

    You can now view the schema for this instance. Save this console again to save these settings. Note the similarities between the schema of an AD LDS instance and the one for an AD DS directory.

NOTE Creating a multi-AD LDS console

If you want to create one console with multiple AD LDS instance schemas, just add additional Schema snap-ins to your console. Use one snap-in for each instance you want to connect to. When you reopen the console, it will link to each instance and save you time.

Using Active Directory Sites and Services to Work with Instances

As with the other Active Directory tools, you can manage AD LDS instances with the Active Directory Sites and Services console. However, before you can do so, you must import the MS-ADLDS-DisplaySpecifiers.ldf file to update the instance's schema to support the appropriate objects. To do so, perform the following steps:

1. Begin by adding the LDIF file to your instance if it hasn't already been done. Open an elevated command prompt.

2. Move to the %SystemRoot%\ADAM folder, cd windows\adam.

3. Import the LDIF file into the instance:

    ```
    ldifde -i -f MS-ADLDS-DisplaySpecifiers.ldf -s servername:portnumber -m -a username
    domainname password
    ```

4. Close the command prompt.

5. Launch Active Directory Sites And Services from the Administrative Tools program group.

6. The console binds to the Active Directory Domain Services directory by default. To bind to an AD LDS instance, right-click Active Directory Sites And Services in the tree pane, and select Change Domain Controller.

7. In the Change Directory Server dialog box, select This Domain Controller Or AD LDS Instance, and click <Type A Directory Server Name[:Port] Here>. Type the server name with the port number separated by a colon, and then press Enter. Click OK.

8. In the warning dialog box, click Yes to change servers.

    You can now work with the replication parameters for the instance. Note that the server name uses the Servername$InstanceName format to illustrate that it is not a domain controller.

MORE INFO   AD LDS tools and instances

For more information on AD LDS tools and instances, go to *http://technet2.microsoft.com/ windowsserver2008/en/library/141900a7-445c-4bd3-9ce3-5ff53d70d10a1033.mspx.*

Exam Tip   Keep in mind that you cannot use graphical tools on Server Core. To manage instances located on Server Core installations, use the graphical tools from a full Windows installation or from a client system running Remote Server Administration Tools (RSAT) to control them remotely.

Working with AD LDS instances requires care and attention because almost every activity is performed either through the command line or by using distinguished names. As you have seen when working with AD DS, typographical errors are the bane of any administrator working with these tools. The same applies to AD LDS. Be sure to double-check all your entries before you run any command or create and manage any object by using its distinguished name.

PRACTICE Working with AD LDS Instances

In this practice, you will create your first AD LDS instance as well as a replica. Then you will manage replication between the two instances. For this, you will need the two servers listed in the "Before you Begin" section of this chapter.

▶ **Exercise 1   Create an AD LDS Instance**

In this exercise, you will create your first AD LDS instance. You previously installed the AD LDS service on both of the member servers mentioned in the "Before You Begin" section of this chapter. You will use the values in Table 14-5 to perform this exercise.

Table 14-5   Instance Creation Values

Item	Value
Instance Name	ADLDSInstance
Ports	50,004 for LDAP 50,005 for Secure LDAP
Application Partition Name	CN=ADLDSInstance,dc=contoso,dc=com
Data Paths	D:\ADLDS\ADLDSInstance\Data
Service Account	Network Service
Administration Account	Contoso\Administrator
LDIF Files for Import	MS-AdamSyncMetadata.ldf MS-ADLDS-DisplaySpecifiers.ldf MS-AZMan.ldf MS-InetOrgPerson.ldf MS-User.ldf MS-UserProxy.ldf MS-UserProxyFull.ldf

Make a practice of filling out a table similar to Table 14-5 each time you create a new instance of AD LDS. Because a server can host a multitude of AD LDS instances, it is a very good practice to document each one.

1. Begin by making sure your domain controller, SERVER01.contoso.com, and your member servers, SERVER03.contoso.com and SERVER04.contoso.com, are running.

2. Log on to SERVER03.contoso.com with the domain Administrator account.

   Remember that, in production, you need only local administrative rights for operations with AD LDS.

3. Launch the Active Directory Lightweight Directory Services Setup Wizard from the Administrative Tools program group.

4. Review the information on the Welcome page, and then click Next.

5. On the Setup Options page, select A Unique Instance, and then click Next.

6. On the Instance Name page, type **ADLDSInstance**, and then click Next.

   When you name the instance, you also name the service that will run that instance. Note that the service name will be ADAM_*instancename*, but the name listed in the Services console will be *instancename* alone.

7. On the Ports page, provide the ports to use to communicate with this instance. Use 50,004 for LDAP and 50,005 for the SSL port number. Click Next.

8. On the Application Directory Partition page, provide the application partition name, in this case, **CN=ADLDSInstance,dc=contoso,dc=com**, and click Next.

   You must always supply a distinguished name.

9. On the File Locations page, change the paths to D:\ADLDS\ADLDSInstance\Data, and then click Next.

   Because this is a directory store, it should be placed on a disk that is separate from the operating system, for example, on a D drive. You can also use separate subfolders for the data files and the data recovery files.

10. On the Service Account Selection page, select Network Service Account, and then click Next.

    Microsoft Windows selects the Network Service account by default. This account has limited local access rights and is a protected account. You should normally use a proper service account, but Network Service will suffice for the purpose of the exercise.

11. On the AD LDS Administrators page, select Currently Logged On User, and then click Next.

    You should normally use a predefined group, but the Administrator account will suffice for the purpose of this exercise.

12. On the Importing LDIF Files page, select all the listed LDIF files, and then click Next.

13. On the Ready To Install page, review your selections, and then click Next.

    AD LDS installs the new instance.

14. Click Finish.

    Your first instance has been created. Open Server Manager and expand the Roles\Active Directory Lightweight Directory Services node to view the results of your operation.

    AD LDS creates log files during the creation of the instance. These files are located in the %SystemRoot%\Debug folder and are named ADAMSetup.log and ADAMSetup_loader.log. You can review them if you find issues during the creation of the instance. Also, creating an instance creates a service for the instance. You can launch the Services console from the Administrative Tools program group to verify the existence of this service.

▶ **Exercise 2   Create an AD LDS Replica Instance**

In this exercise, you will create your first AD LDS replica instance, on the second member server you created.

1. Make sure your domain controller, SERVER01.contoso.com, and your member servers, SERVER03.contoso.com and SERVER04.contoso.com, are running.

2. Log on to SERVER04.contoso.com with the domain Administrator account.

3. Launch the Active Directory Lightweight Directory Services Setup Wizard from the Administrative Tools program group.

4. Review the information on the Welcome page, and then click Next.

5. Under Setup Options, select A Replica Of An Existing Instance, and then click Next.

6. On the Instance Name page, type **ADLDSInstance**, and then click Next.

7. On the Ports page, provide the ports to communicate with this instance. Use 50004 for LDAP and 50005 for the SSL port number. Click Next.

8. On the Joining A Configuration Set page, under Server, click Browse to locate Server 02. Type **SERVER03**, and then click Check Names. Click OK, and then type **50004** into the *LDAP Port* field. Click Next.

9. On the Administrative Credentials For The Configuration Set page, select Currently Logged On User, and then click Next.

   You should normally use a group, but the Administrator account will suffice for the purpose of this exercise.

10. On the Copying Application Directory Partitions page, select the CN=ADLDSInstance,dc=contoso,dc=com partition, and then click Next.

11. On the File Locations page, change the paths to D:\ADLDS\ADLDSInstance\Data, and then click Next.

12. On the Service Account Selection page, select Network Service Account, and then click Next.

    You should normally use a proper service account, but Network Service will suffice for the purpose of the exercise.

13. On the AD LDS Administrators page, select Currently Logged On User, and then click Next.

    You should normally use a group, but the Administrator account will suffice for the purpose of this exercise.

14. On the Ready to Install page, review your selections, and then click Next.

    AD LDS installs the new instance.

15. Click Finish.

    Your replica has been created.

▶ **Exercise 3   Manage Replication Between AD LDS Replicas**

In this exercise, you will view the replication parameters between your two instances. You do not need to update the instances to support Active Directory Sites and Services objects because you imported all LDIF files in the first exercise when you created the source instance.

1. Begin by making sure your domain controller, SERVER01.contoso.com, and your member servers, SERVER03.contoso.com and SERVER04.contoso.com, are running.

2. Log on to SERVER04.contoso.com with the domain Administrator account.

3. Launch Active Directory Sites And Services from the Administrative Tools program group. The console binds to the Active Directory Domain Services directory by default.

4. To bind to the AD LDS instance, right-click Active Directory Sites And Services in the tree pane, and then select Change Domain Controller.

5. In the Change Directory Server dialog box, select This Domain Controller Or AD LDS Instance, and then click <Type A Directory Server Name[:Port] Here>. Type **SERVER03:50004**, and then press Enter. Click OK.

6. In the warning dialog box, click Yes to change servers.

7. Now expand the Active Directory Sites And Services tree completely. You can do so by pressing the asterisk key (*) on your numerical keypad several times. This displays the replication structure for this instance.

   Now, you'll create a new site and move one of the instance objects into this site.

8. Right-click Sites in the tree pane, and then select New Site.

9. Name the site **Replication01**, select the DEFAULTIPSITELINK object, and click OK.

   Your new site link is created, and Active Directory Sites And Services outlines the next steps you must perform. (See Figure 14-6.)

10. Click OK to close the dialog box.

    In this case, you will not perform all activities. You will only move SERVER04 to the new site link. Expand Replication01.

11. Click SERVER04$ADLDSInstance, and drag it to the Servers container under Replication01.

12. In the Moving Objects warning box, click Yes to move the object. The object now appears under the Replication01 site.

This exercise shows you how to work with instances and control replication. In the real world, you will need to perform all the tasks listed in Figure 14-6 to create proper replication partnerships.

MORE INFO   AD LDS replication

For more information on AD LDS replication, go to *http://technet2.microsoft.com/windowsserver2008/ en/library/9d4b4004-9f26-4545-a1e4-8e527102f0a71033.mspx*.

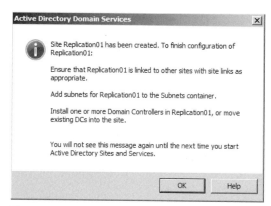

Figure 14-6 Required tasks to complete a replication partnership

Lesson Summary

- The toolset used to control AD LDS instances is very similar to the toolset used for AD DS. Refer to the tools listed in Table 14-3 for a complete list of the tools you can use with AD LDS instances.

- You can create instances both with the graphical interface through the AD LDS Setup tool and through the command line with the *ADAMInstall.exe* command. In both cases, you must plan for all the instance prerequisites beforehand. When using the *ADAMInstall.exe* tool, you will need to prepare an answer file with these values beforehand.

- Working with AD LDS instances means working with distinguished names. Distinguished names use a hierarchical structure that is similar to the hierarchical structure of AD DS forests.

- Working with AD LDS instances means working with server names and port numbers. As a best practice, note each server name and each port number for the instances you create. In fact, always document each instance you create, listing all the values you use to create it.

Lesson Review

You can use the following questions to test your knowledge of the information in Lesson 2, "Configuring and Using AD LDS." The questions are also available on the companion CD if you prefer to review them in electronic form.

NOTE Answers

Answers to these questions and explanations of why each answer choice is right or wrong are located in the "Answers" section at the end of the book.

---

1. You are a local server administrator with *contoso.com*. One of your jobs is to manage AD LDS instances on SERVER03. Recently, you had to install four instances on SERVER03. SERVER03 is a member server of your domain. You began with the default settings for the port selections of each instance. Now, you need to modify the schema of the first instance you installed, Instance01. You register the Active Directory Schema snap-in on the server and create a custom Active Directory Schema console. Yet, when you try to connect to the schema of the first instance, you keep getting an error message. Which of the following is most likely to be the problem?

   A. Instance01 does not include a schema, and you cannot edit it.

   B. You cannot modify the schema of an instance with the Active Directory Schema snap-in. You must use the *LDP.exe* command to do so.

   C. You cannot modify the schema of an instance with the Active Directory Schema snap-in. Modifying the schema of an instance is performed by importing LDIF files with the *LDIFDE.exe* command.

   D. You cannot connect to the instance with the Active Directory Schema snap-in because, by default, it uses the same port as your Active Directory Domain Services directory.

Chapter Review

To further practice and reinforce the skills you learned in this chapter, you can perform the following tasks:

- Review the chapter summary.
- Review the list of key terms introduced in this chapter.
- Complete the case scenario. This scenario sets up a real-world situation involving the topics of this chapter and asks you to create a solution.
- Complete the suggested practices.
- Take a practice test.

Chapter Summary

- As its name suggests, AD LDS is a very portable and malleable directory service. It should always be considered first when you are faced with a schema modification of your network operating system, AD DS. If it is possible to use AD LDS instead of AD DS to integrate an application, then use AD LDS. There are, however, occasions when you cannot replace AD LDS for AD DS. For example, if you implement Exchange Server, you must rely on AD DS. However, Exchange Server 2007 with Service Pack 1 also relies on AD LDS when its server roles are located in a perimeter network.

- AD LDS will run on both the full installation and the Server Core installation of Windows Server 2008. Because of its light weight, AD LDS is a prime candidate for virtualization through Hyper-V.

- AD DS and AD LDS use the same installation process. Begin by installing the role, and then create the directory service instance through a custom wizard or an unattended setup process. To remove AD LDS, you must first remove the instances you create, and then you can remove the role from the server.

- After you have installed the AD LDS service, you can begin to work with it to store directory-related data for different applications. Begin by becoming familiar with the AD LDS tool set. Then, after you understand which tools you can use to manage AD LDS, you can begin to create your first instances. When you've created your instances, you can secure them to ensure that they are properly protected. You'll then move on to the creation of replicas for these instances so that you can install them on various other systems and control replication so that instances located on different computers can be updated through multimaster replication.

Key Terms

Use these key terms to understand better the concepts covered in this chapter.

- **application partitions**   Special directory partitions that control the replication scope for contents of the directory store. They can span several sites and can be assigned to either domain controllers or AD LDS instances.
- **instances**   Discrete directory stores created through AD LDS. Each store is assigned to a particular application and is composed of several objects that include the store itself, the files that make it up, a service contained within the server running the instance, an optional application partition, and an optional replication scope. When created, instances become installed programs on the server.

Case Scenario

In the following case scenario, you will apply what you've learned about Active Directory Lightweight Directory Service. You can find answers to the questions in this scenario in the "Answers" section at the end of this book.

Case Scenario: Determine AD LDS Instance Prerequisites

Contoso, Ltd., has been working with several previous applications until now. Recently, Contoso managers decided to move to Active Directory Domain Services, and they have also decided to standardize on Windows Server 2008 technologies. Because of this, they want to move their former applications to Active Directory Lightweight Directory Services instances.

They turn to you as the potential administrator of AD LDS within the organization to help them address some specific questions in relation to instance prerequisites. Specifically, they want to know:

1. Where should the files for each instance be stored?
2. How should each instance be named?
3. Which ports should be used to connect to the instances?
4. Should application directory partitions be used and why?
5. How should each instance be run?

Suggested Practices

To help you successfully master the exam objectives presented in this chapter, complete the following tasks.

Work with AD LDS Instances

Because there is only one exam objective for this topic, focus on three key tasks to help you prepare for the exam:

- Installing the AD LDS server role.
- Configuring an AD LDS instance.
- Accessing the AD LDS instance through its administration tools.
- **Practice 1** On a server—virtual or physical—that is running either Windows Server 2008 Standard Edition or Windows Server 2008 Enterprise Edition, install the AD LDS server role. This server should not be a domain controller and should be a member server of an Active Directory Domain Services domain.
- **Practice 2** Create an AD LDS instance named **MyADLDSInstance**. Make sure you run through the AD LDS instance prerequisites preparation before you create the instance. Choose ports 50,010 and 50,011 for your instance. Create an application partition within the instance and assign a service account to it. Use an AD DS security group to manage the instance and make sure your account is a member of that group. Store the instance on a data drive that is separate from the operating system. Make sure you import all LDIF files into the instance when you create it.
- **Practice 3** After the instance is created, practice connecting and working with the instance. Use the following tools:
  - ❑ Active Directory Schema snap-in
  - ❑ Active Directory Sites and Services
  - ❑ *LDP.exe*
  - ❑ ADSI Edit

  Use these tools to explore the instance and view its content. You can also practice creating objects within the instance. For example, create an OU and add both a group and a user within the OU.

Take a Practice Test

The practice tests on this book's companion CD offer many options. For example, you can test yourself on just one exam objective, or you can test yourself on all the 70-640 certification exam content. You can set up the test so that it closely simulates the experience of taking a certification exam, or you can set it up in study mode so that you can look at the correct answers and explanations after you answer each question.

MORE INFO   **Practice tests**

For details about all the practice test options available, see the "How to Use the Practice Tests" section in this book's introduction.

Chapter 15

Active Directory Certificate Services and Public Key Infrastructures

Public key infrastructures (PKIs) are becoming core infrastructure elements for all modern organizations. Almost every organization today has some use for public key certificates. Whether it is to secure wireless communications, to offer secure commercial services on Web sites, to integrate Secure Sockets Layer (SSL) virtual private networks, or even just to sign e-mail and identify themselves in Web environments, organizations everywhere are using PKI certificates.

With PKI certificates comes the infrastructure itself—an infrastructure you must first create and then manage. Microsoft has included the ability to generate and maintain PKIs directly in the OS for some years now. In the case of Windows Server 2008, this ability is provided by Active Directory Certificate Services (AD CS), known simply as Certificate Services in previous versions of Microsoft Windows. Because of this, organizations are now choosing to implement and manage their own infrastructures.

MORE INFO Public key infrastructures

For more information on the various aspects of a PKI, look up the PKI white paper series at *http://www.reso-net.com/articles.asp?m=8* under the Advanced Public Key Infrastructures section.

However, the very nature of PKIs is that they are not based on software alone. Because PKI certificates are designed to prove to others that you are who you say you are, you must implement administrative processes that are designed to demonstrate effectively that each person who receives a certificate from you is really who he or she claims to be. By providing certificates to each person in your organization, you provide him or her with an undeniable tool—a tool that guarantees the identity of each person. Public key infrastructures are designed to build a world of trust in an untrustworthy environment.

In fact, PKIs can be used to extend the authority your organization has beyond the borders of the network it controls. Although Active Directory Domain Services (AD DS), as a network operating system (NOS) directory, is primarily aimed at providing authentication and authorization within the corporate network boundaries, AD CS, like the remaining three Active Directory technologies, is designed to provide these services to both internal and external networks. However, when you extend your organization's authority beyond your network boundaries with AD CS, you should rely on a third-party commercial certificate authority (CA) to support the claims you establish through the certificates you publish. (See Figure 15-1.)

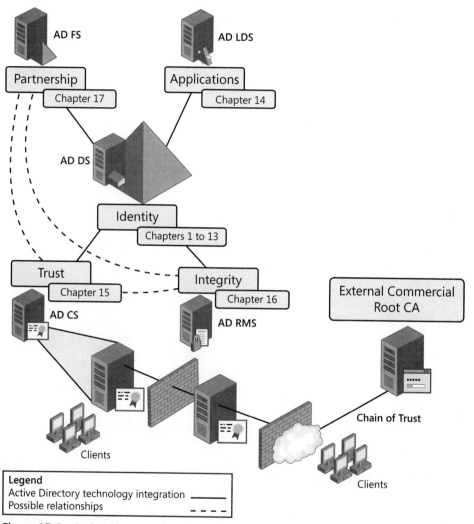

Figure 15-1 Active Directory Certificate Services can provide services both inside and outside your network

For example, when you go to a Web site using the Secure Hypertext Transfer Protocol (HTTPS) that contains an SSL certificate, this certificate proves to you that you really are where you intend to be. When you verify the certificate, you see that it includes the server name, the organization name, and the issuing certificate authority. The certificate works with your browser because browsers such as Microsoft Internet Explorer or Firefox already include a list of trusted commercial CAs that manage the certification process as a business. (See Figure 15-2.)

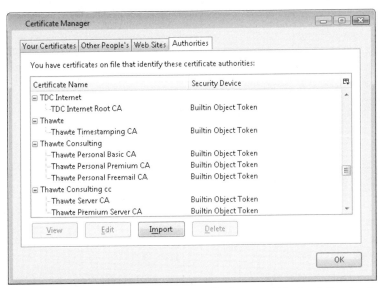

Figure 15-2   Browsers such as Internet Explorer and Firefox listing trusted CAs

The trusted CAs list is automatically updated through the update mechanisms for your selected operating system. In Windows Vista and Windows Server 2008, this update is controlled through a Group Policy setting that is turned on by default. In earlier Windows operating systems, the update of Trusted Root Certificates was a component of Windows, accessed through Control Panel.

MORE INFO   Certificate support in Windows Vista

For more information on Windows Vista certificate support, go to *http://technet2.microsoft.com /WindowsVista/en/library/5b350eae-8b08-4f2c-a09e-a17b1c93f3d01033.mspx?mfr=true*. For a list of Trusted Root Certificates in Windows, go to *http://support.microsoft.com/kb/931125*.

When you issue your own certificates—certificates that do not originate from external CAs— you must include your own organization as a trusted CA on the computers of the people who will be using these certificates. You can do this when you work with the users of your own organization because you control their computers, but when the users are people whose computers you do not control, this becomes problematic. Asking them to accept your certificate is like asking them to trust you when they don't know you.

This is one reason PKI architectures are built the way they are. Essentially, each member of a public key infrastructure is chained together in a hierarchy that ends at the topmost CA. This

CA is ultimately responsible for each of the certificates included in the chain. For example, if you obtain a certificate from your organization and your organization obtained its master certificate from a trusted commercial CA (as shown in Figure 15-3), your certificate will automatically be trusted because each browser already trusts the commercial CA. As you can imagine, this external CA must use a stringent validation program; otherwise, that certificate provider won't be in business for long.

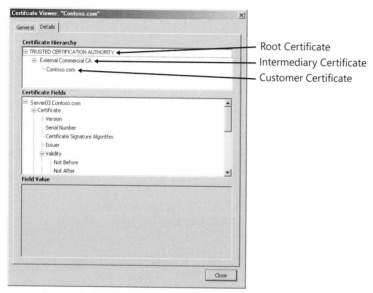

Figure 15-3   A Trusted Certificate chain

Several technologies rely on PKI certificates for operation. One very good example is Microsoft Exchange Server 2007. Because Exchange Server is divided into several roles—Hub Transport, Client Access, Mailbox, and more—and because it transports private information over TCP/IP connections, each server automatically generates a self-signed certificate at installation. Then, through the use of these certificates, e-mail is transported over secure connections. This works well for internal communications, but as soon as you open the doors to communicate with the outside world, for example, providing Microsoft Outlook Web Access (OWA) to employees outside your internal network, you must replace the self-signed certificate with one purchased from a valid vendor. Otherwise, none of your users will be able to access OWA from external Internet locations.

MORE INFO   Learn about Exchange Server 2007

For more information on Exchange Server 2007 and its inner workings, look up *MCITP Self-Paced Training Kit (Exam 70-238): Deploying Messaging Solutions with Microsoft Exchange Server 2007* by Ruest and Ruest (Microsoft Press, 2008).

In some cases, implementing an internal-only PKI makes sense because you are proving who you are only to yourself, but it becomes more difficult and even redundant when dealing with the Internet. How can you prove to others you are who you claim to be when you are the only one saying so? If you are the one who issues the certificates that you use for e-commerce, no one will trust you. You must always keep this in mind whenever you are considering the use of AD CS.

Exam objectives in this chapter:
- Configuring Active Directory Certificate Services
    - ❏ Install Active Directory Certificate Services.
    - ❏ Configure CA server settings.
    - ❏ Manage certificate templates.
    - ❏ Manage enrollments.
    - ❏ Manage certificate revocations.

Lessons in this chapter:
- Lesson 1: Understanding and Installing Active Directory Certificate Services 730
- Lesson 2: Configuring and Using Active Directory Certificate Services 753

Before You Begin

To complete the lessons in this chapter, you must have done the following:

- Installed Windows Server 2008 on a physical or virtual computer. The machine should be named SERVER01 and should be a domain controller in the *Contoso.com* domain. The details for this setup are presented in Chapter 1, "Installation," and Chapter 2, "Administration."
- Installed Windows Server 2008 Enterprise Edition on a physical or virtual computer that should be named SERVER03 and should be a member server within the *Contoso.com* domain. This machine will host the AD CS CAs you will install and create through the exercises in this chapter. Ideally, this computer would also include a D drive to store the data for AD CS. Ten gigabites (GB) is recommended for the size of this drive.
- Installed Windows Server 2008 Enterprise Edition on a physical or virtual computer named SERVER04 and should be a member server within the *Contoso.com* domain. This computer will be used to host an issuing CA for AD CS. Ideally, this computer would also include a D drive to store the data for AD CS. Ten GB is recommended for the size of this drive.

This setup will be sufficient to test basic AD CS installation and configuration. Testing all AD CS capabilities requires up to five computers and might be beyond the laboratory capabilities of most readers.

Real World

Danielle Ruest and Nelson Ruest

In 2003, the Canadian government issued a mandate regarding youthful offenders. Several problems and incorrect decisions had been made when judging youthful offender cases in court because some government representatives—federal, provincial, and municipal police; parole officers; and Ministry of Youth or Social Services representatives—would have information about the youth that was not available to the judging party. To resolve this issue, the government passed a law requiring all parties interacting with youthful offenders to share data among themselves so that the judging party would have all pertinent information on hand to make a more informed decision.

As infrastructure architects, we were hired to develop a system to facilitate this information sharing. Because each party affected by the law did not trust each other, the task held challenges. The police especially did not want their information to transit on the Internet nor even to leave their premises. In addition, each party used different technologies to store the data. We needed to devise a solution that would provide complete security for information transfer yet also provide absolute proof that the data was not compromised in any way.

At the same time, various Canadian governmental entities were in the process of implementing PKIs to provide a secure identity process for their employees and any vendors who interacted with them. We decided to rely on this infrastructure for our solution. In fact, our clients were among the very first to take advantage of this new PKI implementation.

We instructed the developers to use Microsoft SQL Server and the .NET Framework to create the application that would act as a central repository for all the collected information. Then, we created routines in each local data repository to extract the information on a regular basis. That's when the PKI became important. Because we wanted to create extraction files and then send them over the Internet, each partner needed two PKI certificates. The first was a personal certificate that would be used to identify each partner. The second was a server authentication certificate that would be used to identify the start and endpoints of all communication links. To obtain these certificates, each partner had, first, to undergo a training program from the governmental PKI agency to learn about its responsibilities when a certificate was assigned to it and then visit an official governmental representative for an identity verification process before it could obtain the certificates.

When everyone had certificates, we implemented them into the solution. First, we used public and private keys to sign the compressed extraction files digitally. Each partner would sign the compressed file with its private key and then the other partners would use the signing partner's public key to decrypt it. When the file was signed and encrypted, it would be transported over the Internet through an IP Security (IPSec) tunnel that would be created using the server authentication certificates. Each certificate was validated against the Certificate Revocation Lists maintained by the governmental PKI agency every time the process was used. Any invalid certificates would automatically be dropped by the application.

The result was a .NET Web-based application. Because the solution was based on PKI and the PKI agency was a trusted authority, each partner could now trust the other without reservation. This is the value of PKI and certificate services: they provide a foundation for trust in an untrustworthy world. Five years later, the application is still running.

Lesson 1: Understanding and Installing Active Directory Certificate Services

Active Directory Certificate Services provide a variety of services regarding public key infrastructures and certificate usage in general. Using Windows Server 2008 and AD CS, you can support the following certificate usage scenarios:

- You can encrypt all data files. One of the most common problems in IT today is the loss or theft of mobile computer systems. If data is encrypted, the loss is minor, but if data is unprotected, it could affect your ability to do business. With Windows Server 2008 and Windows Vista, you can encrypt all user data files automatically through Group Policy objects and enforce the strong passwords required to protect them further. The Encrypting File System (EFS) relies on certificates to lock and unlock encrypted files.

- You can encrypt all remote communications. Windows Server 2008 includes both IPSec and Secure Sockets Tunnelling Protocol (SSTP) virtual private network connections. Both rely on certificates to authenticate the start and endpoint of the communication.

- You can secure all e-mail messages. Windows Server 2008 includes support for Secure Multipurpose Internet Mail Extensions (S/MIME), the standard e-mail security protocol. Signed messages are protected from tampering and prove they originate from the correct person.

- You can secure all logons. Using smart cards, you can use certificates to support the logon process and ensure that all users, especially administrators, are who they say they are.

- You can secure all Web sites. Using Windows Server 2008 and Internet Information Services (IIS) 7.0, you can secure all communications to your Web sites, ensuring the safety of all your client transactions.

- You can secure servers to validate their authenticity. For example, when you assign certificates to servers in a Network Access Protection (NAP) infrastructure or in any other secure service, computers in your network will know they are working with your own servers and not with other servers trying to impersonate yours.

- You can secure all wireless communications. Using Windows Server 2008 and Windows Vista, you can ensure that all wireless communications originate from trusted endpoints.

- You can protect all data from tampering. Using Active Directory Rights Management Services (AD RMS), you can rely on Windows Server 2008 to protect from tampering or misuse all the information you generate.

In addition, consider issuing a certificate to all your employees to help them certify who they are in all their Internet transactions. Keep in mind that all external certificates should include a trusted CA within them to enable them to work automatically with any browser.

> **After this lesson, you will be able to:**
> - Understand when to use AD CS.
> - Install AD CS.
> - Install an Online Responder.
> - Locate and view the AD CS installation.
>
> **Estimated lesson time: 30 minutes**

Understanding AD CS

Active Directory Certificate Services is the engine Windows Server 2008 relies on to manage public key certificates. By using AD CS, you can build a comprehensive PKI hierarchy that can be used to issue and manage certificates within your organization. AD CS is composed of several components:

- **Certificate authorities**   CAs are the servers you use to issue and manage certificates. Because of the hierarchical nature of a PKI, AD CS supports both root and subordinate or child CAs. The root CA usually issues certificates to subordinate CAs, which enables them in turn to issue certificates to users, computers, and services. The subordinate CA can issue certificates only while its own certificate is valid. When this certificate expires, the subordinate CA must request a certificate renewal from its root CA. For this reason, root CAs often have certificate durations that are much longer than any of their subordinates. In turn, subordinate CAs usually have certificate durations that are longer than those they issue to users, computers, or services.

- **CA Web Enrollment**   Using Web Enrollment, users can connect to the CA through a Web browser to request certificates, perform smart card enrollments, or obtain certificate revocation lists (CRL). CRLs provide users of your public key infrastructure with a list of certificates that have been invalidated or revoked by your organization. Systems relying on PKI poll CA servers to obtain CRLs each time a certificate is presented to them. If the certificate presented to them is on this list, it is automatically refused.

- **Online responder**   This service is designed to respond to specific certificate validation requests through the Online Certificate Status Protocol (OCSP). Using an online responder (OR), the system relying on PKI does not need to obtain a full CRL and can submit a validation request for a specific certificate. The online responder decodes the validation request and determines whether the certificate is valid. When it determines the status of the requested certificate, it sends back an encrypted response containing the information to the requester. Using online responders is much faster and more efficient than using CRLs. AD CS includes online responders as a new feature in Windows Server 2008.

MORE INFO Online responders

Online responders are often an alternative to or an extension of CRLs that support the certificate revocation process. Microsoft online responders comply with request for comments
(RFC) 2560 for OCSP. For more information about this RFC, go to *http://go.microsoft.com*
/fwlink/?LinkID=67082.

- **Network Device Enrollment Service** Devices that use low-level operating systems,
  such as routers and switches, can also participate in a PKI through the Network Device
  Enrollment Service (NDES) by using the Simple Certificate Enrollment Protocol (SCEP),
  a protocol developed by Cisco Systems, Inc. These devices usually do not participate in
  an AD DS directory and, therefore, do not have AD DS accounts. However, through the
  NDES and the SCEP, they can also become part of the PKI hierarchy that is maintained
  and managed by your AD CS installation.

These four components form the core of the AD CS service in Windows Server 2008.

MORE INFO New features in AD CS

For more information on the new features AD CS supports in Windows Server 2008, go to
http://technet2.microsoft.com/windowsserver2008/en/library/171362c0-3773-498d-8cc3-
0ddcd8082bf51033.mspx.

Standalone vs. Enterprise CAs

Your biggest concern when preparing to deploy an AD CS is how you will structure the four
basic services AD CS offers. Initially, you will be concerned about the first role: the CAs you
need to deploy. AD CS supports two CA types:

- **Standalone CA** A CA that is not necessarily integrated in an AD DS directory service.
  Standalone CAs are CAs running on member or standalone servers—servers in a workgroup. Standalone CAs are often used as internal root CAs and are taken offline for security purposes after they have been used to generate certificates for subordinate servers.
  Certificate issuing and approval are performed manually, and certificates are based on
  standard templates, which you cannot modify. The clients of a standalone CA can be
  members of an AD DS directory, but AD DS directory membership is not a requirement.
  Standalone CAs can run Windows Server 2008 Standard Edition, Windows Server 2008
  Enterprise Edition, or Windows Server 2008 Datacenter Edition.
- **Enterprise CA** A CA that is integrated in an AD DS directory service. Enterprise CAs
  are usually member servers and are often used as issuing CAs—CAs that are subordinate to another CA in a hierarchy but that actually provide certificates to end users and
  endpoint devices. Issuing CAs are usually online at all times and must be highly available. Because they are integrated in AD DS directories, enterprise CAs automatically

issue and approve certificates when requested by members of the directory. Certificate templates are more advanced and can be edited to meet specific requirements. All encryption keys are protected through directory integration. Enterprise CAs can run only on Windows Server 2008 Enterprise Edition or Windows Server 2008 Datacenter Edition.

Table 15-1 outlines the different features supported by standalone versus enterprise CAs.

Table 15-1 Comparing Standalone and Enterprise CAs

Feature	Standalone	Enterprise
Publish CA configuration to Active Directory Domain Services directories.	Optional	Mandatory
CA certificate data integration with AD DS forests.	Optional (manual process)	Mandatory and Automatic
Certificate Revocation List publication in AD DS forests.	Optional (manual process)	Mandatory and Automatic; also includes Delta CRLs and cross certificates
AD DS forest publication assigned on a per-template level as an attribute of the template.	n/a	Supported
Web enrollment for certificate requests and validation.	Supported	Supported
Certificate Microsoft Management Console (MMC) for certificate requests and validation.	n/a	Supported
Certificate requests through HTTP or HTTPS.	Supported	Supported
Certificate requests through the remote procedure call (RPC) along with the Distributed Component Object Model (DCOM).	n/a	Default mode
V1 templates with custom object identifiers (OID) as source for certificates.	Default	n/a
V2 and V3 customizable templates as source for certificates. Templates can also be duplicated.	n/a	Default
User input during certificate requests.	Manual	Retrieved from AD DS
Supported enrollment methods.	Automatic or Pending for all templates	Automatic or Pending and applied on a template basis
Certificate approval process.	Manual	Manual or Automatic through AD DS authentication and access control

Table 15-1   Comparing Standalone and Enterprise CAs

Feature	Standalone	Enterprise
Certificate publishing.	Manually to client or CA; can be to AD DS but only through custom policy module	Depends on certificate type and template settings but can be automatically enrolled in client's certificate store and published in AD DS
Certificate publishing and management through AD DS.	n/a	Supported
Deployment options.	Domain controller (DC), member or standalone server	DC or member server only

As you can see in Table 15-1, standalone CAs are focused on delivering specific services and should be considered mostly for standalone environments where automation is not required. Good examples are root CAs or CAs located in a perimeter network and offering services to the Internet.

Enterprise CAs should be considered mostly as issuing CAs in internal networks that also include AD DS forest structures. Enterprise CAs automate the certificate allocation process and are very useful when you need to issue certificates to devices for wireless networks or to users for smart card integration. Imagine managing the entire request and approval process manually when you have thousands of users and devices. It could easily become overwhelming.

Exam Tip   Learn the differences between standalone and enterprise CAs well. These topics are an important part of the AD CS coverage in the exam.

Creating the CA Hierarchy

A second consideration when planning your CA hierarchy is security. Because a CA hierarchy is based on certificate chaining, any compromise of a top-level or root CA automatically compromises all the certificates that are based on it. This is one reason you must secure root CAs as much as possible. In fact, a common practice is to create a tiered CA hierarchy and take the top members of a tiered architecture offline. The logic is that if a server is offline, it is as secure as it can be.

However, determining the number of tiers in your AD CS architecture depends on several other factors as well. You need to consider the size and geographic distribution of your network. You also need to identify the trust relationship you will require between CAs and the certificate holders. Keep in mind that each time a certificate is presented, it must be validated through either a CRL or an online responder, so to use certificates, you must have connectivity of some sort.

Consider also the potential scenarios you intend to support with your AD CS deployment. Will you be interacting with people or partners outside your network? Will you be using smart cards? Will you be using wireless networks? Will you be using IPSec or the new SSTP? Basically, any time you need to certify the identity of a device, an application, or a user, you will need to rely on AD CS and, potentially, third-party commercial certificate authorities.

When you have the answers to these questions, you can proceed with the planning of your AD CS hierarchy. When you do so, consider the following:

- Creating a single tiered hierarchy with a single root CA only in very rare situations in which you feel the root CA cannot be compromised under any circumstance.

- Creating a two-tiered hierarchy with a root CA and issuing CAs when you need to protect the root CA but your organization size and the purpose of the hierarchy does not warrant a more complex hierarchy. In this model, you can take the root CA offline to protect it. (See Figure 15-4.)

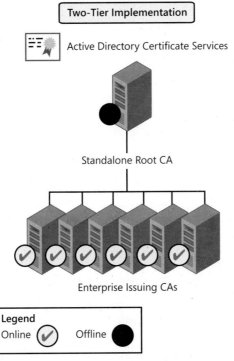

Figure 15-4   A two-tiered hierarchy

- Creating a three-tiered hierarchy with a root CA, intermediate CAs, and issuing CAs when you need higher levels of security and high availability for the issuing CAs, and your administration model, user population, and geographic scope warrant the extra cost of the additional tier. Multiple intermediate CAs are often used to support different policies in different environments in this model. If you use this model, take both the root and intermediate CAs offline to protect them, as shown in Figure 15-5.

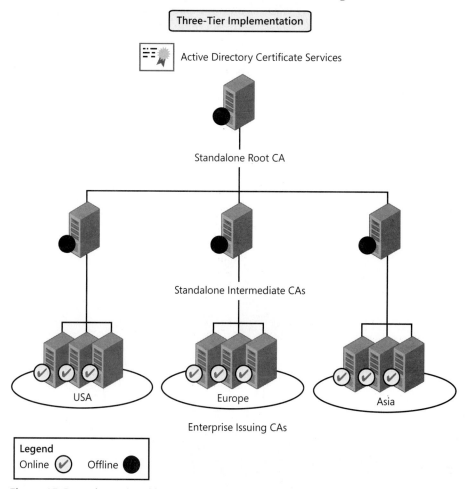

Figure 15-5   A three-tiered hierarchy in a geographic deployment

■ Creating more than three tiers only in highly complex environments that require the utmost security where the CA infrastructure must be protected at all times.

As you can see, the more tiers you create in a hierarchy, the higher the level of complexity in terms of management and administration. However, the more complex your hierarchy, the more secure it can be. In addition, consider which type of CA you need to deploy in each tier. Table 15-2 outlines the CA type based on the tier model.

Table 15-2   Assigning CA Type Based on Tier Model

CA Type	One Tier	Two Tiers	Three Tiers
Root CA	Enterprise CA (online)	Standalone CA (offline)	Standalone CA (offline)
Intermediate CA			Standalone CA (offline)
Issuing CA		Enterprise CA (online)	Enterprise CA (online)

Exam Tip   Keep these different hierarchies in mind when you take the exam. CA hierarchies are an important aspect of any AD CS deployment.

Best Practices for AD CS Deployments

Architectures using two or more tiers represent the most common deployments of AD CS. When you plan for your AD CS infrastructure, keep the following in mind:

- Avoid single-tiered hierarchies as much as possible because they are very difficult to protect.
- Root and intermediate CAs (if implemented) should be taken offline as soon as possible after the infrastructure is in place. For this reason, these CAs are excellent candidates for virtualization through Windows Server 2008 Hyper-V. Create a virtual machine (VM), install the AD CS Standalone CA role, and then save the machine state as soon as you can.
- Consider removing the VM files for the root CA from the host server as soon as it is taken offline. Store the secured VM in a vault of some type.
- If you use virtualization in support of your AD CS deployment, secure the VMs as much as possible. It is a lot easier to walk away with a VM than it is with a physical server.
- Consider creating VMs that do not have or that have disabled network connections for the root and intermediate CAs. This ensures an even higher level of protection. Certificates are transferred from these servers through either USB devices or floppy disks.
- Control the removable devices on root and intermediate CAs through device protection settings in the Local Security Policy console. This adds a further layer of protection.
- Make sure your CA administrators are highly trustworthy individuals. They control the entire CA hierarchy and, because of this, they are in a very high position of trust.
- Secure thoroughly the data center that hosts the CAs. Control access to the data center and use smart card administrative logons as much as possible.
- Consider using a single root CA but adding availability through multiple CA installations as soon as you reach the intermediate and issuing tiers of the hierarchy.
- You cannot change the name of a server after the AD CS service is installed, so plan your server names carefully and make sure you can keep them for a very long time.
- You cannot change a CA from standalone to enterprise or vice versa after AD CS is installed. Once again, plan accordingly.

- As a general practice, do not install AD CS on a DC. Although it can be done, endeavor to keep the AD DS server role independent of all other roles except the Domain Name System (DNS) role.

These guidelines will assist you in your AD CS deployment planning phase.

MORE INFO   Best practices for PKI deployments

For additional information on PKI deployments with Windows infrastructures, look up "Best Practices for Implementing a Microsoft Windows Server 2003 Public Key Infrastructure" at *http://technet2.microsoft.com/windowsserver/en/library/091cda67-79ec-481d-8a96-03e0be7374ed1033.mspx?mfr=true*. It refers to Windows Server 2003 rather than to Windows Server 2008, but its practices are still valid for any version of Windows.

Additional Planning Requirements

You're almost ready to proceed. However, as mentioned earlier, planning and deploying a CA hierarchy is not only a technical activity. You need to have the appropriate administrative processes to support the use of certificates in your network. Three additional considerations need to be covered before you can move on to installing AD CS:

- You must consider how you will support certificate enrollment.
- You must consider how you will renew certificates.
- You must create a certificate practice statement (CPS).

The first focuses on how you plan to support certificate requests and distribution. As mentioned earlier, a certificate is used to identify its holder thoroughly whether it is a user, a machine, or an application. Therefore, you must put in place a requester identification validation process. You don't want to issue a certificate to John Kane when you're not sure the requester is actually John Kane. Third-party certificate authorities use several types of processes for this validation, the most stringent of which will involve a visit to the person requesting the certificate by an authorized legal representative of the CA. This means a face-to-face meeting and then, after the requester is validated, you can provide him or her with a certificate in that name. To protect the certificate further, you can store it on a hardware token such as a smart card and provide that to the requester. It then becomes the responsibility of the requester to protect the certificate and the token that contains it.

However, if you plan to use automatic enrollment through enterprise CAs, you need to make sure that users are properly validated before they are given access to your network. Rely on some form of official identification such as a passport or other governmental ID mechanism. This should already be part of your human resources processes and policies.

The second consideration deals with certificate lifetimes. Certificates usually include two key pairs: a private key and a public key. When you encrypt data, you use the private key to do so.

When others decrypt the data, they usually use your public key to do so. The longer you use a certificate key pair, the more prone it is to attack or compromise. When you renew a certificate, the renewal generates a new key pair for the certificate. Therefore, you must plan certificate lifetimes and renewals carefully. In fact, you must temper key pair life with the risk of compromise.

In addition, you must ensure that your tiered hierarchy also includes tiered lifetimes. Root CAs should have the longest lifetime, then intermediate CAs if you use them, then issuing CAs, and then issued certificates. For example, you might use a gap of 10 years for each tier in your architecture; that is, assign 10 years to each tier. In a three-tier architecture, use 30 years for the root CA, 20 years for the intermediate CAs, and 10 years for issuing CAs. Then you can assign one or two years to the certificates you issue. The reason for this hierarchy of durations is that each time a certificate expires for a server, all subordinate certificates expire as well. To protect against this eventuality, you give very long durations to servers.

Finally, you must plan and prepare your certificate practice statement. CPSs are based on the certificate policies you create. Policies define the issuing organization's responsibilities in terms of each of the certificate types it issues. The issuing organization is ultimately responsible for any wrongdoing or misuse of the certificates it issued. Because of this, involve the legal, human resources, and security departments of your organization to assist you in defining the policies you use for each certificate type and then generate your CPS from that. The CPS should include several items, such as a clear definition of who you are, a list of your certificate policies; a general statement of the procedures you use to issue, assign, and revoke certificates; the way you protect your CAs; and so on.

Another important item that must be included in your CPS is the revocation policy you use. Revocation occurs when you need to cancel a certificate for any reason, usually when someone does not adhere to the policy you defined for that particular certificate type. Keep in mind that revocation is the only method you have of invalidating a certificate when it is misused.

The CPS should be publicly available to both your internal and external CA users. This usually means making it available in some form on the Internet or through intranets.

MORE INFO   **Certificate practice statements**

For more information on defining certificate policies and certificate practice statements, go to *http://technet2.microsoft.com/windowsserver/en/library/78c89e0f-44f8-452a-922c-5dd5b8eaa63b1033.mspx?mfr=true*.

Exam Tip   Familiarize yourself with certificate policies and certificate practice statements because they are a definite part of the exam topics for AD CS.

Quick Check

1. What are the different types of certificate authorities supported by AD CS?
2. You are planning to install a root CA in a two-tier architecture. Which type of CA should you install?
3. How is the trusted CA list updated in Windows Vista and Windows Server 2008?

Quick Check Answers

1. AD CS supports two types of certificate authorities. The standalone CA is used in environments that do not need integration with Active Directory Domain Services because it does not interact with AD DS by default. Enterprise CAs are directly integrated into the AD DS directory and can provide automated user or device enrollment.
2. You should install a standalone CA. Root CAs are usually taken offline as soon as possible after the deployment of your public key infrastructure. Therefore, it makes sense to use the simplest form of CA supported by AD CS.
3. The trusted root CA list in Windows Vista and Windows Server 2008 is updated through Group Policy settings, which are turned on by default. In previous versions of Windows, the trusted root CA list was a component of Windows controlled through Control Panel.

Installing AD CS

Installing AD CS is a much more involved process than installing Active Directory Lightweight Directory Services (AD LDS). This is because of the choice between standalone and enterprise CAs and because of the subsequent choices that ensue from this original selection.

In most cases, you will install at least a two-tiered structure, installing first a standalone, then an enterprise CA. In larger organizations, you will deploy several tiers and install several servers in each tier except for the root.

Servers hosting the AD CS role should be configured with the following capabilities whether they are physical or virtual:

- Multiple processors because they accelerate the certificate allocation process.
- Minimal amounts of RAM because RAM has little effect on certificate processing. VMs can have 512 megabytes (MB) of RAM.
- Separate disks for the certificate store. Ideally, you will have at least one data disk and store the database on it. Issuing servers for large communities should also have a separate disk for log files.

- Key lengths will have an impact on CPU and disk usage. Short keys will require more disk overhead. Long keys will require more CPU usage and lower disk usage. Keep your key lengths to medium sizes to obtain the best performance from the server.
- If using physical systems, use a redundant array of inexpensive disks (RAID) level that is balanced between reliability and improved performance.

IMPORTANT Installation on Windows Server 2008

The AD CS role cannot be installed on Server Core and requires the full installation of Windows Server 2008 to operate. This means that if you install CAs in perimeter networks, you will have to lock down the server thoroughly through the Security Configuration Wizard. In addition, AD CS cannot be installed on Itanium-based systems.

Different editions of Windows Server 2008 will offer different features in support of AD CS. Table 15-3 outlines the supported features based on the selected edition of Windows Server 2008.

Table 15-3 AD CS Features per Windows Server 2008 Edition

Supported Components and Features	Web	Standard	Enterprise	Datacenter
Standalone certificate authority	☐	☑	☑	☑
Enterprise certificate authority	☐	☐	☑	☑
Network Device Enrollment Service (NDES)	☐	☐	☑	☑
Online responder service	☐	☐	☑	☑
Key archival	☐	☐	☑	☑
Role Separation	☐	☐	☑	☑
Certificate Manager restrictions	☐	☐	☑	☑
Delegated enrollment agent restrictions	☐	☐	☑	☑

Preparing for AD CS Installation

You must prepare your environment before installing AD CS. The prerequisites for an AD CS installation include the following:

- An AD DS forest with at least a forest root domain. Preferably, you will also have a child production domain.
- Computers to run the certificate authorities used in your hierarchy. In the simplest deployment, this will mean at least two computers: one for the root CA and one for the issuing CA. The issuing CA can also host the online responder service and NDES. The issuing CA will require the installation of IIS, but the AD CS installation process will

automatically add this feature during installation. Both computers should be members of the production domain.

❏ Keep in mind that the root CA can run Windows Server 2008 Standard Edition. In addition, it should be disconnected from the network after the installation is complete, for security purposes.

❏ The enterprise issuing CA will need to run on either Windows Server 2008 Enterprise Edition or Windows Server 2008 Datacenter Edition.

❏ The root CA needs at least two drives, and the issuing CA should have three drives to store the certificate database and its logs.

■ You will need a special user account if you choose to install the NDES service. Create a domain account and make it a member of the local IIS_IUSRS group on each server that will host this service. For example, you could name this account NDESService.

■ Client computers, ideally running Windows Vista, to request and obtain certificates.

MORE INFO   Deploying AD CS

For more information on deploying AD CS, go to *http://technet2.microsoft.com/windowsserver2008 /en/library/a8f53a9b-f3f6-4b13-8253-dbf183a5aa621033.mspx?mfr=true.*

Now you can move on to the actual installation. To install a standalone root CA, use the procedure outlined in the following practice.

PRACTICE Installing a CA Hierarchy

In this practice, you will create a two-tier AD CS hierarchy and install the NDES feature of AD CS. To perform this practice, you must have prepared at least three virtual servers as outlined in the Before You Begin section at the beginning of this chapter.

▶ **Exercise 1   Install AD CS as a Standalone Root CA**

In this exercise, you will create a standalone root CA, which will be used as the root of your CA hierarchy. This task is performed on SERVER03. Make sure that SERVER01, your DC, is also running and that SERVER03 is a member of the domain.

1. Log on to SERVER03 with the domain Administrator account.

   You need local administrative credentials only, but for the purposes of this exercise, it is all right to use the domain administrator account. This server can be running Windows Server 2008 Standard Edition, Windows Server 2008 Enterprise Edition, or Windows Server 2008 Datacenter Edition.

2. Launch Server Manager from the Administrative Tools program group.

3. Right-click the Roles node in the tree pane and select Add Roles.

4. Review the Before You Begin information and click Next.

5. On the Select Server Roles page, select Active Directory Certificate Services and click Next.

6. On the Introduction to Active Directory Certificate Services page, review the information about the selected role and click Next.

7. On the Select Role Services page, select Certification Authority and click Next.

   Because this will be a root CA and you will take it offline as soon as you create the issuing CA, you do not assign any other role features or services.

8. On the Specify Setup Type page, select Standalone and click Next.

9. On the CA Type page, select Root CA and click Next.

10. On the Set Up Private Key page, select Create A New Private Key and click Next.

    You need to create a new private key because you are creating a new root CA. However, if you were reinstalling a CA because of a system failure, you would use an existing key, one that was generated during the initial installation of the root CA. In addition, if you were creating a root CA to be chained with an external third-party CA, you would use the last option, to use the key provided by the third-party CA. You must install the key on the server before you begin the AD CS installation for the option to be available. Use the instructions provided by your third-party CA to install the certificate.

11. On the Configure Cryptography For CA page, select the suggested cryptographic service provider (CSP). Select a key character length of 2048. Select the sha1 hash algorithm for signing certificates issued by this CA. Also select Use Strong Private Key Protection Features Provided By This CSP.

    There are several options on this page.

    ❑ CSPs are the engines the Microsoft Crypto application programming interface (API) will use to generate the key pair for this root CA. CSPs can be either software or hardware based. For example, the RSA#Microsoft Software Key Storage Provider is software based, and the RSA#Microsoft Smart Card Key Storage Provider is hardware based.

    ❑ Key character length determines the length of the keys in the pair. Four lengths are possible. Remember that the longer the key, the more processing the server will require to decode it.

    ❑ Hash algorithms are used to produce and assign a hash value on the keys in the pair. Because they are assigned to the keys, any tampering of the key will change the hash value and invalidate the key. Hash values provide further key protection. The algorithm you select will simply use a different calculation method to generate the hash value.

    ❑ The last option on the page provides further protection for the root CA because use of the CA will require administrative access and will work with only this level of access. You use this option to provide further protection for this root CA.

12. Click Next.

13. On the Configure CA Name page, type **Contoso-Root-CA**, leave the distinguished name suffix as is, and click Next.

   You use this name because it will be embedded in every subordinate certificate issued by the chain.

14. On the Set Validity Period page, change the year value to **20** and click Next.

15. On the Configure Certificate Database page, specify the storage locations for the certificate database and the certificate database log.

   Because this is a root CA that should be taken offline and should be used only to generate certificates for the issuing CAs, you can place both on the D drive.

16. For the database location, click Browse, navigate to the D drive, click Make New Folder, and name it **CertData**. Click OK. For the logs, create a folder on the D drive and name it **CertLogs**. Click Next.

17. Review the information available on the AD CS page and click Install. When the installation completes, review the installation results and click Close.

   Your root CA is installed.

   Note that you will no longer be able to change the name of this server unless you uninstall AD CS first. This is one more reason for not using a server name in the CA name in step 12.

Exam Tip   Make sure you understand these installation choices well because they are part of the exam.

Your root CA is installed. Return to Server Manager to view the results of the installation. For example, you should have an event ID 103 listed on the summary page of the AD CS role. (See Figure 15-6.) This event shows that the CA name will be added to the Certificate Authorities container in your AD DS domain. It also displays the command you can use to view the information in the directory after the name has been added.

Disconnect this CA from the network after the Group Policy cycle has been updated, to provide further protection for this server. You can now move on to installing your first issuing CA. You should install more than one issuing CA to provide high availability for your AD CS infrastructure, but each installation uses the same process.

NOTE   **Review the AD CS installation process**

For a step-by-step guide to the installation of AD CS, go to *http://go.microsoft.com/fwlink /?LinkId=90856.*

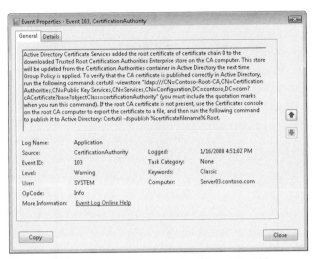

Figure 15-6 Viewing the contents of Event ID 103

▶ **Exercise 2   Install AD CS as an Enterprise Issuing CA**

You can now move on to install your issuing CA. You should normally install more than one issuing CA to provide high availability for your AD CS infrastructure, but for the purposes of this exercise, one issuing CA will be sufficient. Make sure that SERVER01, SERVER03, and SERVER04 are all running.

1. Log on to SERVER04, using the domain Administrator account.

   You need local administrative access rights only, but for the purposes of this exercise, the domain administrator account will also work. This server can be running Windows Server 2008 Enterprise Edition or Windows Server 2008 Datacenter Edition.

2. Launch Server Manager from the Administrative Tools program group.

3. Right-click the Roles node and select Add Roles.

4. Review the Before You Begin information and click Next.

5. On the Select Server Roles page, select Active Directory Certificate Services and click Next.

6. On the Introduction to Active Directory Certificate Services page, review the information about the selected role and click Next.

7. On the Select Role Services page, select Certificate Authority and Online Responder. When you select Online Responder, the wizard will ask you to add the Web Server role with the required features. Click Add Required Role Services.

8. Click Next.

   You do not select the CA Web Enrollment because this is an internal enterprise CA, and enterprise CAs rely on AD DS to distribute certificates to users and devices. If you were installing this CA in an external network, you might consider using Web Enrollment to enable users to request certificates from your CA.

You cannot choose the Network Device Enrollment Service (NDES) installation at this time because AD CS does not support installing a CA at the same time as you install NDES. If you want to install NDES, you must select Add Role Services from Server Manager after the CA installation has completed.

9. On the Specify Setup Type page, select Enterprise and click Next.

10. On the Specify CA Type page, select Subordinate CA and click Next.

11. On the Set Up Private Key page, select Create A New Private Key and click Next.

12. On the Configure Cryptography For CA page, accept the default values and click Next.

13. On the Configure CA Name page, type **Contoso-Issuing-CA01**, leave the default distinguished name suffix as is, and click Next.

    You use a valid name and a number because you should create additional issuing CAs for redundancy purposes.

14. On the Request Certificate From A Parent CA page, select Save A Certificate Request To File And Manually Send It Later To A Parent CA.

15. Select Certificate Request Name from the File Name field and copy it to the clipboard, using Ctrl + C, and then click Browse and navigate to your Documents folder. Paste the name in the *File Name* field, using Ctrl + V; click Save, and then click Next.

16. On the Configure Certificate Database page, specify the storage locations for the certificate database and the certificate database log.

    Because this is an issuing CA that will be used for testing only, you can place the data and the logs on the D drive. However, in a production environment, issuing CAs will be used heavily; this means you should place the data on the D drive and the logs on an E drive.

17. For the database location, click Browse, navigate to the D drive, click Make New Folder, and name it **CertData**. Click OK.

18. For the logs, create a folder on the D drive and name it **CertLogs**. Click Next when ready.

19. Review the installation of IIS. Click Next.

20. On the Web Server Role Services page, review the required services and click Next.

21. Review the information in the Confirm Installation Selections page and click Install. When the installation completes, review the installation results and click Close.

    The subordinate CA setup is not usable until it has been issued a root CA certificate and this certificate has been used to complete the installation of this subordinate CA.

Exam Tip   Keep in mind that you cannot install the CA and the NDES role features at the same time.

▶ **Exercise 3   Obtain and Install the Issuing CA Certificate**

Now, you will obtain the certificate to complete the installation of the issuing CA. You should normally perform this procedure offline using a removable storage device such as a floppy disk or a USB flash drive, but for the purpose of this exercise, you will use a shared folder to transfer the certificate request and the certificate after it is issued.

1. On SERVER04, launch Windows Explorer and navigate to the C drive. Create a new folder and name it **Temp**.
2. Right-click the Temp folder and select Share.
3. In the File Sharing dialog box, select Everyone in the drop-down list, and then click Add.
4. In the Permission Level column, from the drop-down list, assign the Contributor role to Everyone and click Share.
5. Copy the certificate request you generated from your Documents folder to the Temp folder.
6. On SEREVR03, launch the Certificate Authority console from the Administrative Tools program group.
7. In the Certification Authority console, right-click the root CA name in the tree pane, select All Tasks, and then choose Submit New Request.
8. In the Open Request File dialog box, move to the address bar and type **\\SERVER04 \Temp**. When the folder opens, select the request, and then click Open.
9. Move to the Pending Request node in the tree pane, right-click the pending request in the details pane to choose All Tasks, and then choose Issue.
10. Move to the Issued Certificates in the tree pane, right-click the issued certificate in the details pane, and choose Open.
11. In the Certificate dialog box, choose the Details tab and click Copy To File at the bottom of the dialog box.

    This launches the Certificate Export Wizard.
12. Click Next.
13. Select the Cryptographic Message Syntax Standard – PKCS #7 Certificates (P7B), select Include All Certificates In The Certification Path If Possible, and click Next.

    There are several supported formats.

    ❑ Distinguished Encoding Rules (DER) Encoded Binary X.509 is often used for computers that do not run the Windows operating system. This creates certificate files in the CER format.

❑ Base-64 Encoded X.509 supports S/MIME, which is the format used to transfer secured e-mails over the Internet. On servers, it is usually used for non-Windows operating systems. This also creates certificate files in the CER format.

❑ Cryptographic Message Syntax Standard (PKCS #7) is the format used to transfer certificates and their chained path from one computer to another. This format uses the P7B file format.

❑ Personal Information Exchange (PKCS #12) is also used to transfer certificates and their chained path from one computer to another, but in addition, this format supports the transfer of the private key as well as the public key. Use this format with caution because transporting the private key can jeopardize it. This format uses the PFX file format.

❑ Microsoft Serialized Certificate Store is a custom Microsoft format that should be used when you need to transfer root certificates from one computer to another. This uses the SST file format.

14. In the File To Export dialog box, click Browse and save the certificate in the \\SERVER04 \Temp folder. Name it **Issuing-CA01.p7b** and click Save.

15. Click Next when you return to the wizard.

16. Review your settings and click Finish.

17. Click OK when the wizard tells you that the export was successful. Return to SERVER04. Remember that, normally, you would use a removable device to transport this certificate from one server to another.

18. Go to Server Manager and select Contoso-Issuing-CA01 in the tree pane (Server Manager \Roles\Active Directory Certificate Services\Contoso-Issuing-CA01).

19. Right-click Contoso-Issuing-CA01, select All Tasks, and then choose Install CA Certificate.

20. Move to the C:\Temp folder, select the certificate, and click Open.

21. This imports the certificate and enables the server.

22. Right-click the server name, select All Tasks, and then choose Start Service.

    Your issuing CA is ready to issue certificates. At this point, you should really take SERVER03 offline, but because this is a test environment and you need to conserve CPU usage and disk space, keep it running.

IMPORTANT Protect the certificate

Now that the server is ready to work, store the transferred certificate in a safe place. You should also shut down the root CA when you have performed this task for all the issuing CAs you require in your infrastructure. If the root CA is a virtual machine, shut it down, and then remove the VM files from the host server. For example, you could copy them to a DVD and then store the DVD in a very safe place.

▶ **Exercise 4   Prepare to Install the NDES Feature**

Now, you will install the NDES feature. Again, this task is performed on SERVER04, but you must use SERVER01 to create a user account first.

1. Log on to SERVER01, using the domain Administrator account.
2. Launch Active Directory Users And Computers from the Administrative Tools program group.
3. Create the following OU structure: Contoso.com\Admins\Service Identities.
4. Right-click Service Identities, choose New, and then select User.
5. Name the user **NDESService** and use this name for both the logon and the pre-Windows 2000 logon names. Click Next.
6. Assign a strong password. Clear User Must Change Password At Next Logon and select Password Never Expires.
7. Click Next, and then Finish to create the account.
8. Return to SERVER04 and log on as the domain Administrator.
9. Launch Server Manager from the Administrative Tools program group.
10. Expand Configuration\Local Users and Groups\Groups.
11. Double-click the IIS_IUSRS group.
12. Add the NDESService account to this group and click OK.

▶ **Exercise 5   Install the NDES Feature**

Now you're ready to install the NDES service.

1. Right-click Active Directory Certificate Services in the tree pane of Server Manager and select Add Role Services.
2. On the Select Role Services page, select Network Device Enrollment Service.
   This will require the addition of Windows Authentication to your IIS installation.
3. Click Add Required Role Services and click Next.
4. On the Specify User Account page, click Select User, enter **NDESService** with its password, and click OK. Click Next.
5. On the Specify Registration Authority Information page, you need to enter the information for your registration authority or the authority that will assign and manage certificates assigned to network devices. Type **Contoso-MSCEP-RA01**, select your country from the drop-down list, and leave all other information blank. Click Next.
   Normally, you should enter all the required and optional information, but for the purpose of this exercise, leaving them blank is all right.
6. On the Configure Cryptography For Registration Authority page, keep the defaults and click Next.

Keep in mind that key length affects CPU usage; therefore, unless you have stringent security requirements, keep the 2048 key length.

7. Review the information about the installation of IIS. Click Next.

8. On the Web Server Role Services page, review the required services and click Next.

9. On the Confirm Installation Services page, click Install.

10. Review the status and progress of the installation.

11. Click Close.

Your NDES service is now installed and ready to work. Your installation of the issuing server is complete.

MORE INFO   Simple Certificate Enrollment Protocol (SCEP)

For more information on SCEP, go to *http://www3.ietf.org/proceedings/07jul/slides/pkix-3.pdf*.

Lesson Summary

- AD CS is composed of four elements: certificate authorities, CA Web Enrollment, online responders, and Network Device Enrollment Service. These are the core elements of any AD CS deployment.

- Certificate authorities are the servers you use to issue and manage certificates. Because of the hierarchical nature of a PKI, AD CS supports both root and subordinate or child CAs. The root CA usually issues certificates to subordinate CAs, which enables them in turn to issue certificates to users, computers, and services. The subordinate CA can issue certificates only while its own certificate is valid. When this certificate expires, the subordinate CA must request a certificate renewal from its root CA. For this reason, root CAs often have certificate durations that are much longer than any of their subordinates. In turn, subordinate CAs usually have certificate durations that are longer than those they issue to users, computers, or services.

- ORs are designed to respond to specific certificate validation requests through the Online Certificate Status Protocol (OCSP). Using an OR, the system relying on a PKI does not need to obtain a full CRL and can submit a validation request for a specific certificate. The OR decodes the validation request and determines whether the certificate is valid. When it determines the status of the requested certificate, it sends back an encrypted response containing the information to the requester. Using ORs is much faster and more efficient than using CRLs. AD CS includes ORs as a new feature in Windows Server 2008.

- Devices that use low-level operating systems, such as routers and switches, can also participate in a PKI through the NDES by using the SCEP, a protocol developed by Cisco Systems, Inc. These devices usually do not participate in an AD DS directory and, therefore, do not have AD DS accounts. However, through the NDES and the SCEP, they can also become part of the PKI hierarchy that is maintained and managed by your AD CS installation.

- CA server types are tied to the version of Windows Server 2008 you use. Standalone CAs can be created with Windows Server 2008 Standard Edition, Windows Server 2008 Enterprise Edition, or Windows Server 2008 Datacenter Edition. Enterprise CAs can be created with Windows Server 2008 Enterprise Edition or Windows Server 2008 Datacenter Edition only.

Lesson Review

You can use the following questions to test your knowledge of the information in Lesson 1, "Understanding and Installing Active Directory Certificate Services." The questions are also available on the companion CD if you prefer to review them in electronic form.

NOTE Answers

Answers to these questions and explanations of why each answer choice is right or wrong are located in the "Answers" section at the end of the book.

1. You are an administrator for the Contoso domain. Your boss has decided to deploy Active Directory Certificate Services, and he wants it done today. You tell him that you investigated AD CS and, from what you've learned, deploying a public key infrastructure is not usually done in one day. After some discussion, your boss agrees that perhaps you should install this role in a laboratory first, but he wants to be there to see how it works. He wants you to install an enterprise certificate authority. You make sure that the server you are using is running Windows Server 2008 Enterprise Edition, and you launch the installation through Server Manager. When you get to the Specify Setup Type page of the Add Roles Wizard, the Enterprise CA option is not available. (See Figure 15-7.) What could be the problem? (Choose all that apply.)

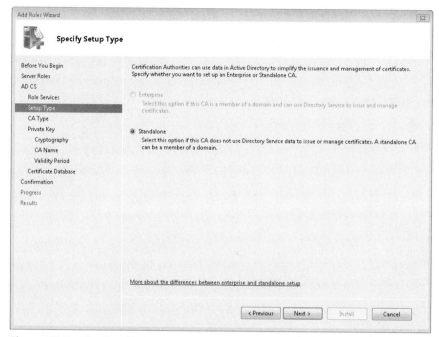

Figure 15-7 The Specify Setup Type page of the AD CS Installation Wizard

A. Your server is not running Windows Server 2008 Enterprise Edition.

B. You are logged on with an account that is not part of the domain.

C. Your server is not a member of an AD DS domain.

D. You cannot install an enterprise CA with Server Manager.

Lesson 2: Configuring and Using Active Directory Certificate Services

After you have deployed your servers, you still need to complete several configurations to begin using them to issue and manage certificates to users and devices. Several activities are required:

- To issue and maintain certificates, you must finalize the configuration of your issuing CAs.
- For your online responder to issue responses to requests, you must finalize the configuration of the online responder.
- To support network device enrollments, you must finish the configuration of the NDES on an issuing CA.
- After all of these configurations are completed, you must test your CA operations to ensure that everything is working correctly.

> **After this lesson, you will be able to:**
> - Create a revocation configuration.
> - Work with CA server configuration settings.
> - Work with certificate templates.
> - Configure the CA to issue OCSP response signing certificates.
> - Manage certificate enrollments.
> - Manage certificate revocations.
> **Estimated lesson time: 40 minutes**

Finalizing the Configuration of an Issuing CA

Finalizing the configuration of an issuing CA includes the following actions:

- Creating a certificate revocation configuration
- Configuring and personalizing certificate templates with specific attention to the following factors:
  - If you want to use the EFS to protect data, you must configure certificates for use with EFS. This also involves planning for the recovery agent or the agent that will be able to recover data if a user's EFS key is lost.
  - If you want to protect your wireless networks with certificates, you must configure wireless network certificates. This will enforce strong authentication and encrypt all communications between wireless devices.
  - If you want to use smart cards to support two-factor authentication, you must configure smart card certificates.

❑ If you want to protect Web sites and enable e-commerce, you must configure Web server certificates. You can also use this certificate type to protect DCs and encrypt all communications to and from them.

■ Configuring enrollment and issuance options

You perform each of these actions on the issuing CA itself or remotely through a workstation, using the Remote Server Administration Tools (RSAT).

Creating a Revocation Configuration for a CA

Revocation is one of the only vehicles available to you to control certificates when they are misused or when you need to cancel deployed certificates. This is one reason your revocation configuration should be completed before you begin to issue certificates.

To create a revocation configuration, perform the following actions:

■ Specify Certificate Revocation List (CRL) distribution points.
■ Configure CRL and Delta CRL overlap periods.
■ Schedule the publication of CRLs.

Begin with the CRL distribution point. Revocation configurations are performed in the Certification Authority console.

1. Log on to an issuing CA with a domain account that has local administrative rights.
2. Launch the Certification Authority console from the Administrative Tools program group.
3. Right-click the issuing CA name and select Properties.
4. In the Properties dialog box, click the Extensions tab and verify that the Select Extension drop-down list is set to CRL Distribution Point (CDP). Also make sure that the Publish CRLs To This Location and the Publish Delta CRLs To This Location check boxes are selected.
5. Click OK.

    If you made any changes to the CAs configuration, you will be prompted to stop and restart the AD CS service. Click Yes to do so.

Now, move on to configuring CRL and Delta CRL overlap periods. This is performed with the *Certutil.exe* command.

1. On the issuing CA, open an elevated command prompt and execute the following commands:

    ```
    certutil -setreg ca\CRLOverlapUnits value
    certutil -setreg ca\CRLOverlapPeriod units
    certutil -setreg ca\CRLDeltaOverlapUnits value
    certutil -setreg ca\CRLDeltaOverlapPeriod units
    ```

    Value is the value you want to use to set the overlap period, and *units* is in minutes, hours, or days. For example, you could set the CRL overlap period to 24 hours and the Delta CRL publication period to 12 hours. For this, you would use the following commands:

```
certutil -setreg ca\CRLOverlapUnits 24
certutil -setreg ca\CRLOverlapPeriod hours
certutil -setreg ca\CRLDeltaOverlapUnits 12
certutil -setreg ca\CRLDeltaOverlapPeriod hours
```

2. Go to the Certification Authority console and right-click the issuing CA server name to stop and restart the service.

Finally, configure the publication of the CRLs.

1. In the Certification Authority console, expand the console tree below the issuing CA server name.
2. Right-click Revoked Certificates and select Properties.
3. On the CRL Publishing Parameters tab, configure the CRL and Delta CRL publication periods.

   By default, both values are set to one week and one day, respectively. If you expect to have a high throughput of certificates and need to ensure high availability of the CRLs, decrease both values. If not, keep the default values.

   You can also view existing CRLs on the View CRLs tab.
4. Click OK.

Your revocation configuration is complete.

Configuring and Personalizing Certificate Templates

Certificate templates are used to generate the certificates you will use in your AD CS configuration. Enterprise CAs use version 2 and 3 templates. These templates are configurable and enable you to personalize them. To prepare templates for various uses, you must first configure each template you intend to use and, after each is configured, deploy each to your CAs. After templates are deployed, you can use them to issue certificates. Begin by identifying which templates you want to use, and then move on to the procedure.

1. Log on to an issuing CA, using domain administrative credentials.
2. Launch Server Manager from the Administrative Tools program group.
3. Expand Roles\Active Directory Certificate Services\Certificate Templates (*servername*).
4. Note that all the existing templates are listed in the details pane.

IMPORTANT **Upgrading certificate authorities**

If you are upgrading an existing CA infrastructure to Windows Server 2008, the first time you log on to a new server running AD CS, you will be prompted to update the existing certificate templates. Answer Yes to do so. This upgrades all templates to Windows Server 2008 versions.

---

5. Note that you are connected to a DC by default.

   To work with templates, you must be connected to a DC so that the templates can be published to AD DS.

6. If you are not connected, use the *Connect To Another Writable Domain Controller* command in the Action pane to do so.

   You are ready to create the templates you require.

7. Select the source template, right-click the template to select Duplicate Template, and select the version of Windows Server to support.

   This should always be Windows Server 2008 unless you are running in a mixed PKI hierarchy.

8. Name the new template, customize it, and save the customizations.

   Customize templates according to the following guidelines:

   ❑ To create an EFS template, select the Basic EFS template as the source, duplicate it for Windows Server 2008, and name it. Use a valid name, for example, **Basic EFS WS08**, and then move through the property tabs to customize its content. Pay particular attention to key archival on the Request Handling tab and make sure you select the Archive Subject Encryption Private Key check box. Also, use encryption to send the key to the CA. Archival storage of the private key enables you to protect it if the user ever loses it. You can also use the Subject Name tab to add information such as Alternate Subject Name values. Click OK.

   ❑ If you plan to use EFS, you must also create an EFS Recovery Agent template. Duplicate it for Windows Server 2008. Name it with a valid name such as **EFS Recovery Agent WS08**. Publish the recovery agent certificate in Active Directory. Note that the recovery agent certificate is valid for a much longer period than the EFS certificate itself. Also, use the same settings on the other property tabs as you assigned to the Basic EFS duplicate.

   MORE INFO   Using EFS

   For more information on the implementation of EFS, look up the "Working with the Encrypting File System" white paper at *http://www.reso-net.com/articles.asp?m=8* under the Advanced Public Key Infrastructures section.

   ❑ If you plan to use wireless networks, create a Network Policy Server (NPS) template for use with your systems. Basically, you create the template and configure it for autoenrollment. Then, the next time the NPS servers in your network update their Group Policy settings, they will be assigned new certificates. Use the RAS and IAS Server templates as the sources for your new NPS template. Duplicate it for Windows Server 2008. Name it appropriately, for example, **NPS Server WS08**. Publish it in Active Directory. Move to the Security tab to select the RAS and IAS Servers group to assign the Autoenroll as well as the Enroll permissions. Review other tabs as needed and save the new template.

❑   If you want to use smart card logons, create duplicates of the Smartcard Logon and Smartcard User templates. Set the duplicates for Windows Server 2008. Name them appropriately and publish them in Active Directory. You do not use Autoenrollment for these certificates because you need to use smart card enrollment stations to distribute the smart cards themselves to the users.

❑   If you want to protect Web servers or DCs, create duplicates of the Web Server and Domain Controller Authentication templates. Do not use the Domain Controller template; it is designed for earlier versions of the operating system. Duplicate them for Windows Server 2008, publish them in Active Directory, and verify their other properties.

NOTE   **Configuring duplicate templates**

The configuration of each template type often includes additional activities that are not necessarily tied to AD CS. Make sure you view the AD CS online help to review the activities associated with the publication of each certificate type.

Now that your templates are ready, you must issue the template to enable the CA to issue certificates based on these personalized templates.

  9.   In Server Manager, expand Roles\Active Directory Certificate Services*Issuing CA Name* \Certificate Templates.

10.   To issue a template, right-click Certificate Templates, choose New, and then select Certificate Template To Issue.

11.   In the Enable Certificate Templates dialog box, use Ctrl + click to select all the templates you want to issue, and then click OK. (See Figure 15-8.)

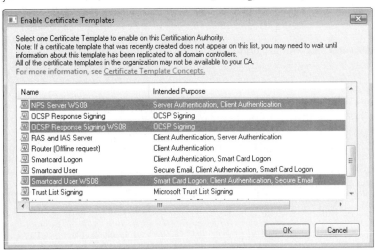

Figure 15-8   Enable Certificate Templates dialog box

Now you're ready to configure enrollment. This is done through Group Policy. You can choose either to create a new Group Policy for this purpose or to modify an existing Group Policy object. This policy must be assigned to all members of the domain; therefore, the Default Domain Policy might be your best choice or, if you do not want to modify this policy, create a new policy and assign it to the entire domain. You use the Group Policy Management Console (GPMC) to do so.

1. Log on to a DC, and then launch Group Policy Management from the Administrative Tools program group.

2. Locate or create the appropriate policy and right-click it to choose Edit.

3. To assign autoenrollment for computers, expand Computer Configuration\Policies \Windows Settings\Security Settings\Public Key Policies.

4. Double-click Certificate Services Client – Auto-Enrollment.

5. Enable the policy and select the Renew Expired Certificates, Update Pending Certificates, And Remove Revoked Certificates check box.

6. Select the Update Certificates That Use Certificate Templates check box if you have already issued some certificates manually for this purpose. Click OK to assign these settings.

7. To assign autoenrollment for users, expand User Configuration\Policies\Windows Settings\Security Settings\Public Key Policies.

8. Enable the policy and select the same options as for computers.

9. Notice that you can enable Expiration Notification for users. Enable it and set an appropriate value.

    This will notify users when their certificates are about to expire.

10. Click OK to assign these settings.

> **IMPORTANT Computer and User Group Policy settings**
>
> Normally, you should not apply both user and computer settings in the same Group Policy object. This is done here only to illustrate the settings you need to apply to enable autoenrollment.

11. Close the GPMC.

12. Return to the issuing CA and move to Server Manager to set the default action your issuing CA will use when it receives certificate requests.

13. Right-click the issuing CA server name under AD CS and choose Properties.

14. Click the Policy Module tab and click the Properties button.

15. To have certificates issued automatically, select Follow The Settings In The Certificate Template, If Applicable. Otherwise, Automatically Issue The Certificate. Click OK.

16. Click OK once again to close the Properties dialog box.

Your issuing CA is now ready for production and will begin to issue certificates automatically when they are requested either by devices or by users.

Finalizing the Configuration of an Online Responder

If you decided to use online responders, you will need to finalize their configuration. Online responders can create an array of systems to provide high availability for the service. An array can be as simple as two CAs acting as ORs, or it can include many more servers.

To finalize the configuration of an online responder, you must configure and install an OCSP Response Signing certificate and configure an Authority Information Access extension to support it. After this is done, you must assign the template to a CA and then enroll the system to obtain the certificate. Use the following procedure to configure the OCSP Response Signing Certificate.

1. Log on to an issuing CA server, using a domain account with local administrative access rights.
2. In Server Manager, expand Roles\Active Directory Certificate Services\ Certificate Templates(*servername*).
3. Right-click the OCSP Response Signing template and click Duplicate Template. Select a Windows Server 2008 Enterprise Edition template and click OK.
4. Type a valid name for the new template, for example, **OCSP Response Signing WS08**.
5. Select the Publish Certificate in Active Directory check box.
6. On the Security tab, under Group Or User Names, click Add, click Object Types to enable the Computer object type, and click OK.
7. Type the name and click Check Names or browse to find the computer that hosts the online responder. Click OK.
8. Click the computer name and then, in the Permissions section of the dialog box, select the Allow: Read, Enroll, and Autoenroll options.
9. Click OK to create the duplicate template.

Your certificate template is ready. Now you must configure the Authority Information Access (AIA) Extension to support the OR.

IMPORTANT   Assigning access rights

Normally, you should assign access rights to groups and not to individual objects in an AD DS directory. Because you will have several ORs, using a group makes sense. Ideally, you will create a group in AD DS, name it appropriately—for example, Online Responders—and add the computer accounts of each OR to this group. After you do that, you will assign the access rights of the OCSP Response Signing template to the group instead of to the individual systems. This way, you will have to do it only once.

---

1. Log on to an issuing CA, using a domain account with local administrative credentials.

2. Launch Server Manager from the Administrative Tools program group.

3. Expand Roles\Active Directory Certificate Services*Issuing CA servername*.

4. In the Actions pane, select Properties.

5. Click the Extensions tab, click the Select Extension drop-down list, and then click Authority Information Access (AIA).

6. Specify the locations to obtain certificate revocation data. In this case, select the location beginning with HTTP://.

7. Select the Include In The AIA Extension Of Issued Certificates and the Include In The Online Certificate Status Protocol (OCSP) Extension check boxes.

8. Click OK to apply the changes.

   Note that you must stop and restart the AD CS service because of the change.

9. Click Yes at the suggested dialog box.

10. Now move to the Certificate Templates node under the issuing CA name and right-click it, select New, and then choose Certificate Template To Issue.

11. In the Enable Certificate Templates dialog box, select the new OCSP Response Signing template you created earlier and click OK.

    The new template should appear in the details pane.

12. To assign the template to the server, reboot it.

    You now need to verify that the OCSP certificate has been assigned to the server. You do so with the Certificates snap-in. By default, this snap-in is not in a console. You must create a new console to use it.

13. Open the Start menu, type **mmc** in the search box, and press Enter.

14. In the MMC, select Add/Remove Snap-in from the File menu to open the Add Or Remove Snap-ins dialog box.

15. Select the Certificates snap-in and click Add.

16. Select Computer Account and click Next.

17. Select Local Computer and click Finish.

18. Click OK to close the Add Or Remove Snap-ins dialog box.

19. Select Save from the File menu to save the console and place it in your Documents folder. Name the console **Computer Certificates** and click Save.

20. Expand Certificates\Personal\Certificates and verify that it contains the new OCSP certificate.

21. If the certificate is not there, install it manually by right-clicking Certificates under Personal, choosing All Tasks, and then selecting Request New Certificate.

22. On the Certificate Enrollment page, click Next.

23. Select the new OCSP certificate and click Enroll.

24. On the next page, click the down arrow to the right of Details, and then click View Certificate. Browse through the tabs to view the certificate details. Click OK.

25. Click Finish to complete this part of the operation.

26. Right-click the Certificate, choose All Tasks, and then select Manage Private Keys.

27. On the Security tab, under User Group Or User Names, click Add.

28. In the Select Users, Computers, or Groups dialog box, click Locations and select the local server name. Click OK.

29. Type **Network Service** and click Check Names.

30. Click OK.

31. Click Network Service, and then, in the Permissions section of the dialog box, select Allow: Full Control.

32. Click OK to close the dialog box.

Your OR is ready to provide certificate validation information.

MORE INFO   Online responder

For more information on the OR service, go to *http://technet2.microsoft.com/windowsserver2008/en /library/045d2a97-1bff-43bd-8dea-f2df7e270e1f1033.mspx?mfr=true.*

You'll note that the Online Responder node in Server Manager also includes an Array Configuration node. When you add other ORs, you can add them to this array configuration to provide high availability of the OR service. Complex environments using multitiered hierarchies will have large OR arrays to ensure that all their users and devices can easily validate their certificates.

Add a Revocation Configuration for an Online Responder

When the OR is ready, add a revocation configuration. Because each CA that is an OR in an array includes its own certificate, each also requires a revocation configuration. The revocation configuration will serve requests for specific CA key pairs and certificates. In addition, you need to update the revocation configuration for a CA each time you renew its key pair. To create a Revocation Configuration, perform the following steps:

1. Log on to an issuing CA, using a domain account that has local administrative rights.

2. Launch Server Manager from the Administrative Tools program group.

3. Expand Roles\Active Directory Certificate Services\Online Responder\Revocation Configuration.

4. Right-click Revocation Configuration and choose Add Revocation Configuration.

5. Click Next at the Welcome page.

6. On the Name The Revocation Configuration page, assign a valid name.

    Because each revocation configuration is tied to a particular CA, it makes sense to include the CA's name in the name of the configuration, for example, RCSERVER04.

7. Click Next.

8. On the Select CA Certificate Location page, identify where the certificate can be loaded from.

    You can choose from Active Directory, from a local certificate store, or from a file.

9. Choose Select A Certificate For An Existing Enterprise CA and click Next.

    Now, the OR must validate that the issuer of the certificate, in this case, the root CA, has a valid certificate. Two choices are possible: Active Directory or Computer Name.

10. Because your root CA is offline, choose Active Directory and click Browse.

11. Locate the certificate for the root CA and click OK.

    After the certificate is selected, the wizard will load the Online Responder signing templates.

12. Click Next.

    On the Select A Signing Certificate page, you must select a signing method because the OR signs each response to clients before it sends it. Three choices are available:

    ❑ Automatic selection will load a certificate from the OCSP template you created earlier.

    ❑ Manually, you can choose the certificate to use.

    ❑ CA Certificate uses the certificate from the CA itself.

13. Choose Automatically Select A Signing Certificate and select Auto-Enroll for an OCSP signing certificate.

14. Browse for a CA and select the issuing CA. Click OK.

    This should automatically select the template you prepared earlier.

15. Click Next.

    Now the wizard will initialize the revocation provider. If, for some reason, it cannot find it, you will need to add the provider manually.

16. Click Provider, and then click Add under Base CRLs. For example, you could use the following HTTP address: **http://localhost/ca.crl**.

17. Click OK. Repeat this step for the Delta CRLs and use the same HTTP address. Click OK.

    However, because you are obtaining the certificate from Active Directory, the listed provider will be an address in ldap:// format and should be provided automatically by the wizard. AD CS relies on Lightweight Directory Access Protocol (LDAP) to obtain information from the AD DS directory store.

18. Click Finish to complete the revocation configuration.

You should now have a new revocation configuration listed in the details pane. Repeat this procedure for each CA that is an OR.

Exam Tip   Take note of the operations you need to enable ORs because they are part of the exam.

Considerations for the Use and Management of AD CS

Active Directory Certificate Services role services are managed by using MMC snap-ins. Table 15-4 lists the tools you have used throughout this chapter, most of which are available from within Server Manager.

Table 15-4   AD CS Management Tools

Tool	Usage	Location
Certification Authority	To manage a certificate authority.	Server Manager
Certificates	To manage certificates. This snap-in is installed by default.	Custom MMC snap-in
Certificate Templates	To manage certificate templates.	Server Manager
Online Responder	To manage an OR.	Server Manager
Enterprise PKI	To manage the entire PKI infrastructure.	Server Manager
Certutil	To manage PKI functions from the command line.	Command prompt

NOTE   Install the snap-ins without installing AD CS

The snap-ins listed in Table 15-4 can be installed by using Server Manager and selecting the AD CS tools under Remote Server Administration Tools. If the computer you want to perform remote administration tasks from is running Windows Vista Service Pack 1, you can obtain the Remote Server Administration Tools Pack from the Microsoft Download Center at *http://go.microsoft.com /fwlink/?LinkID=89361*.

As you work with AD CS, you will see that it provides a great amount of information through the Event Log. Table 15-5 lists the most common events for AD CS certificate authorities.

Table 15-5   Common Certificate Authority Event IDs

Category	Event ID	Description
AD CS Access Control	39, 60, 92	Related to insufficient or inappropriate use of permissions.
AD CS and AD DS	24, 59, 64, 91, 93, 94, 106, 107	Related to access (read or write) for AD DS objects.
AD CS Certificate Request (Enrollment) Processing	3, 7, 10, 21, 22, 23, 53, 56, 57, 79, 80, 97, 108, 109, 128, 132	One element for certificate enrollment to succeed is missing: valid CA certificate, certificate templates with proper configuration, client accounts, or certificate requests.
AD CS Certification Authority Certificate and Chain Validation	27, 31, 42, 48, 49, 51, 58, 64, 100, 103, 104, 105	Related to availability, validity, and chain validation for a CA certificate.

Table 15-5   Common Certificate Authority Event IDs

Category	Event ID	Description
AD CS Certification Authority Upgrade	111, 112, 113, 114, 115, 116, 117, 118, 119, 120, 121, 122, 123, 125, 126	Related to upgrading certificate authorities from an earlier version of Windows to Windows Server 2008 and can indicate configuration options or components that need to be reconfigured.
AD CS Cross-Certification	99, 102	Related to the cross-CA certificates created to establish relationships between the original certificate and the renewed root.
AD CS Database Availability	17	Related to CA database access issues.
AD CS Exit Module Processing	45, 46	Related to the exit module functions: publish or send e-mail notification.
AD CS Key Archival and Recovery	81, 82, 83, 84, 85, 86, 87, 88, 96, 98, 127	Related to key recovery agent certificates, exchange (XCHG) certificates and keys, or that one or all these components are missing.
AD CS Performance Counters Availability	110	Related to performance counters that cannot be started.
AD CS Policy Module Processing	9, 43, 44, 77, 78	Related to problems detected with a policy module.
AD CS Program Resource Availability	15, 16, 26, 30, 33, 34, 35, 38, 40, 61, 63, 89, 90	Related to the availability of system resources and operating system components.
AD CS Registry Settings	5, 19, 20, 28, 95	Related to the corruption or deletion of configuration settings in the registry.
AD CS Online Responder	16, 17, 18, 19, 20, 21, 22, 23, 25, 26, 27, 29, 31, 33, 34, 35	Related to Online Responder service dependencies.

Rely on the contents of Table 15-5 to identify quickly the area an issue relates to so that you can resolve it faster.

MORE INFO   AD CS event IDs

To find more information on event types, read the information at *http://technet2.microsoft.com /windowsserver2008/en/library/688d1449-3086-4a79-95e6-5a7f620681731033.mspx.*

Working with Enterprise PKI

One of the most useful tools in an AD CS infrastructure is Enterprise PKI, or *PKIView* from the command line, which is the Enterprise PKI node under Active Directory Certificate Services in Server Manager. Enterprise PKI can be used for several AD CS management activities. Basically, Enterprise PKI gives you a view of the status of your AD CS deployment and enables you to view the entire PKI hierarchy in your network and drill down into individual CAs to identify quickly issues with the configuration or operation of your AD CS infrastructure.

Enterprise PKI is mostly used as a diagnostic and health view tool because it displays operational information about the members of your PKI hierarchy. In addition, you can use Enterprise PKI to link to each CA quickly by right-clicking the CA name and selecting Manage CA. This launches the Certification Authority console for the targeted CA.

From the Actions pane, you can also gain access to the Templates console (Manage Templates) as well as to the Certificate Containers in Active Directory Domain Services (Manage AD Containers). The latter enables you to view the contents of each of the various containers in a directory that is used to store certificates for your PKI architecture. (See Figure 15-9.)

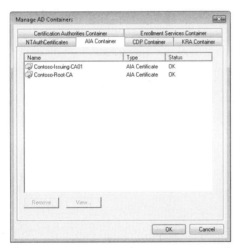

Figure 15-9   Viewing the AD containers through Enterprise PKI

Rely on Enterprise PKI to check AD CS health status visually. Its various icons give you immediate feedback on each component of your infrastructure, showing green when all is healthy, yellow when minor issues are found, and red when critical issues arise.

Protecting Your AD CS Configuration

Along with the security measures you must perform for your root and intermediate CAs, you must also protect each CA, especially issuing CAs through regular backups. Backing up a CA is very simple. In Server Manager, expand Roles\ Active Directory Certificate Services\ *CA Server Name*. Right-click the server name, select All Tasks, and choose Back Up CA. When you launch the backup operation, it launches the Certification Authority Backup Wizard. To back up the CA, use the following operations.

1. Launch the Certification Authority Backup Wizard and click Next.

2. On the Items To Back Up page, select the items you want to back up.
    - ❑ The Private Key And CA Certificate option will protect the certificate for this server.
    - ❑ The Certificate Database And Certificate Database Log option will protect the certificates this CA manages. You can also perform incremental database backups.

3. Identify the location to back up to.

   For example, you could create the backup to a file share on a central server location. Keep in mind, however, that you are backing up highly sensitive data and transporting it over the network, which might not be the best solution. A better choice might be to back up to a local folder and then copy the backup to removable media.

4. Identify the location and click Next. Note that the target location must be empty.

5. Assign a strong password to the backup. Click Next.

6. Review the information and click Finish.

   The wizard performs the backup. Protect the backup media thoroughly because it contains very sensitive information.

You can also perform automated backups through the command line with the *Certutil.exe* command with the appropriate switches to back up and restore the database.

MORE INFO   Using *Certutil.exe* to protect CA data

For more information on the *Certutil.exe* utility for backup and restore, go to *http://support.microsoft.com/kb/185195*.

To restore information, use the Certification Authority Restore Wizard. When you request a restore operation by right-clicking the server name, selecting All Tasks, and choosing Restore CA, the wizard will immediately prompt you to stop the CA service before the restore operation can begin. Click OK. After the service is stopped, the Welcome page of the wizard appears.

1. Click Next.
2. Select the items you want to restore. You can restore the private key and the CA certificate as well as the database and log. Choose the items to restore.
3. Type the location of the backup files or click Browse to locate the backup data. Click Next.
4. Type the password to open the backup and click Next.
5. Verify your settings and click Finish.

   After the restore operation is complete, the wizard will offer to restart the AD CS service.
6. Click Yes. Verify the operation of your CA after the restore is complete.

PRACTICE Configuring and Using AD CS

In this practice, you will perform four key tasks. In the first, you will work with Enterprise PKI to correct the errors in an AD CS implementation. Then you will create a custom certificate template to publish certificates. You will also enable autoenrollment for certificates to ensure that your users can obtain them automatically. Finally, you will ensure that your issuing CA will automatically enroll clients.

▶ **Exercise 1   Correct an AD CS Implementation with Enterprise PKI**

In this exercise, you will rely on Enterprise PKI to identify and then correct configuration issues with your AD CS implementation. This exercise will help you see the value of working with Enterprise PKI.

1. Make sure that SERVER01, SERVER03, and SERVER04 are running.
2. Log on to SERVER04, using the domain Administrator account.
3. Launch Server Manager from the Administrative Tools program group.
4. Expand Roles\Active Directory Certificate Services\Enterprise PKI\Contoso-Root-CA \Contoso-Issuing-CA. Click Contoso-Issuing-CA and note the errors. (See Figure 15-10.)

Errors exist in your configuration. If you navigate to the Contoso-Root-CA, you will see that this CA also includes errors according to Enterprise PKI. These errors refer to the Web-based download locations for the CRL Distribution Point and for the AIA. These errors appear because they refer to locations that do not exist. These locations must be created manually in IIS. However, because you are using an AD DS–integrated AD CS deployment, you do not need to add Web-based download locations even if they are indicated by default in the configuration of AD CS. In an AD DS–integrated deployment, the directory service is responsible for AIA and CRL distribution, and, because this service is highly available, no secondary location is required. In fact, you need to add secondary locations only if you want to make them available to mobile or external users who are outside your internal network. If you do so, your URLs will need to be available externally.

5. Click Contoso-Root-CA under the Enterprise PKI node and select Manage CA.

    This launches the Certificate Authority standalone console with a focus on the root CA. Remember that Server Manager can work with the local server only. Therefore, you need to use the standalone console.

6. Right-click Contoso-Root-CA and select Properties.

7. Click the Extensions tab and verify that CRL Distribution Point (CDP) is selected in the drop-down list.

8. Select http://<ServerDNSName>/CertEnroll/<CaName><CRLNameSuffix><DeltaCRLAllowed>.crl in the locations section of the dialog box and clear Include In CRLs, Clients Use This To Find Delta CRL Locations as well as Include in the CDP extension of issued certificates.

9. Select Authority Information Access (AIA) from the drop-down list.

10. Select http://<ServerDNSName>/CertEnroll/<ServerDNSName>_<CaName><CertificateName>.crt and clear Include in the AIA extension of issued certificates. Click OK to apply your changes.

    AD CS automatically points to a CertEnroll virtual directory under the default Web site for Web as the CDP. However, the installation process for AD CS does not create this virtual directory by default. In addition, because this is a root CA, it does not host IIS and will be taken offline. Pointing to a nonexistent Web server as a CDP location is not good practice, and this location must be removed from the CA's configuration; otherwise, it will be embedded in the certificates it issues.

11. Because you modified the configuration of the AD CS server, the console will ask you to restart AD CS on this server. Click Yes.

12. Close the Certificate Authority console and return to Enterprise PKI in Server Manager.

13. On the toolbar, click the Refresh button to update Enterprise PKI. Note that though there are no longer location errors for the root CA, there are still errors under the issuing CA.

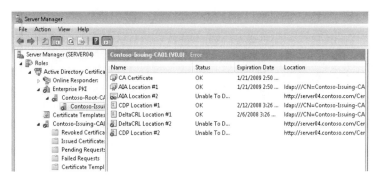

Figure 15-10   Viewing configuration errors in Enterprise PKI

You are ready to correct the errors in the issuing CA.

1. Right-click Contoso-Issuing-CA under AD CS in Server Manager and select Properties.

   In this case, you can use Server Manager because Contoso-Issuing-CA is the local computer.

2. Click the Extensions tab and verify that CRL Distribution Point (CDP) is selected in the drop-down list.

3. Select   http://<ServerDNSName>/CertEnroll/<CaName><CRLNameSuffix><DeltaCRL-Allowed>.crl in the locations section of the dialog box and clear Include In CRLs, Clients Use This To Find Delta CRL Locations as well as Include in the CDP extension of issued certificates.

4. Select Authority Information Access (AIA) from the drop-down list.

5. Select http://<ServerDNSName>/CertEnroll/<ServerDNSName>_<CaName><Certificate-Name>.crt and clear Include in the AIA extension of issued certificates. Click OK to apply your changes.

   Once again, AD CS automatically points to a CertEnroll virtual directory under the default Web site for Web as the CDP. However, the installation process for AD CS does not create this virtual directory by default. If you need to provide Web support for CRLs, even if this is only an internal deployment, you would need to create the virtual directory in IIS. However, in this case, it is not required. Also, as a best practice, you do not remove the HTTP location. If you need to add it later, the proper format for the URL will already be there, and you will need to recheck only the appropriate options.

6. Because you modified the configuration of the AD CS server, the console will ask you to restart AD CS on this server. Click Yes.

7. Return to Enterprise PKI in Server Manager.

8. On the toolbar, click the Refresh button to update Enterprise PKI.

   Note that there is now only one error under the issuing CA. This error stems from the original self-signed certificate that was generated during installation of this CA. This certificate is superseded by the certificate that was issued by the root CA. Because of this, you must revoke the original certificate.

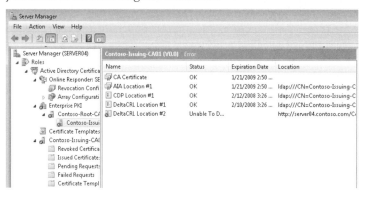

9. To finalize your configuration, move to Contoso-Issuing-CA under AD CS and select Issued Certificates.

   This will list all certificates issued by this CA in the details pane.

10. Locate the first certificate.

    It should be of a CA Exchange type. The certificate type is listed under the Certificate Template column in the details pane.

11. Right-click this certificate, select All Tasks, and then click Revoke Certificate.

12. In the Certificate Revocation dialog box, select Superseded from the drop-down list, verify the date, and click OK.

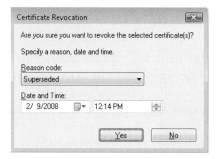

When you revoke the certificate, it is automatically moved to the Revoked Certificates folder and is no longer valid. However, because you newly revoked a certificate, you must update the revocation list.

13. Right-click the Revoked Certificates node and choose All Tasks to select Publish.

14. In the Publish CRL dialog box, select New CRL and click OK.

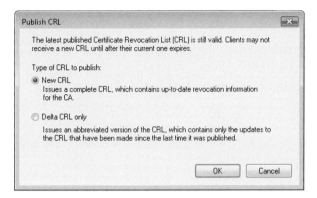

15. Return to Enterprise PKI and click the Refresh button.

    There should no longer be any errors in the Enterprise PKI view.

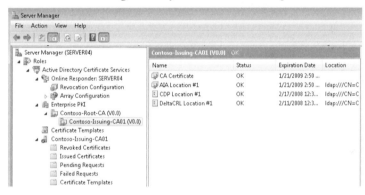

You will need to perform these activities in your network when you implement AD CS; otherwise, your Enterprise PKI views will always display errors.

▶ **Exercise 2   Create a Duplicate Certificate Template for EFS**

In this exercise, you will create a duplicate certificate to enable EFS and publish it so it can use autoenroll and use EFS to protect the system data.

1. Make sure SERVER01 and SERVER04 are both running.
2. Log on to SERVER04, using the domain Administrator account.
3. Launch Server Manager from the Administrative Tools program group.
4. Expand Roles\Active Directory Certificate Services\Certificate Templates (*servername*). Note that all the existing templates are listed in the details pane.

Note also that you are connected to a DC (SERVER01) by default. To work with templates, you must be connected to a DC so that the templates can be published to AD DS. If you are not connected, you must use the *Connect To Another Writable Domain Controller* command in the action pane to do so.

5. Select the Basic EFS template in the details pane, right-click it, and select Duplicate Template.

6. Select the version of Windows Server to support—in this case, Windows Server 2008— and click OK.

7. Name the template **Basic EFS WS08** and set the following options. Leave all other options as is.

   ❏ On the Request Handling tab, select the Archive Subject's Encryption Private Key and the Use Advanced Symmetric Algorithm To Send The Key To The CA check boxes. Archival storage of the private key enables you to protect it if the user loses it.

   ❏ On the Subject Name tab, add information to the Alternate Subject Name values. Select the E-mail Name and User Principal Name (UPN) check boxes.

8. Click OK.

9. Right-click the EFS Recovery Agent template and choose Duplicate.

10. Select the version of Windows Server to support—in this case, Windows Server 2008— and click OK.

11. Name the template **EFS Recovery Agent WS08** and set the following options. Leave all other options as is.

    ❏ On the General tab, select the Publish certificate in the Active Directory check box. Note that the recovery agent certificate is valid for a much longer period than is the EFS certificate itself.

    ❏ On the Request Handling tab, make sure you select the Archive Subject's Encryption Private Key and the Use Advanced Symmetric Algorithm To Send The Key To The CA check boxes. Archival storage of the private key enables you to protect it if the user loses it.

    ❏ On the Subject Name tab, add information to the Alternate Subject Name values. Select the E-mail Name and User Principal Name (UPN) check boxes.

12. Click OK.

13. In Server Manager, expand Roles\Active Directory Certificate Services*Issuing CA Name*\Certificate Templates.

14. To issue a template, right-click Certificate Templates, choose New, and then select Certificate Template To Issue.

15. In the Enable Certificate Templates dialog box, use Ctrl + click to select both Basic EFS WS08 and EFS Recovery Agent WS08 and click OK.

    Your templates are ready.

▶ **Exercise 3   Configure Autoenrollment**

In this exercise, you use Group Policy to configure autoenrollment. This exercise uses the Default Domain policy for simplicity, but in your environment, you should create a custom policy for this purpose and for all other custom settings you need to apply at the entire domain level.

1. Move to SERVER01 and log on as a domain administrator.
2. Launch Group Policy Management from the Administrative Tools program group.
3. Expand all the nodes to locate the Default Domain policy. Right-click it and choose Edit.
4. To assign autoenrollment for computers, expand Computer Configuration\Policies \Windows Settings\Security Settings\Public Key Policies.
5. Double-click Certificate Services Client – Auto-Enrollment.
6. Enable the policy and select the Renew Expired Certificates, Update Pending Certificates, And Remove Revoked Certificates check box.
7. Enable Expiration Notification For Users and leave the value at 10%.
   This will notify users when their certificates are about to expire.
8. Click OK to assign these settings.
9. Close the GPMC.
   Your policy is ready.

▶ **Exercise 4   Enable the CA to Issue Certificates**

Now you need to set the default action the CA will perform when it receives certificate requests.

1. Return to SERVER04 and log on, using the domain Administrator account.
2. Move to Server Manager.
3. Right-click the issuing CA server name under AD CS, Contoso-Issuing-CA01, and choose Properties.
4. Click the Policy Module tab and click the Properties button.
5. To have certificates issued automatically, select Follow The Settings In The Certificate Template, If Applicable. Otherwise, Automatically Issue The Certificate. Click OK. Click OK once again to close the Properties dialog box.
   Your issuing CA is now ready for production and will begin to issue EFS certificates automatically when they are requested either by your users or by computers.

Lesson Summary

- Revocation configurations for issuing CAs include several components. The first is a list of the Certificate Revocation List distribution points. The second is the overlap between the CRL and the Delta CRLs you send to requesters. The third is the schedule you use to publish CRLs.

- Issuing CAs should be enterprise CAs because of their capability to support autoenrollment and modify and personalize certificate templates.

- Online responders can create an array of systems to provide high availability for the service. An array can be as simple as two CAs acting as ORs, or it can include many more servers.

- ORs must rely on the Online Certificate Status Protocol (OCSP) certificates to sign the responses they send to requesters. These certificates encrypt the content of the response sent from the OR.

- ORs also require the configuration of the Authority Information Access extension before they can be fully functional. This extension is part of the properties of the certificate authority.

- Each CA that is an OR must have its own revocation configuration because each has its own certificate. To operate in an array, each of these certificates must be trusted. The revocation configuration is used to allow other array members to trust each particular CA in the array.

- Protection of every CA in your infrastructure is essential. This is why you should perform regular backups of all CA data, including the CA's certificates. Protect these backups very carefully because they contain highly sensitive data.

Lesson Review

You can use the following questions to test your knowledge of the information in Lesson 2, "Configuring and Using Active Directory Certificate Services." The questions are also available on the companion CD if you prefer to review them in electronic form.

NOTE Answers

Answers to these questions and explanations of why each answer choice is right or wrong are located in the "Answers" section at the end of the book.

1. You are a PKI administrator for Contoso, Ltd. You want to configure your OR. You have already configured your OCSP Response Signing certificates, configured the Authority Information Access extension, and rebooted the server. Now you are ready to verify that the certificate has been automatically loaded onto the server. You create a custom console to contain the Certificates snap-in, but when you view the certificates in the Personal node of the computer, the snap-in does not appear. You decide to import the certificate manually, but when you use the Request New Certificate Wizard, you find that the certificate is not available to you. What could be the problem?

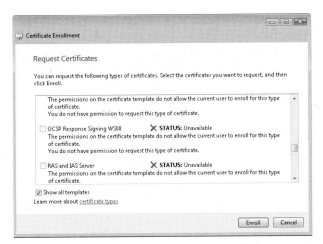

A. You cannot request this certificate through the wizard. You must use the *Certutil.exe* command.

B. The security properties of the certificate template are not set properly.

C. You cannot load an OCSP Response Signing Certificate on this server.

D. You do not need to load this certificate manually. It will be loaded automatically at the next Group Policy refresh cycle.

Chapter Review

To further practice and reinforce the skills you learned in this chapter, you can perform the following tasks:

- Review the chapter summary.
- Review the list of key terms introduced in this chapter.
- Complete the case scenario. This scenario sets up a real-world situation involving the topics of this chapter and asks you to create a solution.
- Complete the suggested practices.
- Take a practice test.

Chapter Summary

- You can use public key infrastructures to extend the authority your organization has beyond the borders of the network it controls. The role of AD DS is focused on network operating system directory services and should really be contained within the internal boundaries of your network. AD CS, however, can run both within a corporate network and outside the corporate network. When used within the network, it can be integrated with AD DS to provide automated certificate enrollment. When used outside your network, it should be installed as standalone certificate authorities and linked to a third-party trusted certificate authority to ensure that your certificates are trusted by computer systems over which you do not have control.

- You can rely on certificates for a variety of purposes, including data encryption on PCs, for communication encryption between two endpoints, for information protection, for two-factor authentications, for wireless communications, and more. All are based on the AD CS role.

- AD CS deployments are hierarchical in nature and form a chain of trust from the lowest to the topmost point of the hierarchy. If certificates are invalidated or expire at any point in the chain, every certificate that is below the invalidated certificate in the chain will be invalidated as well.

- Online Responders (ORs) can be linked to create an array configuration that will provide high availability for the OR service. The more complex your AD CS deployment becomes, the more likely you are to create these arrays to ensure that all users and devices have constant access to the certificate validation services the OR provides.

- When you deploy ORs, you must ensure that each contains its own revocation configuration. This step is necessary because each OR relies on its own certificate for validation purposes. Each revocation configuration will support a specific certificate key pair and will be published to each OR in an array. If you need to renew the OR's certificate, you will need to update its revocation configuration.

■ One of the most useful management tools you have for AD CS is *Certutil.exe*. This tool supports almost every possible operation on a CA and enables you to automate maintenance and administration tasks.

Key Terms

Use these key terms to understand better the concepts covered in this chapter.

■ **hierarchy**   The chain of servers that provide functionality in a PKI implementation. The chain begins with the root server and potentially extends through intermediate and issuing servers until it gets to the endpoint, the user or the endpoint device.

■ **key pair**   PKI certificates usually include a key pair. The private key is used by the owner of the certificate to sign and encrypt information digitally. The public key, which is available to recipients of the information, is used to decrypt it.

■ **revocation**   Certificates are issued for a specific duration of time. When the duration expires, the certificate is invalidated. If you need to deny the use of a certificate before the end of its lifetime, you must revoke it. Revoking a certificate provides immediate invalidation. All revocations are inserted into the Certificate Revocation List, which is used by all devices to validate the certificates they are presented with.

Case Scenario

In the following case scenario, you will apply what you've learned about subjects of this chapter. You can find answers to the questions in this scenario in the "Answers" section at the end of this book.

Case Scenario: Manage Certificate Revocation

You are a systems administrator for Contoso, Ltd. Contoso has deployed an AD CS infrastructure and has published certificates for a wide number of uses. One of these is to create software signing certificates for the software it distributes to its clients. These certificates are used to ensure that the software actually originates from Contoso. Contoso clients are pleased with this new approach because it guarantees that the source of the software is valid and free of malicious code.

As administrator, one of your duties is to perform weekly reviews of the event logs of your servers. Because you're using Windows Server 2008, you have configured event forwarding on each of the certificate authorities in your network. This makes administration easier, eliminating the need to log on to individual servers to view the event logs. You have to verify only one central location.

During a routine check, you notice that the root CA of your AD CS infrastructure has sent events to your central logging server. At first, you think this is very odd because the root CA should be offline at all times except for very rare maintenance operations or in the rare case when you need to issue a certificate for a new subordinate CA. As system administrator, you know that neither event has occurred in the recent past.

You look at the different events that were forwarded and you see that the CA was turned on about a week ago. During that time, it was used to generate two new root certificates under the Contoso name. Fortunately, you also included the security logs in the forwarding configuration. You look them up to see who logged on to the root CA. Because logons require smart cards, your event logs can be used to validate who used the server. You find out to your surprise that the logons belong to two employees who were fired last week. These employees should not have had access to this server.

You check on the Internet and find that the two root certificates are being used to sign software that does not originate from Contoso. In fact, it appears that the two ex-employees are currently offering software signing certificates using the Contoso name for sale on the Internet.

What do you do?

Suggested Practices

To help you successfully master the exam objectives presented in this chapter, complete the following tasks.

Working with AD CS

There are several exam objectives for this topic. Because of this, you should focus your practices on the following areas:

- Identifying the differences between standalone and enterprise CAs
- Working with the installation and configuration process for AD CS CAs
- Installing and configuring the Online Responder service
- Installing Network Device Enrollment Service
- Working with certificate templates

You should also practice using the various management tools and consoles for AD CS. Most of the consoles are available in Server Manager. The only console you need to create is the Certificates console.

Use the following instructions to perform these tasks.

- **Practice 1**   Prepare two servers—virtual or physical—as member servers of an AD DS domain. Then, install a standalone root CA and follow with the installation of an enterprise issuing CA. Run through each of the operations outlined in this chapter for the installation and configuration of both servers. For the purpose of the exercise, keep the root CA online and allow it to communicate with the issuing CA.
- **Practice 2**   Use the issuing CA to install the Online Responder service. Then run through each of the steps outlined in Lesson 2, "Configuring and Using Active Directory Certificate Services," to finalize the configuration of the Online Responder service. Pay attention to each step. ORs are new to AD CS and, therefore, will likely be on the exam.
- **Practice 3**   Follow the instructions in the practice in Lesson 1, "Understanding and Installing Active Directory Certificate Services," to install and configure the NDES. This is also a new feature of AD CS and, thus, will be on the exam.
- **Practice 4**   Modify a few template duplicates. Make sure you review the tabs of each template's property sheets thoroughly. Version 2 and 3 templates include many options and features.
- **Practice 5**   Finally, perform backups and restores and explore both Enterprise PKI and the options available through the *Certutil.exe* tool. Don't forget to study AD CS as well as PKI implementations with Windows Server 2003. The Microsoft TechNet Web site includes much more information on PKI in Windows Server 2003 than in Windows Server 2008.

Take a Practice Test

The practice tests on this book's companion CD offer many options. For example, you can test yourself on just one exam objective, or you can test yourself on all the 70-640 certification exam content. You can set up the test so that it closely simulates the experience of taking a certification exam, or you can set it up in study mode so that you can look at the correct answers and explanations after you answer each question.

MORE INFO   Practice tests

For details about all the practice test options available, see the "How to Use the Practice Tests" section in this book's introduction.

Chapter 16

Active Directory Rights Management Services

Active Directory Rights Management Services (AD RMS), formerly known simply as Rights Management Services, is designed to extend the reach of your internal network to the outside world. However, this time, the extension applies to intellectual property. People have been struggling with Digital Rights Management (DRM) ever since they started working with computers. In the first days of computing, software manufacturers went to great lengths to protect their software from theft. Even today, some vendors require the use of hardware keys for their software to run. Others have resorted to a Web-based approval and validation process. For example, with the release of Windows Vista, Microsoft has introduced a new licensing scheme, one option of which is a Key Management Server (KMS), to validate the licensed versions of Microsoft Windows you use.

Software creation isn't the only industry struggling with rights management. The music industry is also under pressure to determine the best way to protect digital music, sometimes even using questionable methods to do so. For instance, in 2005, Mark Russinovich, now Technical Fellow at Microsoft Corporation, discovered that Sony BMG installed a root kit with its CD player that activated when users load it onto their PCs. This root kit would send playlist information back to a central server managed by Sony through the Internet. This led to a series of articles and a flurry of activity on the Internet about the approaches music vendors were using to protect content.

MORE INFO Mark Russinovich and Sony BMG

For more information on Mark's adventure with Sony, go to *http://blogs.technet.com/markrussinovich /archive/2005/10/31/sony-rootkits-and-digital-rights-management-gone-too-far.aspx.*

Now many record labels have decided to sell their music in MP3 format without data protection. When you buy the song, you become responsible for protecting it; however, you can play it on any device. It might or might not be related to Mark's story with Sony BMG, but the move displays just how complex DRM can become.

Music and software are not the only items that need protection. In data centers everywhere, people are starting to look to new technologies to protect their intellectual property. For example, the nice thing about e-mail is that it automatically keeps a trail of the conversations it includes. Each time you respond to a message, the original message is embedded into yours and so on. Without DRM, anyone can change the content of this embedded response at any time, changing the tone or nature of the conversation. Even worse, anyone can forward the conversation and change its content, and you won't even know about it. Implementing DRM to protect e-mail content ensures that your responses can never be modified even if they are embedded in another message.

The same applies to other intellectual property—Microsoft Office Word documents, Microsoft Office PowerPoint presentations, and other content. Many organizations rely on the value of their intellectual property. Losing this property or having it misused, copied, or stolen can cause untold damages to their operations. You don't have to be a major enterprise to profit from some form of rights management. Whenever you earn a living from the information you generate or you maintain competitive leadership through the use of internal information, consider DRM.

AD RMS enables you to protect your intellectual property through the integration of several features. In fact, in addition to a direct integration with Active Directory Domain Services (AD DS), AD RMS can also rely on both Active Directory Certificate Services (AD CS) and Active Directory Federation Services (AD FS). AD CS can generate the public key infrastructure (PKI) certificates that AD RMS can embed in documents. AD FS extends your AD RMS policies beyond the firewall and supports the protection of your intellectual property among your business partners. (See Figure 16-1.)

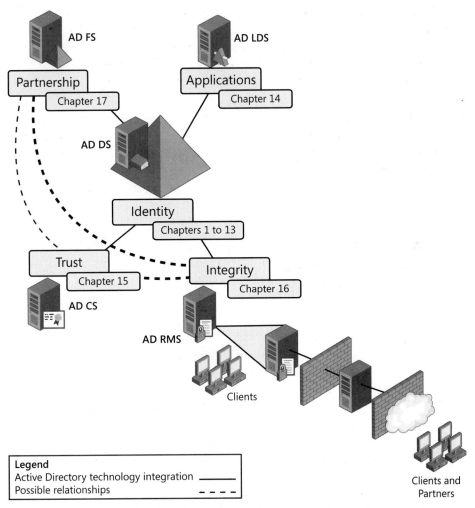

Legend
Active Directory technology integration _____
Possible relationships   - - - -

Figure 16-1   AD RMS extending the reach of authority beyond network boundaries

Exam objectives in this chapter:
- Configuring Additional Active Directory Server Roles
    - Configure Active Directory Rights Management Services (AD RMS).

Lessons in this chapter:

- Lesson 1: Understanding and Installing Active Directory Rights
  Management Services. 786
- Lesson 2: Configuring and Using Active Directory Rights Management Services . . 809

Before You Begin

To complete the lessons in this chapter, you must have done the following:

■ Installed Windows Server 2008 on a physical or virtual computer. The computer should be named SERVER01 and should be a domain controller in the *contoso.com* domain. The details for this setup are presented in Chapter 1, "Installation," and Chapter 2, "Administration."

■ Installed Windows Server 2008 Enterprise Edition on a physical or virtual computer. The computer should be named SERVER03 and should be a member server within the *contoso.com* domain. This computer will host the AD RMS policy servers you will install and create through the exercises in this chapter. Ideally, this computer will also include a D drive to store the data for AD RMS. Forty GB will be sufficient for these exercises, although Microsoft recommends 80 GB for a working AD RMS server.

■ Installed Windows Server 2008 Enterprise Edition on a physical or virtual computer. The computer should be named SERVER04 and should be a member server within the *contoso.com* domain. This computer will host the AD RMS policy servers you will install and create through the exercises in this chapter. Ideally, this computer will also include a D drive to store the data for AD RMS. Forty GB will be sufficient for these exercises, although Microsoft recommends 80 GB for a working AD RMS server.

■ Installed Windows Server 2003 Enterprise Edition on a physical or virtual computer. The computer should be named SERVER05 and should be a member server within the *contoso.com* domain. This computer will host an installation of Microsoft SQL Server 2005, which will be used to run the configuration and logging database for AD RMS. This computer would also include a D drive to store the data for SQL Server. Ten GB is recommended for the size of this drive.

MORE INFO **Create a SQL Server 2005 virtual appliance**

For information on how to create a virtual appliance with SQL Server 2005, go to *http:// itmanagement.earthweb.com/article.php/3718566.*

If you are using Microsoft Virtual PC or Virtual Server, you can also use a preconfigured virtual machine, available in a .vhd format. More information on that at *https://www.microsoft.com /downloads/details.aspx?FamilyID=7b243252-acb7-451b-822b-df639443aeaf&DisplayLang=en.*

As you can see, a thorough test of AD RMS requires quite a few computers. For this reason, using a virtual infrastructure makes the most sense. If you can, you should also add a client computer running Windows Vista and Microsoft Office 2007 so you can use the AD RMS infrastructure after it is deployed.

Real World

Danielle Ruest and Nelson Ruest

In 2007, we were asked to create a book as part of a complete series on a specific technology, covering architectures, deployment, administration, and so on. Several author teams would participate in the project, each focusing on one book.

We rushed to prepare our table of contents (TOC) and to deliver it on the due date. Having recently installed Microsoft Office 2007, we decided to use one of the new templates in Word 2007. It gave our TOC a nice, polished look. The publisher was impressed with our format and sent it to the other teams, asking them to use the same format. When all the TOCs were in, the project was presented to the board and was approved.

The author teams started working on their copy. As it turned out, however, one of the teams was very far behind on its schedule and would not be able to complete its chapters on time. Could we help the team out and write a couple of its chapters? We agreed to look at the team's TOC.

When we received the other authors' TOC, we were not surprised to see our original format. However, as we examined the TOC to determine which chapters we could help with, we found that 33 percent of our content appeared verbatim in the other authors' TOC.

We quickly called our publisher. It was never determined whether they had performed the plagiarism on purpose or by mistake, but if we had used a digital rights management technology such as AD RMS in our own TOC, this could never have happened. Although copyrights protect content ownership, they will never be as far-reaching as DRM, which ensures that content can be used only in the manner it was intended. No other technology or principle can protect information in the same way.

Lesson 1: Understanding and Installing Active Directory Rights Management Services

Many organizations choose to implement AD RMS in stages.

- The first stage focuses on internal use of intellectual property. In this stage, you concentrate on implementing proper access rights for the documentation you produce. Employees can view, read, and manage only content they are involved with. Content cannot be copied except under strict conditions.

- The second stage involves sharing content with partners. Here you begin to provide protected content to partner firms. Partners can view and access protected documents but cannot copy or otherwise share the information.

- The third stage involves a wider audience. Your intellectual property can be distributed outside the boundaries of your network in a protected mode. Because it is protected, it cannot be copied or distributed unless you give the required authorizations.

In each case, you must be sure to communicate your document protection policy fully to the people who will be working with your data. Employees must be fully trained on the solution to understand the impact of divulging information to unauthorized audiences. Partners should be provided with policy statements so they can understand how to protect your information. Then, when you reach wider audiences, you will have to make sure they also fully understand your protection policies so they can work with your information properly.

Each stage of the implementation will require additional components to further the reach of your protection strategies.

After this lesson, you will be able to:
- Understand the components that make up AD RMS services.
- Understand different AD RMS deployment scenarios.
- Understand AD RMS prerequisites for deployment.
- Install AD RMS in various scenarios.

Estimated lesson time: 40 minutes

Understanding AD RMS

As mentioned earlier, AD RMS is an updated version of the Microsoft Windows Rights Management Services available in Microsoft Windows Server 2003. With this release, Microsoft has included several new features that extend the functionality included in AD RMS. However, the scenarios you use to deploy AD RMS remain the same.

AD RMS works with a special AD RMS client to protect sensitive information. Protection is provided through the AD RMS server role, which is designed to provide certificate and licensing management. Information—configuration and logging—is persisted in a database. In test environments, you can rely on the Windows Internal Database (WID) included in Windows Server 2008, but in production environments, you should rely on a formal database engine such as Microsoft SQL Server 2005 or Microsoft SQL Server 2008 running on a separate server. This will provide the ability to load balance AD RMS through the installation of multiple servers running this role. WID does not support remote connections; therefore, only one server can use it. Internet Information Services (IIS) 7.0 provides the Web services upon which AD RMS relies, and the Microsoft Message Queuing service ensures transaction coordination in distributed environments. The AD RMS client provides access to AD RMS features on the desktop. In addition, an AD DS directory provides integrated authentication and administration. AD RMS relies on AD DS to authenticate users and verify that they are allowed to use the service. This makes up the AD RMS infrastructure. (See Figure 16-2.)

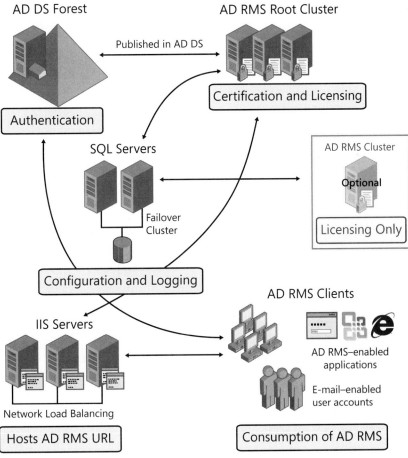

Figure 16-2 A highly available AD RMS infrastructure

The first time you install an AD RMS server, you create an AD RMS root cluster by default. A root cluster is designed to handle both certification and licensing requests. Only one root cluster can exist in an AD DS forest. You can also install licensing-only servers, which automatically form a licensing cluster. Clusters are available only if you deployed the AD RMS database on a separate server. Each time you add a new AD RMS server with either the root or the licensing role, it is automatically integrated into the corresponding existing cluster. Microsoft recommends that you rely on the root role more than on the licensing-only role for two reasons:

- Root clusters handle all AD RMS operations and are, therefore, multifunctional.
- Root and licensing-only clusters are independent; that is, they cannot share load balancing of the service. If you install all your servers as root servers, they automatically load balance each other.

After the infrastructure is in place, you can enable information-producing applications such as word processors, presentation tools, e-mail clients, and custom in-house applications to rely on AD RMS to provide information protection services. As users create the information, they define who will be able to read, write, modify, print, transfer, and otherwise manipulate the information. In addition, you can create policy templates that can apply a given configuration to documents as they are created.

Exam Tip   Keep in mind that any server installation in AD RMS automatically creates a cluster. This cluster is not to be confused with the Failover Clustering or Network Load Balancing services that are included in Windows Server 2008. The AD RMS cluster is designed to provide high availability and load balancing to ensure that the service is always available.

Usage rights are embedded directly within the documents you create so that the information remains protected even if it moves beyond your zone of authority. For example, if a protected document leaves your premises and arrives outside your network, it will remain protected because AD RMS settings are persistent. AD RMS offers a set of Web services, enabling you to extend it and integrate its features in your own information-producing applications. Because they are Web services, organizations can use them to integrate AD RMS features even in non-Windows environments.

MORE INFO   AD RMS

Find out more about AD RMS at *http://go.microsoft.com/fwlink/?LinkId=80907*.

New AD RMS Features

Active Directory Rights Management Services includes several new features:

- AD RMS is now a server role that is integrated into Windows Server 2008. In previous releases, the features supported by AD RMS were in a package that required a separate download. In addition, the Server Manager installation provides all dependencies and required component installations as well. Also, if no remote database is indicated during installation, Server Manager will automatically install Windows Internal Database.

■ As with most of the Windows Server 2008 server roles, AD RMS is administered through a Microsoft Management Console (MMC). Previous versions provided administration only through a Web interface.

■ AD RMS now also includes direct integration with Active Directory Federation Services, enabling you to extend your rights management policies beyond the firewall with your partners. This means your partners do not need their own AD RMS infrastructures and can rely on yours through AD FS to access AD RMS features. In previous releases, you could rely on only Windows Live IDs to federate RMS services. With the integration of AD RMS and AD FS, you no longer need to rely on a third party to protect information. However, to use federation, you must have an established federated trust before you install the AD RMS extension that integrates with AD FS, and you must use the latest RMS client—the Windows Vista client or the RMS client with SP2 for versions of Windows earlier than Windows Vista. For information on AD FS, see Chapter 17, "Active Directory Federation Services."

■ AD RMS servers are also self-enrolled when they are created. Enrollment creates a server licensor certificate (SLC), which grants the server the right to participate in the AD RMS structure. Earlier versions required access to the Microsoft Enrollment Center through the Internet to issue and sign the SLC. AD RMS relies on a self-enrollment certificate that is included in Windows Server 2008. Because of this, you can now run AD RMS in isolated networks without requiring Internet access of any kind.

■ Finally, AD RMS includes new administration roles so that you can delegate specific AD RMS tasks without having to grant excessive administration rights. Four local administrative roles are created:

❏ AD RMS Enterprise Administrators, which can manage all aspects of AD RMS. This group includes the user account used to install the role as well as the local administrators group.

❏ AD RMS Template Administrators, which supports the ability to read information about the AD RMS infrastructure as well as list, create, modify, and export rights policy templates.

❏ AD RMS Auditors, which enables members to manage logs and reports. Auditors have read-only access to AD RMS infrastructure information.

❏ AD RMS Service, which contains the AD RMS service account that is identified during the role installation.

Because each of these groups is local, create corresponding groups in your AD DS directory and insert these groups within the local groups on each AD RMS server. Then, when you need to grant rights to an administrative role, all you need to do is add the user's account to the group in AD DS.

Exam Tip   Delegation is an important aspect of AD RMS administration. Pay close attention to the various delegation roles and the groups that support them.

MORE INFO   **Features available in previous releases**

For information on features released in RMS before Windows Server 2008, go to *http:// go.microsoft.com/fwlink/?LinkId=68637.*

Basically, when you protect information through AD RMS, you rely on the AD RMS server to issue rights account certificates. These certificates identify the trusted entities—users, groups, computers, applications, or services—that can create and publish rights-enabled content. After a content publisher has been trusted, it can assign rights and conditions to the content it creates. Each time a user establishes a protection policy on a document, AD RMS issues a publishing license for the content. By integrating this license in the content, AD RMS binds it so that the license becomes permanently attached and no longer requires access to an AD RMS system to provide document or content protection.

Usage rights are integrated in any form of binary data that supports usage within or outside your network as well as online or offline. When content is protected, it is encrypted with special encryption keys, much like the keys created when using AD CS. To view the data, users must access it through an AD RMS–enabled browser or application. If the application is not AD RMS–enabled, users will not be able to manipulate the information because the application will not be able to read the protection policy to decrypt the data properly.

When other users access the rights-protected content, their AD RMS clients request a usage license from the server. If the user is also a trusted entity, the AD RMS server issues this use license. The use license reads the protection license for this document and applies these usage rights to the document for the duration of its lifetime.

To facilitate the publishing process, trusted users can create protection licenses from predefined templates that can be applied through the tools they are already familiar with—word processors, e-mail clients, and the like. Each template applies a specific predefined usage policy, as shown in Figure 16-3.

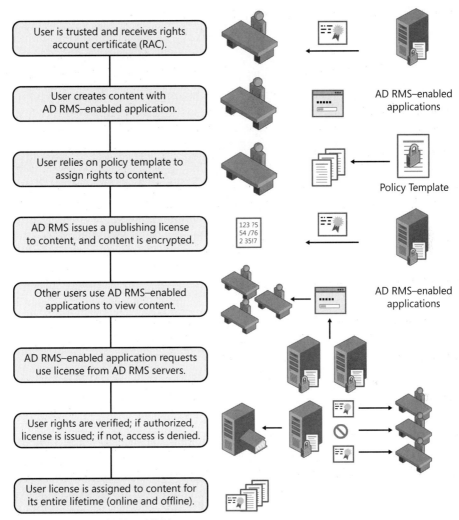

Figure 16-3   AD RMS publishing process

AD RMS Installation Scenarios

Each organization has its own needs and requirements for information protection. For this reason, AD RMS supports several deployment scenarios. These scenarios include:

- **Single server deployment** Install AD RMS on a single server. This installs the WID as the support database. Because all the components are local, you cannot scale this deployment to support high availability. Use the single server deployment only in test environments. If you want to use this deployment to test AD RMS beyond the firewall, you will have to add appropriate AD RMS exceptions.

- **Internal deployment** Install AD RMS on multiple servers tied to an AD DS directory. You must use a separate server to host the AD RMS database; otherwise, you will not be able to load balance the AD RMS role.

- **Extranet deployment** When users are mobile and do not remain within the confines of your network, you must deploy AD RMS in an extranet—a special perimeter network that provides internal services to authorized users. In this scenario, you will need to configure appropriate firewall exceptions and add a special extranet URL on an external-facing Web server to allow external client connections.

MORE INFO   AD RMS configuration in an extranet

For more information on how to configure AD RMS to collaborate outside of the organizational network, see the "Deploying Active Directory Rights Management Services in an Extranet Step-by-Step Guide" at *http://go.microsoft.com/fwlink/?LinkID=72138*.

- **Multiforest deployment** When you have existing partnerships that are based on AD DS forest trusts, you must perform a multiforest deployment. In this case, you must deploy multiple AD RMS installations, one in each forest. Then, assign a Secure Sockets Layer (SSL) certificate to each Web site that hosts the AD RMS clusters in each forest. You must also extend the AD DS forest schema to include AD RMS objects. However, if you are using Microsoft Exchange Server in each forest, the extensions will already exist. Finally, your AD RMS service account—the account that runs the service—will need to be trusted in each forest.

MORE INFO   Multiforest AD RMS deployments

For more information on this deployment model, see *http://go.microsoft.com/fwlink/?LinkId=72139*.

- **AD RMS with AD FS deployment** You can also extend the AD RMS root cluster to other forests through Active Directory Federation Services. To do so, you must prepare the following:

   1. Assign an SSL certificate to the Web site hosting the AD RMS root cluster. This will ensure secure communications between the cluster and the AD FS resource server.

2. Install the root cluster.

3. Prepare a federated trust relationship before you install the Identity Federation Support role service of AD RMS.

4. Create a claims-aware application on the AD FS resource partner server for both the certification and the licensing pipelines of AD RMS.

5. Assign the Generate Security Audits user right to the AD RMS service account.

6. Define the extranet cluster URL in AD RMS and then install the AD RMS Identity Federation Support role service through Server Manager. Have the federation URL on hand during installation.

MORE INFO   AD RMS and AD FS deployment

For more information on the AD RMS and AD FS deployment, see *http://go.microsoft.com /fwlink/?LinkId=72135*.

- **Licensing-only server deployment**   In complex forest environments, you might want to deploy a licensing-only AD RMS cluster in addition to the root cluster. In this case, you must first assign an SSL certificate to the Web site hosting the AD RMS root cluster and then install the root cluster. After you meet these conditions, you can install licensing-only servers.

MORE INFO   Set up a licensing-only AD RMS cluster

For more information on how to set up a licensing-only AD RMS cluster, see *http:// go.microsoft.com/fwlink/?LinkId=72141*.

- **Upgrade Windows RMS to AD RMS**   If you upgrade from an existing Windows RMS installation, you must perform the following activities:

1. Make sure your RMS systems are upgraded to RMS Service Pack 1 prior to the upgrade.

2. Back up all servers, and back up the configuration database. Store it in a secure location.

3. If you are using offline enrollment to set up your Windows RMS environment, make sure the enrollment is complete before the upgrade.

4. If you already have service connection points in Active Directory directory service, make sure you use the same URL for the upgrade.

5. If your Windows RMS database is running Microsoft SQL Server Desktop Engine (MSDE), you must upgrade to SQL Server before you upgrade to AD RMS.

6. Clear the RMS Message Queuing queue to make sure all messages are written to the RMS logging database prior to upgrade.

7.   Upgrade the root cluster before upgrading the licensing-only server. This will provide the root cluster's self-signed SLC to the licensing server when you upgrade it.

8.   Upgrade all other servers in the RMS cluster.

These scenarios provide the most common deployment structures for AD RMS.

Installing Active Directory Rights Management Services

A full installation of AD RMS can be quite complex. Keep in mind that a single cluster can exist within an AD DS forest and make sure you have all the prerequisites in place before you proceed. Also, because of the AD RMS dependencies, these prerequisites are comprehensive. During this preparation process, you'll be deciding how to deploy your AD RMS systems. Will you be using only root cluster members, or will you be dividing tasks between root and licensing-only clusters? Do you need interaction with outside partners? Will your deployment be internal only? Answers to each of these questions will help form the architecture of your AD RMS deployment and implementation.

After you have all the prerequisites in place, you can proceed to the actual installation. This is a multistep operation that requires care and attention.

MORE INFO   AD RMS cluster installation instructions

For more information on the installation of AD RMS clusters, go to *http://technet2.microsoft.com /windowsserver2008/en/library/3f1d6d09-4e85-4ad9-83ff-a8720b5441d61033.mspx?mfr=true*.

Preparing AD RMS Installation Prerequisites

There are several prerequisites to AD RMS installation. If you are setting up only a test environment, you have few items to consider, but when you are ready to deploy AD RMS into a production environment, you will want to take the utmost care to deploy it correctly. For this reason, endeavor to make your test environment match the requirements of your production environment so that no surprises pop up when you perform the actual deployment.

IMPORTANT   Additional AD RMS installation options

Note that AD RMS is not supported and does not run in Server Core installations of Windows Server 2008. However, AD RMS is a good candidate for virtualization under Hyper-V, especially in test environments. Keep this in mind when you plan and prepare your AD RMS deployment.

Begin with the prerequisites. Table 16-1 outlines the basic requirements for an AD RMS deployment. Table 16-2 outlines other considerations you need to keep in mind when preparing for AD RMS.

Table 16-1   RMS System Requirements

Hardware/Software	Requirement	Recommended
Processor	One Pentium, 4.3 GHz or higher	Two Pentium, 4.3 GHz or higher
RAM	512 MB	1024 MB
Hard disk space	40 GB	80 GB
Operating system	Any Windows Server 2008 edition except Windows Server Web Edition and Itanium-based systems	Windows Server Enterprise Edition or Windows Server Datacenter Edition
File system	FAT32 or NTFS	NTFS
Messaging	Message Queuing	
Web Services	IIS with ASP.NET enabled	

Table 16-2   AD RMS Considerations

Component	Consideration
Web Server URL	Reserve URLs that will not change and do not include a computer name nor use localhost. Also, use different URLs for internal and external connections.
Active Directory Domain Services	An AD DS domain running on Windows 2000 SP3, Windows Server 2003, or Windows Server 2008. Upgrade or run a new AD DS domain on Windows Server 2008 if possible.
Installation location	AD RMS must be installed in the same domain as its potential users. If possible, install a multidomain forest and install AD RMS in the child production domain.
Domain User accounts	E-mail address configured in AD DS.
Service Account	Standard domain user account that is a member of the local Administrators group. Domain-based service account that is assigned the Generate Security Audits user right.
Installation Account	A domain-based account. Must not be on a smart card. Must have local administrator privileges. To generate service connection points, must be a member of Enterprise Admins. To use an external database, must be a member of System Administrators role on DB server.

Table 16-2 AD RMS Considerations

Component	Consideration
Database server	Windows Internal Database or SQL Server 2005 with SP2 or later, including stored procedures to perform operations. For fault tolerance, use SQL Server 2005 with SP2 installed on a separate computer.
Database instance	Create and name the AD RMS database instance and start the SQL Server Browser service before installation.
Installation certificate	Obtain an SSL certificate for the AD RMS cluster. Use certificates only in testing environments. Obtain a trusted certificate from an external third-party commercial CA and install the certificate prior to the AD RMS installation.
Cluster key protection	Store the cluster key in the AD RMS configuration database. If possible, use a hardware protection device to store the cluster key and install it on each server before you install the AD RMS role.
DNS configuration	Create custom CNAME records for the root cluster URL and the database server. Use separate CNAME records for the AD RMS cluster URL and for the database server to protect against system loss.
Server licensor certificate name	Prepare an official name before you install. Use an official name, for example, the name of your organization.
AD RMS–enabled client	AD RMS–enabled browser or application (Word, Microsoft Office Outlook, or PowerPoint in Office 2007 Enterprise Edition, Office 2007 Professional Plus, or Office 2007 Ultimate Edition)
Smart card usage	Can be integrated in AD RMS but not for setup. Do not use a smart card for the installation account, or the account will fail.
Client OS	Windows Vista includes AD RMS client by default; XP requires Windows RMS Client with SP2.

Exam Tip Pay attention to the installation prerequisites in Table 16-1 as well as the considerations in Table 16-2. They are complex and, because of this, will certainly appear on the exam.

NOTE AD RMS client for Windows XP

To obtain the AD RMS client for Windows XP, go to *http://www.microsoft.com/downloads/details.aspx? FamilyId=02DA5107-2919-414B-A5A3-3102C7447838&displaylang=en*.

As you can see from Table 16-1, installing AD RMS in a production environment is not a trivial matter.

MORE INFO **Hardware and software considerations for AD RMS**

For more information, see "Pre-installation Information for Active Directory Rights Management Services" at *http://go.microsoft.com/fwlink/?LinkId=84733*.

Understanding AD RMS Certificates

Because it encrypts and signs data, AD RMS, like AD CS, relies on certificates and assigns these certificates to the various users in the AD RMS infrastructure. It also uses licenses that are in an Extensible Rights Markup Language (XrML) format. Because these licenses are embedded in the content users create, they are also a form of certificate. Like AD CS, the AD RMS hierarchy forms a chain of trust that validates the certificate or license when it is used. Table 16-3 outlines the various certificates you require in an AD RMS infrastructure.

Table 16-3   AD RMS Certificates

Certificate	Content
Server licensor certificate (SLC)	The SLC is a self-signed certificate generated during the AD RMS setup of the first server in a root cluster. Other members of the root cluster will share this SLC. If you create a licensing-only cluster, it will generate its own SLC and share it with members of its cluster. The default duration for an SLC is 250 years.
Rights account certificate (RAC)	RACs are issued to trusted users who have an e-mail-enabled account in AD DS. RACs are generated when the user first tries to open rights-protected content. Standard RACs identify users in relation to their computers and have a duration of 365 days. Temporary RACs do not tie the user to a specific computer and are valid for only 15 minutes. The RAC contains the public key of the user as well as his or her private key. The private key is encrypted with the computer's private key. (See "Machine certificate," listed later in this table.)
Client licensor certificate (CLC)	After the user has a RAC and launches an AD RMS–enabled application, the application automatically sends a request for a CLC to the AD RMS cluster. The client computer must be connected for this process to work, but after the CLC is obtained, the user can apply AD RMS policies even offline. Because the CLC is tied to the client's RAC, it is automatically invalidated if the RAC is revoked. The CLC includes the client licensor public key, the client licensor private key that is encrypted by the user's public key, and the AD RMS cluster's public key. The CLC private key is used to encrypt content.

Table 16-3   AD RMS Certificates

Certificate	Content
Machine certificate	The first time an AD RMS–enabled application is used, a machine certificate is created. The AD RMS client in Windows automatically manages this process with the AD RMS cluster. This certificate creates a lockbox on the computer to correlate the machine certificate with the user's profile. The machine certificate contains the public key for the activated computer. The private key is contained within the lockbox on the computer.
Publishing license	The publishing license is created when the user saves content in a rights-protected mode. This license lists which users can use the content and under which conditions as well as the rights each user has to the content. This license includes the symmetric content key for decrypting content as well as the public key of the cluster.
Use license	The use license is assigned to a user who opens rights-protected content. It is tied to the user's RAC and lists the access rights the user has to the content. If the RAC is not available, the user cannot work with rights-protected content. It contains the symmetric key for decrypting content. This key is encrypted with the public key of the user.

Exam Tip   Pay attention to the different certificates and licenses used in AD RMS. They are good candidates for exam questions.

Installation Procedure

Now that you understand the various requirements and processes that make up an AD RMS installation, you are ready to proceed. Ensure that you have prepared all the requirements listed in Table 16-1, and then perform the following steps.

Install AD RMS

1. Log on to a member server running Windows Server 2008, using Enterprise Administrative credentials.

   This server can be running Windows Server 2008 Standard Edition, Windows Server 2008 Enterprise Edition, or Windows Server 2008 Datacenter Edition.

IMPORTANT **Use member servers**

Do not install AD RMS on a domain controller. Use a member server only! With the advent of virtualization, aside from the operating system licensing aspect, there is no longer any reason to create multipurpose domain controllers. Each virtual machine can have its own purpose and run independently of all other services.

---

2. Launch Server Manager from the Administrative Tools program group.

3. Right-click the Roles node in the tree pane, and select Add Roles.

4. Review the Before You Begin information, and click Next.

5. On the Select Server Roles page, select Active Directory Rights Management Services, and click Next.

    The Add Role Wizard will ask you to add the Web Server (IIS) role with the required features, Windows Process Activation Service (WPAS), and Message Queuing.

6. Click Add Required Role Services if these services weren't installed prior to the installation of AD RMS. Click Next when you are ready.

7. On the Active Directory Rights Management Services page, review the information about the selected role, and then click Next.

8. On the Select Role Services page, make sure the Active Directory Rights Management Server check box is selected, and then click Next.

    Do not choose the Identity Federation Support option at this time. You cannot install this option until the AD FS federation relationship has been created.

9. On the Create Or Join An AD RMS Cluster page, select Create A New AD RMS Cluster option, and then click Next.

    If the cluster was already created and you were installing a second server, you would select Join An Existing AD RMS cluster because there can be only one cluster per forest.

10. On the Select Configuration Database page, select the Use A Different Database Server, and then click Next.

    If you choose to use Windows Internal Database to host the AD RMS databases for a single-server installation, steps 11 and 12 are not required. Keep in mind that when you use a WID instance, you will not be able to join other servers to this cluster. Use WID only in test environments if you do not have the resources to create a proper database server.

11. Click Select to locate the server that hosts the database, type the name, and then click Check Names. Click OK.

12. In the Database Instance drop-down list, select the appropriate instance, click Validate, and then click Next.

13. On the Specify Service Account page, click Specify, type the domain user account and password that should be used as the AD RMS service account, click OK, and then click Next.

    Remember that this account must be a member of the local Administrators group.

14. On the Configure AD RMS Cluster Key Storage page, select Use CSP Key Storage, and then click Next.

    You choose to protect the AD RMS cluster key by using a cryptographic storage provider because it is a more secure protection method. You will need to select the storage provider and then install this certificate on each new AD RMS server before you can add them to the root cluster. You can also store the key in the AD RMS database, but doing so is less secure than with a cryptographic service provider (CSP).

15. On the Specify AD RMS Cluster Key page, select the CSP to use. You can select either software or hardware cryptographic service providers. Use the one that best fits your security policy guidelines, and select Create A New Key With The Selected CSP. Click Next.

    You can also use an existing key, but do so only when you are recovering from an unrecoverable configuration database.

16. On the Select AD RMS Cluster Web Site page, select the Web site where you want to install the AD RMS Web services, and click Next. If you did not prepare the Web site beforehand, the name of the Web site will be Default Web Site.

17. On the Specify Cluster Address page, select Use An SSL-Encrypted Connection (https://).

    As a security best practice, the AD RMS cluster should be provisioned by using an SSL-encrypted connection. You should be using a certificate provided by a third-party commercial certification authority (CA) so that it can be automatically trusted by all parties. This certificate should already be installed on the server so that you can select it as you proceed through the installation.

    Do not use an unencrypted connection. You cannot rely on open connections if you intend to use Identity Federation for your AD RMS implementation.

18. In the Internal Address section of the Specify Cluster Address page, type the fully qualified domain name (FQDN) of the AD RMS cluster, and click Validate. If validation succeeds, click Next.

    This must be a valid FQDN, which cannot be changed afterward. If you want to change the default port on which AD RMS communicates, you can do it on this page of the wizard as well. You must do it now because you will not be able to change it at a later date.

19. Click Validate, and then click Next.

20. On the Choose A Server Authentication Certificate For SSL Encryption page, select Choose An Existing Certificate For SSL Encryption (Recommended), select the certificate you installed, and then click Next.

If you did not install the certificate prior to setup, you can click Import to import the certificate now. You can also use a self-signed certificate, or, if you did not obtain the certificate prior to installation, you can select the third option, to choose encryption later. Note, however, that you will not be able to complete your installation until you obtain and install this certificate if you choose the last option.

IMPORTANT   Self-signed certificates

Self-signed certificates should be used for test environments only. In a production environment, use a proper SSL certificate issued from a commercial certification authority.

---

21. On the Name The Server Licensor Certificate page, type a valid name to identify the AD RMS cluster, and then click Next.

22. On the Register AD RMS Service Connection Point page, select Register The AD RMS Service Connection Point Now, and then click Next.

    This action will register the AD RMS service connection point (SCP) in the AD DS.

IMPORTANT   Access rights for SCP creation

To register the AD RMS SCP, you must be logged on to the AD RMS server, using a user account with write access to the Services container in AD DS—that is, a member of the Enterprise Admins group.

If you are preparing the cluster and need to install additional cluster members before it starts servicing requests, select Register The AD RMS Service Connection Point Later. Then join the other cluster member and, when you are ready, create the SCP.

23. On the Web Server (IIS) page, review the information about IIS, and click Next.

    The pages mentioned in steps 23 and 24 are available only if IIS is not preinstalled on the server.

24. On the next page, keep the Web server default selections, and click Next.

25. On the Confirm Installation Selections page, review your choices, and click Install.

26. When the installation is complete, click Finish to close the installation wizard. Log off and log back on to update the permissions granted to the logged-on user account.

    The user account logged on when the AD RMS server role was installed is automatically made a member of the AD RMS Enterprise Administrators group. This gives you access to all AD RMS operations.

    The installation is complete. (See Figure 16-4.)

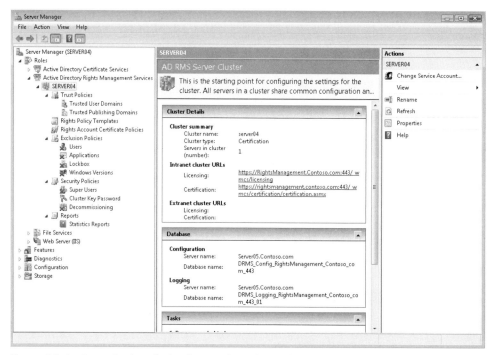

Figure 16-4   Once the installation is complete, the entire AD RMS tree structure becomes available in Service Manager

---

MORE INFO   AD RMS cluster

For more information on how to install an AD RMS cluster, see *http://technet2.microsoft.com /windowsserver2008/en/library/74272acc-0f2d-4dc2-876f-15b156a0b4e01033.mspx?mfr=true*. For a step-by-step installation guide, see *http://go.microsoft.com/fwlink/?LinkId=72134*. To provide high availability for the cluster, you must install additional cluster members. For information on this installation, go to *http://technet2.microsoft.com/windowsserver2008/en/library /1bc393b9-5ce9-4950-acae-63a463ccfc361033.mspx?mfr=true*.

PRACTICE Installing AD RMS

In this practice, you will install AD RMS into a new cluster. First, you must add a DNS record. In the following exercises, you will create the service account and the AD RMS role groups in the directory, create and install a Web Server certificate, and then proceed to the installation. Be sure the computers listed in the "Before You Begin" section of this chapter are running before you proceed. You need SERVER01, SERVER04, and SERVER05 for this practice.

▶ Exercise 1   Prepare the DNS Record

In this exercise, you will create a CNAME record to prepare for the AD RMS cluster URL.

1. Log on to SERVER01, using the domain Administrator account.
2. Launch Server Manager from the Administrative Tools program group.
3. Expand Roles\DNS Server\DNS\SERVER01\Forward Lookup Zones\contoso.com.
4. Right-click in the details pane, and select New Alias (CNAME).
5. In the New Resource Record dialog box, type an alias name of **RightsManagement** and assign it to SERVER04.contoso.com in the Fully Qualified Domain Name (FQDN) For Target Host section of the dialog box. Click OK.

    You have created a new record for the AD RMS cluster URL. It will be updated to other servers as you perform the other exercises.

▶ Exercise 2   Prepare the Directory

In this exercise, you will create a service account and four groups for AD RMS administration delegation.

1. Log on to SERVER01, using the domain Administrator account, if you haven't done so already.
2. Launch Server Manager from the Administrative Tools program group.
3. Expand Roles\Active Directory Domain Services\Active Directory Users and Computers \contoso.com. Create the Admins\Service Identities OU structure.
4. Right-click the Service Identities OU, choose New, and then select User.
5. Name the user **ADRMSService** and use this name for both the logon and the pre–Windows 2000 logon names. Click Next.
6. Assign a complex password, clear User Must Change Password At Next Logon, and select Password Never Expires. Click Next, and then click Finish to create the account.
7. Now create the AD RMS administration groups under Contoso.com\Admins\Admin Groups\Server Delegations OU. Create these OUs if they are not already created.
8. Create four global security groups. Right-click in the details pane, select New, and then choose Group. Type the name, and click OK. Create the following four groups:
    ❑ AD RMS Enterprise Administrators
    ❑ AD RMS Template Administrators
    ❑ AD RMS Auditors
    ❑ AD RMS Service Account
9. Open the AD RMS Service Account group (right-click and choose Properties), and click the Members tab. Add the ADRMSService account to this group, and then click OK.
10. Log on to SERVER03, using the domain Administrator account, if you have not done so already.
11. Launch Server Manager from the Administrative Tools program group.

12. Expand Configuration\Local Users and Groups\Groups.

13. Select the Administrators group, and open it.

14. Add the AD RMS Service Account group to this group, and click OK.

    You are ready to proceed with the installation.

▶ **Exercise 3   Prepare a Web Server Certificate**

Because AD RMS requires SSL-encrypted Web connections, you must create and install a Web server certificate before you can proceed with the installation. Note that for this practice to work, you must have performed the practices in Chapter 15, "Active Directory Certificate Services and Public Key Infrastructures," first.

1. Log on to SERVER04, using the domain Administrator account.

   This will grant you Enterprise Administrator credentials, which are required to create the SCP. These rights are required for Exercise 4.

2. Launch Server Manager from the Administrative Tools program group.

3. Expand Roles\Active Directory Certificate Services\Certificate Templates (SERVER04).

   Note that all the existing templates are listed in the details pane.

4. Select the Web Server template in the details pane, and right-click it to select Duplicate Template.

5. Select the version of Windows Server to support, in this case, Windows Server 2008, and click OK.

6. Name the template **Web Server WS08** and set the following options. Leave all other options as is.

   a. On the General tab, make sure you select Publish Certificate In Active Directory.

   b. On the Security tab, add the computer account for SERVER04. Click Add, click Object Types, select Computers, and then click OK.

   c. Type **SERVER04**, click Check Names, click OK, and then click OK.

   d. Grant SERVER04 the Allow:Read and Enroll permissions, and click OK.

   e. Leave all other settings as is.

7. Click OK.

   Template issuance is performed in the Certification Authority console section of Server Manager.

8. Expand Roles\Active Directory Certificate Services\Contoso-*issuing-serve*\Certificate Templates.

9. To issue a template, right-click Certificate Templates, choose New, and then select Certificate Template To Issue.

10. In the Enable Certificate Templates dialog box, select Web Server WS08, and click OK.

▶ **Exercise 4   Install a Web Server Certificate**

Now, you need to request and install the certificate.

1. Move to the Start menu, type **mmc** in the Search box, and then press Enter.
2. Click Add/Remove Snap-ins from the File menu, select the Certificates snap-in, and click Add.
3. Choose Computer Account, and click Next.
4. Make sure Local Computer is selected, click Finish, and then OK.
5. Click Save As from the File menu, navigate to your Documents folder, and name it **Computer Certificates**.
6. Expand the Certificates (Local Computer)\Persona l\Certificates node.
7. Right-click Certificates, select All Tasks, and then choose Request New Certificate. Click Next.
8. Select the Web Server WS08 certificate, and then click More Information to enroll for this certificate.
9. In the Certificate Properties dialog box, on the Subject tab, add the following values:
   a. In the *Subject Name Value* field, ensure that Full DN is selected, type **CN=SERVER04,DC=Contoso,DC=com**, and then click Add.
   b. Click the Alternative Name section, select URL in the Type drop-down list, enter **RightsManagement.contoso.com** in the *Value* field, and then click Add.
   c. Click the General tab and type **Contoso DRM** in the *Friendly Name* field and **Web Server Certificate** in the *Description* field.
   d. Click the Private Key tab, expand the Key Options section, and select the Make Private Key Exportable and Allow Private Key To Be Archived check boxes.
10. Click OK, and then click Enroll. Click Finish.
11. To verify that the certificate has been issued, click Certificates, and view the certificate in the details pane.
12. Close the Certificates console.

    You are ready to install AD RMS.

▶ **Exercise 5   Install an AD RMS Root Cluster**

Ensure that you have at least SERVER01, SERVER03, and SERVER05 running, and make sure the SQL server on SERVER05 is also running. SERVER03 is the server you used to perform the practice operations in Chapter 15. Because of this, it should include AD CS and already have a certificate that you can use during this operation.

1. Log on to SERVER03, using the domain Administrator account. This will grant you Enterprise Administrator credentials, which are required to create the SCP.
2. Launch Server Manager from the Administrative Tools program group.

3. Right-click the Roles node in the tree pane, and select Add Roles.

4. Review the Before You Begin information, and click Next.

5. On the Select Server Roles page, select Active Directory Rights Management Services.

   The Add Role Wizard will ask you to add the Web Server (IIS) role with the required features, Windows Process Activation Service (WPAS), and Message Queuing.

6. Click Add Required Role Services if these services weren't installed prior to the installation of AD RMS. Click Next.

7. On the Active Directory Rights Management Services page, review the information about the selected role, and then click Next.

8. On the Select Role Services page, ensure that the Active Directory Rights Management Server is selected, and then click Next.

9. On the Create Or Join An AD RMS Cluster page, select Create A New AD RMS Cluster, and then click Next.

10. On the Select Configuration Database page, select the Use A Different Database Server, and then click Next.

    If you choose to use Windows Internal Database to host the AD RMS databases for a single-server installation, steps 11 and 12 are not required. However, using WID is valid for test purposes only.

11. Click Select to locate SERVER05, type the server name, click Check Names, and then click OK.

12. In Database Instance, select the Default instance, click Validate, and then click Next.

13. On the Specify Service Account page, click Specify, type **ADRMSService** and its password, click OK, and then click Next.

14. On the Configure AD RMS Cluster Key Storage page, select Use AD RMS Centrally Managed Key Storage, and then click Next.

    You choose to protect the AD RMS cluster key by using that database because it simplifies the exercise and does not require additional components; however, normally, you should provide the best protection for this key, through a CSP provider.

15. On the Specify AD RMS Cluster Key Password page, type a strong password, confirm it, and then click Next.

16. On the Select AD RMS Cluster Web Site page, select Default Web Site, and then click Next.

17. On the Specify Cluster Address the page, select Use An SSL-Encrypted Connection (https://).

    As a security best practice, the AD RMS cluster should be provisioned by using an SSL-encrypted connection.

18. In the Internal Address section, type **RightsManagement.contoso.com**, leave the port number as is, and click Validate. When the validation succeeds, click Next.

19. On the Choose A Server Authentication Certificate For SSL Encryption page, select Choose An Existing Certificate For SSL Encryption (Recommended), select the SERVER04 certificate, and click Next.

    If you have not run through the practice exercises in Chapter 15 yet, and the server does not include an appropriate certificate or AD CS, use a self-signed certificate.

20. On the Name The Server Licensor Certificate page, type **Contoso DRM** to identify the AD RMS cluster, and then click Next.

21. On the Register AD RMS Service Connection Point page, select Register The AD RMS Service Connection Point Now, and then click Next.

    This action will register the AD RMS service connection point (SCP) in AD DS.

22. On the Web Server (IIS) page, review the information about IIS, and then click Next.

23. On the Select Role Services page, keep the Web server default selections, and click Next.

24. On the Confirm Installation Selections page, review your choices, and then click Install.

25. When the installation is complete, click Finish to close the installation wizard.

26. Log off and log back on to update the permissions granted to the logged-on user account.

    The user account that is logged on when the AD RMS server role is installed is automatically made a member of the AD RMS Enterprise Administrators group. This gives you access to all AD RMS operations. Your installation is complete.

IMPORTANT AD RMS administration groups

To render the administration groups you created in AD DS operational, you must add them to the respective local groups on this server. In a production environment, you need to perform this additional step to complete your setup.

Lesson Summary

- AD RMS is designed to provide support for data protection services through digital rights management. To do so, it relies on a complex infrastructure that requires additional services such as AD DS, SQL Server, Internet Information Services, and, potentially, AD FS for interforest partnerships.

- Users must have an e-mail–enabled account in an AD DS domain to use AD RMS services.

- Users must also rely on AD RMS–enabled applications to protect content. These applications can be productivity tools such as Office Word, Outlook, PowerPoint, Internet Explorer, or a custom AD RMS–enabled application. Without the application, you cannot view or work with protected content.

- Windows Vista includes the AD RMS client by default, but Windows XP does not. In Windows XP, you must download and install Windows Rights Management Client with SP2.

Lesson Review

You can use the following questions to test your knowledge of the information in Lesson 1, "Understanding and Installing Active Directory Rights Management Services." The questions are also available on the companion CD if you prefer to review them in electronic form.

NOTE Answers

Answers to these questions and explanations of why each answer choice is right or wrong are located in the "Answers" section at the end of the book.

1. You are an administrator for the *contoso.com* domain. You have just finished installing AD RMS, and now you want to configure AD RMS. Setup has completed without any errors. However, when you begin working with the AD RMS server, you get an error message. What could be the problem?

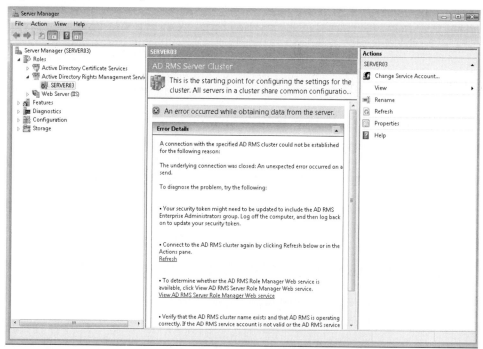

A. Your server is not running AD RMS.

B. The server certificate is invalid, and, because of this, the AD RMS server will not start.

C. Your server is not a member of an AD DS domain.

D. Your account does not have appropriate privileges to manage AD RMS.

Lesson 2: Configuring and Using Active Directory Rights Management Services

AD RMS installations can be complex to prepare, but after you have worked with the proper installation preparation process, your installations will be flawless. After your servers are installed, however, you must complete the configuration of the AD RMS cluster and prepare the usage policies you want to implement in your network. This involves several tasks:

- If you want to make AD RMS available outside your network, you must add an extranet cluster URL to your configuration.
- If you want to integrate AD RMS services with partners, you must configure proxy settings and install Identity Federation Support. Keep in mind that you must have a working AD FS implementation to add these components to your infrastructure. You must also configure trust policies for the interoperation of your AD RMS cluster with other clusters.
- You must configure the various AD RMS certificates to ensure that you set up proper validation periods.
- If your organization has decided that your rights-protection policies will not affect the entire organization and will target only a specific group of users or departments, for example, the legal department, you must configure exclusion policies.
- You must prepare user accounts for integration with AD RMS.
- You must prepare policy templates for your organization to use. These templates will facilitate the rights-protection process for your users.
- You must be familiar with the various AD RMS clients so that you can support them if your users experience problems with it.
- AD RMS relies on three databases for operation. You must be aware of these databases and maintain them for a proper AD RMS operation.

These operations will finalize the deployment of your AD RMS cluster.

After this lesson, you will be able to:
- Configure extranet URLs.
- Prepare for integration with partners.
- Work with AD RMS certificates.
- Prepare user accounts for AD RMS.
- Prepare exclusion policies.
- Work with policy templates.
- Work with the AD RMS databases.

Estimated lesson time: 30 minutes

Configuring AD RMS

AD RMS configuration, unlike Windows Rights Management Services, is performed through the MMC. This console is integrated in Server Manager but is also available as a standalone console through Remote Server Administration Tools (RSAT). Each of the tasks you need to perform to finalize your configuration is available through this console.

MORE INFO   Configure AD RMS

For more information on configuring AD RMS, go to *http://technet2.microsoft.com /windowsserver2008/en/library/73829489-45f1-415b-90ab-061a263d1ef61033.mspx?mfr=true*.

Creating an Extranet URL

When you want to extend your AD RMS infrastructure to mobile users or teleworkers outside your internal network, you must configure an extranet URL. Use the following procedure.

1. Log on to a server that is a member of the root cluster, using AD RMS Enterprise Administrators credentials.
2. Launch Server Manager from the Administrative Tools program group.
3. Expand Roles\Active Directory Rights Management Services*servername*.
4. Right-click the server name, and choose Properties.
5. Click the Cluster URLs tab.
6. On the Cluster URLs page, enable Extranet URLs, and add the appropriate URL data for both Licensing and Certification.

   These URLs must point to a valid IIS installation in the extranet and should be permanent. Proper DNS registration should also be implemented for these URLs. Use SSL encryption for the communication through Secure HTTP or HTTPS connections. Finally, remember to create the appropriate virtual directories to host the AD RMS data.
7. Click OK to close the dialog box and apply the change.

   Your extranet URLs are ready.

Configuring Trust Policies

Although you can't enable federation support until you have a working AD FS infrastructure in place, you can learn about the various models AD RMS supports to provide federation of your DRM policies. AD RMS can support four trust models:

- Trusted user domains enable your AD RMS cluster to process requests for other AD RMS clusters located in different AD DS forests. Trusted user domains are added by importing the server licensor certificate from the AD RMS cluster you want to trust into your own cluster.

- Trusted publishing domains enable your own AD RMS cluster to issue use licenses for content that was protected by another AD RMS cluster. To create a trusted publishing domain, you must import the publishing cluster's SLC as well as its private key into your own cluster.
- Windows Live ID trusts enable users who have a valid Windows Live ID (formerly known as Microsoft Passport) to use rights-protected content but not to create it.
- Federated trusts are established through AD FS and extend the operation of your AD RMS cluster to the forests with which you have established a federated trust.

Each of these trust types extends your AD RMS authority beyond the limits of your own forest.

MORE INFO Create AD RMS trusts

To learn more about working with AD RMS trusts, go to *http://technet2.microsoft.com /windowsserver2008/en/library/67d89efe-28f6-422e-b0e3-e85da40a04f01033.mspx?mfr=true.*

Exporting the Server Licensor Certificate

To work with either trusted publishing domains or trusted user domains, you must export the server licensor certificate from your root cluster or from the root cluster to be trusted. Certificates are exported to be used in establishing trusts. To perform this procedure, you need to be a member of the local AD RMS Enterprise Administrators or its equivalent.

1. Log on to a server that is a member of the root cluster, using AD RMS Enterprise Administrators credentials.
2. Launch Server Manager from the Administrative Tools program group.
3. Expand Roles\Active Directory Rights Management Services*servername*.
4. Right-click the server name, and choose Properties.
5. Click the Server Certificate Tab, and click Export Certificate.
6. In the Export Certificate As dialog box, type a valid name, for example, the name of your cluster, and select a proper location such as your Documents folder to create the .bin file. Click Save.
7. Close the Properties dialog box.
   Protect this certificate thoroughly because it controls access to your AD RMS cluster.

Preparing AD RMS Certificates

Certificates are created by default during the installation of AD RMS. However, you must configure appropriate certificate duration based on your rights-protection policies. Four activities can be performed in terms of certificate administration:

- Specify the duration of rights account certificates.
- Enable certification for mobile devices.

- Enable certification of server services.
- Authenticate clients through smart cards.

Of these, the one you must absolutely set is the validation period for the RAC. Others are optional operations that depend on your rights-protection policies. To modify the duration of the RAC, use the following procedure.

1. Log on to a server that is a member of the root cluster, using AD RMS Enterprise Administrators credentials.
2. Launch Server Manager from the Administrative Tools program group.
3. Expand Roles\Active Directory Rights Management Services*servername*.
4. Click Change Standard RAC Validity Period in the details pane.
5. Click the Standard RAC tab, and set the number of days to enable the certificate in the Standard RAC Validity Period section of the dialog box.
6. Click the Temporary RAC tab and set the number of minutes to enable the certificate in the Temporary RAC Validity Period section of the dialog box.
7. Click OK to close the dialog box.

Note that standard RACs are valid for 365 days by default, and temporary RACs last only 15 minutes. You might want to extend the duration of a temporary RAC, but be careful about extending the validity of a standard RAC because one year is already a considerable time.

Note that if you are using federated trusts, you will need to modify the RAC validity period under the Federated Identity Support node, not under the root cluster node.

MORE INFO   **Managing certificates**

For more information on working with the other certificate types, go to *http://technet2.microsoft.com /windowsserver2008/en/library/5eb527a9-34d8-464f-9735-e7dcd2613ffc1033.mspx.*

Preparing Exclusion Policies

When you decide the scope of your rights-protection policy implementation, you can configure exclusion policies or policies that will exclude users and computers from participating in your AD RMS implementation. You can create exclusion policies for four entities: users, applications, lockboxes, and Windows operating systems. When you do so, the list of the specified exclusion members is included in the use license for the content. You can remove an excluded entity from an exclusion list, but remember that if you remove the entity from the list, it will no longer be added to the use licenses. Existing content, however, will already contain it because use licenses are issued only once, by default. Because of this, keep three items in mind when preparing exclusion lists:

- Assign only exclusions that will be as permanent as possible.
- If you change your mind, wait until existing use licenses have expired before removing entities from an exclusion list.
- Rely on exclusion lists if the credentials of one of the supported entities, such as a user, have been compromised, and your rights protected content is at risk.

When you have decided to create an exclusion list, use the procedure that follows. In this case, you will exclude users from AD RMS.

1. Log on to a server that is a member of the root cluster, using AD RMS Enterprise Administrators credentials.
2. Launch Server Manager from the Administrative Tools program group.
3. Expand Roles\Active Directory Rights Management Services*servername*\Exclusion Policies\Users.
4. Click Enable User Exclusion in the Actions pane. This enables exclusion.
5. To exclude users, click Exclude User in the Actions pane. This launches the Exclude User Account Wizard.

   You can exclude a user either through the e-mail address or through the public key assigned to the user. The first is for users included in your AD DS directory, and the second is for external users who might not have an account in your AD DS directory. If you exclude users in your AD DS directory, make sure you exclude a group so that it is easier to manage as time goes on.
6. Select the appropriate exclusion method, either locate the user account or type in the public key string, and then click Next.
7. Click Finish to close the wizard.

Use the same node to remove the exclusion if you need to. Use the same process for other exclusion types.

Quick Check

1. How many root clusters can you deploy in an Active Directory Domain Services forest?
2. What is the difference between a root cluster and a licensing-only cluster, and which is preferable to use?
3. Which delegation roles does AD RMS support?

Quick Check Answers

1. You can deploy only a single AD RMS root cluster per AD DS forest. This is because AD RMS creates an SCP during installation, and only one SCP can exist per forest.

2. The root cluster offers all AD RMS, whereas the licensing-only cluster simply manages licenses. Licensing-only clusters are designed to support the root cluster role, but if you are given a choice, you should deploy only root clusters. This creates a single AD RMS cluster on your network and simplifies management while providing all the functionality you require. Use licensing-only clusters in rare occasions when root-only deployments are not practical.

3. AD RMS supports four delegation roles:

    ❑ AD RMS Enterprise Administrators can manage every aspect of AD RMS.

    ❑ AD RMS Template Administrators can prepare and modify protection templates.

    ❑ AD RMS Auditors have read-only access to AD RMS logs.

    ❑ AD RMS Service Account is designed to grant proper access rights to the AD RMS service account.

MORE INFO   Exclusion policies

To learn more about exclusion policies, go to *http://technet2.microsoft.com/windowsserver2008/en /library/3a612201-7302-419b-86b2-3bde6d448d4e1033.mspx?mfr=true*.

Preparing Accounts and Access Rights

To ensure that your users can work with AD RMS, you must prepare their accounts. When you do so, AD RMS includes the account within its own database. However, when you remove an account, AD RMS disables the account but does not automatically remove it from its database. Because of this, the database can become large and contain obsolete data. To protect against this, either create a stored procedure in SQL Server that will automatically remove the account when you delete it or create a script that will do so on a scheduled basis.

In addition, you might need to create a special Super Users group that will contain operators that have full access to all the content protected by your AD RMS implementation. Members of this Super Users group are much like the recovery agents you would use for the Encrypting File System (EFS). These users can recover or modify any data that is managed by your AD RMS infrastructure and can, therefore, recover data from users who have left the organization. You should usually assign a Universal Group from your directory to this role. Prepare the Universal Group before enabling Super Users in AD RMS. To configure a Super User group to work with AD RMS, use the following procedure.

1. Log on to a server that is a member of the root cluster, using AD RMS Enterprise Administrators credentials.
2. Launch Server Manager from the Administrative Tools program group.
3. Expand Roles\Active Directory Rights Management Services*servername*\Security Policies.
4. Click Change Super Users Settings in the details pane.
5. In the Actions pane, click Enable Super Users.
6. Click Change Super Users Group in the details pane to view the Super User Group Property sheet.
7. Type the e-mail address of a mail-enabled universal distribution group from your forest or use the Browse button to locate it.
8. Click OK to close the Property sheet.

Members of this group will now have access to all AD RMS content. Select these members very carefully and ensure that they are completely trustworthy. In fact, you might prefer to keep the Super Users group disabled and enable it only when you need it for security purposes.

MORE INFO Account preparation

To learn more about account preparation, go to *http://technet2.microsoft.com/windowsserver2008 /en/library/5d3a2ead-319e-49e7-a1b4-e3f69a1a4f1b1033.mspx?mfr=true*.

Preparing Policy Templates

To facilitate the rights-protection application by your users, prepare policy templates. These templates will save considerable time for your users and ensure that you maintain the standards you set in your rights-protection policies. You must perform several activities with policy templates. First, you must create the template. Next, you must specify a location for the template.

Locations are usually shared folders contained within your network. However, for users to rely on the template to create content, they must have access to it. Offline users will not have access to the templates unless you configure the offline folder settings for the shared folder so that the content of the folder will automatically be available locally to the user. In addition, relying on offline folders will ensure that when you modify, add, or update templates, they will automatically be updated on the client computer the next time the user connects to the network. Offline folders, however, will not work for external users who do not have access to your internal network. You will have to consider an alternate delivery method if you choose to allow external users to create content. Users who have access only to pre-created content do not require access to the policy templates. To create a policy template, use the following procedure:

1. Log on to a server that is a member of the root cluster, using AD RMS Template Administrators credentials.
2. Launch Server Manager from the Administrative Tools program group.

3. Expand Roles\Active Directory Rights Management Services*servername*\Rights Policy Templates.

4. Under the AD RMS node of the console, select Rights Policy Templates (Server Manager \Roles\AD RMS*Servername*).

5. In the Actions pane, select Create Distributed Rights Policy Template. This launches the wizard.

6. On the Add Template Identification Information page, click Add.

7. Specify the language, type the name and description for the new template, click Add, and then click Next.

8. On the Add User Rights page, you must perform several activities:

   a. Click Add to select the user or group that will have access to the template.

      Selecting Anyone will enable any user to request a use license for the content. If you want to select a specific group, use the Browse button.

   b. Under Users And Rights, you must first select the user and then assign the rights to that particular user or group in the Rights For User pane. You can also create a custom right for the user.

   c. Note that the Grant Owner (Author) Full Control right with no expiration option is selected by default.

   d. In the Rights Request URL, type the appropriate URL. This will enable users to request additional rights by going to the URL.

9. Click Next.

10. On the Specify Expiration Policy page, select one of the three available options and type a value in days. If you need to ensure that content expires automatically after a number of days, select Expires After The Following Duration (Days), and type the number of days. Click Next.

11. On the Specify Extended Policy page, you can assign the following settings:

    a. Choose Enable Users to view protected content, using a browser add-on. This enables users who do not have AD RMS–enabled applications to view protected content by automatically installing the required add-on.

    b. Select Request A New Use License Every Time Content Is Consumed (Disable Client-Side Caching) if you need authentication against the AD RMS servers each time content is consumed. Note that this will not work for offline users.

    c. Select If You Would Like To Specify Additional Information For Your AD RMS-Enabled Applications, You Can Specify Them Here As Name-Value Pairs if you need to add specific data to the protected content. This option is usually reserved for developers, however.

12. Click Next. On the Specify Revocation Policy page, you can enable revocation by selecting the Require Revocation option and then:

    a. Selecting Location Where The Revocation List Is Published (URL or UNC) and typing the value for the location of the revocation file.

    Keep in mind that if you use a URL and you have both internal and external users, the URL should be accessible from both network locations.

    b. Selecting Refresh Interval For Revocation List (Days) and typing the number of days the revocation list will be maintained.

    This determines when users must update their revocation list when viewing content.

    c. Selecting File Containing Public Key Corresponding To The Signed Revocation List.

13. Click Finish.

Note that when you implement revocation, you must be careful with its settings. To make revocation practical, you must publish the revocation list on a regular basis.

MORE INFO Policy templates

To learn more about policy templates, go to *http://technet2.microsoft.com/windowsserver2008/en /library/a42680fa-2855-40d9-8e2c-74f72793ca241033.mspx?mfr=true*.

Working with AD RMS Clients

AD RMS relies on a local client to give users access to its capabilities. Two clients exist: the Windows Vista client, which is also included in Windows Server 2008, and a client that runs on Windows 2000, Windows 2003, and Windows XP. The last of these must be downloaded and installed on each client computer to work. Three versions of this client exist: x86, x64, and Itanium to support all Windows version platforms.

Clients automatically discover the AD RMS cluster through one of three methods:

- They can rely on the AD DS Service Connection Point created during the AD RMS installation.
- In complex, multiforest AD RMS deployments, they must rely on registry overrides, which are placed directly on the client computer. This is especially true for earlier versions of Windows operating systems.
- They can rely on the URLs included in the issuance licenses for the content.

Each of these methods provides redundancy to ensure that clients can always access content.

MORE INFO   AD RMS and Windows RMS clients

To learn more about AD RMS clients and obtain the Windows RMS clients, go to *http:// technet2.microsoft.com/windowsserver2008/en/library/3230bca4-51cb-418f-86ba-bb6539 3854181033.mspx?mfr=true.*

Quick Check

1. What is a server licensor certificate?
2. Which trust policies does AD RMS support?

Quick Check Answers

1. A server licensor certificate, or SLC, is a self-signed certificate that is generated during setup of the first server in a root cluster and assigned to the cluster as a whole. Other cluster members will share the SLC when they are installed.
2. AD RMS supports four trust policies:
   - ❏ Trusted user domains enable your AD RMS cluster to process requests for other AD RMS clusters located in different AD DS forests. Trusted user domains are added by importing the server licensor certificate from the AD RMS cluster you want to trust into your own cluster.
   - ❏ Trusted publishing domains enable your own AD RMS cluster to issue use licenses for content that was protected by another AD RMS cluster. To create a trusted publishing domain, you must import the publishing cluster's SLC as well as its private key into your own cluster.
   - ❏ Windows Live ID trusts allow users who have a valid Windows Live ID (formerly known as Microsoft Passport) to use rights-protected content but not to create it.
   - ❏ Federated trusts are established through AD FS and extend the operation of your AD RMS cluster to the forests with which you have established a federated trust.

Managing Databases

AD RMS relies on three databases to operate. Familiarize yourself with these databases and their operation to ensure the proper functioning of your AD RMS cluster. These databases include:

- The configuration database, which is used to store all AD RMS configuration data. This database is accessed by AD RMS servers to provide rights-protection services and information to clients.

- The logging database, which stores data about every activity in either a root or a licensing-only cluster. This database is useful for auditing AD RMS events.

- The directory services database, which stores information about users and all their corresponding data. This information is accessed from AD DS directories through the Lightweight Directory Access Protocol (LDAP). This database requires regular maintenance if you remove users from AD RMS as mentioned earlier in this lesson.

In addition to these databases, AD RMS relies on the Message Queuing service to send events to the logging database. If you are concerned about auditing AD RMS usage, and you should be, perform regular checks and verifications of this service to ensure its proper operation.

In addition to the different functionalities available within the AD RMS console, Microsoft provides a special RMS toolkit that contains a series of utilities for AD RMS administration and operation. Download this toolkit, and add it to your AD RMS administration kit to control your deployment fully.

MORE INFO   Rights Management Services administration toolkit

To download the RMS toolkit with utilities for RMS management, go to *http://www.microsoft.com /downloads/details.aspx?FamilyID=bae62cfc-d5a7-46d2-9063-0f6885c26b98&DisplayLang=en.*

MORE INFO   Additional AD RMS resources

To access additional AD RMS resources, go to *http://technet2.microsoft.com/windowsserver2008/en /library/789533a5-50c5-435d-b06a-37db0ab5666e1033.mspx?mfr=true.*

PRACTICE Creating a Rights Policy Template

In this practice, you will create a customized rights policy template. You will use the AD RMS installation you created in Lesson 1 to create a new template.

▶ **Exercise 1   Create a New Template**

Templates enable users to apply rights policies in a quick, standardized manner. To create a template, you must use the AD RMS Template Administrators access right or the AD RMS Enterprise Administrators access right. To perform this exercise, you should have SERVER01, SERVER04, and SERVER05 running.

1. Log on to a server that is a member of the root cluster, using AD RMS Template Administrators credentials.

2. Launch Server Manager from the Administrative Tools program group.

3. Expand Roles\Active Directory Rights Management Services*servername*\Rights Policy Templates.

4. In the Actions pane, select Create Distributed Rights Policy Template.

    This launches the wizard.

5. On the Add Template Identification Information page, click Add.

6. Specify the language, type **Contoso Legal Template** for the name and **Template to protect legal documents at Contoso Ltd.** for the description for the new template, and click Add. Click Next.

7. On the Add User Rights page, you must perform several activities:

    a. Click Add to select the user or group that will have access to the template. Select Anyone.

        This will enable any user to request a use license for the content.

    b. Under Users And Rights, select Anyone, and then assign the View rights in the Rights For User pane.

    c. Make sure that the Grant Owner (Author) Full Control Right With No Expiration option is selected.

    d. In the Rights request URL, type the following URL: **https://RightsManagement .Contoso.com**.

        This will enable users to request additional rights by going to the URL.

8. Click Next. On the Specify Expiration Policy page, select Never Expires. Make sure you do not select Expires After The Following Duration (Days). Click Next.

9. On the Specify Extended Policy page, you can assign the following settings:

    ❑ Select Enable Users to view protected content, using a browser add-on. This enables users who do not have AD RMS–enabled applications to view protected content by automatically installing the required add-on.

    ❑ Do not select Request A New Use License Every Time Content Is Consumed (Disable Client-Side Caching).

    ❑ Do not select If You Would Like To Specify Additional Information For Your AD RMS-Enabled Applications, You Can Specify Them Here As Name-Value Pairs. This option is usually reserved for developers.

10. Click Next. On the Specify Revocation Policy page, do not enable revocation. Click Finish.

    Note that the template now appears in the details pane. It is ready for distribution.

Lesson Summary

■ When you work with AD RMS, you will need to perform several configuration tasks to complete your installation. These tasks include creating an extranet URL if you want to give external users access to your DRM system. They also include configuring trust policies in support of additional external accesses.

- If you want to work with other AD RMS infrastructures, you must exchange server licensor certificates with each other. This means exporting certificates from the source cluster and importing them in the target cluster.
- If you need to exclude users from your DRM system, you must create exclusion policies.
- To facilitate user content creation, create rights policy templates. These templates will simplify users' work and ensure that your DRM strategy is used in a standard manner.

Lesson Review

You can use the following questions to test your knowledge of the information in Lesson 2, "Configuring and Using Active Directory Rights Management Services." The questions are also available on the companion CD if you prefer to review them in electronic form.

NOTE Answers

Answers to these questions and explanations of why each answer choice is right or wrong are located in the "Answers" section at the end of the book.

---

1. You are an administrator for the *contoso.com* domain. You have just finished installing AD RMS, and now you want to configure AD RMS. You've configured an extranet URL and tested the operation from the AD RMS server you were using to set up the URL. This URL relies on SSL to secure HTTP traffic. However, when users try to access AD RMS from outside your network, they can't. What could be the problem?

    A. Your users should be using a URL address in the HTTP:// format.

    B. The server certificate is invalid, and, because of this, users cannot access the URL.

    C. Users must have AD DS domain accounts to access the URL.

    D. The URL you provided to users is wrong.

Chapter Review

To further practice and reinforce the skills you learned in this chapter, you can perform the following tasks:

- Review the chapter summary.
- Review the list of key terms introduced in this chapter.
- Complete the case scenario. This scenario sets up a real-world situation involving the topics of this chapter and asks you to create a solution.
- Complete the suggested practices.
- Take a practice test.

Chapter Summary

- AD RMS is designed to support the extension of your organization's authority beyond the firewall. The extension applies to the protection of intellectual property.
- To protect your intellectual property, AD RMS must rely on several technologies: Active Directory Domain Services, Active Directory Certificate Services, Active Directory Federation Services, and SQL Server. AD DS provides a central authentication service, AD CS provides the public key infrastructure certificates used in AD RMS, AD FS enables you to integrate AD RMS policies with partners and external users, and SQL Server stores all AD RMS data.
- Many organizations choose to implement AD RMS in stages:
    - The first stage focuses on internal use of intellectual property.
    - The second involves sharing content with partners.
    - The third involves a wider audience where your intellectual property is distributed outside the boundaries of your network in a protected mode.
- When you install AD RMS, you create a root cluster. This cluster can supply both certification and licensing services. Each AD DS forest can host only a single root cluster; however, in large implementations, you can separate the certification and licensing roles by creating an additional licensing cluster. To consume the AD RMS services, you need AD RMS–enabled applications. These can be tools such as word processors, presentation tools, e-mail clients, or custom in-house applications. Each time a user creates new information, AD RMS templates determine usage rights for the information. These include who will be able to read, open, write, modify, print, transfer, and otherwise manipulate the information.

Key Terms

Use these key terms to understand better the concepts covered in this chapter.

- **enrollment**   Servers that must be enrolled to publish certificates. In prior releases, you needed the Microsoft Enrollment Service, but with AD RMS, servers can self-enroll through a self-enrollment certificate.

- **publishing license**   Licenses that are assigned to content when authorized users protect content. This license determines which rights are assigned to the document. When the document is opened by another authorized user, a use license is provided by the server and is permanently embedded into the content.

- **root cluster**   A root cluster that is automatically created with each AD RMS installation. The cluster provides high availability for the AD RMS service as soon as a second server is installed. Only one root cluster can be installed per AD DS forest, but you can also create licensing-only clusters to support AD RMS operations.

Case Scenario

In the following case scenario, you will apply what you've learned about Active Directory Rights Management Services. You can find answers to the questions in this scenario in the "Answers" section at the end of this book.

Case Scenario: Prepare to Work with an External AD RMS Cluster

You are a systems administrator with Contoso, Ltd. You have recently finished implementing an AD RMS deployment within your organization, and everything is running smoothly. Users both inside and outside of your network have access to your rights management policies to ensure the protection of your content.

Now your organization wants to share rights protection policies with a partner organization, but it does not want to put a federation services infrastructure in place. What are your options?

Suggested Practices

To help you successfully master the exam objectives presented in this chapter, complete the following tasks.

Work with AD RMS

There is only a single exam objective for this topic. Because of this, you should focus your practices on the following areas:

- Identifying the requirements for an AD RMS installation
- Working with the installation and configuration process for AD RMS root clusters
- Finalizing the configuration process for a root cluster
- Working with rights policy templates

You should also practice using the various console sections for AD RMS. All of these are available in Server Manager.

- **Practice 1**   Use the instructions in the "Before You Begin" section of this chapter to prepare your test environment. If at all possible, rely on an external database server to support the installation. This will enable you to configure a true root cluster. When you're ready, create the cluster and add a second server to it so that you can see how clusters operate.
- **Practice 2**   After the cluster is installed, use Server Manager to run through all the activities required to create or modify a rights policy template. These templates are an important part of the AD RMS administration process.

Don't forget to study DRM implementations with Windows Server 2008. The Microsoft TechNet Web site includes more information on AD RMS; run through as much of it as you can.

Take a Practice Test

The practice tests on this book's companion CD offer many options. For example, you can test yourself on just one exam objective, or you can test yourself on all the 70-640 certification exam content. You can set up the test so that it closely simulates the experience of taking a certification exam, or you can set it up in study mode so that you can look at the correct answers and explanations after you answer each question.

MORE INFO   Practice tests

For details about all the practice test options available, see the "How to Use the Practice Tests" section in this book's introduction.

Chapter 17
Active Directory Federation Services

Organizations have been struggling with securing their networks from the outside world ever since the Internet was invented. The basic principle is that every organization that has an interface between its network and the Internet also has a perimeter network of some sort. In many cases, organizations spend great effort implementing special security technologies such as intrusion detection systems, and yet, the basic premise of a perimeter network is to keep the firewalls it contains as secure as possible. But how does that affect potential partnerships?

In the early days of Microsoft Windows domains with Microsoft Windows NT, Microsoft provided the capability to create trusts between domains to support domain interactions. With the release of Active Directory Domain Services (AD DS) in Windows 2000, Microsoft brought forward the concept of the trust and supported inter-domain trusts. Domains within the same forest would use automatic transitive trusts, and domains from different forests would use explicit trusts when they wanted to share security contexts. With the release of Microsoft Windows Server 2003, Microsoft extended the concept of the transitive trust to forests with the introduction of forest trusts. Using a forest trust, partners could extend the security contexts of their own internal forest to trust other partner forests. However, implementing forests trusts has two significant impacts:

- First, it requires opening specific ports in a firewall to support Active Directory Domain Services (AD DS) traffic.
- Second, if the partnerships grow too large, it can become extremely cumbersome to manage multiple trusts. (See Figure 17-1.)

Using trusts might not be the best way to implement partnerships.

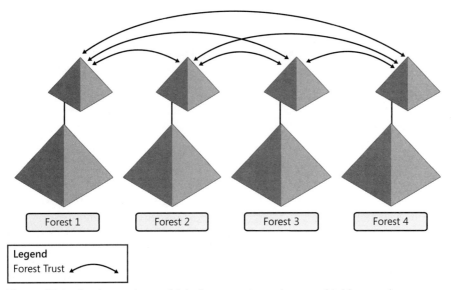

Forest 1 Forest 2 Forest 3 Forest 4

Legend
Forest Trust

Figure 17-1 Implementing multiple forest trusts can become highly complex

The Purpose of a Firewall

Although forest trusts can become highly complex, they also have an impact on your protection mechanisms. For example, AD DS traffic will transit through the Lightweight Directory Access Protocol (LDAP) on TCP/IP port 389 or, preferably, through secure LDAP (LDAP/S) on port 636. In addition, if you need to transit global catalog (GC) traffic, you'll need to use port 3268 or, once again preferably, port 3269 on LDAP/S.

However, firewalls are designed to keep unwanted traffic out. Perforating them by opening endless numbers of TCP/IP ports is not a solution. Traditional perimeter networks will have two layers of protection. The first protects perimeter networks from external access. The second protects internal networks from the perimeter. The perimeter itself provides a series of services such as Active Directory Certificate Services (AD CS), Active Directory Rights Management Services (AD RMS), and, in some circumstances, Active Directory Lightweight Directory Services (AD LDS). AD DS is reserved exclusively for internal networks.

The ideal external firewall will use one set of key ports and this set only. These include:

- Port 53, which is used for Domain Name System (DNS) traffic. DNS traffic is usually provided in a read-only manner.
- Port 80, which is used by open Hypertext Transfer Protocol (HTTP) data. Port 80 is usually used for read-only access because it is not secured.
- Port 443 for Secure HTTP or Hypertext Transfer Protocol Secure (HTTPS). Communications on port 443 are secured through Secure Sockets Layer (SSL) or Transport Layer

Security (TLS), which both rely on Certificate Authority (CA) certificates to encrypt data. Because of this, communications on port 443 support read-write or secure data read operations.

■ Port 25, which is used for Simple Mail Transfer Protocol (SMTP), a necessary risk because no one can work without access to e-mail.

All other ports should ideally be closed. The internal firewall will have a few more open ports, depending on the technologies you have running in the perimeter. (See Figure 17-2.) For example, if you are using AD LDS to provide authentication services for Web applications in the perimeter, you might want to have one-way synchronizations from your internal AD DS directory to provision your own user accounts. If you are using Internet Information Services (IIS), you might want to push and pull data to the Web sites in the perimeter. In addition, you want to get the e-mail messages from your SMTP relays in the perimeter into your internal network. This is the basis of a secure perimeter design.

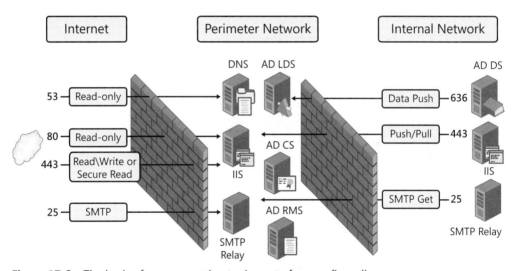

Figure 17-2   The basis of a secure perimeter is a set of secure firewalls

Active Directory Federation Services

In comes Active Directory Federation Services (AD FS), one of the Active Directory technologies included in Windows Server 2008. Once again, this Active Directory technology is designed to extend the authority of your internal network to the outside world. (See Figure 17-3.) AD FS is designed to provide similar functionality to the forest trust or the explicit trust but, this time, not through the traditional LDAP TCP/IP ports but rather through the common HTTP ports. In fact, AD FS uses port 443 because all AD FS trust communications are secured and encrypted. In this manner, it can rely on AD CS to provide certificates for each server in the AD

FS implementation. AD FS can also extend your AD RMS deployment and provide federation services for intellectual property management between partners.

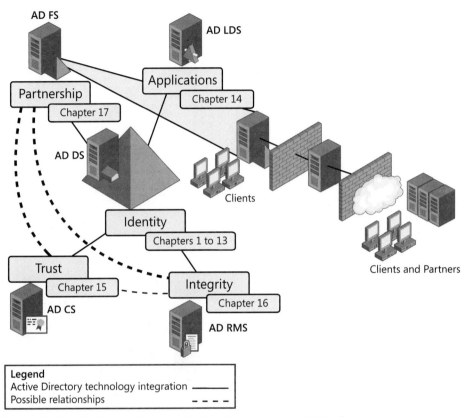

Figure 17-3   AD FS extends the authority of your internal AD DS directory

To extend your internal authority, AD FS provides extensions to internal forests and enables organizations to create partnerships without having to open any additional port on their firewalls. Basically, AD FS relies on each partner's internal AD DS directory to provide authentication for extranet or perimeter services. When a user attempts to authenticate to an application integrated to AD FS, the AD FS engine will poll the internal directory for authentication data. If the user has access provided through the internal directory, he or she will be granted access to the external application. The major advantage of this is that each partner organization needs to manage only authentication data in the internal network. The federation services of AD FS do all the rest.

In short, AD FS should be used whenever you want to implement a partnership with other organizations that also rely on internal AD DS directories. When you need to provide authentication services in your perimeter network, but the users or organizations you want to interact with do not have internal AD DS directories, or the scope of the partnership does not warrant an AD FS deployment, you should rely on AD LDS.

Exam objectives in this chapter:
- Configuring Additional Active Directory Server Roles
  - ❑ Configure Active Directory Federation Services (AD FS).

Lessons in this chapter:

- Lesson 1: Understanding Active Directory Federation Services 832
- Lesson 2: Configuring and Using Active Directory Federation Services 854

Before You Begin

To complete the lessons in this chapter, you must have performed the installations shown in the following list. It is highly recommended that you use virtual machines for this chapter because it requires access to so many computers. If you performed the exercises in the previous chapters, you will already have several of these computers in place.

- Installed Windows Server 2008 on a physical or virtual machine. The machine should be named SERVER01 and should be a domain controller in the *contoso.com* domain. The details for this setup are presented in Chapter 1, "Installation," and Chapter 2, "Administration."

- Installed Windows Server 2008 Enterprise Edition on a physical or virtual machine, which should be named SERVER03 and should be a member server within the *contoso.com* domain. This computer will host the internal AD FS role you will install and create through the exercises in this chapter.

- Installed Windows Server 2008 Enterprise Edition on a physical or virtual machine, which should be named SERVER04 and should be a member server within the *contoso.com* domain. This computer will host an AD FS proxy server.

- Installed Windows Server 2003 Enterprise Edition on a physical or virtual machine, which should be named SERVER05 and should be a member server within the *contoso.com* domain. This computer will host an installation of Microsoft SQL Server 2005, which will run the configuration and logging database for AD RMS. This computer would also include a D drive to store the data for SQL Server. 10 gigabytes (GB) should be enough for the size of this drive. You use Windows Server 2003 because it requires less RAM than Windows Server 2008. Note that this computer is not necessary for the exercises in this chapter, but having it turned on will prevent AD RMS errors from appearing on SERVER04.

- Installed Windows Server 2008 on a physical or virtual machine, which should be named SERVER06 and should be a domain controller in the *woodgrovebank.com* domain and include the DNS server role. No special setup is required other than having a new directory named *woodgrovebank.com*.

■ Installed Windows Server 2008 Enterprise Edition on a physical or virtual machine, which should be named SERVER07 and should be a member server within the *woodgrovebank.com* domain. This computer will host the internal AD FS role you will install and create through the exercises in this chapter.

■ Installed Windows Server 2008 Enterprise Edition on a physical or virtual machine, which should be named SERVER08 and should be a member server within the *woodgrovebank.com* domain. This computer will host an AD FS proxy server.

This setup will be sufficient to test basic AD FS installation and configuration. Testing all of AD FS capabilities requires client machines as well and might be beyond the laboratory capabilities of most readers.

Note that you can create an AD FS environment with fewer computers, as outlined in the *Microsoft Step-by-Step Guide for AD FS*, which is available at *http://www.microsoft.com/downloads/details.aspx?familyid=062F7382-A82F-4428-9BBD-A103B9F27654&displaylang=en*, but it is not recommended to install AD FS on an AD DS domain controller; therefore, the recommended setup is as outlined here.

Real World

Danielle Ruest and Nelson Ruest

In 2005, one of our clients, a major health care organization, needed to put together an identity federation solution. Their goal was to have their entire health care system—doctors, pharmacists, health care workers, hospitals, social services workers, private clinics, and so on—work together through a single integrated identity and access (IDA) solution. Because most of the organizations involved used internal Active Directory for authentication and network access, this solution was to be based on Windows technologies.

The goal was to make sure that all members of the system had a verifiable identity within the system. The challenge was considerable. Although many larger partners had their own internal Active Directory forests, many of the smaller partners did not. For example, pharmacies did not have any way of linking themselves together to have a single identity authority. Private clinics or doctors did not have this capability either.

The initial solution was to create a multitude of forest trusts between each of the existing Active Directory forests. Then, to provide support for the members of the system that did not have their own directory service, a completely new directory would be created that would be located within a perimeter network hosted by a hosting firm as an outsourced service to the health care provider for a per-user fee to maintain the directory service.

The customer had several concerns about the potential solution. The first was long-term costs. When all the members of the system were tallied, they added up to over 500,000 users, more than half of them without a directory service. Maintaining an external directory for these users would become very expensive very quickly. Second, the client did not want to perforate firewalls by supporting all the ports required for forest trusts. However, the cost of a private network was prohibitive. Third, although the client wanted each of the system members to interact through a single IDA, it did not want to be responsible for all the accounts linked to the new solution.

We recommended that, although Windows Server 2008 was not available yet, Windows Server 2003 R2 was, and with it came the initial release of Microsoft Federation Services. In addition, Microsoft had released Active Directory Application Mode (ADAM) a couple of years earlier. This case seemed like a perfect candidate for the integration of the three technologies. We suggested the following:

- Use the Federation Services to link all existing directory services and make centralized applications available through the Web.
- Allow each partner to manage its own internal directory services without external intervention.
- Use ADAM instances to provide authentication services in the perimeter network. The client could even create a self-service portal that would enable members to update their own records, change passwords, and so on.
- Reduce the number of open ports on the firewall down to the most common ports that were already open.

This proposal met the customer's needs and would not cost a fortune to implement. In fact, implementation could start with a pilot project focusing on one or two key applications and then adding new system members as the solution was fleshed out. What's even better is that with the release of Windows Server 2008, Microsoft brought many of the technologies we proposed under a single banner: Active Directory.

Lesson 1: Understanding Active Directory Federation Services

In general terms, AD FS is a single sign-on (SSO) engine that allows users of your external Web-based applications to access and authenticate through a browser. That's not so different from using an external AD LDS directory store that is linked with your internal directory. However, the key feature of AD FS is that to authenticate a client, it uses the internal authentication store of the user's own domain and does not have a store of its own. It also uses the original authentication the client performed in its own network and passes this authentication to all the Web applications that are AD FS–enabled.

The advantages are clear. Organizations need to manage only a single authentication store for their own users and don't need to manage secondary stores at all. Using an AD LDS directory for extranet authentication adds administrative overhead because the organization needs to manage its own internal store and the external store or stores as well. Users also often must remember several access codes and passwords to log on to each of these stores. AD FS simplifies this because it federates the user's internal AD DS identity and projects it to the external world. Users need to authenticate only once: when they log on to their own network.

Using AD FS, you can form business-to-business (B2B) partnerships with very little overhead. In these B2B partnerships, organizations fit into two categories:

- **Resource organization** When organizations that have exposed resources such as Web sites—e-commerce or collaboration—decide to use AD FS to simplify the authentication process to these resources, they form partnerships with other organizations—suppliers, partners, and so on. The organization that forms the partnership is deemed the resource organization because it hosts the shared resources in its perimeter network.
- **Account organization** When organizations enter into an AD FS relationship with resource organizations, they are deemed the account organizations because they manage the accounts used to access the shared resources in SSO designs.

AD FS supports one additional authentication mode. In a Web SSO design, it will authenticate users from anywhere on the Internet. After such users have been authenticated, AD FS examines the users' attributes in AD DS or in AD LDS directories to identify which claims the users have to the application they are authenticating to.

To support this identity federation, AD FS relies on four role services.

- **Federation Service** This service is formed by the servers that share a trust policy. The federation server will route authentication requests to the appropriate source directory to generate security tokens for the user requesting access.
- **Federation Service Proxy** To obtain the authentication requests from the user, the federation server relies on a proxy server that is located in the perimeter network. The proxy collects authentication information from the user's browser through the WS-Federation

Passive Requestor Profile (WS-F PRP), an AD FS Web service, and passes it on to the federation service.

- **Claims-Aware Agent**   An agent sits on the Web server and initiates queries of security token claims to the federation service. Each claim is used to grant or deny access to a given application. ASP.NET applications that can examine the various claims contained in the user's AD FS security token are deemed to be claims-aware applications. These applications can rely on the claims to determine whether the user has access to the application. Two examples of claims-aware applications are AD RMS and Microsoft Office SharePoint Server 2007.

- **Windows Token-Based Agent**   This is an alternate agent that can convert the AD FS security token into an impersonation-level Windows NT access token for applications that rely on Windows authentication mechanisms instead of other Web-based authentication methods.

Because it is based on a standard Web service, AD FS does not need to rely on AD DS alone to support federated identities. Any directory service that adheres to the WS-Federation standard can participate in an AD FS identity federation.

Although Federation Services existed in Windows Server 2003 R2, AD FS has been improved significantly in Windows Server 2008 to facilitate the installation and administration processes. AD FS also supports more Web applications than the original release did.

MORE INFO   **AD FS**

For more information on AD FS, go to *http://technet2.microsoft.com/windowsserver2008/en/server-manager/activedirectoryfederationservices.mspx*

> **After this lesson, you will be able to:**
> - Understand the AD FS authentication process.
> - Understand the components that make up an AD FS implementation.
> - Install AD FS.
>
> **Estimated lesson time: 40 minutes**

The AD FS Authentication Process

After the AD FS partnerships are in place, it becomes transparent for users to log on to external Web applications that are included in the partnership. In a typical AD FS scenario, when a user logs on to a claims-aware application in an extranet, AD FS automatically provisions the user's credentials and outlines the claims included in the user's AD DS account attributes. (See Figure 17-4.)

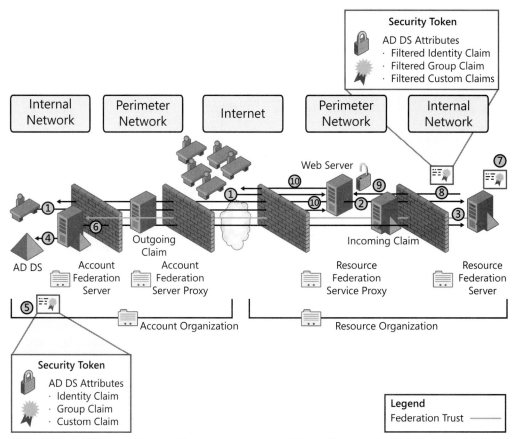

Figure 17-4   Using AD FS to provide access to extranet Web applications through Federated Web SSO

1. A user who is located within an internal network or on the Internet wants to access a claims-aware Web application in an extranet. This user belongs to one of the account organizations that is a member of the AD FS partnership.

2. The claims-aware agent on the Web server verifies with a resource federation server (RFS) in the resource organization to see whether the client is granted access. Because the request must traverse a firewall, the agent first contacts a Federation Service Proxy (FSP), who then contacts the internal federation server.

3. Because it does not have an account for the user but has a federation relationship with the directory store in the account organization—a federation trust, in fact—the federation server in the resource organization checks with an account federation server (AFS) in the account organization's internal network, once again through a proxy, to identify the user's access rights. These access rights are listed in the form of claims, which are attributes linked to the user's account object in AD DS.

4. The federation server in the account organization is directly linked to the organization's internal AD DS and obtains access rights from the directory through an LDAP query. Note that the user account can also reside in an AD LDS directory store.

5. The account organization's federation server constructs the user's AD FS security token. This token includes the user's identifier, the list of claims included in the user's AD DS account, and the digital certificate of the AFS.

6. The AFS responds to the RFS with the client's access rights contained within the signed security token, once again through the proxy server. This is an outgoing claim.

7. The RFS decrypts the token and extracts the claims for the user from the incoming claim. It then maps the claims to the organization claims it maintains and applies a filtering policy for the specific requesting Web application.

8. The filtered claims are then packaged once again into a signed security token, which is sent to the Web server in the resource organization's extranet by posting it to the URL included in the Web application's original request. In this case, the signature for the token is based either on the RFS digital certificate or on a Kerberos session key because the systems are in the same network.

9. The Web server relies on its claims-aware agent to decrypt the user's security token, looks up the user's claims, and then grants access to the application based on the claims in the token.

10. To support single sign-on, the AD FS Web agent on the Web server directs the user's browser to write a local authentication cookie for the user so that it does not need to perform this lookup again the next time it needs to authenticate during this session.

The process is simple after it is in place. However, implementing AD FS must be done with care. Each partner can use its own internal directory stores to grant users access to extranet applications. This simplifies access management, but to do so, each partner must implement federation trusts. Federation trusts rely on the partners having at least one AD FS federation server installed in their networks. The direction of the trust is always from the resource partner to the account partner.

Note that when the user is using either a public or home computer that is not part of the account organization's AD DS domain, he or she can use a special AD FS Web page, which will enable that user to select which account organization to use. This Web page also provides logon screens that can support either forms-based or Windows Integrated authentication. This enables external users to access the extranet applications even if they are not using corporate computers.

If you do not want to create a Web page that includes a list of account organizations because you do not want to publish these organization names for security reasons, you can include the account organization directly within the query string for the resource being accessed. Use the following Web query format:

```
https://webserver/appname/apppage.aspx?whr=urn:federation:accountpartner
```

In this query, you rely on the *whr* parameter to identify the account organization in the federation partnership.

Working with AD FS Designs

AD FS supports three configurations or architectural designs, depending on the type of B2B partnership you need to establish. Each includes its own particularities, and each supports a particular partnership scenario.

- **Federated Web SSO**   This model usually spans several firewalls because it links applications contained within an extranet in a resource organization to the internal directory stores of account organizations. The only trust that exists in this model is the federation trust, which is always a one-way trust from the resource organization to the account organization(s). This is the most common AD FS deployment scenario. (See Figure 17-4, presented earlier.)

- **Federated Web SSO with Forest Trust**   In this model, the organization uses two AD DS forests. One is the internal forest, but the second one is an external forest located within a perimeter network. A forest trust is established between the forest in the perimeter network and the internal forest. In addition, a federation trust is established between the resource federation server, which is located within the perimeter, and the account federation server, located in the internal network. In this scenario, external users have accounts in the perimeter forest, and internal users have accounts in the internal forest. The AD FS systems federate the access rights from the accounts in both forests to the applications in the perimeter. Because of this, internal users have access to the applications from both the internal network and the Internet, whereas external users have access to the applications only from the Internet. (See Figure 17-5.)

IMPORTANT   Using AD DS directories in perimeter networks

Be very wary of this design. The very function of each of the four additional Active Directory technologies—AD LDS, AD CS, AD RMS, and AD FS—is to extend the authority of your internal AD DS deployments without having to host external AD DS forests. Hosting an external AD DS forest is a risk you should avoid as much as possible. In addition, creating a forest trust between an external and an internal forest means opening up ports on a firewall—ports that should normally be closed. Instead, rely on AD LDS and AD FS to perform the same functions.

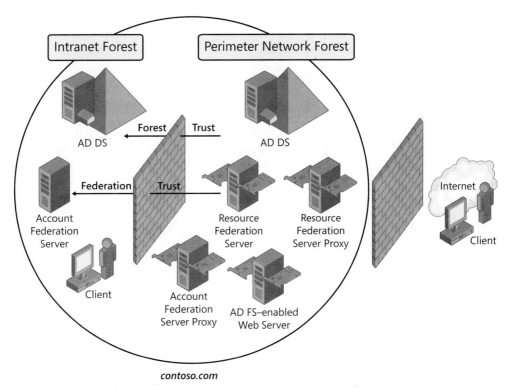

contoso.com

Figure 17-5 Relying on a forest trust as well as a federation trust to provide access to extranet applications

- **Web SSO**   When all the users for an extranet application are external and do not have accounts within an AD DS domain, you must deploy Web SSO only. The Web SSO model allows the users to authenticate only once to multiple Web applications. However, this model relies on multihomed Web servers—servers that include at least two network interface cards (NICs), one that is connected to the external network and one that is connected to the internal network. The Web servers are part of the internal AD DS domain and are connected to it through the internal NIC. Clients access the applications through the external NIC. The Federation Service Proxy is also multihomed to provide access to both the external and the internal network. (See Figure 17-6.)

The most common scenarios are the first and the last but, ideally, all members of your identity federation deployment will have their own AD DS directory and will act as account organizations to simplify your deployment strategy.

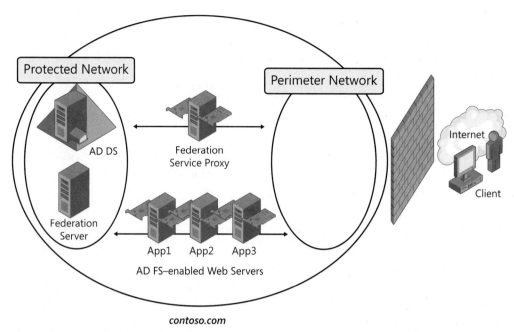

contoso.com

Figure 17-6   Using a Web SSO federation scenario

Exam Tip   Pay attention to the three AD FS deployment scenarios, even the Federated Web SSO with Forest Trust scenario, although it is not recommended. Each of the exam questions will be based on one or the other.

Understanding AD FS Components

In addition to the various role services supported by AD FS, this technology relies on several components. These include:

- Claims
- Cookies
- Certificates

Each of these three components provides additional support to the AD FS process. Also, as you have seen, AD FS relies on a special terminology—a terminology of its own, in fact. To have a better grasp of the AD FS components, it is important to review and understand this terminology.

Understanding AD FS Claims

In their most basic form, claims are statements each partner in an AD FS relationship makes about its users. Claims can be based on several values, for example, user names, certificate keys, group memberships, specific privileges, or more. Claims are the basis of the authorization AD FS sends to the Web application. Claims can be obtained in three ways:

- The account federation server can query the internal directory store for the claims and provide them to a resource partner.
- The account organization can provide the claims to a resource federation server, which then passes them on to the resource application after they have been filtered.
- The federation service queries the directory store (AD DS or AD LDS) for the claims and provides them to the resource application after they have been filtered.

AD FS can support three types of claims:

- **Identity claim type**   Any claim that is based on the user's identity falls within this category. There must be at least one identity claim type in every claim for security tokens to be generated from a list of claims.
    - This can include a user principal name (UPN), which represents the user's identity in a format that resembles an e-mail address (*username@accountdomain*). Keep in mind that even if several UPNs can exist for a user account, only one can be used in an identity claim type. If other UPNs must be communicated in the claim, they must be defined as custom claim types. When included with other identity claim types, the UPN has the highest priority.
    - This can also be an e-mail address (*username@emaildomain*). Like the UPN, only one e-mail address can be communicated as the e-mail claim type. All other e-mail addresses, if they are required, must be listed as custom claim types. When included with other identity claim types, the e-mail address has the second-highest priority.
    - You can also rely on common names, which are really nothing more than arbitrary strings of characters. Note that there is no method you can use to guarantee the uniqueness of a common name; therefore, be careful when using this claim type. When included with other identity claim types, the common name has the lowest priority.
- **Group claim type**   The group memberships a user belongs to can also be used in a claim. Because a user can belong to several groups, you can provide several group claim types in a claim. For example, the same user can belong to the Tester, Developer, and User groups for an application.
- **Custom claim type**   If custom information must be provided for a user, for example, a custom identification number such as bank account number or employee number, you would put it in a custom claim type.

When claims are processed, they are filtered by the federation server. This reduces the overall number of claims an organization needs to have. If filtering was not available, then the organization would be responsible for mapping out each claim for each partner. This would greatly increase the number of claims to manage.

MORE INFO   AD FS claims and claim mapping

For more information on AD FS claims and claim mappings, go to *http://technet2.microsoft.com/ windowsserver2008/en/library/4fd78221-3d2e-4236-a971-18cdb8513d6b1033.mspx?mfr=true.*

Understanding AD FS Cookies

In addition to claims, AD FS works with cookies, which are inscribed in users' browsers during Web sessions that are authenticated through AD FS. Three types of cookies are used by AD FS.

- **Authentication cookies** Because the first instance of an AD FS authentication can require a few transactions, AD FS generates an authentication cookie to be placed within the user's browser to support SSO for additional authentications. This cookie will include all the claims for the user. Authentication cookies are issued by both the AD FS Web agent and the federation service itself. Relying on the Web agent avoids having to place public and private key pairs on the server. When the Web agent creates an authentication cookie, it simply uses the existing security token generated by the federation server. The federation server, however, must have key pairs because it relies on these key pairs to sign security tokens.

  This cookie is signed, but it is not encrypted. This is one more reason all communications in this process are encrypted through either TLS or SSL. Also, because it is a session cookie, it is erased after the session is closed.

- **Account Partner cookies** During the authentication process, the client must announce its account partner membership. If this announcement has a valid token, the AD FS process writes a cookie on the client so that it can rely on this cookie instead of having to perform partner discovery again the next time the client authenticates.

  This cookie is not signed or encrypted. It is a long-lived and persistent cookie.

- **Sign-out cookies** Each time the federation service assigns a token, the resource partner or target server linked to the token is added to a sign-out cookie. The sign-out cookie is then used to facilitate an authentication artifact, for example, cached cookies, clean-up operations at the end of a user session.

  This cookie is not signed or encrypted. It is a session cookie that is deleted as part of the clean-up operations.

MORE INFO AD FS cookies

For more information on AD FS cookies, go to *http://technet2.microsoft.com/windowsserver2008/en/library/0357bdbc-219d-4ec1-a6d0-1a3376bc1eb51033.mspx?mfr=true*.

Understanding AD FS Certificates

To ensure secure communications, the AD FS implementation uses several certificate types. In fact, AD FS can rely on your AD CS deployment to obtain the certificates it needs. Each server role within an AD FS deployment will rely on certificates. The type of certificate required by the role depends on its purpose.

- **Federation servers** The federation server must have both a server authentication certificate and a token-signing certificate installed before it can perform any AD FS operations and become fully functional. In addition, the trust policy that forms the basic tenet of the federation relationship must rely on a verification certificate. The latter is nothing more than the public key of the token-signing certificate.

  ❑ The server authentication certificate is an SSL authentication certificate that secures Web traffic between the federation server and the Federation Service Proxy or the Web clients. SSL certificates are usually requested and installed through IIS Manager.

  ❑ Each time the federation server generates a security token, it must digitally sign the token with its token-signing certificate. Signing certificates ensures that it cannot be tampered with during transit. The token-signing certificate is made up of a private and public key pair.

  ❑ When there is more than one federation server in a deployment, a verification process must take place between servers. To do this, each server must have the verification certificates for all the other servers. As mentioned previously, the verification certificate consists of the public key of the token-signing certificate for a federation server. This means the certificate is installed on the target server without its corresponding private key.

- **Federation Service proxies** Proxies must have a server authentication certificate to support SSL-encrypted communications with Web clients.

  They must also have a client authentication certificate to authenticate the federation server during communications. This certificate can be any client authentication certificate type so long as it relies on extended key usage (EKU). Both the private and the public keys for this certificate are stored on the proxy. The public key is also stored on the federation server(s) and in the trust policy. When you work with this certificate type in the AD FS console, they are called Federation Service Proxy certificates.

- **AD FS Web agents**   Any AD FS–enabled Web server hosting the AD FS Web agent must also have a server authentication certificate to secure its communications with Web clients.

AD FS can easily rely on AD CS to obtain and manage these certificates. Keep in mind, however, that because many of the AD FS roles are outward-facing, your certificates must be from a trusted certification authority; otherwise, you will need to modify the Trusted CA store on each Web client.

MORE INFO   AD FS certificates

For more information on AD FS certificates, go to *http://technet2.microsoft.com/windowsserver2008/en/library/505507c2-db4a-45da-ad1b-082d5484b0c91033.mspx?mfr=true*.

Exam Tip   Pay attention to AD FS certificate exchanges. Because AD FS communications must be encrypted at all times, they are a core part of this exam topic.

Understanding AD FS Terminology

Because of its reliance on several technologies, AD FS uses terminology from a wide range of sources. It is a good idea to ensure your familiarity with these terms so that you understand what is being discussed when a term arises. Table 17-1 outlines the most common terms used in AD FS. Many of these have already been covered.

Table 17-1   Common AD FS Terms

Term	Description
Account federation server	The federation server that is hosted in the account organization's internal network.
Account Federation Service Proxy	The FSP that is hosted in the account organization's perimeter network. The FSP acts as a relay between the perimeter and the federation server. The FSP is sometimes referred to as a Federation Service Proxy.
Account partner or organization	The partner that hosts the AD DS directory that contains the accounts of the users who access extranet applications.
AD FS Web Agent	An agent that is installed on a Web server running IIS. The agent is used to interpret the claims and tokens provided by the federation server. This agent can rely on claims alone or on Windows Integrated authentication to provide access to applications.
Claim	The statement the federation server makes about a user or client.
Claims-aware application	An ASP.NET application that can interpret claims to grant user access.

Table 17-1 Common AD FS Terms

Term	Description
Claim mapping	When a federation server processes an incoming claim and filters it to extract appropriate authorizations for a user, it performs claim mapping.
Client account partner discovery Web page	A Web page that lists partner organizations and allows users to identify their own organization during the logon process.
Client authentication certificate	AD FS uses two-way authentication between the federation server and the proxies. To do this, the proxy relies on a client authentication certificate, and the federation server relies on a server authentication certificate.
Client logon or logoff Web page	AD FS provides custom Web pages to give visual feedback to users when they log on or log off an AD FS session.
Federated application	The same as a claims-aware application. It can rely on federated identities for authentication.
Federated user	Any user who has been granted appropriate claims in the account directory to access applications in the resource organization.
Federation	Any two organizations that have established a federation trust.
Federation trust	The one-way trust between a resource organization and the account organization(s) it wants to partner with.
Organization claims	All claims contained within the organization's namespace.
Passive client	Any HTTP browser that can also use cookies. The client must support the WS-F PRP Web Service specification.
Resource account	If you plan to rely on Windows Integrated authentication, you must create resource accounts for each user you want to grant access to. The Windows NT authentication process requires this account to map credentials for the user.
Resource federation server	The internal server that is used to perform claims mapping and issue access security tokens for users who need to work with an application. This federation server is located within the resource organization's internal network.
Resource Federation Service Proxy	The proxy that is located in the perimeter network of the resource organization. It performs account partner discovery for Internet clients and redirects incoming requests to the internal federation server.
Resource group	Used in the resource forest to map incoming group claims. It can then be used to support Windows NT authentication.
Resource partner or organization	The organization that hosts the federated applications in its perimeter network.

Table 17-1   Common AD FS Terms

Term	Description
Security token	A digitally signed object that contains the claims for a given user. When a security token is issued, it means that the user has successfully authenticated to an account federation server.
Security Token Service (STS)	The AD FS Web Service that is used to issue tokens. To issue tokens, the STS must trust the entire chain of events that leads to the issuance. In AD FS, the federation service itself is an STS.
Server authentication certificate	AD FS uses two-way authentication between the federation server and the proxies. To do this, the proxy relies on a client authentication certificate, and the federation server relies on a server authentication certificate. AD FS–enabled Web servers also require server authentication certificates to authenticate themselves to browser clients.
Server farm	A group of federation servers that act together to provide high availability for the federation service. Server farms can be applied to any of the federation servers, proxies, or AD FS–enabled Web servers, but each farm can include only a single federation server type.
Service-oriented architecture (SOA)	SOAs are standards-based and language-agnostic architectures that rely on Web services to support distributed services on the Internet.
Single sign-on (SSO)	SSO simplifies application access by requiring a single logon from the user.
Token-signing certificate	The certificate that is used to sign the security tokens generated by the resource federation server.
Trust policy	The trust policy defines the set of parameters the federation service requires to identify partners, certificates, account stores, claims, and the various properties of the entities that are associated with the federation service. This policy is in XML file format.
Uniform Resource Identifier (URI)	AD FS relies on URIs to identify partners and account stores.
Verification certificate	The public key of a token-signing certificate loaded on all federation servers in an organization.
Web Services (WS-*)	A standards-based Internet service that forms part of an SOA. Commonly known Web services include the Simple Object Access Protocol (SOAP); the extended markup language (XML); and Universal Description, Discovery, and Integration (UDDI). Web Services are language-agnostic so they can interoperate between different IT infrastructures, for example UNIX, Linux, and Windows.

Table 17-1 Common AD FS Terms

Term	Description
Web Services Security (WS-Security)	The SOA specifications that outline how you digitally sign and encrypt SOAP messages.
Windows NT token-based application	A Windows-based application that relies in Windows NT authentication to process authorizations.
WS-Federation	The Web server specification that outlines the standards to be used when implementing federation.
WS-Federation Passive Requestor Profile (WS-F PRP)	The component of WS-Federation that outlines the standard protocol to be used when passive clients access an application through a federation service.

Installing Active Directory Federation Services

A basic installation of AD FS requires a series of computers. Ideally, you will have two AD DS domains, two perimeter networks, and AD FS servers distributed within each environment. The account organization should host AD DS and at least one federation server internally as well as a Federation Service Proxy in its perimeter network. The resource organization should have an AD DS and at least one internal federation server. Its perimeter network should include at least one AD FS–enabled Web server and one FSP. However, the full deployment you design will be based on considerations such as the number of partner organizations, the type of applications to share, the requirement for high availability and load balancing, and other considerations of this type.

Test environments can be set up with as few as four computers: one client, one AD FS–enabled Web server, and two federation servers to participate in AD FS federation between two organizations. Because of the nature of AD FS, computer clocks should be synchronized to the same time or should never have more than five minutes of difference between one and the other; otherwise, the process will not work because the token time stamps will be invalid. Because many of the computers are not part of an AD DS domain, you cannot rely on the PDC Emulator Operations Master for clock synchronization. The best way to ensure time synchronization is to use the Network Time Protocol (NTP) to link each server to an external clock server and thereby ensure that they all have the same time.

MORE INFO Rely on NTP for time synchronization

For information on how to set up NTP on your servers to ensure time synchronization in the perimeter and the internal networks, look up *Windows Server 2008: The Complete Reference* by Ruest and Ruest (McGraw-Hill Osborne, 2008).

Quick Check

1. Your organization is an account organization in a federation partnership. It wants to support user access from the Internet, but it does not want to list its name within a drop-down list for privacy and security reasons. Which options are available to you to do this?

2. Which are the four role services and features that make up the AD FS server role?

3. Which are the three AD FS deployment designs?

Quick Check Answers

1. When you don't want to include your organization name in the organization drop-down list on the federation server's Web page, you can rely on the *whr* parameter to include your organization name directly within the query used to access the application. The format of the query should be as follows:

   ```
   https://webserver/appname/apppage.aspx?whr=urn:federation:accountpartner
   ```

2. AD FS includes four role services:

   ❑ The Federation Service provides the core AD FS functionality managing resource access, filtering claims, and generating security tokens.

   ❑ The Federation Service Proxy is an Internet relay that passes requests on to internal Federation Service servers.

   ❑ The claims-aware agent supports the integration of Web applications to AD FS processes.

   ❑ The Windows Token-based Agent supports the integration of Windows applications to AD FS processes.

3. AD FS supports three deployment designs: Federated Web Single-Sign-On, Federated Web SSO with Forest Trust, and Web SSO.

AD FS Installation Requirements

To prepare for an AD FS deployment, you must begin with its prerequisites. Table 17-2 outlines the basic requirements for an AD FS deployment. Note that the federation service was first released with Windows Server 2003 R2. Because of this, you can interoperate between Windows Server 2003 R2 and Windows Server 2008 federation systems. Table 17-2, however, lists requirements for AD FS only, which can run only on Windows Server 2008.

Table 17-2 AD FS Deployment Requirements

Hardware/Software	Requirement	Note
Processor	133 MHz for x86-based computers	Because of the low processor, memory, and disk space requirements for AD FS server roles, you can easily virtualize this role through Hyper-V.
RAM	512 MB	Recommended: 1 GB. AD FS is not a memory-intensive process, but it is always best to allocate at least 1 GB.
Hard disk space	10 MB for the AD FS installation	Recommended: a large system volume of at least 50 GB to ensure space for growth.
Operating system	Windows Server 2008 Enterprise Edition or Datacenter Edition	Federation Service, Federation Service Proxy, and AD FS Web Agent role services cannot run on earlier operating systems.
Web Services	IIS with ASP.NET enabled and .NET Framework 2.0	Use IIS 7.0 with ASP.NET 2.0 and .NET Framework 2.0.
Installation location	Default location on the system drive	The federation service and Federation Service Proxy cannot coexist on the same computer.
AD DS and AD LDS account store requirements	At least a single domain forest	Ideally, a minimum of two forests will exist. At worst, use one forest and one AD LDS store.
Installation certificate for TLS/SSL and token signing	Obtain an SSL server authentication certificate for each deployed AD FS server role	Rely on an external third-party commercial CA to obtain a trusted certificate or enterprise CAs. Use self-signed certificates only in testing environments. Each of the federation servers and the Federation Service Proxy and the Web agent servers needs an authentication certificate.
TCP/IP network connectivity	IPv4 or IPv6 connectivity, ideally static address assignments	Network connectivity must exist between client, domain controller, and computers hosting the federation service, the Federation Service Proxy and the AD FS Web agent.
DNS configuration	Create custom CNAME records of the internal server that is running the federation service	Do not use host files with DNS. Use proper DNS registrations.

Table 17-2   AD FS Deployment Requirements

Hardware/Software	Requirement	Note
Web browser	Microsoft Internet Explorer 5 or later, Mozilla Firefox, and Safari on Apple	JScript and at least trusted cookies must be enabled for the federation servers and Web applications.
Client operating system	Windows XP or Windows Vista for the AD FS client	The Vista OS is recommended.

MORE INFO   AD FS step-by-step guides

For access to AD FS step-by-step guides, go to *http://technet2.microsoft.com/windowsserver/en/tech-nologies/featured/adfs/default.mspx*.

Exam Tip   Because of its nature, the AD FS server role is ideal for virtualization through Windows Server 2008 Hyper-V.

Quick Check

1. Which ports must be open in a firewall to support AD FS operations?
2. Which claim types are supported by AD FS?

Quick Check Answers

1. AD FS relies on a single port for all its operations: port 443, the SSL/TLS HTTP or HTTPS port.
2. AD FS supports three claim types:
   - ❑ Identity claims, which can be user principal name, e-mail address, or common name
   - ❑ Group claims, which are nothing more than membership in specific distribution or security groups in AD DS
   - ❑ Custom claims, which can include any custom information such as a bank account number for the user

---

Upgrade Considerations

Many organizations choose to use a specific service account when deploying services such as AD FS. If you opted to do this in your Windows Server 2003 R2 deployment of AD FS, you must make note of which account and password is assigned to which service because the AD FS upgrade process automatically resets all these services, by default, to use the Network Service account. After the upgrade is complete, you can change the service back to the named service account you had previously assigned to it.

Ideally, you will test the upgrade in a laboratory, perhaps a virtual laboratory, before you begin the process in your production networks.

PRACTICE **Prepare an AD FS Deployment**

In this practice, you will create a complex AD FS environment that will consist of several computers. The computers you need for this practice are outlined in the "Before You Begin" section of this chapter. Table 17-3 outlines the roles each domain and computer will play in your AD FS deployment.

Table 17-3   AD FS Computer Roles

Domain Name	Role
contoso.com	Account Domain
woodgrovebank.com	Resource Domain
Computer Name	**Role**
SERVER01	AD DS domain controller for *contoso.com*, the account domain
SERVER03	The federation server for *contoso.com*, the account domain
SERVER04	The Federation Service Proxy for *contoso.com*, the account domain
SERVER05	The SQL Server database server for the AD RMS deployment in *contoso.com*
SERVER06	AD DS domain controller for *woodgrovebank.com*, the resource domain
SERVER07	The federation server for *woodgrovebank.com*, the resource domain
SERVER08	The Federation Service Proxy and AD FS–enabled Web server for *woodgrovebank.com*, the resource domain

Begin by preparing the DNS in each forest and then move on to install the federation servers. Then install the federation service proxies in both forests and AD FS–enable the Web site in the resource forest.

IMPORTANT   Perimeter networks

Note that this layout does not include perimeter networks. Perimeter networks require a complex TCP/IP configuration, which is not required for the purpose of this practice. However, make sure that your AD FS deployments include proper server placement within perimeter networks as outlined in Lesson 1, "Understanding and Installing Active Directory Federation Services."

▶ **Exercise 1   Configure Cross-DNS References**

In this exercise, you will configure the DNS servers in each forest to refer to the servers in the other forest. Because each forest is independent of the other, their DNS servers do not know about the other. To exchange information from one forest to the other, you need to implement cross-DNS references in each forest. The easiest way to do this is to use forwarders from one domain to the other and vice versa. Make sure SERVER01 and SERVER06 are running.

1. Log on to SERVER01 with the domain Administrator account.
2. Launch Server Manager from the Administrative Tools program group.
3. Expand Roles\DNS Serve\DNS\SERVER01.
4. Right-click SERVER01 in the tree pane and select Properties.
5. Click the Forwarders tab and click Edit.
6. Type the IP address of SERVER06 and click OK twice.
7. Repeat the procedure in reverse on SERVER06; that is, add the SERVER01 IP address as a forwarder for SERVER06.
8. Test the operation by pinging each server from the other. For example, use the following command to ping SERVER01 from SERVER06:

   ```
   ping server01.contoso.com
   ```

   You should receive a response stating the IP address of SERVER01.

▶ **Exercise 2   Install the Federation Servers**

In this exercise, you will install the federation servers. This involves the installation of the server role plus the required support services for the role. Make sure SERVER01, SERVER03, SERVER06, and SERVER07 are running.

1. Log on to SERVER07 with the domain Administrator account.

   You do not need as high privileges as the domain administrator to install and work with AD FS, but using these credentials here facilitates the exercise. Local administrative privileges are all that are required to work with AD FS.
2. Launch Server Manager from the Administrative Tools program group.
3. Right-click the Roles node in the tree pane and select Add Roles.
4. Review the Before You Begin information and click Next.
5. On the Select Server Roles page, select Active Directory Federation Services and click Next.
6. Review the information about the role and click Next.
7. On the Select Role Services page, select Federation Service. Server Manager prompts you to add the required role services and features. Click Add Required Role Services. Click Next.

8. On the Choose A Server Authentication Certificate For SSL Encryption page, select Create A Self-Signed Certificate For SSL Encryption and click Next.

   In a production environment, you would need to request certificates from a trusted CA so that all your systems will work together through the Internet.

9. On the Choose A Token-Signing Certificate page, select Create A Self-Signed Token-Signing Certificate and click Next.

10. On the Select Trust Policy page, select Create A New Trust Policy and click Next.

    Make a note of the path used to save this trust policy. Your federation relationship will rely on this policy to work.

11. Review the information on the Web Server (IIS) page and click Next.

12. On the Select Role Services page, accept the default values and click Next.

13. On the Confirm Installation Selections page, review your choices and click Install.

14. When the installation is complete, click Close to close the installation wizard.

15. Repeat the same procedure for SERVER03.

    Note that because SERVER03 is a root CA, the operation is shorter. However, use the same settings as with SERVER07. This means relying on self-signed certificates wherever possible.

IMPORTANT Default Web Site

When the AD FS installation is complete, you must configure the Default Web Site in IIS with TLS/SSL security on both federation servers. This will be done in Lesson 2, "Configuring and Using Active Directory Federation Services."

You begin with SERVER07 because it does not include any role and displays all the installation pages you would see when installing the AD FS role on a new server. Note that because SERVER03 already includes some server roles, the installation process on this server is shorter.

▶ **Exercise 3   Install the Federation Service Proxies**

In this exercise, you will install the federation service proxies. This involves the installation of the server role plus the required support services for the role. Make sure SERVER01, SERVER03, SERVER04, SERVER06, SERVER07, and SERVER08 are running.

1. Log on to SERVER08 with the domain Administrator account.

2. Launch Server Manager from the Administrative Tools program group.

3. Right-click the Roles node in the tree pane and select Add Roles.

4. Review the Before You Begin information and click Next.

5. On the Select Server Roles page, select Active Directory Federation Services and click Next.

6. Review the information about the role and click Next.

7. On the Select Role Services page, select Federation Service Proxy and click Add Required Role Services. Also, select AD FS Web Agents and click Next.

   Note that although you cannot add the Federation Service Proxy on the same server as the federation server, you can combine the FSP and the AD FS Web Agents role services.

8. On the Choose A Server Authentication Certificate For SSL Encryption page, select Create A Self-Signed Certificate For SSL Encryption and click Next.

   In a production environment, you would need to request certificates from a trusted CA so that all your systems will work together through the Internet.

9. On the Specify Federation Server page, type **server07.woodgrovebank.com** and click Validate.

   The validation should fail because you have not yet set up the trust relationship between each computer. This is done by exporting and importing the SSL certificates for each server through IIS. You will perform this task in Lesson 2.

10. Click Next.

11. On the Choose A Client Authentication Certificate page, select Create A Self-Signed Client Authentication Certificate and click Next.

12. Review the information on the Web Server (IIS) page and click Next.

13. On the Select Role Services page, accept the default values and click Next.

14. On the Confirm Installation Selections page, review your choices and click Install.

15. When the installation is complete, click Close to close the installation wizard.

16. Repeat the operation on SERVER04 in the *contoso.com* domain. When asked to input the federation server, type **server03.contoso.com**. Also, use self-signed certificates when prompted and do not install AD FS Web Agents on SERVER04. Its role is only that of an FSP because it is in the account organization.

   You begin with SERVER08 because it does not include any role and displays all the installation pages you would see when installing the AD FS role on a new server. Note that because SERVER04 already includes some server roles, the installation process on this server is shorter.

Exam Tip   Pay attention to the details of each installation type; they are covered on the exam.

Lesson Summary

■ AD FS extends your internal authentication store to external environments through identity federation and federation trusts.

- Federation partnerships always involve a resource and an account organization. A resource organization can be a partner of several account organizations, but an account organization can be a partner with only a single resource organization.
- AD FS relies on secure HTTP communications by using SSL authentication certificates to verify the identity of both the server and the client during communications. Because of this, all communications occur through port 433 over HTTPS.
- AD FS is a Web Services implementation that relies on standards-based implementations to ensure that it can interact with partners using different operating systems, for example, Windows, UNIX, and Linux.

Lesson Review

You can use the following questions to test your knowledge of the information in Lesson 1, "Understanding and Installing Active Directory Federation Services." The questions are also available on the companion CD if you prefer to review them in electronic form.

NOTE Answers

Answers to these questions and explanations of why each answer choice is right or wrong are located in the "Answers" section at the end of the book.

---

1. You are a systems administrator for Contoso, Ltd. Your organization already has a federation relationship with Woodgrove Bank, which was implemented using Federation Services with Windows Server 2003 R2. To improve security, you deployed the federation service with named accounts running the service. Now you're ready to upgrade to AD FS, but when you perform the upgrade, you find out that the named account used to run the service has been removed and replaced with the Network Service account. Why did this happen?

    A. You cannot use named service accounts to run the AD FS service.

    B. The default service account used in an AD FS installation or upgrade is Network Service.

    C. Woodgrove has a policy that states that all federation services must run with the Network Service account.

    D. Microsoft prefers to use the Network Service account to run federation services and resets it as a best practice.

Lesson 2: Configuring and Using Active Directory Federation Services

As you saw in Lesson 1, servers in an AD FS relationship must rely on certificates to create a chain of trust between each other and to ensure that all traffic transported over the trust relationships is encrypted at all times. As discussed in Chapter 15, "Active Directory Certificate Services and Public Key Infrastructures," the best way to ensure that this chain of trust is valid and is trusted in all locations is either to obtain certificates from a trusted third-party CA or obtain them through the creation of a linked AD CS implementation that uses a third-party CA as its root.

This is only one aspect of the AD FS configuration that must be completed. When you deploy AD FS, you will want to configure your AD FS–aware applications, configure trust policies between partner organizations, and configure claims for your users and groups. Then, you can generally begin to run and manage AD FS.

MORE INFO   AD FS operations

For more information on AD FS operations, look up "AD FS Operations Guide" at *http://technet2.microsoft.com/windowsserver/en/library/007d4d62-2e2e-43a9-8652-9108733cbb731033.mspx?mfr=true.*

> **After this lesson, you will be able to:**
> - Manage AD FS certificates.
> - Finalize AD FS server configurations.
> - Work with AD FS trust policies.
>
> **Estimated lesson time: 40 minutes**

Finalize the Configuration of AD FS

When you deploy AD FS, you must perform several activities to complete the configuration. These activities include:

- Configuring the Web service on each server to use SSL/TLS encryption for the Web site that is hosting the AD FS service.
- Exporting certificates from each server and importing them into the other servers that form the relationship. For example, the federation server's token-signing certificate must be installed as a validation certificate in the other servers in the trust relationship to support the AD FS security token exchange processes.
- Configuring IIS on the servers that will host the claims-aware applications. These servers must use HTTPS for application-related communications.

- Creating and configuring the claims-aware applications you will be hosting.
- Configuring the federation servers in each partner organization. This involves several steps, which include:
  - In an account organization, configuring the trust policy, creating claims for your users, and, finally, configuring the AD DS account store for identity federation.
  - In a resource organization, configuring the trust policy creating claims for your users, configuring an AD DS account store for identity federation, and then enabling a claims-aware application.
- Creating the federation trust to enable identity federation. This also involves several steps:
  - Exporting the trust policy from the account organization and importing it into the resource organization
  - Creating and configuring a claim mapping in the resource organization
  - Exporting the partner policy from the resource organization and importing it into the account organization

Much of this effort is related to certificate mapping from one server to another. One important factor is the ability to access the roots or at least the Web sites hosting the Certificate Revocation Lists (CRL) for each certificate. As discussed in Chapter 15, CRLs are the only way you can tell a member of a trust chain whether a certificate is valid. If it is supported, you can use the Microsoft Online Responder service (OCSP) from AD CS to do this as well.

In AD FS, CRL checking is enabled by default. CRL checking is mostly performed for the security token signatures, but it is good policy to rely on it for all digital signatures.

Using and Managing AD FS

When the configuration of the identity federation is complete, you will move on to regular administration and management of the AD FS services and server roles. You will rely on the Active Directory Federation Services console in Server Manager to perform these tasks. Administration tasks will include:

- Configuring the federation service or federation server farm. Remember that you can have up to three farms in an AD FS deployment:
  - A federation server farm that includes several servers hosting the same role
  - A Federation Service Proxy farm
  - A claims-aware application server farm running IIS
- Managing the trust policy that is associated with the federation service by:
  - Administering account stores in either AD DS or AD LDS.
  - Managing the account, resource partners, or both that trust your organization.
  - Managing claims on federation servers.

❑ Managing certificates used by federation servers.

❑ Managing certificates in AD FS–protected Web applications.

Because AD FS relies so heavily on IIS, many of the federation server settings that are configured in the Active Directory Federation Services node of Server Manager are stored in the Web.config file located in the Federation Service virtual directory in IIS. Other configuration settings are stored in the trust policy file. As with other IIS settings, the Web.config file can easily be edited directly because it is nothing more than a text file. The settings you can control through the Web.config file include:

- The path to the trust policy file.
- The local certificate used for signing tokens.
- The location of the ASP.NET Web pages supporting the service.
- The debug logging level for the service as well as the path to the log files directory.
- The ability to control the access type, for example, anonymous access, to group claims you prepare for the organization.

When edited, you can publish the Web.config file to other servers requiring the same configuration settings. After IIS has been reset, the new configuration will take effect.

However, the trust policy file should never be edited manually. This file should always be edited through the controls in the AD FS console or through programmatic settings that rely on the AD FS object model.

MORE INFO   **AD FS object model**

For more information on scripting support and the AD FS object model, see *http://msdn2.microsoft.com/en-us/library/ms674895.aspx*.

When you work with FSPs, you can rely on the AD FS console to configure:

- The federation service with which the FSP is working.
- The manner in which the FSP will collect user credential information from browsers and Web applications.

The settings configured for Federation Service proxies are also stored in a Web.config file, much like the federation server settings. However, because the FSP does not include a trust policy file, all its settings are stored within its Web.config file. These include:

- The Federation Service URL.
- The client authentication certificate to be used by the federation server proxy for TLS/SSL-encrypted communications with the federation service.
- The ASP.NET Web pages supporting the service.

Preparing and putting in place an identity federation through AD FS requires care and planning. Because of this, take the time to practice and prepare thoroughly in a laboratory before you move this technology into production.

PRACTICE **Finalizing the AD FS Configuration**

In this practice, you will finalize the AD FS installation you performed in Lesson 1. You will need to rely on the same computers you used in that practice. Begin by configuring the IIS server on each of the federation servers and then map certificates from one server to the other and configure the Web server. You can also create and configure the Web application that will be claims-aware. Then configure the federation servers for each partner organization. You finish the AD FS configuration by creating the federation trust.

▶ **Exercise 1   Configure SSL for the Federation Servers and the FSPs**

In this exercise, you will configure IIS to require SSL on the Default Web Site of the federation servers and the Federation Service proxies. Make sure that all servers are running. This includes SERVER01, SERVER03, SERVER04, SERVER05, SERVER06, SERVER07, and SERVER08.

1. Log on to SERVER03 with the domain Administrator account.

   You do not need domain administrative credentials; in fact, you need only local administrative credentials to perform this task, but using the domain Administrators account facilitates this exercise.

2. Launch Internet Information Services (IIS) Manager from the Administrative Tools program group.

3. Expand *Servername*\Sites\Default Web Site.

4. In the details pane, in the Features view, move to the IIS section and double-click SSL Settings.

5. On the SSL Settings page, select the Require SSL check box.

   In a production environment, you can also require 128-bit SSL, which is more secure than the default setting but requires additional processing overhead. For the purposes of this practice, the default setting is sufficient.

6. Under Client Certificates, select Accept, and then click Apply in the Actions pane.

7. Repeat this procedure on SERVER04, SERVER07, and SERVER08.

   All your AD FS servers are now configured to rely on SSL-encrypted communications.

▶ **Exercise 2   Export and Import Certificates**

One of the most important factors in setting up federation partnerships is the integration of the certificates from each server to link each server with the ones it needs to communicate with. To do so, you need to perform several tasks.

■ Create a file share that each server can access to simplify the transfer of certificate files from one server to another.

- Export the token-signing certificate from the account federation server (SERVER03) to a file.
- Export the server authentication certificate of the account federation server (SERVER03) to a file.
- Export the server authentication certificate of the resource federation server (SERVER07) to a file.
- Import the server authentication certificate for both federation servers.
- Export the client authentication certificate of the account Federation Service Proxy (SERVER04) to a file.
- Export the client authentication certificate of the resource Federation Service Proxy (SERVER08) to a file.
- Import the client authentication certificate on the respective federation servers.
- First, you need to create the file share you will use to store the certificates.

1. Log on to SERVER03 with the domain Administrator account.
2. Launch Windows Explorer and move to the C drive. Create a new folder and name it **Temp**.
3. Right-click the Temp folder and select Share.
4. In the File Sharing dialog box, select Everyone in the drop-down list, click Add, and from the Permission Level column, assign the Contributor role to Everyone.
5. Click Share.

    Your shared folder is ready. Proceed to the export of the security token signing certificate.

6. Log on to SERVER03 with the domain Administrator account.
7. Launch Active Directory Federation Services from the Administrative Tools program group.
8. Right-click Federation Service and select Properties on the General Tab. Click View.
9. Click the Details tab and click Copy To File.
10. On the Welcome To The Certificate Export Wizard page, click Next.
11. On the Export Private Key page, select No, Do Not Export The Private Key and click Next.

    You do not export the private key file because you are creating a validation certificate that consists only of the certificate's public key.

12. On the Export File Format page, ensure that DER Encoded Binary X.509 (.CER) is selected and click Next.
13. On the File To Export page, type **C:\Temp\SERVER03TokenSigning.cer** and click Next.

    This token-signing certificate will be imported to SERVER07 when the Account Partner Wizard prompts you for the Account Partner Verification Certificate. You can then use the shared TEMP folder to obtain this file over the network.

14. On the Completing The Certificate Export Wizard page, verify the information and click Finish. Click OK when you get the Certificate Export Was Successful message. Click OK twice to close the Federation Service property sheet.

So that successful communications can occur between both of the federation servers (SERVER03 and SERVER07) and their respective FSPs (SERVER04 and SERVER08) as well as with the Web server (SERVER08), each server must trust the root of the federation servers. Because you use self-signed certificates in this practice, you must export and import each certificate. Table 17-4 outlines which certificates must be exported and where they must be imported. (See also Figure 17-7.)

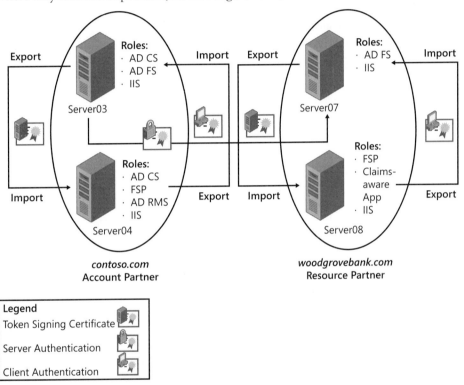

Figure 17-7   Preparing certificate mappings for AD FS

Table 17-4   AD FS Certificate Mappings

Server Name	Certificate to Export	Certificate Name	Location to Import
SERVER03	Token Signing	SERVER03TokenSigning.cer	SERVER07
SERVER03	SSL Server Authentication	SERVER03SSL.cer	SERVER04
SERVER04	SSL Client Authentication	SERVER04SSL.cer	SERVER03
SERVER07	SSL Server Authentication	SERVER07SSL.cer	SERVER08
SERVER08	SSL Client Authentication	SERVER08SSL.cer	SERVER07

▶ **Exercise 3   Export the SSL Server and Client Certificates**

Beginning with SERVER03, you will export the SSL server and client authentication certificates to a file on each server.

1. Log on to SERVER03 with domain Administrator credentials.
2. Launch Internet Information Services (IIS) Manager from the Administrative Tools program group.
3. In the details pane, click the server name.
4. In the Features view, move to the IIS section and double-click Server Certificates.
5. Double-click the Contoso-Root-CA certificate and click the Details tab.
6. On the Details tab, click Copy to File. Click Next.
7. On the Export Private Key page, select No, Do Not Export The Private Key and click Next.
8. On the Export File Format page, ensure that DER Encoded Binary X.509 (.CER) is selected and click Next.
9. On the File To Export page, click Browse and move to the C:\Temp folder. Name the certificate **SERVER03SSL.cer** and click Save. Click Next.
10. On the Completing The Certificate Export Wizard page, verify the information and click Finish. Click OK when you get the Certificate Export Was Successful message. Click OK again to close the dialog box.

Now move to SERVER04 and repeat the procedure.

1. Log on to SERVER04 with domain Administrator credentials.
2. Launch Internet Information Services (IIS) Manager from the Administrative Tools program group.
3. In the details pane, click the server name.
4. In the Features view, move to the IIS section and double-click Server Certificates.
5. Double-click the Contoso-Issuing-CA certificate and move to the Details tab.
6. On the Details tab, click Copy To File. Click Next.
7. On the Export Private Key page, click No, Do Not Export The Private Key and click Next.
8. On the Export File Format page, ensure that DER Encoded Binary X.509 (.CER) is selected and click Next.
9. On the File To Export page, click Browse and move to your Documents folder. Name the certificate **SERVER04SSL.cer**, click Save, and then click Next.
10. On the Completing The Certificate Export Wizard page, verify the information and click Finish.
11. Click OK when you get the Certificate Export Was Successful message. Click OK again to close the dialog box.

Now move to SERVER07 and repeat the procedure.

1. Log on to SERVER07 with domain Administrator credentials.
2. Launch Internet Information Services (IIS) Manager from the Administrative Tools program group.
3. In the details pane, click the server name.
4. In the Features view, move to the IIS section and double-click Server Certificates.
5. Double-click the SERVER07.WoodgroveBank.com certificate and move to the Details tab.
6. On the Details tab, click Copy To File. Click Next.
7. On the Export Private Key page, click No, Do Not Export The Private Key and click Next.
8. On the Export File Format page, ensure that DER Encoded Binary X.509 (.CER) is selected and click Next.
9. On the File To Export page, click Browse and move to your Documents folder. Name the certificate **SERVER07SSL.cer**, click Save, and then click Next.
10. On the Completing The Certificate Export Wizard page, verify the information and click Finish.
11. Click OK when you get the Certificate Export Was Successful message. Click OK again to close the dialog box.

Now move to SERVER08 and repeat the procedure.

1. Log on to SERVER08 with domain Administrator credentials.
2. Launch Internet Information Services (IIS) Manager from the Administrative Tools program group.
3. In the details pane, click the server name.
4. In the Features view, move to the IIS section and double-click Server Certificates.
5. Double-click the SERVER08.WoodgroveBank.com certificate and move to the Details tab.
6. On the Details tab, click Copy To File. Click Next.
7. On the Export Private Key page, click No, Do Not Export The Private Key and click Next.
8. On the Export File Format page, ensure that DER Encoded Binary X.509 (.CER) is selected and click Next.
9. On the File To Export page, click Browse and move to your Documents folder. Name the certificate **SERVER08SSL.cer**, click Save, and then click Next.
10. On the Completing The Certificate Export Wizard page, verify the information and click Finish.
11. Click OK when you get the Certificate Export Was Successful message. Click OK again to close the dialog box.

Because you will need to import these certificates into other servers, you need to copy them to a shared folder.

1. For SERVER04, SERVER07, and SERVER08, launch Windows Explorer and move to your Documents folder.

2. Right-click the certificate and select Copy.

3. Move to the address bar at the top of the Explorer window and type **\\SERVER03.Contoso.com\temp**.

4. If you used the same account name and password for the domain Administrators account in both domains, you will not be prompted for credentials. If not, type **Contoso*AdminAccount*** in the logon name box and type its corresponding password.

5. Paste the certificate into the Minimize Windows Explorer folder.

   Repeat this procedure on each server to place all the certificates in the \\SERVER03.contoso.com\TEMP folder.

▶ **Exercise 4   Import an SSL Authentication Certificate into a Server**

Beginning with SERVER03, you will import an SSL authentication certificate into a server.

1. Log on to SERVER03 with domain administrator credentials.

2. Move to the Start menu, type **mmc** in the Search box, and then press Enter.

3. In the new console, select Add/Remove Snap-in from the File menu, select the Certificate snap-in, and click Add.

4. Choose Computer Account and click Next. Ensure that Local Computer is selected, click Finish, and then click OK.

   Now you will save the console.

5. Select Save As from the File menu, browse to your Documents folder, and name it **Computer Certificates**.

6. Expand Console Root\Certificates (Local Computer) \Trusted Root Certification Authorities.

7. Right-click Trusted Root Certification Authorities, click All Tasks, and then click Import.

8. On the Welcome To The Certificate Import wizard page, click Next.

9. On the File To Import page, click Browse and move to the C:\Temp folder.

10. Select the certificate for SERVER04, SERVER04SSL.cer, and click Open. Click Next.

11. On the Certificate Store page, select Place All Certificates In The Following Store, make sure the selected store is Trusted Root Certification Authorities, and click Next.

12. On the Completing The Certificate Import Wizard page, verify the information and click Finish. Click OK to close the successful import message.

    Repeat these procedures for each certificate to import. Refer to Table 17-4 to see which certificate must be imported where. For each of the other servers, go to the shared TEMP folder on SERVER03 to obtain the certificate. Your certificate mappings are complete.

▶ **Exercise 5   Configure the Web Server**

To set up a claims-aware application on a Web server, you need to configure IIS and create a claims-aware application. To do so, perform the following steps. Make sure SERVER06 and SERVER08 are running.

1. Log on to SERVER08 with the domain Administrator account.

   You do not need domain administrative credentials; in fact, you need only local administrative credentials to perform this task, but using the domain Administrators account facilitates this exercise.

2. Launch Internet Information Services (IIS) Manager from the Administrative Tools program group.

3. In the tree, expand SERVER08\Sites\Default Web Site.

4. In the actions pane, under the Edit Site section, click Bindings.

5. In the Site Bindings dialog box, select the HTTPS binding and click Edit.

6. Verify that the SERVER08.WoodgroveBank.com certificate is bound to port 443. If not, select it and click OK.

7. Click Close to close the Site Bindings dialog box.

8. In the center pane, in the Features view, under the IIS section, double-click SSL Settings.

9. Verify that the settings require SSL and are set to accept client certificates. If not, change these settings and click Apply.

10. In the tree, double-click Default Web Site to return to the Features view.

Perform the following steps to create and configure a claims-aware application.

1. Right-click Default Web Site and select Add Application.

2. In the Add Application dialog box, in the *Alias* field, type **claimapplication01**.

3. Click Select, select Classic .NET AppPool from the drop-down list, and click OK.

4. Click the ellipse button (...) under Physical Path and select the C:\inetpub\wwwroot folder.

5. Click Make A New Folder, type **claimapplication01**, click OK, and then click OK again to close the dialog box.

   Your application has been created; however, it is an empty application. You do not need to actually create an application for the purpose of this exercise, but if you want to, you can.

MORE INFO   Create a sample claims-aware application

To create the three files that make up the sample claims-aware application, use the procedure called "Creating the Sample Claims-aware Application" from *http://207.46.196.114/ windowsserver2008/en/library/5ae6ce09-4494-480b-8816-8897bde359491033.mspx*. After these files are created, copy them into the C:\Inetpub\Wwwroot\Claimapp folder.

▶ **Exercise 6   Configure the Federation Servers**

Both federation servers need to be configured to operate properly. SERVER03, the account federation server, must have a configured trust policy. You must also create claims for your users and identify the AD DS account store. SERVER07, the resource federation server, must have a trust policy, claims for the users in the resource domain, a configured account store, and enabled claims-aware applications. Ensure that SERVER01, SERVER03, SERVER06, and SERVER07 are running.

1. Log on to SERVER03 with the domain Administrator account.

   In this case, you need to use domain administrator credentials to identify the account store.

2. Launch Active Directory Federation Services from the Administrative Tools program group.

3. Expand Federation Service\Trust Policy.

4. Right-click the trust policy to select Properties.

5. On the General tab, under Federation Service URI, type **urn:federation:Contoso**.

   Make sure you type the characters as they appear in your domain name because this value is case sensitive.

6. Ensure that the Federation Service endpoint URL lists https://SERVER03.Contoso.com /adfs/ls/.

7. Click the Display Name tab and, under Display Name For This Trust Policy, type **Contoso** to provide a name that does not depend on a single server. Click OK.

Now move to create claims for your users.

1. Expand Trust Policy\My Organization\Organization Claims.

2. Right-click Organization Claims, select New, and then choose Organization Claim.

3. In the Create A New Organization Claim dialog box, type **Woodgrove Bank Application Claim**.

4. Ensure that Group Claim is selected.

5. Click OK to create the claim.

   It should now be listed in the details pane.

Now, add the account store for *contoso.com*.

1. Move to the Account Stores node in the tree pane under My Organization.

2. Right-click Account Stores, select New, and then choose Account Store.

3. Review the information on the Welcome page and click Next.

4. On the Account Store Type page, ensure that Active Directory Domain Services (AD DS) is selected and click Next.

Note that only one AD DS store can be associated with an AD FS implementation. You can, however, add additional AD LDS stores along with the AD DS store.

5. On the Enable this Account Store page, ensure that the Enable This Account Store check box is selected and click Next. Click Finish to complete the operation.

Note that this adds Active Directory as a valid account store under the Account Stores node.

The last item to configure in the *contoso.com* or account organization is to map a group to the group claim you created earlier.

1. Right-click Active Directory under the Account Stores node, select New, and then choose Group Claim Extraction.
2. Click Add, type **Accounting**, and then click Check Names. Click OK.
3. Ensure that Woodgrove Bank Application Claim is selected in the drop-down list and click OK.

Note that AD FS relies on the e-mail group name to assign the group claim mapping.

The account federation server is now ready. Prepare the resource federation server, SERVER07.

1. Log on to SERVER07 with the domain Administrator account.

In this case, you need to use domain administrator credentials to identify the account store.

2. Launch Active Directory Federation Services from the Administrative Tools program group.
3. Expand Federation Service\Trust Policy.
4. Right-click the trust policy to select Properties.
5. On the General tab, under Federation Service URI, type **urn:federation:Woodgrove-Bank**.

Make sure you type the characters as they appear in your domain name because this value is case sensitive.

6. Make sure the Federation Service endpoint URL lists https://SERVER07.Woodgrove-Bank.com/adfs/ls/.
7. Click the Display Name tab and, under Display Name For This Trust Policy, type **Woodgrove Bank** to provide a name that does not depend on a single server. Click OK.

Now create claims for your users.

1. Expand Trust Policy\My Organization\Organization Claims.
2. Right-click Organization Claims, select New, and choose Organization Claim.
3. In the Create A New Organization Claim dialog box, type **Woodgrove Bank Application Claim**.

4. Ensure that Group Claim is selected.

5. Click OK to create the claim.

    It should now be listed in the details pane.

Now add the account store for *woodgrovebank.com*.

1. Move to the Account Stores node in the tree pane under My Organization.

2. Right-click Account Stores, select New, and choose Account Store.

3. Review the information on the Welcome page and click Next.

4. On the Account Store Type page, ensure that Active Directory Domain Services (AD DS) is selected and click Next.

5. On the Enable This Account Store page, ensure that the Enable This Account Store check box is selected and click Next. Click Finish to complete the operation.

    Note that this adds Active Directory as a valid account store under the Account Stores node.

Now add a claims-aware application to the AD FS resources.

1. Move to the Applications node under My Organization.

2. Right-click Applications, choose New, and then select Application.

3. Review the information on the Welcome page and click Next.

4. On the Application Type page, ensure that Claims-Aware Application is selected and click Next.

5. On the Application Details page, type **Claim Application 01** in the *Application Display Name* field and type the application URL as **https://SERVER08.WoodgroveBank.com/ claimapplication01**. Click Next.

6. On the Accept Identity Claims page, select User Principal Name and click Next.

    Note that you can add several identity claim types, but remember that they are processed in order, as outlined earlier.

7. Ensure that Enable This Application is selected and click Next. Click Finish to create the application.

8. Select the newly created application in the tree pane.

9. Move to the details pane and right-click Woodgrove Bank Application Claim and select Enable.

10. Verify that the new claim you created is enabled in the details pane.

    Your resource federation server is now ready to process claims.

Exam Tip   Make note of this procedure and practice the various operations several times. Configuring trust policies and user and group claim mapping is definitely part of the exam.

▶ **Exercise 7 Configure the Federation Trust**

Now that both federation servers have been configured, you can move on to the configuration of the federation trust. To do so, you must export the trust policy from the account federation server, import it into the resource federation server, create a claim mapping based on this policy, and then export the partner policy from the RFS to import it into the AFS. This will complete the AD FS implementation. Make sure that SERVER01, SERVER03, SERVER06, and SERVER07 are running.

1. Log on to SERVER03 with the domain Administrator account.
2. Launch Active Directory Federation Services from the Administrative Tools program group.
3. Expand Federation Service\Trust Policy.
4. Right-click Trust Policy and select Export Basic Partner Policy.
5. Click Browse, move to the C:\Temp folder, and name the policy **ContosoTrustPolicy.xml**. Click Save. Click OK to close the dialog box.

   In the release of Federation Services in Windows Server 2003 R2, the export and import of polices was done manually and could lead to errors. In AD FS, this process relies on the graphical interface to perform the task, reducing the possibility of error.

Now, import the policy into the RFS in Woodgrove Bank.

1. Log on to SERVER07 with the domain Administrator account.
2. Launch Active Directory Federation Services from the Administrative Tools program group.
3. Expand Federation Service\Trust Policy\Partner Organizations.
4. Right-click Account Partners, select New, and then choose Account Partner.
5. Review the information on the Welcome page and click Next.
6. On the Import Policy File page, select Yes, and then click Browse.
7. In the address bar, type **\\SERVER03.contoso.com\temp** and press Enter. Select the Contoso Trust Policy and click Open. Click Next.
8. On the Account Partner Details page, review the information and click Next.

   This information should be the same information you input when you configured the Trust Policy properties for the *contoso.com* domain.
9. On the Account Partner Verification Certificate page, ensure that Use The Verification Certificate In The Import Policy File is selected and click Next.
10. On the Federation Scenario page, ensure that Federated Web SSO is selected and click Next.
11. On the Account Partner Identity Claims page, ensure that the UPN Claim and the E-mail Claim check boxes are selected and click Next.

Remember that common names are very hard to validate and verify that they are unique. Therefore, avoid using them as much as possible.

12. On the Accepted UPN Suffixes page, type **Contoso.com**, click Add, and then click Next.

13. On the Accepted E-mail Suffixes page, type **Contoso.com**, click Add, and then click Next.

14. On the Enable This Account Partner page, ensure that the Enable This Account Partner check box is selected and click Next.

15. Click Finish to complete the operation.

    The account partner is now set up on the RFS. Note that it is now displayed under the Account Partners node.

Now you will create a claim mapping for this partner.

1. Right-click Contoso under the Account Partners node, select New, and then choose Incoming Group Claim Mapping.

2. In the Create A New Incoming Group Claim Mapping dialog box, type **Woodgrove Bank Application Claim**, ensure that the Woodgrove Bank Application Claim is selected in the drop-down list, and then click OK.

    Note that you must type in the uppercase and lowercase characters exactly as you typed them in the *contoso.com* domain when you created the group claim earlier. Using the same name in both the account and the resource organizations makes this easier.

You are now ready to export the partner policy from the RFS and import it into the AFS.

1. Right-click Contoso under the Account Partners node and select Export Policy.

2. In the Export Partner Policy dialog box, click Browse.

3. In the address bar, type **\\SERVER03.contoso.com\temp** and press Enter.

4. Type **ContosoPartnerPolicy** and click Save.

5. Click OK to complete the operation.

    You can now import this partner policy into the AFS.

6. Log on to SERVER03 with the domain Administrator account.

7. Launch Active Directory Federation Services from the Administrative Tools program group.

8. Expand Federation Service\Trust Policy\Partner Organizations.

9. Right-click Resource Partners, select New, and then choose Resource Partner.

10. Review the information on the Welcome page and click Next.

11. On the Import Policy File page, select Yes, and then click Browse.

12. Move to C:\Temp, select the Contoso Partner Policy and click Open. Click Next.

13. On the Resource Partner Details page, review the information and click Next.

    This information should be the same information you input when you configured the trust policy properties for the Woodgrove Bank domain.

14. On the Federation Scenario page, ensure that Federated Web SSO is selected and click Next.

15. On the Resource Partner Identity Claims page, ensure that the UPN Claim and the E-mail Claim check boxes are selected and click Next.

16. On the Select UPN Suffix page, ensure that Replace All UPN Suffixes With The Following is selected and that *contoso.com* is the UPN suffix listed. Click Next.

    Remember that only one UPN suffix can be used in a partnership even if you can have several in the AD DS forest.

17. On the Select E-mail Suffix page, ensure that Replace All E-Mail Suffixes With is selected and that *contoso.com* is the e-mail suffix that is listed. Click Next.

18. On the Enable This Resource Partner page, ensure that the Enable This Resource Partner check box is selected and click Next.

19. Click Finish to complete the operation.

    Woodgrove Bank should now be listed as a resource partner. Your implementation is complete.

Lesson Summary

- Because AD FS relies on secure communications, you must ensure that each server in an AD FS partnership trusts the root certificate that was used to issue certificates for each of the servers in the deployment. If you use self-signed certificates, you must export each certificate and then import it in the corresponding server's trusted CA stores.

- When you configure a partnership, you must first create claims-aware applications and assign specific claims to each partner in the partnership.

- After the claims have been created, you then identify which directory store will be used by each federation server in the deployment.

- You create a federation trust between the two partners. This involves preparing the trust policy on each server, exporting the trust policy from the account federation server, and importing it in the resource federation server. Then you can use this trust policy to assign claims to the account organization. To complete the federation trust, you export the partner policy from the RFS and then import it into the AFS. At this point, your partnership has been created.

Lesson Review

You can use the following questions to test your knowledge of the information in Lesson 2, "Configuring and Using Active Directory Federation Services." The questions are also available on the companion CD if you prefer to review them in electronic form.

NOTE Answers

Answers to these questions and explanations of why each answer choice is right or wrong are located in the "Answers" section at the end of the book.

---

1. You are an administrator for the *contoso.com* domain. Your organization has decided to create a federation partnership with Woodgrove Bank so that you can use identity federation to access a new application in the bank's perimeter network. The federation servers and Federation Service proxies are already in place, but you need to configure the federation trust to enable identity federation. Which steps must you perform? (Choose all that apply.)

   A. Communicate with your counterpart at Woodgrove Bank to establish how you will exchange information.

   B. Export the partner policy from Woodgrove Bank and import it into Contoso.

   C. Export the partner policy from Contoso and import it into Woodgrove Bank.

   D. Export the trust policy from Contoso and import it into Woodgrove Bank.

   E. Create and configure a claim mapping in Woodgrove Bank.

   F. Export the trust policy from the Woodgrove Bank and import it into Contoso.

Chapter Review

To further practice and reinforce the skills you learned in this chapter, you can perform the following tasks:

- Review the chapter summary.
- Review the list of key terms introduced in this chapter.
- Complete the case scenario. This scenario sets up a real-world situation involving the topics of this chapter and asks you to create a solution.
- Complete the suggested practices.
- Take a practice test.

Chapter Summary

- As a network operating system directory service, AD DS is mainly designed to work within the boundaries of your network. When you need to extend its identity and access (IDA) services to the outside world, you must rely on additional technologies. This is where AD FS comes in. The very purpose of AD FS is to provide external support for the internal IDA services you run, without having to open any special port on the firewall. Because of this, AD FS is an excellent tool for the foundation of partnerships. In the end, organizations partner through AD FS but continue to manage only their internal AD DS service.

- AD FS is composed of four role services: the Federation Service, the Federation Service Proxy, the Claims-aware Agent, and the Windows Token-based Agent. Note that the federation service and Federation Service Proxy cannot coexist on the same server.

- In addition to the basic technologies included in AD FS, the federation processes rely on claims to identify which access has been granted to users, cookies to simplify the logon process and support for single sign-on, and certificates to validate all transactions and secure all communications.

- AD FS supports three designs: Federated Web SSO, Federated Web SSO with Forest Trust, and Web SSO. Of the three, the most common deployment type is Federated Web SSO. In fact, the very existence of AD FS can help avoid the requirement for forest trusts that pass through firewalls.

Key Terms

Use these key terms to understand better the concepts covered in this chapter.

- **claim mapping**   When a federation server processes an incoming claim and filters it to extract appropriate authorizations for a user, it performs claim mapping.
- **federation trust**   The one-way trust between a resource organization and the account organization(s) it wants to partner with.
- **service-oriented architecture (SOA)**   SOAs are standards-based and language-agnostic architectures that rely on Web Services to support distributed services on the Internet.
- **Web services**   Standards-based Internet services that form part of an SOA. Commonly known Web services include the Simple Object Access Protocol (SOAP); the extended markup language (XML); and Universal Description, Discovery, and Integration (UDDI). Web services are language-agnostic, so they can interoperate between different IT infrastructures, for example, among UNIX, Linux, and Windows.
- **WS-Federation Passive Requestor Profile**   The component of WS-Federation that outlines the standard protocol to be used when passive clients access an application through a federation service.

Case Scenario

In the following case scenario, you will apply what you've learned about AD FS. You can find answers to the questions in this scenario in the "Answers" section at the end of this book.

Case Scenario: Choose the Right AD Technology

You are a systems administrator for Contoso, Ltd. Your organization has decided to deploy Windows Server 2008 and wants to implement several of its technologies. Specifically, your implementation goals are:

- To update your central authentication and authorization store.
- To ensure the protection of your intellectual property, especially when you work with partners.
- To support five applications running in the extranet.
    - ❑ Two of the applications are Windows-based and rely on Windows NT authentication.
    - ❑ Three of the applications are Web-based and rely on the authentication models supported by IIS.

- Clients for your extranet applications stem from three locations, which include the internal network, partner organizations, and the general public on the Internet.

- Because you are running applications in the extranet, you must have secure communications at all times.

Your goal is to identify which Windows Server 2008 technologies are required and how they should be implemented. What do you recommend?

Suggested Practices

To help you successfully master the exam objectives presented in this chapter, complete the following tasks.

Prepare for AD FS

The best way to practice for AD FS on the exam is to run through each of the practice exercises included in this chapter. They expose you to each of the elements required to understand the exam objective for this topic.

In addition, you can also run through the exercises outlined in the *Microsoft Step-by-Step Guide for Active Directory Federation Services*, which is available at *http://www.microsoft.com/downloads/details.aspx?familyid=062F7382-A82F-4428-9BBD-A103B9F27654&displaylang=en*.

Keep in mind that it is not recommended to install AD FS on an AD DS domain controller even though this is the method used in the step-by-step guide on the Microsoft Web site.

Take a Practice Test

The practice tests on this book's companion CD offer many options. For example, you can test yourself on just one exam objective, or you can test yourself on all the 70-640 certification exam content. You can set up the test so that it closely simulates the experience of taking a certification exam, or you can set it up in study mode so that you can look at the correct answers and explanations after you answer each question.

MORE INFO   Practice tests

For details about all the practice test options available, see the "How to Use the Practice Tests" section in this book's introduction.

Answers

Chapter 1: Lesson Review Answers

Lesson 1

1. **Correct Answers: A and B**

   A. **Correct:** A domain controller will create or join an Active Directory domain, which must have a valid DNS name.

   B. **Correct:** A domain must have a NetBIOS name to support earlier applications that use NetBIOS names.

   C. **Incorrect:** A DHCP server is not necessary. In fact, a domain controller should have statically assigned IP addresses.

   D. **Incorrect:** Although a DNS server is required for the functionality of a domain, if a DNS server does not exist, the Active Directory Installation Wizard will install and configure DNS service on the domain controller.

2. **Correct Answer: D**

   A. **Incorrect:** Windows Server 2008 forest functional level requires that all domains operate at Windows Server 2008 domain functional level. Because the Litware domain might include Windows Server 2003 domain controllers, that domain must remain at the Windows Server 2003 domain functional level. Therefore, the forest must also remain at Windows Server 2003 forest functional level.

   B. **Incorrect:** Windows Server 2008 forest functional level requires that all domains operate at Windows Server 2008 domain functional level. Because the Litware domain might include Windows Server 2003 domain controllers, that domain must remain at the Windows Server 2003 domain functional level. Therefore, the forest must also remain at Windows Server 2003 forest functional level.

   C. **Incorrect:** A domain operating at Windows Server 2008 domain functional level cannot include Windows Server 2003 domain controllers.

   D. **Correct:** The Litware domain might include Windows Server 2003 domain controllers and, therefore, must operate at Windows Server 2003 domain functional level. The forest functional level cannot be raised until all domains are operating at Windows Server 2008 domain functional level.

Lesson 2

1. **Correct Answer: A**
   A. **Correct:** A password is required so that it can be assigned to the local Administrator account on the server after AD DS is removed.
   B. **Incorrect:** SERVER02 is currently a domain controller, and you are logged on as Administrator. Therefore, you already have the credentials required to perform the demotion operation.
   C. **Incorrect:** SERVER02 is currently a domain controller, and you are logged on as Administrator. Therefore, you already have the credentials required to perform the demotion operation. The Domain Controllers group contains computer accounts for domain controllers.

2. **Correct Answer: D**
   A. **Incorrect:** AD CS is not supported on Server Core.
   B. **Incorrect:** AD FS is not supported on Server Core.
   C. **Incorrect:** AD RMS is not supported on Server Core.
   D. **Correct:** AD CS is not supported on Server Core, so you must reinstall the server with the full installation of Windows Server 2008.

Chapter 1: Case Scenario Answers

Case Scenario: Creating an Active Directory Forest

1. Yes. Server Core supports Active Directory Domain Services. You do not need a full installation of Windows Server 2008 to create a domain controller.
2. Use the *Netsh* command to configure IP addresses.
3. Use *Ocsetup.exe* to add server roles. Alternatively, there are parameters for the *Dcpromo.exe /unattend* command that can install the DNS service.
4. Use *Dcpromo.exe* to add and configure AD DS.

Chapter 2: Lesson Review Answers

Lesson 1

1. **Correct Answer: C**
   A. **Incorrect:** The Active Directory snap-in in Server Manager, if launched, will be run with the same credentials as the custom console. An Access Denied error will continue to occur.

B. **Incorrect:** Although *dsa.msc* is a shortcut to opening the Active Directory Users And Computers console, it will be run with the same credentials as the custom console. An Access Denied error will continue to occur.

C. **Correct:** An Access Denied error indicates that your credentials are not sufficient to perform the requested action. The question indicates that you are certain that you have permission. The answer introduces the assumption that you have a secondary account. Even though that account is not the Administrator, it is administrative. This is the best answer to the question.

D. **Incorrect:** *DSMOD USER* with the *-p* switch can be used to reset a user's password; however, the question is targeting the Access Denied error. There is no suggestion that the command prompt was launched with different credentials; therefore, you will continue to receive Access Denied errors.

Lesson 2

1. **Correct Answer: D**

    A. **Incorrect:** An Active Directory task, whether performed using command-line commands, scripts, or remote server administration tools, can be performed by any user who has been delegated permission to the task.

    B. **Incorrect:** Domain Admins are members of the Administrators group in the domain, so any permissions assigned to Administrators would also be assigned to you as a member of the Domain Admins group.

    C. **Incorrect:** The ability to delete an OU or any object in Active Directory is related to permissions, not to ownership.

    D. **Correct:** New organizational units are created with protection from deletion. You must remove the protection before deleting the OU. Protection can be removed using the Active Directory Users And Computers snap-in, with Advanced Features view, on the Object tab of an OU's properties dialog box.

Lesson 3

1. **Correct Answers: A, B, and D**

    A. **Correct:** Assigning an administrative task requires modifying the DACL of an object such as an OU. The Advanced Security Settings dialog box provides the most direct access to the permissions in the DACL. The Delegation of Control Wizard masks the complexities of object ACEs by stepping you through the assignment of permissions to groups. DSACLS can be used to manage Active Directory permissions from the command prompt.

    B. **Correct:** Assigning an administrative task requires modifying the DACL of an object such as an OU. The Advanced Security Settings dialog box provides the most direct access to the permissions in the DACL. The Delegation of Control Wizard masks the complexities of object ACEs by stepping you through the assignment of permissions to groups. DSACLS can be used to manage Active Directory permissions from the command prompt.

C. **Incorrect:** DSUTIL is used to manage the domain and directory service properties but is not used to manage object permissions.

D. **Correct:** Assigning an administrative task requires modifying the DACL of an object such as an OU. The Advanced Security Settings dialog box provides the most direct access to the permissions in the DACL. The Delegation of Control Wizard masks the complexities of object ACEs by stepping you through the assignment of permissions to groups. DSACLS can be used to manage Active Directory permissions from the command prompt.

Chapter 2: Case Scenario Answers

Case Scenario: Organizational Units and Delegation

1. The best design for computer objects at Contoso would be a single parent OU, within which child OUs would be created for each site. The support team at each site would be delegated control for computer objects in that site's OU. The parent OU would be used to delegate permissions so that the team at headquarters can manage computer objects in any site.

2. Even though each site has only one or two members of support personnel, it is always a best practice to create a group, place the users in that group, and delegate permissions to the group. As the organization and support teams grow and as users enter and leave the organization, managing permissions assigned to user accounts becomes very difficult. After the permission is assigned to a group, support personnel can simply be added to or removed from the group.

3. Because users at any site might request assistance from a support person in another site, users should remain within a single OU. There is no need to divide users into OUs by sites based on delegation or manageability. The OU containing the users would be delegated to a group that includes all support personnel. In fact, you could create a group that includes the groups of each site's support teams.

Chapter 3: Lesson Review Answers

Lesson 1

1. **Correct Answer: C**

A. **Incorrect:** Although a user account template will enable you to copy several dozen attributes of it to a new user account, you would have to copy the template 2,000 times to complete this task.

B. **Incorrect:** The *LDIFDE* command imports objects from LDIF files, which are not the format natively managed by Microsoft Office Excel.

C. **Correct:** The *CSVDE* command imports objects from comma-delimited text files. Excel can open, edit, and save these files.

D. **Incorrect:** The *Dsadd* command enables you to create a user from the command line, but you would need to run the command 2,000 times to complete your task.

2. **Correct Answer: A**

A. **Correct:** *LDIFDE* supports adding, modifying, or deleting Active Directory objects.

B. **Incorrect:** *Dsmod* modifies properties of an existing object.

C. **Incorrect:** *DEL* is a command that erases a file.

D. **Incorrect:** *CSVDE* can import users but cannot delete them.

Lesson 2

1. **Correct Answer: C**

A. **Incorrect:** There is no native cmdlet in Windows PowerShell for creating users.

B. **Incorrect:** ADSI does not provide a *NewUser* method.

C. **Correct:** A container, such as an OU or domain, provides a *Create* method to create objects of a specified class.

D. **Incorrect:** This is VBScript syntax, recognizable by its use of the Set statement.

2. **Correct Answer: D**

A. **Incorrect:** There is no native cmdlet in Windows PowerShell for creating users.

B. **Incorrect:** The *SetInfo* method commits a new user and its properties to Active Directory, but it must be used in conjunction with commands that create the object and its attributes. It cannot be used as a single command.

C. **Incorrect:** A container, such as an OU or domain, provides a *Create* method to create objects of a specified class, but until the *SetInfo* method is used, the object is not saved to Active Directory. Therefore, *Create* is not sufficient as a single command.

D. **Correct:** The *Dsadd* command can create a user with a single command.

3. **Correct Answers: A, B, and D**

A. **Correct:** An object is created by invoking the *Create* method of a container such as an OU.

B. **Correct:** The *SetInfo* method commits a new user and its properties to Active Directory. If the *SetInfo* method is not used, the new object and changes to its properties occur in your local representation of the object only.

    C. **Incorrect:** This code is invalid. It is similar to code that would be used in VBScript, though not in the creation of user objects.

    D. **Correct:** You must connect to the container in which the user will be created.

Lesson 3

1. **Correct Answer: C**

    A. **Incorrect:** You can use the Ctrl key to multiselect users, but they must be in a single OU. The ten users in this scenario are in different OUs.

    B. **Incorrect:** *Dsmod* will enable you to change the Office property, but *Dsget* will not locate the objects. *Dsget* is used to display attributes, not locate objects.

    C. **Correct:** You can use the *Dsquery* command to identify users whose Office property is set to *Miammi* and pipe the results to the *Dsmod* command to change the Office property.

    D. **Incorrect:** These cmdlets are not used with Active Directory objects.

2. **Correct Answers: B and C**

    A. **Incorrect:** Move-Item is a valid Windows PowerShell cmdlet that moves objects in a namespace, but Windows PowerShell does not yet expose Active Directory as a namespace.

    B. **Correct:** VBScript uses the *MoveHere* method of a container to move a user to the container.

    C. **Correct:** You can use the *Dsmove* command to move an object in Active Directory.

    D. **Incorrect:** The *Redirusr.exe* command is used to configure Active Directory so that new user objects created without specifying an OU will go to a container other than the default Users container.

    E. **Incorrect:** The Active Directory Migration Tool is used to migrate accounts between domains.

3. **Correct Answer: A**

    A. **Correct:** Computer restrictions limit the computers that a user can log on to. On the Account tab of her user account, you can click the Log On To button and add the computer by name to the list of allowed workstations.

    B. **Incorrect:** When a computer account is created, you can control who is allowed to join the computer to the domain with this button, but it has nothing to do with who can log on to the computer after it is a domain member.

    C. **Incorrect:** *Dsmove* is used to move an object in Active Directory.

    D. **Incorrect:** Although the user right to log on locally is required, the error message that she reports is not the message that would be received if she did not have the right to log on locally.

Chapter 3: Case Scenario Answers

Case Scenario: Import User Accounts

1. You should use a VBScript or Windows PowerShell script. Both of these scripting languages are capable of taking advantage of a database, such as an Excel file saved as a comma-separated values (.csv) file, as the source of data for user account creation. In the script, you can perform business logic. For example, you can construct the logon name and e-mail address attributes, using the user name information provided in the Excel file. Although *CSVDE* does enable you to import .csv files, it simply imports the attributes in the file; it cannot perform business logic or create new attributes in real time.

2. You can disable the accounts that are created until the students arrive.

3. In the Active Directory Users and Computers snap-in, you can select all users and change the *company* attribute one time. At the command prompt, you can use *Dsquery.exe* to pipe the DNs of all users to *Dsmod.exe*, which can change the company attribute.

Chapter 4: Lesson Review Answers

Lesson 1

1. **Correct Answer: B**
   A. **Incorrect:** Universal security groups cannot contain users or groups from trusted external domains. They can contain users, global groups, and other universal groups from any domain in the forest.
   B. **Correct:** Domain local security groups can contain members from trusted external domains.
   C. **Incorrect:** Global security groups cannot contain users or groups from trusted external domains. They can contain users and other global groups from the same domain only.
   D. **Incorrect:** Distribution groups cannot be assigned permissions to resources.

2. **Correct Answer: D**
   A. **Incorrect:** The group is a distribution group, which cannot be assigned permission. Changing the scope will not address that limitation.
   B. **Incorrect:** The group is a distribution group, which cannot be assigned permission. Changing the scope will not address that limitation.

C. **Incorrect:** The group is a distribution group. Adding it to the Domain Users group will not enable its members to access the shared folder.

D. **Correct:** The *−secgrp yes* switch will change the group type to a security group, after which you can add it to the ACL of the shared folder.

3. **Correct Answers: C, D, E, and F**

A. **Incorrect:** Global groups cannot contain global groups from other domains.

B. **Incorrect:** Global groups cannot contain global groups from other domains.

C. **Correct:** Global groups can contain users in the same forest.

D. **Correct:** Global groups can contain users in trusted domains.

E. **Correct:** Global groups can contain users in the same domain.

F. **Correct:** Global groups can contain global groups in the same domain.

G. **Incorrect:** Global groups cannot contain domain local groups.

H. **Incorrect:** Global groups cannot contain universal groups.

Lesson 2

1. **Correct Answers: B, C, and D**

A. **Incorrect:** The Remove-Item cmdlet in Windows PowerShell cannot be used to remove members of a group because groups are not exposed in a namespace.

B. **Correct:** *Dsrm* is used to delete a group.

C. **Correct:** *Dsmod* with the *−remmbr* option can remove members from a group.

D. **Correct:** *LDIFDE* with a change type of modify and a delete:member operation can remove members from a group.

E. **Incorrect:** *CSVDE* can import new groups. It cannot modify existing groups.

2. **Correct Answer: B**

A. **Incorrect:** *Dsrm* deletes a group. Deleting a group will not solve the problem.

B. **Correct:** You can use *Dsmod* with the *−scope* switch to change the scope of GroupA to a universal group, then to a global group. You will then be able to add GroupA to GroupB. This is a tricky question. Sometimes questions are not quite what they appear to be about on the surface. This question was not about using commands or even about adding one group to another—it was about group scope.

C. **Incorrect:** *Dsquery* searches Active Directory for objects. It cannot make a change, so it will not solve the problem.

D. **Incorrect:** *Dsget* retrieves an attribute of an object. It cannot make a change, so it will not solve the problem.

3. **Correct Answer: D**

   A. **Incorrect:** Get-Members is a Windows PowerShell cmdlet that gets the members of an programmatic object, not of a group.

   B. **Incorrect:** *Dsquery* queries Active Directory for objects matching a search filter. It does not list group membership.

   C. **Incorrect:** *LDIFDE* can be used to export a group and thereby its members, but only direct members.

   D. **Correct:** *Dsget* can return an attribute of an object, including the *member* attribute of group objects. With the *expand* option, *Dsget* can return the full membership of a group.

Lesson 3

1. **Correct Answer: D**

   A. **Incorrect:** The team members already have permission. This permission will not prevent them from accessing the folder from other computers.

   B. **Incorrect:** The team members already have permission. This permission will not prevent them from accessing the folder from other computers.

   C. **Incorrect:** This permission will not prevent users from accessing the folder from other computers.

   D. **Correct:** A Deny permission overrides Allow permissions. If a team member attempts to connect to the folder from another computer, he or she will be a member of the Network special identity group and will be denied access. If the same team member logs on locally to the conference room computer, he will be a member of Interactive and not Network, so the permissions assigned to him as a member of the team will allow access.

2. **Correct Answer: D**

   A. **Incorrect:** The Members tab of the group enables you to add and remove members but not to delegate the administration of membership.

   B. **Incorrect:** The Security tab of Mike Danseglio's user object determines who is delegated the ability to perform tasks on his object, not what Mike is able to do.

   C. **Incorrect:** The Member Of tab of Mike Danseglio's user object determines the groups to which Mike belongs, not the groups to which Mike has been delegated control.

   D. **Correct:** The Managed By tab of a group enables you to specify the group's manager and to allow the manager to update group membership.

3. **Correct Answers: B, C, and D**

    A. **Incorrect:** Account Operators does not have the right to shut down a domain controller.

    B. **Correct:** Print Operators has the right to shut down a domain controller.

    C. **Correct:** Backup Operators has the right to shut down a domain controller.

    D. **Correct:** Server Operators has the right to shut down a domain controller.

    E. **Incorrect:** The Interactive special identity group does not have the right to shut down a domain controller.

Chapter 4: Case Scenario Anwers

Case Scenario: Implementing a Group Strategy

1. Global security groups should be used to represent user roles at both Trey Research and Woodgrove Bank.

2. Domain local security groups should be used to manage Read and Write access to the Sliced Bread folders.

3. The Marketing and Research global groups will be members of the domain local group that manages Write access. The group that manages Read access will have the following members: Finance, the CEO, her assistant, and the Auditors global group from the Woodgrove Bank domain.

Chapter 5: Lesson Review Answers

Lesson 1

1. **Correct Answer: D**

    A. **Incorrect:** *Dsmove* is a command-line utility that moves existing objects in Active Directory. It does not control the default location for new objects.

    B. **Incorrect:** Move-Item is a Windows PowerShell cmdlet that moves existing objects in a namespace.

    C. **Inorrect:** *Netdom* is a command-line utility that enables you to join a domain, rename a computer, and perform other computer-related activities, but it does not control the default location for new computers.

    D. **Correct:** *Redircmp* is a command-line utility that redirects the default computer container to an alternate OU.

2. **Correct Answer: A**

   A. **Correct:** The *ms-DS-MachineAccountQuota* attribute of the domain by default allows all authenticated users the ability to join ten computers to the domain. This quota is checked when a user is joining a computer to the domain without a pre-staged account. Set this attribute to zero.

   B. **Incorrect:** This attribute configures the default quota for all Active Directory objects, not just for new computer accounts.

   C. **Incorrect:** Removing this user right does not prevent Authenticated Users from joining computers to the domain.

   D. **Incorrect:** Setting this permission will prevent all users, including administrators, from creating computer accounts.

3. **Correct Answer: B**

   A. **Incorrect:** *Dsadd* creates new objects, including computer objects, but does not join a computer to the account.

   B. **Correct:** *Netdom Join* can join the local computer or a remote computer to the domain

   C. **Incorrect:** *Dctest* tests various components of a domain controller.

   D. **Incorrect:** *System.cpl* is the System Properties control panel application. It enables you to join the local computer to a domain, but not to join a remote computer to a domain.

Lesson 2

1. **Correct Answer: C**

   A. **Incorrect:** *CSVDE* can import one or more computers but requires you first to create a comma-separated values file.

   B. **Incorrect:** *LDIFDE* can import one or more computers but requires you first to create an LDIF file.

   C. **Correct:** *Dsadd* enables you to create a computer object with a single command.

   D. **Incorrect:** Windows PowerShell enables you to use ADSI to create computers, but it takes several commands to do so.

   E. **Incorrect:** VBScript enables you to use ADSI to create computers, but it requires that you first create a script.

2. **Correct Answers: A, D, and E**

   A. **Correct:** *CSVDE* can import one or more computers from a .csv file, and Excel can save a worksheet as a .csv file.

   B. **Incorrect:** *LDIFDE* can import one or more computers, but the LDIF format cannot be created using Excel.

    C. **Incorrect:** *Dsadd* enables you to create computer objects one at a time.

    D. **Correct:** Windows PowerShell enables you to use ADSI to create computers and can use a .csv file as a data source.

    E. **Correct:** VBScript enables you to use ADSI to create computers and can use a .csv file as a data source.

Lesson 3

1. **Correct Answer: A**

    A. **Correct:** Such events are symptomatic of a broken secure channel. Resetting the computer's account is the correct step to take to address the issue.

    B. **Incorrect:** The event does not reflect user authentication problems.

    C. **Incorrect:** Disabling the server account will prevent the server from authenticating. Enabling it will not fix the problem.

    D. **Incorrect:** The event does not reflect user authentication problems.

2. **Correct Answers: C, D, and E**

    A. **Incorrect:** Deleting the computer account will cause its SID to be removed and its group memberships to be lost. You will be forced to add the new account to the same groups and to assign permissions to the new account.

    B. **Incorrect:** Creating a new account for the new system creates a new SID. Permissions will have to be reassigned and group memberships re-created.

    C. **Correct:** Resetting the computer account makes it available for a system to join the domain using the account. The account's SID and group memberships are preserved.

    D. **Correct:** You must rename the account so that it can be joined by the new system using its name.

    E. **Correct:** After resetting and renaming the account, you must join the new system to the domain.

3. **Correct Answer: C**

    A. **Incorrect:** A down arrow indicates that computer accounts are disabled. It is not necessary to reset the accounts.

    B. **Incorrect:** A down arrow indicates that computer accounts are already disabled.

    C. **Correct:** A down arrow indicates that the accounts are disabled. You need to enable them.

    D. **Incorrect:** A down arrow indicates that computer accounts are disabled. It is not necessary to delete the accounts.

Chapter 5: Case Scenario Answers

Case Scenario 1: Creating Computer Objects and Joining the Domain

1. Computers are added to the Computers container because it is the default computer container. When a computer is joined to the domain and an account has not been pre-staged in a specific OU, Windows creates the account in the default computer container.

2. The *Redircmp.exe* command can redirect the default computer container to the Clients OU.

3. You can reduce the *ms-DS-MachineAccountQuota* attribute to zero. By default, the value is 10, which allows all authenticated users to create computers and join up to ten systems to the domain.

Case Scenario 2: Automating the Creation of Computer Objects

1. *CSVDE* can import .csv files, which can be exported from Excel.

2. *Dsquery* computer "*DN of OU*" | dsmod computer –disabled yes

3. You can select 100 systems, right-click any one system, and choose Properties. You can change the *Description* attribute for all objects at one time in the Properties For Multiple Items dialog box.

Chapter 6: Lesson Review Answers

Lesson 1

1. **Correct Answers: B and D**

   A. **Incorrect:** The central store is used to centralize administrative templates so that they do not have to be maintained on administrators' workstations.

   B. **Correct:** To create GPOs, the business unit administrators must have permission to access the Group Policy Objects container. By default, the Group Policy Creator Owners group has permission, so adding the administrators to this group will allow them to create new GPOs.

   C. **Incorrect:** Business unit administrators require permission to link GPOs only to their business unit OU, not to the entire domain. Therefore, delegating permission to link GPOs to the domain grants too much permission to the administrators.

   D. **Correct:** After creating a GPO, business unit administrators must be able to scope the GPO to users and computers in their OU; therefore, they must have the Link GPOs permission.

2. **Correct Answers: B and D**

   A. **Incorrect:** The central store is used to centralize administrative templates so that they do not have to be maintained on administrators' workstations.

   B. **Correct:** To create GPOs, the business unit administrators must have permission to access the Group Policy Objects container. By default, the Group Policy Creator Owners group has permission, so adding the administrators to this group will allow them to create new GPOs.

   C. **Incorrect:** Business unit administrators require permission to link GPOs only to their business unit OU, not to the entire domain. Therefore, delegating permission to link GPOs to the domain grants too much permission to the administrators.

   D. **Correct:** After creating a GPO, business unit administrators must be able to scope the GPO to users and computers in their OU; therefore, they must have the Link GPOs permission.

3. **Correct Answer: D**

   A. **Incorrect:** A saved report is an HTML or XML description of a GPO and its settings. It cannot be imported into another GPO.

   B. **Incorrect:** The *Restore From Backup* command is used to restore a GPO in its entirety.

   C. **Incorrect:** You cannot paste settings into a GPO.

   D. **Correct:** You can import settings to an existing GPO from the backed-up settings of another GPO.

Lesson 2

1. **Correct Answers: B and C**

   A. **Incorrect:** If you configure a domain to block inheritance, GPOs linked to sites will not be applied to users or computers in the domain. The Northwind Lockdown GPO is linked to the domain and will apply to all users, including those in the Domain Admins group.

   B. **Correct:** By blocking inheritance on the OU that contains all the users in the Domain Admins group, you prevent the policy settings from applying to those users.

   C. **Correct:** The Deny Apply Group Policy permission, assigned to Domain Admins, exempts Domain Admins from the scope of the GPO, which otherwise applies to the Authenticated Users group.

   D. **Incorrect:** All user accounts in the domain belong to the Domain Users group as their primary group. Therefore, the GPO will apply to all users, including those in the Domain Admins group.

2. **Correct Answers: A and D**

   A. **Correct:** Because the desktop restrictions are in the User Configuration node but are being applied when users log on to specific computers, loopback policy processing is required.

   B. **Incorrect:** Linking the GPO to the OU containing user accounts causes the restrictions to apply to all users at all times, not only when they log on to conference and training room systems.

   C. **Incorrect:** The Block Inheritance option is not necessary and will prevent the application of all other GPOs from parent OUs, from the domain, and from sites.

   D. **Correct:** To scope the GPO correctly, you must link it to the OU containing the computer objects of conference and training room systems.

Lesson 3

1. **Correct Answers: B and D**

   A. **Incorrect:** The Group Policy Modeling Wizard is used to simulate Group Policy application, not to report its actual application.

   B. **Correct:** The Group Policy Results Wizard can be used to report Group Policy application on a remote system.

   C. **Incorrect:** *Gpupdate.exe* is used to initiate a manual policy refresh.

   D. **Correct:** *Gpresult.exe* can be used with the */s* switch to gather RSoP information remotely.

   E. **Incorrect:** *Msconfig.exe* is used to gather system information and to control system startup.

2. **Correct Answer: A**

   A. **Correct:** *Gpresult.exe* produces an RSoP report that will indicate when the GPO was applied. Screen saver policy settings are user configuration settings, so you must run *Gpresult.exe* for user settings.

   B. **Incorrect:** There is no *–computer* option for the *Gpresult.exe* command.

   C. **Incorrect:** Screen saver settings are user, not computer, configuration.

   D. **Incorrect:** *Gpupdate.exe* is used to trigger a policy refresh, not to report policy application.

Chapter 6: Case Scenario Answers

Case Scenario: Implementing Group Policy

1. The settings that control the user's desktop environment are found in the User Configuration node.

2. Link the GPO to the OU containing the training computers. If you link the GPO to the OU containing users, the settings will affect users on all computers at Northwind Traders.

3. You must enable loopback policy processing. By linking the GPO to the OU containing training room computers and enabling loopback processing, the training room computers will apply settings in the User Configuration node of the GPO.

4. Loopback policy processing must be configured in the Replace mode. In the Replace mode, user settings in GPOs scoped to the user are ignored. Only the user settings in GPOs scoped to the computer are applied.

5. You must exclude training room computers from the scope of the screen saver GPO. You can do this in one of two ways. You can block inheritance on the training room computer OU. Alternatively, you can use the security group filtering on the domain GPO. Create a group containing training room computers and assign the Deny Apply Group Policy permission to the screen saver GPO to that group.

Chapter 7: Lesson Review Answers

Lesson 1

1. **Correct Answers: A, B, C, and D**

   A. **Correct:** The local Administrator account is a default member of Administrators. It cannot be removed.

   B. **Correct:** Domain Admins is added to Administrators when a computer joins the domain. The Member Of policy settings add specified groups to Administrators and do not remove existing members.

   C. **Correct:** Sydney Support is added to the Administrators group by the Sydney Support GPO. The Member Of policy settings add specified groups to Administrators and do not remove existing members.

   D. **Correct:** Help Desk is added to the Administrators group by the Corporate Help Desk GPO. The Member Of policy settings add specified groups to Administrators and do not remove existing members.

   E. **Incorrect:** The Remote Desktop Users group is not a default member of Administrators and is not added to Administrators by any of the GPOs.

2. **Correct Answers: A and C**

   A. **Correct:** The local Administrator account is a default member of Administrators. It cannot be removed.

   B. **Incorrect:** Domain Admins is added to Administrators when a computer joins the domain but is removed by the Sydney Support GPO, which specifies the authoritative membership of the group.

   C. **Correct:** Sydney Support is added to the Administrators group by the Sydney Support GPO.

   D. **Incorrect:** Help Desk is specified as a member of the Administrators group by the Corporate Help Desk GPO, but the Sydney Support GPO has higher precedence because it is linked to the OU in which DESKTOP234 exists. Therefore, the membership specified by the Sydney Support GPO's Members Of This Group setting is authoritative.

   E. **Incorrect:** The Remote Desktop Users group is not a default member of Administrators and is not added to Administrators by any of the GPOs.

3. **Correct Answers: A, C, and D**

   A. **Correct:** The local Administrator account is a default member of Administrators. It cannot be removed.

   B. **Incorrect:** Domain Admins is added to Administrators when a computer joins the domain but is removed by the Corporate Help Desk GPO, which specifies the membership of Administrators using the Members Of This Group setting.

   C. **Correct:** Sydney Support is added to the Administrators group by the Sydney Support GPO. Because the Sydney Support GPO has higher precedence than the Corporate Help Desk GPO, DESKTOP234 applies the Sydney Support GPO after applying the Corporate Help Desk GPO; thus, the Sydney Support GPO's members are added to the Administrators group.

   D. **Correct:** Help Desk is specified as a member of the Administrators group by the Corporate Help Desk GPO. When this GPO is applied, all other members of Administrators, except the Administrator account itself, are removed.

   E. **Incorrect:** The Remote Desktop Users group is not a default member of Administrators and is not added to Administrators by any of the GPOs.

Lesson 2

1. **Correct Answer: B**

   A. **Incorrect:** Local Security Policy enables you to configure the settings on a single server.

   B. **Correct:** You can use Security Configuration And Analysis to compare the test environment configuration to a template, to reconcile discrepancies, and to export the resulting settings to a security template. The security template can then be imported into a GPO.

   C.   **Incorrect:** The Security Configuration Wizard does not manage user rights.

   D.   **Incorrect:** The Security Templates snap-in can create a security template but cannot export the settings of the test environment server. Security Configuration And Analysis is a better answer.

2. **Correct Answer: C**

   A.   **Incorrect:** Local Security Policy enables you to configure the settings on a single server.

   B.   **Incorrect:** Security Configuration And Analysis enables you to create security templates that can be imported into a GPO, but the tool is not role-based. The Security Configuration Wizard is a better answer.

   C.   **Correct:** The Security Configuration Wizard creates role-based security policies that manage services, firewall rules, and audit policies as well as certain registry settings.

   D.   **Incorrect:** Security Templates enables you to create security templates that can be imported into a GPO, but the tool is not role-based. The Security Configuration Wizard is a better answer.

3. **Correct Answers: A and D**

   A.   **Correct:** The *Scwcmd.exe /transform* command creates a GPO that includes the settings in the specified security policy.

   B.   **Incorrect:** You do not need to create a GPO. The *Scwcmd.exe* command does that automatically.

   C.   **Incorrect:** You do not import settings from a security policy into a GPO. You can import the settings from a security template into a GPO.

   D.   **Correct:** The GPO created must be linked to an appropriate site, domain, or OU before its settings are applied to computers in that container.

Lesson 3

1. **Correct Answers: B and D**

   A.   **Incorrect:** The goal is to deploy the application to computers, not to users. Therefore, the User Configuration node is not the correct place on which to create the software package.

   B.   **Correct:** To deploy the application to computers, the software package must be created in the Computer Configuration node of the GPO.

   C.   **Incorrect:** The software installation extension does not apply settings if a slow link is detected. Because the application is deployed to computers, not to users, configuring the connection speed in the User Configuration node does not change the default connection speed in the Computer Configuration node, 500 kbps. The connection from that branch office is less than 500 kbps, so computers in the branch office will not install the application.

   D. **Correct:** The software installation extension does not apply settings if a slow link is detected. By configuring the slow link detection threshold to 256, you ensure that clients connecting over the 364 kbps connection from the branch office will detect the link as a fast link, so clients will install the application.

   E. **Incorrect:** The software installation extension does not apply settings if a slow link is detected. The connection from that branch office is less than 1,000 kbps, so computers in the branch office will not install the application.

2. **Correct Answers: A and D**

   A. **Correct:** You want to deploy the application to users, so you must create the package in the User Configuration policies of a GPO. The GPO must then be scoped to apply only to sales users. Because all users are in a single OU, you must create a security group with which to filter the GPO.

   B. **Incorrect:** The GPO is not correctly scoped. Only computers exist in the Sales OU of each site. Computers will not process settings in the User Configuration policies under normal Group Policy processing.

   C. **Incorrect:** You want to deploy the application to users. Policies in the Computer Configuration node apply to computers. Because no computers are in the sales group, the policy will not be applied by any system.

   D. **Correct:** If a computer is configured to perform loopback policy processing, it applies settings in the User Configuration policies of GPOs scoped to the computer. The GPO is scoped to the sales computers by being linked to the Sales OU. Loopback processing enables the User Configuration software package to be installed by the computers.

3. **Correct Answers: A, C, D, and E**

   A. **Correct:** The software deployment GPO must be scoped to apply to all users in the four branch offices. Although you could link the GPO to each of the four selected branches, that was not presented as an option.

   B. **Incorrect:** The application must be fully installed before the user launches it for the first time. When you publish an application, the user must install it using Programs And Features in Control Panel on Window Server 2008 and Windows Vista or using Add/Remove Programs in Control Panel on Windows XP.

   C. **Correct:** For the application to be fully installed before the user opens it the first time, you must select the Install This Application At Logon option. Otherwise, the application will be installed when the user opens the application the first time or opens a file type associated with the application.

D. **Correct:** A shadow group is a group that contains users based on a characteristic such as the OU in which the user account exists. Because the GPO is linked to the Employees OU, it must be filtered with a security group that contains the users in the four branches.

E. **Correct:** For the application to be fully installed before the user opens it the first time, you must assign the application.

F. **Incorrect:** The Required Upgrade For Existing Packages option is used only in upgrade scenarios.

Lesson 4

1. **Correct Answer: D**

   A. **Incorrect:** Logon Event auditing is used to capture local interactive and network logon to workstations and servers.

   B. **Incorrect:** Directory Service Access auditing is used to monitor changes to objects and attributes in Active Directory.

   C. **Incorrect:** Privilege Use auditing relates to program execution and termination.

   D. **Correct:** Account Logon Event auditing creates events when a user attempts to log on with a domain user account to any computer in the domain.

   E. **Incorrect:** Account Management auditing creates events related to the creation, deletion, and modification of users, computers, and groups in Active Directory.

2. **Correct Answer: B**

   A. **Incorrect:** Account Management auditing creates events related to the creation, deletion, and modification of users, computers, and groups in Active Directory, but it does not show the previous and changed values of attributes.

   B. **Correct:** The *Auditpol.exe* command can be used to enable Directory Service Changes auditing, which logs the details of changes made to attributes as defined in the SACL of Active Directory objects. The previous and changed values of the attribute are included in the event log entry.

   C. **Incorrect:** Privilege Use auditing relates to program execution and termination.

   D. **Incorrect:** Directory Service Access auditing monitors changes to objects and attributes in Active Directory, but it does not report the previous and changed values of attributes.

3. **Correct Answers: E, F, and G**

   A. **Incorrect:** You have configured permissions that prevent access by consultants. Therefore, there will be no successful access attempts to audit.

   B. **Incorrect:** File system access events will be logged on the file servers, not on the domain controllers.

   C. **Incorrect:** Directory Service Access audit policy relates to changes to objects in Active Directory, not to a folder on a disk subsystem.

   D. **Incorrect:** The audit policy setting must apply to the file servers, not to domain controllers.

   E. **Correct:** You must enable Object Access auditing on the file servers. The Server Configuration GPO is scoped to apply to all file servers.

   F. **Correct:** File system access events will appear in the Security log of each file server.

   G. **Correct:** Auditing entries must be configured on the Confidential Data folder. Auditing failures to Full Control access will create audit events for any type of access that failed.

Chapter 7: Case Scenario Answers

Case Scenario 1: Software Installation with Group Policy Software Installation

1. The application package should be created in the Computer Configuration node so that it is installed on computers used by the mobile sales force. If the package is created in the User Configuration node, the application is associated with users and will be installed on any computer to which the users log on, including conference-room computers.

2. Advanced. Because the application package is created in the Computer Configuration node, Publish is not an available option. The available options are Assign and Advanced. You must choose Advanced to associate a transform with the package.

3. The GPO deploys the application in the Computer Configuration node, so the GPO must be scoped to computers. It can be linked to the domain or, better yet, to the Clients OU in which all client computers exist. The GPO must be further filtered to apply only to the computers used by the mobile sales force. This is accomplished by creating a global security group that contains the computers and using that group to filter the GPO. You must also remove the Authenticated Users group, which is given the Apply Group Policy permission by default.

Case Scenario 2: Security Configuration

1. Add an auditing entry that audits for failed attempts by the Everyone group to access the folder at the Full Control access level, which includes all other access levels. A second auditing entry must audit successful attempts by the Administrators group to access the folder at the Full Control access level, again to capture activities at any access level.

2. Restricted groups policies enable you to manage the membership of groups. A restricted groups policy setting for the Administrators group should be configured to

specify Members Of This Group are your account and the account of the VP of Human Resources. This policy setting is called the Members setting. It lists the final, authoritative membership of the specified group. The Administrator account cannot be removed from the Administrators group.

3. You must enable the Audit Object Access and Audit Privilege Use audit policies. Audit Object Access must be defined to audit Success and Failure events because the auditing entries on the Salaries folder are for both successful and failed access. Audit Privilege Use must be defined to audit Success events to log events when a member of the Administrators group takes ownership of a folder.

4. You can use security templates to manage the configuration of the seven servers. Security templates can be created on one system by using the Security Templates snap-in and imported to a database and thereafter applied to the servers by using the Security Configuration and Analysis snap-in.

5. Policy settings in Active Directory–based GPOs can override your security settings because domain-based GPOs override the configuration of local GPOs. You can monitor your server's configuration by running Resultant Set of Policy (RSoP) reports to identify settings in domain GPOs that conflict with your desired configuration or by using the Security Configuration and Analysis snap-in to compare the servers' configuration against the security template.

Chapter 8: Lesson Review Answers

Lesson 1

1. **Correct Answers: C, D, and E**
   A. **Incorrect:** The password policies in the Default Domain Policy GPO define policies for all users in the domain, not just for service accounts.
   B. **Incorrect:** PSOs cannot be linked to organizational units, only to groups and users.
   C. **Correct:** PSOs can be linked to groups, so you must create a group that contains the service accounts.
   D. **Correct:** The PSO must be applied to the Service Accounts group; otherwise, the settings contained in the PSO will not take effect.
   E. **Correct:** PSOs can be linked to groups, so you must create a group that contains the service accounts.

2. **Correct Answer: D**

A. **Incorrect:** The Account Lockout Duration policy setting is specified in minutes. This setting will lock out an account for 100 minutes, after which time the account will be unlocked automatically.

B. **Incorrect:** The Account Lockout Duration policy setting is specified in minutes. This setting will lock out an account for 1 minute, after which time, the account will be unlocked automatically.

C. **Incorrect:** The Account Lockout Threshold policy setting specifies how many invalid logon attempts result in account lockout. It does not determine the length of time for which an account is locked out.

D. **Correct:** An Account Lockout Duration policy setting of 0 locks the account indefinitely until an administrator unlocks the account.

3. **Correct Answer: C**

A. **Incorrect:** Although PSO1 has the highest precedence value, a PSO that applies to groups is overridden by a PSO that applies directly to the user, even if the user PSO has lower precedence.

B. **Incorrect:** A precedence value of 99 is lower than the precedence value of 1.

C. **Correct:** Although PSO3 does not have the highest precedence value (PSO1 is higher), it is linked to the user account, so it takes precedence.

D. **Incorrect:** PSO4 is a user-linked PSO, but its value, 200, is lower than PSO3.

Lesson 2

1. **Correct Answer: B**

A. **Incorrect:** This setting will generate event log entries when a user successfully logs on with a domain account. A successful logon does not generate account lockout.

B. **Correct:** Failed logons to a domain account can generate account lockout. Auditing for failed account logon events will generate event log entries that identify when the failed logons occur.

C. **Incorrect:** Logon events generate event log entries on the computer to which a user logs on or connects over the network. Local logons are not associated with account lockout.

D. **Incorrect:** Logon events generate event log entries on the computer to which a user logs on or connects over the network. Local logons are not associated with account lockout.

2. **Correct Answer: C**

A. **Incorrect:** Account logon events are generated when a user logs on with a domain account to any computer in the domain.

B. **Incorrect:** Audit policies are settings in the Computer Configuration node of a GPO. These settings do not apply to user accounts.

C. **Correct:** Logon events are generated in the event log of a computer when a user logs on interactively to the computer or connects to the computer over the network, for example, to a shared folder on the computer.

D. **Incorrect:** Account logon events are generated by domain controllers when they authenticate a user logging on to any computer in the domain. This GPO is not scoped to domain controllers.

Lesson 3

1. **Correct Answer: B**

   A. **Incorrect:** An RODC requires only one writable Windows Server 2008 domain controller. Such a domain controller already exists in your domain.

   B. **Correct:** You must run *Adprep /rodcprep* to configure the forest so that the RODC can replicate DNS application partitions.

   C. **Incorrect:** The *Dsmgmt* command is used to configure administrator role separation on an RODC after the RODC has been installed.

   D. **Incorrect:** You use the *Dcpromo* command to perform an installation of a domain controller, including an RODC.

2. **Correct Answer: A**

   A. **Correct:** The Policy Usage tab of the Advanced Password Replication Policy dialog box reports the accounts whose passwords are stored on an RODC.

   B. **Incorrect:** The Allowed RODC Password Replication Group specifies users whose credentials will be cached on all RODCs in the domain.

   C. **Incorrect:** The Denied RODC Password Replication Group specifies users whose credentials will not be cached on any RODC in the domain.

   D. **Incorrect:** The Resultant Policy tab evaluates the password replication policy for a user or computer; it does not indicate whether that user's or computer's credentials are yet cached on the RODC.

3. **Correct Answers: B and D**

   A. **Incorrect:** The Allowed RODC Password Replication Group specifies users whose credentials will be cached on all RODCs in the domain. The five users need to log on to only one of the branch offices.

   B. **Correct:** The Password Replication Policy tab of the branch office RODC is used to specify the credentials that can be cached by the RODC.

   C. **Incorrect:** The users do not require the right to log on locally to the branch office domain controller.

   D. **Correct:** By prepopulating the credentials of the five users, you ensure that the RODC will be able to authenticate the users without forwarding the authentication to the data center on the far side of the WAN link.

Chapter 8: Case Scenario Answers

Case Scenario 1: Increasing the Security of Administrative Accounts

1. Fine-grained password policies can be configured only in a domain at the domain functional level of Windows Server 2008. Before you can raise the domain functional level to Windows Server 2008, you must upgrade all Windows Server 2003 domain controllers to Windows Server 2008.
2. ADSI Edit.
3. You should assign a value between 1 and 9. Values closer to 1 have higher precedence. In addition, ensure that the new PSOs are not directly linked to the user account.
4. Define audit policy settings in the Default Domain Controllers GPO that configure auditing of failed account logon events.

Case Scenario 2: Increasing the Security and Reliability of Branch Office Authentication

1. Ensure that all domains are at the Windows Server 2003 domain functional level and that the forest is at the Windows Server 2003 forest functional level. On the schema master, run *Adprep /rodcprep*. Upgrade at least one Windows Server 2003 domain controller to Windows Server 2008.
2. You can delegate the installation of an RODC by pre-creating the computer accounts of the RODC in the Domain Controllers OU. When you do so, you can specify the user credentials that will be used to attach the RODC to the account, and then that user can successfully install the RODC without domain administrative privileges.
3. You can use the *Dsmgmt.exe* command to give the user local administrative privileges on the RODC.

Chapter 9: Lesson Review Answers

Lesson 1

1. Correct Answer: C
   A. **Incorrect:** You can use the command-line tool to create a domain tree. To do so, it is best to pre-create an answer file so that all values are passed automatically to the command during setup. However, you can also use the wizard to perform this task.
   B. **Incorrect:** Most often, you use standalone servers to create a new domain. This means you must log on with local administrative rights and then provide appropriate forest credentials to add the domain during the installation.

    C. **Correct:** The option to create a domain tree is not available in the wizard unless you select the advanced mode of the wizard at the very beginning.

    D. **Incorrect:** Credentials are requested by the wizard during the preparation process for the installation. Using a standalone or member server has no effect on the operation.

2. **Correct Answers: B and D**

    A. **Incorrect:** You must select the advanced mode of the wizard to create the domain tree, but selecting this mode has no impact on the wizard's ability to create the delegation.

    B. **Correct:** Because the delegation uses a top-level root name (.ms), you must create the delegation manually in your forest root domain. The wizard cannot create it automatically because you do not have credentials for the root DNS server that maintains this name.

    C. **Incorrect:** Because you create the delegation manually, you must tell the wizard to omit the creation.

    D. **Correct:** Because you created a manual delegation, you must tell the wizard to omit the delegation creation.

    E. **Incorrect:** You can create the delegation manually after the domain tree has been installed; however, it is a best practice to create it beforehand and then add components to its configuration after additional domain controllers have been created in the domain tree.

Lesson 2

1. **Correct Answers: A, B, C, D, and E**

    A. **Correct:** Your DNS server administrator might have already configured scavenging for all zones, but it is good practice to validate that it has been applied to your zone.

    B. **Correct:** By default, replication scopes are assigned properly when you create the zone, but it is always a good practice for your zone to use the appropriate replication scope.

    C. **Correct:** You might have other custom records to create, but you should create at least two: a text (TXT) record and a responsible person (RP) record. These will be used to update the Start of Authority record.

    D. **Correct:** The text (TXT) record will contain the information for the DNS operating standards you will apply to the zone.

    E. **Correct:** An e-mail address is assigned to a Responsible Person (RP) record to enable others to communicate with the operator in case of issues or problems with name resolution.

    F. **Incorrect:** Because the zone is new, there should be no unused records in the zone.

    G. **Incorrect**: Reverse lookup zones are required only when your zone hosts secure Web applications. No information about such an application has been provided.

2. **Correct Answers: A and B**

    A. **Correct:** Because all zones are located on domain controllers, you must use domain administrator credentials to manage DNS.

    B. **Correct**: If the server is not enlisted into the partition, the partition will not be available to the server.

    C. **Incorrect**: Enterprise administrator credentials are required only to create the application directory partition, not to assign it.

    D. **Incorrect**: You can use the command line to assign zones to partitions, but it is not mandatory.

    E. **Incorrect**: You can always change the replication scope of a partition in DNS after it has been created. It is one of the basic operations DNS zone administrators must perform.

Chapter 9: Case Scenario Answers

Case Scenario: Block Specific DNS Names

Trey Research can add the two problematic names to the global query block list on their DNS servers. This is done through the command line. The corresponding command is:

```
dnscmd /config /globalqueryblocklist wpad isatap biometrics biology
```

This command ensures that the Web Proxy Automatic Discovery protocol and the Intra-site Automatic Tunneling Addressing Protocol that are blocked by default continue to be blocked as well as adding the two problematic department names. Now, even if the administrative policies are not followed, the possibility of spoofing from these departments will be greatly limited.

Remember that this command affects all the FLZs hosted on a particular DNS server. If you have other DNS servers hosting other zones, for example, a DNS server in a child domain, you must run the command on those servers as well.

Chapter 10: Lesson Review Answers

Lesson 1

1. **Correct Answer: D**

    A. **Incorrect:** Because you are upgrading the operative system of a domain controller, you must perform another step prior to the upgrade.

    B.   **Incorrect:** The *Adprep /domainprep /gpprep* command must be run prior to upgrading the domain controller, but you must perform another step prior to running this command.

    C.   **Incorrect:** The server is already a domain controller, so it is not necessary to run the Active Directory Domain Services Installation Wizard.

    D.   **Correct:** You must run *Adprep /forestprep* on the schema master of the forest as the first step to prepare the forest for a Windows Server 2008 domain controller.

    E.   **Incorrect:** The *Adprep /rodcprep* command must be run prior to installing a read-only domain controller.

2.   **Correct Answers: B, C, and D**

    A.   **Incorrect:** Because the domain was built using only Windows Server 2008 domain controllers, it is not necessary to run *Adprep /rodcprep*.

    B.   **Correct:** To allow a nonadministrative user to attach an RODC to the domain, an account must be prestaged in the Domain Controllers OU.

    C.   **Correct:** The UseExistingAccount option of the *Dcpromo.exe* command enables you to attach a server to a prestaged RODC account.

    D.   **Correct:** To attach a server to a prestaged RODC account, the server must be removed from the domain prior to running *Dcpromo.exe*.

3.   **Correct Answer: C**

    A.   **Incorrect:** *NTBackup* and system state backups are not supported in Windows Server 2008.

    B.   **Incorrect:** Adding the Windows Server Backup Features is not sufficient to create installation media.

    C.   **Correct:** The *Ntdsutil.exe* command enables you to create installation media. The Sysvol and Full options will create installation media that include SYSVOL for a writable domain controller.

    D.   **Incorrect:** A copy of the directory and SYSVOL is not used for installation of a domain controller.

Lesson 2

1.   **Correct Answer: E**

    A.   **Incorrect:** The infrastructure master should not be placed on a domain controller that is a GC server unless all domain controllers in the domain are GC servers.

    B.   **Incorrect:** Although there can be benefits to transferring the RID master role, it is not the required change in this scenario.

    C.   **Incorrect:** Although there can be benefits to transferring the schema master role, it is not the required change in this scenario.

    D. **Incorrect:** Although there can be benefits to transferring the domain naming master role, it is not the required change in this scenario.

    E. **Correct:** The infrastructure master should not be placed on a domain controller that is a GC server unless all domain controllers in the domain are GC servers. Because SERVER02 is not a GC server, you should transfer the infrastructure master role to SERVER02.

2. **Correct Answers: D and E**

    A. **Incorrect:** The infrastructure master role is specific to each domain. You do not need to transfer it and, in fact, you cannot transfer it to a domain controller in another domain.

    B. **Incorrect:** The PDC Emulator role is specific to each domain. You do not need to transfer it and, in fact, you cannot transfer it to a domain controller in another domain.

    C. **Incorrect:** The RID master role is specific to each domain. You do not need to transfer it and, in fact, you cannot transfer it to a domain controller in another domain.

    D. **Correct:** The schema master role is a forest role. It should be transferred to the *contoso.com* domain prior to decommissioning the domain.

    E. **Correct:** The domain naming master role is a forest role. It should be transferred to the *contoso.com* domain prior to decommissioning the domain.

3. **Correct Answers: A, B, and C**

    A. **Correct:** The infrastructure master is a domain operations master.

    B. **Correct:** The PDC emulator is a domain operations master.

    C. **Correct:** The RID master is a domain operations master.

    D. **Incorrect:** The schema master is a forest operations master, not a domain operations master.

    E. **Incorrect:** The domain naming master is a forest operations master, not a domain operations master.

Lesson 3

1. **Correct Answers: C and D**

    A. **Incorrect:** The replication of SYSVOL by using DFS-R within a domain is dependent upon the domain controllers of that domain, not on domain controllers in other domains.

    B. **Incorrect:** The replication of SYSVOL by using DFS-R within a domain is dependent upon the domain functional level of that domain, not on the forest functional level.

    C. **Correct:** All domain controllers must be running Windows Server 2008 before you can replicate SYSVOL by using DFS-R within that domain.

    D. **Correct:** The domain must be at Windows Server 2008 domain functional level before you can replicate SYSVOL by using DFS-R within that domain.

    E. **Incorrect:** The replication of SYSVOL by using DFS-R within a domain is dependent upon the domain functional level of that domain, not on the domain functional level of other domains.

2. **Correct Answer: A**

    A. **Correct:** The *Dfsrmig.exe* command is used to migrate the replication of SYSVOL from FRS to DFS-R.

    B. **Incorrect:** The *Repadmin.exe* command is used to manage Active Directory replication, not SYSVOL replication.

    C. **Incorrect:** The *Dfsutil.exe* command is used to perform administrative tasks on a DFS namespace, not to configure SYSVOL replication.

    D. **Incorrect:** The *Dfscmd.exe* command is used to perform administrative tasks on a DFS namespace, not to configure SYSVOL replication.

Chapter 10: Case Scenario Answers

Case Scenario: Upgrading a Domain

1. You must run *Adprep /forestprep* before installing any Windows Server 2008 domain controllers in a forest.

2. It is not possible for all domain controllers in a domain to be read-only. There must be at least one writable domain controller, so it is not possible to have all three branches served by read-only domain controllers. One DC must be writable. Alternatively, one writable DC could be maintained in a central location, and three RODCs could be deployed to the three branches.

3. When there is planned downtime for a server performing single master operations, you should transfer the operations to another domain controller. When the original master comes back online, you can transfer the operations back to it.

Chapter 11: Lesson Review Answers

Lesson 1

1. **Correct Answer: C**

A. **Incorrect:** Every domain controller is assigned to a site. It might be in the wrong site, but it is reflected as a server object in a site.

B. **Incorrect:** You cannot create a site without a site link, so the branch office site is on a site link. It might be the wrong site link, but it is assigned to a site link.

C. **Correct:** If the branch office IP address range is not represented by a subnet object, which is then associated with the site, then computers might authenticate against domain controllers in another site.

D. **Incorrect:** It is not possible to assign a subnet to two different sites.

2. **Correct Answers: A, D, and E**

A. **Correct:** A subnet object with the IP address range of the branch enables clients to be informed of their site.

B. **Incorrect:** The computer account for each domain controller should be in the Domain Controllers OU.

C. **Incorrect:** Two site link transports are supported by Active Directory: IP and SMTP. No additional site link transport is necessary.

D. **Correct:** A site object for the branch office is required to manage service localization, such as authentication, within the branch office.

E. **Correct:** A server object for the domain controller must be in the site object.

Lesson 2

1. **Correct Answer: D**

A. **Incorrect:** A read-only domain controller must still be able to contact a global catalog server.

B. **Incorrect:** Application directory partitions are not involved with user authentication.

C. **Incorrect:** Intersite replication will not address the problem caused when the branch domain controller cannot contact a global catalog server.

D. **Correct:** Universal group membership caching, implemented for the branch office site, will cause the domain controller to cache users' universal group memberships from a global catalog server, so that logon is not denied.

2. **Correct Answers: D and E**

A. **Incorrect:** The schema partition is replicated to all domain controllers in the forest. However, you should make sure that the domain controller you are demoting is not the schema operations master.

B. **Incorrect:** The configuration partition is replicated to all domain controllers in the forest.

C. **Incorrect:** The domain naming context is replicated to all domain controllers in the domain.

D. **Correct:** A global catalog is on only one domain controller, by default. It is possible that the domain controller you want to demote is the only global catalog server, in which case, you should configure another global catalog server prior to demoting the domain controller.

E. **Correct:** Application directory partitions can be hosted on one or more domain controllers. It is possible for an application directory partition to exist only on the domain controller you are planning to demote.

3. **Correct Answer: C**

A. **Incorrect:** You can use *Dcpromo.exe* to specify that a new domain controller should be a global catalog server, but you cannot use *Dcpromo.exe* to modify existing domain controllers.

B. **Incorrect:** You can use the Active Directory Domain Services Installation Wizard to specify that a new domain controller should be a global catalog server, but you cannot use the wizard to modify existing domain controllers.

C. **Correct:** Use the Active Directory Sites and Services snap-in to configure a global catalog server by opening the properties of the *NTDS Settings* object within the server object representing the domain controller.

D. **Incorrect:** The Active Directory Users and Computers snap-in cannot be used to configure global catalog servers.

E. **Incorrect:** The Active Directory Domains and Trusts snap-in cannot be used to configure global catalog servers.

Lesson 3

1. **Correct Answer: D**

A. **Incorrect:** The total cost of replication from Site A to Site C over the links to Site B would be 350. The cost of replication over link A-C is only 100. Replication will use link A-C.

B. **Incorrect:** The total cost of replication from Site A to Site C over the links to Site B would be 350. The cost of replication over link A-C is only 100. Replication will use link A-C.

C. **Incorrect:** The total cost of replication from Site A to Site C over the links to Site B would be 150. The cost of replication over link A-C is only 100. Replication will use link A-C.

D. **Correct:** The total cost of replication from Site A to Site C over the links to Site B is 200. If the cost of replication over link A-C is over 200, replication will use links A-B and C-B.

2. **Correct Answers: B and C**

A. **Incorrect:** If there is a site link from sites A to C, it is possible that replication might occur between sites on that link. You have not prevented replication directly between Site A and Site C.

B. **Correct:** To prevent replication between Sites A and C, you must delete the site link that contains those two sites.

C. **Correct:** Site links are transitive by default, so Site A can replicate directly with Site C, using links A-B and B-C. You must disable site link transitivity.

D. **Incorrect:** Reducing site link costs will encourage replication to avoid creating a connection over link A-C. However, it does not ensure that changes are sent, first, to Site B.

3. **Correct Answer: A**

A. **Correct:** When IP connectivity is not available, SMTP must be used for replication, and SMTP cannot be used to replicate the domain naming context. Therefore, the ship must be a separate domain in the forest.

B. **Incorrect:** Increasing the cost of the site link will not enable replication between the ship and headquarters.

C. **Incorrect:** Designating a bridgehead server will not enable replication between the ship and headquarters.

D. **Incorrect:** Manually creating a connection object will not enable replication between the ship and headquarters.

4. **Correct Answers: A and B**

A. **Correct:** In the Active Directory Sites And Services snap-in, you can right-click NTDS Settings and force replication.

B. **Correct:** The Replication Diagnostics tool, *Repadmin.exe*, enables you to force replication from the command line.

C. **Incorrect:** The Directory Service Diagnosis tool, *Dcdiag.exe*, is a command-line tool that enables you to test the health of replication and security for Active Directory Domain Services.

D. **Incorrect:** The Active Directory Domains And Trusts snap-in is used to create and manage user, group, and computer objects. It does not enable you to force replication.

Chapter 11: Case Scenario Answers

Case Scenario: Configuring Sites and Subnets

1. Create one Active Directory site for Denver. Intrasite replication topology, created by the KCC, generates a two-way topology with a maximum of three hops. Replication will occur within one minute. If the headquarters and the warehouse are in separate sites,

intersite replication frequency is, at best, every 15 minutes.

2. Designating a preferred bridgehead server is useful to ensure that the role is performed by a server with the most available system resources. It can also be useful if network configuration, such as firewalls, requires that replication traffic be directed to a single IP address. However, if the preferred bridgehead server is not available, the intersite topology generator (ISTG) does not automatically designate a temporary bridgehead. Therefore, replication stops if the preferred bridgehead server is offline.

3. To achieve a true hub-and-spoke topology, you must create five site links. Each site link contains the Denver site and one of the branches. Therefore, the five site links would be: Denver–Portland, Denver–Seattle, Denver–Chicago, Denver–Miami, and Denver–Fort Lauderdale. You must also disable site link transitivity so that replication cannot build connections that skip over the Denver site.

4. Create a manual connection object for the warehouse domain controller so that it receives replication from SERVER01. A manual connection object will not be deleted by the KCC when it builds the intrasite replication topology.

Chapter 12: Lesson Review Answers

Lesson 1

1. **Correct Answers: A and D**

    A. **Correct:** In Active Directory Users And Computers, you can right-click the root node of the snap-in or the domain, and you will find the Raise Domain Functional Level command.

    B. **Incorrect:** Active Directory Schema is not used to raise the domain functional level.

    C. **Incorrect:** Active Directory Sites And Services is not used to raise the domain functional level.

    D. **Correct:** You can right-click the domain in the Active Directory Domains And Trusts snap-in and choose Raise Domain Functional Level.

2. **Correct Answers: B, D, and E**

    A. **Incorrect:** You must have one writable domain controller running Windows Server 2008 before adding an RODC to a domain. You already have a Windows Server 2008 domain controller in the *contoso.com* domain.

    B. **Correct:** The domain functional level must be at least Windows Server 2003 before adding an RODC.

    C. **Incorrect:** You cannot raise the domain functional level to Windows Server 2008 because you have a domain controller running Windows Server 2003.

D. **Correct:** The forest functional level must be at least Windows Server 2003 before adding an RODC.

E. **Correct:** You must run *Adprep /rodcprep* before adding the first RODC to a domain.

F. **Incorrect:** You already have a Windows Server 2008 domain controller, so you have already run *Adprep /forestprep*.

3. **Correct Answer: C**

A. **Incorrect:** RODCs are not required to implement fine-grained password policies.

B. **Incorrect:** The *Dfsrmig.exe* command configures DFS-R of SYSVOL.

C. **Correct:** Windows Server 2008 forest functional level is required for fine-grained password policies.

D. **Incorrect:** Fine-grained password policies are not managed with the GPMC.

Lesson 2

1. **Correct Answers: A, C, and G**

A. **Correct:** The users in *wingtiptoys.com* will authenticate with computers in the *tailspintoys.com* domain. That makes *wingtiptoys.com* the trusted domain. The trust you must configure in *wingtiptoys.com* is an incoming trust.

B. **Incorrect:** An outgoing trust would allow users in *tailspintoys.com* to authenticate with computers in *wingtiptoys.com*.

C. **Correct:** The users in *wingtiptoys.com* are required to log on to computers in *tailspintoys.com*, but there is no requirement for users in *tailspintoys.com* to authenticate with computers in *wingtiptoys.com*.

D. **Incorrect:** The users in *tailspintoys.com* are not required to log on to computers in *wingtiptoys.com*.

E. **Incorrect:** Realm trusts are created with Kerberos v5 realms, not with Windows domains.

F. **Incorrect:** A shortcut trust is used between domains in a multidomain forest.

G. **Correct:** Because users in both the *europe.wingtiptoys.com* and *wingtiptoys.com* domains will authenticate with computers in *tailspintoys.com*, a forest trust is required. Forest trusts are transitive.

H. **Incorrect:** An external trust would not provide the ability for users in the *europe.wingtiptoys.com* domain to authenticate with computers in the *tailspintoys.com* domain.

2. **Correct Answers: C and D**

A. **Incorrect:** Creating duplicate accounts for the users will not enable the users to access resources.

    B. **Incorrect:** Rebuilding the Windows NT 4.0 domain will not enable the users to access resources.

    C. **Correct:** The */verify* parameter verifies the health of an existing trust relationship. Some trusted users are able to access the resources, so the trust relationship is known to be healthy.

    D. **Correct:** The fact that the problematic accounts were migrated from Windows NT 4.0 suggests that there are SIDs in the users' *sIDHistory* attributes that are being filtered out because SID filtering is enabled by default on all external trusts. The */quarantine:no* parameter will disable SID filtering.

3. **Correct Answer: D**

    A. **Incorrect:** Reinstalling the operating systems is unlikely to solve the problem because performance is reasonable for accessing resources in the users' own domains.

    B. **Incorrect:** Whether the IP address is assigned dynamically or statically is not relevant to the problem.

    C. **Incorrect:** Dynamic updates of DNS records is not relevant to the problem.

    D. **Correct:** A shortcut trust can improve performance by allowing domain controllers in one domain to refer clients to the other domain directly rather than through the forest root domain.

Chapter 12: Case Scenario Answers

Case Scenario: Managing Multiple Domains and Forests

1. You must raise the domain and forest functional level to at least Windows Server 2003. Forest trusts are allowed only at forest functional levels of Windows Server 2003 or Windows Server 2008.

2. Because you do not have an account in the *wingtiptoys.com* domain, you can create only one-way incoming and one-way outgoing trusts. Administrators in *wingtiptoys.com* must create the reciprocal one-way outgoing and one-way incoming trusts.

3. You must enable selective authentication on the outgoing trust. Then, you must give those users the Allowed To Authenticate permission on the computer objects of the four servers.

Chapter 13: Lesson Review Answers

Lesson 1

1. **Correct Answer: B**
   A. **Incorrect:** Restartable AD DS is one of the best features of Windows Server 2008.
   B. **Correct**: If someone is working on the other DC in the forest root domain and has stopped the AD DS service, you will not be able to stop it on this server because at least one DC for each domain must be operational before the service will stop.
   C. **Incorrect**: You do not need to use DSRM in Windows Server 2008 to perform database operations on a DC.
   D. **Incorrect**: You can stop the AD DS service either through the command line or through the Services console.

2. **Correct Answers: D and F**
   A. **Incorrect:** If the server has failed, you cannot restart it in DSRM.
   B. **Incorrect**: You do not need to perform an authoritative restore because there is no indication that the server contained lost data that was not found in the other DCs.
   C. **Incorrect**: You do not need to reinstall the OS if you have access to full server backups.
   D. **Correct**: You must restart the server in WinRE to launch the full server recovery operation.
   E. **Incorrect**: You cannot perform a nonauthoritative restore with *Ntdsutil.exe* in Windows Server 2008. You must use Windows Server Backup or *Wbadmin.exe*.
   F. **Correct**: You can perform a full server recovery with either the command line or the graphical interface.

Lesson 2

1. **Correct Answers: C and D**
   A. **Incorrect:** Expiration dates do not cause a collector set to stop. They stop new collections from starting when the expiration date has been reached.
   B. **Incorrect**: To be running, the collector sets must be on a schedule; otherwise, they would stop when the user who created them logged off.
   C. **Correct**: You must set a stop condition on each collector set to ensure that it stops.
   D. **Correct**: You must set a duration on the collector set when you schedule it to run; otherwise, it will not stop.

2. **Correct Answers: A, B, C, and D**

A. **Correct:** Reliability Monitor will reveal whether any changes have been made to the server recently and whether those changes could be tied to performance bottlenecks.

B. **Correct:** Event Viewer, especially the System event log, will reveal any errors or warnings about performance on the system.

C. **Correct:** Task Manager will display a real-time view into resources and enable you to identify potential bottlenecks.

D. **Correct:** Performance Monitor, especially the role-based Data Collector Set templates, will enable you to discover quickly any performance issues with the current server configuration and make recommendations on possible changes to improve performance.

Chapter 13: Case Scenario Answers

Case Scenario: Working with Lost and Found Data

Occasionally, especially in large forests, someone will delete a container at the same time someone else is creating or modifying an object in the same container. This can be on entirely different DCs, but when replication synchronizes data on the DCs, the newly created object no longer has a home. When this happens, AD DS automatically stores these objects within the LostAndFound container. This special container manages lost and found objects within the domain. Another special container, the LostAndFoundConfig container, manages lost and found objects for the entire forest. The LostAndFoundConfig container is in the forest root domain only.

Therefore, you should regularly review the LostAndFound and the LostAndFoundConfig containers for objects to determine whether these objects should be moved to new containers or simply deleted from the directory.

Use the following procedure to verify the LostAndFound container in a child domain:

1. Move to the Active Directory Users And Computers portion of Server Manager.
2. Click View, choose Advanced Features, expand the tree, and then click the LostAndFound container.
3. Identify any objects located within this container. Decide whether they need to be moved to other containers or deleted.

Be careful when deleting objects. Make sure you review the object's properties before doing so. Sometimes, it is best to move the object and deactivate it while you communicate with your peers to determine whether it is a necessary object. Remember that once deleted, SIDs cannot be recovered.

Chapter 14: Lesson Review Answers

Lesson 1

1. **Correct Answer: C**

   A. **Incorrect:** Existing setup processes must complete before you can initiate another setup operation. It is also difficult to tell whether setup processes have completed when you use the command line unless you use the *Start /w* command, which will return the command prompt only when an operation completes. After a reboot, you will find that there are no setup processes currently in operation, yet you still cannot uninstall AD LDS.

   B. **Incorrect:** Using Server Manager does not solve the problem because you must remove all AD LDS instances before you can remove the role.

   C. **Correct:** You must remove all existing AD LDS instances before you can remove the role from the server. After all instances have been removed, you can remove the AD LDS role. This is one more reason why AD LDS instance documentation is so important.

   D. **Incorrect:** *Oclist* will give you the name of all the roles and features to use with the *Ocsetup* command. However, this is a full installation of Windows Server 2008 because you have access to Server Manager. *Oclist* does not work on the full installation.

Lesson 2

1. **Correct Answer: D**

   A. **Incorrect:** All AD LDS instances have a schema, and all instance schemas can be edited. This is one reason you should use AD LDS instead of AD DS to integrate applications.

   B. **Incorrect:** You can make modifications to the instance with the *LDP.exe* command, but schema modifications should be performed through the Active Directory Schema snap-in.

   C. **Incorrect:** You can make modifications to the instance with the LDIF files and the *LDIFDE.exe* command, but schema modifications should be performed through the Active Directory Schema snap-in.

   D. **Correct:** When you use AD LDS Setup to create instances with default port numbers, the first port used on member servers is port 389. For example, to connect to the first instance, you need to use Instance01:389. However, because your Active Directory Domain Services schema also uses port 389, and your server is member of a domain, the Active Directory Schema snap-in will not connect to the instance.

This is one reason you should never use port 389 for AD LDS instances in a domain.

Chapter 14: Case Scenario Answers

Case Scenario: Determine AD LDS Instance Prerequisites

You look up the information on AD LDS on the Microsoft TechNet Center for Active Directory technologies and come up with the following answers:

1. A data drive should be created for each server that will host AD LDS instances. Because these servers will be hosting directory stores, you should place these stores on a drive that is separate from the operating system and into separate folders so that they can be easily identified.

2. You should always use meaningful names to identify instances. For example, the name of the application that will be tied to an instance is a good candidate. Instance names are used to identify the instance on the local computer as well as to identify and name the files that make up the instance and the service that supports it. Names cannot include spaces or special characters.

3. Both AD LDS and AD DS use the same ports for communication. These ports are the default LDAP (389) and LDAP over the Secure Sockets Layer (SSL), or Secure LDAP, (636) ports. AD DS uses two additional ports, 3268, which uses LDAP to access the global catalog, and 3269, which uses Secure LDAP to access the global catalog. Because AD DS and AD LDS use the same ports, you should make it a habit to use other ports, ports beyond the 50,000 range, for your AD LDS instances. This will ensure that they are segregated from AD DS services, especially if the instance is installed within a domain. In addition, you should install PKI certificates on each AD LDS instance to use Secure LDAP for communication and management. This will prevent tampering with or detection of AD LDS data.

4. Ideally, each AD LDS instance should use an application partition, even if no replication is required. Creating an application directory partition will make it easier to manage the instance through a variety of tools.

5. Instances should be run through the use of a service account. You can use the Network Service account, but if you intend to run multiple instances, it is suggested that you use named service accounts for each instance. This way, you know exactly when the instance performs operations because you can view the logon operations of the service account in the Event Viewer.

Chapter 15: Lesson Review Answers

Lesson 1

1. **Correct Answers: B and C**

   A. **Incorrect:** Although it is true that you cannot install enterprise CAs on Windows Server 2008 Standard Edition or Windows Server 2008 Web Edition, you are actually running the Windows Server 2008 Enterprise Edition of Windows Server because you verified this prerequisite at the beginning of the installation.

   B. **Correct:** If you are logged on with a local account, even an account with local administrative privileges, you cannot install an enterprise CA. You must use a domain account to install an enterprise CA.

   C. **Correct:** To install an enterprise CA, your server must be a member of the domain because enterprise CAs rely on the AD DS directory service to publish and issue certificates.

   D. **Incorrect:** Because of all the required components in an enterprise CA installation, you should use Server Manager to install this role.

Lesson 2

1. **Correct Answer: B**

   A. **Incorrect:** Although you can use *Certutil.exe* to load certificates, you should also be able to perform the same operation through the wizard.

   B. **Correct:** The certificate template access rights are not set properly. To load the certificate manually on the server, the user account must have the Allow: Enroll permission set. In addition, the server you load the certificate on should also have the Allow: Enroll permission. You must re-create the template and reissue it to correct its access rights.

   C. **Incorrect:** You should be able to load the OCSP certificate onto this server because it is an OR.

   D. **Incorrect:** Although the certificate should be able to load automatically if it has the Allow: Autoenroll permission set, there is no reason other than access rights that would stop you from loading it manually.

Chapter 15: Case Scenario Answers

Case Scenario: Manage Certificate Revocation

You go to your superiors with the information. They need to undertake a police operation immediately to stop the two ex-employees from selling certificates with the Contoso name embedded in them. In addition, your sales personnel need to initiate some damage-control operations with your clients. Having software on the market that does not originate from Contoso, yet contains Contoso certificates, can be extremely damaging to your company's reputation.

For your part, you immediately move to block the use of the certificates. To do so, you must first bring the root CA online. Then, you use the Certification Authority section of Server Manager to revoke the two stolen certificates. Fortunately, when you cancel these certificates, any certificates that were issued using these as a source will be automatically invalidated.

Then, you force publication of the Certificate Revocation List. To do so, you use the Revoked Certificates node of the Certification Authority console. Unfortunately, you realize that even if you publish this new CRL immediately, clients will not update their CRL until their next refresh cycle, which depends on the refresh configuration.

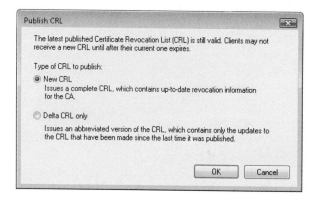

Finally, your organization should issue a public statement about the two lost certificates. All Contoso clients should know that they are at risk and must verify each certificate they receive in the Contoso name until the revocation has taken effect.

As you can see, root CA security is of the utmost importance in a PKI architecture.

Chapter 16: Lesson Review Answers

Lesson 1

1. **Correct Answer: D**

   A. **Incorrect:** The server is running AD RMS because the AD RMS node is available in Server Manager.

   B. **Incorrect:** The server certificate is validated during the installation process. At worst, you can always use a self-signed certificate. This cannot be the problem.

   C. **Incorrect:** To install AD RMS, your server must be a member of the domain because AD RMS relies on the AD DS directory service to publish and issue certificates.

   D. **Correct:** During the installation, your account is added to the AD RMS Enterprise Administrators group on the local computer. To update the privileges of your account, you must log off and then log on again. Without this procedure, your account will not have the required access rights to run AD RMS.

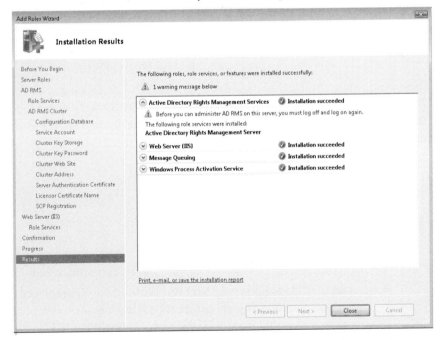

Lesson 2

1. **Correct Answer: B**

   A. **Incorrect:** To access HTTP over SSL, users must use a URL address in the HTTPS:// format.

B. **Correct:** The server certificate is validated when users try to access the URL. If it is not from a trusted CA, it will not work. If you used a self-signed certificate, the URL would have worked when you accessed it from the server because the server trusts its own certificate, but it will not work from user browsers because they do not trust the self-signed certificate.

C. **Incorrect:** To access AD RMS from outside the network, users do not need an AD DS account.

D. **Incorrect:** The URL is correct because you verified it from the server you used to set it up.

Chapter 16: Case Scenario Answers

Case Scenario: Prepare to Work with an External AD RMS Cluster

The best and easiest way to share policy infrastructures without putting federation trusts in place is to rely on cross-certificate publication. This means using trusted publishing domains that enable your own AD RMS cluster to issue use licenses for content that was protected by another AD RMS cluster. To create a trusted publishing domain, you must import the publishing cluster's SLC as well as its private key into your own cluster.

To proceed, you must first export your Server Licensor Certificate and then have it imported into your partner's root cluster. Your partner must also perform the same activity. After the two certificates are imported, both environments will be able to support the issuance of publishing and use certificates for each other.

Chapter 17: Lesson Review Answers

Lesson 1

1. **Correct Answer: B**

A. **Incorrect:** All services can use a named service account to run.

B. **Correct:** The named service account is automatically replaced by the Network Service account during installation. When the upgrade is complete, you must reset the service account for each AD FS service.

C. **Incorrect:** Woodgrove's policies would affect servers in the Woodgrove network and not in your own.

D. **Incorrect:** Although the Network Service account has limited access rights to the local computer and is a good account to use for certain services, it is by no means a best practice and Microsoft does not enforce its use.

Lesson 2

1. **Correct Answers: A, B, D, and E**

    A. **Correct:** You must communicate with your counterpart to determine how you will exchange policy files during the setup of the partnership.

    B. **Correct:** You export the partner policy from the resource organization (Woodgrove Bank) and import it into the account organization (Contoso).

    C. **Incorrect:** The partner policy must be exported from the resource organization (Woodgrove Bank) and imported into the account organization (Contoso). This option proposes the reverse.

    D. **Correct:** You export the trust policy from the account organization (Contoso) and import it into the resource organization (Woodgrove Bank).

    E. **Correct:** You must create and configure a claim mapping in the resource organization (Woodgrove Bank).

    F. **Incorrect:** The trust policy must be exported from the account organization (Contoso) and imported into the resource organization (Woodgrove Bank). This option proposes the reverse.

Chapter 17: Case Scenario Answers

Case Scenario: Choose the Right AD Technology

Answers may vary but should include all the elements presented here.

You look over the requirements and decide that it is a good opportunity to rely on the five Active Directory technologies. You decide to proceed as follows:

- You will use AD DS to upgrade the internal directory service.

- You will implement AD RMS to protect your intellectual property. This means that when you create a partnership, your organization will be the resource organization because you host the AD RMS installation.

- To support the applications in the extranet, you will need to implement identity federation with AD FS. You will implement the AD FS Federated Web Single-Sign-On design, and your organization will be the resource organization. In addition, you will need to add the following elements to support each of the applications:

❑ To support the Windows-based applications in the extranet, you need access to a directory store. Because you do not want to deploy AD DS in an extranet because of the risks involved, you will deploy AD LDS. The instance of AD LDS will provide logon services for the Windows applications through AD FS. You will install the AD FS Windows Token-based Agent to support identity federation.

❑ The Web-based applications will be AD FS–enabled by installing the AD FS Claims-aware Agent.

■ The clients that access your applications will be supported by the AD FS and the AD LDS processes. Specifically, partner organizations and internal users will rely on AD FS, and the general public will rely on instances of AD LDS to gain access to the applications.

■ You will implement Active Directory Certificate Services to provide communication security. To facilitate access to all applications and ensure that all partners can validate the certificates you generate, you will rely on a third-party commercial trusted CA as the root of your AD CS deployment. This way, all your certificates will be trusted at all times because the root certificate is trusted by all.

This is a best practices implementation of the five AD technologies.

Index

Symbols and Numbers

. (dot), 102, 394
$ (dollar sign), 102, 123

A

A (host) record, 413, 517–518
AAAA (host) record, 413
access control entries. *See* ACEs (access control entries)
access control lists. *See* ACLs (access control lists)
access rights
    AD RMS considerations, 814–815
    assigning, 759
    authentication process, 835
    SCP creation, 801
account attributes, 119–121
Account Expires setting, 120
account federation server (AFS), 834, 839, 842
Account Federation Service Proxy, 842
Account Is Disabled setting, 120
Account Is Trusted For Delegation setting, 120
Account Lockout and Management tools, 614–616
Account Lockout Duration policy, 359
account lockout policies. *See* lockout policies
Account Lockout Policy node, 359
Account Lockout Threshold setting, 359
Account Operators group
    characteristics, 177–178
    creating computer objects, 192
    moving computers, 214
account organizations
    configuring AD FS, 855
    defined, 832, 842
    discovery Web page, 843
    organization claims, 843
Account Partner cookies, 840
account policies, 303, 613
Account Policy node, 361
Account property, 117
AcctInfo.dll, 614–616
ACEs (access control entries)
    AD DS administration, 613
    defined, 69
    deleted groups, 171
    effective permissions, 76
    migration considerations, 574
    viewing, 71
ACLs (access control lists)

Active Directory objects, 69–71
AD DS administration, 613, 620
AD RMS support, 7
GPO support, 262
group nesting, 153
group scope, 145
IDA support, 3–4
managing for groups, 141–143
migration considerations, 574
protected groups, 178
securing trust relationships, 591
security translation, 575
actions, 35, 100
Active Directory Application Mode (ADAM), 6, 685, 694, 831
Active Directory Certificate Services. *See* AD CS (Active Directory Certificate Services)
Active Directory data store
    AD DS administration, 620–621
    as identity store, 3
    defined, 9
    LDAP support, 8
Active Directory Diagnostics collector set, 667
Active Directory directory service
    creating computer objects, 52–54
    creating group objects, 50–52, 63–64
    creating organizational units, 46–48, 61
    creating user objects, 48–50, 61–63
    defined, 46
    finding objects, 54–67
Active Directory Domain Services. *See* AD DS (Active Directory Domain Services)
Active Directory Domain Services Installation Wizard
    child domain delegations, 405, 417
    configuring GC servers, 524
    creating domain controllers, 13
    creating instances, 703
    creating RODCs, 379, 470
    installation media, 472
    installing domain controllers, 461–463, 466–467, 474–475
    installing domain trees, 469
    managing domain controllers in sites, 516
    operations master roles, 486
    removing domain controllers, 473
    removing domains, 418
    zone delegations, 412

Active Directory Domains and Trusts snap-in
  AD DS administration, 619
  creating manual trusts, 583
  domain functional levels, 494, 560
  forest functional levels, 377, 563
  functionality, 36
  UPN suffixes, 49
Active Directory Federation Services. *See* AD FS
  (Active Directory Federation Services)
Active Directory Integrated (ADI) zone, 408
Active Directory Lightweight Directory Services. *See*
  AD LDS (Active Directory Lightweight Directory
  Services)
Active Directory Migration Tool (ADMT), 573, 575–576
Active Directory objects
  ACL support, 69
  assigning permissions, 72–73
  control access rights, 72
  creating with Windows PowerShell, 103
  delegating, 69–70
  delegating administrative tasks, 74–75
  deleting, 128, 163
  importing users with CSVDE, 90, 94–95
  importing users with LDIFDE, 90–92, 95–96
  permissions and inheritance, 73–74
  protecting from deletion, 625–626
  restoring, 626–627
  viewing ACLs, 70–71
  viewing permissions, 70–71, 75
Active Directory partitions, 523, 551
Active Directory Rights Management Service. *See* AD RMS
  (Active Directory Rights Management Service)
Active Directory schema, 37, 88
Active Directory Schema Management console, 613
Active Directory Schema snap-in
  AD DS administration, 619, 701
  AD LDS considerations, 701, 704
  working with instances, 712
Active Directory Services Interface. *See* ADSI
  (Active Directory Services Interface)
Active Directory sites. *See* sites
Active Directory Sites and Services snap-in
  AD DS administration, 619, 701
  AD LDS support, 701
  configuring GC servers, 524
  connection objects, 532
  functionality, 36, 512
  Subnets node, 513
  UGMC configuration, 525
  working with instances, 713
Active Directory Users and Computers snap-in
  AD DS administration, 619
  Additional Account Info tab, 614

  assigning permissions, 73
  controlling view of objects, 54
  creating computer objects, 52
  creating group objects, 50
  creating organizational units, 46
  creating RODC accounts, 470
  creating user objects, 48
  default containers, 11
  delegating administrative tasks, 74
  deleting computer accounts, 220
  disabling accounts, 127, 219
  domain functional levels, 560
  functionality, 36
  managing computers, 215
  managing user accounts, 614
  managing user attributes, 114–117
  moving user accounts, 129
  moving/renaming groups, 163
  object protection, 625
  resetting computer accounts, 217
  Saved Queries node, 55
  Specops Gpupdate tool, 616
  user account hidden attributes, 88
  viewing Active Directory object ACLs, 70
AD CS (Active Directory Certificate Services)
  AD RMS support, 782
  additional information, 742, 744
  CA hierarchy, 734–736
  CA Web Enrollment, 731
  certificate authorities, 6, 731
  certificate usage scenarios, 730
  deployment best practices, 737–738
  enterprise CAs, 732–734, 740
  functionality, 6, 723, 731
  installing, 740–742
  installing as enterprise issuing CA, 745–747
  installing as standalone root CA, 742–744
  installing issuing CA certificate, 747–748
  installing NDES, 749–750
  IPSec (Internet Protocol security), 6, 729
  managing, 763–764
  NDES support, 732
  new features, 732
  online responders, 731–732
  planning requirements, 738–740
  protecting configuration, 766–767
  renaming computers, 219
  standalone CAs, 732–734, 740
AD DS (Active Directory Domain Services)
  Access auditing feature, 624
  AD LDS comparison, 691–692
  adding role via Windows interface, 12
  additional information, 6, 9

administration categories, 612–614
auditing directory changes, 626
certificate authorities, 733
communication ports, 703–704
creating baselines, 671
creating domain controllers, 11–13
creating forests, 11–12, 14–21
deployment considerations, 12
DNS support, 393, 414, 417–419
domain-based GPOs, 238–239
functionality, 5, 229
IDA support, 3–7
infrastructure components, 8–11
installing, 420–422, 424–429
installing from media, 472–473
Kerberos protocol, 4
perimeter networks, 836
planning architecture, 572
policy-based administration, 8
protecting objects, 625–626
recovering information, 624–625
replication services, 8
root cluster support, 788
schema support, 8
Server Core installation, 23–29
tools supported, 36–37, 619–622, 701–703
virtual machines, 648
AD DS administration
    AcctInfo.dll, 614–616
    additional information, 622
    administration activities, 612–614
    auditing directory changes, 626
    domain controllers as virtual machines, 648–650
    offline maintenance, 623–624
    online maintenance, 622–623
    proactive restores, 638–648
    protecting objects, 625–626
    Quest Object Restore for Active Directory, 628–629
    recovering information, 624–625
    restoring objects, 626–628
    Specops Gpupdate tool, 616–619
    tools supported, 36–37, 619–622, 701–703
    Windows Server Backup, 629–638
AD FS (Active Directory Federation Services)
    AD RMS support, 782, 789, 792–793, 818
    additional information, 833, 854, 856
    authentication, 827–828, 832–836
    B2B commerce, 832
    certificates, 841–842
    claims, 839–840
    configurations supported, 836–838
    cookies, 840–841
    Federated Web SSO, 836

Federated Web SSO with Forest Trust, 836
finalizing configuration, 854–855, 857–869
firewalls support, 693
functionality, 7, 825, 827–828
installing, 845–848
managing, 855–857
preparing deployment, 849–852
service roles, 832–833, 846
terminology, 842–845
upgrade considerations, 848–849
Web SSO, 837
AD FS Web agent, 840, 842
AD LDS (Active Directory Lightweight Directory
    Services)
    AD DS administration, 619–621
    AD DS comparison, 691–692
    additional information, 694
    auditing support, 703
    communication ports, 703–704
    creating instances, 703–709, 714–716
    Dsbutil.exe command, 620
    functionality, 6, 685–686
    installing, 694–696
    LDAP support, 6, 690, 692
    managing replication, 692, 717–718
    migrating previous LDAP instances, 708–709
    supported scenarios, 692–694
    tools supported, 701–703
    unattended instance creation, 706–707
    working with instances, 709–717
AD LDS Setup tool, 701, 703
AD RMS (Active Directory Rights Management Service)
    AD CS support, 730
    additional information, 788, 790, 794, 810, 819
    best practices, 800
    certificate support, 797–798
    configuration preparation, 809
    configuring trust policies, 810–811
    creating extranet URLs, 810
    exporting SLCs, 811
    functionality, 7, 781–782, 786–788
    implementing in stages, 786
    installation prerequisites, 794–797
    installing, 798–807
    managing databases, 818–819
    new features, 788–790
    preparing access rights, 814–815
    preparing accounts, 814–815
    preparing certificates, 811–812
    preparing exclusion policies, 812–814
    preparing policy templates, 815–817
    RMS toolkit, 819
    system requirements, 795

working with clients, 817–818
AD RMS Auditors role, 789, 814
AD RMS Enterprise Administrators role, 789, 814
AD RMS Identity Federation Support role, 793
AD RMS Service role, 789, 814
AD RMS Template Administrators role, 789, 814
ADAM (Active Directory Application Mode), 6, 685, 694, 831
ADAMInstall.exe command, 701, 706
ADAMSync.exe command, 702
ADAMUninstall.exe command, 702
Add Printer Wizard, 59
Add Roles Wizard, 12, 461
Add To Group command, 152
Add/Remove Columns command, 54
Add/Remove Snap-in command, 303
Address property, 117
ADI (Active Directory Integrated) zone, 408
ADM file extension, 245–246
administrative role separation, 383
administrative tasks. *See also* AD DS administration
    AD DS tools, 36–37, 619–622, 701–703
    AD RMS roles, 789
    adding to Start menu, 37
    best practices for group attributes, 169–170
    creating custom consoles, 38–41
    delegating membership management, 172–175, 181
    delegating restricted groups policies, 294–295
    deleting user accounts, 128–181
    directory service, 610–611
    disabling/enabling user accounts, 127–128
    DNS tools, 448–450
    for computer accounts, 213
    moving user accounts, 129
    protecting groups from accidental deletion, 171
    recycling user accounts, 128
    renaming user accounts, 129–130
    resetting passwords, 125–126, 132
    running with alternate credentials, 37–38
    Server Manager tools, 37
    unlocking user accounts, 126–127, 132
    VBScript support, 108–110
    Windows PowerShell support, 98–108
administrative templates
    adding, 245
    ADM file extension, 245
    ADML file extension, 245
    ADMX file extension, 245
    defined, 245
    exploring, 251–252
    filtering policy settings, 246–247
Administrative Templates node, 243–248
Administrative Tools folder, 35, 40

Administrator account
    delegation considerations, 77
    initial password, 24
    policy settings, 231
    removing domain controllers, 27
Administrators GPO, 238
Administrators role, 383
ADML file extension, 245–246
ADMT (Active Directory Migration Tool), 573, 575–576
Admt.exe command, 573
ADMX file extension, 245–246
Adprep /forestprep command, 469
Adprep /rodcprep command, 378–379, 466, 472, 562
ADSchemaAnalyzer.exe command, 702
ADSI (Active Directory Services Interface)
    AD LDS support, 691
    connecting to containers, 104
    functionality, 8
    managing user attributes, 123
    VBScript support, 109–110
ADSI Edit tool
    AD DS administration, 619, 702
    AD LDS support, 702
    application directory partitions, 526
    managing passwords, 361
    working with instances, 709–711
aDSPath attribute, 164
Advanced Encryption Services (AES), 559
Advanced Security Settings dialog box
    assigning permissions, 72–73
    delegating membership management, 174–175
    removing/resetting permissions, 75
Aelita Enterprise Directory Manager, 688–689
AES (Advanced Encryption Services), 559
AFS (account federation server), 834, 839, 842
aging, 408, 438
AIA (Authority Information Access) extension, 759–760
alias
    CNAME records, 413
    defined, 102
    single-label names, 442
Allow Apply Group Policy permission, 262
allow permissions
    ACE support, 574
    as cumulative, 76
    deny permission comparison, 76, 626
Allow Read permission, 262
Allow Write Member permission, 174
Allowed List attribute, 380–381
Allowed RODC Password Replication Group, 380
alternate credentials, 37–38, 126
Always Wait For Network At Startup And Logon policy
    setting, 236

Analyze Computer Now command, 307
Anonymous Logon group, 179
answer files
    installing child domains, 468
    installing domain trees, 469
    unattended installation, 462–464
APIPA (Automatic Private IP Addressing), 395
application basic groups, 562
application directory partitions
    AD DS administration, 612, 620
    AD LDS considerations, 704, 708–709
    additional information, 448, 527
    customized, 446–448
    defined, 408, 525, 707
    Directory Service Diagnosis tool, 545
    examining, 528–529
    overview, 445–448, 522, 525–527
    replication scope, 404, 408, 414, 445, 447
Application log, 281, 663
applications
    assigning, 323–325
    claims-aware, 842, 855, 863
    federated, 843
    maintaining, 327–329
    publishing, 323–325
    token-based, 845
    upgrading, 331–332
arrow keys, 642
assigning applications, 323–325
Asynchronous Full Transfer (AXFR), 412
Attribute Editor, 88, 116–117
attributes. *See also* specific attributes
    auditing changes, 620
    data protection measures, 624
    redefining, 562
Audit Account Logon Events setting, 336, 368
Audit Account Management setting, 336
Audit Directory Service Access setting, 336, 341–342
Audit Logon Events setting, 336
audit logs, 335, 339
Audit Object Access setting, 337, 340–341
audit policies
    auditing directory changes, 626
    balancing, 337
    configuring, 369–370
    defined, 349
    enabling, 340, 343
    functionality, 335
    scoping, 370
    Security Configuration Wizard, 312
    supported settings, 335–337
Audit Policy Change setting, 336
Audit Privilege Use setting, 336

Audit Process Tracking setting, 337
Audit System Events setting, 336
auditing
    AD DS administration, 620
    AD LDS support, 703
    AD RMS support, 789, 814
    authentication, 368–372
    configuring permissions, 343
    directory changes, 626
    file system access, 337–341
    IDA support, 4
    logging database support, 819
auditpol command, 342
Authenticated Users group
    administrative tasks, 127
    Allow Apply Group Policy permission, 262
    defined, 179
    multiple forests, 572
    securing trust relationships, 591
    selective authentication, 593
authentication
    Account Partner cookies, 840
    AD FS support, 827–828, 832–836
    AD LDS support, 693
    AD RMS support, 786
    auditing, 368–372
    authentication cookies, 840
    computer account problems, 216
    defined, 31, 355
    digital certificates, 6
    for identity, 4
    in branch offices, 374–375
    Kerberos protocol, 4, 9
    security policy support, 312
    selective, 559, 593–595, 600–601
    shortcut trusts, 586
    sign-out cookies, 840
    smart card support, 812
    special identities, 179
    trusts and, 579–582
authentication cookies, 840
authoritative restores
    deleted groups, 171
    overview, 632–645
    restoration scenario, 639
    Windows Server Backup, 630
Authority Information Access (AIA) extension, 759–760
Authorization Manager tool, 559, 562
Automatic Private IP Addressing (APIPA), 395
availability
    directory service, 611
    domain local groups, 147
    global groups, 147

group scope considerations, 146
local groups, 146
universal groups, 148
virtual machines, 650
AXFR (Asynchronous Full Transfer), 412

B

B2B commerce, 832
backlinks, 116, 184
backup functions. *See also* restore functions
    AD CS considerations, 766–767
    additional information, 632
    data protection measures, 624
    virtual hard disks, 636
    Windows Server Backup, 629–638
Backup Operators group, 178, 631
baseline settings, 310
Bcdedit.exe command, 639
Bindview Secure Active Directory LifeCycle Suite, 688
bridgehead servers
    AD DS administration, 612
    polling, 542
    preferred, 539, 546
    replication overview, 538–539
browse lists, 483
Builtin container, 11, 177
business continuity. *See* AD DS administration; backup
    functions; restore functions

C

CA (certificate authority). *See also* specific CAs
    AD CS support, 6, 731
    common event IDs, 763–764
    creating hierarchy, 734–736
    creating revocation configuration, 754–755
    defined, 731
    firewall considerations, 826
    managing, 763
    requester identification validation, 738
    SMTP considerations, 537
    trust considerations, 725, 730
    upgrading, 755, 764
    Web Enrollment process, 731
caching
    credentials, 381–382, 385–386
    DNS support, 431
    universal group membership, 524–525
canonical name (CNAME) record, 413, 803
central store, 246, 252
certificate authority. *See* CA (certificate authority)
certificate chaining, 734, 854

certificate enrollment, 738, 823
certificate practice statement (CPS), 738–739
certificate revocation
    creating configuration, 753–755
    defined, 739, 777
    online responders, 761–762
certificate revocation lists. *See* CRLs (certificate
    revocation lists)
certificate templates
    certificate authorities, 733
    configuring, 755–756
    configuring duplicate, 757
    configuring enrollment, 758–759
    customizing, 756–757
    issuing, 757
    managing, 763
    personalizing, 753–754
certificates
    AD FS support, 841–842
    AD RMS support, 797–798, 811–812
    additional information, 725, 842
    CRL support, 731
    event IDs, 764
    exporting, 854, 857–862
    Federation Server proxies, 841
    federation servers, 841
    importing, 857–859, 862
    lifetime considerations, 738–739
    managing, 763
    online responders, 731
    requester identification validation, 738
    self-signed, 801, 818
    SLC, 789, 797, 810–811, 818
    trust considerations, 725, 734
Certificates snap-in, 760–761
Certification Authority Backup Wizard, 766
Certutil command, 763, 767
CF (conditional forwarders), 417, 440–441
changeType field (LDIFDE), 161, 204
child CAs, 731
child domains
    application directory partitions, 445
    creating, 427–429
    delegations, 405, 417–418
    DNS considerations, 404–405, 414
    installing, 467–468
    replication scope, 404
    shortcut trusts, 586
child objects, 73, 77
Cisco Systems, Inc., 732
claim mapping, 843, 855, 872
claims
    additional information, 840

custom claim type, 839, 848
  defined, 839, 842–843
  group claim type, 839, 848
  identity claim type, 839, 848
claims-aware agent, 833, 846
claims-aware applications, 842, 855, 863
CLC (client licensor certificate), 797
client authentication certificate, 843
client licensor certificate (CLC), 797
client-side extensions. *See* CSEs (client-side extensions)
cloud concept, 398
cmdlets
  alias support, 102
  command shell comparison, 101
  defined, 98
  namespace support, 103
  overview, 99–101
  scripting support, 99
  support for variables, 102, 123
  syntax, 99
CN (common name)
  defined, 60
  identity claim type, 839
  name attributes, 118
  renaming user accounts, 129–130
cn attribute, 118, 129, 144
CNAME (canonical name) record, 413, 803
collision detection and management, 532
colons (::), 395
command prompts, arrow keys, 642
command shell, 101–102
common name. *See* CN (common name)
compaction, 624, 683
computer accounts
  AD DS administration, 612, 621
  administrative tasks, 213
  data protection measures, 624
  deleting, 220
  disabling/enabling, 219
  logon process, 216
  prestaging, 192–193, 196, 206
  recycling, 220
  resetting, 217, 220
  RODC support, 381
  secure channel, 216
  troubleshooting, 216–217, 222
Computer Configuration node
  Administrative Templates node, 243–248
  defined, 231, 241
  Policies node, 241
  Preferences node, 241, 243–244
  Software Installation node, 325
  Software Settings node, 242

  Windows Settings node, 242
Computer Management console, 35
computer objects
  AD DS administration, 613, 620
  checking existence, 194
  configuring attributes with Dsmod, 214
  configuring attributes with VBScript, 214
  configuring attributes with Windows PowerShell, 214
  configuring properties, 213–214
  creating, 52–54, 63–64, 199–200
  creating OUs, 199
  creating with Dsadd, 205, 209
  creating with Netdom, 205
  creating with VBScript, 208, 211
  creating with Windows PowerShell, 206–208, 211
  delegating permissions, 192, 200
  domain requirements, 190
  importing with CSVDE, 203–204, 209–210
  importing with LDIFDE, 204–205
  managing, 215, 221–222
  moving, 214–215
  prestaging, 195–197
  renaming, 218–219
  restrictions creating, 197
  Specops Gpupdate tool, 617–618
computer settings. *See* Computer Configuration node
Computers container
  as default container, 11, 195
  configuring, 195–196
  joining computers to domains, 190
  moving computers, 214
  redirecting, 200, 559
conditional forwarders (CF), 417, 440–441
Conditional Forwarders node, 441
Configuration container, 509
configuration database, 310, 818
configuration management, 176, 613
configuration partition, 522
Configure Computer Now command, 307
connection objects
  creating, 545–546
  defined, 532
  displaying for domain controllers, 544
  forcing replication, 532
constructed attributes, 117
containers
  connecting to, 104
  default, 11
  defined, 11
  OUs and, 46, 190–191
  permission inheritance, 73
cookies
  Account Partner cookies, 840

additional information, 841
authentication cookies, 840
defined, 840
passive clients, 843
sign-out cookies, 840
Copy Object User Wizard, 87
copyrights, 785
CPS (certificate practice statement), 738–739
Create Computer Objects permission, 192
Create method, 104, 109, 206
credential caching, 381–382, 385–386
CRLs (certificate revocation lists)
    AD FS configuration, 855
    CA support, 733
    creating revocation configuration, 754–755
    defined, 731
    online responders, 731
cryptographic storage providers (CSPs), 800
Cscript command, 25–26, 108
CSEs (client-side extensions)
    configuring, 236
    CPSI support, 322
    defined, 235
    GPO support, 240
    policy settings, 242
CSPs (cryptographic storage providers), 800
CSV file extension
    importing computers with Windows PowerShell, 208
    importing groups with CSVDE, 160
    importing users with CSVDE, 90
    importing users with Windows PowerShell, 106
CSVDE tool
    AD DS administration, 619, 702
    AD LDS support, 702
    importing computers, 203–204, 209–210
    importing groups, 160, 165
    importing users, 90, 94–95
custom claim type, 839, 848

D

DACL (discretionary ACL)
    defined, 69
    migration considerations, 574
    property sets, 72
    viewing, 71
Data Collector Set templates, 667
data collector sets
    adding counters, 669
    common counters, 667–669
    creating, 666–667, 675–679
    creating performance baselines, 671
    defined, 683

tracking counters, 669
data management, 611
data protection
    built-in measures, 624–625, 628
    protecting objects, 625–626, 628
    Windows Server Backup, 629–630
data store. *See* Active Directory data store
database management
    AD DS administration, 614, 623–624
    AD RMS support, 818–819
    automating maintenance, 655–657
    performing maintenance, 653–655
Dcdiag.exe (Directory Server Diagnosis), 543–545, 619, 702
DCOM (Distributed Component Object Model), 733
Dcpromo command
    AD DS administration, 620
    adding AD DS to Server Core, 26
    additional information, 463
    configuring GC servers, 524
    creating RODC, 380, 470–471
    demoting domain controllers, 473
    installing child domains, 468
    installing domain controllers, 461–463, 467
    installing domain trees, 469
    installing forests, 464
    operation master roles, 488
    promoting domain controllers, 26
    removing domain controllers, 473
    removing domains, 418
    unattended installation, 462
DDNS (dynamic DNS) servers
    defined, 398, 409
    dynamic IP addresses, 443
    name records, 406
    server scavenging, 411
dedicated forest root domain, 567–568
Default Domain Controller GPO, 239, 301, 370
Default Domain GPO, 238
Default Domain Policy, 360–361, 758
default local groups
    additional information, 179
    defined, 177
    example, 178
    listed, 177–178
defragmentation, 624
delegation
    AD RMS administration, 789–790, 814
    administrative tasks, 74–75, 78–79
    child domains, 405, 417–418
    computer object permissions, 192
    constrained, 559
    defined, 81, 349

domain trees, 418
Group Policy membership, 295–298
information management tasks, 613
membership management, 172–175, 181
OU support, 77–78
overview, 69–70
permission inheritance and, 74
proactive management strategy, 611
restricted groups policies, 294–295
role-based access control, 77
zone, 412, 422–424
Delegation of Control Wizard, 74–75
Delete command, 220
Delete method (Windows PowerShell), 128
deletion
Active Directory objects, 128, 163
computer accounts, 220
GPO links, 257
groups with Dsrm, 163–164
manual trusts, 590
objects, 620
organizational units, 47–48
protecting groups, 171
protecting objects, 625–626
PSOs, 366
user accounts, 128
delimiters in group names, 144
Denied List attribute, 380–381
Denied RODC Password Replication Group, 380
deny permissions
access considerations, 171
ACE support, 574
allow permission comparison, 76, 626
description attribute, 162, 170, 214
DFS (distributed file shares), 612
DFS Namespaces, 510
DFS replication, 644, 663
DFS Replication log, 663
Dfscomd command, 26
DFS-R (Distributed File System Replication)
AD DS administration, 620
compression replication, 648
Directory Service Diagnosis tool, 545
domain functional level, 494–495
GPO replication, 241
migrating SYSVOL replication, 496
migration stages, 495–496
SYSVOL replication, 494–502, 559
timestamp support, 482
DFSRadmin.exe command, 620, 648
Dfsrmig.exe command, 495–496
DHCP (Dynamic Host Configuration Protocol)
DDNS servers, 398

DNS considerations, 443–445
IPv6 support, 395
RID master role and, 480
digital certificates. *See* certificates
Digital Rights Management (DRM), 781
digital signatures, 6, 398
Directory Replication Agent (DRA), 240
Directory Server Diagnosis (Dcdiag.exe), 543–545, 619, 702
Directory Service Access auditing category, 341
Directory Service Changes auditing category, 341–342, 345–346
Directory Service log, 663
Directory Service Remote Procedure Call (DS-RPC), 537
directory services database, 819
Directory Services Repair Mode, 623
Directory Services Restore Mode (DSRM), 639–640
Directory Services Restore Mode password, 464, 631, 639–640
diskpart command, 646
displayName attribute, 119
distinguished name. *See* DN (distinguished name)
Distributed Component Object Model (DCOM), 733
distributed file shares (DFS), 612
Distributed File System Replication. *See* DFS-R (Distributed File System Replication)
distribution groups, 51, 145
DLL (dynamic link library), 614–616
DN (distinguished name)
AD LDS support, 704
defined, 60
Dsget command, 122
Dsmod command, 121–122
member attribute, 480–481
DNS (Domain Name System)
AD DS administration, 417–419, 612, 620–621, 738
AD RMS support, 810, 850
additional information, 400, 406
administration tools, 448–450
application directory partitions, 408, 445–448
configuring, 431, 596
creating baselines, 671
DHCP considerations, 443–445
domain controller requirements, 12, 378
firewall support, 826
forest root domain, 464
forest trusts, 589
forwarders *vs.* root hints, 439–441
functionality, 8, 393, 406
hierarchical naming structure, 394
IP addresses, 393
IPv6 support, 395–396
LDAP support, 690

name resolution process, 393, 406–408
PNRP support, 397–398
record types, 413–414
replication scope, 415
single-label names, 411, 415, 441–443, 450–451
split-brain syndrome, 400–402
TCP/IP port, 394
types of servers, 398–400
virtual machines, 648
Windows Server 2008 features, 414–416
WINS support, 442–443
zone types, 412–413
DNS Manager, 448, 620
DNS Notify process, 409
DNS records, 406, 456, 803. *See also* specific record types
DNS Server log, 663
DNS servers
   AD DS support, 417–419, 620
   administering, 448–450
   dynamic, 398, 406, 409, 411, 443
   primary, 419–420
   read-only, 399, 415
   read-write, 398
   security considerations, 431–432
   working with settings, 432–436
DNS zones. *See also* FLZ (forward lookup zones); RLZ
   (reverse lookup zones)
   ADI, 408
   background loading, 415
   configuring scavenging, 432–433
   DDNS servers, 398
   defined, 456
   domain, 409, 414
   forest, 409, 414
   primary, 410, 412
   RODC support, 399
   secondary, 411–412
   stub, 411–412
Dnscmd command
   AD DS administration, 620
   application directory partitions, 446
   functionality, 26, 448
   single-label names, 441
Dnslint command, 449
dollar sign ($), 102, 123
Domain Admins group
   auditing considerations, 341
   creating computer objects, 192, 194
   creating GPOs, 239
   creating manual trusts, 583
   default groups, 177
   deleting OUs, 48

end user support, 291
forest functional levels, 377
installing RODCs, 470
migration considerations, 576
moving computers, 214
PRP support, 380
restoring objects, 626
scheduled backups, 631
schema masters, 465
domain component, 60
Domain Controller Authentication template, 757
Domain Controller template, 757
domain controllers. *See also* operations masters; RODCs
   (read-only domain controllers)
   AD CS considerations, 738
   AD DS administration, 472–473, 613, 620–621, 623
   AD LDS considerations, 695
   application directory partitions, 527
   as virtual machines, 648–650
   auditing support, 337, 341
   build recommendations, 631–632
   certificate templates, 755
   compacting directory database, 614
   creating, 11–13
   creating from backup data, 651–653
   defined, 2, 9
   demoting, 473, 527
   Directory Service Diagnosis tool, 545
   displaying connection objects, 544
   displaying replication partners, 544
   domain-based GPOs, 238
   functional levels, 557
   functionality, 460
   global catalog, 418, 464
   GPO links, 256
   in sites, 11
   installing, 27–29, 465–466, 474–476
   installing additional, 466–467
   installing child domains, 467–468
   installing domain trees, 468–469
   installing forests, 464
   installing with Windows interface, 461–462
   Kerberos authentication, 4
   managing in sites, 515–516
   multiple-domain forests, 569
   placement in branch offices, 374–375
   placing writable, 378
   preferred bridgehead servers, 539
   recommendations, 461
   removing, 26–27, 473
   renaming, 558
   replication traffic, 510

scoping audit policies, 370
security templates, 304
service locator records, 517
synchronizing with replication partners, 544
unattended installation options, 462–464
Windows Server Backup, 630
WSRM considerations, 673
domain DNS zone, 409, 414, 527
domain functional levels
    AD DS administration, 619
    defined, 10, 557
    deploying RODCs, 377
    installing domain trees, 469
    installing forests, 464
    levels supported, 557–558
    raising, 494, 560, 563–565
    Windows 2000 Native, 558
    Windows Server 2003, 558–559, 565
    Windows Server 2008, 559
domain local groups
    characteristics, 146–147, 149
    defined, 51
    group nesting, 153
    group scope considerations, 150
    RODC support, 380
    securing trust relationships, 591
Domain Name System. *See* DNS (Domain Name System)
domain naming context, 522
domain naming master role
    forest-wide, 479
    functionality, 480
    identifying, 485
    placing, 483
    seizing, 487–488
domain quarantine, 592–593
domain trees
    creating, 424–426
    delegation, 418
    installing, 468–469
Domain Users group, 127, 194
domain-based GPOs, 238–239, 268
domains
    AD DS administration, 621
    authentication within, 579–580
    computers joining, 189–190, 193–195, 201
    default groups, 177–178
    defined, 9, 31
    design considerations, 570
    DFS replication, 663
    external trusts, 587
    forests and, 9
    GPO links, 234, 258

installing additional domain controllers, 465–467
installing first domain controller, 465–466
migration considerations, 575
moving objects, 163, 572–576, 621
naming considerations, 11, 118
operations master roles, 479–483
password policies, 360
removing, 418
renaming, 561
renaming objects, 163
resetting computer accounts, 217
trusts between, 577–578
trusts within, 577
domain-wide authentication, 593
dot (.), 102, 394
DRA (Directory Replication Agent), 240
DRM (Digital Rights Management), 781
DS commands. *See also* specific commands
    defined, 59
    managing user attributes, 132
    manipulating objects, 89
    modifiers, 89
    supported, 88–89
DSACLS.exe command, 75, 620, 702
Dsadd command
    AD DS administration, 620
    creating computers, 205, 209
    creating groups, 159–160, 165
    creating user account, 89, 94
    functionality, 88
    GroupDN parameter, 159
    optional parameters, 160
Dsamain.exe command, 620, 641, 702
Dsbutil.exe command, 620
DSDBUtil.exe command, 702
Dsget command
    AD DS administration, 620
    functionality, 88
    managing user attributes, 122
    manipulating objects, 89
    retrieving group membership, 162, 167
Dsmgmt.exe command, 383, 620, 702
Dsmod command
    AD DS administration, 620
    changing group membership, 162–163, 166
    changing group type/scope, 151
    configuring computer attributes, 214
    disabling accounts, 127
    enabling accounts, 127
    functionality, 88
    managing user attributes, 121–122
    manipulating objects, 89

renaming user accounts, 130
resetting computer accounts, 217
resetting passwords, 126
Dsmove command
    AD DS administration, 620
    functionality, 88
    moving computers, 215
    moving groups, 163
    moving user accounts, 129
    renaming groups, 163
Dsquery command
    AD DS administration, 620
    functionality, 59–60, 88
    manipulating objects, 89
DSRM (Directory Services Restore Mode), 639–640
Dsrm command
    AD DS administration, 620
    deleting computer accounts, 220
    deleting groups, 163–164
    deleting user accounts, 128
    functionality, 88
DSRM password, 464, 631, 639–640
DS-RPC (Directory Service Remote Procedure Call), 537
dynamic DNS servers. *See* DDNS (dynamic DNS) servers
Dynamic Host Configuration Protocol. *See* DHCP
    (Dynamic Host Configuration Protocol)
dynamic link library (DLL), 614–616
dynamic updates, 436
dynamicObject class, 562

E

e-commerce, 754
EDM (Enterprise Directory Manager), 689
EFS (Encrypting File System)
    AD CS support, 6, 753
    certificate templates, 756
    recovery agents, 814
EKU (extended key usage), 841
e-mail, 730, 839
Encrypting File System. *See* EFS (Encrypting File
    System)
encryption
    AD CS support, 730, 754
    AD FS support, 827
    AD RMS support, 800
    certificate authorities, 826
    issuing CAs, 732
Enterprise Admins group
    AD RMS installation, 798
    creating computer objects, 192
    creating manual trusts, 583
    default groups, 177

forest functional levels, 377
moving computers, 214
PRP support, 380
schema masters, 465
Specops Gpupdate tool, 617–618
enterprise CAs
    automatic enrollment, 738
    certificate templates, 755
    defined, 732, 740
    deployment best practices, 737
    hierarchy considerations, 737
    installation considerations, 742, 745–747
    issuing CAs, 734
    standalone CA comparison, 733–734
Enterprise Directory Manager (EDM), 689
Enterprise PKI, 763, 765–766
error messages, 217, 673
Errors events, 663
event IDs, 665, 763–764
event log policies, 303
event logs
    auditing directory changes, 626
    computer account problems, 217
    examining for Group Policy, 281, 283
    GPO replication errors, 241
    new features, 665
    Server Manager support, 663
Event Viewer
    AD DS administration, 620, 702
    AD LDS support, 702
    DNS support, 449
    functionality, 660, 663–665
    location, 35
    viewing Security log, 341
Everyone group, 179
Exchange Server (Microsoft). *See* Microsoft Exchange
    Server
Exclude User Account Wizard, 813
exclusion policies, 812–814
explicit permissions, 74, 198
Export Template feature, 307
exporting
    certificates, 854, 857–862
    information to security templates, 308
    SLCs, 811
    trust policy, 855
extended key usage (EKU), 841
Extensible Markup Language (XML), 349, 844
external trusts, 587–588, 593
extranets
    AD RMS support, 792, 810
    additional information, 792
    Web SSO, 837

F

Failover Clustering service, 788
fault tolerance, 397
federated applications, 843
Federated Identity Support node, 812
federated users, 843
Federated Web SSO, 836
Federated Web SSO with Forest Trust, 836
federation, 843
Federation Server Proxy certificates, 841
federation servers
    AD FS certificates, 841
    configuring, 855, 857, 864–866
    installing, 850–851
    test environments, 845
Federation Service, 832–833, 846
Federation Service proxy. *See* FSP (Federation Service proxy)
federation trust
    configuring, 867–869
    creating, 855
    defined, 834, 843, 872
File Replication Service. *See* FRS (File Replication Service)
file systems
    auditing access, 337–341
    security templates, 303
filtering policy settings, 246–247
Find commands, 58–59
fine-grained password and lockout policy, 360–361
firewalls
    AD FS support, 693
    AD LDS support, 693
    authentication process, 834
    defined, 349
    network security, 311
    ports supported, 826–827
    purpose, 826–827
    split-brain syndrome, 401
Flexible Single Master of Operations (FSMO), 613, 619
FLZ (forward lookup zones)
    creating, 417
    creating custom records, 439
    defined, 409
    finalizing configuration, 433–435
    RLZs and, 436
    WINS support, 443
Folder Redirection node, 242
footprinting the network, 431
ForEach cmdlet, 107
forest DNS zone, 409, 414
forest functional levels

AD DS administration, 619
    defined, 10–11, 557
    deploying RODCs, 377
    installing forests, 464
    levels supported, 560–561
    raising, 563–565
    Windows 2000, 561
    Windows Server 2003, 561–562
    Windows Server 2008, 562
forest root domain
    AD CS installation, 741
    creating, 464
    dedicated, 567–568
    default groups, 177
    defined, 9, 31
    DNS considerations, 404–405, 414
    operations masters, 483
    zone placeholders, 417
forest trusts
    AD FS considerations, 825
    Federated Web SSO with Forest Trust, 836
    functionality, 588–589
    selective authentication, 593
forests
    authentication within, 580–582
    creating, 11–12, 14–21, 420–422, 685
    defined, 9, 31
    design considerations, 570
    DFS replication, 663
    installing, 464
    installing domain controllers, 465–466
    moving objects, 572–576, 621
    multiple, 572
    multiple-domain, 569–570, 586
    operations master roles, 479–480
    root cluster support, 788, 814
    SCP support, 814
    single-domain, 568–569
forest-wide authentication, 593
Format-List cmdlet, 100–101
forward lookup, 409
forward lookup zones. *See* FLZ (forward lookup zones)
Forwarded Events log, 663
forwarders
    conditional, 417, 440–441
    defined, 409
    root hints comparison, 439–441
FQDN (fully qualified domain name)
    AD RMS support, 800
    forward lookup, 409
    global query block lists, 416
    installing domain controllers, 462
    reverse lookup, 410

single-label names and, 415, 442
split-brain syndrome, 401
FRS (File Replication Service)
　AD DS administration, 621
　Directory Service Diagnosis tool, 545
　GPO replication, 241
　migrating SYSVOL replication, 496
　migration stages, 495–496
　SYSVOL replication, 494–502, 559
　timestamp support, 482
FSMO (Flexible Single Master of Operations), 613, 619
FSP (Federation Service proxy)
　Account Federation Service Proxy, 842
　authentication process, 834, 841
　configuring, 856–857
　defined, 832, 846
　federation servers, 841
　installing, 845, 851–852
　Resource Federation Service Proxy, 843
full system backups, 633–638
fully qualified domain name. *See* FQDN (fully qualified domain name)
functional levels. *See also* domain functional levels; forest functional levels
　defined, 10, 31, 557
　raising, 557

G

GC servers
　AD DS administration, 613
　configuring, 524, 527–528
　placing, 523
　UGMC considerations, 524–525
General property, 117
Get-ChildItem cmdlet, 102
Get-Help cmdlet, 101
GetInfo method, 105
GetObject statement, 109, 123
Get-Service cmdlet, 100–101
global catalog
　configuring GC servers, 524
　defined, 8, 31, 551
　domain controllers, 418, 464
　overview, 523
　placing GC servers, 523
　SRV records, 517
global cloud, 398
global groups
　characteristics, 147, 149
　defined, 51
　filtering GPOs, 263
　group nesting, 153

group scope considerations, 150
global query block lists, 415–416, 451–452
global unicast addresses, 396, 398
globally unique identifier (GUID), 240, 362, 481
GNZ (GlobalNames Zone)
　additional information, 442
　defined, 409
　single-label names, 411, 415, 441–443
　WINS comparison, 415
GPC (Group Policy Container), 240–241
GPfixup.exe command, 620
GPMC (Group Policy Management console)
　AD DS administration, 614, 621
　certificate templates, 758
　functionality, 232
　GPO precedence, 257
　Group Policy Inheritance tab, 259
　Group Policy Modeling node, 281
　Linked Group Policy Objects tab, 258
　starter GPOs, 248
GPME (Group Policy Management Editor)
　central store support, 246
　creating filters, 246–247
　editing GPOs, 232, 239, 315
　Extended tab, 243
　PDC Emulator role, 482
　Preference node support, 244
　software deployment GPO, 325
　unmanaged policy settings, 248
　WMI Filters node, 265
GPO Diagnostic Best Practices Analyzer, 620, 622
GPO Editor, 232, 238
GPO links
　defined, 234
　deleting, 257
　disabling, 257
　enforcing, 260–262
　Group Policy client, 256
　implementing Group Policy, 249–250
　joining computers to domains, 190
　managing, 255
　permissions, 239
　precedence, 260
　to domain controllers, 256
　to domains, 258
　to OUs, 234, 257–258, 269
　to sites, 234, 256, 258
GPO scope
　configuring enforced option, 272–273
　defined, 234
　enabling/disabling nodes, 266–267
　GPO inheritance/precedence, 257–262

GPO links, 255–257
Group Policy processing, 268–270
loopback policy processing, 270–271, 274–275
managing, 327
mechanisms supported, 255
password policies, 357
security filters, 234, 262–264, 273
targeting preferences, 267–268
WMI filters, 234
GPOs (Group Policy objects). *See also* local GPOs
AD DS administration, 612, 614, 620–621
applying to specific groups, 263
auditing logon, 369
creating, 232, 239, 249–250
creating with policy settings, 272
defined, 232, 286
Delegation tab, 263
Details tab, 266
domain-based, 238–239, 268
editing, 232, 239, 249–250, 315
enabling/disabling, 266–267
excluding specific groups, 263
exploring, 250–251
group scope, 145
inheritance, 257–259
managing, 232
moving user accounts, 129
OU support, 11, 191
precedence, 257–259
protecting, 657
relinking, 620
replicating, 240–241
Scope tab, 263
security templates, 304
Specops Gpupdate tool, 617
starter, 247–248
storing, 240
targeting preferences, 268
troubleshooting status, 241
Gpotool.exe command, 241
Gpresult.exe command, 277, 279–280, 282–283
GPSI (Group Policy Software Installation)
characteristics, 236, 322–325
maintaining deployed applications, 327–329
managing software, 329–332
preparing SDPs, 325
slow links, 329
software deployment GPO, 325–327, 330–331
software deployment options, 323–325
Windows Installer packages, 322–323
GPT (Group Policy Template), 240–241, 494
GPUpdate command, 235

group accounts, 612, 624
group claim type, 839, 848
group membership
adding members, 54, 56, 65–66
caching for universal groups, 524–525
changing with Dsmod, 162–163, 166
changing with LDIFDE, 161, 166
data protection measures, 624
delegating management, 172–175, 181
delegating with Group Policy, 295–298
domain local groups, 147
global groups, 147
group claim type, 839
group scope considerations, 145, 148–150
infrastructure master role, 481
local groups, 146
managing, 151–153, 164
migration considerations, 575–576
restricted groups policy settings, 291–294
retrieving with Dsget, 162, 167
scripting shadow groups, 363
taking effect quickly, 153
universal groups, 148
group objects, 50–52, 63–64, 620
Group Policy
AD DS support, 8
certificate templates, 758
defined, 231
delegating membership, 295–298
deploying security policies, 314–315
examining event logs, 281
maintaining deployed applications, 327–329
PDC Emulator role, 482
policy settings, 231
processing overview, 268–270
refreshing with GPUpdate, 235
software installation, 236–237
transforming security policies, 319–320
troubleshooting, 280
Group Policy client, 235, 237, 256, 258
Group Policy Container (GPC), 240–241
Group Policy Creator Owners group, 239, 380
Group Policy Management console. *See* GPMC (Group Policy Management console)
Group Policy Management Editor. *See* GPME (Group Policy Management Editor)
Group Policy Modeling Wizard, 277, 280–281, 283–284
Group Policy Objects container, 239, 248, 257
Group Policy Operational Log, 281
Group Policy refresh, 235–236
Group Policy Results Wizard, 277–280, 282

Group Policy Software Installation. *See* GPSI (Group Policy Software Installation)
Group Policy Template (GPT), 240–241, 494
group scope
  converting, 149–151, 156
  membership possibilities, 145, 148–149
  overview, 145–148
  selecting, 51
groups
  administrative role separation, 383
  assigning permissions, 73
  best practices, 169–170
  computer accounts, 220
  converting types, 149–151, 156
  creating, 143–149, 155–156, 180–181
  creating with Dsadd, 159–160, 165
  defaults, 177–179
  defining naming conventions, 143–145
  deleting with Dsrm, 163–164
  group claim type, 839
  importing with CSVDE, 160, 165
  management strategies, 153–155
  managing enterprises, 141–143
  managing membership, 151–153
  managing with LDIFDE, 161
  moving with Dsmove, 163
  nesting, 153–155
  OUs and, 176
  protected, 178
  protecting from accidental deletion, 171
  renaming with Dsmove, 163
  role-based management, 141–143
  shadow, 176, 185, 362–363
  special identities, 179, 185
  types listed, 50–51, 145
GUID (globally unique identifier), 240, 362, 481

H

hash code, 358
hidden attributes, 88, 116
hierarchy
  certificate authority, 734–737, 739–740, 742–750
  defined, 777
  DNS naming structure, 394
  PKI, 731
high availability, 650, 788
HKCU PSDrive, 103
HKLM PSDrive, 103
Holme, Dan, 86, 140, 230, 290, 356, 363, 460, 508, 556
host name, 518
host (A) record, 413, 517–518

HTTP
  AD FS support, 7, 827
  certificate authorities, 733
  firewall support, 826
HTTPS (Secure HTTP)
  AD FS support, 7, 854
  certificate authorities, 733
  firewall support, 826
  SSL certificates, 724
Hyper-V
  certificate authorities, 737
  DC hardening, 444
  domain controller support, 631, 648, 695

I

IDA (identity and access) infrastructure
  AD FS support, 830
  audit trails, 4
  control access, 4
  information storage, 3
  Kerberos authentication, 4
  technologies comprising support, 5–7
identity
  authenticating, 4
  defined, 3
  group management strategies, 153
  identity claim type, 839
  special, 179, 185
identity claim type, 839, 848
Identity Integration Feature Pack (IIFP), 693
identity store, 3–4, 32, 189
IETF (Internet Engineering Task Force), 414
IFM (Install From Media), 630, 633
ifm command, 472
IIFP (Identity Integration Feature Pack), 693
IIS (Internet Information Services)
  AD CS support, 730
  AD FS support, 854, 856
  AD RMS support, 7, 786, 810
  allocating resources, 674
  firewall considerations, 827
IIS Manager, 841
importing certificates, 857–859, 862
importing computers
  CSVDE tool, 203–204, 209–210
  LDIFDE tool, 204–205, 210
  Windows PowerShell, 206–208
importing groups, 160, 165
importing security templates, 308
importing SLCs, 810
importing users

CSVDE tool, 90, 94–95
LDIFDE tool, 90–92, 95–96
Windows PowerShell, 106–108
Incremental Zone Transfer (IXFR), 412
inetOrgPerson object, 119, 562
INF file extension, 302
Information events, 663
information management, 613
infrastructure master role
    domain-wide, 479
    functionality, 480–481
    identifying, 485
    placing, 483–484
    seizing, 487
inheritance
    blocking, 260–262
    disabling, 74
    domain-linked policies, 269
    GPOs, 257–259
    permissions and, 73–74, 77
    policy, 259
initial notification delay, 534
Install From Media (IFM), 630, 633
installation media
    creating, 472–473, 476, 633
    installing AD DS, 472–473
Installing Windows Wizard, 24
instances
    Active Directory Schema snap-in, 712
    Active Directory Sites and Services snap-in, 713
    additional information, 707, 712–713
    ADSI Edit, 709–711
    creating AD LDS, 703–706, 714–716
    defined, 707
    Ldp.exe command, 711–712
    unattended AD LDS, 706–707
intellectual property
    implementing AD RMS, 786
    protecting, 782, 785
Interactive group, 179
inter-forest migration, 572
Internet Engineering Task Force (IETF), 414
Internet Explorer Maintenance node, 242
Internet Information Services. *See* IIS (Internet Information Services)
Internet Protocol security. *See* IPSec (Internet Protocol security)
intersite, 535, 551
Inter-Site MessagingSMTP (ISM-SMTP), 537
intersite replication
    bridgehead servers, 538
    configuring, 539–543, 546–547
    defined, 535

Directory Service Diagnosis tool, 545
    overview, 535–537
    replication frequency, 542
    replication schedules, 542
    replication transport protocols, 537
    intersite topology generator (ISTG), 535–538, 562
Inter-Site Transports container, 537, 540
intra-forest migration, 572–573, 576
intrasite, 551
Intra-site Automatic Tunnel Addressing Protocol
    (ISATAP), 415–416
intrasite replication, 534–535, 537–538
IP addresses
    A records, 517
    DDNS considerations, 443
    DNS support, 393
    domain controller requirements, 12
    RLZ support, 436, 438
    round robin, 411
    subnet objects, 512
Ipconfig command, 449, 621
IPSec (Internet Protocol security)
    AD CS support, 6, 729–730
    security policies, 312
IPv4 protocol
    additional information, 397
    address types, 395–396
    APIPA support, 395
    creating RLZ, 437
    ISATAP support, 416
    security policies, 312
    WINS support, 442
IPv6 protocol
    creating RLZ, 437
    DNS support, 395–396
    ISATAP support, 416
    security policies, 312
ISATAP (Intra-site Automatic Tunnel Addressing
    Protocol), 415–416
ISM-SMTP (Inter-Site MessagingSMTP), 537
ISO files, 645
issuing CAs
    certificate lifetimes, 739
    certificate templates, 755
    defined, 732
    enterprise CAs, 734
    finalizing configuration, 753–759
    hierarchy considerations, 735
    installation considerations, 742, 745–748
ISTG (intersite topology generator), 535–538, 562
item-level targeting, 267–268
IXFR (Incremental Zone Transfer), 412

J

Javelina ADvantage, 688–689

K

KCC (Knowledge Consistency Checker)
    AD DS administration, 612
    Directory Service Diagnosis tool, 545
    forest functional levels, 562
    functionality, 240, 533–534
    intrasite replication, 534
    launching, 544
    site links, 535
KDC (key distribution center), 579, 582
Kerberos Password protocol (KPASSWD), 517
Kerberos protocol
    AD DS administration, 621
    AES support, 559
    authentication support, 4, 9, 579–582
    defined, 32
    multiple-domain forests, 569
    realm trusts, 588
    SRV records, 517
    validating trusts, 590
key distribution center (KDC), 579, 582
Key Management Server (KMS), 781
key pairs
    certificate lifetimes, 738
    defined, 777
    security tokens, 840
KMS (Key Management Server), 781
Ksetup.exe command, 621
Ktpass.exe command, 621

L

LAN Diagnostics collector set, 667
LAN Manager, 312
lastLogonTimestamp attribute, 558
LDAP (Lightweight Directory Access Protocol)
    AD DS administration, 610, 621
    AD LDS support, 6, 690, 692, 703
    AD RMS support, 819
    data store manipulation, 8
    defined, 349
    forest functional levels, 562
    importing computers, 203
    item-level targeting, 268
    populating user attributes, 105
    relational database comparison, 690–691
    security policy support, 312
    SRV records, 517
LDAP over SSL, 703

LDAP query groups, 562
LDIF (LDAP Data Interchange Format)
    AD LDS support, 702, 705–706
    defined, 90–91, 161
    importing computers, 204, 210
    LDIFDE support, 161
LDIFDE tool
    AD DS administration, 621, 702
    AD LDS support, 702, 708, 713
    additional information, 709
    changing group membership, 161, 166
    importing computers, 204–205, 210
    importing passwords, 126
    importing users, 90–92, 95–96
    managing groups, 161
    parameters supported, 92
Ldp.exe command
    AD DS administration, 621, 702
    AD LDS support, 702, 704
    application directory partitions, 527
    functionality, 629
    restoring objects, 626
    working with instances, 711–712
least-privilege security, 192, 569
legacy DNS, 410, 417
licensing clusters, 788, 819
Lightweight Directory Access Protocol. *See* LDAP
    (Lightweight Directory Access Protocol)
linked properties, 54, 56
linked-value replication, 561
link-local addresses, 395–396, 398
link-local cloud, 398
load balancing, 786, 788
local Administrators group
    characteristics, 146, 177
    creating computer objects, 192
    delegating membership, 295
    end user support, 291
    joining computers to domains, 190, 193–194
    migration considerations, 576
    restricted group policies, 295
    scheduled backups, 631
Local Computer GPO, 237–238
local GPOs
    configuring, 300–301
    defined, 349
    RSoP support, 237–238, 268
    security settings, 300–301
local groups, 146, 149
local security authority (LSA), 216
Local Security Authority Subsystem (LSASS), 574
local security policies, 303, 315–316
Local Security Policy console, 307, 314, 737

local Users group, 146, 194
location attribute, 214
lockout policies
    configuring, 363–366
    fine-grained, 360–361
    for domains, 360
    multiple-domain forests, 570
    overview, 359
    unlocking accounts, 126
Log On To property, 119, 121
logging database, 819
Logon Events setting, 368, 371
logon process
    AD CS support, 730
    auditing, 369
    computer accounts, 216
Logon property, 119
loopback addresses, 396
loopback policies, 270–271, 274–275
LostandFound container, 614
LostandFoundConfig container, 614
LSA (local security authority), 216
LSASS (Local Security Authority Subsystem), 574

M
MAC address, 119
machine certificate, 798
mail exchanger (MX) records, 414
maintenance. *See* AD DS administration
Manage command, 190, 193–195, 201, 215
managedBy attribute, 213
manual trusts
    additional information, 586
    creating, 583–586
    defined, 579
    deleting, 590
    external trusts, 587–588, 593
    forest trusts, 588–589, 593
    realm trusts, 583, 588
    shortcut trusts, 586–587
    types listed, 583
Maximum Password Age policy setting, 358
member attribute
    defined, 152
    deleted groups, 171
    global group replication, 147
    group membership management, 172
    importing groups with CSVDE, 160
    infrastructure master role, 480–481
    linked-value replication, 561
    multiple-domain forests, 570
    SID support, 141

Member Of restricted policy setting, 291–295
memberOf attribute, 152, 162, 481
Members attribute, 341
Members restricted policy setting, 291–294
metadata, 473, 544
methods, 100, 135
Microsoft Enrollment Center, 789
Microsoft Exchange Server
    AD LDS support, 685, 692–693
    additional information, 726
    PKI support, 726
Microsoft Federation Services, 831
Microsoft Identity Integration Server (MIIS), 693
Microsoft Identity Lifecycle Manager (MILM), 693
Microsoft Management Console. *See* MMC (Microsoft Management Console)
Microsoft Message Queuing service, 786, 819
Microsoft Office SharePoint Server 2007, 833
Microsoft Passport, 811, 818
Microsoft SharePoint Portal Server, 693
Microsoft SQL Server, 786
Microsoft System Center Configuration Manager, 176, 322, 661
Microsoft Systems Management Server, 322
Microsoft Windows Update, 410
MIIS (Microsoft Identity Integration Server), 693
MILM (Microsoft Identity Lifecycle Manager), 693
Minimum Password Length policy, 358
MMC (Microsoft Management Console)
    Actions pane, 35
    AD CS role, 763
    AD RMS role, 789, 810
    Add/Remove Snap-in command, 303
    certificate authorities, 733
    console modes, 39
    creating/editing local GPOs, 238
    custom consoles, 36, 38–44
    overview, 35–36
    preconfigured consoles, 36
mobile computer systems, 730, 811
Move command, 214
MoveHere method, 129–130
MoveTo method, 129
Movetree.exe command, 621–622
MP3 format, 781
MS-adamschemaw2k3.ldf file, 705
MS-adamschemaw2k8.ldf file, 706
MS-AdamSyncMetadata.ldf file, 705–706
MS-ADAM-Upgrade-1.ldf file, 705
MS-ADLDS-DisplaySpecifiers.ldf file, 706, 713
MS-AZMan.ldf file, 706
MSC file extension, 40
ms-DS-MachineAccountQuota attribute, 197–198

MSI file extension, 322, 349
MS-InetOrgPerson.ldf file, 706
MSP file extension, 323
MST file extension, 323, 349
MS-User.ldf file, 706
MS-UserProxyFull.ldf file, 706
MS-UserProxy.ldf file, 706
Multiple Universal Naming Convention Provider (MUP), 268
multiple-domain forests, 569–570, 586
MUP (Multiple Universal Naming Convention Provider), 268
MX (mail exchanger) records, 414

N

name attribute, 118–119, 129, 144
name recursion, 410
name resolution
    application directory partitions, 445
    DNS servers, 399
    domain controller requirements, 12
    forwarders, 409, 417, 439–441
    overview, 406
    PNRP support, 397–398
    process overview, 393, 406–408
    root hints, 409–410, 439–441
namespaces
    cmdlet support, 103
    defined, 265
    DFS Namespaces, 510
    linking, 440
    multiple-domain forests, 569
    split-brain syndrome, 401–402
    trees and, 9
    zone delegations, 412
naming contexts, 522, 551
naming conventions
    best practices, 169
    for groups, 143–145
    single-label names, 442
NAS (network attached storage), 144
NDES (Network Device Enrollment Service)
    AD CS support, 741
    defined, 732
    installing, 749–750
nesting process, 153–155
net user command, 25
NetBIOS, 11
Netdom command
    AD DS administration, 621
    creating computers, 205
    deleting manual trusts, 590

    managing trusts, 591
    renaming computers, 218
    renaming domain controllers, 558
    resetting computer accounts, 217–218
netdom command, 25
NetIQ Security Administration Suite, 688–689
Netlogon service, 216–217
NetPro Active Directory LifeCycle Suite, 688
netsh command, 25
network attached storage (NAS), 144
Network Device Enrollment Service. *See* NDES (Network Device Enrollment Service)
Network group, 179
Network Load Balancing service, 788
network operating system (NOS), 610, 685
Network Policy Server (NPS), 756
network security, 311, 431–432
Network Service account, 705, 848
Network Time Protocol (NTP), 845
networks, footprinting, 431
New Object Computer Wizard, 192
new object protection option, 624
New Object Site dialog box, 513
New Object Subnet dialog box, 514
New Object User Wizard, 114
New Trust Wizard, 583, 585, 588
New Zone Wizard, 413
Nltest.exe command, 217–218, 621
Non-Administrators GPO, 238
nonauthoritative restores
    deleted groups, 171
    overview, 632–645
    restoration scenario, 639
    Windows Server Backup, 630
NOS (network operating system), 610, 685
notification process, 534
NPS (Network Policy Server), 756
Nslookup command, 449, 621
NT LAN Manager (NTLM), 579
Ntds.dit database
    AD DS administration, 614, 623
    defined, 522, 683
    Windows Server Backup, 630
Ntdsutil.exe command
    AD DS administration, 621, 702
    AD LDS support, 702
    application directory partitions, 527
    backup considerations, 631
    capturing system state data, 650–651
    creating snapshots, 640–641
    IFM subcommand options, 633
    installation media, 472

performing restores, 644
seizing roles, 488
NTLM (NT LAN Manager), 579
NTP (Network Time Protocol), 845

O

object class, 104, 562
object identifiers (OIDs), 733
object reference, 102
objects. *See also* specific object types
    assigning permissions, 72
    auditing changes, 620, 626
    cmdlet support, 99
    computer, 52–54, 63–64
    controlling view, 54
    creating with CSVDE, 160
    data protection measures, 624
    defined, 100, 135
    deleting, 620
    displaying metadata, 544
    DS commands, 89
    finding in Active Directory, 54–67
    finding using Dsquery command, 59–60
    group, 50–52, 63–64
    homeless, 614
    looking up, 54
    migration considerations, 576
    moving, 572–576, 620–621
    new object protection option, 624
    properties, 100
    removing permissions, 75
    renaming, 620
    resetting permissions, 75
    user, 48–50, 61–63
Oclist command, 26
Ocsetup command, 25–26
OCSP (Online Certificate Status Protocol), 731–732, 855
OCSP Response Signing certificate, 759
OIDs (object identifiers), 733
Online Certificate Status Protocol (OCSP), 731–732
online responders
    AD FS configuration, 855
    adding revocation configuration, 761–762
    additional information, 732, 761
    defined, 731–732
    event IDs, 764
    finalizing configuration, 759–762
    managing, 763
operations management, 611
operations masters
    AD DS administration, 620

defined, 478, 504
failover plans, 484
identifying, 484–485, 490
overview, 478–479
placing, 483–484
recognizing failures, 486
returning roles to original holders, 488–489
roles supported, 479
seizing roles, 487–488
transferring roles, 485–486, 489–491
Organization property, 117
organizational units. *See* OUs (organizational units)
OUs (organizational units)
    AD DS administration, 613
    assigning permissions, 73
    computer objects, 214
    containers and, 46, 190–191
    creating, 46–48, 61, 199
    defined, 11, 46
    delegating membership management, 175
    delegation support, 77–78
    deleting, 47–48
    deleting user accounts, 128
    GPO links, 234, 257–258, 269
    groups and, 176
    linking PSOs, 362–363
    permission considerations, 176
    protecting from accidental deletion, 47
    RDN requirements, 118
    shadow groups, 176
    viewing permissions, 72
Outlook Web Access (OWA), 726
OWA (Outlook Web Access), 726

P

parent objects, 73–74
parent-child trust, 580
partial attribute set (PAS), 8, 31, 523, 551
partitions, 523, 551
passive clients, 843
Password Must Meet Complexity Requirements policy, 358
Password Never Expires setting, 120, 360–361
password policies
    AD DS administration, 615
    configuring, 363–366
    domain, 360
    fine-grained, 360–361, 559, 570
    multiple-domain forests, 570
    overview, 357–359

Password Policy Basic by Special Operations Software,
    361
Password Policy node, 357, 361
password replication policy. *See* PRP (password
    replication policy)
password settings object. *See* PSO (password settings
    object)
passwords
    Administrator account, 24
    alternative credentials, 126
    computer accounts, 189
    control access rights, 72
    data protection measures, 624
    Directory Services Restore Mode password, 464, 631
    for service accounts, 121
    migration considerations, 576
    PDC Emulator role, 482
    permission considerations, 73, 76
    resetting, 125–126, 132, 610
    RODC considerations, 375
    setting, 106
    trust, 585
patch files, 323
PDC Emulator role
    AD DS administration, 613
    domain-wide, 479
    functionality, 481–483
    identifying, 484
    placing, 483
    seizing, 487
PDCs (primary domain controllers), 479, 481–483
performance benchmarks, 621
performance counters, 667–670, 764
Performance Log Users group, 667
Performance Logs and Alerts tool, 666
performance management. *See also* Event Viewer
    creating performance baselines, 671
    managing system resources, 660–661
    Performance Monitor, 661, 666–671
    Reliability Monitor, 661, 665
    Task Manager, 660–663
    Windows System Resource Manager, 661, 672–674,
        679–680
Performance Monitor, 661, 666–671
permissions. *See also* specific permissions
    ACE support, 69
    Advanced Security Settings dialog box, 72–73
    assigning to objects, 72
    best practice, 73
    configuring for auditing, 343
    creating AD LDS instances, 705
    creating computer objects, 197

default groups, 177–178
delegating, 69–70
delegating for computer objects, 192, 200
effective, 76–77
explicit, 74, 198
granting, 54, 56
inheritance and, 73–74, 77
least-privilege approach, 192, 569
linking GPOs, 239
managing for groups, 141–143
managing with property sets, 72
moving computers, 214
preparing SDPs, 325
removing from objects, 75
reporting, 75
resetting on objects, 75
security templates, 303
security translation, 575
setting, 75
viewing delegated, 79
viewing for Active Directory objects, 70–71, 75
pipeline variables, 102
PKI (public key infrastructure)
    AD CS support, 6, 731, 782
    additional information, 6
    CRL support, 731
    deployment best practices, 738
    Enterprise PKI, 763, 765–766
    NDES support, 732
    online responders, 731
    trusted CAs, 725
PKIView. *See* Enterprise PKI
PNRP (Peer Name Resolution Protocol), 397–398, 417
pointer (PTR) records, 414, 436
Policies node, 241–242
policy inheritance, 259
policy settings (policy)
    applying, 235–236
    auditing, 335–337, 368
    blocking inheritance, 260
    configuring, 234
    creating GPOs with precedence, 272
    defined, 231, 241, 286
    filtering, 246–247
    GPME support, 232
    managed, 248
    modifying GPO scope, 269–270
    scoping audit policies, 370
    states supported, 234
    testing, 234
    unmanaged, 248
    viewing effects, 250

policy templates
  AD RMS configuration, 809
  creating, 788, 819–820
  manipulating, 789
  preparing, 815–817
Policy-Based QoS node, 242
polling
  bridgehead servers, 542
  defined, 535
  intersite replication, 542
  intrasite replication, 535
precedence
  GPO links, 260
  GPOs, 257–259
  PSOs, 362
Preferences node, 241, 243–244
preferred bridgehead servers, 539, 546
prestaging
  computer accounts, 192–193, 196
  computer objects, 195–197
  defined, 193
primary domain controllers (PDCs), 479, 481–483
primary zone, 410, 412, 415, 417
Print Operators group, 178
private keys, 738, 841
Profile property, 117
properties. *See also* specific properties
  for objects, 100, 116
  multiselecting user objects, 117
  object references, 102
Properties dialog box
  Account tab, 87, 115, 119
  Additional Account Info tab, 615
  Address tab, 87, 115
  Attribute Editor tab, 88, 116–117
  Authentication tab, 594
  Categories tab, 326
  COM+ tab, 116
  Deployment Options section, 326
  Deployment tab, 326
  Dial-in tab, 116
  Environment tab, 115
  Explain tab, 234, 243
  for sites, 514
  for subnets, 515
  General tab, 87, 115, 149, 433, 447, 524
  Managed By tab, 172–173, 213
  Member Of tab, 88, 115, 213
  Members tab, 151
  Modifications tab, 326
  Name Servers tab, 434
  Notes field, 170
  Object tab, 171
  Operating System tab, 213
  Organization tab, 88, 115
  Policy Module tab, 758
  Previous Versions tab, 650
  Profile tab, 87, 115
  Remote Control tab, 115
  Security tab, 70, 434
  Session tab, 115
  Sessions tab, 115
  Shadow Copies tab, 649
  SOA tab, 434
  Telephones tab, 115
  Terminal Services Profile tab, 115
  Upgrades tab, 326
  WINS tab, 434
  Zone Transfers tab, 434
property sets, 72
Protect from Accidental Deletion attribute, 648
protected accounts, 178
protected groups, 178
providers, 103
PRP (password replication policy)
  configuring, 385
  defined, 380, 389
  domain-wide, 380–381
  RODC support, 375, 381
PSDrives, 103
PSO (password settings object)
  creating, 362, 364–365
  defined, 361, 389
  deleting, 366
  linking, 362–363
  managing, 361–362
  precedence, 362
  resultant, 362, 365–366, 390
PTR (pointer) records, 414, 436
public key infrastructure. *See* PKI (public key infrastructure)
public keys, 738, 841
publishing applications, 323–325
publishing license, 790, 798, 823
Put method
  computer objects, 214
  user accounts, 130
  user objects, 105, 109, 123
PutEx method, 106

Q
Quest FastLane Active Roles, 688–689
Quest Object Restore for Active Directory, 628–629

R

RAC (rights account certificate), 797, 812
RAS and IAS Server templates, 756
RC4-HMAC algorithm, 559
RDN (relative distinguished name)
    as Create method parameter, 104, 109
    defined, 60
    name attributes, 118
Read Members permission, 174–175
read-only domain controllers. *See* RODCs (read-only
    domain controllers)
realm trusts, 583, 588
recovery functions. *See* restore functions
Redircmp.exe command, 196, 559
Redirusr.exe command, 196, 559
registry
    adding custom settings, 304
    Administrative Template node policies, 244
    policy settings, 231
    security policy, 312
    tattooing, 248
registry permissions, 303
Regsvr32.exe command, 619, 712
relational databases, 690–691
relative distinguished name. *See* RDN (relative
    distinguished name)
relative identifier (RID), 479–480
Reliability Monitor, 661, 665
remote communication, 278, 730
Remote Installation Services node, 242
remote procedure call (RPC), 733
Remote Procedure Call System Service (RPCSS), 268
Remote Server Administration Tools. *See* RSAT (Remote
    Server Administration Tools)
renaming
    computers, 218–219
    domain controllers, 558
    domains, 561
    groups, 163
    objects, 620
    user accounts, 129–130
Repadmin.exe (Replication Diagnostics Tool), 543–544,
    621, 703
replicas, 522, 551
replication. *See also* DFS-R (Distributed File System
    Replication); intersite replication; intrasite
    replication
    AD DS support, 8, 612
    AD LDS support, 692, 717–718
    configuring, 545–547
    connection objects, 532
    data protection measures, 624

defined, 510
DFS, 644, 663
domain local groups, 147
domain naming context, 522
forcing, 532, 544
global groups, 147
GPOs, 240–241
group membership changes, 153
group scope considerations, 145
KCC support, 533–534
key features, 531–532
linked-value, 561
local groups, 146
monitoring, 543–545
universal groups, 148
Replication Diagnostics Tool (Repadmin.exe), 543–544,
    621, 703
replication scope
    AD DS administration, 619
    application directory partitions, 404, 408, 414, 445
    best practice, 440
    changing, 447
    child domains, 404
    DNS, 415
ReplMon.exe command, 622
reporting
    AD DS administration, 614
    permissions, 75
request for comments. *See* RFC (request for comments)
Reset Account command, 218, 220
Reset Account Lockout Counter After setting, 359
Reset Password command, 127
resource accounts, 843
resource federation server (RFS), 834, 843
Resource Federation Service Proxy, 843
Resource Monitor, 661–663
resource organizations, 832, 843, 855
resource records, 410. *See also* specific records
Responsible Person (RP) records, 434–436
restore functions. *See also* backup functions
    AD CS considerations, 767
    authoritative restores, 171, 630, 632–645
    DSRM password, 464, 631, 639–640
    from complete backups, 645–648
    identifying backup data sets, 640–642
    nonauthoritative restores, 171, 630, 632–645
    Quest Object Restore for Active Directory, 628–629
    restore scenarios, 638–639
    restoring objects, 626–628
restricted groups policies
    delegating administration, 294–295
    overview, 291–294
    security templates, 303

Restricted Groups policy node, 291
resultant PSO
  defined, 362, 390
  identifying, 365–366
  overview, 362
Resultant Set of Policies. *See* RSoP (Resultant Set of
  Policies)
reverse lookup, 410
reverse lookup zones. *See* RLZ (reverse lookup zones)
revocation. *See* certificate revocation
RFC (request for comments), 410, 414
RFC 2052, 517
RFC 2560, 732
RFS (resource federation server), 834, 843
RID (relative identifier), 479–480
RID master role
  domain-wide, 479
  functionality, 480
  identifying, 485
  placing, 483
  seizing, 487–488
rights account certificate (RAC), 797, 812
RLZ (reverse lookup zones)
  creating, 417, 436–438
  defined, 410, 438
RODC accounts, 470
RODCs (read-only domain controllers)
  AD DS administration, 613, 619
  AD LDS considerations, 695
  backup considerations, 631
  configuring, 383–386
  credentials caching, 381–382
  DC hardening, 444
  defined, 375, 390
  deploying, 377–380
  DNS servers, 399
  DNS zones, 415
  forest functional levels, 561
  installing, 379–380, 384–385, 465, 469–472
  PRP support, 375, 380–381
  read-only servers, 417
  replicas, 522
role-based configuration, 304, 310
role-based management, 77, 141–143
rollback process, 314, 560
root CAs
  AD CS support, 731
  certificate lifetimes, 739
  defined, 731
  depicted, 737
  deployment best practices, 737
  hierarchy considerations, 734–735
  installation considerations, 742–744

  securing, 734
  standalone CAs, 732
root clusters
  creating by default, 788
  defined, 788, 823
  deploying, 814
  installing, 805–807
  logging database, 819
root hints, 409–410, 439–441
root kits, 781
round robin, 411
RP (Responsible Person) records, 434–436
RPC (remote procedure call), 733
RPCSS (Remote Procedure Call System Service), 268
RSAT (Remote Server Administration Tools)
  AD CS support, 763
  AD RMS support, 810
  graphical tool support, 713
  installation requirements, 37, 615
  Quest Object Restore for Active Directory, 628
  Specops Gpupdate tool, 617
RSoP (Resultant Set of Policies)
  defined, 235, 277, 286
  Gpresult command support, 279–280
  Group Policy Modeling Wizard support, 280–281
  Group Policy Results Wizard support, 278–280
  local GPOs, 238
Ruest, Danielle, 404, 608, 688, 728, 785, 830
Ruest, Nelson, 404, 608, 688, 728, 785, 830
Russinovich, Mark, 781

S
SACL (system ACL)
  auditing support, 338, 340–342
  defined, 69
  migration considerations, 574
SAM (Security Accounts Manager), 146, 189, 577
sAMAccountName attribute
  computer accounts, 189, 203, 206, 216
  groups, 144, 162
  user accounts, 104, 118, 130
saved queries
  additional information, 56
  creating, 55
  customizing views, 55
  defined, 81
  saving, 55
scavenging
  removing records, 438
  server, 411
  zone, 412, 432–433
SCEP (Simple Certificate Enrollment Protocol), 732, 750

scheduling backups, 631, 635–638, 648
Schema Admins group, 177, 465
schema master role
  forest-wide, 479
  functionality, 480
  identifying, 485
  placing, 483
  seizing, 487–488
schemas
  Active Directory schema, 37, 88
  AD DS administration, 613
  AD LDS support, 694
  defined, 8, 32, 465, 522
  LDAP support, 690
Schtasks.exe command, 650
scope. *See also* GPO scope; group scope
  audit policies, 370
  defined, 234, 286
  GPO, 234
SCP (service connection point), 801, 814
scripting
  cmdlet support, 99
  importing computers, 207–208
  shadow group membership, 363
  VBScript support, 112
  Windows PowerShell support, 108, 111–112
Scripts node, 242
SCWAudit.inf template, 312
Scwcmd.exe command, 309, 314
Scw.exe command, 309
SD (security descriptor), 574
SDP (software distribution point), 323, 325
Secedit.exe utility, 308
secondary zone, 411–412, 415, 417
secure channel, 216–218, 224
Secure HTTP (HTTPS)
  AD FS support, 7, 854
  certificate authorities, 733
  firewall support, 826
  SSL certificates, 724
Secure Multipurpose Internet Mail Extensions (S/
    MIME), 730
Secure Sockets Layer. *See* SSL (Secure Sockets Layer)
Secure Sockets Tunneling Protocol (SSTP), 730
Security Accounts Manager (SAM), 146, 189, 577
Security Configuration and Analysis snap-in, 305–307,
    316–318
security configuration database, 309
Security Configuration Manager, 304
Security Configuration Wizard
  AD CS considerations, 741
  applying security policies, 313
  Audit Policy section, 312

Confirm Service Changes page, 311
  creating security policies, 309–314
  deploying security policies, 314
  editing security policies, 313
  functionality, 309, 318–319
  IPSec limitations, 312
  modifying security policy settings, 314
  Network Security section, 311
  Registry Settings section, 312
  rolling back security policies, 314
  security templates, 313
Security CSE, 236
security descriptor (SD), 574
security filters, 234, 262–264, 273
security groups, 50, 145, 380
security identifier. *See* SID (security identifier)
Security log, 341–342, 344–345, 663
security management. *See also* AD CS (Active Directory
    Certificate Services)
  AD DS administration, 613
  AD LDS considerations, 695
  best practices, 800
  CA hierarchy, 734–736
  DNS server role, 431–432
  domain/forest design, 570
  LDAP considerations, 691
  network security, 311, 431–432
security policies
  applying, 313
  configuring, 303, 315–316
  creating, 309–314
  deploying with Group Policy, 314–315
  editing, 313
  modifying settings, 314
  network security, 311
  rolling back, 314
security principals
  account properties, 119
  AD DS administration, 621
  defined, 69
  effective permissions, 76
  groups as, 141, 145
  RID master role, 480
  viewing, 70
Security Settings node, 237, 242, 304
security templates
  account policies, 303
  analyzing computer configuration, 306–307
  applying to computers, 305
  correcting discrepancies, 307
  creating, 303, 307, 316
  defined, 349
  event log policies, 303

file system permissions, 303
GPO support, 304
importing, 308
local policies, 303
managing configuration, 302–305
registry permissions, 303
restricted groups policies, 303
saving settings, 304
Secedit.exe utility, 308
Security Configuration Wizard, 313
system services, 303
Security Templates snap-in, 303–304
Security Token Service (STS), 844
security tokens
AD FS configuration, 854
authentication process, 835
defined, 844
federation servers, 841
key pairs, 840
security translation, 575
Select dialog box, 56–57
selective authentication, 559, 593–595, 600–601
self-signed certificates, 801, 818
server authentication certificate, 844
Server Core
AD CS considerations, 741
adding AD DS to installation, 26
graphical tool limitations, 713
initial configuration tasks, 25–26
installing, 24
installing AD LDS, 694–699
installing domain controllers, 27–29
installing RODC, 380
optional features, 24
supported roles, 23–24
VSS support, 649
server farms, 844, 855
server licensor certificate. *See* SLC (server licensor
    certificate)
Server Manager
Active Directory Users and Computers node, 614
AD CS support, 763
AD DS administration, 621, 703
AD LDS support, 703
AD RMS support, 788
Add Roles Wizard, 12, 461
adding roles, 12
administrative tools, 37
event logs, 663
functionality, 12
installing Windows PowerShell, 98
Online Responder node, 761
performance considerations, 662

Server Operators group, 177–178
Server Performance Advisor, 666, 670
server scavenging, 411
servers. *See also* DNS servers
AD CS support, 730
AD RMS considerations, 789
bridgehead, 538–539, 542, 546, 612
certificate lifetimes, 739
configuring, 863
deployment best practices, 737
importing certificates, 862
placement considerations, 512
root clusters, 788
securing CAs, 734
security templates, 304
Servers container, 516
service connection point (SCP), 801, 814
service localization, 508, 510, 512, 551
service principal name (SPN), 580
service records. *See* SRV (service) records
service-oriented architecture (SOA), 844, 872
services
defined, 349, 361
naming, 397
Services tool, 35
session initiation protocol (SIP), 414
Set statement, 123
SetInfo method
committing changes, 105, 124
computer objects, 214
populating attributes, 105
SetPassword method and, 106
SetPassword method, 106, 126
Setup log, 663
shadow groups
additional information, 363
defined, 176, 185, 362
maintaining dynamically, 176
overview, 176
shared folders, 613, 815
shortcut trusts, 586–587
SID (security identifier)
AD DS administration, 615
computer accounts, 189, 194, 219
data protection measures, 624
defined, 574
deleted groups and, 171
group support, 141, 145
migration considerations, 574–575
recycling accounts, 128
RID master role, 480
stored information, 3
tokenGroups attribute, 117

user object support, 105
SID filtering, 592–593
sIDHistory attribute, 574–575, 592
sign-out cookies, 840
Simple Certificate Enrollment Protocol (SCEP), 732, 750
Simple Mail Transport Protocol (SMTP), 537, 827
Simple Object Access Protocol (SOAP), 844
single sign-on. *See* SSO (single sign-on)
single-domain forests, 568–569
single-label names
    creating, 451
    defined, 411
    DNS support, 415
    managing, 441–443, 450–451
SIP (session initiation protocol), 414
site link bridges, 540, 612
site links
    AD DS administration, 612
    cost considerations, 541
    creating, 546
    defined, 509, 535
    overview, 535–537
    replication schedules, 543
    transitivity, 539–540
site objects, 513–514
site planning
    connection speed, 511
    criteria summarized, 512
    server placement, 512
    service placement, 511
    user population, 511
site-local addresses, 396
sites
    AD DS administration, 612
    configuring, 519–520
    defined, 11, 32, 509
    defining, 512–515
    domain controller locations, 516–519
    GPO links, 234, 256, 258
    managing domain controllers, 515–516
    planning, 510–512
    replication traffic, 510
    service localization, 510, 512
    site coverage, 519
    UGMC considerations, 524–525
SLC (server licensor certificate)
    defined, 789, 797, 818
    exporting, 811
    importing, 810
Smart Card Is Required For Interactive Logon setting, 120
smart cards
    AD CS support, 730–731, 737–738, 753

AD RMS support, 796, 812
    certificate templates, 757
SmartCard Logon template, 757
SmartCard User template, 757
S/MIME (Secure Multipurpose Internet Mail Extensions), 730
SMTP (Simple Mail Transport Protocol), 537, 827
snap-ins, 35. *See also* specific snap-ins
snapshots
    AD DS administration, 620
    creating, 640–641
    deleted groups, 171
SOA (service-oriented architecture), 844, 872
SOA (Start of Authority) record, 411, 434–435
SOAP (Simple Object Access Protocol), 844
software deployment GPOs
    creating, 325–326, 330–331
    managing scope, 327
software distribution point (SDP), 323
Software Installation node, 325, 327
Software Settings node, 242
Sony BMG, 781
special characters in user names, 49
special identities, 179, 185
Special Operations Software, 616
Specops Gpupdate tool, 616–619
split-brain syndrome, 400–402
SPN (service principal name), 580
spoofing, 415
SRV (service) records
    contents, 517–518
    defined, 414
    domain controllers, 517
    functionality, 393, 417
    site coverage, 519
SSL (Secure Sockets Layer)
    AD DS support, 703
    AD FS configuration, 857
    AD RMS support, 792
    authentication certificates, 841
    authentication cookies, 840
    exporting certificates, 860–862
    firewall support, 826
    HTTPS support, 724
    importing certificates, 862
SSO (single sign-on)
    AD FS support, 832, 835
    defined, 7, 844
    Federated Web SSO, 836
    Federated Web SSO with Forest Trust, 836
    Web SSO, 837
SSTP (Secure Sockets Tunneling Protocol), 730
standalone CAs

defined, 732, 740
deployment best practices, 737
enterprise CA comparison, 733–734
hierarchy considerations, 737
installing AD CS, 742–744
Start of Authority (SOA) record, 411, 434–435
starter GPOs, 247–248
storage
  cryptographic storage providers, 800
  GPOs, 240
Store Passwords Using Reversible Encryption setting,
  120
STS (Security Token Service), 844
stub zone, 411–412
subnets, 512, 515, 612
Subnets node, 513
subordinate CAs, 731
subsequent notification delay, 534
Super Users group, 814–815
System Diagnostics collector set, 667
System log, 281, 663
System Monitor, 449, 621, 666
System Performance collector set, 667
System Properties dialog box, 193
system resource management. *See* performance
  management
system services, 303
system state data, 632, 650–651
SYSVOL (system volume)
  central store, 246
  configuring DFS replication, 494–502, 559
  domain controller requirements, 12
  GPO replication, 241
  migrating replication to DFS-R, 496
  migration stages, 495–496
  raising domain functional level, 494

T

Task Manager
  Event Log support, 665
  functionality, 660–663
Task Scheduler tool, 35, 650
tattooing the registry, 248
TCP protocol, 518
TCP/IP (Transmission Control Protocol/Internet
  Protocol), 7, 394
templates
  administrative, 245, 251–252
  creating user accounts, 87–88, 93–94
  disabling, 87
test environments, 845
testing

Dcdiag.exe support, 544–545
policy settings, 234
trusts, 591
TGT (ticket granting ticket), 4, 579
ticket granting ticket (TGT), 4, 579
time synchronization, 845
Time to Live setting. *See* TTL (Time to Live) setting
timestamps, 845
TLS (Transport Layer Security), 826, 840
tokenGroups attribute, 117, 481
token-signing certificate, 844
tombstone container, 624, 628, 683
tombstone lifetime, 128, 624
transform command, 314
transitivity
  realm trusts, 588
  securing trust relationships, 592
  site links, 539–540
  trust relationships, 578
Transmission Control Protocol/Internet Protocol (TCP/
  IP), 7, 394
Transport Layer Security (TLS), 826, 840
tree-root trust, 580
trees, 9, 571
troubleshooting
  AD DS administration, 621
  computer accounts, 216–217, 222
  Gpotool.exe support, 241
  Group Policy, 280
  operations master roles, 486–488
  WSRM, 673
trust flow, 580–581, 586
trust passwords, 585
trust path, 580–581, 586
trust policy, 844, 855
trust relationships. *See also* forest trusts; manual trusts
  AD DS administration, 619, 621
  AD FS support, 827, 854
  AD RMS considerations, 789–790, 810–811, 818
  administering, 590–591, 595–601
  authentication protocols and, 579–582
  between domains, 577–578
  certificate authorities, 725, 730, 734
  characteristics, 578–579
  computers joining domains, 189
  creating, 597–599
  defined, 145
  managing, 591
  providing access, 599–600
  resetting computer accounts, 217
  securing relationships, 591–595
  selective authentication, 559, 593–595, 600–601
  testing, 591

validating, 590, 599
within domains, 577
Trusted Root Certificates, 725
TTL (Time to Live) setting
defined, 408, 411
false positive record results, 432
SOA records, 435
type adapter, 104, 123

U

UDDI (Universal Description, Discovery, and
Integration), 844
UDP protocol, 518
UGMC (universal group membership caching),
524–525, 528
Ultrasound.exe command, 621–622
unattended installation
answer files, 462–464
domain controllers, 462–464
listing of parameters, 26
Uniform Resource Identifier (URI), 844
Universal Description, Discovery, and Integration
(UDDI), 844
universal group membership caching (UGMC), 524–
525, 528
universal groups
AD RMS support, 814–815
characteristics, 148–149
defined, 51, 524
Universal Time Coordinate (UTC), 482
Update Sequence Number (USN), 632, 691
UPN (user principle name)
AD DS administration, 619
creating user objects, 49
identity claim type, 839
name attributes, 118
split-brain syndrome, 402
URI (Uniform Resource Identifier), 844
URLs, 810
use license, 790, 798, 812
user accounts
AD DS administration, 612
AD LDS support, 693
AD RMS considerations, 789, 809
administering, 124–130
automating creation, 93–96
certificate authorities, 742
creating with Dsadd command, 89, 94
creating with templates, 87–88, 93–94
data protection measures, 624
deleting, 128
disabling templates, 87

disabling/enabling, 127–128
group management strategies, 153
lockout policies, 126
managing, 614
migration considerations, 576
moving, 129
name attributes, 118–119
object protection, 626
recycling, 128
renaming, 129–130
resetting passwords, 125–126
unlocking, 126–127, 132
User Cannot Change Password setting, 120
User Configuration node
Administrative Templates node, 243–248
defined, 231, 241
Folder Redirection node, 242
Internet Explorer Maintenance node, 242
loopback policy processing, 270
Policies node, 241
Preferences node, 241, 243–244
Remote Installation Services node, 242
Software Settings node, 242
Windows Settings node, 242
User Must Change Password At Next Logon setting,
120, 125
user objects
account properties, 119–120
AD DS administration, 613, 620
creating, 48–50, 61–63
creating with VBScript, 109
creating with Windows PowerShell, 103–106, 110–111
hidden attributes, 88, 116–117
importing with CSVDE tool, 90, 94–95
importing with LDIFDE command, 90–92, 95–96
importing with Windows PowerShell, 106–108
managing attributes, 114–117, 121–124
multiselecting, 117, 131
name attributes, 118–119
populating attributes, 104–106
viewing attributes, 116–117, 130–131
user principle name. *See* UPN (user principle name)
user settings. *See* User Configuration node
userAccountControl attribute, 203
userPassword attribute, 558
userPrincipalName attribute, 118
Users container
as default container, 11
default groups, 177
domain local groups, 380
redirecting, 196, 559
userWorkstations attribute, 119

USN (Update Sequence Number), 632, 691
UTC (Universal Time Coordinate), 482

V
variables
  in cmdlets, 102, 123
  pipeline, 102
VBScript language
  ADMT support, 573
  configuring computer attributes, 214
  creating computers, 208, 211
  creating users, 109
  disabling accounts, 127
  enabling accounts, 128
  managing group membership, 164
  managing user attributes, 123–124
  moving computers, 215
  moving user accounts, 129
  overview, 108
  renaming user accounts, 130
  resetting passwords, 126
  unlocking user accounts, 127
  Windows PowerShell comparison, 109–110
verification certificate, 844
VHDs (virtual hard disks), 636
virtual appliances, 784
virtual machines
  AD LDS considerations, 695
  AD RMS considerations, 799
  additional information, 784
  certificate authorities, 737
  domain controllers as, 648–650
  high availability, 650
  restoring from complete backups, 645
Volume Shadow Copy Service (VSS), 648–650
VPNs (virtual private networks), 6
VSS (Volume Shadow Copy Service), 648–650
vssadmin command, 649

W
W32tm.exe command, 621
WAIK (Windows Automated Installation Kit), 631
Warning events, 663
Wbadmin.exe command
  AD DS administration, 630
  full system backup, 635
  performing restores, 643, 647
  scheduling backups, 636–638
Web browsers, 416, 731, 843
Web pages, 843

Web Proxy Automatic Discovery Protocol (WPAD),
  415–416
Web server certificates, 804–805
Web Server template, 757
Web services
  AD FS support, 832, 854
  AD RMS support, 788
  defined, 844, 872
  division of responsibilities, 610
Web SSO, 837
Web.config file, 856
what-if analyses, 280–281
Where-Object cmdlet, 102
WID (Windows Internal Database), 786, 799
Win32_OperatingSystem class, 265
Windows 2000
  domain functional levels, 558
  forest functional levels, 561
Windows Automated Installation Kit (WAIK), 631
Windows Domain Manager, 591
Windows event IDs, 665
Windows Explorer, 618
Windows Installer package (.msi file), 322, 349
Windows Installer transform (.mst file), 323, 349
Windows Integrated authentication, 835
Windows Internal Database (WID), 786, 799
Windows Internet Name Service. *See* WINS (Windows
  Internet Name Service)
Windows Live ID, 811, 818
Windows Logs node, 281
Windows Management Interface. *See* WMI (Windows
  Management Interface)
Windows NT, 845
Windows Performance Monitor, 661, 666–670
  functionality, 671
Windows PowerShell
  cmdlet support, 99–103
  configuring computer attributes, 214
  console depicted, 99
  creating computers, 206–208, 211
  creating users, 103–106, 110–111
  deleting user accounts, 128
  disabling accounts, 127
  enabling accounts, 128
  importing computers, 206–208
  importing users, 106–108
  installing, 110
  managing group membership, 164
  managing user attributes, 123–124
  moving computers, 215
  moving user accounts, 129
  overview, 98–99

renaming user accounts, 130
resetting passwords, 126
script support, 108
VBScript comparison, 109–110
Windows Recovery Environment (WinRE), 631, 639
Windows Reliability and Performance Monitor (WRPM), 666
Windows Reliability and Performance node, 671
Windows Reliability Monitor, 661, 665
Windows RMS, 793–794, 818
Windows Scripting Host (WSH), 109
Windows Security log, 335
Windows Server 2003
   AD DS administration tools, 622
   domain functional levels, 558–559, 565
   forest functional levels, 561–562
Windows Server 2008
   AD DS administration tools, 622
   domain functional levels, 559
   forest functional levels, 562
   installing AD CS, 741
   system resource tools, 660–661
Windows Server Backup
   AD DS administration, 621, 703
   AD LDS support, 703
   creating installation media, 633
   data protection measures, 624, 629–630
   full system backups, 633–638
   operations supported, 630–632
   scheduling backups, 631, 635–638, 648
   system state data, 632
Windows Settings node, 242
Windows System Resource Manager (WSRM)
   functionality, 661, 672–674
   installing, 679–680
Windows Time, 621

Windows Token-Based Agent, 833, 846
Windows XP, 796
WinRE (Windows Recovery Environment), 631, 639
WINS (Windows Internet Name Service)
   DNS support, 442–443
   functionality, 409
   single-label names, 411
wireless communications, 730
wireless networks, 6, 753, 756
WMI (Windows Management Interface), 110, 264, 621
WMI filters, 234, 264–266
WMI Filters node, 265
workgroups, 189, 380, 470
WPAD (Web Proxy Automatic Discovery Protocol), 415–416
WRPM (Windows Reliability and Performance Monitor), 666
Wscript command, 108
WS-Federation Passive Requestor Profile, 832, 845, 872
WSH (Windows Scripting Host), 109
WSRM (Windows System Resource Manager)
   functionality, 661, 672–674
   installing, 679–680
WS-Security, 845

X

XML (Extensible Markup Language), 349, 844
XML Notepad tool, 327

Z

zone delegation, 412, 422–424
zone scavenging, 412, 432–433
zone transfers, 412
zones. *See* DNS zones

Windows Server 2008— Resources for Administrators

Prepare for Certification with Self-Paced Training Kits

Official Exam Prep Guides—
Plus Practice Tests

Ace your preparation for the skills measured by the MCP exams—and on the job. With official *Self-Paced Training Kits* from Microsoft, you'll work at your own pace through a system of lessons, hands-on exercises, troubleshooting labs, and review questions. Then test yourself with the Readiness Review Suite on CD, which provides hundreds of challenging questions for in-depth self-assessment and practice.

- **MCSE Self-Paced Training Kit (Exams 70-290, 70-291, 70-293, 70-294): Microsoft® Windows Server™ 2003 Core Requirements.** 4-Volume Boxed Set. ISBN: 0-7356-1953-0. (Individual volumes are available separately.)

- **MCSA/MCSE Self-Paced Training Kit (Exam 70-270): Installing, Configuring, and Administering Microsoft Windows® XP Professional, Second Edition.** ISBN: 0-7356-2152-7.

- **MCSE Self-Paced Training Kit (Exam 70-298): Designing Security for a Microsoft Windows Server 2003 Network.** ISBN: 0-7356-1969-7.

- **MCSA/MCSE Self-Paced Training Kit (Exam 70-350): Implementing Microsoft Internet Security and Acceleration Server 2004.** ISBN: 0-7356-2169-1.

- **MCSA/MCSE Self-Paced Training Kit (Exam 70-284): Implementing and Managing Microsoft Exchange Server 2003.** ISBN: 0-7356-1899-2.

For more information about Microsoft Press® books, visit: **www.microsoft.com/mspress**

For more information about learning tools such as online assessments, e-learning, and certification, visit:
www.microsoft.com/mspress *and* **www.microsoft.com/learning**

Windows Server 2008 Resource Kit—
Your Definitive Resource!

**Windows Server® 2008
Resource Kit**

Microsoft® MVPs with
Microsoft Windows Server Team

ISBN 9780735623613

Your definitive reference for deployment and operations—from the experts who know the technology best. Get in-depth technical information on Active Directory®, Windows PowerShell™ scripting, advanced administration, networking and network access protection, security administration, IIS, and other critical topics—plus an essential toolkit of resources on CD.

Also available as single volumes

**Windows Server 2008
Security Resource Kit**

Jesper M. Johansson et al. with
Microsoft Security Team

ISBN 9780735625044

**Windows Server 2008
Networking and Network
Access Protection (NAP)**

Joseph Davies, Tony Northrup,
Microsoft Networking Team

ISBN 9780735624221

**Windows Server 2008
Active Directory Resource Kit**

Stan Reimer et al. with
Microsoft Active Directory Team

ISBN 9780735625150

**Windows® Administration
Resource Kit: Productivity
Solutions for IT Professionals**

Dan Holme

ISBN 9780735624313

**Windows Powershell
Scripting Guide**

Ed Wilson

ISBN 9780735622791

**Internet Information
Services (IIS) 7.0
Resource Kit**

Mike Volodarsky et al. with
Microsoft IIS Team

ISBN 9780735624412

See our complete line of books at: **microsoft.com/mspress**